# THE
# HOME BOOK OF VERSE

# THE HOME BOOK OF VERSE

AMERICAN AND ENGLISH

With an Appendix Containing a Few Well-Known Poems in Other Languages

Selected and Arranged
By

BURTON EGBERT STEVENSON
Editor of "The Home Book of Modern Verse"
"The Home Book of Verse for Young Folks"
"The Home Book of Quotations"

NINTH EDITION
(Extended in The Home Book of Modern Verse)

HOLT, RINEHART AND WINSTON
NEW YORK

In Canada, Holt, Rinehart and Winston of Canada, Limited

Ninth Edition
Published, June, 1953
Second Printing, October, 1955
Third Printing, November, 1957
Fourth Printing, March, 1959
Fifth Printing, September, 1962

88141–0412

PRINTED IN THE UNITED STATES OF AMERICA

# SONS OF THE EMERALD ISLE

## FATHER O'FLYNN

Of priests we can offer a charmin' variety,
Far renowned for larnin' and piety;
Still, I'd advance ye widout impropriety,
Father O'Flynn as the flower of them all.

Here's a health to you, Father O'Flynn,
*Sláinte*, and *sláinte*, and *sláinte* agin;
Powerfulest preacher, and
Tinderest teacher, and
Kindliest creature in ould Donegal.

Don't talk of your Provost and Fellows of Trinity,
Famous forever at Greek and Latinity,
Faix! and the divels and all at Divinity—
Father O'Flynn 'd make hares of them all!
Come, I vinture to give ye my word,
Niver the likes of his logic was heard,
Down from mythology
Into thayology,
Troth! and conchology if he'd the call.

Och! Father O'Flynn, you've the wonderful way wid you,
All ould sinners are wishful to pray wid you,
All the young childer are wild for to play wid you,
You've such a way wid you, Father avick!
Still, for all you've so gentle a soul,
Gad, you've your flock in the grandest control,
Checking the crazy ones,
Coaxin' onaisy ones,
Liftin' the lazy ones on wid the stick.

And, though quite avoidin' all foolish frivolity,
Still, at all seasons of innocent jollity,
Where was the play-boy could claim an equality
At comicality, Father, wid you?
Once the Bishop looked grave at your jest,
Till this remark set him off wid the rest:
"Is it lave gaiety
All to the laity?
Cannot the clargy be Irishmen too?"

Here's a health to you, Father O'Flynn,
*Sláinte*, and *sláinte*, and *sláinte* agin;
Powerfulest preacher, and
Tinderest teacher, and
Kindliest creature in ould Donegal.

*Alfred Perceval Graves* [1846–1931]

## FATHER MOLLOY

### OR, THE CONFESSION

PADDY McCABE was dying one day,
And Father Molloy he came to confess him;
Paddy prayed hard he would make no delay,
But forgive him his sins and make haste for to bless him
"First tell me your sins," says Father Molloy,
"For I'm thinking you've not been a very good boy."
"Oh," says Paddy, "so late in the evenin', I fear
'Twould throuble you such a long story to hear,
For you've ten long miles o'er the mountains to go,
While the road *I've* to travel 's much longer you know.
So give us your blessin' and get in the saddle;
To tell all my sins my poor brain it would addle;
And the docther gave ordhers to keep me so quiet—
'Twould disturb me to tell all my sins, if I'd thry it;
And your Riverence has towld us, unless we tell *all*,
'Tis worse than not makin' confession at all.
So I'll say in a word I'm no very good boy—
And, therefore, your blessin', sweet Father Molloy."

"Well, I'll read from a book," says Father Molloy,
"The manifold sins that humanity's heir to;
And when you hear those that your conscience annoy,
You'll just squeeze my hand, as acknowledging thereto."
Then the father began the dark roll of iniquity,
And Paddy, thereat, felt his conscience grow rickety,
And he gave such a squeeze that the priest gave a roar—
"Oh, murdher!" says Paddy, "don't read any more,
For, if you keep readin', by all that is thrue,
Your Riverence's fist will be soon black and blue;
Besides, to be throubled my conscience begins,
That your Riverence should have any hand in my sins;
So you'd betther suppose I committed them all,
For whether they're great ones, or whether they're small,
Or if they're a dozen, or if they're fourscore,
'Tis your Riverence knows how to absolve them, astore;
So I'll say in a word, I'm no very good boy—
And, therefore, your blessin', sweet Father Molloy."

"Well," says Father Molloy, "if your sins I forgive,
So you must forgive all your enemies truly;
And promise me also that, if you should live,
You'll leave off your old tricks, and begin to live newly."
"I forgive ev'rybody," says Pat, with a groan,
"Except that big vagabone Micky Malone;
And him I will murdher if ever I can—"
"Tut, tut!" says the priest, "you're a very bad man;
For without your forgiveness, and also repentance,
You'll ne'er go to Heaven, and that is my sentence."
"Poo!" says Paddy McCabe, "that's a very hard case—
With your Riverence and Heaven I'm content to make pace;
But with Heaven and your Riverence I wondher—*Och hone*—
You would think of comparin' that blackguard Malone—
But since I'm hard pressed and that I *must* forgive,
I forgive—if I die—but as sure as I live
That ugly blackguard I will surely desthroy!—
So, *now* for your blessin', sweet Father Molloy."

*Samuel Lover* [1797-1868]

## PADDY O'RAFTHER

PADDY, in want of a dinner one day,
Credit all gone, and no money to pay,
Stole from a priest a fat pullet, they say,
And went to confession just after;
"Your riv'rince," says Paddy, "I stole this fat hen."
"What, what!" says the priest, "at your ould thricks again?
Faith, you'd rather be stalin' than sayin' *amen*,
Paddy O'Rafther!"

"Sure, you wouldn't be angry," says Pat, "if you knew
That the best of intintions I had in my view—
For I stole it to make it a prisint to you,
And you can absolve me afther."
"Do you think," says the priest, "I'd partake of your theft?
Of your seven small senses you must be bereft—
You're the biggest blackguard that I know, right and left,
Paddy O'Rafther."

"Then what shall I do with the pullet," says Pat,
"If your riv'rince won't take it? By this and by that
I don't know no more than a dog or a cat
What your riv'rince would have me be afther."
"Why, then," says his rev'rence, "you sin-blinded owl,
Give back to the man that you stole from his fowl:
For if you do not, 'twill be worse for your sowl,
Paddy O'Rafther."

Says Paddy, "I asked him to take it—'tis thrue
As this minit I'm talkin', your riv'rince, to you;
But he wouldn't resaive it—so what can I do?"
Says Paddy, nigh choken with laughter.
"By my throth," says the priest, "but the case is absthruse;
If he won't take his hen, why the man is a goose:
'Tis not the first time my advice was no use,
Paddy O'Rafther.

"But, for sake of your sowl, I would sthrongly advise
To some one in want you would give your supplies—
Some widow, or orphan, with tears in their eyes;

And *then* you may come to *me* afther."
So Paddy went off to the brisk Widow Hoy,
And the pullet between them was eaten with joy,
And, says she, " 'Pon my word, you're the cleverest boy,
Paddy O'Rafther!"

Then Paddy went back to the priest the next day,
And told him the fowl he had given away
To a poor lonely widow, in want and dismay,
The loss of her spouse weeping afther.
"Well, now," says the priest, "I'll absolve you, my lad,
For repentantly making the best of the bad,
In feeding the hungry and cheering the sad,
Paddy O'Rafther!"

*Samuel Lover* [1797–1868]

## LARRIE O'DEE

Now the Widow McGee,
And Larrie O'Dee,
Had two little cottages out on the green,
With just room enough for two pig-pens between.
The widow was young and the widow was fair,
With the brightest of eyes and the brownest of hair,
And it frequently chanced, when she came in the morn,
With the swill for her pig, Larrie came with the corn,
And some of the ears that he tossed from his hand
In the pen of the widow were certain to land.

One morning said he:
"Och! Misthress McGee,
It's a waste of good lumber, this runnin' two rigs,
Wid a fancy purtition betwane our two pigs!"
"Indade, sir, it is!" answered Widow McGee,
With the sweetest of smiles upon Larrie O'Dee.
"And thin, it looks kind o' hard-hearted and mane.
Kapin' two friendly pigs so exsaidenly near
That whiniver one grunts the other can hear,
And yit kape a cruel purtition betwane."

"Schwate Widow McGee,"
Answered Larrie O'Dee,
"If ye fale in your heart we are mane to the pigs,
Ain't we mane to ourselves to be runnin' two rigs?
Och! it made me heart ache when I paped through the cracks
Of me shanty, lasht March, at yez swingin' yer axe;
An' a bobbin' yer head an a-shtompin' yer fate,
Wid yer purty white hands jisht as red as a bate,
A-shplittin' yer kindlin'-wood out in the shtorm,
When one little shtove it would kape us both warm!"

"Now, piggy," says she,
"Larrie's courtin' o' me,
Wid his dilicate tinder allusions to you;
So now yez must tell me jisht what I must do:
For, if I'm to say yes, shtir the swill wid yer snout,
But if I'm to say no, ye must kape yer nose out.
Now, Larrie, for shame! to be bribin' a pig
By tossin' a handful of corn in its shwig!"
"Me darlint, the piggy says yes," answered he.
And that was the courtship of Larrie O'Dee.

*William W. Fink* [18 -

## THE IRISHMAN AND THE LADY

THERE was a lady lived at Leith,
A lady very stylish, man;
And yet, in spite of all her teeth,
She fell in love with an Irishman—
A nasty, ugly Irishman,
A wild, tremendous Irishman,
A tearing, swearing, thumping, bumping, ranting, roaring Irishman.

His face was no ways beautiful,
For with small-pox 'twas scarred across;
And the shoulders of the ugly dog
Were almost double a yard across.

Oh, the lump of an Irishman,
The whiskey-devouring Irishman,
The great he-rogue with his wonderful brogue—the fighting, rioting Irishman.

One of his eyes was bottle-green,
And the other eye was out, my dear;
And the calves of his wicked-looking legs
Were more than two feet about, my dear.
Oh, the great big Irishman,
The rattling, battling Irishman—
The stamping, ramping, swaggering, staggering, leathering swash of an Irishman.

He took so much of Lundy-foot
That he used to snort and snuffle—O!
And in shape and size the fellow's neck
Was as bad as the neck of a buffalo.
Oh, the horrible Irishman,
The thundering, blundering Irishman—
The slashing, dashing, smashing, lashing, thrashing, hashing Irishman.

His name was a terrible name, indeed,
Being Timothy Thady Mulligan;
And whenever he emptied his tumbler of punch
He'd not rest till he filled it full again.
The boozing, bruising Irishman,
The 'toxicated Irishman—
The whiskey, frisky, rummy, gummy, brandy, no dandy Irishman.

This was the lad the lady loved,
Like all the girls of quality;
And he broke the skulls of the men of Leith,
Just by the way of jollity.
Oh, the leathering Irishman,
The barbarous, savage Irishman—
The hearts of the maids, and the gentlemen's heads, were bothered I'm sure by this Irishman.

*William Maginn* [1793–1842]

## IRISH ASTRONOMY

### A VERITABLE MYTH, TOUCHING THE CONSTELLATION OF O'RYAN, IGNORANTLY AND FALSELY SPELLED ORION

O'RYAN was a man of might
Whin Ireland was a nation,
But poachin' was his heart's delight
And constant occupation.
He had an ould militia gun,
And sartin sure his aim was;
He gave the keepers many a run
And wouldn't mind the game laws.

St. Pathrick wanst was passin' by
O'Ryan's little houldin',
And, as the saint felt wake and dhry,
He thought he'd enther bould in.
"O'Ryan," says the saint, "avick!
To praich at Thurles I'm goin',
So let me have a rasher quick,
And a dhrop of Innishowen."

"No rasher will I cook for you,
While betther is to spare, sir,
But here's a jug of mountain dew,
And there's a rattlin' hare, sir."
St. Pathrick he looked mighty sweet,
And says he, "Good luck attind you,
And, when you're in your windin' sheet,
It's up to heaven I'll sind you."

O'Ryan gave his pipe a whiff—
"Them tidin's is thransportin';
But may I ax your saintship if
There's any kind of sportin'?"
St. Pathrick said, "A Lion's there,
Two Bears, a Bull, and Cancer"—
"Bedad," says Mick, "the huntin's rare;
St. Pathrick, I'm your man, sir."

So, to conclude my song aright,
For fear I'd tire your patience,
You'll see O'Ryan any night
Amid the constellations.
And Venus follows in his track,
Till Mars grows jealous raally,
But, faith, he fears the Irish knack
Of handling the shillaly.

*Charles Graham Halpine* [1829–1868]

## THE FIDDLER OF DOONEY

When I play on my fiddle in Dooney,
Folk dance like a wave of the sea;
My cousin is priest in Kilvarnet,
My brother in Moharabuiee.

I passed my brother and cousin:
They read in their books of prayer;
I read in my book of songs
I bought at the Sligo fair.

When we come at the end of time,
To Peter sitting in state,
He will smile on the three old spirits,
But call me first through the gate;

For the good are always the merry,
Save by an evil chance,
And the merry love the fiddle,
And the merry love to dance:

And when the folk there spy me,
They all come up to me,
With "Here is the fiddler of Dooney!"
And dance like a wave of the sea.

*William Butler Yeats* [1865–1939]

## THE BIRTH OF ST. PATRICK

On the eighth day of March it was, some people say,
That Saint Pathrick at midnight he first saw the day;
While others declare 'twas the ninth he was born,
And 'twas all a mistake between midnight and morn;
For mistakes will occur in a hurry and shock,
And some blamed the babby—and some blamed the clock—
Till with all their cross-questions sure no one could know
If the child was too fast, or the clock was too slow.

Now the first faction-fight in owld Ireland, they say,
Was all on account of Saint Pathrick's birthday:
Some fought for the eighth—for the ninth more would die,
And who wouldn't see right, sure they blackened his eye!
At last, both the factions so positive grew,
That each kept a birthday, so Pat then had two,
Till Father Mulcahy, who showed them their sins,
Said, "No one could have two birthdays, but a twins."

Says he, "Boys, don't be fightin' for eight or for nine,
Don't be always dividin'—but sometimes combine;
Combine eight with nine, and seventeen is the mark,
So let that be his birthday."—"Amen," says the clerk.
"If he wasn't a twins, sure our hist'ry will show
That, at least, he's worth any two saints that we know!"
Then they all got blind dhrunk—which complated their bliss,
And we keep up the practice from that day to this.

*Samuel Lover* [1797–1864]

## SAINT PATRICK

St. Patrick was a gentleman,
Who came of decent people;
He built a church in Dublin town,
And on it put a steeple.
His father was a Gallagher;
His mother was a Brady;
His aunt was an O'Shaughnessy,
His uncle an O'Grady.

So, success attend St. Patrick's fist,
For he's a saint so clever;
Oh! he gave the snakes and toads a twist,
And bothered them forever!

The Wicklow hills are very high,
And so's the Hill of Howth, sir;
But there's a hill, much bigger still,
Much higher nor them both, sir:
'Twas on the top of this high hill
St. Patrick preached his sarmint
That drove the frogs into the bogs,
And banished all the varmint.

There's not a mile in Ireland's isle
Where dirty varmin musters,
But where he put his dear fore-foot,
And murdered them in clusters.
The toads went pop, the frogs went hop,
Slap-dash into the water;
And the snakes committed suicide
To save themselves from slaughter.

Nine hundred thousand reptiles blue
He charmed with sweet discourses,
And dined on them at Killaloe
In soups and second courses.
Where blind-worms crawling in the grass
Disgusted all the nation,
He gave them a rise, which opened their eyes
To a sense of their situation.

No wonder that those Irish lads
Should be so gay and frisky,
For sure St. Pat he taught them that,
As well as making whiskey;
No wonder that the saint himself
Should understand distilling,
Since his mother kept a shebeen-shop
In the town of Enniskillen.

O, was I but so fortunate
As to be back in Munster,
'Tis I'd be bound that from that ground
I never more would once stir.
For there St. Patrick planted turf,
And plenty of the praties,
With pigs galore, ma gra, ma 'store,
And cabbages—and ladies!
So, success attend St. Patrick's fist,
For he's a saint so clever;
O, he gave the snakes and toads a twist
And bothered them forever!

*Henry Bennett* [1785– ? ]

## MR. MOLONY'S ACCOUNT OF THE BALL

### GIVEN TO THE NEPAULESE AMBASSADOR BY THE PENINSULAR AND ORIENTAL COMPANY

O WILL ye choose to hear the news?
Bedad, I cannot pass it o'er:
I'll tell you all about the Ball
To the Naypaulase Ambassador.
Begor! this fête all balls does bate,
At which I've worn a pump, and I
Must here relate the splendthor great
Of th' Oriental Company.

These men of sinse dispoised expinse,
To fête these black Achilleses.
"We'll show the blacks," says they, "Almack's,
And take the rooms at Willis's."
With flags and shawls, for these Nepauls,
They hung the rooms of Willis up,
And decked the walls, and stairs, and halls
With roses and with lilies up.

And Jullien's band it tuck its stand
So sweetly in the middle there,
And soft bassoons played heavenly chunes,
And violins did fiddle there.

And when the Coort was tired of spoort,
  I'd lave you, boys, to think there was
A nate buffet before them set,
  Where lashins of good dhrink there was!

At ten before the ball-room door,
  His moighty Excellency was;
He smoiled and bowed to all the crowd,
  So gorgeous and immense he was.
His dusky shuit, sublime and mute,
  Into the doorway followed him;
And O the noise of the blackguard boys,
  As they hurrood and hollowed him!

The noble Chair stud at the stair,
  And bade the dthrums to thump; and he
Did thus evince, to that Black Prince,
  The welcome of his Company.
O fair the girls, and rich the curls,
  And bright the oys, you saw there, was;
And fixed each oye ye there could spoi,
  On Gineral Jung Bahawther was!

This Gineral great then tuck his sate,
  With all the other ginerals,
(Bedad, his troat, his belt, his coat,
  All bleezed with precious minerals);
And as he there, with princely air,
  Recloinin on his cushion was,
All round about his royal chair,
  The squeezin and the pushin was.

O Pat, such girls, such Jukes and Earls,
  Such fashion and nobilitee!
Just think of Tim, and fancy him
  Amidst the hoigh gentility!
There was Lord De L'Huys, and the Portygeese
  Ministher and his lady there,
And I reckonized, with much surprise,
  Our messmate, Bob O'Grady, there;

There was Baroness Brunow, that looked like Juno,
And Baroness Rehausen there,
And Countess Roullier, that looked peculiar
Well, in her robes of gauze in there.
There was Lord Crowhurst (I knew him first
When only Mr. Pips he was),
And Mick O'Toole, the great big fool,
That after supper tipsy was.

There was Lord Fingall and his ladies all,
And Lords Killeen and Dufferin,
And Paddy Fife, with his fat wife,—
I wondther how he could stuff her in.
There was Lord Belfast, that by me passed,
And seemed to ask how should *I* go there?
And the Widow Macrae, and Lord A. Hay,
And the Marchioness of Sligo there.

Yes, Jukes and Earls, and diamonds and pearls,
And pretty girls, was spoorting there;
And some beside (the rogues!) I spied,
Behind the windies, coorting there.
O, there's one I know, bedad, would show
As beautiful as any there;
And I'd like to hear the pipers blow,
And shake a fut with Fanny there!

*William Makepeace Thackeray* [1811–1863]

## BACHELOR'S HALL

BACHELOR'S HALL! what a quare-lookin' place it is!
Kape me from sich all the days of me life!
Sure, but I think what a burnin' disgrace it is,
Niver at all to be gettin' a wife.

Say the old bachelor, gloomy an' sad enough,
Placin' his tay-kettle over the fire;
Soon it tips over—Saint Patrick! he's mad enough,
If he were prisent, to fight with the squire!

Now, like a pig in a mortar-bed wallowin',
  Say the old bachelor kneading his dough;
Troth, if his bread he could ate without swallowin',
  How it would favor his palate, ye know!

He looks for the platter—Grimalkin is scourin' it!
  Sure, at a baste like that, swearin' 's no sin;
His dishcloth is missing; the pigs are devourin' it—
  Thunder and turf! what a pickle he's in!

When his male's over, the table's left sittin' so;
  Dishes, take care of yourselves, if ye can;
Divil a drop of hot water will visit ye,—
  Och, let him alone for a baste of a man!

Pots, dishes, pans, an' such grasy commodities,
  Ashes and praty-skins, kiver the floor;
His cupboard's a storehouse of comical oddities,
  Sich as had niver been neighbors before.

Late in the night, when he goes to bed shiverin',
  Niver a bit is the bed made at all;
He crapes like a terrapin under the kiverin';—
  Bad luck to the pictur of Bachelor's Hall!

*John Finley* [1796–1866]

## THE SABINE FARMER'S SERENADE

'Twas on a windy night,
  At two o'clock in the morning,
An Irish lad so tight,
  All wind and weather scorning,
At Judy Callaghan's door,
  Sitting upon the palings,
His love-tale he did pour,
  And this was part of his wailings:—
    *Only say*
  *You'll be Mrs. Brallaghan;*
    *Don't say nay,*
  *Charming Judy Callaghan.*

Oh! list to what I say,
  Charms you've got like Venus;
Own your love you may,
  There's but the wall between us.
You lie fast asleep
  Snug in bed and snoring;
Round the house I creep,
  Your hard heart imploring.

I've got a pig and a sow,
  I've got a sty to sleep 'em
A calf and a brindled cow,
  And a cabin too, to keep 'em;
Sunday hat and coat,
  An old gray mare to ride on,
Saddle and bridle to boot,
  Which you may ride astride on.

I've got an acre of ground,
  I've got it set with praties;
I've got of 'baccy a pound,
  I've got some tea for the ladies;
I've got the ring to wed,
  Some whiskey to make us gaily;
I've got a feather bed
  And a handsome new shillelagh.

You've got a charming eye,
  You've got some spelling and reading
You've got, and so have I,
  A taste for genteel breeding;
You're rich, and fair, and young,
  As everybody's knowing;
You've got a decent tongue
  Whene'er 'tis set a-going.

For a wife till death
  I am willing to take ye;
But, och! I waste my breath,
  The devil himself can't wake ye.

'Tis just beginning to rain,
So I'll get under cover;
To-morrow I'll come again,
And be your constant lover.
*Only say*
*You'll be Mrs. Brallaghan;*
*Don't say nay,*
*Charming Judy Callaghan.*

*Francis Sylvester Mahony* [1804–1866]

## THE WIDOW MALONE

Did ye hear of the Widow Malone,
Ohone!
Who lived in the town of Athlone,
Alone?
Oh! she melted the hearts
Of the swains in them parts,
So lovely the Widow Malone,
Ohone!
So lovely the Widow Malone.

Of lovers she had a full score,
Or more;
And fortunes they all had galore,
In store;
From the minister down
To the Clerk of the Crown,
All were courting the Widow Malone,
Ohone!
All were courting the Widow Malone.

But so modest was Mistress Malone,
'Twas known
No one ever could see her alone,
Ohone!
Let them ogle and sigh,
They could ne'er catch her eye,
So bashful the Widow Malone,
Ohone!
So bashful the Widow Malone.

Till one Mister O'Brien from Clare,—
How quare!
It's little for blushing they care
Down there—
Put his arm round her waist,
Took ten kisses at laste—
"Oh," says he, "you're my Molly Malone,
My own;—
"Oh," says he, "you're my Molly Malone!"

And the widow they all thought so shy,
My eye!
Ne'er thought of a simper or sigh—
For why?
But, "Lucius," says she,
"Since you've now made so free,
You may marry your Molly Malone,
Ohone!
You may marry your Molly Malone."

There's a moral contained in my song,
Not wrong;
And, one comfort, it's not very long,
But strong:
If for widows you die,
Learn *to kiss*, not to sigh,
For they're all like sweet Mistress Malone,
Ohone!
Oh! they're very like Mistress Malone!

*Charles James Lever* [1806-1872]

## WIDOW MACHREE

**From "Handy Andy"**

WIDOW MACHREE, it's no wonder you frown,
Och hone! Widow Machree,
Faith, it ruins your looks, that same dirty black gown,
Och hone! Widow Machree.
How altered your air,
With that close cap you wear—
'Tis destroying your hair

Which should be flowing free;
Be no longer a churl
Of its black silken curl,
Och hone! Widow Machree!

Widow Machree, now the summer is come,
Och hone! Widow Machree,
When everything smiles, should a beauty look glum?
Och hone! Widow Machree.
See, the birds go in pairs,
And the rabbits and hares,—
Why, even the bears
Now in couples agree;
And the mute little fish,
Though they can't spake, they wish,—
Och hone! Widow Machree.

Widow Machree, and when winter comes in,
Och hone! Widow Machree,
To be poking the fire all alone is a sin,
Och hone! Widow Machree.
Sure the shovel and tongs
To each other belongs,
And the kettle sings songs
Full of family glee;
While alone with your cup,
Like a hermit, you sup,
Och hone! Widow Machree.

And how do you know, with the comforts I've towld,
Och hone! Widow Machree,
But you're keeping some poor fellow out in the cowld?
Och hone! Widow Machree.
With such sins on your head
Sure your peace would be fled,
Could you sleep in your bed
Without thinking to see
Some ghost or some sprite,
That would wake you each night,
Crying, "Och hone! Widow Machree"?

Then take my advice, darling Widow Machree,
Och hone! Widow Machree,
And, with my advice, faith, I wish you'd take me,
Och hone! Widow Machree.
You'd have me to desire
Then to stir up the fire,
And sure Hope is no liar
In whispering to me,
That the ghosts would depart,
When you'd me near your heart,
Och hone! Widow Machree!

*Samuel Lover* [1797-1868]

## THE PEACEABLE RACE

"Who says that the Irish are fighters be birth?"
Says little Dan Crone.
"Faix, there's not a more peaceable race on th' earth,
If ye l'ave 'em alone.

"Tim O'Toole? Well, I grant ye now, there is a lad
That's beset wid the curse o' pugnacity bad,
But he's jisht th' ixciption that's provin' the rule;
An' what else could ye ask from a lad like O'Toole?
Shure, he's sich a big mountain o' muscle and bone,
Sizin' up to the heft o' some siventeen stone,
That he fair aggravates iv'ry other bould buck
To be wishful to thump him a little for luck,
An' to prove that there's others as clever as him.
Now, I ask ye, suppose ye was sturdy as Tim,
Don't ye think 'twould be right ye should take a delight
In defindin' yer title an' testin' yer might?"
Says little Dan Crone.

"Is it me? Arrah! now it is jokin' ye are.
But I bid ye be careful an' not go too far.
Shure, it's true I'm no more nor the height o' yer waist,
But there's many a bigger has sampled a taste
O' the knuckles that's bunched in this little ould fisht.
Where's the dog wouldn't fight whin his tail gets a twisht?

Do I hunt fur the throuble? Mayhap, now, it's thrue
Upon certain occasions that's jisht what I do.
Shure, how else would they know—I'm that stunted an' small—
I'd the heart of a man in me body at all?"
Says little Dan Crone.

"Well, thin, keep yer opinion. 'Tis little it's worth,"
Says little Dan Crone.
"Faix, we're jisht the most peaceable race on the earth,
If ye l'ave us alone."

*Thomas Augustin Daly* [1871–1948]

## THE RECRUIT

Sez Corporal Madden to Private McFadden:
"Bedad, yer a bad 'un!
Now turn out yer toes!
Yer belt is unhookit,
Yer cap is on crookit,
Ye may not be dhrunk,
But, be jabers, ye look it!
Wan—two!
Wan—two!
Ye monkey-faced divil, I'll jolly ye through!
Wan—two!—
Time! Mark!
Ye march like the aigle in Cintheral Parrk!"

Sez Corporal Madden to Private McFadden:
"A saint it ud sadden
To dhrill such a mug!
Eyes front!—ye baboon, ye!—
Chin up!—ye gossoon, ye!
Ye've jaws like a goat—
Halt! ye leather-lipped loon, ye!
Wan—two!
Wan—two!

Ye whiskered orang-outang, I'll fix you!
Wan—two!—
Time! Mark!
Ye've eyes like a bat!—can ye see in the dark?"

Sez Corporal Madden to Private McFadden:
"Yer figger wants padd'n'—
Sure, man, ye've no shape!
Behind ye yer shoulders
Stick out like two bowlders;
Yer shins is as thin
As a pair of pen-holders!
Wan—two!
Wan—two!
Yer belly belongs on yer back, ye Jew!
Wan—two!—
Time! Mark!
I'm dhry as a dog—I can't shpake but I bark!"

Sez Corporal Madden to Private McFadden:
"Me heart it ud gladden
To blacken yer eye.
Ye're gettin' too bold, ye
Compel me to scold ye,—
'Tis halt! that I say,—
Will ye heed what I told ye?
Wan—two!
Wan—two!
Be jabers, I'm dhryer than Brian Boru!
Wan—two!—
Time! Mark!
What's wur-ruk for chickens is sport for the lark!"

Sez Corporal Madden to Private McFadden:
"I'll not stay a gadd'n
Wid dagoes like you!
I'll travel no farther,
I'm dyin' for—wather;—
Come on, if ye like,—
Can ye loan me a quather?

Ya-as, you,
What,—two?
And ye'll pay the potheen? Ye're a daisy! Whurroo!
You'll do!
Whist! Mark!
The Rigiment's flatthered to own ye, me spark!"

*Robert William Chambers* [1865–1933]

## FINNIGIN TO FLANNIGAN

Superintindint wuz Flannigan;
Boss av the siction wuz Finnigin;
Whiniver the kyars got offen the thrack
An' muddled up things t' th' divil an' back,
Finnigin writ it to Flannigan,
Afther the wreck wuz all on agin;
That is, this Finnigin
Repoorted to Flannigan.

Whin Finnigin furst writ to Flannigan,
He writed tin pages—did Finnigin,
An' he tould jist how the smash occurred;
Full minny a tajus, blunderin' wurrd
Did Finnigin write to Flannigan
Afther the kyars had gone on agin.
That wuz how Finnigin
Repoorted to Flannigan.

Now Flannigan knowed more than Finnigin—
He'd more idjucation—had Flannigan;
An' it wore'm clane an' complatcly out
To tell what Finnigin writ about
In his writin' to Musther Flannigan.
So he writed back to Finnigin:
"Don't do sich a sin agin;
Make 'em brief, Finnigin!"

Whin Finnigin got this from Flannigan,
He blushed rosy rid—did Finnigin;
An' he said: "I'll gamble a whole month's pa-ay
That it will be minny an' minny a da-ay

Befoore Sup'rintindint, that's Flannigan,
Gits a whack at this very same sin agin.
From Finnigin to Flannigan
Repoorts won't be long agin."

. . . . . .

Wan da-ay on the siction av Finnigin,
On the road sup'rintinded be Flannigan,
A rail give way on a bit av a curve
An' some kyars wint off as they made the shwerve.
"There's nobody hurted," sez Finnigin,
"But repoorts must be made to Flannigan."
An' he winked at McGorrigan,
As married a Finnigin.

He wuz shantyin' thin, wuz Finnigin,
As minny a railroader's been agin,
An' the shmoky ol' lamp wuz burnin' bright
In Finnigin's shanty all that night—
Bilin' down his repoort, wuz Finnigin!
An' he writed this here: "Musther Flannigan:
Off agin, on agin,
Gone agin.—Finnigin."

*Strickland W. Gillilan* [1869-

## BARNEY McGEE

BARNEY McGEE, there's no end of good luck in you,
Will-o'-the-wisp, with a flicker of Puck in you,
Wild as a bull-pup and all of his pluck in you,—
Let a man tread on your coat and he'll see!—
Eyes like the lakes of Killarney for clarity,
Nose that turns up without any vulgarity,
Smile like a cherub, and hair that is carroty,—
Wow, you're a rarity, Barney McGee!
Mellow as Tarragon, prouder than Aragon—
Hardly a paragon, you will agree—
Here's all that's fine to you!
Books and old wine to you!
Girls be divine to you, Barney McGee!

Lucky the day when I met you unwittingly,
Dining where vagabonds came and went flittingly.
Here's some *Barbera* to drink it befittingly,
That day at *Silvio's*, Barney McGee!
Many's the time we have quaffed our Chianti there,
Listened to Silvio quoting us Dante there,—
Once more to drink *Nebiolo spumante* there,
How we'd pitch Pommery into the sea!
There where the gang of us met ere Rome rang of us,
They had the hang of us to a degree.
How they would trust to you!
That was but just to you.
Here's o'er their dust to you, Barney McGee!

Barney McGee, when you're sober you scintillate,
But when you're in drink you're the pride of the intellect;
Divil a one of us ever came in till late,
Once at the bar where you happened to be—
Every eye there like a spoke in you centering,
You with your eloquence, blarney, and bantering—
All Vagabondia shouts at your entering,
King of the Tenderloin, Barney McGee!
There's no satiety in your society
With the variety of your *esprit*.
Here's a long purse to you,
And a great thirst to you!
Fate be no worse to you, Barney McGee!

Och, and the girls whose poor hearts you deracinate,
Whirl and bewilder and flutter and fascinate!
Faith, it's so killing you are, you assassinate,—
Murder's the word for you, Barney McGee!
Bold when they're sunny and smooth when they're showery,—
Oh, but the style of you, fluent and flowery!
Chesterfield's way, with a touch of the Bowery!
How would they silence you, Barney *machree?*
Naught can your gab allay, learned as Rabelais
(You in his abbey lay once on a spree).
Here's to the smile of you
(Oh, but the guile of you!)
And a long while of you, Barney McGee!

Facile with phrases of length and Latinity,
Like *honorificabilitudinity*,
Where is the maid could resist your vicinity,
Wiled by the impudent grace of your plea?
Then your vivacity and pertinacity
Carry the day with the divil's audacity;
No mere veracity robs your sagacity
Of perspicacity, Barney McGee.
When all is new to them, what will you do to them?
Will you be true to them? Who shall decree?
Here's a fair strife to you!
Health and long life to you!
And a great wife to you, Barney McGee!

Barney McGee, you're the pick of gentility;
Nothing can phase you, you've such a facility;
Nobody ever yet found your utility,—
That is the charm of you, Barney McGee;
Under conditions that others would stammer in,
Still unperturbed as a cat or a Cameron,
Polished as somebody in the Decameron,
Putting the glamor on prince or Pawnee!
In your meanderin', love, and philanderin',
Calm as a mandarin sipping his tea!
Under the art of you,
Parcel and part of you,
Here's to the heart of you, Barney McGee!

You who were ever alert to befriend a man,
You who were ever the first to defend a man,
You who had always the money to lend a man,
Down on his luck and hard up for a V!
Sure, you'll be playing a harp in beatitude
(And a quare sight you will be in that attitude)—
Some day, where gratitude seems but a platitude,
You'll find your latitude, Barney McGee.
That's no flim-flam at all, frivol or sham at all,
Just the plain— Damn it all, have one with me!
Here's luck and more to you!
Friends by the score to you,
True to the core to you, Barney McGee!

*Richard Hovey* [1864–1900]

# PIPE AND CAN

## A RELIGIOUS USE OF TOBACCO

The Indian weed now withered quite;
Green at morn, cut down at night;
Shows thy decay: all flesh is hay:
Thus think, then drink Tobacco.

And when the smoke ascends on high,
Think thou behold'st the vanity
Of worldly stuff, gone with a puff:
Thus think, then drink Tobacco.

But when the pipe grows foul within,
Think of thy soul defiled with sin,
And that the fire doth it require:
Thus think, then drink Tobacco.

The ashes, that are left behind,
May serve to put thee still in mind
That unto dust return thou must:
Thus think, then drink Tobacco.

*Robert Wisdome (?)* [?–1568]

## ODE TO TOBACCO

Thou who, when fears attack,
Bid'st them avaunt, and Black
Care, at the horseman's back
Perching, unseatest;
Sweet when the morn is gray;
Sweet, when they've cleared away
Lunch; and at close of day
Possibly sweetest:

I have a liking old
For thee, though manifold
Stories, I know, are told,

Not to thy credit;
How one (or two at most)
Drops make a cat a ghost—
Useless, except to roast—
Doctors have said it:

How they who use fusees
All grow by slow degrees
Brainless as chimpanzees,
Meagre as lizards;
Go mad, and beat their wives;
Plunge (after shocking lives)
Razors and carving-knives
Into their gizzards.

Confound such knavish tricks!
Yet know I five or six
Smokers who freely mix
Still with their neighbors;
Jones—(who, I'm glad to say,
Asked leave of Mrs. J.)—
Daily absorbs a clay
After his labors.

Cats may have had their goose
Cooked by tobacco-juice;
Still why deny its use
Thoughtfully taken?
We're not as tabbies are:
Smith, take a fresh cigar!
Jones, the tobacco-jar!
Here's to thee, Bacon!

*Charles Stuart Calverley* [1831–1884]

## THE PIPE OF TOBACCO

Let the toper regale in his tankard of ale,
Or with alcohol moisten his thrapple,—
Only give me, I pray, a good pipe of soft clay,
Nicely tapered and thin in the stapple;—

And I shall puff, puff—let who will say enough!
No luxury else I'm in lack o',—
No malice I hoard 'gainst Queen, Prince, Duke, or Lord,
While I pull at my Pipe of Tobacco.

When I feel the hot strife of the battle of life,
And the prospect is aught but enticin'—
Mayhap some real ill, like a protested bill,
Dims the sunshine that tinged the horizon,—
Only let me puff, puff—be they ever so rough,
All the sorrows of life I lose track o';
The mists disappear, and the vista is clear,
With a soothing mild Pipe of Tobacco.

And when joy after pain, like the sun after rain,
Stills the waters long turbid and troubled,
That life's current may flow with a ruddier glow,
And the sense of enjoyment be doubled,—
Oh! let me puff, puff—till I feel *quantum suff.*
Such luxury still I'm in lack o'!
Be joy ever so sweet, it would be incomplete
Without a good Pipe of Tobacco.

Should my recreant muse—sometimes apt to refuse
The guidance of bit and of bridle—
Still blankly demur, spite of whip and of spur,
Unimpassioned, inconstant, or idle,—
Only let me puff, puff—till the brain cries enough;—
Such excitement is all I'm in lack o';
And the poetic vein soon to fancy gives rein,
Inspired by a Pipe of Tobacco.

And when with one accord, round the jovial board,
In friendship our bosoms are glowing,
While with toast and with song we the evening prolong,
And with nectar the goblets are flowing—
Still let us puff, puff—be life smooth, be it rough,
Such enjoyment we're ever in lack o':
The more peace and good-will will abound as we fill
A jolly good Pipe of Tobacco!

*John Usher* [?]

## INTER SODALES

OVER a pipe the Angel of Conversation
Loosens with glee the tassels of his purse,
And, in a fine spiritual exaltation,
Hastens, a rosy spendthrift, to disburse
The coins new-minted of imagination.

An amiable, a delicate animation
Informs our thought, and earnest we rehearse
The sweet old farce of mutual admiration
Over a pipe.

Heard in this hour's delicious divagation
How soft the song! the epigram how terse!
With what a genius for administration
We rearrange the rumbling universe,
And map the course of man's regeneration
Over a pipe!

*William Ernest Henley* [1849-1903]

## THE MENU

I BEG you come tonight and dine.
A welcome waits you, and sound wine,—
The Roederer chilly to a charm,
As Juno's breath the claret warm,
The sherry of an ancient brand.
No Persian pomp, you understand,—
A soup, a fish, two meats, and then
A salad fit for aldermen
(When aldermen, alas the days!
Were really worth their *mayonnaise*);
A dish of grapes whose clusters won
Their bronze in Carolinian sun;
Next, cheese—for you the Neufchâtel,
A bit of Cheshire likes me well;
*Café au lait* or coffee black,
With Kirsch or Kümmel or Cognac

(The German band in Irving Place
By this time purple in the face);
Cigars and pipes. These being through,
Friends shall drop in, a very few—
Shakespeare and Milton, and no more.
When these are guests I bolt the door,
With "Not at Home" to anyone
Excepting Alfred Tennyson.

*Thomas Bailey Aldrich* [1836–1907]

## AD MINISTRAM*

### AFTER HORACE

Dear Lucy, you know what my wish is,—
  I hate all your Frenchified fuss;
Your silly entrées and made dishes
  Were never intended for us.
No footman in lace and in ruffles
  Need dangle behind my arm-chair;
And never mind seeking for truffles,
  Although they be ever so rare.

But a plain leg of mutton, my Lucy,
  I prithee get ready at three:
Have it smoking, and tender and juicy,
  And what better meat can there be?
And when it has feasted the master,
  'Twill amply suffice for the maid;
Meanwhile I will smoke my canaster,
  And tipple my ale in the shade.

*William Makepeace Thackeray* [1811–1863]

## A SALAD

To make this condiment, your poet begs
The pounded yellow of two hard-boiled eggs;
Two boiled potatoes, passed through kitchen sieve,
Smoothness and softness to the salad give;
Let onion atoms lurk within the bowl,
And, half-suspected, animate the whole.
Of mordant mustard add a single spoon,
Distrust the condiment that bites so soon;

* For the original of this poem see page 3827.

But deem it not, thou man of herbs, a fault,
To add a double quantity of salt;
Four times the spoon with oil from Lucca drown,
And twice with vinegar procured from town;
And, lastly, o'er the flavored compound toss
A magic soupçon of anchovy sauce.
Oh, green and glorious! Oh, herbaceous treat!
'Twould tempt the dying anchorite to eat:
Back to the world he'd turn his fleeting soul,
And plunge his fingers in the salad-bowl!
Serenely full, the epicure would say,
Fate cannot harm me, I have dined to-day.

*Sydney Smith* [1771–1845]

## VERSES PLACED OVER THE DOOR AT THE ENTRANCE INTO THE APOLLO ROOM AT THE DEVIL TAVERN

Welcome all who lead or follow,
To the Oracle of Apollo—
Here he speaks out of his pottle,
Or the tripos, his tower bottle:
All his answers are divine,
Truth itself doth flow in wine.
Hang up all the poor hop-drinkers,
Cries old Sim, the king of skinkers;
He the half of life abuses,
That sits watering with the Muses.
Those dull girls no good can mean us;
Wine it is the milk of Venus,
And the poet's horse accounted:
Ply it, and you all are mounted.
'Tis the true Phœbian liquor,
Cheers the brain, makes wit the quicker,
Pays all debts, cures all diseases,
And at once three senses pleases.
Welcome all who lead or follow,
To the Oracle of Apollo.

*Ben Jonson* [1573?–1637]

## LINES ON THE MERMAID TAVERN

Souls of Poets dead and gone,
What Elysium have ye known,
Happy field or mossy cavern,
Choicer than the Mermaid Tavern?
Have ye tippled drink more fine
Than mine host's Canary wine?
Or are fruits of Paradise
Sweeter than those dainty pies
Of venison? O generous food!
Dressed as though bold Robin Hood
Would, with his Maid Marian,
Sup and bowse from horn and can.

I have heard that on a day
Mine host's sign-board flew away
Nobody knew whither, till
An Astrologer's old quill
To a sheepskin gave the story,—
Said he saw you in your glory,
Underneath a new-old Sign
Sipping beverage divine,
And pledging with contented smack
The Mermaid in the Zodiac!

Souls of Poets dead and gone,
What Elysium have ye known—
Happy field or mossy cavern—
Choicer than the Mermaid Tavern?

*John Keats* [1795–1821]

## "GIVE ME ALE"

When as the chill Sirocco blows,
And Winter tells a heavy tale;
When pyes and daws and rooks and crows
Sit cursing of the frosts and snows;
Then give me ale.

Ale in a Saxon rumkin then,
  Such as will make grimalkin prate;
Bids valor burgeon in tall men,
Quickens the poet's wit and pen,
    Despises fate.

Ale, that the absent battle fights,
  And frames the march of Swedish drum,
Disputes with princes, laws, and rights,
What's done and past tells mortal wights,
    And what's to come.

Ale, that the plowman's heart up-keeps
  And equals it with tyrants' thrones,
That wipes the eye that over-weeps,
And lulls in sure and dainty sleeps
    The o'er-wearied bones.

Grandchild of Ceres, Bacchus' daughter,
  Wine's emulous neighbor, though but stale,
Ennobling all the nymphs of water,
And filling each man's heart with laughter—
    Ha! give me ale!

*Unknown*

## "JOLLY GOOD ALE AND OLD"

**From "Gammer Gurton's Needle"**

I CANNOT eat but little meat,
  My stomach is not good;
But sure I think that I can drink
  With him that wears a hood.
Though I go bare, take ye no care,
  I nothing am a-cold;
I stuff my skin so full within
  Of jolly good ale and old.
    Back and side go bare, go bare;
    Both foot and hand go cold;
    But, belly, God send thee good ale enough,
    Whether it be new or old.

I love no roast but a nut-brown toast,
  And a crab laid in the fire;
A little bread shall do me stead;
  Much bread I not desire.
No frost nor snow, no wind, I trow,
  Can hurt me if I wold;
I am so wrapped and thoroughly lapped
  Of jolly good ale and old.

And Tib, my wife, that as her life
  Loveth well good ale to seek,
Full oft drinks she till ye may see
  The tears run down her cheek:
Then doth she trowl to me the bowl
  Even as a maltworm should,
And saith, "Sweetheart, I took my part
  Of this jolly good ale and old."

Now let them drink till they nod and wink,
  Even as good fellows should do;
They shall not miss to have the bliss
  Good ale doth bring men to;
And all poor souls that have scoured bowls
  Or have them lustily trolled,
God save the lives of them and their wives,
  Whether they be young or old.
    Back and side go bare, go bare;
    Both foot and hand go cold;
    But, belly, God send thee good ale enough,
    Whether it be new or old.

*John Still* [1543?–1608]

## DRINK TO-DAY

From "The Bloody Brother"

DRINK to-day, and drown all sorrow;
You shall perhaps not do it to-morrow:
Best, while you have it, use your breath;
There is no drinking after death.

Wine works the heart up, wakes the wit,
There is no cure 'gainst age but it:
It helps the headache, cough, and phthisic,
And is for all diseases physic.

Then let us swill, boys, for our health;
Who drinks well, loves the commonwealth.
And he that will to bed go sober
Falls with the leaf still in October.

*John Fletcher* [1579-1625]

## CORONEMUS NOS ROSIS ANTEQUAM MARCESCANT

LET us drink and be merry, dance, joke, and rejoice,
With claret and sherry, theorbo and voice!
The changeable world to our joy is unjust,
All treasure's uncertain,
Then down with your dust!
In frolics dispose your pounds, shillings, and pence,
For we shall be nothing a hundred years hence.

We'll sport and be free with Moll, Betty, and Dolly,
Have oysters and lobsters to cure melancholy:
Fish-dinners will make a man spring like a flea,
Dame Venus, love's lady,
Was born of the sea:
With her and with Bacchus we'll tickle the sense,
For we shall be past it a hundred years hence.

Your most beautiful bride who with garlands is crowned
And kills with each glance as she treads on the ground,
Whose lightness and brightness doth shine in such splendor
That none but the stars
Are thought fit to attend her,
Though now she be pleasant and sweet to the sense,
Will be damnable mouldy a hundred years hence.

Then why should we turmoil in cares and in fears,
Turn all our tranquill'ty to sighs and to tears?

Let's eat, drink, and play till the worms do corrupt us,
'Tis certain, *Post mortem*
*Nulla voluptas.*
For health, wealth and beauty, wit, learning and sense,
Must all come to nothing a hundred years hence.

*Thomas Jordan* [1612?–1685]

## THE EPICURE

### AFTER ANACREON

Fill the bowl with rosy wine,
Around our temples roses twine,
And let us cheerfully awhile,
Like the wine and roses, smile.
Crowned with roses, we contemn
Gyges' wealthy diadem.

To-day is ours; what do we fear?
To-day is ours; we have it here!
Let's treat it kindly, that it may
Wish, at least, with us to stay.
Let's banish business, banish sorrow,
To the gods belongs to-morrow.

*Abraham Cowley* [1618–1667]

## DRINKING

### AFTER ANACREON

The thirsty earth soaks up the rain,
And drinks, and gapes for drink again;
The plants suck in the earth, and are,
With constant drinking, fresh and fair;
The sea itself (which one would think
Should have but little need of drink),
Drinks twice ten thousand rivers up,
So filled that they o'erflow the cup.
The busy sun (and one would guess
By's drunken fiery face no less),

Drinks up the sea, and, when he's done,
The moon and stars drink up the sun:
They drink and dance by their own light;
They drink and revel all the night.
Nothing in nature's sober found,
But an eternal "health" goes round.
Fill up the bowl then, fill it high—
Fill all the glasses there; for why
Should every creature drink but I?
Why, men of morals, tell me why?

*Abraham Cowley* [1618–1667]

## THE WINTER GLASS

THEN let the chill Sirocco blow,
And gird us round with hills of snow;
Or else go whistle to the shore,
And make the hollow mountains roar.

Whilst we together jovial sit
Careless, and crowned with mirth and wit;
Where though bleak winds confine us home,
Our fancies round the world shall roam.

We'll think of all the friends we know,
And drink to all worth drinking to:
When having drank all thine and mine,
We rather shall want health than wine.

But where friends fail us, we'll supply
Our friendships with our charity.
Men that remote in sorrows live,
Shall by our lusty brimmers thrive.

We'll drink the wanting into wealth,
And those that languish into health,
The afflicted into joy, the oppressed
Into security and rest.

The worthy in disgrace shall find
Favor return again more kind,
And in restraint who stifled lie,
Shall taste the air of liberty.

The brave shall triumph in success,
The lovers shall have mistresses,
Poor unregarded virtue praise,
And the neglected poet bays.

Thus shall our healths do others good,
Whilst we ourselves do all we would;
For freed from envy and from care,
What would we be but what we are?

'Tis the plump grape's immortal juice
That does this happiness produce,
And will preserve us free together,
Maugre mischance, or wind and weather.

Then let old Winter take his course,
And roar abroad till he be hoarse,
And his lungs crack with ruthless ire,
It shall but serve to blow our fire.

Let him our little castle ply
With all his loud artillery,
Whilst sack and claret man the fort,
His fury shall become our sport.

Or, let him Scotland take, and there
Confine the plotting Presbyter;
His zeal may freeze, whilst we, kept warm
With love and wine, can know no harm.

*Charles Cotton* [1630–1687]

## HARRY CAREY'S GENERAL REPLY, TO THE LIBELLING GENTRY, WHO ARE ANGRY AT HIS WELFARE

With an honest old friend and a merry old song,
And a flask of old port, let me sit the night long,
And laugh at the malice of those who repine
That they must swig porter while I can drink wine.

I envy no mortal though ever so great,
Nor scorn I a wretch for his lowly estate;
But what I abhor and esteem as a curse
Is poorness of Spirit, not poorness of Purse.

Then dare to be generous, dauntless, and gay,
Let's merrily pass life's remainder away;
Upheld by our friends, we our foes may despise,
For the more we are envied, the higher we rise.

*Henry Carey* [ ? –1743]

## GAFFER GRAY

"Ho! why dost thou shiver and shake,
Gaffer Gray,
And why doth thy nose look so blue?"
" 'Tis the weather that's cold,
'Tis I'm grown very old,
And my doublet is not very new,
Well-a-day!"

"Then line that warm doublet with ale,
Gaffer Gray,
And warm thy old heart with a glass."
"Nay, but credit I've none,
And my money's all gone;
Then say how may that come to pass?
Well-a-day!"

"Hie away to the house on the brow,
Gaffer Gray,
And knock at the jolly priest's door."
"The priest often preaches
Against worldly riches,
But ne'er gives a mite to the poor,
Well-a-day!"

"The lawyer lives under the hill,
Gaffer Gray,
Warmly fenced both in back and in front."

"He will fasten his locks,
And will threaten the stocks,
Should he evermore find me in want.
Well-a-day!"

"The squire has fat beeves and brown ale,
Gaffer Gray,
And the season will welcome you there."
"His fat beeves and his beer,
And his merry new year,
Are all for the flush and the fair,
Well-a-day!"

"My keg is but low, I confess,
Gaffer Gray,
What then? While it lasts, man, we'll live."
"The poor man alone,
When he hears the poor moan,
Of his morsel a morsel will give,
Well-a-day."

*Thomas Holcroft* [1745–1809]

## "A REASON FAIR TO FILL MY GLASS"

I've oft been asked by prosing souls
And men of sober tongue,
What joys there are in draining bowls
And tippling all night long?
But though these cautious knaves I scorn,
For once I'll not disdain
To tell them why I drink till morn
And fill my glass again.

'Tis by the glow my bumper gives
Life's picture's mellow made;
The fading light then brightly lives,
And softly sinks the shade:
Some happier tint still rises there
With every drop I drain,
And that I think's a reason fair
To fill my glass again.

My muse, too, when her wings are dry,
No frolic flight will take,
But round the bowl she'll dip and fly
Like swallows round a lake;
Then if the nymphs will have their share
Before they'll bless their swain,
Why that I think's a reason fair
To fill my glass again.

In life I've rung all changes through,
Run every pleasure down
'Mid each extreme of folly, too,
And lived with half the town;
For me there's nothing new or rare
Till wine deceives my brain,
And that I think's a reason fair
To fill my glass again.

There's many a lad I knew is dead,
And many a lass grown old,
And as the lesson strikes my head
My weary heart grows cold;
But wine awhile drives off despair,
Nay, bids a hope remain,
Why, that I think's a reason fair
To fill my glass again.

I find too when I stint my glass
And sit with sober air,
I'm posed by some dull reasoning ass
Who treads the path of care;
Or, harder still, am doomed to bear
Some coxcomb's fribbling strain,
And that I'm sure's a reason fair
To fill my glass again.

Though hipped and vexed at England's fate
In these convulsive days,
I can't endure the ruined state
My sober eye surveys;

But through the bottle's dazzling glare
The gloom is seen less plain,
And that I think's a reason fair
To fill my glass again.

*Charles Morris* [1745–1838]

## "LET THE TOAST PASS"

From "The School for Scandal"

HERE'S to the maiden of bashful fifteen,
Here's to the widow of fifty;
Here's to the flaunting extravagant quean,
And here's to the housewife that's thrifty.

*Let the toast pass,*
*Drink to the lass,*
*I'll warrant she'll prove an excuse for the glass.*

Here's to the charmer whose dimples we prize,
Now to the maid who has none, sir;
Here's to the girl with a pair of blue eyes,
And here's to the nymph with but one, sir.

Here's to the maid with a bosom of snow,
And to her that's as brown as a berry;
Here's to the wife, with a face full of woe,
And now to the girl that is merry.

For let 'em be clumsy, or let 'em be slim,
Young or ancient, I care not a feather;
So fill the pint bumper quite up to the brim,
So fill up your glasses, nay fill to the brim,
And let us e'en toast them together.

*Let the toast pass,*
*Drink to the lass,*
*I'll warrant she'll prove an excuse for the glass.*

*Richard Brinsley Sheridan* [1751–1816]

## THE YEAR THAT'S AWA'

HERE's to the year that's awa'!
We will drink it in strong and in sma';
And here's to ilk bonnie young lassie we lo'ed,
While swift flew the year that's awa'.

Here's to the sodger who bled,
And the sailor who bravely did fa';
Their fame is alive though their spirits are fled
On the wings of the year that's awa'.

Here's to the friends we can trust
When storms of adversity blaw;
May they live in our songs and be nearest our hearts,
Nor depart like the year that's awa'.

*John Dunlop* [1755–1820]

## JOHN BARLEYCORN

THERE were three kings into the east,
Three kings both great and high;
And they hae sworn a solemn oath
John Barleycorn should die.

They took a plough and ploughed him down,
Put clods upon his head;
And they hae sworn a solemn oath
John Barleycorn was dead.

But the cheerful spring came kindly on,
And showers began to fall:
John Barleycorn got up again,
And sore surprised them all.

The sultry suns of summer came,
And he grew thick and strong;
His head weel armed wi' pointed spears,
That no one should him wrong.

The sober autumn entered mild,
  When he grew wan and pale;
His bending joints and drooping head
  Showed he began to fail.

His color sickened more and more,
  He faded into age;
And then his enemies began
  To show their deadly rage.

They've ta'en a weapon, long and sharp,
  And cut him by the knee;
Then tied him fast upon a cart,
  Like a rogue for forgerie.

They laid him down upon his back,
  And cudgelled him full sore;
They hung him up before the storm,
  And turned him o'er and o'er.

They fillèd up a darksome pit
  With water to the brim:
They heavèd in John Barleycorn,
  There let him sink or swim.

They laid him out upon the floor,
  To work him further woe:
And still, as signs of life appeared,
  They tossed him to and fro.

They wasted o'er a scorching flame
  The marrow of his bones;
But a miller used him worst of all,
  For he crushed him 'tween two stones.

And they hae ta'en his very heart's blood,
  And drank it round and round,
And still the more and more they drank,
  Their joy did more abound.

John Barleycorn was a herc bold,
Of noble enterprise;
For if you do but taste his blood,
'Twill make your courage rise.

'Twill make a man forget his woe;
'Twill heighten all his joy:
'Twill make the widow's heart to sing,
Though the tear were in her eye.

Then let us toast John Barleycorn,
Each man a glass in hand;
And may his great posterity
Ne'er fail in old Scotland!

*Robert Burns* [1759-1796]

## "FILL THE BUMPER FAIR"

FILL the bumper fair!
Every drop we sprinkle
O'er the brow of Care
Smooths away a wrinkle.
Wit's electric flame
Ne'er so swiftly passes
As when through the frame
It shoots from brimming glasses.
*Fill the bumper fair!*
*Every drop we sprinkle*
*O'er the brow of Care*
*Smooths away a wrinkle.*

Sages can, they say,
Grasp the lightning's pinions,
And bring down its ray
From the starred dominions:—
So we, Sages, sit,
And, 'mid bumpers bright'ning,
From the Heaven of Wit
Draw down all its lightning.

Wouldst thou know what first
Made our souls inherit
This ennobling thirst
From wine's celestial spirit?
It chanced upon that day,
When, as bards inform us,
Prometheus stole away
The living fires that warm us:

The careless Youth, when up
To Glory's fount aspiring,
Took nor urn nor cup
To hide the pilfered fire in.—
But, oh his joy, when, round
The halls of Heaven spying,
Among the stars he found
A bowl of Bacchus lying!

Some drops were in that bowl,
Remains of last night's pleasure,
With which the Sparks of Soul
Mixed their burning treasure.
Hence the goblet's shower
Hath such spells to win us;
Hence its mighty power
O'er the flame within us.
*Fill the bumper fair!*
*Every drop we sprinkle*
*O'er the brow of Care*
*Smooths away a wrinkle.*

*Thomas Moore* [1779-1852]

## "WREATHE THE BOWL"

Wreathe the bowl
With flowers of soul,
The brightest Wit can find us;
We'll take a flight
Towards heaven to-night,

And leave dull earth behind us!
Should Love amid
The wreaths be hid
That Joy, the enchanter, brings us,
No danger fear
While wine is near—
We'll drown him if he stings us.
Then, wreathe the bowl
With flowers of soul,
The brightest Wit can find us;
We'll take a flight
Towards heaven to-night,
And leave dull earth behind us!

'Twas nectar fed
Of old, 'tis said,
Their Junos, Joves, Apollos;
And man may brew
His nectar too;
The rich receipt's as follows:—
Take wine like this;
Let looks of bliss
Around it well be blended;
Then bring Wit's beam
To warm the stream,
And there's your nectar splendid!
So wreathe the bowl
With flowers of soul,
The brightest Wit can find us;
We'll take a flight
Towards heaven to-night,
And leave dull earth behind us!

Say, why did Time
His glass sublime
Fill up with sands unsightly,
When wine, he knew,
Runs brisker through,
And sparkles far more brightly?
Oh, lend it us,
And, smiling thus,

The glass in two we'd sever,
Make pleasure glide
In double tide,
And fill both ends forever!
Then wreathe the bowl
With flowers of soul,
The brightest Wit can find us;
We'll take a flight
Towards heaven to-night,
And leave dull earth behind us!

*Thomas Moore* [1779-1852]

## SAINT PERAY

When to any saint I pray,
It shall be to Saint Peray.
He alone, of all the brood,
Ever did me any good:
Many I have tried that are
Humbugs in the calendar.

On the Atlantic, faint and sick,
Once I prayed Saint Dominick:
He was holy, sure, and wise;—
Was 't not he that did devise
Auto da Fès and rosaries?—
But for one in my condition
This good saint was no physician.

Next, in pleasant Normandie,
I made a prayer to Saint Denis,
In the great cathedral, where
All the ancient kings repose;
But, how I was swindled there
At the "Golden Fleece,"—he knows!

In my wanderings, vague and various,
Reaching Naples—as I lay
Watching Vesuvius from the bay,
I besought Saint Januarius.
But I was a fool to try him;

Naught I said could liquefy him;
And I swear he did me wrong,
Keeping me shut up so long
In that pest-house, with obscene
Jews and Greeks and things unclean—
What need had I of quarantine?

In Sicily at least a score,—
In Spain about as many more,—
And in Rome almost as many
As the loves of Don Giovanni,
Did I pray to—sans reply;
Devil take the tribe!—said I.

Worn with travel, tired and lame,
To Assisi's walls I came:
Sad and full of homesick fancies,
I addressed me to Saint Francis:
But the beggar never did
Anything as he was bid,
Never gave me aught—but fleas,—
Plenty had I at Assise.

But in Pròvence, near Vaucluse
  Hard by the Rhone, I found a Saint
Gifted with a wondrous juice,
  Potent for the worst complaint.

'Twas at Avignon that first—
In the witching time of thirst—
To my brain the knowledge came
Of this blessed Catholic's name;
Forty miles of dust that day
Made me welcome Saint Peray.

Though till then I had not heard
Aught about him, ere a third
Of a litre passed my lips,
All saints else were in eclipse.
For his gentle spirit glided
  With such magic into mine,
That methought such bliss as I did
  Poet never drew from wine.

Rest he gave me and refection,—
Chastened hopes, calm retrospection,—
Softened images of sorrow,
Bright forebodings for the morrow,—
Charity for what is past,—
Faith in something good at last.

Now, why should any almanack
The name of this good creature lack?
Or wherefore should the breviary
Omit a saint so sage and merry?
The Pope himself should grant a day
Especially to Saint Peray.
But, since no day hath been appointed,
On purpose, by the Lord's anointed,
Let us not wait—we'll do him right;
Send round your bottles, Hal—and set your night.

*Thomas William Parsons* [1819-1892]

## SPARKLING AND BRIGHT

SPARKLING and bright in liquid light,
Does the wine our goblets gleam in;
With hue as red as the rosy bed
Which a bee would choose to dream in.
*Then fill to-night, with hearts as light,*
*To loves as gay and fleeting*
*As bubbles that swim on the beaker's brim.*
*And break on the lips while meeting.*

Oh! if Mirth might arrest the flight
Of Time through Life's dominions,
We here a while would now beguile
The graybeard of his pinions,
*To drink to-night, with hearts as light,*
*To loves as gay and fleeting*
*As bubbles that swim on the beaker's brim,*
*And break on the lips while meeting.*

But since Delight can't tempt the wight,
  Nor fond Regret delay him,
Nor Love himself can hold the elf,
  Nor sober Friendship stay him,
    *We'll drink to-night, with hearts as light,*
      *To loves as gay and fleeting*
    *As bubbles that swim on the beaker's brim,*
      *And break on the lips while meeting.*

*Charles Fenno Hoffman* [1806–1884]

## THE MAHOGANY TREE

Christmas is here:
Winds whistle shrill,
Icy and chill,
Little care we:
Little we fear
Weather without,
Sheltered about
The Mahogany Tree.

Once on the boughs
Birds of rare plume
Sang, in its bloom;
Night-birds are we:
Here we carouse,
Singing like them,
Perched round the stem
Of the jolly old tree.

Here let us sport,
Boys, as we sit;
Laughter and wit
Flashing so free.
Life is but short—
When we are gone,
Let them sing on
Round the old tree.

Evenings we knew,
Happy as this;

Faces we miss,
Pleasant to see.
Kind hearts and true,
Gentle and just,
Peace to your dust!
We sing round the tree.

Care, like a dun,
Lurks at the gate:
Let the dog wait;
Happy we'll be!
Drink, every one;
Pile up the coals,
Fill the red bowls
Round the old tree!

Drain we the cup.—
Friend, art afraid?
Spirits are laid
In the Red Sea.
Mantle it up;
Empty it yet;
Let us forget,
Round the old tree.

Sorrows, begone!
Life and its ills,
Duns and their bills,
Bid we to flee.
Come with the dawn,
Blue-devil sprite,
Leave us to-night
Round the old tree.

*William Makepeace Thackeray* [1811–1863]

## TODLIN' HAME

When I ha'e a saxpence under my thoom,
Then I get credit in ilka toun;
But aye when I'm puir they bid me gang by,
Oh, poverty parts gude company!

Todlin' hame, todlin' hame,
Couldna' my love come todlin' hame?

Fair fa' the gudewife, and send her gude sale;
She gi'es us white bannocks to relish her ale;
Syne, if that her tippeny chance to be sma',
We tak' a gude scour o't, and ca't awa.
  Todlin' hame, todlin' hame,
  As round as a neep come todlin' hame.

My kimmer and I lay down to sleep,
Wi' twa pint-stoups at our bed's feet;
And aye when we wakened, we drank them dry.
What think ye o' my wee kimmer and I?
  Todlin' butt, and todlin' ben,
  Sae round as my love comes todlin' hame.

Leeze me on liquor, my todlin' dow,
Ye're aye gude-humored when weetin' your mou'!
When sober sae sour, ye'll fecht wi' a flea,
That 'tis a blithe nicht to the bairns and me,
  When, todlin' hame, todlin' hame,
  When, round as a neep, ye come todlin' hame.

*Unknown*

## THE CRUISKEEN LAWN

Let the farmer praise his grounds,
Let the huntsman praise his hounds,
  The shepherd his dew-scented lawn;
But I, more blest than they,
Spend each happy night and day
  With my charming little cruiskeen lawn, lawn, lawn,
  My charming little cruiskeen lawn.

Gra machree ma cruiskeen,
Slainté geal mavourneen,
  's gra machree a cooleen bawn.
Gra machree ma cruiskeen,
Slainté geal mavourneen,
Gra machree a cooleen bawn, bawn, bawn,
  's gra machree a cooleen bawn.

Immortal and divine,
Great Bacchus, god of wine,
  Create me by adoption your son;
In hope that you'll comply,
My glass shall ne'er run dry,
  Nor my smiling little cruiskeen lawn.

And when grim death appears,
In a few but pleasant years,
  To tell me that my glass has run;
I'll say, Begone, you knave,
For bold Bacchus gave me leave
  To take another cruiskeen lawn.

Then fill your glasses high,
Let's not part with lips a-dry,
  Though the lark now proclaims it is dawn;
And since we can't remain,
May we shortly meet again,
  To fill another cruiskeen lawn.

*Unknown*

## GIVE ME THE OLD

Old wine to drink!
  Ay, give the slippery juice
That drippeth from the grape thrown loose
  Within the tun;
Plucked from beneath the cliff
Of sunny-sided Teneriffe,
 And ripened 'neath the blink
  Of India's sun!
  Peat whiskey hot,
Tempered with well-boiled water!
These make the long night shorter,—
  Forgetting not
Good stout old English porter.

Old wood to burn!
Ay, bring the hill-side beech
From where the owlets meet and screech,

And ravens croak;
The crackling pine, and cedar sweet;
Bring too a clump of fragrant peat,
Dug 'neath the fern;
The knotted oak,
A fagot too, perhap,
Whose bright flame, dancing, winking,
Shall light us at our drinking;
While the oozing sap
Shall make sweet music to our thinking.

Old books to read!
Ay, bring those nodes of wit,
The brazen-clasped, the vellum writ,
Time-honored tomes!
The same my sire scanned before,
The same my grandsire thumbèd o'er,
The same his sire from college bore,
The well-earned meed
Of Oxford's domes:
Old Homer blind,
Old Horace, rake Anacreon, by
Old Tully, Plautus, Terence lie;
Mort Arthur's olden minstrelsie,
Quaint Burton, quainter Spenser, ay!
And Gervase Markham's venerie—
Nor leave behind
The Holye Book by which we live and die.

Old friends to talk!
Ay, bring those chosen few,
The wise, the courtly, and the true,
So rarely found;
Him for my wine, him for my stud,
Him for my easel, distich, bud
In mountain-walk!
Bring Walter good,
With soulful Fred, and learnèd Will,
And thee, my alter ego (dearer still
For every mood).

These add a bouquet to my wine!
These add a sparkle to my pine!
  If these I tine,
Can books, or fire, or wine be good?

*Robert Hinckley Messinger* [1811-1874]

## THE SPIRIT OF WINE

*The Spirit of Wine*
*Sang in my glass, and I listened*
*With love to his odorous music,*
*His flushed and magnificent song.*

—"I am health, I am heart, I am life!
For I give for the asking
The fire of my father, the Sun,
And the strength of my mother, the Earth.
Inspiration in essence,
I am wisdom and wit to the wise,
His visible muse to the poet,
The soul of desire to the lover,
  The genius of laughter to all.

"Come, lean on me, ye that are weary!
Rise, ye faint-hearted and doubting!
Haste, ye that lag by the way!
I am Pride, the consoler;
Valor and Hope are my henchmen;
I am the Angel of Rest.

"I am life, I am wealth, I am fame:
For I captain an army
Of shining and generous dreams;
And mine, too, all mine, are the keys
Of that secret spiritual shrine,
Where, his work-a-day soul put by,
Shut in with his saint of saints—
With his radiant and conquering self—
Man worships, and talks, and is glad.

"Come, sit with me, ye that are lonely,
Ye that are paid with disdain,
Ye that are chained, and would soar!
I am beauty and love;
I am friendship, the comforter;
I am that which forgives and forgets."—

*The Spirit of Wine*
*Sang in my heart, and I triumphed*
*In the savor and scent of his music,*
*His magnetic and mastering song.*

*William Ernest Henley* [1849–1903]

## "DAY AND NIGHT MY THOUGHTS INCLINE"

Day and night my thoughts incline
To the blandishments of wine:
Jars were made to drain, I think,
Wine, I know, was made to drink.

When I die, (the day be far!)
Should the potters make a jar
Out of this poor clay of mine,
Let the jar be filled with wine!

*Richard Henry Stoddard* [1825–1903]

## FALSTAFF'S SONG

Where's he that died o' Wednesday?
  What place on earth hath he?
A tailor's yard beneath, I wot,
  Where worms approaching be;
For the wight that died o' Wednesday,
  Just laid the light below,
Is dead as the varlet turned to clay
  A score of years ago.

Where's he that died o' Sabba' day?
  Good Lord, I'd not be he!
The best of days is foul enough
  From this world's fare to flee;

And the saint that died o' Sabba' day,
With his grave turf yet to grow,
Is dead as the sinner brought to pray
A hundred years ago.

Where's he that died o' yesterday?
What better chance hath he
To clink the can and toss the pot
When this night's junkets be?
For the lad that died o' yesterday
Is just as dead—ho! ho!—
As the whoreson knave men laid away
A thousand years ago.

*Edmund Clarence Stedman* [1833-1908]

## THE MALTWORM'S MADRIGAL

I DRINK of the Ale of Southwark, I drink of the Ale of Chepe;
At noon I dream on the settle; at night I cannot sleep;
For my love, my love it groweth; I waste me all the day;
And when I see sweet Alison, I know not what to say.

The sparrow when he spieth his Dear upon the tree,
He beateth-to his little wing; he chirketh lustily;
But when I see sweet Alison, the words begin to fail;
I wot that I shall die of Love—an I die not of Ale.

Her lips are like the muscadel; her brows are black as ink;
Her eyes are bright as beryl stones that in the tankard wink;
But when she sees me coming, she shrilleth out—"Te-Hee!
Fye on thy ruddy nose, Cousin, what lackest thou of me?

"Fye on thy ruddy nose, Cousin! Why be thine eyes so small?
Why go thy legs tap-lappetty like men that fear to fall?
Why is thy leathern doublet besmeared with stain and spot?
Go to. Thou art no man (she saith)—thou art a Pottle-pot!"

"No man," i' faith. "No man!" she saith. And "Pottle-
pot" thereto!
"Thou sleepest like our dog all day; thou drink'st as fishes
do."
I would that I were Tibb the dog; he wags at her his tail;
Or would that I were fish, in truth, and all the sea were Ale!

So I drink of the Ale of Southwark, I drink of the Ale of
Chepe;
All day I dream in the sunlight; I dream and eke I weep,
But little lore of loving can any flagon teach,
For when my tongue is loosèd most, then most I lose my
speech.

*Austin Dobson* [1840–1921]

## THE POWER OF MALT

Why, if 'tis dancing you would be,
There's brisker pipes than poetry.
Say, for what were hop-yards meant,
Or why was Burton built on Trent?
Oh, many a peer of England brews
Livelier liquor than the Muse,
And malt does more than Milton can
To justify God's ways to man.
Ale, man, ale's the stuff to drink
For fellows whom it hurts to think:
Look into the pewter pot
To see the world as the world's not.

*Alfred Edward Housman* [1859–1936]

## A STEIN SONG

From "Spring"

Give a rouse, then, in the Maytime
For a life that knows no fear!
Turn night-time into daytime
With the sunlight of good cheer!
For it's always fair weather
When good fellows get together.
With a stein on the table and a good song ringing clear.

When the wind comes up from Cuba,
And the birds are on the wing,
And our hearts are patting juba
To the banjo of the spring,
Then it's no wonder whether
The boys will get together,
With a stein on the table and a cheer for everything.

For we're all frank-and-twenty
When the spring is in the air;
And we've faith and hope a-plenty,
And we've life and love to spare;
And it's birds of a feather
When we all get together,
With a stein on the table and a heart without a care

For we know the world is glorious,
And the goal a golden thing,
And that God is not censorious
When his children have their fling;
And life slips its tether
When the boys get together,
With a stein on the table in the fellowship of spring.

*Richard Hovey* [1864–1900]

## THE KAVANAGH

A STONE jug and a pewter mug,
And a table set for three!
A jug and a mug at every place,
And a biscuit or two with Brie!
Three stone jugs of Cruiskeen Lawn,
And a cheese like crusted foam!
The Kavanagh receives to-night!
McMurrough is at home!

We three and the barley-bree!
And a health to the one away,
Who drifts down careless Italy,
God's wanderer and estray!

For friends are more than Arno's store
Of garnered charm, and he
Were blither with us here the night
Than Titian bids him be.

Throw ope the window to the stars,
And let the warm night in!
Who knows what revelry in Mars
May rhyme with rouse akin?
Fill up and drain the loving cup
And leave no drop to waste!
The moon looks in to see what's up—
Begad, she'd like a taste!

What odds if Leinster's kingly roll
Be now an idle thing?
The world is his who takes his toll,
A vagrant or a king.
What though the crown be melted down,
And the heir a gypsy roam?
The Kavanagh receives to-night!
McMurrough is at home!

We three and the barley-bree!
And the moonlight on the floor!
Who were a man to do with less?
What emperor has more?
Three stone jugs of Cruiskeen Lawn,
And three stout hearts to drain
A slanter to the truth in the heart of youth
And the joy of the love of men.

*Richard Hovey* [1864-1900]

# GLINTS O' SUNSHINE

## SONG

From "Love's Labor's Lost"

### I—SPRING

When daisies pied, and violets blue,
  And lady-smocks all silver-white,
And cuckoo-buds of yellow hue,
  Do paint the meadows with delight,
The cuckoo then, on every tree,
Mocks married men; for thus sings he,
    Cuckoo;
Cuckoo, cuckoo, — O word of fear,
Unpleasing to a married ear!

When shepherds pipe on oaten straws,
  And merry larks are ploughmen's clocks,
When turtles tread, and rooks, and daws,
  And maidens bleach their summer smocks
The cuckoo then, on every tree,
Mocks married men; for thus sings he,
    Cuckoo;
Cuckoo, cuckoo, — O word of fear,
Unpleasing to a married ear!

### II — WINTER

When icicles hang by the wall,
  And Dick the shepherd blows his nail,
And Tom bears logs into the hall,
  And milk comes frozen home in pail,
When blood is nipped, and ways be foul,
Then nightly sings the staring owl,
    Tu-who;
Tu-whit, tu-who,—a merry note,
While greasy Joan doth keel the pot.

When all aloud the wind doth blow,
  And coughing drowns the parson's saw,
And birds sit brooding in the snow,
  And Marian's nose looks red and raw,
When roasted crabs hiss in the bowl,
Then nightly sings the staring owl,
        Tu-who;
Tu-whit, tu-who,—a merry note,
While greasy Joan doth keel the pot.

*William Shakespeare* [1564–1616]

## THE WIDOW

The widow can bake, and the widow can brew,
The widow can shape, an' the widow can sew,
An' mony braw things the widow can do;
  Then have at the widow, my laddie.
Wi' courage attack her baith early an' late;
To kiss her an' clap her ye maunna be blate:
Speak weel, an' do better: for that's the best gate
  To win a young widow, my laddie.

The widow she's youthfu', an' never ae hair
The waur o' the wearing, an' has a good skair
O' everything lovely; she's witty an' fair,
  An' has a rich jointure, my laddie.
What could ye wish better, your pleasure to crown,
Than a widow, the bonniest toast in the town,
Wi' naithing but draw in your stool and sit down,
  An' sport wi' the widow, my laddie.

Then till her, an' kill her wi' courtesy dead,
Though stark love an' kindness be a' ye can plead;
Be heartsome an' airy, an' hope to succeed
  Wi' a bonny gay widow, my laddie.
Strike iron while it's het, if ye'd have it to wald;
For fortune ay favors the active an' bauld,
But ruins the wooer that's thoughtless an' cauld,
  Unfit for the widow, my laddie.

*Allan Ramsay* [1686–1758]

## SNEEZING

What a moment, what a doubt!
All my nose is inside out, —
All my thrilling, tickling caustic,
Pyramid rhinocerostic,
  Wants to sneeze and cannot do it!
How it yearns me, thrills me, stings me,
How with rapturous torment wrings me!
  Now says, "Sneeze, you fool,—get through it."
Shee—shee—oh! 'tis most del-ishi—
Ishi—ishi—most del-ishi!
(Hang it, I shall sneeze till spring!)
Snuff is a delicious thing.

*Leigh Hunt* [1784–1859]

## CAUTIONARY VERSES TO YOUTH OF BOTH SEXES

My little dears, who learn to read, pray early learn to shun
That very silly thing indeed which people call a pun;
Read Entick's rules, and 'twill be found how simple an offence
It is to make the self-same sound afford a double sense.

For instance, ale may make you ail, your aunt an ant may kill,
You in a vale may buy a veil, and Bill may pay the bill.
Or if to France your bark you steer, at Dover, it may be
A peer appears upon the pier, who, blind, still goes to sea.

Thus one might say, when to a treat good friends accept our greeting,
'Tis meet that men who meet to eat should eat their meat when meeting.
Brawn on the board's no bore indeed, although from boar prepared;
Nor can the fowl, on which we feed, foul feeding be declared.

Thus one ripe fruit may be a pear, and yet be pared again,
And still be one, which seemeth rare until we do explain.

It therefore should be all your aim to speak with ample care:
For who, however fond of game, would choose to swallow
hair?

A fat man's gait may make us smile, who have no gate to
close:
The farmer sitting on his stile no stylish person knows:
Perfumers men of scents must be; some Scilly men are
bright;
A brown man oft deep read we see, a black a wicked wight.

Most wealthy men good manors have, however vulgar they;
And actors still the harder slave, the oftener they play;
So poets can't the baize obtain, unless their tailors choose;
While grooms and coachmen, not in vain, each evening seek
the Mews.

The dyer who by dyeing lives, a dire life maintains;
The glazier, it is known, receives his profits from his panes:
By gardeners thyme is tied, 'tis true, when spring is in its
prime;
But time or tide won't wait for you, if you are tied for time.

Then now you see, my little dears, the way to make a pun;
A trick which you, through coming years, should sedulously
shun:
The fault admits of no defence; for wheresoe'er 'tis found,
You sacrifice for sound the sense: the sense is never sound.

So let your words and actions too, one single meaning prove,
And, just in all you say or do, you'll gain esteem and love:
In mirth and play no harm you'll know, when duty's task
is done;
But parents ne'er should let you go unpunished for a pun.

*Theodore Edward Hook* [1788–1841]

## A CREDO

For the sole edification
Of this decent congregation,
Goodly people, by your grant
I will sing a holy chant—

I will sing a holy chant.
If the ditty sound but oddly,
'Twas a father, wise and godly,
Sang it so long ago--
Then sing as Martin Luther sang,
As Doctor Martin Luther sang:
"Who loves not wine, woman, and song,
He is a fool his whole life long!"

He, by custom patriarchal,
Loved to see the beaker sparkle;
And he thought the wine improved,
Tasted by the lips he loved—
By the kindly lips he loved.
Friends, I wish this custom pious
Duly were observèd by us,
To combine love, song, wine,
And sing as Martin Luther sang,
As Doctor Martin Luther sang:
"Who loves not wine, woman, and song,
He is a fool his whole life long!"

Who refuses this our Credo,
And who will not sing as we do,
Were he holy as John Knox,
I'd pronounce him heterodox!
I'd pronounce him heterodox,
And from out this congregation,
With a solemn commination,
Banish quick the heretic,
Who will not sing as Luther sang,
As Doctor Martin Luther sang:
"Who loves not wine, woman, and song,
He is a fool his whole life long!"

*William Makepeace Thackeray* [1811-1863]

## THE LAY OF THE LEVITE

THERE is a sound that's dear to me,
It haunts me in my sleep;
I wake, and, if I hear it not,
I cannot choose but weep.

Above the roaring of the wind,
  Above the river's flow,
Methinks I hear the mystic cry
  Of "Clo!—old Clo!"

The exile's song, it thrills among
  The dwellings of the free;
Its sound is strange to English ears,
  But 'tis not strange to me;
For it hath shook the tented field
  In ages long ago,
And hosts have quailed before the cry
  Of "Clo!—old Clo!"

O, lose it not! forsake it not.
  And let no time efface
The memory of that solemn sound,
  The watchword of our race;
For not by dark and eagle eye,
  The Hebrew shall ye know,
So well as by the plaintive cry
  Of "Clo!—old Clo!"

Even now, perchance, by Jordan's banks,
  Or Sidon's sunny walls,
Where, dial-like, to portion time
  The palm-tree's shadow falls,
The pilgrims, wending on their way,
  Will linger as they go,
And listen to the distant cry
  Of "Clo!—old Clo!"

*William Edmondstoune Aytoun* [1813–1865]

## EARLY RISING

"God bless the man who first invented sleep!"
  So Sancho Panza said, and so say I:
And bless him, also, that he didn't keep
  His great discovery to himself; nor try
To make it—as the lucky fellow might—
A close monopoly by patent-right!

Yes; bless the man who first invented sleep
 (I really can't avoid the iteration);
But blast the man, with curses loud and deep,
 Whate'er the rascal's name, or age, or station,
Who first invented, and went round advising,
That artificial cut-off,—Early Rising!

"Rise with the lark, and with the lark to bed,"
 Observes some solemn, sentimental owl;
Maxims like these are very cheaply said:
 But, ere you make yourself a fool or fowl,
Pray, just inquire about his rise and fall,
And whether larks have any beds at all!

The time for honest folks to be abed
 Is in the morning, if I reason right;
And he who cannot keep his precious head
 Upon his pillow till it's fairly light,
And so enjoy his forty morning winks,
Is up to knavery, or else—he drinks!

Thomson, who sang about the "Seasons," said
 It was a glorious thing to *rise* in season;
But then he said it—lying—in his bed,
 At ten o'clock, A. M.,—the very reason
He wrote so charmingly. The simple fact is,
His preaching wasn't sanctioned by his practice.

'Tis, doubtless, well to be sometimes awake,—
 Awake to duty, and awake to truth,—
But when, alas! a nice review we take
 Of our best deeds and days, we find, in sooth,
The hours that leave the slightest cause to weep
Are those we passed in childhood, or asleep!

'Tis beautiful to leave the world awhile
 For the soft visions of the gentle night;
And free, at last, from mortal care or guile,
 To live as only in the angels' sight,
In sleep's sweet realm so cozily shut in,
Where, at the worst, we only *dream* of sin!

So let us sleep and give the Maker praise.
  I like the lad who, when his father thought
To clip his morning nap by hackneyed phrase
  Of vagrant worm by early songster caught,
Cried, "Served him right!—it's not at all surprising;
The worm was punished, sir, for early rising!"

*John Godfrey Saxe* [1816–1887]

## EL CAPITAN-GENERAL

There was a captain-general who ruled in Vera Cruz,
And what we used to hear of him was always evil news:
He was a pirate on the sea—a robber on the shore,
The Señor Don Alonzo Estabán San Salvador.

There was a Yankee skipper who round about did roam;
His name was Stephen Folger, and Nantucket was his home:
And having gone to Vera Cruz, he had been skinned full sore
By the Señor Don Alonzo Estabán San Salvador.

But having got away alive, though all his cash was gone,
He said, "If there is vengeance, I will surely try it on!
And I do wish I may be damned if I don't clear the score
With Señor Don Alonzo Estabán San Salvador!"

He shipped a crew of seventy men—well-armèd men were
  they,
And sixty of them in the hold he darkly stowed away;
And, sailing back to Vera Cruz, was sighted from the shore
By the Señor Don Alonzo Estabán San Salvador.

With twenty-five soldados he came on board so pleased,
And said, "*Maldito* Yankee—again your ship is seized.
How many sailors have you got?" Said Folger, "Ten—or
  more,"
To the Captain Don Alonzo Estabán San Salvador.

"But come into my cabin and take a glass of wine.
I do suppose, as usual, I'll have to pay a fine:

I have got some old Madeira, and we'll talk the matter o'er—
My Captain Don Alonzo Estabán San Salvador."

And as over that Madeira the captain-general boozed,
It seemed to him as if his head was getting quite confused;
For it happened that some morphine had travelled from
"the store"
To the glass of Don Alonzo Estabán San Salvador.

"What is it makes the vessel roll? What sounds are these
I hear?
It seems as if the rising waves were beating on my ear!"—
"Oh, it is the breaking of the surf—just that and nothing
more,
My Captain Don Alonzo Estabán San Salvador!"

The governor was in a sleep which muddled all his brains;
The seventy men had got his gang and put them all in chains;
And when he woke the following day he could not see the
shore,
For he was out on the blue water—the Don San Salvador.

"Now do you see that yard-arm—and understand the
thing?"
Said Captain Folger. "For all from that yard-arm you
shall swing,
Or forty thousand dollars you shall pay me from your store,
My Captain Don Alonzo Estabán San Salvador."

The Capitano took a pen—the order he did sign—
"O Señor Yankee! but you charge amazing high for wine!"
But 'twas not till the draft was paid they let him go ashore,
El Señor Don Alonzo Estabán San Salvador.

The greatest sharp some day will find another sharper wit;
It always makes the Devil laugh to see a biter bit;
It takes two Spaniards any day to come a Yankee o'er—
Even two like Don Alonzo Estabán San Salvador.

*Charles Godfrey Leland* [1824-1903]

## THE LEGEND OF HEINZ VON STEIN

Out rode from his wild, dark castle
  The terrible Heinz von Stein;
He came to the door of a tavern,
  And gazed on the swinging sign.

He sat himself down at a table,
  And growled for a bottle of wine;
Up came with a flask and a corkscrew
  A maiden of beauty divine.

Then, seized with a deep love-longing,
  He uttered, "O damosel mine,
Suppose you just give a few kisses
  To the valorous Ritter von Stein!"

But she answered, "The kissing business
  Is entirely out of my line;
And I certainly will not begin it
  On a countenance ugly as thine!"

Oh, then the bold knight was angry,
  And cursed both coarse and fine;
And asked, "How much is the swindle
  For your sour and nasty wine?"

And fiercely he rode to the castle,
  And sat himself down to dine;
And this is the dreadful legend
  Of the terrible Heinz von Stein.

*Charles Godfrey Leland* [1824–1903]

## HALLOWE'EN

Of a' the festivals we hear,
Frae Handsel-Monday till New Year,
There's few in Scotland held mair dear
  For mirth, I ween,
Or yet can boast o' better cheer,
  Than Hallowe'en.

Langsyne indeed, as now in climes
Where priests for siller pardon crimes,
The kintry 'round in Popish rhymes
  Did pray and graen;
But customs vary wi' the times
  At Hallowe'en.

Ranged round a bleezing ingleside,
Where nowther cauld nor hunger bide,
The farmer's house, wi' secret pride,
  Will a' convene;
For that day's wark is thrown aside
  At Hallowe'en.

Placed at their head the gudewife sits,
And deals round apples, pears, and nits;
Syne tells her guests, how, at sic bits
  Where she has been,
Bogle's ha'e gart folk tyne their wits
  At Hallowe'en.

Grieved, she recounts how, by mischance,
Puir pussy's forced a' night to prance
Wi' fairies, wha in thousands dance
  Upon the green,
Or sail wi' witches owre to France
  At Hallowe'en.

Syne, issued frae the gardy-chair,
For that's the seat of empire there,
To co'er the table wi' what's rare,
  Commands are gi'en;
That a' fu' daintily may fare
  At Hallowe'en.

And when they've toomed ilk heapit plate,
And a' things are laid out o' gate,
To ken their matrimonial mate,
  The youngsters keen
Search a' the dark decrees o' fate
  At Hallowe'en.

A' things prepared in order due,
Gosh guide's! what fearfu' pranks ensue!
Some i' the kiln-pat thraw a clew,
At whilk, bedene,
Their sweethearts by the far end pu'
At Hallowe'en.

Ithers, wi' some uncanny gift,
In an auld barn a riddle lift,
Where, thrice pretending corn to sift,
Wi' charms between,
Their joy appears, as white as drift,
At Hallowe'en.

But 'twere a langsome tale to tell
The gates o' ilka charm and spell;
Ance, gaen to saw hampseed himsel',
Puir Jock Maclean,
Plump in a filthy peat-pot fell
At Hallowe'en.

Half filled wi' fear, and droukit weel,
He frae the mire dught hardly speel;
But frae that time the silly chiel
Did never grien
To cast his cantrips wi' the Deil
At Hallowe'en.

O Scotland! famed for scenes like this,
That thy sons walk where wisdom is,
Till death in everlasting bliss
Shall steek their e'en,
Will ever be the constant wish
of
Jockie Mein.

*John Mayne* [1759-1836]

## YAW, DOT IS SO!

YAW, dot is so! yaw, dot is so!
"Dis vorldt vas all a fleeting show!"
I shmokes mine pipe,
I trinks mine bier,

Und efry day to vork I go;
"Dis vorldt vas all a fleeting show;"
Yaw, dot is so!

Yaw, dot is so! yaw, dot is so!
I don't got mooch down here below.
I eadt und trink,
I vork und sleep,
Und find out, as I oldter grow,
I haf a hardter row to hoe;
Yaw, dot is so!

Yaw, dot is so! yaw, dot is so!
Dis vorldt don't gife me half a show;
Somedings to vear,
Some food to eadt;
Vot else? Shust vait a minude, dough;
Katrina, und der poys! oho!
Yaw, dot is so!

Yaw, dot is so! yaw, dot is so!
Dis vorldt don't been a fleeting show.
I haf mine frau,
I haf mine poys
To sheer me, daily, as I go;
Dot's pest as anydings I know;
Yaw, dot is so!

*Charles Follen Adams* [1842–1918]

## TWO HUNDRED YEARS AGO

Two honder year ago de worl' is purty slow,
Even folk upon dis countree 's not so smart,
Den who is travel roun' an' look out de pleasan' groun'
For geev' de Yankee peop' a leetle start?
I'll tole you who dey were, de beeg, rough voyageurs,
Wit' deir cousin w'at you call coureurs de bois,
Dat's fightin' all de tam, an' never care a dam,
An' ev'ry wan dem feller he's come from Canadaw
Baptême!
He's comin' all de way from Canadaw.

But He watch dem, le bon Dieu, for He's got some work to do,
An' He won't trust ev'rybody, no siree!
Only full-blood Canadien, lak Marquette an' Hennepin,
An' w'at you t'ink of Louis Verandrye?
On church of Bonsecours! makin' ready for de tour,
See dem down upon de knee, all prayin' dere—
Wit' de paddle on de han' ev'ry good Canadien man,
An' affer dey be finish, hooraw for anyw'ere.
Yass, sir!
Dey're ready now for goin' anyw'ere.

De nort' win' know dem well, an' de prairie grass can tell
How offen it is trample by de ole tam botte sauvage—
An' gray wolf on hees den kip very quiet, w'en
He hear dem boy a' singin' upon de long portage,
An' de night would fin' dem lie wit' deir faces on de sky,
An' de breeze would come an' w'isper on deir ear
'Bout de wife an' sweetheart dere on Soreal an' Trois Rivieres
Dey may never leev to see anoder year.
Dat's true,
Dey may never leev to kiss anoder year.

An' you'll know de place dey go, from de canyon down below,
Or de mountain wit' hees nose above de cloud,
De lak among de hill, w'ere de grizzly drink hees fill,
Or de rapid on de reever roarin' loud.
Ax de wil' deer if de flash of de ole Tree Reever sash
He don't see it on de woods of Illinois,
An' de musk-ox as he go, w'ere de camp-fire melt de snow,
De smell he still remember of tabac Canadien!
Ha! Ha!
It's hard forgettin' smell of tabac Canadien!

So, ma frien', de Yankee man, he mus' try an' understan',
W'en he holler for dat flag de Star an' Stripe,
If he's little win' still lef' an' no danger hurt hese'f,
Den he better geev anoder cheer, ba cripe!
For de flag of la belle France, dat show de way across
From Louisbourg to Florida an' back.

So raise it ev'ryw'ere, lak' de ole tam voyageurs,
W'en you hear of de la Salle an' Cadillac—
Hooraw!
For de flag of de la Salle an' Cadillac.

*William Henry Drummond* [1854-1907]

## WRECK OF THE "JULIE PLANTE"

On wan dark night on Lac St. Pierre,
De win' she blow, blow, blow,
An' de crew of de wood scow "Julie Plante"
Got scar't an' run below;
For de win' she blow lak hurricane,
Bimeby she blow some more,
An' de scow bus' up on Lac St. Pierre,
Wan arpent from de shore.

De Captinne walk on de fronte deck,
An' walk de hin' deck, too—
He call de crew from up de hole
He call de cook also.
De cook she's name was Rosie,
She come from Montreal,
Was chambre maid on lumber barge,
On de Grande Lachine Canal.

De win' she blow from nor'—eas'—wes'—
De sout' win' she blow, too,
W'en Rosie cry, "Mon cher Captinne,
Mon cher, w'at I shall do?"
Den de Captinne t'row de big ankerre,
But still de scow she dreef,
De crew he can't pass on de shore,
Becos' he los' hees skeef.

De night was dark, lak' one black cat,
De wave run high an' fas',
W'en de Captinne tak' de Rosie girl
An' tie her to de mas'.

Den he also tak' de life preserve,
An' jomp off on de lak',
An' say, "Good by, ma Rosie dear,
I go drown for your sak'."

Nex' mornin' very early,
'Bout ha'f-pas' two—t'ree—four—
De Captinne, scow, an' de poor Rosie
Was corpses on de shore;
For de win' she blow lak' hurricane
Bimeby she blow some more,
An' de scow bus' up on Lac St. Pierre,
Wan arpent from de shore.

MORAL

Now, all good wood scow sailor man
Tak' warning by dat storm,
An' go an' marry some nice French girl
An' leev on wan beeg farm;
De win' can blow lak' hurricane,
An' s'pose she blow some more,
You can't get drown on Lac St. Pierre,
So long you stay on shore.

*William Henry Drummond* [1854–1907]

## HUMPTY DUMPTY

*"Humpty Dumpty sat on a wall;*
*Humpty Dumpty had a great fall:*
*Not all the king's horses nor all the king's men*
*Could set Humpty Dumpty up again."*

Full many a project that never was hatched
Falls down, and gets shattered beyond being patched;
And luckily, too! for if all came to chickens,
Then things without feathers might go to the dickens.

If each restless unit that moves among men
Might climb to a place with the privileged "ten,"
Pray tell us where all the commotion would stop!
Must the whole pan of milk, forsooth, rise to the top?

If always the statesman attained to his hopes,
And grasped the great helm, who would stand by the ropes?
Or if all dainty fingers their duties might choose,
Who would wash up the dishes, and polish the shoes?

Suppose every aspirant writing a book
Contrived to get published, by hook or by crook;
Geologists then of a later creation
Would be startled, I fancy, to find a formation
Proving how the poor world did most woefully sink
Beneath mountains of paper, and oceans of ink!

Or even suppose all the women were married;
By whom would superfluous babies be carried?
Where would be the good aunts that should knit all the stockings?
Or nurses, to do up the singings and rockings?
Wise spinsters, to lay down their wonderful rules,
And with theories rare to enlighten the fools,—
Or to look after orphans, and primary schools?

No! Failure's a part of the infinite plan;
Who finds that he can't, must give way to who can;
And as one and another drops out of the race.
Each stumbles at last to his suitable place.

So the great scheme works on,—though, like eggs from the wall,
Little single designs to such ruin may fall,
That not all the world's might, of its horses or men,
Could set their crushed hopes at the summit again.

*Adeline D. T. Whitney* [1824-1906]

## STRICTLY GERM-PROOF

The Antiseptic Baby and the Prophylactic Pup
Were playing in the garden when the Bunny gamboled up;
They looked upon the Creature with a loathing undisguised;—
It wasn't Disinfected and it wasn't Sterilized.

They said it was a Microbe and a Hotbed of Disease;
They steamed it in a vapor of a thousand-odd degrees;
They froze it in a freezer that was cold as Banished Hope
And washed it in permanganate with carbolated soap.

In sulphrueted hydrogen they steeped its wiggly ears;
They trimmed its frisky whiskers with a pair of hard-boiled
    shears;
They donned their rubber mittens and they took it by the
    hand
And 'lected it a member of the Fumigated Band.

There's not a Micrococcus in the garden where they play;
They bathe in pure iodoform a dozen times a day;
And each imbibes his rations from a Hygienic Cup—
The Bunny and the Baby and the Prophylactic Pup.

*Arthur Guiterman* [1871–1943]

## CAVE SEDEM!

BEWARE the deadly Sitting habit,
Or, if you sit, be like the rabbit,
Who keepeth ever on the jump
By springs concealed beneath his rump.

A little ginger 'neath the tail
Will oft for lack of brains avail;
Eschew the dull and slothful Seat,
And move about with willing feet!

Man was not made to sit a-trance,
And press, and press, and press his pants;
But rather, with an open mind,
To circulate among his kind.

And so, my son, avoid the snare
Which lurks within a cushioned chair;
To run like hell, it has been found,
Both feet must be upon the ground.

*Theodore F. MacManus* [1872–

## REVIVAL HYMN

From "Uncle Remus"

OH, whar shill we go w'en de great day comes,
Wid de blowin' er de trumpits en de bangin' er de drums?
How many po' sinners'll be kotched out late
En fine no latch ter de golden gate?
No use fer ter wait twel ter-morrer!
De sun mustn't set on yo' sorrer,
Sin's es sharp ez a bamboo-brier—
Oh, Lord! fetch the mo'ners up higher!

W'en de nashuns er de earf is a-stan'in' all aroun',
Who's a gwine ter be choosen fer ter w'ar de glory-crown?
Who's gwine fer ter stan' stiff-kneed en bol',
En answer to der name at de callin' er de roll?
You better come now ef you comin'—
Ole Satun is loose en a bummin'—
De wheels er distruckshun is a hummin'—
Oh, come 'long, sinner, ef you comin'!

De song er salvashun is a mighty sweet song,
En de Pairidise win' blow fur en blow strong,
En Aberham's bosom, hit's saft en hit's wide,
En right dar's de place whar de sinners oughter hide!
Oh, you nee'nter be a stoppin' en a lookin';
Ef you fool wid ole Satun you'll git took in;
You'll hang on de aidge en get shook in,
Ef you keep on a stoppin' en a lookin'.

De time is right now, en dish yer's de place—
Let de sun er salvashun shine squar' in yo' face;
Fight de battles er de Lord, fight soon en fight late,
En you'll allers fine a latch ter de golden gate.
No use fer ter wait twel ter-morrer,
De sun mustn't set on yo' sorrer—
Sin's es sharp ez a bamboo-brier,
Ax de Lord fer ter fetch you up higher!

*Joel Chandler Harris* [1848–1908]

## THE POWER OF PRAYER

### THE FIRST STEAMBOAT UP THE ALABAMA

YOU, Dinah! Come and set me whar de ribber-roads does meet.
De Lord, *He* made dese black-jack roots to twis' into a seat.
Umph, dar! De Lord have mussy on dis blin' ole nigger's feet.

It pear to me dis mornin' I kin smell de fust o' June,
I 'clar, I b'lieve dat mockin'-bird could play de fiddle soon!
Dem yonder town-bells sounds like dey was ringin' in de moon.

Well, ef dis nigger *is* been blin' for fo'ty years or mo',
Dese ears dey sees de world, like th'u' de cracks dat's in de do';
For de Lord has built dis cabin wid de winders hind and 'fo'.

I know my front ones *is* stopped up, and things is sort o' dim;
But den, th'u' *dem* temptations vain won't leak in on ole Jim!
De back ones shows me earth enough, aldo' dey's mons'ous slim.

And as for Hebben—bless de Lord, and praise His holy name!
*Dat* shines in all de co'ners o' dis cabin jes' de same
As ef dat cabin hadn't nar a plank upon de frame!

Who *call* me? Listen down the ribber, Dinah! Don't you hyar
Somebody holl'in' "*Hoo, Jim, hoo?*" My Sarah died las' y'ar;
*Is* dat black angel done come back to call ole Jim from hyar?

My stars! dat can't be Sarah—shuh, jes' listen, Dinah, *now!*
What kin be comin' up dat bend, a-makin' sich a row?
Fus' bellerin', like a pawin' bull, den squealin' like a sow!

De Lord 'a' massy sakes alive! jes' hear—*Ker-woof! Ker-*
*woof!*
De Debble's comin' round dat bend—he's comin', shuh enuff,
A-splashin' up de water wid his tail and wid his hoof!

I'se pow'ful skeered; but neversomeless I ain't gwine run
away;
I'm gwine to stan' stiff-legged for de Lord dis blessed day;
*You* screech, and howl, and swish de water, Satan! Let us
pray:

*O hebbenly Mahs'r, what Thou willest dat mus' be jes' so,*
*And ef Thou hast bespoke de word, some nigger's boun' to go.*
*Den, Lord, please take ole Jim, and lef young Dinah hyar be-*
*low!*

*Scuse Dinah, scuse her, Mahs'r; for she's sich a little chile,*
*She hardly jes' begin to scramble up the home-yard stile;*
*But dis old traveller's feet been tired dis many an' many a mile.*

*I'se wufless as de rotten pole o' las' year's fodder-stack;*
*De rheumatiz done bit my bones: you hyar 'em crack and crack?*
*I can't sit down 'dout gruntin' like 'twas breakin' o' my back.*

*What use de wheel when hub and spokes is warped and split*
*and rotten?*
*What use dis dried up cotton-stalk when Life done picked my*
*cotton?*
*I'se like a word, dat somebody done said, and den forgotten.*

*But Dinah! Shuh! dat gal jes' like dis little hick'ry-tree,*
*De sap 's jis risin' in her; she do grow owdaciouslee—*
*Lord, ef you's clarin' de underbrush, don't cut her down—cut*
*me!*

*I would not proud presume—but yet I'll boldly make reques',*
*Sence Jacob had dat wastlin' match, I, too, gwine do my bes';*
*When Jacob got all underholt, de Lord He answered, Yes!*

*And what for waste de wittles now, and th'ow away de bread?*
*Jes' for to strength dese idle hands to scratch dis ole bald head?*
*Tink of de 'conomy, Mahs'r, ef dis ole Jim was dead!*

Stop; ef I don't believe de Debble's gone on up de stream!
Jes' now he squealed down dar: — hush; dat's a mighty
  weakly scream!
Yes, sir, he's gone, he's gone; — he snort 'way off, like in a
  dream!

O glory, hallelujah to de Lord dat reigns on high!
De Debble's fa'rly skeered to def; he done gone flyin' by;
I know'd he could'n' stan' dat pra'r, I felt my Mahs'r nigh!

You, Dinah, ain't you' shamed now dat you didn't trust to
  grace?
I heerd you thrashin' th'u' de bushes when he showed his
  face!
You fool, you t'ink de Debble couldn't beat *you* in a race?

I tell you, Dinah, jes' as sure as you is standin' dar,
When folks start prayin', answer-angels drops down th'u'
  de a'r;
Yea, Dinah, whar 'ould you be now, exceptin' fur dat pra'r?

*Sidney and Clifford Lanier*

## NEBUCHADNEZZAR

You, Nebuchadnezzah, whoa, sah!
Whar is you tryin' to go, sah?
I'd hab you fur to know, sah,
  *I's* a-holdin' ob de lines.
You better stop dat prancin',
You's paw'ful fond ob dancin',
But I'll bet my yeah's advancin'
  Dat I'll cure you ob yo' shines.

Look heah, mule! Better min' out;
Fus' t'ing you know you'll fin' out
How quick I'll w'ar dis line out
  On yo' ugly stubbo'n back;
You needn't try to steal up
An' lif' dat precious heel up;
You's got to plough dis fiel' up,
  You has, sah, fur a fac'.

Dar, *dat's* de way to do it!
He's comin' right down to it;
Jes' watch him ploughin' troo it!
  Dis nigger ain't no fool.
Some folks dey would 'a' beat him:
Now, dat would only heat him;
I know jes' how to treat him:
  You mus' *reason* wid a mule.

He minds me like a nigger.
If he wuz only bigger
He'd fotch a mighty figger,
  He would, I *tell* you! Yes, sah!
See how he keeps a-clickin'!
He's as gentle as a chicken,
And nebber thinks o' kickin'—
  *Whoa, dar! Nebuchadnezzah!*

. . . . . . .

Is dis heah me, or not me?
Or is de debbil got me?
Wuz dat a cannon shot me?
  Hab I laid heah more'n a week?
Dat mule do kick amazin'—
De beast was sp'iled in raisin'!
By now I 'spect he's grazin'
  On de odder side de creek.

*Irwin Russell* [1853-1879]

## KENTUCKY PHILOSOPHY

You Wi'yum, come 'ere, suh, dis minute. Wut dat you got under dat box?
I don't want no foolin'—you hear me? Wut you say? Ain't nu'h'n but *rocks?*
'Peahs ter me you's owdashus pertickler. S'posin' dey's uv a new kine.
I'll des take a look at dem rocks. Hi yi! does you think dat I's bline?

I calls dat a plain watermillion, you scamp, en I knows
whah it growed;
It come fum de Jimmerson cawn fiel', dah on t'er side er de
road.
You stole it, you rascal—you stole it! I watched you fum
down in de lot.
En time I gits th'ough wid you, nigger, you won't eb'n be a
grease spot!

*I'll* fix you. Mirandy! *Mirandy!* go cut me a hick'ry—make
'ase!
En cut me de toughes' an keenes' you c'n fine anywhah on
de place.
I'll l'arn you, Mr. Wi'yum Joe Vetters, ter steal en ter lie,
you young sinner,
Disgracin' yo' ole Christian mammy, en makin' her leave
cookin' dinner!

Now ain't you ashamed er yo'se'f, suh? I is. I's ashamed
you's my son!
En de holy accorjun angel he's ashamed er wut you has
done;
En he done tuk it down up yander in coal-black, blood-red
letters—
"One watermillion stoled by Wi'yum Josephus Vetters."

En wut you s'posin' Brer Bascom, yo' teacher at Sunday
school,
'Ud say ef he knowed how you's broke de good Lawd's Gol'n
Rule?
Boy, whah's de raisin' I give you? Is you boun' fuh ter be a
black villiun?
I's s'prised dat a chile er yo' mammy 'ud steal any man's
watermillion.

En I's now gwiner cut it right open, en you shain't have
narry bite,
Fuh a boy who'll steal watermillions—en dat in de day's
broad light—

Ain't—*Lawdy!* it's GREEN! Mirandy! Mi-ran-dy! come on
wi' dat switch!
*Well*, stealin' a g-r-e-e-n watermillion! who ever heerd tell
er des sich?
Cain't tell w'en dey's ripe? W'y, you thump 'um, en w'en
dey go pank dey is green;
But when dey go *punk*, now you mine me, dey's ripe—en
dat's des wut I mean.
En nex' time you hooks watermillions—*you* heered me, you
ign'ant young hunk,
Ef you don't want a lickin' all over, be sho dat dey allers
go "punk!"

*Harrison Robertson* [1856-1939]

## A PLANTATION DITTY

DE gray owl sing fum de chimbly top:
"Who—who—is—you-oo?"
En I say: "Good Lawd, hit's des po' me,
En I ain't quite ready fer de Jasper Sea;
I'm po' en sinful, en you 'lowed I'd be;
Oh, wait, good Lawd, 'twell ter-morrer!"

De gray owl sing fum de cypress tree:
"Who—who—is—you-oo?"
En I say: "Good Lawd, ef you look you'll see
Hit ain't nobody but des po' me,
En I like ter stay 'twell my time is free;
Oh, wait, good Lawd, 'twell ter-morrer!"

*Frank L. Stanton* [1857-1927]

## ANGELINA

WHEN de fiddle gits to singin' out a ol' Vahginny reel,
An' you 'mence to feel a ticklin' in yo' toe an' in yo' heel;
Ef you t'ink you got 'uligion an' you wants to keep it, too,
You jes' bettah tek a hint an' git yo'self clean out o' view.
Case de time is mighty temptin' when de chune is in de swing,
Fu' a darky, saint or sinner man, to cut de pigeon-wing.
An' you couldn't he'p f'om dancin' ef yo' feet was boun' wif
twine,
When Angelina Johnson comes a-swingin' down de line

Don't you know Miss Angelina? She's de da'lin' of de place.
W'y, dey ain't no high-toned lady wif sich mannahs an' sich grace.
She kin move across de cabin, wif its planks all rough an' wo',
Jes' de same's ef she was dancin' on ol' mistus' ball-room flo'.
Fact is, you do' see no cabin—evaht'ing you see look grand,
An' dat one ol' squeaky fiddle soun' to you jes' lak a ban';
Cotton britches look lak broadclof an' a linsey dress look fine,
When Angelina Johnson comes a-swingin' down de line.

Some folks say dat dancin's sinful, an' de blessed Lawd, dey say,
Gwine to punish us fu' steppin' w'en we hyeah de music play.
But I tell you I don' b'lieve it, fu' de Lawd is wise and good,
An' he made de banjo's metal an' he made de fiddle's wood,
An' he made de music in dem, so I don' quite t'ink he'll keer
Ef our feet keeps time a little to de melodies we hyeah.
W'y, dey's somep'n downright holy in de way our faces shine,
When Angelina Johnson comes a-swingin' down de line.

Angelina steps so gentle, Angelina bows so low,
An' she lif' huh sku't so dainty dat huh shoetop skacely show:
An' dem teef o' huh'n a-shinin', ez she tek you by de han'—
Go 'way, people, d' ain't anothah sich a lady in de lan'!
When she's movin' thoo de figgers er a-dancin' by huhse'f,
Folks jes' stan' stock-still a-sta'in', an' dey mos' nigh hol's dey bref;
An' de young mens, dey's a-sayin', "I's gwine mek dat damsel mine,"
When Angelina Johnson comes a-swingin' down de line.

*Paul Laurence Dunbar* [1872–1906]

## LAY OF ANCIENT ROME

Oh, the Roman was a rogue,
He erat was, you bettum;
He ran his automobilis
And smoked his cigarettum;

He wore a diamond studibus
  And elegant cravattum,
A maxima cum laude shirt,
  And such a stylish hattum!

He loved the luscious hic-hæc-hoc,
  And bet on games and equi;
At times he won; at others, though,
  He got it in the nequi;
He winked (quo usque tandem?)
  At puellas on the Forum,
And sometimes even made
  Those goo-goo oculorum!

He frequently was seen
  At combats gladiatorial,
And ate enough to feed
  Ten boarders at Memorial;
He often went on sprees
  And said, on starting homus,
"Hic labor—opus est,
  Oh, where's my hic—hic—domus?"

Although he lived in Rome—
  Of all the arts the middle—
He was (excuse the phrase)
  A horrid individ'l;
Ah! what a different thing
  Was the homo (dative, hominy)
Of far away B. C.
  From us of Anno Domini.

*Thomas Ybarra* [1880-

## THE WISDOM OF FOLLY

THE cynics say that every rose
Is guarded by a thorn that grows
    To spoil our posies:
But I no pleasure therefore lack;
I keep my hands behind my back
    When smelling roses.

'Tis proved that Sodom's appletarts
Have ashes as component parts
For those that steal them:
My soul no disillusion seeks;
I love my apples' rosy cheeks,
But never peel them.

Though outwardly a gloomy shroud,
The inner half of every cloud
Is bright and shining:
I therefore turn my clouds about
And always wear them inside out
To show the lining.

Our idols' feet are made of clay;
So stony-hearted critics say
With scornful mockings:
My images are deified
Because I keep them well supplied
With shoes and stockings.

My *modus operandi* this—
To take no heed of what's amiss;
And not a bad one:
Because as Shakespeare used to say
A merry heart goes twice the way
That tires a sad one.

*Ellen Thorneycroft Fowler* [1860–1929]

## THE POST THAT FITTED

**Though tangled and twisted the course of true love.**
**This ditty explains**
**No tangle's so tangled it cannot improve**
**If the Lover has brains.**

Ere the steamer bore him Eastward, Sleary was engaged to marry
An attractive girl at Tunbridge, whom he called "my little Carrie."
Sleary's pay was very modest; Sleary was the other way.
Who can cook a two-plate dinner on eight paltry dibs a day?

Long he pondered o'er the question in his scantly furnished
quarters—
Then proposed to Minnie Boffkin, eldest of Judge Boffkin's
daughters.
Certainly an impecunious Subaltern was not a catch,
But the Boffkins knew that Minnie mightn't make another
match.

So they recognized the business, and, to feed and clothe the
bride,
Got him made a Something Something somewhere on the
Bombay side,
Anyhow, the billet carried pay enough for him to marry—
As the artless Sleary put it: "Just the thing for me and
Carrie."

Did he, therefore, jilt Miss Boffkin—impulse of a baser
mind?
No! He started epileptic fits of an appalling kind.
(Of his *modus operandi* only this much I could gather:—
"Pears' shaving sticks will give you little taste and lots of
lather.")

Frequently in public places his affliction used to smite
Sleary with distressing vigor—always in the Boffkins' sight.
Ere a week was over, Minnie weepingly returned his ring,
Told him his "unhappy weakness" stopped all thought of
marrying.

Sleary bore the information with a chastened holy joy,—
Epileptic fits don't matter in Political employ,—
Wired three short words to Carrie—took his ticket, packed
his kit—
Bade farewell to Minnie Boffkin in one last, long, lingering fit.

Four weeks later, Carrie Sleary read—and laughed until she
wept—
Mrs. Boffkin's warning letter on the "wretched epilept."
Year by year, in pious patience, vengeful Mrs. Boffkin sits
Waiting for the Sleary babies to develop Sleary's fits.

*Rudyard Kipling* [1865–1936]

# JUST NONSENSE

## NO!

No sun—no moon!
No morn—no noon—
  No dawn—no dusk—no proper time of day—
No sky—no earthly view—
No distance looking blue—
  No road—no street—no "t'other side the way"—
No end to any Row—
No indications where the Crescents go—
No top to any steeple—
  No recognitions of familiar people—
No courtesies for showing 'em—
No knowing 'em!
  No travelling at all—no locomotion,
  No inkling of the way—no notion—
"No go"—by land or ocean—
No mail—no post—
No news from any foreign coast—
  No park—no ring—no afternoon gentility—
No company—no nobility—
  No warmth, no cheerfulness, no healthful ease,
    No comfortable feel in any member—
    No shade, no shine, no butterflies, no bees,
      No fruits, no flowers, no leaves, no birds,
        November!

*Thomas Hood* [1799–1845]

## TO MINERVA

FROM THE GREEK

My temples throb, my pulses boil,
  I'm sick of Song, and Ode, and Ballad—
So, Thyrsis, take the Midnight Oil,
  And pour it on a lobster salad.

My brain is dull, my sight is foul,
I cannot write a verse, or read,—
Then, Pallas, take away thine Owl,
And let us have a lark instead.

*Thomas Hood* [1799–1845]

## THE ALPHABET

A is an Angel of blushing eighteen;
B is the Ball where the Angel was seen;
C is the Chaperon, who cheated at cards;
D is the Deuxtemps with Frank of the Guards;
E is the Eye, killing slowly but surely;
F is the Fan whence it peeped so demurely;
G is the Glove of superlative kid;
H is the Hand which it spitefully hid;
I is the Ice which the fair one demanded;
J is the Juvenile that dainty who handed;
K is the Kerchief, a rare work of art;
L is the Lace which composed the chief part;
M is the old Maid who watched the chits dance;
N is the Nose she turned up at each glance;
O is the Olga (just then in its prime);
P is the Partner who wouldn't keep time;
Q is a Quadrille put instead of the Lancers;
R is the Remonstrances made by the dancers;
S is the Supper where all went in pairs;
T is the Twaddle they talked on the stairs;
U is the Uncle who "thought we'd be goin'";
V is the Voice which his niece replied "No" in
W is the Waiter who sat up till eight;
X is the exit, not rigidly straight;
Y is the Yawning fit caused by the Ball;
Z stands for Zero, or nothing at all.

*Charles Stuart Calverley* [1831–1884]

## A TRAGIC STORY

There lived a sage in days of yore,
And he a handsome pigtail wore;
But wondered much, and sorrowed more,
Because it hung behind him.

He mused upon this curious case,
And swore he'd change the pigtail's place,
And have it hanging at his face,
Not dangling there behind him.

Says he, "The mystery I've found,—
I'll turn me round,"—he turned him round;
But still it hung behind him.

Then round and round, and out and in,
All day the puzzled sage did spin;
In vain—it mattered not a pin,—
The pigtail hung behind him.

And right, and left, and round about,
And up, and down, and in, and out
He turned; but still the pigtail stout
Hung steadily behind him.

And though his efforts never slack,
And though he twist, and twirl, and tack,
Alas! still faithful to his back,
The pigtail hangs behind him.

*William Makepeace Thackeray* [1811-1863]

## THE JUMBLIES

THEY went to sea in a sieve, they did;
In a sieve they went to sea;
In spite of all their friends could say,
On a winter's morn, on a stormy day,
In a sieve they went to sea.
And when the sieve turned round and round,
And every one cried, "You'll all be drowned!"
They called aloud, "Our sieve ain't big;
But we don't care a button; we don't care a fig:
In a sieve we'll go to sea!"
Far and few, far and few,
Are the lands where the Jumblies live:
Their heads are green, and their hands are blue;
And they went to sea in a sieve.

They sailed away in a sieve, they did,
  In a sieve they sailed so fast,
With only a beautiful pea-green veil
Tied with a ribbon, by way of a sail,
  To a small tobacco-pipe mast.
And every one said who saw them go,
"Oh! won't they be soon upset, you know?
For the sky is dark, and the voyage is long;
And, happen what may, it's extremely wrong
  In a sieve to sail so fast."

The water it soon came in, it did;
  The water it soon came in:
So, to keep them dry, they wrapped their feet
In a pinky paper all folded neat:
  And they fastened it down with a pin.
And they passed the night in a crockery-jar;
And each of them said, "How wise we are!
Though the sky be dark, and the voyage be long
Yet we never can think we were rash or wrong,
  While round in our sieve we spin."

And all night long they sailed away;
  And, when the sun went down,
They whistled and warbled a moony song
To the echoing sound of a coppery gong,
  In the shade of the mountains brown,
"O Timballoo! How happy we are
When we live in a sieve and a crockery-jar!
And all night long, in the moonlight pale,
We sail away with a pea-green sail
  In the shade of the mountains brown."

They sailed to the Western Sea, they did,—
  To a land all covered with trees:
And they bought an owl, and a useful cart,
And a pound of rice, and a cranberry-tart,
  And a hive of silvery bees;
And they bought a pig, and some green jackdaws
And a lovely monkey with lollipop paws,

And forty bottles of ring-bo-ree,
  And no end of Stilton cheese:

And in twenty years they all came back,—
  In twenty years or more;
And every one said, "How tall they've grown!
For they've been to the Lakes, and the Torrible Zone,
  And the hills of the Chankly Bore."
And they drank their health, and gave them a feast
Of dumplings made of beautiful yeast;
And every one said, "If we only live,
We, too, will go to sea in a sieve,
  To the hills of the Chankly Bore."
    Far and few, far and few,
      Are the lands where the Jumblies live:
    Their heads are green, and their hands are blue;
      And they went to sea in a sieve.

*Edward Lear* [1812–1888]

## THE OWL AND THE PUSSY-CAT

The Owl and the Pussy-cat went to sea
  In a beautiful pea-green boat:
They took some honey, and plenty of money
  Wrapped up in a five-pound note.
The Owl looked up to the stars above,
  And sang to a small guitar,
"O lovely Pussy, O Pussy, my love,
  What a beautiful Pussy you are,
      You are,
      You are!
  What a beautiful Pussy you are!"

Pussy said to the Owl, "You elegant fowl,
  How charmingly sweet you sing!
Oh! let us be married; too long we have tarried:
  But what shall we do for a ring?"
They sailed away, for a year and a day,
  To the land where the bong-tree grows;
And there in a wood a Piggy-wig stood,

With a ring at the end of his nose,
His nose,
His nose,
With a ring at the end of his nose.

"Dear Pig, are you willing to sell for one shilling
Your ring?" Said the Piggy, "I will."
So they took it away, and were married next day
By the Turkey who lives on the hill.
They dined on mince and slices of quince,
Which they ate with a runcible spoon;
And hand in hand, on the edge of the sand,
They danced by the light of the moon,
The moon,
The moon,
They danced by the light of the moon.

*Edward Lear* [1812–1888]

## THE POBBLE WHO HAS NO TOES

The Pobble who has no toes
Had once as many as we;
When they said, "Some day you may lose them all;"
He replied, "Fish fiddle-de-dee!"
And his Aunt Jobiska made him drink
Lavender water tinged with pink,
For she said, "The World in general knows
There's nothing so good for a Pobble's toes!"

The Pobble who has no toes
Swam across the Bristol Channel;
But before he set out he wrapped his nose
In a piece of scarlet flannel.
For his Aunt Jobiska said, "No harm
Can come to his toes if his nose is warm;
And it's perfectly known that a Pobble's toes
Are safe,—provided he minds his nose."

The Pobble swam fast and well,
And when boats or ships came near him,
He tinkledy-binkledy-winkled a bell,
So that all the world could hear him.

And all the Sailors and Admirals cried,
When they saw him nearing the further side,—
"He has gone to fish, for his Aunt Jobiska's
Runcible Cat with crimson whiskers!"

But before he touched the shore,--
  The shore of the Bristol Channel,—
A sea-green Porpoise carried away
  His wrapper of scarlet flannel.
And when he came to observe his feet,
Formerly garnished with toes so neat,
His face at once became forlorn
On perceiving that all his toes were gone!

And nobody ever knew,
  From that dark day to the present,
Whoso had taken the Pobble's toes,
  In a manner so far from pleasant.
Whether the shrimps or crawfish gray,
Or crafty Mermaids stole them away—
Nobody knew; and nobody knows
How the Pobble was robbed of his twice five toes!

The Pobble who has no toes
  Was placed in a friendly Bark,
And they rowed him back, and carried him up
  To his Aunt Jobiska's Park.
And she made him a feast, at his earnest wish,
Of eggs and buttercups fried with fish;
And she said, "It's a fact the whole world knows,
That Pobbles are happier without their toes."

*Edward Lear* [1812-1888]

## THE COURTSHIP OF THE YONGHY-BONGHY-BÒ

On the Coast of Coromandel
  Where the early pumpkins blow,
    In the middle of the woods
  Lived the Yonghy-Bonghy-Bò.

Two old chairs, and half a candle,
One old jug without a handle,—
    These were all his worldly goods:
    In the middle of the woods,
    These were all the worldly goods,
Of the Yonghy-Bonghy-Bò,
Of the Yonghy-Bonghy-Bò.

Once, among the Bong-trees walking
  Where the early pumpkins blow,
    To a little heap of stones
  Came the Yonghy-Bonghy-Bò.
There he heard a Lady talking
To some milk-white Hens of Dorking,—
    "'Tis the Lady Jingly Jones!
    On that little heap of stones
    Sits the Lady Jingly Jones!"
  Said the Yonghy-Bonghy-Bò.

"Lady Jingly! Lady Jingly!
  Sitting where the pumpkins blow,
    Will you come and be my wife?"
  Said the Yonghy-Bonghy-Bò.
"I am tired of living singly,—
On this coast so wild and shingly,—
    I'm a-weary of my life;
    If you'll come and be my wife,
    Quite serene would be my life!"
  Said the Yonghy-Bonghy-Bò.

"On this Coast of Coromandel,
  Shrimps and water-cresses grow,
    Prawns are plentiful and cheap,"
  Said the Yonghy-Bonghy-Bò.
"You shall have my chairs and candle,
And my jug without a handle!
    Gaze upon the rolling deep
    (Fish is plentiful and cheap);
    As the sea, my love is deep!"
  Said the Yonghy-Bonghy-Bò.

Lady Jingly answered sadly,
And her tears began to flow,—
"Your proposal comes too late,
Mr. Yonghy-Bonghy-Bò!
I would be your wife most gladly!"
(Here she twirled her fingers madly,)
"But in England I've a mate!
Yes! you've asked me far too late,
For in England I've a mate,
Mr. Yonghy-Bonghy-Bò.

"Mr. Jones—(his name is Handel,—
Handel Jones, Esquire, & Co.)
Dorking fowls delights to send,
Mr. Yonghy-Bonghy-Bò!
Keep, oh! keep your chairs and candle,
And your jug without a handle,—
I can merely be your friend!
—Should my Jones more Dorkings send,
I will give you three, my friend!
Mr. Yonghy-Bonghy-Bò.

"Though you've such a tiny body,
And your head so large doth grow,—
Though your hat may blow away,
Mr. Yonghy-Bonghy-Bò!
Though you're such a Hoddy Doddy,—
Yet I wish that I could modi-
fy the words I needs must say!
Will you please to go away?
That is all I have to say,
Mr. Yonghy-Bonghy-Bò!"

Down the slippery slopes of Myrtle,
Where the early pumpkins blow,
To the calm and silent sea
Fled the Yonghy-Bonghy-Bò.
There, beyond the Bay of Gurtle,
Lay a large and lively Turtle;—

"You're the Cove," he said, "for me;
On your back beyond the sea,
Turtle, you shall carry me!"
Said the Yonghy-Bonghy-Bò.

Through the silent-roaring ocean
Did the Turtle swiftly go;
Holding fast upon his shell
Rode the Yonghy-Bonghy-Bò.
With a sad primeval motion
Towards the sunset isles of Boshen
Still the Turtle bore him well.
Holding fast upon his shell,
"Lady Jingly Jones, farewell!"
Sang the Yonghy-Bonghy-Bò.

From the Coast of Coromandel,
Did that Lady never go;
On that heap of stones she moans
For the Yonghy-Bonghy-Bò.
On that Coast of Coromandel,
In his jug without a handle,
Still she weeps and daily mourns;
On that little heap of stones
To her Dorking Hens she moans
For the Yonghy-Bonghy-Bò,
For the Yonghy-Bonghy-Bò.

*Edward Lear* [1812–1888]

## NONSENSE VERSES

There was an Old Man with a beard,
Who said, "It is just what I feared!
Two Owls and a Hen,
Four Larks and a Wren,
Have all built their nests in my beard!"

There was an Old Man in a tree,
Who was horribly bored by a bee;
When they said, "Does it buzz?"
He replied, "Yes, it does!
It's a regular brute of a bee!"

There was an Old Man in a boat,
Who said, "I'm afloat! I'm afloat!"
  When they said, "No, you ain't!"
  He was ready to faint,
That unhappy Old Man in a boat.

There was an Old Man with a poker,
Who painted his face with red ochre;
  When they said, "You're a Guy!"
  He made no reply,
But knocked them all down with his poker.

There was an Old Man who said, "Hush!
I perceive a young bird in this bush!"
  When they said, "Is it small?"
  He replied, "Not at all!
It is four times as big as the bush!"

*Edward Lear* [1812–1888]

## THE TURTLE AND FLAMINGO

A LIVELY young turtle lived down by the banks
Of a dark rolling stream called the Jingo,
And one summer day, as he went out to play,
Fell in love with a charming flamingo—
An enormously genteel flamingo!
An expansively crimson flamingo!
A beautiful, bouncing flamingo!

Spake the turtle in tones like a delicate wheeze:
"To the water I've oft seen you in go,
And your form has impressed itself deep on my shell,
You perfectly modeled flamingo!
You tremendously 'A 1' flamingo!
You inex-pres-*si*-ble flamingo!

"To be sure I'm a turtle, and you are a belle,
And *my* language is not your fine lingo;
But smile on me, tall one, and be my bright flame,
You miraculous, wondrous flamingo!
You blazingly beauteous flamingo!

You turtle-absorbing flamingo!
You inflammably gorgeous flamingo!"

Then the proud bird blushed redder than ever before,
And that was quite un-nec-es-*sa*-ry,
And she stood on one leg and looked out of one eye,
The position of things for to vary,—
This aquatical, musing flamingo!
This dreamy, uncertain flamingo!
This embarrassing, harassing flamingo!

Then she cried to the quadruped, greatly amazed:
"Why your passion toward *me* do you hurtle?
I'm an ornithological wonder of grace,
And you're an illogical turtle,—
A waddling, impossible turtle!
A low-minded, grass-eating turtle!
A highly improbable turtle!"

Then the turtle sneaked off with his nose to the ground,
And never more looked at the lasses;
And falling asleep, while indulging his grief,
Was gobbled up whole by Agassiz,—
The peripatetic Agassiz!
The turtle-dissecting Agassiz!
The illustrious, industrious Agassiz!

Go with me to Cambridge some cool, pleasant day,
And the skeleton lover I'll show you:
He's in a hard case, but he'll look in your face,
Pretending (the rogue!) he don't know you!
Oh, the deeply deceptive young turtle!
The double-faced, glassy-cased turtle!
The *green*, but a very *mock*-turtle!

*James Thomas Fields* [1816–1881]

## JABBERWOCKY

'Twas brillig, and the slithy toves
Did gyre and gimble in the wabe;
All mimsy were the borogoves,
And the mome raths outgrabe.

"Beware the Jabberwock, my son!
  The jaws that bite, the claws that catch!
Beware the Jubjub bird, and shun
  The frumious Bandersnatch!"

He took his vorpal sword in hand:
  Long time the manxome foe he sought.—
So rested he by the Tumtum tree,
  And stood awhile in thought.

And as in uffish thought he stood,
  The Jabberwock, with eyes of flame,
Came whiffling through the tulgey wood,
  And burbled as it came!

One, two! One, two! And through and through
  The vorpal blade went snicker-snack!
He left it dead, and with its head
  He went galumphing back.

"And hast thou slain the Jabberwock?
  Come to my arms, my beamish boy!
O frabjous day! Callooh! Callay!"
  He chortled in his joy.

'Twas brillig, and the slithy toves
  Did gyre and gimble in the wabe;
All mimsy were the borogoves,
  And the mome raths outgrabe.

*Lewis Carroll* [1832-1898]

## THE GARDENER'S SONG

From "Sylvie and Bruno"

He thought he saw an Elephant,
  That practised on a fife:
He looked again, and found it was
  A letter from his wife.
"At length I realize," he said,
  "The bitterness of life!"

He thought he saw a Buffalo
  Upon the chimney-piece:
He looked again, and found it was
  His Sister's Husband's Niece.
"Unless you leave this house," he said,
  "I'll send for the Police!"

He thought he saw a Rattlesnake
  That questioned him in Greek:
He looked again, and found it was
  The Middle of Next Week.
"The one thing I regret," he said,
  "Is that it cannot speak!"

He thought he saw a Banker's Clerk
  Descending from the 'bus:
He looked again, and found it was
  A Hippopotamus.
"If this should stay to dine," he said,
  "There won't be much for us!"

He thought he saw a Kangaroo
  That worked a coffee-mill:
He looked again, and found it was
  A Vegetable-Pill.
"Were I to swallow this," he said,
  "I should be very ill!"

He thought he saw a Coach-and-Four
  That stood beside his bed:
He looked again, and found it was
  A Bear without a Head.
"Poor thing," he said, "poor silly thing!
  It's waiting to be fed!"

He thought he saw an Albatross
  That fluttered round the lamp·
He looked again, and found it was
  A Penny-Postage-Stamp.
"You'd best be getting home," he said:
  "The nights are very damp!"

He thought he saw a Garden Door
  That opened with a key:
He looked again, and found it was
  A Double-Rule-of-Three:
"And all its mystery," he said,
  "Is clear as day to me!"

*Lewis Carroll* [1832–1898]

## THE WALRUS AND THE CARPENTER

**From "Through the Looking-Glass"**

The sun was shining on the sea,
  Shining with all his might:
He did his very best to make
  The billows smooth and bright—
And this was odd, because it was
  The middle of the night.

The moon was shining sulkily,
  Because she thought the sun
Had got no business to be there
  After the day was done—
"It's very rude of him," she said,
  "To come and spoil the fun!"

The sea was wet as wet could be,
  The sands were dry as dry.
You could not see a cloud, because
  No cloud was in the sky:
No birds were flying overhead—
  There were no birds to fly.

The Walrus and the Carpenter
  Were walking close at hand:
They wept like anything to see
  Such quantities of sand.
"If this were only cleared away,"
  They said, "it *would* be grand!"

"If seven maids with seven mops
  Swept it for half a year,
Do you suppose," the Walrus said,
  "That they could get it clear?"
"I doubt it," said the Carpenter,
  And shed a bitter tear.

"O Oysters, come and walk with us!"
  The Walrus did beseech.
"A pleasant talk, a pleasant walk,
  Along the briny beach:
We cannot do with more than four,
  To give a hand to each."

The eldest Oyster looked at him,
  But never a word he said:
The eldest Oyster winked his eye,
  And shook his heavy head—
Meaning to say he did not choose
  To leave the oyster-bed.

But four young Oysters hurried up,
  All eager for the treat:
Their coats were brushed, their faces washed,
  Their shoes were clean and neat—
And this was odd, because, you know,
  They hadn't any feet.

Four other Oysters followed them,
  And yet another four;
And thick and fast they came at last,
  And more, and more, and more—
All hopping through the frothy waves,
  And scrambling to the shore.

The Walrus and the Carpenter
  Walked on a mile or so,
And then they rested on a rock
  Conveniently low:
And all the little Oysters stood
  And waited in a row.

"The time has come," the Walrus said,
  "To talk of many things:
Of shoes—and ships—and sealing-wax—
  Of cabbages—and kings—
And why the sea is boiling hot—
  And whether pigs have wings."

"But wait a bit," the Oysters cried,
  "Before we have our chat;
For some of us are out of breath,
  And all of us are fat!"
"No hurry!" said the Carpenter.
  They thanked him much for that.

"A loaf of bread," the Walrus said,
  "Is what we chiefly need:
Pepper and vinegar besides
  Are very good indeed—
Now, if you're ready, Oysters dear,
  We can begin to feed."

"But not on us!" the Oysters cried,
  Turning a little blue.
"After such kindness, that would be
  A dismal thing to do!"
"The night is fine," the Walrus said.
  "Do you admire the view?

"It was so kind of you to come!
  And you are very nice!"
The Carpenter said nothing but
  "Cut us another slice.
I wish you were not quite so deaf—
  I've had to ask you twice!"

"It seems a shame," the Walrus said,
  "To play them such a trick,
After we've brought them out so far,
  And made them trot so quick!"
The Carpenter said nothing but
  "The butter's spread too thick!"

"I weep for you," the Walrus said:
  "I deeply sympathize."
With sobs and tears he sorted out
  Those of the largest size,
Holding his pocket-handkerchief
  Before his streaming eyes.

"O Oysters," said the Carpenter,
  "You've had a pleasant run!
Shall we be trotting home again?"
  But answer came there none—
And this was scarcely odd, because
  They'd eaten every one.

*Lewis Carroll* [1832-1898]

## CLEAN CLARA

What! not know our Clean Clara?
Why, the hot folks in Sahara,
And the cold Esquimaux,
Our little Clara know!
Clean Clara, the Poet sings,
Cleaned a hundred thousand things!

She cleaned the keys of the harpsichord,
She cleaned the hilt of the family sword,
She cleaned my lady, she cleaned my lord;
All the pictures in their frames,
Knights with daggers, and stomachered dames—
Cecils, Godfreys, Montforts, Graemes,
Winifreds—all those nice old names!

She cleaned the works of the eight-day clock,
She cleaned the spring of a secret lock,
She cleaned the mirror, she cleaned the cupboard;
All the books she India-rubbered!

She cleaned the Dutch-tiles in the place,
She cleaned some very old-fashioned lace;
The Countess of Miniver came to her,
"Pray, my dear, will you clean my fur?"

All her cleanings are admirable;
To count your teeth you will be able,
If you look in the walnut table!

She cleaned the tent-stitch and the sampler;
She cleaned the tapestry, which was ampler;
Joseph going down into the pit,
And the Shunammite woman with the boy in a fit;

You saw the reapers, *not* in the distance,
And Elisha coming to the child's assistance,
With the house on the wall that was built for the prophet,
The chair, the bed, and the bolster of it;

The eyebrows all had a twirl reflective,
Just like an eel; to spare invective,
There was plenty of color, but no perspective.
However, Clara cleaned it all,
With a curious lamp, that hangs in the hall!
She cleaned the drops of the chandeliers,—
Madam, in mittens, was moved to tears!

She cleaned the cage of the cockatoo,
The oldest bird that ever grew;
I should say a thousand years old would do—
I'm sure he looked it; but nobody knew;
She cleaned the china, she cleaned the delf,
She cleaned the baby, she cleaned herself!

To-morrow morning she means to try
To clean the cobwebs from the sky;
Some people say the girl will rue it,
But my belief is she will do it.

So I've made up my mind to be there to see:
There's a beautiful place in the walnut tree;
The bough is as firm as a solid rock;
She brings out her broom at six o'clock.

*William Brighty Rands* [1823–1882]

## THE LOVERS

SALLY SALTER, she was a young teacher who taught,
And her friend, Charley Church, was a preacher who praught,
Though his enemies called him a screecher who scraught.

His heart, when he saw her, kept sinking and sunk,
And his eye, meeting hers, began winking, and wunk;
While she, in her turn, kept thinking, and thunk.

He hastened to woo her, and sweetly he wooed,
For his love grew until to a mountain it grewed,
And what he was longing to do then he doed.

In secret he wanted to speak, and he spoke,
To seek with his lips what his heart long had soke;
So he managed to let the truth leak, and it loke.

He asked her to ride to the church, and they rode;
They so sweetly did glide that they both thought they glode,
And they came to the place to be tied, and were toed.

Then homeward, he said, let us drive, and they drove,
And as soon as they wished to arrive, they arrove,
For whatever he couldn't contrive, she controve.

The kiss he was dying to steal, then he stole;
At the feet where he wanted to kneel then he knole;
And he said, "I feel better than ever I fole."

So they to each other kept clinging, and clung,
While Time his swift circuit was winging, and wung;
And this was the thing he was bringing, and brung:

The man Sally wanted to catch, and had caught;
That she wanted from others to snatch, and had snaught;
Was the one that she now liked to scratch, and she scraught.

And Charley's warm love began freezing, and froze,
While he took to teazing, and cruelly toze
The girl he had wished to be squeezing, and squoze.

"Wretch!" he cried, when she threatened to leave him, and
left,
"How could you deceive me, as you have deceft?"
And she answered, "I promised to cleave, and I've cleft."

*Phœbe Cary* (?) [1824-1871]

## THE TWINS

In form and feature, face and limb,
I grew so like my brother,
That folks got taking me for him,
And each for one another.
It puzzled all our kith and kin,
It reached a fearful pitch;
For one of us was born a twin,
Yet not a soul knew which.

One day, to make the matter worse,
Before our names were fixed,
As we were being washed by nurse,
We got completely mixed;
And thus, you see, by fate's decree,
Or rather nurse's whim,
My brother John got christened me,
And I got christened him.

This fatal likeness even dogged
My footsteps when at school,
And I was always getting flogged,
For John turned out a fool.
I put this question, fruitlessly,
To every one I knew,
"What *would* you do, if you were me,
To prove that you were *you?*"

Our close resemblance turned the tide
Of my domestic life,
For somehow, my intended bride
Became my brother's wife.

In fact, year after year the same
  Absurd mistakes went on,
And when I died, the neighbors came
  And buried brother John.

*Henry Sambrooke Leigh* [1837-1883]

## A THRENODY

The Ahkoond of Swat is dead—*London Papers*

WHAT, what, what,
What's the news from Swat?
  Sad news,
  Bad news,
Comes by the cable led
Through the Indian Ocean's bed,
Through the Persian Gulf, the Red
Sea and the Med-
Iterranean—he's dead;
The Ahkoond is dead!

For the Ahkoond I mourn,
  Who wouldn't?
He strove to disregard the message stern,
  But he Ahkoodn't.
Dead, dead, dead;
    (Sorrow, Swats!)
Swats wha hae wi' Ahkoond bled,
Swats whom he hath often led
Onward to a gory bed,
  Or to victory,
  As the case might be,
    Sorrow, Swats!
Tears shed,
  Shed tears like water.
Your great Ahkoond is dead!
  That Swats the matter!

Mourn, city of Swat!
Your great Ahkoond is not,
But lain 'mid worms to rot.
His mortal part alone, his soul was caught

(Because he was a good Ahkoond)
Up to the bosom of Mahound.
Though earthy walls his frame surround
(Forever hallowed be the ground!)
And sceptics mock the lowly mound
And say "He's now of no Ahkoond!"
His soul is in the skies,—
The azure skies that bend above his loved
Metropolis of Swat.
He sees with larger, other eyes,
Athwart all earthly mysteries—
He knows what's Swat.

Let Swat bury the great Ahkoond
With a noise of mourning and of lamentation!
Let Swat bury the great Ahkoond
With the noise of the mourning
Of the Swattish nation!
Fallen is at length
Its tower of strength,
Its sun is dimmed ere it had nooned;
Dead lies the great Ahkoond,
The great Ahkoond of Swat
Is not!

*George Thomas Lanigan* [1845-1886]

## THE FASTIDIOUS SERPENT

THERE was a snake that dwelt in Skye,
Over the misty sea, oh;
He lived upon nothing but gooseberry-pie
For breakfast, dinner, and tea, oh.

Now gooseberry-pie—as is very well known—
Over the misty sea, oh,
Is not to be found under every stone,
Nor yet upon every tree, oh.

And being so ill to please with his meat,
Over the misty sea, oh,
The snake had sometimes nothing to eat,
And an angry snake was he, oh.

Then he'd flick his tongue and his head he'd shake,
  Over the misty sea, oh,
Crying, "Gooseberry-pie! For goodness' sake
  Some gooseberry-pie for me, oh!"

And if gooseberry-pie was not to be had,
  Over the misty sea, oh,
He'd twine and twist like an eel gone mad,
  Or a worm just stung by a bee, oh.

But though he might shout and wriggle about,
  Over the misty sea, oh,
The snake had often to go without
  His breakfast, dinner, and tea, oh.

*Henry Johnstone* [1844–

## MY RECOLLECTEST THOUGHTS

From "Davy and the Goblin"

My recollectest thoughts are those
  Which I remember yet;
And bearing on, as you'd suppose,
  The things I don't forget.

But my resemblest thoughts are less
  Alike than they should be;
A state of things, as you'll confess,
  You very seldom see.

And yet the mostest thought I love
  Is what no one believes—
That I'm the sole survivor of
  The famous Forty Thieves!

*Charles Edward Carryl* [1841–1920]

## MR. FINNEY'S TURNIP

Mr. Finney had a turnip
  And it grew behind the barn;
And it grew and it grew,
  And that turnip did no harm.

There it grew and it grew
  Till it could grow no longer;
Then his daughter Lizzie picked it
  And put it in the cellar.

There it lay and it lay
  Till it began to rot;
And his daughter Susie took it
  And put it in the pot.

And they boiled it and boiled it
  As long as they were able;
And then his daughters took it
  And put it on the table.

Mr. Finney and his wife
  They sat them down to sup;
And they ate and they ate
  And they ate that turnip up.

*Unknown*

## THE SIEGE OF BELGRADE

An Austrian army, awfully arrayed,
Boldly by battery besieged Belgrade;
Cossack commanders cannonading come,
Dealing destruction's devastating doom.
Every endeavor engineers essay
For fame, for fortune,—fighting furious fray:
Generals 'gainst generals grapple—gracious God
How honors Heaven heroic hardihood!
Infuriate, indiscriminate in ill,
Kindred kill kinsmen—kinsmen kindred kill!
Labor low levels loftiest, longest lines;
Men march 'mid mounds, 'mid moles, 'mid murderous mines.
Now noisy, noxious numbers notice naught
Of outward obstacles opposing ought:
Poor patriots, partly purchased, partly pressed,
Quite quailing, quaking, quickly quarter quest.

Reason returns, religious right redounds,
Suwarrow stops such sanguinary sounds:
Truce to thee, Turkey—triumph to thy train!
Unjust, unwise, unmerciful Ukraine!
Vanish vain victory! vanish victory vain!
Why wish we warfare? Wherefore welcome were
Xerxes, Ximenes, Xanthus, Xaviere?
Yield, yield, ye youths! ye yeomen, yield your yell!
Zeno's, Zarpatus', Zoroaster's zeal,
All, all arouse! all against arms appeal!

*Alaric Alexander Watts* [1797–1864]

## ELLEN M'JONES ABERDEEN

Macphairson Clonglocketty Angus M'Clan
Was the son of an elderly laboring man.
You've guessed him a Scotchman, shrewd reader, at sight,
And p'r'aps altogether, shrewd reader, you're right.

From the bonnie blue Forth to the lovely Deeside,
Round by Dingwall and Wrath to the mouth of the Clyde,
There wasn't a child, or woman, or man
Who could pipe with Clonglocketty Angus M'Clan.

No other could wake such detestable groans,
With reed and with chanter—with bag and with drones:
All day and all night he delighted the chiels
With sniggering pibrochs and jiggety reels.

He'd clamber a mountain and squat on the ground,
And the neighboring maidens would gather around
To list to his pipes and to gaze in his een,
Especially Ellen M'Jones Aberdeen.

All loved their M'Clan, save a Sassenach brute,
Who came to the Highlands to fish and to shoot;
He dressed himself up in a Highlander way,
Though his name it was Pattison Corby Torbay.

Torbay had incurred a good deal of expense
To make him a Scotchman in every sense;
But this is a matter, you'll readily own,
That isn't a question of tailors alone.

A Sassenach chief may be bonily built,
He may purchase a sporran, a bonnet, and kilt;
Stick a skeän in his hose—wear an acre of stripes—
But he cannot assume an affection for pipes.

Clonglocketty's pipings all night and all day
Quite frenzied poor Pattison Corby Torbay:
The girls were amused at his singular spleen,
Especially Ellen M'Jones Aberdeen.

"Macphairson Clonglocketty Angus, my lad,
With pibrochs and reels you are driving me mad.
If you really must play on that cursed affair,
My goodness! play something resembling an air."

Boiled over the blood of Macphairson M'Clan—
The Clan of Clonglocketty rose as one man:
For all were enraged at the insult, I ween!—
Especially Ellen M'Jones Aberdeen.

"Let's show," said M'Clan, "to this Sassenach loon
That the bagpipes *can* play him a regular tune.
Let's see," said M'Clan, as he thoughtfully sat,
"'In My Cottage' is easy—I'll practice at that."

He blew at his "Cottage," and blew with a will,
For a year, seven months, and a fortnight, until
(You'll hardly believe it) M'Clan, I declare,
Elicited something resembling an air.

It was wild—it was fitful—as wild as the breeze—
It wandered about into several keys;
It was jerky, spasmodic, and harsh, I'm aware,
But still it distinctly suggested an air.

The Sassenach screamed and the Sassenach danced,
He shrieked in his agony, bellowed and pranced;
And the maidens who gathered rejoiced at the scene,
Especially Ellen M'Jones Aberdeen.

"Hech gather, hech gather, hech gather around:
And fill a' yer lugs wi' the exquisite sound.

An air frae the bagpipes—beat that if ye can!
Hurrah for Clonglocketty Angus M'Clan!"

The fame of his piping spread over the land;
Respectable widows proposed for his hand,
And maidens came flocking to sit on the green,
Especially Ellen M'Jones Aberdeen.

One morning the fidgety Sassenach swore
He'd stand it no longer—he drew his claymore,
And (this was, I think, in extremely bad taste),
Divided Clonglocketty close to the waist.

Oh! loud were the wailings for Angus M'Clan,
Oh! deep was the grief for that excellent man,
The maids stood aghast at the horrible scene,
Especially Ellen M'Jones Aberdeen.

It sorrowed poor Pattison Corby Torbay
To find them "take on" in this serious way.
He pitied the poor little fluttering birds,
And solaced their souls with the following words:—

"Oh, maidens," said Pattison, touching his hat,
"Don't blubber, my dears, for a fellow like that;
Observe, I'm a very superior man,
A much better fellow than Angus M'Clan."

They smiled when he winked and addressed them as "dears,"
And they all of them vowed, as they dried up their tears,
A pleasanter gentleman never was seen—
Especially Ellen M'Jones Aberdeen.

*William Schwenck Gilbert* [1836–1911]

## TO THE TERRESTRIAL GLOBE

### BY A MISERABLE WRETCH

Roll on, thou ball, roll on!
Through pathless realms of Space
Roll on!
What though I'm in a sorry case?

What though I cannot meet my bills?
What though I suffer toothache's ills?
What though I swallow countless pills?
Never *you* mind!
Roll on!

Roll on, thou ball, roll on!
Through seas of inky air
Roll on!
It's true I've got no shirts to wear;
It's true my butcher's bill is due;
It's true my prospects all look blue—
But don't let that unsettle you!
Never *you* mind!
Roll on. (*It rolls on*)

*William Schwenck Gilbert* [1836–1911]

## HIS HEART WAS TRUE TO POLL

I'LL sing you a song, not very long,
But the story somewhat new,
Of William Kidd, who, whatever he did,
To his Poll was always true.
He sailed away in a gallant ship
From the port of old Bris*tol*,
And the last words he uttered,
As his handkercher he fluttered,
Were, "My heart is true to Poll."

His heart was true to Poll,
His heart was true to Poll.
It's no matter what you do,
If your heart be only true:
And his heart *was* true to Poll.

'Twas a wreck. Willi*am*, on shore he swam,
And looked about for an inn;
When a noble savage lady, of a color rather shady,
Came up with a kind of grin:

"Oh, marry *me*, and a king you'll be,
And in a palace loll;
Or we'll eat you willy-nilly."
So he gave his *hand*, did Billy,
But his *heart* was true to Poll.

Away a twelvemonth sped, and a happy life he led
As the King of the Kikeryboos;
His paint was red and yellow, and he used a big umbrella,
And he wore a pair of over-*shoes;*
He'd corals and knives, and twenty-six wives,
Whose beauties I cannot here extol:
One day they all revolted,
So he back to Bristol bolted,
For his *heart* was true to Poll.

*Francis Cowley Burnand* [1837–1917]

## RED RIDING HOOD

MOST worthy of praise were the virtuous ways
Of Little Red Riding Hood's ma,
And no one was ever more cautious and clever
Than Little Red Riding Hood's pa.
They never misled, for they meant what they said,
And frequently said what they meant:
They were careful to show her the way she should go,
And the way that they showed her she went.
For obedience she was effusively thanked,
And for anything else she was carefully spanked.

It thus isn't strange that Red Riding Hood's range
Of virtues so steadily grew,
That soon she won prizes of various sizes,
And golden encomiums too.
As a general rule she was head of her school,
And at six was so notably smart
That they gave her a check for reciting The Wreck
Of the Hesperus wholly by heart.
And you all will applaud her the more, I am sure,
When I add that the money she gave to the poor.

At eleven this lass had a Sunday-school class,
At twelve wrote a volume of verse,
At fourteen was yearning for glory, and learning
To be a professional nurse.
To a glorious height the young paragon might
Have climbed, if not nipped in the bud,
But the following year struck her smiling career
With a dull and a sickening thud!
(I have shed a great tear at the thought of her pain,
And must copy my manuscript over again!)

Not dreaming of harm, one day on her arm
A basket she hung. It was filled
With drinks made of spices, and jellies, and ices,
And chicken-wings, carefully grilled,
And a savory stew, and a novel or two
She persuaded a neighbor to loan,
And a Japanese fan, and a hot-water can,
And a bottle of eau de cologne,
And the rest of the things that your family fill
Your room with whenever you chance to be ill.

She expected to find her decrepit but kind
Old grandmother waiting her call,
Exceedingly ill. Oh, that face on the pillow
Did not look familiar at all!
With a whitening cheek she started to speak,
But her peril she instantly saw:
Her grandma had fled and she'd tackled instead
Four merciless paws and a maw!
When the neighbors came running the wolf to subdue,
He was licking his chops—and Red Riding Hood's, too!

At this terrible tale some readers will pale,
And others with horror grow dumb,
And yet it was better, I fear, he should get her:—
Just think what she might have become!
For an infant so keen might in future have been
A woman of awful renown,
Who carried on fights for her feminine rights,
As the Mayor of an Arkansas town,

Or she might have continued the sins of her 'teens
And come to write verse for the Big Magazines!

THE MORAL: There's nothing much glummer
Than children whose talents appal.
One much prefers those that are dumber.
And as for the paragons small—
If a swallow cannot make a summer,
It can bring on a summary fall!

*Guy Wetmore Carryl* [1873-1904]

## A NAUTICAL BALLAD

From "Davy and the Goblin"

A CAPITAL ship for an ocean trip
Was the "Walloping Window-blind,"
No gale that blew dismayed her crew
Or troubled the captain's mind.
The man at the wheel was taught to feel
Contempt for the wildest blow,
And it often appeared, when the weather had cleared,
That he'd been in his bunk below.

The boatswain's mate was very sedate,
Yet fond of amusement, too;
And he played hop-scotch with the starboard watch
While the captain tickled the crew.
And the gunner we had was apparently mad,
For he sat on the after rail,
And fired salutes with the captain's boots,
In the teeth of the booming gale.

The captain sat in a commodore's hat
And dined in a royal way
On toasted pigs and pickles and figs
And gummery bread each day.
But the cook was Dutch and behaved as such;
For the food that he gave the crew
Was a number of tons of hot-cross buns
Chopped up with sugar and glue.

And we all felt ill as mariners will
  On a diet that's cheap and rude;
And we shivered and shook as we dipped the cook
  In a tub of his gluesome food.
Then nautical pride we laid aside,
  And we cast the vessel ashore
On the Gulliby Isles, where the Poohpooh smiles,
  And the Anagazanders roar.

Composed of sand was that favored land,
  And trimmed with cinnamon straws;
And pink and blue was the pleasing hue
  Of the Tickletoeteaser's claws.
And we sat on the edge of a sandy ledge
  And shot at the whistling bee;
And the Binnacle-bats wore water-proof hats,
  As they danced in the sounding sea.

On rubagub bark, from dawn to dark,
  We fed, till we all had grown
Uncommonly shrunk—when a Chinese junk
  Came by from the torriby zone.
She was stubby and square, but we didn't much care
  And we cheerily put to sea;
And we left the crew of the junk to chew
  The bark of the rubagub tree.

*Charles Edward Carryl* [1841–1920]

## THE PLAINT OF THE CAMEL

From "The Admiral's Caravan"

"Canary-birds feed on sugar and seed,
  Parrots have crackers to crunch;
And as for the poodles, they tell me the noodles
  Have chickens and cream for their lunch.
    But there's never a question
    About MY digestion—
  ANYTHING does for me!

"Cats, you're aware, can repose in a chair,
  Chickens can roost upon rails;
Puppies are able to sleep in a stable,
  And oysters can slumber in pails.

But no one supposes
A poor Camel dozes—
ANY PLACE does for me!

"Lambs are enclosed where it's never exposed.
Coops are constructed for hens;
Kittens are treated to houses well heated,
And pigs are protected by pens.
But a Camel comes handy
Wherever it's sandy—
ANYWHERE does for me!

"People would laugh if you rode a giraffe,
Or mounted the back of an ox;
It's nobody's habit to ride on a rabbit,
Or try to bestraddle a fox.
But as for a Camel, he's
Ridden by families—
ANY LOAD does for me!

"A snake is as round as a hole in the ground,
And weasels are wavy and sleek;
And no alligator could ever be straighter
Than lizards that live in a creek,
But a Camel's all lumpy
And bumpy and humpy—
ANY SHAPE does for me!"

*Charles Edward Carryl* [1841–1920]

## THE FROG

Be kind and tender to the Frog,
And do not call him names,
As "Slimy-skin," or "Polly-wog,"
Or likewise, "Uncle James,"
Or "Gape-a-grin," or "Toad-gone-wrong,"
Or "Billy Bandy-knees:"
The Frog is justly sensitive
To epithets like these.

No animal will more repay
A treatment kind and fair,

At least so lonely people say
Who keep a frog (and, by the way,
They are extremely rare).

*Hilaire Belloc* [1870–1953]

## SAGE COUNSEL

The lion is the beast to fight:
He leaps along the plain,
And if you run with all your might,
He runs with all his mane.
I'm glad I'm not a Hottentot,
But if I were, with outward cal-lum
I'd either faint upon the spot
Or hie me up a leafy pal-lum.

The chamois is the beast to hunt:
He's fleeter than the wind,
And when the chamois is in front
The hunter is behind.
The Tyrolese make famous cheese
And hunt the chamois o'er the chaz-zums;
I'd choose the former, if you please,
For precipices give me spaz-zums.

The polar bear will make a rug
Almost as white as snow:
But if he gets you in his hug,
He rarely lets you go.
And polar ice looks very nice,
With all the colors of a prissum:
But, if you'll follow my advice,
Stay home and learn your catechissum.

*Arthur Quiller-Couch* [1863–1944]

## CHILD'S NATURAL HISTORY

### GEESE

Ev-er-y child who has the use
Of his sen-ses knows a goose.
Sees them un-der-neath the tree
Gath-er round the goose-girl's knee,

While she reads them by the hour
From the works of Scho-pen-hau-er.
How pa-tient-ly the geese at-tend!
But do they re-al-ly com-pre-hend
What Scho-pen-hau-er's driv-ing at?
Oh, not at all; but what of that?
Nei-ther do I; nei-ther does she;
And, for that mat-ter, nor does he.

### A SEAL

See, Chil-dren, the Fur-bear-ing Seal;
Ob-serve his mis-di-rect-ed zeal;
He dines with most ab-ste-mi-ous care
On Fish, Ice Water and Fresh Air
A-void-ing cond-i-ments or spice
For fear his fur should not be nice
And fine and soft and smooth and meet
For Broad-way or for Re-gent Street.
And yet some-how I often feel
(Though for the kind Fur-bear-ing Seal
I harbor a Re-spect Pro-found)
He runs Fur-bear-ance in the ground.

### THE YAK

This is the Yak, so neg-li-gee;
His coif-fure's like a stack of hay;
He lives so far from Any-where,
I fear the Yak neg-lects his hair,
And thinks, since there is none to see,
What mat-ter how un-kempt he be:
How would he feel if he but knew
That in this Pic-ture-book I drew
His Phys-i-og-no-my un-shorn,
For chil-dren to de-ride and scorn?

### THE MON-GOOS

This, Children, is the famed Mon-goos.
He has an ap-pe-tite ab-struse:
Strange to re-late, this crea-ture takes
A cu-ri-ous joy in eat-ing snakes—

All kinds—though, it must be con-fessed,
He likes the poi-son-ous ones the best.
From him we learn how ve-ry small
A thing can bring a-bout a Fall.
O Mon-goos, where were you that day
When Mistress Eve was led a-stray?
If you'd but seen the ser-pent first,
Our parents would not have been cursed,
And so there would be no ex-cuse
For MILTON, but for you—Mon-goos!

*Oliver Herford* [1863–1935]

## IN FOREIGN PARTS

WHEN I lived in Singapore,
It was something of a bore
To receive the bulky Begums who came trundling to my door;
They kept getting into tangles
With their bingle-bongle-bangles,
And the tiger used to bite them as he sat upon the floor.

When I lived in Timbuctoo,
Almost everyone I knew
Used to play upon the sackbut, singing "toodle-doodle-doo,"
And they made ecstatic ballads,
And consumed seductive salads,
Made of chicory and hickory and other things that grew.

When I lived at Rotterdam,
I possessed a spotted ram,
Who would never feed on anything but hollyhocks and ham;
But one day he butted down
All the magnates of the town,
So they slew him, though I knew him to be gentle as a lamb.

*But!*
When I got to Kandahar,
It was very, very far,

And the people came and said to me, "How *very* plain you are!"
So I sailed across the foam,
And I toddle-waddled home,
And no more I'll go a-rovering beyond the harbor bar.

*Laura E. Richards* [1850–1943]

## "SAID OPIE READ"

Said Opie Read to E. P. Roe,
"How do you like Gaboriau?"
"I like him very much indeed,"
Said E. P. Roe to Opie Read.

*Julian Street* [1879–1947] *and James Montgomery Flagg* [1877–1960]

## THE LAUGHING WILLOW

To see the Kaiser's epitaph
Would make a weeping willow laugh.

*Oliver Herford* [1863–1935]

## A GRAIN OF SALT

Of all the wimming doubly blest
The sailor's wife's the happiest,
For all she does is stay to home
And knit and darn—and let 'im roam.

Of all the husbands on the earth
The sailor has the finest berth,
For in 'is cabin he can sit
And sail and sail—and let 'er knit.

*Wallace Irwin* [1875–1959]

## THE PURPLE COW

Reflections on a Mythic Beast,
Who's Quite Remarkable, at Least.

I never saw a Purple Cow;
I never Hope to See One;
But I can Tell you, Anyhow,
I'd rather See than Be One.

### CINQ ANS APRÈS

(Confession: and a portrait, Too,
Upon a Background that I Rue!)

Ah, yes, I wrote the "Purple Cow"—
  I'm sorry, now, I Wrote it!
But I can Tell you, Anyhow,
  I'll Kill you if you Quote it!

*Gelett Burgess* [1866–1951]

### NONSENSE VERSES

The Window has Four little Panes:
  But One have I:
The Window-Panes are in its Sash,—
  I wonder why!

My Feet they haul me 'round the House:
  They hoist me up the Stairs:
I only have to steer them and
  They ride me everywheres.

Remarkable truly, is Art!
See—Elliptical wheels on a Cart!
  It looks very fair
  In the Picture up there:
But imagine the Ride when you start!

I'd rather have Fingers than Toes:
I'd rather have Eyes than a Nose:
  And as for my hair,
  I'm glad it's all there,
I'll be awfully sad when it goes!

I wish that my Room had a Floor;
I don't so much care for a Door,
  But this walking around
  Without touching the ground
Is getting to be quite a bore!

*Gelett Burgess* [1866–1951]

## VERS NONSENSIQUES

I AM gai. I am poet. I dvell
Rupert Street, at the fifth. I am svell.
  And I sing tralala
  And I love my mamma,
And the English, I speaks him quite vell!

"Cassez-vous, cassez-vous, cassez-vous,
O mer, sur vos froids gris cailloux!"
  Ainsi tradusit Laure
  Au profit d'Isadore
(Bon jeune homme, et son future époux.)

Il existe une espinstere à Tours
Un peu vite, et qui portait toujours
  Un ulster peau-de-phoque,
  Un chapeau biliqoque,
Et des nicreboquers en velours.

Un marin naufragé (de Doncastre)
Pour prière, au milieu du désastre
  Repetait à genoux
  Ces mots simples et doux:—
"Scintellez, scintellez, petits astres!"

*George du Maurier* [1834-1896]

## HOME

A MELANCHOLY little man was seated on the ground;
He showed supreme indifference to everything around.
"Why do you not run home," I cried, "and tumble into bed?"
He looked at me expressively, and presently he said:

"One rubber plant can never make a home,
Not even when combined with brush and comb,
  And spoon, and fork, and knife,
  And graphophone, and wife.
No! Something more is needed for a home."

I said: "What does your dwelling lack? The pretty hearth-side tone?
The note of domesticity?" He gave a fearful groan.
"Alas!" he cried, while from his seat he slowly upward bobbed
And seized his hat, "a flat's a flat!" Together then we sobbed:

"One rubber plant can never make a home;
One day did not suffice for building Rome.
  One gas-log and a cat
  Can't civilize a flat.
No! Something more is needed for a home."

*Unknown*

## TWO LIMERICKS

A CANNER, exceedingly canny,
One morning remarked to his granny,
  "A canner can can
  Anything that he can;
But a canner can't can a can, can he?"

A TUTOR who tooted a flute
Tried to teach two young tutors to toot.
  Said the two to the tutor,
  "Is it harder to toot, or
To tutor two tutors to toot?"

*Carolyn Wells* [18  -1942]

## MORE LIMERICKS

A BRIGHT little maid of St. Thomas
One day found a suit of pajamas;
  Said the maiden, "Well, well,
  What these are, I can't tell,
But I'm certain the garments ain't mama's."

THERE was a young fellow named Tait,
Who dined with his girl at 8:08;
  As Tait did not state,
  I cannot relate
What Tait and his tête-à-tête ate at 8:08.

THERE was an old man of Tarentum,
Who gnashed his false teeth till he bent 'em:
And when asked for the cost
Of what he had lost,
Said, "I really can't tell, for I rent 'em!"

A LADY there was of Antigua,
Who said to her spouse, "What a pig you are!"
He answered, "My queen,
Is it manners you mean,
Or do you refer to my figure?"

THE poor benighted Hindoo,
He does the best he kindoo;
He sticks to caste
From first to last;
For pants he makes his skindoo.

THERE were three young women of Birmingham,
And I know a sad story concerning 'em:
They stuck needles and pins
In the reverend shins
Of the Bishop engaged in confirming 'em.

THERE was a young lady of Niger
Who smiled as she rode on a tiger;
They returned from the ride
With the lady inside,
And the smile on the face of the tiger.

THERE was a young lady of Wilts,
Who walked up to Scotland on stilts;
When they said it was shocking
To show so much stocking,
She answered: "Then what about kilts?"

THERE was a young girl of Lahore,
The same shape behind as before.
As no one knew where
To offer a chair,
She had to sit down on the floor.

*Cosmo Monkhouse* [1840–1901]

As a beauty I'm not a great star,
There are others more handsome by far.
But my face—I don't mind it,
Because I'm behind it—
It's the people in front that I jar.

*Anthony Euwer* [1877-

THERE was a small boy of Quebec,
Who was buried in snow to his neck;
When they said, "Are you friz?"
He replied, "Yes, I is—
But we don't call this cold in Quebec."

*Rudyard Kipling* [1865-1936]

THERE was a young man so benighted
He didn't know when he was slighted,
But went to the party
And ate just as hearty
As if he'd been duly invited!

---

THERE was an old man of Nantucket
Who kept all his cash in a bucket;
But his daughter, named Nan,
Ran away with a man—
And as for the bucket, Nantucket.

*Dayton Voorhees*, in *Princeton Tiger*, 1902

He followed the pair to Pawtucket,
Nan, and the man—and the bucket;
And he said to the man,
"You're quite welcome to Nan,"—
But as for the bucket, Pawtucket.

## THE SAD TALE OF MR. MEARS

THERE was a man who had a clock,
His name was Matthew Mears;
And every day he wound that clock
For eight and twenty years.

And then one day he found that clock
An eight-day clock to be,
And a madder man than Matthew Mears
You would not wish to see.

*Unknown*

# OLD FAVORITES

## AN ELEGY ON THE DEATH OF A MAD DOG

From "The Vicar of Wakefield"

Good people all, of every sort,
  Give ear unto my song;
And if you find it wondrous short,—
  It cannot hold you long.

In Islington there was a man
  Of whom the world might say,
That still a godly race he ran,—
  Whene'er he went to pray.

A kind and gentle heart he had,
  To comfort friends and foes:
The naked every day he clad,—
  When he put on his clothes.

And in that town a dog was found,
  As many dogs there be,
Both mongrel, puppy, whelp, and hound,
  And curs of low degree.

This dog and man at first were friends;
  But when a pique began,
The dog, to gain some private ends,
  Went mad, and bit the man.

Around from all the neighboring streets
  The wondering neighbors ran,
And swore the dog had losts his wits,
  To bite so good a man.

The wound it seemed both sore and sad
  To every Christian eye:
And while they swore the dog was mad,
  They swore the man would die.

But soon a wonder came to light,
  That showed the rogues they lied:—
The man recovered of the bite,
  The dog it was that died.

*Oliver Goldsmith* [1728-1774]

## AN ELEGY

### ON THAT GLORY OF HER SEX, MRS. MARY BLAIZE

Good people all, with one accord,
  Lament for Madam Blaize,
Who never wanted a good word—
  From those who spoke her praise.

The needy seldom passed her door,
  And always found her kind;
She freely lent to all the poor—
  Who left a pledge behind.

She strove the neighborhood to please
  With manners wondrous winning;
And never followed wicked ways—
  Unless when she was sinning.

At church, in silks and satins new
  With hoop of monstrous size,
She never slumbered in her pew—
  But when she shut her eyes.

Her love was sought, I do aver,
  By twenty beaux and more;
The King himself has followed her—
  When she has walked before.

But now, her wealth and finery fled,
  Her hangers-on cut short all;
The doctors found, when she was dead—
  Her last disorder mortal.

Let us lament, in sorrow sore,
  For Kent Street well may say,
That had she lived a twelvemonth more—
  She had not died to-day.

*Oliver Goldsmith* [1728–1774]

## THE DIVERTING HISTORY OF JOHN GILPIN

### SHOWING HOW HE WENT FARTHER THAN HE INTENDED AND CAME SAFE HOME AGAIN

John Gilpin was a citizen
  Of credit and renown,
A train-band captain eke was he
  Of famous London town.

John Gilpin's spouse said to her dear,
  "Though wedded we have been
These twice ten tedious years, yet we
  No holiday have seen.

"To-morrow is our wedding-day,
  And we will then repair
Unto the Bell at Edmonton,
  All in a chaise and pair.

"My sister, and my sister's child,
  Myself, and children three,
Will fill the chaise; so you must ride
  On horseback after we."

He soon replied, "I do admire
  Of womankind but one,
And you are she, my dearest dear,
  Therefore it shall be done.

"I am a linen-draper bold,
As all the world doth know,
And my good friend the calender
Will lend his horse to go."

Quoth Mrs. Gilpin, "That's well said;
And for that wine is dear,
We will be furnished with our own,
Which is both bright and clear."

John Gilpin kissed his loving wife;
O'erjoyed was he to find,
That though on pleasure she was bent,
She had a frugal mind.

The morning came, the chaise was brought,
But yet was not allowed
To drive up to the door, lest all
Should say that she was proud.

So three doors off the chaise was stayed,
Where they did all get in;
Six precious souls, and all agog
To dash through thick and thin.

Smack went the whip, round went the wheels,
Were never folk so glad,
The stones did rattle underneath,
As if Cheapside were mad.

John Gilpin at his horse's side
Seized fast the flowing mane,
And up he got, in haste to ride,
But soon came down again;

For saddle-tree scarce reached had he,
His journey to begin,
When, turning round his head, he saw
Three customers come in.

So down he came; for lcss of time,
  Although it grieved him sore,
Yet loss of pence, full well he knew,
  Would trouble him much more.

'Twas long before the customers
  Were suited to their mind,
When Betty screaming came downstairs,
  "The wine is left behind!"

"Good lack!" quoth he—"yet bring it me,
  My leathern belt likewise,
In which I bear my trusty sword,
  When I do exercise."

Now Mistress Gilpin (careful soul!)
  Had two stone bottles found,
To hold the liquor that she loved,
  And keep it safe and sound.

Each bottle had a curling ear,
  Through which the belt he drew,
And hung a bottle on each side,
  To make his balance true.

Then over all, that he might be
  Equipped from top to toe,
His long red cloak, well brushed and neat,
  He manfully did throw.

Now see him mounted once again
  Upon his nimble steed,
Full slowly pacing o'er the stones,
  With caution and good heed.

But finding soon a smoother road
  Beneath his well-shod feet,
The snorting beast began to trot,
  Which galled him in his seat.

So, "Fair and softly," John he cried,
  But John he cried in vain;
That trot become a gallop soon,
  In spite of curb and rein.

So stooping down, as needs he must
  Who cannot sit upright,
He grasped the mane with both his hands,
  And eke with all his might.

His horse, who never in that sort
  Had handled been before,
What thing upon his back had got
  Did wonder more and more.

Away went Gilpin, neck or naught;
  Away went hat and wig:
He little dreamt, when he set out,
  Of running such a rig.

The wind did blow, the cloak did fly,
  Like streamer long and gay,
Till, loop and button failing both,
  At last it flew away.

Then might all people well discern
  The bottles he had slung;
A bottle swinging at each side,
  As hath been said or sung.

The dogs did bark, the children screamed,
  Up flew the windows all;
And every soul cried out, "Well done!"
  As loud as he could bawl.

Away went Gilpin—who but he?
  His fame soon spread around;
"He carries weight!" "He rides a race!"
  "'Tis for a thousand pound!"

And still, as fast as he drew near,
'Twas wonderful to view,
How in a trice the turnpike-men
Their gates wide open threw.

And now, as he went bowing down
His reeking head full low,
The bottles twain behind his back
Were shattered at a blow.

Down ran the wine into the road,
Most piteous to be seen,
Which made his horse's flanks to smoke
As they had basted been.

But still he seemed to carry weight,
With leathern girdle braced;
For all might see the bottle-necks
Still dangling at his waist.

Thus all through merry Islington
These gambols he did play,
Until he came unto the Wash
Of Edmonton so gay;

And there he threw the Wash about
On both sides of the way,
Just like unto a trundling mop,
Or a wild goose at play.

At Edmonton his loving wife
From the balcony spied
Her tender husband, wondering much
To see how he did ride.

"Stop, stop, John Gilpin!—Here's the house!"
They all at once did cry;
"The dinner waits, and we are tired;"—
Said Gilpin—"So am I."

But yet his horse was not a whit
  Inclined to tarry there!
For why?—his owner had a house
  Full ten miles off, at Ware,

So like an arrow swift he flew,
  Shot by an archer strong;
So did he fly—which brings me to
  The middle of my song.

Away went Gilpin, out of breath,
  And sore against his will,
Till at his friend the calender's
  His horse at last stood still.

The calender, amazed to see
  His neighbor in such trim,
Laid down his pipe, flew to the gate,
  And thus accosted him:

"What news? what news? your tidings tell;
  Tell me you must and shall—
Say why bareheaded you are come,
  Or why you come at all?"

Now Gilpin had a pleasant wit
  And loved a timely joke;
And thus unto the calender
  In merry guise he spoke:

"I came because your horse would come,
  And, if I well forbode,
My hat and wig will soon be here.—
  They are upon the road."

The calender, right glad to find
  His friend in merry pin,
Returned him not a single word
  But to the house went in;

Whence straight he came with hat and wig;
  A wig that flowed behind,
A hat not much the worse for wear,
  Each comely in its kind.

He held them up, and in his turn
  Thus showed his ready wit,
"My head is twice as big as yours,
  They therefore needs must fit.

"But let me scrape the dirt away
  That hangs upon your face;
And stop and eat, for well you may
  Be in a hungry case."

Said John, "It is my wedding-day,
  And all the world would stare,
If wife should dine at Edmonton,
  And I should dine at Ware."

So turning to his horse, he said,
  "I am in haste to dine;
'Twas for your pleasure you came here,
  You shall go back for mine."

Ah, luckless speech, and bootless boast!
  For which he paid full dear;
For, while he spake, a braying ass
  Did sing most loud and clear;

Whereat his horse did snort, as he
  Had heard a lion roar,
And galloped off with all his might.
  As he had done before.

Away went Gilpin, and away
  Went Gilpin's hat and wig:
He lost them sooner than at first;
  For why?—they were too big.

Now Mistress Gilpin, when she saw
  Her husband posting down
Into the country far away,
  She pulled out half-a-crown;

And thus unto the youth she said
  That drove them to the Bell,
"This shall be yours, when you bring back
  My husband safe and well."

The youth did ride, and soon did meet
  John coming back amain:
Whom in a trice he tried to stop,
  By catching at his rein;

But not performing what he meant,
  And gladly would have done,
The frighted steed he frighted more,
  And made him faster run.

Away went Gilpin, and away
  Went postboy at his heels,
The postboy's horse right glad to miss
  The lumbering of the wheels.

Six gentlemen upon the road,
  Thus seeing Gilpin fly,
With postboy scampering in the rear,
  They raised the hue and cry:

"Stop thief! stop thief!—a highwayman!"
  Not one of them was mute;
And all and each that passed that way
  Did join in the pursuit.

And now the turnpike gates again
  Flew open in short space;
The toll-men thinking, as before,
  That Gilpin rode a race.

And so he did, and won it too,
  For he got first to town;
Nor stopped till where he had got up
  He did again get down.

Now let us sing, Long live the king!
  And Gilpin, long live he!
And when he next doth ride abroad
  May I be there to see!

*William Cowper* [1731–1800]

## THE RAZOR-SELLER

A FELLOW in a market-town,
Most musical, cried "Razors!" up and down,
  And offered twelve for eighteen pence;
Which certainly seemed wondrous cheap,
And, for the money, quite a heap,
  As every man should buy, with cash and sense.

A country bumpkin the great offer heard,—
Poor Hodge, who suffered by a thick black beard,
  That seemed a shoe-brush stuck beneath his nose:
With cheerfulness the eighteen pence he paid,
And proudly to himself in whispers said,
  "This rascal stole the razors, I suppose!

"No matter if the fellow *be* a knave,
Provided that the razors *shave;*
  It *sartinly* will be a monstrous prize."
So home the clown, with his good fortune, went,
Smiling, in heart and soul content,
  And quickly soaped himself to ears and eyes.

Being well lathered from a dish or tub,
Hodge now began with grinning pain to grub,
  Just like a hedger cutting furze;
'Twas a vile razor!—then the rest he tried,—
All were impostors. "Ah!" Hodge sighed,
  "I wish my eighteen pence were in my purse."

In vain, to chase his beard, and bring the graces,
He cut, and dug, and winced, and stamped, and swore;
Brought blood, and danced, blasphemed, and made wry faces,
And cursed each razor's body o'er and o'er:

His muzzle, formed of *opposition* stuff,
Firm as a Foxite, would not lose its ruff;
So kept it,—laughing at the steel and suds.
Hodge, in a passion, stretched his angry jaws,
Vowing the direst vengeance, with clenched claws,
On the vile cheat that sold the goods.
"Razors! a base, confounded dog!
Not fit to scrape a hog!"

Hodge sought the fellow,—found him,—and begun:
"P'rhaps, Master Razor-rogue, to you 'tis fun
That people flay themselves out of their lives.
You rascal! for an hour have I been grubbing,
Giving my whiskers here a scrubbing,
With razors just like oyster-knives.
Sirrah! I tell you you're a knave,
To cry up razors that can't shave!"

"Friend," quoth the razor-man, "I'm not a knave;
As for the razors you have bought,
Upon my soul, I never thought
That they would *shave*."
"Not think they'd *shave!*" quoth Hodge, with wondering eyes,
And voice not much unlike an Indian yell;
"What were they made for, then, you dog?" he cries.
"*Made*," quoth the fellow, with a smile,— "*to sell*."

*John Wolcot* [1738–1819]

## THE THREE WARNINGS

The tree of deepest root is found
Least willing still to quit the ground:
'Twas therefore said by ancient sages,
That love of life increased with years

So much, that in our later stages,
When pains grow sharp, and sickness rages,
The greatest love of life appears.
This great affection to believe,
Which all confess, but few perceive,—
If old assertions can't prevail,—
Be pleased to hear a modern tale.
When sports went round, and all were gay,
On neighbor Dodson's wedding-day,
Death called aside the jocund groom
With him into another room,
And looking grave—"You must," says he,
"Quit your sweet bride, and come with me."
"With you! and quit my Susan's side!
With you!" the hapless husband cried;
"Young as I am, 'tis monstrous hard!
Besides, in truth, I'm not prepared:
My thoughts on other matters go;
This is my wedding-day, you know."
What more he urged, I have not heard,
His reasons could not well be stronger;
So Death the poor delinquent spared,
And left to live a little longer.
Yet calling up a serious look—
His hour-glass trembled while he spoke—
"Neighbor," he said, "farewell! No more
Shall Death disturb your mirthful hour;
And farther, to avoid all blame
Of cruelty upon my name,
To give you time for preparation,
And fit you for your future station,
Three several warnings you shall have,
Before you're summoned to the grave.
Willing for once I'll quit my prey,
And grant a kind reprieve,
In hopes you'll have no more to say,
But, when I call again this way,
Well-pleased the world will leave."
To these conditions both consented,
And parted perfectly contented.

What next the hero of our tale befell,
How long he lived, how wise, how well,
How roundly he pursued his course,
And smoked his pipe, and stroked his horse
  The willing Muse shall tell.
He chaffered then, he bought, he sold,
Nor once perceived his growing old,
   Nor thought of Death as near;
His friends not false, his wife no shrew,
Many his gains, his children few,
  He passed his hours in peace.
But while he viewed his wealth increase,
While thus along Life's dusty road
The beaten track content he trod,
Old Time, whose haste no mortal spares,
Uncalled, unheeded, unawares,
  Brought on his eightieth year.
And now, one night, in musing mood
  As all alone he sat,
The unwelcome messenger of Fate
   Once more before him stood.
Half killed with anger and surprise,
"So soon returned!" old Dodson cried.
"So soon, d' ye call it?" Death replies.
"Surely, my friend, you're but in jest!
  Since I was here before
'Tis six-and-thirty years at least,
  And you are now fourscore."
  "So much the worse," the clown rejoined,
"To spare the agèd would be kind:
However, see your search be legal;
And your authority—is 't regal?
Else you are come on a fool's errand,
With but a secretary's warrant.
Besides, you promised me Three Warnings,
Which I have looked for nights and mornings;
But for that loss of time and ease,
I can recover damages."
  "I know," cries Death, "that at the best
I seldom am a welcome guest;

But don't be captious, friend, at least:
I little thought you'd still be able
To stump about your farm and stable;
Your years have run to a great length;
I wish you joy, though, of your strength!"
"Hold," says the farmer, "not so fast!
I have been lame these four years past."
"And no great wonder," Death replies:
"However, you still keep your eyes;
And sure, to see one's loves and friends,
For legs and arms would make amends."
"Perhaps," says Dodson, "so it might,
But latterly I've lost my sight."
"This is a shocking tale, 'tis true,
But still there's comfort left for you:
Each strives your sadness to amuse;
I warrant you hear all the news."
"There's none," cries he; "and if there were,
I'm grown so deaf I could not hear."
"Nay, then," the spectre stern rejoined,
"These are unwarrantable yearnings;
If you are lame, and deaf, and blind,
You've had your three sufficient warnings.
So, come along, no more we'll part."
He said, and touched him with his dart.
And now old Dodson, turning pale,
Yields to his fate—so ends my tale.

*Hester Thrale Piozzi* [1741-1821]

## THE SAILOR'S CONSOLATION

ONE night came on a hurricane,
The sea was mountains rolling,
When Barney Buntline turned his quid,
And said to Billy Bowling:
"A strong nor'wester's blowing, Bill;
Hark! don't ye hear it roar, now?
Lord help 'em, how I pities them
Unhappy folks on shore now!

"Foolhardy chaps who live in towns,
  What danger they are all in,
And now lie quaking in their beds,
  For fear the roof should fall in;
Poor creatures! how they envies us,
  And wishes, I've a notion,
For our good luck, in such a storm,
  To be upon the ocean!

"And as for them who're out all day
  On business from their houses,
And late at night are coming home,
  To cheer their babes and spouses,—
While you and I, Bill, on the deck
  Are comfortably lying,
My eyes! what tiles and chimney-pots
  About their heads are flying!

"And very often have we heard
  How men are killed and undone
By overturns of carriages,
  By thieves, and fires in London;
We know what risks all landsmen run,
  From noblemen to tailors;
Then, Bill, let us thank Providence
  That you and I are sailors."

*Charles Dibdin* [1745–1814]

## TAM O' SHANTER

WHEN chapman billies leave the street,
And drouthy neibors, neibors meet,
As market-days are wearing late,
And folk begin to tak the gate;
While we sit bousing at the nappy,
And gettin' fou and unco happy,
We think na on the lang Scots miles,
The mosses, waters, slaps, and stiles,
That lie between us and our hame,
Whare sits our sulky sullen dame,

Gathering her brows like gathering storm,
Nursing her wrath to keep it warm.

This truth fand honest Tam o' Shanter,
As he frae Ayr ae night did canter
(Auld Ayr, wham ne'er a town surpasses,
For honest men and bonnie lasses).

O Tam! hadst thou but been sae wise,
As ta'en thy ain wife Kate's advice!
She tauld thee weel thou wast a skellum,
A blethering, blustering, drunken blellum;
That frae November till October,
Ae market-day thou wast na sober;
That ilka melder, wi' the miller,
Thou sat as lang as thou had siller;
That every naig was ca'd a shoe on,
The smith and thee gat roaring fou on;
That at the Lord's house, even on Sunday,
Thou drank wi' Kirkton Jean till Monday.
She prophesied that, late or soon,
Thou would be found deep drowned in Doon;
Or catched wi' warlocks i' the mirk,
By Alloway's auld haunted kirk.

Ah, gentle dames! it gars me greet,
To think how monie counsels sweet,
How monie lengthened, sage advices,
The husband frae the wife despises!

But to our tale:—Ae market-night,
Tam had got planted unco right,
Fast by an ingle, bleezing finely,
Wi' reaming swats, that drank divinely;
And at his elbow, Souter Johnny,
His ancient, trusty, drouthy crony;
Tam lo'ed him like a vera brither;—
They had been fou for weeks thegither!

The night drave on wi' sangs and clatter;
And aye the ale was growing better:

The landlady and Tam grew gracious,
Wi' favors secret, sweet, and precious:
The Souter tauld his queerest stories;
The landlord's laugh was ready chorus:
The storm without might rair and rustle,—
Tam did na mind the storm a whistle.

Care, mad to see a man sae happy,
E'en drowned himself amang the nappy!
As bees flee hame wi' lades o' treasure,
The minutes winged their way wi' pleasure:
Kings may be blessed, but Tam was glorious,
O'er a' the ills o' life victorious!

But pleasures are like poppies spread,—
You seize the flower, its bloom is shed:
Or like the snowfall in the river,—
A moment white—then melts forever;
Or like the borealis race,
That flit ere you can point their place;
Or like the rainbow's lovely form,
Evanishing amid the storm.
Nae man can tether time or tide;
The hour approaches Tam maun ride;
That hour, o' night's black arch the key-stane,
That dreary hour he mounts his beast in;
And sic a night he taks the road in,
As ne'er poor sinner was abroad in.

The wind blew as 'twad blawn its last;
The rattling showers rose on the blast;
The speedy gleams the darkness swallowed;
Loud, deep, and lang, the thunder bellowed:
That night, a child might understand,
The Deil had business on his hand.

Weel mounted on his gray mare, Meg,
(A better never lifted leg,)
Tam skelpit on through dub and mire,
Despising wind, and rain, and fire;

Whiles holding fast his guid blue bonnet;
Whiles crooning o'er some auld Scots sonnet;
Whiles glowering round wi' prudent cares,
Lest bogles catch him unawares;—
Kirk-Alloway was drawing nigh,
Whare ghaists and houlets nightly cry.

By this time he was cross the ford,
Whare in the snaw the chapman smoored;
And past the birks and meikle stane,
Whare drunken Charlie brak's neckbane;
And through the whins, and by the cairn,
Whare hunters fand the murdered bairn;
And near the thorn, aboon the well,
Whare Mungo's mither hanged hersel.
Before him Doon pours all his floods;
The doubling storm roars through the woods;
The lightnings flash from pole to pole;
Near and more near the thunders roll;
When, glimmering through the groaning trees,
Kirk-Alloway seemed in a bleeze;
Through ilka bore the beams were glancing,
And loud resounded mirth and dancing.

Inspiring bold John Barleycorn,
What dangers thou canst make us scorn!
Wi' tippenny, we fear nae evil;
Wi' usquebae, we'll face the Devil!
The swats sae reamed in Tammie's noddle,
Fair play, he cared na deils a boddle.
But Maggie stood right sair astonished,
Till, by the heel and hand admonished,
She ventured forward on the light;
And, wow! Tam saw an unco sight!
Warlocks and witches in a dance;
Nae cotillion brent new frae France,
But hornpipes, jigs, strathspeys, and reels,
Put life and mettle in their heels.
A winnock-bunker in the east,
There sat auld Nick, in shape o' beast;

A towzie tyke, black, grim, and large,
To gie them music was his charge:
He screwed the pipes and gart them skirl,
Till roof and rafters a' did dirl,
Coffins stood round, like open presses,
That shawed the dead in their last dresses;
And by some devilish cantrip slight,
Each in its cauld hand held a light:
By which heroic Tam was able
To note upon the haly table,
A murderer's banes in gibbet airns;
Twa span-lang, wee, unchristened bairns;
A thief, new-cutted frae a rape,
Wi' his last gasp his gab did gape;
Five tomahawks, wi' bluid red-rusted;
Five scimitars, wi' murder crusted;
A garter, which a babe had strangled;
A knife, a father's throat had mangled,
Whom his ain son o' life bereft,—
The gray hairs yet stack to the heft;
Wi' mair o' horrible and awfu',
Which even to name wad be unlawfu'.

As Tammie glowered, amazed and curious,
The mirth and fun grew fast and furious:
The piper loud and louder blew;
The dancers quick and quicker flew;
They reeled, they set, they crossed, they cleekit,
Till ilka carline swat and reekit,
And coost her duddies to the wark,
And linket at it in her sark!

Now Tam, O Tam! had thae been queans,
A' plump and strappin' in their teens;
Their sarks, instead o' creeshie flannen,
Been snaw-white seventeen-hunder linen!
Thir breeks o' mine, my only pair,
That ance were plush o' guid blue hair,
I wad hae gi'en them off my hurdies,
For ae blink o' the bonnie burdies!

But withered beldams, auld and droll,
Rigwoodie hags, wad spean a foal,
Louping and flinging on a crummock,
I wonder didna turn thy stomach.

But Tam kenned what was what fu' brawlie;
There was ae winsome wench and walie,
That night enlisted in the core,
(Lang after kenned on Carrick shore;
For monie a beast to dead she shot,
And perished monie a bonnie boat,
And shook baith meikle corn and bear,
And kept the country-side in fear.)
Her cutty-sark, o' Paisley harn,
That, while a lassie, she had worn,
In longitude though sorely scanty,
It was her best, and she was vauntie.
Ah! little kenned thy reverend grannie,
That sark she coft for her wee Nannie,
Wi' two pund Scots, ('twas a' her riches,)
Wad ever graced a dance o' witches!

But here my Muse her wing maun cour;
Sic flights are far beyond her power;
To sing how Nannie lap and flang
(A souple jade she was, and strang),
And how Tam stood, like ane bewitched,
And thought his very e'en enriched;
Even Satan glowered, and fidged fu' fain,
And hotched and blew wi' might and main
Till first ae caper, syne anither,
Tam tint his reason a' thegither,
And roars out, "Weel done, Cutty-sark!"
And in an instant all was dark;
And scarcely had he Maggie rallied,
When out the hellish legion sallied.
As bees bizz out wi' angry fyke,
When plundering herds assail their byke;
As open pussie's mortal foes,
When, pop! she starts before their nose;

As eager runs the market-crowd,
When, "Catch the thief!" resounds aloud;
So Maggie runs, the witches follow,
Wi' monie an eldritch screech and hollow.

Ah, Tam! ah, Tam! thou'll get thy fairin'!
In hell they'll roast thee like a herrin'!
In vain thy Kate awaits thy comin'!
Kate soon will be a woefu' woman!
Now, do thy speedy utmost, Meg,
And win the key-stane o' the brig;
There at them thou thy tail may toss;
A running stream they dare na cross.
But ere the key-stane she could make,
The fient a tail she had to shake!
For Nannie, far before the rest,
Hard upon noble Maggie pressed,
And flew at Tam wi' furious ettle;
But little wist she Maggie's mettle!
Ae spring brought off her master hale,
But left behind her ain gray tail;
The carline caught her by the rump,
And left poor Maggie scarce a stump.

Now, wha this tale o' truth shall read,
Ilk man and mother's son, tak heed!
Whene'er to drink you are inclined,
Or cutty-sarks run in your mind,
Think, ye may buy the joys owre dear:—
Remember Tam o' Shanter's mare.

*Robert Burns* [1759–1796]

## GLUGGITY GLUG

From "The Myrtle and the Vine"

A JOLLY fat friar loved liquor good store,
  And he had drunk stoutly at supper;
He mounted his horse in the night at the door,
  And sat with his face to the crupper:

"Some rogue," quoth the friar, "quite dead to remorse,
Some thief, whom a halter will throttle,
Some scoundrel has cut off the head of my horse,
While I was engaged at the bottle,
Which went gluggity, gluggity—glug—glug—glug."

The tail of the steed pointed south on the dale,
'Twas the friar's road home, straight and level;
But, when spurred, a horse follows his nose, not his tail,
So he scampered due north, like a devil:
"This new mode of docking," the friar then said,
"I perceive doesn't make a horse trot ill;
And 'tis cheap,—for he never can eat off his head
While I am engaged at the bottle,
Which goes gluggity, gluggity—glug—glug—glug."

The steed made a stop,—in a pond he had got,
He was rather for drinking than grazing;
Quoth the friar, "'Tis strange headless horses should trot
But to drink with their tails is amazing!"
Turning round to see whence this phenomenon rose,
In the pond fell this son of a pottle;
Quoth he, "The head's found, for I'm under his nose,—
I wish I were over a bottle,
Which goes gluggity, gluggity—glug—glug—glug!"

*George Colman the Younger* [1762–1836

## THE LAIRD O' COCKPEN

THE Laird o' Cockpen, he's proud and he's great
His mind is ta'en up wi' things o' the State;
He wanted a wife, his braw house to keep;
But favor wi' wooin' was fashous to seek.

Doun by the dyke-side a lady did dwell.
At his table-head he thought she'd look well,—
M'Clish's ae daughter o' Claverse-ha' Lee,
A penniless lass wi' a lang pedigree.

His wig was well-pouthered, as guid as when new,
His waistcoat was white, his coat it was blue;

He put on a ring, a sword, and cocked hat,—
And wha could refuse the Laird wi' a' that!

He took the gray mare, and rade cannily,
And rapped at the yett o' Claverse-ha' Lee;
"Gae tell Mistress Jean to come speedily ben,—
She's wanted to speak wi' the Laird o' Cockpen."

Mistress Jean she was makin' the elder-flower wine.
"And what brings the Laird at sic a like time?"
She put aff her apron, and on her silk goun,
Her mutch wi' red ribbons, and gaed awa' doun.

And when she cam' ben, he bowed fu' low;
And what was his errand he soon let her know.
Amazed was the Laird when the lady said, "Na,"
And wi' a laigh curtsie she turnèd awa'.

Dumfoundered he was, but nae sigh did he gi'e;
He mounted his mare, and rade cannily;
And aften he thought, as he gaed through the glen,
"She's daft to refuse the Laird o' Cockpen!"

And now that the Laird his exit had made,
Mistress Jean she reflected on what she had said;
"Oh, for ane I'll get better, it's waur I'll get ten,—
I was daft to refuse the Laird o' Cockpen."

Neist time that the Laird and the Lady were seen,
They were gaun arm-in-arm to the kirk on the green;
Now she sits in the ha' like a weel-tappit hen,
But as yet there's nae chickens appeared at Cockpen.

*The first seven stanzas by Carolina Nairne* [1766–1845]
*The last two by Susan Ferrier* [1782–1854]

## THE WELL OF ST. KEYNE

A Well there is in the west country,
  And a clearer one never was seen;
There is not a wife in the west country
  But has heard of the Well of St. Keyne.

An oak and an elm tree stand beside,
  And behind doth an ash-tree grow,
And a willow from the bank above
  Droops to the water below.

A traveller came to the Well of St. Keyne;
  Joyfully he drew nigh;
For from cock-crow he had been travelling,
  And there was not a cloud in the sky.

He drank of the water so cool and clear,
  For thirsty and hot was he,
And he sat down upon the bank,
  Under the willow-tree.

There came a man from the house hard by,
  At the Well to fill his pail,
On the Well-side he rested it,
  And bade the Stranger hail.

"Now, art thou a bachelor, Stranger?" quoth he,
  "For, an if thou hast a wife,
The happiest draught thou hast drank this day
  That ever thou didst in thy life.

"Or has thy good woman, if one thou hast,
  Ever here in Cornwall been?
For, an if she have, I'll venture my life
  She has drunk of the Well of St. Keyne."

"I have left a good woman who never was here,"
  The Stranger he made reply;
"But that my draught should be better for that,
  I pray you answer me why."

"St. Keyne," quoth the Cornish-man, "many a time
  Drank of this crystal Well;
And, before the angel summoned her,
  She laid on the water a spell,—

"If the Husband, of this gifted Well
Shall drink before his Wife,
A happy man henceforth is he,
For he shall be Master for life;—

"But, if the Wife should drink of it first,
Heaven help the Husband then!"—
The Stranger stooped to the Well of St. Keyne,
And drank of the water again.

"You drank of the Well, I warrant, betimes?"
He to the Cornish-man said;
But the Cornish-man smiled as the Stranger spake,
And sheepishly shook his head:—

"I hastened, as soon as the wedding was done,
And left my Wife in the porch;
But i' faith, she had been wiser than me,
For she took a bottle to church."

*Robert Southey* [1774–1843]

## ADDRESS TO A MUMMY

And thou hast walked about (how strange a story!)
In Thebes's streets three thousand years ago,
When the Memnonium was in all its glory,
And time had not begun to overthrow
Those temples, palaces, and piles stupendous
Of which the very ruins are tremendous.

Speak! for thou long enough hast acted dummy.
Thou hast a tongue,—come, let us hear its tune;
Thou'rt standing on thy legs, above ground, mummy!
Revisiting the glimpses of the moon,—
Not like thin ghosts or disembodied creatures,
But with thy bones and flesh, and limbs and features.

Tell us—for doubtless thou canst recollect—
To whom should we assign the Sphinx's fame?
Was Cheops or Cephrenes architect
Of either pyramid that bears his name?

Is Pompey's Pillar really a misnomer?
Had Thebes a hundred gates, as sung by Homer?

Perhaps thou wert a Mason, and forbidden
By oath to tell the secrets of thy trade,—
Then say what secret melody was hidden
In Memnon's statue, which at sunrise played?
Perhaps thou wert a Priest,—if so, my struggles
Are vain, for priestcraft never owns its juggles.

Perhaps that very hand, now pinioned flat,
Has hob-a-nobbed with Pharaoh, glass to glass;
Or dropped a halfpenny in Homer's hat;
Or doffed thine own to let Queen Dido pass;
Or held, by Solomon's own invitation,
A torch at the great temple's dedication.

I need not ask thee if that hand, when armed,
Has any Roman soldier mauled and knuckled;
For thou wert dead and buried and embalmed
Ere Romulus and Remus had been suckled:
Antiquity appears to have begun
Long after thy primeval race was run.

Thou couldst develop—if that withered tongue
Might tell us what those sightless orbs have seen—
How the world looked when it was fresh and young,
And the great deluge still had left it green;
Or was it then so old that history's pages
Contained no record of its early ages?

Still silent! incommunicative elf!
Art sworn to secrecy? then keep thy vows;
But prithee tell us something of thyself,—
Reveal the secrets of thy prison-house;
Since in the world of spirits thou hast slumbered,
What hast thou seen, what strange adventures numbered?

Since first thy form was in this box extended,
We have, above ground, seen some strange mutations:
The Roman empire has begun and ended,
New worlds have risen, we have lost old nations;

And countless kings have into dust been humbled,
While not a fragment of thy flesh has crumbled.

Didst thou hear not the pother o'er thy head,
When the great Persian conqueror, Cambyses,
Marched armies o'er thy tomb with thundering tread,—
O'erthrew Osiris, Orus, Apis, Isis;
And shook the pyramids with fear and wonder,
When the gigantic Memnon fell asunder?

If the tomb's secrets may not be confessed,
The nature of thy private life unfold:
A heart has throbbed beneath that leathern breast,
And tears adown that dusty cheek have rolled;
Have children climbed those knees, and kissed that face?
What was thy name and station, age and race?

Statue of flesh,—Immortal of the dead!
Imperishable type of evanescence!
Posthumous man,—who quit'st thy narrow bed,
And standest undecayed within our presence!
Thou wilt hear nothing till the Judgment morning,
When the great trump shall thrill thee with its warning.

Why should this worthless tegument endure,
If its undying guest be lost for ever?
O, let us keep the soul embalmed and pure
In living virtue, that when both must sever,
Although corruption may our frame consume,
The immortal spirit in the skies may bloom!

*Horace Smith* [1779-1849]

## JOHN GRUMLIE

John Grumlie swore by the light o' the moon
And the green leaves on the tree,
That he could do more work in a day
Than his wife could do in three.

His wife rose up in the morning
  Wi' cares and troubles enow—
John Grumlie bide at hame, John,
  And I'll go haud the plow.

First ye maun dress your children fair,
  And put them a' in their gear;
And ye maun turn the malt, John,
  Or else ye'll spoil the beer;
And ye maun reel the tweel, John,
  That I span yesterday;
And ye maun ca' in the hens, John,
  Else they'll all lay away.

O he did dress his children fair,
  And put them a' in their gear;
But he forgot to turn the malt,
  And so he spoiled the beer:
And he sang loud as he reeled the tweel
  That his wife span yesterday;
But he forgot to put up the hens,
  And the hens all layed away.

The hawket crummie loot down nae milk;
  He kirned, nor butter gat;
And a' gade wrang, and naught gade right;
  He danced wi' rage, and grat;
Then up he ran to the head o' the knowe
  Wi' mony a wave and shout—
She heard him as she heard him not,
  And steered the stots about.

John Grumlie's wife cam hame at e'en,
  A weary wife and sad,
And burst into a laughter loud,
  And laughed as she'd been mad:
While John Grumlie swore by the light o' the moon
  And the green leaves on the tree,
If my wife should na win a penny a day
  She's aye her will for me.

*Allan Cunningham* [1784–1842]

## THE NEEDLE

THE gay belles of fashion may boast of excelling
In waltz or cotillion, at whist or quadrille;
And seek admiration by vauntingly telling
Of drawing, and painting, and musical skill;
But give me the fair one, in country or city,
Whose home and its duties are dear to her heart,
Who cheerfully warbles some rustical ditty,
While plying the needle with exquisite art:
The bright little needle—the swift-flying needle,
The needle directed by beauty and art.

If Love have a potent, a magical token,
A talisman, ever resistless and true—
A charm that is never evaded or broken,
A witchery certain the heart to subdue—
'Tis this—and his armory never has furnished
So keen and unerring, or polished a dart;
Let Beauty direct it, so pointed and burnished,
And, oh! it is certain of touching the heart:
The bright little needle—the swift-flying needle,
The needle directed by beauty and art.

Be wise, then, ye maidens, nor seek admiration
By dressing for conquest, and flirting with all;
You never, whate'er be your fortune or station,
Appear half so lovely at rout or at ball,
As gayly convened at a work-covered table,
Each cheerfully active and playing her part,
Beguiling the task with a song or a fable,
And plying the needle with exquisite art:
The bright little needle—the swift-flying needle,
The needle directed by beauty and art.

*Samuel Woodworth* [1784–1842]

## MISADVENTURES AT MARGATE

MR. SIMPKINSON (*loquitur*)

I WAS in Margate last July, I walked upon the pier,
I saw a little vulgar Boy,—I said, "What make you here?

The gloom upon your youthful cheek speaks anything but joy;"
Again I said, "What make you here, you little vulgar Boy?"

He frowned, that little vulgar Boy,—he deemed I meant to scoff,—
And when the little heart is big, a little "sets it off."
He put his finger in his mouth, his little bosom rose,—
He had no little handkerchief to wipe his little nose!

"Hark! don't you hear, my little man?—it's striking nine," I said,
"An hour when all good little boys and girls should be in bed.
Run home and get your supper, else your Ma will scold,—O fie!
It's very wrong indeed for little boys to stand and cry!"

The tear-drop in his little eye again began to spring,
His bosom throbbed with agony,—he cried like anything!
I stooped, and thus amidst his sobs I heard him murmur,—"Ah!
I have n't got no supper! and I have n't got no Ma!

"My father, he is on the seas,—my mother's dead and gone!
And I am here, on this here pier, to roam the world alone;
I have not had, this livelong day, one drop to cheer my heart,
Nor '*brown*' to buy a bit of bread with,—let alone a tart.

"If there's a soul will give me food, or find me in employ,
By day or night, then blow me tight!" (he was a vulgar Boy;)
"And now I'm here, from this here pier it is my fixed intent
To jump, as Mister Levi did from off the Monument!"

"Cheer up! cheer up! my little man,—cheer up!" I kindly said,
"You are a naughty boy to take such things into your head;
If you should jump from off the pier, you'd surely break your legs,
Perhaps your neck,—then Bogey'd have you, sure as eggs are eggs!

"Come home with me, my little man, come home with me and sup!
My landlady is Mrs. Jones,—we must not keep her up,—
There's roast potatoes at the fire,—enough for me and you,—
Come home, you little vulgar Boy,—I lodge at Number 2."

I took him home to Number 2, the house beside "The Foy."
I bad him wipe his dirty shoes,—that little vulgar Boy,—
And then I said to Mistress Jones, the kindest of her sex,
"Pray be so good as go and fetch a pint of double X!"

But Mrs. Jones was rather cross, she made a little noise,
She said she "did not like to wait on little vulgar Boys."
She with her apron wiped the plates, and, as she rubbed the delf,
Said I might "go to Jericho, and fetch my beer myself!"

I did not go to Jericho,—I went to Mr. Cobb,—
I changed a shilling (which in town the people call a Bob)—
It was not so much for myself as for that vulgar child,—
And I said, "A pint of double X, and please to draw it mild!"

When I came back I gazed about,—I gazed on stool and chair,—
I could not see my little friend,—because he was not there!
I peeped beneath the table-cloth, beneath the sofa, too,—
I said, "You little vulgar Boy! why, what's become of you?"

I could not see my table-spoons.—I looked, but could not see
The little fiddle-patterned ones I use when I'm at tea;
I could not see my sugar-tongs, my silver watch,—oh, dear!
I know 'twas on the mantel-piece when I went out for beer.

I could not see my mackintosh,—it was not to be seen!
Nor yet my best white beaver hat, broad-brimmed and lined with green;
My carpet-bag,—my cruet-stand, that holds my sauce and soy,—
My roast potatoes!—all are gone!—and so's that vulgar Boy!

I rang the bell for Mrs. Jones, for she was down below,
"Oh, Mrs. Jones, what *do* you think?—ain't this a pretty go?
That horrid little vulgar Boy whom I brought here to-night
He's stolen my things and run away!" Says she, "And sarve you right!"

Next morning I was up betimes,—I sent the Crier round,
All with his bell and gold-laced hat, to say I'd give a pound
To find that little vulgar Boy, who'd gone and used me so;
But when the Crier cried, "O Yes!" the people cried, "O No!"

I went to "Jarvis' Landing-place," the glory of the town,
There was a common sailor-man a walking up and down;
I told my tale,—he seemed to think I'd not been treated well,
And called me "Poor old Buffer"—what that means I cannot tell.

That sailor-man, he said he'd seen that morning on the shore
A son of—something—'twas a name I'd never heard before,—
A little "gallows-looking chap,"—dear me, what could he mean?—
With a "carpet-swab" and "mucking-togs," and a hat turned up with green.

He spoke about his "precious eyes," and said he'd seen him "sheer,"—
It's very odd that sailor-men should talk so very queer;
And then he hitched his trousers up, as is, I'm told, their use,—
It's very odd that sailor-men should wear those things so loose.

I did not understand him well, but think he meant to say
He'd seen that little vulgar Boy, that morning, swim away
In Captain Large's Royal George, about an hour before,
And they were now, as he supposed, "some*wheres*" about the Nore.

A landsman said, "I *twig* the chap,—he's been upon the
Mill,—
And 'cause he *gammons* so the *flats*, ve calls him Veeping
Bill!"
He said "he'd done me werry brown," and "nicely *stowed*
the *swag*,"—
That's French, I fancy, for a hat, or else a carpet-bag.

I went and told the constable my property to track;
He asked me if "I did not wish that I might get it back?"
I answered, "To be sure I do!—it's what I'm come about."
He smiled and said, "Sir, does your mother know that you
are out?"

Not knowing what to do, I thought I'd hasten back to town,
And beg our own Lord Mayor to catch the Boy who'd "done
me brown."
His Lordship very kindly said he'd try and find him out,
But he "rather thought that there were several vulgar boys
about."

He sent for Mr. Whithair then, and I described "the swag,"
My mackintosh, my sugar-tongs, my spoons, and carpet-bag;
He promised that the New Police should all their powers
employ,
But never to this hour have I beheld that vulgar Boy!

MORAL

Remember, then, that when a boy I've heard my Grandma
tell,
"BE WARNED IN TIME BY OTHERS' HARM, AND YOU SHALL DO
FULL WELL!"
Don't link yourself with vulgar folks, who've got no fixed
abode,
Tell lies, use naughty words, and say they "wish they may be
blowed!"

Don't take too much of double X!—and don't at night go out
To fetch your beer yourself, but make the pot-boy bring your
stout!

And when you go to Margate next, just stop and ring the bell,
Give my respects to Mrs. Jones, and say I'm pretty well!

*Richard Harris Barham* [1788–1845]

## "THE CAPTAIN STOOD ON THE CARRONADE"

THE Captain stood on the Carronade—"First lieutenant," says he,
"Send all my merry men aft here, for they must list to me:
I haven't the gift of the gab, my sons, because I'm bred to the sea;
That ship there is a Frenchman, who means to fight with we.
Odds blood, hammer and tongs, long as I've been to sea,
I've fought 'gainst every odds—but I've gained the victory.

"That ship there is a Frenchman, and if we don't take *she*,
'Tis a thousand bullets to one, that she will capture *we;*
I haven't the gift of the gab, my boys; so each man to his gun;
If she's not mine in half an hour, I'll flog each mother's son.
Odds bobs, hammer and tongs, long as I've been to sea,
I've fought 'gainst every odds—and I've gained the victory."

We fought for twenty minutes, when the Frenchman had enough;
"I little thought," said he, "that your men were of such stuff;"
The Captain took the Frenchman's sword, a low bow made to he;
"I haven't the gift of the gab, monsieur, but polite I wish to be.
Odds bobs, hammer and tongs, long as I've been to sea,
I've fought 'gainst every odds—and I've gained the victory."

Our Captain sent for all of us; "My merry men," said he,
"I haven't the gift of the gab, my lads, but yet I thankful be;

You've done your duty handsomely, each man stood to his
gun;
If you hadn't, you villains, as sure as day, I'd have flogged
each mother's son.
Odds bobs, hammer and tongs, as long as I'm at sea,
I'll fight 'gainst every odds—and I'll gain the victory."

*Frederick Marryat* [1792-1848]

## FAITHLESS NELLY GRAY

### A PATHETIC BALLAD

BEN BATTLE was a soldier bold,
And used to war's alarms;
But a cannon-ball took off his legs,
So he laid down his arms!

Now as they bore him off the field,
Said he, "Let others shoot,
For here I leave my second leg,
And the Forty-second Foot!"

The army-surgeons made him limbs:
Said he, "They're only pegs;
But there's as wooden members quite
As represent my legs!"

Now Ben he loved a pretty maid,
Her name was Nelly Gray;
So he went to pay her his devours
When he'd devoured his pay!

But when he called on Nelly Gray,
She made him quite a scoff;
And when she saw his wooden legs,
Began to take them off!

"O Nelly Gray! O Nelly Gray!
Is this your love so warm?
The love that loves a scarlet coat,
Should be more uniform!"

She said, "I loved a soldier once,
For he was blithe and brave;
But I will never have a man
With both feet in the grave!

"Before you had those timber toes,
Your love I did allow,
But then, you know, you stand upon
Another footing now!"

"O Nelly Gray! O Nelly Gray!
For all your jeering speeches,
At duty's call I left my legs
In Badajoz's *breaches!*"

"Why, then," said she, "you've lost the feet
Of legs in war's alarms,
And now you cannot wear your shoes
Upon your feats of arms!"

"Oh, false and fickle Nelly Gray,
I know why you refuse:—
Though I've no feet, some other man
Is standing in my shoes!

"I wish I ne'er had seen your face;
But now a long farewell!
For you will be my death:—alas!
You will not be my *Nell!*"

Now when he went from Nelly Gray,
His heart so heavy got,
And life was such a burthen grown,
It made him take a knot!

So round his melancholy neck
A rope he did entwine,
And, for his second time in life,
Enlisted in the Line!

One end he tied around a beam,
 And then removed his pegs,
And, as his legs were off,—of course
 He soon was off his legs!

And there he hung till he was dead
 As any nail in town,—
For though distress had cut him up,
 It could not cut him down!

A dozen men sat on his corpse,
 To find out why he died—
And they buried Ben at four cross-roads,
 With a *stake* in his inside!

*Thomas Hood* [1799–1845]

## FAITHLESS SALLY BROWN

YOUNG Ben he was a nice young man,
 A carpenter by trade;
And he fell in love with Sally Brown,
 That was a lady's maid.

But as they fetched a walk one day,
 They met a press-gang crew;
And Sally she did faint away,
 Whilst Ben he was brought to.

The boatswain swore with wicked words
 Enough to shock a saint,
That, though she did seem in a fit,
 'Twas nothing but a feint.

"Come, girl," said he, "hold up your head,
 He'll be as good as me;
For when your swain is in our boat
 A boatswain he will be."

So when they'd made their game of her,
 And taken off her elf,
She roused, and found she only was
 A coming to herself.

"And is he gone, and is he gone?"
She cried, and wept outright;
"Then I will to the water-side,
And see him out of sight."

A waterman came up to her;
"Now, young woman," said he,
"If you weep on so, you will make
Eye-water in the sea."

"Alas! they've taken my beau, Ben,
To sail with old Benbow;"
And her woe began to run afresh,
As if she'd said, Gee woe!

Says he, "They've only taken him
To the tender-ship, you see."
"The tender-ship," cried Sally Brown,
"What a hardship that must be!

"O, would I were a mermaid now,
For then I'd follow him!
But O, I'm not a fish-woman,
And so I cannot swim.

"Alas! I was not born beneath
The Virgin and the Scales,
So I must curse my cruel stars,
And walk about in Wales."

Now Ben had sailed to many a place
That's underneath the world;
But in two years the ship came home,
And all her sails were furled.

But when he called on Sally Brown,
To see how she got on,
He found she'd got another Ben,
Whose Christian name was John.

"O Sally Brown! O Sally Brown!
How could you serve me so?
I've met with many a breeze before,
But never such a blow!"

Then, reading on his 'bacco box,
He heaved a heavy sigh,
And then began to eye his pipe,
And then to pipe his eye.

And then he tried to sing, "All's Well!"
But could not, though he tried;
His head was turned,—and so he chewed
His pigtail till he died.

His death, which happened in his berth,
At forty-odd befell;
They went and told the sexton, and
The sexton tolled the bell.

*Thomas Hood* [1799-1845]

## "PLEASE TO RING THE BELLE"

I'LL tell you a story that's not in Tom Moore:
Young Love likes to knock at a pretty girl's door:
So he called upon Lucy—'twas just ten o'clock—
Like a spruce single man, with a smart double knock.

Now a hand-maid, whatever her fingers be at,
Will run like a puss when she hears a *rat*-tat:
So Lucy ran up—and in two seconds more
Had questioned the stranger and answered the door.

The meeting was bliss, but the parting was woe;
For the moment will come when such comers must go.
So she kissed him, and whispered—poor innocent thing—
"The next time you come, love, pray come with a ring."

*Thomas Hood* [1799-1845]

## OLD GRIMES

OLD Grimes is dead; that good old man
  We never shall see more:
He used to wear a long black coat,
  All buttoned down before.

His heart was open as the day,
  His feelings all were true;
His hair was some inclined to gray—
  He wore it in a queue.

Whene'er he heard the voice of pain,
  His breast with pity burned;
The large, round head upon his cane
  From ivory was turned.

Kind words he ever had for all;
  He knew no base design:
His eyes were dark and rather small,
  His nose was aquiline.

He lived at peace with all mankind,
  In friendship he was true;
His coat had pocket-holes behind,
  His pantaloons were blue.

Unharmed, the sin which earth pollutes
  He passed securely o'er,
And never wore a pair of boots
  For thirty years or more.

But good old Grimes is now at rest,
  Nor fears misfortune's frown:
He wore a double-breasted vest—
  The stripes ran up and down.

He modest merit sought to find,
  And pay it its desert:
He had no malice in his mind,
  No ruffles on his shirt.

His neighbors he did not abuse—
  Was sociable and gay:
He wore large buckles on his shoes,
  And changed them every day.

His knowledge, hid from public gaze,
  He did not bring to view,
Nor made a noise, town-meeting days,
  As many people do.

His worldly goods he never threw
  In trust to fortune's chances,
But lived (as all his brothers do)
  In easy circumstances.

Thus undisturbed by anxious cares,
  His peaceful moments ran;
And everybody said he was
  A fine old gentleman.

*Albert Gorton Greene* [1802–1868]

## THE ANNUITY

I GAED to spend a week in Fife—
  An unco week it proved to be—
For there I met a waesome wife
  Lamentin' her viduity.
Her grief brak out sae fierce and fell,
I thought her heart wad burst the shell,
And,—I was sae left tae mysel,—
  I sell't her an annuity.

The bargain lookit fair eneugh—
  She just was turned o' saxty-three;
I couldna guessed she'd prove sae teugh,
  By human ingenuity.
But years have come, and years have gane,
And there she's yet as stieve 's a stane—
The limmer's growin' young again,
  Since she got her annuity.

She's crined awa' to bane and skin,
  But that, it seems, is naught to me;
She's like to live—although she's in
  The last stage o' tenuity.
She munches wi' her wizened gums,
An' stumps about on legs o' thrums;
But comes, as sure as Christmas comes,
  To ca' for her annuity.

She jokes her joke, an' cracks her crack,
  As spunkie as a growin' flea—
An' there she sits upon my back,
  A livin' perpetuity.
She hurkles by her ingle side,
An' toasts an' toasts her wrunkled hide—
Lord kens how lang she yet may bide
  To ca' for her annuity.

I read the tables drawn wi' care
  For an insurance company;
Her chance o' life was stated there,
  Wi' perfect perspicuity.
But tables here or tables there,
She's lived ten years beyond her share,
An's like to live a dizzen mair,
  To ca' for her annuity.

I got the loun that drew the deed—
  We spelled it o'er right carefully;—
In vain he yerked his souple head,
  To find an ambiguity:
It's dated—tested—a' complete—
The proper stamp—nae word delete—
And diligence, as on decreet,
  May pass for her annuity.

Last Yule she had a fearfu' hoast,—
  I thought a kink might set me free;
I led her out, 'mang snaw and frost,
  Wi' constant assiduity.

But deil ma' care—the blast gaed by,
And missed the auld anatomy—
It just cost me a tooth, forbye
  Discharging her annuity.

I thought that grief might gar her quit—
  Her only son was lost at sea—
But aff her wits behoved to flit,
  An' leave her in fatuity!
She threeps, an' threeps, he's livin' yet,
For a' the tellin' she can get;
But catch the doited runt forget
  To ca' for her annuity!

If there's a sough o' cholera,
  Or typhus,—wha sae gleg as she?
She buys up baths, an' drugs, an' a',
  In siccan superfluity!
She doesna need—she's fever proof—
The pest gaed owre her very roof—
She tauld me sae—an' then her loof
  Held out for her annuity.

Ae day she fell, her arm she brak—
  A compound fracture as could be—
Nae leech the cure wad undertak,
  Whate'er was the gratuity.
It's cured! She handles 't like a flail—
It does as weel in bits as hale—
But I'm a broken man mysel
  Wi' her and her annuity.

Her broozled flesh and broken banes
  Are weel as flesh and banes can be;
She beats the tades that live in stanes,
  An' fatten in vacuity!
They die when they're exposed to air,
They canna thole the atmosphere—
But her! expose her onywhere,
  She lives for her annuity.

If mortal means could nick her thread,
  Sma' crime it wad appear to me;
Ca' t murder—or ca' t homicide—
  I'd justify 't—an' do it tae.
But how to fell a withered wife
That's carved out o' the tree of life—
The timmer limmer dares the knife
  To settle her annuity.

I'd try a shot—but whar's the mark?
  Her vital parts are hid frae me;
Her backbone wanders through her sark
  In an unkenned corkscrewity.
She's palsified, an' shakes her head
Sae fast about, ye scarce can see 't;
It's past the power o' steel or lead
  To settle her annuity.

She might be drowned; but go she'll not
  Within a mile o' loch or sea;
Or hanged—if cord could grip a throat
  O' siccan exiguity.
It's fitter far to hang the rope—
It draws out like a telescope;
'Twad tak' a dreadfu' length o' drop
  To settle her annuity.

Will poison do 't? It has been tried,
  But, be't in hash or fricassee,
That's just the dish she can't abide,
  Whatever kind o' *goût* it hae.
It's needless to assail her doubts,—
She gangs by instinct, like the brutes,—
An' only eats an' drinks what suits
  Hersel an' her annuity.

The Bible says the age o' man
  Threescore and ten, perchance, may be;
She's ninety-four. Let them wha can,
  Explain the incongruity.

She should hae lived afore the flood—
She's come o' patriarchal blood,
She's some auld Pagan, mummified
  Alive for her annuity.

She's been embalmed inside and oot—
  She's sauted to the last degree—
There's pickle in her very snoot
  Sae caper-like an' cruety.
Lot's wife was fresh compared to her—
They've kyanized the useless knir,—
She canna decompose—nae mair
  Than her accursed annuity.

The water-drap wears out the rock,
  As this eternal jaud wears me;
I could withstand the single shock,
  But not the continuity.
It's pay me here, an' pay me there,
An' pay me, pay me, evermair—
I'll gang demented wi' despair—
  I'm *charged* for her annuity!

*George Outram* [1805-1856]

## THE SMACK IN SCHOOL

A DISTRICT school, not far away,
Mid Berkshire's hills, one winter's day,
Was humming with its wonted noise
Of threescore mingled girls and boys;
Some few upon their tasks intent,
But more on furtive mischief bent.
The while the master's downward look
Was fastened on a copy-book;
When suddenly, behind his back,
Rose sharp and clear a rousing smack,
As 'twere a battery of bliss
Let off in one tremendous kiss!
"What's that?" the startled master cries;
"That, thir," a little imp replies,

"Wath William Willith, if you pleathe,—
I thaw him kith Thuthanna Peathe!"
With frown to make a statue thrill,
The master thundered, "Hither, Will!"
Like wretch o'ertaken in his track,
With stolen chattels on his back,
Will hung his head in fear and shame,
And to the awful presence came,—
A great, green, bashful simpleton,
The butt of all good-natured fun.
With smile suppressed, and birch upraised,
The threatener faltered,—"I'm amazed
That you, my biggest pupil, should
Be guilty of an act so rude!
Before the whole set school to boot—
What evil genius put you to't?"
"'Twas she herself, sir," sobbed the lad,
"I did not mean to be so bad;
But when Susannah shook her curls,
And whispered, I was 'fraid of girls
And dursn't kiss a baby's doll,
I couldn't stand it, sir, at all,
But up and kissed her on the spot!
I know—boo-hoo—I ought to not.
But, somehow, from her looks—boo-hoo—
I thought she kind o' wished me to!"

*William Pitt Palmer* [1805-1884]

## "THE POPE HE LEADS A HAPPY LIFE"

From "Harry Lorrequer"

The Pope he leads a happy life,
He fears not married care nor strife,
He drinks the best of Rhenish wine,—
I would the Pope's gay lot were mine.

But yet all happy's not his life,
He has no maid, nor blooming wife;
Nor child has he to raise his hope—
I would not wish to be the Pope.

The Sultan better pleases me,
His is a life of jollity;
He's wives as many as he will—
I would the Sultan's throne then fill.

But even he's a wretched man,
He must obey the Alcoran;
He dare not drink one drop of wine—
I would not change his lot for mine.

So here I take my lowly stand,
I'll drink my own, my native land;
I'll kiss my maiden fair and fine,
And drink the best of Rhenish wine.

And when my maiden kisses me,
I'll think that I the Sultan be;
And when my cheery glass I tope,
I'll fancy then I am the Pope.

*Charles Lever* [1806–1872]

## THE HEIGHT OF THE RIDICULOUS

I WROTE some lines once on a time
  In wondrous merry mood,
And thought, as usual, men would say
  They were exceeding good.

They were so queer, so very queer,
  I laughed as I would die;
Albeit, in the general way,
  A sober man am I.

I called my servant, and he came;
  How kind it was of him,
To mind a slender man like me,
  He of the mighty limb!

"These to the printer," I exclaimed,
  And, in my humorous way,
I added (as a trifling jest),
  "There'll be the devil to pay."

He took the paper, and I watched,
And saw him peep within;
At the first line he read, his face
Was all upon the grin.

He read the next; the grin grew broad,
And shot from ear to ear;
He read the third; a chuckling noise
I now began to hear.

The fourth; he broke into a roar;
The fifth; his waistband split;
The sixth; he burst five buttons off,
And tumbled in a fit.

Ten days and nights, with sleepless eye,
I watched that wretched man,
And since, I never dare to write
As funny as I can.

*Oliver Wendell Holmes* [1809–1894]

## THE BALLAD OF THE OYSTERMAN

It was a tall young oysterman lived by the river-side,
His shop was just upon the bank, his boat was on the tide;
The daughter of a fisherman, that was so straight and slim,
Lived over on the other bank, right opposite to him.

It was the pensive oysterman that saw a lovely maid,
Upon a moonlight evening, a-sitting in the shade;
He saw her wave a handkerchief, as much as if to say,
"I'm wide awake, young oysterman, and all the folks away."

Then up arose the oysterman, and to himself said he,
"I guess I'll leave the skiff at home, for fear that folks should see;
I read it in the story-book, that, for to kiss his dear,
Leander swam the Hellespont,—and I will swim this here."

And he has leaped into the waves, and crossed the shining stream,
And he has clambered up the bank, all in the moonlight gleam;
Oh, there are kisses sweet as dew, and words as soft as rain—
But they have heard her father's step, and in he leaps again!

Out spoke the ancient fisherman: "Oh, what was that, my daughter?"
"'Twas nothing but a pebble, sir, I threw into the water."
"And what is that, pray tell me, love, that paddles off so fast?"
"It's nothing but a porpoise, sir, that's been a swimming past."

Out spoke the ancient fisherman: "Now bring me my harpoon!
I'll get into my fishing-boat, and fix the fellow soon."
Down fell that pretty innocent, as falls a snow-white lamb;
Her hair drooped round her pallid cheeks, like seaweed on a clam.

Alas for those two loving ones! she waked not from her swound,
And he was taken with the cramp, and in the waves was drowned;
But Fate has metamorphosed them, in pity of their woe,
And now they keep an oyster-shop for mermaids down below

*Oliver Wendell Holmes* [1809–1894]

## LITTLE BILLEE

THERE were three sailors of Bristol city
Who took a boat and went to sea.
But first with beef and captain's biscuits
And pickled pork they loaded she.

There was gorging Jack and guzzling Jimmy,
And the youngest he was little Billee.
Now when they got as far as the Equator
They'd nothing left but one split pea.

Says gorging Jack to guzzling Jimmy,
"I am extremely hungaree."
To gorging Jack says guzzling Jimmy,
"We've nothing left, us must eat we."

Says gorging Jack to guzzling Jimmy,
"With one another we shouldn't agree!
There's little Bill, he's young and tender,
We're old and tough, so let's eat he."

"Oh! Billy, we're going to kill and eat you,
So undo the button of your chemie."
When Bill received this information
He used his pocket handkerchie.

"First let me say my catechism,
Which my poor mammy taught to me."
"Make haste, make haste," says guzzling Jimmy,
While Jack pulled out his snickersnee.

So Billy went up to the main-top gallant mast,
And down he fell on his bended knee.
He scarce had come to the twelfth commandment
When up he jumps. "There's land I see:

"Jerusalem and Madagascar,
And North and South Amerikee:
There's the British flag a-riding at anchor,
With Admiral Napier, K. C. B."

So when they got aboard of the Admiral's,
He hanged fat Jack and flogged Jimmee:
But as for little Bill he made him
The Captain of a Seventy three.

*William Makepeace Thackeray* [1811-1863]

## THE JACKDAW OF RHEIMS

THE Jackdaw sat on the Cardinal's chair:
Bishop and abbot and prior were there;
Many a monk, and many a friar,
Many a knight, and many a squire,

With a great many more of lesser degree,—
In sooth, a goodly company;
And they served the Lord Primate on bended knee.
    Never, I ween,
    Was a prouder seen,
Read of in books, or dreamt of in dreams,
Than the Cardinal Lord Archbishop of Rheims!

    In and out
    Through the motley rout,
That little Jackdaw kept hopping about;
    Here and there
    Like a dog in a fair,
    Over comfits and cates,
    And dishes and plates,
Cowl and cope, and rochet and pall,
Mitre and crosier, he hopped upon all!
    With a saucy air,
    He perched on the chair
Where, in state, the great Lord Cardinal sat,
In the great Lord Cardinal's great red hat;
    And he peered in the face
    Of his Lordship's Grace,
With a satisfied look, as if he would say,
"We two are the greatest folks here to-day!"
    And the priests, with awe,
    As such freaks they saw,
Said, "The Devil must be in that little Jackdaw!"

The feast was over, the board was cleared,
The flawns and the custards had all disappeared,
And six little Singing-boys,—dear little souls!
In nice clean faces, and nice white stoles,—
    Came in order due,
    Two by two,
Marching that grand refectory through.
A nice little boy held a golden ewer,
Embossed and filled with water, as pure
As any that flows between Rheims and Namur

Which a nice little boy stood ready to catch
In a fine golden hand-basin made to match.
Two nice little boys, rather more grown,
Carried lavender-water and eau-de-Cologne;
And a nice little boy had a nice cake of soap,
Worthy of washing the hands of the Pope.
    One little boy more
    A napkin bore,
Of the best white diaper, fringed with pink,
And a Cardinal's hat marked in "permanent ink."

The great Lord Cardinal turns at the sight
Of these nice little boys dressed all in white:
    From his finger he draws
    His costly turquoise;
And, not thinking at all about little Jackdaws,
    Deposits it straight
    By the side of his plate,
While the nice little boys on his Eminence wait;
Till, when nobody's dreaming of any such thing,
That little Jackdaw hops off with the ring!

. . . . . . . . .

    There's a cry and a shout,
    And a deuce of a rout,
And nobody seems to know what they're about,
But the monks have their pockets all turned inside out;
    The friars are kneeling,
    And hunting, and feeling
The carpet, the floor, and the walls, and the ceiling.
    The Cardinal drew
    Off each plum-colored shoe,
And left his red stockings exposed to the view;
    He peeps, and he feels
    In the toes and the heels;
They turn up the dishes,—they turn up the plates,—
They take up the poker and poke out the grates,
    —They turn up the rugs,
    They examine the mugs:

But no!—no such thing;
They can't find THE RING!
And the Abbot declared that, "when nobody twigged it,
Some rascal or other had popped in and prigged it!"

The Cardinal rose with a dignified look,
He called for his candle, his bell, and his book:
In holy anger, and pious grief,
He solemnly cursed that rascally thief!
He cursed him at board, he cursed him in bed,
From the sole of his foot to the crown of his head!
He cursed him in sleeping, that every night
He should dream of the devil, and wake in a fright;
He cursed him in eating, he cursed him in drinking,
He cursed him in coughing, in sneezing, in winking;
He cursed him in sitting, in standing, in lying;
He cursed him in walking, in riding, in flying;
He cursed him in living, he cursed him in dying!
Never was heard such a terrible curse!
But what gave rise
To no little surprise,
Nobody seemed one penny the worse!

The day was gone,
The night came on,
The monks and the friars they searched till dawn;
When the sacristan saw,
On crumpled claw
Come limping a poor little lame Jackdaw.
No longer gay,
As on yesterday;
His feathers all seemed to be turned the wrong way;
His pinions drooped—he could hardly stand,
His head was as bald as the palm of your hand;
His eye so dim,
So wasted each limb,
That, heedless of grammar, they all cried, "THAT'S HIM!
That's the scamp that has done this scandalous thing!
That's the thief that has got my Lord Cardinal's Ring!"

The poor little Jackdaw,
When the monks he saw,
Feebly gave vent to the ghost of a caw;
And turned his bald head, as much as to say,
"Pray, be so good as to walk this way!"
Slower and slower
He limped on before,
Till they came to the back of the belfry-door,
Where the first thing they saw,
Midst the sticks and the straw,
Was the RING, in the nest of that little Jackdaw.

Then the great Lord Cardinal called for his book,
And off that terrible curse he took;
The mute expression
Served in lieu of confession,
And, being thus coupled with full restitution,
The Jackdaw got plenary absolution!
—When those words were heard,
That poor little bird
Was so changed in a moment, 'twas really absurd.
He grew sleek and fat;
In addition to that,
A fresh crop of feathers came thick as a mat.
His tail waggled more
Even than before;
But no longer it wagged with an impudent air,
No longer he perched on the Cardinal's chair.
He hopped now about
With a gait devout;
At matins, at vespers, he never was out;
And, so far from any more pilfering deeds,
He always seemed telling the Confessor's beads.
If any one lied, or if any one swore,
Or slumbered in prayer-time, and happened to snore,
That good Jackdaw
Would give a great "Caw!"
As much as to say, "Don't do so any more!"
While many remarked, as his manners they saw,
That they "never had known such a pious Jackdaw!"

He long lived the pride
Of that countryside,
And at last in the odor of sanctity died;
When, as words were too faint
His merits to paint,
The Conclave determined to make him a Saint;
And on newly-made Saints and Popes, as you know,
It's the custom, at Rome, new names to bestow,
So they canonized him by the name of Jem Crow!

*Richard Harris Barham* [1788–1845]

## THE ALARMED SKIPPER

MANY a long, long year ago,
Nantucket skippers had a plan
Of finding out, though "lying low,"
How near New York their schooners ran.

They greased the lead before it fell,
And then by sounding, through the night.
Knowing the soil that stuck so well,
They always guessed their reckoning right.

A skipper gray, whose eyes were dim,
Could tell, by tasting, just the spot;
And so below he 'd "douse the glim,"—
After, of course, his "something hot."

Snug in his berth, at eight o'clock,
This ancient skipper might be found;
No matter how his craft would rock,
He slept,—for skippers' naps are sound.

The watch on deck would now and then
Run down and wake him, with the lead;
He'd up and taste, and tell the men
How many miles they went ahead.

One night 'twas Jotham Marden's watch,
A curious wag—the peddler's son;
And so he mused (the wanton wretch!)
"To-night I'll have a grain of fun.

"We're all a set of stupid fools,
  To think the skipper knows, by tasting,
What ground he's on; Nantucket schools
  Don't teach such stuff, with all their basting!"

And so he took the well-greased lead,
  And rubbed it o'er a box of earth
That stood on deck—a parsnip-bed,—
  And then he sought the skipper's berth.

"Where are we now, sir? Please to taste."
  The skipper yawned, put out his tongue,
Opened his eyes in wondrous haste,
  And then upon the floor he sprung.

The skipper stormed, and tore his hair,
  Hauled on his boots, and roared to Marden,
"Nantucket's sunk, and here we are
  Right over old Marm Hackett's garden!"

*James Thomas Fields* [1816–1881]

## THE PUZZLED CENSUS TAKER

"Got any boys?" the Marshal said
  To a lady from over the Rhine;
And the lady shook her flaxen head,
  And civilly answered, "*Nein!*"

"Got any girls?" the Marshal said
  To the lady from over the Rhine;
And again the lady shook her head,
  And civilly answered, "*Nein!*"

"But some are dead?" the Marshal said
  To the lady from over the Rhine;
And again the lady shook her head,
  And civilly answered, "*Nein!*"

"Husband of course?" the Marshal said
  To the lady from over the Rhine;
And again she shook her flaxen head,
  And civilly answered, "*Nein!*"

"The devil you have!" the Marshal said
  To the lady from over the Rhine;
And again she shook her flaxen head,
  And civilly answered, "*Nein!*"

"Now what do you mean by shaking your head,
  And always answering 'Nine'?"
"*Ich kann nicht Englisch!*" civilly said
  The lady from over the Rhine.

*John Godfrey Saxe* [1816–1887]

## PYRAMUS AND THISBE

This tragical tale, which, they say, is a true one,
Is old; but the manner is wholly a new one.
One Ovid, a writer of some reputation,
Has told it before in a tedious narration;
In a style, to be sure, of remarkable fullness,
But which nobody reads on account of its dullness.

Young Peter Pyramus,—*I* call him Peter,
Not for the sake of the rhyme or the meter,
But merely to make the name completer,—
For Peter lived in the olden times,
And in one of the worst of pagan climes
That flourish now in classical fame,
Long before either noble or boor
Had such a thing as a *Christian* name,—
Young Peter, then, was a nice young beau
As any young lady would wish to know;
In years, I ween, he was rather green,
That is to say, he was just eighteen,—
A trifle too short, and a shaving too lean,
But "a nice young man" as ever was seen,
And fit to dance with a May-day queen!

Now Peter loved a beautiful girl
As ever ensnared the heart of an earl
In the magical trap of an auburn curl,—

A little Miss Thisbe, who lived next door
(They slept, in fact, on the very same floor,
With a wall between them, and nothing more,—
Those double dwellings were common of yore),
And they loved each other, the legends say,
In that very beautiful, bountiful way,
That every young maid and every young blade
Are wont to do before they grow staid,
And learn to love by the laws of trade.
But (alack-a-day, for the girl and the boy!)
A little impediment checked their joy,
And gave them, awhile, the deepest annoy.—
For some good reason, which history cloaks,
The match didn't happen to please the old folks!

So Thisbe's father and Peter's mother
Began the young couple to worry and bother,
And tried their innocent passion to smother
By keeping the lovers from seeing each other!
But who ever heard of a marriage deterred
Or even deferred
By any contrivance so very absurd
As scolding the boy, and caging his bird?

Now, Peter, who wasn't discouraged at all
By obstacles such as the timid appal,
Contrived to discover a hole in the wall,
Which wasn't so thick but removing a brick
Made a passage,—though rather provokingly small.
Through this little chink the lover could greet her,
And secrecy made their courting the sweeter,
While Peter kissed Thisbe, and Thisbe kissed Peter,—
For kisses, like folks with diminutive souls,
Will manage to creep through the smallest of holes!

'Twas here that the lovers, intent upon love,
Laid a nice little plot to meet at a spot
Near a mulberry-tree in a neighboring grove;
For the plan was all laid by the youth and the maid,

Whose hearts, it would seem, were uncommonly bold ones,
To run off and get married in spite of the old ones.

In the shadows of evening, as still as a mouse,
The beautiful maiden slipped out of the house,
The mulberry-tree impatient to find;
While Peter, the vigilant matrons to blind,
Strolled leisurely out some minutes behind.

While waiting alone by the trysting-tree,
A terrible lion as e'er you set eye on
Came roaring along quite horrid to see,
And caused the young maiden in terror to flee;
(A lion's a creature whose regular trade is
Blood,—and "a terrible thing among ladies,")
And, losing her veil as she ran from the wood,
The monster bedabbled it over with blood.

Now Peter, arriving, and seeing the veil
All covered o'er and reeking with gore,
Turned, all of a sudden, exceedingly pale,
And sat himself down to weep and to wail;
For, soon as he saw the garment, poor Peter
Made up his mind in very short meter
That Thisbe was dead, and the lion had eat her!
So breathing a prayer, he determined to share
The fate of his darling, "the loved and the lost,"
And fell on his dagger, and gave up the ghost!

Now Thisbe returning, and viewing her beau
Lying dead by her veil (which she happened to know),
She guessed in a moment, the cause of his erring,
And, seizing the knife, that had taken his life,
In less than a jiffy was dead as a herring!

MORAL

Young gentlemen: Pray recollect, if you please,
Not to make assignations near mulberry-trees;
Should your mistress be missing, it shows a weak head
To be stabbing yourself, till you know she is dead.

Young ladies: You shouldn't go strolling about
When your anxious mammas don't know you are out;
And remember that accidents often befall
From kissing young fellows through holes in the wall.

*John Godfrey Saxe* [1816-1887]

## MY FAMILIAR

*Ecce iterum Crispinus!*

Again I hear that creaking step!—
He's rapping at the door!—
Too well I know the boding sound
That ushers in a bore.
I do not tremble when I meet
The stoutest of my foes,
But Heaven defend me from the friend
Who comes—but never goes!

He drops into my easy chair,
And asks about the news,
He peers into my manuscript,
And gives his candid views;
He tells me where he likes the line,
And where he's forced to grieve;
He takes the strangest liberties,—
But never takes his leave!

He reads my daily paper through
Before I've seen a word;
He scans the lyric (that I wrote),
And thinks it quite absurd;
He calmly smokes my last cigar,
And coolly asks for more;
He opens everything he sees—
Except the entry door!

He talks about his fragile health,
And tells me of the pains
He suffers from a score of ills
Of which he ne'er complains;

And how he struggled once with Death
  To keep the fiend at bay;
On themes like those away he goes—
  But never goes away!

He tells me of the carping words
  Some shallow critic wrote;
And every precious paragraph
  Familiarly can quote;
He thinks the writer did me wrong;
  He'd like to run him through!
He says a thousand pleasant things—
  But never says, "Adieu!"

Whene'er he comes—that dreadful man—
  Disguise it as I may,
I know that, like an autumn rain,
  He'll last throughout the day.
In vain I speak of urgent tasks;
  In vain I scowl and pout;
A frown is no extinguisher—
  It does not put him out!

I mean to take the knocker off,
  Put crape upon the door,
Or hint to John that I am gone
  To stay a month or more.
I do not tremble when I meet
  The stoutest of my foes,
But Heaven defend me from the friend
  Who never, never goes!

*John Godfrey Saxe* [1816–1887]

## HANS BREITMANN'S PARTY.

HANS BREITMANN gife a barty,
  Dey had biano-blayin;
I felled in lofe mit a Merican frau,
  Her name was Madilda Yane.

She hat haar as prown ash a pretzel,
Her eyes vas himmel-plue,
Und ven dey looket indo mine,
Dey shplit mine heart in two.

Hans Breitmann gife a barty,
I vent dere you'll pe pound.
I valset mit Madilda Yane
Und vent shpinnen round und round.
De pootiest Frauelein in de House,
She vayed 'pout dwo hoondred pound,
Und efery dime she give a shoomp
She make de vindows sound.

Hans Breitmann gife a barty,
I dells you it cost him dear.
Dey rolled in more ash sefen kecks
Of foost-rate Lager Beer.
Und venefer dey knocks de shpicket in
De Deutschers gifes a cheer.
I dinks dat so vine a barty
Nefer coom to a het dis year.

Hans Breitmann gife a barty;
Dere all vas Souse und Brouse,
Ven de sooper coomed in, de gompany
Did make demselfs to house;
Dey ate das Brot und Gensy broost,
De Bratwurst und Braten fine,
Und vash der Abendessen down
Mit four parrels of Neckarwein.

Hans Breitmann gife a barty;
We all cot troonk ash bigs.
I poot mine mout to a parrel of bier,
Und emptied it oop mit a schwigs.
Und denn I gissed Madilda Yane
Und she shlog me on de kop,
Und de gompany fited mit daple-lecks
Dill de coonshtable made oos shtop.

Hans Breitmann gife a barty—
  Where ish dat barty now?
Where ish de lofely golden cloud
  Dat float on de moundains' prow?
Where ish de himmelstrahlende Stern—
  De shtar of de shpirit's light?
All goned afay mit de Lager Beer—
  Afay in de Ewigkeit!

*Charles Godfrey Leland* [1824-1903]

## "NOTHING TO WEAR"

### AN EPISODE OF CITY LIFE

Miss Flora McFlimsey, of Madison Square,
Has made three separate journeys to Paris,
And her father assures me, each time she was there,
That she and her friend Mrs. Harris
(Not the lady whose name is so famous in history,
But plain Mrs. H., without romance or mystery)
Spent six consecutive weeks without stopping
In one continuous round of shopping,—
Shopping alone, and shopping together,
At all hours of the day, and in all sorts of weather,—
For all manner of things that a woman can put
On the crown of her head or the sole of her foot,
Or wrap round her shoulders, or fit round her waist,
Or that can be sewed on, or pinned on, or laced,
Or tied on with a string, or stitched on with a bow,
In front or behind, above or below;
For bonnets, mantillas, capes, collars, and shawls;
Dresses for breakfasts and dinners and balls;
Dresses to sit in and stand in and walk in;
Dresses to dance in and flirt in and talk in;
Dresses in which to do nothing at all;
Dresses for winter, spring, summer, and fall;
All of them different in color and pattern,
Silk, muslin, and lace, crape, velvet, and satin,
Brocade, and broadcloth, and other material,
Quite as expensive and much more ethereal;

In short, for all things that could ever be thought of,
Or milliner, *modiste*, or tradesman be bought of,
  From ten-thousand-francs robes to twenty-sous frills;
In all quarters of Paris, and to every store,
While McFlimsey in vain stormed, scolded, and swore,
  They footed the streets, and he footed the bills.

The last trip, their goods shipped by the steamer Arago,
Formed, McFlimsey declares, the bulk of her cargo,
Not to mention a quantity kept from the rest,
Sufficient to fill the largest-sized chest,
Which did not appear on the ship's manifest,
But for which the ladies themselves manifested
Such particular interest, that they invested
Their own proper persons in layers and rows
Of muslins, embroideries, worked under-clothes,
Gloves, handkerchiefs, scarfs, and such trifles as those;
Then, wrapped in great shawls, like Circassian beauties,
Gave *good-by* to the ship, and *go-by* to the duties.
Her relations at home all marvelled, no doubt,
Miss Flora had grown so enormously stout
  For an actual belle and a possible bride;
But the miracle ceased when she turned inside out,
  And the truth came to light, and the dry-goods beside,
Which, in spite of collector and custom-house sentry,
Had entered the port without any entry.

And yet, though scarce three months have passed since the
    day
This merchandise went, on twelve carts, up Broadway,
This same Miss McFlimsey, of Madison Square,
The last time we met was in utter despair,
Because she had nothing whatever to wear!

NOTHING TO WEAR! Now, as this is a true ditty,
  I do not assert—this, you know, is between us—
That she's in a state of absolute nudity,
  Like Powers' Greek Slave, or the Medici Venus;
But I do mean to say, I have heard her declare,

When, at the same moment, she had on a dress
Which cost five hundred dollars, and not a cent less
And jewelry worth ten times more, I should guess,
That she had not a thing in the wide world to wear!

I should mention just here, that out of Miss Flora's
Two hundred and fifty or sixty adorers,
I had just been selected as he who should throw all
The rest in the shade, by the gracious bestowal
On myself, after twenty or thirty rejections,
Of those fossil remains which she called her "affections,"
And that rather decayed, but well-known work of art,
Which Miss Flora persisted in styling "her heart."
So we were engaged. Our troth had been plighted,
Not by moonbeam or starbeam, by fountain or grove,
But in a front parlor, most brilliantly lighted,
Beneath the gas-fixtures we whispered our love.
Without any romance or raptures or sighs,
Without any tears in Miss Flora's blue eyes,
Or blushes, or transports, or such silly actions,
It was one of the quietest business transactions,
With a very small sprinkling of sentiment, if any,
And a very large diamond imported by Tiffany.
On her virginal lips while I printed a kiss,
She exclaimed, as a sort of parenthesis,
And by way of putting me quite at my ease,
"You know, I'm to polka as much as I please,
And flirt when I like,—now, stop, don't you speak,—
And you must not come here more than twice in the week,
Or talk to me either at party or ball,
But always be ready to come when I call;
So don't prose to me about duty and stuff,
If we don't break this off, there will be time enough
For that sort of thing; but the bargain must be
That, as long as I choose, I am perfectly free,
For this is a sort of engagement, you see,
Which is binding on you but not binding on me."

Well, having thus wooed Miss McFlimsey and gained her,
With the silks, crinolines, and hoops that contained her,

I had, as I thought, a contingent remainder
At least in the property, and the best right
To appear as its escort by day and by night;
And it being the week of the Stuckups' grand ball,—
  Their cards had been out for a fortnight or so,
  And set all the Avenue on the tiptoe,—
I considered it only my duty to call,
  And see if Miss Flora intended to go.
I found her,—as ladies are apt to be found,
When the time intervening between the first sound
Of the bell and the visitor's entry is shorter
Than usual,—I found—I won't say, I caught her,—
Intent on the pier-glass, undoubtedly meaning
To see if perhaps it didn't need cleaning.
She turned as I entered,—"Why, Harry, you sinner,
I thought that you went to the Flashers' to dinner!"
"So I did," I replied; "but the dinner is swallowed
  And digested, I trust, for 'tis now nine and more,
So being relieved from that duty, I followed
  Inclination, which led me, you see, to your door;
And now will your ladyship so condescend
As just to inform me if you intend
Your beauty and graces and presence to lend
(All of which, when I own, I hope no one will borrow)
To the Stuckups', whose party, you know, is to-morrow?"

The fair Flora looked up with a pitiful air,
And answered quite promptly, "Why, Harry, *mon cher*,
I should like above all things to go with you there;
But really and truly—I've nothing to wear."

"Nothing to wear! go just as you are;
Wear the dress you have on, and you'll be by far,
I engage, the most bright and particular star
  On the Stuckup horizon"—I stopped—for her eye,
Notwithstanding this delicate onset of flattery,
Opened on me at once a most terrible battery
  Of scorn and amazement. She made no reply,
But gave a slight turn to the end of her nose
  (That pure Grecian feature), as much as to say,

"How absurd that any sane man should suppose
That a lady would go to a ball in the clothes,
No matter how fine, that she wears every day!"

So I ventured again: "Wear your crimson brocade,"
(Second turn-up of nose)—"That's too dark by a shade."
"Your blue silk"—"That's too heavy." "Your pink"—
"That's too light."
"Wear tulle over satin"—"I can't endure white."
"Your rose-colored, then, the best of the batch"—
"I haven't a thread of point lace to match."
"Your brown *moire antique*"—"Yes, and look like a
Quaker."
'The pearl-colored"—"I would, but that plaguey dress-
maker
Has had it a week." "Then that exquisite lilac
In which you would melt the heart of a Shylock."
(Here the nose took again the same elevation)—
"I wouldn't wear that for the whole of creation."
"Why not? It's my fancy, there's nothing could strike
it
As more *comme il faut*"—"Yes, but, dear me! that lean
Sophronia Stuckup has got one just like it,
And I won't appear dressed like a chit of sixteen."
"Then that splendid purple, that sweet Mazarine,
That superb *point d'aiguille*, that imperial green,
That zephyr-like tarlatan, that rich *grenadine*"—
"Not one of all which is fit to be seen,"
Said the lady, becoming excited and flushed.
"Then wear," I exclaimed, in a tone which quite crushed
Opposition, "that gorgeous *toilette* which you sported
In Paris last spring, at the grand presentation,
When you quite turned the head of the head of the
nation;
And by all the grand court were so very much courted."
The end of the nose was portentously tipped up,
And both the bright eyes shot forth indignation,
As she burst upon me with the fierce exclamation,
"I have worn it three times at the least calculation,
And that and the most of my dresses are ripped up!"

Here I ripped *out* something, perhaps rather rash,
  Quite innocent, though; but, to use an expression
More striking than classic, it "settled my hash,"
  And proved very soon the last act of our session.
"Fiddlesticks, it is, sir? I wonder the ceiling
Doesn't fall down and crush you—oh! you men have no
    feeling;
You selfish, unnatural, illiberal creatures,
Who set yourselves up as patterns and preachers,
Your silly pretense,—why, what a mere guess it is!
Pray, what do you know of a woman's necessities!
I have told you and shown you I've nothing to wear,
And it's perfectly plain you not only don't care,
But you do not believe me" (here the nose went still
    higher).
"I suppose, if you dared, you would call me a liar.
Our engagement is ended, sir—yes, on the spot;
You're a brute and a monster, and—I don't know what."
I mildly suggested the words—Hottentot,
Pickpocket, and cannibal, Tartar, and thief,
As gentle expletives which might give relief;
But this only proved as spark to the powder,
And the storm I had raised came faster and louder;
It blew and it rained, thundered, lightened, and hailed
Interjections, verbs, pronouns, till language quite failed
To express the abusive, and then its arrears
Were brought up all at once by a torrent of tears,
And my last faint, despairing attempt at an obs-
Ervation was lost in a tempest of sobs.

Well, I felt for the lady, and felt for my hat, too,
Improvised on the crown of the latter a tattoo,
In lieu of expressing the feelings which lay
Quite too deep for words, as Wordsworth would say;
Then, without going through the form of a bow,
Found myself in the entry—I hardly knew how,—
On doorstep and sidewalk, past lamp-post and square,
At home and up stairs, in my own easy-chair;
  Poked my feet into slippers, my fire into blaze,
And said to myself, as I lit my cigar,

Supposing a man had the wealth of the Czar
Of the Russias to boot, for the rest of his days,
On the whole, do you think he would have much to spare,
If he married a woman with nothing to wear?

Since that night, taking pains that it should not be bruited
Abroad in society, I've instituted
A course of inquiry, extensive and thorough,
On this vital subject, and find, to my horror,
That the fair Flora's case is by no means surprising,
But that there exists the greatest distress
In our female community, solely arising
From this unsupplied destitution of dress,
Whose unfortunate victims are filling the air
With the pitiful wail of "Nothing to wear."
Researches in some of the "Upper Ten" districts
Reveal the most painful and startling statistics,
Of which let me mention only a few:
In one single house, on Fifth Avenue,
Three young ladies were found, all below twenty-two,
Who have been three whole weeks without anything new
In the way of flounced silks, and, thus left in the lurch,
Are unable to go to ball, concert, or church.
In another large mansion, near the same place,
Was found a deplorable, heartrending case
Of entire destitution of Brussels point lace.
In a neighboring block there was found, in three calls,
Total want, long continued, of camel's-hair shawls;
And a suffering family, whose case exhibits
The most pressing need of real ermine tippets;
One deserving young lady almost unable
To survive for the want of a new Russian sable;
Another confined to the house, when it's windier
Than usual, because her shawl isn't India.
Still another, whose tortures have been most terrific
Ever since the sad loss of the steamer Pacific,
In which were engulfed, not friend or relation
(For whose fate she perhaps might have found consolation
Or borne it, at least, with serene resignation),

But the choicest assortment of French sleeves and collars
Ever sent out from Paris, worth thousands of dollars,
And all as to style most *recherche* and rare,
The want of which leaves her with nothing to wear,
And renders her life so drear and dyspeptic
That she's quite a recluse, and almost a sceptic;
For she touchingly says that this sort of grief
Cannot find in Religion the slightest relief,
And Philosophy has not a maxim to spare
For the victims of such overwhelming despair.
But the saddest by far of all these sad features
Is the cruelty practised upon the poor creatures
By husbands and fathers, real Bluebeards and Timons,
Who resist the most touching appeals made for diamonds
By their wives and their daughters, and leave them for days
Unsupplied with new jewelry, fans, or bouquets,
Even laugh at their miseries whenever they have a chance,
And deride their demands as useless extravagance;
One case of a bride was brought to my view,
Too sad for belief, but, alas! 'twas too true,
Whose husband refused, as savage as Charon,
To permit her to take more than ten trunks to Sharon.
The consequence was, that when she got there,
At the end of three weeks she had nothing to wear,
And when she proposed to finish the season
  At Newport, the monster refused out and out,
For his infamous conduct alleging no reason,
  Except that the waters were good for his gout.
Such treatment as this was too shocking, of course,
And proceedings are now going on for divorce.

But why harrow the feelings by lifting the curtain
From these scenes of woe? Enough, it is certain,
Has here been disclosed to stir up the pity
Of every benevolent heart in the city,
And spur up Humanity into a canter
To rush and relieve these sad cases instanter.
Won't somebody, moved by this touching description,
Come forward to-morrow and head a subscription?

Won't some kind philanthropist, seeing that aid is
So needed at once by these indigent ladies,
Take charge of the matter? Or won't Peter Cooper
The corner-stone lay of some spendid super-
Structure, like that which to-day links his name
In the Union unending of honor and fame;
And found a new charity just for the care
Of these unhappy women with nothing to wear,
Which, in view of the cash which would daily be claimed,
The *Laying-out* Hospital well might be named?
Won't Stewart, or some of our dry-goods importers,
Take a contract for clothing our wives and our daughters?
Or, to furnish the cash to supply these distresses,
And life's pathway strew with shawls, collars, and dresses,
Ere the want of them makes it much rougher and thornier,
Won't someone discover a new California?

Oh ladies, dear ladies, the next sunny day
Please trundle your hoops just out of Broadway,
From its whirl and its bustle, its fashion and pride,
And the temples of Trade which tower on each side,
To the alleys and lanes, where Misfortune and Guilt
Their children have gathered, their city have built;
Where Hunger and Vice, like twin beasts of prey,
  Have hunted their victims to gloom and despair;
Raise the rich, dainty dress, and the fine broidered skirt,
Pick your delicate way through the dampness and dirt,
  Grope through the dark dens, climb the rickety stair
To the garret, where wretches, the young and the old,
Half-starved, and half-naked, lie crouched from the cold.
  See those skeleton limbs, those frost-bitten feet,
All bleeding and bruised by the stones of the street;
Hear the sharp cry of childhood, the deep groans that swell
  From the poor dying creature who writhes on the floor,
Hear the curses that sound like the echoes of Hell,
  As you sicken and shudder and fly from the door;
Then home to your wardrobes, and say, if you dare,—
Spoiled children of Fashion,—you've nothing to wear!

And oh, if perchance there should be a sphere
Where all is made right which so puzzles us here,

Where the glare and the glitter and tinsel of Time
Fade and die in the light of that region sublime,
Where the soul, disenchanted of flesh and of sense,
Unscreened by its trappings and shows and pretence,
Must be clothed for the life and the service above,
With purity, truth, faith, meekness, and love;
O daughters of Earth! foolish virgins, beware!
Lest in that upper realm you have nothing to wear!

*William Allen Butler* [1825–1902]

## DARIUS GREEN AND HIS FLYING-MACHINE

If ever there lived a Yankee lad,
Wise or otherwise, good or bad,
Who, seeing the birds fly, didn't jump
With flapping arms from stake or stump,
Or, spreading the tail of his coat for a sail,
Take a soaring leap from post or rail,
And wonder why *he* couldn't fly,
And flap and flutter and wish and try,—
If ever you knew a country dunce
Who didn't try that as often as once,
All I can say is, that's a sign
He never would do for a hero of mine.

An aspiring genius was D. Green:
The son of a farmer,—age fourteen;
His body was long and lank and lean,—
Just right for flying, as will be seen;
He had two eyes as bright as a bean,
And a freckled nose that grew between,
A little awry;—for I must mention
That he had riveted his attention
Upon his wonderful invention,
Twisting his tongue as he twisted the strings,
And working his face as he worked the wings,
And with every turn of gimlet and screw
Turning and screwing his mouth round too,
Till his nose seemed bent to catch the scent,

Around some corner, of new-baked pies,
And his wrinkled cheeks and his squinting eyes
Grew puckered into a queer grimace,
That made him look very droll in the face,
And also very wise.

And wise he must have been, to do more
Than ever a genius did before,
Excepting Daedalus of yore
And his son Icarus, who wore
Upon their backs those wings of wax
He had read of in the old almanacs.
Darius was clearly of the opinion,
That the air was also man's dominion,
And that, with paddle or fin or pinion,
We soon or late should navigate
The azure as now we sail the sea.
The thing looks simple enough to me;
And, if you doubt it,
Hear how Darius reasoned about it:

"The birds can fly, an' why can't I?
Must we give in," says he with a grin,
" 'T the bluebird an' phoebe are smarter'n we be?
Jest fold our hands, an' see the swaller
An' blackbird an' catbird beat us holler?
Does the leetle chatterin', sassy wren,
No bigger'n my thumb, know more than men?
Jest show me that! er prove 't the bat
Hez got more brains than's in my hat,
An' I'll back down, an' not till then!"

He argued further: "Ner I can't see
What's th' use o' wings to a bumble-bee,
Fer to git a livin' with, more'n to me;—
Ain't my business importanter'n his'n is?
That Icarus was a silly cuss,—
Him an' his daddy Daedalus;
They might 'a' knowed wings made o' wax
Wouldn't stan' sun-heat an' hard whacks:
I'll make mine o' luther, er suthin' er other."

And he said to himself, as he tinkered and planned:
"But I ain't goin' to show my hand
To nummies that never can understand
The fust idee that's big an' grand.
They'd 'a' laft an' made fun
O' Creation itself afore 'twas done!"
So he kept his secret from all the rest,
Safely buttoned within his vest;
And in the loft above the shed
Himself he locks, with thimble and thread
And wax and hammer and buckles and screws,
And all such things as geniuses use;—
Two bats for patterns, curious fellows!
A charcoal-pot and a pair of bellows;
An old hoop-skirt or two, as well as
Some wire, and several old umbrellas;
A carriage-cover, for tail and wings;
A piece of harness; and straps and strings;
And a big strong box, in which he locks
These and a hundred other things.

His grinning brothers, Reuben and Burke
And Nathan and Jotham and Solomon, lurk
Around the corner to see him work,—
Sitting cross-leggèd, like a Turk,
Drawing the waxed-end through with a jerk,
And boring the holes with a comical quirk
Of his wise old head, and a knowing smirk.
But vainly they mounted each other's backs,
And poked through knot-holes and pried through cracks;
With wood from the pile and straw from the stacks
He plugged the knot-holes and calked the cracks;
And a bucket of water, which one would think
He had brought up into the loft to drink
When he chanced to be dry,
Stood always nigh, for Darius was sly!
And, whenever at work he happened to spy
At chink or crevice a blinking eye,
He let a dipper of water fly:

"Take that! an', ef ever ye git a peep,
Guess ye'll ketch a weasel asleep!"
And he sings as he locks his big strong box:
"The weasel's head is small an' trim,
An' he is leetle an' long an' slim,
An' quick of motion an' nimble of limb,
An', ef yeou'll be advised by me,
Keep wide awake when ye're ketchin' him!"

So day after day
He stitched and tinkered and hammered away,
Till at last 'twas done,—
The greatest invention under the sun!
"An' now," says Darius, "hooray fer some fun!"

'Twas the Fourth of July, and the weather was dry,
And not a cloud was on all the sky,
Save a few light fleeces, which here and there,
Half mist, half air,
Like foam on the ocean went floating by,—
Just as lovely a morning as ever was seen
For a nice little trip in a flying-machine.

Thought cunning Darius, "Now I shan't go
Along 'ith the fellers to see the show:
I'll say I've got sich a terrible cough!
An' then, when the folks 'ave all gone off,
I'll hev full swing fer to try the thing,
An' practyse a little on the wing."

"Ain't goin' to see the celebration?"
Says brother Nate. "No; botheration!
I've got sich a cold—a toothache—I—
My gracious!—feel's though I should fly!"
Said Jotham, "'Sho! guess ye better go."
But Darius said, "No!
Shouldn't wonder 'f yeou might see me, though,
'Long 'bout noon, ef I git red
O' this jumpin', thumpin' pain 'n my head."
For all the while to himself he said,—
"I tell ye what!

I'll fly a few times around the lot,
To see how 't seems, then soon's I've got
The hang o' the thing, ez likely's not,
I'll astonish the nation, an' all creation,
By flyin' over the celebration!
Over their heads I'll sail like an eagle;
I'll balance myself on my wings like a sea-gull;
I'll dance on the chimbleys; I'll stan' on the steeple;
I'll flop up to winders an' scare the people!
I'll light on the libbe'ty-pole, an' crow;
An I'll say to the gawpin' fools below,
'What world's this 'ere that I've come near?'
Fer I'll make 'em b'lieve I'm a chap f'm the moon;
An' I'll try a race 'ith their ol' balloon!"

He crept from his bed;
And, seeing the others were gone, he said,
"I'm a-gittin' over the cold 'n my head."
And away he sped,
To open the wonderful box in the shed.

His brothers had walked but a little way,
When Jotham to Nathan chanced to say,
"What on airth is he up to, hey?"
"Don'o',—the' 's suthin' er other to pay,
Er he wouldn't 'a' stayed to hum to-day."
Says Burke, "His toothache's all 'n his eye!
*He* never'd miss a Fo'th-o'-July,
Ef he hedn't got some machine to try."
Then Sol, the little one, spoke: "By darn!
Le's hurry back, an' hide 'n the barn,
An' pay him fer tellin' us that yarn!"
"Agreed!" Through the orchard they creep back,
Along by the fences, behind the stack,
And one by one, through a hole in the wall,
In under the dusty barn they crawl,
Dressed in their Sunday garments all;
And a very astonishing sight was that,
When each in his cobwebbed coat and hat
Came up through the floor like an ancient rat.

And there they hid; and Reuben slid
The fastenings back, and the door undid.
"Keep dark!" said he,
"While I squint an' see what the' is to see."

As knights of old put on their mail,—
From head to foot an iron suit,
Iron jacket and iron boot,
Iron breeches, and on the head
No hat, but an iron pot instead,
And under the chin the bail,—
(I believe they called the thing a helm,)—
And, thus accoutred, they took the field,
Sallying forth to overwhelm
The dragons and pagans that plagued the realm:
So this modern knight prepared for flight,
Put on his wings and strapped them tight,—
Jointed and jaunty, strong and light,—
Buckled them fast to shoulder and hip,—
Ten feet they measured from tip to tip!
And a helm had he, but that he wore,
Not on his head, like those of yore,
But more like the helm of a ship.

"Hush!" Reuben said, "he's up in the shed!
He's opened the winder,—I see his head!
He stretches it out, an' pokes it about,
Lookin' to see 'f the coast is clear,
An' nobody near;—
Guess he don'o' who's hid in here!
He's riggin' a spring-board over the sill!
Stop laffin', Solomon! Burke, keep still!
He's a climbin' out now—Of all the things!
What's he got on? I van, it's wings!
An' that t'other thing? I vum, it's a tail!
An' there he sets like a hawk on a rail!
Steppin' careful, he travels the length
Of his spring-board, and teeters to try its strength.
Now he stretches his wings, like a monstrous bat;
Peeks over his shoulder, this way an' that,

Fer to see 'f the' 's any one passin' by;
But the' 's on'y a ca'f an' a goslin' nigh.
*They* turn up at him a wonderin' eye,
To see—The dragon! he's goin' to fly!
Away he goes! Jimminy! what a jump!
Flop—flop—an' plump to the ground with a thump!
Flutt'rin' an' flound'rin', all 'n a lump!"

As a demon is hurled by an angel's spear,
Heels over head, to his proper sphere,—
Heels over head, and head over heels,
Dizzily down the abyss he wheels,—
So fell Darius. Upon his crown,
In the midst of the barn-yard, he came down,
In a wonderful whirl of tangled strings,
Broken braces and broken springs,
Broken tail and broken wings,
Shooting-stars, and various things,—
Barn-yard litter of straw and chaff,
And much that wasn't so sweet by half.
Away with a bellow fled the calf,
And what was that? Did the gosling laugh?
'Tis a merry roar from the old barn-door,
And he hears the voice of Jotham crying;
"Say, D'rius! how de yeou like flyin'?"

Slowly, ruefully, where he lay,
Darius just turned and looked that way,
As he stanched his sorrowful nose with his cuff,
"Wal, I like flyin' well enough,"
He said; "but the' ain't sich a thunderin' sight
O' fun in 't when ye come to light."

I just have room for the Moral here:
And this is the moral,—Stick to your sphere;
Or, if you insist, as you have the right,
On spreading your wings for a loftier flight,
The moral is,—Take care how you light.

*John Townsend Trowbridge* [1827–1916]

## THE SOCIETY UPON THE STANISLAUS

I RESIDE at Table Mountain, and my name is Truthful James;
I am not up to small deceit, or any sinful games;
And I'll tell in simple language what I know about the row
That broke up our Society upon the Stanislow.

But first I would remark, that it is not a proper plan
For any scientific gent to whale his fellow-man,
And, if a member don't agree with his peculiar whim,
To lay for that same member for to "put a head" on him.

Now nothing could be finer or more beautiful to see
Than the first six months' proceedings of that same Society,
Till Brown of Calaveras brought a lot of fossil bones
That he found within a tunnel near the tenement of Jones.

Then Brown he read a paper, and he reconstructed there,
From those same bones, an animal that was extremely rare;
And Jones then asked the Chair for a suspension of the rules,
Till he could prove that those same bones was one of his lost
mules.

Then Brown he smiled a bitter smile, and said he was at
fault,—
It seemed he had been trespassing on Jones's family vault:
He was a most sarcastic man, this quiet Mr. Brown,
And on several occasions he had cleaned out the town.

Now I hold it is not decent for a scientific gent
To say another is an ass,—at least, to all intent;
Nor should the individual who happens to be meant
Reply by heaving rocks at him, to any great extent.

Then Abner Dean of Angel's raised a point of order—when
A chunk of old red sandstone took him in the abdomen,
And he smiled a kind of sickly smile, and curled up on the
floor,
And the subsequent proceedings interested him no more.

For, in less time than I write it, every member did engage
In a warfare with the remnants of a palæozoic age;
And the way they heaved those fossils in their anger was a sin,
Till the skull of an old mammoth caved the head of Thompson in.

And this is all I have to say of these improper games,
For I live at Table Mountain, and my name is Truthful James;
And I've told in simple language what I know about the row
That broke up our Society upon the Stanislow.

*Bret Harte* [1839–1902]

## DOW'S FLAT

1856

Dow's Flat. That's its name:
And I reckon that you
Are a stranger? The same?
Well, I thought it was true,—
For thar isn't a man on the river as can't spot the place at first view.

It was called after Dow,—
Which the same was an ass;
And as to the how
Thet the thing kem to pass,—
Jest tie up your hoss to that buckeye, and sit ye down here in the grass.

You see this 'yer Dow
Hed the worst kind of luck;
He slipped up somehow
On each thing thet he struck.
Why, ef he'd a-straddled thet fence-rail, the derned thing 'ed get up and buck.

He mined on the bar
  Till he couldn't pay rates;
He was smashed by a car
  When he tunnelled with Bates;
And right on the top of his trouble kem his wife and five kids from the States.

It was rough,—mighty rough;
  But the boys they stood by,
And they brought him the stuff
  For a house, on the sly;
And the old woman,—well, she did washing, and took on when no one was nigh.

But this 'yer luck of Dow's
  Was so powerful mean
That the spring near his house
  Dried right up on the green;
And he sunk forty feet down for water, but nary a drop to be seen.

Then the bar petered out,
  And the boys wouldn't stay;
And the chills got about,
  And his wife fell away;
But Dow in his well kept a peggin' in his usual ridikilous way.

One day,—it was June,—
  And a year ago, jest,—
This Dow kem at noon
  To his work like the rest,
With a shovel and pick on his shoulder, and a derringer hid in his breast.

He goes to the well,
  And he stands on the brink,
And stops for a spell
  Jest to listen and think:
For the sun in his eyes (jest like this, sir!), you see, kinder made the cuss blink.

His two ragged gals
  In the gulch were at play,
And a gownd that was Sal's
  Kinder flapped on a bay:
Not much for a man to be leavin', but his all,—as I've heer'd
  the folks say.

And—That's a peart hoss
  Thet you've got—ain't it now?
What might be her cost?
  Eh? Oh!—Well, then, Dow—
Let's see,—well, that forty-foot grave wasn't his, sir, that
  day, anyhow.

For a blow of his pick
  Sorter caved in the side,
And he looked and turned sick,
  Then he trembled and cried.
For you see the dern cuss had struck—"Water?"—beg your
  parding, young man,—there you lied!

It was *gold*,—in the quartz,
  And it ran all alike;
And I reckon five oughts
  Was the worth of that strike;
And that house with the coopilow's his'n,—which the same
  isn't bad for a Pike.

Thet's why it's Dow's Flat;
  And the thing of it is
That he kinder got that
  Through sheer contrairiness:
For 'twas *water* the derned cuss was seekin', and his luck
  made him certain to miss.

Thet's so! Thar's your way,
  To the left of yon tree;
But—a—look h'yur, say?
  Won't you come up to tea?
No? Well, then the next time you're passin'; and ask after
  Dow,— and thet's *me*.

*Bret Harte* [1839–1902]

## PLAIN LANGUAGE FROM TRUTHFUL JAMES

TABLE MOUNTAIN, 1870

WHICH I wish to remark,
And my language is plain,
That for ways that are dark
And for tricks that are vain,
The heathen Chinee is peculiar:
Which the same I would rise to explain.

Ah Sin was his name;
And I shall not deny,
In regard to the same,
What that name might imply;
But his smile it was pensive and childlike.
As I frequent remarked to Bill Nye.

It was August the third,
And quite soft was the skies;
Which it might be inferred
That Ah Sin was likewise;
Yet he played it that day upon William
And me in a way I despise.

Which we had a small game,
And Ah Sin took a hand:
It was Euchre. The same
He did not understand;
But he smiled, as he sat by the table,
With the smile that was childlike and bland

Yet the cards they were stocked
In a way that I grieve,
And my feelings were shocked
At the state of Nye's sleeve,
Which was stuffed full of aces and bowers,
And the same with intent to deceive.

But the hands that were played
By that heathen Chinee,
And the points that he made,
Were quite frightful to see,—

Till at last he put down a right bower,
  Which the same Nye had dealt unto me.

Then I looked up at Nye,
  And he gazed upon me;
And he rose with a sigh,
  And said, "Can this be?
We are ruined by Chinese cheap labor,"—
  And he went for that heathen Chinee.

In the scene that ensued
  I did not take a hand,
But the floor it was strewed,
  Like the leaves on the strand,
With the cards that Ah Sin had been hiding,
  In the game "he did not understand."

In his sleeves, which were long,
  He had twenty-four jacks,—
Which was coming it strong,
  Yet I state but the facts;
And we found on his nails, which were taper,
  What is frequent in tapers,—that's wax.

Which is why I remark,
  And my language is plain,
That for ways that are dark,
  And for tricks that are vain,
The heathen Chinee is peculiar,—
  Which the same I am free to maintain.

*Bret Harte* [1839-1902]

## THE RETORT

OLD Birch, who taught the village school,
  Wedded a maid of homespun habit;
He was as stubborn as a mule,
  And she as playful as a rabbit.

Poor Kate had scarce become a wife
  Before her husband sought to make her
The pink of country-polished life,
  And prim and formal as a Quaker.

One day the tutor went abroad,
And simple Katie sadly missed him;
When he returned, behind her lord
She shyly stole, and fondly kissed him.

The husband's anger rose, and red
And white his face alternate grew:
"Less freedom, ma'am!" Kate sighed and said,
"O, dear! I *didn't know 'twas you!*"

*George Pope Morris* [1802–1864]

## THE FLITCH OF DUNMOW

Come, Micky and Molly and dainty Dolly,
Come, Betty and blithesome Bill;
Ye gossips and neighbors, away with your labors!
Come to the top of the hill.
For there are Jenny and jovial Joe;
Jolly and jolly, jolly they go,
Jogging over the hill.

By apple and berry, 'tis twelve months merry
Since Jenny and Joe were wed!
And never a bother or quarrelsome pother
To trouble the board or bed.
So Joe and Jenny are off to Dunmow:
Happy and happy, happy they go,
Young and rosy and red.

Oh, Jenny's as pretty as doves in a ditty;
And Jenny, her eyes are black;
And Joey's a fellow as merry and mellow
As ever shouldered a sack.
So quick, good people, and come to the show
Merry and merry, merry they go,
Bumping on Dobbin's back.

They've pranked up old Dobbin with ribbons and bobbin,
And tethered his tail in a string!
The fat flitch of bacon is not to be taken
By many that wear the ring!

Good luck, good luck, to Jenny and Joe!
Jolly and jolly, jolly they go.
  Hark! how merry they sing:

"O, merry, merry, merry are we,
Happy as birds that sing in a tree!
All of the neighbors are merry to-day,
Merry are we, and merry are they.
O merry are we! for love, you see,
Fetters a heart and sets it free.

"O happy, happy, happy is life
For Joe (that's me) and Jenny my wife!
All of the neighbors are happy, and say—
'Never were folk so happy as they!'
O happy are we! for love, you see,
Fetters a heart and sets it free.

"O jolly, jolly, jolly we go,
I and my Jenny, and she and her Joe.
All of the neighbors are jolly, and sing—
'She is a queen, and he is a king!'
O jolly are we! for love, you see,
Fetters a heart and sets it free."

*James Carnegie* [1827–1905]

## THE YARN OF THE "NANCY BELL"

'TWAS on the shores that round our coast
  From Deal to Ramsgate span,
That I found alone, on a piece of stone,
  An elderly naval man.

His hair was weedy, his beard was long,
    And weedy and long was he;
And I heard this wight on the shore recite
    In a singular minor key:

"Oh, I am a cook and a captain bold,
    And the mate of the *Nancy* brig,
And a bo'sun tight, and a midshipmite,
    And the crew of the captain's gig."

And he shook his fists and he tore his hair,
    Till I really felt afraid,
For I couldn't help thinking the man had been drinking,
    And so I simply said:

"Oh, elderly man, it's little I know
    Of the duties of men of the sea,
And I'll eat my hand if I understand
    However you can be

"At once a cook, and a captain bold,
    And the mate of the *Nancy* brig,
And a bo'sun tight, and a midshipmite,
    And the crew of the captain's gig."

Then he gave a hitch to his trousers, which
    Is a trick all seamen larn,
And having got rid of a thumping quid,
    He spun this painful yarn:

"'Twas in the good ship *Nancy Bell*
    That we sailed to the Indian Sea,
And there on a reef we come to grief,
    Which has often occurred to me.

"And pretty nigh all o' the crew was drowned
    (There was seventy-seven o' soul),
And only ten of the *Nancy's* men
    Said 'Here!' to the muster-roll.

"There was me, and the cook, and the captain bold,
    And the mate of the *Nancy* brig,
And the bo'sun tight, and a midshipmite,
    And the crew of the captain's gig.

"For a month we'd neither wittles nor drink,
    Till a-hungry we did feel,
So we drawed a lot, and, accordin', shot
    The captain for our meal.

"The next lot fell to the *Nancy's* mate,
And a delicate dish he made;
Then our appetite with the midshipmite
We seven survivors stayed.

"And then we murdered the bo'sun tight,
And he much resembled pig;
Then we wittled free, did the cook and me,
On the crew of the captain's gig.

"Then only the cook and me was left,
And the delicate question, 'Which
Of us two goes to the kettle?' arose,
And we argued it out as sich.

"For I loved that cook as a brother, I did,
And the cook he worshipped me;
But we'd both be blowed if we'd either be stowed
In the other chap's hold, you see.

"'I'll be eat if you dines off me,' says Tom.
'Yes, that,' says I, 'you'll be,—
I'm boiled if I die, my friend,' quoth I;
And 'Exactly so,' quoth he.

"Says he: 'Dear James, to murder me
Were a foolish thing to do,
For don't you see that you can't cook *me*,
While I can—and will—cook *you!*'

"So he boils the water, and takes the salt
And the pepper in portions true
(Which he never forgot), and some chopped shalot,
And some sage and parsley too.

"'Come here,' says he, with a proper pride,
Which his smiling features tell,
''Twill soothing be if I let you see
How extremely nice you'll smell.'

"And he stirred it round and round and round,
And he sniffed at the foaming froth;
When I ups with his heels, and smothers his squeals
In the scum of the boiling broth.

"And I eat that cook in a week or less,
And—as I eating be
The last of his chops, why, I almost drops,
For a wessel in sight I see.

. . . . . . . .

"And I never larf, and I never smile,
And I never lark nor play;
But sit and croak, and a single joke
I have—which is to say:

"Oh, I am a cook and a captain bold
And the mate of the *Nancy* brig,
And a bo'sun tight, and a midshipmite,
And the crew of the captain's gig!"

*William Schwenck Gilbert* [1836–1911]

## CAPTAIN REECE

Of all the ships upon the blue,
No ship contained a better crew
Than that of worthy Captain Reece,
Commanding of the *Mantelpiece.*

He was adored by all his men,
For worthy Captain Reece, R. N.,
Did all that lay within him to
Promote the comfort of his crew.

If ever they were dull or sad,
Their captain danced to them like mad,
Or told, to make the time pass by,
Droll legends of his infancy.

A feather-bed had every man,
Warm slippers and hot-water can,
Brown windsor from the captain's store,
A valet, too, to every four.

Did they with thirst in summer burn,
Lo, seltzogenes at every turn,
And on all very sultry days
Cream ices handed round on trays.

Then currant wine and ginger pops
Stood handily on all the "tops":
And, also, with amusement rife,
A "Zoetrope, or Wheel of Life."

New volumes came across the sea
From Mister Mudie's libraree;
The *Times* and *Saturday Review*
Beguiled the leisure of the crew.

Kind-hearted Captain Reece, R. N.,
Was quite devoted to his men;
In point of fact, good Captain Reece
Beatified the *Mantelpiece*.

One summer eve, at half past ten,
He said (addressing all his men),
"Come, tell me, please, what I can do,
To please and gratify my crew.

"By any reasonable plan
I'll make you happy if I can;
My own convenience count as *nil;*
It is my duty, and I will."

Then up and answered William Lee
(The kindly captain's coxswain he,
A nervous, shy, low-spoken man);
He cleared his throat, and thus began:

"You have a daughter, Captain Reece,
Ten female cousins and a niece,
A ma, if what I'm told is true,
Six sisters, and an aunt or two.

"Now, somehow, sir, it seems to me,
More friendly-like we all shall be,
If you united of 'em to
Unmarried members of the crew.

"If you'd ameliorate our life,
Let each select from them a wife;
And as for nervous me, old pal,
Give me your own enchanting gal!"

Good Captain Reece, that worthy man,
Debated on his coxswain's plan:
"I quite agree," he said, "O Bill;
It is my duty, and I will.

"My daughter, that enchanting girl.
Has just been promised to an earl,
And all my other familee
To peers of various degree.

"But what are dukes and viscounts to
The happiness of all my crew?
The word I gave you I'll fulfil;
It is my duty, and I will.

"As you desire it shall befall,
I'll settle thousands on you all,
And I shall be, despite my hoard,
The only bachelor on board."

The boatswain of the *Mantelpiece*,
He blushed and spoke to Captain Reece:
"I beg your honor's leave," he said,
"If you would wish to go and wed,

"I have a widowed mother who
Would be the very thing for you—
She long has loved you from afar,
She washes for you, Captain R."

The captain saw the dame that day—
Addressed her in his playful way—
"And did it want a wedding-ring?
It was a tempting ickle sing!

"Well, well, the chaplain I will seek,
We'll all be married this day week
At yonder church upon the hill;
It is my duty, and I will!"

The sisters, cousins, aunts, and niece,
And widowed ma of Captain Reece,
Attended there as they were bid;
It was their duty, and they did.

*William Schwenck Gilbert* [1836–1911]

## "'SPĂCIALLY JIM"

I wus mighty good-lookin' when I wus young,
  Peert an' black-eyed an' slim,
With fellers a-courtin' me Sunday nights,
  'Spăcially Jim.

The likeliest one of 'em all wus he,
  Clipper an' han'som' an' trim;
But I tossed up my head an' made fun o' the crowd,
  'Spăcially Jim.

I said I hadn't no 'pinion o' men,
  An' I wouldn't take stock in him!
But they kep' on a-comin' in spite o' my talk,
  'Spăcially Jim.

I got so tired o' havin' 'em roun'
  ('Spăcially Jim!)
I made up my mind I'd settle down
  An' take up with him.

So we wus married one Sunday in church,
  'Twas crowded full to the brim;
'Twas the only way to git rid of 'em all,
  'Spăcially Jim.

*Bessie Morgan* [18 –

## ROBINSON CRUSOE

From "Davy and the Goblin"

THE night was thick and hazy,
When the "Piccadilly Daisy"
Carried down the crew and captain in the sea;
And I think the water drowned 'em,
For they never, never found 'em,
And I know they did n't come ashore with me.

Oh! 'twas very sad and lonely
When I found myself the only
Population on this cultivated shore;
But I've made a little tavern
In a rocky little cavern,
And I sit and watch for people at the door.

I spent no time in looking
For a girl to do my cooking,
As I'm quite a clever hand at making stews;
But I had that fellow Friday
Just to keep the tavern tidy,
And to put a Sunday polish on my shoes.

I have a little garden
That I'm cultivating lard in,
As the things I eat are rather tough and dry;
For I live on toasted lizards,
Prickly pears, and parrot gizzards,
And I'm really very fond of beetle-pie.

The clothes I had were furry,
And it made me fret and worry
When I found the moths were eating off the hair;
And I had to scrape and sand 'em,
And I boiled 'em and I tanned 'em,
Till I got the fine morocco suit I wear.

I sometimes seek diversion
In a family excursion

With the few domestic animals you see;
    And we take along a carrot
    As refreshments for the parrot,
And a little can of jungleberry tea.

    Then we gather as we travel
    Bits of moss and dirty gravel,
And we chip off little specimens of stone;
    And we carry home as prizes
    Funny bugs of handy sizes,
Just to give the day a scientific tone.

    If the roads are wet and muddy,
    We remain at home and study,—
For the Goat is very clever at a sum,—
    And the Dog, instead of fighting,
    Studies ornamental writing,
While the Cat is taking lessons on the drum.

    We retire at eleven,
    And we rise again at seven;
And I wish to call attention, as I close,
    To the fact that all the scholars
    Are correct about their collars,
And particular in turning out their toes.

*Charles Edward Carryl* [1841-1920]

## CASEY AT THE BAT

THE outlook wasn't brilliant for the Mudville nine that day;
The score stood four to two, with but one inning more to
    play;
And so, when Cooney died at first, and Barrows did the same,
A sickly silence fell upon the patrons of the game.

A straggling few got up to go in deep despair. The rest
Clung to the hope which springs eternal in the human breast;
They thought, if only Casey could but get a whack, at that,
They'd put up even money now, with Casey at the bat.

But Flynn preceded Casey, as did also Jimmy Blake,
And the former was a pudding and the latter was a fake;
So upon that stricken multitude grim melancholy sat,
For there seemed but little chance of Casey's getting to the bat.

But Flynn let drive a single, to the wonderment of all,
And Blake, the much despisèd, tore the cover off the ball;
And when the dust had lifted, and they saw what had occurred,
There was Jimmy safe on second, and Flynn a-hugging third.

Then from the gladdened multitude went up a joyous yell,
It bounded from the mountain-top, and rattled in the dell;
It struck upon the hillside, and recoiled upon the flat;
For Casey, mighty Casey, was advancing to the bat.

There was ease in Casey's manner as he stepped into his place,
There was pride in Casey's bearing, and a smile on Casey's face;
And when, responding to the cheers, he lightly doffed his hat,
No stranger in the crowd could doubt 'twas Casey at the bat.

Ten thousand eyes were on him as he rubbed his hands with dirt,
Five thousand tongues applauded when he wiped them on his shirt;
Then while the writhing pitcher ground the ball into his hip,
Defiance gleamed in Casey's eye, a sneer curled Casey's lip.

And now the leather-covered sphere came hurtling through the air,
And Casey stood a-watching it in haughty grandeur there;
Close by the sturdy batsman the ball unheeded sped.
"That ain't my style," said Casey. "Strike one," the umpire said.

From the benches, black with people, there went up a muffled roar,
Like the beating of the storm-waves on a stern and distant shore;

"Kill him! kill the umpire!" shouted some one on the stand.
And it's likely they'd have killed him had not Casey raised
his hand.

With a smile of Christian charity great Casey's visage shone;
He stilled the rising tumult; he bade the game go on;
He signalled to the pitcher, and once more the spheroid flew,
But Casey still ignored it, and the umpire said, "Strike two."

"Fraud!" cried the maddened thousands, and the echo
answered, "Fraud!"
But a scornful look from Casey, and the audience was awed;
They saw his face grow stern and cold, they saw his muscles
strain,
And they knew that Casey wouldn't let that ball go by again.

The sneer is gone from Casey's lips, his teeth are clenched in
hate,
He pounds with cruel violence his bat upon the plate;
And now the pitcher holds the ball, and now he lets it go,
And now the air is shattered by the force of Casey's blow.

Oh! somewhere in this favored land the sun is shining bright,
The band is playing somewhere, and somewhere hearts are
light;
And somewhere men are laughing, and somewhere children
shout,
But there is no joy in Mudville—mighty Casey has struck
out.

*Ernest Lawrence Thayer* [1863-1940]

## AT A COWBOY DANCE

GIT yer little sage hens ready,
Trot 'em out upon the floor—
Line up there, you cusses! Steady!
Lively, now! One couple more.
Shorty, shed that old sombrero;
Bronco, douse that cigarette;
Stop that cussin', Casimero,
'Fore the ladies! Now, all set!

S'lute yer ladies, all together!
  Ladies opposite the same—
Hit the lumber with yer leathers!
  Balance all, an' swing yer dame!
Bunch the heifers in the middle;
  Circle stags an' do-se-do!
Pay attention to the fiddle!
  Swing her round an' off you go!

First four forward! Back to places!
  Second follow—shuffle back!
Now you've got it down to cases—
  Swing 'em till their trotters crack!
Gents all right a-heel-and-toein'!
  Swing 'em, kiss 'em if you kin—
On to next an' keep a-goin'
  Till you hit yer pards ag'in!

Gents to center; ladies round 'em,
  Form a basket; balance all!
Whirl yer gals to where you found 'em!
  Promenade around the hall!
Balance to yer pards an' trot 'em
  Round the circle double quick!
Grab an' kiss 'em while you've got 'em—
  Hold 'em to it if they kick!

Ladies, left hand to yer sonnies!
  Alaman! Grand right an' left!
Balance all, an' swing yer honeys—
  Pick 'em up an' feel their heft!
Promenade like skeery cattle—
  Balance all an' swing yer sweets!
Shake yer spurs an' make 'em rattle!
  Keno! Promenade to seats.

*James Barton Adams* [1843–1918]

## BEHOLD THE DEEDS

(Being the Plaint of Adolphe Culpepper Ferguson, Salesman of Fancy Notions, held in durance of his Landlady for a failure to connect on Saturday Night.)

I WOULD that all men my hard case might know,
  How grievously I suffer for no sin:
I, Adolphe Culpepper Ferguson, for lo!
  I of my landlady am lockèd in
For being short on this sad Saturday,
Nor having shekels of silver wherewith to pay:
She has turned and is departed with my key;
Wherefore, not even as other boarders free,
  I sing, (as prisoners to their dungeon-stones
When for ten days they expiate a spree):
  Behold the deeds that are done of Mrs. Jones!

One night and one day have I wept my woe;
  Nor wot I, when the morrow doth begin,
If I shall have to write to Briggs & Co.,
  To pray them to advance the requisite tin
For ransom of their salesman, that he may
Go forth as other boarders go alway—
As those I hear now flocking from their tea,
Led by the daughter of my landlady
  Piano-ward. This day, for all my moans,
Dry bread and water have been servèd me.
  Behold the deeds that are done of Mrs. Jones!

Miss Amabel Jones is musical, and so
  The heart of the young he-boarder doth win,
Playing "The Maiden's Prayer," *adagio*—
  That fetcheth him, as fetcheth the "bunko skin"
The innocent rustic. For my part, I pray
That Badarjewska maid may wait for aye
Ere sits she with a lover, as did we
Once sit together, Amabel! Can it be
  That all that arduous wooing not atones
For Saturday's shortness of trade dollars three?
  *Behold* the deeds that are done of Mrs. Jones!

Yea! she forgets the arm that was wont to go
  Around her waist. She wears a buckle, whose pin
Galleth the crook of her young man's elbow.
  *I* forget not, for I that youth have been.
Smith was aforetime the Lothario gay.
Yet once, I mind me, Smith was forced to stay
Close in his room. Not calm, as I, was he;
But his noise brought no pleasaunce, verily.
  Small ease he got of playing on the bones
Or hammering on the stove-pipe, that I see.
  Behold the deeds that are done of Mrs. Jones!

Thou, for whose fear the figurative crow
  I eat, accursed be thou and all thy kin!
Thee will I show up—yea, up will I show
  Thy too thick buckwheats, and thy tea too thin.
Ay! here I dare thee, ready for the fray:
Thou dost *not* "keep a first-class house," I say!
It dost not with the advertisements agree.
Thou lodgest a Briton with a puggaree.
  And thou hast harbored Jacobses and Cohns,
Also a Mulligan. Thus denounce I thee!
  Behold the deeds that are done of Mrs. Jones!

ENVOY

Boarders! the worst I have not told to ye:
She hath stolen my trousers, that I may not flee
  Privily by the window. Hence these groans.
There is no fleeing in a *robe de nuit*.
  Behold the deeds that are done of Mrs. Jones!

*Henry Cuyler Bunner* [1855-1896]

## DE FUST BANJO

From "Christmas Night in the Quarters"

Go 'way, fiddle! folks is tired o' hearin' you a-squawkin'.
Keep silence fur yo' betters!—don't you heah de banjo
  talkin?
About de 'possum's tail she's gwine to lecter—ladies, listen!
About de ha'r whut is n't dar, an' why de ha'r is missin'

"Dar's gwine to be a' oberflow," said Noah, lookin' solemn—
Fur Noah tuk the "Herald," an' he read de ribber column—
An' so he sot his hands to wuk a-cl'arin' timber-patches,
An' 'lowed he's gwine to build a boat to beat the steamah
*Natchez.*

Ol' Noah kep' a-nailin' an' a-chippin' an' a-sawin';
An' all de wicked neighbors kep' a-laughin' an' a-pshawin';
But Noah didn't min' 'em, knowin' whut wuz gwine to
happen:
An' forty days an' forty nights de rain it kep' a-drappin'.

Now, Noah had done cotched a lot ob ebry sort o' beas'es—
Ob all de shows a-trabbelin', it beat 'em all to pieces!
He had a Morgan colt an' sebral head o' Jarsey cattle—
An' druv 'em 'board de Ark as soon's he heered de thunder
rattle.

Den sech anoder fall ob rain!—it come so awful hebby,
De ribber riz immejitly, an' busted troo de lebbee;
De people all wuz drownded out—'cep' Noah an' de critters,
An' men he'd hired to work de boat—an' one to mix de
bitters.

De Ark she kep' a-sailin' an' a-sailin' *an'* a-sailin';
De lion got his dander up, an' like to bruk de palin';
De sarpints hissed; de painters yelled; tel , whut wid all de
fussin',
You c'u'dn't hardly heah de mate a-bossin' 'roun' an'
cussin'.

Now Ham, de only nigger whut wuz runnin' on de packet,
Got lonesome in de barber-shop, an' c'u'dn't stan' de racket:
An' so, fur to amuse he-se'f, he steamed some wood an'
bent it,
An' soon he had a banjo made—de fust dat wuz invented.

He wet de ledder, stretched it on: made bridge an' screws
an' aprin:
An' fitted in a proper neck—'twuz berry long an' tap'rin';
He tuk some tin, an' twisted him a thimble fur to ring it:
An' den de mighty question riz: how wuz he gwine to string
it?

De 'possum had as fine a tail as dis dat I's a-singin';
De ha'r's so long an' thick an' strong,—des fit fur banjo-
stringin';
Dat nigger shaved 'em off as short as washday-dinner graces:
An' sorted ob 'em by de size, f'om little E's to basses.

He strung her, tuned her, struck a jig,—'twuz "Nebber
min' de wedder,"—
She soun' like forty-lebben bands a-playin' all togedder:
Some went to pattin'; some to dancin': Noah called de
figgers;
An' Ham he sot an' knocked de tune, de happiest ob niggers!

Now, sence dat time—it's mighty strange—dere's not de
slightes' showin'
Ob any ha'r at all upon de 'possum's tail a-growin';
An' curi's, too, dat nigger's ways: his people nebber los'
'em—
Fur whar you finds de nigger— dar's de banjo an' de 'possum!

*Irwin Russell* [1853-1879]

# PART V

# POEMS OF PATRIOTISM, HISTORY AND LEGEND

## "HOW SLEEP THE BRAVE"

How sleep the brave, who sink to rest
By all their country's wishes blest!
When Spring, with dewy fingers cold,
Returns to deck their hallowed mould,
She there shall dress a sweeter sod
Than Fancy's feet have ever trod.

By fairy hands their knell is rung;
By forms unseen their dirge is sung;
There Honor comes, a pilgrim gray,
To bless the turf that wraps their clay;
And Freedom shall awhile repair
To dwell, a weeping hermit, there!

*William Collins* [1721–1759]

# MY COUNTRY

## AMERICA

MY country, 'tis of thee,
Sweet land of liberty,
    Of thee I sing;
Land where my fathers died,
Land of the pilgrims' pride,
From every mountain-side
    Let Freedom ring.

My native country, thee,
Land of the noble free,—
    Thy name I love;
I love thy rocks and rills,
Thy woods and templed hills;
My heart with rapture thrills
    Like that above.

Let music swell the breeze,
And ring from all the trees
    Sweet Freedom's song;
Let mortal tongues awake,
Let all that breathe partake,
Let rocks their silence break,
    The sound prolong.

Our fathers' God, to Thee,
Author of liberty,
    To Thee we sing;
Long may our land be bright
With Freedom's holy light;
Protect us by Thy might,
    Great God, our King.

*Samuel Francis Smith* [1808–1895]

## THE STAR-SPANGLED BANNER

O SAY, can you see, by the dawn's early light,
What so proudly we hailed at the twilight's last gleaming?
Whose broad stripes and bright stars, through the perilous fight,
O'er the ramparts we watched, were so gallantly streaming!
And the rockets' red glare, the bombs bursting in air,
Gave proof through the night that our flag was still there:
O say, does that star-spangled banner yet wave
O'er the land of the free and the home of the brave?

On the shore, dimly seen through the mists of the deep,
Where the foe's haughty host in dread silence reposes,
What is that which the breeze, o'er the towering steep,
As it fitfully blows, now conceals, now discloses?
Now it catches the gleam of the morning's first beam,
In full glory reflected now shines on the stream:
'Tis the star-spangled banner! O long may it wave
O'er the land of the free and the home of the brave!

And where is that band who so vauntingly swore
That the havoc of war and the battle's confusion
A home and a country should leave us no more?
Their blood has washed out their foul footsteps' pollution.
No refuge could save the hireling and slave
From the terror of flight, or the gloom of the grave:
And the star-spangled banner in triumph doth wave
O'er the land of the free and the home of the brave!

Oh! thus be it ever, when freemen shall stand
Between their loved homes and the war's desolation!
Blest with victory and peace, may the heaven-rescued land
Praise the Power that hath made and preserved us a nation.
Then conquer we must, for our cause it is just,
And this be our motto: "In God is our trust."
And the star-spangled banner in triumph shall wave
O'er the land of the free and the home of the brave!

*Francis Scott Key* [1780–1843]

## THE AMERICAN FLAG

I

When Freedom, from her mountain height,
  Unfurled her standard to the air,
She tore the azure robe of night,
  And set the stars of glory there;
She mingled with its gorgeous dyes
The milky baldric of the skies,
And striped its pure, celestial white
With streakings of the morning light;
Then, from his mansion in the sun,
She called her eagle bearer down,
And gave into his mighty hand,
The symbol of her chosen land.

II

Majestic monarch of the cloud!
  Who rear'st aloft thy regal form,
To hear the tempest-trumpings loud,
And see the lightning-lances driven,
  When strive the warriors of the storm,
And rolls the thunder-drum of heaven—
Child of the sun! to thee 'tis given
To guard the banner of the free,
To hover in the sulphur smoke,
To ward away the battle-stroke,
And bid its blendings shine afar,
Like rainbows on the cloud of war,
  The harbingers of victory!

III

Flag of the brave! thy folds shall fly,
The sign of hope and triumph high,
When speaks the signal-trumpet tone,
And the long line comes gleaming on:
Ere yet the life-blood, warm and wet,
Has dimmed the glistening bayonet,

Each soldier eye shall brightly turn
To where thy sky-born glories burn,
And, as his springing steps advance,
Catch war and vengeance from the glance;
And when the cannon-mouthings loud
Heave in wild wreaths the battle-shroud,
And gory sabres rise and fall,
Like shoots of flame on midnight's pall;
Then shall thy meteor-glances glow,
And cowering foes shall sink beneath
Each gallant arm that strikes below
That lovely messenger of death.

IV

Flag of the seas! on ocean wave
Thy stars shall glitter o'er the brave;
When death, careering on the gale,
Sweeps darkly round the bellied sail,
And frighted waves rush wildly back
Before the broadside's reeling rack,
Each dying wanderer of the sea
Shall look at once to heaven and thee,
And smile to see thy splendors fly
In triumph o'er his closing eye.

V

Flag of the free heart's hope and home,
By angel hands to valor given;
Thy stars have lit the welkin dome,
And all thy hues were born in heaven.
Forever float that standard sheet!
Where breathes the foe but falls before us,
With Freedom's soil beneath our feet,
And Freedom's banner streaming o'er us?

*Joseph Rodman Drake* [1795-1820]

## YANKEE DOODLE

FATHER and I went down to camp,
Along with Captain Gooding,
And there we see the men and boys,
As thick as hasty pudding.

*Chorus*—Yankee Doodle, keep it up,
Yankee Doodle, dandy,
Mind the music and the step,
And with the girls be handy.

And there we see a thousand men,
As rich as 'Squire David;
And what they wasted every day
I wish it could be savèd.

The 'lasses they eat every day
Would keep our house a winter;
They have so much that, I'll be bound,
They eat whene'er they're a mind to.

And there we see a swamping gun,
As big as a log of maple,
Upon a deucèd little cart,
A load for father's cattle.

And every time they shoot it off,
It takes a horn of powder,
And makes a noise like father's gun,
Only a nation louder.

I went as nigh to one myself
As Siah's underpinning;
And father went as nigh again,
I thought the deuce was in him.

Cousin Simon grew so bold,
I thought he would have cocked it;
It scared me so, I shrinked it off,
And hung by father's pocket.

And Captain Davis had a gun,
He kind of clapped his hand on't,
And stuck a crooked stabbing-iron
Upon the little end on't.

And there I see a pumpkin shell
As big as mother's basin;
And every time they touched it off,
They scampered like the nation.

I see a little barrel, too,
The heads were made of leather,
They knocked upon 't with little clubs
To call the folks together.

And there was Captain Washington,
And gentlefolks about him,
They say he's grown so tarnal proud
He will not ride without 'em.

He had got on his meeting clothes,
And rode a strapping stallion,
And gave his orders to the men,—
I guess there was a million.

The flaming ribbons in his hat,
They looked so tearing fine ah,
I wanted peskily to get,
To give to my Jemima.

And then I see a snarl of men
A digging graves, they told me.
So tarnal long, so tarnal deep,
They 'tended they should hold me.

It scared me so, I hooked it off,
Nor stopped, as I remember,
Nor turned about, till I got home,
Locked up in mother's chamber.

*Edward Bangs (?)* [fl. 1776]

## HAIL! COLUMBIA

HAIL! Columbia, happy land!
Hail! ye heroes, heaven-born band,
Who fought and bled in freedom's cause,
And when the storm of war was gone,

Enjoyed the peace your valor won;
Let independence be your boast,
Ever mindful what it cost,
Ever grateful for the prize,
Let its altar reach the skies.

*Chorus*—Firm, united let us be,
Rallying round our liberty,
As a band of brothers joined,
Peace and safety we shall find.

Immortal patriots, rise once more!
Defend your rights, defend your shore;
Let no rude foe, with impious hand,
Invade the shrine where sacred lies
Of toil and blood the well-earned prize;
While offering peace, sincere and just,
In heaven we place a manly trust,
That truth and justice will prevail,
And every scheme of bondage fail.

Sound, sound the trump of fame!
Let Washington's great name
Ring through the world with loud applause!
Let every clime to freedom dear
Listen with a joyful ear;
With equal skill, with steady power,
He governs in the fearful hour
Of horrid war, or guides with ease
The happier time of honest peace.

Behold the chief, who now commands,
Once more to serve his country stands,
The rock on which the storm will beat!
But, armed in virtue, firm and true,
His hopes are fixed on heaven and you.
When hope was sinking in dismay,
When gloom obscured Columbia's day,
His steady mind, from changes free,
Resolved on death or liberty.

*Joseph Hopkinson* [1770–1842]

## COLUMBIA

Columbia, Columbia, to glory arise,
The queen of the world, and the child of the skies;
Thy genius commands thee; with rapture behold,
While ages on ages thy splendor unfold,
Thy reign is the last and the noblest of time,
Most fruitful thy soil, most inviting thy clime;
Let the crimes of the east ne'er encrimson thy name,
Be freedom, and science, and virtue thy fame.

To conquest and slaughter let Europe aspire;
Whelm nations in blood, and wrap cities in fire;
Thy heroes the rights of mankind shall defend,
And triumph pursue them, and glory attend.
A world is thy realm: for a world be thy laws,
Enlarged as thine empire, and just as thy cause;
On Freedom's broad basis, that empire shall rise,
Extend with the main, and dissolve with the skies.

Fair science her gates to thy sons shall unbar,
And the east see the morn hide the beams of her star.
New bards, and new sages, unrivalled shall soar
To fame unextinguished, when time is no more;
To thee, the last refuge of virtue designed,
Shall fly from all nations the best of mankind;
Here, grateful to heaven, with transport shall bring
Their incense, more fragrant than odors of spring.

Nor less shall thy fair ones to glory ascend,
And genius and beauty in harmony blend;
The graces of form shall awake pure desire,
And the charms of the soul ever cherish the fire;
Their sweetness unmingled, their manners refined,
And virtue's bright image, instamped on the mind,
With peace and soft rapture shall teach life to glow,
And light up a smile in the aspect of woe.

Thy fleets to all regions thy power shall display,
The nations admire and the ocean obey;
Each shore to thy glory its tribute unfold,
And the east and the south yield their spices and gold.

As the day-spring unbounded, thy splendor shall flow,
And earth's little kingdoms before thee shall bow;
While the ensigns of union, in triumph unfurled,
Hush the tumult of war and give peace to the world.

Thus, as down a lone valley, with cedars o'erspread,
From war's dread confusion I pensively strayed,
The gloom from the face of fair heaven retired;
The winds ceased to murmur; the thunders expired;
Perfumes as of Eden flowed sweetly along,
And a voice as of angels, enchantingly sung:
"Columbia, Columbia, to glory arise,
The queen of the world, and the child of the skies."

*Timothy Dwight* [1752-1817]

## "OH MOTHER OF A MIGHTY RACE"

Oh mother of a mighty race,
Yet lovely in thy youthful grace!
The elder dames, thy haughty peers,
Admire and hate thy blooming years.
  With words of shame
And taunts of scorn they join thy name.

For on thy cheeks the glow is spread
That tints thy morning hills with red;
Thy step—the wild deer's rustling feet
Within thy woods are not more fleet;
  Thy hopeful eye
Is bright as thine own sunny sky.

Ay, let them rail—those haughty ones,
While safe thou dwellest with thy sons.
They do not know how loved thou art,
How many a fond and fearless heart
  Would rise to throw
Its life between thee and the foe.

They know not, in their hate and pride,
What virtues with thy children bide;
How true, how good, thy graceful maids
Make bright, like flowers, the valley-shades;

What generous men
Spring, like thine oaks, by hill and glen;—

What cordial welcomes greet the guest
By thy lone rivers of the West;
How faith is kept, and truth revered,
And man is loved, and God is feared,
In woodland homes,
And where the ocean border foams.

There's freedom at thy gates and rest
For Earth's down-trodden and oppressed,
A shelter for the hunted head,
For the starved laborer toil and bread.
Power, at thy bounds,
Stops and calls back his baffled hounds.

Oh, fair young mother! on thy brow
Shall sit a nobler grace than now.
Deep in the brightness of the skies
The thronging years in glory rise,
And, as they fleet,
Drop strength and riches at thy feet.

*William Cullen Bryant* [1794–1878]

## HYMN OF THE WEST

WORLD'S FAIR, ST. LOUIS, MO., 1904

O THOU, whose glorious orbs on high
Engird the earth with splendor round,
From out Thy secret place draw nigh
The courts and temples of this ground;
Eternal Light,
Fill with Thy might
These domes that in Thy purpose grew,
And lift a nation's heart anew!

Illumine Thou each pathway here,
To show the marvels God hath wrought!
Since first Thy people's chief and seer
Looked up with that prophetic thought.

Bade Time unroll
The fateful scroll,
And empire unto Freedom gave
From cloudland height to tropic wave.

Poured through the gateways of the North
Thy mighty rivers join their tide,
And, on the wings of morn sent forth,
Their mists the far-off peaks divide.
By Thee unsealed,
The mountains yield
Ores that the wealth of Ophir shame,
And gems enwrought of seven-hued flame.

Lo, through what years the soil hath lain,
At Thine own time to give increase—
The greater and the lesser grain,
The ripening boll, the myriad fleece!
Thy creatures graze
Appointed ways;
League after league across the land
The ceaseless herds obey Thy hand.

Thou, whose high archways shine most clear
Above the plenteous Western plain,
Thine ancient tribes from round the sphere
To breathe its quickening air are fain:
And smiles the sun
To see made one
Their brood throughout Earth's greenest space,
Land of the new and lordlier race!

*Edmund Clarence Stedman* [1833-1908]

## CONCORD HYMN

SUNG AT THE COMPLETION OF THE BATTLE MONUMENT, APRIL 19, 1836

By the rude bridge that arched the flood,
Their flag to April's breeze unfurled,
Here once the embattled farmers stood,
And fired the shot heard round the world.

The foe long since in silence slept;
  Alike the conqueror silent sleeps;
And Time the ruined bridge has swept
  Down the dark stream which seaward creeps.

On this green bank, by this soft stream,
  We set to-day a votive stone;
That memory may their deed redeem,
  When, like our sires, our sons are gone.

Spirit, that made those heroes dare
  To die, and leave their children free,
Bid Time and Nature gently spare
  The shaft we raise to them and thee.

*Ralph Waldo Emerson* [1803–1882]

## BATTLE-HYMN OF THE REPUBLIC

MINE eyes have seen the glory of the coming of the Lord;
He is trampling out the vintage where the grapes of wrath are stored;
He hath loosed the fateful lightning of His terrible swift sword;
    His truth is marching on.

I have seen Him in the watch-fires of a hundred circling camps;
They have builded Him an altar in the evening dews and damps;
I can read his righteous sentence by the dim and flaring lamps;
    His day is marching on.

I have read a fiery gospel, writ in burnished rows of steel:
"As ye deal with my contemners, so with you my grace shall deal;
Let the Hero, born of woman, crush the serpent with his heel,
    Since God is marching on."

He has sounded forth the trumpet that shall never call re-
treat;
He is sifting out the hearts of men before His judgment-seat:
Oh, be swift, my soul, to answer Him! be jubilant, my feet!
Our God is marching on.

In the beauty of the lilies Christ was born across the sea,
With a glory in His bosom that transfigures you and me:
As He died to make men holy, let us die to make men free,
While God is marching on.

*Julia Ward Howe* [1819–1910]

## THE EAGLE'S SONG

THE lioness whelped, and the sturdy cub
Was seized by an eagle and carried up,
And homed for a while in an eagle's nest,
And slept for a while on an eagle's breast;
And the eagle taught it the eagle's song:
"To be staunch, and valiant, and free, and strong!"

The lion-whelp sprang from the eyrie nest,
From the lofty crag where the queen birds rest;
He fought the King on the spreading plain,
And drove him back o'er the foaming main.
He held the land as a thrifty chief,
And reared his cattle, and reaped his sheaf,
Nor sought the help of a foreign hand,
Yet welcomed all to his own free land!

Two were the sons that the country bore
To the Northern lakes and the Southern shore;
And Chivalry dwelt with the Southern son,
And Industry lived with the Northern one.
Tears for the time when they broke and fought!
Tears was the price of the union wrought!
And the land was red in a sea of blood,
Where brother for brother had swelled the flood!

And now that the two are one again,
Behold on their shield the word "Refrain!"

And the lion cubs twain sing the eagle's song:
"To be staunch, and valiant, and free, and strong!"
For the eagle's beak, and the lion's paw,
And the lion's fangs, and the eagle's claw,
And the eagle's swoop, and the lion's might,
And the lion's leap, and the eagle's sight,
Shall guard the flag with the word "Refrain!"
Now that the two are one again!

*Richard Mansfield* [1857–1907]

## THE FLAG GOES BY

HATS off!
Along the street there comes
A blare of bugles, a ruffle of drums,
A flash of color beneath the sky:
Hats off!
The flag is passing by!

Blue and crimson and white it shines,
Over the steel-tipped, ordered lines.
Hats off!
The colors before us fly;
But more than the flag is passing by:

Sea-fights and land-fights, grim and great,
Fought to make and to save the State:
Weary marches and sinking ships;
Cheers of victory on dying lips;

Days of plenty and years of peace;
March of a strong land's swift increase;
Equal justice, right and law,
Stately honor and reverend awe;

Sign of a nation, great and strong
To ward her people from foreign wrong:
Pride and glory and honor,—all
Live in the colors to stand or fall.

Hats off!
Along the street there comes
A blare of bugles, a ruffle of drums;
And loyal hearts are beating high:
Hats off!
The flag is passing by!

*Henry Holcomb Bennett* [1863–1924]

## UNMANIFEST DESTINY

To what new fates, my country, far
And unforeseen of foe or friend,
Beneath what unexpected star,
Compelled to what unchosen end,

Across the sea that knows no beach
The Admiral of Nations guides
Thy blind obedient keels to reach
The harbor where thy future rides!

The guns that spoke at Lexington
Knew not that God was planning then
The trumpet word of Jefferson
To bugle forth the rights of men.

To them that wept and cursed Bull Run,
What was it but despair and shame?
Who saw behind the cloud the sun?
Who knew that God was in the flame?

Had not defeat upon defeat.
Disaster on disaster come,
The slave's emancipated feet
Had never marched behind the drum.

There is a Hand that bends our deeds
To mightier issues than we planned;
Each son that triumphs, each that bleeds
My country, serves Its dark command.

I do not know beneath what sky
  Nor on what seas shall be thy fate;
I only know it shall be high,
  I only know it shall be great.

*Richard Hovey* [1864-1900]

## ON A SOLDIER FALLEN IN THE PHILIPPINES

STREETS of the roaring town,
Hush for him, hush, be still!
He comes, who was stricken down
Doing the word of our will.
Hush! Let him have his state.
Give him his soldier's crown,
The grists of trade can wait
Their grinding at the mill,
But he cannot wait for his honor, now the trumpet has been blown.
Wreathe pride now for his granite brow, lay love on his breast of stone.

Toll! Let the great bells toll
Till the clashing air is dim,
Did we wrong this parted soul?
We will make it up to him.
Toll! Let him never guess
What work we set him to.
Laurel, laurel, yes;
He did what we bade him do.
Praise, and never a whispered hint but the fight he fought was good;
Never a word that the blood on his sword was his country's own heart's-blood.

A flag for the soldier's bier
Who dies that his land may live;
O, banners, banners here,
That he doubt not nor misgive!

That he heed not from the tomb
The evil days draw near
When the nation, robed in gloom,
With its faithless past shall strive.
Let him never dream that his bullet's scream went wide of its island mark,
Home to the heart of his darling land where she stumbled and sinned in the dark.

*William Vaughn Moody* [1869–1910]

## AN ODE IN TIME OF HESITATION

WRITTEN AFTER SEEING AT BOSTON THE STATUE OF ROBERT GOULD SHAW, KILLED WHILE STORMING FORT WAGNER, JULY 18, 1863, AT THE HEAD OF THE FIRST ENLISTED NEGRO REGIMENT, THE 54th MASSACHUSETTS

### I

BEFORE the solemn bronze Saint Gaudens made
To thrill the heedless passer's heart with awe,
And set here in the city's talk and trade
To the good memory of Robert Shaw,
This bright March morn I stand,
And hear the distant spring come up the land;
Knowing that what I hear is not unheard
Of this boy soldier and his negro band,
For all their gaze is fixed so stern ahead,
For all the fatal rhythm of their tread.
The land they died to save from death and shame
Trembles and waits, hearing the spring's great name,
And by her pangs these resolute ghosts are stirred.

### II

Through street and mall the tides of people go
Heedless; the trees upon the Common show
No hint of green; but to my listening heart
The still earth doth impart
Assurance of her jubilant emprise,
And it is clear to my long-searching eyes

That love at last has might upon the skies.
The ice is runneled on the little pond;
A telltale patter drips from off the trees;
The air is touched with southland spiceries,
As if but yesterday it tossed the frond
Of pendant mosses where the live-oaks grow
Beyond Virginia and the Carolines,
Or had its will among the fruits and vines
Of aromatic isles asleep beyond
Florida and the Gulf of Mexico.

III

Soon shall the Cape Ann children shout in glee,
Spying the arbutus, spring's dear recluse;
Hill lads at dawn shall hearken the wild goose
Go honking northward over Tennessee;
West from Oswego to Sault Sainte-Marie,
And on to where the Pictured Rocks are hung,
And yonder where, gigantic, willful, young,
Chicago sitteth at the northwest gates,
With restless violent hands and casual tongue
Moulding her mighty fates,
The Lakes shall robe them in ethereal sheen;
And like a larger sea, the vital green
Of springing wheat shall vastly be outflung
Over Dakota and the prairie states.
By desert people immemorial
On Arizonan mesas shall be done
Dim rites unto the thunder and the sun;
Nor shall the primal gods lack sacrifice
More splendid, when the white Sierras call
Unto the Rockies straightway to arise
And dance before the unveiled ark of the year,
Sounding their windy cedars as for shawms,
Unrolling rivers clear
For flutter of broad phylacteries;
While Shasta signals to Alaskan seas
That watch old sluggish glaciers downward creep
To fling their icebergs thundering from the steep,

And Mariposa through the purple calms
Gazes at far Hawaii crowned with palms
Where East and West are met,—
A rich seal on the ocean's bosom set
To say that East and West are twain,
With different loss and gain:
The Lord hath sundered them; let them be sundered yet.

IV

Alas! what sounds are these that come
Sullenly over the Pacific seas,—
Sounds of ignoble battle, striking dumb
The season's half-awakened ecstasies?
Must I be humble, then,
Now when my heart hath need of pride?
Wild love falls on me from these sculptured men;
By loving much the land for which they died
I would be justified.
My spirit was away on pinions wide
To soothe in praise of her its passionate mood
And ease it of its ache of gratitude.
Too sorely heavy is the debt they lay
On me and the companions of my day.
I would remember now
My country's goodliness, make sweet her name.
Alas! what shade art thou
Of sorrow or of blame
Liftest the lyric leafage from her brow,
And pointest a slow finger at her shame?

V

Lies! lies! It cannot be! The wars we wage
Are noble, and our battles still are won
By justice for us, ere we lift the gage.
We have not sold our loftiest heritage.
The proud republic hath not stooped to cheat
And scramble in the market-place of war;
Her forehead weareth yet its solemn star.

Here is her witness: this, her perfect son,
This delicate and proud New England soul
Who leads despisèd men, with just-unshackled feet,
Up the large ways where death and glory meet,
To show all peoples that our shame is done,
That once more we are clean and spirit-whole.

VI

Crouched in the sea fog on the moaning sand
All night he lay, speaking some simple word
From hour to hour to the slow minds that heard,
Holding each poor life gently in his hand
And breathing on the base rejected clay
Till each dark face shone mystical and grand
Against the breaking day;
And lo, the shard the potter cast away
Was grown a fiery chalice, crystal-fine,
Fulfilled of the divine
Great wine of battle wrath by God's ring-finger stirred.
Then upward, where the shadowy bastion loomed
Huge on the mountain in the wet sea light,
Whence now, and now, infernal flowerage bloomed,
Bloomed, burst, and scattered down its deadly seed,—
They swept, and died like freemen on the height,
Like freemen, and like men of noble breed;
And when the battle fell away at night
By hasty and contemptuous hands were thrust
Obscurely in a common grave with him
The fair-haired keeper of their love and trust.
Now limb doth mingle with dissolvèd limb
In nature's busy old democracy
To flush the mountain laurel when she blows
Sweet by the southern sea,
And heart with crumpled heart climbs in the rose:—
The untaught hearts with the high heart that knew
This mountain fortress for no earthly hold
Of temporal quarrel, but the bastion old
Of spiritual wrong,
Built by an unjust nation sheer and strong,

Expugnable but by a nation's rue
And bowing down before that equal shrine
By all men held divine,
Whereof his band and he were the most holy sign.

VII

O bitter, bitter shade!
Wilt thou not put the scorn
And instant tragic question from thine eyes?
Do thy dark brows yet crave
That swift and angry stave—
Unmeet for this desirous morn—
That I have striven, striven to evade?
Gazing on him, must I not deem they err
Whose careless lips in street and shop aver
As common tidings, deeds to make his cheek
Flush from the bronze, and his dead throat to speak?
Surely some elder singer would arise,
Whose harp hath leave to threaten and to mourn
Above this people when they go astray.
Is Whitman, the strong spirit, overworn?
Has Whittier put his yearning wrath away?
I will not and I dare not yet believe!
Though furtively the sunlight seems to grieve,
And the spring-laden breeze
Out of the gladdening west is sinister
With sounds of nameless battle overseas;
Though when we turn and question in suspense
If these things be indeed after these ways,
And what things are to follow after these,
Our fluent men of place and consequence
Fumble and fill their mouths with hollow phrase,
Or for the end-all of deep arguments
Intone their dull commercial liturgies—
I dare not yet believe! My ears are shut!
I will not hear the thin satiric praise
And muffled laughter of our enemies,
Bidding us never sheathe our valiant sword
Till we have changed our birthright for a gourd
Of wild pulse stolen from a barbarian's hut;

Showing how wise it is to cast away
The symbols of our spiritual sway,
That so our hands with better ease
May wield the driver's whip and grasp the jailer's keys.

VIII

Was it for this our fathers kept the law?
This crown shall crown their struggle and their ruth?
Are we the eagle nation Milton saw
Mewing its mighty youth,
Soon to possess the mountain winds of truth,
And be a swift familiar of the sun
Where aye before God's face His trumpets run?
Or have we but the talons and the maw,
And for the abject likeness of our heart
Shall some less lordly bird be set apart?—
Some gross-billed wader where the swamps are fat?
Some gorger in the sun? Some prowler with the bat?

IX

Ah no!
We have not fallen so.
We are our fathers' sons: let those who lead us know!
'Twas only yesterday sick Cuba's cry
Came up the tropic wind, "Now help us, for we die!"
Then Alabama heard,
And rising, pale, to Maine and Idaho
Shouted a burning word.
Proud state with proud impassioned state conferred,
And at the lifting of a hand sprang forth,
East, west, and south, and north,
Beautiful armies. Oh, by the sweet blood and young
Shed on the awful hill slope of San Juan,
By the unforgotten names of eager boys
Who might have tasted girls' love and been stung
With the old mystic joys
And starry griefs, now the spring nights come on,
But that the heart of youth is generous,—
We charge you, ye who lead us,
Breathe on their chivalry no hint of stain!
Turn not their new-world victories to gain!

One least leaf plucked for chaffer from the bays
Of their dear praise,
One jot of their pure conquest put to hire,
The implacable republic will require;
With clamor, in the glare and gaze of noon,
Or subtly, coming as a thief at night,
But surely, very surely, slow or soon
That insult deep we deeply will requite.
Tempt not our weakness, our cupidity!
For save we let the island men go free,
Those baffled and dislaureled ghosts
Will curse us from the lamentable coasts
Where walk the frustrate dead.
The cup of trembling shall be drainèd quite,
Eaten the sour bread of astonishment,
With ashes of the hearth shall be made white
Our hair, and wailing shall be in the tent;
Then on your guiltier head
Shall our intolerable self-disdain
Wreak suddenly its anger and its pain;
For manifest in the disastrous light
We shall discern the right
And do it, tardily.—O ye who lead,
Take heed!
Blindness we may forgive, but baseness we will smite.

*William Vaughn Moody* [1869–1910]

## THE PARTING OF THE WAYS

Untrammelled Giant of the West,
   With all of Nature's gifts endowed,
With all of Heaven's mercies blessed,
   Nor of thy power unduly proud—
Peerless in courage, force, and skill,
And godlike in thy strength of will,—

Before thy feet the ways divide:
   One path leads up to heights sublime;
Downward the other slopes, where bide
   The refuse and the wrecks of Time.

Choose then, nor falter at the start,
O choose the nobler path and part!

Be thou the guardian of the weak,
Of the unfriended, thou the friend;
No guerdon for thy valor seek,
No end beyond the avowèd end.
Wouldst thou thy godlike power preserve,
Be godlike in the will to serve!

*Joseph B. Gilder* [1858–1936]

## DIXIE

[THE ORIGINAL VERSION]

I WISH I was in de land ob cotton,
Old times dar am not forgotten;
Look away, look away, look away, Dixie land!
In Dixie land whar I was born in,
Early on one frosty mornin',
Look away, look away, look away, Dixie land!

*Chorus*—Den I wish I was in Dixie! Hooray! Hooray!
In Dixie's land we'll took our stand, to lib an' die in Dixie,
Away, away, away down south in Dixie!
Away, away, away down south in Dixie!

Old missus marry Will de weaber,
William was a gay deceaber,
When he put his arm around 'er,
He looked as fierce as a forty-pounder.

His face was sharp as a butcher cleaber,
But dat did not seem to greab 'er;
Will run away, missus took a decline, O,
Her face was the color of bacon rhine, O.

While missus libbed, she libbed in clover,
When she died, she died all over;
How could she act de foolish part,
An' marry a man to break her heart?

Buckwheat cakes an' stony batter
Makes you fat or a little fatter;
Here's a health to de next old missus,
An' all de gals dat want to kiss us.

Now if you want to drive 'way sorrow,
Come an' hear dis song to-morrow;
Den hoe it down an' scratch your grabble,
To Dixie's land I'm bound to trabble.

*Daniel Decatur Emmett* [1815–1904]

## DIXIE

SOUTHRONS, hear your country call you!
Up, lest worse than death befall you!
To arms! To arms! To arms, in Dixie!
Lo! all the beacon-fires are lighted,—
Let all hearts be now united!
To arms! To arms! To arms, in Dixie!
Advance the flag of Dixie!
Hurrah! hurrah!
For Dixie's land we take our stand,
And live or die for Dixie!
To arms! To arms!
And conquer peace for Dixie!
To arms! To arms!
And conquer peace for Dixie!

Hear the Northern thunders mutter!
Northern flags in South winds flutter!
Send them back your fierce defiance!
Stamp upon the accursed alliance!

Fear no danger! Shun no labor!
Lift up rifle, pike, and saber!
Shoulder pressing close to shoulder,
Let the odds make each heart bolder!

How the South's great heart rejoices
At your cannons' ringing voices!

For faith betrayed, and pledges broken,
Wrongs inflicted, insults spoken.

Strong as lions, swift as eagles,
Back to their kennels hunt these beagles!
Cut the unequal bonds asunder!
Let them hence each other plunder!

Swear upon your country's altar
Never to submit or falter,
Till the spoilers are defeated,
Till the Lord's work is completed!

Halt not till our Federation
Secures among earth's powers its station!
Then at peace, and crowned with glory,
Hear your children tell the story!

If the loved ones weep in sadness,
Victory soon shall bring them gladness,—
        To arms!
Exultant pride soon vanquish sorrow;
Smiles chase tears away to-morrow.
  To arms! To arms! To arms, in Dixie!
    Advance the flag of Dixie!
        Hurrah! hurrah!
For Dixie's land we take our stand,
    And live or die for Dixie!
        To arms! To arms!
    And conquer peace for Dixie!
        To arms! To arms!
    And conquer peace for Dixie!

*Albert Pike* [1809–1891]

## MY MARYLAND

THE despot's heel is on thy shore,
    Maryland!
His torch is at thy temple door,
    Maryland!

Avenge the patriotic gore
That flecked the streets of Baltimore,
And be the battle-queen of yore,
Maryland, my Maryland!

Hark to an exiled son's appeal,
Maryland!
My Mother State, to thee I kneel,
Maryland!
For life or death, for woe or weal,
Thy peerless chivalry reveal,
And gird thy beauteous limbs with steel,
Maryland, my Maryland!

Thou wilt not cower in the dust,
Maryland!
Thy beaming sword shall never rust,
Maryland!
Remember Carroll's sacred trust,
Remember Howard's warlike thrust,
And all thy slumberers with the just,
Maryland, my Maryland!

Come! 'tis the red dawn of the day,
Maryland!
Come with thy panoplied array,
Maryland!
With Ringgold's spirit for the fray,
With Watson's blood at Monterey,
With fearless Lowe and dashing May,
Maryland, my Maryland!

Dear Mother, burst the tyrant's chain,
Maryland!
Virginia should not call in vain,
Maryland!
She meets her sisters on the plain,—
"*Sic semper!*" 'tis the proud refrain

That baffles minions back amain,
    Maryland!
Arise in majesty again,
    Maryland, my Maryland!

Come! for thy shield is bright and strong,
    Maryland!
Come! for thy dalliance does thee wrong,
    Maryland!
Come to thine own heroic throng
Stalking with Liberty along,
And chant thy dauntless slogan-song,
    Maryland, my Maryland!

I see the blush upon thy cheek,
    Maryland!
For thou wast ever bravely meek,
    Maryland!
But lo! there surges forth a shriek,
From hill to hill, from creek to creek,
Potomac calls to Chesapeake,
    Maryland, my Maryland!

Thou wilt not yield the Vandal toll,
    Maryland!
Thou wilt not crook to his control,
    Maryland!
Better the fire upon thee roll,
Better the shot, the blade, the bowl,
Than crucifixion of the soul,
    Maryland, my Maryland!

I hear the distant thunder hum,
    Maryland!
The Old Line's bugle, fife, and drum,
    Maryland!
She is not dead, nor deaf, nor dumb;
Huzza! she spurns the Northern scum!
She breathes! She burns! She'll come! She'll come!
    Maryland, my Maryland!

*James Ryder Randall* [1839–1908]

## THE VIRGINIANS OF THE VALLEY

The knightliest of the knightly race
That, since the days of old,
Have kept the lamp of chivalry
Alight in hearts of gold;
The kindliest of the kindly band
That, rarely hating ease,
Yet rode with Spotswood round the land,
And Raleigh round the seas;

Who climbed the blue Virginian hills
Against embattled foes,
And planted there, in valleys fair,
The lily and the rose;
Whose fragrance lives in many lands,
Whose beauty stars the earth,
And lights the hearths of happy homes
With loveliness and worth.

We thought they slept!—the sons who kept
The names of noble sires,—
And slumbered while the darkness crept
Around their vigil-fires;
But aye the "Golden Horseshoe" knights
Their old Dominion keep,
Whose foes have found enchanted ground,
But not a knight asleep!

*Francis Orray Ticknor* [1822–1874]

## AMERICA TO GREAT BRITAIN

All hail! thou noble land,
Our Fathers' native soil!
Oh, stretch thy mighty hand,
Gigantic grown by toil,
O'er the vast Atlantic wave to our shore!
For thou, with magic might,
Canst reach to where the light
Of Phœbus travels bright
The world o'er!

The Genius of our clime,
From his pine-embattled steep,
Shall hail the guest sublime;
While the Tritons of the deep
With their conchs the kindred league shall proclaim
Then let the world combine,—
O'er the main our naval line,
Like the milky-way shall shine,
Bright in fame!

Though ages long have passed
Since our Fathers left their home,
Their pilot in the blast,
O'er untravelled seas to roam,
Yet lives the blood of England in our veins!
And shall we not proclaim
That blood of honest fame
Which no tyranny can tame
By its chains?

While the language free and bold
Which the bard of Avon sung,
In which our Milton told
How the vault of heaven rung
When Satan, blasted, fell with his host;—
While this, with reverence meet,
Ten thousand echoes greet,
From rock to rock repeat
Round our coast;—

While the manners, while the arts,
That mould a nation's soul,
Still cling around our hearts,—
Between let Ocean roll,
Our joint communion breaking with the Sun:
Yet, still, from either beach
The voice of blood shall reach,
More audible than speech,
"We are One!"

*Washington Allston* [1779-1843]

## TO ENGLAND

I

Lear and Cordelia! 'twas an ancient tale
Before thy Shakespeare gave it deathless fame;
The times have changed, the moral is the same.
So like an outcast, dowerless and pale,
Thy daughter went; and in a foreign gale
Spread her young banner, till its sway became
A wonder to the nations. Days of shame
Are close upon thee; prophets raise their wail.
When the rude Cossack with an outstretched hand
Points his long spear across the narrow sea,—
"Lo! there is England!" when thy destiny
Storms on thy straw-crowned head, and thou dost stand
Weak, helpless, mad, a by-word in the land,—
God grant thy daughter a Cordelia be!

II

Stand, thou great bulwark of man's liberty!
Thou rock of shelter, rising from the wave,
Sole refuge to the overwearied brave
Who planned, arose, and battled to be free,
Fell, undeterred, then sadly turned to thee,—
Saved the free spirit from their country's grave,
To rise again, and animate the slave,
When God shall ripen all things. Britons, ye
Who guard the sacred outpost, not in vain
Hold your proud peril! Freemen undefiled,
Keep watch and ward! Let battlements be piled
Around your cliffs; fleets marshalled, till the main
Sink under them; and if your courage wane,
Through force or fraud, look westward to your child!

*George Henry Boker* [1823–1890]

## AMERICA

Nor force nor fraud shall sunder us! Oh ye
Who north or south, on east or western land,
Native to noble sounds, say truth for truth,
Freedom for freedom, love for love, and God

For God; Oh ye who in eternal youth
Speak with a living and creative flood
This universal English, and do stand
Its breathing book; live worthy of that grand
Heroic utterance—parted, yet a whole,
Far, yet unsevered,—children brave and free
Of the great Mother-tongue, and ye shall be
Lords of an Empire wide as Shakespeare's soul,
Sublime as Milton's immemorial theme,
And rich as Chaucer's speech, and fair as Spenser's dream.

*Sydney Dobell* [1824–1874]

## TO AMERICA

### ON A PROPOSED ALLIANCE BETWEEN TWO GREAT NATIONS

What is the voice I hear
  On the winds of the western sea?
Sentinel, listen from out Cape Clear
  And say what the voice may be.
  'Tis a proud free people calling loud to a people proud and free.

And it says to them: "Kinsmen, hail;
  We severed have been too long.
Now let us have done with a worn-out tale—
  The tale of ancient wrong—
  And our friendship last long as our love doth last, and be stronger than death is strong."

Answer them, sons of the self-same race,
  And blood of the self-same clan;
Let us speak with each other face to face
  And answer as man to man,
  And loyally love and trust each other as none but free men can.

Now fling them out to the breeze,
  Shamrock, Thistle, and Rose,
And the Star-spangled Banner unfurl with these—
  A message to friends and foes
  Wherever the sails of peace are seen and wherever the war wind blows—

A message to bond and thrall to wake,
For whenever we come, we twain,
The throne of the tyrant shall rock and quake,
And his menace be void and vain,
For you are lords of a strong land and we are lords of the main.

Yes, this is the voice of the bluff March gale;
We severed have been too long,
But now we have done with a worn-out tale—
The tale of an ancient wrong—
And our friendship shall last as love doth last and be stronger than death is strong.

*Alfred Austin* [1835–1913]

## SAXON GRIT

Worn with the battle of Stamford town,
Fighting the Norman by Hastings bay,
Harold the Saxon's sun went down,
While the acorns were falling one autumn day.
Then the Norman said, "I am lord of the land:
By tenor of conquest here I sit;
I will rule you now with the iron hand;"
But he had not thought of the Saxon grit.

He took the land, and he took the men,
And burnt the homesteads from Trent to Tyne,
Made the freemen serfs by a stroke of the pen,
Eat up the corn and drank the wine,
And said to the maiden, pure and fair,
"You shall be my leman, as is most fit,
Your Saxon churl may rot in his lair;"
But he had not measured the Saxon grit.

To the merry greenwood went bold Robin Hood,
With his strong-hearted yeomanry ripe for the fray,
Driving the arrow into the marrow
Of all the proud Normans who came in his way;

Scorning the fetter, fearless and free,
  Winning by valor, or foiling by wit,
Dear to our Saxon folk ever is he,
  This merry old rogue with the Saxon grit.

And Kett the tanner whipped out his knife,
  And Watt the smith his hammer brought down,
For ruth of the maid he loved better than life,
  And by breaking a head, made a hole in the Crown.
From the Saxon heart rose a mighty roar,
  "Our life shall not be by the King's permit;
We will fight for the right, we want no more;"
  Then the Norman found out the Saxon grit.

For slow and sure as the oaks had grown
  From acorns falling that autumn day,
So the Saxon manhood in thorpe and town
  To a nobler stature grew alway;
Winning by inches, holding by clinches,
  Standing by law and the human right,
Many times failing, never once quailing,
  So the new day came out of the night.

. . . . . . .

Then rising afar in the Western sea,
  A new world stood in the morn of the day,
Ready to welcome the brave and free,
  Who would wrench out the heart and march away
From the narrow, contracted, dear old land,
  Where the poor are held by a cruel bit,
To ampler spaces for heart and hand—
  And here was a chance for the Saxon grit.

Steadily steering, eagerly peering,
  Trusting in God your fathers came,
Pilgrims and strangers, fronting all dangers,
  Cool-headed Saxons, with hearts aflame.
Bound by the letter, but free from the fetter,
  And hiding their freedom in Holy Writ,
They gave Deuteronomy hints in economy,
  And made a new Moses of Saxon grit.

They whittled and waded through forest and fen,
  Fearless as ever of what might befall;
Pouring out life for the nurture of men,
  In faith that by manhood the world wins all.
Inventing baked beans and no end of machines;
  Great with the rifle and great with the axe—
Sending their notions over the oceans,
  To fill empty stomachs and straighten bent backs.

Swift to take chances that end in the dollar,
  Yet open of hand when the dollar is made,
Maintaining the meetin', exalting the scholar,
  But a little too anxious about a good trade;
This is young Jonathan, son of old John,
  Positive, peaceable, firm in the right,
Saxon men all of us, may we be one,
  Steady for freedom, and strong in her might.

Then, slow and sure, as the oaks have grown
  From the acorns that fell on that autumn day,
So this new manhood in city and town,
  To a nobler stature will grow alway;
Winning by inches, holding by clinches,
  Slow to contention, and slower to quit,
Now and then failing, never once quailing,
  Let us thank God for the Saxon grit.

*Robert Collyer* [1823-1912]

## AT GIBRALTAR

### I

ENGLAND, I stand on thy imperial ground,
  Not all a stranger; as thy bugles blow,
  I feel within my blood old battles flow,—
The blood whose ancient founts in thee are found.
Still surging dark against the Christian bound
  While Islam presses; well its peoples know
  Thy heights that watch them wandering below;
I think how Lucknow heard their gathering sound.

I turn, and meet the cruel, turbaned face.
  England! 'tis sweet to be so much thy son!
I feel the conqueror in my blood and race;
  Last night Trafalgar awed me, and to-day
Gibraltar wakened; hark, thy evening gun
  Startles the desert over Africa!

*George Edward Woodberry* [1855-1930]

## GIBRALTAR

SEVEN weeks of sea, and twice seven days of storm
Upon the huge Atlantic, and once more
We ride into still water and the calm
Of a sweet evening screened by either shore
Of Spain and Barbary. Our toils are o'er,
Our exile is accomplished. Once again
We look on Europe, mistress as of yore
Of the fair earth and of the hearts of men.
Ay, this is the famed rock, which Hercules
And Goth and Moor bequeathed us. At this door
England stands sentry. God! to hear the shrill
Sweet treble of her fifes upon the breeze
And at the summons of the rock gun's roar
To see her red coats marching from the hill.

*Wilfrid Scawen Blunt* [1840-1922]

## MOTHER ENGLAND

I

THERE was a rover from a western shore,
England! whose eyes the sudden tears did drown,
Beholding the white cliff and sunny down
Of thy good realm, beyond the sea's uproar.
I, for a moment, dreamed that, long before,
I had beheld them thus, when, with the frown
Of sovereignty, the victor's palm and crown
Thou from the tilting-field of nations bore.
Thy prowess and thy glory dazzled first;
But when in fields I saw the tender flame
Of primroses, and full-fleeced lambs at play,
Meseemed I at thy breast, like these, was nursed;

Then mother—Mother England!—home I came
Like one who hath been all too long away!

II

As nestling at thy feet in peace I lay,
A thought awoke and restless stirred in me:
"My land and congeners are beyond the sea,
Theirs is the morning and the evening day.
Wilt thou give ear while this of them I say:—
'Haughty art thou, and they are bold and free,
As well befits who have descent from thee,
And who have trodden brave the forlorn way.
Children of thine, but grown to strong estate;
Nor scorn from thee would they be slow to pay,
Nor check from thee submissly would they bear;
Yet, Mother England! yet their hearts are great,
And if for thee should dawn some darkest day,
At cry of thine, how proudly would they dare!'"

*Edith M. Thomas* [1854–1925]

## "GOD SAVE THE KING"

God save our gracious King,
Long live our noble King,
  God save the King!
Send him victorious,
Happy and glorious,
Long to reign over us,
  God save the King!

O Lord our God, arise,
Scatter his enemies,
  And make them fall.
Confound their politics,
Frustrate their knavish tricks;
On Thee our hearts we fix,
  God save us all!

Thy choicest gifts in store,
On him be pleased to pour,
  Long may he reign.
May he defend our laws,
And ever give us cause,
To sing with heart and voice,
  God save the King!

*Henry Carey* (?) [ ? –1743]

## RULE, BRITANNIA

From "Alfred"

When Britain first, at Heaven's command,
  Arose from out the azure main,
This was the charter of the land,
  And guardian angels sung the strain:
    *Rule, Britannia, rule the waves,*
    *Britons never will be slaves.*

The nations not so blest as thee
  Must, in their turns, to tyrants fall,
Whilst thou shalt flourish, great and free,
  The dread and envy of them all.

Still more majestic shalt thou rise,
  More dreadful from each foreign stroke;
As the loud blast that tears the skies
  Serves but to root thy native oak.

Thee haughty tyrants ne'er shall tame;
  All their attempts to bend thee down
Will but arouse thy generous flame,
  But work their woe, and thy renown.

To thee belongs the rural reign;
  Thy cities shall with commerce shine;
All thine shall be the subject main,
  And every shore it circles, thine.

The Muses, still with Freedom found,
  Shall to thy happy coast repair:
Blest Isle! with matchless beauty crowned,
  And manly hearts to guard the fair.
    *Rule, Britannia, rule the waves,*
    *Britons never will be slaves.*

*James Thomson* [1700–1748]

## "YE MARINERS OF ENGLAND"

Ye Mariners of England
  That guard our native seas!
Whose flag has braved, a thousand years,
  The battle and the breeze!
Your glorious standard launch again
  To match another foe;
And sweep through the deep,
  While the stormy winds do blow!
While the battle rages loud and long,
  And the stormy winds do blow.

The spirits of your fathers
  Shall start from every wave!—
For the deck it was their field of fame,
  And Ocean was their grave:
Where Blake and mighty Nelson fell
  Your manly hearts shall glow,
As ye sweep through the deep,
  While the stormy winds do blow!
While the battle rages loud and long,
  And the stormy winds do blow.

Britannia needs no bulwarks,
  No towers along the steep;
Her march is o'er the mountain-waves,
  Her home is on the deep.
With thunders from her native oak
  She quells the floods below,

As they roar on the shore,
When the stormy winds do blow!
When the battle rages loud and long,
And the stormy winds do blow.

The meteor flag of England
Shall yet terrific burn;
Till danger's troubled night depart
And the star of peace return.
Then, then, ye ocean-warriors!
Our song and feast shall flow
To the fame of your name,
When the storm has ceased to blow!
When the fiery fight is heard no more,
And the storm has ceased to blow.

*Thomas Campbell* [1777-1844]

## "READY, AY, READY"

OLD England's sons are English yet,
Old England's hearts are strong;
And still she wears her coronet
Aflame with sword and song.
As in their pride our fathers died,
If need be, so die we;
So wield we still, gainsay who will,
The sceptre of the sea.
England, stand fast; let heart and hand be steady;
Be thy first word thy last,—Ready, ay, ready!

We've Raleighs still for Raleigh's part,
We've Nelsons yet unknown;
The pulses of the Lion Heart
Beat on through Wellington.
Hold, Britain, hold thy creed of old,
Strong foe and steadfast friend,
And, still unto thy motto true,
Defy not, but defend.
England, stand fast; let heart and hand be steady;
Be thy first word thy last,—Ready, ay, ready!

Men whispered that our arm was weak,
  Men said our blood was cold,
And that our hearts no longer speak
  The clarion-note of old;
But let the spear and sword draw near
  The sleeping lion's den,
His island shore shall start once more
  To life with armèd men.
England, stand fast; let heart and hand be steady;
Be thy first word thy last,—Ready, ay, ready!

*Herman Charles Merivale* [1806–1874]

## "OF OLD SAT FREEDOM ON THE HEIGHTS"

From "On a Mourner"

Of old sat Freedom on the heights,
  The thunders breaking at her feet;
Above her shook the starry lights,
  She heard the torrents meet.

There in her place she did rejoice,
  Self-gathered in her prophet-mind,
But fragments of her mighty voice
  Came rolling on the wind.

Then stepped she down through town and field
  To mingle with the human race,
And part by part to men revealed
  The fullness of her face—

Grave mother of majestic works,
  From her isle-altar gazing down,
Who, God-like, grasps the triple forks,
  And, king-like, wears the crown.

Her open eyes desire the truth.
  The wisdom of a thousand years
Is in them. May perpetual youth
  Keep dry their light from tears;

That her fair form may stand and shine,
    Make bright our days and light our dreams,
Turning to scorn with lips divine
    The falsehood of extremes!

*Alfred Tennyson* [1809–1892]

## AN ODE

### IN IMITATION OF ALCÆUS

    WHAT constitutes a State?
Not high-raised battlement or labored mound,
    Thick wall or moated gate;
Not cities proud with spires and turrets crowned;
    Not bays and broad-armed ports,
Where, laughing at the storm, rich navies ride;
    Not starred and spangled courts,
Where low-browed baseness wafts perfume to pride.
    No:—men, high-minded men,
With powers as far above dull brutes endued
    In forest, brake, or den,
As beasts excel cold rocks and brambles rude,—
    Men who their duties know,
But know their rights, and, knowing, dare maintain;
    Prevent the long-aimed blow,
And crush the tyrant while they rend the chain:—
    These constitute a State;
And sovereign Law, that State's collected will,
    O'er thrones and globes elate
Sits empress, crowning good, repressing ill.
    Smit by her sacred frown,
The fiend, Dissension, like a vapor sinks;
    And e'en the all-dazzling Crown
Hides his faint rays, and at her bidding shrinks.

    Such was this heaven-loved isle,
Than Lesbos fairer and the Cretan shore!
    No more shall Freedom smile?
Shall Britons languish, and be men no more?

Since all must life resign,
Those sweet rewards which decorate the brave
'Tis folly to decline,
And steal inglorious to the silent grave.

*William Jones* [1746–1794]
(*The last four lines are said to have been added by Dr. Samuel Johnson.*)

## ENGLAND, 1802

I

O FRIEND! I know not which way I must look
For comfort, being, as I am, oppressed,
To think that now our life is only dressed
For show; mean handy-work of craftsman, cook,
Or groom!—We must run glittering like a brook
In the open sunshine, or we are unblest:
The wealthiest man among us is the best:
No grandeur now in nature or in book
Delights us. Rapine, avarice, expense,
This is idolatry; and these we adore:
Plain living and high thinking are no more:
The homely beauty of the good old cause
Is gone; our peace, our fearful innocence,
And pure religion breathing household laws.

II

Milton! thou shouldst be living at this hour:
England hath need of thee: she is a fen
Of stagnant waters: altar, sword, and pen,
Fireside, the heroic wealth of hall and bower,
Have forfeited their ancient English dower
Of inward happiness. We are selfish men;
Oh! raise us up, return to us again,
And give us manners, virtue, freedom, power.
Thy soul was like a Star, and dwelt apart;
Thou hadst a voice whose sound was like the sea
Pure as the naked heavens, majestic, free,
So didst thou travel on life's common way,
In cheerful godliness; and yet thy heart
The lowliest duties on herself did lay.

III

Great men have been among us; hands that penned
And tongues that uttered wisdom—better none:
The later Sidney, Marvell, Harrington,
Young Vane, and others who called Milton friend.
These moralists could act and comprehend:
They knew how genuine glory was put on;
Taught us how rightfully a nation shone
In splendor: what strength was, that would not bend
But in magnanimous meekness. France, 'tis strange,
Hath brought forth no such souls as we had then.
Perpetual emptiness! unceasing change!
No single volume paramount, no code,
No master spirit, no determined road;
But equally a want of books and men!

IV

It is not to be thought of that the flood
Of British freedom, which, to the open sea
Of the world's praise, from dark antiquity
Hath flowed, "with pomp of waters, unwithstood,"—
Roused though it be full often to a mood
Which spurns the check of salutary bands,—
That this most famous stream in bogs and sands
Should perish; and to evil and to good
Be lost for ever. In our halls is hung
Armory of the invincible Knights of old:
We must be free or die, who speak the tongue
That Shakespeare spake; the faith and morals hold
Which Milton held.—In everything we are sprung
Of Earth's first blood, have titles manifold.

V

When I have borne in memory what has tamed
Great Nations, how ennobling thoughts depart
When men change swords for ledgers, and desert
The student's bower for gold, some fears unnamed
I had, my Country—am I to be blamed?

Now, when I think of thee, and what thou art,
Verily, in the bottom of my heart,
Of those unfilial fears I am ashamed.
For dearly must we prize thee; we who find
In thee a bulwark for the cause of men;
And I by my affection was beguiled:
What wonder if a Poet now and then,
Among the many movements of his mind,
Felt for thee as a lover or a child!

*William Wordsworth* [1770–1850]

## "ENGLAND, MY ENGLAND"

WHAT have I done for you,
England, my England?
What is there I would not do,
England, my own?
With your glorious eyes austere,
As the Lord were walking near,
Whispering terrible things and dear
As the Song on your bugles blown,
England—
Round the world on your bugles blown!

Where shall the watchful Sun,
England, my England,
Match the master-work you've done,
England, my own?
When shall he rejoice agen
Such a breed of mighty men
As come forward, one to ten,
To the Song on your bugles blown,
England—
Down the years on your bugles blown?

Ever the faith endures,
England, my England:—
"Take and break us: we are yours,
England, my own!

Life is good, and joy runs high
Between English earth and sky:
Death is death; but we shall die
  To the Song on your bugles blown,
    England—
  To the stars on your bugles blown!"

They call you proud and hard,
  England, my England:
You with worlds to watch and ward,
  England, my own!
You whose mailed hand keeps the keys
Of such teeming destinies,
You could know nor dread nor ease
  Were the Song on your bugles blown,
    England,
  Round the Pit on your bugles blown!

Mother of Ships whose might
  England, my England,
Is the fierce old Sea's delight,
  England, my own,
Chosen daughter of the Lord,
Spouse-in-Chief of the ancient Sword,
There's the menace of the Word
  In the Song on your bugles blown,
    England—
  Out of heaven on your bugles blown!

*William Ernest Henley* [1849–1903]

## ENGLAND

THERE she sits in her Island-home,
  Peerless among her Peers!
And Liberty oft to her arms doth come,
  To ease its poor heart of tears.
Old England still throbs with the muffled fire
  Of a past she can never forget:
And again shall she herald the world up higher·
  For there's life in the Old Land yet.

They would mock at her now, who of old looked forth
  In their fear, as they heard her afar;
But loud will your wail be, O Kings of the Earth!
  When the Old Land goes down to the war.
The Avalanche trembles, half-launched, and half-riven,
  Her voice will in motion set:
O ring out the tidings, wide-reaching as Heaven!
  There's life in the Old Land yet.

The old nursing Mother's not hoary yet,
  There is sap in her ancient tree:
She lifteth a bosom of glory yet,
  Through her mists, to the Sun and the Sea—
Fair as the Queen of Love, fresh from the foam,
  Or a star in a dark cloud set;
Ye may blazon her shame,—ye may leap at her name,—
  But there's life in the Old Land yet.

Let the storm burst, you will find the Old Land
  Ready-ripe for a rough, red fray!
She will fight as she fought when she took her stand
  For the Right in the olden day.
Rouse the old royal soul; Europe's best hope
  Is her sword-edge for Victory set!
She shall dash Freedom's foes down Death's bloody slope;
  For there's life in the Old Land yet.

*Gerald Massey* [1828–1907]

## THE SONG OF THE BOW

From "The White Company"

WHAT of the bow?
  The bow was made in England:
Of true wood, of yew-wood,
  The wood of English bows;
    So men who are free
    Love the old yew-tree
And the land where the yew-tree grows.

What of the cord?
  The cord was made in England:
A rough cord, a tough cord,
  A cord that bowmen love;

And so we will sing
Of the hempen string
And the land where the cord was wove.

What of the shaft?
The shaft was cut in England:
A long shaft, a strong shaft,
Barbed and trim and true;
So we'll drink all together
To the gray goose-feather
And the land where the gray goose flew.

What of the mark?
Ah, seek it not in England:
A bold mark, our old mark,
Is waiting over-sea.
When the strings harp in chorus,
And the lion flag is o'er us,
It is there that our mark will be.

What of the men?
The men were bred in England:
The bowmen—the yeomen,
The lads of dale and fell.
Here's to you—and to you!
To the hearts that are true
And the land where the true hearts dwell.

*Arthur Conan Doyle* [1859–1930]

## AN ENGLISH MOTHER

EVERY week of every season out of English ports go forth,
White of sail or white of trail, East, or West, or South, or North,
Scattering like a flight of pigeons, half a hundred home-sick ships,
Bearing half a thousand striplings—each with kisses on his lips
Of some silent mother, fearful lest she show herself too fond,
Giving him to bush or desert as one pays a sacred bond,

—Tell us, you who hide your heartbreak, which is sadder, when all's done,
To repine, an English mother, or to roam, an English son?

You who shared your babe's first sorrow when his cheek no longer pressed
On the perfect, snow-and-roseleaf beauty of your mother-breast,
In the rigor of his nurture was your woman's mercy mute,
Knowing he was doomed to exile with the savage and the brute?
Did you school yourself to absence all his adolescent years,
That, though you be torn with parting, he should never see the tears?
Now his ship has left the offing for the many-mouthèd sea,
This your guerdon, empty heart, by empty bed to bend the knee!

And if he be but the latest thus to leave your dwindling board,
Is a sorrow less for being added to a sorrow's hoard?
Is the mother-pain the duller that to-day his brothers stand,
Facing ambuscades of Congo or alarms of Zululand?
Toil, where blizzards drift the snow like smoke across the plains of death?
Faint, where tropic fens at morning steam with fever-laden breath?
Die, that in some distant river's veins the English blood may run—
Mississippi, Yangtze, Ganges, Nile, Mackenzie, Amazon?

Ah! you still must wait and suffer in a solitude untold
While your sisters of the nations call you passive, call you cold—
Still must scan the news of sailings, breathless search the slow gazette,
Find the dreadful name . . . and, later, get his blithe farewell! And yet—

Shall the lonely at the hearthstone shame the legions who have died
Grudging not the price their country pays for progress and for pride?
—Nay; but, England, do not ask us thus to emulate your scars
Until women's tears are reckoned in the budgets of your wars.

*Robert Underwood Johnson* [1853-1937]

## AVE IMPERATRIX!

SET in this stormy Northern sea,
Queen of these restless fields of tide,
England! what shall men say of thee,
Before whose feet the worlds divide?

The earth, a brittle globe of glass,
Lies in the hollow of thy hand,
And through its heart of crystal pass,
Like shadows through a twilight land,

The spears of crimson-suited war,
The long white-crested waves of fight,
And all the deadly fires which are
The torches of the lords of Night.

The yellow leopards, strained and lean,
The treacherous Russian knows so well,
With gaping blackened jaws are seen
To leap through hail of screaming shell.

The strong sea-lion of England's wars
Hath left his sapphire cave of sea,
To battle with the storm that mars
The star of England's chivalry.

The brazen-throated clarion blows
Across the Pathan's reedy fen,
And the high steeps of Indian snows
Shake to the tread of armèd men.

And many an Afghan chief, who lies
  Beneath his cool pomegranate-trees,
Clutches his sword in fierce surmise
  When on the mountain-side he sees

The fleet-foot Marri scout, who comes
  To tell how he hath heard afar
The measured roll of English drums
  Beat at the gates of Kandahar.

For southern wind and east wind meet
  Where, girt and crowned by sword and fire,
England with bare and bloody feet
  Climbs the steep road of wide empire.

O lonely Himalayan height,
  Gray pillar of the Indian sky,
Where saw'st thou last in clanging fight
  Our wingèd dogs of Victory?

The almond groves of Samarcand,
  Bokhara, where red lilies blow,
And Oxus, by whose yellow sand
  The grave white-turbaned merchants go;

And on from thence to Ispahan,
  The gilded garden of the sun,
Whence the long dusty caravan
  Brings cedar and vermilion;

And that dread city of Cabul
  Set at the mountain's scarpèd feet,
Whose marble tanks are ever full
  With water for the noonday heat;

Where through the narrow straight Bazaar
  A little maid Circassian
Is led, a present from the Czar
  Unto some old and bearded Khan,—

Here have our wild war-eagles flown,
  And flapped wide wings in fiery fight;
But the sad dove, that sits alone
  In England—she hath no delight.

In vain the laughing girl will lean
  To greet her love with love-lit eyes:
Down in some treacherous black ravine,
  Clutching his flag, the dead boy lies.

And many a moon and sun will see
  The lingering wistful children wait
To climb upon their father's knee;
  And in each house made desolate,

Pale women who have lost their lord
  Will kiss the relics of the slain—
Some tarnished epaulette,—some sword—
  Poor toys to soothe such anguished pain.

For not in quiet English fields
  Are these, our brothers, lain to rest,
Where we might deck their broken shields
  With all the flowers the dead love best.

For some are by the Delhi walls,
  And many in the Afghan land,
And many where the Ganges falls
  Through seven mouths of shifting sand.

And some in Russian waters lie,
  And others in the seas which are
The portals to the East, or by
  The wind-swept heights of Trafalgar.

O wandering graves! O restless sleep!
  O silence of the sunless day!
O still ravine! O stormy deep!
  Give up your prey! Give up your prey!

And thou whose wounds are never healed,
Whose weary race is never won,
O Cromwell's England! must thou yield
For every inch of ground a son?

Go! crown with thorns thy gold-crowned head,
Change thy glad song to song of pain;
Wind and wild wave have got thy dead,
And will not yield them back again.

Wave and wild wind and foreign shore
Possess the flower of English land!—
Lips that thy lips shall kiss no more,
Hands that shall never clasp thy hand.

What profit now that we have bound
The whole round world with nets of gold,
If hidden in our heart is found
The care that groweth never old?

What profit that our galleys ride,
Pine-forest-like, on every main?
Ruin and wreck are at our side,
Grim warders of the House of Pain.

Where are the brave, the strong, the fleet?
Where is our English chivalry?
Wild grasses are their burial-sheet,
And sobbing waves their threnody.

O loved ones lying far away,
What word of love can dead lips send!
O wasted dust! O senseless clay!
Is this the end? Is this the end?

Peace, peace! we wrong the noble dead
To vex their solemn slumber so;
Though childless, and with thorn-crowned head,
Up the steep road must England go,

Yet when this fiery web is spun,
  Her watchmen shall descry from far
The young Republic like a sun
  Rise from these crimson seas of war.

*Oscar Wilde* [1856–1900]

## RECESSIONAL

God of our fathers, known of old—
  Lord of our far-flung battle line—
Beneath whose awful hand we hold
  Dominion over palm and pine—
Lord God of Hosts, be with us yet,
Lest we forget—lest we forget!

The tumult and the shouting dies—
  The Captains and the Kings depart—
Still stands Thine ancient sacrifice,
  An humble and a contrite heart.
Lord God of Hosts, be with us yet,
Lest we forget—lest we forget!

Far-called, our navies melt away—
  On dune and headland sinks the fire—
Lo, all our pomp of yesterday
  Is one with Nineveh and Tyre!
Judge of the Nations, spare us yet,
Lest we forget—lest we forget!

If, drunk with sight of power, we loose
  Wild tongues that have not Thee in awe—
Such boastings as the Gentiles use,
  Or lesser breeds without the Law—
Lord God of Hosts, be with us yet,
Lest we forget—lest we forget!

For heathen heart that puts her trust
  In reeking tube and iron shard—
All valiant dust that builds on dust,
  And guarding calls not Thee to guard,—
For frantic boast and foolish word,
Thy Mercy on Thy People, Lord! AMEN.

*Rudyard Kipling* [1865–1936]

## THE WEARIN' O' THE GREEN

O, PADDY dear, an' did ye hear the news that's goin' round?
The shamrock is by law forbid to grow on Irish ground!
No more St. Patrick's Day we'll keep, his color can't be seen,
For there's a cruel law agin the wearin' o' the Green!
I met wid Napper Tandy, and he took me by the hand,
And he said, "How's poor Ould Ireland, and how does she stand?"
She's the most disthressful country that iver yet was seen,
For they're hangin' men and women there for wearin' o' the Green.

An' if the color we must wear is England's cruel Red,
Let it remind us of the blood that Ireland has shed;
Then pull the shamrock from your hat, and throw it on the sod,—
And never fear, 'twill take root there, though under foot 'tis trod!
When law can stop the blades of grass from growin' as they grow,
And when the leaves in summer-time their color dare not show,
Then I will change the color, too, I wear in my caubeen,
But till that day, plaze God, I'll stick to wearin' o' the Green.

*Unknown*

## DARK ROSALEEN

O MY dark Rosaleen,
  Do not sigh, do not weep!
The priests are on the ocean green,
  They march along the deep.
There's wine from the royal Pope
  Upon the ocean green,
And Spanish ale shall give you hope,
  My dark Rosaleen!
  My own Rosaleen!

Shall glad your heart, shall give you hope,
Shall give you health, and help, and hope,
My dark Rosaleen!

Over hills and through dales
Have I roamed for your sake;
All yesterday I sailed the sails
On river and on lake.
The Erne, at its highest flood,
I dashed across unseen,
For there was lightning in my blood,
My dark Rosaleen!
My own Rosaleen!
Oh! there was lightning in my blood,
Red lightning lightened through my blood
My dark Rosaleen!

All day long, in unrest,
To and fro do I move.
The very soul within my breast
Is wasted for you, love!
The heart in my bosom faints
To think of you, my Queen,
My life of life, my saint of saints,
My dark Rosaleen!
My own Rosaleen!
To hear your sweet and sad complaints,
My life, my love, my saint of saints,
My dark Rosaleen!

Woe and pain, pain and woe,
Are my lot, night and noon,
To see your bright face clouded so,
Like to the mournful moon.
But yet will I rear your throne
Again in golden sheen;
'Tis you shall reign, shall reign alone
My dark Rosaleen!
My own Rosaleen!

'Tis you shall have the golden throne,
'Tis you shall reign, and reign alone,
  My dark Rosaleen!

Over dews, over sands,
  Will I fly for your weal:
Your holy, delicate white hands
  Shall girdle me with steel.
At home in your emerald bowers,
  From morning's dawn till e'en,
You'll pray for me, my flower of flowers,
  My dark Rosaleen!
  My own Rosaleen!
You'll think of me through daylight's hours,
My virgin flower, my flower of flowers,
  My dark Rosaleen!

I could scale the blue air,
  I could plough the high hills,
Oh, I could kneel all night in prayer,
  To heal your many ills!
And one beamy smile from you
  Would float like light between
My toils and me, my own, my true,
  My dark Rosaleen!
  My own Rosaleen!
Would give me life and soul anew,
A second life, a soul anew,
  My dark Rosaleen!

Oh! the Erne shall run red
  With redundance of blood,
The earth shall rock beneath our tread,
  And flames wrap hill and wood,
And gun-peal and slogan-cry
  Wake many a glen serene,
Ere you shall fade, ere you shall die,
  My dark Rosaleen!
  My own Rosaleen!

The Judgment Hour must first be nigh,
Ere you shall fade, ere you can die,
My dark Rosaleen!

*James Clarence Mangan* [1803–1849]

## EXILE OF ERIN

There came to the beach a poor exile of Erin,
The dew on his thin robe was heavy and chill;
For his country he sighed, when at twilight repairing
To wander alone by the wind-beaten hill.
But the day-star attracted his eye's sad devotion,
For it rose o'er his own native isle of the ocean,
Where once, in the fire of his youthful emotion,
He sang the bold anthem of Erin go bragh.

Sad is my fate! said the heart-broken stranger;
The wild deer and wolf to a covert can flee,
But I have no refuge from famine and danger,
A home and a country remain not to me.
Never again, in the green sunny bowers
Where my forefathers lived, shall I spend the sweet hours
Or cover my harp with the wild-woven flowers,
And strike to the numbers of Erin go bragh!

Erin, my country! though sad and forsaken,
In dreams I revisit thy sea-beaten shore;
But, alas! in a far foreign land I awaken,
And sigh for the friends who can meet me no more!
O cruel fate! wilt thou never replace me
In a mansion of peace, where no perils can chase me?
Never again shall my brothers embrace me?
They died to defend me, or live to deplore!

Where is my cabin-door, fast by the wildwood?
Sisters and sire, did ye weep for its fall?
Where is the mother that looked on my childhood?
And where is the bosom-friend, dearer than all?

O my sad heart! long abandoned by pleasure,
Why did it dote on a fast-fading treasure?
Tears, like the rain-drop, may fall without measure,
But rapture and beauty they cannot recall.

Yet, all its sad recollections suppressing,
One dying wish my lone bosom can draw,—
Erin, an exile bequeaths thee his blessing!
Land of my forefathers, Erin go bragh!
Buried and cold, when my heart stills her motion,
Green be thy fields, sweetest isle of the ocean!
And thy harp-striking bards sing aloud with devotion,—
Erin mavournin, Erin go bragh!

*Thomas Campbell* [1777–1844]

## ANDROMEDA

THEY chained her fair young body to the cold and cruel stone;
The beast begot of sea and slime had marked her for his own;
The callous world beheld the wrong, and left her there alone.
Base caitiffs who belied her, false kinsmen who denied her,
Ye left her there alone!

My Beautiful, they left thee in thy peril and thy pain;
The night that hath no morrow was brooding on the main:
But, lo! a light is breaking of hope for thee again;
'Tis Perseus' sword a-flaming, thy dawn of day proclaiming
Across the western main.
O Ireland! O my country! he comes to break thy chain!

*James Jeffrey Roche* [1847–1908]

## IRELAND

Si oblitus fuero tui Ierusalem: oblivioni detur dextera mea.

THY sorrow, and the sorrow of the sea,
Are sisters; the sad winds are of thy race:
The heart of melancholy beats in thee,
And the lamenting spirit haunts thy face,

Mournful and mighty Mother! who art kin
  To the ancient earth's first woe,
When holy Angels wept, beholding sin.
For not in penance do thy true tears flow,
Not thine the long transgression: at thy name,
  We sorrow not with shame,
But proudly: for thy soul is as the snow.

Old as the sorrow for lost Paradise
Seems thine old sorrow: thou in the mild West,
Who wouldst thy children upon earth suffice
For Paradise, and pure Hesperian rest;
Had not the violent and bitter fates
  Burned up with fiery feet
The greenness of thy pastures; had not hates,
Envies, and desolations, with fierce heat
Wasted thee, and consumed the land of grace,
  Beauty's abiding place;
And vexed with agony bright joy's retreat.

Swift at the word of the Eternal Will,
Upon thee the malign armed Angels came.
Flame was their winging, flame that laps thee still;
And in the anger of their eyes was flame.
One was the Angel of the field of blood,
  And one of lonelier death:
One saddened exiles on the ocean flood,
And famine followed on another's breath.
Angels of evil, with incessant sword,
  Smote thee, O land adored!
And yet smite: for the Will of God so saith.

A severing and sundering they wrought,
A rending of the soul. They turned to tears
The laughter of thy waters: and they brought,
To sow upon thy fields, quick seed of fears;
That brother should hate brother, and one roof
  Shelter unkindly hearts;
Friend from his ancient friendship hold aloof,
And comrades learn to play sad alien parts,

Province from noble province dwell estranged,
  And all old trusts be changed;
And treason teach true men her impious arts.

But yet in their reluctant hands they bore
Laurel, and palm, and crown, and bay: an host,
Heartened by wrath and sorrow more and more,
Strove ever, giving up the mighty ghost;
The field well fought, the song well sung, for sake,
  Mother! of thee alone:
Sorrow and wrath bade deathless courage wake,
And struck from burning harps a deathless tone.
With palm and laurel won, with crown and bay,
  Went proudly down death's way
Children of Ireland, to their deathless throne.

Proud and sweet habitation of thy dead!
Throne upon throne, its thrones of sorrow filled:
Prince on prince coming with triumphant tread,
All passion, save the love of Ireland, stilled.
By the forgetful waters they forget
  Not thee, O Inisfail!
Upon thy fields their dreaming eyes are set,
They hear thy winds call ever through each vale.
Visions of victory exalt and thrill
  Their hearts' whole hunger still:
High beats their longing for the living Gael.

Sarsfield is sad there with his last desire;
FitzGerald mourns with Emmet; ancient chiefs
Dream on their saffron-mantled hosts, afire
Against the givers of their Mother's griefs.
*Was it for naught*, captain asks captain old,
  *Was it in vain, we fell?*
*Shall we have fallen like the leaves of gold,*
*And no green spring wake from the long dark spell?*
*Shall never a crown of summer fruitage come*
  *From blood of martyrdom?*
*Yet to our faith will we not say farewell!*

There the white soul of Davis, there the worn,
Waste soul of Mangan, there the surging soul
Of Grattan, hunger for thy promised morn:
There the great legion of thy martyr roll,
Filled with the fames of seven hundred years,
  Hunger to hear the voice,
Sweeter than marriage music in their ears,
That shall bid thee and all thy sons rejoice.
There bide the spirits who for thee yet burn:
  *Ah! might we but return,*
*And make once more for thee the martyr choice!*

*No swordsmen are the Christians!* Oisin cried:
*O Patrick! thine is but a little race.*
Nay, ancient Oisin! they have greatly died
In battle glory and with warrior grace.
Signed with the Cross, they conquered and they fell;
  Sons of the Cross, they stand:
The Prince of Peace loves righteous warfare well,
And loves thine armies, O our Holy Land!
The Lord of Hosts is with thee, and thine eyes
  Shall see upon thee rise
His glory, and the blessing of His Hand.

Thou hast no fear: with immemorial pride,
Bright as when Oscar ran the morning glades;
The knightly Fenian hunters at his side,
The sunlight through green leaves glad on their blades
The heart in thee is full of joyous faith.
  Not in the bitter dust
Thou crouchest, heeding what the coward saith:
But, radiant with an everlasting trust,
Hearest thine ancient rivers in their glee
  Sing themselves on to sea,
Thy winds make melody: O joy most just!

Nay! we insult thee not with tears, although
With thee we sorrow: not as for one dead
We mourn, for one in the cold earth laid low.
Still is the crown upon thy sovereign head,

Still is the scepter within thy strong hand,
  Still is the kingdom thine:
The armies of thy sons on thy command
Wait, and thy starry eyes through darkness shine.
Tears for the dear and dead! For thee, *All hail!*
  Unconquered Inisfail!
Tears for the lost: thou livest, O divine!

Thou passest not away: the sternest powers
Spoil not all beauty of thy face, nor mar
All peace of thy great heart, O pulse of ours!
The darkest cloud dims thee not all, O star!
Ancient and proud thy sorrows, and their might
  That of the murmuring waves:
They hearten us to fight the unceasing fight,
Filled with the grace, that flows from holy graves.
Sons pass away, and thou hast sons as true
  To fight the fight anew:
Thy welfare, all the gain their warfare craves.

Sweet Mother! in what marvellous dear ways
Close to thine heart thou keepest all thine own!
Far off, they yet can consecrate their days
To thee, and on the swift winds westward blown,
Send thee the homage of their hearts, their vow
  Of one most sacred care:
To thee devote all passionate power, since thou
Vouchsafest them, O land of love! to bear
Sorrow and joy with thee. Each far son thrills
  Toward thy blue dreaming hills,
And longs to kiss thy feet upon them, Fair!

*If death come swift upon me, it will be*
*Because of the great love I bear the Gael!*
So sang upon the separating sea
Columba, while his boat sped out of hail,
And all grew lonely. But some sons thou hast,
  Whose is an heavier lot,
Close at thy side: they see thy torment last,
And all their will to help thee helps thee not.

Mother! their grief, to look on thy dear face,
  Worn with each weary trace
Of fresh woes, and of old woes unforgot!

And yet great spirits ride thy winds: thy ways
Are haunted and enchanted evermore.
Thy children hear the voices of old days
In music of the sea upon thy shore,
In falling of the waters from thine hills,
  In whispers of thy trees:
A glory from the things eternal fills
Their eyes, and at high noon thy people sees
Visions, and wonderful is all the air.
  So upon earth they share
Eternity: they learn it at thy knees.

Eternal is our faith in thee: the sun
Shall sooner fall from Heaven, than from our lives
That faith; and the great stars fade one by one,
Ere fade that light in which thy people strives.
Strong in the everlasting righteousness
  Triumphs our faith: the fight
Hath holiest hosts to inspire it and to bless;
Thy children lift true faces to the light.
Theirs are the visitations from on high,
  Voices that call and cry:
Celestial comfort in the deeps of night.

Charmed upon waters three, forlorn and cold,
The swans, Children of Lir, endured their doom:
From off their white wings flashed the morning gold,
And round their white wings closed the twilight gloom.
Yet on their stormy weird the Christian bell
  Broke, and they stirred with dread:
The Coming of the Saints upon them fell;
They woke to joy, and found their white wings fled.
And thou, in these last days, shalt thou not hear
  A sound of sacred fear?
God's bells shall ring, and all sad days be dead.

But desolate be the houses of thy foes:
Sorrow encompass them, and vehement wrath
Besiege them: be their hearts cold as the snows:
Let lamentation keen about their path,
The fires of God burn round them, and His night
  Lie on their blinded eyes:
And when they call to the Eternal Light,
None shall make answer to their stricken cries.
Mercy and pity shall not know them more:
  God shall shut to the door,
And close on them His everlasting skies.

How long? Justice of Very God! How long?
The Isle of Sorrows from of old hath trod
The stony road of unremitting wrong,
The purple winepress of the wrath of God:
Is then the Isle of Destiny indeed
  To grief predestinate;
Ever foredoomed to agonize and bleed,
Beneath the scourging of eternal fate?
Yet against hope shall we still hope, and still
  Beseech the Eternal Will:
Our lives to this one service dedicate.

Ah, tremble into passion, Harp! and sing
War song, O Sword! Fill the fair land, great Twain!
Wake all her heavy heart to triumphing:
To vengeance, and armed trampling of the plain!
And you, white spirits on the mountain wind,
  Cry between eve and morn!
Cry, mighty Dead! until the people find
Their souls a furnace of desire and scorn.
Call to the hosting upon Tara, call
  The tribes of Eire all:
Trump of the Champions! immemorial Horn!

Shall not the Three Waves thunder for their King,
The Captain of thy people? Shall not streams
Leap from thy mountains' heart, and many a spring
Gladden thy valleys, for the joy of dreams

Fulfilled, for glory of the battle won?
  Hast thou no prophet left?
Is all thy Druid wizardry undone,
And thou of thy foreknowledge quite bereft?
Nay! but the power of faith is prophecy,
  Vision, and certainty:
Faith, that hath walked the waves, and mountains cleft.

As haunting Tirnanoge within the sea,
So hid within the Eyes of God thy fate
Lies dreaming: and when God shall bid it be,
Ah, then the fair perfection of thy state!
Bravely the gold and silver bells shall chime,
  When thou art wed with peace:
Far to the desert of their own sad clime
Shall fly the ill Angels, when God bids them cease.
Thine shall be only a majestic joy,
  No evil can destroy:
The sorrows of thy soul shall have release.

Thy blood of martyrs to the martyrs' Home
Cries from the earth: the altar of high Heaven
Is by their cries besieged and overcome:
The Rainbow Throne and flaming Spirits Seven
Know well the music of that agony,
  That surge of a long sigh,
That voice of an unresting misery,
That ardor of anguish unto the Most High.
Thou from thy wronged earth pleadest with the Just,
  Whose loving mercy must
Hear, and command thy death in life to die.

Golden allies are thine, bright souls of Saints,
Glad choirs of intercession for the Gael:
Their flame of prayer ascends, their stream of plaints
Flows to the wounded feet, for Inisfail.
Victor, the Angel of thy Patrick, pleads;
  Mailed Michael with his sword
Kneels there, the champion of thy bitter needs,
Prince of the shining armies of the Lord:

And there, Star of the Morning and the Sea,
  Mary pours prayer for thee:
And unto Mary be thy prayers outpoured.

*O Rose! O Lily! O Lady full of grace!*
*O Mary Mother! O Mary Maid! hear thou.*
*Glory of Angels! Pity, and turn thy face,*
*Praying thy Son, even as we pray thee now,*
*For thy dear sake to set thine Ireland free:*
  *Pray thou thy little Child!*
*Ah! who can help her, but in mercy He?*
*Pray then, pray thou for Ireland, Mother mild!*
*O Heart of Mary! pray the Sacred Heart:*
  *His, at Whose word depart*
*Sorrows and hates, home to Hell's waste and wild.*

*Lionel Johnson* [1867–1902]

## TO THE DEAD OF '98

God rest you, rest you, rest you, Ireland's dead!
  Peace be upon you shed,
Peace from the Mercy of the Crucified,
  You, who for Ireland died!
Soft fall on you the dews and gentle airs
  Of interceding prayers,
From lowly cabins of our ancient land,
  Yours yet, O Sacred Band!
God rest you, rest you: for the fight you fought
  Was His; the end you sought,
His; from His altar fires you took your flame,
  Hailing His Holy Name.
Triumphantly you gave yourselves to death:
  And your last breath
Was one last sigh for Ireland, sigh to Him,
  As the loved land grew dim.

And still, blessèd and martyr souls! you pray
  In the same faith this day:
From forth your dwelling beyond sun and star,
  Where only spirits are,

Your prayers in a perpetual flight arise,
  To fold before God's Eyes
Their tireless wings, and wait the Holy Word
  That one day shall be heard.
*Not unto us*, they plead, *Thy goodness gave*
  *Our mother to enslave;*
*To us Thou gavest death for love of her:*
  *Ah, what death lovelier?*
*But to our children's children give to see*
  *The perfect victory!*
*Thy dead beseech thee: to Thy living give*
  *In liberty to live!*

*Lionel Johnson* [1867–1902]

## THE MEMORY OF THE DEAD

Who fears to speak of Ninety-Eight?
  Who blushes at the name?
When cowards mock the patriot's fate,
  Who hangs his head for shame?
He's all a knave, or half a slave,
  Who slights his country thus;
But a true man, like you, man,
  Will fill your glass with us.

We drink the memory of the brave,
  The faithful and the few—
Some lie far off beyond the wave,
  Some sleep in Ireland, too;
All, all are gone—but still lives on
  The fame of those who died;
All true men, like you, men,
  Remember them with pride.

Some on the shores of distant lands
  Their weary hearts have laid,
And by the stranger's heedless hands
  Their lonely graves were made:

But, though their clay be far away
  Beyond the Atlantic foam,
In true men, like you, men,
  Their spirit's still at home.

The dust of some is Irish earth;
  Among their own they rest;
And the same land that gave them birth
  Has caught them to her breast;
And we will pray that from their clay
  Full many a race may start
Of true men, like you, men,
  To act as brave a part.

They rose in dark and evil days
  To right their native land;
They kindled here a living blaze
  That nothing shall withstand.
Alas! that Might can vanquish Right—
  They fell and passed away;
But true men, like you, men,
  Are plenty here to-day.

Then here's their memory—may it be
  For us a guiding light,
To cheer our strife for liberty,
  And teach us to unite.
Through good and ill, be Ireland's still,
  Though sad as theirs your fate;
And true men be you, men,
  Like those of Ninety-Eight!

*John Kells Ingram* [1823–1907]

## CUSHLA MA CHREE

DEAR Erin, how sweetly thy green bosom rises!
  An emerald set in the ring of the sea!
Each blade of thy meadows my faithful heart prizes,
  Thou queen of the west! the world's cushla ma chree!

Thy gates open wide to the poor and the stranger—
  There smiles hospitality hearty and free;
Thy friendship is seen in the moment of danger,
  And the wanderer is welcomed with cushla ma chree.

Thy sons they are brave; but, the battle once over,
  In brotherly peace with their foes they agree;
And the roseate cheeks of thy daughters discover
  The soul-speaking blush that says cushla ma chree.

Then flourish forever, my dear native Erin!
  While sadly I wander an exile from thee;
And, firm as thy mountains, no injury fearing,
  May heaven defend its own cushla ma chree!

*John Philpot Curran* [1750–1817]

## THE GREEN LITTLE SHAMROCK OF IRELAND

There's a dear little plant that grows in our isle,
  'Twas Saint Patrick himself sure that set it;
And the sun on his labor with pleasure did smile,
  And with dew from his eye often wet it.
It thrives through the bog, through the brake, and the mireland;
And he called it the dear little shamrock of Ireland—
  The sweet little shamrock, the dear little shamrock,
  The sweet little, green little, shamrock of Ireland!

This dear little plant still grows in our land,
  Fresh and fair as the daughters of Erin,
Whose smiles can bewitch, whose eyes can command,
  In each climate that they may appear in;
And shine through the bog, through the brake, and the mireland,
Just like their own dear little shamrock of Ireland.
  The sweet little shamrock, the dear little shamrock,
  The sweet little, green little, shamrock of Ireland!

This dear little plant that springs from our soil,
  When its three little leaves are extended,
Denotes on one stalk we together should toil,
  And ourselves by ourselves be befriended;

And still through the bog, through the brake, and the
mireland,
From one root should branch, like the shamrock of Ireland,
The sweet little shamrock, the dear little shamrock,
The sweet little, green little, shamrock of Ireland!

*Andrew Cherry* [1762–1812]

## MY LAND

SHE is a rich and rare land;
Oh! she's a fresh and fair land,
She is a dear and rare land—
This native land of mine.

No men than hers are braver—
Her women's hearts ne'er waver;
I'd freely die to save her,
And think my lot divine.

She's not a dull or cold land;
No! she's a warm and bold land;
Oh! she's a true and old land—
This native land of mine.

Could beauty ever guard her,
And virtue still reward her,
No foe would cross her border—
No friend within it pine.

Oh! she's a fresh and fair land,
Oh! she's a true and rare land!
Yes, she's a rare and fair land—
This native land of mine.

*Thomas Osborne Davis* [1814–1845]

## FAINNE GAEL AN LAE

**"Until the day break and the shadows flee away"**

ERE the long roll of the ages end
And the days of time are done,
The Lord shall unto Erin send
His own appointed One,

Whose soul must wait the hour of Fate,
His name be known to none;
But his feet shall stand on the Irish land
In the rising of the sun.

In darkness of our captive night,
Whilst storms the watch-tower shake,
Some shall not sleep, but vigil keep
Until the morning break;
Until through clouds of threatening hate,
The seas of sorrow o'er,
The first red beam of the sun-burst gleam
Illumines Erin's shore.

Oh! perfect, pure, exalted One,
For whom in prayer we wait,
Of Irish-born thou happiest son
And noblest of the great;
As night to noon goes swift and soon,
May years now roll away
And bring the hour of thy conquering power
And the dawning of the day!

*Alice Milligan* [18 -

## IRELAND

IRELAND, O Ireland, center of my longings,
Country of my fathers, home of my heart!
Overseas you call me: *Why an exile from me?*
*Wherefore sea-severed, long leagues apart?*

As the shining salmon, homeless in the sea-depths,
Hears the river call him, scents out the land,
Leaps and rejoices in the meeting of the waters,
Breasts weir and torrent, nests in the sand;

Lives there and loves; yet with the year's returning,
Rusting in the river, pines for the sea,
Sweeps back again to the ripple of the tideway,
Roamer of the waters, vagabond and free;—

Wanderer am I like the salmon of the rivers;
  London is my ocean, murmurous and deep,
Tossing and vast; yet through the roar of London
  Comes to me thy summons, calls me in sleep.

Pearly are the skies in the country of my fathers,
  Purple are thy mountains, home of my heart.
Mother of my yearning, love of all my longings,
  Keep me in remembrance, long leagues apart.

*Stephen Lucius Gwynne* [1865–1950]

## "HILLS O' MY HEART"

Hills o' my heart!
I have come to you at calling of my one love and only,
  I have left behind the cruel scarlet wind of the east,
The hearth of my fathers wanting me is lonely,
  And empty is the place I filled at gathering of the feast.

Hills o' my heart!
You have cradled him I love in your green quiet hollows,
  Your wavering winds have hushed him to soft forgetful sleep,
Below dusk boughs where bird-voice after bird-voice follows
  In shafts of silver melody that split the hearkening deep.

Hills o' my heart!
Let the herdsman who walks in your high haunted places
  Give him strength and courage, and weave his dreams alway:
Let your cairn-heaped hero-dead reveal their grand exultant faces,
  And the Gentle Folk be good to him betwixt the dark and day.

Hills o' my heart!
And I would the Green Harper might wake his soul to singing
  With music of the golden wires heard when the world was new,
That from his lips an echo of its sweetness may come ringing,
  A song of pure and noble hopes—a song of all things true.

Hills o' my heart!
For sake of the yellow head that drew me wandering over
Your misty crests from my own home where sorrow bided then,
I set my seven blessings on your kindly heather cover,
On every starry moorland loch, and every shadowy glen,
Hills o' my heart!

*Ethna Carbery* [1866–1902]

## SCOTLAND YET

GAE bring my guid auld harp ance mair,
Gae bring it free and fast,
For I maun sing anither sang,
Ere a' my glee be past;
And trow ye as I sing, my lads,
The burden o't shall be,
Auld Scotland's howes and Scotland's knowes,
And Scotland's hills for me;
We'll drink a cup to Scotland yet,
Wi' a' the honors three.

The heath waves wild upon her hills,
And, foaming frae the fells,
Her fountains sing o' freedom still,
As they dance doun the dells;
And weel I lo'e the land, my lads,
That's girded by the sea;
Then Scotland's vales and Scotland's dales,
And Scotland's hills for me;
We'll drink a cup to Scotland yet,
Wi' a' the honors three.

The thistle wags upon the fields,
Where Wallace bore his blade,
That gave her foemen's dearest bluid
To dye her auld gray plaid;
And looking to the lift, my lads,
He sang this doughty glee,

Auld Scotland's right and Scotland's might,
And Scotland's hills for me;
We'll drink a cup for Scotland yet,
Wi' a' the honors three.

They tell o' lands wi' brighter skies,
Where freedom's voice ne'er rang;
Gie me the hills where Ossian lies,
And Coila's minstrel sang;
For I've nae skill o' lands, my lads,
That kenna to be free;
Then Scotland's right and Scotland's might,
And Scotland's hills for me;
We'll drink a cup to Scotland yet,
Wi' a' the honors three.

*Henry Scott Riddell* [1798-1870]

## THE WATCH ON THE RHINE *

A VOICE resounds like thunder-peal,
'Mid clashing waves and clang of steel:—
"The Rhine, the Rhine, the German Rhine!
Who guards to-day my stream divine?"

*Chorus*—Dear Fatherland, no danger thine:
Firm stand thy sons to watch the Rhine!

They stand a hundred thousand strong,
Quick to avenge their country's wrong;
With filial love their bosoms swell,
They'll guard the sacred landmark well!

The dead of a heroic race
From heaven look down and meet their gaze;
They swear with dauntless heart, "O Rhine,
Be German as this breast of mine!

"While flows one drop of German blood,
Or sword remains to guard thy flood,
While rifle rests in patriot hand,—
No foe shall tread thy sacred strand!

* For the original of this poem see page 3833.

"Our oath resounds, the river flows,
In golden light our banner glows;
Our hearts will guard thy stream divine:
The Rhine, the Rhine, the German Rhine!"
*After the German of Max Schneckenburger* [1819–1849]

## THE GERMAN FATHERLAND *

WHICH is the German's fatherland?
Is't Prussia's or Swabia's land?
Is't where the Rhine's rich vintage streams?
Or where the Northern sea-gull screams?—
Ah, no, no, no!
His fatherland's not bounded so!

Which is the German's fatherland?
Bavaria's or Styria's land?
Is't where the Marsian ox unbends?
Or where the Marksman iron rends?—
Ah, no, no, no!
His fatherland's not bounded so!

Which is the German's fatherland?
Pomerania's or Westphalia's land?
Is it where sweep the Dunian waves?
Or where the thundering Danube raves?—
Ah, no, no, no!
His fatherland's not bounded so!

Which is the German's fatherland?
O, tell me now the famous land!
Is't Tyrol, or the land of Tell?
Such lands and people please me well.—
Ah, no, no, no!
His fatherland's not bounded so!

Which is the German's fatherland?
Come, tell me now the famous land.
Doubtless, it is the Austrian state,
In honors and in triumphs great.—

* For the original of this poem see page 3834

Ah, no, no!
His fatherland's not bounded so!

Which is the German's fatherland?
So tell me now at last the land!—
As far's the German accent rings
And hymns to God in heaven sings,—
That is the land,—
There, brother, is thy fatherland!

There is the German's fatherland,
Where oaths attest the graspèd hand,—
Where truth beams from the sparkling eyes,
And in the heart love warmly lies;—
That is the land,—
There, brother, is thy fatherland!

That is the German's fatherland,
Where wrath pursues the foreign band,—
Where every Frank is held a foe,
And Germans all as brothers glow;—
That is the land,—
All Germany's thy fatherland!

All Germany, then, the land shall be;
Watch o'er it, God, and grant that we
With German hearts, in deed and thought,
May love it truly as we ought.
Be this the land,
All Germany shall be the land!

*From the German of Ernst Moritz Arndt* [1769–1860]

## THE MARSEILLAISE *

Ye sons of freedom, wake to glory!
Hark! hark! what myriads bid you rise!
Your children, wives, and grandsires hoary,
Behold their tears and hear their cries!
Shall hateful tyrants, mischief breeding,

* For the original of this poem see page 3836

With hireling hosts, a ruffian band,
Affright and desolate the land,
While peace and liberty lie bleeding?
To arms! to arms, ye brave!
The avenging sword unsheathe;
March on! march on! all hearts resolved
On victory or death.

Now, now the dangerous storm is rolling,
Which treacherous kings, confederate, raise;
The dogs of war, let loose, are howling,
And lo! our fields and cities blaze;
And shall we basely view the ruin,
While lawless force, with guilty stride,
Spreads desolation far and wide,
With crimes and blood his hands imbruing?

With luxury and pride surrounded,
The vile, insatiate despots dare,
Their thirst of power and gold unbounded,
To meet and vend the light and air;
Like beasts of burden would they load us,
Like gods would bid their slaves adore:
But man is man, and who is more?
Then, shall they longer lash and goad us?

O Liberty! can man resign thee,
Once having felt thy generous flame?
Can dungeons, bolts, or bars confine thee?
Or whips thy noble spirit tame?
Too long the world has wept, bewailing
That falsehood's dagger tyrants wield,
But freedom is our sword and shield,
And all their arts are unavailing.
To arms! to arms, ye brave!
The avenging sword unsheathe;
March on! march on! all hearts resolved
On victory or death.

*Adapted from the French of Rouget de Lisle* [1760–1836]

# SOLDIER SONGS

## "CHARLIE IS MY DARLING"

'TWAS on a Monday morning
  Richt early in the year,
That Charlie cam' to our toun,
  The young Chevalier.

*And Charlie he's my darling,*
  *My darling, my darling;*
*Charlie he's my darling,*
  *The young Chevalier!*

As he was walking up the street,
  The city for to view,
Oh, there he spied a bonny lass
  The window looking through.

Say licht's he jumped up the stair,
  And tirled at the pin;
And wha sae ready as hersel'
  To let the laddie in?

He set his Jenny on his knee,
  All in his Highland dress;
For brawly weel he kenned the way
  To please a bonny lass.

It's up yon heathery mountain,
  And down yon scroggy glen,
We daurna gang a-milking,
  For Charlie and his men.

*And Charlie he's my darling,*
  *My darling, my darling;*
*Charlie he's my darling,*
  *The young Chevalier!*

*Unknown.*

## THE FAREWELL

It was a' for our rightfu' King
  We left fair Scotland's strand;
It was a' for our rightfu' King
  We e'er saw Irish land,
      My dear—
  We e'er saw Irish land.

Now a' is done that men can do,
  And a' is done in vain;
My love and native land, farewell,
  For I maun cross the main,
      My dear—
  For I maun cross the main.

He turned him right and round about
  Upon the Irish shore,
And gae his bridle-reins a shake,
  With, Adieu for evermore,
      My dear—
  With, Adieu for evermore!

The sodger frae the wars returns,
  The sailor frae the main;
But I hae parted frae my love,
  Never to meet again,
      My dear—
  Never to meet again.

When day is gane, and night is come,
  And a' folk bound to sleep,
I think on him that's far awa',
  The lee-lang night, and weep,
      My dear—
  The lee-lang night, and weep.

*Robert Burns* [1759-1796]

## "HERE'S A HEALTH TO THEM THAT'S AWA'"

Here's a health to them that's awa',
Here's a health to them that's awa';
And wha winna wish guid-luck to our cause,
May never guid-luck be their ſa'!
It's guid to be merry and wise,
It's guid to be honest and true,
It's guid to support Caledonia's cause,
And bide by the buff and the blue.

Here's a health to them that's awa',
Here's a health to them that's awa';
Here's a health to Charlie, the chief o' the clan,
Although that his band be sma'.
May Liberty meet wi' success!
May Prudence protect her frae evil!
May tyrants and Tyranny tine in the mist,
And wander their way to the devil!

Here's a health to them that's awa',
Here's a health to them that's awa';
Here's a health to Tammie, the Norland laddie,
That lives at the lug o' the law!
Here's freedom to him that wad read!
Here's freedom to him that wad write!
There's nane ever feared that the truth should be heard,
But they wham the truth wad indite.

Here's a health to them that's awa',
Here's a health to them that's awa';
Here's Maitland and Wycombe, and who does na like 'em
We'll build in a hole o' the wa'.
Here's timmer that's red at the heart,
Here's fruit that's sound at the core!
May he that would turn the buff and blue coat
Be turned to the back o' the door.

Here's a health to them that's awa',
Here's a health to them that's awa';
Here's Chieftain McLeod, a chieftain worth gowd,
Though bred amang mountains o' snaw!
Here's friends on baith sides o' the Forth,
And friends on baith sides o' the Tweed;
And wha wad betray Old Albion's rights,
May they never eat of her bread!

*Robert Burns* [1759-1796]

## THE BLUE BELLS OF SCOTLAND

Oh where! and oh where! is your Highland laddie gone?
He's gone to fight the French for King George upon the
throne;
And it's oh! in my heart how I wish him safe at home.

Oh where! and oh where! does your Highland laddie dwell!
He dwells in merry Scotland at the sign of the Blue Bell;
And it's oh! in my heart that I love my laddie well.

What clothes, in what clothes is your Highland laddie clad?
His bonnet's of the Saxon green, his waistcoat's of the plaid;
And it's oh! in my heart that I love my Highland lad.

Suppose, oh suppose, that your Highland lad should die?
The bagpipes shall play over him, I'll lay me down and cry;
And it's oh! in my heart that I wish he may not die!

*Unknown*

## THE BONNY EARL OF MURRAY

Ye Highlands and ye Lawlands,
O where hae ye been?
They hae slain the Earl of Murray,
And hae laid him on the green.

Now wae be to thee, Huntly!
And wherefore did ye sae?
I bade you bring him wi' you,
But forbade you him to slay.

He was a braw gallant,
  And he rid at the ring;
And the bonny Earl of Murray,
  O he might hae been a king!

He was a braw gallant,
  And he played at the ba';
And the bonny Earl of Murray
  Was the flower amang them a'!

He was a braw gallant,
  And he played at the gluve;
And the bonny Earl of Murray,
  O he was the Queen's luve!

O lang will his Lady
  Look owre the Castle Doune,
Ere she see the Earl of Murray
  Come sounding through the toun!

*Unknown*

## PIBROCH OF DONALD DHU

Pibroch of Donuil Dhu,
  Pibroch of Donuil,
Wake thy wild voice anew,
  Summon Clan-Conuil!
Come away, come away,
  Hark to the summons!
Come in your war array,
  Gentles and commons.

Come from deep glen, and
  From mountain so rocky;
The war-pipe and pennon
  Are at Inverlochy.
Come every hill-plaid, and
  True heart that wears one;
Come every steel blade, and
  Strong hand that bears one.

Leave untended the herd,
  The flock without shelter;
Leave the corpse uninterred,
  The bride at the altar;
Leave the deer, leave the steer,
  Leave nets and barges:
Come with your fighting gear,
  Broadswords and targes.

Come as the winds come, when
  Forests are rended:
Come as the waves come, when
  Navies are stranded!
Faster come, faster come,
  Faster and faster—
Chief, vassal, page, and groom,
  Tenant and master!

Fast they come, fast they come—
  See how they gather!
Wide waves the eagle plume,
  Blended with heather.
Cast your plaids, draw your blades,
  Forward each man set!
Pibroch of Donuil Dhu,
  Kneel for the onset!

*Walter Scott* [1771–1832]

## BORDER BALLAD

From "The Monastery"

March, march, Ettrick and Teviotdale;
  Why the de'il dinna ye march forward in order?
March, march, Eskdale and Liddesdale!
  All the Blue Bonnets are bound for the Border!
    Many a banner spread
    Flutters above your head,
Many a crest that is famous in story.
    Mount and make ready, then,
    Sons of the mountain glen,
Fight for the Queen and our old Scottish glory.

Come from the hills where the hirsels are grazing;
  Come from the glen of the buck and the roe;
Come to the crag where the beacon is blazing;
  Come with the buckler, the lance, and the bow.
    Trumpets are sounding;
    War-steeds are bounding;
Stand to your arms, then, and march in good order.
    England shall many a day
    Tell of the bloody fray
When the Blue Bonnets came over the Border.

*Walter Scott* [1771–1832]

## "WHEN BANNERS ARE WAVING"

When banners are waving, and lances are pushing;
When captains are shouting, and war-horses rushing;
When cannon are roaring, and hot bullets flying,
He that would honor win, must not fear dying.

Though shafts fly so quick that it seems to be snowing;
Though streamlets with blood more than water are flowing;
Though with sabre and bullet our bravest are dying,
We speak of revenge, but we ne'er speak of flying.

Come, stand to it, heroes! The heathen are coming;
Horsemen are round the walls, riding and running;
Maidens and matrons all Arm! arm! are crying,
From petards the wildfire's flashing and flying.

The trumpets from turrets high loudly are braying;
The steeds for the onset are snorting and neighing;
As waves in the ocean, the dark plumes are dancing;
As stars in the blue sky, the helmets are glancing.

Their ladders are planting, their sabres are sweeping;
Now swords from our sheaths by the thousand are leaping;
Like the flash of the levin, ere men hearken thunder,
Swords gleam, and the steel caps are cloven asunder.

The shouting has ceased, and the flashing of cannon!
I looked from the turret for crescent and pennon:
As flax touched by fire, as hail in the river,
They were smote, they were fallen, and had melted for ever.

*Unknown*

## THE BRITISH GRENADIERS

SOME talk of Alexander, and some of Hercules;
Of Hector and Lysander, and such great names as these;
But of all the world's brave heroes, there's none that can compare,
With a tow, row, row, row, row, row, to the British Grenadier.

Those heroes of antiquity ne'er saw a cannon ball,
Or knew the force of powder to slay their foes withal;
But our brave boys do know it, and banish all their fears,
Sing tow, row, row, row, row, row, for the British Grenadiers.

Whene'er we are commanded to storm the palisades,
Our leaders march with fusees, and we with hand grenades;
We throw them from the glacis, about the enemies' ears;
Sing tow, row, row, row, row, row, for the British Grenadiers.

And when the seige is over, we to the town repair,
The townsmen cry "Hurra, boys, here comes a grenadier,
Here comes the grenadiers, my boys, who know no doubts or fears,
Then sing tow, row, row, row, row, row, for the British Grenadiers."

Then let us fill a bumper, and drink a health to those
Who carry cups and pouches, and wear the loupèd clothes;
May they and their commanders live happy all their years,
With a tow, row, row, row, row, row, for the British Grenadiers.

*Unknown*

## HEART OF OAK

COME, cheer up, my lads! 'tis to glory we steer,
To add something more to this wonderful year:
To honor we call you, not press you like slaves;
For who are so free as the sons of the waves?

Heart of oak are our ships,
Heart of oak are our men,
We always are ready:
Steady, boys, steady!
We'll fight and we'll conquer again and again.

We ne'er see our foes but we wish them to stay,
They never see us but they wish us away;
If they run, why, we follow, or run them ashore;
For if they won't fight us we cannot do more.

They swear they'll invade us, these terrible foes!
They frighten our women, our children and beaux;
But should their flat bottoms in darkness get o'er,
Still Britons they'll find to receive them on shore.

Britannia triumphant, her ships sweep the sea;
Her standard is Justice—her watchword, "Be free."
Then cheer up, my lads! with one heart let us sing,
"Our soldiers, our sailors, our statesmen, our King,"

*David Garrick* [1717–1779]

## THE SOLDIER'S DREAM

Our bugles sang truce, for the night-cloud had lowered,
And the sentinel stars set their watch in the sky;
And thousands had sunk on the ground overpowered,
The weary to sleep, and the wounded to die.

When reposing that night on my pallet of straw
By the wolf-scaring faggot that guarded the slain,
At the dead of the night a sweet Vision I saw;
And thrice ere the morning I dreamt it again.

Methought from the battle-field's dreadful array,
Far, far I had roamed on a desolate track:
'Twas Autumn,—and sunshine arose on the way
To the home of my fathers, that welcomed me back

I flew to the pleasant fields traversed so oft
  In life's morning march, when my bosom was young;
I heard my own mountain-goats bleating aloft,
  And knew the sweet strain that the corn-reapers sung.

Then pledged we the wine-cup, and fondly I swore
  From my home and my weeping friends never to part;
My little ones kissed me a thousand times o'er,
  And my wife sobbed aloud in her fulness of heart.

"Stay, stay with us!—rest!—thou art weary and worn!"
  And fain was their war-broken soldier to stay;—
But sorrow returned with the dawning of morn,
  And the voice in my dreaming ear melted away.

*Thomas Campbell* [1777–1844]

## THE CAVALIER'S SONG

A STEED, a steed of matchless speed!
  A sword of metal keen!
All else to noble hearts is dross,
  All else on earth is mean.
The neighing of the war-horse proud,
  The rolling of the drum,
The clangor of the trumpet loud,
  Be sounds from heaven that come;
And oh! the thundering press of knights,
  Whenas their war-cries swell,
May tole from heaven an angel bright,
  And rouse a fiend from hell.

Then mount! then mount, brave gallants all,
  And don your helms amain;
Death's couriers, Fame and Honor, call
  Us to the field again.
No shrewish fears shall fill our eye
  When the sword-hilt's in our hand—
Heart-whole we'll part, and no whit sigh
  For the fairest of the land!

Let piping swain, and craven wight,
  Thus weep and puling cry;
Our business is like men to fight,
  And hero-like to die!

*William Motherwell* [1797–1835]

## CAVALIER TUNES

### I—MARCHING ALONG

KENTISH Sir Byng stood for his King,
Bidding the crop-headed Parliament swing:
And, pressing a troop unable to stoop,
And see the rogues flourish and honest folk droop,
Marched them along, fifty-score strong,
Great-hearted gentlemen, singing this song.

God for King Charles! Pym and such carles
To the Devil that prompts 'em their treasonous parles!
Cavaliers, up! Lips from the cup,
Hands from the pasty, nor bite take nor sup
Till you're—

*Chorus.*—Marching along, fifty-score strong,
  Great-hearted gentlemen, singing this song.

Hampton to hell, and his obsequies' knell.
Serve Hazelrig, Fiennes, and young Harry as well!
England, good cheer! Rupert is near!
Kentish and loyalists, keep we not here,

*Chorus.*—Marching along, fifty-score strong,
  Great-hearted gentlemen, singing this song?

Then, God for King Charles! Pym and his snarls
To the Devil that pricks on such pestilent carles!
Hold by the right, you double your might;
So, onward to Nottingham, fresh from the fight,

*Chorus.*—March we along, fifty-score strong,
  Great-hearted gentlemen, singing this song!

### II—GIVE A ROUSE

King Charles, and who'll do him right now?
King Charles, and who's ripe for fight now?
Give a rouse: here's, in hell's despite now,
King Charles!

Who gave me the goods that went since?
Who raised me the house that sank once?
Who helped me to gold I spent since?
Who found me in wine you drank once?

*Cho.*—King Charles, and who'll do him right now?
King Charles, and who's ripe for fight now?
Give a rouse: here's, in hell's despite now,
King Charles!

To whom used my boy George quaff else,
By the old fool's side that begot him?
For whom did he cheer and laugh else,
While Noll's damned troopers shot him?

*Cho.*—King Charles, and who'll do him right now?
King Charles, and who's ripe for fight now?
Give a rouse: here's, in hell's despite now,
King Charles!

### III—BOOT AND SADDLE

Boot, saddle, to horse, and away!
Rescue my castle before the hot day
Brightens to blue from its silvery gray.

*Cho.*—Boot, saddle, to horse, and away!

Ride past the suburbs, asleep as you'd say;
Many's the friend there, will listen and pray
"God's luck to gallants that strike up the lay—

*Cho.*—Boot, saddle, to horse, and away!"

Forty miles off, like a roebuck at bay,
Flouts Castle Brancepeth the Roundheads' array:
Who laughs, "Good fellows ere this, by my fay,

*Cho.*—Boot, saddle, to horse, and away!"

Who? My wife Gertrude, that, honest and gay,
Laughs when you talk of surrendering, "Nay!
I've better counsellors; what counsel they?

*Cho.*—Boot, saddle, to horse, and away!"

*Robert Browning* [1812–1889]

## THE SONG OF THE CAMP

"Give us a song!" the soldiers cried,
The outer trenches guarding,
When the heated guns of the camps allied
Grew weary of bombarding.

The dark Redan, in silent scoff,
Lay, grim and threatening, under;
And the tawny mound of the Malakoff
No longer belched its thunder.

There was a pause. A guardsman said,
"We storm the forts to-morrow;
Sing while we may, another day
Will bring enough of sorrow."

They lay along the battery's side,
Below the smoking cannon:
Brave hearts, from Severn and from Clyde,
And from the banks of Shannon.

They sang of love, and not of fame;
Forgot was Britain's glory:
Each heart recalled a different name,
But all sang "Annie Laurie."

Voice after voice caught up the song,
Until its tender passion
Rose like an anthem, rich and strong,—
Their battle-eve confession.

Dear girl, her name he dared not speak,
But, as the song grew louder,
Something upon the soldier's cheek
Washed off the stains of powder.

Beyond the darkening ocean burned
The bloody sunset's embers,
While the Crimean valleys learned
How English love remembers.

And once again a fire of hell
Rained on the Russian quarters,
With scream of shot, and burst of shell,
And bellowing of the mortars!

And Irish Nora's eyes are dim
For a singer, dumb and gory;
And English Mary mourns for him
Who sang of "Annie Laurie."

Sleep, soldiers! still in honored rest
Your truth and valor wearing:
The bravest are the tenderest,—
The loving are the daring.

*Bayard Taylor* [1825–1878]

## REVEILLE

The morning is cheery, my boys, arouse!
The dew shines bright on the chestnut boughs,
And the sleepy mist on the river lies,
Though the east is flushing with crimson dyes.
Awake! awake! awake!
O'er field and wood and brake,
With glories newly born,
Comes on the blushing morn.
Awake! awake!

You have dreamed of your homes and friends all night;
You have basked in your sweethearts' smiles so bright;
Come, part with them all for a while again,—
Be lovers in dreams; when awake, be men.
Turn out! turn out! turn out!
You have dreamed full long, I know.
Turn out! turn out! turn out!
The east is all aglow.
Turn out! turn out!

From every valley and hill there come
The clamoring voices of fife and drum;
And out in the fresh, cool morning air
The soldiers are swarming everywhere.
Fall in! fall in! fall in!
Every man in his place,
Fall in! fall in! fall in!
Each with a cheerful face,
Fall in! fall in!

*Michael O'Connor* [1837–1862]

## "I GIVE MY SOLDIER BOY A BLADE"

I GIVE my soldier boy a blade,
In fair Damascus fashioned well:
Who first the glittering falchion swayed,
Who first beneath its fury fell,
I know not; but I hope to know,
That, for no mean or hireling trade,
To guard no feeling base or low—
I give my soldier boy the blade!

Cool, calm, and clear—the lucid flood
In which its tempering work was done;—
As calm, as clear, in wind and wood,
Be thou where'er it sees the sun!
For country's claim at honor's call,
For outraged friend, insulted maid,
At mercy's voice to bid it fall—
I give my soldier boy the blade!

The eye which marked its peerless edge,
The hand that weighed its balanced poise,
Anvil and pincers, forge and wedge,
Are gone with all their flame and noise;
Yet still the gleaming sword remains!
So, when in dust I low am laid,
Remember by these heartfelt strains,
I give my soldier boy the blade!

*William Maginn* [1793–1842]

## STONEWALL JACKSON'S WAY

Come, stack arms, men! Pile on the rails,
Stir up the camp-fire bright;
No growling if the canteen fails,
We'll make a roaring night.
Here Shenandoah brawls along,
There burly Blue Ridge echoes strong,
To swell the Brigade's rousing song
Of "Stonewall Jackson's way."

We see him now—the queer slouched hat
Cocked o'er his eye askew;
The shrewd, dry smile; the speech so pat,
So calm, so blunt, so true.
The "Blue-Light Elder" knows 'em well;
Says he, "That's Banks—he's fond of shell;
Lord save his soul! we'll give him—" well!
That's "Stonewall Jackson's way."

Silence! ground arms! kneel all! caps off!
Old Massa's goin' to pray.
Strangle the fool that dares to scoff!
Attention! it's his way.
Appealing from his native sod,
*In forma pauperis* to God:
"Lay bare Thine arm: stretch forth Thy rod!
Amen!" That's "Stonewall's way."

He's in the saddle now. Fall in!
Steady! the whole brigade!
Hill's at the ford, cut off; we'll win
His way out, ball and blade!
What matter if our shoes are worn?
What matter if our feet are torn?
"Quick step! we're with him before morn!"
That's "Stonewall Jackson's way."

The sun's bright lances rout the mists
Of morning, and, by George!
Here's Longstreet, struggling in the lists,
Hemmed in an ugly gorge.
Pope and his Dutchmen, whipped before;
"Bay'nets and grape!" hear Stonewall roar;
"Charge, Stuart! Pay off Ashby's score!"
In "Stonewall Jackson's way."

Ah! Maiden, wait and watch and yearn
For news of Stonewall's band!
Ah! Widow, read, with eyes that burn,
That ring upon thy hand.
Ah! Wife, sew on, pray on, hope on;
Thy life shall not be all forlorn;
The foe had better ne'er been born
That gets in "Stonewall's way."

*John Williamson Palmer* [1825-1906]

## MUSIC IN CAMP

Two armies covered hill and plain,
Where Rappahannock's waters
Ran deeply crimsoned with the stain
Of battle's recent slaughters.

The summer clouds lay pitched like tents
In meads of heavenly azure;
And each dread gun of the elements
Slept in its high embrasure.

The breeze so softly blew, it made
No forest leaf to quiver;
And the smoke of the random cannonade
Rolled slowly from the river.

And now, where circling hills looked down
With cannon grimly planted,
O'er listless camp and silent town
The golden sunset slanted.

When on the fervid air there came
  A strain,—now rich, now tender;
The music seemed itself aflame
  With day's departing splendor.

A Federal band, which, eve and morn,
  Played measures brave and nimble,
Had just struck up with flute and horn
  And lively clash of cymbal.

Down flocked the soldiers to the banks;
  Till, margined by its pebbles,
One wooded shore was blue with "Yanks,"
  And one was gray with "Rebels."

Then all was still; and then the band,
  With movement light and tricksy,
Made stream and forest, hill and strand,
  Reverberate with "Dixie."

The conscious stream, with burnished glow,
  Went proudly o'er its pebbles,
But thrilled throughout its deepest flow
  With yelling of the Rebels.

Again a pause; and then again
  The trumpets pealed sonorous,
And "Yankee Doodle" was the strain
  To which the shore gave chorus.

The laughing ripple shoreward flew
  To kiss the shining pebbles;
Loud shrieked the swarming Boys in Blue
  Defiance to the Rebels.

And yet once more the bugles sang
  Above the stormy riot;
No shout upon the evening rang—
  There reigned a holy quiet.

The sad, slow stream, its noiseless flood
  Poured o'er the glistening pebbles;
All silent now the Yankees stood,
  All silent stood the Rebels.

No unresponsive soul had heard
  That plaintive note's appealing,
So deeply "Home, Sweet Home" had stirred
  The hidden founts of feeling.

Or Blue or Gray, the soldier sees,
  As by the wand of fairy,
The cottage 'neath the live-oak trees,
  The cabin by the prairie.

Or cold or warm, his native skies
  Bend in their beauty o'er him;
Seen through the tear-mist in his eyes,
  His loved ones stand before him.

As fades the iris after rain
  In April's tearful weather,
The vision vanished, as the strain
  And daylight died together.

But Memory, waked by Music's art,
  Expressed in simplest numbers,
Subdued the sternest Yankee's heart—
  Made light the Rebel's slumbers.

And fair the form of Music shines—
  That bright, celestial creature,
Who still, 'mid War's embattled lines,
  Gave this one touch of Nature.

*John Reuben Thompson* [1823-1873]

## THE "GREY HORSE TROOP"

All alone on the hillside—
Larry an' Barry an' me;
Nothin' to see but the sky an' the plain,
Nothin' to see but the drivin' rain,

Nothin' to see but the painted Sioux,
Galloping, galloping: "Whoop—whuroo!
The divil in yellow is down in the mud!"
Sez Larry to Barry, "I'm losin' blood."

"Cheers for the Greys!" yells Barry;
"Second Dragoons!" groans Larry;
Hurrah! hurrah! for Egan's Grey Troop!
Whoop! ye divils—ye've got to whoop;
Cheer for the troopers who die: sez I—
"Cheer for the troop that never shall die!

All alone on the hillside—
Larry an' Barry an' me;
Flat on our bellies, an' pourin' in lead—
Seven rounds left, an' the horses dead—
Barry a-cursin' at every breath;
Larry beside him, as white as death;
Indians galloping, galloping by,
Wheelin' and squealin' like hawks in the sky!

"Cheers for the Greys!" yells Barry;
"Second Dragoons!" groans Larry;
Hurrah! hurrah! for Egan's Grey Troop!
Whoop! ye divils—ye've got to whoop;
Cheer for the troopers who die: sez I—
"Cheer for the troop that never shall die!"

All alone on the hillside—
Larry an' Barry an' me;
Two of us livin' and one of us dead—
Shot in the head, and God!—how he bled!
"Larry's done up," sez Barry to me;
"Divvy his cartridges! Quick! gimme three!"
While nearer an' nearer an' plainer in view,
Galloped an' galloped the murderin' Sioux.

"Cheers for the Greys!" yells Barry;
"Cheer—" an' he falls on Larry.
Alas! alas! for Egan's Grey Troop!
The Red Sioux, hovering stoop to swoop;

Two out of three lay dead, while I
Cheered for the troop that never shall die.

All alone on the hillside—
Larry an' Barry an' me;
An' I fired an' yelled till I lost my head,
Cheerin' the livin, cheerin' the dead,
Swingin' my cap, I cheered until
I stumbled and fell. Then over the hill
There floated a trumpeter's silvery call,
An' Egan's Grey Troop galloped up, that's all.

Drink to the Greys,—an' Barry!
Second Dragoons,—an' Larry!
Here's a bumper to Egan's Grey Troop!
Let the crape on the guidons droop;
Drink to the troopers who die, while I
Drink to the troop that never shall die!

*Robert William Chambers* [1865–1933]

## DANNY DEEVER

"WHAT are the bugles blowin' for?" said Files-on-Parade.
"To turn you out, to turn you out," the Color-Sergeant said.
"What makes you look so white, so white?" said Files-on-Parade.
"I'm dreadin' what I've got to watch," the Color-Sergeant said.
For they're hangin' Danny Deever, you can 'ear the Dead March play,
The regiment's in 'ollow square—they're hangin' him to-day;
They've taken of his buttons off an' cut his stripes away,
An' they're hangin' Danny Deever in the mornin'.

"What makes the rear-rank breathe so 'ard?" said Files-on-Parade.
"It's bitter cold, it's bitter cold," the Color-Sergeant said.
"What makes that front-rank man fall down?" says Files-on-Parade.
"A touch o' sun, a touch o' sun," the Color-Sergeant said.

They're hangin' Danny Deever, they are marchin' of 'im round,
They 'ave 'alted Danny Deever by 'is coffin on the ground;
An' 'e'll swing in 'arf a minute for a sneakin' shootin' hound—
O they're hangin' Danny Deever in the mornin'!

"'Is cot was right-'and cot to mine," said Files-on-Parade.
"'E's sleepin' out an' far to-night," the Color-Sergeant said.
"I've drunk 'is beer a score o' times," said Files-on-Parade.
"'E's drinkin' bitter beer alone," the Color-Sergeant said.
They are hangin' Danny Deever, you must mark 'im to 'is place,
For 'e shot a comrade sleepin'—you must look 'im in the face;
Nine 'undred of 'is county an' the regiment's disgrace,
While they're hangin' Danny Deever in the mornin'.

"What's that so black agin the sun?" said Files-on-Parade.
"It's Danny fightin' 'ard fur life," the Color-Sergeant said.
"What's that that whimpers over'ead?" said Files-on-Parade.
"It's Danny's soul that's passin' now," the Color-Sergeant said.
For they're done with Danny Deever, you can 'ear the quickstep play,
The regiment's in column, an' they're marchin' us away;
Ho! the young recruits are shakin', an' they'll want their beer to-day,
After hangin' Danny Deever in the mornin'.

*Rudyard Kipling* [1865–1936]

## GUNGA DIN

You may talk o' gin an' beer
When you're quartered safe out 'ere,
An' you're sent to penny-fights an' Aldershot it;
But when it comes to slaughter

You will do your work on water,
An' you'll lick the bloomin' boots of 'im that's got it.
Now in Injia's sunny clime,
Where I used to spend my time
A-servin' of 'Er Majesty the Queen,
Of all them black-faced crew
The finest man I knew
Was our regimental *bhisti,* Gunga Din.
He was "Din! Din! Din!
You limpin' lump o' brick-dust, Gunga Din!
Hi! *slippey hitherao!*
Water! get it! *Panee lao!*
You squidgy-nosed old idol, Gunga Din!"

The uniform 'e wore
Was nothin' much before,
An' rather less than 'arf o' that be'ind,
For a piece o' twisty rag
An' a goatskin water-bag
Was all the field-equipment 'e could find.
When the sweatin' troop-train lay
In a sidin' through the day,
Where the 'eat would make your bloomin' eye-brows crawl,
We shouted "*Harry By!*"
Till our throats were bricky-dry,
Then we wopped 'im cause 'e couldn't serve us all.
It was "Din! Din! Din!
You 'eathen, where the mischief 'ave you been?
You put some *juldee* in it
Or I'll *marrow* you this minute,
If you don't fill up my helmet, Gunga Din!"

'E would dot an' carry one
Till the longest day was done;
An' 'e didn't seem to know the use o' fear.
If we charged or broke or cut,
You could bet your bloomin' nut,
'E'd be waitin' fifty paces right flank rear.
With 'is *mussick* on 'is back,
'E would skip with our attack,

An' watch us till the bugles made "Retire,"
An' for all 'is dirty 'ide
'E was white, clear white, inside
When 'e went to tend the wounded under fire!
    It was "Din! Din! Din!"
    With the bullets kickin' dust-spots on the green
    When the cartridges ran out,
    You could 'ear the front-files shout,
    "Hi! ammunition-mules an' Gunga Din!"

I sha'n't forgit the night
When I dropped be'ind the fight
With a bullet where my belt-plate should 'a' been,
I was chokin' mad with thirst,
An' the man that spied me first
Was our good old grinnin', gruntin' Gunga Din.
'E lifted up my 'ead,
An' 'e plugged me where I bled,
An' 'e guv me 'arf-a-pint o' water—green:
It was crawlin' an' it stunk,
But of all the drinks I've drunk,
I'm gratefullest to one from Gunga Din.
    It was "Din! Din! Din!
    'Ere's a beggar with a bullet through 'is spleen
    'E's chawin' up the ground,
    An' 'e's kickin' all around:
    For Gawd's sake git the water, Gunga Din!"

'E carried me away
To where a *dooli* lay,
An' a bullet come an' drilled the beggar clean.
'E put me safe inside,
An' just before 'e died:
"I 'ope you liked your drink," sez Gunga Din.
So I'll meet 'im later on
At the place where 'e is gone—
Where it's always double drill an' no canteen;
'E'll be squattin' on the coals,
Givin' drink to pore damned souls,
An' I'll git a swig in hell from Gunga Din!

Yes, Din! Din! Din!
You Lazarushian-leather Gunga Din!
Though I've belted you an' flayed you,
By the livin' Gawd that made you,
You're a better man than I am, Gunga Din!

*Rudyard Kipling* [1865–1936]

## THE MEN BEHIND THE GUNS

A CHEER and salute for the Admiral, and here's to the Captain bold,
And never forget the Commodore's debt when the deeds of might are told!
They stand to the deck through the battle's wreck when the great shells roar and screech—
And never they fear when the foe is near to practice what they preach:
But off with your hat and three times three for Columbia's true-blue sons,
The men below who batter the foe—the men behind the guns!

Oh, light and merry of heart are they when they swing into port once more,
When, with more than enough of the "green-backed stuff," they start for their leave-o'-shore;
And you'd think, perhaps, that the blue-bloused chaps who loll along the street
Are a tender bit, with salt on it, for some fierce "mustache" to eat—
Some warrior bold, with straps of gold, who dazzles and fairly stuns
The modest worth of the sailor boys—the lads who serve the guns.

But say not a word till the shot is heard that tells that the fight is on,
Till the long, deep roar grows more and more from the ships of "Yank" and "Don,"

Till over the deep the tempests sweep of fire and bursting shell,
And the very air is a mad Despair in the throes of a living hell;
Then down, deep down, in the mighty ship, unseen by the midday suns,
You'll find the chaps who are giving the raps—the men behind the guns!

Oh, well they know how the cyclones blow that they loose from their cloud of death,
And they know is heard the thunder-word their fierce ten-incher saith!
The steel decks rock with the lightning shock, and shake with the great recoil,
And the sea grows red with the blood of the dead and reaches for his spoil—
But not till the foe has gone below or turns his prow and runs,
Shall the voice of peace bring sweet release to the men behind the guns!

*John Jerome Rooney* [1866–1934]

## THE FIGHTING RACE

"Read out the names!" and Burke sat back,
And Kelly drooped his head,
While Shea—they call him Scholar Jack—
Went down the list of the dead.
Officers, seamen, gunners, marines,
The crews of the gig and yawl,
The bearded man and the lad in his teens,
Carpenters, coal-passers—all.
Then, knocking the ashes from out his pipe,
Said Burke in an offhand way:
"We're all in that dead man's list, by Cripe!
Kelly and Burke and Shea."
"Well, here's to the Maine, and I'm sorry for Spain,"
Said Kelly and Burke and Shea.

"Wherever there's Kellys there's trouble," said Burke.
  "Wherever fighting's the game,
Or a spice of danger in grown man's work,"
  Said Kelly, "you'll find my name."
"And do we fall short," said Burke, getting mad,
  "When it's touch-and-go for life?"
Said Shea, "It's thirty-odd years, bedad,
  Since I charged to drum and fife
Up Marye's Heights, and my old canteen
  Stopped a rebel ball on its way;
There were blossoms of blood on our sprigs of green—
  Kelly and Burke and Shea—
And the dead didn't brag." "Well, here's to the flag!"
  Said Kelly and Burke and Shea.

"I wish 'twas in Ireland, for there's the place,"
  Said Burke, "that we'd die by right,
In the cradle of our soldier race,
  After one good stand-up fight.
My grandfather fell on Vinegar Hill,
  And fighting was not his trade;
But his rusty pike's in the cabin still,
  With Hessian blood on the blade."
"Aye, aye," said Kelly, "the pikes were great
  When the word was 'clear the way!'
We were thick on the roll in ninety-eight—
  Kelly and Burke and Shea."
"Well, here's to the pike and the sword and the like!"
  Said Kelly and Burke and Shea.

And Shea, the scholar, with rising joy,
  Said, "We were at Ramillies;
We left our bones at Fontenoy
  And up in the Pyrenees;
Before Dunkirk, on Landen's plain,
  Cremona, Lille, and Ghent;
We're all over Austria, France, and Spain,
  Wherever they pitched a tent.
We've died for England from Waterloo
  To Egypt and Dargai;

And still there's enough for a corps or crew,
  Kelly and Burke and Shea."
"Well, here's to good honest fighting-blood!"
  Said Kelly and Burke and Shea.

"Oh, the fighting races don't die out,
  If they seldom die in bed,
For love is first in their hearts, no doubt,"
  Said Burke; then Kelly said:
"When Michael, the Irish Archangel, stands,
  The Angel with the sword,
And the battle-dead from a hundred lands
  Are ranged in one big horde,
Our line, that for Gabriel's trumpet waits,
  Will stretch three deep that day,
From Jehoshaphat to the Golden Gates—
  Kelly and Burke and Shea."
"Well, here's thank God for the race and the sod!"
  Said Kelly and Burke and Shea.

*Joseph I. C. Clarke* [1846-1925]

# "HOW SLEEP THE BRAVE"

## "SOLDIER, REST! THY WARFARE O'ER"

From "The Lady of the Lake"

Soldier, rest! thy warfare o'er,
  Sleep the sleep that knows not breaking;
Dream of battled fields no more,
  Days of danger, nights of waking.
In our isle's enchanted hall,
  Hands unseen thy couch are strewing,
Fairy strains of music fall,
  Every sense in slumber dewing.
Soldier, rest! thy warfare o'er,
Dream of fighting fields no more:
Sleep the sleep that knows not breaking,
Morn of toil, nor night of waking.

No rude sound shall reach thine ear,
  Armor's clang, or war-steed champing,
Trump nor pibroch summon here
  Mustering clan, or squadron tramping.
Yet the lark's shrill fife may come
  At the daybreak from the fallow,
And the bittern sound his drum,
  Booming from the sedgy shallow.
Ruder sounds shall none be near,
Guards nor warders challenge here,
Here's no war-steed's neigh and champing,
Shouting clans, or squadrons stamping.

Huntsman, rest! the chase is done;
  While our slumbrous spells assail ye,
Dream not, with the rising sun,
  Bugles here shall sound reveille.

Sleep! the deer is in his den;
  Sleep! thy hounds are by thee lying;
Sleep! nor dream in yonder glen,
  How thy gallant steed lay dying.
Huntsman, rest! thy chase is done,
Think not of the rising sun,
For at dawning to assail ye
Here no bugles sound reveille.

*Walter Scott* [1771–1832]

## "PEACE TO THE SLUMBERERS"

Peace to the slumberers!
  They lie on the battle-plain,
With no shroud to cover them;
  The dew and the summer rain
And all that sweep over them.
    Peace to the slumberers!

Vain was their bravery!—
  The fallen oak lies where it lay
Across the wintry river;
  But brave hearts, once swept away,
Are gone, alas! forever.
    Vain was their bravery!

Woe to the conqueror!
  Our limbs shall lie as cold as theirs
Of whom his sword bereft us,
  Ere we forget the deep arrears
Of vengeance they have left us!
    Woe to the conqueror!

*Thomas Moore* [1779–1852]

## THE MINSTREL-BOY

The Minstrel-Boy to the war is gone,
  In the ranks of death you'll find him;
His father's sword he has girded on,
  And his wild harp slung behind him.

"Land of song!" said the warrior-bard,
  "Though all the world betrays thee,
*One* sword, at least, thy rights shall guard,
  *One* faithful harp shall praise thee!"

The Minstrel fell!—but the foeman's chain
  Could not bring his proud soul under;
The harp he loved ne'er spoke again,
  For he tore its chords asunder,
And said, "No chains shall sully thee,
  Thou soul of love and bravery!
Thy songs were made for the pure and free,
  They shall never sound in slavery!"

*Thomas Moore* [1779–1852]

## "IT IS GREAT FOR OUR COUNTRY TO DIE"

O, IT is great for our country to die, where ranks are contending!
  Bright is the wreath of our fame; Glory awaits us for aye,—
Glory, that never is dim, shining on with light never ending,—
  Glory that never shall fade, never, O never, away!

O, it is sweet for our country to die! How softly reposes
  Warrior-youth on his bier, wet by the tears of his love,
Wet by a mother's warm tears. They crown him with garlands of roses,
  Weep, and then joyously turn, bright where he triumphs above.

Not to the shades shall the youth descend, who for country hath perished;
  Hebe awaits him in heaven, welcomes him there with her smile;
There, at the banquet divine, the patriot spirit is cherished;
  Gods love the young who ascend pure from the funeral pile.

Not to Elysian fields, by the still, oblivious river;
  Not to the isles of the blest, over the blue, rolling sea;
But on Olympian heights shall dwell the devoted forever;
  There shall assemble the good, there the wise, valiant, and free.

O, then, how great for our country to die, in the front rank to perish,
  Firm with our breast to the foe, Victory's shout in our ear!
Long they our statues shall crown, in songs our memory cherish;
  We shall look forth from our heaven, pleased the sweet music to hear.

*James Gates Percival* [1795-1856]

## A BALLAD OF HEROES

*Now all your victories are in vain*—A. Mary F. Robinson

Because you passed, and now are not,—
  Because, in some remoter day,
Your sacred dust from doubtful spot
  Was blown of ancient airs away,—
  Because you perished,—must men say
Your deeds were naught, and so profane
  Your lives with that cold burden? Nay,
The deeds you wrought are not in vain!

Though, it may be, above the plot
  That hid your once imperial clay,
No greener than o'er men forgot
  The unregarding grasses sway;—
  Though there no sweeter is the lay
From careless bird,—though you remain
  Without distinction of decay,—
The deeds you wrought are not in vain!

No. For while yet in tower or cot
  Your story stirs the pulses' play;
And men forget the sordid lot—
  The sordid care, of cities gray;
  While yet, beset in homelier fray,
They learn from you the lesson plain

That Life may go, so Honor stay,—
The deeds you wrought are not in vain!

ENVOY

Heroes of old! I humbly lay
The laurel on your graves again;
Whatever men have done, men may,—
The deeds you wrought are not in vain!

*Austin Dobson* [1840-1921]

## WAR IS KIND

Do not weep, maiden, for war is kind.
Because your lover threw wild hands toward the sky
And the affrighted steed ran on alone,
Do not weep.
War is kind.

Hoarse, booming drums of the regiment,
Little souls who thirst for fight—
These men were born to drill and die.
The unexplained glory flies above them;
Great is the battle-god, great—and his kingdom
A field where a thousand corpses lie.

Do not weep, babe, for war is kind.
Because your father tumbled in the yellow trenches,
Raged at his breast, gulped and died,
Do not weep.
War is kind.

Swift-blazing flag of the regiment,
Eagle with crest of red and gold,
These men were born to drill and die.
Point for them the virtue of slaughter,
Make plain to them the excellence of killing,
And a field where a thousand corpses lie.

Mother whose heart hung humble as a button
On the bright splendid shroud of your son,
Do not weep.
War is kind.

*Stephen Crane* [1870-1900]

## ENGLAND'S DEAD

Son of the ocean isle!
Where sleep your mighty dead?
Show me what high and stately pile
Is reared o'er Glory's bed.

Go, stranger! track the deep,
Free, free, the white sail spread!
Wave may not foam, nor wild wind sweep,
Where rest not England's dead.

On Egypt's burning plains,
By the pyramid o'erswayed,
With fearful power the noonday reigns,
And the palm-trees yield no shade.

But let the angry sun
From heaven look fiercely red,
Unfelt by those whose task is done,—
*There* slumber England's dead.

The hurricane hath might
Along the Indian shore,
And far, by Ganges' banks at night
Is heard the tiger's roar.

But let the sound roll on!
It hath no tone of dread
For those that from their toils are gone;—
*There* slumber England's dead!

Loud rush the torrent-floods
The western wilds among,
And free, in green Columbia's woods
The hunter's bow is strung.

But let the floods rush on!
Let the arrow's flight be sped!
Why should *they* reck whose task is done?—
*There* slumber England's dead!

The mountain-storms rise high
In the snowy Pyrenees,
And toss the pine-boughs through the sky,
Like rose-leaves on the breeze.

But let the storm rage on!
Let the forest-wreaths be shed:
For the Roncesvalles' field is won,—
*There* slumber England's dead.

On the frozen deep's repose,
'Tis a dark and dreadful hour,
When round the ship the ice-fields close,
To chain her with their power.

But let the ice drift on!
Let the cold-blue desert spread!
*Their* course with mast and flag is done,—
Even *there* sleep England's dead.

The warlike of the isles,
The men of field and wave!
Are not the rocks their funeral piles,
The seas and shores their grave?

Go, stranger! track the deep,
Free, free the white sail spread!
Wave may not foam, nor wild wind sweep,
Where rest not England's dead.

*Felicia Dorothea Hemans* [1793–1835]

## THE PIPES O' GORDON'S MEN

HOME comes a lad with the bonnie hair,
And the kilted plaid that the hill-clans wear;
And you hear the mother say,
"Whear ha' ye ben, wee Laddie; whear ha' ye ben th' day?"
"O! I ha' ben wi' Gordon's men;
Dinna ye hear th' bagpipes play?
And I followed th' soldiers across the green,
And doon th' road ta Aberdeen.

And when I'm a man, my Mother,
And th' Hielanders parade,
I'll be marchin' there, wi' my Father's pipes,
And I'll wear th' red cockade."

Beneath the Soudan's sky ye ken the smoke,
As the clans reply when the tribesmen spoke.
Then the charge roars by!
The death-sweat clings to the kilted form that the stretcher brings,
And the iron-nerved surgeons say,
"Whear ha' ye ben, my Laddie; whear ha' ye ben th' day?"
"O, I ha' ben wi' Gordon's men;
Dinna ye hear th' bagpipes play?
And I piped th' clans from the river barge
Across the sands, and through the charge.
And I—skirled—th' pibroch—keen—an' high,
But th' pipes—ben broke—an' —my—lips—ben—dry."

### CORONACH

Upon the hill-side, high and steep,
Where rank on rank the soldiers sleep,—
Where the silent cannons beside the path,
Point the last forced-march that the soldier hath,—
Where the falling grave-grass has partly hid
The round-shot, heaped in a pyramid—
A white stone rises. Across its face
You can read the words that the chisels trace:
"Whear ha' ye ben, wee Laddie; whear ha' ye ben th' day?"
"O, I ha' ben wi' Gordon's men;
Dinna ye hear th' bagpipes play?"

*J. Scott Glasgow* [18 -

## THE BLUE AND THE GRAY

By the flow of the inland river,
Whence the fleets of iron have fled,
Where the blades of the grave-grass quiver,
Asleep are the ranks of the dead:—

Under the sod and the dew,
Waiting the Judgment Day:—
Under the one, the Blue;
Under the other, the Gray.

These in the robings of glory,
Those in the gloom of defeat,
All with the battle-blood gory,
In the dusk of eternity meet:—
Under the sod and the dew,
Waiting the Judgment Day:—
Under the laurel, the Blue;
Under the willow, the Gray.

From the silence of sorrowful hours
The desolate mourners go,
Lovingly laden with flowers,
Alike for the friend and the foe:—
Under the sod and the dew,
Waiting the Judgment Day:—
Under the roses, the Blue;
Under the lilies, the Gray.

So, with an equal splendor
The morning sun-rays fall,
With a touch impartially tender,
On the blossoms blooming for all:—
Under the sod and the dew,
Waiting the Judgment Day:—
Broidered with gold, the Blue;
Mellowed with gold, the Gray.

So, when the summer calleth,
On forest and field of grain,
With an equal murmur falleth
The cooling drip of the rain:—
Under the sod and the dew,
Waiting the Judgment Day:—
Wet with the rain, the Blue;
Wet with the rain, the Gray.

Sadly, but not with upbraiding,
  The generous deed was done.
In the storms of the years that are fading
  No braver battle was won:—
    Under the sod and the dew,
      Waiting the Judgment Day:—
    Under the blossoms, the Blue;
      Under the garlands, the Gray.

No more shall the war-cry sever,
  Or the winding rivers be red:
They banish our anger forever
  When they laurel the graves of our dead!
    Under the sod and the dew,
      Waiting the Judgment Day:—
    Love and tears for the Blue;
      Tears and love for the Gray.

*Francis Miles Finch* [1827-1907]

## THE BIVOUAC OF THE DEAD

THE muffled drum's sad roll has beat
  The soldier's last tattoo;
No more on Life's parade shall meet
  That brave and fallen few.
On Fame's eternal camping-ground
  Their silent tents are spread,
And Glory guards, with solemn round,
  The bivouac of the dead.

No rumor of the foe's advance
  Now swells upon the wind;
No troubled thought at midnight haunts
  Of loved ones left behind;
No vision of the morrow's strife
  The warrior's dream alarms;
No braying horn nor screaming fife
  At dawn shall call to arms.

Their shivered swords are red with rust;
  Their plumèd heads are bowed;
Their haughty banner, trailed in dust,
  Is now their martial shroud.
And plenteous funeral tears have washed
  The red stains from each brow,
And the proud forms, by battle gashed,
  Are free from anguish now.

The neighing troop, the flashing blade,
  The bugle's stirring blast,
The charge, the dreadful cannonade,
  The din and shout, are past;
Nor war's wild note, nor glory's peal,
  Shall thrill with fierce delight
Those breasts that nevermore may feel
  The rapture of the fight.

Like the fierce northern hurricane
  That sweeps his great plateau,
Flushed with the triumph yet to gain,
  Came down the serried foe.
Who heard the thunder of the fray
  Break o'er the field beneath,
Knew well the watchword of that day
  Was "Victory or Death."

Long had the doubtful conflict raged
  O'er all that stricken plain,
For never fiercer fight had waged
  The vengeful blood of Spain;
And still the storm of battle blew,
  Still swelled the gory tide;
Not long, our stout old chieftain knew,
  Such odds his strength could bide.

'Twas in that hour his stern command
  Called to a martyr's grave
The flower of his belovèd land,
  The nation's flag to save.

By rivers of their fathers' gore
  His first-born laurels grew,
And well he deemed the sons would pour
  Their lives for glory too.

Full many a norther's breath has swept
  O'er Angostura's plain,
And long the pitying sky has wept
  Above its mouldered slain.
The raven's scream, or eagle's flight,
  Or shepherd's pensive lay,
Alone awakes each sullen height
  That frowned o'er that dread fray.

Sons of the Dark and Bloody Ground,
  Ye must not slumber there,
Where stranger steps and tongues resound
  Along the heedless air.
Your own proud land's heroic soil
  Shall be your fitter grave;
She claims from war his richest spoil—
  The ashes of her brave.

Thus 'neath their parent turf they rest,
  Far from the gory field,
Borne to a Spartan mother's breast
  On many a bloody shield;
The sunshine of their native sky
  Smiles sadly on them here,
And kindred eyes and hearts watch by
  The heroes' sepulchre.

Rest on, embalmed and sainted dead!
  Dear as the blood ye gave;
No impious footstep here shall tread
  The herbage of your grave;
Nor shall your story be forgot,
  While Fame her record keeps,
Or Honor points the hallowed spot
  Where Valor proudly sleeps.

Yon marble minstrel's voiceless stone
In deathless song shall tell,
When many a vanished age hath flown,
The story how ye fell;
Nor wreck, nor change, nor winter's blight,
Nor Time's remorseless doom,
Shall dim one ray of glory's light
That gilds your deathless tomb.

*Theodore O'Hara* [1820–1867]

## ROLL-CALL

"CORPORAL GREEN!" the Orderly cried;
"Here!" was the answer loud and clear,
From the lips of a soldier standing near,—
And "Here!" was the word the next replied.

"Cyrus Drew!"—then a silence fell;
This time no answer followed the call;
Only his rear-man had seen him fall:
Killed or wounded—he could not tell.

There they stood in the failing light,
These men of battle, with grave, dark looks,
As plain to be read as open books,
While slowly gathered the shades of night.

The fern on the hill-sides was splashed with blood,
And down in the corn, where the poppies grew,
Were redder stains than the poppies knew,
And crimson-dyed was the river's flood.

For the foe had crossed from the other side,
That day, in the face of a murderous fire
That swept them down in its terrible ire;
And their life-blood went to color the tide.

"Herbert Cline!"—At the call there came
Two stalwart soldiers into the line,
Bearing between them this Herbert Cline,
Wounded and bleeding, to answer his name.

"Ezra Kerr!"—and a voice answered "Here!"
"Hiram Kerr!"—but no man replied.
They were brothers, these two; the sad wind sighed,
And a shudder crept through the cornfield near.

"Ephraim Deane!"—then a soldier spoke:
"Deane carried our regiment's colors," he said,
"When our ensign was shot; I left him dead
Just after the enemy wavered and broke.

"Close to the roadside his body lies;
I paused a moment and gave him to drink;
He murmured his mother's name, I think,
And Death came with it and closed his eyes."

'Twas a victory,—yes; but it cost us dear:
For that company's roll, when called at night,
Of a hundred men who went into the fight,
Numbered but twenty that answered "*Here!*"

*Nathaniel Graham Shepherd* [1835–1869]

## DIRGE

### FOR ONE WHO FELL IN BATTLE

Room for a Soldier! lay him in the clover;
He loved the fields, and they shall be his cover;
Make his mound with hers who called him once her lover:
Where the rain may rain upon it,
Where the sun may shine upon it,
Where the lamb hath lain upon it,
And the bee will dine upon it.

Bear him to no dismal tomb under city churches;
Take him to the fragrant fields, by the silver birches,
Where the whippoorwill shall mourn, where the oriole perches:
Make his mound with sunshine on it,
Where the bee will dine upon it,
Where the lamb hath lain upon it,
And the rain will rain upon it.

Busy as the busy bee, his rest should be the clover;
Gentle as the lamb was he, and the fern should be his cover:
Fern and rosemary shall grow my soldier's pillow over:
Where the rain may rain upon it,
Where the sun may shine upon it,
Where the lamb hath lain upon it,
And the bee will dine upon it.

Sunshine in his heart, the rain would come full often
Out of those tender eyes which evermore did soften;
He never could look cold, till we saw him in his coffin:
Make a mound with sunshine on it,
Where the wind may sigh upon it,
Where the moon may stream upon it,
And Memory shall dream upon it.

"Captain or Colonel,"—whatever invocation
Suit our hymn the best, no matter for thy station,—
On thy grave the rain shall fall from the eyes of a mighty nation!
Long as the sun doth shine upon it
Shall grow the goodly pine upon it,
Long as the stars do gleam upon it
Shall Memory come to dream upon it.

*Thomas William Parsons* [1819–1892]

## DIRGE FOR A SOLDIER

Close his eyes; his work is done!
What to him is friend or foeman,
Rise of moon, or set of sun,
Hand of man, or kiss of woman?
Lay him low, lay him low,
In the clover or the snow!
What cares he? he cannot know:
Lay him low!

As man may, he fought his fight,
Proved his truth by his endeavor;
Let him sleep in solemn night,
Sleep forever and forever.

Lay him low, lay him low,
In the clover or the snow!
What cares he? he cannot know:
Lay him low!

Fold him in his country's stars,
Roll the drum and fire the volley!
What to him are all our wars,
What but death-bemocking folly?
Lay him low, lay him low,
In the clover or the snow!
What cares he? he cannot know:
Lay him low!

Leave him to God's watching eye;
Trust him to the hand that made him.
Mortal love weeps idly by:
God alone has power to aid him.
Lay him low, lay him low,
In the clover or the snow!
What cares he? he cannot know:
Lay him low!

*George Henry Boker* [1823–1890]

## "BLOW, BUGLES, BLOW"

BLOW, bugles, blow, soft and sweet and low,
Sing a good-night song for them who bravely faced the foe;
Sing a song of truce to pain,
Where they sleep nor wake again,
'Neath the sunshine or the rain—
Blow, bugles, blow.

Wave, banners, wave, above each hero's grave,
Fold them, O thou stainless flag that they died to save;
All thy stars with glory bright,
Bore they on through Treason's night,
Through the darkness to the light—
Wave, banners, wave.

Fall, blossoms, fall, over one and all,
They who heard their country's cry and answered to the call;
'Mid the shock of shot and shell,
Where they bled and where they fell,
They who fought so long and well—
Fall, blossoms, fall.

Sigh, breezes, sigh, so gently wandering by,
Bend above them tenderly, blue of summer sky;
All their weary marches done,
All their battles fought and won,
Friend and lover, sire and son—
Sigh, breezes, sigh.

*John S. McGroarty* [1862–1944]

## "SUCH IS THE DEATH THE SOLDIER DIES"

Such is the death the soldier dies:
He falls,—the column speeds away;
Upon the dabbled grass he lies,
His brave heart following, still, the fray.

The smoke-wraiths drift among the trees,
The battle storms along the hill;
The glint of distant arms he sees;
He hears his comrades shouting still.

A glimpse of far-borne flags, that fade
And vanish in the rolling din:
He knows the sweeping charge is made,
The cheering lines are closing in.

Unmindful of his mortal wound,
He faintly calls and seeks to rise;
But weakness drags him to the ground:—
Such is the death the soldier dies.

*Robert Burns Wilson* [1850–1916]

## THE BRAVE AT HOME

From "The Wagoner of the Alleghanies"

THE maid who binds her warrior's sash
  With smile that well her pain dissembles,
The while beneath her drooping lash
  One starry tear-drop hangs and trembles,
Though Heaven alone records the tear,
  And Fame shall never know her story,
Her heart has shed a drop as dear
  As e'er bedewed the field of glory.

The wife who girds her husband's sword,
  Mid little ones who weep or wonder,
And bravely speaks the cheering word,
  What though her heart be rent asunder,
Doomed nightly in her dreams to hear
  The bolts of death around him rattle,
Hath shed as sacred blood as e'er
  Was poured upon the field of battle!

The mother who conceals her grief
  While to her breast her son she presses,
Then breathes a few brave words and brief,
  Kissing the patriot brow she blesses,
With no one but her secret God
  To know the pain that weighs upon her,
Sheds holy blood as e'er the sod
  Received on Freedom's field of honor!

*Thomas Buchanan Read* [1822–1872]

## SOMEBODY'S DARLING

INTO a ward of the whitewashed walls
  Where the dead and the dying lay—
Wounded by bayonets, shells, and balls—
  Somebody's darling was borne one day.

Somebody's darling! so young and so brave,
  Wearing still on his pale, sweet face—
Soon to be hid by the dust of the grave—
  The lingering light of his boyhood's grace.

Matted and damp are the curls of gold
  Kissing the snow of that fair young brow;
Pale are the lips of delicate mould—
  Somebody's darling is dying now.
Back from the beautiful blue-veined brow
  Brush the wandering waves of gold;
Cross his hands on his bosom now—
  Somebody's darling is still and cold.

Kiss him once for Somebody's sake;
  Murmur a prayer, soft and low;
One bright curl from the cluster take—
  They were Somebody's pride, you know.
Somebody's hand hath rested there;
  Was it a mother's, soft and white?
And have the lips of a sister fair
  Been baptized in those waves of light?

God knows best. He has Somebody's love;
  Somebody's heart enshrined him there;
Somebody wafted his name above,
  Night and morn, on the wings of prayer.
Somebody wept when he marched away,
  Looking so handsome, brave, and grand;
Somebody's kiss on his forehead lay;
  Somebody clung to his parting hand;—

Somebody's watching and waiting for him,
  Yearning to hold him again to her heart;
There he lies—with the blue eyes dim,
  And the smiling, child-like lips apart.
Tenderly bury the fair young dead,
  Pausing to drop on his grave a tear;
Carve on the wooden slab at his head,
  "*Somebody's darling slumbers here!*"

*Marie R. La Coste* [1842–1936]

## LITTLE GIFFEN

OUT of the focal and foremost fire,
Out of the hospital walls as dire,
Smitten of grape-shot and gangrene
(Eighteenth battle and *he* sixteen!)—
Spectre such as you seldom see,
Little Giffen of Tennessee.

"Take him and welcome!" the surgeon said;
"Little the doctor can help the dead!"
So we took him and brought him where
The balm was sweet on the summer air;
And we laid him down on a wholesome bed—
Utter Lazarus, heel to head!

And we watched the war with bated breath—
Skeleton Boy against skeleton Death.
Months of torture, how many such!
Weary weeks of the stick and crutch;
And still a glint in the steel-blue eye
Told of a spirit that wouldn't die,—

And didn't. Nay, more! in death's despite
The crippled skeleton learned to write.
"Dear Mother," at first, of course; and then,
"Dear Captain," inquiring about "the men."
Captain's answer: "Of eighty-and-five,
Giffen and I are left alive."

Word of gloom from the war, one day:
"Johnston's pressed at the front, they say!"
Little Giffen was up and away;
A tear—his first—as he bade good-by,
Dimmed the glint of his steel-blue eye.
"I'll write, if spared." There was news of the fight;
But none of Giffen.—He did not write.

I sometimes fancy that, were I king
Of the princely Knights of the Golden Ring,
With the song of the minstrel in mine ear,
And the tender legend that trembles here,
I'd give the best on his bended knee,
The whitest soul of my chivalry,
For Little Giffen of Tennessee.

*Francis Orray Ticknor* [1822–1874]

## ODE

Sung on the occasion of decorating the graves of the Confederate dead, at Magnolia Cemetery, Charleston, S. C., 1867.

SLEEP sweetly in your humble graves,
  Sleep, martyrs of a fallen cause;
Though yet no marble column craves
  The pilgrim here to pause.

In seeds of laurel in the earth
  The blossom of your fame is blown,
And somewhere, waiting for its birth,
  The shaft is in the stone!

Meanwhile, behalf the tardy years
  Which keep in trust your storied tombs,
Behold! your sisters bring their tears,
  And these memorial blooms.

Small tributes! but your shades will smile
  More proudly on these wreaths to-day,
Than when some cannon-moulded pile
  Shall overlook this bay.

Stoop, angels, hither from the skies!
  There is no holier spot of ground
Than where defeated valor lies,
  By mourning beauty crowned!

*Henry Timrod* [1829–1867]

## SENTINEL SONGS

WHEN falls the soldier brave,
Dead at the feet of wrong,
The poet sings and guards his grave
With sentinels of song.

Songs, march! he gives command,
Keep faithful watch and true;
The living and dead of the Conquered Land
Have now no guards save you.

Gray Ballads! mark ye well!
Thrice holy is your trust!
Go! halt by the fields where warriors fell;
Rest arms! and guard their dust.

List! Songs! your watch is long,
The soldiers' guard was brief;
Whilst right is right, and wrong is wrong,
Ye may not seek relief.

Go! wearing the gray of grief!
Go! watch o'er the Dead in Gray!
Go! guard the private and guard the chief,
And sentinel their clay!

And the songs, in stately rhyme,
And with softly-sounding tread,
Go forth, to watch for a time—a time—
Where sleep the Deathless Dead.

And the songs, like funeral dirge,
In music soft and low,
Sing round the graves, whilst hot tears surge
From hearts that are homes of woe.

What though no sculptured shaft
Immortalize each brave?
What though no monument epitaphed
Be built above each grave?

When marble wears away,
  And monuments are dust,
The songs that guard our soldiers' clay
  Will still fulfil their trust.

With lifted head, and steady tread,
  Like stars that guard the skies,
Go watch each bed, where rest the dead,
  Brave Songs, with sleepless eyes.

*Abram J. Ryan* [1839–1888]

## HEROES

The winds that once the Argo bore
  Have died by Neptune's ruined shrines,
And her hull is the drift of the deep-sea floor,
  Though shaped of Pelion's tallest pines.
You may seek her crew on every isle
  Fair in the foam of Ægean seas,
But, out of their rest, no charm can wile
  Jason and Orpheus and Hercules.

And Priam's wail is heard no more
  By windy Ilion's sea-built walls;
Nor great Achilles, stained with gore,
  Shouts, "O ye gods, 'tis Hector falls!"
On Ida's mount is the shining snow,
  But Jove has gone from its brow away;
And red on the plain the poppies grow
  Where Greek and Trojan fought that day.

Mother Earth, are the heroes dead?
  Do they thrill the soul of the years no more?
Are the gleaming snows and the poppies red
  All that is left of the brave of yore?
Are there none to fight as Theseus fought,
  Far in the young world's misty dawn?
Or to teach as gray-haired Nestor taught?
  Mother Earth, are the heroes gone?

Gone? In a grander form they rise.
  Dead? We may clasp their hands in ours,
And catch the light of their clearer eyes,
  And wreathe their brows with immortal flowers.
Wherever a noble deed is done,
  'Tis the pulse of a hero's heart is stirred;
Wherever Right has a triumph won,
  There are the heroes' voices heard.

Their armor rings on a fairer field
  Than Greek and Trojan fiercely trod;
For Freedom's sword is the blade they wield,
  And the gleam above is the smile of God.
So, in his isle of calm delight,
  Jason may sleep the years away;
For the heroes live, and the sky is bright,
  And the world is a braver world to-day.

*Edna Dean Proctor* [1838-1923]

## THE ONLY SON

O BITTER wind toward the sunset blowing,
  What of the dales to-night?
In yonder gray old hall what fires are glowing,
  What ring of festal light?

"*In the great window as the day was dwindling*
  *I saw an old man stand;*
*His head was proudly held and his eyes kindling,*
  *But the list shook in his hand.*"

O wind of twilight, was there no word uttered,
  No sound of joy or wail?
"'*A great fight and a good death,' he muttered;*
  *'Trust him, he would not fail.'*"

What of the chamber dark where she was lying
  For whom all life is done?
"*Within her heart she rocks a dead child, crying*
  *'My son, my little son.'*"

*Henry Newbolt* [1862-1938]

## YOUNG WINDEBANK

THEY shot young Windebank just here,
By Merton, where the sun
Strikes on the wall. 'Twas in a year
Of blood the deed was done.

At morning from the meadows dim
He watched them dig his grave.
Was this in truth the end for him,
The well beloved and brave?

He marched with soldier scarf and sword,
Set free to die that day,
And free to speak once more the word
That marshalled men obey.

But silent on the silent band
That faced him stern as death,
He looked and on the summer land,
And on the grave beneath.

Then with a sudden smile and proud
He waved his plume and cried,
"The king! the king!" and laughed aloud,
'The king! the king!" and died.

Let none affirm he vainly fell,
And paid the barren cost
Of having loved and served too well
A poor cause and a lost.

He in the soul's eternal cause
Went forth as martyrs must—
The kings who make the spirit laws
And rule us from the dust.

Whose wills unshaken by the breath
Of adverse Fate endure,
To give us honor strong as death
And loyal love as sure.

*Margaret L. Woods* [1856–1945]

## A HARROW GRAVE IN FLANDERS

HERE in the marshland, past the battered bridge,
One of a hundred grains untimely sown,
Here, with his comrades of the hard-won ridge,
He rests, unknown.

His horoscope had seemed so plainly drawn:
School triumphs earned apace in work and play;
Friendships at will; then love's delightful dawn
And mellowing day.

Home fostering hope; some service to the State;
Benignant age; then the long tryst to keep
Where in the yew-tree shadow congregate
His fathers sleep.

Was here the one thing needful to distil
From life's alembic, through this holier fate,
The man's essential soul, the hero-will?
We ask: and wait.

*Robert Offley Ashburton* [1858–1945]

## V. D. F.

YOU from Givenchy, since no years can harden
The beautiful dead, when holy twilight reaches
The sleeping cedar and the copper beeches,
Return to walk again in Wadham Garden.
We, growing old, grow stranger to the College,
Symbol of youth, where we were young together,
But you, beyond the reach of time and weather,
Of youth in death forever keep the knowledge.
We hoard our youth, we hoard our youth, and fear it,
But you, who freely gave what we have hoarded,
Are with the final goal of youth rewarded—
The road to travel and the traveler's spirit.
And therefore, when for us the stars go down,
Your star is steady over Oxford Town.

*Unknown*

# POEMS OF HISTORY

## THE DESTRUCTION OF SENNACHERIB

[710 B. C.]

THE Assyrian came down like the wolf on the fold,
And his cohorts were gleaming in purple and gold;
And the sheen of their spears was like stars on the sea,
When the blue wave rolls nightly on deep Galilee.

Like the leaves of the forest when Summer is green,
That host with their banners at sunset were seen:
Like the leaves of the forest when Autumn hath blown,
That host on the morrow lay withered and strown.

For the Angel of Death spread his wings on the blast,
And breathed in the face of the foe as he passed;
And the eyes of the sleepers waxed deadly and chill,
And their hearts but once heaved, and for ever grew still!

And there lay the steed with his nostril all wide,
But through it there rolled not the breath of his pride:
And the foam of his gasping lay white on the turf,
And cold as the spray of the rock-beating surf.

And there lay the rider distorted and pale,
With the dew on his brow, and the rust on his mail;
And the tents were all silent, the banners alone,
The lances unlifted, the trumpet unblown.

And the widows of Ashur are loud in their wail,
And the idols are broke in the temple of Baal;
And the might of the Gentile, unsmote by the sword,
Hath melted like snow in the glance of the Lord!

*George Gordon Byron* [1788–1824]

## THE VISION OF BELSHAZZAR

[538 B. C.]

The King was on his throne,
The Satraps thronged the hall;
A thousand bright lamps shone
O'er that high festival.
A thousand cups of gold,
In Judah deemed divine,—
Jehovah's vessels hold
The godless Heathen's wine!

In that same hour and hall,
The fingers of a hand
Came forth against the wall,
And wrote as if on sand:
The fingers of a man;—
A solitary hand
Along the letters ran,
And traced them like a wand.

The monarch saw, and shook,
And bade no more rejoice;
All bloodless waxed his look,
And tremulous his voice.
"Let the men of lore appear,
The wisest of the earth,
And expound the words of fear,
Which mar our royal mirth."

Chaldea's seers are good,
But here they have no skill;
And the unknown letters stood,
Untold and awful still.
And Babel's men of age
Are wise and deep in lore;
But now they were not sage,
They saw,—but knew no more.

A captive in the land,
  A stranger and a youth,
He heard the King's command,
  He saw that writing's truth.
The lamps around were bright,
  The prophecy in view:
He read it on that night,—
  The morrow proved it true.

"Belshazzar's grave is made,
  His kingdom passed away,
He, in the balance weighed,
  Is light and worthless clay;
The shroud, his robe of state,
  His canopy, the stone:
The Mede is at his gate!
  The Persian on his throne!"

*George Gordon Byron* [1788–1824]

## HORATIUS AT THE BRIDGE

[C. 496 B. C.]

LARS PORSENA of Clusium
  By the Nine Gods he swore
That the great house of Tarquin
  Should suffer wrong no more.
By the Nine Gods he swore it,
  And named a trysting-day,
And bade his messengers ride forth,
East and west and south and north,
  To summon his array.

East and west and south and north
  The messengers ride fast,
And tower and town and cottage
  Have heard the trumpet's blast.
Shame on the false Etruscan
  Who lingers in his home,
When Porsena of Clusium
  Is on the march for Rome.

The horsemen and the footmen
  Are pouring in amain
From many a stately market-place,
  From many a fruitful plain,
From many a lonely hamlet,
  Which, hid by beech and pine,
Like an eagle's nest, hangs on the crest
  Of purple Apennine;

From lordly Volaterræ
  Where scowls the far-famed hold
Piled by the hands of giants
  For godlike kings of old;
From sea-girt Populonia,
  Whose sentinels descry
Sardinia's snowy mountain-tops
  Fringing the southern sky;

From the proud mart of Pisæ,
  Queen of the western waves,
Where ride Massilia's triremes
  Heavy with fair-haired slaves,
From where sweet Clanis wanders
  Through corn and vines and flowers,
From where Cortona lifts to heaven
  Her diadem of towers.

Tall are the oaks whose acorns
  Drop in dark Auser's rill;
Fat are the stags that champ the boughs
  Of the Ciminian hill;
Beyond all streams, Clitumnus
  Is to the herdsman dear;
Best of all pools the fowler loves
  The great Volsinian mere.

But now no stroke of woodman
  Is heard by Auser's rill;
No hunter tracks the stag's green path
  Up the Ciminian hill;

Unwatched along Clitumnus
  Grazes the milk-white steer;
Unharmed the water-fowl may dip
  In the Volsinian mere.

The harvests of Arretium,
  This year, old men shall reap;
This year, young boys in Umbro
  Shall plunge the struggling sheep;
And in the vats of Luna,
  This year, the must shall foam
Round the white feet of laughing girls
  Whose sires have marched to Rome.

There be thirty chosen prophets,
  The wisest of the land,
Who alway by Lars Porsena
  Both morn and evening stand:
Evening and morn the Thirty
  Have turned the verses o'er,
Traced from the right on linen white
  By mighty seers of yore.

And with one voice the Thirty
  Have their glad answer given:
"Go forth, go forth, Lars Porsena,-
  Go forth, beloved of Heaven!
Go, and return in glory
  To Clusium's royal dome,
And hang round Nurscia's altars
  The golden shields of Rome!"

And now hath every city
  Sent up her tale of men;
The foot are fourscore thousand,
  The horse are thousands ten.
Before the gates of Sutrium
  Is met the great array;
A proud man was Lars Porsena
  Upon the trysting-day.

For all the Etruscan armies
  Were ranged beneath his eye,
And many a banished Roman,
  And many a stout ally;
And with a mighty following,
  To join the muster, came
The Tusculan Mamilius,
  Prince of the Latian name.

But by the yellow Tiber
  Was tumult and affright:
From all the spacious champaign
  To Rome men took their flight.
A mile around the city,
  The throng stopped up the ways;
A fearful sight it was to see
  Through two long nights and days.

For agèd folk on crutches,
  And women great with child,
And mothers, sobbing over babes
  That clung to them and smiled,
And sick men borne in litters
  High on the necks of slaves,
And troops of sunburned husbandmen
  With reaping-hooks and staves,

And droves of mules and asses
  Laden with skins of wine,
And endless flocks of goats and sheep,
  And endless herds of kine,
And endless trains of wagons,
  That creaked beneath the weight
Of corn-sacks and of household goods,
  Choked every roaring gate.

Now, from the rock Tarpeian,
  Could the wan burghers spy
The line of blazing villages
  Red in the midnight sky.

The Fathers of the City,
They sat all night and day,
For every hour some horseman came
With tidings of dismay.

To eastward and to westward
Have spread the Tuscan bands,
Nor house, nor fence, nor dovecote
In Crustumerium stands.
Verbenna down to Ostia
Hath wasted all the plain;
Astur hath stormed Janiculum,
And the stout guards are slain.

I wis, in all the Senate
There was no heart so bold
But sore it ached, and fast it beat,
When that ill news was told.
Forthwith up rose the Consul,
Up rose the Fathers all;
In haste they girded up their gowns,
And hied them to the wall.

They held a council, standing
Before the River-Gate;
Short time was there, ye well may guess,
For musing or debate.
Out spake the Consul roundly:
"The bridge must straight go down;
For, since Janiculum is lost,
Naught else can save the town."

Just then a scout came flying,
All wild with haste and fear:
"To arms! to arms! Sir Consul,—
Lars Porsena is here."
On the low hills to westward
The Consul fixed his eye,
And saw the swarthy storm of dust
Rise fast along the sky.

And nearer fast and nearer
  Doth the red whirlwind come;
And louder still, and still more loud,
From underneath that rolling cloud,
Is heard the trumpet's war-note proud,
  The trampling and the hum.
And plainly and more plainly
  Now through the gloom appears,
Far to left and far to right,
In broken gleams of dark-blue light,
The long array of helmets bright,
  The long array of spears.

And plainly and more plainly,
  Above that glimmering line,
Now might ye see the banners
  Of twelve fair cities shine;
But the banner of proud Clusium
  Was highest of them all,—
The terror of the Umbrian,
  The terror of the Gaul.

And plainly and more plainly
  Now might the burghers know,
By port and vest, by horse and crest,
  Each warlike Lucumo:
There Cilnius of Arretium
  On his fleet roan was seen;
And Astur of the fourfold shield,
Girt with the brand none else may wield;
Tolumnius with the belt of gold,
And dark Verbenna from the hold
  By reedy Thrasymene.

Fast by the royal standard,
  O'erlooking all the war,
Lars Porsena of Clusium
  Sat in his ivory car.

By the right wheel rode Mamilius,
  Prince of the Latian name;
And by the left false Sextus,
  That wrought the deed of shame.

But when the face of Sextus
  Was seen among the foes,
A yell that rent the firmament
  From all the town arose.
On the house-tops was no woman
  But spat towards him and hissed,
No child but screamed out curses,
  And shook its little fist.

But the Consul's brow was sad,
  And the Consul's speech was low,
And darkly looked he at the wall,
  And darkly at the foe:
"Their van will be upon us
  Before the bridge goes down;
And if they once may win the bridge,
  What hope to save the town?"

Then out spake brave Horatius,
  The Captain of the Gate:
"To every man upon this earth
  Death cometh soon or late.
And how can man die better
  Than facing fearful odds
For the ashes of his fathers
  And the temples of his Gods,

"And for the tender mother
  Who dandled him to rest,
And for the wife who nurses
  His baby at her breast,
And for the holy maidens
  Who feed the eternal flame,—
To save them from false Sextus
  That wrought the deed of shame?

"Hew down the bridge, Sir Consul,
  With all the speed ye may;
I, with two more to help me,
  Will hold the foe in play.
In yon strait path a thousand
  May well be stopped by three:
Now who will stand on either hand,
  And keep the bridge with me?"

Then out spake Spurius Lartius,—
  A Ramnian proud was he:
"Lo, I will stand at thy right hand,
  And keep the bridge with thee."
And out spake strong Herminius,—
  Of Titian blood was he:
"I will abide on thy left side,
  And keep the bridge with thee."

"Horatius," quoth the Consul,
  "As thou sayest so let it be."
And straight against that great array
  Forth went the dauntless Three.
For Romans in Rome's quarrel
  Spared neither land nor gold,
Nor son nor wife, nor limb nor life,
  In the brave days of old.

Then none was for a party;
  Then all were for the state;
Then the great man helped the poor,
  And the poor man loved the great:
Then lands were fairly portioned;
  Then spoils were fairly sold:
The Romans were like brothers
  In the brave days of old.

Now Roman is to Roman
  More hateful than a foe,
And the Tribunes beard the high,
  And the Fathers grind the low.

As we wax hot in faction,
  In battle we wax cold;
Wherefore men fight not as they fought
  In the brave days of old.

Now while the Three were tightening
  Their harness on their backs,
The Consul was the foremost man
  To take in hand an axe;
And Fathers, mixed with Commons,
  Seized hatchet, bar, and crow,
And smote upon the planks above,
  And loosed the props below.

Meanwhile the Tuscan army,
  Right glorious to behold,
Came flashing back the noonday light,
Rank behind rank, like surges bright
  Of a broad sea of gold.
Four hundred trumpets sounded
  A peal of warlike glee,
As that great host with measured tread,
And spears advanced, and ensigns spread,
Rolled slowly towards the bridge's head,
  Where stood the dauntless Three.

The Three stood calm and silent,
  And looked upon the foes,
And a great shout of laughter
  From all the vanguard rose;
And forth three chiefs came spurring
  Before that deep array,
To earth they sprang, their swords they drew,
And lifted high their shields, and flew
  To win the narrow way:

Aunus, from green Tifernum,
  Lord of the Hill of Vines;
And Seius, whose eight hundred slaves
  Sicken in Ilva's mines;
And Picus, long to Clusium
  Vassal in peace and war,

Who led to fight his Umbrian powers
From that gray crag where, girt with towers,
The fortress of Nequinum lowers
O'er the pale waves of Nar.

Stout Lartius hurled down Aunus
Into the stream beneath;
Herminius struck at Seius;
And clove him to the teeth;
At Picus brave Horatius
Darted one fiery thrust,
And the proud Umbrian's gilded arms
Clashed in the bloody dust.

Then Ocnus of Falerii
Rushed on the Roman Three;
And Lausulus of Urgo,
The rover of the sea;
And Aruns of Volsinium,
Who slew the great wild boar,—
The great wild boar that had his den
Amidst the reeds of Cosa's fen,
And wasted fields, and slaughtered men,
Along Albinia's shore.

Herminius smote down Aruns;
Lartius laid Ocnus low;
Right to the heart of Lausulus
Horatius sent a blow:
"Lie there," he cried, "fell pirate!
No more, aghast and pale,
From Ostia's walls the crowd shall mark
The track of thy destroying bark;
No more Campania's hinds shall fly
To woods and caverns, when they spy
Thy thrice-accursèd sail!"

But now no sound of laughter
Was heard among the foes;
A wild and wrathful clamor
From all the vanguard rose.

Six spears' lengths from the entrance,
  Halted that deep array,
And for a space no man came forth
  To win the narrow way.

But, hark! the cry is Astur:
  And lo! the ranks divide;
And the great Lord of Luna
  Comes with his stately stride.
Upon his ample shoulders
  Clangs loud the fourfold shield,
And in his hand he shakes the brand
  Which none but he can wield.

He smiled on those bold Romans,
  A smile serene and high;
He eyed the flinching Tuscans,
  And scorn was in his eye.
Quoth he, "The she-wolf's litter
  Stand savagely at bay;
But will ye dare to follow,
  If Astur clears the way?"

Then, whirling up his broadsword
  With both hands to the height,
He rushed against Horatius,
  And smote with all his might.
With shield and blade Horatius
  Right deftly turned the blow.
The blow, though turned came yet too nigh;
It missed his helm, but gashed his thigh.
The Tuscans raised a joyful cry
  To see the red blood flow.

He reeled, and on Herminius
  He leaned one breathing-space,
Then, like a wild-cat mad with wounds,
  Sprang right at Astur's face.
Through teeth, and skull, and helmet
  So fierce a thrust he sped,
The good sword stood a hand-breadth out
  Behind the Tuscan's head.

And the great lord of Luna
  Fell at that deadly stroke,
As falls on Mount Avernus
  A thunder-smitten oak.
Far o'er the crashing forest
  The giant arms lie spread;
And the pale augurs, muttering low,
  Gaze on the blasted head.

On Astur's throat Horatius
  Right firmly pressed his heel,
And thrice and four times tugged amain,
  Ere he wrenched out the steel.
"And see," he cried, "the welcome,
  Fair guests, that waits you here!
What noble Lucumo comes next
  To taste our Roman cheer?"

But at his haughty challenge
  A sullen murmur ran,
Mingled of wrath, and shame, and dread,
  Along that glittering van.
There lacked not men of prowess,
  Nor men of lordly race,
For all Etruria's noblest
  Were round the fatal place.

But all Etruria's noblest
  Felt their hearts sink to see
On the earth the bloody corpses,
  In the path the dauntless Three;
And, from the ghastly entrance
  Where those bold Romans stood,
All shrank, like boys who, unaware,
Ranging the woods to start a hare,
Come to the mouth of the dark lair
Where, growling low, a fierce old bear
  Lies amidst bones and blood.

Was none who would be foremost
  To lead such dire attack;

But those behind cried "Forward!"
  And those before cried "Back!"
And backward now and forward
  Wavers the deep array;
And on the tossing sea of steel
To and fro the standards reel,
And the victorious trumpet-peal
  Dies fitfully away.

Yet one man for one moment
  Stood out before the crowd;
Well known was he to all the Three,
  And they gave him greeting loud:
"Now welcome, welcome, Sextus!
  Now welcome to thy home!
Why dost thou stay, and turn away?
  Here lies the road to Rome."

Thrice looked he at the city;
  Thrice looked he at the dead;
And thrice came on in fury,
  And thrice turned back in dread;
And, white with fear and hatred,
  Scowled at the narrow way
Where, wallowing in a pool of blood,
  The bravest Tuscans lay.

But meanwhile axe and lever
  Have manfully been plied;
And now the bridge hangs tottering
  Above the boiling tide.
"Come back, come back, Horatius!"
  Loud cried the Fathers all.—
"Back, Lartius! back, Herminius!
  Back, ere the ruin fall!"

Back darted Spurius Lartius;—
  Herminius darted back;
And, as they passed, beneath their feet
  They felt the timbers crack.

But when they turned their faces,
  And on the farther shore
Saw brave Horatius stand alone,
  They would have crossed once more;

But with a crash like thunder
  Fell every loosened beam,
And, like a dam, the mighty wreck
  Lay right athwart the stream:
And a long shout of triumph
  Rose from the walls of Rome,
As to the highest turret-tops
  Was splashed the yellow foam.

And, like a horse unbroken,
  When first he feels the rein,
The furious river struggled hard,
  And tossed his tawny mane,
And burst the curb, and bounded,
  Rejoicing to be free;
And whirling down, in fierce career,
Battlement, and plank, and pier,
  Rushed headlong to the sea.

Alone stood brave Horatius,
  But constant still in mind,—
Thrice thirty thousand foes before,
  And the broad flood behind.
"Down with him!" cried false Sextus,
  With a smile on his pale face;
"Now yield thee," cried Lars Porsena,
  "Now yield thee to our grace."

Round turned he, as not deigning
  Those craven ranks to see;
Naught spake he to Lars Porsena,
  To Sextus naught spake he;
But he saw on Palatinus
  The white porch of his home;
And he spake to the noble river
  That rolls by the towers of Rome:

"O Tiber! Father Tiber!
 To whom the Romans pray,
A Roman's life, a Roman's arms,
 Take thou in charge this day!"
So he spake, and, speaking, sheathed
 The good sword by his side,
And, with his harness on his back,
 Plunged headlong in the tide.

No sound of joy or sorrow
 Was heard from either bank,
But friends and foes in dumb surprise,
With parted lips and straining eyes,
 Stood gazing where he sank;
And when above the surges
 They saw his crest appear,
All Rome sent forth a rapturous cry,
And even the ranks of Tuscany
 Could scarce forbear to cheer.

But fiercely ran the current,
 Swollen high by months of rain;
And fast his blood was flowing,
 And he was sore in pain,
And heavy with his armor,
 And spent with changing blows;
And oft they thought him sinking,
 But still again he rose.

Never, I ween, did swimmer,
 In such an evil case,
Struggle through such a raging flood
 Safe to the landing-place;
But his limbs were borne up bravely
 By the brave heart within,
And our good Father Tiber
 Bore bravely up his chin.

"Curse on him!" quoth false Sextus;—
 "Will not the villain drown?
But for this stay, ere close of day
 We should have sacked the town!"

"Heaven help him!" quoth Lars Porsena,
"And bring him safe to shore;
For such a gallant feat of arms
Was never seen before."

And now he feels the bottom;
Now on dry earth he stands;
Now round him throng the Fathers
To press his gory hands;
And now, with shouts and clapping,
And noise of weeping loud,
He enters through the River-Gate,
Borne by the joyous crowd.

They gave him of the corn-land,
That was of public right,
As much as two strong oxen
Could plough from morn till night;
And they made a molten image,
And set it up on high,
And there it stands unto this day
To witness if I lie.

It stands in the Comitium,
Plain for all folk to see,—
Horatius in his harness,
Halting upon one knee;
And underneath is written,
In letters all of gold,
How valiantly he kept the bridge
In the brave days of old.

And still his name sounds stirring
Unto the men of Rome,
As the trumpet-blast that cries to them
To charge the Volscian home;
And wives still pray to Juno
For boys with hearts as bold
As his who kept the bridge so well
In the brave days of old.

And in the nights of winter
  When the cold north-winds blow,
And the long howling of the wolves
  Is heard amidst the snow;
When round the lonely cottage
  Roars loud the tempest's din,
And the good logs of Algidus
  Roar louder yet within;

When the oldest cask is opened,
  And the largest lamp is lit;
When the chestnuts glow in the embers,
  And the kid turns on the spit;
When young and old in circle
  Around the firebrands close;
When the girls are weaving baskets,
  And the lads are shaping bows;

When the goodman mends his armor,
  And trims his helmet's plume;
When the goodwife's shuttle merrily
  Goes flashing through the loom;
With weeping and with laughter
  Still is the story told,
How well Horatius kept the bridge
  In the brave days of old.

*Thomas Babington Macaulay* [1800-1859]

## LEONIDAS

[480 B. C.]

SHOUT for the mighty men
  Who died along this shore,
Who died within this mountain's glen!
For never nobler chieftain's head
Was laid on valor's crimson bed,
  Nor ever prouder gore
Sprang forth, than theirs who won the day
Upon thy strand, Thermopylæ!

Shout for the mighty men
  Who on the Persian tents,

Like lions from their midnight den
Bounding on the slumbering deer,
Rushed—a storm of sword and spear;
  Like the roused elements,
Let loose from an immortal hand
To chasten or to crush a land!

But there are none to hear—
  Greece is a hopeless slave.
Leonidas! no hand is near
To lift thy falchion now;
No warrior makes the warrior's vow
  Upon thy sea-washed grave.
The voice that should be raised by men
Must now be given by wave and glen.

And it is given! The surge,
  The tree, the rock, the sand
On freedom's kneeling spirit urge,
In sounds that speak but to the free,
The memory of thine and thee!
  The vision of thy band
Still gleams within the glorious dell
Which their gore hallowed as it fell!

And is thy grandeur done?
  Mother of men like these!
Has not thy outcry gone
Where justice has an ear to hear?
Be holy! God shall guide thy spear,
  Till in thy crimsoned seas
Are plunged the chain and scimitar.
Greece shall be a new-born star!

*George Croly* [1780–1860]

## ANTONY TO CLEOPATRA

[AUGUST, 30 B. C.]

I AM dying, Egypt, dying!
  Ebbs the crimson life-tide fast,
And the dark Plutonian shadows
  Gather on the evening blast;

Let thine arms, O Queen, enfold me,
  Hush thy sobs and bow thine ear,
Listen to the great heart-secrets
  Thou, and thou alone, must hear.

Though my scarred and veteran legions
  Bear their eagles high no more,
And my wrecked and scattered galleys
  Strew dark Actium's fatal shore;
Though no glittering guards surround me,
  Prompt to do their master's will,
I must perish like a Roman,
  Die the great Triumvir still.

Let not Cæsar's servile minions
  Mock the lion thus laid low;
'Twas no foeman's arm that felled him,
  'Twas his own that struck the blow:
His who, pillowed on thy bosom,
  Turned aside from glory's ray—
His who, drunk with thy caresses,
  Madly threw a world away.

Should the base plebeian rabble
  Dare assail my name at Rome,
Where the noble spouse, Octavia,
  Weeps within her widowed home,
Seek her; say the gods bear witness,—
  Altars, augurs, circling wings,—
That her blood, with mine commingled,
  Yet shall mount the throne of kings.

And for thee, star-eyed Egyptian—
  Glorious sorceress of the Nile!—
Light the path to Stygian horrors,
  With the splendor of thy smile;
Give the Cæsar crowns and arches,
  Let his brow the laurel twine:
I can scorn the Senate's triumphs,
  Triumphing in love like thine.

I am dying, Egypt, dying!
  Hark! the insulting foeman's cry;
They are coming—quick, my falchion!
  Let me front them ere I die.
Ah, no more amid the battle
  Shall my heart exulting swell;
Isis and Osiris guard thee—
  Cleopatra—Rome—farewell!

*William Haines Lytle* [1826-1863]

## BOADICEA: AN ODE

[62 A. D.]

When the British warrior queen,
  Bleeding from the Roman rods,
Sought, with an indignant mien,
  Counsel of her country's gods,

Sage beneath a spreading oak
  Sat the Druid, hoary chief,
Every burning word he spoke
  Full of rage and full of grief:

"Princess! if our agèd eyes
  Weep upon thy matchless wrongs,
'Tis because resentment ties
  All the terrors of our tongues.

"Rome shall perish:—write that word
  In the blood that she has spilt;
Perish, hopeless and abhorred,
  Deep in ruin as in guilt.

"Rome, for empire far renowned,
  Tramples on a thousand states;
Soon her pride shall kiss the ground,—
  Hark! the Gaul is at her gates.

"Other Romans shall arise
  Heedless of a soldier's name;
Sounds, not arms, shall win the prize,
  Harmony the path to fame.

"Then the progeny that springs
From the forests of our land,
Armed with thunder, clad with wings,
Shall a wider world command.

"Regions Cæsar never knew
Thy posterity shall sway;
Where his eagles never flew,
None invincible as they."

Such the bard's prophetic words,
Pregnant with celestial fire,
Bending as he swept the chords
Of his sweet but awful lyre.

She, with all a monarch's pride,
Felt them in her bosom glow,
Rushed to battle, fought and died;
Dying, hurled them at the foe.

"Ruffians! pitiless as proud,
Heaven awards the vengeance due;
Empire is on us bestowed,
Shame and ruin wait for you!"

*William Cowper* [1731–1800]

## "HE NEVER SMILED AGAIN"

[NOVEMBER, 1120]

THE bark that held the prince went down,
The sweeping waves rolled on;
And what was England's glorious crown
To him that wept a son?
He lived—for life may long be borne,
Ere sorrow break its chain;—
Why comes not death to those who mourn?—
He never smiled again!

There stood proud forms around his throne,
The stately and the brave;
But which could fill the place of one,
That one beneath the wave?

Before him passed the young and fair,
In pleasure's reckless train;
But seas dashed o'er his son's bright hair—
He never smiled again!

He sat where festal bowls went round,
He heard the minstrel sing;
He saw the tourney's victor crowned
Amidst the knightly ring;
A murmur of the restless deep
Was blent with every strain,
A voice of winds that would not sleep—
He never smiled again!

Hearts, in that time, closed o'er the trace
Of vows once fondly poured,
And strangers took the kinsman's place
At many a joyous board;
Graves, which true love had bathed with tears,
Were left to heaven's bright rain,
Fresh hopes were born for other years—
*He* never smiled again!

*Felicia Dorothea Hemans* [1793-1835]

## BRUCE TO HIS MEN AT BANNOCKBURN

[JUNE 24, 1314]

SCOTS, wha hae wi' Wallace bled,
Scots, wham Bruce has aften led;
Welcome to your gory bed,
Or to victory!

Now's the day, and now's the hour:
See the front o' battle lour:
See approach proud Edward's power,—
Chains and slavery!

Wha will be a traitor knave?
Wha can fill a coward's grave?
Wha sae base as be a slave?
Let him turn and flee!

Wha for Scotland's king and law
Freedom's sword will strongly draw,
Freeman stand, or freeman fa',
    Let him follow me!

By oppression's woes and pains!
By your sons in servile chains,
We will drain our dearest veins,
    But they shall be free!

Lay the proud usurpers low!
Tyrants fall in every foe!
Liberty's in every blow!—
    Let us do or die!

*Robert Burns* [1759–1796]

## CORONACH

**From "The Lady of the Lake"**

He is gone on the mountain,
    He is lost to the forest,
Like a summer-dried fountain,
    When our need was the sorest.
The font, reappearing
    From the raindrops shall borrow,
But to us comes no cheering,
    To Duncan no morrow!

The hand of the reaper
    Takes the ears that are hoary,
But the voice of the weeper
    Wails manhood in glory.
The autumn winds rushing
    Waft the leaves that are serest.
But our flower was in flushing,
    When blighting was nearest.

Fleet foot on the correi,
    Sage counsel in cumber,
Red hand in the foray,
    How sound is thy slumber!

Like the dew on the mountain,
Like the foam on the river,
Like the bubble on the fountain,
Thou art gone, and for ever!

*Walter Scott* [1771-1832]

## CREÇY

[AUGUST 26, 1346]

AT Creçy by Somme in Ponthieu
High up on a windy hill
A mill stands out like a tower:
King Edward stands on the mill.
The plain is seething below,
As Vesuvius seethes with flame,
But O! not with fire, but gore,
Earth incarnadined o'er,
Crimson with shame and with fame.
To the King run the messengers, crying,
"Thy Son is hard pressed to the dying!"
"Let alone: for to-day will be written in story
To the great world's end and for ever:
So let the boy have the glory."

Erin and Gwalia there
With England are ranked against France;
Out-facing the oriflamme red
The red dragons of Merlin advance;
As a harvest in autumn renewed
The lances bend over the fields;
Snow-thick our arrow-heads white
Level the foe as they light;
Knighthood to yeomanry yields:
Proud heart, the King watches, as higher
Goes the blaze of the battle, and nigher:
"To-day is a day will be written in story
To the great world's end, and for ever!
Let the boy alone have the glory."

Harold at Senlac-on-Sea
  By Norman arrow laid low,
When the shield-wall was breached by the shaft,
  Thou art avenged by the bow!
Chivalry! name of romance!
  Thou art henceforth but a name;
Weapon that none can withstand,
Yew in the Englishman's hand,
  Flight-shaft unerring in aim!
As a lightning-struck forest the foemen
Shiver down to the stroke of the bowmen;
"O to-day is a day will be written in story
To the great world's end, and for ever!
So, let the boy have the glory."

Pride of Liguria's shore
  Genoa wrestles in vain;
Vainly Bohemia's king
  King-like is laid with the slain.
The Blood-lake is wiped out in blood,
  The shame of the centuries o'er;
Where the pride of the Norman had sway,
The lions lord over the fray,
  The legions of France are no more:
The Prince to his father kneels lowly:
"His is the battle—his wholly!
For to-day is a day will be written in story
To the great world's end, and for ever!
So, let him have the spurs and the glory."

*Francis Turner Palgrave* [1824–1897]

## THE PATRIOT'S PASS-WORD

[JULY 9, 1386]

"MAKE way for Liberty!" he cried,
Made way for Liberty, and died.

In arms the Austrian phalanx stood,
A living wall, a human wood;

A wall,—where every conscious stone
Seemed to its kindred thousands grown;
A rampart all assaults to bear,
Till time to dust their frames should wear:
A wood,—like that enchanted grove
In which with fiends Rinaldo strove,
Where every silent tree possessed
A spirit prisoned in its breast,
Which the first stroke of coming strife
Might startle into hideous life:
So still, so dense, the Austrians stood,
A living wall, a human wood.
Impregnable their front appears,
All-horrent with projected spears,
Whose polished points before them shine,
From flank to flank, one brilliant line,
Bright as the breakers' splendors run
Along the billows to the sun.

Opposed to these, a hovering band
Contended for their father-land:
Peasants, whose new-found strength had broke
From manly necks the ignoble yoke,
And forged their fetters into swords,
On equal terms to fight their lords,
And what insurgent rage had gained
In many a mortal fray maintained.
Marshalled once more, at Freedom's call,
They came to conquer or to fall,
Where he who conquered, he who fell,
Was deemed a dead, or living, Tell;
Such virtue had that patriot breathed,
So to the soil his soul bequeathed,
That wheresoe'er his arrows flew,
Heroes in his own likeness grew,
And warriors sprang from every sod,
Which his awakening footstep trod.

And now the work of life and death
Hung on the passing of a breath;

The fire of conflict burned within,
The battle trembled to begin;
Yet, while the Austrians held their ground,
Point for assault was nowhere found;
Where'er the impatient Switzers gazed,
The unbroken line of lances blazed:
That line 'twere suicide to meet,
And perish at their tyrants' feet:
How could they rest within their graves,
And leave their homes the haunts of slaves?
Would they not feel their children tread
With clanging chains, above their head?

It must not be: this day, this hour,
Annihilates the invader's power:
All Switzerland is in the field,
She will not fly, she cannot yield,
She must not fall; her better fate
Here gives her an immortal date.
Few were the number she could boast,
Yet every freeman was a host,
And felt as 'twere a secret known
That one should turn the scale alone,
While each unto himself were he
On whose sole arm hung victory.

It did depend on *one* indeed;
Behold him,—Arnold Winkelried!
There sounds not to the trump of fame
The echo of a nobler name.
Unmarked he stood amid the throng,
In rumination deep and long,
Till you might see, with sudden grace,
The very thought come o'er his face,
And by the motion of his form
Anticipate the bursting storm,
And by the uplifting of his brow
Tell where the bolt would strike, and how.

But 'twas no sooner thought than done,
The field was in a moment won;

"Make way for Liberty!" he cried,
Then ran, with arms extended wide,
As if his dearest friend to clasp;
Ten spears he swept within his grasp;
"Make way for Liberty!" he cried;
Their keen points met from side to side;
He bowed amidst them, like a tree,
And thus made way for Liberty.

Swift to the breach his comrades fly;
"Make way for Liberty!" they cry,
And through the Austrian phalanx dart,
As rushed the spears through Arnold's heart;
While, instantaneous as his fall,
Rout, ruin, panic seized them all;
An earthquake could not overthrow
A city with a surer blow.

Thus Switzerland again was free;
Thus Death made way for Liberty!

*James Montgomery* [1771–1854]

## THE BATTLE OF OTTERBURN

[AUGUST 10, 1388]

It fell about the Lammas tide,
When muir-men win their hay,
That the doughty Earl of Douglas rade
Into England, to take a prey.

He chose the Gordons and the Græmes,
With them the Lindsays gay;
But the Jardines wald not with him ride,
And they rue it to this day.

And they hae harried the dales o' Tyne,
And half o' Bambrough-shire,
And the Otter-dale they burned it hale,
And set it a' on fire.

Then he cam' up to Newcastle,
  And rade it round about:
"O wha's the lord of this castle?
  Or wha's the lady o't?"

But up spake proud Lord Percy then,
  And O but he spake hie!
"I am the lord of this castle,
  My wife's the lady gay."

"If thou'rt the lord of this castle,
  Sae weel it pleases me,
For, ere I cross the Border fells,
  The tane of us shall dee."

He took a lang spear in his hand,
  Shod with the metal free,
And for to meet the Douglas there
  He rode right furiouslie.

But O how pale his lady looked,
  Frae aff the castle-wa',
As down before the Scottish spear
  She saw proud Percy fa'.

"Had we twa been upon the green,
  And never an eye to see,
I wad hae had you, flesh and fell;
  But your sword sall gae wi me."

"Now gae ye up to Otterbourne,
  And wait there dayis three,
And gin I come not ere they end,
  A fause knight ca' ye me."

"The Otterbourne's a bonnie burn;
  'Tis pleasant there to be;
But there is naught at Otterbourne
  To feed my men and me.

"The deer rins wild on hill and dale,
The birds fly wild frae tree to tree;
But there is neither bread nor kale
To fend my men and me.

"Yet I will stay at Otterbourne,
Where you sall welcome be;
And, if ye come not at three days' end,
A fause lord I'll ca' thee."

"Thither will I come," proud Percy said,
"By the might of Our Ladye;"
"There will I bide thee," said the Douglas,
"My troth I plight to thee."

They licted high on Otterbourne,
Upon the bent sae broun;
They licted high on Otterbourne,
And pitched their pallions doun.

And he that had a bonnie boy,
He sent his horse to grass;
And he that had not a bonnie boy,
His ain servant he was.

But up then spak' a little page,
Before the peep o' dawn:
"O waken ye, waken ye, my good lord,
For Percy's hard at hand."

"Ye lie, ye lie, ye liar loud!
Sae loud I hear ye lie:
For Percy had not men yestreen
To dight my men and me.

"But I hae dreamed a dreary dream,
Beyond the Isle of Sky;
I saw a deid man win a fight,
And I think that man was I."

He belted on his gude braid-sword,
  And to the field he ran,
But he forgot the hewmont strong,
  That should have kept his brain.

When Percy wi' the Douglas met,
  I wot he was fu' fain;
They swakkit swords, till sair they swat,
  And the blud ran down like rain.

But Percy wi' his gude braid-sword,
  That could sae sharply wound,
Has wounded Douglas on the brow,
  Till he fell to the ground.

And then he called his little foot-page,
  And said, "Run speedily,
And fetch my ain dear sister's son,
  Sir Hugh Montgomery.

"My nephew gude," the Douglas said,
  "What recks the death of ane?
Last night I dreamed a dreary dream,
  And I ken the day's thy ain!

"My wound is deep; I fain wad sleep;
  Tak' thou the vanguard o' the three,
And bury me by the braken-bush,
  That grows on yonder lilye lea.

"O bury me by the braken-bush,
  Beneath the blumin' brier;
Let never living mortal ken
  That a kindly Scot lies here."

He lifted up that noble lord,
  Wi' the saut tear in his e'e;
He hid him by the braken-bush,
  That his merrie men might not see.

The moon was clear, the day drew near,
  The spears in flinders flew,
And mony a gallant Englishman
  Ere day the Scotsmen slew.

The Gordons gude, in English blude
  They wat their hose and shoon;
The Lindsays flew like fire about,
  Till a' the fray was dune.

The Percy and Montgomery met,
  That either of other was fain;
They swakkit swords, and sair they swat,
  And the blude ran down between.

"Now yield thee, yield thee, Percy," he said,
  "Or else I will lay thee low!"
"To whom maun I yield," quoth Earl Percy,
  "Since I see it maun be so?"

"Thou shalt not yield to lord or loun,
  Nor yet shalt thou yield to me;
But yield thee to the braken-bush,
  That grows upon yon lilye lea."

"I will not yield to a braken-bush,
  Nor yet will I yield to a brier;
But I would yield to Earl Douglas,
  Or Sir Hugh the Montgomery, if he were here."

As soon as he knew it was Montgomery,
  He struck his sword's point in the gronde;
The Montgomery was a courteous knight,
  And quickly took him by the honde.

This deed was done at the Otterbourne,
  About the breaking o' the day;
Earl Douglas was buried at the braken-bush,
  And the Percy led captive away.

*Unknown*

## AGINCOURT

[OCTOBER 25, 1415]

FAIR stood the wind for France
When we our sails advance,
Nor now to prove our chance
Longer will tarry;
But putting to the main,
At Caux, the mouth of Seine,
With all his martial train
Landed King Harry.

And taking many a fort,
Furnished in warlike sort,
Marcheth towards Agincourt
In happy hour;
Skirmishing day by day
With those that stopped his way
Where the French general lay
With all his power.

Which, in his height of pride,
King Henry to deride,
His ransom to provide
Unto him sending;
Which he neglects the while
As from a nation vile,
Yet with an angry smile
Their fall portending.

And turning to his men,
Quoth our brave Henry then,
"Though they to one be ten
Be not amazèd:
Yet have we well begun:
Battles so bravely won
Have ever to the sun
By fame been raisèd.

"And for myself (quoth he)
This my full rest shall be:
England ne'er mourn for me
Nor more esteem me:
Victor I will remain
Or on this earth lie slain,
Never shall she sustain
Loss to redeem me.

"Poitiers and Cressy tell,
When most their pride did swell,
Under our swords they fell:
No less our skill is
Than when our grandsire great
Claiming the regal seat,
By many a warlike feat
Lopped the French lilies."

The Duke of York so dread
The eager vanguard led;
With the main Henry sped
Among his henchmen.
Excester had the rear,
A braver man not there;
O Lord, how hot they were
On the false Frenchmen!

They now to fight are gone,
Armor on armor shone,
Drum now to drum did groan,
To hear was wonder;
That with the cries they make
The very earth did shake:
Trumpet to trumpet spake,
Thunder to thunder.

Well it thine age became,
O noble Erpingham,
Which didst the signal aim
To our hid forces!

When from a meadow by,
Like a storm suddenly
The English archery
  Struck the French horses.

With Spanish yew so strong,
Arrows a cloth-yard long
That like to serpents stung,
  Piercing the weather;
None from his fellow starts,
But playing manly parts,
And like true English hearts
  Stuck close together.

When down their bows they threw,
And forth their bilbos drew,
And on the French they flew,
  Not one was tardy;
Arms were from shoulders sent,
Scalps to the teeth were rent,
Down the French peasants went—
  Our men were hardy.

This while our noble king,
His broadsword brandishing,
Down the French host did ding
  As to o'erwhelm it;
And many a deep wound lent,
His arms with blood besprent,
And many a cruel dent
  Bruisèd his helmet.

Gloster, that duke so good,
Next of the royal blood,
For famous England stood
  With his brave brother;
Clarence, in steel so bright,
Though but a maiden knight,
Yet in that furious fight
  Scarce such another.

Warwick in blood did wade,
Oxford the foe invade,
And cruel slaughter made
    Still as they ran up;
Suffolk his axe did ply,
Beaumont and Willoughby
Bare them right doughtily,
    Ferrers and Fanhope.

Upon Saint Crispin's Day
Fought was this noble fray,
Which fame did not delay
    To England to carry.
O when shall English men
With such acts fill a pen?
Or England breed again
    Such a King Harry?

*Michael Drayton* [1563–1631]

## A BALLAD OF ORLEANS

[1429]

The fray began at the middle-gate,
  Between the night and the day;
Before the matin bell was rung
  The foe was far away.
There was no knight in the land of France
  Could gar that foe to flee,
Till up there rose a young maiden,
  And drove them to the sea.

*Sixty forts around Orleans town,*
  *And sixty forts of stone!*
*Sixty forts at our gates last night—*
  *To-day there is not one!*

Talbot, Suffolk, and Pole are fled
  Beyond the Loire, in fear—
Many a captain who would not drink,
  Hath drunken deeply there—

Many a captain is fallen and drowned,
  And many a knight is dead,
And many die in the misty dawn
  While forts are burning red.

The blood ran off our spears all night
  As the rain runs off the roofs—
God rest their souls that fell i' the fight
  Among our horses' hoofs!
They came to rob us of our own
  With sword and spear and lance,
They fell and clutched the stubborn earth,
  And bit the dust of France!

We fought across the moonless dark
  Against their unseen hands—
A knight came out of Paradise
  And fought among our bands.
Fight on, O maiden knight of God,
  Fight on and do not tire—
For lo! the misty break o' the day
  Sees all their forts on fire!

*Sixty forts around Orleans town,*
  *And sixty forts of stone!*
*Sixty forts at our gates last night—*
  *To-day there is not one!*

*A. Mary F. Robinson* [1857-

## COLUMBUS

[JANUARY, 1487]

St. Stephen's cloistered hall was proud
  In learning's pomp that day,
For there a robed and stately crowd
  Pressed on in long array.
A mariner with simple chart
  Confronts that conclave high,
While strong ambition stirs his heart,
And burning thoughts of wonder part
  From lip and sparkling eye.

What hath he said? With frowning face,
  In whispered tones they speak,
And lines upon their tablets trace,
  Which flush each ashen cheek;
The Inquisition's mystic doom
  Sits on their brows severe,
And bursting forth in visioned gloom,
Sad heresy from burning tomb
  Groans on the startled ear.

Courage, thou Genoese! Old Time
  Thy splendid dream shall crown;
Yon Western Hemisphere sublime,
  Where unshorn forests frown,
The awful Andes' cloud-wrapped brow,
  The Indian hunter's bow,
Bold streams untamed by helm or prow,
And rocks of gold and diamonds, thou
  To thankless Spain shalt show.

Courage, World-finder! Thou hast need!
  In Fate's unfolding scroll,
Dark woes and ingrate wrongs I read,
  That rack the noble soul.
On! on! Creation's secrets probe,
  Then drink thy cup of scorn,
And wrapped in fallen Cæsar's robe,
Sleep like that master of the globe,
  All glorious,—yet forlorn.

*Lydia Huntly Sigourney* [1791-1865]

## COLUMBUS

[AUGUST 3—OCTOBER 12, 1492]

BEHIND him lay the gray Azores,
  Behind the Gates of Hercules;
Before him not the ghost of shores,
  Before him only shoreless seas.

The good mate said: "Now must we pray,
  For lo! the very stars are gone.
Brave Admiral, speak, what shall I say?"
  "Why, say 'Sail on! sail on! and on!'"

"My men grow mutinous day by day;
  My men grow ghastly wan and weak."
The stout mate thought of home; a spray
  Of salt wave washed his swarthy cheek.
"What shall I say, brave Admiral, say,
  If we sight naught but seas at dawn?"
"Why, you shall say at break of day,
  'Sail on! sail on! sail on! and on!'"

They sailed and sailed, as winds might blow,
  Until at last the blanched mate said:
"Why, now not even God would know
  Should I and all my men fall dead.
These very winds forget their way,
  For God from these dread seas is gone.
Now speak, brave Admiral, speak and say"—
  He said: "Sail on! sail on! and on!"

They sailed. They sailed. Then spake the mate:
  "This mad sea shows his teeth to-night.
He curls his lip, he lies in wait,
  With lifted teeth, as if to bite!
Brave Admiral, say but one good word:
  What shall we do when hope is gone?"
The words leapt like a leaping sword:
  "Sail on! sail on! sail on! and on!"

Then, pale and worn, he kept his deck,
  And peered through darkness. Ah, that night
Of all dark nights! And then a speck—
  A light! a light! a light! a light!
It grew, a starlit flag unfurled!
  It grew to be Time's burst of dawn.
He gained a world; he gave that world
  Its grandest lesson: "On! sail on!"

*Joaquin Miller* [1839-1913]

## A LAMENT FOR FLODDEN

[SEPTEMBER 9, 1513]

I'VE heard them lilting at our ewe-milking,
  Lasses a-lilting before dawn o' day;
But now they are moaning on ilka green loaning:
  "The Flowers of the Forest are a' wede away."

At buchts, in the morning, nae blithe lads are scorning,
  Lasses are lanely and dowie and wae;
Nae daffing, nae gabbing, but sighing and sabbing,
  Ilk ane lifts her leglen and hies her away.

In har'st, at the shearing, nae youths now are jeering,
  The bandsters are lyart, and runkled, and gray:
At fair or at preaching, nae wooing, nae fleeching—
  The Flowers of the Forest are a' wede away.

At e'en, in the gloaming, nae swankies are roaming
  'Bout stacks wi' the lasses at bogle to play;
But ilk ane sits eerie, lamenting her dearie—
  The Flowers of the Forest are a' wede away.

Dool and wae for the order sent our lads to the Border!
  The English, for ance, by guile wan the day;
The Flowers of the Forest, that fought aye the foremost
  The prime o' our land, lie cauld in the clay.

We'll hear nae mair lilting at our ewe-milking;
  Women and bairns are heartless and wae;
Sighing and moaning on ilka green loaning:
  "The Flowers of the Forest are a' wede away."

*Jane Elliot* [1727–1805]

## SIR HUMPHREY GILBERT

[1583]

SOUTHWARD with fleet of ice
  Sailed the corsair Death;
Wild and fast blew the blast,
  And the east-wind was his breath.

His lordly ships of ice
  Glisten in the sun;
On each side, like pennons wide,
  Flashing crystal streamlets run.

His sails of white sea-mist
  Dripped with silver rain;
But where he passed there was cast
  Leaden shadows o'er the main.

Eastward from Campobello
  Sir Humphrey Gilbert sailed;
Three days or more seaward he bore.
  Then, alas! the land-wind failed.

Alas! the land-wind failed,
  And ice-cold grew the night;
And nevermore, on sea or shore,
  Should Sir Humphrey see the light.

He sat upon the deck,
  The Book was in his hand;
"Do not fear! Heaven is as near,"
  He said, "by water as by land!"

In the first watch of the night,
  Without a signal's sound,
Out of the sea, mysteriously,
  The fleet of Death rose all around.

The moon and the evening star
  Were hanging in the shrouds;
Every mast, as it passed,
  Seemed to rake the passing clouds.

They grappled with their prize,
  At midnight black and cold!
As of a rock was the shock;
  Heavily the ground-swell rolled.

Southward through day and dark,
  They drift in close embrace,
With mist and rain, o'er the open main;
  Yet there seems no change of place.

Southward, forever southward,
  They drift through dark and day;
And like a dream, in the Gulf-Stream,
  Sinking, vanish all away.

*Henry Wadsworth Longfellow* [1807-1882]

## THE ARMADA: A FRAGMENT

[JULY 21-29, 1588]

ATTEND, all ye who list to hear our noble England's praise;
I sing of the thrice famous deeds she wrought in ancient days,
When that great fleet invincible against her bore, in vain,
The richest spoils of Mexico, the stoutest hearts of Spain.

It was about the lovely close of a warm summer day,
There came a gallant merchant-ship full sail to Plymouth
  Bay;
The crew had seen Castile's black fleet, beyond Aurigny's
  isle,
At earliest twilight, on the waves lie heaving many a mile.
At sunrise she escaped their van, by God's especial grace;
And the tall Pinta, till the noon, had held her close in chase.
Forthwith a guard at every gun was placed along the wall;
The beacon blazed upon the roof of Edgecumbe's lofty hall;
Many a light fishing-bark put out to pry along the coast;
And with loose rein and bloody spur rode inland many a post.

With his white hair unbonneted, the stout old sheriff comes;
Behind him march the halberdiers; before him sound the
  drums:
His yeomen round the market cross make clear an ample
  space;
For there behooves him to set up the standard of Her Grace.
And haughtily the trumpets peal, and gaily dance the bells,
As slow upon the laboring wind the royal blazon swells.

Look how the Lion of the sea lifts up his ancient crown,
And underneath his deadly paw treads the gay lilies down.
So stalked he when he turned to flight, on that famed Picard field,
Bohemia's plume, and Genoa's bow, and Cæsar's eagle shield.
So glared he when at Agincourt in wrath he turned to bay,
And crushed and torn beneath his claws the princely hunters lay.
Ho! strike the flagstaff deep, Sir Knight: ho! scatter flowers, fair maids:
Ho! gunners, fire a loud salute: ho! gallants, draw your blades:
Thou sun, shine on her joyously; ye breezes, waft her wide;
Our glorious *Semper Eadem*, the banner of our pride.

The freshening breeze of eve unfurled that banner's massy fold;
The parting gleam of sunshine kissed that haughty scroll of gold;
Night sank upon the dusky beach, and on the purple sea,
Such night in England ne'er had been, nor e'er again shall be.
From Eddystone to Berwick bounds, from Lynn to Milford Bay,
That time of slumber was as bright and busy as the day;
For swift to east and swift to west the ghastly war-flame spread,
High on St. Michael's Mount it shone: it shone on Beachy Head.
Far o'er the deep the Spaniard saw, along each southern shire,
Cape beyond cape, in endless range, those twinkling points of fire.
The fisher left his skiff to rock on Tamar's glittering waves:
The rugged miners poured to war from Mendip's sunless caves:
O'er Longleat's towers, o'er Cranbourne's oaks, the fiery herald flew:
He roused the shepherds of Stonehenge, the rangers of Beaulieu.

Right sharp and quick the bells all night rang out from Bristol town,
And ere the day three hundred horse had met on Clifton Down;
The sentinel on Whitehall gate looked forth into the night,
And saw, o'erhanging Richmond Hill, the streak of blood-red light:
Then bugle's note and cannon's roar the deathlike silence broke,
And with one start, and with one cry, the royal city woke.

At once on all her stately gates arose the answering fires;
At once the wild alarum clashed from all her reeling spires;
From all the batteries of the Tower pealed loud the voice of fear;
And all the thousand masts of Thames sent back a louder cheer:
And from the furthest wards was heard the rush of hurrying feet,
And the broad streams of pikes and flags rushed down each roaring street:
And broader still became the blaze, and louder still the din,
As fast from every village round the horse came spurring in;
And eastward straight from wild Blackheath the warlike errand went,
And roused in many an ancient hall the gallant squires of Kent.
Southward from Surrey's pleasant hills flew those bright couriers forth;
High on bleak Hampstead's swarthy moor they started for the north;
And on, and on, without a pause, untired they bounded still:
All night from tower to tower they sprang; they sprang from hill to hill;
Till the proud Peak unfurled the flag o'er Darwin's rocky dales;
Till like volcanoes flared to heaven the stormy hills of Wales;

Till twelve fair counties saw the blaze on Malvern's lonely
height;
Till streamed in crimson on the wind the Wrekin's crest of
light;
Till broad and fierce the star came forth on Ely's stately
fane,
And tower and hamlet rose in arms o'er all the boundless
plain;
Till Belvoir's lordly terraces the sign to Lincoln sent,
And Lincoln sped the message on o'er the wide vale of Trent:
Till Skiddaw saw the fire that burned on Gaunt's embattled
pile,
And the red glare on Skiddaw roused the burghers of Carlisle.

*Thomas Babington Macaulay* [1800–1859]

## "GOD SAVE ELIZABETH!"

Let them come, come never so proudly,
O'er the green waves as giants ride;
Silver clarions menacing loudly,
"All the Spains" on their banners wide;
High on deck of the gilded galleys
Our light sailors they scorn below:—
We will scatter them, plague, and shatter them,
Till their flag hauls down to their foe!
For our oath we swear
By the name we bear,
By England's Queen, and England free and fair,—
Her's ever and her's still, come life, come death!
God save Elizabeth!

Sidonia, Recalde, and Leyva
Watch from their bulwarks in swarthy scorn,
Lords and Princes by Philip's favor;—
We by birthright are noble born!
Freemen born of the blood of freemen:
Sons of Creçy and Flodden are we!
We shall sunder them, fire, and plunder them;
English boats on the English sea!

Drake and Frobisher, Hawkins and Howard,
Raleigh, Cavendish, Cecil, and Brooke,
Hang like wasps by the flagships towered,
Sting their way through the thrice-piled oak!
Let them range their seven-mile crescent,
Giant galleons, canvas wide!
Ours will harry them, board, and carry them,
Plucking the plumes of the Spanish pride.

Has God risen in wrath and scattered?
Have His tempests smote them in scorn?
Past the Orcades, dumb and tattered,
'Mong sea-beasts do they drift forlorn?
We were as lions hungry for battle;
God has made our battle His own!
God has scattered them, sunk, and shattered them:
Give the glory to Him alone!
While our oath we swear
By the name we bear,
By England's Queen, and England free and fair,—
Her's ever and her's still, come life, come death!
God save Elizabeth!

*Francis Turner Palgrave* [1824–1897]

## IVRY

[MARCH 14, 1590]

Now glory to the Lord of Hosts, from whom all glories are!
And glory to our Sovereign Liege, King Henry of Navarre!
Now let there be the merry sound of music and of dance,
Through thy corn-fields green, and sunny vines, oh pleasant land of France!
And thou, Rochelle, our own Rochelle, proud city of the waters,
Again let rapture light the eyes of all thy mourning daughters.
As thou wert constant in our ills, be joyous in our joy;
For cold, and stiff, and still are they who wrought thy walls annoy.

Hurrah! hurrah! a single field hath turned the chance of war.
Hurrah! hurrah! for Ivry, and Henry of Navarre.

Oh! how our hearts were beating, when, at the dawn of day
We saw the army of the League drawn out in long array;
With all its priest-led citizens, and all its rebel peers,
And Appenzel's stout infantry, and Egmont's Flemish spears.
There rode the brood of false Lorraine, the curses of our land;
And dark Mayenne was in the midst, a truncheon in his hand;
And, as we looked on them, we thought of Seine's empurpled flood,
And good Coligni's hoary hair all dabbled with his blood;
And we cried unto the living God, who rules the fate of war,
To fight for His own holy name, and Henry of Navarre.

The King is come to marshal us, in all his armor dressed;
And he has bound a snow-white plume upon his gallant crest.
He looked upon his people, and a tear was in his eye;
He looked upon the traitors, and his glance was stern and high.
Right graciously he smiled on us, as rolled from wing to wing,
Down all our line, a deafening shout: "God save our Lord the King!"
"And if my standard-bearer fall, as fall full well he may,
For never saw I promise yet of such a bloody fray,
Press where ye see my white plume shine, amidst the ranks of war,
And be your oriflamme to-day the helmet of Navarre."

Hurrah! the foes are moving. Hark to the mingled din,
Of fife, and steed, and trump, and drum, and roaring culverin.
The fiery Duke is pricking fast across Saint André's plain,
With all the hireling chivalry of Guelders and Almayne.
Now by the lips of those ye love, fair gentlemen of France,
Charge for the golden lilies,—upon them with the lance!
A thousand spurs are striking deep, a thousand spears in rest,
A thousand knights are pressing close behind the snow-white crest;

And in they burst, and on they rushed, while, like a guiding star,
Amidst the thickest carnage blazed the helmet of Navarre.

Now, God be praised, the day is ours. Mayenne hath turned his rein;
D'Aumale hath cried for quarter; the Flemish count is slain.
Their ranks are breaking like thin clouds before a Biscay gale;
The field is heaped with bleeding steeds, and flags, and cloven mail.
And then we thought on vengeance, and, all along our van,
"Remember Saint Bartholomew!" was passed from man to man.
But out spake gentle Henry, "No Frenchman is my foe:
Down, down with every foreigner, but let your brethren go."
Oh! was there ever such a knight, in friendship or in war,
As our Sovereign Lord, King Henry, the soldier of Navarre?

Right well fought all the Frenchmen who fought for France to-day;
And many a lordly banner God gave them for a prey.
But we of the religion have borne us best in fight;
And the good Lord of Rosny hath ta'en the cornet white.
Our own true Maximilian the cornet white hath ta'en,
The cornet white with crosses black, the flag of false Lorraine.
Up with it high; unfurl it wide; that all the host may know
How God hath humbled the proud house which wrought His Church such woe.
Then on the ground, while trumpets sound their loudest point of war,
Fling the red shreds, a footcloth meet for Henry of Navarre.

Ho! maidens of Vienna; ho! matrons of Lucerne;
Weep, weep, and rend your hair for those who never shall return.
Ho! Philip, send, for charity, thy Mexican pistoles,
That Antwerp monks may sing a mass for thy poor spearmen's souls.

Ho! gallant nobles of the League, look that your arms be
bright;
Ho! burghers of St. Genevieve, keep watch and ward to-
night;
For our God hath crushed the tyrant, our God hath raised
the slave,
And mocked the counsel of the wise, and the valor of the
brave.
Then glory to His holy name, from whom all glories are;
And glory to our Sovereign Lord, King Henry of Navarre!

*Thomas Babington Macaulay* [1800–1859]

## THE "REVENGE"

### A BALLAD OF THE FLEET [SEPTEMBER, 1591]

At Florés in the Azores Sir Richard Grenville lay,
And a pinnace, like a fluttered bird, came flying from far
away:
"Spanish ships of war at sea! we have sighted fifty-three!"
Then sware Lord Thomas Howard: "'Fore God I am no
coward;
But I cannot meet them here, for my ships are out of gear,
And the half my men are sick. I must fly, but follow quick.
We are six ships of the line; can we fight with fifty-three?"

Then spake Sir Richard Grenville: "I know you are no
coward;
You fly them for a moment to fight with them again.
But I've ninety men and more that are lying sick ashore.
I should count myself the coward if I left them, my Lord
Howard,
To these Inquisition dogs and the devildoms of Spain."

So Lord Howard passed away with five ships of war that
day,
Till he melted like a cloud in the silent summer heaven;
But Sir Richard bore in hand all his sick men from the land
Very carefully and slow,
Men of Bideford in Devon,

And we laid them on the ballast down below;
For we brought them all aboard,
And they blessed him in their pain, that they were not left
to Spain,
To the thumbscrew and the stake, for the glory of the Lord.

He had only a hundred seamen to work the ship and to fight,
And he sailed away from Florés till the Spaniard came in
sight,
With his huge sea-castles heaving upon the weather bow.
"Shall we fight or shall we fly?
Good Sir Richard, tell us now,
For to fight is but to die!
There'll be little of us left by the time this sun be set."
And Sir Richard said again: "We be all good English men.
Let us bang these dogs of Seville, the children of the devil,
For I never turned my back upon Don or devil yet."

Sir Richard spoke and he laughed, and we roared a hurrah,
and so
The little *Revenge* ran on sheer into the heart of the foe,
With her hundred fighters on deck, and her ninety sick below;
For half of their fleet to the right and half to the left were
seen,
And the little *Revenge* ran on through the long sea-lane
between.

Thousands of their soldiers looked down from their decks
and laughed,
Thousands of their seamen made mock at the mad little craft
Running on and on, till delayed
By their mountain-like *San Philip* that, of fifteen hundred
tons,
And up-shadowing high above us with her yawning tiers of
guns,
Took the breath from our sails, and we stayed.

And while now the great *San Philip* hung above us like a cloud
Whence the thunderbolt will fall
Long and loud,
Four galleons drew away
From the Spanish fleet that day,

And two upon the larboard and two upon the starboard lay,
And the battle-thunder broke from them all.

But anon the great *San Philip*, she bethought herself and went,
Having that within her womb that had left her ill content;
And the rest they came aboard us, and they fought us hand to hand,
For a dozen times they came with their pikes and musqueteers,
And a dozen times we shook 'em off as a dog that shakes his ears
When he leaps from the water to the land.

And the sun went down, and the stars came out far over the summer sea,
But never a moment ceased the fight of the one and the fifty-three,
Ship after ship, the whole night long, their high-built galleons came,
Ship after ship, the whole night long, drew back with her dead and her shame.
For some were sunk and many were shattered, and so could fight us no more—
God of battles, was ever a battle like this in the world before?

For he said, "Fight on! fight on!"
Though his vessel was all but a wreck;
And it chanced that, when half of the short summer night was gone,
With a grisly wound to be dressed he had left the deck,
But a bullet struck him that was dressing it suddenly dead,
And himself he was wounded again in the side and the head,
And he said, "Fight on! fight on!"

And the night went down, and the sun smiled out far over the summer sea,
And the Spanish fleet with broken sides lay round us all in a ring;
But they dared not touch us again, for they feared that we still could sting.

So they watched what the end would be.
And we had not fought them in vain,
But in perilous plight were we,
Seeing forty of our poor hundred were slain,
And half of the rest of us maimed for life
In the crash of the cannonades and the desperate strife;
And the sick men down in the hold were most of them stark
and cold,
And the pikes were all broken or bent, and the powder was
all of it spent;
And the masts and the rigging were lying over the side;
But Sir Richard cried in his English pride,
"We have fought such a fight for a day and a night
As may never be fought again!
We have won great glory, my men!
And a day less or more
At sea or ashore,
We die—does it matter when?
Sink me the ship, Master Gunner—sink her, split her in
twain!
Fall into the hands of God, not into the hands of Spain!"

And the gunner said, "Ay, ay," but the seamen made re-
ply:
"We have children, we have wives,
And the Lord hath spared our lives.
We will make the Spaniard promise, if we yield, to let us go;
We shall live to fight again and to strike another blow."
And the lion there lay dying, and they yielded to the foe.

And the stately Spanish men to their flagship bore him then,
Where they laid him by the mast, old Sir Richard caught at
last,
And they praised him to his face with their courtly foreign
grace;
But he rose upon their decks, and he cried:
"I have fought for Queen and Faith like a valiant man and
true;
I have only done my duty as a man is bound to do.
With a joyful spirit I Sir Richard Grenville die!"
And he fell upon their decks, and he died.

And they stared at the dead that had been so valiant and true,
And had holden the power and glory of Spain so cheap
That he dared her with one little ship and his English few;
Was he devil or man? He was devil for aught they knew,
But they sank his body with honor down into the deep,
And they manned the *Revenge* with a swarthier alien crew,
And away she sailed with her loss and longed for her own;
When a wind from the lands they had ruined awoke from sleep,
And the water began to heave and the weather to moan,
And or ever that evening ended a great gale blew,
And a wave like the wave that is raised by an earthquake grew,
Till it smote on their hulls and their sails and their masts and their flags,
And the whole sea plunged and fell on the shot-shattered navy of Spain,
And the little *Revenge* herself went down by the island crags
To be lost evermore in the main.

*Alfred Tennyson* [1809–1892]

## THE SONG OF THE SPANISH MAIN

Out in the south, when the day is done,
And the gathered winds go free,
Where golden-sanded rivers run,
Fair islands fade in the setting sun,
And the great ships stagger, one by one,
Up from the windy sea.

Out in the south, where a twilight shroud
Hangs o'er the ocean's rim,
Sail on sail, like a floating cloud,
Galleon, brigantine, cannon-browed,
Rich from the Indies, homeward crowd,
Singing a Spanish hymn.

Out in the south, when the sun has set
And the lightning flickers pale,
The cannon bellow their steady threat,

The ships grind, all in a crimson sweat,
And hoarse throats call, "Have ye stricken yet?"
  Across the quarter-rail.

Out in the south, in the dead of night,
  When I hear the thunder speak,
'Tis the Englishmen in their pride and might
Mad with glory and blind with fight,
Locked with the Spaniards, left and right,
  Fighting them cheek to cheek.

Out in the south, when the dawn's pale light
  Walks cold on the beaten shore,
And the mists of night, like clouds of fight,
Silvery violet, blinding bright,
Drift in glory from height to height
  Where the white-tailed eagles soar;

There comes a song through the salt and spray,
  Blood-kin to the ocean's roar,
"All day long down Florez way
Richard Grenville stands at bay.
Come and take him if ye may!"
  Then hush, forevermore.

*John Bennett* [1865–1956]

## HENRY HUDSON'S QUEST

[1609]

Out from the harbor of Amsterdam
  The Half Moon turned her prow to sea;
The coast of Norway dropped behind,
  Yet Northward still kept she
Through the drifting fog and the driving snow,
Where never before man dared to go:
"O Pilot, shall we find the strait that leads to the Eastern
    Sea?"
"A waste of ice before us lies—we must turn back," said he.

Westward they steered their tiny bark,
  Westward through weary weeks they sped,
Till the cold gray strand of a stranger-land
  Loomed through the mist ahead.
League after league they hugged the coast,
And their Captain never left his post:
"O Pilot, see you yet the strait that leads to the Eastern
    Sea?"
"I see but the rocks and the barren shore; no strait is
    there," quoth he.

They sailed to the North—they sailed to the South—
  And at last they rounded an arm of sand
Which held the sea from a harbor's mouth—
  The loveliest in the land;
They kept their course across the bay,
And the shore before them fell away:
"O Pilot, see you not the strait that leads to the Eastern
    sea?"
"Hold the rudder true! Praise Christ Jesu! the strait is
    here," said he.

Onward they glide with wind and tide,
  Past marshes gray and crags sun-kissed;
They skirt the sills of green-clad hills,
  And meadows white with mist—
But alas! the hope and the brave, brave dream!
For rock and shallow bar the stream:
"O Pilot, can this be the strait that leads to the Eastern
    Sea?"
"Nay, Captain, nay; 'tis not this way; turn back we must,"
    said he.

Full sad was Hudson's heart as he turned
  The Half Moon's prow to the South once more;
He saw no beauty in crag or hill,
  No beauty in curving shore;
For they shut him away from that fabled main
He sought his whole life long,—in vain:

"O Pilot, say, can there be a strait that leads to the Eastern Sea?"
"God's crypt is sealed! 'Twill stand revealed in His own good time," quoth he.

*Burton Egbert Stevenson* [1872–

## TO THE VIRGINIAN VOYAGE

[1611]

You brave heroic minds,
Worthy your country's name,
That honor still pursue;
Go and subdue!
Whilst loitering hinds
Lurk here at home, with shame.

Britons, you stay too long:
Quickly aboard bestow you,
And with a merry gale
Swell your stretched sail,
With vows as strong
As the winds that blow you.

Your course securely steer,
West and by south forth keep!
Rocks, lee-shores, nor shoals,
When Eolus scowls,
You need not fear,
So absolute the deep.

And cheerfully at sea,
Success you still entice,
To get the pearl and gold,
And ours to hold
Virginia,
Earth's only paradise;

Where nature hath in store
Fowl, venison, and fish,

And the fruitful'st soil,
Without your toil,
Three harvests more,
All greater than your wish

And the ambitious vine
Crowns with his purple mass
The cedar reaching high
To kiss the sky,
The cypress, pine,
And useful sassafras;

To whom the Golden Age
Still nature's laws doth give,
No other cares attend,
But them to defend
From winter's rage,
That long there doth not live.

When as the luscious smell
Of that delicious land,
Above the seas that flows,
The clear wind throws,
Your hearts to swell
Approaching the dear strand;

In kenning of the shore
(Thanks to God first given)
O you the happiest men,
Be frolic then!
Let cannons roar,
Frighting the wide heaven;

And in regions far,
Such heroes bring ye forth
As those from whom we came,
And plant our name
Under that star
Not known unto our North;

And as there plenty grows
Of laurel everywhere,—
  Apollo's sacred tree,—
  You it may see,
A poet's brows
To crown, that may sing there.

Thy *Voyages* attend
Industrious Hakluyt,
  Whose reading shall inflame
  Men to seek fame,
And much commend
To after-times thy wit.

*Michael Drayton* [1563–1631]

## "THE WORD OF GOD TO LEYDEN CAME"

[AUGUST 15, 1620]

THE word of God to Leyden came,
  Dutch town by Zuyder Zee:
Rise up, my children of no name,
  My kings and priests to be.
There is an empire in the West,
  Which I will soon unfold;
A thousand harvests in her breast,
  Rocks ribbed with iron and gold.

Rise up, my children, time is ripe!
  Old things are passed away.
Bishops and kings from earth I wipe;
  Too long they've had their day.
A little ship have I prepared
  To bear you o'er the seas;
And in your souls, my will declared,
  Shall grow by slow degrees.

Beneath my throne the martyrs cry:
  I hear their voice, How long?
It mingles with their praises high,
  And with their victor song.

The thing they longed and waited for.
But died without the sight;
So, this shall be! I wrong abhor,
The world I'll now set right.

Leave, then, the hammer and the loom,
You've other work to do;
For Freedom's commonwealth there's room,
And you shall build it too.
I'm tired of bishops and their pride,
I'm tired of kings as well;
Henceforth I take the people's side,
And with the people dwell.

Tear off the mitre from the priest,
And from the king, his crown;
Let all my captives be released;
Lift up, whom men cast down.
Their pastors let the people choose,
And choose their rulers too;
Whom they select, I'll not refuse,
But bless the work they do.

The Pilgrims rose, at this, God's word,
And sailed the wintry seas:
With their own flesh nor blood conferred,
Nor thought of wealth or ease.
They left the towers of Leyden town,
They left the Zuyder Zee;
And where they cast their anchor down,
Rose Freedom's realm to be.

*Jeremiah Eames Rankin* [1828–1904]

## THE LANDING OF THE PILGRIM FATHERS

[NOVEMBER 19, 1620]

THE breaking waves dashed high
On a stern and rock-bound coast,
And the woods, against a stormy sky,
Their giant branches tossed;

And the heavy night hung dark
  The hills and waters o'er,
When a band of exiles moored their bark
  On the wild New England shore.

Not as the conqueror comes,
  They, the true-hearted, came:
Not with the roll of the stirring drums,
  And the trumpet that sings of fame;

Not as the flying come,
  In silence and in fear,—
They shook the depths of the desert's gloom
  With their hymns of lofty cheer.

Amidst the storm they sang,
  And the stars heard, and the sea;
And the sounding aisles of the dim woods rang
  To the anthem of the free!

The ocean-eagle soared
  From his nest by the white wave's foam,
And the rocking pines of the forest roared;
  This was their welcome home!

There were men with hoary hair
  Amidst that pilgrim-band;
Why had they come to wither there,
  Away from their childhood's land?

There was woman's fearless eye,
  Lit by her deep love's truth;
There was manhood's brow, serenely high,
  And the fiery heart of youth.

What sought they thus afar?
  Bright jewels of the mine?
The wealth of seas, the spoils of war?—
  They sought a faith's pure shrine!

Aye, call it holy ground,
  The soil where first they trod!
They have left unstained what there they found—
  Freedom to worship God!

*Felicia Dorothea Hemans* [1793-1835]

## THE MAYFLOWER

[DECEMBER 21, 1620]

Down in the bleak December bay
The ghostly vessel stands away;
Her spars and halyards white with ice,
Under the dark December skies.
A hundred souls, in company,
Have left the vessel pensively,—
Have reached the frosty desert there,
And touched it with the knees of prayer.
  And now the day begins to dip,
The night begins to lower
  Over the bay, and over the ship
    Mayflower.

Neither the desert nor the sea
Imposes rites: their prayers are free;
Danger and toil the wild imposes,
And thorns must grow before the roses.
And who are these?—and what distress
The savage-acred wilderness
On mother, maid, and child may bring,
Beseems them for a fearful thing;
  For now the day begins to dip,
The night begins to lower
  Over the bay, and over the ship
    Mayflower.

But Carver leads (in heart and health
A hero of the commonwealth)
The axes that the camp requires,
To build the lodge, and heap the fires.
And Standish from his warlike store
Arrays his men along the shore,

Distributes weapons resonant,
And dons his harness militant;
For now the day begins to dip,
The night begins to lower
Over the bay, and over the ship
Mayflower;

And Rose, his wife, unlocks a chest—
She sees a Book, in vellum dressed,
She drops a tear, and kisses the tome,
Thinking of England and of home:
Might they—the Pilgrims, there and then
Ordained to do the work of men—
Have seen, in visions of the air,
While pillowed on the breast of prayer
(When now the day began to dip,
The night began to lower
Over the bay, and over the ship
Mayflower),

The Canaan of their wilderness
A boundless empire of success;
And seen the years of future nights
Jewelled with myriad household lights;
And seen the honey fill the hive;
And seen a thousand ships arrive;
And heard the wheels of travel go;
It would have cheered a thought of woe,
When now the day began to dip,
The night began to lower
Over the bay, and over the ship
Mayflower.

*Erastus Wolcott Ellsworth* [1822-1902]

## THE PILGRIM FATHERS

The Pilgrim Fathers,—where are they?
The waves that brought them o'er
Still roll in the bay, and throw their spray
As they break along the shore;

Still roll in the bay, as they rolled that day
  When the Mayflower moored below;
When the sea around was black with storms,
  And white the shore with snow.

The mists that wrapped the Pilgrim's sleep
  Still brood upon the tide;
And his rocks yet keep their watch by the deep
  To stay its waves of pride.
But the snow-white sail that he gave to the gale,
  When the heavens looked dark, is gone,—
As an angel's wing through an opening cloud
  Is seen, and then withdrawn.

The pilgrim exile,—sainted name!
  The hill whose icy brow
Rejoiced, when he came, in the morning's flame,
  In the morning's flame burns now.
And the moon's cold light, as it lay that night
  On the hillside and the sea,
Still lies where he laid his houseless head,—
  But the Pilgrim,—where is he?

The Pilgrim Fathers are at rest:
  When summer's throned on high,
And the world's warm breast is in verdure dressed,
  Go, stand on the hill where they lie.
The earliest ray of the golden day
  On that hallowed spot is cast;
And the evening sun, as he leaves the world,
  Looks kindly on that spot last.

The Pilgrim spirit has not fled:
  It walks in noon's broad light;
And it watches the bed of the glorious dead,
  With the holy stars, by night.
It watches the bed of the brave who have bled,
  And still guard this ice-bound shore,
Till the waves of the bay, where the Mayflower lay,
  Shall foam and freeze no more.

*John Pierpont* [1785-1866]

## THE BATTLE OF NASEBY

BY OBADIAH BIND-THEIR-KINGS-IN-CHAINS-AND-THEIR-NOBLES-WITH-LINKS-OF-IRON; SERGEANT IN IRETON'S REGIMENT.

[JUNE 14, 1645]

OH, WHEREFORE come ye forth, in triumph from the North,
With your hands, and your feet, and your raiment all red?
And wherefore doth your rout send forth a joyous shout?
And whence be the grapes of the wine-press that ye tread?

Oh, evil was the root, and bitter was the fruit,
And crimson was the juice of the vintage that we trod;
For we trampled on the throng of the haughty and the strong,
Who sate in the high places and slew the saints of God.

It was about the noon of a glorious day of June,
That we saw their banners dance and their cuirasses shine,
And the Man of Blood was there, with his long essenced hair,
And Astley, and Sir Marmaduke, and Rupert of the Rhine.

Like a servant of the Lord, with his Bible and his sword,
The General rode along us to form us for the fight;
When a murmuring sound broke out, and swelled into a shout
Among the godless horsemen upon the tyrant's right.

And hark! like the roar of the billows on the shore,
The cry of battle rises along their charging line:
For God! for the Cause! for the Church! for the Laws!
For Charles, King of England, and Rupert of the Rhine!

The furious German comes, with his clarions and his drums,
His bravoes of Alsatia, and pages of Whitehall;
They are bursting on our flanks! Grasp your pikes! Close your ranks!
For Rupert never comes but to conquer or to fall.

They are here! They rush on! We are broken! We are
gone!
Our left is borne before them like stubble on the blast.
O Lord, put forth Thy might! O Lord, defend the right!
Stand back to back, in God's name, and fight it to the last!

Stout Skippon hath a wound; the centre hath given ground:
Hark! hark! what means the trampling of horsemen on
our rear?
Whose banner do I see, boys? 'Tis he! thank God! 'tis he,
boys!
Bear up another minute! Brave Oliver is here.

Their heads all stooping low, their points all in a row,
Like a whirlwind on the trees, like a deluge on the dykes,
Our cuirassiers have burst on the ranks of the Accursed,
And at a shock have scattered the forest of his pikes.

Fast, fast the gallants ride, in some safe nook to hide
Their coward heads, predestined to rot on Temple Bar;
And he,—he turns, he flies:—shame on those cruel eyes
That bore to look on torture, and dare not look on war!

Ho! comrades, scour the plain; and, ere ye strip the slain,
First give another stab to make your search secure;
Then shake from sleeves and pockets their broad-pieces and
lockets,
The tokens of the wanton, the plunder of the poor.

Fools! your doublets shone with gold, and your hearts were
gay and bold,
When you kissed your lily hands to your lemans to-day;
And to-morrow shall the fox, from her chamber in the rocks,
Lead forth her tawny cubs to howl above the prey.

Where be your tongues that late mocked at heaven, and hell,
and fate?
And the fingers that once were so busy with your blades?
Your perfumed satin clothes, your catches and your oaths,
Your stage-plays and your sonnets, your diamonds and
your spades?

Down! down! forever down, with the mitre and the crown!
With the Belial of the Court, and the Mammon of the Pope!
There is woe in Oxford halls; there is wail in Durham's stalls;
The Jesuit smites his bosom; the Bishop rends his cope.

And she of the Seven Hills shall mourn her children's ills,
And tremble when she thinks on the edge of England's sword;
And the kings of earth in fear shall shudder when they hear
What the hand of God hath wrought for the Houses and the Word!

*Thomas Babington Macaulay* [1800–1859]

## THE EXECUTION OF MONTROSE

[MAY 21, 1650]

COME hither, Evan Cameron!
Come, stand beside my knee:
I hear the river roaring down
Towards the wintry sea.
There's shouting on the mountain-side,
There's war within the blast;
Old faces look upon me,
Old forms go trooping past:
I hear the pibroch wailing
Amidst the din of fight,
And my dim spirit wakes again
Upon the verge of night.

'Twas I that led the Highland host
Through wild Lochaber's snows,
What time the plaided clans came down
To battle with Montrose.
I've told thee how the Southrons fell
Beneath the broad claymore,
And how we smote the Campbell clan
By Inverlochy's shore.

I've told thee how we swept Dundee,
  And tamed the Lindsays' pride;
But never have I told thee yet
  How the great Marquis died.

A traitor sold him to his foes;—
  O deed of deathless shame!
I charge thee, boy, if e'er thou meet
  With one of Assynt's name—
Be it upon the mountain's side,
  Or yet within the glen,
Stand he in martial gear alone,
  Or backed by armèd men—
Face him, as thou wouldst face the man
  Who wronged thy sire's renown;
Remember of what blood thou art,
  And strike the caitiff down!

They brought him to the Watergate,
  Hard bound with hempen span,
As though they held a lion there,
  And not a fenceless man.
They set him high upon a cart,—
  The hangman rode below,—
They drew his hands behind his back,
  And bared his noble brow.
Then, as a hound is slipped from leash,
  They cheered the common throng,
And blew the note with yell and shout,
  And bade him pass along.

It would have made a brave man's heart
  Grow sad and sick that day,
To watch the keen malignant eyes
  Bent down on that array.
There stood the Whig west-country lords,
  In balcony and bow;
There sat their gaunt and withered dames,
  And their daughters all a-row.

And every open window
  Was full as full might be
With black-robed Covenanting carles,
  That goodly sport to see!

But when he came, though pale and wan,
  He looked so great and high,
So noble was his manly front,
  So calm his steadfast eye,
The rabble rout forebore to shout,
  And each man held his breath,
For well they knew the hero's soul
  Was face to face with death.
And then a mournful shudder
  Through all the people crept,
And some that came to scoff at him
  Now turned aside and wept.

But onwards—always onwards,
  In silence and in gloom,
The dreary pageant labored,
  Till it reached the house of doom.
Then first a woman's voice was heard
  In jeer and laughter loud,
And an angry cry and a hiss arose
  From the heart of the tossing crowd:
Then, as the Graeme looked upwards,
  He saw the ugly smile
Of him who sold his king for gold,—
  The master-fiend Argyle!

The Marquis gazed a moment,
  And nothing did he say,
But Argyle's cheek grew ghastly pale
  And he turned his eyes away.
The painted harlot by his side,
  She shook through every limb,
For a roar like thunder swept the street,
  And hands were clenched at him;

And a Saxon soldier cried aloud,
 "Back, coward, from thy place!
For seven long years thou hast not dared
 To look him in the face."

Had I been there with sword in hand,
 And fifty Camerons by,
That day through high Dunedin's streets
 Had pealed the slogan-cry.
Not all their troops of trampling horse,
 Nor might of mailèd men,
Not all the rebels in the south
 Had borne us backwards then!
Once more his foot on Highland heath
 Had trod as free as air,
Or I, and all who bore my name,
 Been laid around him there!

It might not be. They placed him next
 Within the solemn hall,
Where once the Scottish kings were throned
 Amidst their nobles all.
But there was dust of vulgar feet
 On that polluted floor,
And perjured traitors filled the place
 Where good men sate before.
With savage glee came Warriston
 To read the murderous doom;
And then uprose the great Montrose
 In the middle of the room.

"Now, by my faith as belted knight,
 And by the name I bear,
And by the bright Saint Andrew's cross
 That waves above us there,
Yea, by a greater, mightier oath—
 And oh, that such should be!—
By that dark stream of royal blood
 That lies 'twixt you and me,—

I have not sought in battle-field
  A wreath of such renown,
Nor dared I hope on my dying day
  To win the martyr's crown!

'There is a chamber far away
  Where sleep the good and brave,
But a better place ye have named for me
  Than by my fathers' grave.
For truth and right, 'gainst treason's might,
  This hand hath always striven,
And ye raise it up for a witness still
  In the eye of earth and heaven.
Then nail my head on yonder tower,
  Give every town a limb,—
And God who made shall gather them:
  I go from you to Him!"

The morning dawned full darkly,
  The rain came flashing down,
And the jagged streak of the levin-bolt
  Lit up the gloomy town:
The thunder crashed across the heaven,
  The fatal hour was come;
Yet aye broke in, with muffled beat,
  The 'larum of the drum.
There was madness on the earth below
  And anger in the sky,
And young and old, and rich and poor,
  Came forth to see him die.

Ah, God! that ghastly gibbet!
  How dismal 'tis to see
The great tall spectral skeleton,
  The ladder and the tree!
Hark! hark! it is the clash of arms—
  The bells begin to toll—
"He is coming! he is coming!
  God's mercy on his soul!"

One last long peal of thunder:
  The clouds are cleared away,
And the glorious sun once more looks down
  Amidst the dazzling day.

"He is coming! he is coming!"
  Like a bridegroom from his room,
Came the hero from his prison
  To the scaffold and the doom.
There was glory on his forehead,
  There was luster in his eye,
And he never walked to battle
  More proudly than to die;
There was color in his visage,
  Though the cheeks of all were wan,
And they marvelled as they saw him pass,
  That great and goodly man!

He mounted up the scaffold,
  And he turned him to the crowd;
But they dared not trust the people,
  So he might not speak aloud.
But he looked upon the heavens,
  And they were clear and blue,
And in the liquid ether
  The eye of God shone through;
Yet a black and murky battlement
  Lay resting on the hill,
As though the thunder slept within—
  All else was calm and still.

The grim Geneva ministers
  With anxious scowl drew near,
As you have seen the ravens flock
  Around the dying deer.
He would not deign them word nor sign,
  But alone he bent the knee,
And veiled his face for Christ's dear grace
  Beneath the gallows-tree.

Then radiant and serene he rose,
  And cast his cloak away:
For he had ta'en his latest look
  Of earth and sun and day.

A beam of light fell o'er him,
  Like a glory round the shriven,
And he climbed the lofty ladder
  As it were the path to heaven.
Then came a flash from out the cloud,
  And a stunning thunder-roll;
And no man dared to look aloft,
  For fear was on every soul.
There was another heavy sound,
  A hush and then a groan;
And darkness swept across the sky—
  The work of death was done!

*William Edmondstoune Aytoun* [1813–1865]

## AN HORATIAN ODE UPON CROMWELL'S RETURN FROM IRELAND

[1650]

The forward youth that would appear
Must now forsake his Muses dear,
  Nor in the shadows sing
  His numbers languishing.

'Tis time to leave the books in dust,
And oil the unused armor's rust,
  Removing from the wall
  The corselet of the hall.

So restless Cromwell could not cease
In the inglorious arts of peace,
  But through adventurous war
  Urged his active star;

And, like the three-forked lightning, first
Breaking the clouds where it was nursed,

Did through his own side
His fiery way divide;

For 'tis all one to courage high,
The emulous, or enemy,
And with such, to enclose
Is more than to oppose;—

Then burning through the air he went,
And palaces and temples rent;
And Cæsar's head at last
Did through his laurels blast.

'Tis madness to resist or blame
The face of angry Heaven's flame;
And if we would speak true,
Much to the man is due,

Who, from his private gardens, where
He lived reservèd and austere
(As if his highest plot
To plant the bergamot),

Could by industrious valor climb
To ruin the great work of time,
And cast the Kingdoms old
Into another mould;

Though Justice against Fate complain,
And plead the ancient rights in vain—
But those do hold or break
As men are strong or weak—

Nature, that hateth emptiness,
Allows of penetration less,
And therefore must make room
Where greater spirits come.

What field of all the civil war
Where his were not the deepest scar?
And Hampton shows what part
He had of wiser art;

Where, twining subtle fears with hope,
He wove a net of such a scope
    That Charles himself might chase
    To Caresbrooke's narrow case;

That thence the Royal actor borne
The tragic scaffold might adorn:
    While round the armèd bands
    Did clap their bloody hands.

He nothing common did or mean
Upon that memorable scene,
    But with his keener eye
    The axe's edge did try;

Nor called the gods, with vulgar spite,
To vindicate his helpless right;
    But bowed his comely head
    Down, as upon a bed.

This was that memorable hour
Which first assured the forcèd power:
    So when they did design
    The Capitol's first line,

A Bleeding Head, where they begun,
Did fright the architects to run;
    And yet in that the State
    Foresaw its happy fate!

And now the Irish are ashamed
To see themselves in one year tamed;
    So much one man can do
    That does both act and know.

They can affirm his praises best,
And have, though overcome, confessed
    How good he is, how just
    And fit for highest trust.

Nor yet grown stiffer with command,
But still in the republic's hand—

How fit he is to sway
That can so well obey!

He to the Commons' feet presents
A Kingdom for his first year's rents,
And, what he may, forbears
His fame, to make it theirs:

And has his sword and spoils ungirt
To lay them at the public's skirt.
So when the falcon high
Falls heavy from the sky,

She, having killed, no more doth search
But on the next green bough to perch;
Where, when he first does lure,
The falconer has her sure.

What may not then our Isle presume,
While victory his crest does plume?
What may not others fear,
If thus he crowns each year?

As Cæsar, he, ere long, to Gaul,
To Italy an Hannibal,
And to all States not free
Shall Climacteric be.

The Pict no shelter now shall find
Within his parti-colored mind,
But, from this valor, sad,
Shrink underneath the plaid

Happy, if in the tufted brake
The English hunter him mistake,
Nor lay his hounds in near
The Caledonian deer.

But thou, the war's and fortune's son,
March indefatigably on,
And for the last effect,
Still keep the sword erect:

Besides the force it has to fright
The spirits of the shady night;
The same arts that did gain
A power, must it maintain.

*Andrew Marvell* [1621–1678]

## ON THE LATE MASSACRE IN PIEDMONT

[1655]

Avenge, O Lord, thy slaughtered saints, whose bones
Lie scattered on the Alpine mountains cold;
Even them who kept thy truth so pure of old,
When all our fathers worshipped stocks and stones,
Forget not: in thy book record their groans
Who were thy sheep, and in their ancient fold
Slain by the bloody Piemontese, that rolled
Mother with infant down the rocks. Their moans
The vales redoubled to the hills, and they
To Heaven. Their martyred blood and ashes sow
O'er all the Italian fields, where still doth sway
The triple Tyrant; that from these may grow
A hundred-fold, who, having learnt thy way,
Early may fly the Babylonian woe.

*John Milton* [1608–1674]

## MORGAN

[1668]

Oh, what a set of Vagabundos,
Sons of Neptune, sons of Mars,
Raked from todos otros mundos,
Lascars, Gascons, Portsmouth tars,
Prison mate and dock-yard fellow,
Blades to Meg and Molly dear,
Off to capture Porto Bello
Sailed with Morgan the Buccaneer!

Out they voyaged from Port Royal
(Fathoms deep its ruins be,
Pier and convent, fortress loyal,
Sunk beneath the gaping sea);

On the Spaniard's beach they landed,
  Dead to pity, void of fear,—
Round their blood-red flag embanded,
  Led by Morgan the Buccaneer.

Dawn till dusk they stormed the castle,
  Beat the gates and gratings down;
Then, with ruthless rout and wassail,
  Night and day they sacked the town,
Staved the bins its cellars boasted,
  Port and Lisbon, tier on tier,
Quaffed to heart's content, and toasted
  Harry Morgan the Buccaneer:

Stripped the church and monastery,
  Racked the prior for his gold,
With the traders' wives made merry,
  Lipped the young and mocked the old,
Diced for hapless señoritas
  (Sire and brother bound anear),—
Juanas, Lolas, Manuelitas,
  Cursing Morgan the Buccaneer.

Lust and rapine, flame and slaughter,
  Forayed with the Welshman grim:
"Take my pesos, spare my daughter!"
  "Ha! ha!" roared that devil's limb,
"These shall jingle in our pouches,
  She with us shall find good cheer."
"Lash the graybeard till he crouches!"
  Shouted Morgan the Buccaneer.

Out again through reef and breaker,
  While the Spaniard moaned his fate,
Back they voyaged to Jamaica,
  Flush with doubloons, coins of eight,
Crosses wrung from Popish varlets,
  Jewels torn from arm and ear,—
Jesu! how the Jews and harlots
  Welcomed Morgan the Buccaneer!

*Edmund Clarence Stedman* [1833–1908]

## THE LAMENTABLE BALLAD OF THE BLOODY BROOK

[SEPTEMBER 18, 1675]

COME listen to the Story of brave Lathrop and his Men,—
How they fought, how they died,
When they marched against the Red Skins in the Autumn Days, and then
How they fell, in their pride,
By Pocumtuck Side.

"Who will go to Deerfield Meadows and bring the ripened Grain?"
Said old Mosely to his men in Array.
"Take the Wagons and the Horses, and bring it back again:
But be sure that no Man stray
All the Day, on the Way."

Then the Flower of Essex started, with Lathrop at their head,
Wise and brave, bold and true.
He had fought the Pequots long ago, and now to Mosely said,
"Be there Many, be there Few,
I will bring the Grain to you."

They gathered all the Harvest, and marched back on their Way,
Through the Woods which blazed like Fire.
No Soldier left the Line of march to wander or to stray,
Till the Wagons were stalled in the Mire,
And the Beasts began to tire.

The Wagons have all forded the Brook as it flows,
And then the Rear-Guard stays
To pick the purple Grapes that are hanging from the Boughs,
When, crack!—to their Amaze,
A hundred Fire-locks blaze!

Brave Lathrop, he lay dying; but as he fell he cried,
"Each Man to his Tree," said he,
"Let no one yield an Inch;" and so the Soldier died;
And not a Man of all can see
Where the Foe can be.

And Philip and his Devils pour in their Shot so fast,
From behind and before,
That Man after Man is shot down and breathes his last.
Every Man lies dead in his Gore
To fight no more,—no more!

Oh, weep, ye Maids of Essex, for the Lads who have died,-
The Flower of Essex they!
The Bloody Brook still ripples by the black Mountain-side,
But never shall they come again to see the ocean-tide,
And never shall the Bridegroom return to his Bride,
From that dark and cruel Day,—cruel Day!

*Edward Everett Hale* [1822–1909]

## THE SONG OF THE WESTERN MEN

[1688]

A GOOD sword and a trusty hand!
A merry heart and true!
King James's men shall understand
What Cornish lads can do.

And have they fixed the where and when?
And shall Trelawny die?
Here's twenty thousand Cornish men
Will know the reason why!

Out spake their captain brave and bold,
A merry wight was he:
"If London Tower were Michael's hold,
We'll set Trelawny free!

"We'll cross the Tamar, land to land,
The Severn is no stay,
With 'One and all!' and hand in hand,
And who shall bid us nay?

"And when we come to London Wall,
A pleasant sight to view,
Come forth! come forth, ye cowards all,
Here's men as good as you!

"Trelawny he's in keep and hold,
Trelawny he may die;
But here's twenty thousand Cornish bold
Will know the reason why!"

*Robert Stephen Hawker* [1803–1875]

## BONNIE DUNDEE

From "The Doom of Devoirgoil"

[1689]

To the Lords of Convention 'twas Claver'se who spoke,
"Ere the King's crown shall fall, there are crowns to be broke;
So let each Cavalier who loves honor and me
Come follow the bonnet of Bonnie Dundee!

*"Come fill up my cup, come fill up my can,*
*Come saddle your horses, and call up your men;*
*Come open the West Port and let me gang free,*
*And it's room for the bonnets of Bonnie Dundee!"*

Dundee he is mounted, he rides up the street,
The bells are rung backward, the drums they are beat;
But the Provost, douce man, said, "Just e'en let him be,
The Gude Town is well quit of that deil of Dundee!"

As he rode doun the sanctified bends of the Bow,
Ilk carline was flyting and shaking her pow;
But the young plants of grace they looked couthie and slee,
Thinking, Luck to thy bonnet, thou Bonnie Dundee!

With sour-featured Whigs the Grass-market was thranged,
As if half the West had set tryst to be hanged;
There was spite in each look, there was fear in each e'e,
As they watched for the bonnets of Bonnie Dundee.

These cowls of Kilmarnock had spits and had spears,
And lang-hafted gullies to kill cavaliers;
But they shrunk to close-heads, and the causeway was free
At the toss of the bonnet of Bonnie Dundee.

He spurred to the foot of the proud Castle rock,
And with the gay Gordon he gallantly spoke:
"Let Mons Meg and her marrows speak twa words or three,
For the love of the bonnet of Bonnie Dundee."

The Gordon demands of him which way he goes.
"Where'er shall direct me the shade of Montrose!
Your Grace in short space shall hear tidings of me,
Or that low lies the bonnet of Bonnie Dundee.

"There are hills beyond Pentland, and lands beyond Forth;
If there's lords in the Lowlands, there's chiefs in the North;
There are wild Duniewassals three thousand times three
Will cry 'Hoigh!' for the bonnet of Bonnie Dundee.

"There's brass on the target of barkened bull-hide,
There's steel in the scabbard that dangles beside;
The brass shall be burnished, the steel shall flash free,
At a toss of the bonnet of Bonnie Dundee.

"Away to the hills, to the caves, to the rocks,—
Ere I own an usurper, I'll couch with the fox;
And tremble, false Whigs, in the midst of your glee,
You have not seen the last of my bonnet and me!"

He waved his proud hand, and the trumpets were blown,
The kettle-drums clashed, and the horsemen rode on,
Till on Ravelston's cliffs and on Clermiston's lea
Died away the wild war-notes of Bonnie Dundee.

*Walter Scott* [1771–1832]

## A BALLAD OF SARSFIELD

[1690]

Sarsfield went out the Dutch to rout,
And to take and break their cannon;
To Mass went he at half-past three,
And at four he crossed the Shannon.

Tirconnel slept. In dream his thoughts
Old fields of victory ran on;
And the chieftains of Thomond in Limerick's towers
Slept well by the banks of Shannon.

He rode ten miles and he crossed the ford,
And couched in the wood and waited;
Till, left and right, on marched in sight
That host which the true men hated.

"Charge!" Sarsfield cried; and the green hill-side
As they charged replied in thunder;
They rode o'er the plain and they rode o'er the slain
And the rebel rout lay under.

The spark flashed out—like a sailor's shout
The sound into heaven ascended;
The hosts of the sky made to earth reply,
And the thunders twain were blended!

Sarsfield went out the Dutch to rout,
And to take and break their cannon;—
A century after, Sarsfield's laughter
Was echoed from Dungannon.

*Aubrey Thomas De Vere* [1814–1902]

## THE BATTLE OF BLENHEIM

[August 13, 1704]

It was a summer evening;
Old Kaspar's work was done,
And he before his cottage-door
Was sitting in the sun;
And by him sported on the green
His little grandchild, Wilhelmine.

She saw her brother Peterkin
Roll something large and round,
That he beside the rivulet,
In playing there, had found:
She ran to ask what he had found,
That was so large and smooth and round.

Old Kaspar took it from the boy,
Who stood expectant by;
And then the old man shook his head,
And with a natural sigh,
"'Tis some poor fellow's skull," said he
"Who fell in the great victory.

"I find them in my garden,
For there's many here about;
And often, when I go to plough,
The ploughshare turns them out;
For many thousand men," said he,
"Were slain in that great victory."

"Now tell us what 'twas all about,"
Young Peterkin, he cries;
And little Wilhelmine looks up
With wonder-waiting eyes;
"Now tell us all about the war,
And what they fought each other for."

"It was the English," Kaspar cried,
"Who put the French to rout;
But what they fought each other for
I could not well make out;
But everybody said," quoth he,
"That 'twas a famous victory.

"My father lived at Blenheim then,
Yon little stream hard by;
They burned his dwelling to the ground,
And he was forced to fly;
So with his wife and child he fled,
Nor had he where to rest his head.

"With fire and sword the country round
Was wasted far and wide,
And many a childing mother then,
And new-born baby, died;
But things like that, you know, must be
At every famous victory.

"They say it was a shocking sight
After the field was won;
For many thousand bodies here
Lay rotting in the sun:
But things like that, you know, must be
After a famous victory.

"Great praise the Duke of Marlborough won
And our good Prince Eugene."
"Why, 'twas a very wicked thing!"
Said little Wilhelmine.
"Nay, nay, my little girl," quoth he,
"It was a famous victory.

"And everybody praised the Duke,
Who this great fight did win."
"But what good came of it at last?"
Quoth little Peterkin.
"Why, that I cannot tell," said he;
"But 'twas a famous victory."

*Robert Southey* [1774-1843]

## LOVEWELL'S FIGHT

[MAY 8, 1725]

Of worthy Captain Lovewell I purpose now to sing,
How valiantly he served his country and his King;
He and his valiant soldiers did range the woods full wide,
And hardships they endured to quell the Indian's pride.

'Twas nigh unto Pigwacket, on the eighth day of May,
They spied a rebel Indian soon after break of day;
He on a bank was walking, upon a neck of land,
Which leads into a pond, as we're made to understand.

Our men resolved to have him, and travelled two miles round
Until they met the Indian, who boldly stood his ground;
Then spake up Captain Lovewell, "Take you good heed," says he,
"This rogue is to decoy us, I very plainly see.

"The Indians lie in ambush, in some place nigh at hand,
In order to surround us upon this neck of land;
Therefore we'll march in order, and each man leave his pack
That we may briskly fight them, when they make their attack."

They came unto this Indian, who did them thus defy,
As soon as they came nigh him, two guns he did let fly,
Which wounded Captain Lovewell, and likewise one man more,
But when this rogue was running, they laid him in his gore.

Then having scalped the Indian, they went back to the spot
Where they had laid their packs down, but there they found them not,
For the Indians having spied them, when they them down did lay,
Did seize them for their plunder, and carry them away.

These rebels lay in ambush, this very place hard by,
So that an English soldier did one of them espy,
And cried out, "Here's an Indian!" With that they started out,
As fiercely as old lions, and hideously did shout.

With that our valiant English all gave a loud huzza,
To show the rebel Indians they feared them not a straw:
So now the fight began, and as fiercely as could be,
The Indians ran up to them, but soon were forced to flee.

Then spake up Captain Lovewell, when first the fight began:
"Fight on, my valiant heroes! you see they fall like rain."
For as we are informed, the Indians were so thick
A man could scarcely fire a gun and not some of them hit.

Then did the rebels try their best our soldiers to surround,
But they could not accomplish it, because there was a pond
To which our men retreated, and covered all the rear;
The rogues were forced to face them, although they skulked
for fear.

Two logs there were behind them, that close together lay,
Without being discovered, they could not get away;
Therefore our valiant English they travelled in a row,
And at a handsome distance, as they were wont to go.

'Twas ten o'clock in the morning when first the fight begun,
And fiercely did continue until the setting sun;
Excepting that the Indians some hours before 'twas night
Drew off into the bushes and ceased awhile to fight;

But soon again returned, in fierce and furious mood,
Shouting as in the morning, but yet not half so loud;
For as we are informed, so thick and fast they fell,
Scarce twenty of their number at night did get home well.

And that our valiant English till midnight there did stay,
To see whether the rebels would have another fray;
But they no more returning, they made off towards their
home,
And brought away their wounded as far as they could come.

Of all our valiant English there were but thirty-four,
And of the rebel Indians there were about fourscore.
And sixteen of our English did safely home return,
The rest were killed and wounded, for which we all must
mourn.

Our worthy Captain Lovewell among them there did die,
They killed Lieutenant Robbins, and wounded good young
Frye,
Who was our English Chaplain; he many Indians slew,
And some of them he scalped when bullets round him flew.

Young Fullam, too, I'll mention, because he fought so well;
Endeavoring to save a man, a sacrifice he fell:

But yet our valiant Englishmen in fight were ne'er dismayed,
But still they kept their motion, and Wymans Captain made,

Who shot the old chief Paugus, which did the foe defeat,
Then set his men in order, and brought off the retreat;
And, braving many dangers and hardships in the way,
They safe arrived at Dunstable, the thirteenth day of May

*Unknown*

## ADMIRAL HOSIER'S GHOST

### WRITTEN ON THE TAKING OF CARTHAGENA FROM THE SPANIARDS, 1739

As near Portobello lying
On the gently-swelling flood,
At midnight, with streamers flying,
Our triumphant navy rode;
There while Vernon sat all-glorious
From the Spaniards' late defeat,
And his crews, with shouts victorious,
Drank success to England's fleet:

On a sudden, shrilly sounding,
Hideous yells and shrieks were heard;
Then, each heart with fear confounding,
A sad troop of ghosts appeared;
All in dreary hammocks shrouded,
Which for winding-sheets they wore,
And, with looks by sorrow clouded,
Frowning on that hostile shore.

On them gleamed the moon's wan lustre,
When the shade of Hosier brave
His pale bands was seen to muster,
Rising from their watery grave:
O'er the glimmering wave he hied him,
Where the Burford reared her sail,
With three thousand ghosts beside him,
And in groans did Vernon hail.

"Heed, oh, heed our fatal story!
  I am Hosier's injured ghost;
You who now have purchased glory
  At this place where I was lost:
Though in Portobello's ruin,
  You now triumph free from fears,
When you think on our undoing,
  You will mix your joys with tears.

"See these mournful spectres sweeping
  Ghastly o'er this hated wave,
Whose wan cheeks are stained with weeping;
  These were English captains brave.
Mark those numbers, pale and horrid,
  Who were once my sailors bold;
Lo! each hangs his drooping forehead,
  While his dismal tale is told.

"I, by twenty sail attended,
  Did this Spanish town affright;
Nothing then its wealth defended
  But my orders—not to fight!
Oh! that in this rolling ocean
  I had cast them with disdain,
And obeyed my heart's warm motion,
  To have quelled the pride of Spain!

"For resistance I could fear none;
  But with twenty ships had done
What thou, brave and happy Vernon,
  Hast achieved with six alone.
Then the Bastimentos never
  Had our foul dishonor seen,
Nor the sea the sad receiver
  Of this gallant train had been.

"Thus, like thee, proud Spain dismaying,
  And her galleons leading home,
Though condemned for disobeying,
  I had met a traitor's doom:

To have fallen, my country crying,
'He has played an English part,'
Had been better far than dying
Of a grieved and broken heart.

"Unrepining at thy glory,
Thy successful arms we hail;
But remember our sad story,
And let Hosier's wrongs prevail.
Sent in this foul clime to languish,
Think what thousands fell in vain,
Wasted with disease and anguish,
Not in glorious battle slain.

"Hence with all my train attending,
From their oozy tombs below,
Through the hoary foam ascending,
Here I feed my constant woe.
Here the Bastimentos viewing,
We recall our shameful doom,
And, our plaintive cries renewing,
Wander through the midnight gloom.

"O'er these waves forever mourning
Shall we roam, deprived of rest,
If, to Britain's shores returning,
You neglect my just request;
After this proud foe subduing,
When your patriot friends you see,
Think on vengeance for my ruin,
And for England—shamed in me."

*Richard Glover* [1712–1785]

## FONTENOY

[APRIL 30, 1745]

THRICE at the huts of Fontenoy the English column failed,
And twice the lines of Saint Antoine the Dutch in vain assailed;
For town and slope were filled with fort and flanking battery,
And well they swept the English ranks and Dutch auxiliary.

As vainly through De Barri's wood the British soldiers burst,
The French artillery drove them back, diminished and dispersed.
The bloody Duke of Cumberland beheld with anxious eye,
And ordered up his last reserve, his latest chance to try.
On Fontenoy, on Fontenoy, how fast his generals ride!
And mustering come his chosen troops, like clouds at eventide.

Six thousand English veterans in stately column tread;
Their cannon blaze in front and flank, Lord Hay is at their head.
Steady they step a-down the slope, steady they climb the hill,
Steady they load, steady they fire, moving right onward still,
Betwixt the wood and Fontenoy, as through a furnace-blast,
Through rampart, trench, and palisade, and bullets showering fast;
And on the open plain above they rose and kept their course,
With ready fire and grim resolve that mocked at hostile force:
Past Fontenoy, past Fontenoy, while thinner grow their ranks,
They break, as broke the Zuyder Zee through Holland's ocean-banks.

More idly than the summer flies, French tirailleurs rush round;
As stubble to the lava-tide, French squadrons strew the ground;
Bombshell and grape and round-shot tore, still on they marched and fired;
Fast, from each volley, grenadier and voltigeur retired.
"Push on my household cavalry!" King Louis madly cried.
To death they rush, but rude their shock; not unavenged they died.
On through the camp the column trod—King Louis turns his rein.
"Not yet, my liege," Saxe interposed; "the Irish troops remain."

And Fontenoy, famed Fontenoy, had been a Waterloo,
Had not these exiles ready been, fresh, vehement, and true.

"Lord Clare," he said, "you have your wish; there are your Saxon foes!"
The Marshal almost smiles to see, so furiously he goes.
How fierce the look these exiles wear, who're wont to be so gay!
The treasured wrongs of fifty years are in their hearts to-day:
The treaty broken, ere the ink wherewith 'twas writ could dry;
Their plundered homes, their ruined shrines, their women's parting cry;
Their priesthood hunted down like wolves, their country overthrown—
Each looks as if revenge for all were staked on him alone.
On Fontenoy, on Fontenoy, nor ever yet elsewhere,
Rushed on to fight a nobler band than these proud exiles were.

O'Brien's voice is hoarse with joy, as, halting, he commands:
"Fix bayonets—charge!" Like mountain-storm rush on those fiery bands.
Thin is the English column now, and faint their volleys grow,
Yet, mustering all the strength they have, they make a gallant show.
They dress their ranks upon the hill, to face that battle-wind!
Their bayonets the breakers' foam, like rocks the men behind!
One volley crashes from their line, when, through the surging smoke,
With empty guns clutched in their hands, the headlong Irish broke.
On Fontenoy, on Fontenoy, hark to that fierce huzza:
"Revenge! remember Limerick! dash down the Sacsanagh!"

Like lions leaping at a fold, when mad with hunger's pang,
Right up against the English line the Irish exiles sprang;
Bright was their steel, 'tis bloody now, their guns are filled with gore;
Through shattered ranks and severed files and trampled flags they tore.
The English strove with desperate strength, paused, rallied, staggered, fled;
The green hillside is matted close with dying and with dead.
Across the plain and far away passed on that hideous wrack,
While cavalier and fantassin dash in upon their track.
On Fontenoy, on Fontenoy, like eagles in the sun,
With bloody plumes, the Irish stand—the field is fought and won!

*Thomas Osborne Davis* [1814–1845]

## LAMENT FOR CULLODEN

[APRIL 16, 1746]

THE lovely lass o' Inverness,
Nae joy nor pleasure can she see;
For e'en and morn she cries, Alas!
And aye the saut tear blins her e'e:
Drumossie moor—Drumossie day—
A waefu' day it was to me!
For there I lost my father dear,
My father dear, and brethren three.

Their winding-sheet the bluidy clay,
Their graves are growing green to see:
And by them lies the dearest lad
That ever blest a woman's e'e!
Now wae to thee, thou cruel lord,
A bluidy man I trow thou be;
For mony a heart thou hast made sair
That ne'er did wrang to thine or thee.

*Robert Burns* [1759–1796]

## A BALLAD OF THE FRENCH FLEET

[OCTOBER 15, 1746]

MR. THOMAS PRINCE, *loquitur*

A FLEET with flags arrayed
Sailed from the port of Brest,
And the Admiral's ship displayed
The signal: "Steer southwest."
For this Admiral D'Anville
Had sworn by cross and crown
To ravage with fire and steel
Our helpless Boston Town.

There were rumors in the street,
In the houses there was fear
Of the coming of the fleet,
And the danger hovering near.
And while from mouth to mouth
Spread the tidings of dismay,
I stood in the Old South,
Saying humbly: "Let us pray!

"O Lord! we would not advise;
But if in thy Providence
A tempest should arise
To drive the French Fleet hence,
And scatter it far and wide,
Or sink it in the sea,
We should be satisfied,
And thine the glory be."

This was the prayer I made,
For my soul was all on flame,
And even as I prayed
The answering tempest came;
It came with a mighty power,
Shaking the windows and walls,
And tolling the bell in the tower,
As it tolls at funerals.

The lightning suddenly
  Unsheathed its flaming sword,
And I cried: "Stand still, and see
  The salvation of the Lord!"
The heavens were black with cloud,
  The sea was white with hail,
And ever more fierce and loud
  Blew the October gale.

The fleet it overtook,
  And the broad sails in the van
Like the tents of Cushan shook,
  Or the curtains of Midian.
Down on the reeling decks
  Crashed the o'erwhelming seas:
Ah, never were there wrecks
  So pitiful as these!

Like a potter's vessel broke
  The great ships of the line;
They were carried away as a smoke,
  Or sank like lead in the brine.
O Lord! before thy path
  They vanished and ceased to be,
When thou didst walk in wrath
  With thine horses through the sea!

*Henry Wadsworth Longfellow* [1807–1882]

## PAUL REVERE'S RIDE

From "Tales of a Wayside Inn"

[APRIL 18–19, 1775]

LISTEN, my children, and you shall hear
Of the midnight ride of Paul Revere,
On the eighteenth of April, in seventy-five;
Hardly a man is now alive
Who remembers that famous day and year.

He said to his friend, "If the British march
By land or sea from the town to-night,
Hang a lantern aloft in the belfry arch
Of the North Church tower as a signal light,—
One, if by land, and two, if by sea;
And I on the opposite shore will be,
Ready to ride and spread the alarm
Through every Middlesex village and farm,
For the country folk to be up and to arm."

Then he said, "Good night!" and with muffled oar
Silently rowed to the Charlestown shore,
Just as the moon rose over the bay,
Where swinging wide at her moorings lay
The Somerset, British man-of-war;
A phantom ship, with each mast and spar
Across the moon like a prison bar,
And a huge black hulk, that was magnified
By its own reflection in the tide.

Meanwhile, his friend, through alley and street,
Wanders and watches with eager ears,
Till in the silence around him he hears
The muster of men at the barrack door,
The sound of arms, and the tramp of feet,
And the measured tread of the grenadiers,
Marching down to their boats on the shore.

Then he climbed the tower of the Old North Church
By the wooden stairs, with stealthy tread,
To the belfry-chamber overhead,
And startled the pigeons from their perch
On the sombre rafters, that round him made
Masses and moving shapes of shade,—
By the trembling ladder, steep and tall,
To the highest window in the wall,
Where he paused to listen and look down
A moment on the roofs of the town,
And the moonlight flowing over all.

Beneath in the churchyard, lay the dead,
In their night-encampment on the hill,
Wrapped in silence so deep and still
That he could hear, like a sentinel's tread,
The watchful night-wind, as it went
Creeping along from tent to tent,
And seeming to whisper, "All is well!"
A moment only he feels the spell
Of the place and the hour, and the secret dread
Of the lonely belfry and the dead;
For suddenly all his thoughts are bent
On a shadowy something far away,
Where the river widens to meet the bay,—
A line of black that bends and floats
On the rising tide, like a bridge of boats.

Meanwhile, impatient to mount and ride,
Booted and spurred, with a heavy stride
On the opposite shore walked Paul Revere.
Now he patted his horse's side,
Now gazed at the landscape far and near,
Then, impetuous, stamped the earth,
And turned and tightened his saddle-girth;
But mostly he watched with eager search
The belfry-tower of the Old North Church,
As it rose above the graves on the hill,
Lonely and spectral and sombre and still.
And lo! as he looks, on the belfry's height
A glimmer, and then a gleam of light!
He springs to the saddle, the bridle he turns,
But lingers and gazes, till full on his sight
A second lamp in the belfry burns!

A hurry of hoofs in a village street,
A shape in the moonlight, a bulk in the dark,
And beneath, from the pebbles, in passing, a spark
Struck out by a steed flying fearless and fleet:
That was all! And yet, through the gloom and the light,
The fate of a nation was riding that night;
And the spark struck out by that steed, in his flight
Kindled the land into flame with its heat.

He has left the village and mounted the steep,
And beneath him, tranquil and broad and deep,
Is the Mystic, meeting the ocean tides;
And under the alders that skirt its edge,
Now soft on the sand, now loud on the ledge,
Is heard the tramp of his steed as he rides.

It was twelve by the village clock,
When he crossed the bridge into Medford town.
He heard the crowing of the cock,
And the barking of the farmer's dog,
And felt the damp of the river fog,
That rises after the sun goes down.

It was one by the village clock,
When he galloped into Lexington.
He saw the gilded weathercock
Swim in the moonlight as he passed.
And the meeting-house windows, blank and bare,
Gaze at him with a spectral glare,
As if they already stood aghast
At the bloody work they would look upon.

It was two by the village clock,
When he came to the bridge in Concord town.
He heard the bleating of the flock,
And the twitter of birds among the trees,
And felt the breath of the morning breeze
Blowing over the meadows brown.
And one was safe and asleep in his bed
Who at the bridge would be first to fall,
Who that day would be lying dead,
Pierced by a British musket-ball.

You know the rest. In the books you have read,
How the British Regulars fired and fled,—
How the farmers gave them ball for ball,
From behind each fence and farmyard wall,
Chasing the red-coats down the lane,
Then crossing the fields to emerge again
Under the trees at the turn of the road,
And only pausing to fire and load.

So through the night rode Paul Revere;
And so through the night went his cry of alarm
To every Middlesex village and farm,—
A cry of defiance and not of fear,
A voice in the darkness, a knock at the door,
And a word that shall echo forevermore!
For, borne on the night-wind of the Past,
Through all our history, to the last,
In the hour of darkness and peril and need,
The people will waken and listen to hear
The hurrying hoof-beats of that steed,
And the midnight message of Paul Revere.

*Henry Wadsworth Longfellow* [1807–1882]

## NEW ENGLAND'S CHEVY CHASE

[APRIL 19, 1775]

'TWAS the dead of the night. By the pineknot's red light
Brooks lay, half-asleep, when he heard the alarm,—
Only this, and no more, from a voice at the door:
"The Red-Coats are out, and have passed Phips's farm."

Brooks was booted and spurred; he said never a word:
Took his horn from its peg, and his gun from the rack;
To the cold midnight air he led out his white mare,
Strapped the girths and the bridle, and sprang to her back.

Up the North County road at her full pace she strode,
Till Brooks reined her up at John Tarbell's to say,
"We have got the alarm,—they have left Phips's farm;
You rouse the East Precinct, and I'll go this way."

John called his hired man, and they harnessed the span;
They roused Abram Garfield, and Abram called me:
"Turn out right away; let no minute-man stay;
The Red-Coats have landed at Phips's," says he.

By the Powder-House Green seven others fell in;
At Nahum's the men from the Saw-Mill came down;
So that when Jabez Bland gave the word of command,
And said, "Forward, march!" there marched forward THE TOWN.

Parson Wilderspin stood by the side of the road,
And he took off his hat, and he said, "Let us pray!
O Lord, God of might, let thine angels of light
Lead thy children to-night to the glories of day!
And let thy stars fight all the foes of the Right
As the stars fought of old against Sisera."

And from heaven's high arch those stars blessed our march,
Till the last of them faded in twilight away;
And with morning's bright beam, by the banks of the stream
Half the county marched in, and we heard Davis say:

"On the King's own highway I may travel all day,
And no man hath warrant to stop me," says he;
"I've no man that's afraid, and I'll march at their head."
Then he turned to the boys, "Forward, march! Follow me."

And we marched as he said, and the Fifer he played
The old "White Cockade," and he played it right well.
We saw Davis fall dead, but no man was afraid;
That bridge we'd have had, though a thousand men fell.

This opened the play, and it lasted all day.
We made Concord too hot for the Red-Coats to stay;
Down the Lexington way we stormed, black, white, and gray
We were first in the feast, and were last in the fray.

They would turn in dismay, as red wolves turn at bay.
They levelled, they fired, they charged up the road.
Cephas Willard fell dead; he was shot in the head
As he knelt by Aunt Prudence's well-sweep to load.

John Danforth was hit just in Lexington Street,
John Bridge at that lane where you cross Beaver Falls,
And Winch and the Snows just above John Munroe's—
Swept away by one swoop of the big cannon-balls.

I took Bridge on my knee, but he said, "Don't mind me;
Fill your horn from mine,—let me lie where I be.
Our fathers," says he, "that their sons might be free,
Left their king on his throne, and came over the sea;
And that man is a knave, or a fool who, to save
His life for a minute, would live like a slave."

Well, all would not do! There were men good as new,—
From Rumford, from Saugus, from towns far away,--
Who filled up quick and well for each soldier that fell;
And we drove them, and drove them, and drove them, all day.
We knew, every one, it was war that begun,
When that morning's marching was only half done.

In the hazy twilight, at the coming of night,
I crowded three buckshot and one bullet down.
'Twas my last charge of lead; and I aimed her and said,
"Good luck to you, lobsters, in old Boston Town."

In a barn at Milk Row, Ephraim Bates and Munroe,
And Baker, and Abram, and I made a bed.
We had mighty sore feet, and we'd nothing to eat;
But we'd driven the Red-Coats, and Amos, he said:
"It's the first time," says he, "that it's happened to me
To march to the sea by this road where we've come;
But confound this whole day, but we'd all of us say
We'd rather have spent it this way than to home."

The hunt had begun with the dawn of the sun,
And night saw the wolf driven back to his den.
And never since then, in the memory of men,
Has the Old Bay State seen such a hunting again.

*Edward Everett Hale* [1822-1909]

## WARREN'S ADDRESS AT BUNKER HILL

[JUNE 16-17, 1775]

STAND! the ground's your own, my braves!
Will ye give it up to slaves?
Will ye look for greener graves?

Hope ye mercy still?
What's the mercy despots feel?
Hear it in that battle-peal!
Read it on yon bristling steel!
Ask it,—ye who will.

Fear ye foes who kill for hire?
Will ye to your homes retire?
Look behind you!—they're afire!
And, before you, see
Who have done it! From the vale
On they come—and will ye quail?
Leaden rain and iron hail
Let their welcome be!

In the God of battles trust!
Die we may,—and die we must:
But, O, where can dust to dust
Be consigned so well,
As where heaven its dews shall shed
On the martyred patriot's bed,
And the rocks shall raise their head,
Of his deeds to tell?

*John Pierpont* [1785–1866]

## THE MARYLAND BATTALION

[BATTLE OF LONG ISLAND, AUGUST 27, 1776]

SPRUCE Macaronis, and pretty to see,
Tidy and dapper and gallant were we;
Blooded fine gentlemen, proper and tall,
Bold in a fox-hunt, and gay at a ball;
Prancing soldados, so martial and bluff,
Billets for bullets, in scarlet and buff—
But our cockades were clasped with a mother's low prayer,
And the sweethearts that braided the swordknots were fair.

There was grummer of drums humming hoarse in the hills,
And the bugles sang fanfaron down by the mills;
By Flatbush the bagpipes were droning amain,
And keen cracked the rifles in Martense's lane;
For the Hessians were flecking the hedges with red,
And the grenadiers' tramp marked the roll of the dead.

Three to one, flank and rear, flashed the files of St. George,
The fierce gleam of their steel as the glow of a forge.
The brutal boom-boom of their swart cannoneers
Was sweet music compared with the taunt of their cheers—
For the brunt of their onset, our crippled array,
And the light of God's leading gone out in the fray!

Oh, the rout on the left and the tug on the right!
The mad plunge of the charge and the wreck of the flight!
When the cohorts of Grant held stout Stirling at strain,
And the mongrels of Hesse went tearing the slain;
When at Freeke's Mill the flumes and the sluices ran red,
And the dead choked the dyke and the marsh choked the
dead!

"Oh, Stirling, good Stirling! how long must we wait?
Shall the shout of your trumpet unleash us too late?
Have you never a dash for brave Mordecai Gist,
With his heart in his throat, and his blade in his fist?
Are we good for no more than to prance in a ball,
When the drums beat the charge and the clarions call?"

Tralára, Tralára! Now praise we the Lord,
For the clang of His call and the flash of His sword!
Tralára! Tralára! Now forward to die;
For the banner, hurrah! and for sweethearts, good-by!
"Four hundred wild lads!" Maybe so. I'll be bound
'Twill be easy to count us, face up, on the ground.
If we hold the road open, though Death take the toll,
We'll be missed on parade when the States call the roll—
When the flags meet in peace and the guns are at rest,
And fair Freedom is singing Sweet Home in the West.

*John Williamson Palmer* [1825–1906]

## SEVENTY-SIX

WHAT heroes from the woodland sprung,
When, through the fresh-awakened land,
The thrilling cry of freedom rung
And to the work of warfare strung
The yeoman's iron hand!

Hills flung the cry to hills around,
And ocean-mart replied to mart,
And streams, whose springs were yet unfound,
Pealed far away the startling sound
Into the forest's heart.

Then marched the brave from rocky steep,
From mountain-river swift and cold;
The borders of the stormy deep,
The vales where gathered waters sleep,
Sent up the strong and bold,—

As if the very earth again
Grew quick with God's creating breath,
And, from the sods of grove and glen,
Rose ranks of lion-hearted men
To battle to the death.

The wife, whose babe first smiled that day,
The fair fond bride of yestereve,
And agèd sire and matron gray,
Saw the loved warriors haste away,
And deemed it sin to grieve.

Already had the strife begun;
Already blood, on Concord's plain,
Along the springing grass had run,
And blood had flowed at Lexington,
Like brooks of April rain.

That death-stain on the vernal sward
  Hallowed to freedom all the shore;
In fragments fell the yoke abhorred—
The footstep of a foreign lord
  Profaned the soil no more.

*William Cullen Bryant* [1794-1878]

## SONG OF MARION'S MEN

[1780-1781]

Our band is few, but true and tried,
  Our leader frank and bold;
The British soldier trembles
  When Marion's name is told.
Our fortress is the good greenwood,
  Our tent the cypress-tree;
We know the forest round us
  As seamen know the sea.
We know its walls of thorny vines,
  Its glades of reedy grass,
Its safe and silent islands
  Within the dark morass.

Woe to the English soldiery
  That little dread us near!
On them shall light at midnight
  A strange and sudden fear:
When, waking to their tents on fire,
  They grasp their arms in vain,
And they who stand to face us
  Are beat to earth again;
And they who fly in terror deem
  A mighty host behind,
And hear the tramp of thousands
  Upon the hollow wind.

Then sweet the hour that brings release
  From danger and from toil;
We talk the battle over,
  We share the battle's spoil.

The woodland rings with laugh and shout
  As if a hunt were up,
And woodland flowers are gathered
  To crown the soldier's cup.
With merry songs we mock the wind
  That in the pine-top grieves,
And slumber long and sweetly
  On beds of oaken leaves.

Well knows the fair and friendly moon
  The band that Marion leads—
The glitter of their rifles,
  The scampering of their steeds.
'Tis life to guide the fiery barb
  Across the moonlight plain;
'Tis life to feel the night-wind
  That lifts his tossing mane.
A moment in the British camp—
  A moment—and away,
Back to the pathless forest
  Before the peep of day.

Grave men there are by broad Santee,
  Grave men with hoary hairs;
Their hearts are all with Marion,
  For Marion are their prayers.
And lovely ladies greet our band
  With kindliest welcoming,
With smiles like those of summer,
  And tears like those of spring.
For them we wear these trusty arms,
  And lay them down no more
Till we have driven the Briton,
  Forever, from our shore.

*William Cullen Bryant* [1794-1878]

## CARMEN BELLICOSUM

In their ragged regimentals
Stood the old Continentals,
    Yielding not,

While the grenadiers were lunging,
And like hail fell the plunging
Cannon-shot;
When the files
Of the isles,
From the smoky night-encampment, bore the banner of the rampant
Unicorn;
And grummer, grummer, grummer, rolled the roll of the drummer,
Through the morn!

Then with eyes to the front all,
And with guns horizontal,
Stood our sires;
And the balls whistled deadly,
And in streams flashing redly
Blazed the fires;
As the roar
On the shore,
Swept the strong battle-breakers o'er the green-sodded acres
Of the plain;
And louder, louder, louder, cracked the black gunpowder,
Cracking amain!

Now like smiths at their forges
Worked the red St. George's
Cannoneers;
And the villainous saltpetre
Rung a fierce, discordant metre
Round their ears;
As the swift
Storm-drift,
With hot sweeping anger, came the horseguards' clangor
On our flanks;
Then higher, higher, higher, burned the old-fashioned fire
Through the ranks!

Then the bare-headed colonel
Galloped through the white infernal
Powder-cloud;

And his broad-sword was swinging,
And his brazen throat was ringing
Trumpet-loud.
Then the blue
Bullets flew,
And the trooper-jackets redden at the touch of the leaden
Rifle-breath;
And rounder, rounder, rounder, roared the iron six-pounder,
Hurling death!

*Guy Humphreys McMaster* [1829–1887]

## ON THE LOSS OF THE "ROYAL GEORGE"

[AUGUST 29, 1782]

TOLL for the brave!
The brave that are no more!
All sunk beneath the wave,
Fast by their native shore!

Eight hundred of the brave,
Whose courage well was tried,
Had made the vessel heel,
And laid her on her side.

A land-breeze shook the shrouds,
And she was overset;
Down went the "Royal George,"
With all her crew complete.

Toll for the brave!
Brave Kempenfelt is gone;
His last sea-fight is fought,
His work of glory done.

It was not in the battle;
No tempest gave the shock;
She sprang no fatal leak;
She ran upon no rock.

His sword was in its sheath;
His fingers held the pen,
When Kempenfelt went down
With twice four hundred men.

Weigh the vessel up,
Once dreaded by our foes!
And mingle with our cup
The tear that England owes.

Her timbers yet are sound,
And she may float again,
Full charged with England's thunder,
And plough the distant main.

But Kempenfelt is gone,
His victories are o'er;
And he and his eight hundred
Shall plough the wave no more.

*William Cowper* [1731–1800]

## CREMONA

[FEBRUARY 1, 1702]

THE Grenadiers of Austria are proper men and tall;
The Grenadiers of Austria have scaled the city wall;
They have marched from far away
Ere the dawning of the day,
And the morning saw them masters of Cremona.

There's not a man to whisper, there's not a horse to neigh,
Of the footmen of Lorraine and the riders of Duprés;
They have crept up every street,
In the market-place they meet,
They are holding every vantage in Cremona.

The Marshal Villeroy he has started from his bed;
The Marshal Villeroy has no wig upon his head;
"I have lost my men!" quoth he,
"And my men they have lost me,
And I sorely fear we both have lost Cremona."

Prince Eugène of Austria is in the market-place;
Prince Eugène of Austria has smiles upon his face;
    Says he, "Our work is done,
    For the Citadel is won,
And the black and yellow flag floats o'er Cremona."

Major Dan O'Mahony is in the barrack square,
And just six hundred Irish lads are waiting for him there;
    Says he, "Come in your shirt,
    And you won't take any hurt,
For the morning air is pleasant in Cremona."

Major Dan O'Mahony is at the barrack gate,
And just six hundred Irish lads will neither stay nor wait;
    There's Dillon and there's Burke,
    And there'll be some bloody work
Ere the Kaiserlics shall boast they hold Cremona.

Major Dan O'Mahony has reached the river fort,
And just six hundred Irish lads are joining in the sport;
    "Come, take a hand!" says he,
    "And if you will stand by me,
Then it's glory to the man who takes Cremona!"

Prince Eugène of Austria has frowns upon his face,
And loud he calls his Galloper of Irish blood and race:
    "MacDonnell, ride, I pray,
    To your countrymen, and say
That only they are left in all Cremona!"

MacDonnell he has reined his mare beside the river dike,
And he has tied the parley flag upon a sergeant's pike;
    Six companies were there
    From Limerick and Clare,
The last of all the guardians of Cremona.

"Now, Major Dan O'Mahony, give up the river gate,
Or, Major Dan O'Mahony, you'll find it is too late;
    For when I gallop back
    'Tis the signal for attack,
And no quarter for the Irish in Cremona!"

And Major Dan he laughed: "Faith, if what you say be true,
And if they will not come until they hear again from you,
Then there will be no attack,
For you're never going back,
And we'll keep you snug and safely in Cremona."

All the weary day the German stormers came,
All the weary day they were faced by fire and flame;
They have filled the ditch with dead,
And the river's running red,
But they cannot win the gateway of Cremona.

All the weary day, again, again, again,
The horsemen of Duprés and the footmen of Lorraine,
Taafe and Herberstein,
And the riders of the Rhine;
It's a mighty price they're paying for Cremona.

Time and time they came with the deep-mouthed German
roar,
Time and time they broke like the wave upon the shore;
For better men were there
From Limerick and Clare,
And who will take the gateway of Cremona?

Prince Eugène has watched, and he gnaws his nether lip;
Prince Eugène has cursed as he saw his chances slip:
"Call off! Call off!" he cried,
"It is nearing eventide,
And I fear our work is finished in Cremona."

Says Wauchop to McAuliffe, "Their fire is growing slack."
Says Major Dan O'Mahony, "It is their last attack·
But who will stop the game
While there's light to play the same,
And to walk a short way with them from Cremona?"

And so they snarl behind them, and beg them turn and come,
They have taken Neuberg's standard, they have taken
Diak's drum:

And along the winding Po,
Beard on shoulder, stern and slow,
The Kaiserlics are riding from Cremona.

Just two hundred Irish lads are shouting on the wall;
Four hundred more are lying who can hear no slogan call;
But what's the odds of that,
For it's all the same to Pat
If he pays his debt in Dublin or Cremona.

Says General de Vaudray, "You've done a soldier's work!
And every tongue in France shall talk of Dillon and of Burke!
Ask what you will this day,
And be it what it may,
It is granted to the heroes of Cremona."

"Why, then," says Dan O'Mahony, "one favor we entreat,
We were called a little early, and our toilet's not complete.
We've no quarrel with the shirt,
But the breeches wouldn't hurt,
For the evening air is chilly in Cremona."

*Arthur Conan Doyle* [1859-1930]

## CASABIANCA

[BATTLE OF THE NILE, AUGUST, 1798]

THE boy stood on the burning deck,
Whence all but him had fled;
The flame that lit the battle's wreck
Shone round him o'er the dead.

Yet beautiful and bright he stood,
As born to rule the storm;
A creature of heroic blood,
A proud, though child-like form.

The flames rolled on; he would not go
Without his father's word;
That father, faint in death below,
His voice no longer heard.

He called aloud, "Say, father, say,
If yet my task be done!"
He knew not that the chieftain lay
Unconscious of his son.

"Speak, father!" once again he cried,
"If I may yet be gone!"
And but the booming shots replied,
And fast the flames rolled on.

Upon his brow he felt their breath,
And in his waving hair,
And looked from that lone post of death
In still, yet brave despair;

And shouted but once more aloud,
"My father! must I stay?"
While o'er him, fast, through sail and shroud,
The wreathing fires made way.

They wrapped the ship in splendor wild,
They caught the flag on high,
And streamed above the gallant child,
Like banners in the sky.

There came a burst of thunder sound;
The boy,—oh! where was he?
Ask of the winds, that far around
With fragments strewed the sea,—

With mast, and helm, and pennon fair,
That well had borne their part,—
But the noblest thing that perished there,
Was that young, faithful heart.

*Felicia Dorothea Hemans* [1793-1835]

## HOHENLINDEN

[DECEMBER 3, 1800]

On Linden, when the sun was low,
All bloodless lay the untrodden snow;
And dark as winter was the flow
Of Iser, rolling rapidly.

But Linden saw another sight,
When the drum beat, at dead of night,
Commanding fires of death to light
The darkness of her scenery.

By torch and trumpet fast arrayed
Each horseman drew his battle-blade,
And furious every charger neighed
To join the dreadful revelry.

Then shook the hills with thunder riven;
Then rushed the steed, to battle driven;
And louder than the bolts of heaven
Far flashed the red artillery.

But redder yet that light shall glow
On Linden's hills of stainèd snow;
And bloodier yet the torrent flow
Of Iser, rolling rapidly.

'Tis morn; but scarce yon level sun
Can pierce the war-clouds, rolling dun,
Where furious Frank and fiery Hun
Shout in their sulphurous canopy.

The combat deepens. On, ye Brave,
Who rush to glory, or the grave!
Wave, Munich! all thy banners wave,
And charge with all thy chivalry!

Few, few shall part, where many meet!
The snow shall be their winding-sheet,
And every turf beneath their feet
Shall be a soldier's sepulchre.

*Thomas Campbell* [1777–1844]

## BATTLE OF THE BALTIC

[APRIL 2, 1801]

OF Nelson and the North,
Sing the glorious day's renown,
When to battle fierce came forth
All the might of Denmark's crown,

And her arms along the deep proudly shone;
By each gun the lighted brand,
In a bold determined hand,
And the Prince of all the land
Led them on.

Like leviathans afloat,
Lay their bulwarks on the brine;
While the sign of battle flew
On the lofty British line;
It was ten of April morn by the chime:
As they drifted on their path,
There was silence deep as death;
And the boldest held his breath,
For a time.—

But the might of England flushed
To anticipate the scene;
And her van the fleeter rushed
O'er the deadly space between.
"Hearts of oak!" our captain cried; when each gun
From its adamantine lips
Spread a death-shade round the ships,
Like the hurricane eclipse
Of the sun.

Again! again! again!
And the havoc did not slack,
Till a feeble cheer the Dane
To our cheering sent us back;—
Their shots along the deep slowly boom:--
Then ceased—and all is wail,
As they strike the shattered sail;
Or, in conflagration pale,
Light the gloom.—

Outspoke the victor then,
As he hailed them o'er the wave:
"Ye are brothers! ye are men!
And we conquer but to save:—

So peace instead of death let us bring.
But yield, proud foe, thy fleet,
With the crews, at England's feet,
And make submission meet
To our King."—

Then Denmark blessed our chief,
That he gave her wounds repose;
And the sounds of joy and grief,
From her people wildly rose,
As death withdrew his shades from the day;
While the sun looked smiling bright
O'er a wide and woful sight,
Where the fires of funeral light
Died away.

Now joy, Old England, raise!
For the tidings of thy might,
By the festal cities' blaze,
Whilst the wine-cup shines in light;
And yet, amidst that joy and uproar,
Let us think of them that sleep,
Full many a fathom deep,
By thy wild and stormy steep,
Elsinore!—

Brave hearts! to Britain's pride
Once so faithful and so true,
On the deck of fame that died;—
With the gallant good Riou:
Soft sigh the winds of Heaven o'er their grave!
While the billow mournful rolls,
And the mermaid's song condoles,
Singing glory to the souls
Of the brave!

*Thomas Campbell* [1777–1844]

## THE FIGHTING TÉMÉRAIRE

[OCTOBER 21, 1805]

It was eight bells ringing,
 For the morning watch was done,
And the gunner's lads were singing
 As they polished every gun.
It was eight bells ringing,
And the gunner's lads were singing,
For the ship she rode a-swinging,
 As they polished every gun.

*Oh! to see the linstock lighting,*
 *Téméraire! Téméraire!*
*Oh! to hear the round shot biting,*
 *Téméraire! Téméraire!*
*Oh! to see the linstock lighting,*
*And to hear the round shot biting,*
*For we're all in love with fighting*
 *On the Fighting Téméraire.*

It was noontide ringing,
 And the battle just begun,
When the ship her way was winging,
 As they loaded every gun,
It was noontide ringing,
When the ship her way was winging,
And the gunner's lads were singing,
 As they loaded every gun.

*There'll be many grim and gory,*
 *Téméraire! Téméraire!*
*There'll be few to tell the story,*
 *Téméraire! Téméraire!*
*There'll be many grim and gory,*
*There'll be few to tell the story,*
*But we'll all be one in glory*
 *With the Fighting Téméraire.*

There's a far bell ringing
  At the setting of the sun,
And a phantom voice is singing
  Of the great days done.
There's a far bell ringing,
And a phantom Voice is singing
Of renown for ever clinging
  To the great days done.

*Now the sunset breezes shiver,*
  *Téméraire! Téméraire!*
*And she's fading down the river,*
  *Téméraire! Téméraire!*
*Now the sunset breezes shiver,*
*And she's fading down the river,*
*But in England's song for ever*
  *She's the Fighting Téméraire.*

*Henry Newbolt* [1862–1938]

## SKIPPER IRESON'S RIDE

[1808]

Of all the rides since the birth of time,
Told in story or sung in rhyme,—
On Apuleius's Golden Ass,
Or one-eyed Calender's horse of brass,
Witch astride of a human back,
Islam's prophet on Al-Borák,—
The strangest ride that ever was sped
Was Ireson's, out from Marblehead!
  Old Floyd Ireson, for his hard heart,
Tarred and feathered and carried in a cart
    By the women of Marblehead!

Body of turkey, head of fowl,
Wings a-droop like a rained-on fowl,
Feathered and ruffled in every part,
Skipper Ireson stood in the cart.
Scores of women, old and young,
Strong of muscle, and glib of tongue,

Pushed and pulled up the rocky lane,
Shouting and singing the shrill refrain:
"Here's Flud Oirson, fur his horrd horrt,
Torr'd an' futherr'd an' corr'd in a corrt
By the women o' Morble'ead!"

Wrinkled scolds with hands on hips,
Girls in bloom of cheek and lips,
Wild-eyed, free-limbed, such as chase
Bacchus round some antique vase,
Brief of skirt, with ankles bare,
Loose of kerchief and loose of hair,
With conch-shells blowing and fish-horns' twang,
Over and over the Mænads sang:
"Here's Flud Oirson, fur his horrd horrt,
Torr'd an' futherr'd an' corr'd in a corrt
By the women o' Morble'ead!"

Small pity for him!—He sailed away
From a leaking ship in Chaleur Bay,—
Sailed away from a sinking wreck,
With his own town's-people on her deck!
"Lay by! lay by!" they called to him.
Back he answered, "Sink or swim!
Brag of your catch of fish again!"
And off he sailed through the fog and rain!
Old Floyd Ireson, for his hard heart,
Tarred and feathered and carried in a cart
By the women of Marblehead!

Fathoms deep in dark Chaleur
That wreck shall lie forevermore.
Mother and sister, wife and maid,
Looked from the rocks of Marblehead
Over the moaning and rainy sea,—
Looked for the coming that might not be!
What did the winds and the sea-birds say
Of the cruel captain who sailed away?—
Old Floyd Ireson, for his hard heart,
Tarred and feathered and carried in a cart
By the women of Marblehead!

Through the street, on either side,
Up flew windows, doors swung wide;
Sharp-tongued spinsters, old wives gray,
Treble lent the fish-horn's bray.
Sea-worn grandsires, cripple-bound,
Hulks of old sailors run aground,
Shook head, and fist, and hat, and cane,
And cracked with curses the hoarse refrain:
"Here's Flud Oirson, fur his horrd horrt,
Torr'd an' futherr'd an' corr'd in a corrt
By the women o' Morble'ead!"

Sweetly along the Salem road
Bloom of orchard and lilac showed.
Little the wicked skipper knew
Of the fields so green and the sky so blue.
Riding there in his sorry trim,
Like an Indian idol glum and grim,
Scarcely he seemed the sound to hear
Of voices shouting, far and near:
"Here's Flud Oirson, fur his horrd horrt,
Torr'd an' futherr'd an' corr'd in a corrt
By the women o' Morble'ead!"

"Hear me, neighbors!" at last he cried,—
"What to me is this noisy ride?
What is the shame that clothes the skin
To the nameless horror that lives within?
Waking or sleeping, I see a wreck,
And hear a cry from a reeling deck!
Hate me and curse me,—I only dread
The hand of God and the face of the dead!"
Said old Floyd Ireson, for his hard heart,
Tarred and feathered, and carried in a cart
By the women of Marblehead!

Then the wife of the skipper lost at sea
Said, "God has touched him! why should we!"
Said an old wife mourning her only son,
"Cut the rogue's tether and let him run!"

So with soft relentings and rude excuse,
Half scorn, half pity, they cut him loose,
And gave him a cloak to hide him in,
And left him alone with his shame and sin.
Poor Floyd Ireson, for his hard heart,
Tarred and feathered and carried in a cart
By the women of Marblehead!

*John Greenleaf Whittier* [1807-1892]

## THE BURIAL OF SIR JOHN MOORE AFTER CORUNNA

[JANUARY 16, 1809]

NOT a drum was heard, not a funeral note,
As his corse to the rampart we hurried;
Not a soldier discharged his farewell shot
O'er the grave where our hero we buried.

We buried him darkly at dead of night,
The sods with our bayonets turning,
By the struggling moonbeam's misty light
And the lanthorn dimly burning.

No useless coffin enclosed his breast,
Not in sheet or in shroud we wound him;
But he lay like a warrior taking his rest
With his martial cloak around him.

Few and short were the prayers we said,
And we spoke not a word of sorrow;
But we steadfastly gazed on the face that was dead,
And we bitterly thought of the morrow.

We thought, as we hollowed his narrow bed
And smoothed down his lonely pillow,
That the foe and the stranger would tread o'er his head,
And we far away on the billow!

Lightly they'll talk of the spirit that's gone,
And o'er his cold ashes upbraid him—
But little he'll reck, if they let him sleep on
In the grave where a Briton has laid him.

But half of our heavy task was done
When the clock struck the hour for retiring;
And we heard the distant and random gun
That the foe was sullenly firing.

Slowly and sadly we laid him down,
From the field of his fame fresh and gory;
We carved not a line, and we raised not a stone,
But we left him alone with his glory.

*Charles Wolfe* [1791–1823]

## INCIDENT OF THE FRENCH CAMP

[APRIL 23, 1809]

You know, we French stormed Ratisbon:
A mile or so away,
On a little mound, Napoleon
Stood on our storming-day;
With neck out-thrust, you fancy how,
Legs wide, arms locked behind,
As if to balance the prone brow
Oppressive with its mind.

Just as perhaps he mused, "My plans
That soar, to earth may fall,
Let once my army-leader Lannes
Waver at yonder wall,"—
Out 'twixt the battery-smokes there flew
A rider, bound on bound
Full-galloping; nor bridle drew
Until he reached the mound.

Then off there flung in smiling joy,
And held himself erect
By just his horse's mane, a boy:
You hardly could suspect—

(So tight he kept his lips compressed,
  Scarce any blood came through),
You looked twice ere you saw his breast
  Was all but shot in two.

"Well," cried he, "Emperor, by God's grace
  We've got you Ratisbon!
The Marshal's in the market-place,
  And you'll be there anon
To see your flag-bird flap his vans
  Where I, to heart's desire,
Perched him!" The chief's eye flashed; his plans
  Soared up again like fire.

The chief's eye flashed; but presently
  Softened itself, as sheathes
A film the mother-eagle's eye
  When her bruised eaglet breathes;
"You're wounded!" "Nay," the soldier's pride
  Touched to the quick, he said:
"I'm killed, Sire!" And his chief beside,
  Smiling the boy fell dead.

*Robert Browning* [1812-1889]

## THE EVE OF WATERLOO

From "Childe Harold's Pilgrimage"

[JUNE 18, 1815]

THERE was a sound of revelry by night,
And Belgium's capital had gathered then
Her Beauty and her Chivalry, and bright
The lamps shone o'er fair women and brave men;
A thousand hearts beat happily; and when
Music arose with its voluptuous swell,
Soft eyes looked love to eyes which spake again,
And all went merry as a marriage bell;—
But hush! hark! a deep sound strikes like a rising knell!

Did ye not hear it?—No; 'twas but the wind,
Or the car rattling o'er the stony street;
On with the dance! let joy be unconfined;
No sleep till morn, when Youth and Pleasure meet
To chase the glowing Hours with flying feet—
But hark!—that heavy sound breaks in once more,
As if the clouds its echo would repeat;
And nearer, clearer, deadlier than before!
Arm! Arm! it is—it is—the cannon's opening roar!

Within a windowed niche of that high wall
Sate Brunswick's fated chieftain; he did hear
That sound the first amidst the festival,
And caught its tone with Death's prophetic ear;
And when they smiled because he deemed it near,
His heart more truly knew that peal too well
Which stretched his father on a bloody bier,
And roused the vengeance blood alone could quell:
He rushed into the field, and, foremost fighting, fell.

Ah! then and there was hurrying to and fro,
And gathering tears, and tremblings of distress,
And cheeks all pale, which but an hour ago
Blushed at the praise of their own loveliness;
And there were sudden partings, such as press
The life from out young hearts, and choking sighs
Which ne'er might be repeated; who could guess
If ever more should meet those mutual eyes,
Since upon night so sweet such awful morn could rise!

And there was mounting in hot haste: the steed,
The mustering squadron, and the clattering car,
Went pouring forward with impetuous speed,
And swiftly forming in the ranks of war;
And the deep thunder peal on peal afar;
And near, the beat of the alarming drum
Roused up the soldier ere the morning star;
While thronged the citizens with terror dumb,
Or whispering, with white lips—"The foe! they come! they come!"

And wild and high the "Cameron's gathering" rose!
The war-note of Lochiel, which Albyn's hills
Have heard, and heard, too, have her Saxon foes:—
How in the noon of night that pibroch thrills,
Savage and shrill! But with the breath which fills
Their mountain-pipe, so fill the mountaineers
With the fierce native daring which instils
The stirring memory of a thousand years,
And Evan's, Donald's fame rings in each clansman's ears!

And Ardennes waves above them her green leaves,
Dewy with nature's tear-drops as they pass,
Grieving, if aught inanimate e'er grieves,
Over the unreturning brave,—alas!
Ere evening to be trodden like the grass
Which now beneath them, but above shall grow
In its next verdure, when this fiery mass
Of living valor, rolling on the foe
And burning with high hope, shall moulder cold and low.

Last noon beheld them full of lusty life,
Last eve in Beauty's circle proudly gay,
The midnight brought the signal-sound of strife,
The morn the marshalling in arms,—the day
Battle's magnificently stern array!
The thunder-clouds close o'er it, which when rent
The earth is covered thick with other clay,
Which her own clay shall cover, heaped and pent,
Rider and horse,—friend, foe,—in one red burial blent!

*George Gordon Byron* [1788–1824]

## WATERLOO

Why have the Mighty lived—why have they died?
Is it ever thus with idle wreck to strew
Fields such as thine, remorseless Waterloo?
Hopeless the lesson! Vainly hath ever cried
Stern Fate to man—"So perish human pride!"
Still must the Many combat for the Few:
Still must the noblest blood fair earth bedew:
Tyrants, slaves, freemen, mouldering side by side!

On such a day the World was lost, and won,
By Pompey at Pharsalia: such a day
Saw glorious Hannibal a fugitive:
So faded 'neath the Macedonian Sun
Persia's pale star: so empire passed away
From Harold's brow,—but He disdained to live!

*Aubrey De Vere* [1788–1846]

## MARCO BOZZARIS

[APRIL 20, 1823]

AT midnight, in his guarded tent,
  The Turk was dreaming of the hour
When Greece, her knee in suppliance bent,
  Should tremble at his power:
In dreams, through camp and court, he bore
The trophies of a conqueror;
  In dreams his song of triumph heard;
Then wore his monarch's signet ring:
Then pressed that monarch's throne—a king;
As wild his thoughts, and gay of wing,
  As Eden's garden bird.

At midnight, in the forest shades,
  Bozzaris ranged his Suliote band,
True as the steel of their tried blades,
  Heroes in heart and hand.
There had the Persian's thousands stood,
There had the glad earth drunk their blood
  On old Platæa's day;
And now there breathed that haunted air
The sons of sires who conquered there,
With arm to strike, and soul to dare,
  As quick, as far as they.

An hour passed on—the Turk awoke;
  That bright dream was his last;
He woke—to hear his sentries shriek,
"To arms! they come! the Greek! the Greek!"

He woke—to die midst flame, and smoke,
And shout, and groan, and sabre-stroke,
  And death-shots falling thick and fast
As lightnings from the mountain-cloud;
And heard, with voice as trumpet loud,
  Bozzaris cheer his band:
"Strike—till the last armed foe expires;
Strike—for your altars and your fires;
Strike—for the green graves of your sires;
  God—and your native land!"

They fought—like brave men, long and well;
  They piled that ground with Moslem slain,
They conquered—but Bozzaris fell,
  Bleeding at every vein.
His few surviving comrades saw
His smile when rang their proud hurrah,
  And the red field was won;
Then saw in death his eyelids close
Calmly, as to a night's repose,
  Like flowers at set of sun.

Come to the bridal-chamber, Death!
  Come to the mother's, when she feels,
For the first time, her first-born's breath;
  Come when the blessèd seals
That close the pestilence are broke,
And crowded cities wail its stroke;
Come in consumption's ghastly form,
The earthquake shock, the ocean storm;
Come when the heart beats high and warm
  With banquet-song, and dance, and wine;
And thou art terrible,—the tear,
The groan, the knell, the pall, the bier,
And all we know, or dream, or fear
  Of agony, are thine.

But to the hero, when his sword
  Has won the battle for the free,
Thy voice sounds like a prophet's word;
And in its hollow tones are heard

The thanks of millions yet to be.
Come, when his task of fame is wrought—
Come, with her laurel-leaf, blood-bought-
Come in her crowning hour—and then
Thy sunken eye's unearthly light
To him is welcome as the sight
Of sky and stars to prisoned men:
Thy grasp is welcome as the hand
Of brother in a foreign land;
Thy summons welcome as the cry
That told the Indian isles were nigh
To the world-seeking Genoese,
When the land wind, from woods of palm,
And orange groves, and fields of balm,
Blew o'er the Haytian seas.

Bozzaris! with the storied brave
Greece nurtured in her glory's time,
Rest thee—there is no prouder grave,
Even in her own proud clime.
She wore no funeral-weeds for thee,
Nor bade the dark hearse wave its plume
Like torn branch from death's leafless tree
In sorrow's pomp and pageantry,
The heartless luxury of the tomb:
But she remembers thee as one
Long loved, and for a season gone;
For thee her poet's lyre is wreathed,
Her marble wrought, her music breathed;
For thee she rings the birthday bells;
Of thee her babes' first lisping tells;
For thine her evening prayer is said
At palace-couch and cottage-bed;
Her soldier, closing with the foe,
Gives for thy sake a deadlier blow;
His plighted maiden, when she fears
For him, the joy of her young years,
Thinks of thy fate, and checks her tears:
And she, the mother of thy boys,

Though in her eye and faded cheek
Is read the grief she will not speak,
  The memory of her buried joys,
And even she who gave thee birth,
Will, by their pilgrim-circled hearth,
  Talk of thy doom without a sigh:
For thou art Freedom's now, and Fame's:
One of the few, the immortal names,
  That were not born to die.

*Fitz-Greene Halleck* [1790–1867]

## OLD IRONSIDES

[SEPTEMBER 14, 1830]

AY, tear her tattered ensign down!
  Long has it waved on high,
And many an eye has danced to see
  That banner in the sky;
Beneath it rung the battle shout,
  And burst the cannon's roar;—
The meteor of the ocean air
  Shall sweep the clouds no more.

Her deck, once red with heroes' blood,
  Where knelt the vanquished foe,
When winds were hurrying o'er the flood,
  And waves were white below,
No more shall feel the victor's tread,
  Or know the conquered knee;—
The harpies of the shore shall pluck
  The eagle of the sea!

Oh, better that her shattered hulk
  Should sink beneath the wave;
Her thunders shook the mighty deep,
  And there should be her grave;
Nail to the mast her holy flag,
  Set every threadbare sail,
And give her to the god of storms,
  The lightning and the gale!

*Oliver Wendell Holmes* [1809–1894]

## THE VALOR OF BEN MILAM

[DECEMBER 5–11, 1835]

*Oh, who will follow old Ben Milam into San Antonio?*
Such was the thrilling word we heard in the chill December glow;
Such was the thrilling word we heard, and a ringing, answering cry
Went up from the dun adobe walls to the cloudless Texas sky.

He had won from the reek of a Mexique jail back without map or chart,
With his mother-wit and his hero-grit and his stanch Kentucky heart;
He had trudged by vale and by mountain trail, and by thorn and thirsty plain,
And now, with joy on his grizzled brow, he had come to his own again.

*They're the spawn of Hell!* we heard him tell; *they will knife and lie and cheat*
*At the board of none of the swarthy horde would I deign to sit at meat;*
*They hold it naught that I bled and fought when Spain was their ruthless foe;*
*Oh, who will follow old Ben Milam into San Antonio?*

It was four to one, not gun for gun, but never a curse cared we,
Three hundred faithful and fearless men who had sworn to make Texas free.
It was mighty odds, by all the gods, this brute of the Mexique dam,
But it was not much for heroes such as followed old Ben Milam!

With rifle-crack and sabre-hack we drove them back in the street;
From house to house in the red carouse we hastened their flying feet;

And ever that shout kept pealing out with a swift and sure
death-blow:
*Oh, who will follow old Ben Milam into San Antonio?*

Behind the walls from the hurtling balls Cos cowered and
swore in his beard,
While we slashed and slew from dawn till dew, and, Bexar,
how we cheered!
But ere failed each ruse, and the white of truce on the fail-
ing day was thrown,
Our fearless soul had gone to the goal, the Land of the Great
Unknown.

Death brought the darksome boon too soon to this truest
one of the true,
Or, men of the fated Alamo, Milam had died with you!
So when their names that now are Fame's—the scorners of
braggard sham;—
In song be praised, let a rouse be raised for the name of Ben
Milam! *Clinton Scollard* [1860–1932]

## THE DEFENCE OF THE ALAMO

[MARCH 6, 1836]

SANTA ANA came storming, as a storm might come;
There was rumble of cannon; there was rattle of blade;
There was cavalry, infantry, bugle and drum,—
Full seven thousand, in pomp and parade,
The chivalry, flower of Mexico;
And a gaunt two hundred in the Alamo!

And thirty lay sick, and some were shot through;
For the siege had been bitter, and bloody, and long.
"Surrender, or die!"—"Men, what will *you* do?"
And Travis, great Travis, drew sword, quick and strong;
Drew a line at his feet . . . "Will you come? Will you go?
*I* die with my wounded, in the Alamo."

Then Bowie gasped, "Lead me over that line!"
Then Crockett, one hand to the sick, one hand to his gun,
Crossed with him; then never a word or a sign
Till all, sick or well, all, all save but one,

One man. Then a woman stepped, praying, and slow
Across; to die at her post in the Alamo.

Then that one coward fled, in the night, in that night
  When all men silently prayed and thought
Of home; of to-morrow; of God and the right,
  Till dawn: and with dawn came Travis's cannon-shot,
In answer to insolent Mexico,
From the old bell-tower of the Alamo.

Then came Santa Ana; a crescent of flame!
  Then the red escalade; then the fight hand to hand;
Such an unequal fight as never had name
  Since the Persian hordes butchered that doomed Spartan
    band.
All day—all day and all night; and the morning? so slow,
Through the battle-smoke mantling the Alamo.

Now silence! Such silence! Two thousand lay dead
  In a crescent outside! And within? Not a breath
Save the gasp of a woman, with gory gashed head,
  All alone, all alone there, waiting for death;
And she but a nurse. Yet when shall we know
Another like this of the Alamo?

Shout "Victory, victory, victory ho!"
  I say 'tis not always to the hosts that win!
I say that the victory, high or low,
  Is given the hero who grapples with sin,
Or legion or single; just asking to know
When duty fronts death in his Alamo.

*Joaquin Miller* [1839-1913]

## THE FIGHT AT SAN JACINTO

[APRIL 21, 1836]

"Now for a brisk and cheerful fight!"
  Said Harman, big and droll,
As he coaxed his flint and steel for a light,
  And puffed at his cold clay bowl;

"For we are a skulking lot," says he,
"Of land-thieves hereabout,
And the bold señores, two to one,
Have come to smoke us out."

Santa Anna and Castrillon,
Almonte brave and gay,
Portilla red from Goliad,
And Cos with his smart array.
Dulces and cigaritos,
And the light guitar, ting-tum!
Sant' Anna courts siesta—
And Sam Houston taps his drum.

The buck stands still in the timber—
"Is it patter of nuts that fall?"
The foal of the wild mare whinnies—
Did he hear the Comanche call?
In the brake by the crawling bayou
The slinking she-wolves howl,
And the mustang's snort in the river sedge
Has startled the paddling fowl.

A soft, low tap, and a muffled tap,
And a roll not loud nor long—
We would not break Sant' Anna's nap,
Nor spoil Almonte's song.
Saddles and knives and rifles!
Lord! but the men were glad
When Deaf Smith muttered "Alamo!"
And Karnes hissed "Goliad!"

The drummer tucked his sticks in his belt,
And the fifer gripped his gun.
Oh, for one free, wild, Texan yell,
As we took the slope in a run!
But never a shout nor a shot we spent,
Nor an oath nor a prayer, that day,
Till we faced the bravos, eye to eye,
And then we blazed away.

Then we knew the rapture of Ben Milam,
  And the glory that Travis made,
With Bowie's lunge, and Crockett's shot,
  And Fannin's dancing blade;
And the heart of the fighter, bounding free
  In his joy so hot and mad—
When Millard charged for Alamo,
  Lamar for Goliad.

Deaf Smith rode straight, with reeking spur,
  Into the shock and rout:
"I've hacked and burned the bayou bridge,
  There's no sneak's back-way out!"
Muzzle or butt for Goliad,
  Pistol and blade and fist!
Oh, for the knife that never glanced,
  And the gun that never missed!

Dulces and cigaritos,
  Song and the mandolin!
That gory swamp was a gruesome grove
  To dance fandangos in.
We bridged the bog with the sprawling herd
  That fell in that frantic rout;
We slew and slew till the sun set red,
  And the Texan star flashed out.

*John Williamson Palmer* [1825–1906]

## THE WRECK OF THE HESPERUS

[DECEMBER 17, 1839]

It was the schooner Hesperus,
  That sailed the wintry sea;
And the skipper had taken his little daughtèr,
  To bear him company.

Blue were her eyes as the fairy-flax,
  Her cheeks like the dawn of day,
And her bosom white as the hawthorn buds
  That ope in the month of May.

The skipper he stood beside the helm,
His pipe was in his mouth,
And he watched how the veering flaw did blow
The smoke now West, now South.

Then up and spake an old Sailòr,
Had sailed to the Spanish main,
"I pray thee, put into yonder port,
For I fear a hurricane.

"Last night, the moon had a golden ring,
And to-night no moon we see!"
The skipper, he blew a whiff from his pipe,
And a scornful laugh laughed he.

Colder and louder blew the wind,
A gale from the Northeast,
The snow fell hissing in the brine,
And the billows frothed like yeast.

Down came the storm, and smote amain
The vessel in its strength;
She shuddered and paused, like a frighted steed,
Then leaped her cable's length.

"Come hither! come hither! my little daughtèr,
And do not tremble so;
For I can weather the roughest gale
That ever wind did blow."

He wrapped her warm in his seaman's coat
Against the stinging blast;
He cut a rope from a broken spar,
And bound her to the mast.

"O father! I hear the church-bells ring,
Oh say, what may it be?"
"'Tis a fog-bell on a rock-bound coast!"—
And he steered for the open sea.

"O father! I hear the sound of guns,
  Oh say, what may it be?"
"Some ship in distress, that cannot live
  In such an angry sea!"

"O father! I see a gleaming light,
  Oh say, what may it be!"
But the father answered never a word,
  A frozen corpse was he.

Lashed to the helm, all stiff and stark,
  With his face turned to the skies,
The lantern gleamed through the gleaming snow
  On his fixed and glassy eyes.

Then the maiden clasped her hands and prayed
  That savèd she might be;
And she thought of Christ, who stilled the wave,
  On the Lake of Galilee.

And fast through the midnight dark and drear,
  Through the whistling sleet and snow,
Like a sheeted ghost, the vessel swept
  Towards the reef of Norman's Woe.

And ever the fitful gusts between
  A sound came from the land;
It was the sound of the trampling surf
  On the rocks and the hard sea-sand.

The breakers were right beneath her bows,
  She drifted a dreary wreck,
And a whooping billow swept the crew
  Like icicles from her deck.

She struck where the white and fleecy waves
  Looked soft as carded wool,
But the cruel rocks, they gored her side
  Like the horns of an angry bull.

Her rattling shrouds, all sheathed in ice,
With the masts, went by the board;
Like a vessel of glass, she stove and sank,
Ho! ho! the breakers roared!

At daybreak, on the bleak sea-beach,
A fisherman stood aghast,
To see the form of a maiden fair,
Lashed close to a drifting mast.

The salt sea was frozen on her breast,
The salt tears in her eyes;
And he saw her hair, like the brown sea-weed,
On the billows fall and rise.

Such was the wreck of the Hesperus,
In the midnight and the snow!
Christ save us all from a death like this,
On the reef of Norman's Woe!

*Henry Wadsworth Longfellow* [1807-1882]

## THE LOST COLORS

[1843]

FROWNING, the mountain stronghold stood,
Whose front no mortal could assail;
For more than twice three hundred years
The terror of the Indian vale.
By blood and fire the robber band
Answered the helpless village wail.

Hot was his heart and cool his thought,
When Napier from his Englishmen
Up to the bandits' rampart glanced,
And down upon his ranks again.
Summoned to dare a deed like that,
Which of them all would answer then?

What sullen regiment is this
That lifts its eyes to dread Cutchee?

Abased, its standard bears no flag.
For thus the punishment shall be
That England metes to Englishmen
Who shame her once by mutiny.

From out the disgraced Sixty-Fourth
There stepped a hundred men of might.
Cried Napier: "Now prove to me
I read my soldiers' hearts aright!
Form! Forward! Charge, my volunteers!
*Your colors are on yonder height!"*

So sad is shame, so wise is trust!
The challenge echoed bugle-clear.
Like fire along the Sixty-Fourth
From rank to file rang cheer on cheer.
In death and glory up the pass
They fought for all to brave men dear.

Old is the tale, but read anew
In every warring human heart,
What rebel hours, what coward shame,
Upon the aching memory start!
To find the ideal forfeited,
—What tears can teach the holy art?

Thou great Commander! leading on
Through weakest darkness to strong light;
By any anguish, give us back
Our life's young standard, pure and bright.
O fair, lost Colors of the soul!
For your sake storm we any height.

*Elizabeth Stuart Phelps Ward* [1844-1911]

## A BALLAD OF SIR JOHN FRANKLIN

[1845-47]

O, WHITHER sail you, Sir John Franklin?
  Cried a whaler in Baffin's Bay.
To know if between the land and the pole
  I may find a broad sea-way

I charge you back, Sir John Franklin,
  As you would live and thrive;
For between the land and the frozen pole
  No man may sail alive.

But lightly laughed the stout Sir John,
  And spoke unto his men:
Half England is wrong, if he be right;
  Bear off to westward then.

O, whither sail you, brave Englishman?
  Cried the little Esquimau.
Between your land and the polar star
  My goodly vessels go.

Come down, if you would journey there,
  The little Indian said;
And change your cloth for fur clothing,
  Your vessel for a sled.

But lightly laughed the stout Sir John,
  And the crew laughed with him too:—
A sailor to change from ship to sled,
  I ween, were something new.

All through the long, long polar day,
  The vessels westward sped;
And wherever the sail of Sir John was blown,
  The ice gave way and fled:—

Gave way with many a hollow groan,
  And with many a surly roar,
But it murmured and threatened on every side,
  And closed where he sailed before.

Ho! see ye not, my merry men,
  The broad and open sea?
Bethink ye what the whaler said,
Think of the little Indian's sled!
  The crew laughed out in glee.

Sir John, Sir John, 'tis bitter cold,
  The scud drives on the breeze,
The ice comes looming from the north,
  The very sunbeams freeze.

Bright summer goes, dark winter comes,—
  We cannot rule the year;
But long ere summer's sun goes down,
  On yonder sea we'll steer.

The dripping icebergs dipped and rose,
  And floundered down the gale;
The ships were stayed, the yards were manned,
  And furled the useless sail.

The summer's gone, the winter's come,—
  We sail not on yonder sea:
Why sail we not, Sir John Franklin?—
  A silent man was he.

The summer goes, the winter comes,—
  We cannot rule the year:
I ween we cannot rule the ways,
  Sir John, wherein we'd steer.

The cruel ice came floating on,
  And closed beneath the lee,
Till the thickening waters dashed no more:
'Twas ice around, behind, before—
  My God! there is no sea!

What think you of the whaler now?
  What of the Esquimau?
A sled were better than a ship,
  To cruise through ice and snow.

Down sank the baleful crimson sun,
  The northern light came out,
And glared upon the ice-bound ships,
  And shook its spears about.

The snow came down, storm breeding storm,
  And on the decks was laid,
Till the weary sailor, sick at heart,
  Sank down beside his spade.

Sir John, the night is black and long,
  The hissing wind is bleak,
The hard, green ice as strong as death:—
  I prithee, Captain, speak!

The night is neither bright nor short,
  The singing breeze is cold,—
The ice is not so strong as hope,
  The heart of man is bold!

What hope can scale this icy wall,
  High over the main flag-staff?
Above the ridges the wolf and bear
Look down, with a patient, settled stare,
  Look down on us and laugh.

The summer went, the winter came,—
  We could not rule the year;
But summer will melt the ice again,
And open a path to the sunny main,
  Whereon our ships shall steer.

The winter went, the summer went,
  The winter came around;
But the hard, green ice was strong as death,
And the voice of hope sank to a breath,
  Yet caught at every sound.

Hark! heard you not the noise of guns?—
  And there, and there, again?
'Tis some uneasy iceberg's roar,
  As he turns in the frozen main.

Hurra! Hurra! the Esquimaux
  Across the ice-fields steal:
God give them grace for their charity!—
  Ye pray for the silly seal.

Sir John, where are the English fields,
  And where are the English trees,
And where are the little English flowers
  That open in the breeze?

Be still, be still, my brave sailors!
  You shall see the fields again,
And smell the scent of the opening flowers,
  The grass, and the waving grain.

Oh! when shall I see my orphan child?
  My Mary waits for me.
Oh! when shall I see my old mother,
  And pray at her trembling knee?

Be still, be still, my brave sailors!
  Think not such thoughts again.
But a tear froze slowly on his cheek:
  He thought of Lady Jane.

Ah! bitter, bitter grows the cold,
  The ice grows more and more;
More settled stare the wolf and bear,
  More patient than before.

Oh, think you, good Sir John Franklin,
  We'll ever see the land?
'Twas cruel to send us here to starve,
  Without a helping hand.

'Twas cruel, Sir John, to send us here,
  So far from help or home,
To starve and freeze on this lonely sea:
I ween the lords of the Admiralty
  Would rather send than come.

Oh! whether we starve to death alone,
  Or sail to our own country,
We have done what man has never done—
The truth is founded, the secret won—
  We passed the Northern Sea!

*George Henry Boker* [1823–1890]

## MONTEREY

[SEPTEMBER 23, 1846]

We were not many, we who stood
Before the iron sleet that day:
Yet many a gallant spirit would
Give half his years if but he could
Have been with us at Monterey.

Now here, now there, the shot it hailed
In deadly drifts of fiery spray,
Yet not a single soldier quailed
When wounded comrades round them wailed
Their dying shout at Monterey.

And on—still on our column kept
Through walls of flame its withering way;
Where fell the dead, the living stepped,
Still charging on the guns which swept
The slippery streets of Monterey.

The foe himself recoiled aghast,
When, striking where he strongest lay,
We swooped his flanking batteries past,
And braving full their murderous blast,
Stormed home the towers of Monterey.

Our banners on those turrets wave,
And there our evening bugles play:
Where orange-boughs above their grave
Keep green the memory of the brave
Who fought and fell at Monterey.

We are not many—we who pressed
Beside the brave who fell that day—
But who of us has not confessed
He'd rather share their warrior rest
Than not have been at Monterey?

*Charles Fenno Hoffman* [1806–1884]

## PESCHIERA

[MAY, 1848]

WHAT voice did on my spirit fall,
Peschiera, when thy bridge I crossed?
"'Tis better to have fought and lost,
Than never to have fought at all."

The tricolor—a trampled rag
Lies, dirt and dust; the lines I track
By sentry boxes, yellow-black,
Lead up to no Italian flag.

I see the Croat soldier stand
Upon the grass of your redoubts;
The eagle with his black wing flouts
The breadth and beauty of your land.

Yet not in vain, although in vain,
O men of Brescia, on the day
Of loss past hope, I heard you say
Your welcome to the noble pain.

You said: "Since so it is, good-bye,
Sweet life, high hope; but whatsoe'er
May be, or must, no tongue shall dare
To tell, 'The Lombard feared to die!'"

You said (there shall be answer fit):
"And if our children must obey,
They must; but, thinking on this day,
'Twill less debase them to submit."

You said (O not in vain you said):
"Haste, brothers, haste, while yet we may
The hours ebb fast of this one day,
While blood may yet be nobly shed."

Ah! not for idle hatred, not
For honor, fame, nor self-applause,
But for the glory of the cause,
You did, what will not be forgot.

And though the stranger stand, 'tis true,
By force and fortune's right he stands:
By fortune, which is in God's hands,
And strength, which yet shall spring in you.

This voice did on my spirit fall,
Peschiera, when thy bridge I crossed:
"'Tis better to have fought and lost,
Than never to have fought at all."

*Arthur Hugh Clough* [1819–1861]

## THE LOSS OF THE BIRKENHEAD

SUPPOSED TO BE TOLD BY A SOLDIER WHO SURVIVED

[FEBRUARY 26, 1852]

Right on our flank the crimson sun went down;
The deep sea rolled around in dark repose;
When, like the wild shriek from some captured town,
A cry of women rose.

The stout ship *Birkenhead* lay hard and fast,
Caught without hope upon a hidden rock;
Her timbers thrilled as nerves, when through them passed
The spirit of that shock.

And ever like base cowards, who leave their ranks
In danger's hour, before the rush of steel,
Drifted away disorderly the planks
From underneath her keel.

So calm the air, so calm and still the flood,
That low down in its blue translucent glass
We saw the great fierce fish, that thirst for blood,
Pass slowly, then repass.

They tarried, the waves tarried, for their prey!
The sea turned one clear smile! Like things asleep
Those dark shapes in the azure silence lay,
As quiet as the deep.

Then amidst oath, and prayer, and rush, and wreck,
Faint screams, faint questions waiting no reply,
Our Colonel gave the word, and on the deck
Formed us in line to die.

To die!—'twas hard, whilst the sleek ocean glowed
Beneath a sky as fair as summer flowers:—
*All to the boats!* cried one:—he was, thank God,
No officer of ours!

Our English hearts beat true:—we would not stir:
That base appeal we heard, but heeded not:
On land, on sea, we had our Colors, sir,
To keep without a spot!

They shall not say in England, that we fought
With shameful strength, unhonored life to seek;
Into mean safety, mean deserters, brought
By trampling down the weak.

So we made women with their children go,
The oars ply back again, and yet again;
Whilst, inch by inch, the drowning ship sank low,
Still under steadfast men.

—What follows, why recall?—The brave who died,
Died without flinching in the bloody surf,
They sleep as well beneath that purple tide,
As others under turf:—

They sleep as well! and, roused from their wild grave,
Wearing their wounds like stars, shall rise again,
Joint-heirs with Christ, because they bled to save
His weak ones, not in vain.

*Francis Hastings Doyle* [1810–1888]

## THE CHARGE OF THE LIGHT BRIGADE

[BALACLAVA, OCTOBER 25, 1852]

HALF a league, half a league,
Half a league onward,
All in the valley of Death
Rode the six hundred.

"Forward, the Light Brigade!
Charge for the guns!" he said:
Into the valley of Death
  Rode the six hundred.

"Forward, the Light Brigade!"
Was there a man dismayed?
Not though the soldier knew
  Some one had blundered:
Theirs not to make reply,
Theirs not to reason why,
Theirs but to do and die:
Into the valley of Death
  Rode the six hundred.

Cannon to right of them,
Cannon to left of them,
Cannon in front of them
  Volleyed and thundered;
Stormed at with shot and shell,
Boldly they rode and well,
Into the jaws of Death,
Into the mouth of Hell
  Rode the six hundred.

Flashed all their sabres bare,
Flashed as they turned in air
Sabring the gunners there,
Charging an army, while
  All the world wondered:
Plunged in the battery-smoke
Right through the line they broke;
Cossack and Russian
Reeled from the sabre-stroke,
  Shattered and sundered.
Then they rode back, but not,
  Not the six hundred.

Cannon to right of them,
Cannon to left of them,
Cannon behind them

Volleyed and thundered;
Stormed at with shot and shell,
While horse and hero fell,
They that had fought so well
Came through the jaws of Death,
Back from the mouth of Hell,
All that was left of them,
Left of six hundred.

When can their glory fade?
O the wild charge they made!
All the world wondered.
Honor the charge they made!
Honor the Light Brigade,
Noble six hundred!

*Alfred Tennyson* [1809-1892]

## THE RELIEF OF LUCKNOW

[SEPTEMBER 26, 1857]

OH, that last day in Lucknow fort!
We knew that it was the last;
That the enemy's lines crept surely on,
And the end was coming fast.

To yield to that foe meant worse than death;
And the men and we all worked on;
It was one day more of smoke and roar,
And then it would all be done.

There was one of us, a corporal's wife,
A fair, young, gentle thing,
Wasted with fever in the siege,
And her mind was wandering.

She lay on the ground, in her Scottish plaid,
And I took her head on my knee;
"When my father comes hame frae the pleugh," she said,
"Oh! then please wauken me."

She slept like a child on her father's floor,
In the flecking of woodbine-shade,
When the house-dog sprawls by the open door,
And the mother's wheel is stayed.

It was smoke and roar and powder-stench,
And hopeless waiting for death;
And the soldier's wife, like a full-tired child,
Seemed scarce to draw her breath.

I sank to sleep; and I had my dream
Of an English village-lane,
And wall and garden;—but one wild scream
Brought me back to the roar again.

There Jessie Brown stood listening
Till a sudden gladness broke
All over her face; and she caught my hand
And drew me near as she spoke:—

"The Hielanders! O! dinna ye hear
The slogan far awa'?
The McGregor's. O! I ken it weel;
It's the grandest o' them a'!

"God bless the bonny Hielanders!
We're saved! we're saved!" she cried;
And fell on her knees; and thanks to God
Flowed forth like a full flood-tide.

Along the battery-line her cry
Had fallen among the men,
And they started back;—they were there to die;
But was life so near them, then?

They listened for life; the rattling fire
  Far off, and the far-off roar,
Were all; and the colonel shook his head,
  And they turned to their guns once more.

But Jessie said, "The slogan's done;
  But winna ye hear it noo,—
*The Campbells are comin'?* It's no a dream;
  Our succors hae broken through!"

We heard the roar and the rattle afar,
  But the pipes we could not hear;
So the men plied their work of hopeless war,
  And knew that the end was near.

It was not long ere it made its way,—
  A thrilling, ceaseless sound:
It was no noise from the strife afar,
  Or the sappers under ground.

It *was* the pipes of the Highlanders!
  And now they played *Auld Lang Syne*,
It came to our men like the voice of God,
  And they shouted along the line.

And they wept, and shook one another's hands,
  And the women sobbed in a crowd;
And every one knelt down where he stood,
  And we all thanked God aloud.

That happy time, when we welcomed them,
  Our men put Jessie first;
And the general gave her his hand, and cheers
  Like a storm from the soldiers burst.

And the pipers' ribbons and tartans streamed,
  Marching round and round our line;
And our joyful cheers were broken with tears,
  As the pipes played *Auld Lang Syne*.

*Robert Traill Spence Lowell* [1816–1891]

## THE PRIVATE OF THE BUFFS; OR, THE BRITISH SOLDIER IN CHINA

[1857]

Last night, among his fellow roughs,
He jested, quaffed, and swore;
A drunken private of the Buffs,
Who never looked before.
To-day, beneath the foeman's frown,
He stands in Elgin's place,
Ambassador from Britain's crown,
And type of all her race.

Poor, reckless, rude, low-born, untaught,
Bewildered, and alone,
A heart, with English instinct fraught,
He yet can call his own.
Ay, tear his body limb from limb,
Bring cord, or axe, or flame,
He only knows that not through him
Shall England come to shame.

Far Kentish hop-fields round him seemed,
Like dreams, to come and go;
Bright leagues of cherry-blossom gleamed,
One sheet of living snow;
The smoke above his father's door
In gray soft eddyings hung;
Must he then watch it rise no more,
Doomed by himself, so young?

Yes, honor calls!—with strength like steel
He put the vision by;
Let dusky Indians whine and kneel,
An English lad must die.
And thus, with eyes that would not shrink,
With knee to man unbent,
Unfaltering on its dreadful brink,
To his red grave he went.

Vain, mightiest fleets of iron framed,
  Vain, those all-shattering guns,
Unless proud England keep, untamed,
  The strong heart of her sons;
So let his name through Europe ring,—
  A man of mean estate,
Who died, as firm as Sparta's king,
  Because his soul was great.

*Francis Hastings Doyle* [1810–1888]

## HOW OLD BROWN TOOK HARPER'S FERRY

[OCTOBER 16, 1859]

JOHN BROWN in Kansas settled, like a steadfast Yankee farmer,
  Brave and godly, with four sons, all stalwart men of might.
There he spoke aloud for freedom, and the Border-strife grew warmer,
  Till the Rangers fired his dwelling, in his absence, in the night;
    And Old Brown,
    Osawatomie Brown,
Came homeward in the morning—to find his house burned down.

Then he grasped his trusty rifle and boldly fought for freedom;
  Smote from border unto border the fierce, invading band;
And he and his brave boys vowed—so might Heaven help and speed 'em!—
  They would save those grand old prairies from the curse that blights the land;
    And Old Brown,
    Osawatomie Brown,
Said, "Boys, the Lord will aid us!" and he shoved his ramrod down.

And the Lord *did* aid these men, and they labored day and even,
Saving Kansas from its peril; and their very lives seemed charmed,
Till the ruffians killed one son, in the blessèd light of Heaven:
In cold blood the fellows slew him, as he journeyed all unarmed;
Then Old Brown,
Osawatomie Brown,
Shed not a tear, but shut his teeth, and frowned a terrible frown!

Then they seized another brave boy,—not amid the heat of battle,
But in peace, behind his ploughshare,—and they loaded him with chains,
And with pikes, before their horses, even as they goad their cattle,
Drove him cruelly, for their sport, and at last blew out his brains;
Then Old Brown,
Osawatomie Brown,
Raised his right hand up to Heaven, calling Heaven's vengeance down.

And he swore a fearful oath, by the name of the Almighty,
He would hunt this ravening evil that had scathed and torn him so;
He would seize it by the vitals; he would crush it day and night; he
Would so pursue its footsteps, so return it blow for blow,
That Old Brown,
Osawatomie Brown,
Should be a name to swear by, in backwoods or in town!

Then his beard became more grizzled, and his wild blue eye grew wilder,
And more sharply curved his hawk's-nose, snuffing battle from afar;

And he and the two boys left, though the Kansas strife
    waxed milder,
  Grew more sullen, till was over the bloody Border War,
        And Old Brown,
        Osawatomie Brown,
Had gone crazy, as they reckoned by his fearful glare and
    frown.

So he left the plains of Kansas and their bitter woes behind
    him,
  Slipped off into Virginia, where the statesmen all are born.
Hired a farm by Harper's Ferry, and no one knew where to
    find him,
  Or whether he'd turned parson, or was jacketed and shorn;
        For Old Brown,
        Osawatomie Brown,
Mad as he was, knew texts enough to wear a parson's gown.

He bought no ploughs and harrows, spades and shovels,
    and such trifles;
  But quietly to his rancho there came, by every train,
Boxes full of pikes and pistols, and his well-beloved Sharp's
    rifles;
  And eighteen other madmen joined their leader there again.
        Says Old Brown,
        Osawatomie Brown,
"Boys, we've got an army large enough to march and take
    the town!

"Take the town, and seize the muskets, free the negroes,
    and then arm them;
  Carry the County and the State, ay, and all the potent
    South.
On their own heads be the slaughter, if their victims rise to
    harm them—
  These Virginians! who believed not, nor would heed the
    warning mouth."
        Says Old Brown,
        Osawatomie Brown,
"The world shall see a Republic, or my name is not John
    Brown."

'Twas the sixteenth of October, on the evening of a Sunday.
"This good work," declared the captain, "shall be on a holy night!"
It was on a Sunday evening, and before the noon of Monday,
With two sons, and Captain Stephens, fifteen privates—black and white,
Captain Brown,
Osawatomie Brown,
Marched across the bridged Potomac, and knocked the sentry down;

Took the guarded armory-building, and the muskets and the cannon;
Captured all the county majors and the colonels, one by one;
Scared to death each gallant scion of Virginia they ran on,
And before the noon of Monday, I say, the deed was done.
Mad Old Brown,
Osawatomie Brown,
With his eighteen other crazy men, went in and took the town.

Very little noise and bluster, little smell of powder made he;
It was all done in the midnight, like the Emperor's *coup d'etat*.
"Cut the wires! Stop the rail-cars! Hold the streets and bridges!" said he,
Then declared the new Republic, with himself for guiding star,—
This Old Brown,
Osawatomie Brown,
And the bold two thousand citizens ran off and left the town.

Then was riding and railroading and expressing here and thither;
And the Martinsburg Sharpshooters and the Charlestown Volunteers,
And the Shepherdstown and Winchester Militia hastened whither
Old Brown was said to muster his ten thousand grenadiers.

General Brown!
Osawatomie Brown!
Behind whose rampant banner all the North was pouring down.

But at last, 'tis said, some prisoners escaped from Old Brown's durance,
And the effervescent valor of the Chivalry broke out,
When they learned that nineteen madmen had the marvellous assurance—
Only nineteen—thus to seize the place and drive them straight about;
And Old Brown,
Osawatomie Brown,
Found an army come to take him, encamped around the town.

But to storm, with all the forces I have mentioned, was too risky;
So they hurried off to Richmond for the Government Marines,
Tore them from their weeping matrons, fired their souls with Bourbon whiskey,
Till they battered down Brown's castle with their ladders and machines;
And Old Brown,
Osawatomie Brown,
Received three bayonet stabs, and a cut on his brave old crown.

Tallyho! the old Virginia gentry gather to the baying!
In they rushed and killed the game, shooting lustily away;
And whene'er they slew a rebel, those who came too late for slaying,
Not to lose a share of glory, fired their bullets in his clay;
And Old Brown,
Osawatomie Brown,
Saw his sons fall dead beside him, and between them laid him down.

How the conquerors wore their laurels; how they hastened on the trial;
How Old Brown was placed, half dying, on the Charlestown court-house floor;
How he spoke his grand oration, in the scorn of all denial;
What the brave old madman told them,—these are known the country o'er.
"Hang Old Brown,
Osawatomie Brown,"
Said the judge, "and all such rebels!" with his most judicial frown.

But, Virginians, don't do it! for I tell you that the flagon,
Filled with blood of Old Brown's offspring, was first poured by Southern hands;
And each drop from Old Brown's life-veins, like the red gore of the dragon,
May spring up a vengeful Fury, hissing through your slave-worn lands!
And Old Brown,
Osawatomie Brown,
May trouble you more than ever, when you've nailed his coffin down!

*Edmund Clarence Stedman* [1833–1908]

## BROWN OF OSSAWATOMIE

[DECEMBER 2, 1859]

John Brown of Ossawatomie spake on his dying day:
"I will not have to shrive my soul a priest in Slavery's pay.
But let some poor slave-mother whom I have striven to free,
With her children, from the gallows-stair put up a prayer for me!"

John Brown of Ossawatomie, they led him out to die;
And lo! a poor slave-mother with her little child pressed nigh.

Then the bold, blue eye grew tender, and the old harsh face
grew mild,
As he stooped between the jeering ranks and kissed the
negro's child!

The shadows of his stormy life that moment fell apart;
And they who blamed the bloody hand forgave the loving
heart.
That kiss from all its guilty means redeemed the good intent,
And round the grisly fighter's hair the martyr's aureole bent!

Perish with him the folly that seeks through evil good!
Long live the generous purpose unstained with human blood!
Not the raid of midnight terror, but the thought which un-
derlies;
Not the borderer's pride of daring, but the Christian's sacri-
fice.

Nevermore may yon Blue Ridges the Northern rifle hear,
Nor see the light of blazing homes flash on the negro's spear;
But let the free-winged angel Truth their guarded passes
scale,
To teach that right is more than might, and justice more
than mail!

So vainly shall Virginia set her battle in array;
In vain her trampling squadrons knead the winter snow with
clay.
She may strike the pouncing eagle, but she dares not harm
the dove;
And every gate she bars to Hate, shall open wide to Love!

*John Greenleaf Whittier* [1807–1892]

## BROTHER JONATHAN'S LAMENT FOR SISTER CAROLINE

[DECEMBER 20, 1860]

SHE has gone,—she has left us in passion and pride,—
Our stormy-browed sister, so long at our side!
She has torn her own star from our firmament's glow,
And turned on her brother the face of a foe!

Oh, Caroline, Caroline, child of the sun,
We can never forget that our hearts have been one,—
Our foreheads both sprinkled in Liberty's name,
From the fountain of blood with the finger of flame!

You were always too ready to fire at a touch;
But we said: "She is hasty,—she does not mean much."
We have scowled when you uttered some turbulent threat;
But Friendship still whispered: "Forgive and forget!"

Has our love all died out? Have its altars grown cold?
Has the curse come at last which the fathers foretold?
Then Nature must teach us the strength of the chain
That her petulant children would sever in vain.

They may fight till the buzzards are gorged with their spoil,
Till the harvest grows black as it rots in the soil,
Till the wolves and the catamounts troop from their caves,
And the shark tracks the pirate, the lord of the waves:

In vain is the strife! When its fury is past,
Their fortunes must flow in one channel at last,
As the torrents that rush from the mountains of snow
Roll mingled in peace through the valleys below.

Our Union is river, lake, ocean, and sky;
Man breaks not the medal, when God cuts the die!
Though darkened with sulphur, though cloven with steel,
The blue arch will brighten, the waters will heal!

Oh, Caroline, Caroline, child of the sun,
There are battles with Fate that can never be won!
The star-flowering banner must never be furled,
For its blossoms of light are the hope of the world!

Go, then, our rash sister! afar and aloof,
Run wild in the sunshine away from our roof;
But when your heart aches and your feet have grown sore,
Remember the pathway that leads to our door!

*Oliver Wendell Holmes* [1809–1894]

## THE REVEILLE

[April, 1861]

Hark! I hear the tramp of thousands,
And of armèd men the hum;
Lo! a nation's hosts have gathered
Round the quick alarming drum,—
Saying, "Come,
Freemen, come!
Ere your heritage be wasted," said the quick alarming drum.

"Let me of my heart take counsel:
War is not of life the sum;
Who shall stay and reap the harvest
When the autumn days shall come?"
But the drum
Echoed, "Come!
Death shall reap the braver harvest," said the solemn-sounding drum.

"But when won the coming battle,
What of profit springs therefrom?
What if conquest, subjugation,
Even greater ills become?"
But the drum
Answered, "Come!
You must do the sum to prove it," said the Yankee answering drum.

"What if, 'mid the cannons' thunder,
Whistling shot and bursting bomb,
When my brothers fall around me,
Should my heart grow cold and numb?"
But the drum
Answered, "Come!
Better there in death united, than in life a recreant.—Come!"

Thus they answered,—hoping, fearing,
Some in faith, and doubting some,

Till a trumpet-voice proclaiming,
Said, "My chosen people, come!"
Then the drum,
Lo! was dumb,
For the great heart of the nation, throbbing, answered,
"Lord, we come!"

*Bret Harte* [1839-1902]

## THE WASHERS OF THE SHROUD

[OCTOBER, 1861]

ALONG a river-side, I know not where,
I walked one night in mystery of dream;
A chill creeps curdling yet beneath my hair,
To think what chanced me by the pallid gleam
Of a moon-wraith that waned through haunted air.

Pale fireflies pulsed within the meadow-mist
Their halos, wavering thistledowns of light;
The loon, that seemed to mock some goblin tryst,
Laughed; and the echoes, huddling in affright,
Like Odin's hounds, fled baying down the night.

Then all was silent, till there smote my ear
A movement in the stream that checked my breath:
Was it the slow plash of a wading deer?
But something said, "This water is of Death!
The Sisters wash a shroud,—ill thing to hear!"

I, looking then, beheld the ancient Three
Known to the Greek's and to the Northman's creed,
That sit in shadow of the mystic Tree,
Still crooning, as they weave their endless brede,
One song: "Time was, Time is, and Time shall be."

No wrinkled crones were they, as I had deemed,
But fair as yesterday, to-day, to-morrow,
To mourner, lover, poet, ever seemed;
Something too high for joy, too deep for sorrow,
Thrilled in their tones, and from their faces gleamed.

"Still men and nations reap as they have strawn,"
So sang they, working at their task the while;
"The fatal raiment must be cleansed ere dawn:
For Austria? Italy? the Sea-Queen's isle?
O'er what quenched grandeur must our shroud be drawn?

"Or is it for a younger, fairer corse,
That gathered States like children round his knees,
That tamed the wave to be his posting-horse,
Feller of forests, linker of the seas,
Bridge-builder, hammerer, youngest son of Thor's?

"What make we, murmurest thou? and what are we?
When empires must be wound, we bring the shroud,
The time-old web of the implacable Three:
Is it too coarse for him, the young and proud?
Earth's mightiest deigned to wear it,—why not he?"

"Is there no hope?" I moaned, "so strong, so fair!
Our Fowler whose proud bird would brook erewhile
No rival's swoop in all our western air!
Gather the ravens, then, in funeral file
For him, life's morn yet golden in his hair?

"Leave me not hopeless, ye unpitying dames!
I see, half seeing. Tell me, ye who scanned
The stars, Earth's elders, still must noblest aims
Be traced upon oblivious ocean-sands?
Must Hesper join the wailing ghosts of names?"

"When grass-blades stiffen with red battle-dew,
Ye deem we choose the victor and the slain:
Say, choose we them that shall be leal and true
To the heart's longing, the high faith of brain?
Yet there the victory lies, if ye but knew.

"Three roots bear up Dominion: Knowledge, Will,—
These twain are strong, but stronger yet the third,—
Obedience,—'tis the great tap-root that still,
Knit round the rock of Duty, is not stirred,
Though Heaven-loosed tempests spend their utmost skill

"Is the doom sealed for Hesper? 'Tis not we
Denounce it, but the Law before all time:
The brave makes danger opportunity;
The waverer, paltering with the chance sublime,
Dwarfs it to peril: which shall Hesper be?

"Hath he let vultures climb his eagle's seat
To make Jove's bolts purveyors of their maw?
Hath he the Many's plaudits found more sweet
Than Wisdom? held Opinion's wind for Law?
Then let him hearken for the doomster's feet!

"Rough are the steps, slow-hewn in flintiest rock,
States climb to power by; slippery those with gold
Down which they stumble to eternal mock:
No chafferer's hand shall long the sceptre hold,
Who, given a Fate to shape, would sell the block.

"We sing old Sagas, songs of weal and woe,
Mystic because too cheaply understood;
Dark sayings are not ours; men hear and know,
See Evil weak, see strength alone in Good,
Yet hope to stem God's fire with walls of tow.

"Time Was unlocks the riddle of Time Is,
That offers choice of glory or of gloom;
The solver makes Time Shall Be surely his.
But hasten, Sisters! for even now the tomb
Grates its slow hinge and calls from the abyss."

"But not for him," I cried, "not yet for him,
Whose large horizon, westering, star by star
Wins from the void to where on Ocean's rim
The sunset shuts the world with golden bar,
Nor yet his thews shall fail, his eye grow dim!

"His shall be larger manhood, saved for those
That walk unblenching through the trial-fires;
Not suffering, but faint heart, is worst of woes,
And he no base-born son of craven sires,
Whose eye need blench confronted with his foes.

"Tears may be ours, but proud, for those who win
Death's royal purple in the foeman's lines;
Peace, too, brings tears; and mid the battle-din,
The wiser ear some text of God divines,
For the sheathed blade may rust with darker sin.

"God, give us peace! not such as lulls to sleep,
But sword on thigh, and brow with purpose knit!
And let our Ship of State to harbor sweep,
Her ports all up, her battle-lanterns lit,
And her leashed thunders gathering for their leap!"

So cried I with clenched hands and passionate pain,
Thinking of dear ones by Potomac's side;
Again the loon laughed mocking, and again
The echoes bayed far down the night and died,
While waking I recalled my wandering brain.

*James Russell Lowell* [1819-1891]

## THE PICKET-GUARD

[NOVEMBER, 1861]

"ALL quiet along the Potomac," they say,
"Except now and then a stray picket
Is shot, as he walks on his beat to and fro,
By a rifleman hid in the thicket.
'Tis nothing: a private or two, now and then,
Will not count in the news of the battle;
Not an officer lost—only one of the men,
Moaning out, all alone, the death-rattle."

All quiet along the Potomac to-night,
Where the soldiers lie peacefully dreaming;
Their tents in the rays of the clear autumn moon,
Or the light of the watch-fire, are gleaming.
A tremulous sigh of the gentle night-wind
Through the forest leaves softly is creeping,
While the stars up above, with their glittering eyes,
Keep guard, for the army is sleeping.

There's only the sound of the lone sentry's tread,
As he tramps from the rock to the fountain,
And thinks of the two in the low trundle-bed
Far away in the cot on the mountain.
His musket falls slack; his face, dark and grim,
Grows gentle with memories tender,
As he mutters a prayer for the children asleep—
For their mother—may Heaven defend her!

The moon seems to shine just as brightly as then,
That night, when the love yet unspoken
Leaped up to his lips—when low-murmured vows
Were pledged to be ever unbroken.
Then drawing his sleeve roughly over his eyes,
He dashes off tears that are welling,
And gathers his gun closer up to its place
As if to keep down the heart-swelling.

He passes the fountain, the blasted pine-tree;
The footstep is lagging and weary;
Yet onward he goes, through the broad belt of light,
Towards the shade of the forest so dreary.
Hark! was it the night-wind that rustled the leaves?
Was it moonlight so wondrously flashing?
It looked like a rifle . . . "Ha! Mary, good-by!"
The red life-blood is ebbing and plashing.

All quiet along the Potomac to-night;
No sound save the rush of the river;
While soft falls the dew on the face of the dead—
The picket's off duty forever.

*Ethel Lynn Beers* [1827–1879]

## CIVIL WAR

[1861]

"Rifleman, shoot me a fancy shot
Straight at the heart of yon prowling vidette;
Ring me a ball in the glittering spot
That shines on his breast like an amulet!"

"Ah, captain! here goes for a fine-drawn bead,
There's music around when my barrel's in tune!"
Crack! went the rifle, the messenger sped,
And dead from his horse fell the ringing dragoon.

"Now, rifleman, steal through the bushes, and snatch
From your victim some trinket to handsel first blood;
A button, a loop, or that luminous patch
That gleams in the moon like a diamond stud!"

"O captain! I staggered, and sunk on my track,
When I gazed on the face of that fallen vidette,
For he looked so like you, as he lay on his back,
That my heart rose upon me, and masters me yet.

"But I snatched off the trinket,—this locket of gold;
An inch from the center my lead broke its way,
Scarce grazing the picture, so fair to behold,
Of a beautiful lady in bridal array."

"Ha! rifleman, fling me the locket!—'tis she,
My brother's young bride,—and the fallen dragoon
Was her husband—Hush! soldier, 'twas Heaven's decree;
We must bury him there, by the light of the moon!

"But, hark! the far bugles their warnings unite;
War is a virtue,—weakness a sin;
There's a lurking and loping around us to-night;
Load again, rifleman, keep your hand in!"

*Charles Dawson Shanly* [1811-1875]

## KEARNY AT SEVEN PINES

[MAY 31, 1862]

So that soldierly legend is still on its journey,—
That story of Kearny who knew not to yield!
'Twas the day when with Jameson, fierce Berry, and Birney,
Against twenty thousand he rallied the field.

Where the red volleys poured, where the clamor rose highest,
  Where the dead lay in clumps through the dwarf oak and pine,
Where the aim from the thicket was surest and nighest,—
  No charge like Phil Kearny's along the whole line.

When the battle went ill, and the bravest were solemn,
  Near the dark Seven Pines, where we still held our ground,
He rode down the length of the withering column,
  And his heart at our war-cry leapt up with a bound;
He snuffed, like his charger, the wind of the powder,—
  His sword waved us on and we answered the sign;
Loud our cheer as we rushed, but his laugh rang the louder,
  "There's the devil's own fun, boys, along the whole line!"

How he strode his brown steed! How we saw his blade brighten
  In the one hand still left,—and the reins in his teeth!
He laughed like a boy when the holidays heighten,
  But a soldier's glance shot from his visor beneath.
Up came the reserves to the mellay infernal,
  Asking where to go in,—through the clearing or pine?
"Oh, anywhere! Forward! 'Tis all the same, Colonel:
  You'll find lovely fighting along the whole line!"

Oh, evil the black shroud of night at Chantilly,
  That hid him from sight of his brave men and tried!
Foul, foul sped the bullet that clipped the white lily,
  The flower of our knighthood, the whole army's pride!
Yet we dream that he still,—in that shadowy region
  Where the dead form their ranks at the wan drummer's sign,—
Rides on, as of old, down the length of his legion,
  And the word still is "Forward!" along the whole line.

*Edmund Clarence Stedman* [1833–1908]

## BARBARA FRIETCHIE

[SEPTEMBER 13, 1862]

Up from the meadows rich with corn,
Clear in the cool September morn,

The clustered spires of Frederick stand
Green-walled by the hills of Maryland.

Round about them orchards sweep,
Apple and peach tree fruited deep,

Fair as the garden of the Lord
To the eyes of the famished rebel horde,

On that pleasant morn of the early fall
When Lee marched over the mountain-wall;

Over the mountains winding down,
Horse and foot, into Frederick town.

Forty flags with their silver stars,
Forty flags with their crimson bars,

Flapped in the morning wind: the sun
Of noon looked down, and saw not one.

Up rose old Barbara Frietchie then,
Bowed with her fourscore years and ten;

Bravest of all in Frederick town,
She took up the flag the men hauled down;

In her attic window the staff she set,
To show that one heart was loyal yet.

Up the street came the rebel tread,
Stonewall Jackson riding ahead.

Under his slouched hat left and right
He glanced; the old flag met his sight.

"Halt!"—the dust-brown ranks stood fast.
"Fire!"—out blazed the rifle-blast.

It shivered the window, pane and sash;
It rent the banner with seam and gash

Quick as it fell, from the broken staff
Dame Barbara snatched the silken scarf.

She leaned far out on the window-sill,
And shook it forth with a royal will.

"Shoot, if you must, this old gray head,
But spare your country's flag," she said.

A shade of sadness, a blush of shame,
Over the face of the leader came;

The nobler nature within him stirred
To life at that woman's deed and word;

"Who touches a hair of yon gray head
Dies like a dog! March on!" he said.

All day long through Frederick street
Sounded the tread of marching feet:

All day long that free flag tossed
Over the heads of the rebel host.

Ever its torn folds rose and fell
On the loyal winds that loved it well;

And through the hill-gaps sunset light
Shone over it with a warm good-night.

Barbara Frietchie's work is o'er,
And the Rebel rides on his raids no more

Honor to her! and let a tear
Fall, for her sake, on Stonewall's bier.

Over Barbara Frietchie's grave,
Flag of Freedom and Union, wave!

Peace and order and beauty draw
Round thy symbol of light and law:

And ever the stars above look down
On thy stars below in Frederick town!

*John Greenleaf Whittier* [1807-1892]

## KEENAN'S CHARGE

[MAY 2, 1863]

I

THE sun had set;
The leaves with dew were wet:—
Down fell a bloody dusk
On the woods, that second of May,
Where "Stonewall's" corps, like a beast of prey,
Tore through, with angry tusk.

"They've trapped us, boys!"
Rose from our flank a voice.
With rush of steel and smoke
On came the rebels straight,
Eager as love and wild as hate;
And our line reeled and broke;

Broke and fled.
Not one stayed,— but the dead!
With curses, shrieks, and cries,
Horses and wagons and men
Tumbled back through the shuddering glen.
And above us the fading skies.

There's one hope, still,—
Those batteries, parked on the hill!
"Battery, wheel!" ('mid the roar),
"Pass pieces; fix prolonge to fire
Retiring. Trot!" In the panic dire
A bugle rings "Trot!"—and no more.

The horses plunged,
The cannon lurched and lunged.

To join the hopeless rout.
But suddenly rose a form
Calmly in front of the human storm,
With a stern, commanding shout:

"Align those guns!"
(We knew it was Pleasonton's.)
The cannoneers bent to obey,
And worked with a will at his word,
And the black guns moved as if *they* had heard.
But, ah, the dread delay!

"To wait is crime;
O God, for ten minutes' time!"
The General looked around.
There Keenan sat, like a stone,
With his three hundred horse alone,
Less shaken than the ground.

"Major, your men?"
"Are soldiers, General." "Then,
Charge, Major! Do your best;
Hold the enemy back, at all cost,
Till my guns are placed;—else the army is lost.
You die to save the rest!"

II

By the shrouded gleam of the western skies,
Brave Keenan looked into Pleasonton's eyes
For an instant—clear, and cool, and still;
Then, with a smile, he said: "I will."

"Cavalry, charge!" Not a man of them shrank.
Their sharp, full cheer, from rank on rank,
Rose joyously, with a willing breath,—
Rose like a greeting hail to death.

Then forward they sprang, and spurred, and clashed;
Shouted the officers, crimson-sashed;
Rode well the men, each brave as his fellow,
In their faded coats of the blue and yellow:

And above in the air, with an instinct true,
Like a bird of war their pennon flew.

With clank of scabbards and thunder of steeds,
And blades that shine like sunlit reeds,
And strong brown faces bravely pale
For fear their proud attempt shall fail,
Three hundred Pennsylvanians close
On twice ten thousand gallant foes.

Line after line the troopers came
To the edge of the wood that was ringed with flame;
Rode in, and sabred, and shot,—and fell:
Nor came one back his wounds to tell.
And full in the midst rose Keenan, tall,
In the gloom, like a martyr awaiting his fall,
While the circle-stroke of his sabre, swung
'Round his head, like a halo there, luminous hung.

Line after line, aye, whole platoons,
Struck dead in their saddles, of brave dragoons
By the maddened horses were onward borne
And into the vortex flung, trampled and torn;
As Keenan fought with his men, side by side.

So they rode, till there were no more to ride.

But over them, lying there shattered and mute,
What deep echo rolls? 'Tis a death-salute
From the cannon in place; for, heroes, you braved
Your fate not in vain: the army was saved!

Over them now,—year following year,—
Over their graves the pine-cones fall,
And the whippoorwill chants his spectre-call;
But they stir not again; they raise no cheer;
They have ceased. But their glory shall never cease
Nor their light be quenched in the light of peace.
The rush of their charge is resounding still,
That saved the army at Chancellorsville.

*George Parsons Lathrop* [1851–1898]

## THE BLACK REGIMENT

[PORT HUDSON, MAY 27, 1863]

DARK as the clouds of even,
Ranked in the western heaven,
Waiting the breath that lifts
All the dead mass, and drifts
Tempest and falling brand
Over a ruined land,—
So still and orderly,
Arm to arm, knee to knee,
Waiting the great event,
Stands the black regiment.

Down the long dusky line
Teeth gleam and eyeballs shine;
And the bright bayonet,
Bristling and firmly set,
Flashed with a purpose grand,
Long ere the sharp command
Of the fierce rolling drum
Told them their time had come,
Told them what work was sent
For the black regiment.

"Now," the flag-sergeant cried,
"Though death and hell betide,
Let the whole nation see
If we are fit to be
Free in this land; or bound
Down, like the whining hound,—
Bound with red stripes of pain
In our old chains again!"
Oh, what a shout there went
From the black regiment!

"Charge!" Trump and drum awoke;
Onward the bondmen broke;
Bayonet and saber-stroke

Vainly opposed their rush.
Through the wild battle's crush,
With but one thought aflush,
Driving their lords like chaff,
In the guns' mouths they laugh;
Or at the slippery brands,
Leaping with open hands,
Down they tear man and horse,
Down in their awful course;
Trampling with bloody heel
Over the crashing steel,
All their eyes forward bent,
Rushed the black regiment.

"Freedom!" their battle-cry,—
"Freedom! or leave to die!"
Ah! and they meant the word,
Not as with us 'tis heard,
Not a mere party shout:
They gave their spirits out;
Trusted the end to God,
And on the gory sod
Rolled in triumphant blood.
Glad to strike one free blow,
Whether for weal or woe;
Glad to breathe one free breath,
Though on the lips of death;
Praying,—alas! in vain!—
That they might fall again,
So they could once more see
That burst to liberty!
This was what "freedom" lent
To the black regiment.

Hundreds on hundreds fell;
But they are resting well;
Scourges and shackles strong
Never shall do them wrong.
Oh, to the living few,
Soldiers, be just and true!

Hail them as comrades tried;
Fight with them side by side;
Never, in field or tent,
Scorn the black regiment!

*George Henry Boker* [1823–1890]

## THE HIGH TIDE AT GETTYSBURG

[JULY 3, 1863]

A CLOUD possessed the hollow field,
The gathering battle's smoky shield:
  Athwart the gloom the lightning flashed,
  And through the cloud some horsemen dashed,
And from the heights the thunder pealed.

Then, at the brief command of Lee,
Moved out that matchless infantry,
  With Pickett leading grandly down,
  To rush against the roaring crown
Of those dread heights of destiny.

Far heard above the angry guns,
A cry across the tumult runs:
  The voice that rang through Shiloh's woods,
  And Chickamauga's solitudes:
The fierce South cheering on her sons!

Ah, how the withering tempest blew
Against the front of Pettigrew!
  A Khamsin wind that scorched and singed,
  Like that infernal flame that fringed
The British squares at Waterloo!

A thousand fall where Kemper led;
A thousand died where Garnett bled;
  In blinding flame and strangling smoke,
  The remnant through the batteries broke,
And crossed the works with Armistead.

"Once more in Glory's van with me!"
Virginia cried to Tennessee:
"We two together, come what may,
Shall stand upon those works to-day!"
The reddest day in history.

Brave Tennessee! In reckless way
Virginia heard her comrade say:
"Close round this rent and riddled rag!"
What time she set her battle-flag
Amid the guns of Doubleday.

But who shall break the guards that wait
Before the awful face of Fate?
The tattered standards of the South
Were shrivelled at the cannon's mouth,
And all her hopes were desolate.

In vain the Tennesseean set
His breast against the bayonet;
In vain Virginia charged and raged,
A tigress in her wrath uncaged,
Till all the hill was red and wet!

Above the bayonets, mixed and crossed,
Men saw a gray, gigantic ghost
Receding through the battle-cloud,
And heard across the tempest loud
The death-cry of a nation lost!

The brave went down! Without disgrace
They leaped to Ruin's red embrace;
They only heard Fame's thunders wake,
And saw the dazzling sun-burst break
In smiles on Glory's bloody face!

They fell, who lifted up a hand
And bade the sun in heaven to stand;
They smote and fell, who set the bars
Against the progress of the stars,
And stayed the march of Motherland!

They stood, who saw the future come
On through the fight's delirium;
  They smote and stood, who held the hope
  Of nations on that slippery slope,
Amid the cheers of Christendom!

God lives! He forged the iron will,
That clutched and held that trembling hill!
  God lives and reigns! He built and lent
  The heights for Freedom's battlement,
Where floats her flag in triumph still!

Fold up the banners! Smelt the guns!
Love rules. Her gentler purpose runs.
  A mighty mother turns in tears,
  The pages of her battle years,
Lamenting all her fallen sons!

*Will Henry Thompson* [1848–1918]

## JOHN BURNS OF GETTYSBURG

Have you heard the story that gossips tell
Of Burns of Gettysburg? No? Ah, well:
Brief is the glory that hero earns,
Briefer the story of poor John Burns:
He was the fellow who won renown,—
The only man who didn't back down
When the rebels rode through his native town;
But held his own in the fight next day,
When all his townsfolk ran away.
That was in July, sixty-three,—
The very day that General Lee,
Flower of Southern chivalry,
Baffled and beaten, backward reeled
From a stubborn Meade and a barren field.

I might tell how, but the day before,
John Burns stood at his cottage door,
Looking down the village street,

Where, in the shade of his peaceful vine,
He heard the low of his gathered kine,
And felt their breath with incense sweet;
Or I might say, when the sunset burned
The old farm gable, he thought it turned
The milk that fell like a babbling flood
Into the milk-pail, red as blood!
Or how he fancied the hum of bees
Were bullets buzzing among the trees.
But all such fanciful thoughts as these
Were strange to a practical man like Burns,
Who minded only his own concerns,
Troubled no more by fancies fine
Than one of his calm-eyed, long-tailed kine,—
Quite old-fashioned and matter-of-fact,
Slow to argue, but quick to act.
That was the reason, as some folks say,
He fought so well on that terrible day.

And it was terrible. On the right
Raged for hours the heady fight,
Thundered the battery's double bass,—
Difficult music for men to face;
While on the left—where now the graves
Undulate like the living waves
That all that day unceasing swept
Up to the pits the rebels kept—
Round-shot ploughed the upland glades,
Sown with bullets, reaped with blades;
Shattered fences here and there
Tossed their splinters in the air;
The very trees were stripped and bare;
The barns that once held yellow grain
Were heaped with harvests of the slain;
The cattle bellowed on the plain,
The turkeys screamed with might and main,
The brooding barn-fowl left their rest
With strange shells bursting in each nest.

Just where the tide of battle turns,
Erect and lonely, stood old John Burns.

How do you think the man was dressed?
He wore an ancient long buff vest,
Yellow as saffron,—but his best;
And, buttoned over his manly breast,
Was a bright blue coat, with a rolling collar,
And large gilt buttons,—size of a dollar,—
With tails that the country-folk called "swaller."
He wore a broad-brimmed, bell-crowned hat,
White as the locks on which it sat.
Never had such a sight been seen
For forty years on the village green,
Since old John Burns was a country beau,
And went to the "quiltings" long ago.

Close at his elbows all that day,
Veterans of the Peninsula,
Sunburnt and bearded, charged away;
And striplings, downy of lip and chin,—
Clerks that the Home-Guard mustered in,—
Glanced, as they passed, at the hat he wore,
Then at the rifle his right hand bore;
And hailed him, from out their youthful lore,
With scraps of a slangy repertoire:
"How are you, White Hat?" "Put her through!"
"Your head's level!" and "Bully for you!"
Called him "Daddy,"—begged he'd disclose
The name of the tailor who made his clothes,
And what was the value he set on those;
While Burns, unmindful of jeer or scoff,
Stood there picking the rebels off,—
With his long brown rifle, and bell-crowned hat,
And the swallow-tails they were laughing at.

'Twas but a moment, for that respect
Which clothes all courage their voices checked;
And something the wildest could understand
Spake in the old man's strong right hand,
And his corded throat, and the lurking frown
Of his eyebrows under his old bell-crown;
Until, as they gazed, there crept an awe
Through the ranks in whispers, and some men saw,

In the antique vestments and long white hair,
The Past of the Nation in battle there;
And some of the soldiers since declare
That the gleam of his old white hat afar,
Like the crested plume of the brave Navarre,
That day was their oriflamme of war.

So raged the battle. You know the rest:
How the rebels, beaten and backward pressed,
Broke at the final charge and ran.
At which John Burns—a practical man—
Shouldered his rifle, unbent his brows,
And then went back to his bees and cows.

That is the story of old John Burns;
This is the moral the reader learns:
In fighting the battle, the question's whether
You'll show a hat that's white, or a feather!

*Bret Harte* [1839-1902]

## FARRAGUT

[MOBILE BAY, AUGUST 5, 1864]

FARRAGUT, Farragut,
    Old Heart of Oak,
Daring Dave Farragut,
    Thunderbolt stroke,
Watches the hoary mist
    Lift from the bay,
Till his flag, glory-kissed,
    Greets the young day.

Far, by gray Morgan's walls,
    Looms the black fleet.
Hark, deck to rampart calls
    With the drums' beat!
Buoy your chains overboard,
    While the steam hums;
Men! to the battlement,
    Farragut comes.

See, as the hurricane
  Hurtles in wrath
Squadrons of clouds amain
  Back from its path!
Back to the parapet,
  To the guns' lips,
Thunderbolt Farragut
  Hurls the black ships.

Now through the battle's roar
  Clear the boy sings,
"By the mark fathoms four,"
  While his lead swings.
Steady the wheelmen five
  "Nor' by East keep her,"
"Steady," but two alive:
  How the shells sweep her!

Lashed to the mast that sways
  Over red decks,
Over the flame that plays
  Round the torn wrecks,
Over the dying lips
  Framed for a cheer,
Farragut leads his ships,
  Guides the line clear.

On by heights cannon-browed,
  While the spars quiver;
Onward still flames the cloud
  Where the hulks shiver.
See, yon fort's star is set,
  Storm and fire past.
Cheer him, lads—Farragut,
  Lashed to the mast!

Oh! while Atlantic's breast
  Bears a white sail,
While the Gulf's towering crest
  Tops a green vale,

Men thy bold deeds shall tell,
  Old Heart of Oak,
Daring Dave Farragut,
  Thunderbolt stroke!

*William Tucker Meredith* [1839-?]

## CRAVEN

[MOBILE BAY, AUGUST 5, 1864]

OVER the turret, shut in his ironclad tower,
  Craven was conning his ship through smoke and flame;
Gun to gun he had battered the fort for an hour,
  Now was the time for a charge to end the game.

There lay the narrowing channel, smooth and grim,
  A hundred deaths beneath it, and never a sign:
There lay the enemy's ships, and sink or swim
  The flag was flying, and he was head of the line.

The fleet behind was jamming: the monitor hung
  Beating the stream; the roar for a moment hushed;
Craven spoke to the pilot; slow she swung;
  Again he spoke, and right for the foe she rushed

Into the narrowing channel, between the shore
  And the sunk torpedoes lying in treacherous rank;
She turned but a yard too short; a muffled roar,
  A mountainous wave, and she rolled, righted, and sank.

Over the manhole, up in the ironclad tower,
  Pilot and captain met as they turned to fly:
The hundredth part of a moment seemed an hour,
  For one could pass to be saved, and one must die.

They stood like men in a dream; Craven spoke,—
  Spoke as he lived and fought, with a captain's pride:
"After you, Pilot." The pilot woke,
  Down the ladder he went, and Craven died.

All men praise the deed and the manner; but we—
  We set it apart from the pride that stoops to the proud,
The strength that is supple to serve the strong and free,
  The grave of the empty hands and promises loud;

Sidney thirsting a humbler need to slake,
  Nelson waiting his turn for the surgeon's hand,
Lucas crushed with chains for a comrade's sake,
  Outram coveting right before command,

These were paladins, these were Craven's peers,
  These with him shall be crowned in story and song,
Crowned with the glitter of steel and the glimmer of tears,
  Princes of courtesy, merciful, proud, and strong.

*Henry Newbolt* [1862-1938]

## SHERIDAN'S RIDE

[OCTOBER 19, 1864]

Up from the South, at break of day,
Bringing to Winchester fresh dismay,
The affrighted air with a shudder bore,
Like a herald in haste, to the chieftain's door,
The terrible grumble, and rumble, and roar,
Telling the battle was on once more,
    And Sheridan twenty miles away.

And wider still those billows of war
Thundered along the horizon's bar;
And louder yet into Winchester rolled
The roar of that red sea uncontrolled,
Making the blood of the listener cold,
As he thought of the stake in that fiery fray,
    And Sheridan twenty miles away.

But there is a road from Winchester town,
A good, broad highway leading down:
And there, through the flush of the morning light,
A steed as black as the steeds of night
Was seen to pass, as with eagle flight;

As if he knew the terrible need,
He stretched away with his utmost speed;
Hills rose and fell, but his heart was gay,
With Sheridan fifteen miles away.

Still sprang from those swift hoofs, thundering south,
The dust, like smoke from the cannon's mouth,
Or the trail of a comet, sweeping faster and faster,
Foreboding to traitors the doom of disaster.
The heart of the steed and the heart of the master
Were beating like prisoners assaulting their walls,
Impatient to be where the battle-field calls;
Every nerve of the charger was strained to full play,
With Sheridan only ten miles away.

Under his spurning feet, the road
Like an arrowy Alpine river flowed,
And the landscape sped away behind
Like an ocean flying before the wind;
And the steed, like a bark fed with furnace ire,
Swept on, with his wild eye full of fire;
But, lo! he is nearing his heart's desire;
He is snuffing the smoke of the roaring fray,
With Sheridan only five miles away.

The first that the general saw were the groups
Of stragglers, and then the retreating troops;
What was done? what to do? a glance told him both,
Then, striking his spurs, with a terrible oath,
He dashed down the line, 'mid a storm of huzzas,
And the wave of retreat checked its course there, because
The sight of the master compelled it to pause.
With foam and with dust the black charger was gray;
By the flash of his eye, and the red nostril's play,
He seemed to the whole great army to say:
"I have brought you Sheridan all the way
From Winchester town to save the day!"

Hurrah! hurrah for Sheridan!
Hurrah! hurrah for horse and man!

And when their statues are placed on high,
Under the dome of the Union sky,
The American soldier's Temple of Fame,
There, with the glorious general's name,
Be it said, in letters both bold and bright:
"Here is the steed that saved the day
By carrying Sheridan into the fight,
From Winchester—twenty miles away!"

*Thomas Buchanan Read* [1822–1872]

## SONG OF SHERMAN'S MARCH TO THE SEA

[NOVEMBER, 1864]

Our camp-fires shone bright on the mountains
That frowned on the river below,
While we stood by our guns in the morning,
And eagerly watched for the foe;
When a rider came out from the darkness
That hung over mountain and tree,
And shouted: "Boys, up and be ready,
For Sherman will march to the sea."

Then cheer upon cheer for bold Sherman
Went up from each valley and glen,
And the bugles reëchoed the music
That came from the lips of the men:
For we knew that the stars in our banner
More bright in their splendor would be,
And that blessings from Northland would greet us
When Sherman marched down to the sea.

Then forward, boys, forward to battle!
We marched on our wearisome way,
And we stormed the wild hills of Resaca;
God bless those who fell on that day!
Then Kenesaw, dark in its glory,
Frowned down on the flag of the free,
But the East and the West bore our standards,
And Sherman marched on to the sea.

Still onward we pressed, till our banners
  Swept out from Atlanta's grim walls,
And the blood of the patriot dampened
  The soil where the traitor flag falls;
Yet we paused not to weep for the fallen,
  Who slept by each river and tree;
We twined them a wreath of the laurel
  As Sherman marched down to the sea.

Oh! proud was our army that morning,
  That stood where the pine darkly towers,
When Sherman said: "Boys, you are weary;
  This day fair Savannah is ours!"
Then sang we a song for our chieftain,
  That echoed o'er river and lea,
And the stars in our banner shone brighter
  When Sherman marched down to the sea.

*Samuel H. M. Byers* [1838-1933]

## A SECOND REVIEW OF THE GRAND ARMY

[MAY 24, 1865]

I READ last night of the Grand Review
In Washington's chiefest avenue,—
Two hundred thousand men in blue,
  I think they said was the number,—
Till I seemed to hear their trampling feet,
The bugle blast and the drum's quick beat,
The clatter of hoofs in the stony street,
The cheers of people who came to greet,
And the thousand details that to repeat
  Would only my verse encumber,—
Till I fell in a revery, sad and sweet,
  And then to a fitful slumber.

When, lo! in a vision I seemed to stand
In the lonely Capitol. On each hand
Far stretched the portico, dim and grand
Its columns ranged like a martial band

Of sheeted spectres, whom some command
  Had called to a last reviewing.
And the streets of the city were white and bare;
No footfall echoed across the square;
But out of the misty midnight air
I heard in the distance a trumpet blare,
And the wandering night-winds seemed to bear
  The sound of a far tattooing.

Then I held my breath with fear and dread;
For into the square, with a brazen tread,
There rode a figure whose stately head
  O'erlooked the review that morning,
That never bowed from its firm-set seat
When the living column passed its feet,
Yet now rode steadily up the street
  To the phantom bugle's warning:

Till it reached the Capitol square, and wheeled,
And there in the moonlight stood revealed
A well-known form that in State and field
  Had led our patriot sires:
Whose face was turned to the sleeping camp,
Afar through the river's fog and damp,
That showed no flicker, nor waning lamp,
  Nor wasted bivouac fires.

And I saw a phantom army come,
With never a sound of fife or drum,
But keeping time to a throbbing hum
  Of wailing and lamentation:
The martyred heroes of Malvern Hill,
Of Gettysburg and Chancellorsville,
The men whose wasted figures fill
  The patriot graves of the nation.

And there came the nameless dead,—the men
Who perished in fever-swamp and fen,
The slowly-starved of the prison-pen;
  And, marching beside the others,

Came the dusky martyrs of Pillow's fight,
With limbs enfranchised and bearing bright;
I thought—perhaps 'twas the pale moonlight—
  They looked as white as their brothers!

And so all night marched the Nation's dead,
With never a banner above them spread,
Nor a badge, nor a motto brandishèd;
No mark—save the bare uncovered head
  Of the silent bronze Reviewer;
With never an arch save the vaulted sky;
With never a flower save those that lie
On the distant graves—for love could buy
  No gift that was purer or truer.

So all night long swept the strange array;
So all night long, till the morning gray,
I watched for one who had passed away,
  With a reverent awe and wonder,—
Till a blue cap waved in the lengthening line,
And I knew that one who was kin of mine
Had come; and I spake—and lo! that sign
  Awakened me from my slumber.

*Bret Harte* [1839–1902]

## THE CONQUERED BANNER

FURL that Banner, for 'tis weary;
Round its staff 'tis drooping dreary;
  Furl it, fold it—it is best;
For there's not a man to wave it,
And there's not a sword to save it,
And there's not one left to lave it
In the blood which heroes gave it;
And its foes now scorn and brave it;
  Furl it, hide it—let it rest!

Take that Banner down! 'tis tattered;
Broken is its shaft and shattered;
And the valiant hosts are scattered

Over whom it floated high.
Oh, 'tis hard for us to fold it,
Hard to think there's none to hold it,
Hard that those who once unrolled it
Now must furl it with a sigh!

Furl that Banner—furl it sadly;
Once ten thousands hailed it gladly,
And ten thousands wildly, madly,
Swore it should forever wave—
Swore that foeman's sword should never
Hearts like theirs entwined dissever,
And that flag should float forever
O'er their freedom, or their grave!

Furl it! for the hands that grasped it,
And the hearts that fondly clasped it,
Cold and dead are lying low;
And that Banner—it is trailing,
While around it sounds the wailing
Of its people in their woe.

For, though conquered, they adore it—
Love the cold, dead hands that bore it!
Weep for those who fell before it!
Pardon those who trailed and tore it!
But, oh, wildly they deplore it,
Now who furl and fold it so!

Furl that Banner! True, 'tis gory,
Yet 'tis wreathed around with glory,
And 'twill live in song and story
Though its folds are in the dust!
For its fame on brightest pages,
Penned by poets and by sages,
Shall go sounding down the ages—
Furl its folds though now we must!

Furl that Banner, softly, slowly;
Treat it gently—it is holy,

For it droops above the dead;
Touch it not—unfold it never;
Let it droop there, furled forever,—
For its people's hopes are fled.

*Abram J. Ryan* [1839-1888]

## DRIVING HOME THE COWS

Out of the clover and blue-eyed grass,
He turned them into the river-lane;
One after another he let them pass,
Then fastened the meadow-bars again.

Under the willows, and over the hill,
He patiently followed their sober pace;
The merry whistle for once was still,
And something shadowed the sunny face.

Only a boy! and his father had said
He never could let his youngest go:
Two already were lying dead
Under the feet of the trampling foe.

But after the evening work was done,
And the frogs were loud in the meadow-swamp,
Over his shoulder he slung his gun,
And stealthily followed the foot-path damp,

Across the clover, and through the wheat,
With resolute heart and purpose grim,
Though cold was the dew on his hurrying feet,
And the blind bat's flitting startled him.

Thrice since then had the lanes been white,
And the orchards sweet with apple-bloom;
And now, when the cows came back at night,
The feeble father drove them home.

For news had come to the lonely farm
That three were lying where two had lain;
And the old man's tremulous, palsied arm
Could never lean on a son's again.

The summer day grew cold and late.
  He went for the cows when the work was done;
But down the lane, as he opened the gate,
  He saw them coming, one by one,—

Brindle, Ebony, Speckle, and Bess,
  Shaking their horns in the evening wind;
Cropping the buttercups out of the grass,—
  But who was it following close behind?

Loosely swung in the idle air
  The empty sleeve of army blue;
And worn and pale, from the crisping hair,
  Looked out a face that the father knew.

For Southern prisons will sometimes yawn,
  And yield their dead unto life again;
And the day that comes with a cloudy dawn
  In golden glory at last may wane.

The great tears sprang to their meeting eyes;
  For the heart must speak when the lips are dumb;
And under the silent evening skies,
  Together they followed the cattle home.

*Kate Putnam Osgood* [1841–1910]

## ODE RECITED AT THE HARVARD COMMEMORATION

JULY 21, 1865

I

WEAK-WINGED is song,
Nor aims at that clear-ethered height
Whither the brave deed climbs for light:
  We seem to do them wrong,
Bringing our robin's-leaf to deck their hearse
Who in warm life-blood wrote their nobler verse,
Our trivial song to honor those who come
With ears attuned to strenuous trump and drum,
And shaped in squadron-strophes their desire,
Live battle-odes whose lines were steel and fire:
  Yet sometimes feathered words are strong,

A gracious memory to buoy up and save
From Lethe's dreamless ooze, the common grave
Of the unventurous throng.

II

To-day our Reverend Mother welcomes back
Her wisest Scholars, those who understood
The deeper teaching of her mystic tome,
And offered their fresh lives to make it good:
No lore of Greece or Rome,
No science peddling with the names of things,
Or reading stars to find inglorious fates,
Can lift our life with wings
Far from Death's idle gulf that for the many waits,
And lengthen out our dates
With that clear fame whose memory sings
In manly hearts to come, and nerves them and dilates:
Nor such thy teaching, Mother of us all!
Not such the trumpet-call
Of thy diviner mood,
That could thy sons entice
From happy homes and toils, the fruitful nest
Of those half-virtues which the world calls best,
Into War's tumult rude;
But rather far that stern device
The sponsors chose that round thy cradle stood
In the dim, unventured wood,
The VERITAS that lurks beneath
The letter's unprolific sheath,
Life of whate'er makes life worth living,
Seed-grain of high emprise, immortal food,
One heavenly thing whereof earth hath the giving.

III

Many loved Truth, and lavished life's best oil
Amid the dust of books to find her,
Content at last, for guerdon of their toil,
With the cast mantle she hath left behind her.
Many in sad faith sought for her;
Many with crossed hands sighed for her;

But these, our brothers, fought for her;
At life's dear peril wrought for her,
So loved her that they died for her,
Tasting the raptured fleetness
Of her divine completeness:
Their higher instinct knew
Those love her best who to themselves are true,
And what they dare to dream of, dare to do;
They followed her and found her
Where all may hope to find,
Not in the ashes of the burnt-out mind,
But beautiful, with danger's sweetness round her.
Where faith made whole with deed
Breathes its awakening breath
Into the lifeless creed,
They saw her plumed and mailed,
With sweet, stern face unveiled,
And all-repaying eyes, look proud on them in death.

IV

Our slender life runs rippling by, and glides
Into the silent hollow of the past;
What is there that abides
To make the next age better for the last?
Is earth too poor to give us
Something to live for here that shall outlive us?
Some more substantial boon
Than such as flows and ebbs with Fortune's fickle moon?
The little that we see
From doubt is never free;
The little that we do
Is but half-nobly true;
With our laborious hiving
What men call treasure, and the gods call dross,
Life seems a jest of Fate's contriving,
Only secure in every one's conniving,
A long account of nothings paid with loss,
Where we poor puppets, jerked by unseen wires,
After our little hour of strut and rave,
With all our pasteboard passions and desires,

Loves, hates, ambitions, and immortal fires,
Are tossed pell-mell together in the grave.
But stay! no age was e'er degenerate,
Unless men held it at too cheap a rate,
For in our likeness still we shape our fate.
Ah, there is something here
Unfathomed by the cynic's sneer,
Something that gives our feeble light
A high immunity from Night,
Something that leaps life's narrow bars
To claim its birthright with the hosts of heaven;
A seed of sunshine that can leaven
Our earthly dulness with the beams of stars,
And glorify our clay
With light from fountains elder than the Day;
A conscience more divine than we,
A gladness fed with secret tears,
A vexing, forward-reaching sense
Of some more noble permanence;
A light across the sea,
Which haunts the soul and will not let it be,
Still beaconing from the heights of undegenerate years.

V

Whither leads the path
To ampler fates that leads?
Not down through flowery meads,
To reap an aftermath
Of youth's vainglorious weeds,
But up the steep, amid the wrath
And shock of deadly-hostile creeds,
Where the world's best hope and stay
By battle's flashes gropes a desperate way,
And every turf the fierce foot clings to bleeds.
Peace hath her not ignoble wreath,
Ere yet the sharp, decisive word
Light the black lips of cannon, and the sword
Dreams in its easeful sheath;
But some day the live coal behind the thought,
Whether from Baäl's stone obscene,

Or from the shrine serene
Of God's pure altar brought,
Bursts up in flame; the war of tongue and pen
Learns with what deadly purpose it was fraught,
And, helpless in the fiery passion caught,
Shakes all the pillared state with shock of men:
Some day the soft Ideal that we wooed
Confronts us fiercely, foe-beset, pursued,
And cries reproachful: "Was it, then, my praise,
And not myself was loved? Prove now thy truth;
I claim of thee the promise of thy youth;
Give me thy life, or cower in empty phrase,
The victim of thy genius, not its mate!"
Life may be given in many ways,
And loyalty to Truth be sealed
As bravely in the closet as the field,
So bountiful is Fate;
But then to stand beside her,
When craven churls deride her,
To front a lie in arms and not to yield,
This shows, methinks, God's plan
And measure of a stalwart man,
Limbed like the old heroic breeds,
Who stands self-poised on manhood's solid earth
Not forced to frame excuses for his birth,
Fed from within with all the strength he needs.

VI

Such was he, our Martyr-Chief,
Whom late the Nation he had led,
With ashes on her head,
Wept with the passion of an angry grief:
Forgive me, if from present things I turn
To speak what in my heart will beat and burn,
And hang my wreath on his world-honored urn.
Nature, they say, doth dote,
And cannot make a man
Save on some worn-out plan,
Repeating us by rote:
For him her Old-World moulds aside she threw,
And, choosing sweet clay from the breast

Of the unexhausted West,
With stuff untainted shaped a hero new,
Wise, steadfast in the strength of God, and true.
How beautiful to see
Once more a shepherd of mankind indeed,
Who loved his charge, but never loved to lead;
One whose meek flock the people joyed to be,
Not lured by any cheat of birth,
But by his clear-grained human worth,
And brave old wisdom of sincerity!
They knew that outward grace is dust;
They could not choose but trust
In that sure-footed mind's unfaltering skill,
And supple-tempered will
That bent like perfect steel to spring again and thrust.
His was no lonely mountain-peak of mind,
Thrusting to thin air o'er our cloudy bars,
A sea-mark now, now lost in vapors blind;
Broad prairie rather, genial, level-lined,
Fruitful and friendly for all human kind,
Yet also nigh to heaven and loved of loftiest stars.
Nothing of Europe here,
Or, then, of Europe fronting mornward still,
Ere any names of Serf and Peer
Could Nature's equal scheme deface
And thwart her genial will;
Here was a type of the true elder race,
And one of Plutarch's men talked with us face to face.
I praise him not; it were too late;
And some innative weakness there must be
In him who condescends to victory
Such as the Present gives, and cannot wait,
Safe in himself as in a fate.
So always firmly he:
He knew to bide his time,
And can his fame abide,
Still patient in his simple faith sublime,
Till the wise years decide.
Great captains, with their guns and drums,
Disturb our judgment for the hour,
But at last silence comes;

These all are gone, and, standing like a tower,
  Our children shall behold his fame,
    The kindly-earnest, brave, foreseeing man,
Sagacious, patient, dreading praise, not blame,
  New birth of our new soil, the first American.

VII

Long as man's hope insatiate can discern
  Or only guess some more inspiring goal
  Outside of Self, enduring as the pole,
Along whose course the flying axles burn
Of spirits bravely-pitched, earth's manlier brood;
    Long as below we cannot find
  The meed that stills the inexorable mind;
  So long this faith to some ideal Good,
  Under whatever mortal names it masks,
  Freedom, Law, Country, this ethereal mood
That thanks the Fates for their severer tasks,
  Feeling its challenged pulses leap,
  While others skulk in subterfuges cheap,
And, set in Danger's van, has all the boon it asks,
  Shall win man's praise and woman's love,
  Shall be a wisdom that we set above
All other skills and gifts to culture dear,
  A virtue round whose forehead we inwreathe
  Laurels that with a living passion breathe
When other crowns grow, while we twine them, sear.
  What brings us thronging these high rites to pay,
And seal these hours the noblest of our year,
  Save that our brothers found this better way?

VIII

  We sit here in the Promised Land
  That flows with Freedom's honey and milk;
  But 'twas they won it, sword in hand,
Making the nettle danger soft for us as silk.
  We welcome back our bravest and our best;—
  Ah me! not all! some come not with the rest,
Who went forth brave and bright as any here!
I strive to mix some gladness with my strain,
        But the sad strings complain,
        And will not please the ear:

I sweep them for a pæan, but they wane
Again and yet again
Into a dirge, and die away, in pain.
In these brave ranks I only see the gaps,
Thinking of dear ones whom the dumb turf wraps,
Dark to the triumph which they died to gain:
Fitlier may others greet the living,
For me the past is unforgiving;
I with uncovered head
Salute the sacred dead,
Who went, and who return not.—Say not so!
'Tis not the grapes of Canaan that repay,
But the high faith that failed not by the way;
Virtue treads paths that end not in the grave;
No ban of endless night exiles the brave;
And to the saner mind
We rather seem the dead that stayed behind.
Blow, trumpets, all your exultations blow!
For never shall their aureoled presence lack:
I see them muster in a gleaming row,
With ever-youthful brows that nobler show;
We find in our dull road their shining track;
In every nobler mood
We feel the orient of their spirit glow,
Part of our life's unalterable good,
Of all our saintlier aspiration;
They come transfigured back,
Secure from change in their high-hearted ways,
Beautiful evermore, and with the rays
Of morn on their white Shields of Expectation!

IX

But is there hope to save
Even this ethereal essence from the grave?
What ever 'scaped Oblivion's subtle wrong
Save a few clarion names, or golden threads of song?
Before my musing eye
The mighty ones of old sweep by,
Disvoicëd now and insubstantial things,
As noisy once as we; poor ghosts of kings,

Shadows of empire wholly gone to dust,
And many races, nameless long ago,
To darkness driven by that imperious gust
Of ever-rushing Time that here doth blow:
O visionary world, condition strange,
Where naught abiding is but only Change,
Where the deep-bolted stars themselves still shift and range!
Shall we to more continuance make pretence?
Renown builds tombs; a life-estate is Wit;
And, bit by bit,
The cunning years steal all from us but woe;
Leaves are we, whose decays no harvest sow.
But, when we vanish hence,
Shall they lie forceless in the dark below,
Save to make green their little length of sods,
Or deepen pansies for a year or two,
Who now to us are shining-sweet as gods?
Was dying all they had the skill to do?
That were not fruitless: but the Soul resents
Such short-lived service, as if blind events
Ruled without her, or earth could so endure;
She claims a more divine investiture
Of longer tenure than Fame's airy rents;
Whate'er she touches doth her nature share;
Her inspiration haunts the ennobled air,
Gives eyes to mountains blind,
Ears to the deaf earth, voices to the wind,
And her clear trump sings succor everywhere
By lonely bivouacs to the wakeful mind;
For soul inherits all that soul could dare:
Yea, Manhood hath a wider span
And larger privilege of life than man.
The single deed, the private sacrifice,
So radiant now through proudly-hidden tears,
Is covered up erelong from mortal eyes
With thoughtless drift of the deciduous years;
But that high privilege that makes all men peers,
That leap of heart whereby a people rise
Up to a noble anger's height,
And, flamed on by the Fates, not shrink, but grow more bright,

That swift validity in noble veins,
Of choosing danger and disdaining shame,
Of being set on flame
By the pure fire that flies all contact base,
But wraps its chosen with angelic might,
These are imperishable gains,
Sure as the sun, medicinal as light,
These hold great futures in their lusty reins
And certify to earth a new imperial race.

X

Who now shall sneer?
Who dare again to say we trace
Our lines to a plebeian race?
Roundhead and Cavalier!
Dumb are those names erewhile in battle loud;
Dream-footed as the shadow of a cloud,
They flit across the ear:
That is best blood that hath most iron in't.
To edge resolve with, pouring without stint
For what makes manhood dear.
Tell us not of Plantagenets,
Hapsburgs, and Guelfs, whose thin bloods crawl
Down from some victor in a border-brawl!
How poor their outworn coronets,
Matched with one leaf of that plain civic wreath
Our brave for honor's blazon shall bequeath,
Through whose desert a rescued Nation sets
Her heel on treason, and the trumpet hears
Shout victory, tingling Europe's sullen ears
With vain resentments and more vain regrets!

XI

Not in anger, not in pride,
Pure from passion's mixture rude
Ever to base earth allied,
But with far-heard gratitude,
Still with heart and voice renewed,
To heroes living and dear martyrs dead,
The strain should close that consecrates our brave.
Lift the heart and lift the head!
Lofty be its mood and grave,

Not without a martial ring,
Not without a prouder tread
And a peal of exultation:
Little right has he to sing
Through whose heart in such an hour
Beats no march of conscious power,
Sweeps no tumult of elation!
'Tis no Man we celebrate,
By his country's victories great,
A hero half, and half the whim of Fate,
But the pith and marrow of a Nation
Drawing force from all her men,
Highest, humblest, weakest, all,
For her time of need, and then
Pulsing it again through them,
Till the basest can no longer cower,
Feeling his soul spring up divinely tall,
Touched but in passing by her mantle-hem.
Come back, then, noble pride, for 'tis her dower!
How could poet ever tower,
If his passions, hopes, and fears,
If his triumphs and his tears,
Kept not measure with his people?
Boom, cannon, boom to all the winds and waves!
Clash out, glad bells, from every rocking steeple!
Banners, advance with triumph, bend your staves!
And from every mountain-peak
Let beacon-fire to answering beacon speak,
Katahdin tell Monadnock, Whiteface he,
And so leap on in light from sea to sea,
Till the glad news be sent
Across a kindling continent,
Making earth feel more firm and air breathe braver:
"Be proud! for she is saved, and all have helped to save her
She that lifts up the manhood of the poor,
She of the open soul and open door,
With room about her hearth for all mankind!
The fire is dreadful in her eyes no more;
From her bold front the helm she doth unbind
Sends all her handmaid armies back to spin

And bids her navies, that so lately hurled
Their crashing battle, hold their thunders in,
Swimming like birds of calm along the unharmful shore.
No challenge sends she to the elder world,
That looked askance and hated; a light scorn
Plays o'er her mouth, as round her mighty knees
She calls her children back, and waits the morn
Of nobler day, enthroned between her subject seas."

XII

Bow down, dear Land, for thou hast found release!
Thy God, in these distempered days,
Hath taught thee the sure wisdom of His ways,
And through thine enemies hath wrought thy peace!
Bow down in prayer and praise!
No poorest in thy borders but may now
Lift to the juster skies a man's enfranchised brow.
O Beautiful! my Country! ours once more!
Smoothing thy gold of war-dishevelled hair
O'er such sweet brows as never other wore,
And letting thy set lips,
Freed from wrath's pale eclipse,
The rosy edges of their smile lay bare,
What words divine of lover or of poet
Could tell our love and make thee know it,
Among the Nations bright beyond compare?
What were our lives without thee?
What all our lives to save thee?
We reck not what we gave thee;
We will not dare to doubt thee,
But ask whatever else, and we will dare!

*James Russell Lowell* [1819–1891]

## CUSTER'S LAST CHARGE

(June 25, 1876)

Dead! Is it possible? He, the bold rider,
Custer, our hero, the first in the fight,
Charming the bullets of yore to fly wider,
Far from our battle-king's ringlets of light!

Dead, our young chieftain, and dead, all forsaken!
No one to tell us the way of his fall!
Slain in the desert, and never to waken,
Never, not even to victory's call!

Proud for his fame that last day that he met them!
All the night long he had been on their track,
Scorning their traps and the men that had set them,
Wild for a charge that should never give back.
There on the hilltop he halted and saw them.—
Lodges all loosened and ready to fly;
Hurrying scouts with the tidings to awe them,
Told of his coming before he was nigh.

All the wide valley was full of their forces,
Gathered to cover the lodges' retreat!—
Warriors running in haste to their horses,
Thousands of enemies close to his feet!
Down in the valleys the ages had hollowed,
There lay the Sitting Bull's camp for a prey!
Numbers! What recked he? What recked those who
followed—
Men who had fought ten to one ere that day?

Out swept the squadrons, the fated three hundred.
Into the battle-line steady and full;
Then down the hillside exultingly thundered,
Into the hordes of the old Sitting Bull!
Wild Ogalallah, Arapahoe, Cheyenne,
Wild Horse's braves, and the rest of their crew,
Shrank from that charge like a herd from a lion,—
Then closed around, the grim horde of wild Sioux!

Right to their centre he charged, and then facing—
Hark to those yells! and around them, O see!
Over the hilltops the Indians come racing,
Coming as fast as the waves of the sea!
Red was the circle of fire around them;
No hope of victory, no ray of light,
Shot through that terrible black cloud without them,
Brooding in death over Custer's last fight.

Then did he blench? Did he die like a craven,
  Begging those torturing fiends for his life?
Was there a soldier who carried the Seven
  Flinched like a coward or fled from the strife?
No, by the blood of our Custer, no quailing!
  There in the midst of the Indians they close,
Hemmed in by thousands, but ever assailing,
  Fighting like tigers, all bayed amid foes!

Thicker and thicker the bullets came singing;
  Down go the horses and riders and all;
Swiftly the warriors round them were ringing,
  Circling like buzzards awaiting their fall.
See the wild steeds of the mountain and prairie,
  Savage eyes gleaming from forests of mane;
Quivering lances with pennons so airy,
  War-painted warriors charging amain.

Backward, again and again, they were driven,
  Shrinking to close with the lost little band;
Never a cap that had worn the bright Seven
  Bowed till its wearer was dead on the strand.
Closer and closer the death-circle growing,
  Ever the leader's voice, clarion clear,
Rang out his words of encouragement glowing,
  "We can but die once, boys,—we'll sell our lives dear!"

Dearly they sold them like Berserkers raging,
  Facing the death that encircled them round;
Death's bitter pangs by their vengeance assuaging,
  Marking their tracks by their dead on the ground.
Comrades, our children shall yet tell their story,—
  Custer's last charge on the old Sitting Bull;
And ages shall swear that the cup of his glory
  Needed but that death to render it full.

*Frederick Whittaker* [1838–1917]

## THE LAST REDOUBT

[SEPTEMBER, 1877]

KACELYEVO's slope still felt
The cannons' bolts and the rifles' pelt;

For the last redoubt up the hill remained,
By the Russ yet held, by the Turk not gained.

Mehemet Ali stroked his beard;
His lips were clinched and his look was weird;
Round him were ranks of his ragged folk,
Their faces blackened with blood and smoke.

"Clear me the Muscovite out!" he cried;
Then the name of "Allah!" echoed wide,
And the fezzes were waved and the bayonets lowered,
And on to the last redoubt they poured.

One fell, and a second quickly stopped
The gap that he left when he reeled and dropped;
The second,—a third straight filled his place;
The third,—and a fourth kept up the race.

Many a fez in the mud was crushed,
Many a throat that cheered was hushed,
Many a heart that sought the crest
Found Allah's arms and a houri's breast.

Over their corpses the living sprang,
And the ridge with their musket-rattle rang,
Till the faces that lined the last redoubt
Could see their faces and hear their shout.

In the redoubt a fair form towered,
That cheered up the brave and chid the coward;
Brandishing blade with a gallant air;
His head erect and his bosom bare.

"Fly! they are on us!" his men implored;
But he waved them on with his waving sword.
"It cannot be held; 'tis no shame to go!"
But he stood with his face set hard to the foe.

Then clung they about him, and tugged, and knelt;
He drew a pistol from out his belt,
And fired it blank at the first that set
Foot on the edge of the parapet

Over that first one toppled; but on
Clambered the rest till their bayonets shone,
As hurriedly fled his men dismayed,
Not a bayonet's length from the length of his blade.

"Yield!" But aloft his steel he flashed,
And down on their steel it ringing clashed;
Then back he reeled with a bladeless hilt,
His honor full, but his life-blood spilt.

They lifted him up from the dabbled ground;
His limbs were shapely and soft and round,
No down on his lip, on his cheek no shade,—
"Bismillah!" they cried, "'tis an infidel maid!"

Mehemet Ali came and saw
The riddled breast and the tender jaw.
"Make her a bier of your arms," he said,
"And daintily bury this dainty dead!

"Make her a grave where she stood and fell,
'Gainst the jackal's scratch and the vulture's smell
Did the Muscovite men like their maidens fight,
In their lines we had scarcely supped to-night."

So a deeper trench 'mong the trenches there
Was dug, for the form as brave as fair;
And none, till the judgment trump and shout,
Shall drive her out of the last redoubt.

*Alfred Austin* [1835–1913]

## "FUZZY-WUZZY"

### (SOUDAN EXPEDITIONARY FORCE, 1889)

WE'VE fought with many men acrost the seas,
    An' some of em' was brave an' some was not:
The Paythan an' the Zulu an' Burmese;
    But the Fuzzy was the finest o' the lot.

We never got a ha' porth's change of 'im:
'E squatted in the scrub an' 'ocked our 'orses,
'E cut our sentries up at Sua*kim*,
An' 'e played the cat an' banjo with our forces.
So 'ere's *to* you, Fuzzy-Wuzzy, at your 'ome in the Sowdan;
You're a pore benighted 'eathen but a first-class fightin' man;
We gives you your certifikit, an' if you want it signed
We'll come an' 'ave a romp with you whenever you're inclined.

We took our chanst among the Kyber 'ills,
The Boers knocked us silly at a mile,
The Burman guv us Irriwaddy chills,
An' a Zulu *impi* dished us up in style:
But all we ever got from such as they
Was pop to what the Fuzzy made us swaller;
We 'eld our bloomin' own, the papers say,
But man for man the Fuzzy knocked us 'oller.
Then 'ere's *to* you, Fuzzy-Wuzzy, an' the missis and the kid;
Our orders was to break you, an' of course we went and did.
We sloshed you with Martinis, an' it wasn't 'ardly fair;
But for all the odds agin you, Fuzzy-Wuz, you bruk the square.

'E 'asn't got no papers of 'is own,
'E 'asn't got no medals nor rewards,
So we most certify the skill 'e's shown
In usin' of 'is long two-'anded swords:
When 'e's 'oppin' in an' out among the bush
With 'is coffin-'eaded shield an' shovel-spear,
A 'appy day with Fuzzy on the rush
Will last a 'ealthy Tommy for a year.
So 'ere's *to* you, Fuzzy-Wuzzy, an' your friends which is no more,

If we 'adn't lost some messmates we would 'elp
you to deplore;
But give an' take's the gospel, an' we'll call the
bargain fair,
For if you 'ave lost more than us, you crumpled
up the square!

'E rushes at the smoke when we let drive,
An', before we know, 'e's 'ackin' at our 'ead;
'E's all 'ot sand an' ginger when alive,
An' 'e's generally shammin' when 'e's dead.
'E's a daisy, 'e's a ducky, 'e's a lamb!
'E's a injia-rubber idiot on the spree,
'E's the only thing that doesn't give a damn
For the Regiment o' British Infantree.
So here's *to* you, Fuzzy-Wuzzy, at your 'ome in
the Sowdan;
You're a pore benighted 'eathen but a first-class
fightin' man;
An' 'ere's *to* you, Fuzzy-Wuzzy, with your 'ayrick
'ead of hair—
You big black boundin' beggar—for you bruk a
British square.

*Rudyard Kipling* [1865–1936]

## THE WORD OF THE LORD FROM HAVANA

[FEBRUARY 16, 1898]

THUS spake the Lord:
Because ye have not heard,
Because ye have given no heed
To my people in their need,

Because the oppressed cried
From the dust where he died,
And ye turned your face away
From his cry in that day,

Because ye have bought and sold
That which is above gold,

Because your brother is slain
While ye get you drunk with gain,

(Behold, these are my people, I have brought them to birth
On whom the mighty have trod,
The kings of the earth,
Saith the Lord God!)

Because ye fawned and bowed down
Lest the spoiler frown,
And the wrongs that the spoiled have borne
Ye have held in scorn,

Therefore with rending and flame
I have marred and smitten you,
Therefore I have given you to shame,
That the nations shall spit on you.

Therefore my Angel of Death
Hath stretched out his hand on you,
Therefore I speak in my wrath,
Laying command on you;

(Once have I bared my sword,
And the kings of the earth gave a cry;
Twice have I bared my sword,
That the kings of the earth should die;
Thrice shall I bare my sword,
And ye shall know my name, that it is I!)

Ye who held peace less than right
When a king laid a pitiful tax on you,
Hold not your hand from the fight
When freedom cries under the axe on you!

(I who called France to you, call you to Cuba in turn!
Repay—lest I cast you adrift and you perish astern!)

Ye who made war that your ships
Should lay to at the beck of no nation,
Make war now on Murder, that slips
The leash of her hounds of damnation!

Ye who remembered the Alamo,
Remember the Maine!

*Richard Hovey* [1864-1900]

## DEWEY AT MANILA

[MAY 1, 1898]

'TWAS the very verge of May
When the bold Olympia led
Into Bocagrande Bay
Dewey's squadron, dark and dread,—
Creeping past Corregidor,
Guardian of Manila's shore.

Do they sleep who wait the fray?
Is the moon so dazzling bright
That our cruisers' battle-gray
Melts into the misty light? . . .
Ah! the red flash and the roar!
Wakes at last Corregidor!

All too late their screaming shell
Tears the silence with its track;
This is but the *gate* of hell,
We've no leisure to turn back.
Answer, Concord!—then once more
Slumber on, Corregidor!

And as, like a slowing tide,
Onward still the vessels creep,
Dewey, watching, falcon-eyed,
Orders,—"Let the gunners sleep;
For we meet a foe at four
Fiercer than Corregidor."

Well they slept, for well they knew
What the morrow taught us all,—
He was wise (as well as true)
Thus upon the foe to fall.
Long shall Spain the day deplore
Dewey ran Corregidor.

May is dancing into light
As the Spanish Admiral
From a dream of phantom fight
Wakens at his sentry's call.
Shall he leave Cavité's lee,
Hunt the Yankee fleet at sea?

O Montojo, to thy deck,
That to-day shall float its last!
Quick! To quarters! Yonder speck
Grows a hull of portent vast.
Hither, toward Cavité's lee
Comes the Yankee hunting thee!

Not for fear of hidden mine
Halts our doughty Commodore.
He, of old heroic line,
Follows Farragut once more,
Hazards all on victory,
Here within Cavité's lee.

If he loses, all is gone;
He will win because he must.
And the shafts of yonder dawn
Are not quicker than his thrust.
Soon, Montojo, he shall be
With thee in Cavité's lee.

Now, Manila, to the fray!
Show the hated Yankee host
This is not a holiday,—
Spanish blood is more than boast.
Fleet and mine and battery,
Crush him in Cavité's lee!

Lo, hell's geysers at our fore
Pierce the plotted path—in vain
Nerving every man the more
With the memory of the Maine!
Now at last our guns are free
Here within Cavité's lee.

"Gridley," says the Commodore,
"You may fire when ready." Then
Long and loud, like lions' roar
When a rival dares the den,
Breaks the awful cannonry
Full across Cavité's lee.

Who shall tell the daring tale
Of our Thunderbolt's attack,
Finding, when the chart should fail,
By the lead his dubious track,
Five ships following faithfully
Five times o'er Cavité's lee;

Of our gunners' deadly aim;
Of the gallant foe and brave
Who, unconquered, faced with flame,
Seek the mercy of the wave,—
Choosing honor in the sea
Underneath Cavité's lee?

Let the meed the victors gain
Be the measure of their task.
Less of flinching, stouter strain,
Fiercer combat—who could ask?
And "surrender,"—'twas a word
That Cavité ne'er had heard.

Noon,—the woful work is done!
Not a Spanish ship remains;
But, of their eleven, none
Ever was so truly Spain's!
Which is prouder, they or we,
Thinking of Cavité's lee?

ENVOY

But remember, when we've ceased
Giving praise and reckoning odds,
Man shares courage with the beast,
Wisdom cometh from the gods:

Who would win, on land or wave,
Must be wise as well as brave.

*Robert Underwood Johnson* [1853-1937]

## DEEDS OF VALOR AT SANTIAGO

[JULY 1, 1898]

WHO cries that the days of daring are those that are faded far,
That never a light burns planet-bright to be hailed as the hero's star?
Let the deeds of the dead be laureled, the brave of the elder years,
But a song, we say, for the men of to-day, who have proved themselves their peers!

High in the vault of the tropic sky is the garish eye of the sun,
And down with its crown of guns afrown looks the hilltop to be won;
There is the trench where the Spaniard lurks, his hold and his hiding-place,
And he who would cross the space between must meet death face to face.

The black mouths belch and thunder, and the shrapnel shrieks and flies;
Where are the fain and the fearless, the lads with the dauntless eyes?
Will the moment find them wanting! Nay, but with valor stirred!
Like the leashed hound on the coursing-ground they wait but the warning word.

"Charge!" and the line moves forward, moves with a shout and a swing,
While sharper far than the cactus-thorn is the spiteful bullet's sting.

Now they are out in the open, and now they are breasting
the slope,
While into the eyes of death they gaze as into the eyes of
hope.

Never they wait nor waver, but on they clamber and on,
With "Up with the flag of the Stripes and Stars, and down
with the flag of the Don!"
What should they bear through the shot-rent air but rout
to the ranks of Spain,
For the blood that throbs in their hearts is the blood of the
boys of Anthony Wayne!

See, they have taken the trenches! Where are the foemen?
Gone!
And now "Old Glory" waves in the breeze from the heights
of San Juan!
And so, while the dead are laureled, the brave of the elder
years,
A song, we say, for the men of to-day, who have proved
themselves their peers.

*Clinton Scollard* [1860–1932]

## BREATH ON THE OAT

FREE are the Muses, and where freedom is
They follow, as the thrushes follow spring,
Leaving the old lands songless there behind;
Parnassus disenchanted suns its woods,
Empty of every nymph; wide have they flown;
And now on new sierras think to set
Their wandering court, and thrill the world anew,
Where the Republic babbling waits its speech;
For but the prelude of its mighty song
As yet has sounded. Therefore, would I woo
Apollo to the land I love, 'tis vain;
Unknown he spies on us; and if my verse
Ring not the empyrean round and round,
'Tis that the feeble oat is few of stops.

The noble theme awaits the nobler bard.
Then how all air will quire to it, and all
The great dead listen, America!—For lo,
Diana of the nations hath she lived
Remote, and hoarding her own happiness
In her own land, the land that seemed her first
An exile, where her bark was cast away,
Till maiden grew the backward-hearted child,
And on that sea whose waves were memories
Turned her young shoulder, looked with steadfast eyes
Upon her wilderness, her woods, her streams;
Inland she ran, and gathering virgin joy
Followed her shafts afar from humankind.
And if sometimes her isolation drooped
And yearning woke in her, she put it forth
With a high boast and with a sick disdain;
Actæons fleeing, into antlers branched
The floating tresses of her fancy, and far
Her arrows smote them with a bleeding laugh.
O vain and virgin, O the fool of love!
Now children not her own are at her knee.
For stricken by her path lay one that vexed
Her maiden calm; she reached a petulant hand;
And the old nations drew sharp breath and looked.
The two-edged sword, how came it in her hand?
The sword that slays the holder if he withhold,
That none can take, or having taken drop,
The sword is in thy hand, America!
The wrath of God, that fillets thee with lightnings,
America! Strike then; the sword departs.
Ah God, once more may men crown drowsy days
With glorious death, upholding a great cause!
I deemed it fable; not of them am I.
Yet if they loved thee on the loud May-day
Who with unexultant thunder wreathed the flag,
With thunder and with victory, if they
Who on the third most famous of our Fourths
Along the seaboard mountains swept, a storm
Unleashed, whose tread spurned not the wrecks of Spain,
If these thy sons have loved thee, and have set

Santiago and Manila like new stars
Crowding thy field of blue, new terror perched
Like eagles on thy banners, oh, not less
I love thee, who but prattle in the prime
Of birds of passage over river and wood
Thine also, piping little charms to lure,
Uncaptured and unflying, the wings of song.

*Joseph Russell Taylor* [1868–1933]

## WHEN THE GREAT GRAY SHIPS COME IN

[NEW YORK HARBOR, AUGUST 20, 1898]

To eastward ringing, to westward winging, o'er mapless miles of sea,
On winds and tides the gospel rides that the furthermost isles are free,
And the furthermost isles make answer, harbor, and height, and hill,
Breaker and beach cry each to each, "'Tis the Mother who calls! Be still!"
Mother! new-found, belovèd, and strong to hold from harm,
Stretching to these across the seas the shield of her sovereign arm,
Who summoned the guns of her sailor sons, who bade her navies roam,
Who calls again to the leagues of main, and who calls them this time Home!

And the great gray ships are silent, and the weary watchers rest,
The black cloud dies in the August skies, and deep in the golden west
Invisible hands are limning a glory of crimson bars,
And far above is the wonder of a myriad wakened stars!
Peace! As the tidings silence the strenuous cannonade,
Peace at last! is the bugle blast the length of the long blockade,
And eyes of vigil weary are lit with the glad release,
From ship to ship and from lip to lip it is "Peace! Thank God for peace."

Ah, in the sweet hereafter Columbia still shall show
The sons of these who swept the seas how she bade them rise and go,—
How, when the stirring summons smote on her children's ear,
South and North at the call stood forth, and the whole land answered, "Here!"
For the soul of the soldier's story and the heart of the sailor's song
Are all of those who meet their foes as right should meet with wrong,
Who fight their guns till the foeman runs, and then, on the decks they trod,
Brave faces raise, and give the praise to the grace of their country's God!

Yes, it is good to battle, and good to be strong and free,
To carry the hearts of a people to the uttermost ends of the sea,
To see the day steal up the bay where the enemy lies in wait,
To run your ship to the harbor's lip and sink her across the strait:—
But better the golden evening when the ships round heads for home,
And the long gray miles slip swiftly past in a swirl of seething foam,
And the people wait at the haven's gate to greet the men who win!
Thank God for peace! Thank God for peace, when the great gray ships come in!

*Guy Wetmore Carryl* [1873–1904]

## 1914

### I—Peace

Now, God be thanked Who has matched us with His hour,
And caught our youth, and wakened us from sleeping,
With hand made sure, clear eye, and sharpened power,
To turn, as swimmers into cleanness leaping,
Glad from a world grown old and cold and weary,
Leave the sick hearts that honor could not move,
And half-men, and their dirty songs and dreary,
And all the little emptiness of love!

Oh! we, who have known shame, we have found release there,
Where there's no ill, no grief, but sleep has mending,
Naught broken save this body, lost but breath;
Nothing to shake the laughing heart's long peace there
But only agony, and that has ending;
And the worst friend and enemy is but Death.

### II—Safety

Dear! of all happy in the hour, most blest
He who has found our hid security,
Assured in the dark tides of the world that rest,
And heard our word, "Who is so safe as we?"
We have found safety with all things undying,
The winds, and morning, tears of men and mirth,
The deep night, and birds singing, and clouds flying,
And sleep, and freedom, and the autumnal earth.
We have built a house that is not for Time's throwing.
We have gained a peace unshaken by pain for ever.
War knows no power. Safe shall be my going,
Secretly armed against all death's endeavor;
Safe though all safety's lost; safe where men fall;
And if these poor limbs die, safest of all.

### III—The Dead

Blow out, you bugles, over the rich Dead!
There's none of these so lonely and poor of old,
But, dying, has made us rarer gifts than gold.
These laid the world away; poured out the red
Sweet wine of youth; gave up the years to be
Of work and joy, and that unhoped serene,
That men call age; and those who would have been,
Their sons, they gave, their immortality.
Blow, bugles, blow! They brought us, for our dearth,
Holiness, lacked so long, and Love, and Pain.
Honor has come back, as a king, to earth,
And paid his subjects with a royal wage;
And Nobleness walks in our ways again;
And we have come into our heritage.

### IV—The Dead

These hearts were woven of human joys and cares,
Washed marvellously with sorrow, swift to mirth.

The years had given them kindness. Dawn was theirs,
And sunset, and the colors of the earth.
These had seen movement, and heard music; known
Slumber and waking; loved; gone proudly friended;
Felt the quick stir of wonder; sat alone;
Touched flowers and furs and cheeks. All this is ended.
There are waters blown by changing winds to laughter
And lit by the rich skies, all day. And after,
Frost, with a gesture, stays the waves that dance
And wandering loveliness. He leaves a white
Unbroken glory, a gathered radiance,
A width, a shining peace, under the night.

### V—The Soldier

If I should die, think only this of me:
That there's some corner of a foreign field
That is forever England. There shall be
In that rich earth a richer dust concealed;
A dust whom England bore, shaped, made aware,
Gave, once, her flowers to love, her ways to roam;
A body of England's, breathing English air,
Washed by the rivers, blest by suns of home.
And think, this heart, all evil shed away,
A pulse in the eternal mind, no less
Gives somewhere back the thoughts by England given;
Her sights and sounds; dreams happy as her day;
And laughter, learnt of friends; and gentleness,
In hearts at peace, under an English heaven.

*Rupert Brooke* [1887–1915]

## AUGUST, 1914

How still this quiet cornfield is to-night!
By an intenser glow the evening falls,
Bringing, not darkness, but a deeper light;
Among the stooks a partridge covey calls.

The windows glitter on the distant hill;
Beyond the hedge the sheep-bells in the fold
Stumble on sudden music and are still;
The forlorn pinewoods droop above the wold.

An endless quiet valley reaches out
  Past the blue hills into the evening sky;
Over the stubble, cawing, goes a rout
  Of rooks from harvest, flagging as they fly.

So beautiful it is, I never saw
  So great a beauty on these English fields,
Touched by the twilight's coming into awe,
  Ripe to the soul and rich with summer's yields. . . .

These homes, this valley spread below me here,
  The rooks, the tilted stacks, the beasts in pen,
Have been the heartfelt things, past-speaking dear
  To unknown generations of dead men,

Who, century after century, held these farms,
  And, looking out to watch the changing sky,
Heard, as we hear, the rumors and alarms
  Of war at hand and danger pressing nigh.

And knew, as we know, that the message meant
  The breaking off of ties, the loss of friends,
Death, like a miser getting in his rent,
  And no new stones laid where the trackway ends.

The harvest not yet won, the empty bin,
  The friendly horses taken from the stalls,
The fallow on the hill not yet brought in,
  The cracks unplastered in the leaking walls.

Yet heard the news, and went discouraged home,
  And brooded by the fire with heavy mind,
With such dumb loving of the Berkshire loam
  As breaks the dumb hearts of the English kind,

Then sadly rose and left the well-loved Downs,
  And so by ship to sea, and knew no more
The fields of home, the byres, the market towns,
  Nor the dear outline of the English shore.

But knew the misery of the soaking trench,
  The freezing in the rigging, the despair

In the revolting second of the wrench
  When the blind soul is flung upon the air,

And died (uncouthly, most) in foreign lands
  For some idea but dimly understood
Of an English city never built by hands
  Which love of England prompted and made good. . .

If there be any life beyond the grave,
  It must be near the men and things we love,
Some power of quick suggestion how to save,
  Touching the living soul as from above.

An influence from the Earth from those dead hearts
  So passionate once, so deep, so truly kind,
That in the living child the spirit starts,
  Feeling companioned still, not left behind.

Surely above these fields a spirit broods,
  A sense of many watchers muttering near
Of the lone Downland with the forlorn woods
  Loved to the death, inestimably dear.

A muttering from beyond the veils of Death
  From long-dead men, to whom this quiet scene
Came among blinding tears with the last breath,
  The dying soldier's vision of his queen.

All the unspoken worship of those lives
  Spent in forgotten wars at other calls
Glimmers upon these fields where evening drives
  Beauty like breath, so gently darkness falls.

Darkness that makes the meadows holier still,
  The elm-trees sadden in the hedge, a sigh
Moves in the beech-clump on the haunted hill,
  The rising planets deepen in the sky,

And silence broods like spirit on the brae,
  A glimmering moon begins, the moonlight runs
Over the grasses of the ancient way
  Rutted this morning by the passing guns.

*John Masefield* [1878-

## A CHANT OF HATE AGAINST ENGLAND*

FRENCH and Russian they matter not,
A blow for a blow and a shot for a shot,
We love them not,
We hate them not,
We hold the Weichsel and Vosges gate,
We have but one and only hate,
We love as one, we hate as one,
We have one foe and one alone:—

He is known to you all, he is known to you all,
He crouches behind the dark gray flood,
Full of envy, of rage, of craft, of gall,
Cut off by waves that are thicker than blood.
Come let us stand at the Judgment place
An oath to swear to, face to face.
An oath of bronze no wind can shake,
An oath for our sons and their sons to take,
Come hear the word, repeat the word,
Throughout the Fatherland make it heard:
We will never forego our hate,
We have all but a single hate,
We love as one, we hate as one,
We have one foe and one alone,
England!

At the Captain's mess, in the Banquet-hall,
Sat feasting the officers, one and all,—
Like a sabre-blow, like the swing of a sail,
One raised his glass, held high to hail;
Sharp-snapped like the stroke of a rudder's play,
Spoke three words only: "To the day!"
Whose glass this fate?
They had all but a single hate.
Who was thus known?
They had one foe and one alone,
England!

Take you the folk of the earth in pay,
With bars of gold your ramparts lay,
Bedeck the ocean with bow on bow,
Ye reckon well, but not well enough now.

*For the original of this poem see page 3846.

French and Russian they matter not.
A blow for a blow, a shot for a shot,
We fight the battle with bronze and steel,
And the time that is coming, Peace will seal.

*You* will we hate with a lasting hate,
We will never forego our hate.
Hate by water and hate by land,
Hate of the head and hate of the hand,
Hate of the hammer and hate of the Crown.
Hate of seventy *millions* choking down.
We love as one, we hate as one,
We have one foe and one alone:
England!

*From the German of Ernst Lissauer by Barbara Henderson* [18

## SONNETS WRITTEN IN THE FALL OF 1914

Awake, ye nations, slumbering supine,
Who round enring the European fray!
Heard ye the trumpet sound? "The Day! the Day!
The last that shall on England's empire shine!
The Parliament that broke the Right Divine
Shall see her realm of reason swept away,
And lesser nations shall the sword obey—
The sword o'er all carve the great world's design!"
So on the English Channel boasts the foe
On whose imperial brow death's helmet nods.
Look where his hosts o'er bloody Belgium go,
And mix a nation's past with blazing sods!
A kingdom's waste! a people's homeless woe!
Man's broken Word, and violated gods!

Far fall the day when England's realm shall see
The sunset of dominion! Her increase
Abolishes the man-dividing seas,
And frames the brotherhood on earth to be!
She, in free peoples planting sovereignty,
Orbs half the civil world in British peace;
And though time dispossess her, and she cease,
Rome-like she greatens in man's memory.
Oh, many a crown shall sink in war's turmoil,
And many a new republic light the sky,

Fleets sweep the ocean, nations till the soil,
Genius be born and generations die,
Orient and Occident together toil,
Ere such a mighty work man rears on high!

Hearken, the feet of the Destroyer tread
The wine-press of the nations; fast the blood
Pours from the side of Europe; in full flood
On the Septentrional watershed
The rivers of fair France are running red!
England, the mother-eyrie of our brood,
That on the summit of dominion stood,
Shakes in the blast: heaven battles overhead!
Lift up thy head, O Rheims, of ages heir
That treasured up in thee their glorious sum;
Upon whose brow, prophetically fair,
Flamed the great morrow of the world to come;
Haunt with thy beauty this volcanic air
Ere yet thou close, O Flower of Christendom!

As when the shadow of the sun's eclipse
Sweeps on the earth, and spreads a spectral air,
As if the universe were dying there,
On continent and isle the darkness dips,
Unwonted gloom, and on the Atlantic slips;
So in the night the Belgian cities flare
Horizon-wide; the wandering people fare
Along the roads, and load the fleeing ships.
And westward borne that planetary sweep,
Darkening o'er England and her times to be,
Already steps upon the ocean-deep!
Watch well, my country, that unearthly sea,
Lest when thou thinkest not, and in thy sleep,
Unapt for war, that gloom enshadow thee!

I pray for peace; yet peace is but a prayer.
How many wars have been in my brief years!
All races and all faiths, both hemispheres,
My eyes have seen embattled everywhere
The wide earth through; yet do I not despair
Of peace, that slowly through far ages nears,

Though not to me the golden morn appears;
My faith is perfect in time's issue fair.
For man doth build on an eternal scale,
And his ideals are framed of hope deferred;
And millennium came not; yet Christ did not fail,
Though ever unaccomplished is His word;
Him Prince of Peace, though unenthroned, we hail,
Supreme when in all bosoms He be heard.

This is my faith, and my mind's heritage,
Wherein I toil, though in a lonely place,
Who yet world-wide survey the human race
Unequal from wild nature disengage
Body and soul, and life's old strife assuage;
Still must abide, till heaven perfect its grace,
And love grown wisdom sweeten in man's face,
Alike the Christian and the heathen rage.
The tutelary genius of mankind
Ripens by slow degrees the final State,
That in the soul shall its foundations find
And only in victorious love grow great;
Patient the heart must be, humble the mind,
That doth the greater births of time await!

Whence not unmoved I see the nations form
From Dover to the fountains of the Rhine,
A hundred leagues, the scarlet battle-line,
And by the Vistula great armies swarm,
A vaster flood; rather my breast grows warm,
Seeing all peoples of the earth combine
Under one standard, with one countersign,
Grown brothers in the universal storm.
And never through the wide world yet there rang
A mightier summons! O Thou who from the side
Of Athens and the loins of Cæsar sprang,
Strike, Europe, with half the coming world allied,
For those ideals for which, since Homer sang,
The hosts of thirty centuries have died.

*George Edward Woodberry* [1855-1930]

## ABRAHAM LINCOLN WALKS AT MIDNIGHT

[In Springfield, Illinois]

It is portentous, and a thing of state
That here at midnight, in our little town,
A mourning figure walks, and will not rest,
Near the old court-house pacing up and down.

Or by his homestead, or in shadowed yards
He lingers where his children used to play;
Or through the market, on the well-worn stones
He stalks until the dawn-stars burn away.

A bronzed, lank man! His suit of ancient black,
A famous high top-hat and plain worn shawl
Make him the quaint great figure that men love,
The prairie-lawyer, master of us all.

He cannot sleep upon his hillside now.
He is among us:—as in times before!
And we who toss and lie awake for long
Breathe deep, and start, to see him pass the door.

His head is bowed. He thinks on men and kings,
Yea, when the sick world cries, how can he sleep?
Too many peasants fight, they know not why,
Too many homesteads in black terror weep.

The sins of all the war-lords burn his heart.
He sees the dreadnaughts scouring every main.
He carries on his shawl-wrapped shoulders now
The bitterness, the folly and the pain.

He cannot rest until a spirit-dawn
Shall come;—the shining hope of Europe free:
The league of sober folk, the Workers' Earth
Bringing long peace to Cornland, Alp, and Sea.

It breaks his heart that kings must murder still,
That all his hours of travail here for men
Seem yet in vain. And who will bring white peace
That he may sleep upon his hill again?

*Vachel Lindsay* [1879–1931]

## MAGPIES IN PICARDY

THE magpies in Picardy
  Are more than I can tell.
They flicker down the dusty roads
  And cast a magic spell
On the men who march through Picardy,
  Through Picardy to hell.

(The blackbird flies with panic,
  The swallow goes like light,
The finches move like ladies,
  The owl floats by at night;
But the great and flashing magpie
  He flies as artists might.)

A magpie in Picardy
  Told me secret things—
Of the music in white feathers,
  And the sunlight that sings
And dances in deep shadows—
  He told me with his wings.

(The hawk is cruel and rigid,
  He watches from a height;
The rook is slow and somber,
  The robin loves to fight;
But the great and flashing magpie
  He flies as lovers might.)

He told me that in Picardy,
  An age ago or more,
While all his fathers still were eggs,
  These dusty highways bore
Brown, singing soldiers marching out
  Through Picardy to war.

He said that still through chaos
  Works on the ancient plan,
And two things have altered not
  Since first the world began—
The beauty of the wild green earth
  And the bravery of man.

(For the sparrow flies unthinking
And quarrels in his flight,
The heron trails his legs behind,
The lark goes out of sight;
But the great and flashing magpie
He flies as poets might.)

*T. P. Cameron Wilson* [1889–1918]

## SONGS FROM AN EVIL WOOD

I

There is no wrath in the stars,
They do not rage in the sky;
I look from the evil wood
And find myself wondering why.

Why do they not scream out
And grapple star against star,
Seeking for blood in the wood
As all things round me are?

They do not glare like the sky
Or flash like the deeps of the wood;
But they shine softly on
In their sacred solitude.

To their high, happy haunts
Silence from us has flown,
She whom we loved of old
And know it now she is gone.

When will she come again,
Though for one second only?
She whom we loved is gone
And the whole world is lonely.

II

Somewhere lost in the haze
The sun goes down in the cold,
And birds in this evil wood
Chirrup home as of old;

Chirrup, stir, and are still
  On the high twigs frozen and thin.
There is no more noise of them now,
  And the long night sets in.

Of all the wonderful things
  That I have seen in the wood,
I marvel most at the birds
  And their wonderful quietude.

For a giant smites with his club
  All day the tops of the hill,
Sometimes he rests at night,
  Oftener he beats them still.

And a dwarf with a grim black mane
  Raps with repeated rage
All night in the valley below
  On the wooden walls of his cage.

And the elder giants come
  Sometimes, tramping from far
Through the weird and flickering light
  Made by an earthly star.

And the giant with his club,
  And the dwarf with rage in his breath,
And the elder giants from far,
  They are all the children of Death.

They are all abroad to-night
  And are breaking the hills with their brood,
And the birds are all asleep
  Even in Plug Street Wood!

III

The great guns of England, they listen mile on mile
To the boasts of a broken War-Lord; they lift their throats and smile;
    But the old woods are fallen
      For a while.

The old woods are fallen; yet will they come again,
They will come back some springtime with the warm winds and the rain,
For Nature guardeth her children
Never in vain.

They will come back some season; it may be a hundred years;
It is all one to Nature with the centuries that are hers;
She shall bring back her children
And dry all their tears.

But the tears of a would-be War-Lord shall never cease to flow,
He shall weep for the poisoned armies whenever the gas-winds blow,
He shall always weep for his widows,
And all Hell shall know.

The tears of a pitiless Kaiser shallow they'll flow and wide,
Wide as the desolation made by his silly pride
When he slaughtered a little people
To stab France in her side.

Over the ragged cinders they shall flow on and on
With the listless falling of streams that find not Oblivion,
For ages and ages of years
Till the last star is gone.

IV

I met with Death in his country,
With his scythe and his hollow eye,
Walking the roads of Belgium.
I looked and he passed me by.

Since he passed me by in Plug Street,
In the wood of the evil name,
I shall not now lie with the heroes,
I shall not share their fame,

I shall never be as they are,
A name in the lands of the Free,
Since I looked on Death in Flanders
And he did not look at me.

*Edward J. M. D. Plunkett* [1878–1957]

## INTO BATTLE

THE naked earth is warm with spring,
And with green grass and bursting trees
Leans to the sun's gaze glorying,
And quivers in the sunny breeze;

And life is color and warmth and light,
And a striving evermore for these;
And he is dead who will not fight;
And who dies fighting has increase.

The fighting man shall from the sun
Take warmth, and life from the glowing earth;
Speed with the light-foot winds to run,
And with the trees to newer birth;
And find, when fighting shall be done,
Great rest, and fullness after dearth.

All the bright company of Heaven
Hold him in their high comradeship,
The Dog Star and the Sisters Seven,
Orion's Belt and sworded hip.

The woodland trees that stand together,
They stand to him each one a friend;
They gently speak in the windy weather;
They guide to valley and ridge's end.

The kestrel hovering by day,
And the little owls that call by night,
Bid him be swift and keen as they,
As keen of ear, as swift of sight.

The blackbird sings to him, "Brother, brother,
If this be the last song you shall sing,
Sing well, for you may not sing another;
Brother, sing."

In dreary, doubtful, waiting hours,
Before the brazen frenzy starts,
The horses show him nobler powers;
O patient eyes, courageous hearts!

And when the burning moment breaks,
And all things else are out of mind,
And only joy of battle takes
Him by the throat, and makes him blind,

Through joy and blindness he shall know,
Not caring much to know, that still
Nor lead nor steel shall reach him, so
That it be not the Destined Will.

The thundering line of battle stands,
And in the air Death moans and sings;
But Day shall clasp him with strong hands,
And Night shall fold him in soft wings.

*Julian Grenfell* [1888–1915]

## "I HAVE A RENDEZVOUS WITH DEATH"

I HAVE a rendezvous with Death
At some disputed barricade,
When Spring comes back with rustling shade
And apple-blossoms fill the air—
I have a rendezvous with Death
When Spring brings back blue days and fair.

It may be he shall take my hand
And lead me into his dark land
And close my eyes and quench my breath—
It may be I shall pass him still.
I have a rendezvous with Death
On some scarred slope of battered hill,
When Spring comes round again this year
And the first meadow-flowers appear.

God knows 'twere better to be deep
Pillowed in silk and scented down,
Where Love throbs out in blissful sleep,
Pulse nigh to pulse, and breath to breath,
Where hushed awakenings are dear . . .
But I've a rendezvous with Death
At midnight in some flaming town,
When Spring trips north again this year,
And I to my pledged word am true,
I shall not fail that rendezvous.

*Alan Seeger* [1888–1916]

## THE SPIRES OF OXFORD

(AS SEEN FROM THE TRAIN)

I SAW the spires of Oxford
  As I was passing by,
The gray spires of Oxford
  Against a pearl-gray sky.
My heart was with the Oxford men
  Who went abroad to die.

The years go fast in Oxford,
  The golden years and gay,
The hoary Colleges look down
  On careless boys at play.
But when the bugles sounded war
  They put their games away.

They left the peaceful river,
  The cricket-field, the quad,
The shaven lawns of Oxford
  To seek a bloody sod—
They gave their merry youth away
  For country and for God.

God rest you, happy gentlemen,
  Who laid your good lives down,
Who took the khaki and the gun
  Instead of cap and gown.
God bring you to a fairer place
  Than even Oxford town.

*Winifred M. Letts* [1882–

## IN FLANDERS FIELDS

In Flanders fields the poppies blow
Between the crosses, row on row,
  That mark our place; and in the sky
  The larks, still bravely singing, fly
Scarce heard amid the guns below.

We are the Dead. Short days ago
We lived, felt dawn, saw sunset glow,
  Loved and were loved, and now we lie
  In Flanders fields.

Take up our quarrel with the foe:
To you from failing hands we throw
The torch; be yours to hold it high.
If ye break faith with us who die
We shall not sleep, though poppies grow
In Flanders fields.

*John McCrae* [1872–1918]

## REVEILLÉ

[APRIL 6, 1917]

WHAT sudden bugle calls us in the night
And wakes us from a dream that we had shaped;
Flinging us sharply up against a fight
We thought we had escaped?

It is no easy waking, and we win
No final peace; our victories are few
But still imperative forces pull us in
And sweep us somehow through.

Summoned by a supreme and confident power
That wakes our sleeping courage like a blow,
We rise, half-shaken, to the challenging hour,
And answer it—and go. . . .

*Louis Untermeyer* [1885–

## TO THE UNITED STATES OF AMERICA

BROTHERS in blood! They who this wrong began
To wreck our commonwealth, will rue the day
When first they challenged freemen to the fray,
And with the Briton dared the American.
Now are we pledged to win the Rights of man;
Labor and Justice now shall have their way,
And in a League of Peace—God grant we may—
Transform the earth, not patch up the old plan.

Sure is our hope since he who led your nation
Spake for mankind, and ye arose in awe
Of that high call to work the world's salvation;
Clearing your minds of all estranging blindness
In the vision of Beauty and the Spirit's law,
Freedom and Honor and sweet Loving kindness.

*Robert Bridges* [1844–1930]

## THE ROAD TO FRANCE

THANK God our liberating lance
Goes flaming on the way to France
To France—the trail the Gurkhas found!
To France—old England's rallying ground!
To France—the path the Russians strode!
To France—the Anzacs' glory road!
To France—where our Lost Legion ran
To fight and die for God and man!
To France—with every race and breed
That hates Oppression's brutal creed!

Ah France—how could our hearts forget
The path by which came Lafayette?
How could the haze of doubt hang low
Upon the road of Rochambeau?
At last, thank God! At last we see
There is no tribal Liberty!
No beacon lighting just our shores,
No Freedom guarding but our doors.
The flame she kindled for our sires
Burns now in Europe's battle-fires.
The soul that led our fathers west
Turns back to free the world's oppressed.

Allies, you have not called in vain;
We share your conflict and your pain.
"Old Glory," through new stains and rents,
Partakes of Freedom's sacraments.
Into that hell his will creates
We drive the foe—his lusts, his hates.
Last ccme, we will be last to stay,
Till Right has had her crowning day.
Replenish, comrades, from our veins
The blood the sword of despot drains,
And make our eager sacrifice
Part of the freely rendered price
You pay to lift humanity—
You pay to make our brothers free.
See, with what proud hearts we advance
To France!

*Daniel Henderson* [1880–1955]

## ROUGE BOUQUET

[March 7, 1918]

In a wood they call the Rouge Bouquet
There is a new-made grave to-day,
Built by never a spade nor pick
Yet covered with earth ten metres thick.
There lie many fighting men,
  Dead in their youthful prime,
Never to laugh nor love again
  Nor taste the Summertime.
For Death came flying through the air
And stopped his flight at the dugout stair,
Touched his prey and left them there,
  Clay to clay.
He hid their bodies stealthily
In the soil of the land they fought to free
  And fled away.
Now over the grave abrupt and clear
  Three volleys ring;
And perhaps their brave young spirits hear
  The bugle sing:
"Go to sleep!
Go to sleep!
Slumber well where the shell screamed and fell.
Let your rifles rest on the muddy floor,
You will not need them any more.
Danger's past;
Now at last,
Go to sleep!"

There is on earth no worthier grave
To hold the bodies of the brave
Than this place of pain and pride
Where they nobly fought and nobly died.
Never fear but in the skies
  Saints and angels stand
Smiling with their holy eyes
  On this new-come band.
St. Michael's sword darts through the air
And touches the aureole on his hair
As he sees them stand saluting there,
  His stalwart sons:

And Patrick, Brigid, Columkill
Rejoice that in veins of warriors still
The Gael's blood runs.
And up to Heaven's doorway floats,
From the wood called Rouge Bouquet,
A delicate cloud of bugle notes
That softly say:
"Farewell! Farewell.
Comrades true, born anew, peace to you!
Your souls shall be where the heroes are
And your memory shine like the morning-star.
Brave and dear,
Shield us here.
Farewell!"

*Joyce Kilmer* [1886–1918]

## VICTORY BELLS

[November 11, 1918]

I HEARD the bells across the trees,
I heard them ride the plunging breeze
Above the roofs from tower and spire.
And they were leaping like a fire,
And they were shining like a stream
With sun to make its music gleam.
Deep tones as though the thunder tolled
Cool voices thin as tinkling gold,
They shook the spangled autumn down
From out the tree-tops of the town;
They left great furrows in the air
And made a clangor everywhere
As of metallic wings. They flew
Aloft in spirals to the blue
Tall tent of heaven and disappeared.
And others, swift as though they feared
The people might not heed their cry
Went shouting VICTORY up the sky.
They did not say that war is done,
Only that glory has begun
Like sunrise, and the coming day
Will burn the clouds of war away.
There will be time for dreams again,
And home-coming for weary men.

*Grace Hazard Conkling* [1878–1958]

# POEMS OF PLACES

## ON THE PROSPECT OF PLANTING ARTS AND LEARNING IN AMERICA

THE Muse, disgusted at an age and clime
  Barren of every glorious theme,
In distant lands now waits a better time,
  Producing subjects worthy fame:

In happy climes, where from the genial sun
  And virgin earth such scenes ensue,
The force of Art by Nature seems outdone,
  And fancied beauties by the true:

In happy climes, the seat of Innocence,
  Where Nature guides and Virtue rules,
Where men shall not impose, for truth and sense,
  The pedantry of courts and schools:

There shall be sung another golden age,
  The rise of empire and of arts,
The good and great inspiring epic rage,
  The wisest heads and noblest hearts.

Not such as Europe breeds in her decay:
  Such as she bred when fresh and young,
When heavenly flame did animate her clay,
  By future poets shall be sung.

Westward the course of empire takes its way;
  The first four acts already past,
A fifth shall close the drama with the day;
  Time's noblest offspring is the last.

*George Berkeley* [1685–1753]

## BERMUDAS

WHERE the remote Bermudas ride
In the ocean's bosom unespied,
From a small boat that rowed along
The listening winds received this song:

"What should we do but sing His praise
That led us through the watery maze
Unto an isle so long unknown,
And yet far kinder than our own?
Where He the huge sea-monsters wracks,
That lift the deep upon their backs,
He lands us on a grassy stage,
Safe from the storms' and prelates' rage:
He gave us this eternal Spring
Which here enamels everything,
And sends the fowls to us in care
On daily visits through the air:
He hangs in shades the orange bright
Like golden lamps in a green night,
And does in the pomegranates close
Jewels more rich than Ormus shows:
He makes the figs our mouths to meet
And throws the melons at our feet;
But apples plants of such a price,
No tree could ever bear them twice.
With cedars chosen by His hand
From Lebanon He stores the land;
And makes the hollow seas that roar
Proclaim the ambergris on shore.
He cast (of which we rather boast)
The Gospel's pearl upon our coast;
And in these rocks for us did frame
A temple where to sound His name.
O, let our voice His praise exalt
Till it arrive at Heaven's vault,
Which thence (perhaps) rebounding may
Echo beyond the Mexique bay!"

Thus sung they in the English boat
A holy and a cheerful note:
And all the way, to guide their chime,
With falling oars they kept the time.

*Andrew Marvell* [1621-1678]

## INDIAN NAMES

Ye say, they all have passed away,
  That noble race and brave;
That their light canoes have vanished
  From off the crested wave;
That, 'mid the forests where they roamed,
  There rings no hunter's shout;
But their name is on your waters,—
  Ye may not wash it out.

'Tis where Ontario's billow
  Like Ocean's surge is curled;
Where strong Niagara's thunders wake
  The echo of the world;
Where red Missouri bringeth
  Rich tribute from the West,
And Rappahannock sweetly sleeps
  On green Virginia's breast.

Ye say, their cone-like cabins,
  That clustered o'er the vale,
Have fled away, like withered leaves
  Before the Autumn gale;
But their memory liveth on your hills
  Their baptism on your shore,
Your everlasting rivers speak
  Their dialect of yore.

Old Massachusetts wears it
  Within her lordly crown,
And broad Ohio bears it
  Amid his young renown;

Connecticut hath wreathed it
  Where her quiet foliage waves,
And bold Kentucky breathes it hoarse
  Through all her ancient caves.

Wachuset hides its lingering voice
  Within its rocky heart.
And Alleghany graves its tone
  Throughout his lofty chart;
Monadnock, on his forehead hoar,
  Doth seal the sacred trust;
Your mountains build their monument,
  Though ye destroy their dust.

*Lydia Huntly Sigourney* [1791–1865]

## MANNAHATTA

I WAS asking for something specific and perfect for my city,
Whereupon lo! upsprang the aboriginal name.

Now I see what there is in a name, a word, liquid, sane, unruly, musical, self-sufficient,
I see that the word of my city is that word from of old,
Because I see that word nested in nests of water-bays, superb,
Rich, hemmed thick all around with sail-ships and steamships, an island sixteen miles long, solid-founded,
Numberless crowded streets, high growths of iron, slender, strong, light, splendidly uprising toward clear skies,
Tides swift and ample, well-loved by me, toward sundown,
The flowing sea-currents, the little islands, larger adjoining islands, the heights, the villas,
The countless masts, the white shore-steamers, the lighters, the ferry-boats, the black sea-steamers well-modelled,
The down-town streets, the jobbers' houses of business, the houses of business of the ship-merchants and money-brokers, the river-streets,
Immigrants arriving, fifteen or twenty thousand in a week,
The carts hauling goods, the manly race of drivers of horses, the brown-faced sailors,

The summer air, the bright sun shining, and the sailing
 clouds aloft,
The winter snows, the sleigh-bells, the broken ice in the river,
 passing along up or down with the flood-tide or ebb-tide,
The mechanics of the city, the masters, well-formed, beauti-
 ful-faced, looking you straight in the eyes,
Trottoirs thronged, vehicles, Broadway, the women, the
 shops and shows,
A million people—manners free and superb—open voices—
 hospitality—the most courageous and friendly young
 men,
City of hurried and sparkling waters! city of spires and
 masts!
City nested in bays! my city!

*Walt Whitman* [1819–1892]

## GLOUCESTER MOORS

A MILE behind is Gloucester town
Where the fishing fleets put in,
A mile ahead the land dips down
And the woods and farms begin.
Here, where the moors stretch free
In the high blue afternoon,
Are the marching sun and talking sea,
And the racing winds that wheel and flee
On the flying heels of June.

Jill-o'er-the-ground is purple blue,
Blue is the quaker-maid,
The wild geranium holds its dew
Long in the boulder's shade.
Wax-red hangs the cup
From the huckleberry boughs,
In barberry bells the gray moths sup,
Or where the choke-cherry lifts high up
Sweet bowls for their carouse.

Over the shelf of the sandy cove
Beach-peas blossom late.
By copse and cliff the swallows rove
Each calling to his mate.

Seaward the sea-gulls go,
And the land-birds all are here;
That green-gold flash was a vireo,
And yonder flame where the marsh-flags grow
Was a scarlet tanager.

This earth is not the steadfast place
We landsmen build upon;
From deep to deep she varies pace,
And while she comes is gone.
Beneath my feet I feel
Her smooth bulk heave and dip;
With velvet plunge and soft upreel
She swings and steadies to her keel
Like a gallant, gallant ship.

These summer clouds she sets for sail,
The sun is her masthead light,
She tows the moon like a pinnace frail
Where her phosphor wake churns bright.
Now hid, now looming clear,
On the face of the dangerous blue
The star fleets tack and wheel and veer,
But on, but on does the old earth steer
As if her port she knew.

God, dear God! Does she know her port,
Though she goes so far about?
Or blind astray, does she make her sport
To brazen and chance it out?
I watched when her captains passed:
She were better captainless.
Men in the cabin, before the mast,
But some were reckless and some aghast,
And some sat gorged at mess.

By her battened hatch I leaned and caught
Sounds from the noisome hold,—
Cursing and sighing of souls distraught
And cries too sad to be told.
Then I strove to go down and see;
But they said, "Thou art not of us!"

I turned to those on the deck with me
And cried, "Give help!" But they said, "Let be:
Our ship sails faster thus."

Jill-o'er-the-ground is purple blue,
Blue is the quaker-maid,
The alder-clump where the brook comes through
Breeds cresses in its shade.
To be out of the moiling street
With its swelter and its sin!
Who has given to me this sweet,
And given my brother dust to eat?
And when will his wage come in?

Scattering wide or blown in ranks,
Yellow and white and brown,
Boats and boats from the fishing banks
Come home to Gloucester town.
There is cash to purse and spend,
There are wives to be embraced,
Hearts to borrow and hearts to lend,
And hearts to take and keep to the end,—
O little sails, make haste!

But thou, vast outbound ship of souls,
What harbor town for thee?
What shapes, when thy arriving tolls,
Shall crowd the banks to see?
Shall all the happy shipmates then
Stand singing brotherly?
Or shall a haggard ruthless few
Warp her over and bring her to,
While the many broken souls of men
Fester down in the slaver's pen,
And nothing to say or do?

*William Vaughn Moody* [1869–1910]

## THE SONG OF THE COLORADO

FROM the heart of the mighty mountains strong-souled for my fate I came,
My far-drawn track to a nameless sea through a land without a name;

And the earth rose up to hold me, to bid me linger and stay;
And the brawn and bone of my mother's race were set to
bar my way.

Yet I stayed not, I could not linger; my soul was tense to
the call
The wet winds sing when the long waves leap and beat on
the far sea wall.
I stayed not, I could not linger; patient, resistless, alone,
I hewed the trail of my destiny deep in the hindering stone.

How narrow that first dim pathway—yet deepening hour by
hour!
Years, ages, eons, spent and forgot, while I gathered me
might and power
To answer the call that led me, to carve my road to the sea,
Till my flood swept out with that greater tide as tireless and
tameless and free.

From the far, wild land that bore me, I drew my blood as
wild—
I, born of the glacier's glory, born of the uplands piled
Like stairs to the door of heaven, that the Maker of all
might go
Down from his place with honor, to look on the world and
know
That the sun and the wind and the waters, and the white ice
cold and still,
Were moving aright in the plan he had made, shaping his
wish and will.
When the spirit of worship was on me, turning alone,
apart,
I stayed and carved me temples deep in the mountain's
heart,
Wide-domed and vast and silent, meet for the God I knew,
With shrines that were shadowed and solemn and altars of
richest hue;
And out of my ceaseless striving I wrought a victor's
hymn,
Flung up to the stars in greeting from my far track deep and
dim.

For the earth was put behind me; I reckoned no more with them
That come or go at her bidding, and cling to her garment's hem.
Apart in my rock-hewn pathway, where the great cliffs shut me in,
The storm-swept clouds were my brethren, and the stars were my kind and kin.

Tireless, alone, unstaying, I went as one who goes
On some high and strong adventure that only his own heart knows.
Tireless, alone, unstaying, I went in my chosen road—
I trafficked with no man's burden—I bent me to no man's load.

On my tawny, sinuous shoulders no salt-gray ships swung in;
I washed no feet of cities, like a slave whipped out and in;
My will was the law of my moving in the land that my strife had made—
As a man in the house he has builded, master and unafraid.

O ye that would hedge and bind me—remembering whence I came!
I, that was, and was mighty, ere your race had breath or name!
Play with your dreams in the sunshine—delve and toil and plot—
Yet I keep the way of my will to the sea, when ye and your race are not!

*Sharlot M. Hall* [1870–1944]

## NOW

### YOSEMITE VALLEY

It is creation's morning—
Freshly the rivers run;
The cliffs, white brows adorning,
Sing to the shining sun.

The forest, plumed and crested,
Scales the steep granite wall.

The ranged peaks, glacier-breasted,
March to the festival.

The mountains dance together,
Lifting their domed heads high.
The cataract's foamy feather
Flaunts in the streaming sky.

Somewhere a babe is borning,
Somewhere a maid is won.
It is creation's morning—
Now is the world begun.

*Harriet Monroe* [1860–1936]

## OUT WHERE THE WEST BEGINS

OUT where the handclasp's a little stronger,
Out where the smile dwells a little longer,
That's where the West begins;
Out where the sun is a little brighter,
Where the snows that fall are a trifle whiter,
Where the bonds of home are a wee bit tighter,
That's where the West begins.

Out where the skies are a trifle bluer,
Out where friendship's a little truer,
That's where the West begins;
Out where a fresher breeze is blowing,
Where there's laughter in every streamlet flowing,
Where there's more of reaping and less of sowing,
That's where the West begins.

Out where the world is in the making,
Where fewer hearts in despair are aching,
That's where the West begins;
Where there's more of singing and less of sighing,
Where there's more of giving and less of buying,
And a man makes friends without half trying—
That's where the West begins.

*Arthur Chapman* [1873–1935]

## THE LAW OF THE YUKON

This is the law of the Yukon, and ever she makes it plain:
"Send not your foolish and feeble; send me your strong and your sane—
Strong for the red rage of battle; sane, for I harry them sore,
Send me men girt for the combat, men who are grit to the core;
Swift as the panther in triumph, fierce as the bear in defeat,
Sired of a bulldog parent, steeled in the furnace heat.
Send me the best of your breeding, lend me your chosen ones;
Them will I take to my bosom, them will I call my sons;
Them will I gild with my treasure, them will I glut with my meat;
But the others—the misfits, the failures—I trample under my feet.
Dissolute, damned and despairful, crippled and palsied and slain,
Ye would send me the spawn of your gutters—Go! take back your spawn again.

"Wild and wide are my borders, stern as death is my sway;
From my ruthless throne I have ruled alone for a million years and a day;
Hugging my mighty treasure, waiting for man to come,
Till he swept like a turbid torrent, and after him swept— the scum.
The pallid pimp of the dead-line, the enervate of the pen,
One by one I weeded them out, for all that I sought was— Men.
One by one I dismayed them, frighting them sore with my glooms;
One by one I betrayed them unto my manifold dooms.
Drowned them like rats in my rivers, starved them like curs on my plains,
Rotted the flesh that was left them, poisoned the blood in their veins;
Burst with my winter upon them, searing forever their sight,
Lashed them with fungus-white faces, whimpering wild in the night;

Staggering blind through the storm-whirl, stumbling mad
through the snow,
Frozen stiff in the ice-pack, brittle and bent like a bow;
Featureless, formless, forsaken, scented by wolves in their
flight,
Left for the wind to make music through ribs that are glit-
tering white;
Gnawing the black crust of failure, searching the pit of de-
spair,
Crooking the toe in the trigger, trying to patter a prayer;
Going outside with an escort, raving with lips all afoam,
Writing a cheque for a million, driveling feebly of home;
Lost like a louse in the burning . . . or else in the tented
town
Seeking a drunkard's solace, sinking and sinking down;
Steeped in the slime at the bottom, dead to a decent world,
Lost 'mid the human flotsam, far on the frontier hurled;
In the camp at the bend of the river, with its dozen saloons
aglare,
Its gambling dens ariot, its gramophones all ablare;
Crimped with the crimes of a city, sin-ridden and bridled
with lies,
In the hush of my mountained vastness, in the flush of my
midnight skies.
Plague-spots, yet tools of my purpose, so natheless I suffer
them thrive,
Crushing my Weak in their clutches, that only my Strong
may survive.

"But the others, the men of my mettle, the men who would
'stablish my fame
Unto its ultimate issue, winning me honor, not shame;
Searching my uttermost valleys, fighting each step as they go,
Shooting the wrath of my rapids, scaling my ramparts of
snow;
Ripping the guts of my mountains, looting the beds of my
creeks,
Them will I take to my bosom, and speak as a mother speaks
I am the land that listens, I am the land that broods;
Steeped in eternal beauty, crystalline waters and woods.

Long have I waited lonely, shunned as a thing accurst,
Monstrous, moody, pathetic, the last of the lands and the first;
Visioning camp-fires at twilight, sad with a longing forlorn,
Feeling my womb o'er-pregnant with the seed of cities unborn.
Wild and wide are my borders, stern as death is my sway,
And I wait for the men who will win me—and I will not be won in a day;
And I will not be won by weaklings, subtle, suave and mild,
But by men with the hearts of vikings, and the simple faith of a child;
Desperate, strong and resistless, unthrottled by fear or defeat,
Them will I gild with my treasure, them will I glut with my meat.

"Lofty I stand from each sister land, patient and wearily wise,
With the weight of a world of sadness in my quiet, passionless eyes;
Dreaming alone of a people, dreaming alone of a day,
When men shall not rape my riches, and curse me and go away;
Making a bawd of my bounty, fouling the hand that gave—
Till I rise in my wrath and I sweep on their path and I stamp them into a grave.
Dreaming of men who will bless me, of women esteeming me good,
Of children born in my borders of radiant motherhood.
Of cities leaping to stature, of fame like a flag unfurled,
As I pour the tide of my riches in the eager lap of the world."

This is the Law of the Yukon, that only the Strong shall thrive;
That surely the Weak shall perish, and only the Fit survive.
Dissolute, damned and despairful, crippled and palsied and slain,
This is the Will of the Yukon.—Lo, how she makes it plain!

*Robert W. Service* [1874–1958]

## LINES COMPOSED A FEW MILES ABOVE TINTERN ABBEY, ON REVISITING THE BANKS OF THE WYE, DURING A TOUR, JULY 13, 1798

FIVE years have passed; five summers, with the length
Of five long winters! and again I hear
These waters, rolling from their mountain-springs
With a soft inland murmur.—Once again
Do I behold these steep and lofty cliffs,
Which on a wild secluded scene impress
Thoughts of more deep seclusion; and connect
The landscape with the quiet of the sky.
The day is come when I again repose
Here, under this dark sycamore, and view
These plots of cottage-ground, these orchard-tufts
Which at this season, with their unripe fruits,
Are clad in one green hue, and lose themselves
'Mid groves and copses. Once again I see
These hedge-rows, hardly hedge-rows, little lines
Of sportive wood run wild: these pastoral farms,
Green to the very door; and wreaths of smoke
Sent up, in silence, from among the trees!
With some uncertain notice, as might seem
Of vagrant dwellers in the houseless woods,
Or of some Hermit's cave, where by his fire
The Hermit sits alone.

These beauteous forms,
Through a long absence, have not been to me
As is a landscape to a blind man's eye:
But oft, in lonely rooms, and 'mid the din
Of towns and cities, I have owed to them,
In hours of weariness, sensations sweet,
Felt in the blood, and felt along the heart;
And passing even into my purer mind,
With tranquil restoration:—feelings too
Of unremembered pleasure: such, perhaps,
As have no slight or trivial influence

On that best portion of a good man's life,
His little, nameless, unremembered, acts
Of kindness and of love. Nor less, I trust,
To them I may have owed another gift,
Of aspect more sublime; that blessèd mood,
In which the burthen of the mystery,
In which the heavy and the weary weight
Of all this unintelligible world,
Is lightened:—that serene and blessèd mood,
In which the affections gently lead us on,—
Until, the breath of this corporeal frame
And even the motion of our human blood
Almost suspended, we are laid asleep
In body, and become a living soul:
While with an eye made quiet by the power
Of harmony, and the deep power of joy,
We see into the life of things.
If this
Be but a vain belief, yet, oh! how oft—
In darkness and amid the many shapes
Of joyless daylight; when the fretful stir
Unprofitable, and the fever of the world,
Have hung upon the beatings of my heart—
How oft, in spirit, have I turned to thee,
O sylvan Wye! thou wanderer through the woods,
How often has my spirit turned to thee!
And now, with gleams of half-extinguished thought,
With many recognitions dim and faint,
And somewhat of a sad perplexity,
The picture of the mind revives again:
While here I stand, not only with the sense
Of present pleasure, but with pleasing thoughts
That in this moment there is life and food
For future years. And so I dare to hope,
Though changed no doubt, from what I was when first
I came among these hills; when like a roe
I bounded o'er the mountains, by the sides
Of the deep rivers, and the lonely streams,
Wherever Nature led: more like a man
Flying from something that he dreads, than one

Who sought the thing he loved. For Nature then
(The coarser pleasures of my boyish days,
And their glad animal movements all gone by)
To me was all in all.—I cannot paint
What then I was. The sounding cataract
Haunted me like a passion: the tall rock,
The mountain, and the deep and gloomy wood,
Their colors and their forms, were then to me
An appetite; a feeling and a love,
That had no need of a remoter charm,
By thought supplied, or any interest
Unborrowed from the eye.—That time is past,
And all its aching joys are now no more,
And all its dizzy raptures. Not for this
Faint I, nor mourn nor murmur; other gifts
Have followed; for such loss, I would believe,
Abundant recompense. For I have learned
To look on Nature, not as in the hour
Of thoughtless youth; but hearing oftentimes
The still, sad music of humanity,
Nor harsh nor grating, though of ample power
To chasten and subdue. And I have felt
A presence that disturbs me with the joy
Of elevated thoughts; a sense sublime
Of something far more deeply interfused,
Whose dwelling is the light of setting suns,
And the round ocean and the living air,
And the blue sky, and in the mind of man;
A motion and a spirit, that impels
All thinking things, all objects of all thought,
And rolls through all things. Therefore am I still
A lover of the meadows and the woods,
And mountains; and of all that we behold
From this green earth; of all the mighty world
Of eye, and ear,—both what they half create,
And what perceive; well pleased to recognize
In Nature and the language of the sense,
The anchor of my purest thoughts, the nurse,
The guide, the guardian of my heart, and soul
Of all my moral being.

Nor perchance,
If I were not thus taught, should I the more
Suffer my genial spirits to decay:
For thou art with me here, upon the banks
Of this fair river; thou, my dearest Friend,
My dear, dear Friend; and in thy voice I catch
The language of my former heart, and read
My former pleasure in the shooting lights
Of thy wild eyes. Oh! yet a little while
May I behold in thee what I was once,
My dear, dear Sister! and this prayer I make,
Knowing that Nature never did betray
The heart that loved her; 'tis her privilege,
Through all the years of this our life, to lead
From joy to joy: for she can so inform
The mind that is within us, so impress
With quietness and beauty, and so feed
With lofty thoughts, that neither evil tongues,
Rash judgments, nor the sneers of selfish men,
Nor greetings where no kindness is, nor all
The dreary intercourse of daily life,
Shall e'er prevail against us, or disturb
Our cheerful faith, that all which we behold
Is full of blessings. Therefore let the moon
Shine on thee in thy solitary walk;
And let the misty mountain-winds be free
To blow against thee: and, in after years,
When these wild ecstasies shall be matured
Into a sober pleasure; when thy mind
Shall be a mansion for all lovely forms,
Thy memory be as a dwelling-place
For all sweet sounds and harmonies; oh! then,
If solitude, or fear, or pain, or grief,
Should be thy portion, with what healing thoughts
Of tender joy wilt thou remember me,
And these my exhortations! Nor, perchance—
If I should be where I no more can hear
Thy voice, nor catch from thy wild eyes these gleams
Of past existence—wilt thou then forget
That on the banks of this delightful stream

We stood together; and that I, so long
A worshipper of Nature, hither came
Unwearied in that service: rather say
With warmer love—oh! with far deeper zeal
Of holier love. Nor wilt thou then forget,
That after many wanderings, many years
Of absence, these steep woods and lofty cliffs,
And this green pastoral landscape, were to me
More dear, both for themselves and for thy sake!

*William Wordsworth* [1770–1850]

## THE PASS OF KIRKSTONE

Within the mind strong fancies work.
A deep delight the bosom thrills
Oft as I pass along the fork
Of these fraternal hills:
Where, save the rugged road, we find
No appanage of human kind,
Nor hint of man; if stone or rock
Seem not his handiwork to mock
By something cognizably shaped;
Mockery—or model roughly hewn,
And left as if by earthquake strewn,
Or from the Flood escaped:
Altars for Druid service fit;
(But where no fire was ever lit,
Unless the glow-worm to the skies
Thence offer nightly sacrifice)
Wrinkled Egyptian monument;
Green moss-grown tower; or hoary tent;
Tents of a camp that never shall be razed—
On which four thousand years have gazed!

Ye plough-shares sparkling on the slopes!
Ye snow-white lambs that trip
Imprisoned 'mid the formal props
Of restless ownership!
Ye trees, that may to-morrow fall
To feed the insatiate Prodigal!

Lawns, houses, chattels, groves, and fields,
All that the fertile valley shields;
Wages of folly—baits of crime,
Of life's uneasy game the stake,
Playthings that keep the eyes awake
Of drowsy, dotard Time;—
O care! O guilt!—O vales and plains,
Here, 'mid his own unvexed domains,
A Genius dwells, that can subdue
At once all memory of You,—
Most potent when mists veil the sky,
Mists that distort and magnify;
While the coarse rushes, to the sweeping breeze,
Sigh forth their ancient melodies!

List to those shriller notes!—*that* march
Perchance was on the blast,
When, through this Height's inverted arch,
Rome's earliest legion passed!
—They saw, adventurously impelled,
And older eyes than theirs beheld,
This block—and yon, whose churchlike frame
Gives to this savage Pass its name.
Aspiring Road! that lov'st to hide
Thy darling in a vapory bourn,
Not seldom may the hour return
When thou shalt be my guide:
And I (as all men may find cause,
When life is at a weary pause,
And they have panted up the hill
Of duty with reluctant will)
Be thankful, even though tired and faint,
For the rich bounties of constraint;
Whence oft invigorating transports flow
That choice lacked courage to bestow!

My Soul was grateful for delight
That wore a threatening brow;
A veil is lifted—can she slight
The scene that opens now?

Though habitation none appear,
The greenness tells, man must be there;
The shelter—that the perspective
Is of the clime in which we live;
Where Toil pursues his daily round;
Where Pity sheds sweet tears—and Love,
In woodbine bower or birchen grove,
Inflicts his tender wound.
—Who comes not hither ne'er shall know
How beautiful the world below;
Nor can he guess how lightly leaps
The brook adown the rocky steeps.
Farewell, thou desolate Domain!
Hope, pointing to the cultured plain,
Carols like a shepherd-boy;
And who is she?—Can that be Joy!
Who, with a sunbeam for her guide,
Smoothly skims the meadows wide;
While Faith, from yonder opening cloud,
To hill and vale proclaims aloud,
"Whate'er the weak may dread, the wicked dare,
Thy lot, O Man, is good, thy portion, fair!"

*William Wordsworth* [1770-1850]

## YARROW UNVISITED

From Stirling Castle we had seen
The mazy Forth unravelled,
Had trod the banks of Clyde and Tay,
And with the Tweed had travelled;
And when we came to Clovenford,
Then said my "winsome Marrow,"
"Whate'er betide, we'll turn aside,
And see the Braes of Yarrow."

"Let Yarrow folk, frae Selkirk town,
Who have been buying, selling,
Go back to Yarrow, 'tis their own,
Each maiden to her dwelling!

On Yarrow's banks let herons feed,
Hares couch, and rabbits burrow;
But we will downward with the Tweed,
Nor turn aside to Yarrow.

"There's Galla Water, Leader Haughs,
Both lying right before us;
And Dryburgh, where with chiming Tweed
The lintwhites sing in chorus;
There's pleasant Tiviotdale, a land
Made blithe with plow and harrow:
Why throw away a needful day
To go in search of Yarrow?

"What's Yarrow but a river bare
That glides the dark hills under?
There are a thousand such elsewhere
As worthy of your wonder."
—Strange words they seemed of slight and scorn:
My True-love sighed for sorrow,
And looked me in the face, to think
I thus could speak of Yarrow!

"O green," said I, "are Yarrow's holms,
And sweet is Yarrow flowing!
Fair hangs the apple frae the rock,
But we will leave it growing.
O'er hilly path, and open strath
We'll wander Scotland thorough;
But, though so near, we will not turn
Into the dale of Yarrow.

"Let beeves and home-bred kine partake
The sweets of Burn-mill meadow;
The swan on still Saint Mary's Lake
Float double, swan and shadow!
We will not see them; will not go
To-day, nor yet to-morrow;
Enough if in our hearts we know
There's such a place as Yarrow.

"Be Yarrow stream unseen, unknown!
It must, or we shall rue it:
We have a vision of our own,
Ah! why should we undo it?
The treasured dreams of times long past,
We'll keep them, winsome Marrow!
For when we're there, although 'tis fair,
'Twill be another Yarrow!

"If Care with freezing years should come
And wandering seem but folly,—
Should we be loth to stir from home,
And yet be melancholy;
Should life be dull, and spirits low,
'Twill soothe us in our sorrow
That earth has something yet to show,
The bonny Holms of Yarrow!"

*William Wordsworth* [1770 1850]

## YARROW VISITED

And is this—Yarrow?—*This* the Stream
Of which my fancy cherished
So faithfully, a waking dream?
An image that hath perished!
O that some minstrel's harp were near
To utter notes of gladness
And chase this silence from the air,
That fills my heart with sadness!

Yet why?—a silvery current flows
With uncontrolled meanderings;
Nor have these eyes by greener hills
Been soothed, in all my wanderings.
And, through her depths, Saint Mary's Lake
Is visibly delighted;
For not a feature of those hills
Is in the mirror slighted.

A blue sky bends o'er Yarrow vale,
Save where that pearly whiteness
Is round the rising sun diffused,
A tender hazy brightness;
Mild dawn of promise! that excludes
All profitless dejection;
Though not unwilling here to admit
A pensive recollection.

Where was it that the famous Flower
Of Yarrow Vale lay bleeding?
His bed perchance was yon smooth mound
On which the herd is feeding:
And haply from this crystal pool,
Now peaceful as the morning,
The water-wraith ascended thrice,
And gave his doleful warning.

Delicious is the lay that sings
The haunts of happy lovers,
The path that leads them to the grove,
The leafy grove that covers:
And pity sanctifies the verse
That paints, by strength of sorrow,
The unconquerable strength of love;
Bear witness, rueful Yarrow!

But thou, that didst appear so fair
To fond imagination,
Dost rival in the light of day
Her delicate creation:
Meek loveliness is round thee spread,
A softness still and holy:
The grace of forest charms decayed,
And pastoral melancholy.

That region left, the vale unfolds
Rich groves of lofty stature,
With Yarrow winding through the pomp
Of cultivated nature;

And, rising from those lofty groves,
Behold a ruin hoary,
The shattered front of Newark's towers,
Renowned in Border story.

Fair scenes for childhood's opening bloom,
For sportive youth to stray in,
For manhood to enjoy his strength,
And age to wear away in!
Yon cottage seems a bower of bliss,
A covert for protection
Of tender thoughts that nestle there—
The brood of chaste affection.

How sweet, on this autumnal day,
The wildwood fruits to gather,
And on my True-love's forehead plant
A crest of blooming heather!
And what if I enwreathed my own?
'Twere no offence to reason;
The sober hills thus deck their brows
To meet the wintry season.

I see,—but not by sight alone,
Loved Yarrow, have I won thee;
A ray of fancy still survives—
Her sunshine plays upon thee!
Thy ever-youthful waters keep
A course of lively pleasure;
And gladsome notes my lips can breathe
Accordant to the measure.

The vapors linger round the heights,
They melt, and soon must vanish;
One hour is theirs, nor more is mine—
Sad thought, which I would banish,
But that I know, where'er I go,
Thy genuine image, Yarrow!
Will dwell with me,—to heighten joy,
And cheer my mind in sorrow.

*William Wordsworth* [1770–1850]

## ON A DISTANT PROSPECT OF ETON COLLEGE

Ye distant spires, ye antique towers,
 That crown the watery glade,
Where grateful Science still adores
 Her Henry's holy shade;
And ye, that from the stately brow
Of Windsor's heights the expanse below
 Of grove, of lawn, of mead survey,
Whose turf, whose shade, whose flowers among
Wanders the hoary Thames along
 His silver-winding way:

Ah, happy hills! ah, pleasing shade!
 Ah, fields beloved in vain!
Where once my careless childhood strayed,
 A stranger yet to pain!
I feel the gales that from ye blow
A momentary bliss bestow,
 As waving fresh their gladsome wing,
My weary soul they seem to soothe,
And, redolent of joy and youth,
 To breathe a second spring.

Say, Father Thames, for thou hast seen
 Full many a sprightly race
Disporting on thy margent green
 The paths of pleasure trace;
Who foremost now delight to cleave,
With pliant arm, thy glassy wave?
 The captive linnet which enthral?
What idle progeny succeed
To chase the rolling circle's speed,
 Or urge the flying ball?

While some on earnest business bent
 Their murmuring labors ply
'Gainst graver hours, that bring constraint
 To sweeten liberty:

Some bold adventurers disdain
The limits of their little reign,
  And unknown regions dare descry:
Still as they run they look behind,
They hear a voice in every wind,
  And snatch a fearful joy.

Gay Hope is theirs by fancy fed,
  Less pleasing when possessed;
The tear forgot as soon as shed,
  The sunshine of the breast:
Theirs buxom Health, of rosy hue,
Wild Wit, Invention ever new,
  And lively Cheer, of Vigor born;
The thoughtless day, the easy night,
The spirits pure, the slumbers light
  That fly the approach of morn.

Alas! regardless of their doom
  The little victims play;
No sense have they of ills to come,
  Nor care beyond to-day:
Yet see, how all around them wait
The ministers of human fate
  And black Misfortune's baleful train!
Ah, show them where in ambush stand,
To seize their prey, the murderous band!
  Ah, tell them they are men!

These shall the fury Passions tear,
  The vultures of the mind,
Disdainful Anger, pallid Fear,
  And Shame that sculks behind;
Or pining Love shall waste their youth,
Or Jealousy, with rankling tooth,
  That inly gnaws the secret heart,
And Envy wan, and faded Care,
Grim-visaged comfortless Despair,
  And Sorrow's piercing dart.

Ambition this shall tempt to rise,
  Then whirl the wretch from high,
To bitter Scorn a sacrifice,
  And grinning Infamy.
The stings of Falsehood those shall try
And hard Unkindness' altered eye,
  That mocks the tear it forced to flow;
And keen Remorse with blood defiled,
And moody Madness laughing wild
  Amid severest woe.

Lo! in the Vale of Years beneath
  A grisly troop are seen,
The painful family of Death,
  More hideous than their Queen:
This racks the joints, this fires the veins,
That every laboring sinew strains,
  Those in the deeper vitals rage:
Lo! Poverty, to fill the band,
That numbs the soul with icy hand,
  And slow-consuming Age.

To each his sufferings: all are men,
  Condemned alike to groan;
The tender for another's pain,
  The unfeeling for his own.
Yet, ah! why should they know their fate,
Since sorrow never comes too late,
  And happiness too swiftly flies?
Thought would destroy their paradise!
No more;—where ignorance is bliss,
  'Tis folly to be wise.

*Thomas Gray* [1716–1771]

## A SONG OF SHERWOOD

SHERWOOD in the twilight, is Robin Hood awake?
Gray and ghostly shadows are gliding through the brake;
Shadows of the dappled deer, dreaming of the morn,
Dreaming of a shadowy man that winds a shadowy horn.

Robin Hood is here again: all his merry thieves
Hear a ghostly bugle-note shivering through the leaves,
Calling as he used to call, faint and far away,
In Sherwood, in Sherwood, about the break of day.

Merry, merry England has kissed the lips of June:
All the wings of fairyland were here beneath the moon
Like a flight of rose-leaves fluttering in a mist
Of opal and ruby and pearl and amethyst.

Merry, merry England is waking as of old,
With eyes of blither hazel and hair of brighter gold:
For Robin Hood is here again beneath the bursting spray
In Sherwood, in Sherwood, about the break of day.

Love is in the greenwood building him a house
Of wild rose and hawthorn and honeysuckle boughs:
Love is in the greenwood: dawn is in the skies;
And Marian is waiting with a glory in her eyes.

Hark! The dazzled laverock climbs the golden steep:
Marian is waiting: is Robin Hood asleep?
Round the fairy grass-rings frolic elf and fay,
In Sherwood, in Sherwood, about the break of day.

Oberon, Oberon, rake away the gold,
Rake away the red leaves, roll away the mould,
Rake away the gold leaves, roll away the red,
And wake Will Scarlett from his leafy forest bed.

Friar Tuck and Little John are riding down together
With quarter-staff and drinking-can and gray goose-feather;
The dead are coming back again; the years are rolled away
In Sherwood, in Sherwood, about the break of day.

Softly over Sherwood the south wind blows;
All the heart of England hid in every rose
Hears across the greenwood the sunny whisper leap,
Sherwood in the red dawn, is Robin Hood asleep?

Hark, the voice of England wakes him as of old
And, shattering the silence with a cry of brighter gold,
Bugles in the greenwood echo from the steep,
*Sherwood in the red dawn, is Robin Hood asleep?*

Where the deer are gliding down the shadowy glen
All across the glades of fern he calls his merry men;
Doublets of the Lincoln green glancing through the May
In Sherwood, in Sherwood, about the break of day;

Calls them and they answer: from aisles of oak and ash
Rings the *Follow! Follow!* and the boughs begin to crash;
The ferns begin to flutter and the flowers begin to fly;
And through the crimson dawning the robber band goes by.

*Robin! Robin! Robin!* All his merry thieves
Answer as the bugle-note shivers through the leaves:
Calling as he used to call, faint and far away,
In Sherwood, in Sherwood, about the break of day.

*Alfred Noyes* [1880–1958]

## GODIVA

*I waited for the train at Coventry:*
*I hung with grooms and porters on the bridge,*
*To watch the three tall spires; and there I shaped*
*The city's ancient legend into this:—*
Not only we, the latest seed of Time,
New men, that in the flying of a wheel
Cry down the past, not only we, that prate
Of rights and wrongs, have loved the people well,
And loathed to see them overtaxed; but she
Did more, and underwent, and overcame,
The woman of a thousand summers back,
Godiva, wife to that grim Earl, who ruled
In Coventry; for when he laid a tax
Upon his town, and all the mothers brought
Their children, clamoring, "If we pay, we starve!"
She sought her lord, and found him, where he strode

About the hall, among his dogs, alone,
His beard a foot before him, and his hair
A yard behind. She told him of their tears,
And prayed him, "If they pay this tax, they starve."
Whereat he stared, replying, half-amazed,
"You would not let your little finger ache
For such as *these?*"—"But I would die," said she.
He laughed, and swore by Peter and by Paul:
Then filliped at the diamond in her ear:
"O, ay, ay, ay, you talk!"—"Alas!" she said,
"But prove me what it is I would not do."
And from a heart as rough as Esau's hand,
He answered, "Ride you naked through the town,
And I repeal it"; and, nodding, as in scorn,
He parted, with great strides among his dogs.
 So left alone, the passions of her mind,
As winds from all the compass shift and blow,
Made war upon each other for an hour,
Till pity won. She sent a herald forth,
And bade him cry, with sound of trumpet, all
The hard condition, but that she would loose
The people; therefore, as they loved her well,
From then till noon no foot should pace the street,
No eye look down, she passing, but that all
Should keep within, door shut, and window barred.
 Then fled she to her inmost bower, and there
Unclasped the wedded eagles of her belt,
The grim Earl's gift; but ever at a breath
She lingered, looking like a summer moon
Half-dipped in cloud. Anon she shook her head,
And showered the rippled ringlets to her knee;
Unclad herself in haste; adown the stair
Stole on; and, like a creeping sunbeam, slid
From pillar unto pillar, until she reached
The gateway; there she found her palfrey trapped
In purple blazoned with armorial gold.
 Then she rode forth, clothed on with chastity:
The deep air listened round her as she rode,
And all the low wind hardly breathed for fear.
The little wide-mouthed heads upon the spout

Had cunning eyes to see: the barking cur
Made her cheek flame: her palfrey's footfall shot
Light horrors through her pulses: the blind walls
Were full of chinks and holes; and overhead
Fantastic gables, crowding, stared: but she
Not less through all bore up, till, last, she saw
The white-flowered elder-thicket from the field
Gleam through the Gothic archway in the wall.
  Then she rode back, clothed on with chastity:
And one low churl, compact of thankless earth,
The fatal byword of all years to come,
Boring a little auger-hole in fear,
Peeped—but his eyes, before they had their will,
Were shrivelled into darkness in his head,
And dropped before him. So the Powers, who wait
On noble deeds, cancelled a sense misused;
And she, that knew not, passed; and all at once,
With twelve great shocks of sound, the shameless noon
Was clashed and hammered from a hundred towers,
One after one; but even then she gained
Her bower; whence reissuing, robed and crowned,
To meet her lord, she took the tax away
And built herself an everlasting name.

*Alfred Tennyson* [1809–1892]

## DOVER BEACH

The sea is calm to-night.
The tide is full, the moon lies fair
Upon the straits;—on the French coast the light
Gleams and is gone; the cliffs of England stand,
Glimmering and vast, out in the tranquil bay.
Come to the window, sweet is the night-air!
Only, from the long line of spray
Where the sea meets the moon-blanched land,
Listen! you hear the grating roar
Of pebbles which the waves draw back, and fling,
At their return, up the high strand,
Begin, and cease, and then again begin,
With tremulous cadence slow, and bring
The eternal note of sadness in.

Sophocles long ago
Heard it on the Ægean, and it brought
Into his mind the turbid ebb and flow
Of human misery; we
Find also in the sound a thought,
Hearing it by this distant northern sea.

The sea of faith
Was once, too, at the full, and round earth's shore
Lay like the folds of a bright girdle furled.
But now I only hear
Its melancholy, long, withdrawing roar,
Retreating, to the breath
Of the night-wind, down the vast edges drear
And naked shingles of the world.

Ah, love, let us be true
To one another! for the world, which seems
To lie before us like a land of dreams,
So various, so beautiful, so new,
Hath really neither joy, nor love, nor light,
Nor certitude, nor peace, nor help for pain;
And we are here as on a darkling plain
Swept with confused alarms of struggle and flight,
Where ignorant armies clash by night.

*Matthew Arnold* [1822-1888]

## ST. MICHAEL'S MOUNT

St. Michael's Mount, the tidal isle,
In May with daffodils and lilies
Is kirtled gorgeously a while
As ne'er another English hill is:
About the precipices cling
The rich renascence robes of Spring.

Her gold and silver, nature's gifts,
The prodigal with both hands showers;
O not in patches, not in drifts
But round and round a mount of flowers—

Of lilies and of daffodils,
The envy of all other hills.

And on the lofty summit looms
  The castle: None could build or plan it.
The four-square foliage springs and blooms,
  The piled elaborate flower of granite,
That not the sun can wither; no,
Nor any tempest overthrow.

*John Davidson* [1857–1909]

## SONNET

### COMPOSED UPON WESTMINSTER BRIDGE, SEPTEMBER 3, 1802

EARTH has not anything to show more fair:
Dull would he be of soul who could pass by
A sight so touching in its majesty:
This City now doth, like a garment, wear
The beauty of the morning; silent, bare,
Ships, towers, domes, theaters, and temples lie
Open unto the fields, and to the sky;
All bright and glittering in the smokeless air.
Never did sun more beautifully steep
In his first splendor, valley, rock, or hill;
Ne'er saw I, never felt, a calm so deep!
The river glideth at his own sweet will:
Dear God! the very houses seem asleep;
And all that mighty heart is lying still!

*William Wordsworth* [1770–1850]

## A SONG OF FLEET STREET

FLEET STREET! Fleet Street! Fleet Street in the morning,
  With the old sun laughing out behind the dome of Paul's,
Heavy wains a-driving, merry winds a-striving,
  White clouds and blue sky above the smoke-stained walls.

Fleet Street! Fleet Street! Fleet Street in the noontide,
East and west the streets packed close, and roaring like the sea;
With laughter and with sobbing we feel the world's heart throbbing,
And know that what is throbbing is the heart of you and me.

Fleet Street! Fleet Street! Fleet Street in the evening,
Darkness set with golden lamps down Ludgate Hill a-row:
Oh! hark the voice o' th' city that breaks our hearts with pity,
That crazes us with shame and wrath, and makes us love her so.

Fleet Street! Fleet Street! morning, noon, and starlight,
Through the never-ceasing roar come the great chimes clear and slow;
"Good are life and laughter, though we look before and after,
And good to love the race of men a little ere we go."

*Alice Werner* [1859–1935]

## SONG

Closes and courts and lanes,
Devious, clustered thick,
The thoroughfare, mains and drains,
People and mortar and brick,
Wood, metal, machinery, brains,
Pen and composing stick:
Fleet Street, but exquisite flame
In the nebula once ere day and night
Began their travail, or earth became,
And all was passionate light.

Networks of wire overland,
Conduits under the sea,
Aerial message from strand to strand
By lightning that travels free,
Hither in haste to hand
Tidings of destiny,

These tingling nerves of the world's affairs
  Deliver remorseless, rendering still
The fall of empires, the price of shares,
  The record of good and ill.

Tidal the traffic goes
  Citywards out of the town;
Townwards the evening ebb o'erflows
  This highway of old renown,
When the fog-woven curtains close,
  And the urban night comes down,
    Where souls are spilt and intellects spent
      O'er news vociferant near and far,
    From Hesperus hard to the Orient,
      From dawn to the evening star.

This is the royal refrain
  That burdens the boom and the thud
Of omnibus, mobus, wain,
  And the hoofs on the beaten mud,
From the Griffin at Chancery Lane
  To the portal of old King Lud—
    Fleet Street, diligent night and day,
      Of news of the mart and the burnished hearth,
    Seven hundred paces of narrow way,
      A notable bit of the earth.

*John Davidson* [1857–1909]

## ST. JAMES'S STREET

ST. JAMES'S STREET, of classic fame,
  For Fashion still is seen there:
St. James's Street? I know the name,
  I almost think I've been there!
Why, that's where Sacharissa sighed
  When Waller read his ditty;
Where Byron lived, and Gibbon died,
  And Alvanley was witty.

A famous Street! To yonder Park
  Young Churchill stole in class-time;
Come, gaze on fifty men of mark,
  And then recall the past time.
The *plats* at White's, the play at Crock's,
  The bumpers to Miss Gunning;
The *bonhomie* of Charley Fox,
  And Selwyn's ghastly funning.

The dear old Street of clubs and cribs,
  As north and south it stretches,
Still seems to smack of Rolliad squibs,
  And Gillray's fiercer sketches;
The quaint old dress, the grand old style,
  The *mots*, the racy stories;
The wine, the dice, the wit, the bile—
  The hate of Whigs and Tories.

At dusk, when I am strolling there,
  Dim forms will rise around me;
Lepel flits past me in her chair,
  And Congreve's airs astound me!
And once Nell Gwynne, a frail young Sprite
  Looked kindly when I met her;
I shook my head, perhaps,—but quite
  Forgot to quite forget her.

The Street is still a lively tomb
  For rich, and gay, and clever;
The crops of dandies bud and bloom,
  And die as fast as ever.
Now gilded youth loves cutty pipes,
  And slang that's rather scaring;
It can't approach its prototypes
  In taste, or tone, or bearing.

In Brummell's day of buckle shoes,
  Lawn cravats, and roll collars,
They'd fight, and woo, and bet—and lose,
  Like gentlemen and scholars:

I'm glad young men should go the pace,
  I half forgive Old Rapid!
These louts disgrace their name and race—
  So vicious and so vapid!

Worse times may come. *Bon ton*, indeed,
  Will then be quite forgotten,
And all we much revere will speed
  From ripe to worse than rotten:
Let grass then sprout between yon stones,
  And owls then roost at Boodle's,
For Echo will hurl back the tones
  Of screaming Yankee Doodles.

I love the haunts of old Cockaigne,
  Where wit and wealth were squandered;
The halls that tell of hoop and train,
  Where grace and rank have wandered;
Those halls where ladies fair and leal
  First ventured to adore me!
Something of that old love I feel
  For this old Street before me.

*Frederick Locker-Lampson* [1821–1895]

## THE SOUTH COUNTRY

When I am living in the Midlands
  That are sodden and unkind,
I light my lamp in the evening:
  My work is left behind;
And the great hills of the South Country
  Come back into my mind.

The great hills of the South Country
  They stand along the sea;
And it's there walking in the high woods
  That I could wish to be,
And the men that were boys when I was a boy
  Walking along with me.

The men that live in North England
  I saw them for a day:
Their hearts are set upon the waste fells,
  Their skies are fast and gray;
From their castle-walls a man may see
  The mountains far away.

The men that live in West England
  They see the Severn strong,
A-rolling on rough water brown
  Light aspen leaves along.
They have the secret of the Rocks,
  And the oldest kind of song.

But the men that live in the South Country
  Are the kindest and most wise,
They get their laughter from the loud surf,
  And the faith in their happy eyes
Comes surely from our Sister the Spring
  When over the sea she flies;
The violets suddenly bloom at her feet,
  She blesses us with surprise.

I never get between the pines
  But I smell the Sussex air;
Nor I never come on a belt of sand
  But my home is there.
And along the sky the line of the Downs
  So noble and so bare.

A lost thing could I never find,
  Nor a broken thing mend:
And I fear I shall be all alone
  When I get towards the end.
Who will there be to comfort me
  Or who will be my friend?

I will gather and carefully make my friends
  Of the men of the Sussex Weald,
They watch the stars from silent folds,
  They stiffly plough the field

By them and the God of the South Country
My poor soul shall be healed.

If I ever become a rich man,
Or if ever I grow to be old,
I will build a house with deep thatch
To shelter me from the cold,
And there shall the Sussex songs be sung
And the story of Sussex told.

I will hold my house in the high wood
Within a walk of the sea,
And the men that were boys when I was a boy
Shall sit and drink with me.

*Hilaire Belloc* [1870–1953]

## EDINBURGH

City of mist and rain and blown gray spaces,
Dashed with wild wet color and gleam of tears,
Dreaming in Holyrood halls of the passionate faces
Lifted to one Queen's face that has conquered the years,
Are not the halls of thy memory haunted places?
Cometh there not as a moon (where the blood-rust sears
Floors a-flutter of old with silks and laces),
Gliding, a ghostly Queen, through a mist of tears?

Proudly here, with a loftier pinnacled splendor,
Throned in his northern Athens, what spells remain
Still on the marble lips of the Wizard, and render
Silent the gazer on glory without a stain!
Here and here, do we whisper, with hearts more tender,
Tusitala wandered through mist and rain;
Rainbow-eyed and frail and gallant and slender,
Dreaming of pirate-isles in a jewelled main.

Up the Cannongate climbeth, cleft asunder
Raggedly here, with a glimpse of the distant sea
Flashed through a crumbling alley, a glimpse of wonder,
Nay, for the City is throned on Eternity!

Hark! from the soaring castle a cannon's thunder
    Closes an hour for the world and an æon for me,
Gazing at last from the martial heights whereunder
    Deathless memories roll to an ageless sea.

*Alfred Noyes* [1880–1958]

## CORRYMEELA

Over here in England I'm helpin' wi' the hay,
An' I wisht I was in Ireland the livelong day;
Weary on the English hay, an' sorra take the wheat!
  *Och! Corrymeela an' the blue sky over it.*

There's a deep dumb river flowin' by beyont the heavy trees,
This livin' air is moithered wi' the hummin' o' the bees;
I wisht I'd hear the Claddagh burn go runnin' through the heat
  *Past Corrymeela, wi' the blue sky over it.*

The people that's in England is richer nor the Jews,
There's not the smallest young gosoon but thravels in his shoes!
I'd give the pipe between me teeth to see a barefut child,
  *Och! Corrymeela an' the low south wind.*

Here's hands so full o' money an' hearts so full o' care,
By the luck o' love! I'd still go light for all I did go bare.
"God save ye, *colleen dhas*," I said: the girl she thought me wild.
  *Far Corrymeela, an' the low south wind.*

D'ye mind me now, the song at night is mortail hard to raise,
The girls are heavy goin' here, the boys are ill to plase;
When one'st I'm out this workin' hive, 'tis I'll be back again—
  *Ay, Corrymeela, in the same soft rain.*

The puff o' smoke from one ould roof before an English town!
For a *shaugh* wid Andy Feelan here I'd give a silver crown,
For a curl o' hair like Mollie's ye'll ask the like in vain.
  *Sweet Corrymeela, an' the same soft rain.*

*Moira O'Neill* [18

## THE LITTLE WAVES OF BREFFNY

THE grand road from the mountain goes shining to the sea,
And there is traffic in it, and many a horse and cart;
But the little roads of Cloonagh are dearer far to me,
And the little roads of Cloonagh go rambling through my heart.

A great storm from the ocean goes shouting o'er the hill,
And there is glory in it, and terror on the wind;
But the haunted air of twilight is very strange and still,
And the little winds of twilight are dearer to my mind.

The great waves of the Atlantic sweep storming on their way,
Shining green and silver with the hidden herring shoal;
But the little waves of Breffny have drenched my heart in spray,
And the little waves of Breffny go stumbling through my soul.

*Eva Gore-Booth* [1872-1926]

## A SONG OF GLENANN

OCH, when we lived in ould Glenann
Meself could lift a song!
An' ne'er an hour by day or dark
Would I be thinkin' long.

The weary wind might take the roof,
The rain might lay the corn;
We'd up an' look for betther luck
About the morrow's morn.

But since we come away from there
An' far across the say,
I still have wrought, an' still have thought
The way I'm doin' the day.

An' now we're quarely betther fixed,
In troth! there's nothin' wrong:
But me an' mine, by rain an' shine
We do be thinkin' long.

*Moira O'Neill* [18

## THE MAIDEN CITY

WHERE Foyle his swelling waters rolls northward to the main,
Here, Queen of Erin's daughters, fair Derry fixed her reign.
A holy temple crowned her, and commerce graced her street,
A rampart wall was round her, the river at her feet;
And here she sat alone, boys, and looking from the hill
Vowed The Maiden on her throne, boys, would be a maiden still.

From Antrim crossing over in famous eighty-eight
A plumed and belted lover came to the Ferry gate:
She summoned to defend her our sires—a beardless race—
Who shouted NO SURRENDER! and slammed it in his face.
Then in a quiet tone, boys, they told him 'twas their will
That The Maiden on her throne, boys, should be a maiden still.

Next, crushing all before him, a kingly wooer came
(The royal banner o'er him blushed crimson deep for shame);
He showed the Pope's commission, nor dreamed to be refused.
She pitied his condition, but begged to stand excused.
In short, the fact is known, boys, she chased him from the hill,
For The Maiden on her throne, boys, would be a maiden still.

On our brave sires descending, 'twas then the tempest broke,
Their peaceful dwellings rending, 'mid blood and flame and smoke.
That hallowed graveyard yonder swells with the slaughtered dead—
Oh! brothers! pause and ponder, it was for us they bled;
And while their gift we own, boys—the fane that tops our hill,
Oh, The Maiden on her throne, boys, shall be a maiden still.

Nor wily tongue shall move us, nor tyrant arm affright,
We'll look to One above us Who ne'er forsook the right;
Who will, may crouch and tender the birthright of the free,
But, brothers, NO SURRENDER, no compromise for me!

We want no barrier stone, boys, no gates to guard the hill,
Yet The Maiden on her throne, boys, shall be a maiden still.

*Charlotte Elizabeth Tonna* [1790–1846]

## THE DEAD AT CLONMACNOIS

In a quiet watered land, a land of roses,
Stands Saint Kieran's city fair;
And the warriors of Erin in their famous generations
Slumber there.

There beneath the dewy hillside sleep the noblest
Of the clan of Conn,
Each below his stone with name in branching Ogham
And the sacred knot thereon.

There they laid to rest the seven Kings of Tara,
There the sons of Cairbré sleep—
Battle-banners of the Gael that in Kieran's plain of crosses
Now their final hosting keep.

And in Clonmacnois they laid the men of Teffia,
And right many a lord of Breagh;
Deep the sod above Clan Creidé and Clan Conaill,
Kind in hall and fierce in fray.

Many and many a son of Conn the Hundred-Fighter
In the red earth lies at rest;
Many a blue eye of Clan Colman the turf covers,
Many a swan-white breast.

*Thomas William Rolleston* [1857–1920]

## SWEET INNISFALLEN

Sweet Innisfallen, fare thee well,
May calm and sunshine long be thine!
How fair thou art let others tell,—
To *feel* how fair shall long be mine.

Sweet Innisfallen, long shall dwell
In memory's dream that sunny smile,
Which o'er thee on that evening fell,
When first I saw thy fairy isle.

'Twas light, indeed, too blest for one,
Who had to turn to paths of care—
Through crowded haunts again to run,
And leave thee bright and silent there;

No more unto thy shores to come,
But, on the world's rude ocean tossed,
Dream of thee sometimes, as a home
Of sunshine he had seen and lost.

Far better in thy weeping hours
To part from thee, as I do now,
When mist is o'er thy blooming bowers,
Like sorrow's veil on beauty's brow.

For, though unrivalled still thy grace,
Thou dost not look, as then, *too* blest,
But thus in shadow seem'st a place
Where erring man might hope to rest.—

Might hope to rest, and find in thee
A gloom like Eden's, on the day
He left its shade, when every tree,
Like thine, hung weeping o'er his way.

Weeping or smiling, lovely isle!
And all the lovelier for thy tears,
For though but rare thy sunny smile,
'Tis heaven's own glance when it appears.

Like feeling hearts, whose joys are few,
But, when indeed they come, divine—
The brightest light the sun e'er threw
Is lifeless to one gleam of thine!

*Thomas Moore* [1779-1852]

## "AH, SWEET IS TIPPERARY"

Ah, sweet is Tipperary in the springtime of the year,
When the hawthorn's whiter than the snow,
When the feathered folk assemble and the air is all a-tremble
With their singing and their winging to and fro;

When queenly Slievenamon puts her verdant vesture on,
  And smiles to hear the news the breezes bring;
When the sun begins to glance on the rivulets that dance—
  Ah, sweet is Tipperary in the spring!

Ah, sweet is Tipperary in the springtime of the year,
  When the mists are rising from the lea,
When the Golden Vale is smiling with a beauty all beguiling,
  And the Suir goes crooning to the sea;
When the shadows and the showers only multiply the flowers
  That the lavish hand of May will fling;
When in unfrequented ways, fairy music softly plays—
  Ah, sweet is Tipperary in the spring!

Ah, sweet is Tipperary in the springtime of the year,
  When life like the year is young,
When the soul is just awaking like a lily blossom breaking,
  And love words linger on the tongue;
When the blue of Irish skies is the hue of Irish eyes,
  And love-dreams cluster and cling
Round the heart and round the brain, half of pleasure, half
    of pain—
  Ah, sweet is Tipperary in the spring!

*Denis Aloysius McCarthy* [1870–1931]

## THE GROVES OF BLARNEY

THE groves of Blarney they look so charming,
  Down by the purling of sweet, silent brooks,
All decked with posies, that spontaneous grow there
  Planted in order in the rocky nooks.
'Tis there the daisy, and the sweet carnation,
  The blooming pink, and the rose so fair;
Likewise the lily, and the daffodilly—
  All flowers that scent the sweet, fragrant air.

'Tis Lady Jeffers owns this plantation,
  Like Alexander, or like Helen fair;
There's no commander in all the nation
  For regulation can with her compare.

Such walls surround her, that no nine-pounder
Could ever plunder her place of strength;
But Oliver Cromwell, he did her pommel,
And made a breach in her battlement.

There's gravel walks there for speculation
And conversation, in sweet solitude;
'Tis there the lover may hear the dove, or
The gentle plover, in the afternoon.
And if a lady should be so engaging
As to walk alone in those shady bowers,
'Tis there her courtier, he may transport her
Into some fort, or all under ground.

For 'tis there's a cave where no daylight enters,
But cats and badgers are forever bred;
Being mossed by nature which makes it sweeter
Than a coach-and-six, or a feather bed.
'Tis there the lake is, well-stored with perches,
And comely eels in the verdant mud;
Besides the leeches, and the groves of beeches,
All standing in order for to guard the flood.

There's statues gracing this noble place in,
All heathen gods and nymphs so fair:
Bold Neptune, Plutarch, and Nicodemus,
All standing naked in the open air.
So now to finish this brave narration,
Which my poor genii could not entwine;
But were I Homer or Nebuchadnezzar,
'Tis in every feature I would make it shine.

*Richard Alfred Millikin* [1767–1815]

## THE BELLS OF SHANDON

Sabbata pango;
Funera plango;
Solemnia clango.

INSCRIPTION ON AN OLD BELL

WITH deep affection and recollection
I often think of the Shandon bells,
Whose sounds so wild would, in the days of childhood,
Fling round my cradle their magic spells.

On this I ponder where'er I wander,
And thus grow fonder, Sweet Cork, of thee,—
With thy bells of Shandon,
That sound so grand on
The pleasant waters of the river Lee.

I've heard bells chiming full many a clime in,
Tolling sublime in cathedral shrine,
While at a glib rate brass tongues would vibrate;
But all their music spoke naught to thine.
For memory, dwelling on each proud swelling
Of thy belfry, knelling its bold notes free,
Made the bells of Shandon
Sound far more grand on
The pleasant waters of the river Lee.

I've heard bells tolling "Old Adrian's Mole" in,
Their thunder rolling from the Vatican,—
And cymbals glorious, swinging uproarious
In the gorgeous turrets of Notre Dame;
But thy sounds were sweeter than the dome of Peter
Flings o'er the Tiber, pealing solemnly.
O, the bells of Shandon
Sound far more grand on
The pleasant waters of the river Lee.

There's a bell in Moscow, while on tower and Kiosko
In St. Sophia the Turkman gets,
And loud in air, calls men to prayer,
From the tapering summit of tall minarets.
Such empty phantom I freely grant them;
But there's an anthem more dear to me,—
'Tis the bells of Shandon,
That sound so grand on
The pleasant waters of the river Lee.

*Francis Sylvester Mahony* [1804–1866]

## "DE GUSTIBUS—"

YOUR ghost will walk, you lover of trees,
(If our loves remain)
In an English lane,

By a cornfield-side a-flutter with poppies.
Hark, those two in the hazel coppice—
A boy and a girl, if the good fates please,
  Making love, say,—
  The happier they!
Draw yourself up from the light of the moon
And let them pass, as they will too soon,
  With the beanflowers' boon,
  And the blackbird's tune,
  And May, and June!

What I love best in all the world
Is a castle, precipice-encurled,
In a gash of the wind-grieved Apennine.
Or look for me, old fellow of mine,
(If I get my head from out the mouth
O' the grave, and loose my spirit's bands,
And come again to the land of lands)—
In a sea-side house to the farther South,
Where the baked cicala dies of drouth,
And one sharp tree—'tis a cypress—stands,
By the many hundred years red-rusted,
Rough iron-spiked, ripe fruit-o'ercrusted,
My sentinel to guard the sands
To the water's edge. For, what expands
Before the house, but the great opaque
Blue breadth of sea without a break?
While, in the house, forever crumbles
Some fragment of the frescoed walls,
From blisters where a scorpion sprawls.
A girl bare-footed brings, and tumbles
Down on the pavement, green-flesh melons,
And says there's news to-day—the king
Was shot at, touched in the liver-wing,
Goes with his Bourbon arm in a sling:
—She hopes they have not caught the felons
Italy, my Italy!
Queen Mary's saying serves for me—
  (When fortune's malice
  Lost her Calais)

Open my heart and you will see
Graved inside of it, "Italy."
Such lovers old are I and she:
So it always was, so shall ever be!

*Robert Browning* [1812-1889]

## ITALIAN RHAPSODY

Dear Italy! The sound of thy soft name
Soothes me with balm of Memory and Hope.
Mine, for the moment, height and sweep and slope
That once were mine. Supreme is still the aim
To flee the cold and gray
Of our December day,
And rest where thy clear spirit burns with unconsuming flame.

There are who deem remembered beauty best,
And thine, imagined, fairer is than sight
Of all the charms of other realms confessed,
Thou miracle of sea and land and light.
Was it lest, envying thee,
The world unhappy be,
Benignant Heaven gave to all the all-consoling Night?

Remembered beauty best? Who reason so?
Not lovers, yearning to the same dumb star
That doth disdain their passion—who, afar,
Seek touch and voice in velvet winds and low.
No, storied Italy,
Not thine that heresy,
Thou who thyself art fairer far than Fancy e'er can show.

To me thou art an ever-brooding spell;
An old enchantment, exorcised of wrong;
A beacon, where-against the wings of Song
Are bruisèd so, they cannot fly to tell;
A mistress, at whose feet
A myriad singers meet,
To find thy beauty the despair of measures full and sweet.

Of old, ere caste or custom froze the heart,
  What tales of thine did Chaucer re-indite,—
  Of Constance, and Griselda, and the plight
Of pure Cecilia,—all with joyous art!
    Oh, to have journeyed down
    To Canterbury town,
And known, from lips that touched thy robe, that triad of renown!

Fount of Romance whereat our Shakespeare drank!
  Through him the loves of all are linked to thee
  By Romeo's ardor, Juliet's constancy.
He sets the peasant in the royal rank;
    Shows under mask and paint
    Kinship of knave and saint,
And plays on stolid man with Prospero's wand and Ariel's prank.

Another English foster-child hadst thou
  When Milton from the breast of thy delight
Drew inspiration. With a vestal's vow
  He fed the flame caught from thy sacred light.
    And when upon him lay
    The long eclipse of day,
Thou wert the memory-hoarded treasure of his doomèd sight.

Name me a poet who has trod thy soil:
  He is thy lover, ever hastening back,
With thee forgetting weariness and toil,
  The nightly sorrow for the daily lack.
    How oft our lyric race
    Looked last upon thy face!
Oh, would that I were worthy thus to die in thine embrace!

Oh, to be kin to Keats as urn with urn
  Shares the same Roman earth!—to sleep, apart,
  Near to the bloom that once was Shelley's heart,
Where bees, like lingering lovers, re-return;
    Where the proud pyramid,
    To brighter glory bid,
Gives Cestius his longed-for fame, marking immortal Art.

Or, in loved Florence, to repose beside
  Our trinity of singers! Fame enough
  To neighbor lordly Landor, noble Clough,
And her, our later sibyl, sorrow-eyed.
    Oh, tell me—not their arts,
    But their Italian hearts
Won for their dust that narrow oval, than the world more
      wide!

So might I lie where Browning should have lain,
  My "Italy" for all the world to read,
Like his on the palazzo. For thy pain
  In losing from thy rosary that bead,
    England accords thee room
    Around his minster tomb—
A province conquered of thy soul, and not an Arab slain!

Then take these lines, and add to them the lay,
  All inarticulate, I to thee indite:
The sudden longing on the sunniest day,
  The happy sighing in the stormiest night,
    The tears of love that creep
    From eyes unwont to weep,
Full with remembrance, blind with joy, and with devotion
      deep.

Absence from thee is such as men endure
  Between the glad betrothal and the bride;
Or like the years that Youth, intense and sure,
  From his ambition to his goal must bide.
    And if no more I may
    Mount to Fiesole . . .
Oh, then were Memory meant for those to whom is Hope
      denied.

Show me a lover who hath drunk by night
  Thy beauty-potion, as the grape the dew:
  'Twere little wonder he were poet too,
With wine of song in unexpected might,
    While moonlit cloister calls
    With plashy fountain-falls,
Or darkened Arno moves to music with its mirrored light.

Who can withstand thee? What distress or care
  But yields to Naples, or that long day-dream
We know as Venice, where alone more fair
  Noon is than night; where every lapping stream
    Wooes with a soft caress
    Our new-world weariness,
And every ripple smiles with joy at sight of scene so rare.

The mystery of thy charm—ah, who hath guessed?
  'Twas ne'er divined by day or shown in sleep;
  Yet sometimes Music, floating from her steep,
Holds to our lips a chalice brimmed and blest:
    Then know we that thou art
    Of the Ideal part—
Of Man's one thirst that is not quenched, drink he howe'er so deep.

Thou human-hearted land, whose revels hold
  Man in communion with the antique days,
  And summon him from prosy greed to ways
Where Youth is beckoning to the Age of Gold;
    How thou dost hold him near
    And whisper in his ear
Of the lost Paradise that lies beyond the alluring haze!

In tears I tossed my coin from Trevi's edge,—
  A coin unsordid as a bond of love,—
  And, with the instinct of the homing dove,
I gave to Rome my rendezvous and pledge.
    And when imperious Death
    Has quenched my flame of breath,
Oh, let me join the faithful shades that throng that fount above.

*Robert Underwood Johnson* [1853-1937]

## ABOVE SALERNO

SILVERY the olives on Ravello's steeps,
  Terraced the verdure of her nurtured hills;
Far, far below the blue Salerno sweeps,
  And on the shore her emerald largesse spills.

Lost in the haze of melting hills and skies
Sad Pæstum's plain in shadowy distance lies.

How the Spring flings her tribute to the breeze
  Through every slit in these long, winding walls!
Shunning the screen of flowery tapestries,
  The slim gray lizard, turquoise-vested, crawls—
Blind worshipper of the unconscious sun,
His pagan shrine, his splendid eidolon.

Here Scala lifts upon her furrowed breast
  Twin cities of the living and the dead,
Where toil the quick and where the buried rest,
  With Roman tombs low vaulted overhead:
In these strange dwellings life must surely seem
To hold the secret of its final dream.

The nectarine, peach and almond trees in flower,
  Play on the hues from deep to palest rose.
Shy druid birches guard a secret bower
  Where many a home-like English blossom blows;
With daisy, primrose, and narcissus shine
The lavish stars of Wordsworth's celandine.

On rocky, wave-girt slopes, where buds the vine,
  Golden and green the trellised orchards grow.
Beyond the beach's pale, receding line
  Roam dusky herds of sullen buffalo.
The distant Apennines' dark ranges wear
Halos of snow and amethystine air.

Can this be Italy, or but a dream
  Emerging from the broken waves of sleep?
Since even the rudest works of peasants seem
  Some spell of ancient miracles to keep:
As when against old Barbarossa's power
The Romans threw the grim rock of this tower.

More exquisite than our imagining,
  In silent hours how often shall arise—
From the dim waters of that mystic spring
  Where the soul keeps her anchored memories—

This world of beauty, color, and perfume;
Hoary with age, yet of unaging bloom.

*Ada Foster Murray* [1857–1936]

## VENICE

**From "Childe Harold's Pilgrimage"**

I STOOD in Venice on the Bridge of Sighs,
A palace and a prison on each hand:
I saw from out the wave her structures rise
As from the stroke of the enchanter's wand;
A thousand years their cloudy wings expand
Around me, and a dying Glory smiles
O'er the far times, when many a subject land
Looked to the wingèd Lion's marble piles,
Where Venice sate in state, throned on her hundred isles!

She looks a sea Cybele, fresh from ocean,
Rising with her tiara of proud towers
At airy distance, with majestic motion,
And such she was; her daughters had their dowers
From spoils of nations, and the exhaustless East
Poured in her lap all gems in sparkling showers:
In purple was she robed, and of her feast
Monarchs partook, and deemed their dignity increased.

In Venice Tasso's echoes are no more,
And silent rows the songless gondolier;
Her palaces are crumbling to the shore,
And music meets not always now the ear:
Those days are gone, but Beauty still is here;
States fall, arts fade, but Nature doth not die,
Nor yet forget how Venice once was dear,
The pleasant place of all festivity,
The revel of the earth, the masque of Italy!

But unto us she hath a spell beyond
Her name is story, and her long array
Of mighty shadows, whose dim forms despond
Above the Dogeless city's vanished sway:

Ours is a trophy which will not decay
With the Rialto; Shylock and the Moor,
And Pierre, cannot be swept or worn away,—
The keystones of the arch!—though all were o'er,
For us repeopled were the solitary shore.

*George Gordon Byron* [1788–1824]

## VENICE

VENICE, thou Siren of sea-cities, wrought
By mirage, built on water, stair o'er stair,
Of sunbeams and cloud-shadows, phantom-fair,
With naught of earth to mar thy sea-born thought!
Thou floating film upon the wonder-fraught
Ocean of dreams! Thou hast no dream so rare
As are thy sons and daughters, they who wear
Foam-flakes of charm from thine enchantment caught!
O dark brown eyes! O tangles of dark hair!
O heaven-blue eyes, blonde tresses where the breeze
Plays over sun-burned cheeks in sea-blown air!
Firm limbs of moulded bronze! frank debonair
Smiles of deep-bosomed women! Loves that seize
Man's soul, and waft her on storm-melodies!

*John Addington Symonds* [1840–1893]

## ON THE EXTINCTION OF THE VENETIAN REPUBLIC

ONCE did She hold the gorgeous East in fee,
And was the safeguard of the West; the worth
Of Venice did not fall below her birth,
Venice, the eldest child of liberty.
She was a maiden city, bright and free;
No guile seduced, no force could violate;
And, when she took unto herself a mate,
She must espouse the everlasting Sea.
And what if she had seen those glories fade,
Those titles vanish, and that strength decay;

Yet shall some tribute of regret be paid
When her long life hath reached its final day:
Men are we, and must grieve when even the shade
Of that which once was great, is passed away.

*William Wordsworth* [1770–1850]

## THE GUARDIAN-ANGEL

### A PICTURE AT FANO

DEAR and great Angel, wouldst thou only leave
That child, when thou hast done with him, for me!
Let me sit all the day here, that when eve
Shall find performed thy special ministry,
And time come for departure, thou, suspending
Thy flight, may'st see another child for tending,
Another still, to quiet and retrieve.

Then I shall feel thee step one step, no more,
From where thou standest now, to where I gaze,
—And suddenly my head is covered o'er
With those wings, white above the child who prays
Now on that tomb—and I shall feel thee guarding
Me, out of all the world; for me, discarding
Yon heaven thy home, that waits and opes its door.

I would not look up thither past thy head
Because the door opes, like that child, I know,
For I should have thy gracious face instead,
Thou bird of God! And wilt thou bend me low
Like him, and lay, like his, my hands together,
And lift them up to pray, and gently tether
Me, as thy lamb there, with thy garment's spread?

If this was ever granted, I would rest
My head beneath thine, while thy healing hands
Close-covered both my eyes beside thy breast,
Pressing the brain, which too much thought expands,
Back to its proper size again, and smoothing
Distortion down till every nerve had soothing,
And all lay quiet, happy and suppressed.

How soon all worldly wrong would be repaired!
  I think how I should view the earth and skies
And sea, when once again my brow was bared
  After thy healing, with such different eyes.
O world, as God has made it! All is beauty:
And knowing this, is love, and love is duty.
  What further may be sought for or declared?

Guercino drew this angel I saw teach
  (Alfred, dear friend!)—that little child to pray,
Holding the little hands up, each to each
  Pressed gently,—with his own head turned away
Over the earth where so much lay before him
Of work to do, though heaven was opening o'er him,
  And he was left at Fano by the beach.

We were at Fano, and three times we went
  To sit and see him in his chapel there,
And drink his beauty to our souls' content
  —My angel with me too: and since I care
For dear Guercino's fame (to which in power
And glory comes this picture for a dower,
  Fraught with a pathos so magnificent)—

And since he did not work thus earnestly
  At all times, and has else endured some wrong—
I took one thought his picture struck from me,
  And spread it out, translating it to song.
My love is here. Where are you, dear old friend?
How rolls the Wairoa at your world's far end?
  This is Ancona, yonder is the sea.

*Robert Browning* [1812–1889]

## PERUGIA

For the sake of a weathered gray city set high on a hill
To the northward I go,
Where Umbria's valley lies mile upon emerald mile
Outspread like a chart.
The wind in her steep narrow streets is eternally chill
From the neighboring snow,

But linger who will in the lure of a southerly smile,
Here is my heart.

Wrought to a mutual blueness are mountains and sky;
Intermingling they meet.
Little gray breathings of olive arise from the plain
Like sighs that are seen,
For man and his maker harmonious toil, and the sigh
Of such labor is sweet,
And the fruits of their patience are vistas of vineyards and
grain
In a glory of green.

No wind from the valley that passes the casement but flings
Invisible flowers.
The carol of birds is a gossamer tissue of gold
On a background of bells.
Sweetest of all in the silence the nightingale sings
Through the silver-pure hours,
Till the stars disappear like a dream that may never be told,
That the dawning dispels.

Never so darkling an alley but opens at last
On unlimited space,
Each gate is the frame of a vision that stretches away
To the rims of the sky.
Never a scar that was left by the pitiless past
But has taken a grace
Like the mark of a smile that was turned upon children at
play
In a summer gone by.

Many the tyrants, my city, that held thee in thrall.
What remains of them now?
Names whispered back from the dark through a portal ajar—
They come not again.
By men thou wert made and wert marred, but outlasting
them all
Is the soul that is thou—
A soul that shall speak to my soul till I too pass afar,
And perchance, even then.

*Amelia Josephine Burr* [1878-

## "THERE IS A POOL ON GARDA"

THERE is a pool on Garda,
'Tis fashioned by the moon
That climbs above the mountain's crest
What time the night birds croon;
The pool is paved with silver
Inwrought with burnished gold,
And in its deeps a treasure sleeps
The goblins stored of old.

There is a pool on Garda,
It will elude you still
Ply you the oar from shore to shore
With howe'er strong a will;
'Twill flee you like a phantom,
'Twill lead you on and on;
A luring light, 'twill fade from sight
What time the moon is gone.

There is a pool on Garda,
You'll see it in your dreams;
'Tis shaped of silvery glamor,
'Tis fused of golden beams.
Once you have caught the vision,
The fair elusive ray,
Twill haunt your brain like some sweet strain
Forever and a day!

*Clinton Scollard* [1860–1932]

## CHORUS

From "Hellas"

THE world's great age begins anew,
The golden years return,
The earth doth like a snake renew
Her winter weeds outworn:

Heaven smiles, and faiths and empires gleam
Like wrecks of a dissolving dream.

A brighter Hellas rears its mountains
From waves serener far;
A new Peneus rolls his fountains
Against the morning-star;
Where fairer Tempes bloom, there sleep
Young Cyclads on a sunnier deep.

A loftier Argo cleaves the main,
Fraught with a later prize;
Another Orpheus sings again,
And loves, and weeps, and dies;
A new Ulysses leaves once more
Calypso for his native shore.

O write no more the tale of Troy,
If earth Death's scroll must be!
Nor mix with Laian rage the joy
Which dawns upon the free,
Although a subtler Sphinx renew
Riddles of death Thebes never knew.

Another Athens shall arise,
And to remoter time
Bequeath, like sunset to the skies,
The splendor of its prime;
And leave, if naught so bright may live,
All earth can take or Heaven can give.

Saturn and Love their long repose
Shall burst, more bright and good
Than all who fell, than One who rose,
Than many unsubdued:
Not gold, not blood, their altar dowers,
But votive tears and symbol flowers.

O cease! must hate and death return?
Cease! must men kill and die?
Cease! drain not to its dregs the urn
Of bitter prophecy!

The world is weary of the past—
O might it die or rest at last!

*Percy Bysshe Shelley* [1792–1822]

## THE ISLES OF GREECE

**From "Don Juan"**

The isles of Greece! the isles of Greece!
  Where burning Sappho loved and sung,
Where grew the arts of war and peace,
  Where Delos rose, and Phœbus sprung!
Eternal summer gilds them yet,
But all, except their sun, is set,

The Scian and the Teian muse,
  The hero's harp, the lover's lute,
Have found the fame your shores refuse:
  Their place of birth alone is mute
To sounds which echo further west
Than your sires' "Islands of the Blest."

The mountains look on Marathon—
  And Marathon looks on the sea;
And musing there an hour alone,
  I dreamed that Greece might still be free;
For standing on the Persians' grave,
I could not deem myself a slave.

A king sate on the rocky brow
  Which looks o'er sea-born Salamis;
And ships, by thousands, lay below,
  And men in nations;—all were his!
He counted them at break of day—
And when the sun set, where were they?

And where are they? and where art thou
  My country? On thy voiceless shore
The heroic lay is tuneless now—
  The heroic bosom beats no more!
And must thy lyre, so long divine,
Degenerate into hands like mine?

'Tis something, in the dearth of fame,
 Though linked among a fettered race,
To feel at least a patriot's shame,
 Even as I sing, suffuse my face;
For what is left the poet here?
For Greeks a blush—for Greece a tear.

Must *we* but weep o'er days more blest?
 Must *we* but blush?—Our fathers bled.
Earth! render back from out thy breast
 A remnant of our Spartan dead!
Of the three hundred grant but three.
To make a new Thermopylæ!

What, silent still? and silent all?
 Ah! no;—the voices of the dead
Sound like a distant torrent's fall,
 And answer, "Let one living head,
But one, arise,—we come, we come!"
'Tis but the living who are dumb.

In vain—in vain: strike other chords;
 Fill high the cup with Samian wine!
Leave battles to the Turkish hordes,
 And shed the blood of Scio's vine!
Hark! rising to the ignoble call—
How answers each bold Bacchanal!

You have the Pyrrhic dance as yet;
 Where is the Pyrrhic phalanx gone?
Of two such lessons, why forget
 The nobler and the manlier one?
You have the letters Cadmus gave—
Think ye he meant them for a slave?

Fill high the bowl with Samian wine!
 We will not think of themes like these
It made Anacreon's song divine:
 He served—but served Polycrates—
A tyrant; but our masters then
Were still, at least, our countrymen.

The tyrant of the Chersonese
  Was freedom's best and bravest friend;
*That* tyrant was Miltiades!
  O that the present hour would lend
Another despot of the kind!
Such chains as his were sure to bind.

Fill high the bowl with Samian wine!
  On Suli's rock, and Parga's shore,
Exists the remnant of a line
  Such as the Doric mothers bore;
And there, perhaps, some seed is sown,
The Heracleidan blood might own.

Trust not for freedom to the Franks—
  They have a king who buys and sells;
In native swords and native ranks
  The only hope of courage dwells:
But Turkish force and Latin fraud
Would break your shield, however broad.

Fill high the bowl with Samian wine!
  Our virgins dance beneath the shade—
I see their glorious black eyes shine;
  But, gazing on each glowing maid,
My own the burning tear-drop laves,
To think such breasts must suckle slaves.

Place me on Sunium's marbled steep,
  Where nothing, save the waves and I,
May hear our mutual murmurs sweep;
  There, swan-like, let me sing and die:
A land of slaves shall ne'er be mine—
Dash down yon cup of Samian wine!

*George Gordon Byron* [1788–1824]

## THE BELFRY OF BRUGES

### CARILLON

In the ancient town of Bruges,
In the quaint old Flemish city,
As the evening shades descended,
Low and loud and sweetly blended,

Low at times and loud at times,
And changing like a poet's rhymes,
Rang the beautiful wild chimes
From the Belfry in the market
Of the ancient town of Bruges.

Then, with deep sonorous clangor
Calmly answering their sweet anger,
When the wrangling bells had ended,
Slowly struck the clock eleven,
And, from out the silent heaven,
Silence on the town descended.
Silence, silence everywhere,
On the earth and in the air,
Save that footsteps here and there
Of some burgher home returning,
By the street lamps faintly burning,
For a moment woke the echoes
Of the ancient town of Bruges.

But amid my broken slumbers
Still I heard those magic numbers,
As they loud proclaimed the flight
And stolen marches of the night;
Till their chimes in sweet collision
Mingled with each wandering vision,
Mingled with the fortune-telling
Gypsy-bands of dreams and fancies,
Which amid the waste expanses
Of the silent land of trances
Have their solitary dwelling;
All else seemed asleep in Bruges,
In the quaint old Flemish city.

And I thought how like these chimes
Are the poet's airy rhymes,
All his rhymes and roundelays,
His conceits, and songs, and ditties,
From the belfry of his brain,
Scattered downward, though in vain,

On the roofs and stones of cities!
For by night the drowsy ear
Under its curtains cannot hear,
And by day men go their ways,
Hearing the music as they pass,
But deeming it no more, alas!
Than the hollow sound of brass.

Yet perchance a sleepless wight,
Lodging at some humble inn
In the narrow lanes of life,
When the dusk and hush of night
Shut out the incessant din
Of daylight and its toil and strife,
May listen with a calm delight
To the poet's melodies,
Till he hears, or dreams he hears,
Intermingled with the song,
Thoughts that he has cherished long;
Hears amid the chime and singing
The bells of his own village ringing,
And wakes, and finds his slumberous eyes
Wet with most delicious tears.

Thus dreamed I, as by night I lay
In Bruges, at the Fleur-de-Blé,
Listening with a wild delight
To the chimes that, through the night,
Rang their changes from the Belfry
Of that quaint old Flemish city.

## THE BELFRY OF BRUGES

In the market-place of Bruges stands the belfry old and brown;
Thrice consumed and thrice rebuilded, still it watches o'er the town.

As the summer morn was breaking, on that lofty tower I stood,
And the world threw off its darkness, like the weeds of widowhood.

Thick with towns and hamlets studded, and with streams
and vapors gray,
Like a shield embossed with silver, round and vast the landscape lay.

At my feet the city slumbered. From its chimneys, here
and there,
Wreaths of snow-white smoke, ascending, vanished, ghost-
like, into air.

Not a sound rose from the city at that early morning hour,
But I heard a heart of iron beating in the ancient tower.

From their nests beneath the rafters sang the swallows wild
and high
And the world, beneath me sleeping, seemed more distant
than the sky.

Then most musical and solemn, bringing back the olden
times,
With their strange, unearthly changes, rang the melancholy
chimes.

Like the psalms from some old cloister, when the nuns sing
in the choir;
And the great bell tolled among them, like the chanting of a
friar.

Visions of the days departed, shadowy phantoms filled my
brain;
They who live in history only seemed to walk the earth
again;

All the Foresters of Flanders,—mighty Baldwin Bras de Fer,
Lyderick du Bucq and Cressy, Philip, Guy de Dampierre.

I beheld the pageants splendid that adorned those days of
old;
Stately dames, like queens attended, knights who bore the
Fleece of Gold:

Lombard and Venetian merchants with deep-laden argosies;
Ministers from twenty nations; more than royal pomp and
ease.

I beheld proud Maximilian, kneeling humbly on the ground;
I beheld the gentle Mary, hunting with her hawk and hound;

And her lighted bridal-chamber, where a duke slept with the
queen,
And the armèd guard around them, and the sword unsheathed between.

I beheld the Flemish weavers, with Namur and Juliers bold,
Marching homeward from the bloody battle of the Spurs
of Gold;

Saw the fight at Minnewater, saw the White Hoods moving
west,
Saw great Artevelde victorious scale the Golden Dragon's
nest.

And again the whiskered Spaniard all the land with terror
smote;
And again the wild alarum sounded from the tocsin's throat;

Till the bell of Ghent responded o'er lagoon and dike of sand,
"I am Roland! I am Roland! there is victory in the land!"

Then the sound of drums aroused me. The awakened city's
roar
Chased the phantoms I had summoned back into their graves
once more.

Hours had passed away like minutes; and, before I was
aware,
Lo! the shadow of the belfry crossed the sun-illumined
square.

*Henry Wadsworth Longfellow* [1807-1882]

## NUREMBERG

In the valley of the Pegnitz, where across broad meadow-lands
Rise the blue Franconian mountains, Nuremberg, the ancient, stands.

Quaint old town of toil and traffic, quaint old town of art and song,
Memories haunt thy pointed gables, like the rooks that round them throng:

Memories of the Middle Ages, when the emperors, rough and bold,
Had their dwelling in thy castle, time-defying, centuries old;

And thy brave and thrifty burghers boasted, in their uncouth rhyme,
That their great imperial city stretched its hand through every clime.

In the court-yard of the castle, bound with many an iron band,
Stands the mighty linden planted by Queen Cunigunde's hand;

On the square, the oriel window, where in old heroic days
Sat the poet Melchior singing Kaiser Maximilian's praise.

Everywhere I see around me rise the wondrous world of Art:
Fountains wrought with richest sculpture standing in the common mart;

And above cathedral doorways saints and bishops carved in stone,
By a former age commissioned as apostles to our own.

In the church of sainted Sebald sleeps enshrined his holy dust,
And in bronze the Twelve Apostles guard from age to age their trust;

In the church of sainted Lawrence stands a pix of sculpture rare,
Like the foamy sheaf of fountains, rising through the painted air.

Here, when Art was still religion, with a simple, reverent heart,
Lived and labored Albrecht Dürer, the Evangelist of Art;

Hence in silence and in sorrow, toiling still with busy hand,
Like an emigrant he wandered, seeking for the Better Land.

*Emigravit* is the inscription on the tombstone where he lies;
Dead he is not, but departed,--for the artist never dies.

Fairer seems the ancient city, and the sunshine seems more fair
That he once has trod its pavement, that he once has breathed its air!

Through these streets so broad and stately, these obscure and dismal lanes,
Walked of yore the Mastersingers, chanting rude poetic strains.

From remote and sunless suburbs came they to the friendly guild,
Building nests in Fame's great temple, as in spouts the swallows build.

As the weaver plied the shuttle, wove he too the mystic rhyme,
And the smith his iron measures hammered to the anvil's chime;

Thanking God, whose boundless wisdom makes the flowers of poesy bloom
In the forge's dust and cinders, in the tissues of the loom.

Here Hans Sachs, the cobbler-poet, laureate of the gentle craft,
Wisest of the Twelve Wise Masters, in huge folios sang and laughed.

But his house is now an alehouse, with a nicely sanded floor,
And a garland in the window, and his face above the door,

Painted by some humble artist, as in Adam Puschman's song,
As the old man gray and dovelike, with his great beard white and long.

And at night the swart mechanic comes to drown his cark and care,
Quaffing ale from pewter tankards, in the master's antique chair.

Vanished is the ancient splendor, and before my dreamy eye
Wave these mingled shapes and figures, like a faded tapestry.

Not thy Councils, not thy Kaisers, win for thee the world's regard,
But thy painter, Albrecht Dürer, and Hans Sachs, thy cobbler-bard.

Thus, O Nuremberg, a wanderer from a region far away,
As he paced thy streets and court-yards, sang in thought his careless lay:

Gathering from the pavement's crevice, as a floweret of the soil,
The nobility of labor,—the long pedigree of toil.

*Henry Wadsworth Longfellow* [1807-1882]

## BINGEN ON THE RHINE

A SOLDIER of the Legion lay dying in Algiers,
There was lack of woman's nursing, there was dearth of woman's tears;
But a comrade stood beside him, while his life-blood ebbed away,
And bent, with pitying glances, to hear what he might say.
The dying soldier faltered, as he took that comrade's hand,
And he said, "I nevermore shall see my own, my native land;

Take a message, and a token, to some distant friends of mine,
For I was born at Bingen,—at Bingen on the Rhine.

"Tell my brothers and companions, when they meet and crowd around,
To hear my mournful story, in the pleasant vineyard ground,
That we fought the battle bravely, and when the day was done,
Full many a corse lay ghastly pale beneath the setting sun:
And, 'mid the dead and dying, were some grown old in wars,—
The death-wound on their gallant breasts, the last of many scars;
And some were young, and suddenly beheld life's morn decline,—
And one had come from Bingen,—fair Bingen on the Rhine.

"Tell my mother that her other sons shall comfort her old age;
For I was aye a truant bird, that thought his home a cage;
For my father was a soldier, and even as a child
My heart leaped forth to hear him tell of struggles fierce and wild;
And when he died, and left us to divide his scanty hoard,
I let them take whate'er they would,—but kept my father's sword;
And with boyish love I hung it where the bright light used to shine,
On the cottage wall at Bingen,—calm Bingen on the Rhine.

"Tell my sister not to weep for me, and sob with drooping head,
When the troops come marching home again with glad and gallant tread,
But to look upon them proudly, with a calm and steadfast eye,
For her brother was a soldier too, and not afraid to die;
And if a comrade seek her love, I ask her in my name
To listen to him kindly, without regret or shame,

And to hang the old sword in its place (my father's sword
and mine),
For the honor of old Bingen—dear Bingen on the Rhine.

"There's another,—not a sister; in the happy days gone by
You'd have known her by the merriment that sparkled in
her eye;
Too innocent for coquetry,—too fond for idle scorning,—
O friend! I fear the lightest heart makes sometimes heaviest
mourning!
Tell her the last night of my life (for, ere the moon be risen,
My body will be out of pain, my soul be out of prison),—
I dreamed I stood with *her*, and saw the yellow sunlight shine
On the vine-clad hills of Bingen,—fair Bingen on the Rhine.

"I saw the blue Rhine sweep along,—I heard, or seemed to
hear,
The German songs we used to sing, in chorus sweet and clear;
And down the pleasant river, and up the slanting hill,
The echoing chorus sounded, through the evening calm and
still;
And her glad blue eyes were on me, as we passed, with
friendly talk,
Down many a path beloved of yore, and well-remembered
walk,
And her little hand lay lightly, confidingly in mine,—
But we'll meet no more at Bingen,—loved Bingen on the
Rhine."

His trembling voice grew faint and hoarse,—his grasp was
childish weak,—
His eyes put on a dying look,—he sighed and ceased to speak;
His comrade bent to lift him, but the spark of life had fled,—
The soldier of the Legion in a foreign land was dead!
And the soft moon rose up slowly, and calmly she looked
down
On the red sand of the battle-field, with bloody corses strown;
Yes, calmly on that dreadful scene her pale light seemed to
shine,
As it shone on distant Bingen,—fair Bingen on the Rhine.

*Caroline Elizabeth Sarah Norton* [1808–1877]

## "AS I CAME DOWN FROM LEBANON"

As I came down from Lebanon,
Came winding, wandering slowly down
Through mountain-passes bleak and brown,
The cloudless day was well-nigh done.
The city, like an opal, set
In emerald, showed each minaret
Afire with radiant beams of sun,
And glistened orange, fig, and lime,
Where song-birds made melodious chime,
As I came down from Lebanon.

As I came down from Lebanon,
Like lava in the dying glow,
Through olive orchards far below
I saw the murmuring river run;
And 'neath the wall upon the sand
Swart sheiks from distant Samarcand,
With precious spices they had won,
Lay long and languidly in wait
Till they might pass the guarded gate,
As I came down from Lebanon.

As I came down from Lebanon,
I saw strange men from lands afar,
In mosque and square and gay bazar,
The Magi that the Moslem shun,
And grave Effendi from Stamboul,
Who sherbet sipped in corners cool;
And, from the balconies o'errun
With roses, gleamed the eyes of those
Who dwell in still seraglios,
As I came down from Lebanon.

As I came down from Lebanon,
The flaming flower of daytime died,
And Night, arrayed as is a bride
Of some great king, in garments spun

Of purple and the finest gold,
Outbloomed in glories manifold!
Until the moon, above the dun
And darkening desert, void of shade,
Shone like a keen Damascus blade,
As I came down from Lebanon.

*Clinton Scollard* [1860–1932]

## CEYLON

I HEAR a whisper in the heated air—
"Rest! Rest! give over care!"
Long level breakers on the golden beach
Murmur in silver speech—
"Sleep in the palm-tree shadows on the shore—
Work, work no more!
Rest here and work no more."

Where half unburied cities of dead kings
Breed poisonous creeping things
I learn the poor mortality of man—
Seek vainly for some plan—
Know that great empires pass as I must pass
Like withered blades of grass—
Dead blades of Patna grass.

"Breathe—breathe the odorous sweetness that is ours,"
Cry Frangipani flowers.
"Forget! Forget! and know no more distress,
But languorous idleness:
Dream where dead leaves fall ever from green trees
To float on sapphire seas—
Dream! and be one with these."

*A. Hugh Fisher* [1867–1945]

## MANDALAY

BY the old Moulmein Pagoda, lookin' eastward to the sea,
There's a Burma girl a-settin', an' I know she thinks o' me;
For the wind is in the palm trees, an' the temple bells they
say:
"Come you back, you British soldier; come you back to
Mandalay!"

Come you back to Mandalay,
Where the old Flotilla lay:
Can't you 'ear their paddles chunkin' from Rangoon to Mandalay?
On the road to Mandalay,
Where the flyin'-fishes play,
An' the dawn comes up like thunder outer China 'crost the Bay!

'Er petticut was yaller an' 'er little cap was green,
An' 'er name was Supi-yaw-lat—jes' the same as Theebaw's Queen,
An' I seed her fust a-smokin' of a whackin' white cheroot,
An' a-wastin' Christian kisses on an 'eathen idol's foot:
Bloomin' idol made o' mud—
Wot they called the Great Gawd Budd—
Plucky lot she cared for idols when I kissed 'er where she stud!
On the road to Mandalay—

When the mist was on the rice-fields an' the sun was droppin' slow,
She'd git 'er little banjo an' she'd sing "*Kulla-lo-lo!*"
With 'er arm upon my shoulder, an' 'er cheek agin my cheek,
We useter watch the steamers an' the *hathis* pilin' teak.
Elephints a-pilin' teak
In the sludgy, squdgy creek,
Where the silence 'ung that 'eavy you was 'arf afraid to speak!
On the road to Mandalay—

But that's all shove be'ind me—long ago an' fur away,
An' there ain't no 'buses runnin' from the Benk to Mandalay;
An' I'm learnin' 'ere in London what the ten-year sodger tells:
"If you've 'eard the East a-callin', why, you won't 'eed nothin' else."
No! you won't 'eed nothin' else
But them spicy garlic smells
An' the sunshine an' the palm trees an' the tinkly temple bells!
On the road to Mandalay—

I am sick o' wastin' leather on these gritty pavin'-stones,
An' the blasted Henglish drizzle wakes the fever in my bones;
Though I walks with fifty 'ousemaids outer Chelsea to the Strand,
An' they talks a lot o' lovin', but wot do they understand?
Beefy face an' grubby 'and—
Law! wot *do* they understand?
I've a neater, sweeter maiden in a cleaner, greener land!
On the road to Mandalay—

Ship me somewheres east of Suez where the best is like the worst,
Where there aren't no Ten Commandments, an' a man can raise a thirst;
For the temple bells are callin', an' it's there that I would be—
By the old Moulmein Pagoda, lookin' lazy at the sea—
On the road to Mandalay,
Where the old Flotilla lay,
With our sick beneath the awnings when we went to Mandalay!
Oh, the road to Mandalay,
Where the flyin'-fishes play,
An' the dawn comes up like thunder outer China crost the Bay!

*Rudyard Kipling* [1865–1936]

## NUBIA

A LAND of Dreams and Sleep,—a poppied land!
With skies of endless calm above her head,
The drowsy warmth of summer noonday shed
Upon her hills, and silence stern and grand
Throughout her Desert's temple-burying sand.
Before her threshold, in their ancient place,
With closéd lips, and fixed, majestic face,
Noteless of Time, her dumb colossi stand.
Oh, pass them not with light, irreverent tread;
Respect the dream that builds her fallen throne,
And soothes her to oblivion of her woes.
Hush! for she does but sleep; she is not dead:
Action and Toil have made the world their own,
But she hath built an altar to Repose.

*Bayard Taylor* [1825–1878]

# BALLADS OLD AND NEW

## THOMAS THE RHYMER

TRUE Thomas lay on Huntlie bank;
  A ferlie he spied wi' his e'e;
And there he saw a lady bright,
  Come riding down by the Eildon Tree.

Her skirt was o' the grass-green silk,
  Her mantle o' the velvet fine;
At ilka tett o' her horse's mane
  Hung fifty siller bells and nine.

True Thomas he pu'd aff his cap,
  And louted low down on his knee:
"Hail to thee, Mary, Queen of Heaven!
  For thy peer on earth could never be."

"O no, O no, Thomas!" she said,
  "That name does not belang to me;
I'm but the Queen o' fair Elfland,
  That am hither come to visit thee.

"Harp and carp, Thomas!" she said,
  "Harp and carp along wi' me;
And if ye dare to kiss my lips,
  Sure of your body I will be."

"Betide me weal, betide me woe,
  That weird shall never daunten me."
Syne he has kissed her rosy lips,
  All underneath the Eildon Tree.

"Now, ye maun go wi' me," she said;
  "True Thomas, ye maun go wi' me;
And ye maun serve me seven years,
  Through weal or woe as may chance to be."

She's mounted on her milk-white steed;
She's ta'en true Thomas up behind;
And aye, whene'er her bridle rang,
The steed gaed swifter than the wind.

O they rade on, and farther on,
The steed gaed swifter than the wind;
Until they reached a desert wide,
And living land was left behind.

"Light down, light down now, true Thomas,
And lean your head upon my knee;
Abide ye there a little space,
And I will show you ferlies three.

"O see ye not yon narrow road,
So thick beset wi' thorns and briers?
That is the Path of Righteousness,
Though after it but few inquires.

"And see ye not yon braid, braid road,
That lies across the lily leven?
That is the Path of Wickedness,
Though some call it the Road to Heaven.

"And see yet not yon bonny road,
That winds about the fernie brae?
That is the Road to fair Elfland,
Where thou and I this night maun gae.

"But, Thomas, ye sall haud your tongue,
Whatever ye may hear or see;
For speak ye word in Elfyn-land,
Ye'll ne'er win back to your ain countrie."

O they rade on, and farther on,
And they waded rivers abune the knee;
And they saw neither sun nor moon,
But they heard the roaring of the sea.

It was mirk, mirk night, there was nae starlight,
  They waded through red blude to the knee;
For a' the blude that's shed on earth
  Rins through the springs o' that countrie.

Syne they came to a garden green,
  And she pu'd an apple frae a tree:
"Take this for thy wages, true Thomas;
  It will give thee tongue that can never lee."

"My tongue is mine ain," true Thomas he said;
  "A gudely gift ye wad gie to me!
I neither dought to buy nor sell,
  At fair or tryst where I might be.

"I dought neither speak to prince or peer,
  Nor ask of grace from fair lady!"
"Now haud thy peace!" the lady said,
  "For as I say, so must it be."

He has gotten a coat of the even cloth,
  And a pair o' shoon of the velvet green;
And till seven years were gane and past,
  True Thomas on earth was never seen.

*Unknown*

## EARL MAR'S DAUGHTER

It was intill a pleasant time,
  Upon a simmer's day,
The noble Earl Mar's daughter
  Went forth to sport and play.

And as she played and sported
  Below a green aik tree,
There she saw a sprightly doo
  Set on a branch sae hie.

"O Coo-my-doo, my love sae true,
  If ye'll come doun to me,
Ye'se hae a cage o' gude red gowd
  Instead o' simple tree.

"I'll tak' ye hame and pet ye weel,
Within my bower and ha';
I'll gar ye shine as fair a bird
As ony o' them a'!"

And she had nae these words weel spoke,
Nor yet these words weel said,
Till Coo-my-doo flew frae the branch,
And lighted on her head.

Then she has brought this pretty bird
Hame to her bower and ha',
And made him shine as fair a bird
As ony o' them a'.

When day was gane, and night was come,
About the evening-tide,
This lady spied a bonny youth
Stand straight up by her side.

"Now whence come ye, young man," she said,
"To put me into fear?
My door was bolted right secure,
And what way cam' ye here?"

"O haud your tongue, my lady fair,
Lat a' your folly be;
Mind ye not o' your turtle-doo
Ye wiled from aff the tree?"

"O wha are ye, young man?" she said,
"What country come ye frae?"
"I flew across the sea," he said,
"'Twas but this verra day.

"My mither is a queen," he says,
"Likewise of magic skill;
'Twas she that turned me in a doo,
To fly where'er I will.

"And it was but this verra day
That I cam' owre the sea:
I loved you at a single look;
With you I'll live and dee."

"O Coo-my-doo, my love sae true,
Nae mair frae me ye'se gae."
"That's never my intent, my love;
As ye said, it sall be sae."

There he has lived in bower wi' her,
For six lang years and ane;
Till sax young sons to him she bare,
And the seventh she's brought hame.

But aye, as soon's a child was barn,
He carried them away,
And brought them to his mither's care,
As fast as he could fly.

When he had stayed in bower wi' her
For seven lang years an' mair;
There cam' a lord o' hie renown
To court that lady fair.

But still his proffer she refused,
And a' his presents too;
Says, "I'm content to live alane
Wi' my bird Coo-my-doo!"

Her father sware a michty oath,
He sware it wi' ill-will:
"To-morrow, ere I eat or drink,
That bird I'll surely kill."

The bird was sitting in his cage,
And heard what he did say;
He jumped upon the window-sill:
"'Tis time I was away."

Then Coo-my-doo took flight and flew
  Beyond the raging sea,
And lichted at his mither's castle,
  Upon a tower sae hie.

The Queen his mither was walking out,
  To see what she could see,
And there she saw her darling son
  Set on the tower sae hie.

"Get dancers here to dance," she said,
  "And minstrels for to play;
For here's my dear son Florentine
  Come back wi' me to stay."

"Get nae dancers to dance, mither,
  Nor minstrels for to play;
For the mither o' my seven sons,
  The morn's her wedding day."

"Now tell me, dear son Florentine,
  O tell, and tell me true;
Tell me this day, without delay,
  What sall I do for you?"

"Instead of dancers to dance, mither,
  Or minstrels for to play,
Turn four-and-twenty well-wight men,
  Like storks, in feathers gray;

"My seven sons in seven swans,
  Aboon their heads to flee;
And I mysel' a gay gos-hawk,
  A bird o' high degree."

Then, sighing, said the Queen to hersel',
  "That thing's too high for me!"
But she applied to an auld woman,
  Wha had mair skill than she.

Instead o' dancers to dance a dance,
  Or minstrels for to play,
Were four-and-twenty well-wight men
  Turned birds o' feathers gray;

Her seven sons in seven swans,
  Aboon their heads to flee;
And he himsel' a gay gos-hawk,
  A bird o' high degree.

This flock o' birds took flight and flew
  Beyond the raging sea;
They landed near the Earl Mar's castle,
  And took shelter in every tree.

They were a flock o' pretty birds,
  Right wondrous to be seen;
The weddin'eers they looked at them
  Whilst walking on the green.

These birds flew out frae bush and tree,
  And lichted on the ha';
And, when the wedding-train cam' forth,
  Flew down amang them a'.

The storks they seized the boldest men,
  That they could not fight or flee;
The swans they bound the bridegroom fast
  Unto a green aik tree.

They flew around the bride-maidens,
  Around the bride's own head;
And, wi' the twinkling o' an ee,
  The bride and they were fled.

There's ancient men at weddings been
  For eighty years or more;
But siccan a curious wedding-day
  They never saw before.

For naething could the company do,
Nor naething could they say;
But they saw a flock o' pretty birds
That took their bride away.

*Unknown*

## THE TWA SISTERS

THERE was twa sisters in a bower,
*Binnorie, O Binnorie;*
There was twa sisters in a bower,
*Binnorie, O Binnorie;*
There was twa sisters in a bower,
There came a knight to be their wooer,
*By the bonny mill-dams o' Binnorie.*

He courted the eldest wi' glove and ring,
But he lo'ed the youngest abune a' thing;

He courted the eldest wi' brooch and knife,
But he lo'ed the youngest abune his life;

The eldest she is vexèd sair,
And much envied her sister fair.

Into her bower she couldna rest,
Wi' grief and spite she almost brast.

Upon a morning fair and clear,
She cried upon her sister dear:

"O sister, come to yon sea-strand,
And see our father's ships come to iand."

She's ta'en her by the lily hand,
And led her down to yon sea-strand;

The youngest stude upon a stane,
The eldest came and pushed her in;

She took her by the middle sma',
And dashed her bonny back to the jaw.

"O sister, sister, reach your hand,
And ye shall be heir of half my land."

"O sister, I'll not reach my hand,
And I'll be heir of a' your land;

"Shame fa' the hand that I should take,
It's twinèd me and my world's mate."

"O sister, reach me but your glove,
And sweet William shall be your love."

"Sink on, nor hope for hand or glove!
And sweet William shall be my love.

"Your cherry cheeks and your yellow hair,
Garred me gang maiden evermair."

Sometimes she sunk, and sometimes she swam,
Until she cam to the miller's dam.

O, out it cam the miller's son,
And saw the fair maid swimmin' in.

"O father, father, draw your dam!
Here's either a mermaid, or a milk-white swan."

The miller hasted and drew his dam,
And there he found a drowned woman;

You couldna see her yellow hair,
For gowd and pearls that were so rare;

You couldna see her middle sma',
Her gowden girdle was sae bra';

You couldna see her fingers white,
For gowden rings that were sae gryte.

A famous harper passing by,
The sweet pale face he chanced to spy;

And when he looked that lady on,
He sighed and made a heavy moan;

He made a harp of her breast-bane,
Whose sounds would melt a heart of stane;

The strings he framed of her yellow hair,
Whose notes made sad the listening ear;

He brought it to her father's ha',
And there was the court assembled a';

He laid his harp upon a stane,
And straight it began to play alane:

"O yonder sits my father, the king,
And yonder sits my mother, the queen;

"And yonder stands my brother Hugh,
And by him my William, sweet and true."

But the last tune that the harp played then,
*Binnorie, O Binnorie;*
Was—"Wae to my sister, false Helen!"
*By the bonny mill-dams o' Binnorie.*

*Unknown*

## THE WIFE OF USHER'S WELL

THERE lived a wife at Usher's Well,
And a wealthy wife was she;
She had three stout and stalwart sons,
And sent them o'er the sea.

They hadna been a week from her
A week but barely ane,
Whan word came to the carline wife,
That her three sons were gane.

They hadna been a week from her,
A week but barely three,
Whan word came to the carline wife,
That her sons she'd never see.

"I wish the wind may never cease,
Nor fashes in the flood,
Till my three sons come hame to me,
In earthly flesh and blood!"

It fell about the Martinmas,
When nights are lang and mirk,
The carline wife's three sons came hame,
And their hats were o' the birk.

It neither grew in syke nor ditch,
Nor yet in ony sheugh;
But at the gates o' Paradise,
That birk grew fair eneugh.

"Blow up the fire, my maidens!
Bring water from the well!
For a' my house shall feast this night,
Since my three sons are well."

And she had made to them a bed,
She's made it large and wide;
And she's ta'en her mantle her about,
Sat down at the bed-side.

Up then crew the red, red cock,
And up and crew the gray;
The eldest to the youngest said,
"'Tis time we were awa'."

The cock he hadna crawed but once,
And clapped his wings at a',
Whan the youngest to the eldest said,
"Brother, we must awa'.

"The cock doth craw, the day doth daw',
The channerin' worm doth chide;
Gin we be missed out o' our place,
A sair pain we maun bide."

"Lie still, lie still, a little wee while,
  Lie still but if we may;
Gin my mother should miss us when she wakes,
  She'll go mad ere it be day."

O they've ta'en up their mother's mantle,
  And they've hinged it on the pin:
"O lang may ye hing, my mother's mantle,
  Ere ye hap us again!

"Fare-ye-weel, my mother dear!
  Fareweel to barn and byre!
And fare-ye-weel, the bonny lass
  That kindles my mother's fire."

*Unknown*

## A LYKE-WAKE DIRGE

This ae nighte, this ae nighte,
  *—Every nighte and alle,*
Fire and sleet and candle-lighte,
  *And Christe receive thy saule.*

When thou from hence away art passed,
  *—Every nighte and alle,*
To Whinny-muir thou com'st at last;
  *And Christe receive thy saule.*

If ever thou gavest hosen and shoon,
  *—Every nighte and alle,*
Sit thee down and put them on;
  *And Christe receive thy saule.*

If hosen and shoon thou ne'er gav'st nane,
  *—Every nighte and alle,*
The whinnes sall prick thee to the bare bane;
  *And Christe receive thy saule.*

From Whinny-muir when thou may'st pass,
  *—Every nighte and alle,*
To Brig o' Dread thou com'st at last;
  *And Christe receive thy saule.*

From Brig o' Dread when thou may'st pass,
*—Every nighte and alle,*
To Purgatory fire thou com'st at last;
*And Christe receive thy saule.*

If ever thou gavest meat or drink,
*—Every nighte and alle,*
The fire sall never make thee shrink;
*And Christe receive thy saule.*

If meat or drink thou ne'er gav'st nane,
*—Every nighte and alle,*
The fire will burn thee to the bare bane;
*And Christe receive thy saule.*

This ae nighte, this ae nighte,
*—Every nighte and alle,*
Fire and sleet and candle-lighte,
*And Christe receive thy saule.*

*Unknown*

## THE DOUGLAS TRAGEDY

"Rise up, rise up, now, Lord Douglas," she says,
"And put on your armor so bright;
Let it never be said that a daughter of thine
Was married to a lord under night.

"Rise up, rise up, my seven bold sons,
And put on your armor so bright,
And take better care of your youngest sister,
For your eldest's awa the last night."

He's mounted her on a milk-white steed,
And himself on a dapple gray,
With a bugelet-horn hung down by his side,
And lightly they rode away.

Lord William lookit o'er his left shoulder,
To see what he could see,
And there he spied her seven brethren bold,
Come riding o'er the lea.

"Light down, light down, Lady Marg'ret," he said,
"And hold my steed in your hand,
Until that against your seven brethren bold,
And your father, I mak' a stand."

She held his steed in her milk-white hand,
And never did shed one tear,
Until that she saw her seven brethren fa',
And her father hard fighting, who loved her so dear.

"O haud your hand, Lord William!" she said,
"For your strokes they are wondrous sair;
True lovers I can get many an ane,
But a father I can never get mair."

O she's ta'en out her handkerchief,
It was o' the Holland sae fine,
And aye she dighted her father's wounds,
That were redder than the wine.

"O chuse, O chuse, Lady Marg'ret," he said,
"O whether will ye gang or bide?"
"I'll gang, I'll gang, Lord William," she said,
"For ye've left me no other guide."

He's lifted her on a milk-white steed,
And himself on a dapple gray,
With a bugelet-horn hung down by his side,
And slowly they baith rade away.

O they rade on, and on they rade,
And a' by the light of the moon,
Until they cam' to yon wan water,
And there they lighted doun.

They lighted doun to tak' a drink
Of the spring that ran sae clear;
And doun the stream ran his gude heart's blood,
And sair she gan to fear.

"Haud up, haud up, Lord William," she says,
  "For I fear that you are slain!"
"'Tis naething but the shadow of my scarlet cloak,
  That shines in the water sae plain."

O they rade on, and on they rade,
  And a' by the light of the moon,
Until they cam' to his mother's ha' door,
  And there they lighted doun.

"Get up, get up, lady mother," he says,
  "Get up and let me in!—
Get up, get up, lady mother," he says,
  "For this night my fair lady I've win.

"O mak my bed, lady mother," he says,
  "O mak it braid and deep!
And lay Lady Marg'ret close at my back,
  And the sounder I will sleep."

Lord William was dead lang ere midnight,
  Lady Marg'ret lang ere day;
And all true lovers that go thegither,
  May they have mair luck than they!

Lord William was buried in St. Mary's kirk,
  Lady Marg'ret in Mary's quire;
Out o' the lady's grave grew a bonny red rose,
  And out o' the knight's a brier.

And they twa met, and they twa plat,
  And fain they wad be near;
And a' the warld might ken right weel
  They were twa lovers dear.

But by and rade the Black Douglas,
  And wow but he was rough!
For he pu'ed up the bonny brier,
  And flang't in St. Mary's Lough.

*Unknown*

## FAIR ANNIE

THE reivers they stole Fair Annie,
  As she walked by the sea;
But a noble knight was her ransom soon,
  Wi' gowd and white monie.

She bided in strangers' land wi' him,
  And none knew whence she cam;
She lived in the castle wi' her love,
  But never told her name.

"It's narrow, narrow, mak your bed,
  And learn to lie your lane;
For I'm gaun owre the sea, Fair Annie,
  A braw Bride to bring hame.
Wi' her I will get gowd and gear,
  Wi' you I ne'er gat nane.

"But wha will bake my bridal bread,
  Or brew my bridal ale?
And wha will welcome my bright Bride,
  That I bring owre the dale?"

"It's I will bake your bridal bread,
  And brew your bridal ale;
And I will welcome your bright Bride,
  That you bring owre the dale."

"But she that welcomes my bright Bride
  Maun gang like maiden fair;
She maun lace on her robe sae jimp,
  And comely braid her hair.

"Bind up, bind up your yellow hair,
  And tie it on your neck;
And see you look as maiden-like
  As the day that first we met."

"O how can I gang maiden-like,
  When maiden I am nane?
Have I not borne six sons to thee,
  And am wi' child again?"

"I'll put cooks into my kitchen,
  And stewards in my hall,
And I'll have bakers for my bread,
  And brewers for my ale;
But you're to welcome my bright Bride,
  That I bring owre the dale."

Three months and a day were gane and past,
  Fair Annie she gat word
That her love's ship was come at last,
  Wi' his bright young Bride aboard.

She's ta'en her young son in her arms,
  Anither in her hand;
And she's gane up to the highest tower,
  Looks owre sea and land.

"Come doun, come doun, my mother dear,
  Come aff the castle wa'!
I fear if langer ye stand there,
  Ye'll let yoursell doun fa'."

She's ta'en a cake o' the best bread,
  A stoup o' the best wine,
And a' the keys upon her arm,
  And to the yett is gane.

"O ye're welcome hame, my ain gude lord,
  To your castles and your towers;
Ye're welcome hame, my ain gude lord,
  To your ha's, but and your bowers.
And welcome to your hame, fair lady!
  For a' that's here is yours."

"O whatna lady's that, my lord,
  That welcomes you and me?
Gin I be lang about this place,
  Her friend I mean to be."

Fair Annie served the lang tables
  Wi' the white bread and the wine;
But ay she drank the wan water
  To keep her color fine.

And she gaed by the first table,
  And smiled upon them a';
But ere she reached the second table,
  The tears began to fa'.

She took a napkin lang and white,
  And hung it on a pin;
It was to wipe away the tears,
  As she gaed out and in.

When bells were rung and mass was sung,
  And a' men bound for bed,
The bridegroom and the bonny Bride
  In ae chamber were laid.

Fair Annie's ta'en a harp in her hand,
  To harp thir twa asleep;
But ay, as she harpit and she sang,
  Fu' sairly did she weep.

"O gin my sons were seven rats,
  Rinnin' on the castle wa'.
And I mysell a great gray cat,
  I soon wad worry them a'!

"O gin my sons were seven hares,
  Rinnin' owre yon lily lea,
And I mysell a good greyhound,
  Soon worried they a' should be!"

Then out and spak the bonny young Bride,
  In bride-bed where she lay:
"That's like my sister Annie," she says;
  "Wha is it doth sing and play?

"I'll put on my gown," said the new-come Bride,
  "And my shoes upon my feet;
I will see wha doth sae sadly sing,
  And what is it gars her greet.

"What ails you, what ails you, my housekeeper,
  That ye mak sic a mane?
Has ony wine-barrel cast its girds,
  Or is a' your white bread gane?"

"It isna because my wine is spilt,
  Or that my white bread's gane;
But because I've lost my true love's love,
  And he's wed to anither ane."

"Noo tell me wha was your father?" she says,
  "Noo tell me wha was your mither?
And had ye ony sister?" she says,
  "And had ye ever a brither?"

"The Earl of Wemyss was my father,
  The Countess of Wemyss my mither,
Young Elinor she was my sister dear,
  And Lord John he was my brither."

"If the Earl of Wemyss was your father,
  I wot sae was he mine;
And it's O my sister Annie!
  Your love ye sallna tyne.

"Tak your husband, my sister dear;
  You ne'er were wranged for me,
Beyond a kiss o' his merry mouth
  As we cam owre the sea.

"Seven ships, loaded weel,
  Cam owre the sea wi' me;
Ane o' them will tak me hame,
  And six I'll gie to thee."

*Unknown*

## THE LASS OF LOCHROYAN

"O WHA will shoe my bonny foot?
  And wha will glove my hand?
And wha will bind my middle jimp
  Wi' a lang, lang linen band?

"O wha will kame my yellow hair,
  With a haw bayberry kame?
And wha will be my babe's father
  Till Gregory come hame?"

"Thy father, he will shoe thy foot,
  Thy brother will glove thy hand,
Thy mither will bind thy middle jimp
  Wi' a lang, lang linen band.

"Thy sister will kame thy yellow hair,
  Wi' a haw bayberry kame;
The Almighty will be thy babe's father
  Till Gregory come hame."

"And wha will build a bonny ship,
  And set it on the sea?
For I will go to seek my love,
  My ain love Gregory."

Up then spak her father dear,
  A wafu' man was he:
"And I will build a bonny ship,
  And set her on the sea.

"And I will build a bonny ship,
  And set her on the sea,
And ye sal gae and seek your love,
  Your ain love Gregory."

Then he's gart build a bonny ship,
  And set it on the sea,
Wi' four-and-twenty mariners,
  To bear her company.

O he's gart build a bonny ship,
  To sail on the salt sea;
The mast was o' the beaten gold,
  The sails o' cramoisie.

The sides were o' the gude stout aik,
  The deck o' mountain pine,
The anchor o' the silver shene,
  The ropes o' silken twine.

She hadna sailed but twenty leagues,
  But twenty leagues and three,
When she met wi' a rank reiver,
  And a' his companie.

"Now are ye Queen of Heaven hie,
  Come to pardon a' our sin?
Or are ye Mary Magdalane,
  Was born in Bethlehem?"

"I'm no the Queen of Heaven hie,
  Come to pardon ye your sin,
Nor am I Mary Magdalane,
  Was born in Bethlehem.

"But I'm the lass of Lochroyan,
  That's sailing on the sea
To see if I can find my love,
  My ain love Gregory."

"O see na ye yon bonny bower?
  It's a' covered owre wi' tin;
When thou hast sailed it round about,
  Lord Gregory is within."

And when she saw the stately tower,
Shining both clear and bright,
Whilk stood aboon the jawing wave,
Built on a rock of height,

Says, "Row the boat, my mariners,
And bring me to the land,
For yonder I see my love's castle,
Close by the salt sea strand."

She sailed it round, and sailed it round,
And loud and loud cried she,
"Now break, now break your fairy charms,
And set my true-love free."

She's ta'en her young son in her arms,
And to the door she's gane,
And long she knocked, and sair she ca'd,
But answer got she nane.

"O open, open, Gregory!
O open! if ye be within;
For here's the lass of Lochroyan,
Come far frae kith and kin.

"O open the door, Lord Gregory!
O open and let me in!
The wind blows loud and cauld, Gregory,
The rain drops frae my chin.

"The shoe is frozen to my foot,
The glove unto my hand,
The wet drops frae my yellow hair,
Na langer dow I stand."

O up then spak his ill mither,
—An ill death may she dee!
"Ye're no the lass of Lochroyan,
She's far out-owre the sea.

"Awa', awa', ye ill woman,
Ye're no come here for gude;
Ye're but some witch or wil' warlock,
Or mermaid o' the flood."

"I am neither witch nor wil' warlock,
Nor mermaid o' the sea,
But I am Annie of Lochroyan,
O open the door to me!"

"Gin ye be Annie of Lochroyan,
As I trow thou binna she,
Now tell me of some love-tokens
That passed 'tween thee and me."

"O dinna ye mind, love Gregory,
As we sat at the wine,
We changed the rings frae our fingers?
And I can shew thee thine.

"O yours was gude, and gude enough,
But ay the best was mine,
For yours was o' the gude red gowd,
But mine o' the diamond fine.

"Yours was o' the gude red gowd,
Mine o' the diamond fine;
Mine was o' the purest troth,
But thine was false within."

"If ye be the lass of Lochroyan,
As I kenna thou be,
Tell me some mair o' the love-tokens
Passed between thee and me."

"And dinna ye mind, love Gregory!
As we sat on the hill,
Thou twined me o' my maidenheid,
Right sair against my will?

"Now open the door, love Gregory!
Open the door! I pray;
For thy young son is in my arms,
And will be dead ere day."

"Ye lee, ye lee, ye ill woman,
So loud I hear ye lee;
For Annie of the Lochroyan
Is far out-owre the sea."

Fair Annie turned her round about:
"Weel, syne that it be sae,
May ne'er woman that has borne a son
Hae a heart sae fu' o' wae!

"Tak down, tak down that mast o' gowd,
Set up a mast o' tree;
It disna become a forsaken lady
To sail sae royallie."

When the cock had crawn, and the day did dawn,
And the sun began to peep,
Up then raise Lord Gregory,
And sair, sair did he weep.

"O I hae dreamed a dream, mither,
I wish it may bring good!
That the bonny lass of Lochroyan
At my bower window stood.

"O I hae dreamed a dream, mither,
The thought o't gars me greet!
That fair Annie of Lochroyan
Lay dead at my bed-feet."

"Gin it be for Annie of Lochroyan
That ye mak a' this mane,
She stood last night at your bower-door,
But I hae sent her hame."

"O wae betide ye, ill woman,
  An ill death may ye dee!
That wadna open the door yoursell
  Nor yet wad waken me."

O he's gane down to yon shore-side,
  As fast as he could dree,
And there he saw fair Annie's bark
  A rowing owre the sea.

"O Annie, Annie," loud he cried,
  "O Annie, O Annie, bide!"
But ay the mair he cried "Annie,"
  The braider grew the tide.

"O Annie, Annie, dear Annie,
  Dear Annie, speak to me!"
But ay the louder he gan call,
  The louder roared the sea.

The wind blew loud, the waves rose hie
  And dashed the boat on shore;
Fair Annie's corse was in the faem,
  The babe rose never more.

Lord Gregory tore his gowden locks
  And made a wafu' mane;
Fair Annie's corpse lay at his feet,
  His bonny son was gane.

"O cherry, cherry was her cheek,
  And gowden was her hair,
And coral, coral was her lips,
  Nane might with her compare."

Then first he kissed her pale, pale cheek,
  And syne he kissed her chin,
And syne he kissed her wane, wane lips,
  There was na breath within.

"O wae betide my ill mither,
An ill death may she dee!
She turned my true-love frae my door,
Wha cam so far to me.

"O wae betide my ill mither,
An ill death may she dee!
She has no been the deid o' ane,
But she's been the deid o' three."

Then he's ta'en out a little dart,
Hung low down by his gore,
He thrust it through and through his heart,
And word spak never more.

*Unknown*

## YOUNG BEICHAN AND SUSIE PYE

In London was young Beichan born,
He longed strange countries for to see;
But he was ta'en by a savage Moor,
Who handled him right cruellie;

For he viewed the fashions of that land:
Their way of worship viewèd he;
But to Mahound, or Termagant,
Would Beichan never bend a knee.

So in every shoulder they've putten a bore,
In every bore they've putten a tree,
And they have made him trail the wine
And spices on his fair bodie.

They've casten him in a dungeon deep,
Where he could neither hear nor see;
And fed him on naught but bread and water,
Till he for hunger's like to dee.

This Moor he had but ae daughter,
Her name was callèd Susie Pye;
And every day as she took the air,
Near Beichan's prison she passed by.

And so it fell upon a day,
  About the middle time of Spring,
As she was passing by that way,
  She heard young Beichan sadly sing:

"My hounds they all run masterless,
  My hawks they fly frae tree to tree;
My youngest brother will heir my lands;
  Fair England again I'll never see.

"Oh were I free as I hae been,
  And my ship swimming once more on sea,
I'd turn my face to fair England,
  And sail no more to a strange countrie!"

All night long no rest she got,
  Young Beichan's song for thinking on;
She's stown the keys from her father's head,
  And to the prison strang is gone.

And she has opened the prison doors,
  I wot she opened two or three,
Ere she could come young Beichan at,
  He was locked up so curiouslie.

But when she cam' young Beichan till,
  Sore wondered he that may to see;
He took her for some fair captive:
  "Fair lady, I pray, of what countrie?"

"O have ye any lands," she said,
  "Or castles in your ain countrie,
That ye could give a lady fair,
  From prison strang to set you free?"

"Near London town I have a hall,
  And other castles two or three;
I'll give them all to the lady fair
  That out of prison will set me free."

"Give me the truth of your right hand,
The truth of it give unto me,
That for seven years ye'll no lady wed,
Unless it be alang wi' me."

"I'll give thee the truth of my right hand,
The truth of it I'll freely gie,
That for seven years I'll stay unwed,
For the kindness thou dost show to me."

And she has bribed the proud warder
Wi' mickle gold and white monie;
She's gotten the keys of the prison strang,
And she has set young Beichan free.

She's gi'en him to eat the good spice-cake;
She's gi'en him to drink the blude-red wine;
She's bidden him sometimes think on her
That sae kindly freed him out o' pine.

And she has broken her finger ring,
And to Beichan half of it gave she;
"Keep it to mind you of that love
The lady bore that set you free.

"And set your foot on good ship-board,
And haste ye back to your ain countrie;
And before that seven years have an end,
Come back again, love, and marry me."

But lang ere seven years had an end,
She longed full sore her love to see;
So she's set her foot on good ship-board.
And turned her back to her ain countrie.

She sailèd east, she sailèd west,
Till to fair England's shore she came;
Where a bonny shepherd she espied,
Feeding his sheep upon the plain.

"What news, what news, thou bonny shepherd?
What news has thou to tell to me?"
"Such news I hear, ladie," he says,
"The like was never in this countrie.

"There is a wedding in yonder hall,
And ever the bells ring merrilie;
It is Lord Beichan's wedding-day
Wi' a lady fair o' high degree."

She's putten her hand in her pocket,
Gi'en him the gold and white monie;
"Here, take ye that, my bonny boy,
All for the news thou tell'st to me."

When she came to young Beichan's gate,
She tirlèd softly at the pin:
So ready was the proud porter
To open and let this lady in.

"Is this young Beichan's hall," she said,
"Or is that noble lord within?"
"Yea, he's in the hall among them all,
And this is the day o' his weddin'."

"And has he wed anither love?
And has he clean forgotten me?"
And, sighin', said that ladie gay,
"I wish I were in my ain countrie."

And she has ta'en her gay gold ring,
That with her love she brake sae free;
Says, "Gie him that, ye proud porter,
And bid the bridegroom speak wi' me."

When the porter came his lord before,
He kneelèd low upon his knee—
"What aileth thee, my proud porter,
Thou art so full of courtesie?"

"I've been porter at your gates,
It's now for thirty years and three;
But there stands a lady at them now,
The like o' her did I never see;

"For on every finger she has a ring,
And on her mid-finger she has three;
And meikle gold aboon her brow.
Sae fair a may did I never see."

It's out then spak the bride's mother,
Aye and an angry woman was she:
"Ye might have excepted our bonny bride,
And twa or three of our companie."

"O haud your tongue, thou bride's mother,
Of all your folly let me be;
She's ten times fairer nor the bride,
And all that's in your companie.

"And this golden ring that's broken in twa,
This half o' a golden ring sends she:
'Ye'll carry that to Lord Beichan,' she says,
'And bid him come an' spak wi' me.'

"She begs one sheave of your white bread,
But and a cup of your red wine;
And to remember the lady's love,
That last relieved you out of pine."

"O well-a-day!" said Beichan then,
"That I so soon have married me!
For it can be none but Susie Pye,
That for my love has sailed the sea."

And quickly hied he down the stair;
Of fifteen steps he made but three;
He's ta'en his bonny love in his arms,
And kist, and kist her tenderlie.

"O hae ye ta'en anither bride?
  And hae ye quite forgotten me?
And hae ye quite forgotten her,
  That gave you life and libertie?"

She lookit o'er her left shoulder,
  To hide the tears stood in her e'e;
"Now fare thee well, young Beichan," she says,
  "I'll try to think no more on thee."

"O never, never, Susie Pye,
  For surely this can never be;
Nor ever shall I wed but her
  That's done and dreed so much for me."

Then out and spak the forenoon bride:
  "My lord, your love it changeth soon;
This morning I was made your bride,
  And another's chose ere it be noon."

"O haud thy tongue, thou forenoon bride;
  Ye're ne'er a whit the worse for me;
And whan ye return to your own land,
  A double dower I'll send wi' thee."

He's ta'en Susie Pye by the white hand,
  And gently led her up and down;
And ay, as he kist her red rosy lips,
  "Ye're welcome, jewel, to your own."

He's ta'en her by her milk-white hand,
  And led her to yon fountain stane;
He's changed her name from Susie Pye,
  And called her his bonny love, Lady Jane.

*Unknown*

## THE GAY GOS-HAWK

"O WELL is me, my gay gos-hawk,
  That you can speak and flee;
For you can carry a love-letter
  To my true love frae me."

"O how can I carry a letter to her,
Or how should I her know?
I bear a tongue ne'er wi' her spak',
And eyes that ne'er her saw."

"The white o' my love's skin is white
As down o' dove or maw;
The red o' my love's cheek is red
As blood that's spilt on snaw.

"When ye come to the castle,
Light on the tree of ash,
And sit ye there and sing our loves
As she comes frae the mass.

"Four and twenty fair ladies
Will to the mass repair;
And weel may ye my lady ken,
The fairest lady there."

When the gos-hawk flew to that castle,
He lighted on the ash;
And there he sat and sang their loves
As she came frae the mass.

"Stay where ye be, my maidens a',
And sip red wine anon,
Till I go to my west window
And hear a birdie's moan."

She's gane unto her west window,
The bolt she fainly drew;
And unto that lady's white, white neck
The bird a letter threw.

"Ye're bidden to send your love a send,
For he has sent you twa;
And tell him where he may see you soon,
Or he cannot live ava."

"I send him the ring from my finger,
The garland off my hair,
I send him the heart that's in my breast;
What would my love have mair?
And at the fourth kirk in fair Scotland,
Ye'll bid him wait for me there."

She hied her to her father dear
As fast as gang could she:
"I'm sick at the heart, my father dear;
An asking grant you me!"
"Ask ye na for that Scottish lord,
For him ye'll never see!"

"An asking, an asking, dear father!" she says,
"An asking grant you me;
That if I die in fair England,
In Scotland ye'll bury me.

"At the first kirk o' fair Scotland,
Ye cause the bells be rung;
At the second kirk o' fair Scotland,
Ye cause the mass be sung;

"At the third kirk o' fair Scotland,
Ye deal gold for my sake;
At the fourth kirk o' fair Scotland,
O there ye'll bury me at!

"This is all my asking, father,
I pray ye grant it me!"
"Your asking is but small," he said;
"Weel granted it shall be.
But why do ye talk o' suchlike things?
For ye arena going to dee."

The lady's gane to her chamber,
And a moanfu' woman was she,
As gin she had ta'en a sudden brash,
And were about to dee.

The lady's gane to her chamber
  As fast as she could fare;
And she has drunk a sleepy draught
  She mixed wi' mickle care.

She's fallen into a heavy trance,
  And pale and cold was she;
She seemed to be as surely dead
  As any corpse could be.

Out and spak' an auld witch-wife,
  At the fireside sat she:
"Gin she has killed herself for love,
  I wot it weel may be:

"But drap the het lead on her cheek,
  And drap it on her chin,
And drap it on her bosom white,
  And she'll maybe speak again.
'Tis much that a young lady will do
  To her true love to win."

They drapped the het lead on her cheek,
  They drapped it on her chin,
They drapped it on her bosom white,
  But she spake none again.

Her brothers they went to a room,
  To make to her a bier;
The boards were a' o' the cedar wood,
  The edges o' silver clear.

Her sisters they went to a room,
  To make to her a sark;
The cloth was a' o' the satin fine,
  And the stitching silken-wark.

"Now well is me, my gay gos-hawk,
  That ye can speak and flee!
Come show me any love-tokens
  That ye have brought to me."

"She sends ye her ring frae her finger white,
The garland frae her hair;
She sends ye the heart within her breast;
And what would ye have mair?
And at the fourth kirk o' fair Scotland,
She bids ye wait for her there."

"Come hither, all my merry young men!
And drink the good red wine;
For we must on towards fair England
To free my love frae pine."

The funeral came into fair Scotland,
And they gart the bells be rung;
And when it came to the second kirk,
They gart the mass be sung.

And when it came to the third kirk,
They dealt gold for her sake;
And when it came to the fourth kirk,
Her love was waiting thereat.

At the fourth kirk in fair Scotland
Stood spearmen in a row;
And up and started her ain true love,
The chieftain over them a'.

"Set down, set down the bier," he says,
"Till I look upon the dead;
The last time that I saw her face,
Its color was warm and red."

He stripped the sheet from off her face
A little below the chin;
The lady then she opened her eyes,
And lookèd full on him.

"O give me a shive o' your bread, love,
O give me a cup o' your wine!
Long have I fasted for your sake,
And now I fain would dine.

"Gae hame, gae hame, my seven brothers,
Gae hame and blow the horn!
And ye may say that ye sought my skaith,
And that I hae gi'en ye the scorn.

"I cam' na here to bonny Scotland
To lie down in the clay;
But I cam' here to bonny Scotland,
To wear the silks sae gay!

"I cam' na here to bonny Scotland,
Amang the dead to rest;
But I cam' here to bonny Scotland
To the man that I lo'e best!"

*Unknown*

## SWEET WILLIAM AND MAY MARG'RET

THERE came a ghost to Marg'ret's door,
With many a grievous groan,
And aye he tirlèd at the pin,
But answer made she none.

"Is that my father Philip,
Or is't my brother John?
Or is't my true-love Willie,
From Scotland new come home?"

"'Tis not thy father Philip,
Nor yet thy brother John
But 'tis thy true-love Willie,
From Scotland new come home.

"O sweet Marg'ret, O dear Marg'ret,
I pray thee speak to me:
Give me my faith and troth, Marg'ret,
As I gave it to thee."

"Thy faith and troth thou'lt never get,
Of me shalt never win,
Till that thou come within my bower,
And kiss me cheek and chin."

"If I should come within thy bower,
I am no earthly man:
And should I kiss thy rosy lips
Thy days would not be lang.

"O sweet Marg'ret, O dear Mar'gret,
I pray thee speak to me:
Give me my faith and troth, Marg'ret,
As I gave it to thee."

"Thy faith and troth thou'lt never get,
Of me shalt never win,
Till you take me to yon kirk-yard,
And wed me with a ring."

"My bones are buried in yon kirk-yard
Afar beyond the sea,
And it is but my spirit, Marg'ret,
That's now speaking to thee."

She stretched out her lily-white hand,
And for to do her best:
"Ha'e there your faith and troth, Willie,
God send your soul good rest."

Now she has kilted her robe o' green
A piece below her knee,
And a' the live-lang winter night
The dead corp followed she.

"Is there any room at your head, Willie,
Or any room at your feet?
Or any room at your side, Willie,
Wherein that I may creep?"

"There's nae room at my head, Marg'ret,
There's nae room at my feet;
There's nae room at my side, Marg'ret,
My coffin's made so meet."

Then up and crew the red, red cock,
And up and crew the gray;
"'Tis time, 'tis time, my dear Marg'ret,
That you were gane awa'."

*Unknown*

## WILLY REILLY

"Oh! rise up, Willy Reilly, and come along with me,
I mean for to go with you and leave this counterie,
To leave my father's dwelling, his houses and free land;"
And away goes Willy Reilly and his dear Coolen Ban.

They go by hills and mountains, and by yon lonesome plain,
Through shady groves and valleys, all dangers to refrain;
But her father followed after with a well-armed band,
And taken was poor Reilly and his dear Coolen Ban.

It's home then she was taken, and in her closet bound;
Poor Reilly all in Sligo jail lay on the stony ground,
Till at the bar of justice, before the Judge he'd stand,
For nothing but the stealing of his dear Coolen Ban.

"Now in the cold, cold iron my hands and feet are bound,
I'm handcuffed like a murderer, and tied unto the ground.
But all the toil and slavery I'm willing for to stand,
Still hoping to be succoured by my dear Coolen Ban."

The jailer's son to Reilly goes, and thus to him did say:
"Oh! get up, Willy Reilly, you must appear this day,
For great Squire Foillard's anger you never can withstand:
I'm afeered you'll suffer sorely for your dear Coolen Ban.

"This is the news, young Reilly, last night that I did hear:
The lady's oath will hang you or else will set you clear."
"If that be so," says Reilly, "her pleasure I will stand,
Still hoping to be succoured by my dear Coolen Ban."

Now Willy's dressed from top to toe all in a suit of green,
His hair hangs o'er his shoulders most glorious to be seen;
He's tall and straight, and comely as any could be found;
He's fit for Foillard's daughter, was she heiress to a crown.

The Judge he said: "This lady being in her tender youth,
If Reilly has deluded her she will declare the truth."
Then, like a moving beauty bright, before him she did stand,
"You're welcome there, my heart's delight and dear Coolen Ban."

"Oh, gentlemen," Squire Foillard said, "with pity look on me,
This villain came amongst us to disgrace our family,
And by his base contrivances this villainy was planned;
If I don't get satisfaction I'll quit this Irish land."

The lady with a tear began, and thus replied she:
"The fault is none of Reilly's, the blame lies all on me,
I forced him for to leave this place and come along with me;
I loved him out of measure, which wrought our destiny."

Out bespoke the noble Fox, at the table he stood by:
"Oh, gentlemen, consider on this extremity;
To hang a man for love is a murder, you may see:
So spare the life of Reilly, let him leave this counterie."

"Good my lord, he stole from her her diamonds and her rings,
Gold watch and silver buckles, and many precious things,
Which cost me in bright guineas more than five hundred pounds,
I'll have the life of Reilly should I lose ten thousand pounds."

"Good my lord, I gave them him as tokens of true love,
And when we are a-parting I will them all remove;
If you have got them, Reilly, pray send them home to me."
"I will, my loving lady, with many thanks to thee."

"There is a ring among them I allow yourself to wear,
With thirty locket diamonds well set in silver fair,
And as a true-love token wear it on your right hand,
That you'll think on my poor broken heart when you're in foreign land."

Then out spoke noble Fox: "You may let the prisoner go;
The lady's oath has cleared him, as the Jury all may know.
She has released her own true love, she has renewed his name;
May her honor bright gain high estate, and her offspring rise to fame!"

*Unknown*

## THE TWA CORBIES

As I was walking all alane
I heard twa corbies making a mane;
The tane unto the t'other did say,
"Where sall we gang and dine to-day?"

"—In behint yon auld fail dyke
I wot there lies a new-slain Knight;
And naebody kens that he lies there,
But his hawk, his hound, and lady fair.

"His hound is to the hunting gane,
His hawk to fetch the wild-fowl hame,
His lady's ta'en another mate,
So we may mak our dinner sweet.

"Ye'll set on his white hause-bane,
And I'll pick out his bonnie blue een:
Wi' ae lock o' his gowden hair
We'll theek our nest when it grows bare.

"Mony a one for him make mane,
But nane sall ken whar he is gane;
O'er his white banes, when they are bare,
The wind sall blaw for evermair."

*Unknown*

## THE THREE RAVENS

THERE were three ravens sat on a tree,
They were as black as they might be.

The one of them said to his mate,
"Where shall we our breakfast take?"

"Down in yonder greenè field
There lies a knight slain under his shield;

"His hounds they lie down at his feet,
So well do they their master keep;

"His hawks they fly so eagerly,
There's no fowl dare come him nigh.

"Down there comes a fallow doe
As great with young as she might goe.

"She lifted up his bloudy head
And kist his wounds that were so red.

"She gat him up upon her back
And carried him to earthen lake.

"She buried him before the prime,
She was dead herself ere evensong time.

"God send every gentleman
Such hounds, such hawks, and such a leman."

*Unknown*

## LORD RANDAL

"O WHERE hae ye been, Lord Randal, my son?
O where hae ye been, my handsome young man?"
"I hae been to the wild wood; mother, make my bed soon;
For I'm weary wi' hunting, and fain wald lie doun."

"Where gat ye your dinner, Lord Randal, my son?
Where gat ye your dinner, my handsome young man?"
"I dined wi' my true-love; mother, make my bed soon;
For I'm weary wi' hunting, and fain wald lie doun."

"What gat ye to your dinner, Lord Randal, my son?
What gat ye to your dinner, my handsome young man?"
"I gat eels boiled in broo; mother, make my bed soon;
For I'm weary wi' hunting, and fain wald lie doun."

"What became of your bloodhounds, Lord Randal, my son?
What became of your bloodhounds, my handsome young man?"
"O they swelled and they died; mother, make my bed soon;
For I'm weary wi' hunting, and fain wald lie doun."

"O I fear ye are poisoned, Lord Randal, my son!
O I fear ye are poisoned, my handsome young man!"
"O yes! I am poisoned; mother, make my bed soon;
For I'm sick at the heart, and I fain wald lie doun."

*Unknown*

## EDWARD, EDWARD

"Why does your brand sae drop wi' blude,
Edward, Edward?
Why does your brand sae drop wi' blude,
And why sae sad gang ye, O?"
"O I hae killed my hawk sae gude,
Mither, mither;
O I hae killed my hawk sae gude,
And I had nae mair but he, O."

"Your hawk's blude was never sae red,
Edward, Edward;
Your hawk's blude was never sae red,
My dear son, I tell thee, O."
"O I hae killed my red-roan steed,
Mither, mither;
O I hae killed my red-roan steed,
That erst was sae fair and free, O."

"Your steed was auld, and ye hae got mair,
Edward, Edward;
Your steed was auld, and ye hae got mair;
Some other dule ye dree, O."
"O I hae killed my father dear,
Mither, mither;
O I hae killed my father dear,
Alas, and wae is me, O!"

"And whatten penance will ye dree for that,
Edward, Edward?
Whatten penance will ye dree for that?
My dear son, now tell me, O."
"I'll set my feet in yonder bcat,
Mither, mither;
I'll set my feet in yonder boat,
And I'll fare over the sea, O."

"And what will ye do wi' your towers and your ha',
Edward, Edward?
And what will ye do wi' your towers and your ha',
That were sae fair to see, O?"
"I'll let them stand till they doun fa',
Mither, mither;
I'll let them stand till they doun fa',
For here never mair maun I be, O."

"And what will ye leave to your bairns and your wife,
Edward, Edward?
And what will ye leave to your bairns and your wife,
When ye gang owre the sea, O?"
"The warld's room: let them beg through life,
Mither, mither;
The warld's room: let them beg through life;
For them never mair will I see, O."

"And what will ye leave to your ain mither dear,
Edward, Edward?
And what will ye leave to your ain mither dear,
My dear son, now tell me, O?"
"The cursc of hell frae me sall ye bear,
Mither, mither;
The curse of hell frae me sall ye bear:
Sic counsels ye gave to me, O!"

*Unknown*

## RIDDLES WISELY EXPOUNDED

THERE was a knicht riding frae the east,
*Jennifer gentle an' rosemaree.*
Who had been wooing at monie a place,
*As the doo flies owre the mulberry tree.*

He cam' unto a widow's door,
And speird whare her three dochters were.

"The auldest ane's to a washing gane,
The second's to a baking gane.

"The youngest ane's to a wedding gane,
And it will be nicht or she be hame."

He sat him doun upon a stane,
Till thir three lasses cam' tripping hame.

The auldest ane she let him in,
And pinned the door wi' a siller pin.

The second ane she made his bed,
And laid saft pillows unto his head.

The youngest ane was bauld and bricht,
And she tarried for words wi' this unco knicht.

"Gin ye will answer me questions ten,
The morn ye sall be made my ain.

"O what is higher nor the tree?
And what is deeper nor the sea?

"Or what is heavier nor the lead?
And what is better nor the breid?

"Or what is whiter nor the milk?
Or what is safter nor the silk?

"Or what is sharper nor a thorn?
Or what is louder nor a horn?

"Or what is greener nor the grass?
Or what is waur nor a woman was?"

"O heaven is higher nor the tree,
And hell is deeper nor the sea.

"O sin is heavier nor the lead,
The blessing's better nor the breid.

"The snaw is whiter nor the milk,
And the down is safter nor the silk.

"Hunger is sharper nor a thorn,
And shame is louder nor a horn.

"The pies are greener nor the grass,
And Clootie's waur nor a woman was."

As sune as she the fiend did name,
*Jennifer gentle an' rosemaree,*
He flew awa in a blazing flame,
*As the doo flies owre the mulberry tree.*

*Unknown*

## SIR PATRICK SPENS

### I.—THE SAILING

The King sits in Dunfermline toun,
Drinking the blude-red wine:
"O whaur will I get a skeely skipper
To sail this gude ship of mine?"

Then up an' spak an eldern knight,
Sat at the King's right knee:
"Sir Patrick Spens is the best sailor
That ever sailed the sea."

The King has written a braid letter,
And sealed it wi' his hand,
And sent it to Sir Patrick Spens
Was walking on the strand.

"To Noroway, to Noroway,
To Noroway o'er the faem;
The King's daughter to Noroway,
'Tis thou maun tak' her hame!"

The first line that Sir Patrick read,
  A loud laugh laughèd he;
The neist line that Sir Patrick read,
  The tear blindit his e'e.

"O wha is this hae dune this deed,
  And tauld the King o' me,
To send us out, at this time o' year,
  To sail upon the sea?

"Be it wind or weet, be it hail or sleet,
  Our ship maun sail the faem;
The King's daughter to Noroway,
  'Tis we maun tak' her hame."

They hoysed their sails on Monday morn
  Wi' a' the speed they may;
And they hae landed in Noroway
  Upon the Wodensday.

### II.—THE RETURN

"Mak ready, mak ready, my merry men a'!
  Our gude ship sails the morn."
"Now, ever alack! my master dear,
  I fear a deadly storm!

"I saw the new moon late yestreen,
  Wi' the auld moon in her arm;
And I fear, I fear, my master dear,
  That we sall come to harm!"

They hadna sailed a league, a league,
  A league but barely three,
When the lift grew dark, and the wind blew loud,
  And gurly grew the sea.

The ropes they brak, and the topmast lap,
  It was sic a deadly storm;
And the waves cam owre the broken ship
  Till a' her sides were torn.

"O whaur will I get a gude sailor
  To tak' the helm in hand,
Until I win to the tall topmast
  And see if I spy the land?"

"It's here am I, a sailor gude,
  To tak' the helm in hand,
Till ye win up to the tall topmast,
  But I fear ye'll ne'er spy land."

He hadna gane a step, a step,
  A step but barely ane,
When a bolt flew out of the gude ship's side,
  And the saut sea it cam' in.

"Gae fetch a web o' the silken claith,
  Anither o' the twine,
And wap them into the gude ship's side
  And let na the sea come in."

They fetched a web o' the silken claith,
  Anither o' the twine,
And they wapped them into that gude ship's side,
  But aye the sea cam' in.

O laith, laith were our gude Scots lords
  To weet their cock-heeled shoon!
But lang ere a' the play was played,
  They wat their hats aboon.

And mony was the feather-bed
  That floated on the faem;
And mony was the gude lord's son
  That never mair cam hame.

O lang, lang, may the ladies sit,
  Wi' their fans into their hand,
Or ever they see Sir Patrick Spens
  Come sailing to the strand!

And lang, lang may the maidens sit,
  Wi' their gowd kaims in their hair,
A-waiting for their ain dear loves,
  For them they'll see nae mair.

Half-owre, half-owre to Aberdour,
  'Tis fifty fathoms deep,
And there lies gude Sir Patrick Spens
  Wi' the Scots lords at his feet.

*Unknown*

## EDOM O' GORDON

It fell about the Martinmas,
  When the wind blew shrill and cauld,
Said Edom o' Gordon to his men,
  "We maun draw to a hauld.

"And what a hauld sall we draw to,
  My merry men and me?
We will gae to the house o' the Rodes,
  To see that fair ladye."

The lady stood on her castle wa',
  Beheld baith dale and down;
There she was ware of a host of men
  Cam riding towards the town.

"O see ye not, my merry men a',
  O see ye not what I see?
Methinks I see a host of men;
  I marvel wha they be."

She weened it had been her lovely lord,
  As he cam riding hame;
It was the traitor, Edom o' Gordon,
  Wha recked nae sin nor shame.

She had nae sooner buskit hersell,
  And putten on her gown,
But Edom o' Gordon an' his men
  Were round about the town.

They had nae sooner supper set,
Nae sooner said the grace,
But Edom o' Gordon an' his men
Were lighted about the place.

The lady ran up to her tower-head,
Sae fast as she could hie,
To see if by her fair speeches
She could wi' him agree.

"Come doun to me, ye lady gay,
Come doun, come doun to me;
This night sall ye lig within myne arms,
To-morrow my bride sall be."

"I winna come doun, ye fals Gordon,
I winna come doun to thee;
I winna forsake my ain dear lord,
That is sae far frae me."

"Gie owre your house, ye lady fair,
Gie owre your house to me;
Or I sall brenn yoursell therein,
But and your babies three."

"I winna gie owre, ye fals Gordon,
To nae sic traitor as ye;
And if ye brenn my ain dear babes,
My lord sall mak ye dree.

"Now reach my pistol, Glaud, my man,
And charge ye weel my gun;
For, but an I pierce that bluidy butcher,
My babes, we been undone!"

She stood upon her castle wa',
And let twa bullets flee:
She missed that bluidy butcher's heart,
And only razed his knee.

"Set fire to the house!" quo' fals Gordon,
All wud wi' dule and ire:
"Fals lady, ye sall rue this deid
As ye brenn in the fire!"

"Wae worth, wae worth ye, Jock, my man!
I paid ye weel your fee;
Why pu' ye out the grund-wa' stane,
Lets in the reek to me?

"And e'en wae worth ye, Jock, my man!
I paid ye weel your hire;
Why pu' ye out the grund-wa' stane,
To me lets in the fire?"

"Ye paid me weel my hire, ladye,
Ye paid me weel my fee:
But now I'm Edom o' Gordon's man—
Maun either do or dee."

O then bespake her little son,
Sat on the nurse's knee:
Says, "Mither dear, gie owre this house,
For the reek it smithers me."

"I wad gie a' my gowd, my bairn,
Sae wad I a' my fee,
For ae blast o' the western wind,
To blaw the reek frae thee."

O then bespake her dochter dear—
She was baith jimp and sma':
"O row me in a pair o' sheets,
And tow me owre the wa'!"

They rowed her in a pair o' sheets,
And towed her owre the wa';
But on the point o' Gordon's spear
She gat a deadly fa'.

O bonnie, bonnie was her mouth,
  And cherry were her cheiks,
And clear, clear was her yellow hair,
  Whereon the red blood dreips.

Then wi' his spear he turned her owre;
  O gin her face was wane!
He said, "Ye are the first that e'er
  I wished alive again."

He turned her owre and owre again;
  O gin her skin was white!
"I might hae spared that bonnie face
  To hae been some man's delight.

"Busk and boun, my merry men a',
  For ill dooms I do guess;
I canna look in that bonnie face
  As it lies on the grass."

"Wha looks to freits, my master dear,
  It's freits will follow them;
Let it ne'er be said that Edom o' Gordon
  Was daunted by a dame."

But when the lady saw the fire
  Come flaming owre her head,
She wept, and kissed her children twain,
  Says, "Bairns, we been but dead."

The Gordon then his bugle blew.
  And said, "Awa', awa'!
This house o' the Rodes is a' in a flame;
  I hauld it time to ga'."

And this way lookit her ain dear lord,
  As he cam owre the lea;
He saw his castle a' in a lowe,
  As far as he could see.

Then sair, O sair, his mind misgave,
  And all his heart was wae:
"Put on, put on, my wighty men,
  Sae fast as ye can gae.

"Put on, put on, my wighty men,
  Sae fast as ye can drie!
For he that's hindmost o' the thrang
  Sall ne'er get good o' me."

Then some they rade, and some they ran,
  Out-owre the grass and bent;
But ere the foremost could win up,
  Baith lady and babes were brent.

And after the Gordon he is gane,
  Sae fast as he might drie;
And soon i' the Gordon's foul heart's blude
  He's wroken his dear ladye.

*Unknown*

## ROBIN HOOD AND ALLEN-A-DALE

Come listen to me, you gallants so free,
  All you that love mirth for to hear,
And I will tell you of a bold outlăw.
  That lived in Nottinghamshire.

As Robin Hood in the forest stood,
  All under the greenwood tree,
There was he aware of a brave young man,
  As fine as fine might be.

The youngster was clad in scarlet red,
  In scarlet fine and gay;
And he did frisk it over the plain,
  And chanted a roundelay.

As Robin Hood next morning stood
  Amongst the leaves so gay,
There did he espy the same young man
  Come drooping along the way.

The scarlet he wore the day before
  It was clean cast away;
And at every step he fetched a sigh,
  "Alas! and well-a-day!"

Then steppèd forth brave Little John,
  And Midge, the miller's son;
Which made the young man bend his bow
  When as he see them come.

"Stand off! stand off!" the young man said,
  "What is your will with me?"
"You must come before our master straight,
  Under yon greenwood tree."

And when he came bold Robin before,
  Robin asked him courteously,
"O, hast thou any money to spare,
  For my merry men and me?"

"I have no money," the young man said,
  "But five shillings and a ring;
And that I have kept these seven long years,
  To have at my wedding.

"Yesterday I should have married a maid,
  But she was from me ta'en,
And chosen to be an old knight's delight,
  Whereby my poor heart is slain."

"What is thy name?" then said Robin Hood,
  "Come tell me, without any fail."
"By the faith of my body," then said the young man,
  "My name it is Allen-a-Dale."

"What wilt thou give me," said Robin Hood,
  "In ready gold or fee,
To help thee to thy true-love again,
  And deliver her unto thee?"

"I have no money," then quoth the young man,
"No ready gold nor fee,
But I will swear upon a book
Thy true servant for to be."

"How many miles is it to thy true-love?
Come tell me without guile."
"By the faith of my body," then said the young man,
"It is but five little mile."

Then Robin he hasted over the plain;
He did neither stint nor lin,
Until he came unto the church
Where Allen should keep his weddin'.

"What dost thou here?" the bishop then said;
"I prithee now tell unto me."
"I am a bold harper," quoth Robin Hood,
"And the best in the north country."

"Oh welcome, oh welcome," the bishop he said;
"That music best pleaseth me."
"You shall have no music," quoth Robin Hood,
"Till the bride and the bridegroom I see."

With that came in a wealthy knight,
Which was both grave and old;
And after him a finikin lass,
Did shine like glistering gold.

"This is no fit match," quoth Robin Hood,
"That you do seem to make here;
For since we are come into the church,
The bride shall chuse her own dear."

Then Robin Hood put his horn to his mouth,
And blew blasts two or three;
When four-and-twenty yeomen bold
Came leaping over the lea.

And when they came into the church-yard,
Marching all in a row,
The first man was Allen-a-Dale,
To give bold Robin his bow.

"This is thy true love," Robin he said.
"Young Allen, as I hear say:
And you shall be married at this same time,
Before we depart away."

"That shall not be," the bishop he cried,
"For thy word it shall not stand;
They shall be three times asked in the church,
As the law is of our land."

Robin Hood pulled off the bishop's coat,
And put it upon Little John;
"By the faith of my body," then Robin said,
"This cloth doth make thee a man."

When Little John went into the quire,
The people began to laugh;
He asked them seven times into church,
Lest three times should not be enough.

"Who gives me this maid?" then said Little John,
Quoth Robin Hood, "That do I;
And he that takes her from Allen-a-Dale,
Full dearly he shall her buy."

And then having ended this merry wedding,
The bride looked as fresh as a queen;
And so they returned to the merry greenwood,
Amongst the leaves so green.

*Unknown*

## CHEVY-CHASE

God prosper long our noble king,
Our lives and safeties all;
A woful hunting once there did
In Chevy-Chase befall.

To drive the deer with hound and horn
  Earl Percy took his way;
The child may rue that is unborn
  The hunting of that day.

The stout Earl of Northumberland
  A vow to God did make,
His pleasure in the Scottish woods
  Three summer days to take;

The chiefest harts in Chevy-Chase
  To kill and bear away.
These tidings to Earl Douglas came,
  In Scotland where he lay;

Who sent Earl Percy present word
  He would prevent his sport.
The English earl, not fearing that,
  Did to the woods resort,

With fifteen hundred bowmen bold,
  All chosen men of might,
Who knew full well in time of need
  To aim their shafts aright.

The gallant greyhounds swiftly ran
  To chase the fallow deer;
On Monday they began to hunt,
  When daylight did appear;

And long before high noon they had
  A hundred fat bucks slain;
Then, having dined, the drovers went
  To rouse the deer again.

The bowmen mustered on the hills,
  Well able to endure;
And all their rear, with special care,
  That day was guarded sure.

The hounds ran swiftly through the woods
  The nimble deer to take,
That with their cries the hills and dales
  An echo shrill did make.

Lord Percy to the quarry went,
  To view the slaughtered deer;
Quoth he, "Earl Douglas promisèd
  This day to meet me here;

"But if I thought he would not come,
  No longer would I stay;"
With that, a brave young gentleman
  Thus to the earl did say:—

"Lo, yonder doth Earl Douglas come,—
  His men in armor bright;
Full twenty hundred Scottish spears
  All marching in our sight;

"All men of pleasant Teviotdale,
  Fast by the river Tweed;"
"Then cease your sports," Earl Percy said,
  "And take your bows with speed;

"And now with me, my countrymen,
  Your courage forth advance;
For never was there champion yet,
  In Scotland or in France,

"That ever did on horseback come,
  But if my hap it were,
I durst encounter man for man,
  With him to break a spear."

Earl Douglas on his milk-white steed,
  Most like a baron bold,
Rode foremost of his company.
  Whose armor shone like gold.

"Show me," said he, "whose men you be,
  That hunt so boldly here,
That, without my consent, do chase
  And kill my fallow-deer."

The first man that did answer make,
  Was noble Percy, he—
Who said, "We list not to declare,
  Nor show whose men we be:

"Yet will we spend our dearest blood
  Thy chiefest harts to slay."
Then Douglas swore a solemn oath,
  And thus in rage did say:—

"Ere thus I will out-bravèd be,
  One of us two shall die;
I know thee well, an earl thou art,—
  Lord Percy, so am I.

"But trust me, Percy, pity it were,
  And great offense, to kill
Any of these our guiltless men,
  For they have done no ill.

"Let you and I the battle try,
  And set our men aside."
"Accursed be he," Earl Percy said,
  "By whom this is denied."

Then stepped a gallant squire forth,
  Witherington was his name,
Who said, "I would not have it told
  To Henry, our king, for shame,

"That e'er my captain fought on foot,
  And I stood looking on.
You two be earls," said Witherington,
  "And I a squire alone;

"I'll do the best that do I may,
While I have power to stand;
While I have power to wield my sword,
I'll fight with heart and hand."

Our English archers bent their bows,—
Their hearts were good and true;
At the first flight of arrows sent,
Full fourscore Scots they slew.

Yet stays Earl Douglas on the bent,
As chieftain stout and good;
As valiant captain, all unmoved,
The shock he firmly stood.

His host he parted had in three,
As leader ware and tried;
And soon his spearmen on their foes
Bore down on every side.

Throughout the English archery
They dealt full many a wound;
But still our valiant Englishmen
All firmly kept their ground.

And throwing straight their bows away,
They grasped their swords so bright;
And now sharp blows, a heavy shower,
On shields and helmets light.

They closed full fast on every side,
No slackness there was found;
And many a gallant gentleman
Lay gasping on the ground.

In truth, it was a grief to see
How each one chose his spear,
And how the blood out of their breasts
Did gush like water clear.

At last these two stout earls did meet;
Like captains of great might,
Like lions wode, they laid on lode,
And made a cruel fight.

They fought until they both did sweat,
With swords of tempered steel,
Until the blood, like drops of rain,
They trickling down did feel.

"Yield thee, Lord Percy," Douglas said,
"In faith I will thee bring
Where thou shalt high advancèd be
By James, our Scottish king.

"Thy ransom I will freely give.
And this report of thee,—
Thou art the most courageous knight
That ever I did see."

"No, Douglas," saith Earl Percy then,
"Thy proffer I do scorn;
I will not yield to any Scot
That ever yet was born."

With that there came an arrow keen
Out of an English bow,
Which struck Earl Douglas to the heart,—
A deep and deadly blow;

Who never spake more words than these:
"Fight on, my merry men all;
For why, my life is at an end;
Lord Percy sees my fall."

Then leaving life, Earl Percy took
The dead man by the hand;
And said, "Earl Douglas, for thy life
Would I had lost my hand.

"In truth, my very heart doth bleed
With sorrow for thy sake;
For sure a more redoubted knight
Mischance did never take."

A knight amongst the Scots there was
Who saw Earl Douglas die,
Who straight in wrath did vow revenge
Upon the Earl Percy.

Sir Hugh Mountgomery was he called,
Who, with a spear full bright,
Well-mounted on a gallant steed,
Ran fiercely through the fight;

And past the English archers all,
Without a dread or fear;
And through Earl Percy's body then
He thrust his hateful spear.

With such vehement force and might
He did his body gore,
The staff ran through the other side
A large cloth-yard and more.

So thus did both these nobles die,
Whose courage none could stain.
An English archer then perceived
The noble earl was slain;

He had a bow bent in his hand,
Made of a trusty tree;
An arrow of a cloth-yard long
To the hard head drew he.

Against Sir Hugh Mountgomery
So right the shaft he set,
The gray goose-wing that was thereon
In his heart's blood was wet.

This fight did last from break of day
  Till setting of the sun;
For when they rung the evening-bell
  The battle scarce was done.

With stout Earl Percy there were slain
  Sir John of Egerton,
Sir Robert Ratcliff, and Sir John,
  Sir James, that bold baròn.

And with Sir George and stout Sir James,
  Both Knights of good account,
Good Sir Ralph Raby there was slain,
  Whose prowess did surmount.

For Witherington my heart is woe
  That ever he slain should be,
For when his legs were hewn in two,
  He knelt and fought on his knee.

And with Earl Douglas there were slain
  Sir Hugh Mountgomery,
Sir Charles Murray, that from the field
  One foot would never flee;

Sir Charles Murray of Ratcliff, too,—
  His sister's son was he;
Sir David Lamb, so well esteemed,
  But saved he could not be.

And the Lord Maxwell in like case
  Did with Earl Douglas die:
Of twenty hundred Scottish spears,
  Scarce fifty-five did fly.

Of fifteen hundred Englishmen,
  Went home but fifty-three;
The rest in Chevy-Chase were slain,
  Under the greenwood tree.

Next day did many widows come,
  Their husbands to bewail;
They washed their wounds in brinish tears,
  But all would not prevail.

Their bodies, bathed in purple blood,
  They bore with them away;
They kissed them dead a thousand times,
  Ere they were clad in clay.

The news was brought to Edinburgh,
  Where Scotland's king did reign,
That brave Earl Douglas suddenly
  Was with an arrow slain:

"O heavy news," King James did say;
  "Scotland can witness be
I have not any captain more
  Of such account as he."

Like tidings to King Henry came
  Within as short a space,
That Percy of Northumberland
  Was slain in Chevy-Chase:

"Now God be with him," said our King,
  "Since 'twill no better be;
I trust I have within my realm
  Five hundred as good as he.

"Yet shall not Scots or Scotland say
  But I will vengeance take;
I'll be revengèd on them all
  For brave Earl Percy's sake."

This vow full well the king performed
  After at Humbledown;
In one day fifty knights were slain
  With lords of high renown;

And of the rest, of small account,
  Did many hundreds die:
Thus endeth the hunting of Chevy-Chase,
  Made by the Earl Percy.

God save the king, and bless this land,
  With plenty, joy, and peace;
And grant, henceforth, that foul debate
  'Twixt noblemen may cease.

*Unknown*

## BARBARA ALLEN'S CRUELTY

In Scarlet town, where I was born,
  There was a fair maid dwellin',
Made every youth cry *Well-a-way!*
  Her name was Barbara Allen.

All in the merry month of May,
  When green buds they were swellin',
Young Jemmy Grove on his death-bed lay,
  For love of Barbara Allen.

He sent his man in to her then,
  To the town where she was dwellin',
"O haste and come to my master dear,
  If your name be Barbara Allen."

So slowly, slowly rase she up,
  And slowly she came nigh him,
And when she drew the curtain by—
  "Young man, I think you're dyin'."

"O it's I am sick and very very sick,
  And it's all for Barbara Allen."
"O the better for me ye'se never be,
  Though your heart's blood were a-spillin'!

"O dinna ye mind, young man," says she,
"When the red wine ye were fillin',
That ye made the healths go round and round,
And slighted Barbara Allen?"

He turned his face unto the wall,
And death was with him dealin':
"Adieu, adieu, my dear friends all,
And be kind to Barbara Allen!"

As she was walking o'er the fields,
She heard the dead-bell knellin';
And every jow the dead-bell gave
Cried "Woe to Barbara Allen."

"O mother, mother, make my bed,
O make it saft and narrow:
My love has died for me to-day,
I'll die for him to-morrow.

"Farewell," she said, "ye virgins all,
And shun the fault I fell in:
Henceforth take warning by the fall
Of cruel Barbara Allen."

*Unknown*

## THE BAILIFF'S DAUGHTER OF ISLINGTON

There was a youth, a well-belovèd youth,
And he was a squire's son,
He loved the bailiff's daughter dear,
That lived in Islington.

Yet she was coy and would not believe
That he did love her so,
No, nor at any time would she
Any countenance to him show.

But when his friends did understand
  His fond and foolish mind,
They sent him up to fair London
  An apprentice for to bind.

And when he had been seven long years,
  And never his love could see:
Many a tear have I shed for her sake,
  When she little thought of me.

Then all the maids of Islington
  Went forth to sport and play,
All but the bailiff's daughter dear;
  She secretly stole away.

She pulled off her gown of green,
  And put on ragged attire,
And to fair London she would go
  Her true-love to enquire.

As she went along the high road,
  The weather being hot and dry,
She sat her down upon a green bank,
  And her true-love came riding by.

She started up, with a color so red,
  Catching hold of his bridle-rein;
One penny, one penny, kind sir, she said,
  Will ease me of much pain.

Before I give you one penny, sweet-heart
  Pray tell me where you were born.
At Islington, kind sir, said she,
  Where I have had many a scorn.

I prithee, sweet-heart, then tell to me,
  O tell me, whether you know,
The bailiff's daughter of Islington.
  She is dead, sir, long ago.

If she be dead, then take my horse,
My saddle and bridle also;
For I will unto some far country,
Where no man shall me know.

O stay, O stay, thou goodly youth,
She standeth by thy side;
She is here, alive, she is not dead,
And ready to be thy bride.

O farewell grief, and welcome joy,
Ten thousand times therefor;
For now I have found mine own true-love,
Whom I thought I should never see more.

*Unknown*

## KING JOHN AND THE ABBOT OF CANTERBURY

An ancient story I'll tell you anon
Of a notable prince that was called King John;
And he rulèd England with main and with might,
For he did great wrong, and maintained little right.

And I'll tell you a story, a story so merry,
Concerning the Abbot of Canterbury;
How for his house-keeping and high renown,
They rode post for him to fair London town.

An hundred men the king did hear say,
The abbot kept in his house every day;
And fifty gold chains without any doubt,
In velvet coats waited the abbot about.

"How now, father abbot, I hear it of thee,
Thou keepest a far better house than me;
And for thy house-keeping and high renown,
I fear thou work'st treason against my own crown"

"My liege," quo' the abbot, "I would it were known
I never spend nothing, but what is my own;
And I trust your grace will do me no deere,
For spending of my own true-gotten gear."

"Yes, yes, father abbot, thy fault it is high,
And now for the same thou needest must die;
For except thou canst answer me questions three,
Thy head shall be smitten from thy bodie.

"And first," quo' the king, "when I'm in this stead,
With my crown of gold so fair on my head,
Among all my liege-men so noble of birth,
Thou must tell me to one penny what I am worth.

"Secondly, tell me, without any doubt,
How soon I may ride the whole world about;
And at the third question thou must not shrink,
But tell me here truly what I do think."

"O these are hard questions for my shallow wit,
Nor I cannot answer your grace as yet:
But if you will give me but three weeks' space,
I'll do my endeavor to answer your grace."

"Now three weeks' space to thee will I give,
And that is the longest time thou hast to live;
For if thou dost not answer my questions three,
Thy lands and thy livings are forfeit to me."

Away rode the abbot all sad at that word,
And he rode to Cambridge, and Oxenford;
But never a doctor there was so wise,
That could with his learning an answer devise.

Then home rode the abbot of comfort so cold,
And he met his shepherd a-going to fold:
"How now, my lord abbot, you are welcome home;
What news do you bring us from good King John?"

"Sad news, sad news, shepherd, I must give,
That I have but three days more to live;
For if I do not answer him questions three,
My head will be smitten from my bodie.

"The first is to tell him, there in that stead,
With his crown of gold so fair on his head,
Among all his liege-men so noble of birth,
To within one penny of what he is worth.

"The second, to tell him without any doubt,
How soon he may ride this whole world about;
And at the third question I must not shrink,
But tell him there truly what he does think."

"Now cheer up, sire abbot, did you never hear yet,
That a fool he may learn a wise man wit?
Lend me horse, and serving-men, and your apparel,
And I'll ride to London to answer your quarrel.

"Nay, frown not, if it hath been told unto me,
I am like your lordship, as ever may be;
And if you will but lend me your gown,
There is none shall know us at fair London town."

"Now horses and serving-men thou shalt have,
With sumptuous array most gallant and brave,
With crozier, and mitre, and rochet, and cope,
Fit to appear 'fore our Father the Pope."

"Now welcome, sire abbot," the king he did say,
"'Tis well thou'rt come back to keep thy day:
For and if thou canst answer my questions three,
Thy life and thy living both saved shall be.

"And first, when thou seest me here in this stead,
With my crown of gold so fair on my head,
Among all my liege-men so noble of birth,
Tell me to one penny what I am worth."

"For thirty pence our Saviour was sold
Among the false Jews, as I have been told,
And twenty-nine is the worth of thee,
For I think thou art one penny worser than he."

The king he laughed, and swore by St. Bittel,
"I did not think I had been worth so little!
—Now secondly tell me, without any doubt,
How soon I may ride this whole world about."

"You must rise with the sun, and ride with the same
Until the next morning he riseth again;
And then your grace need not make any doubt
But in twenty-four hours you'll ride it about."

The king he laughed, and swore by St. Jone,
"I did not think it could be done so soon!
—Now from the third question thou must not shrink,
But tell me here truly what I do think."

"Yea, that shall I do, and make your grace merry;
You think I'm the Abbot of Canterbury;
But I'm his poor shepherd, as plain you may see,
That am come to beg pardon for him and for me."

The king he laughed, and swore by the Mass,
"I'll make thee lord abbot this day in his place!"
"Now nay, my liege, be not in such speed,
For alack I can neither write nor read."

"Four nobles a week, then, I will give thee,
For this merry jest thou hast shown unto me;
And tell the old abbot when thou comest home,
Thou hast brought him a pardon from good King John."

*Unknown*

## THE FRIAR OF ORDERS GRAY

It was a friar of orders gray
Walked forth to tell his beads;
And he met with a lady fair
Clad in a pilgrim's weeds.

"Now Christ thee save, thou reverend friar;
I pray thee tell to me,
If ever at yon holy shrine
My true-love thou didst see."

"And how should I know your true-love
From many another one?"
"O, by his cockle hat, and staff,
And by his sandal shoon.

"But chiefly by his face and mien,
That were so fair to view;
His flaxen locks that sweetly curled,
And eyes of lovely blue."

"O lady, he is dead and gone!
Lady, he's dead and gone!
And at his head a green grass turf,
And at his heels a stone.

"Within these holy cloisters long
He languished, and he died,
Lamenting of a lady's love,
And 'plaining of her pride.

"Here bore him barefaced on his bier
Six proper youths and tall,
And many a tear bedewed his grave
Within yon kirkyard wall."

"And art thou dead, thou gentle youth?
And art thou dead and gone?
And didst thou die for love of me?
Break, cruel heart of stone!"

"O, weep not, lady, weep not so;
Some ghostly comfort seek;
Let not vain sorrow rive thy heart,
Nor tears bedew thy cheek."

"O, do not, do not, holy friar,
My sorrow now reprove;
For I have lost the sweetest youth
That e'er won lady's love.

"And now, alas! for thy sad loss
I'll evermore weep and sigh;
For thee I only wished to live,
For thee I wish to die."

"Weep no more, lady, weep no more,
Thy sorrow is in vain;
For violets plucked, the sweetest showers
Will ne'er make grow again.

"Our joys as wingèd dreams do fly;
Why then should sorrow last?
Since grief but aggravates thy loss,
Grieve not for what is past."

"O, say not so, thou holy friar;
I pray thee, say not so;
For since my true-love died for me,
'Tis meet my tears should flow.

"And will he never come again?
Will he ne'er come again?
Ah, no! he is dead, and laid in his grave,
Forever to remain.

"His cheek was redder than the rose;
The comeliest youth was he!
But he is dead and laid in his grave:
Alas, and woe is me!"

"Sigh no more, lady, sigh no more,
Men were deceivers ever:
One foot on sea and one on shore,
To one thing constant never.

"Hadst thou been fond, he had been false,
And left thee sad and heavy;
For young men ever were fickle found,
Since summer trees were leafy."

"Now say not so, thou holy friar,
I pray thee say not so;
My love he had the truest heart,
O, he was ever true!

"And art thou dead, thou much-loved youth,
And didst thou die for me?
Then farewell home; for evermore
A pilgrim I will be.

"But first upon my true-love's grave
My weary limbs I'll lay,
And thrice I'll kiss the green-grass turf
That wraps his breathless clay."

"Yet stay, fair lady; rest awhile
Beneath this cloister wall;
The cold wind through the hawthorn blows,
And drizzly rain doth fall."

"O, stay me not, thou holy friar,
O, stay me not, I pray;
No drizzly rain that falls on me
Can wash my fault away."

"Yet stay, fair lady, turn again,
And dry those pearly tears;
For see, beneath this gown of gray
Thy own true-love appears.

"Here forced by grief and hopeless love,
These holy weeds I sought;
And here, amid these lonely walls,
To end my days I thought.

"But haply, for my year of grace
 Is not yet passed away,
Might I still hope to win thy love,
 No longer would I stay."

"Now farewell grief, and welcome joy
 Once more unto my heart;
For since I have found thee, lovely youth,
 We nevermore will part."

*Adapted from old ballads by Thomas Percy* [1729-1811]

## BONNIE GEORGE CAMPBELL

HIE upon Hielands,
 And low upon Tay,
Bonnie George Campbell
 Rade out on a day.
Saddled and bridled
 And gallant rade he;
Hame cam his gude horse,
 But never cam he!

Out cam his auld mither
 Greeting fu' sair,
And out cam his bonnie bride
 Rivin' her hair.
Saddled and bridled
 And booted rade he;
Toom hame cam the saddle
 But never cam he!

"My meadow lies green,
 And my corn is unshorn,
My barn is to bigg,
 And my babie's unborn."
Saddled and bridled
 And booted rade he;
Toom hame cam the saddle,
 But never cam he!

*Unknown*

## ROSABELLE

From "The Lay of the Last Minstrel"

O LISTEN, listen, ladies gay!
No haughty feat of arms I tell;
Soft is the note, and sad the lay,
That mourns the lovely Rosabelle.

"Moor, moor the barge, ye gallant crew!
And, gentle Lady, deign to stay!
Rest thee in Castle Ravensheuch,
Nor tempt the stormy firth to-day.

"The blackening wave is edged with white;
To inch and rock the sea-mews fly:
The fishers have heard the Water-Sprite,
Whose screams forebode that wreck is nigh.

"Last night the gifted Seer did view
A wet shroud swathed round lady gay;
Then stay thee, Fair, in Ravensheuch;
Why cross the gloomy firth to-day?"

"'Tis not because Lord Lindesay's heir
To-night at Roslin leads the ball,
But that my lady-mother there
Sits lonely in her castle-hall.

"'Tis not because the ring they ride,
And Lindesay at the ring rides well,
But that my sire the wine will chide
If 'tis not filled by Rosabelle."

O'er Roslin all that dreary night
A wondrous blaze was seen to gleam;
'Twas broader than the watch-fire's light,
And redder than the bright moonbeam.

It glared on Roslin's castled rock,
It ruddied all the copse-wood glen;
'Twas seen from Dryden's groves of oak,
And seen from caverned Hawthornden.

Seemed all on fire that chapel proud
  Where Roslin's chiefs uncoffined lie,
Each Baron, for a sable shroud,
  Sheathed in his iron panoply.

Seemed all on fire within, around,
  Deep sacristy and altar's pale;
Shone every pillar foliage-bound,
  And glimmered all the dead men's mail.

Blazed battlement and pinnet high,
  Blazed every rose-carved buttress fair,—
So still they blaze, when fate is nigh
  The lordly line of high Saint Clair.

There are twenty of Roslin's barons bold
  Lie buried within that proud chapelle;
Each one the holy vault doth hold,—
  But the sea holds lovely Rosabelle!

And each Saint Clair was buried there
  With candle, with book, and with knell;
But the sea-caves rung, and the wild winds sung
  The dirge of lovely Rosabelle!

*Walter Scott* [1771–1832]

## ALICE BRAND

**From "The Lady of the Lake"**

I

MERRY it is in the good greenwood,
  When the mavis and merle are singing,
When the deer sweeps by, and the hounds are in cry,
  And the hunter's horn is ringing.

"O Alice Brand, my native land
  Is lost for love of you;
And we must hold by wood and wold,
  As outlaws wont to do.

"O Alice, 'twas all for thy locks so bright,
And 'twas all for thine eyes so blue,
That on the night of our luckless flight,
Thy brother bold I slew.

"Now must I teach to hew the beech
The hand that held the glaive,
For leaves to spread our lowly bed,
And stakes to fence our cave.

"And for vest of pall, thy fingers small,
That wont on harp to stray,
A cloak must shear from the slaughtered deer,
To keep the cold away."

"O Richard! if my brother died,
'Twas but a fatal chance;
For darkling was the battle tried,
And fortune sped the lance.

"If pall and vair no more I wear,
Nor thou the crimson sheen,
As warm, we'll say, is the russet gray,
As gay the forest green.

"And, Richard, if our lot be hard,
And lost thy native land,
Still Alice has her own Richard,
And he his Alice Brand."

II

'Tis merry, 'tis merry, in good greenwood,
So blithe Lady Alice is singing;
On the beech's pride, and oak's brown side,
Lord Richard's ax is ringing.

Up spoke the moody Elfin King,
Who woned within the hill,—
Like wind in the porch of a ruined church,
His voice was ghostly shrill.

"Why sounds yon stroke on beech and oak,
  Our moonlight circle's screen?
Or who comes here to chase the deer,
  Beloved of our Elfin Queen?
Or who may dare on wold to wear
  The fairies' fatal green?

"Up, Urgan, up! to yon mortal hie,
  For thou wert christened man;
For cross or sign thou wilt not fly,
  For muttered word or ban.

"Lay on him the curse of the withered heart,
  The curse of the sleepless eye;
Till he wish and pray that his life would part,
  Nor yet find leave to die!"

III

'Tis merry, 'tis merry, in good greenwood,
  Though the birds have stilled their singing;
The evening blaze doth Alice raise,
  And Richard is fagots bringing.

Up Urgan starts, that hideous dwarf,
  Before Lord Richard stands,
And, as he crossed and blessed himself,
"I fear not sign," quoth the grisly elf,
  "That is made with bloody hands."

But out then spoke she, Alice Brand,
  That woman void of fear,—
"And if there's blood upon his hand,
  'Tis but the blood of deer."

"Now loud thou liest, thou bold of mood!
  It cleaves unto his hand,
The stain of thine own kindly blood,
  The blood of Ethert Brand."

Then forward stepped she, Alice Brand,
  And made the holy sign,—
"And if there's blood on Richard's hand,
  A spotless hand is mine.

"And I conjure thee, Demon elf,
  By Him whom Demons fear,
To show us whence thou art thyself,
  And what thine errand here?"

IV

"'Tis merry, 'tis merry, in Fairy-land,
  When fairy birds are singing,
When the court doth ride by the monarch's side,
  With bit and bridle ringing.

"And gaily shines the Fairy-land—
  But all is glistening show,
Like the idle gleam that December's beam
  Can dart on ice and snow.

"And fading, like that varied gleam,
  Is our inconstant shape,
Who now like knight and lady seem,
  And now like dwarf and ape.

"It was between the night and day,
  When the Fairy King has power,
That I sunk down in a sinful fray,
And, 'twixt life and death, was snatched away
  To the joyless Elfin bower.

"But wist I of a woman bold,
  Who thrice my brow durst sign,
I might regain my mortal mold,
  As fair a form as thine."

She crossed him once—she crossed him twice—
  That lady was so brave;
The fouler grew his goblin hue,
  The darker grew the cave.

She crossed him thrice, that lady bold;
He rose beneath her hand
The fairest knight on Scottish mold,
Her brother, Ethert Brand!

Merry it is in good greenwood,
When the mavis and merle are singing,
But merrier were they in Dunfermline gray,
When all the bells were ringing.

*Walter Scott* [1771–1832]

## SONG

From "Rokeby"

O Brignall banks are wild and fair,
And Greta woods are green,
And you may gather garlands there
Would grace a summer-queen.
And as I rode by Dalton-Hall
Beneath the turrets high,
A Maiden on the castle-wall
Was singing merrily:
"O Brignall banks are fresh and fair,
And Greta woods are green;
I'd rather rove with Edmund there
Than reign our English queen."

"O Maiden, wouldst thou wend with me,
To leave both tower and town,
Thou first must guess what life lead we
That dwell by dale and down.
And if thou canst that riddle read,
As read full well you may,
Then to the greenwood shalt thou speed,
As blithe as Queen of May."
Yet sung she, "Brignall banks are fair,
And Greta woods are green;
I'd rather rove with Edmund there
Than reign our English queen.

"I read you, by your bugle-horn
 And by your palfrey good,
I read you for a Ranger sworn
 To keep the king's greenwood."
"A Ranger, lady, winds his horn,
 And 'tis at peep of light;
His blast is heard at merry morn,
 And mine at dead of night."
Yet sung she, "Brignall banks are fair,
 And Greta woods are gay;
I would I were with Edmund there
 To reign his Queen of May!

"With burnished brand and musketoon
 So gallantly you come,
I read you for a bold Dragoon
 That lists the tuck of drum."
"I list no more the tuck of drum,
 No more the trumpet hear;
But when the beetle sounds his hum
 My comrades take the spear.
And O! though Brignall banks be fair
 And Greta woods be gay,
Yet mickle must the maiden dare
 Would reign my Queen of May!

"Maiden! a nameless life I lead,
 A nameless death I'll die;
The fiend, whose lantern lights the mead,
 Were better mate than I!
And when I'm with my comrades met
 Beneath the greenwood bough,—
What once we were we all forget,
 Nor think what we are now.
Yet Brignall banks are fresh and fair,
 And Greta woods are green,
And you may gather garlands there
 Would grace a summer queen."

*Walter Scott* [1771–1832]

## GLENARA

Oh, heard ye yon pibroch sound sad in the gale,
Where a band cometh slowly with weeping and wail?
'Tis the Chief of Glenara laments for his dear,
And her sire, and her people, are called to her bier.

Glenara came first with the mourners and shroud;
His kinsmen they followed, but mourned not aloud:
Their plaids all their bosoms were folded around;
They marched all in silence,—they looked on the ground

In silence they went, over mountain and moor,
To a heath, where the oak-tree grew lonely and hoar;
"Now here let us place the gray stone of her cairn:
Why speak ye no word?" said Glenara the stern.

"And tell me, I charge you, ye clan of my spouse,
Why fold ye your mantles, why cloud ye your brows?"
So spake the rude chieftain:—no answer is made,
But each mantle unfolding, a dagger displayed.

"I dreamt of my lady, I dreamt of her shroud,"
Cried a voice from the kinsmen, all wrathful and loud:
"And empty that shroud and that coffin did seem;
Glenara! Glenara! now read me my dream!"

Oh, pale grew the cheek of that chieftain, I ween,
When the shroud was unclosed and no lady was seen;
When a voice from the kinsmen spoke louder in scorn,—
'Twas the youth who had loved the fair Ellen of Lorn,—

"I dreamt of my lady, I dreamt of her grief;
I dreamt that her lord was a barbarous chief;
On a rock of the ocean fair Ellen did seem!
Glenara! Glenara! now read me my dream!"

In dust, low the traitor has knelt to the ground,
And the desert revealed where his lady was found;
From a rock of the ocean that beauty is borne,—
Now joy to the house of fair Ellen of Lorn!

*Thomas Campbell* [1777-1844]

## LORD ULLIN'S DAUGHTER

A CHIEFTAIN, to the Highlands bound,
Cries, "Boatman, do not tarry!
And I'll give thee a silver pound,
To row us o'er the ferry."

"Now who be ye, would cross Lochgyle,
This dark and stormy water?"
"O, I'm the chief of Ulva's Isle,
And this Lord Ullin's daughter.

"And fast before her father's men
Three days we've fled together,
For should he find us in the glen,
My blood would stain the heather.

"His horsemen hard behind us ride;
Should they our steps discover,
Then who will cheer my bonny bride
When they have slain her lover?"

Outspoke the hardy Highland wight,
"I'll go, my chief,—I'm ready:—
It is not for your silver bright;
But for your winsome lady:

"And by my word! the bonny bird
In danger shall not tarry:
So, though the waves are raging white
I'll row you o'er the ferry."

By this the storm grew loud apace,
The water-wraith was shrieking;
And in the scowl of heaven each face
Grew dark as they were speaking.

But still as wilder blew the wind,
And as the night grew drearer,
Adown the glen rode armèd men,—
Their trampling sounded nearer.

"O, haste thee, haste!" the lady cries,
"Though tempests round us gather;
I'll meet the raging of the skies,
But not an angry father."

The boat has left a stormy land,
A stormy sea before her,—
When, O, too strong for human hand,
The tempest gathered o'er her.

And still they rowed amidst the roar
Of waters fast prevailing:
Lord Ullin reached that fatal shore,—
His wrath was changed to wailing.

For sore dismayed, through storm and shade,
His child he did discover:
One lovely hand she stretched for aid,
And one was round her lover.

"Come back! come back!" he cried in grief,
"Across this stormy water:
And I'll forgive your Highland chief,
My daughter!—O my daughter!"

'Twas vain;—the loud waves lashed the shore,
Return or aid preventing;—
The waters wild went o'er his child,
And he was left lamenting.

*Thomas Campbell* [1777-1844]

## SIR GALAHAD

My good blade carves the casques of men,
My tough lance thrusteth sure,
My strength is as the strength of ten,
Because my heart is pure.

The shattering trumpet shrilleth high,
  The hard brands shiver on the steel,
The splintered spear-shafts crack and fly,
  The horse and rider reel:
They reel, they roll in clanging lists,
  And when the tide of combat stands,
Perfume and flowers fall in showers,
  That lightly rain from ladies' hands.

How sweet are looks that ladies bend
  On whom their favors fall!
For them I battle till the end,
  To save from shame and thrall:
But all my heart is drawn above,
  My knees are bowed in crypt and shrine:
I never felt the kiss of love,
  Nor maiden's hand in mine.
More bounteous aspects on me beam,
  Me mightier transports move and thrill;
So keep I fair through faith and prayer
  A virgin heart in work and will.

When down the stormy crescent goes,
  A light before me swims,
Between dark stems the forest glows,
  I hear a noise of hymns:
Then by some secret shrine I ride;
  I hear a voice, but none are there;
The stalls are void, the doors are wide.
  The tapers burning fair.
Fair gleams the snowy altar-cloth,
  The silver vessels sparkle clean,
The shrill bell rings, the censer swings,
  And solemn chaunts resound between.

Sometimes on lonely mountain-meres
  I find a magic bark;
I leap on board; no helmsman steers:
  I float till all is dark.

A gentle sound, an awful light!
  Three angels bear the Holy Grail:
With folded feet, in stoles of white,
  On sleeping wings they sail.
Ah, blessed vision! blood of God!
  My spirit beats her mortal bars,
As down dark tides the glory slides,
  And star-like mingles with the stars.

When on my goodly charger borne
  Through dreaming towns I go,
The cock crows ere the Christmas morn,
  The streets are dumb with snow.
The tempest crackles on the leads,
  And, ringing, springs from brand and mail;
But o'er the dark a glory spreads,
  And gilds the driving hail.
I leave the plain, I climb the height;
  No branchy thicket shelter yields;
But blessed forms in whistling storms
  Fly o'er waste fens and windy fields.

A maiden knight—to me is given
  Such hope, I know not fear;
I yearn to breathe the airs of heaven
  That often meet me here.
I muse on joy that will not cease,
  Pure spaces clothed in living beams,
Pure lilies of eternal peace,
  Whose odors haunt my dreams;
And, stricken by an angel's hand,
  This mortal armor that I wear,
This weight and size, this heart and eyes,
  Are touched, are turned to finest air.

The clouds are broken in the sky,
  And through the mountain-walls
A rolling organ-harmony
  Swells up, and shakes and falls.

Then move the trees, the copses nod,
 Wings flutter, voices hover clear:
"O just and faithful knight of God!
 Ride on! the prize is near."
So pass I hostel, hall, and grange;
 By bridge and ford, by park and pale,
All-armed I ride, whate'er betide,
 Until I find the Holy Grail.

*Alfred Tennyson* [1809-1892]

## LADY CLARE

It was the time when lilies blow,
 And clouds are highest up in air,
Lord Ronald brought a lily-white doe
 To give his cousin, Lady Clare.

I trow they did not part in scorn:
 Lovers long-betrothed were they:
They two will wed the morrow morn,—
 God's blessing on the day!

"He does not love me for my birth,
 Nor for my lands so broad and fair;
He loves me for my own true worth,
 And that is well," said Lady Clare.

In there came old Alice the nurse,
 Said, "Who was this that went from thee?"
"It was my cousin," said Lady Clare,
 "To-morrow he weds with me."

"O God be thanked!" said Alice the nurse,
 "That all comes round so just and fair:
Lord Ronald is heir of all your lands,
 And you are *not* the Lady Clare."

"Are ye out of your mind, my nurse, my nurse,"
 Said Lady Clare, "that ye speak so wild?"
"As God's above," said Alice the nurse,
 "I speak the truth: you are my child.

"The old earl's daughter died at my breast;
I speak the truth, as I live by bread!
I buried her like my own sweet child,
And put my child in her stead."

"Falsely, falsely have ye done,
O mother," she said, "if this be true,
To keep the best man under the sun
So many years from his due."

"Nay now, my child," said Alice the nurse,
"But keep the secret for your life,
And all you have will be Lord Ronald's,
When you are man and wife."

"If I'm a beggar born," she said,
"I will speak out, for I dare not lie.
Pull off, pull off, the brooch of gold,
And fling the diamond necklace by."

"Nay now, my child," said Alice the nurse,
"But keep the secret all you can."
She said, "Not so: but I will know
If there be any faith in man."

"Nay now, what faith?" said Alice the nurse,
"The man will cleave unto his right."
"And he shall have it," the lady replied,
"Though I should die to-night."

"Yet give one kiss to your mother dear
Alas, my child, I sinned for thee."
"O mother, mother, mother," she said,
" So strange it seems to me.

"Yet here's a kiss for my mother dear,
My mother dear, if this be so,
And lay your hand upon my head,
And bless me, mother, ere I go."

She clad herself in a russet gown,
  She was no longer Lady Clare:
She went by dale, and she went by down,
  With a single rose in her hair.

The lily-white doe Lord Ronald had brought
  Leaped up from where she lay,
Dropped her head in the maiden's hand,
  And followed her all the way.

Down stepped Lord Ronald from his tower:
  "O Lady Clare, you shame your worth!
Why come you dressed like a village maid,
  That are the flower of the earth?"

"If I come dressed like a village maid,
  I am but as my fortunes are:
I am a beggar born," she said,
  "And not the Lady Clare."

"Play me no tricks," said Lord Ronald,
  "For I am yours in word and in deed.
Play me no tricks," said Lord Ronald,
  "Your riddle is hard to read."

O, and proudly stood she up!
  Her heart within her did not fail;
She looked into Lord Ronald's eyes,
  And told him all her nurse's tale.

He laughed a laugh of merry scorn:
  He turned and kissed her where she stood:
"If you are not the heiress born,
  And I," said he, "the next in blood—

"If you are not the heiress born,
  And I," said he, "the lawful heir,
We two will wed to-morrow morn,
  And you shall still be Lady Clare."

*Alfred Tennyson* [1809–1892]

## GLENKINDIE

ABOUT Glenkindie and his man,
A false ballant hath long been writ;
Some bootless loon had written it,
Upon a bootless plan:
But I have found the true at last,
And here it is, so hold it fast!
'Twas made by a kind damosel
Who loved him and his man right well:

Glenkindie, best of harpers, came
Unbidden to our town;
And he was sad, and sad to see,
For love had worn him down.

It was love, as all men know,
The love that brought him down,
The hopeless love for the King's daughter,
The dove that heired a crown.

Now he wore not that collar of gold,
His dress was forest green,
His wondrous fair and rich mantle
Had lost its silvery sheen.

But still by his side walked Rafe, his boy,
In goodly cramoisie:
Of all the boys that ever I saw,
The goodliest boy was he.

O Rafe the page! O Rafe the page!
Ye stole the heart frae me:
O Rafe the page! O Rafe the page!
I wonder where ye be;
We ne'er may see Glenkindie more,
But may we never see thee?

Glenkindie came within the hall,
We set him on the dais,
And gave him bread, and gave him wine,
The best in all the place.

We set for him the guest's high chair,
  And spread the naperie:
Our Dame herself would serve for him,
  And I for Rafe, perdie!

But down he sat on a low, low stool,
  And thrust his long legs out,
And leaned his back to the high chair,
  And turned his harp about.

He turned it round, he stroked the strings,
  He touched each tirling-pin,
He put his mouth to the sounding-board
  And breathed his breath therein.

And Rafe sat over against his face,
  And looked at him wistfullie:
I almost grat ere he began,
  They were so sad to see.

The very first stroke he strack that day,
  We all came crowding near;
And the second stroke he strack that day,
  We all were smit with fear.

The third stroke that he strack that day,
  Full fain we were to cry;
The fourth stroke that he strack that day,
  We thought that we would die.

No tongue can tell how sweet it was,
  How far, and yet how near,
We saw the saints in Paradise,
  And bairnies on their bier.

And our sweet Dame saw her good lord—
  She told me privilie—
She saw him as she saw him last,
  On his ship upon the sea.

Anon he laid his little harp by,
He shut his wondrous eyes;
We stood a long time like dumb things,
Stood in a dumb surprise.

Then all at once we left that trance,
And shouted where we stood;
We clasped each other's hands and vowed
We would be wise and good.

Soon he rose up and Rafe rose too,
He drank wine and broke bread;
He clasped his hands with our trembling Dame,
But never a word he said.
They went,—Alack and lack-a-day!
They went the way they came.

I followed them all down the floor,
And oh but I had drouth
To touch his cheek, to touch his hand,
To kiss Rafe's velvet mouth!

But I knew such was not for me.
They went straight from the door;
We saw them fade within the mist,
And never saw them more.

*William Bell Scott* [1811–1890]

## "HOW THEY BROUGHT THE GOOD NEWS FROM GHENT TO AIX"

[16—]

I SPRANG to the stirrup, and Joris, and he;
I galloped, Dirck galloped, we galloped all three;
"Good speed!" cried the watch, as the gate-bolts undrew;
"Speed!" echoed the wall to us galloping through;
Behind shut the postern, the lights sank to rest,
And into the midnight we galloped abreast.

Not a word to each other; we kept the great pace
Neck by neck, stride by stride, never changing our place;
I turned in my saddle and made its girths tight,
Then shortened each stirrup, and set the pique right,
Rebuckled the cheek-strap, chained slacker the bit,
Nor galloped less steadily Roland a whit.

'Twas moonset at starting; but while we drew near
Lokeren, the cocks crew and twilight dawned clear;
At Boom, a great yellow star came out to see;
At Düffeld, 'twas morning as plain as could be;
And from Mecheln church-steeple we heard the half-chime,
So Joris broke silence with, "Yet there is time!"

At Aershot, up leaped of a sudden the sun,
And against him the cattle stood black every one,
To stare through the mist at us galloping past,
And I saw my stout galloper Roland at last
With resolute shoulders, each butting away
The haze, as some bluff river headland its spray:

And his low head and crest, just one sharp ear bent back
For my voice, and the other pricked out on his track;
And one eye's black intelligence,—ever that glance
O'er its white edge at me, his own master, askance!
And the thick heavy spume-flakes which aye and anon
His fierce lips shook upwards in galloping on.

By Hasselt, Dirck groaned; and cried Joris "Stay spur!
Your Roos galloped bravely, the fault's not in her,
We'll remember at Aix"—for one heard the quick wheeze
Of her chest, saw the stretched neck and staggering knees,
And sunk tail, and horrible heave of the flank,
As down on her haunches she shuddered and sank.

So, we were left galloping, Joris and I,
Past Looz and past Tongres, no cloud in the sky;
The broad sun above laughed a pitiless laugh,
'Neath our feet broke the brittle bright stubble like chaff;
Till over by Dalhem a dome-spire sprang white,
And "Gallop," gasped Joris, "for Aix is in sight!

"How they'll greet us!"—and all in a moment his roan
Rolled neck and croup over, lay dead as a stone;
And there was my Roland to bear the whole weight
Of the news which alone could save Aix from her fate,
With his nostrils like pits full of blood to the brim,
And with circles of red for his eye-sockets' rim.

Then I cast loose my buffcoat, each holster let fall,
Shook off both my jack-boots, let go belt and all,
Stood up in the stirrup, leaned, patted his ear,
Called my Roland his pet-name, my horse without peer;
Clapped my hands, laughed and sang, any noise, bad or
good,
Till at length into Aix Roland galloped and stood.

And all I remember is,—friends flocking round
As I sat with his head 'twixt my knees on the ground;
And no voice but was praising this Roland of mine,
As I poured down his throat our last measure of wine,
Which (the burgesses voted by common consent)
Was no more than his due who brought good news from
Ghent.

*Robert Browning* [1812–1889]

## THE OLD SCOTTISH CAVALIER

Come listen to another song,
Should make your heart beat high,
Bring crimson to your forehead,
And the luster to your eye;—
It is the song of the olden time,
Of days long since gone by,
And of a Baron stout and bold
As e'er wore sword on thigh!
Like a brave old Scottish cavalier,
All of the olden time!

He kept his castle in the north,
Hard by the thundering Spey;
And a thousand vassals dwelt around,
All of his kindred they.

And not a man of all that clan
Had ever ceased to pray
For the Royal race they loved so well,
Though exiled far away
From the steadfast Scottish cavaliers,
All of the olden time!

His father drew the righteous sword
For Scotland and her claims,
Among the loyal gentlemen
And chiefs of ancient names,
Who swore to fight or fall beneath
The standard of King James,
And died at Killiecrankie Pass
With the glory of the Græmes;
Like a true old Scottish cavalier
All of the olden time!

He never owned the foreign rule,
No master he obeyed,
But kept his clan in peace at home,
From foray and from raid;
And when they asked him for his oath,
He touched his glittering blade,
And pointed to his bonnet blue,
That bore the white cockade:
Like a leal old Scottish cavalier,
All of the olden time!

At length the news ran through the land—
THE PRINCE had come again!
That night the fiery cross was sped
O'er mountain and through glen;
And our old Baron rose in might,
Like a lion from his den,
And rode away across the hills
To Charlie and his men,
With the valiant Scottish cavaliers,
All of the olden time!

He was the first that bent the knee
  When the STANDARD waved abroad,
He was the first that charged the foe
  On Preston's bloody sod;
And ever, in the van of fight,
  The foremost still he trod,
Until on bleak Culloden's heath,
  He gave his soul to God,
    Like a good old Scottish cavalier,
      All of the olden time!

Oh, never shall we know again
  A heart so stout and true—
The olden times have passed away,
  And weary are the new:
The fair White Rose has faded
  From the garden where it grew,
And no fond tears, save those of heaven,
  The glorious bed bedew
    Of the last old Scottish cavalier
      All of the olden time!

*William Edmondstoune Aytoun* [1813–1865]

## THE BALLAD OF KEITH OF RAVELSTON

From "A Nuptial Eve"

THE murmur of the mourning ghost
  That keeps the shadowy kine,
"O Keith of Ravelston,
  The sorrows of thy line!"

Ravelston, Ravelston,
  The merry path that leads
Down the golden morning hill,
  And through the silver meads;

Ravelston, Ravelston,
  The stile beneath the tree,
The maid that kept her mother's kine,
  The song that sang she!

She sang her song, she kept her kine,
  She sat beneath the thorn,
When Andrew Keith of Ravelston
  Rode through the Monday morn.

His henchmen sing, his hawk-bells ring,
  His belted jewels shine;
O Keith of Ravelston,
  The sorrows of thy line!

Year after year, where Andrew came,
  Comes evening down the glade,
And still there sits a moonshine ghost
  Where sat the sunshine maid.

Her misty hair is faint and fair,
  She keeps the shadowy kine;
O Keith of Ravelston,
  The sorrows of thy line!

I lay my hand upon the stile,
  The stile is lone and cold,
The burnie that goes babbling by
  Says naught that can be told.

Yet, stranger! here, from year to year,
  She keeps her shadowy kine;
O Keith of Ravelston,
  The sorrows of thy line!

Step out three steps, where Andrew stood—
  Why blanch thy cheeks for fear?
The ancient stile is not alone,
  'Tis not the burn I hear!

She makes her immemorial moan,
  She keeps her shadowy kine;
O Keith of Ravelston,
  The sorrows of thy line!

*Sydney Dobell* [1824-1874]

## THE MISTLETOE BOUGH

THE mistletoe hung in the castle hall,
The holly branch shone on the old oak wall;
And the baron's retainers were blithe and gay,
And keeping their Christmas holiday.
The baron beheld with a father's pride
His beautiful child, young Lovell's bride;
While she with her bright eyes seemed to be
The star of the goodly company.

"I'm weary of dancing now," she cried;
"Here tarry a moment,—I'll hide, I'll hide!
And, Lovell, be sure thou'rt first to trace
The clew to my secret lurking-place."
Away she ran,—and her friends began
Each tower to search, and each nook to scan;
And young Lovell cried, "O, where dost thou hide?
I'm lonesome without thee, my own dear bride."

They sought her that night, and they sought her next day,
And they sought her in vain while a week passed away;
In the highest, the lowest, the loneliest spot,
Young Lovell sought wildly,—but found her not.
And years flew by, and their grief at last
Was told as a sorrowful tale long past;
And when Lovell appeared, the children cried,
"See! the old man weeps for his fairy bride."

At length an oak chest, that had long lain hid,
Was found in the castle,—they raised the lid,
And a skeleton form lay moldering there
In the bridal wreath of that lady fair!
O, sad was her fate!—in sportive jest
She hid from her lord in the old oak chest.
It closed with a spring!—and, dreadful doom,
The bride lay clasped in her living tomb!

*Thomas Haynes Bayly* [1797-1839]

## THE ABBOT OF INISFALEN

I

THE Abbot of Inisfalen
  Awoke ere dawn of day;
Under the dewy green leaves
  Went he forth to pray.

The lake around his island
  Lay smooth and dark and deep,
And, wrapped in a misty stillness,
  The mountains were all asleep.

Low kneeled the Abbot Cormac,
  When the dawn was dim and gray;
The prayers of his holy office
  He faithfully 'gan say.

Low kneeled the Abbot Cormac,
  When the dawn was waxing red,
And for his sins' forgiveness
  A solemn prayer he said.

Low kneeled that holy Abbot
  When the dawn was waxing clear;
And he prayed with loving-kindness
  For his convent brethren dear.

Low kneeled that blessed Abbot,
  When the dawn was waxing bright;
He prayed a great prayer for Ireland,
  He prayed with all his might.

Low kneeled that good old father,
  While the sun began to dart;
He prayed a prayer for all mankind.
  He prayed it from his heart.

II

The Abbot of Inisfalen
  Arose upon his feet;
He heard a small bird singing,
  And, oh, but it sung sweet!

He heard a white bird singing well
  Within a holly-tree;
A song so sweet and happy
  Never before heard he.

It sung upon a hazel,
  It sung upon a thorn;
He had never heard such music
  Since the hour that he was born.

It sung upon a sycamore,
  It sung upon a briar;
To follow the song and hearken
  This Abbot could never tire.

Till at last he well bethought him
  He might no longer stay;
So he blessed the little white singing-bird,
  And gladly went his way.

III

But when he came to his Abbey walls,
  He found a wondrous change;
He saw no friendly faces there,
  For every face was strange.

The stranger spoke unto him;
  And he heard from all and each
The foreign tone of the Sassenach,
  Not wholesome Irish speech.

Then the oldest monk came forward,
  In Irish tongue spake he:
"Thou wearest the holy Augustine's dress
  And who hath given it thee?"

"I wear the holy Augustine's dress,
And Cormac is my name,
The Abbot of this good Abbey
By grace of God I am.

"I went forth to pray, at the dawn of day;
And when my prayers were said,
I hearkened awhile to a little bird
That sung above my head."

The monks to him made answer,
"Two hundred years have gone o'er,
Since our Abbot Cormac went through the gate,
And never was heard of more.

"Matthias now is our Abbot,
And twenty have passed away.
The stranger is lord of Ireland;
We live in an evil day."

IV

"Now give me absolution;
For my time is come," said he.
And they gave him absolution
As speedily as might be.

Then, close outside the window,
The sweetest song they heard
That ever yet since the world began
Was uttered by any bird.

The monks looked out and saw the bird,
Its feathers all white and clean;
And there in a moment, beside it,
Another white bird was seen.

Those two they sang together,
Waved their white wings, and fled;
Flew aloft, and vanished;
But the good old man was dead.

They buried his blessed body
  Where lake and greensward meet;
A carven cross above his head,
  A holly-bush at his feet;

Where spreads the beautiful water
  To gay or cloudy skies,
And the purple peaks of Killarney
  From ancient woods arise.

*William Allingham* [1824-1889]

## THE CAVALIER'S ESCAPE

TRAMPLE! trample! went the roan,
  Trap! trap! went the gray;
But pad! *pad!* PAD! like a thing that was mad,
  My chestnut broke away.
It was just five miles from Salisbury town,
  And but one hour to day.

Thud! THUD! came on the heavy roan,
  Rap! RAP! the mettled gray;
But my chestnut mare was of blood so rare,
  That she showed them all the way.
Spur on! spur on!—I doffed my hat,
  And wished them all good-day.

They splashed through miry rut and pool,—
  Splintered through fence and rail;
But chestnut Kate switched over the gate,—
  I saw them droop and trail.
To Salisbury town—but a mile of down,
  Once over this brook and rail.

Trap! trap! I heard their echoing hoofs
  Past the walls of mossy stone;
The roan flew on at a staggering pace,
  But blood is better than bone.
I patted old Kate, and gave her the spur,
  For I knew it was all my own.

But trample! trample! came their steeds,
And I saw their wolf's eyes burn;
I felt like a royal hart at bay,
And made me ready to turn.
I looked where highest grew the may,
And deepest arched the fern.

I flew at the first knave's sallow throat;
One blow, and he was down.
The second rogue fired twice, and missed;
I sliced the villain's crown,—
Clove through the rest, and flogged brave Kate,
*Fast, fast to Salisbury town!*

Pad! pad! they came on the level sward,
Thud! thud! upon the sand,—
With a gleam of swords and a burning match,
And a shaking of flag and hand;
But one long bound, and I passed the gate,
Safe from the canting band.

*Walter Thornbury* [1828–1876]

## THE THREE TROOPERS

### DURING THE PROTECTORATE

INTO the Devil tavern
Three booted troopers strode,
From spur to feather spotted and splashed
With the mud of a winter road.
In each of their cups they dropped a crust,
And stared at the guests with a frown;
And drew their swords, and roared for a toast,
"God send this Crum-well-down!"

A blue smoke rose from their pistol locks,
Their sword blades were still wet;
There were long red smears on their jerkins of buff,
As the table they overset.

Then into their cups they stirred the crusts,
  And cursed old London town;
Then waved their swords, and drank with a stamp,
  "God send this Crum-well-down!"

The 'prentice dropped his can of beer,
  The host turned pale as a clout;
The ruby nose of the toping squire
  Grew white at the wild men's shout.
Then into their cups they flung the crusts,
  And showed their teeth with a frown;
They flashed their swords as they gave the toast,
  "God send this Crum-well-down!"

The gambler dropped his dog's-eared cards,
  The waiting-women screamed,
As the light of the fire, like stains of blood,
  On the wild men's sabers gleamed.
Then into their cups they splashed the crusts,
  And cursed the fool of a town,
And leaped on the table, and roared a toast,
  "God send this Crum-well-down!"

Till on a sudden fire-bells rang,
  And the troopers sprang to horse;
The eldest muttered between his teeth,
  Hot curses—deep and coarse.
In their stirrup cups they flung the crusts,
  And cried as they spurred through the town,
With their keen swords drawn and their pistols cocked,
  "God send this Crum-well-down!"

Away they dashed through Temple Bar,
  Their red cloaks flowing free,
Their scabbards clashed, each back-piece shone—
  None liked to touch the three.
The silver cups that held the crusts
  They flung to the startled town,
Shouting again, with a blaze of swords,
  "God send this Crum-well-down!"

*Walter Thornbury* [1828-1876]

## THE SALLY FROM COVENTRY

"PASSION o' me!" cried Sir Richard Tyrone,
Spurning the sparks from the broad paving-stone,
"Better turn nurse and rock children to sleep,
Than yield to a rebel old Coventry Keep.
No, by my halidom, no one shall say,
Sir Richard Tyrone gave a city away!"

Passion o' me! how he pulled at his beard!
Fretting and chafing if any one sneered,
Clapping his breastplate and shaking his fist,
Giving his grizzly moustachios a twist,
Running the protocol through with his steel,
Grinding the letter to mud with his heel.

Then he roared out for a pottle of sack,
Clapped the old trumpeter twice on the back,
Leaped on his bay with a dash and a swing,
Bade all the bells in the city to ring,
And when the red flag from the steeple went down,
Open they flung every gate in the town.

To boot! and to horse! and away like a flood,
A fire in their eyes, and a sting in their blood;
Hurrying out with a flash and a flare,
A roar of hot guns, a loud trumpeter's blare,
And first, sitting proud as a king on his throne,
At the head of them all dashed Sir Richard Tyrone.

Crimson, and yellow, and purple, and dun,
Fluttering scarf, flowing bright in the sun,
Steel like a mirror on brow and on breast,
Scarlet and white on their feather and crest,
Banner that blew in a torrent of red,
Borne by Sir Richard, who rode at their head.

The "trumpet" went down—with a gash on his poll,
Struck by the parters of body and soul.
Forty saddles were empty; the horses ran red
With foul Puritan blood from the slashes that bled.

Curses and cries and a gnashing of teeth,
A grapple and stab on the slippery heath,
And Sir Richard leaped up on the fool that went down,
Proud as a conqueror donning his crown.

They broke them away through a flooding of fire,
Trampling the best blood of London to mire,
When suddenly rising a smoke and a blaze,
Made all "the dragon's sons" stare in amaze:
"O ho!" quoth Sir Richard, "my city grows hot:
I've left it rent-paid to the villainous Scot!"

*Walter Thornbury* [1828–1876]

## SHAMEFUL DEATH

THERE were four of us about that bed;
 The mass-priest knelt at the side,
I and his mother stood at the head,
 Over his feet lay the bride;
We were quite sure that he was dead,
 Though his eyes were open wide.

He did not die in the night,
 He did not die in the day,
But in the morning twilight
 His spirit passed away;
When neither sun nor moon was bright,
 And the trees were merely gray.

He was not slain with the sword,
 Knight's axe, or the knightly spear,
Yet spoke he never a word
 After he came in here;
I cut away the cord
 From the neck of my brother dear.

He did not strike one blow,
 For the recreants came behind,
In a place where the hornbeams grow,
 A path right hard to find,
For the hornbeam boughs swing so
 That the twilight makes it blind.

They lighted a great torch then,
When his arms were pinioned fast;
Sir John, the Knight of the Fen,
Sir Guy, of the Dolorous Blast,
With knights threescore and ten,
Hung brave Sir Hugh at last.

I am threescore and ten,
And my hair is all turned gray,
But I met Sir John of the Fen
Long ago on a summer day,
And am glad to think of the moment when
I took his life away.

I am threescore and ten,
And my strength is mostly passed,
But long ago I and my men,
When the sky was overcast,
And the smoke rolled over the reeds of the fen,
Slew Guy of the Dolorous Blast.

And now, Knights, all of you,
I pray you, pray for Sir Hugh,
A good knight and a true,
And for Alice, his wife, pray too.

*William Morris* [1834-1896]

## THE RIME OF THE ANCIENT MARINER

### ARGUMENT

How a Ship, having passed the Line, was driven by storms to the cold Country towards the South Pole; and how from thence she made her course to the tropical Latitude of the Great Pacific Ocean; and of the strange things that befell; and in what manner the Ancyent Marinere came back to his own Country.

### PART I

**An ancient Mariner meeteth three gallants bidden to a wedding-feast, and detaineth one.**

It is an ancient Mariner,
And he stoppeth one of three.
"By thy long gray beard and glittering eye,
Now wherefore stopp'st thou me?

"The Bridegroom's doors are opened wide,
And I am next of kin;
The guests are met, the feast is set:
May'st hear the merry din."

He holds him with his skinny hand,
"There was a ship," quoth he.
"Hold off! unhand me, gray-beard loon!"
Eftsoons his hand dropped he.

The Wedding-Guest is spellbound by the eye of the old seafaring man, and constrained to hear his tale.

He holds him with his glittering eye—
The Wedding-Guest stood still,
And listens like a three years' child:
The Mariner hath his will.

The Wedding-Guest sat on a stone:
He cannot choose but hear;
And thus spake on that ancient man,
The bright-eyed Mariner.

"The ship was cheered, the harbor cleared,
Merrily did we drop
Below the kirk, below the hill,
Below the lighthouse top.

The Mariner tells how the ship sailed southward with a good wind and fair weather, till it reached the Line.

"The Sun came up upon the left,
Out of the sea came he!
And he shone bright, and on the right
Went down into the sea.

"Higher and higher every day,
Till over the mast at noon——"
The Wedding-Guest here beat his breast,
For he heard the loud bassoon.

The Wedding-Guest heareth the bridal music; but the Mariner continueth his tale.

The bride hath paced into the hall,
Red as a rose is she;
Nodding their heads before her goes
The merry minstrelsy.

The Wedding-Guest he beat his breast,
Yet he cannot choose but hear;
And thus spake on that ancient man,
The bright-eyed Mariner.

"And now the Storm-blast came, and he
Was tyrannous and strong:
He struck with his o'ertaking wings,
And chased us south along.

**The ship driven by a storm toward the South Pole.**

"With sloping masts and dipping prow,
As who pursued with yell and blow
Still treads the shadow of his foe,
And forward bends his head,
The ship drove fast, loud roared the blast,
And southward aye we fled.

"And now there came both mist and snow,
And it grew wondrous cold:
And ice, mast-high, came floating by,
As green as emerald.

"And through the drifts the snowy clifts
Did send a dismal sheen:
Nor shapes of men, nor beasts we ken—
The ice was all between.

**The land of ice, and of fearful sounds, where no living thing was to be seen.**

"The ice was here, the ice was there,
The ice was all around:
It cracked and growled, and roared and howled,
Like noises in a swound!

"At length did cross an Albatross,
Thorough the fog it came;
As if it had been a Christian soul,
We hailed it in God's name.

**Till a great sea-bird, called the Albatross, came through the snow-fog, and was received with great joy and hospitality.**

"It ate the food it ne'er had eat,
And round and round it flew.
The ice did split with a thunder-fit;
The helmsman steered us through!

And lo! the Albatross proveth a bird of good omen, and followeth the ship as it returned northward through fog and floating ice.

"And a good south wind sprung up behind;
The Albatross did follow,
And every day, for food or play,
Came to the mariners' hollo!

"In mist or cloud, on mast or shroud,
It perched for vespers nine;
Whiles all the night, through fog-smoke white,
Glimmered the white moonshine."

The ancient Mariner inhospitably killeth the pious bird of good omen.

"God save thee, ancient Mariner,
From the fiends, that plague thee thus!—
Why look'st thou so?" "With my crossbow
I shot the Albatross.

### PART II

"The Sun now rose upon the right:
Out of the sea came he,
Still hid in mist, and on the left
Went down into the sea.

"And the good south wind still blew behind,
But no sweet bird did follow,
Nor any day for food or play
Came to the mariners' hollo!

His shipmates cry out against the ancient Mariner for killing the bird of good luck.

"And I had done a hellish thing,
And it would work 'em woe:
For all averred I had killed the bird
That made the breeze to blow.
Ah wretch! said they, the bird to slay,
That made the breeze to blow!

But when the fog cleared off, they justify the same, and thus make themselves accomplices in the crime.

"Nor dim nor red, like God's own head,
The glorious Sun uprist:
Then all averred I had killed the bird
That brought the fog and mist.
'Twas right, said they, such birds to slay,
That bring the fog and mist.

"The fair breeze blew, the white foam flew,
The furrow followed free;
We were the first that ever burst
Into that silent sea.

The fair breeze continues; the ship enters the Pacific Ocean, and sails northward, even till it reaches the Line.

"Down dropped the breeze, the sails dropped down,
'Twas sad as sad could be;
And we did speak only to break
The silence of the sea!

The ship hath been suddenly becalmed.

"All in a hot and copper sky,
The bloody Sun, at noon,
Right up above the mast did stand,
No bigger than the Moon.

"Day after day, day after day,
We stuck, nor breath nor motion;
As idle as a painted ship
Upon a painted ocean.

"Water, water, everywhere,
And all the boards did shrink;
Water, water, everywhere,
Nor any drop to drink.

And the Albatross begins to be avenged.

"The very deep did rot: O Christ!
That ever this should be!
Yea, slimy things did crawl with legs
Upon the slimy sea.

"About, about, in reel and rout
The death-fires danced at night;
The water, like a witch's oils,
Burnt green, and blue, and white.

"And some in dreams assurèd were
Of the Spirit that plagued us so;
Nine fathom deep he had followed us
From the land of mist and snow.

A Spirit had followed them; one of the invisible inhabitants of this planet, neither departed souls nor angels; concerning whom the learned Jew, Josephus, and the Platonic Constantinopolitan Michael Psellus, may be consulted. They are very numerous, and there is no climate or element without one or more.

"And every tongue, through utter drought,
Was withered at the root;
We could not speak, no more than if
We had been choked with soot.

The shipmates in their sore distress, would fain throw the whole guilt on the ancient Mariner: in sign whereof they hang the dead sea-bird round his neck.

"Ah! well-a-day! what evil looks
Had I from old and young!
Instead of the cross, the Albatross
About my neck was hung.

PART III

"There passed a weary time. Each throat
Was parched, and glazed each eye.
A weary time! a weary time!
How glazed each weary eye!
When looking westward, I beheld
A something in the sky.

The ancient Mariner beholdeth a sign in the element afar off.

"At first it seemed a little speck,
And then it seemed a mist;
It moved and moved, and took at last
A certain shape, I wist.

"A speck, a mist, a shape, I wist!
And still it neared and neared:
As if it dodged a water-sprite,
It plunged, and tacked, and veered.

At its nearer approach, it seemeth him to be a ship; and at a dear ransom he freeth his speech from the bonds of thirst.

"With throats unslaked, with black lips baked,
We could nor laugh nor wail;
Through utter drought all dumb we stood!
I bit my arm, I sucked the blood,
And cried, A sail! a sail!

"With throats unslaked, with black lips baked,
Agape they heard me call:
Gramercy! they for joy did grin,
And all at once their breath drew in,
As they were drinking all.

A flash of joy;

"See! see! (I cried) she tacks no more
Hither to work us weal—
Without a breeze, without a tide,
She steadies with upright keel!

And horror follows. For can it be a ship that comes onward without wind or tide?

"The western wave was all aflame,
The day was wellnigh done!
Almost upon the western wave
Rested the broad, bright Sun;
When that strange shape drove suddenly
Betwixt us and the Sun.

"And straight the Sun was flecked with bars
(Heaven's Mother send us grace!),
As if through a dungeon-grate he peered
With broad and burning face.

It seemeth him but the skeleton of a ship.

"Alas! (thought I, and my heart beat loud)
How fast she nears and nears!
Are those her sails that glance in the Sun,
Like restless gossameres?

"Are those her ribs through which the Sun
Did peer, as through a grate?
And is that Woman all her crew?
Is that a Death? and are there two?
Is Death that Woman's mate?

And its ribs are seen as bars on the face of the setting Sun. The Specter-Woman and her Death-mate, and no other, on board the skeleton ship. Like vessel, like crew!

"Her lips were red, her looks were free,
Her locks were yellow as gold:
Her skin was as white as leprosy,
The Nightmare Life-in-Death was she,
Who thicks man's blood with cold.

"The naked hulk alongside came,
And the twain were casting dice;
'The game is done! I've won! I've won!'
Quoth she, and whistles thrice.

Death and Life-in-Death have diced for the ship's crew, and she (the latter) winneth the ancient Mariner.

No twilight within the courts of the Sun.

"The Sun's rim dips; the stars rush out
At one stride comes the dark;
With far-heard whisper, o'er the sea,
Off shot the specter-bark.

"We listened and looked sideways up!
Fear at my heart, as at a cup,
My life-blood seemed to sip!
The stars were dim, and thick the night,
The steersman's face by his lamp gleamed white
From the sails the dew did drip—

At the rising of the Moon,

Till clomb above the eastern bar
The hornèd Moon, with one bright star
Within the nether tip.

One after another,

"One after one, by the star-dogged Moon,
Too quick for groan or sigh,
Each turned his face with a ghastly pang,
And cursed me with his eye.

His shipmates drop down dead.

"Four times fifty living men
(And I heard nor sigh nor groan),
With heavy thump, a lifeless lump,
They dropped down one by one.

But Life-in-Death begins her work on the ancient Mariner.

"The souls did from their bodies fly—
They fled to bliss or woe!
And every soul, it passed me by
Like the whizz of my crossbow!"

PART IV

The Wedding-Guest feareth that a spirit is talking to him.

"I fear thee, ancient Mariner!
I fear thy skinny hand!
And thou art long, and lank, and brown,
As is the ribbed sea-sand.

But the ancient Mariner assureth him of his bodily life, and proceedeth to relate his horrible penance.

"I fear thee and thy glittering eye,
And thy skinny hand so brown."—
"Fear not, fear not, thou Wedding-Guest!
This body dropped not down.

"Alone, alone, all, all alone,
Alone on a wide, wide sea!
And never a saint took pity on
My soul in agony.

"The many men, so beautiful!
And they all dead did lie:
And a thousand thousand slimy things
Lived on; and so did I.

**He despiseth the creatures of the calm.**

"I looked upon the rotting sea,
And drew my eyes away;
I looked upon the rotting deck,
And there the dead men lay.

**And envieth that they should live, and so many be dead.**

"I looked to heaven, and tried to pray;
But or ever a prayer had gushed,
A wicked whisper came, and made
My heart as dry as dust.

"I closed my lids, and kept them close,
And the balls like pulses beat;
For the sky and the sea, and the sea and the sky,
Lay like a load on my weary eye,
And the dead were at my feet.

"The cold sweat melted from their limbs,
Nor rot nor reek did they:
The look with which they looked on me
Had never passed away.

**But the curse liveth for him in the eyes of the dead men.**

"An orphan's curse would drag to hell
A spirit from on high;
But oh! more horrible than that
Is a curse in a dead man's eye!
Seven days, seven nights, I saw that curse,
And yet I could not die.

"The moving Moon went up the sky,
And nowhere did abide;
Softly she was going up,
And a star or two beside—

**In his loneliness and fixedness he yearneth towards the journeying Moon, and the stars that still sojourn, yet still move onward; and everywhere the blue sky belongs to them, and is their appointed rest and their native country and their own natural homes, which they enter unannounced, as lords that are certainly expected, and yet there is a silent joy at their arrival.**

"Her beams bemocked the sultry main,
Like April hoar-frost spread;
But where the ship's huge shadow lay,
The charmèd water burnt alway
A still and awful red.

By the light of the Moon he beholdeth God's creatures of the great calm.

"Beyond the shadow of the ship,
I watched the water-snakes:
They moved in tracks of shining white,
And when they reared, the elfish light
Fell off in hoary flakes.

"Within the shadow of the ship
I watched their rich attire:
Blue, glossy green, and velvet black,
They coiled and swam; and every track
Was a flash of golden fire.

Their beauty and their happiness.

"O happy living things! no tongue
Their beauty might declare:
A spring of love gushed from my heart,
And I blessed them unaware:
Sure my kind saint took pity on me,
And I blessed them unaware.

He blesseth them in his heart.

The spell begins to break.

"The selfsame moment I could pray;
And from my neck so free
The Albatross fell off, and sank
Like lead into the sea.

PART V

"O sleep! it is a gentle thing,
Beloved from pole to pole!
To Mary Queen the praise be given!
She sent the gentle sleep from Heaven,
That slid into my soul.

By grace of the Holy Mother, the ancient Mariner is refreshed with rain.

"The silly buckets on the deck,
That had so long remained,
I dreamt that they were filled with dew;
And when I awoke, it rained.

"My lips were wet, my throat was cold,
My garments all were dank;
Sure I had drunken in my dreams,
And still my body drank.

"I moved, and could not feel my limbs:
I was so light—almost
I thought that I had died in sleep,
And was a blessed ghost.

"And soon I heard a roaring wind:
It did not come anear;
But with its sound it shook the sails,
That were so thin and sere.

**He heareth sounds and seeth strange sights and commotions in the sky and the element.**

"The upper air burst into life;
And a hundred fire-flags sheen;
To and fro they were hurried about;
And to and fro, and in and out,
The wan stars danced between.

"And the coming wind did roar more loud,
And the sails did sigh like sedge;
And the rain poured down from one black cloud;
The Moon was at its edge.

"The thick black cloud was cleft, and still
The Moon was at its side;
Like waters shot from some high crag,
The lightning fell with never a jag,
A river steep and wide.

"The loud wind never reached the ship,
Yet now the ship moved on!
Beneath the lightning and the Moon
The dead men gave a groan.

**The bodies of the ship's crew are inspired, and the ship moves on;**

"They groaned, they stirred, they all uprose,
Nor spake, nor moved their eyes;
It had been strange, even in a dream,
To have seen those dead men rise.

"The helmsman steered, the ship moved on;
Yet never a breeze up-blew;
The mariners all 'gan work the ropes,
Where they were wont to do;
They raised their limbs like lifeless tools—
We were a ghastly crew.

"The body of my brother's son
Stood by me, knee to knee:
The body and I pulled at one rope,
But he said naught to me."

But not by the souls of the men, nor by demons of earth or middle air, but by a blessed troop of angelic spirits, sent down by the invocation of the guardian saint.

"I fear thee, ancient Mariner!"
"Be calm, thou Wedding-Guest:
'Twas not those souls that fled in pain,
Which to their corses came again,
But a troop of spirits blest:

"For when it dawned—they dropped their arms,
And clustered round the mast;
Sweet sounds rose slowly through their mouths,
And from their bodies passed.

"Around, around, flew each sweet sound,
Then darted to the Sun;
Slowly the sounds came back again,
Now mixed, now one by one.

"Sometimes a-dropping from the sky
I heard the skylark sing;
Sometimes all little birds that are,
How they seemed to fill the sea and air
With their sweet jargoning!

"And now 'twas like all instruments,
Now like a lonely flute;
And now it is an angel's song,
That makes the Heavens be mute.

"It ceased: yet still the sails made on
A pleasant noise till noon,
A noise like of a hidden brook
In the leafy month of June,
That to the sleeping woods all night
Singeth a quiet tune.

"Till noon we quietly sailed on,
Yet never a breeze did breathe:
Slowly and smoothly went the ship,
Moved onward from beneath.

"Under the keel nine fathom deep,
From the land of mist and snow,
The Spirit slid: and it was he
That made the ship to go.
The sails at noon left off their tune,
And the ship stood still also.

The lonesome Spirit from the South Pole carries on the ship as far as the Line, in obedience to the angelic troop, but still requireth vengeance.

"The Sun, right up above the mast,
Had fixed her to the ocean:
But in a minute she 'gan stir,
With a short uneasy motion—
Backwards and forwards half her length
With a short uneasy motion.

"Then like a pawing horse let go,
She made a sudden bound:
It flung the blood into my head,
And I fell down in a swound.

**The Polar Spirit's fellow-demons, the invisible inhabitants of the element, take part in his wrong; and two of them relate, one to the other, that penance long and heavy for the ancient Mariner hath been accorded to the Polar Spirit, who returneth southward.**

"How long in that same fit I lay,
I have not to declare;
But ere my living life returned,
I heard, and in my soul discerned
Two voices in the air.

"'Is it he?' quoth one, 'is this the man?
By Him who died on cross,
With his cruel bow he laid full low
The harmless Albatross.

"'The Spirit who bideth by himself
In the land of mist and snow,
He loved the bird that loved the man
Who shot him with his bow.'

"The other was a softer voice,
As soft as honey-dew:
Quoth he, 'The man hath penance done,
And penance more will do.'

**PART VI**

*First Voice:*
"'But tell me, tell me! speak again,
Thy soft response renewing—
What makes that ship drive on so fast?
What is the Ocean doing?'

*Second Voice:*
" 'Still as a slave before his lord,
The Ocean hath no blast;
His great bright eye most silently
Up to the Moon is cast—

" 'If he may know which way to go;
For she guides him smooth or grim.
See, brother, see! how graciously
She looketh down on him.'

*First Voice:*
" 'But why drives on that ship so fast,
Without or wave or wind?'

The Mariner hath been cast into a trance; for the angelic power causeth the vessel to drive northward faster than human life could endure.

*Second Voice:*
" 'The air is cut away before,
And closes from behind.

" 'Fly, brother, fly! more high, more high
Or we shall be belated:
For slow and slow that ship will go,
When the Mariner's trance is abated "

"I woke, and we were sailing on
As in a gentle weather:
'Twas night, calm night, the Moon was high;
The dead men stood together.

The supernatural motion is retarded; the Mariner awakes, and his penance begins anew.

"All stood together on the deck,
For a charnel-dungeon fitter:
All fixed on me their stony eyes,
That in the Moon did glitter.

"The pang, the curse, with which they died,
Had never passed away:
I could not draw my eyes from theirs,
Nor turn them up to pray.

"And now this spell was snapped: once more
I viewed the ocean green,
And looked far forth, yet little saw
Of what had else been seen—

The curse is finally expiated.

"Like one that on a lonesome road
Doth walk in fear and dread,
And having once turned round, walks on,
And turns no more his head;
Because he knows a frightful fiend
Doth close behind him tread.

"But soon there breathed a wind on me,
Nor sound nor motion made:
Its path was not upon the sea,
In ripple or in shade.

"It raised my hair, it fanned my cheek
Like a meadow-gale of spring—
It mingled strangely with my fears,
Yet it felt like a welcoming.

"Swiftly, swiftly flew the ship,
Yet she sailed softly too:
Sweetly, sweetly blew the breeze—
On me alone it blew.

And the ancient Mariner beholdeth his native country.

"O dream of joy! is this indeed
The lighthouse top I see?
Is this the hill? is this the kirk?
Is this mine own countree?

"We drifted o'er the harbor-bar,
And I with sobs did pray—
O let me be awake, my God!
Or let me sleep alway.

"The harbor-bay was clear as glass,
So smoothly it was strewn!
And on the bay the moonlight lay,
And the shadow of the Moon.

"The rock shone bright, the kirk no less,
That stands above the rock:
The moonlight steeped in silentness
The steady weathercock.

The angelic spirits leave the dead bodies.

"And the bay was white with silent light
Till rising from the same,
Full many shapes, that shadows were,
In crimson colors came.

And appear in their own forms of light.

"A little distance from the prow
Those crimson shadows were;
I turned my eyes upon the deck—
O Christ! what saw I there!

"Each corse lay flat, lifeless and flat,
And, by the holy rood!
A man all light, a seraph-man,
On every corse there stood.

"This seraph-band, each waved his hand:
It was a heavenly sight!
They stood as signals to the land,
Each one a lovely light;

"This seraph-band, each waved his hand,
No voice did they impart—
No voice; but O, the silence sank
Like music on my heart.

"But soon I heard the dash of oars,
I heard the Pilot's cheer;
My head was turned perforce away,
And I saw a boat appear.

"The Pilot and the Pilot's boy,
I heard them coming fast:
Dear Lord in Heaven! it was a joy
The dead men could not blast.

"I saw a third—I heard his voice:
It is the Hermit good!
He singeth loud his godly hymns
That he makes in the wood.
He'll shrieve my soul, he'll wash away
The Albatross's blood.

PART VII

**The Hermit of the Wood**

"This Hermit good lives in that wood
Which slopes down to the sea.
How loudly his sweet voice he rears!
He loves to talk with marineres
That come from a far countree.

"He kneels at morn, and noon, and eve—
He hath a cushion plump:
It is the moss that wholly hides
The rotted old oak-stump.

"The skiff-boat neared: I heard them talk,
'Why, this is strange, I trow!
Where are those lights so many and fair,
That signal made but now?'

Approacheth the ship with wonder.

"'Strange, by my faith!' the Hermit said—
'And they answered not our cheer!
The planks look warped! and see those sails,
How thin they are and sere!
I never saw aught like to them,
Unless perchance it were

"'Brown skeletons of leaves that lag
My forest-brook along;
When the ivy-tod is heavy with snow,
And the owlet whoops to the wolf below,
That eats the she-wolf's young.'

"'Dear Lord! it hath a fiendish look—
(The Pilot made reply)
I am a-feared.'—'Push on, push on!'
Said the Hermit cheerily.

"The boat came closer to the ship,
But I nor spake nor stirred;
The boat came close beneath the ship,
And straight a sound was heard.

The ship suddenly sinketh.

"Under the water it rumbled on,
Still louder and more dread:
It reached the ship, it split the bay;
The ship went down like lead.

The ancient Mariner is saved in the Pilot s boat.

"Stunned by that loud and dreadful sound,
Which sky and ocean smote,
Like one that hath been seven days drowned
My body lay afloat;
But swift as dreams, myself I found
Within the Pilot's boat.

"Upon the whirl, where sank the ship,
The boat spun round and round;
And all was still, save that the hill
Was telling of the sound.

"I moved my lips—the Pilot shrieked
And fell down in a fit;
The holy Hermit raised his eyes,
And prayed where he did sit.

"I took the oars: the Pilot's boy,
Who now doth crazy go,
Laughed loud and long, and all the while
His eyes went to and fro.
'Ha! ha!' quoth he, 'full plain I see
The Devil knows how to row.'

"And now, all in my own countree,
I stood on the firm land!
The Hermit stepped forth from the boat,
And scarcely he could stand.

" 'O shrieve me, shrieve me, holy man!'
The Hermit crossed his brow.
'Say quick,' quoth he, 'I bid thee say—
What manner of man art thou?'

The ancient Mariner earnestly entreateth the Hermit to shrieve him; and the penance of life falls on him.

"Forthwith this frame of mine was wrenched
With a woful agony,
Which forced me to begin my tale;
And then it left me free.

"Since then, at an uncertain hour,
That agony returns:
And till my ghastly tale is told,
This heart within me burns.

And ever and anon throughout his future life an agony constraineth him to travel from land to land;

"I pass, like night, from land to land;
I have strange power of speech;
That moment that his face I see,
I know the man that must hear me:
To him my tale I teach.

"What loud uproar bursts from that door!
The wedding-guests are there:
But in the garden-bower the bride
And bride-maids singing are·

And hark, the little vesper bell,
Which biddeth me to prayer!

"O Wedding-Guest! this soul hath been
Alone on a wide, wide sea:
So lonely 'twas, that God Himself
Scarce seemèd there to be.

"O sweeter than the marriage-feast,
'Tis sweeter far to me,
To walk together to the kirk
With a goodly company!—

"To walk together to the kirk,
And all together pray,
While each to his great Father bends,
Old men, and babes, and loving friends,
And youths and maidens gay!

And to teach, by his own example, love and reverence to all things that God made and loveth.

"Farewell, farewell! but this I tell
To thee, thou Wedding-Guest!
He prayeth well, who loveth well
Both man and bird and beast.

"He prayeth best, who loveth best
All things both great and small;
For the dear God, who loveth us,
He made and loveth all."

The Mariner, whose eye is bright,
Whose beard with age is hoar,
Is gone: and now the Wedding-Guest
Turned from the bridegroom's door.

He went like one that hath been stunned,
And is of sense forlorn:
A sadder and a wiser man
He rose the morrow morn.

*Samuel Taylor Coleridge* [1772–1834]

## THE DREAM OF EUGENE ARAM

'Twas in the prime of summer time,
An evening calm and cool,
And four-and-twenty happy boys
Came bounding out of school:
There were some that ran and some that leaped,
Like troutlets in a pool.

Away they sped with gamesome minds,
And souls untouched by sin;
To a level mead they came, and there
They drave the wickets in:
Pleasantly shone the setting sun
Over the town of Lynn.

Like sportive deer they coursed about,
And shouted as they ran,
Turning to mirth all things of earth,
As only boyhood can;
But the Usher sat remote from all,
A melancholy man!

His hat was off, his vest apart,
To catch heaven's blessed breeze;
For a burning thought was in his brow,
And his bosom ill at ease:
So he leaned his head on his hands, and read
The book between his knees.

Leaf after leaf, he turned it o'er,
Nor ever glanced aside,
For the peace of his soul he read that book
In the golden eventide:
Much study had made him very lean,
And pale, and leaden-eyed.

At last he shut the ponderous tome,
With a fast and fervent grasp

He strained the dusky covers close,
  And fixed the brazen hasp:
"Oh, God! could I so close my mind,
  And clasp it with a clasp!"

Then leaping on his feet upright,
  Some moody turns he took,—
Now up the mead, then down the mead,
  And past a shady nook,—
And, lo! he saw a little boy
  That pored upon a book.

"My gentle lad, what is't you read—
  Romance or fairy fable?
Or is it some historic page,
  Of kings and crowns unstable?"
The young boy gave an upward glance,
  "It is 'The Death of Abel.'"

The Usher took six hasty strides,
  As smit with sudden pain,
Six hasty strides beyond the place,
  Then slowly back again;
And down he sat beside the lad,
  And talked with him of Cain;

And, long since then, of bloody men,
  Whose deeds tradition saves;
Of lonely folk cut off unseen,
  And hid in sudden graves;
Of horrid stabs, in groves forlorn,
  And murders done in caves;

And how the sprites of injured men
  Shriek upward from the sod;
Aye, how the ghostly hand will point
  To show the burial clod;
And unknown facts of guilty acts
  Are seen in dreams from God!

He told how murderers walk the earth
  Beneath the curse of Cain,
With crimson clouds before their eyes,
  And flames about their brain:
For blood has left upon their souls
  Its everlasting stain.

"And well," quoth he, "I know for truth,
  Their pangs must be extreme,—
Woe, woe, unutterable woe,—
  Who spill life's sacred stream!
For why? Methought, last night, I wrought
  A murder, in a dream!

"One that had never done me wrong,
  A feeble man and old:
I led him to a lonely field;
  The moon shone clear and cold:
Now here, said I, this man shall die,
  And I will have his gold!

"Two sudden blows with a ragged stick,
  And one with a heavy stone,
One hurried gash with a hasty knife,—
  And then the deed was done;
There was nothing lying at my foot
  But lifeless flesh and bone!

"Nothing but lifeless flesh and bone,
  That could not do me ill;
And yet I feared him all the more,
  For lying there so still:
There was a manhood in his look,
  That murder could not kill.

"And, lo! the universal air
  Seemed lit with ghastly flame;
Ten thousand thousand dreadful eyes
  Were looking down in blame:
I took the dead man by his hand
  And called upon his name!

"Oh, God! it made me quake to see
  Such sense within the slain!
But when I touched the lifeless clay,
  The blood gushed out amain!
For every clot, a burning spot
  Was scorching in my brain!

"My head was like an ardent coal,
  My heart as solid ice;
My wretched, wretched soul, I knew,
  Was at the Devil's price;
A dozen times I groaned: the dead
  Had never groaned but twice!

"And now, from forth the frowning sky
  From the Heaven's topmost height,
I heard a voice—that awful voice
  Of the blood-avenging sprite:
'Thou guilty man! take up thy dead
  And hide it from my sight!'

"I took the dreary body up,
  And cast it in a stream,
A sluggish water, black as ink,
  The depth was so extreme:—
My gentle Boy, remember this
  Is nothing but a dream!

"Down went the corse with a hollow plunge
  And vanished in the pool;
Anon I cleansed my bloody hands,
  And washed my forehead cool,
And sat among the urchins young,
  That evening in the school.

"Oh, Heaven! to think of their white souls
  And mine so black and grim!
I could not share in childish prayer
  Nor join in Evening Hymn:
Like a Devil of the Pit I seemed,
  'Mid holy Cherubim!

"And peace went with them, one and all,
And each calm pillow spread:
But Guilt was my grim Chamberlain
That lighted me to bed,
And drew my midnight curtains round,
With fingers bloody red!

"All night I lay in agony,
In anguish dark and deep,
My fevered eyes I dared not close,
But stared aghast at Sleep:
For Sin had rendered unto her
The keys of hell to keep.

"All night I lay in agony,
From weary chime to chime,
With one besetting horrid hint,
That racked me all the time;
A mighty yearning, like the first
Fierce impulse unto crime;

"One stern tyrannic thought, that made
All other thoughts its slave:
Stronger and stronger every pulse
Did that temptation crave,
Still urging me to go and see
The Dead Man in his grave!

"Heavily I rose up, as soon
As light was in the sky,
And sought the black accursèd pool
With a wild misgiving eye:
And I saw the Dead in the river bed,
For the faithless stream was dry!

"Merrily rose the lark, and shook
The dew-drop from its wing;
But I never marked its morning flight,
I never heard it sing,
For I was stooping once again
Under the horrid thing.

"With breathless speed, like a soul in chase,
I took him up and ran;
There was no time to dig a grave
Before the day began:
In a lonesome wood, with heaps of leaves,
I hid the murdered man.

"And all that day I read in school,
But my thought was otherwhere;
As soon as the mid-day task was done,
In secret I was there;
And a mighty wind had swept the leaves,
And still the corse was bare!

"Then down I cast me on my face,
And first began to weep,
For I knew my secret then was one
That earth refused to keep:
Or land or sea, though it should be
Ten thousand fathoms deep.

"So wills the fierce avenging Sprite,
Till blood for blood atones!
Aye, though he's buried in a cave,
And trodden down with stones,
And years have rotted off his flesh,—
The world shall see his bones!

"Oh, God! that horrid, horrid dream
Besets me now awake!
Again—again, with dizzy brain,
The human life I take;
And my red right hand grows raging hot,
Like Cranmer's at the stake.

"And still no peace for the restless clay
Will wave or mold allow;
The horrid thing pursues my soul,—
It stands before me now!"
The fearful Boy looked up, and saw
Huge drops upon his brow.

That very night, while gentle sleep
  The urchin eyelids kissed,
Two stern-faced men set out from Lynn,
  Through the cold and heavy mist;
And Eugene Aram walked between,
  With gyves upon his wrist.

*Thomas Hood* [1799–1845]

## THE BALLAD OF READING GAOL

### I

He did not wear his scarlet coat,
  For blood and wine are red,
And blood and wine were on his hands
  When they found him with the dead,
The poor dead woman whom he loved,
  And murdered in her bed.

He walked amongst the Trial Men
  In a suit of shabby gray;
A cricket cap was on his head,
  And his step seemed light and gay;
But I never saw a man who looked
  So wistfully at the day.

I never saw a man who looked
  With such a wistful eye
Upon that little tent of blue
  Which prisoners call the sky,
And at every drifting cloud that went
  With sails of silver by.

I walked, with other souls in pain,
  Within another ring,
And was wondering if the man had done
  A great or little thing,
When a voice behind me whispered low,
  "*That fellow's got to swing.*"

Dear Christ! the very prison walls
  Suddenly seemed to reel,
And the sky above my head became
  Like a casque of scorching steel;
And, though I was a soul in pain,
  My pain I could not feel.

I only knew what hunted thought
  Quickened his step, and why
He looked upon the garish day
  With such a wistful eye;
The man had killed the thing he loved,
  And so he had to die.

Yet each man kills the thing he loves,
  By each let this be heard,
Some do it with a bitter look,
  Some with a flattering word,
The coward does it with a kiss,
  The brave man with a sword!

Some kill their love when they are young,
  And some when they are old;
Some strangle with the hands of Lust,
  Some with the hands of Gold:
The kindest use a knife, because
  The dead so soon grow cold.

Some love too little, some too long,
  Some sell, and others buy;
Some do the deed with many tears,
  And some without a sigh:
For each man kills the thing he loves,
  Yet each man does not die.

He does not die a death of shame
  On a day of dark disgrace,
Nor have a noose about his neck,
  Nor a cloth upon his face,
Nor drop feet foremost through the floor
  Into an empty space.

He does not sit with silent men
  Who watch him night and day;
Who watch him when he tries to weep,
  And when he tries to pray;
Who watch him lest himself should rob
  The prison of its prey.

He does not wake at dawn to see
  Dread figures throng his room,
The shivering Chaplain robed in white,
  The Sheriff stern with gloom,
And the Governor all in shiny black,
  With the yellow face of Doom.

He does not rise in piteous haste
  To put on convict-clothes,
While some coarse-mouthed Doctor gloats, and notes
  Each new and nerve-twitched pose,
Fingering a watch whose little ticks
  Are like horrible hammer-blows.

He does not know that sickening thirst
  That sands one's throat, before
The hangman with his gardener's gloves
  Slips through the padded door,
And binds one with three leathern thongs,
  That the throat may thirst no more.

He does not bend his head to hear
  The Burial Office read,
Nor, while the terror of his soul
  Tells him he is not dead,
Cross his own coffin, as he moves
  Into the hideous shed.

He does not stare upon the air
  Through a little roof of glass:
He does not pray with lips of clay
  For his agony to pass;
Nor feel upon his shuddering cheek
  That kiss of Caiaphas.

II

Six weeks our guardsman walked the yard,
  In the suit of shabby gray:
His cricket cap was on his head,
  And his step seemed light and gay,
But I never saw a man who looked
  So wistfully at the day.

I never saw a man who looked
  With such a wistful eye
Upon that little tent of blue
  Which prisoners call the sky,
And at every wandering cloud that trailed
  Its raveled fleeces by.

He did not wring his hands, as do
  Those witless men who dare
To try to rear the changeling Hope
  In the cave of black Despair:
He only looked upon the sun,
  And drank the morning air.

He did not wring his hands nor weep,
  Nor did he peek or pine,
But he drank the air as though it held
  Some healthful anodyne;
With open mouth he drank the sun
  As though it had been wine!

And I and all the souls in pain,
  Who tramped the other ring,
Forgot if we ourselves had done
  A great or little thing,
And watched with gaze of dull amaze
  The man who had to swing.

And strange it was to see him pass
  With a step so light and gay,
And strange it was to see him look
  So wistfully at the day,
And strange it was to think that he
  Had such a debt to pay.

For oak and elm have pleasant leaves
  That in the spring-time shoot:
But grim to see is the gallows-tree,
  With its adder-bitten root,
And, green or dry, a man must die
  Before it bears its fruit!

The loftiest place is that seat of grace
  For which all wordlings try:
But who would stand in hempen band
  Upon a scaffold high,
And through a murderer's collar take
  His last look at the sky?

It is sweet to dance to violins
  When Love and Life are fair:
To dance to flutes, to dance to lutes
  Is delicate and rare:
But it is not sweet with nimble feet
  To dance upon the air!

So with curious eyes and sick surmise
  We watched him day by day,
And wondered if each one of us
  Would end the self-same way,
For none can tell to what red Hell
  His sightless soul may stray.

At last the dead men walked no more
  Amongst the Trial Men,
And I knew that he was standing up
  In the black dock's dreadful pen,
And that never would I see his face
  In God's sweet world again.

Like two doomed ships that pass in storm,
  We had crossed each other's way:
But we made no sign, we said no word,
  We had no word to say;
For we did not meet in the holy night,
  But in the shameful day.

A prison wall was round us both,
  Two outcast men we were:
The world had thrust us from its heart,
  And God from out his care:
And the iron gin that waits for Sin
  Had caught us in its snare.

III

In Debtor's Yard the stones are hard,
  And the dripping wall is high,
So it was there he took the air
  Beneath the leaden sky,
And by each side a Warder walked,
  For fear the man might die.

Or else he sat with those who watched
  His anguish night and day;
Who watched him when he rose to weep,
  And when he crouched to pray;
Who watched him lest himself should rob
  Their scaffold of its prey.

The Governor was strong upon
  The Regulations Act:
The Doctor said that Death was but
  A scientific fact:
And twice a day the Chaplain called,
  And left a little tract.

And twice a day he smoked his pipe,
  And drank his quart of beer:
His soul was resolute, and held
  No hiding-place for fear;
He often said that he was glad
  The hangman's hands were near.

But why he said so strange a thing
  No Warder dared to ask:
For he to whom a watcher's doom
  Is given as his task,
Must set a lock upon his lips,
  And make his face a mask.

Or else he might be moved, and try
  To comfort or console:
And what should Human Pity do
  Pent up in Murderers' Hole?
What word of grace in such a place
  Could help a brother's soul?

With slouch and swing around the ring
  We trod the Fools' Parade!
We did not care: we knew we were
  The Devil's Own Brigade:
And shaven head and feet of lead
  Make a merry masquerade.

We tore the tarry rope to shreds
  With blunt and bleeding nails;
We rubbed the doors, and scrubbed the floors,
  And cleaned the shining rails:
And, rank by rank, we soaped the plank,
  And clattered with the pails.

We sewed the sacks, we broke the stones,
  We turned the dusty drill:
We banged the tins, and bawled the hymns,
  And sweated on the mill:
But in the heart of every man
  Terror was lying still.

So still it lay that every day
  Crawled like a weed-clogged wave:
And we forgot the bitter lot
  That waits for fool and knave,
Till once, as we tramped in from work,
  We passed an open grave.

With yawning mouth the yellow hole
  Gaped for a living thing;
The very mud cried out for blood
  To the thirsty asphalt ring:
And we knew that ere one dawn grew fair,
  Some prisoner had to swing.

Right in we went, with soul intent
  On Death and Dread and Doom:
The hangman, with his little bag,
  Went shuffling through the gloom:
And each man trembled as he crept
  Into his numbered tomb.

That night the empty corridors
  Were full of forms of Fear,
And up and down the iron town
  Stole feet we could not hear,
And through the bars that hide the stars
  White faces seemed to peer.

He lay as one who lies and dreams
  In a pleasant meadow-land,
The watchers watched him as he slept,
  And could not understand
How one could sleep so sweet a sleep
  With a hangman close at hand.

But there is no sleep when men must weep
  Who never yet have wept:
So we—the fool, the fraud, the knave—
  That endless vigil kept,
And through each brain on hands of pain
  Another's terror crept.

Alas! it is a fearful thing
  To feel another's guilt!
For, right within, the sword of Sin
  Pierced to its poisoned hilt,
And as molten lead were the tears we shed
  For the blood we had not spilt.

The Warders with their shoes of felt
  Crept by each padlocked door,
And peeped and saw, with eyes of awe,
  Gray figures on the floor,
And wondered why men knelt to pray
  Who never prayed before.

All through the night we knelt and prayed,
  Mad mourners of a corse!
The troubled plumes of midnight were
  The plumes upon a hearse:
And bitter wine upon a sponge
  Was the savor of Remorse.

The gray cock crew, the red cock crew,
  But never came the day;
And crooked shapes of terror crouched
  In the corners where we lay:
And each evil sprite that walks by night
  Before us seemed to play.

They glided past, they glided fast,
  Like travelers through a mist:
They mocked the moon in a rigadoon
  Of delicate turn and twist,
And with formal pace and loathsome grace
  The phantoms kept their tryst.

With mop and mow, we saw them go,
  Slim shadows hand and hand:
About, about, in ghostly rout
  They trod a saraband:
And the damned grotesques made arabesques,
  Like the wind upon the sand!

With the pirouettes of marionettes
  They tripped on pointed tread:
But with flutes of Fear they filled the ear,
  As their grisly masque they led,
And loud they sang, and long they sang,
  For they sang to wake the dead.

"*Oho!*" they cried, "*The world is wide,*
  *But fettered limbs go lame!*
*And once, or twice, to throw the dice*
  *Is a gentlemanly game,*
*But he does not win who plays with Sin*
  *In the Secret House of Shame.*"

No things of air these antics were,
  That frolicked with such glee:
To men whose lives were held in gyves,
  And whose feet might not go free,
Ah! wounds of Christ! they were living things
  Most terrible to see.

Around, around, they waltzed and wound;
  Some wheeled in smirking pairs;
With the mincing step of a demirep
  Some sidled up the stairs:
And with subtle sneer, and fawning leer,
  Each helped us at our prayers.

The morning wind began to moan,
  But still the night went on;
Through its giant loom the web of gloom
  Crept till each thread was spun:
And, as we prayed, we grew afraid
  Of the Justice of the Sun.

The moaning wind went wandering round
  The weeping prison-wall:
Till like a wheel of turning steel
  We felt the minutes crawl:
O moaning wind! what had we done
  To have such a seneschal?

At last I saw the shadowed bars,
  Like a lattice wrought in lead,
Move right across the whitewashed wall
  That faced my three-planked bed,
And I knew that somewhere in the world
  God's dreadful dawn was red.

At six o'clock we cleaned our cells,
  At seven all was still,
But the sough and swing of a mighty wing
  The prison seemed to fill,
For the Lord of Death with icy breath,
  Had entered in to kill.

He did not pass in purple pomp,
  Nor ride a moon-white steed.
Three yards of cord and a sliding board
  Are all the gallows' need:
So with rope of shame the Herald came
  To do the secret deed.

We were as men who through a fen
  Of filthy darkness grope:
We did not dare to breathe a prayer,
  Or to give our anguish scope:
Something was dead in each of us,
  And what was dead was Hope.

For Man's grim Justice goes its way,
  And will not swerve aside:
It slays the weak, it slays the strong,
  It has a deadly stride:
With iron heel it slays the strong,
  The monstrous parricide!

We waited for the stroke of eight:
  Each tongue was thick with thirst:
For the stroke of eight is the stroke of Fate
  That makes a man accursed,
And Fate will use a running noose
  For the best man and the worst.

We had no other thing to do,
  Save to wait for the sign to come:
So, like things of stone in a valley lone,
  Quiet we sat and dumb:
But each man's heart beat thick and quick,
  Like a madman on a drum!

With sudden shock, the prison-clock
  Smote on the shivering air,
And from all the jail rose up a wail
  Of impotent despair,
Like the sound that frightened marshes hear
  From some leper in his lair.

And as one sees most dreadful things
  In the crystal of a dream,
We saw the greasy hempen rope
  Hooked to the blackened beam,
And heard the prayer the hangman's snare
  Strangled into a scream.

And all the woe that moved him so
  That he gave that bitter cry,
And the wild regrets, and the bloody sweats,
  None knew so well as I:
For he who lives more lives than one
  More deaths than one must die.

IV

There is no chapel on the day
  On which they hang a man:
The Chaplain's heart is far too sick,
  Or his face is far too wan,
Or there is that written in his eyes
  Which none should look upon.

So they kept us close till nigh on noon,
  And then they rang the bell,
And the Warders with their jingling keys
  Opened each listening cell,
And down the iron stair we tramped,
  Each from his separate Hell.

Out into God's sweet air we went,
  But not in wonted way,
For this man's face was white with fear,
  And that man's face was gray,
And I never saw sad men who looked
  So wistfully at the day.

I never saw sad men who looked
  With such a wistful eye
Upon that little tent of blue
  We prisoners call the sky,
And at every careless cloud that passed
  In happy freedom by.

But there were those amongst us all
  Who walked with downcast head,
And knew that, had each got his due,
  They should have died instead:
He had but killed a thing that lived,
  Whilst they had killed the dead.

For he who sins a second time
  Wakes a dead soul to pain,
And draws it from its spotted shroud,
  And makes it bleed again,
And makes it bleed great gouts of blood,
  And makes it bleed in vain!

Like ape or clown, in monstrous garb
  With crooked arrows starred,
Silently we went round and round
  The slippery asphalt yard;
Silently we went round and round,
  And no man spoke a word.

Silently we went round and round,
  And through each hollow mind
The Memory of dreadful things
  Rushed like a dreadful wind,
And Horror stalked before each man,
  And Terror crept behind.

The Warders strutted up and down,
  And kept their herd of brutes,
Their uniforms were spick and span,
  They wore their Sunday suits,
But we knew the work they had been at,
  By the quicklime on their boots.

For where a grave had opened wide,
  There was no grave at all:
Only a stretch of mud and sand
  By the hideous prison-wall,
And a little heap of burning lime,
  That the man should have his pall.

For he has a pall, this wretched man,
  Such as few men can claim:
Deep down below a prison-yard,
  Naked for greater shame,
He lies, with fetters on each foot,
  Wrapped in a sheet of flame!

And all the while the burning lime
  Eats flesh and bone away,
It eats the brittle bone by night,
  And the soft flesh by day,
It eats the flesh and bone by turns,
  But it eats the heart alway.

For three long years they will not sow
  Or root or seedling there:
For three long years the unblessed spot
  Will sterile be and bare,
And look upon the wondering sky
  With unreproachful stare.

They think a murderer's heart would taint
  Each simple seed they sow.
It is not true! God's kindly earth
  Is kindlier than men know,
And the red rose would but blow more red,
  The white rose whiter blow.

Out of his mouth a red, red rose!
  Out of his heart a white!
For who can say by what strange way
  Christ brings his will to light,
Since the barren staff the pilgrim bore
  Bloomed in the great Pope's sight?

But neither milk-white rose nor red
  May bloom in prison air;
The shard, the pebble, and the flint,
  Are what they give us there:
For flowers have been known to heal
  A common man's despair.

So never will wine-red rose or white
  Petal by petal, fall
On that stretch of mud and sand that lies
  By that hideous prison-wall,
To tell the men who tramp the yard
  That God's Son died for all.

Yet though the hideous prison-wall
  Still hems him round and round,
And a spirit may not walk by night
  That is with fetters bound,
And a spirit may but weep that lies
  In such unholy ground,

He is at peace—this wretched man—
  At peace, or will be soon:
There is no thing to make him mad,
  Nor does Terror walk at noon,
For the lampless Earth in which he lies
  Has neither Sun nor Moon.

They hanged him as a beast is hanged:
  They did not even toll
A requiem that might have brought
  Rest to his startled soul,
But hurriedly they took him out,
  And hid him in a hole.

They stripped him of his canvas clothes,
  And gave him to the flies:
They mocked the swollen purple throat,
  And the stark and staring eyes:
And with laughter loud they heaped the shroud
  In which their convict lies.

The Chaplain would not kneel to pray
  By his dishonored grave:
Nor mark it with that blessed Cross
  That Christ for sinners gave,
Because the man was one of those
  Whom Christ came down to save.

Yet all is well; he has but passed
  To Life's appointed bourne:
And alien tears will fill for him
  Pity's long-broken urn,
For his mourners will be outcast men,
  And outcasts always mourn.

V

I know not whether Laws be right,
  Or whether Laws be wrong;
All that we know who lie in jail
  Is that the wall is strong;
And that each day is like a year,
  A year whose days are long.

But this I know, that every Law
  That men have made for Man,
Since first Man took his brother's life,
  And this sad world began,
But straws the wheat and saves the chaff
  With a most evil fan.

This too I know—and wise it were
  If each could know the same—
That every prison that men build
  Is built with bricks of shame,
And bound with bars lest Christ should see
  How men their brothers maim.

With bars they blur the gracious moon,
  And blind the goodly sun:
And they do well to hide their Hell,
  For in it things are done
That Son of God nor son of Man
  Ever should look upon!

The vilest deeds like poison weeds
  Bloom well in prison-air:
It is only what is good in Man
  That wastes and withers there:
Pale Anguish keeps the heavy gate,
  And the Warder is Despair.

For they starve the little frightened child,
  Till it weeps both night and day:
And they scourge the weak, and flog the fool,
  And gibe the old and gray,
And some grow mad, and all grow bad,
  And none a word may say.

Each narrow cell in which we dwell
  Is a foul and dark latrine,
And the fetid breath of living Death
  Chokes up each grated screen,
And all, but Lust, is turned to dust
  In Humanity's machine.

The brackish water that we drink
  Creeps with a loathsome slime,
And the bitter bread they weigh in scales
  Is full of chalk and lime,
And Sleep will not lie down, but walks
  Wild-eyed, and cries to Time.

But though lean Hunger and green Thirst
  Like asp with adder fight,
We have little care of prison fare,
  For what chills and kills outright
Is that every stone one lifts by day
  Becomes one's heart by night.

With midnight always in one's heart,
  And twilight in one's cell,
We turn the crank, or tear the rope,
  Each in his separate Hell,
And the silence is more awful far
  Than the sound of a brazen bell.

And never a human voice comes near
  To speak a gentle word:
And the eye that watches through the door
  Is pitiless and hard:
And by all forgot, we rot and rot,
  With soul and body marred.

And thus we rust Life's iron chain,
  Degraded and alone:
And some men curse, and some men weep
  And some men make no moan:
But God's eternal Laws are kind
  And break the heart of stone.

And every human heart that breaks,
  In prison-cell or yard,
Is as that broken box that gave
  Its treasure to the Lord,
And filled the unclean leper's house
  With the scent of costliest nard.

Ah! happy they whose hearts can break
  And peace of pardon win!
How else may man make straight his plan
  And cleanse his soul from Sin?
How else but through a broken heart
  May Lord Christ enter in?

And he of the swollen purple throat,
  And the stark and staring eyes,
Waits for the holy hands that took
  The Thief to Paradise;
And a broken and a contrite heart
  The Lord will not despise.

The man in red who reads the Law
  Gave him three weeks of life,
Three little weeks in which to heal
  His soul of his soul's strife,
And cleanse from every blot of blood
  The hand that held the knife.

And with tears of blood he cleansed the hand,
  The hand that held the steel:
For only blood can wipe out blood,
  And only tears can heal:
And the crimson stain that was of Cain
  Became Christ's snow-white seal.

VI

In Reading gaol by Reading town
  There is a pit of shame,
And in it lies a wretched man
  Eaten by teeth of flame,
In a burning winding-sheet he lies,
  And his grave has got no name.

And there, till Christ call forth the dead,
  In silence let him lie:
No need to waste the foolish tear,
  Or heave the windy sigh:
The man had killed the thing he loved,
  And so he had to die.

And all men kill the thing they love,
  By all let this be heard,
Some do it with a bitter look,
  Some with a flattering word,
The coward does it with a kiss,
  The brave man with a sword!

*Oscar Wilde* [1856–1900]

## THE BALLAD OF JUDAS ISCARIOT

'Twas the body of Judas Iscariot
  Lay in the Field of Blood;
'Twas the soul of Judas Iscariot
  Beside the body stood.

Black was the earth by night,
  And black was the sky;
Black, black were the broken clouds,
  Though the red Moon went by.

'Twas the body of Judas Iscariot
  Strangled and dead lay there;
'Twas the soul of Judas Iscariot
  Looked on it in despair.

The breath of the World came and went
  Like a sick man's in rest;
Drop by drop on the World's eyes
  The dews fell cool and blest.

Then the soul of Judas Iscariot
  Did make a gentle moan—
"I will bury underneath the ground
  My flesh and blood and bone.

"I will bury deep beneath the soil,
  Lest mortals look thereon,
And when the wolf and raven come
  The body will be gone!

"The stones of the field are sharp as steel.
  And hard and bold, God wot;
And I must bear my body hence
  Until I find a spot!"

'Twas the soul of Judas Iscariot
  So grim, and gaunt, and gray,
Raised the body of Judas Iscariot,
  And carried it away.

And as he bare it from the field
  Its touch was cold as ice,
And the ivory teeth within the jaw
  Rattled aloud, like dice.

As the soul of Judas Iscariot
  Carried its load with pain,
The Eye of Heaven, like a lantern's eye,
  Opened and shut again.

Half he walked, and half he seemed
  Lifted on the cold wind;
He did not turn, for chilly hands
  Were pushing from behind.

The first place that he came unto
  It was the open wold,
And underneath were prickly whins,
  And a wind that blew so cold.

The next place that he came unto
  It was a stagnant pool,
And when he threw the body in
  It floated light as wool.

He drew the body on his back,
  And it was dripping chill,
And the next place that he came unto
  Was a Cross upon a hill.

A Cross upon the windy hill,
  And a Cross on either side,
Three skeletons that swing thereon,
  Who had been crucified.

And on the middle cross-bar sat
  A white Dove slumbering;
Dim it sat in the dim light,
  With its head beneath its wing.

And underneath the middle Cross
  A grave yawned wide and vast,
But the soul of Judas Iscariot
  Shivered, and glided past.

The fourth place that he came unto
  It was the Brig of Dread,
And the great torrents rushing down
  Were deep, and swift, and red.

He dared not fling the body in
  For fear of faces dim,
And arms were waved in the wild water
  To thrust it back to him.

'Twas the soul of Judas Iscariot
  Turned from the Brig of Dread,
And the dreadful foam of the wild water
  Had splashed the body red.

For days and nights he wandered on
  Upon an open plain,
And the days went by like blinding mist,
  And the nights like rushing rain.

For days and nights he wandered on,
  All through the Wood of Woe;
And the nights went by like moaning wind,
  And the days like drifting snow.

'Twas the soul of Judas Iscariot
  Came with a weary face—
Alone, alone, and all alone,
  Alone in a lonely place!

He wandered east, he wandered west,
  And heard no human sound;
For months and years, in grief and tears,
  He wandered round and round.

For months and years, in grief and tears,
  He walked the silent night;
Then the soul of Judas Iscariot
  Perceived a far-off light.

A far-off light across the waste,
  As dim as dim might be,
That came and went like a lighthouse gleam
  On a black night at sea.

'Twas the soul of Judas Iscariot
  Crawled to the distant gleam;
And the rain came down, and the rain was blown
  Against him with a scream.

For days and nights he wandered on,
  Pushed on by hands behind;
And the days went by like black, black rain,
  And the nights like rushing wind.

'Twas the soul of Judas Iscariot,
  Strange, and sad, and tall,
Stood all alone at dead of night
  Before a lighted hall.

And the wold was white with snow,
  And his foot-marks black and damp,
And the ghost of the silver Moon arose,
  Holding her yellow lamp.

And the icicles were on the eaves,
  And the walls were deep with white,
And the shadows of the guests within
  Passed on the window light.

The shadows of the wedding guests
  Did strangers come and go,
And the body of Judas Iscariot
  Lay stretched along the snow.

The body of Judas Iscariot
  Lay stretched along the snow;
'Twas the soul of Judas Iscariot
  Ran swiftly to and fro.

To and fro, and up and down,
  He ran so swiftly there,
As round and round the frozen Pole
  Glideth the lean white bear.

'Twas the Bridegroom sat at the table-head,
  And the lights burned bright and clear—
"Oh, who is that?" the Bridegroom said,
  "Whose weary feet I hear?"

'Twas one looked from the lighted hall,
And answered soft and slow,
"It is a wolf runs up and down
With a black track in the snow."

The Bridegroom in his robe of white
Sat at the table-head—
"Oh, who is that who moans without?"
The blessed Bridegroom said.

'Twas one looked from the lighted hall,
And answered fierce and low,
"'Tis the soul of Judas Iscariot
Gliding to and fro."

'Twas the soul of Judas Iscariot
Did hush itself and stand,
And saw the Bridegroom at the door
With a light in his hand.

The Bridegroom stood in the open door,
And he was clad in white,
And far within the Lord's Supper
Was spread so long and bright.

The Bridegroom shaded his eyes and looked,
And his face was bright to see—
"What dost thou here at the Lord's Supper
With thy body's sins?" said he.

'Twas the soul of Judas Iscariot
Stood black, and sad, and bare—
"I have wandered many nights and days;
There is no light elsewhere."

'Twas the wedding guests cried out within,
And their eyes were fierce and bright—
"Scourge the soul of Judas Iscariot
Away into the night!"

The Bridegroom stood in the open door,
  And he waved hands still and slow,
And the third time that he waved his hands
  The air was thick with snow.

And of every flake of falling snow,
  Before it touched the ground,
There came a dove, and a thousand doves
  Made sweet sound.

'Twas the body of Judas Iscariot
  Floated away full fleet,
And the wings of the doves that bare it off
  Were like its winding-sheet.

'Twas the Bridegroom stood at the open door,
  And beckoned, smiling sweet;
'Twas the soul of Judas Iscariot
  Stole in, and fell at his feet.

"The Holy Supper is spread within,
  And the many candles shine,
And I have waited long for thee
  Before I poured the wine!"

The supper wine is poured at last,
  The lights burn bright and fair,
Iscariot washes the Bridegroom's feet,
  And dries them with his hair.

*Robert Buchanan* [1841–1901]

## HE FELL AMONG THIEVES

"Ye have robbed," said he, "ye have slaughtered and made
    an end,
  Take your ill-got plunder, and bury the dead:
What will ye more of your guest and sometime friend?"
  "Blood for our blood," they said.

He laughed: "If one may settle the score for five,
I am ready; but let the reckoning stand till day:
I have loved the sunlight as dearly as any alive."
"You shall die at dawn," said they.

He flung his empty revolver down the slope,
He climbed alone to the Eastward edge of the trees;
All night long in a dream untroubled of hope
He brooded, clasping his knees.

He did not hear the monotonous roar that fills
The ravine where the Yassîn river sullenly flows;
He did not see the starlight on the Laspur hills,
Or the far Afghan snows.

He saw the April noon on his books aglow,
The wistaria trailing in at the window wide;
He heard his father's voice from the terrace below
Calling him down to ride.

He saw the gray little church across the park,
The mounds that hid the loved and honored dead;
The Norman arch, the chancel softly dark,
The brasses black and red.

He saw the School Close, sunny and green,
The runner beside him, the stand by the parapet wall,
The distant tape, and the crowd roaring between,
His own name over all.

He saw the dark wainscot and timbered roof,
The long tables, and the faces merry and keen;
The College Eight and their trainer dining aloof,
The Dons on the daïs serene.

He watched the liner's stem plowing the foam,
He felt her trembling speed and the thrash of her screw;
He heard the passengers' voices talking of home,
He saw the flag she flew.

And now it was dawn. He rose strong on his feet,
And strode to his ruined camp below the wood;
He drank the breath of the morning cool and sweet;
His murderers round him stood.

Light on the Laspur hills was broadening fast,
The blood-red snow-peaks chilled to a dazzling white;
He turned, and saw the golden circle at last,
Cut by the Eastern height.

"O glorious Life, Who dwellest in earth and sun,
I have lived, I praise and adore Thee."
A sword swept.
Over the pass the voices one by one
Faded, and the hill slept.

*Henry Newbolt* [1862–1938]

## THE LAST HUNT

Oh, it's twenty gallant gentlemen
Rode out to hunt the deer,
With mirth upon the silver horn
And gleam upon the spear;
They galloped through the meadow-grass,
They sought the forest's gloom,
And loudest rang Sir Morven's laugh,
And lightest tossed his plume.
There's no delight by day or night
Like hunting in the morn;
So busk ye, gallant gentlemen,
And sound the silver horn!

They rode into the dark greenwood
By ferny dell and glade,—
And now and then upon their cloaks
The yellow sunshine played;
They heard the timid forest-birds
Break off amid their glee,
They saw the startled leveret,
But not a stag did see.

Wind, wind the horn, on summer morn!
Though ne'er a buck appear,
There's health for horse and gentleman
A-hunting of the deer!

They panted up Ben Lomond's side
Where thick the leafage grew,
And when they bent the branches back
The sunbeams darted through;
Sir Morven in his saddle turned,
And to his comrades spake,
"Now quiet! we shall find a stag
Beside the Brownies' Lake."
Then sound not on the bugle-horn,
Bend bush and do not break,
Lest ye should start the timid hart
A-drinking at the lake.

Now they have reached the Brownies' Lake,
A blue eye in the wood,—
And on its brink a moment's space
All motionless they stood:
When, suddenly, the silence broke
With fifty bowstrings' twang,
And hurtling through the drowsy air
Full fifty arrows sang.
Ah, better for those gentlemen,
Than horn and slender spear,
Were morion and buckler true,
A-hunting of the deer.

Not one of that brave company
Shall hunt the deer again;
Some fell beside the Brownies' Pool,
Some dropped in dell or glen;
An arrow pierced Sir Morven's breast,
His horse plunged in the lake,
And swimming to the farther bank
He left a bloody wake.

Ah, what avails the silver horn,
And what the slender spear?
There's other quarry in the wood
Beside the fallow deer!

O'er ridge and hollow sped the horse
Besprent with blood and foam,
Nor slackened pace until at eve
He brought his master home.
How tenderly the Lady Ruth
The cruel dart withdrew!
"False Tirrell shot the bolt," she said,
"That my Sir Morven slew!"
Deep in the forest lurks the foe,
While gayly shines the morn:
Hang up the broken spear, and blow
A dirge upon the horn.

*William Roscoe Thayer* [1859–1923]

## ANDRÉ'S RIDE

When André rode to Pont-du-lac,
With all his raiders at his back,
Mon Dieu! the tumult in the town!
Scarce clanged the great portcullis down
Ere in the sunshine gleamed his spears,
And up marched all his musketeers,
And far and fast in haste's array
Sped men to fight and priests to pray:
In every street a barricade
Of aught that lay to hand was made;
From every house a man was told,
Nor quittance given to young or old:
Should youth be spared or age be slack
When André rode to Pont-du-lac?

When André rode to Pont-du-lac,
With all his ravening reiver-pack,
The mid lake was a frozen road
Unbending to the cannon's load;

No warmth the sun had as it shone;
The kine were stalled, the birds were gone;
Like wild things seemed the shapes of fur
With which was every street astir,
And over all the huddling crowd
The thick breath hung—a solid cloud,—
Roof, road, and river, all were white;
Men moved benumbed by day—by night
The boldest durst not bivouac,
When André rode to Pont-du-lac.

When André rode to Pont-du-lac,
We scarce could stem his swift attack;
A halt, a cheer, a bugle-call,—
Like wild-cats they were up the wall:
But still as each man won the town,
We tossed him from the ramparts down;
And when at last the stormers quailed,
And back the assailants shrank assailed,
Like wounded wasps that still could sting,
Or tigers that had missed their spring,
They would not fly, but turned at bay
And fought out all the dying day;—
Sweet saints! it was a curious track
That André left by Pont-du-lac.

When André rode to Pont-du-lac,
Said he, "A troop of girls could sack
This huckster town, that hugs its hoard
But wists not how to wield a sword."
It makes my blood warm now to know
How soon Sir Cockerel ceased to crow,
And how 'twas my sure dagger-point
In André's harness found a joint:
For I, who now am old, was young,
And strong the thews were, now unstrung,
And deadly though our danger then,
I would that day were back again;
Ay, would to God that day were back
When André rode to Pont-du-lac!

*A. H. Beesly* [18 -1909]

## THE BALLAD OF FATHER GILLIGAN

THE old priest Peter Gilligan
Was weary night and day;
For half his flock were in their beds,
Or under green sods lay.

Once, while he nodded on a chair,
At the moth-hour of eve,
Another poor man sent for him,
And he began to grieve.

"I have no rest, nor joy, nor peace,
For people die and die";
And after cried he, "God forgive!
My body spake, not I!"

He knelt, and leaning on the chair
He prayed and fell asleep;
And the moth-hour went from the fields,
And stars began to peep.

They slowly into millions grew,
And leaves shook in the wind;
And God covered the world with shade,
And whispered to mankind.

Upon the time of sparrow chirp
When the moths came once more,
The old priest Peter Gilligan
Stood upright on the floor.

"Mavrone, mavrone! the man has died,
While I slept on the chair";
He roused his horse out of his sleep,
And rode with little care.

He rode now as he never rode,
By rocky lane and fen;
The sick man's wife opened the door:
"Father! you come again!"

"And is the poor man dead?" he cried.
"He died an hour ago."
The old priest Peter Gilligan
In grief swayed to and fro.

"When you were gone, he turned and died
As merry as a bird."
The old priest Peter Gilligan
He knelt him at the word.

"He who hath made the night of stars
For souls, who tire and bleed,
Sent one of His great angels down
To help me in my need.

"He who is wrapped in purple robes,
With planets in His care,
Had pity on the least of things
Asleep upon a chair."

*William Butler Yeats* [1865-1939]

## HERVÉ RIEL

I

On the sea and at the Hogue, sixteen hundred ninety-two,
Did the English fight the French,—woe to France!
And, the thirty-first of May, helter-skelter through the blue,
Like a crowd of frightened porpoises a shoal of sharks pursue,
Came crowding ship on ship to Saint Malo on the Rance,
With the English fleet in view.

II

'Twas the squadron that escaped, with the victor in full chase;
First and foremost of the drove, in his great ship, Damfreville;
Close on him fled, great and small,
Twenty-two good ships in all;

And they signalled to the place
"Help the winners of a race!
  Get us guidance, give us harbor, take us quick—or, quicker still,
  Here's the English can and will!"

III

  Then the pilots of the place put out brisk and leapt on board;
  "Why, what hope or chance have ships like these to pass?" laughed they:
"Rocks to starboard, rocks to port, all the passage scarred and scored,
Shall the *Formidable* here, with her twelve-and-eighty guns,
  Think to make the river-mouth by the single narrow way,
Trust to enter where 'tis ticklish for a craft of twenty tons,
    And with flow at full beside?
    Now, 'tis slackest ebb of tide.
  Reach the mooring? Rather say,
While rock stands or water runs,
  Not a ship will leave the bay!"

IV

Then was called a council straight.
Brief and bitter the debate:
"Here's the English at our heels; would you have them take in tow
All that's left us of the fleet, linked together stern and bow,
For a prize to Plymouth Sound?
Better run the ships aground!"
  (Ended Damfreville his speech).
"Not a minute more to wait!
  Let the Captains all and each
  Shove ashore, then blow up, burn the vessels on the beach!
France must undergo her fate.

V

"Give the word!" But no such word
Was ever spoke or heard;
  For up stood, for out stepped, for in struck amid all these

—A Captain? A Lieutenant? A Mate—first, second, third?
No such man of mark, and meet
With his betters to compete!
But a simple Breton sailor pressed by Tourville for the fleet,
A poor coasting-pilot he, Hervé Riel the Croisickese.

VI

And "What mockery or malice have we here?" cries Hervé Riel:
"Are you mad, you Malouins? Are you cowards, fools, or rogues?
Talk to me of rocks and shoals, me who took the soundings, tell
On my fingers every bank, every shallow, every swell
'Twixt the offing here and Grève where the river disembogues?
Are you bought by English gold? Is it love the lying's for?
Morn and eve, night and day,
Have I piloted your bay,
Entered free and anchored fast at the foot of Solidor.
Burn the fleet and ruin France? That were worse than fifty Hogues!
Sirs, they know I speak the truth! Sirs, believe me there's a way!
Only let me lead the line,
Have the biggest ship to steer,
Get this *Formidable* clear,
Make the others follow mine,
And I lead them, most and least, by a passage I know well,
Right to Solidor past Grève,
And there lay them safe and sound;
And if one ship misbehave,—
—Keel so much as grate the ground,
Why, I've nothing but my life,—here's my head!" cries Hervé Riel.

VII

Not a minute more to wait.
"Steer us in, then, small and great!
Take the helm, lead the line, save the squadron!" cried its chief.

Captions, give the sailor place!
He is Admiral, in brief.
Still the north-wind, by God's grace!
See the noble fellow's face
As the big ship, with a bound,
Clears the entry like a hound,
Keeps the passage, as its inch of way were the wide seas profound!
See, safe through shoal and rock,
How they follow in a flock,
Not a ship that misbehaves, not a keel that grates the ground,
Not a spar that comes to grief!
The peril, see, is past.
All are harbored to the last,
And just as Hervé Riel hollas "Anchor!"—sure as fate,
Up the English come,—too late!

### VIII

So, the storm subsides to calm:
They see the green trees wave
On the heights o'erlooking Grève.
Hearts that bled are stanched with balm.
"Just our rapture to enhance,
Let the English rake the bay,
Gnash their teeth and glare askance
As they cannonade away!
'Neath rampired Solidor pleasant riding on the Rance!"
How hope succeeds despair on each Captain's countenance!
Out burst all with one accord,
"This is Paradise for Hell!
Let France, let France's King
Thank the man that did the thing!"
What a shout, and all one word,
"Hervé Riel!"
As he stepped in front once more,
Not a symptom of surprise
In the frank blue Breton eyes,
Just the same man as before.

IX

Then said Damfreville, "My friend,
I must speak out at the end,
  Though I find the speaking hard.
Praise is deeper than the lips:
You have saved the King his ships,
  You must name your own reward.
'Faith, our sun was near eclipse!
Demand whate'er you will,
France remains your debtor still.
Ask to heart's content and have! or my name's not Damfreville."

X

Then a beam of fun outbroke
On the bearded mouth that spoke,
As the honest heart laughed through
Those frank eyes of Breton blue:
"Since I needs must say my say,
  Since on board the duty's done,
  And from Malo Roads to Croisic Point, what is it but a run?—
Since 'tis ask and have, I may—
  Since the others go ashore—
Come! A good whole holiday!
  Leave to go and see my wife, whom I call the Belle Aurore!"
  That he asked and that he got,—nothing more.

XI

Name and deed alike are lost:
Not a pillar or a post
  In his Croisic keeps alive the feat as it befell;
Not a head in white and black
On a single fishing-smack,
In memory of the man but for whom had gone to wrack
  All that France saved from the fight whence England bore the bell:

Go to Paris: rank on rank
  Search the heroes flung pell-mell
On the Louvre, face and flank!
  You shall look long enough ere you come to Hervé Riel.
So, for better and for worse,
Hervé Riel, accept my verse!
In my verse, Hervé Riel, do thou once more
Save the squadron, honor France, love thy wife the Belle
    Aurore!

*Robert Browning* [1812–1889]

## THE HIGHWAYMAN

### PART I

THE wind was a torrent of darkness among the gusty trees,
The moon was a ghostly galleon tossed upon cloudy seas,
The road was a ribbon of moonlight over the purple moor,
And the highwayman came riding—
    Riding—riding—
The highwayman came riding, up to the old inn-door.

He'd a French cocked-hat on his forehead, a bunch of lace
  at his chin,
A coat of the claret velvet, and breeches of brown doe-skin;
They fitted with never a wrinkle: his boots were up to the
  thigh!
And he rode with a jeweled twinkle,
    His pistol butts a-twinkle,
His rapier hilt a-twinkle, under the jeweled sky.

Over the cobbles he clattered and clashed in the dark inn-
  yard,
And he tapped with his whip on the shutters, but all was
  locked and barred;
He whistled a tune to the window, and who should be wait-
  ing there
But the landlord's black-eyed daughter,
    Bess, the landlord's daughter,
Plaiting a dark red love-knot into her long black hair.

And dark in the dark old inn-yard a stable-wicket creaked
Where Tim the ostler listened; his face was white and peaked;
His eyes were hollows of madness, his hair like moldy hay,
But he loved the landlord's daughter,
        The landlord's red-lipped daughter,
Dumb as a dog he listened, and he heard the robber say—

"One kiss, my bonny sweetheart, I'm after a prize to-night,
But I shall be back with the yellow gold before the morning
    light;
Yet, if they press me sharply, and harry me through the
    day,
Then look for me by moonlight,
        Watch for me by moonlight,
I'll come to thee by moonlight, though hell should bar the
    way."

He rose upright in the stirrups; he scarce could reach her
    hand,
But she loosened her hair i' the casement! His face burnt
    like a brand
As the black cascade of perfume came tumbling over his
    breast;
And he kissed its waves in the moonlight,
        (Oh, sweet black waves in the moonlight!)
Then he tugged at his rein in the moonlight, and galloped
    away to the West.

## PART II

He did not come in the dawning; he did not come at noon;
And out o' the tawny sunset, before the rise o' the moon,
When the road was a gipsy's ribbon, looping the purple
    moor,
A red-coat troop came marching—
        Marching—marching—
King George's men came marching, up to the old inn-door.

They said no word to the landlord, they drank his ale instead,
But they gagged his daughter and bound her to the foot of
    her narrow bed;

Two of them knelt at her casement, with muskets at their side!
There was death at every window;
And hell at one dark window;
For Bess could see, through her casement, the road that *he* would ride.

They had tied her up to attention, with many a sniggering jest;
They had bound a musket beside her, with the barrel beneath her breast!
"Now keep good watch!" and they kissed her. She heard the dead man say—
*Look for me by moonlight;*
*Watch for me by moonlight;*
*I'll come to thee by moonlight, though hell should bar the way!*

She twisted her hands behind her; but all the knots held good!
She writhed her hands till her fingers were wet with sweat or blood!
They stretched and strained in the darkness, and the hours crawled by like years,
Till, now, on the stroke of midnight,
Cold, on the stroke of midnight,
The tip of one finger touched it! The trigger at least was hers!

The tip of one finger touched it; she strove no more for the rest!
Up, she stood up to attention, with the barrel beneath her breast,
She would not risk their hearing: she would not strive again;
For the road lay bare in the moonlight;
Blank and bare in the moonlight;
And the blood of her veins in the moonlight throbbed to her love's refrain.

*Tlot-tlot; tlot-tlot!* Had they heard it? The horse-hoofs ringing clear;
*Tlot-tlot, tlot-tlot,* in the distance? Were they deaf that they did not hear?

Down the ribbon of moonlight, over the brow of the hill,
The highwayman came riding,
Riding, riding!
The red-coats looked to their priming! She stood up, straight and still!

*Tlot-tlot*, in the frosty silence! *Tlot-tlot*, in the echoing night!
Nearer he came and nearer! Her face was like a light!
Her eyes grew wide for a moment; she drew one last deep breath,
Then her finger moved in the moonlight,
Her musket shattered the moonlight,
Shattered her breast in the moonlight and warned him—with her death.

He turned; he spurred to the Westward; he did not know who stood
Bowed, with her head o'er the musket, drenched with her own red blood!
Not till the dawn he heard it, his face grew gray to hear
How Bess, the landlord's daughter,
The landlord's black-eyed daughter,
Had watched for her love in the moonlight, and died in the darkness there.

Back, he spurred like a madman, shrieking a curse to the sky,
With the white road smoking behind him, and his rapier brandished high!
Blood-red were his spurs in the golden noon; wine-red was his velvet coat,
When they shot him down on the highway,
Down like a dog on the highway,
And he lay in his blood on the highway, with the bunch of lace at his throat.

. . . . . . . . . . . .

*And still of a winter's night, they say, when the wind is in the trees,*
*When the moon is a ghostly galleon tossed upon cloudy seas,*

*When the road is a ribbon of moonlight over the purple moor,*
*A highwayman comes riding—*
*Riding—riding—*
*A highwayman comes riding, up to the old inn-door.*

*Over the cobbles he clatters and clangs in the dark inn-yard;*
*And he taps with his whip on the shutters, but all is locked and barred;*
*He whistles a tune to the window, and who should be waiting there*
*But the landlord's black-eyed daughter,*
*Bess, the landlord's daughter,*
*Plaiting a dark red love-knot into her long black hair.*

*Alfred Noyes* [1880–1958]

## LANCELOT AND GUINEVERE

Sir Lancelot beside the mere
Rode at the golden close of day,
And the sad eyes of Guinevere
Went with him, with him, all the way.

The golden light to silver turned,
The mist came up out of the mere,
And steadily before him burned
The sombre gaze of Guinevere.

A dreadful chill about him crept,
The pleasant air to winter turned;
Like the wan eyes of one that wept
Far through the mist the faint stars burned.

All that had sinned in days gone by
Like pale companions round him crept—
All that beneath the morning sky
Had called the night to mind and wept.

But strangest showed his own offence
Of all the shadows creeping by;
The star of his magnificence
Fell from its station in the sky.

The lean wind robbed him of his pride;
  Keen grew the sting of his offence;
And like a lamp within him died
  The flame of his magnificence.

The drifting phantoms of the mere
  Were death to pleasure and to pride;
The joy he had of Guinevere
  Faded into the dark and died.

Oh loss of hope with loss of day
  In mist and shadow of the mere!—
Where with him, with him, all the way,
  Went the sad eyes of Guinevere.

*Gerald Gould* [1885–1936]

## BALLAD OF THE GOODLY FERE

SIMON ZELOTES SPEAKETH IT SOMEWHILE AFTER THE CRUCIFIXION

Ha' we lost the goodliest fere o' all
For the priests and the gallows tree?
Aye lover he was of brawny men,
O' ships and the open sea.

When they came wi' a host to take Our Man
His smile was good to see,
"First let these go!" quo' our Goodly Fere,
"Or I'll see ye damned," says he.

Aye he sent us out through the crossed high spears
And the scorn of his laugh rang free,
"Why took ye not me when I walked about
Alone in the town?" says he.

Oh we drunk his "Hale" in the good red wine
When we last made company.
No capon priest was the Goodly Fere,
But a man o' men was he.

I ha' seen him drive a hundred men
Wi' a bundle o' cords swung free;

That they took the high and holy house
For their pawn and treasury.

They'll nc' get him a' in a book, I think,
Though they write it cunningly;
No mouse of the scrolls was the Goodly Fere
But aye loved the open sea.

If they think they ha' snared our Goodly Fere
They are fools to the last degree.
"I'll go the feast," quo' our Goodly Fere,
"Though I go the gallows tree.

"Ye ha' seen me heal the lame and blind,
And wake the dead," says he.
"Ye shall see one thing to master all:
'Tis how a brave man dies on the tree."

A son of God was the Goodly Fere
That bade us his brothers be.
I ha' seen him cow a thousand men.
I have seen him upon the tree.

He cried no cry when they drave the nails
And the blood gushed hot and free.
The hounds of the crimson sky gave tongue,
But never a cry cried he.

I ha' seen him cow a thousand men
On the hills o' Galilee.
They whined as he walked out calm between,
Wi' his eyes like the gray o' the sea.

Like the sea that brooks no voyaging,
With the winds unleashed and free,
Like the sea that he cowed at Genseret
Wi' twey words spoke suddently.

A master of men was the Goodly Fere,
A mate of the wind and sea.
If they think they ha' slain our Goodly Fere
They are fools eternally.

I ha' seen him eat o' the honey-comb
Sin' they nailed him to the tree.

*Ezra Pound* [1885–

## EVE

Eve, with her basket, was
Deep in the bells and grass,
Wading in bells and grass
Up to her knees,
Picking a dish of sweet
Berries and plums to eat,
Down in the bells and grass
Under the trees.

Mute as a mouse in a
Corner the cobra lay,
Curled round a bough of the
Cinnamon tall. . . .
Now to get even and
Humble proud heaven and
Now was the moment or
Never at all.

"Eva!" Each syllable
Light as a flower fell,
"Eva!" he whispered the
Wondering maid,
Soft as a bubble sung
Out of a linnet's lung,
Soft and most silverly
"Eva!" he said.

Picture that orchard sprite,
Eve, with her body white,
Supple and smooth to her
Slim finger tips,
Wondering, listening,
Listening, wondering,
Eve with a berry
Half-way to her lips

Oh, had our simple Eve
Seen through the make-believe!
Had she but known the
Pretender he was!

Out of the boughs he came,
Whispering still her name,
Tumbling in twenty rings
Into the grass.

Here was the strangest pair
In the world anywhere,
Eve in the bells and grass
Kneeling, and he
Telling his story low. . . .
Singing birds saw them go
Down the dark path to
The Blasphemous Tree.

Oh, what a clatter when
Titmouse and Jenny Wren
Saw him successful and
Taking his leave!
How the birds rated him,
How they all hated him!
How they all pitied
Poor motherless Eve!

Picture her crying
Outside in the lane,
Eve, with no dish of sweet
Berries and plums to eat,
Haunting the gate of the
Orchard in vain. . . .
Picture the lewd delight
Under the hill to-night—
"Eva!" the toast goes round,
"Eva!" again. *Ralph Hodgson* [1871-

## "TIME, YOU OLD GIPSY MAN"

TIME, you old gipsy man,
Will you not stay,
Put up your caravan
Just for one day?

All things I'll give you
Will you be my guest,

Bells for your jennet
Of silver the best,
Goldsmiths shall beat you
A great golden ring,
Peacocks shall bow to you,
Little boys sing,
Oh, and sweet girls will
Festoon you with may.
Time, you old gipsy,
Why hasten away?

Last week in Babylon,
Last night in Rome,
Morning, and in the crush
Under Paul's dome;
Under Paul's dial
You tighten your rein—
Only a moment,
And off once again;
Off to some city
Now blind in the womb,
Off to another
Ere that's in the tomb.

Time, you old gipsy man,
Will you not stay,
Put up your caravan
Just for one day?

*Ralph Hodgson* [1871-

## CHANSON OF THE BELLS OF OSENEY

(THIRTEENTH CENTURY)

The bells of Oseney
(*Hautclère*, *Doucement*, *Austyn*)
Chant sweetly every day,
And sadly, for our sin.
The bells of Oseney
(*John*, *Gabriel*, *Marie*)
Chant lowly,
        Chant slowly,

Chant wistfully and holy
Of Christ, our Paladin.

Hautclère chants to the East
(His tongue is silvery high),
And Austyn like a priest
Sends West a weighty cry;
But Doucement set between
(Like an appeasive nun)
Chants cheerly,
          Chants clearly,
As if Christ heard her nearly,
A plea to every sky.

A plea that John takes up
(He is the evangelist)
Till Gabriel's angel cup
Pours sound to sun or mist.
And last of all Marie
(The virgin-voice of God)
Peals purely,
          Demurely,
And with a tone so surely
Divine that all must hear.

The bells of Oseney
(*Doucement*, *Austyn*, *Hautclère*)
Pour ever day by day
Their peals on the rapt air;
And with their mellow mates
(*John*, *Gabriel*, *Marie*)
Tell slowly,
          Tell lowly,
Of Christ the High and Holy,
Who makes the whole world fair.

*Cale Young Rice* [1872–1943]

## THE WASTE PLACES

I

As a naked man I go
  Through the desert sore afraid,

Holding up my head although
  I'm as frightened as a maid.

The couching lion there I saw
  From barren rocks lift up his eye;
He parts the cactus with his paw,
  He stares at me as I go by.

He would follow on my trace
  If he knew I was afraid,
If he knew my hardy face
  Hides the terrors of a maid.

In the night he rises and
  He stretches forth, he snuffs the air;
He roars and leaps along the sand,
  He creeps and watches everywhere.

His burning eyes, his eyes of bale,
  Through the darkness I can see;
He lashes fiercely with his tail,
  He would love to spring at me.

I am the lion in his lair;
  I am the fear that frightens me;
I am the desert of despair
  And the nights of agony.

Night or day, whate'er befall,
  I must walk that desert land,
Until I can dare to call
  The lion out to lick my hand.

II

As a naked man I tread
  The gloomy forests, ring on ring,
Where the sun that's overhead
  Cannot see what's happening.

There I go: the deepest shade,
  The deepest silence pressing me;
And my heart is more afraid
  Than a maiden's heart would be.

Every day I have to run
  Underneath the demon tree,
Where the ancient wrong is done
  While I shrink in agony.

There the demon held a maid
  In his arms, and as she, daft,
Screamed again in fear, he laid
  His lips upon her lips and laughed.

And she beckoned me to run,
  And she called for help to me,
And the ancient wrong was done
  Which is done eternally.

I am the maiden and the fear;
  I am the sunless shade, the strife;
I the demon lips, the sneer
  Showing under every life.

I must tread that gloomy way
  Until I shall dare to run
And bear the demon with his prey
  From the forest to the sun.

*James Stephens* [1882–1950]

## THE WARRIOR MAID

THEY bade me to my spinning
Because I was a maid,
But down into the battle
I marshalled unafraid.

Brightly against the sunbeams
I shook the flaming lance.
Then out I swept to gather
With the red and royal dance.

The war was stately in me,
And in my heart was pride—
Fierce moods like neighing horses
Most terribly did ride.

Deep as a sea of scarlet
I saw the banners roll—
And then the great war terror
Laid hold upon my soul.

I laughed aloud to feel it
And royally did cheer:
I strode amid my tremblings
And did not fear to fear.

A warrior rode against me.
I laid him to his rest.
I could not stop to gather
The bright sword from his breast.

But on I drove in splendor,
I—that was but a maid—
With piercing calls of triumph
And I was not afraid.

But once, beneath my charging,
A face shone up below.
Dead in the bloody furrow,
A stranger white as snow!

The foe rode close behind me!
I lost the day for this—
I sprang from off my stallion
And left on him a kiss.

The sword that pierced his bosom
With jewelled splendor shone.
I snatched it from him bleeding,
And lo, it was my own.

The spears blazed thick around me
When I leaped forth again.
But jubilant they found me
To face a thousand men.

Bright-voicéd was my laughter,
I—that was but a maid!
And when the sharp gyve bound me,
Then was I not afraid.

Ah, hadst thou lived, my warrior,
Among the glorious ones,
I had borne thee savage daughters
And beautiful fierce sons.

*Anna Hempstead Branch* [18 –1937]

## THE SONGS OF GUTHRUM AND ALFRED

From "The Ballad of the White Horse"

He took the great harp wearily,
Even Guthrum of the Danes,
With wide eyes bright as the one long day
On the long polar plains.

For he sang of a wheel returning,
And the mire trod back to mire,
And how red hells and golden heavens
Are castles in the fire.

"It is good to sit where the good tales go,
To sit as our fathers sat;
But the hour shall come after his youth,
When a man shall know not tales but truth,
And his heart fail thereat.

"When he shall read what is written
So plain in clouds and clods,
When he shall hunger without hope
Even for evil gods.

"For this is a heavy matter,
And the truth is cold to tell;
Do we not know, have we not heard,
The soul is like a lost bird,
The body a broken shell?

"And a man hopes, being ignorant,
Till in white woods apart,
He finds at last the lost bird dead:
And a man may still lift up his head,
But never more his heart.

"There comes no noise but weeping
Out of the ancient sky,
And a tear is in the tiniest flower,
Because the gods must die.

"The little brooks are very sweet
Like a girl's ribbons curled,
But the great sea is bitter
That washes all the world.

"Strong are the Roman roses
Or the free flowers of the heath,
But every flower, like a flower of the sea,
Smelleth with the salt of death.

"And the heart of the locked battle
Is the happiest place for men;
When shrieking souls as shafts go by
And many have died and all may die;
Though this word be a mystery,
Death is most distant then.

"Death blazes bright above the cup,
And clear above the crown;
But in that dream of battle
We seem to tread it down.

"Wherefore I am a great King
And waste the world in vain,
Because man hath not other power,
Save that in dealing death for dower,
He may forget it for an hour
To remember it again."

And slowly his hands and thoughtfully
Fell from the lifted lyre,
And the owls moaned from the mighty trees
Till Alfred caught it to his knees
And smote it as in ire.

He heaved the head of the harp on high,
And swept the frame-work barred,

And his stroke had all the rattle and spark
  Of horses flying hard.

"When God put man in a garden
  He girt him with a sword,
And sent him forth a free knight,
  That might betray his lord;

"He brake Him and betrayed Him
  And fast and far he fell
Till you and I may stretch our necks
  And burn our beards in hell.

"But though I lie on the floor of the world
  With the seven sins for rods,
I would rather fall with Adam
  Than rise with all your gods.

"What have the strong gods given?
  Where have the glad gods led?
When Guthrum sits on a hero's throne
  And asks if he is dead?

"Sirs, I am but a nameless man,
  A rhymester without home,
Yet since I come to the Wessex clay
  And carry the cross of Rome,

"I will even answer the mighty earl
  That asked of Wessex men
Why they be meek and monkish folk,
And bow to the White Lord's broken yoke;
What sign have we save blood and smoke?
  Here is my answer then.

"That on you is fallen the shadow,
  And not upon the Name;
That though we scatter and though we fly
And you hang over us like the sky
You are more tired of victory,
  Than we are tired of shame.

"That though you hunt the Christian man
  Like a hare in the hill-side
The hare has still more heart to run
  Than you have heart to ride.

"That though all lances split on you,
  All swords be heaved in vain,
We have more lust again to lose
  Than you to win again.

"Your lord sits high in the saddle,
  A broken-hearted king,
But our King Alfred, lost from fame,
Fallen among foes or bonds of shame,
In I know not what mean trade or name,
  Has still some song to sing;

"Our monks go robed in rain and snow
  But the heart of flame therein,
But you go clothed in feasts and flames
  When all is ice within;

"Nor shall all iron dooms make dumb
  Men wondering ceaselessly,
If it be not better to fast for joy
  Than feast for misery.

"Nor monkish order only
  Slides down, as field to fen,
All things achieved and chosen pass
As the White Horse fades in the grass,
  No work of Christian men.

"Ere the sad gods that made your gods
  Saw their sad sunrise pass,
The White Horse of the White Horse Vale,
That you have left to darken and fail,
  Was cut out of the grass.

"Therefore your end is on you,
  Is on you and your kings,
Not for a fire in Ely fen,

Not that your gods are nine or ten,
But because it is only Christian men
Guard even heathen things,

"For our God hath blessed creation,
Calling it good. I know—
What spirit with whom you blindly band
Hath blessed destruction with this hand;
But by God's death the stars shall stand
And the small apples grow."

And the King, with harp on shoulder,
Stood up and ceased his song;
And the owls moaned from the mighty trees,
And the Danes laughed loud and long.

*Gilbert Keith Chesterton* [1874–1936]

## THE PAGEANT OF SEAMEN

THE song of the sea-adventurers, that never were known to fame,
The roving, roistering mariners that builded our England's name:
Foolhardy, reckless, undaunted,
Death they courted and taunted:
In the jaws of hell their flag they flaunted, answering flame with flame.

An endless pageant of power and pride, they steer from the long-ago
From quays that moulder beneath the tide, from cities whose walls lie low:
Carrack and sloop and galley,
Out of the dark they rally,
As homing birds over hill and valley, back to the land they know.

The crews of the Bristol Guinea-men, that traded to Old Calabar,
Fading for years out of English ken in sweltering seas afar;
The Danes and the Dutch they raced there,

The Brandenburgers they chased there,
They bid the Portingale cargoes waste there, under an evil star.

Their ships came back from the Cameroons, ragged and patched and old,
With decks roof-thatched from the Accra noons—but down in their sultry hold,
Battened from wind and weather,
Were coral and ostrich feather,
Jasper and ivory heaped together, amber and dust of gold.

The Greenland skippers that speared the whale at the edge of the grinding floe,
Icicles fringing sheet and sail, and decks in a smother of snow:
Men of Clyde and of Humber,
Cold is their Arctic slumber,
But their deeds of daring that none may number shall live while the north winds blow.

The stately captains of barque and brig, in the days of the good Queen Anne;
Under each powdered periwig was the brain of a sea-bred man.
Was there work to be done? they did it:
Was there danger? they pressed amid it:
Wounded to death, with a smile they hid it, and perished as sailors can.

The filibusters of Tudor years, that held the ocean in fee,
The buccaneers and the privateers, the outlawed sons of the sea:
Terrible, swift, unsleeping,
Like bolts from the azure leaping,
Like birds of prey on their quarry sweeping, foraging far and free.

The pigtailed bo's'ns of Anson and Cook, and the seafaring men they led—
Who has counted in song or book the roll of those glorious dead?

On the desolate isles uncharted
Their valorous souls departed:
They fought—they fell—and in death, blithe-hearted, cheered as the foeman fled.

The men that talked with a Devon twang, as they hoisted the sails of Drake—
All through the West their rumor rang, the pride of the Dons to break,
Fierce to seize and to sunder
The golden argosies' plunder,
The New World's dread and the Old World's wonder, splendid for England's sake.

The coasting-craft and the fishing-craft, lugger and ketch and hoy,
With a duck-gun fore and a blunderbuss aft, served by a man and a boy;
Their tiny armaments flinging
On frigate and gun-boat—bringing
Prizes and prisoners home with singing, fired with a desperate joy.

Ruffed to the chin, or laced to the knee, or stripped to the waist for fight,
Herding the alien hordes of the sea to fields of defeat and flight,
Or, lit by the lightning's flashing,
Close-hauled through the hurricane thrashing,
With decks a-wash and with spars a-crashing, they swoop on the reeling sight.

The sea-dogs sturdy, the sea-hawks bold, that were never known to fame—
The grim adventurers, young and old, that builded our England's name—
Over the waters of dreaming,
Their bows are rocking and gleaming,
To the sun unsetting their flag is streaming, answering flame with flame.

*May Byron* [1861–1936]

## THE BALLAD OF EAST AND WEST

*Oh, East is East, and West is West, and never the twain shall meet,*
*Till Earth and Sky stand presently at God's great Judgment Seat:*
*But there is neither East nor West, Border, nor Breed, nor Birth,*
*When two strong men stand face to face, though they come from the ends of the earth!*

KAMAL is out with twenty men to raise the Border-side,
And he has lifted the Colonel's mare that is the Colonel's pride:
He has lifted her out of the stable-door between the dawn and the day,
And turned the calkins upon her feet, and ridden her far away.
Then up and spoke the Colonel's son that led a troop of the Guides:
"Is there never a man of all my men can say where Kamal hides?"
Then up and spoke Mohammed Khan, the son of the Ressaldar:
"If ye know the track of the morning-mist, ye know where his pickets are.
At dusk he harries the Abazai—at dawn he is into Bonair,
But he must go by Fort Bukloh to his own place to fare,
So if ye gallop to Fort Bukloh as fast as a bird can fly,
By the favor of God ye may cut him off ere he win to the Tongue of Jagai.
But if he be past the Tongue of Jagai, right swiftly turn ye then,
For the length and the breadth of that grisly plain is sown with Kamal's men.
There is rock to the left, and rock to the right, and low lean thorn between,
And ye may hear a breech-bolt snick where never a man is seen."
The Colonel's son has taken a horse, and a raw rough dun was he,
With the mouth of a bell and the heart of Hell and the head of a gallows-tree.

The Colonel's son to the Fort has won, they bid him stay to eat—
Who rides at the tail of a Border thief, he sits not long at his meat.
He's up and away from Fort Bukloh as fast as he can fly,
Till he was aware of his father's mare in the gut of the Tongue of Jagai,
Till he was aware of his father's mare with Kamal upon her back,
And when he could spy the white of her eye, he made the pistol crack.
He has fired once, he has fired twice, but the whistling ball went wide.
"Ye shoot like a soldier," Kamal said. "Show now if ye can ride."
It's up and over the Tongue of Jagai, as blown dust-devils go.
The dun he fled like a stag of ten, but the mare like a barren doe.
The dun he leaned against the bit and slugged his head above,
But the red mare played with the snaffle-bars, as a maiden plays with a glove.
There was rock to the left and rock to the right, and low lean thorn between,
And thrice he heard a breech-bolt snick though never a man was seen.
They have ridden the low moon out of the sky, their hoofs drum up the dawn,
The dun he went like a wounded bull, but the mare like a new-roused fawn.
The dun he fell at a water-course—in a woeful heap fell he,
And Kamal has turned the red mare back, and pulled the rider free.
He has knocked the pistol out of his hand—small room was there to strive,
" 'Twas only by favor of mine," quoth he, "ye rode so long alive:
There was not a rock for twenty mile, there was not a clump of tree,
But covered a man of my own men with his rifle cocked on his knee.
If I had raised my bridle-hand, as I have held it low,
The little jackals that flee so fast were feasting all in a row:

If I had bowed my head on my breast, as I have held it high,
The kite that whistles above us now were gorged till she
could not fly."
Lightly answered the Colonel's son: "Do good to bird and
beast,
But count who come for the broken meats before thou
makest a feast.
If there should follow a thousand swords to carry my bones
away,
Belike the price of a jackal's meal were more than a thief
could pay.
They will feed their horse on the standing crop, their men
on the garnered grain.
The thatch of the byres will serve their fires when all the
cattle are slain.
But if thou thinkest the price be fair,—thy brethren wait
to sup,
The hound is kin to the jackal-spawn,—howl, dog, and call
them up!
And if thou thinkest the price be high, in steer and gear
and stack,
Give me my father's mare again, and I'll fight my own
way back!"
Kamal has gripped him by the hand and set him upon his feet.
"No talk shall be of dogs," said he, "when wolf and gray
wolf meet.
May I eat dirt if thou hast hurt of me in deed or breath;
What dam of lances brought thee forth to jest at the dawn
with Death?"
Lightly answered the Colonel's son: "I hold by the blood
of my clan:
Take up the mare for my father's gift—by God, she has
carried a man!"
The red mare ran to the Colonel's son, and nuzzled against
his breast;
"We be two strong men," said Kamal then, "but she loveth
the younger best.
So she shall go with a lifter's dower, my turquoise-studded rein,
My broidered saddle and saddle-cloth, and silver stirrups
twain."

The Colonel's son a pistol drew, and held it muzzle-end,
"Ye have taken the one from a foe," said he; "will ye take the mate from a friend?"
"A gift for a gift," said Kamal straight; "a limb for the risk of a limb.
Thy father has sent his son to me, I'll send my son to him!"
With that he whistled his only son, that dropped from a mountain-crest—
He trod the ling like a buck in spring, and he looked like a lance in rest.
"Now here is thy master," Kamal said, "who leads a troop of the Guides,
And thou must ride at his left side as shield on shoulder rides.
Till Death or I cut loose the tie, at camp and board and bed,
Thy life is his—thy fate it is to guard him with thy head.
So thou must eat the White Queen's meat, and all her foes are thine,
And thou must harry thy father's hold for the peace of the Border-line,
And thou must make a trooper tough and hack thy way to power—
Belike they will raise thee to Ressaldar when I am hanged in Peshawur."

They have looked each other between the eyes, and there they found no fault,
They have taken the Oath of the Brother-in-Blood on leavened bread and salt:
They have taken the Oath of the Brother-in-Blood on fire and fresh-cut sod,
On the hilt and the haft of the Khyber knife, and the Wondrous Names of God.
The Colonel's son he rides the mare and Kamal's boy the dun,
And two have come back to Fort Bukloh where there went forth but one.
And when they drew to the Quarter-Guard, full twenty swords flew clear—
There was not a man but carried his feud with the blood of the mountaineer.

"Ha' done! ha' done!" said the Colonel's son. "Put up
the steel at your sides!
Last night ye had struck at a Border thief—to-night 'tis
a man of the Guides!"

*Oh, East is East, and West is West, and never the twain shall
meet,*
*Till Earth and Sky stand presently at God's great Judgment Seat;*
*But there is neither East nor West, Border, nor Breed, nor Birth,*
*When two strong men stand face to face, though they come from
the ends of the earth!*

*Rudyard Kipling* [1865–1936]

## THE MAID

THUNDER of riotous hoofs over the quaking sod;
Clash of reeking squadrons, steel-capped, iron-shod;
The White Maid and white horse, and the flapping banner
of God.

Black hearts riding for money; red hearts riding for fame;
The Maid who rides for France and the King who rides for
shame—
Gentlemen, fools, and a saint riding in Christ's high name!

"Dust to dust!" it is written. Wind-scattered are lance
and bow.
Dust, the Cross of Saint George; dust, the banner of snow.
The bones of the King are crumbled, and rotted the shafts
of the foe.

Forgotten, the young knight's valor; forgotten, the captain's
skill;
Forgotten, the fear and the hate and the mailed hands
raised to kill;
Forgotten, the shields that clashed and the arrows that
cried so shrill.

Like a story from some old book, that battle of long ago:
Shadows, the poor French King and the might of his English
foe;
Shadows, the charging nobles and the archers kneeling
a-row—
But a flame in my heart and my eyes, the Maid with her
banner of snow!

*Theodore Roberts* [1877–1953]

# PART VI

# POEMS OF SENTIMENT AND REFLECTION

## THE NOBLE NATURE

**From "An Ode to Sir Lucius Cary and Sir H. Morison"**

It is not growing like a tree
In bulk, doth make man better be;
Or standing long an oak, three hundred year,
To fall a log at last, dry, bald, and sear:
A lily of a day
Is fairer far in May,
Although it fall and die that night,—
It was the plant and flower of Light.
In small proportions we just beauties see,
And in short measures life may perfect be.

*Ben Jonson* [1573?-1637]

# THE PHILOSOPHY OF LIFE

## SWEET AND SOUR

From "Amoretti"

SWEET is the rose, but grows upon a brier;
Sweet is the juniper, but sharp his bough;
Sweet is the eglantine, but pricketh near;
Sweet is the fir-bloom, but his branches rough;
Sweet is the cypress, but his rind is tough;
Sweet is the nut, but bitter is his pill;
Sweet is the broom-flower, but yet sour enough;
And sweet is moly, but his root is ill:
So every sweet with sour is tempered still.
That maketh it be coveted the more;
For easy things, that may be got at will,
Most sorts of men do set but little store.
Why then should I account of little pain,
That endless pleasure shall unto me gain?

*Edmund Spenser* [1552?–1599]

## SIC VITA

LIKE to the falling of a Star;
Or as the flights of Eagles are;
Or like the fresh Spring's gaudy hue;
Or silver drops of morning Dew;
Or like a Wind that chafes the Flood;
Or Bubbles which on water stood;
Even such is Man, whose borrow'd light
Is straight call'd in, and paid to night.

The Wind blows out; the Bubble dies;
The Spring entomb'd in Autumn lies;
The Dew dries up; the Star is shot;
The Flight is past; and Man forgot.

*Henry King* [1592–1669]

## ALL IS VANITY

WHETHER men do laugh or weep,
Whether they do wake or sleep,
Whether they die young or old,
Whether they feel heat or cold;
There is underneath the sun
Nothing in true earnest done.

All our pride is but a jest,
None are worst and none are best,
Grief and joy, and hope and fear
Play their pageants everywhere:
Vain Opinion all doth sway,
And the world is but a play.

Powers above in clouds do sit,
Mocking our poor apish wit,
That so lamely with such state
Their high glory imitate.
No ill can be felt but pain,
And that happy men disdain.

*Philip Rosseter* [1575?–1623]

## TIMES GO BY TURNS

THE loppèd tree in time may grow again,
Most naked plants renew both fruit and flower;
The sorriest wight may find release of pain,
The driest soil suck in some moistening shower;
Times go by turns, and chances change by course,
From foul to fair, from better hap to worse.

The sea of Fortune doth not ever flow,
She draws her favors to the lowest ebb;
Her tides have equal times to come and go,
Her loom doth weave the fine and coarsest web;
No joy so great but runneth to an end,
No hap so hard but may in fine amend.

Not always fall of leaf, nor ever spring,
No endless night, yet not eternal day;
The saddest birds a season find to sing,
The roughest storm a calm may soon allay:
Thus, with succeeding turns, God tempereth all,
That man may hope to rise, yet fear to fall.

A chance may win that by mischance was lost;
That net that holds no great, takes little fish;
In some things all, in all things none are crossed;
Few all they need, but none have all they wish.
Unmingled joys here to no man befall:
Who least, hath some; who most, hath never all.

*Robert Southwell* [1561?–1595]

## "SAY NOT, THE STRUGGLE NAUGHT AVAILETH"

Say not, the struggle naught availeth,
  The labor and the wounds are vain,
The enemy faints not, nor faileth,
  And as things have been they remain.

If hopes were dupes, fears may be liars;
  It may be, in yon smoke concealed,
Your comrades chase e'en now the fliers,
  And, but for you, possess the field.

For while the tired waves, vainly breaking,
  Seem here no painful inch to gain,
Far back, through creeks and inlets making,
  Comes silent, flooding in, the main.

And not by eastern windows only,
  When daylight comes, comes in the light;
In front, the sun climbs slow, how slowly,
  But westward, look, the land is bright.

*Arthur Hugh Clough* [1819–1861]

## KYRIELLE

A LARK in the mesh of the tangled vine,
A bee that drowns in the flower-cup's wine,
A fly in the sunshine,—such is man.
All things must end, as all began.

A little pain, a little pleasure,
A little heaping up of treasure;
Then no more gazing upon the sun.
All things must end that have begun.

Where is the time for hope or doubt?
A puff of the wind, and life is out;
A turn of the wheel, and rest is won.
All things must end that have begun.

Golden morning and purple night,
Life that fails with the failing light;
Death is the only deathless one.
All things must end that have begun.

Ending waits on the brief beginning;
Is the prize worth the stress of winning?
E'en in the dawning the day is done.
All things must end that have begun.

Weary waiting and weary striving,
Glad outsetting and sad arriving;
What is it worth when the goal is won?
All things must end that have begun.

Speedily fades the morning glitter;
Love grows irksome and wine grows bitter.
Two are parted from what was one.
All things must end that have begun.

Toil and pain and the evening rest;
Joy is weary and sleep is best;
Fair and softly the day is done.
All things must end that have begun.

*John Payne* [1842–1916]

## "LET ME ENJOY"

LET me enjoy the earth no less
Because the all-enacting Might
That fashioned forth its loveliness
Had other aims than my delight.

About my path there flits a Fair,
Who throws me not a word or sign;
I will find charm in her uncare,
And laud those lips not meant for mine.

From manuscripts of moving song
Inspired by scenes and souls unknown,
I'll pour out raptures that belong
To others, as they were my own.

Perhaps some day, toward Paradise
And all its blest—if such should be—
I shall lift glad, afar-off eyes,
Though it contain no place for me.

*Thomas Hardy* [1840–1928]

## SONG

BECAUSE the rose must fade,
  Shall I not love the rose?
Because the summer shade
  Passes when winter blows,
Shall I not rest me there
In the cool air?

Because the sunset sky
  Makes music in my soul,
Only to fail and die,
  Shall I not take the whole
Of beauty that it gives
While yet it lives?

Because the sweet of youth
  Doth vanish all too soon,
Shall I forget, forsooth,
  To learn its lingering tune;
My joy to memorize
In those young eyes?

If, like the summer flower
  That blooms—a fragrant death,
Keen music hath no power
  To live beyond its breath,
Then of this flood of song
Let me drink long!

Ah, yes, because the rose
  Fades like the sunset skies;
Because rude winter blows
  All bare, and music dies—
Therefore, now is to me
Eternity!

*Richard Watson Gilder* [1844-1909]

## "WHERE RUNS THE RIVER"

WHERE runs the river? Who can say
Who hath not followed all the way
By alders green and sedges gray
  And blossoms blue?

Where runs the river? Hill and wood
Curve round to hem the eager flood;
It cannot straightly as it would
  Its path pursue.

Yet this we know: O'er whatso plains
Or rocks or waterfalls it strains,
At last the Vast the stream attains;
  And I, and you.

*Francis William Bourdillon* [1852-1921]

## SELF-DEPENDENCE

WEARY of myself, and sick of asking
What I am, and what I ought to be,
At this vessel's prow I stand, which bears me
Forwards, forwards, o'er the starlit sea.

And a look of passionate desire
O'er the sea and to the stars I send:
"Ye who from my childhood up have calmed me,
Calm me, ah, compose me to the end!

"Ah, once more," I cried, "ye stars, ye waters,
On my heart your mighty charm renew;
Still, still let me, as I gaze upon you,
Feel my soul becoming vast like you!"

From the intense, clear, star-sown vault of heaven,
Over the lit sea's unquiet way,
In the rustling night-air came the answer:
"Wouldst thou *be* as these are? *Live* as they.

"Unaffrighted by the silence round them,
Undistracted by the sights they see,
These demand not that the things without them
Yield them love, amusement, sympathy.

"And with joy the stars perform their shining,
And the sea its long moon-silvered roll;
For self-poised they live, nor pine with noting
All the fever of some differing soul.

"Bounded by themselves, and unregardful
In what state God's other works may be,
In their own tasks all their powers pouring,
These attain the mighty life you see."

O air-born voice! long since, severely clear,
A cry like thine in mine own heart I hear:
"Resolve to be thyself; and know, that he,
Who finds himself, loses his misery!"

*Matthew Arnold* [1822–1888]

## HOPE AND FEAR

BENEATH the shadow of dawn's aerial cope,
With eyes enkindled as the sun's own sphere,
Hope from the front of youth in godlike cheer
Looks Godward, past the shades where blind men grope
Round the dark door that prayers nor dreams can ope,
And makes for joy the very darkness dear
That gives her wide wings play; nor dreams that Fear
At noon may rise and pierce the heart of Hope.
Then, when the soul leaves off to dream and yearn,
May Truth first purge her eyesight to discern
What once being known leaves time no power to appall;
Till youth at last, ere yet youth be not, learn
The kind wise word that falls from years that fall—
"Hope not thou much, and fear thou not at all."

*Algernon Charles Swinburne* [1837–1909]

## ON HIS BLINDNESS

WHEN I consider how my light is spent
Ere half my days in this dark world and wide,
And that one talent, which is death to hide,
Lodged with me useless, though my soul more bent
To serve therewith my Maker, and present
My true account, lest He returning chide;
"Doth God exact day-labor, light denied?"
I fondly ask. But Patience, to prevent
That murmur, soon replies, "God doth not need
Either man's work or his own gifts; who best
Bear his mild yoke, they serve him best; his state
Is kingly; thousands at his bidding speed,
And post o'er land and ocean without rest;
They also serve who only stand and wait."

*John Milton* [1608–1674]

## OZYMANDIAS OF EGYPT

I MET a traveler from an antique land
Who said: Two vast and trunkless legs of stone

Stand in the desert. Near them, on the sand,
Half sunk, a shattered visage lies, whose frown
And wrinkled lip and sneer of cold command
Tell that its sculptor well those passions read
Which yet survive, stamped on these lifeless things,
The hand that mocked them and the heart that fed;
And on the pedestal these words appear:
"My name is Ozymandias, king of kings:
Look on my works, ye Mighty, and despair!"
Nothing beside remains. Round the decay
Of that colossal wreck, boundless and bare,
The lone and level sands stretch far away.

*Percy Bysshe Shelley* [1792–1822]

## A TURKISH LEGEND

A CERTAIN Pasha, dead five thousand years,
Once from his harem fled in sudden tears,

And had this sentence on the city's gate
Deeply engraven, "Only God is great."

So these four words above the city's noise
Hung like the accents of an angel's voice,

And evermore, from the high barbican,
Saluted each returning caravan.

Lost is that city's glory. Every gust
Lifts, with dead leaves, the unknown Pasha's dust,

And all is ruin,—save one wrinkled gate
Whereon is written, "Only God is great."

*Thomas Bailey Aldrich* [1837–1907]

## "EVEN THIS SHALL PASS AWAY"

ONCE in Persia reigned a King,
Who upon his signet ring
'Graved a maxim true and wise,
Which, if held before the eyes,

Gave him counsel at a glance,
Fit for every change and chance.
Solemn words, and these are they:
"Even this shall pass away."

Trains of camels through the sand
Brought him gems from Samarcand;
Fleets of galleys through the seas
Brought him pearls to match with these.
But he counted not his gain
Treasures of the mine or main;
"What is wealth?" the King would say;
"Even this shall pass away."

In the revels of his court
At the zenith of the sport,
When the palms of all his guests
Burned with clapping at his jests,
He, amid his figs and wine,
Cried: "Oh, loving friends of mine!
Pleasure comes, but not to stay;
Even this shall pass away."

Fighting on a furious field,
Once a javelin pierced his shield;
Soldiers with a loud lament
Bore him bleeding to his tent;
Groaning from his tortured side,
"Pain is hard to bear," he cried,
"But with patience, day by day—
Even this shall pass away."

Towering in the public square,
Twenty cubits in the air,
Rose his statue, carved in stone.
Then the King, disguised, unknown,
Stood before his sculptured name,
Musing meekly, "What is fame?
Fame is but a slow decay—
Even this shall pass away."

Struck with palsy, sere and old,
Waiting at the gates of gold,
Said he, with his dying breath:
"Life is done, but what is death?"
Then, in answer to the King,
Fell a sunbeam on his ring,
Showing by a heavenly ray—
"Even this shall pass away."

*Theodore Tilton* [1835–1907]

## SESOSTRIS

Sole Lord of Lords and very King of Kings,
He sits within the desert, carved in stone;
Inscrutable, colossal, and alone,
And ancienter than memory of things.
Graved on his front the sacred beetle clings;
Disdain sits on his lips; and in a frown
Scorn lives upon his forehead for a crown.
The affrighted ostrich dare not dust her wings
Anear this Presence. The long caravan's
Dazed camels pause, and mute the Bedouins stare.
This symbol of past power more than man's
Presages doom. Kings look—and Kings despair:
Their scepters tremble in their jeweled hands
And dark thrones totter in the baleful air!

*Lloyd Mifflin* [1846–1921]

## THREE SONNETS ON OBLIVION

### OBLIVION

Her eyes have seen the monoliths of kings
Upcast like foam of the effacing tide;
She has beheld the desert stars deride
The monuments of power's imaginings:
About their base the wind Assyrian flings
The dust that throned the satrap in his pride;
Cambyses and the Memphian pomps abide

As in the flame the moth's presumptuous wings.
There gleams no glory that her hand shall spare,
Nor any sun whose rays shall cross her night,
Whose realm enfolds man's empire and its end.
No armor of renown her sword shall dare,
No council of the gods withstand her might—
Stricken at last Time's lonely Titans bend.

### THE DUST DETHRONED

Sargon is dust, Semiramis a clod.
In crypts profaned the moon at midnight peers;
The owl upon the Sphinx hoots in her ears,
And scant and sere the desert grasses nod
Where once the armies of Assyria trod,
With younger sunlight splendid on the spears;
The lichens cling the closer with the years,
And seal the eyelids of the weary god.
Where high the tombs of royal Egypt heave,
The vulture shadows with arrested wings
The indecipherable boasts of kings,
Till Arab children hear their mother's cry
And leave in mockery their toy—they leave
The skull of Pharaoh staring at the sky.

### THE NIGHT OF GODS

Their mouths have drunken Death's eternal wine—
The draught that Baal in oblivion sips.
Unseen about their courts the adder slips,
Unheard the sucklings of the leopard whine;
The toad has found a resting-place divine,
And bloats in stupor between Ammon's lips.
O Carthage and the unreturning ships,
The fallen pinnacle, the shifting Sign!
Lo! when I hear from voiceless court and fane
Time's adoration of Eternity,—
The cry of kingdoms past and gods undone,—
I stand as one whose feet at noontide gain
A lonely shore; who feels his soul set free,
And hears the blind sea chanting to the sun.

*George Sterling* [1869–1926]

## THE MAGIC MIRROR

THE Magic Mirror makes not nor unmakes,
Charms none to sleep nor any from sleep wakes;
It only giveth back the thing it takes.

It is the heart's own cheer that makes it glad,
And one's own bitterness will drive him mad;
It needeth not that other help be had.

The Mirror maketh none to rise or fall;
To him that hath not doth no portion call;
To him that hath is freely given all.

They see themselves who look in Fortune's face;
Unto the sad is sadness Heaven's grace,
And to the souls that love is love's embrace.

*Henry Mills Alden* [1836–1919]

## EBB AND FLOW

I WALKED beside the evening sea,
And dreamed a dream that could not be;
The waves that plunged along the shore
Said only—"Dreamer, dream no more!"

But still the legions charged the beach;
Loud rang their battle-cry, like speech;
But changed was the imperial strain:
It murmured—"Dreamer, dream again!"

I homeward turned from out the gloom,—
That sound I heard not in my room;
But suddenly a sound, that stirred
Within my very breast, I heard.

It was my heart, that like a sea
Within my breast beat ceaselessly:
But like the waves along the shore,
It said—"Dream on!" and "Dream no more!"

*George William Curtis* [1824–1892]

## THE KING OF DREAMS

Some must delve when the dawn is nigh;
  Some must toil when the noonday beams;
But when night comes, and the soft winds sigh,
  Every man is a King of Dreams!

One must plod while another must ply
  At plow or loom till the sunset streams,
But when night comes, and the moon rides high,
  Every man is a King of Dreams!

One is slave to a master's cry,
  Another serf to a despot seems,
But when night comes, and the discords die,
  Every man is a King of Dreams!

This you may sell and that may buy,
  And this you may barter for gold that gleams,
But there's one domain that is fixed for aye,—
  Every man is a King of Dreams!

*Clinton Scollard* [1860–1932]

## IF ONLY THE DREAMS ABIDE

If the things of earth must pass
Like the dews upon the grass,
Like the mists that break and run
At the forward sweep of the sun,
I shall be satisfied
If only the dreams abide.

Nay, I would not be shorn
Of gold from the mines of morn!
I would not be bereft
Of the last blue flower in the cleft,—
Of the haze that haunts the hills,
Or the moon that the midnight fills!
Still would I know the grace
Upon love's uplifted face,

And the slow, sweet joy-dawn there
Under the dusk of her hair.

I pray thee, spare me, Fate,
The woeful, wearying weight
Of a heart that feels no pain
At the sob of the autumn rain,
And takes no breath of glee
From the organ-surge of the sea,—
Of a mind where memory broods
Over songless solitudes!
I shall be satisfied
If only the dreams abide.

*Clinton Scollard* [1860–1932]

## NEW DREAMS FOR OLD

**Is** there no voice in the world to come crying,
"New dreams for old!
New for old!" ?
Many have long in my heart been lying,
Faded, weary, and cold.
All of them, all, would I give for a new one.
(Is there no seeker
Of dreams that were?)
Nor would I ask if the new were a true one:
Only for new dreams!
New for old!

For I am here, halfway of my journey,
Here with the old!
All so old!
And the best heart with death is at tourney,
If naught new it is told.
Will there no voice, then, come—or a vision—
Come with the beauty
That ever blows
Out of the lands that are called Elysian?
I must have new dreams!
New for old!

*Cale Young Rice* [1872–1943]

## "LORD OF MY HEART'S ELATION"

LORD of my heart's elation,
Spirit of things unseen,
Be thou my aspiration
Consuming and serene!

Bear up, bear out, bear onward,
This mortal soul alone,
To selfhood or oblivion,
Incredibly thine own,—

As the foamheads are loosened
And blown along the sea,
Or sink and merge forever
In that which bids them be.

I, too, must climb in wonder,
Uplift at thy command,—
Be one with my frail fellows
Beneath the wind's strong hand,

A fleet and shadowy column
Of dust or mountain rain,
To walk the earth a moment
And be dissolved again.

Be thou my exaltation
Or fortitude of mien,
Lord of the world's elation,
Thou breath of things unseen!

*Bliss Carman* [1861–1929]

## THE HIGHER PANTHEISM

THE sun, the moon, the stars, the seas, the hills and the plains—
Are not these, O Soul, the Vision of Him who reigns?

Is not the Vision he? though He be not that which He
seems?
Dreams are true while they last, and do we not live in
dreams?

Earth, these solid stars, this weight of body and limb,
Are they not sign and symbol of thy division from Him?

Dark is the world to thee: thyself art the reason why;
For is He not all but thou, that hast power to feel "I am I"?

Glory about thee, without thee; and thou fulfillest thy doom,
Making Him broken gleams, and a stifled splendor and
gloom.

Speak to Him, thou, for He hears, and Spirit with Spirit can
meet—
Closer is He than breathing, and nearer than hands and feet.

God is law, say the wise; O Soul, and let us rejoice,
For if He thunder by law the thunder is yet His voice.

Law is God, say some: no God at all, says the fool;
For all we have power to see is a straight staff bent in a pool;

And the ear of man cannot hear, and the eye of man cannot
see;
But if we could see and hear, this Vision—were it not He?

*Alfred Tennyson* [1809–1892]

## THE WHITE PEACE

It lies not on the sunlit hill
Nor on the sunlit plain:
Nor ever on any running stream
Nor on the unclouded main—

But sometimes, through the Soul of Man,
Slow moving o'er his pain,
The moonlight of a perfect peace
Floods heart and brain.

*William Sharp* [1855–1905]

## THE MYSTIC'S PRAYER

LAY me to sleep in sheltering flame,
  O Master of the Hidden Fire!
Wash pure my heart, and cleanse for me
  My soul's desire.

In flame of sunrise bathe my mind,
  O Master of the Hidden Fire,
That, when I wake, clear eyed may be
  My soul s desire.

*William Sharp* [1855–1905]

## THE PLAY

THE endless mime goes on; new faces come,
  New mummers babble in each other's ears;
And some wear masks of woe, of laughter some,
  Nor know they play Life's Comedy of Tears.

*James B. Kenyon* [1858–1924]

## TRIFLES

THE massive gates of Circumstance
  Are turned upon the smallest hinge,
And thus some seeming pettiest chance
  Oft gives our life its after-tinge.

The trifles of our daily lives,
  The common things scarce worth recall,
Whereof no visible trace survives,
  These are the mainsprings, after all.

*Unknown*

## BOOKRA

As I lay asleep in Italy.—SHELLEY

ONE night I lay asleep in Africa,
In a closed garden by the city gate;
A desert horseman, furious and late,
Came wildly thundering at the massive bar,

"Open in Allah's name! Wake, Mustapha!
Slain is the Sultan,—treason, war, and hate
Rage from Fez to Tetuan! Open straight."
The watchman heard as thunder from afar:
"Go to! In peace this city lies asleep;
To all-knowing Allah 'tis no news you bring;"
Then turned in slumber still his watch to keep.
At once a nightingale began to sing,
In oriental calm the garden lay,—
Panic and war postponed another day.

*Charles Dudley Warner* [1829–1900]

## INTO THE TWILIGHT

Out-worn heart, in a time out-worn,
Come clear of the nets of wrong and right;
Laugh, heart, again in the gray twilight,
Sigh, heart, again in the dew of the morn

Your mother Eire is always young,
Dew ever shining and twilight gray;
Though hope fall from you and love decay,
Burning in fires of a slanderous tongue.

Come, heart, where hill is heaped upon hill:
For there the mystical brotherhood
Of sun and moon and hollow and wood
And river and stream work out their will;

And God stands winding His lonely horn,
And time and the world are ever in flight;
And love is less kind than the gray twilight,
And hope is less dear than the dew of the morn.

*William Butler Yeats* [1865–1939]

## TEARS

When I consider Life and its few years—
A wisp of fog betwixt us and the sun;
A call to battle, and the battle done
Ere the last echo dies within our ears;

A rose choked in the grass; an hour of fears;
The gusts that past a darkening shore do beat;
The burst of music down an unlistening street—
I wonder at the idleness of tears.
Ye old, old dead, and ye of yesternight,
Chieftains, and bards, and keepers of the sheep,
By every cup of sorrow that you had,
Loose me from tears, and make me see aright
How each hath back what once he stayed to weep;
Homer his sight, David his little lad!

*Lizette Woodworth Reese* [1856–1935]

## VERS LA VIE

**The statue by Victor Rosseau in the Palais des Beaux Arts, Brussels**

ANGEL, hast thou betrayed me? Long ago
In the Forgotten Land of souls that wait,
Thou leddest me to the outward-folding gate,
Bidding me live. I leaned into the flow
Of earthward-rushing spirits, fain to know
What are humanity and human fate
Of which the rumor reached to where we sate
In our cool, hidden, dreamless ante-glow.
But I learn not, and am bewildered here
To know why thou with seeming-kindly hands
Didst let me forth, explorer of a star
Where all is strange, and very often Fear
Urges retreat to that Forgotten Land's
Unthoughtful shores where thou and Silence are!

*Arthur Upson* [1877–1908]

## LEAVES

ONE by one, like leaves from a tree,
All my faiths have forsaken me;
But the stars above my head
Burn in white and delicate red,
And beneath my feet the earth
Brings the sturdy grass to birth.

**I** who was content to be
But a silken-singing tree,
But a rustle of delight
In the wistful heart of night—
I have lost the leaves that knew
Touch of rain and weight of dew.
Blinded by a leafy crown,
I looked neither up nor down—
But the little leaves that die
Have left me room to see the sky;
Now for the first time I know
Stars above and earth below.

*Sara Teasdale* [1884–1933]

## PRE-EXISTENCE

WHILE sauntering through the crowded street,
Some half-remembered face I meet,

Albeit upon no mortal shore
That face, methinks, has smiled before.

Lost in a gay and festal throng,
I tremble at some tender song,

Set to an air whose golden bars
I must have heard in other stars.

In sacred aisles I pause to share
The blessing of a priestly prayer,—

When the whole scene which greets mine eyes
In some strange mode I recognize,

As one whose every mystic part
I feel prefigured in my heart.

At sunset, as I calmly stand,
A stranger on an alien strand,

Familiar as my childhood's home
Seems the long stretch of wave and foam.

One sails toward me o'er the bay,
And what he comes to do and say

I can foretell. A prescient lore
Springs from some life outlived of yore.

O swift, instinctive, startling gleams
Of deep soul-knowledge! not as *dreams*

For aye ye vaguely dawn and die,
But oft with lightning certainty

Pierce through the dark, oblivious brain,
To make old thoughts and memories plain—

Thoughts which perchance must travel back
Across the wild, bewildering track

Of countless æons; memories far,
High-reaching as yon pallid star,

Unknown, scarce seen, whose flickering grace
Faints on the outmost rings of space!

*Paul Hamilton Hayne* [1830–1886]

## ENVOY

From "Songs from Vagabondia"

I

HAVE little care that Life is brief,
And less that Art is long.
Success is in the silences
Though Fame is in the song.

II

With the Orient in her eyes,
Life my mistress lured me on.
"Knowledge," said that look of hers,
"Shall be yours when all is done."

Like a pomegranate in halves,
"Drink me," said that mouth of hers,
And I drank who now am here
Where my dust with dust confers.

*Bliss Carman* [1861–1929]

## THE PETRIFIED FERN

In a valley, centuries ago,
Grew a little fern-leaf, green and slender,
Veining delicate and fibers tender;
Waving when the wind crept down so low.
Rushes tall, and moss, and grass grew round it,
Playful sunbeams darted in and found it,
Drops of dew stole in by night, and crowned it,
But no foot of man e'er trod that way;
Earth was young, and keeping holiday.

Monster fishes swam the silent main,
Stately forests waved their giant branches,
Mountains hurled their snowy avalanches,
Mammoth creatures stalked across the plain;
Nature reveled in grand mysteries,
But the little fern was not of these,
Did not number with the hills and trees;
Only grew and waved its wild sweet way,—
No one came to note it day by day.

Earth, one time, put on a frolic mood,
Heaved the rocks and changed the mighty motion
Of the deep, strong currents of the ocean;
Moved the plain and shook the haughty wood,
Crushed the little fern in soft moist clay,
Covered it, and hid it safe away.
Oh, the long, long centuries since that day!
Oh, the changes! Oh, life's bitter cost,
Since that useless little fern was lost!

Useless? Lost? There came a thoughtful man
Searching Nature's secrets, far and deep;
From a fissure in a rocky steep
He withdrew a stone, o'er which there ran

Fairy pencilings, a quaint design,
Veinings, leafage, fibers clear and fine.
And the fern's life lay in every line!
So, I think, God hides some souls away,
Sweetly to surprise us, the last day.

*Mary Bolles Branch* [1840–1922]

## THE QUESTION WHITHER

When we have thrown off this old suit,
So much in need of mending,
To sink among the naked mute,
Is that, think you, our ending?
We follow many, more we lead,
And you who sadly turf us,
Believe not that all living seed
Must flower above the surface.

Sensation is a gracious gift,
But were it cramped to station,
The prayer to have it cast adrift,
Would spout from all sensation.
Enough if we have winked to sun,
Have sped the plow a season;
There is a soul for labor done,
Endureth fixed as reason.

Then let our trust be firm in Good,
Though we be of the fasting;
Our questions are a mortal brood,
Our work is everlasting.
We children of Beneficence
Are in its being sharers;
And Whither vainer sounds than Whence,
For word with such wayfarers.

*George Meredith* [1828–1909]

## THE GOOD GREAT MAN

How seldom, friend, a good great man inherits
Honor or wealth, with all his worth and pains!

It sounds like stories from the land of spirits
If any man obtain that which he merits
  Or any merit that which he obtains.

### REPLY TO THE ABOVE

For shame, dear friend! renounce this canting strain!
What wouldst thou have a good great man obtain?
Wealth, title, dignity, a gilded chain,
Or throne of corses which his sword hath slain?
Greatness and goodness are not means, but ends.
Hath he not always treasures, always friends,—
The good great man? Three treasures,—love, and light
  And calm thoughts, equable as infant's breath;
And three firm friends, more sure than day and night,—
  Himself, his Maker, and the Angel Death.

*Samuel Taylor Coleridge* [1772–1834]

## HUMAN FRAILTY

WEAK and irresolute is man;
  The purpose of to-day,
Woven with pains into his plan,
  To-morrow rends away.

The bow well bent, and smart the spring,
  Vice seems already slain;
But Passion rudely snaps the string,
  And it revives again.

Some foe to his upright intent
  Finds out his weaker part;
Virtue engages his assent,
  But Pleasure wins his heart.

'Tis here the folly of the wise
  Through all his art we view:
And while his tongue the charge denies,
  His conscience owns it true.

Bound on a voyage of awful length
  And dangers little known,
A stranger to superior strength,
  Man vainly trusts his own.

But oars alone can ne'er prevail
  To reach the distant coast;
The breath of Heaven must swell the sail,
  Or all the toil is lost.

*William Cowper* [1731-1800]

## STANZAS

Where forlorn sunsets flare and fade
  On desolate sea and lonely sand,
Out of the silence and the shade
  What is the voice of strange command
Calling you still, as friend calls friend
  With love that cannot brook delay,
To rise and follow the ways that wend
  Over the hills and far away?

Hark to the city, street on street
  A roaring reach of death and life,
Of vortices that clash and fleet
  And ruin in appointed strife;
Hark to it calling, calling clear,
  Calling until you cannot stay,
From dearer things than your own most dear
  Over the hills and far away.

Out of the sound of the ebb-and-flow,
  Out of the sight of lamp and star,
It calls you where the good winds blow,
  And the unchanging meadows are;
From faded hopes and hopes agleam,
  It calls you, calls you night and day
Beyond the dark, into the dream
  Over the hills and far away.

*William Ernest Henley* [1849-1903]

## THE SEEKERS

Friends and loves we have none, nor wealth, nor blest
abode,
But the hope, the burning hope, and the road, the lonely
road.

Not for us are content, and quiet, and peace of mind,
For we go seeking a city that we shall never find.

There is no solace on earth for us—for such as we—
Who search for a hidden city that we shall never see.

Only the road and the dawn, the sun, the wind, the rain,
And the watch-fire under stars, and sleep, and the road
again.

We seek the City of God, and the haunt where beauty
dwells,
And we find the noisy mart and the sound of burial bells.

Never the golden city, where radiant people meet,
But the dolorous town where mourners are going about the
street.

We travel the dusty road till the light of the day is dim
And sunset shows us spires away on the world's rim.

We travel from dawn till dusk, till the day is past and by,
Seeking the Holy City beyond the rim of the sky.

Friends and loves we have none, nor wealth, nor blest abode,
But the hope, the burning hope, and the road, the lonely
road.

*John Masefield* [1878–

## THE AGNOSTIC'S CREED

At last I have ceased repining, at last I accept my fate;
I have ceased to beat at the Portal, I have ceased to knock
at the Gate;
I have ceased to work at the Puzzle, for the Secret has ended
my search,
And I know that the Key is entrusted to never a creed nor
church.

They have threatened with lakes of fire, they have threatened with fetters of hell;
They have offered me heights of heaven with their fields of asphodel;
But the Threat and the Bribe are useless if Reason be strong and stout,
And an honest man can never surrender an honest doubt.

The fables of hell and of heaven are but worn-out Christmas toys
To coax or to bribe or to frighten the grown-up girls and boys;
I have ceased to be an infant, I have travelled beyond their span—
It may do for women and children, but it never will do for a man.

They are all alike, these churches: Mohammedan, Christian, Parsee;
You are vile, you are curst, you are outcast, if you be not as they be;
But my Reason stands against them, and I go as it bids me go;
Its commands are as calls of a trumpet, and I follow for weal or woe.

But oh! it is often cheerless, and oh! it is often chill,
And I often sigh to heaven as my path grows steep and still.
I have left behind my comrades, with their prattle and childish noise;
My boyhood now is behind me, with all of its broken toys!

Oh! that God of gods is glorious, the emperor of every land;
He carries the moon and the planets in the palm of His mighty hand;
He is girt with the belt of Orion, he is Lord of the suns and stars,
A wielder of constellations, of Canopus, Arcturus, and Mars!

I believe in Love and Duty, I believe in the True and Just;
I believe in the common kinship of everything born from dust.

I hope that the Right will triumph, that the sceptered
Wrong will fall;
That Death will at last be defeated, that the Grave will not
end all.

I believe in the martyrs and heroes who have died for the
sake of Right;
And I promise, like them, to follow in my Reason's faithful
light;
If my Reason errs in Judgment, I but honestly strive as
I can;
If a God decrees my downfall, I shall stand it like a man.

*Walter Malone* [1866–1915]

## A DOUBTING HEART

WHERE are the swallows fled?
Frozen and dead
Perchance upon some bleak and stormy shore.
O doubting heart!
Far over purple seas
They wait, in sunny ease,
The balmy southern breeze,
To bring them to their northern homes once more.

Why must the flowers die?
Prisoned they lie
In the cold tomb, heedless of tears or rain.
O doubting heart!
They only sleep below
The soft white ermine snow
While winter winds shall blow,
To breathe and smile upon you soon again.

The sun has hid its rays
These many days;
Will dreary hours never leave the earth?
O doubting heart!
The stormy clouds on high
Veil the same sunny sky
That soon (for spring is nigh),
Shall wake the summer into golden mirth.

Fair hope is dead, and light
Is quenched in night.
What sound can break the silence of despair?
O doubting heart!
The sky is overcast,
Yet stars shall rise at last,
Brighter for darkness past,
And angels' silver voices stir the air.

*Adelaide Anne Procter* [1825–1864]

## VAIN VIRTUES

From "The House of Life"

What is the sorriest thing that enters Hell?
None of the sins,—but this and that fair deed
Which a soul's sin at length could supersede.
These yet are virgins, whom death's timely knell
Might once have sainted; whom the fiends compel
Together now, in snake-bound shuddering sheaves
Of anguish, while the pit's pollution leaves
Their refuse maidenhood abominable.
Night sucks them down, the tribute of the pit,
Whose names, half entered in the book of Life,
Were God's desire at noon. And as their hair
And eyes sink last, the Torturer deigns no whit
To gaze, but, yearning, waits his destined wife,
The Sin still blithe on earth that sent them there

*Dante Gabriel Rossetti* [1828–1882]

## EVOLUTION

Out of the dusk a shadow,
Then, a spark;
Out of the cloud a silence,
Then, a lark;
Out of the heart a rapture,
Then, a pain;
Out of the dead, cold ashes,
Life again.

*John Banister Tabb* [1845–1909]

## EACH IN HIS OWN TONGUE

A FIRE-MIST and a planet,—
  A crystal and a cell,—
A jellyfish and a saurian,
  And caves where the cave-men dwell;
Then a sense of law and beauty,
  And a face turned from the clod,—
Some call it Evolution,
  And others call it God.

A haze on the far horizon,
  The infinite, tender sky,
The ripe, rich tint of the cornfields,
  And the wild geese sailing high,—
And all over upland and lowland
  The charm of the goldenrod,—
Some of us call it Autumn,
  And others call it God.

Like tides on a crescent sea-beach,
  When the moon is new and thin,
Into our hearts high yearnings
  Come welling and surging in,—
Come from the mystic ocean,
  Whose rim no foot has trod,—
Some of us call it Longing,
  And others call it God.

A picket frozen on duty,—
  A mother starved for her brood,—
Socrates drinking the hemlock,
  And Jesus on the rood;
And millions who, humble and nameless,
  The straight, hard pathway plod,—
Some call it Consecration,
  And others call it God.

*William Herbert Carruth* [1859-1924]

## THE NAME

It shifts and glides from form to form,
 It drifts and darkles, gleams and glows;
It is the passion of the storm,
 The poignance of the rose;—
Through changing shapes, through devious ways,
 By noon or night, in cloud or flame,
My heart has followed all my days
 Something I cannot name!

In sunlight on some woman's hair,
 Or starlight in some woman's eyne,
Or in low laughter smothered where
 Her red lips wedded mine,
My heart hath known, and thrilled to know,
 This unnamed presence that it sought;
And when my heart hath found it so,
 "*Love is the name*," I thought.

Sometimes when sudden afterglows
 In futile glory storm the skies,
Within their transient gold and rose
 The secret stirs and dies;
Or when the trampling morn walks o'er
 The troubled seas, with feet of flame,
My awed heart whispers, "*Ask no more,*
 *For Beauty is the name!*"

Or dreaming in old chapels where
 The dim aisles pulse with murmurings
That part are music, part are prayer—
 (Or rush of hidden wings),
Sometimes I lift a startled head
 To some saint's carven countenance,
Half fancying that the lips have said,
 "*All names mean God, perchance!*"

*Don Marquis* [1878–1937]

## "IN GOD'S ETERNAL STUDIOS"

From "The Studios Photographic"

By every light, in every pose,
In God's Eternal Studios,
The human heart, with frown or laugh,
Is posing for its photograph.
Sweet smile; sad, serious expression;
Honor triumphant over passion:
Oh! wonderful are the effects
He through Truth's living lens detects,
As, instant, watchful for the best,
Behind the curtain without rest,
In loving eagerness He waits
To catch our souls on deathless plates!

Fear not the darkness that surrounds
Thy character. On dark backgrounds,
With light from Heaven in thy face,
What tones He gets! With what fine grace
He molds and modulates and blends
The history of face and hands:
Revealing through what grief and bliss
The spirit came to look like this!
To look like Him Who long ago
For His good pleasure planned it so,
That He in His Eternal Home
Might treasure them in Time to Come!

Through unknown fortunes yet to be,
Beneath the stars, beside the sea,
Between the birthday and the grave,
Teaching the tender heart be brave,
He woos our better from our worse,
The Artist of the Universe!
The undiscouraged Connoisseur
Of priceless human character!
The glory of Whose presence fills
With master might the steadfast hills!
While deep within our souls it glows
From all His starry studios!

*Paul Shivell* [1874-

## INDIRECTION

FAIR are the flowers and the children, but their subtle suggestion is fairer;
Rare is the roseburst of dawn, but the secret that clasps it is rarer;
Sweet the exultance of song, but the strain that precedes it is sweeter;
And never was poem yet writ, but the meaning outmastered the meter.

Never a daisy that grows, but a mystery guideth the growing;
Never a river that flows, but a majesty scepters the flowing;
Never a Shakespeare that soared, but a stronger than he did enfold him,
Nor ever a prophet foretells, but a mightier seer hath foretold him.

Back of the canvas that throbs the painter is hinted and hidden;
Into the statue that breathes the soul of the sculptor is bidden;
Under the joy that is felt lie the infinite issues of feeling;
Crowning the glory revealed is the glory that crowns the revealing.

Great are the symbols of being, but that which is symboled is greater;
Vast the create and beheld, but vaster the inward creator;
Back of the sound broods the silence, back of the gift stands the giving;
Back of the hand that receives thrill the sensitive nerves of receiving.

Space is as nothing to spirit, the deed is outdone by the doing;
The heart of the wooer is warm, but warmer the heart of the wooing;

And up from the pits where these shiver, and up from the
heights where those shine,
Twin voices and shadows swim starward, and the essence
of life is divine.

*Richard Realf* [1834-1878]

## A GRAMMARIAN'S FUNERAL

SHORTLY AFTER THE REVIVAL OF LEARNING IN EUROPE

LET us begin and carry up this corpse,
Singing together.
Leave we the common crofts, the vulgar thorpes
Each in its tether
Sleeping safe on the bosom of the plain,
Cared-for till cock-crow:
Look out if yonder be not day again
Rimming the rock-row!
That's the appropriate country; there, man's thought,
Rarer, intenser,
Self-gathered for an outbreak, as it ought,
Chafes in the censer.
Leave we the unlettered plain its herd and crop;
Seek we sepulture
On a tall mountain, citied to the top,
Crowded with culture!
All the peaks soar, but one the rest excels;
Clouds overcome it;
No! yonder sparkle is the citadel's
Circling its summit.
Thither our path lies; wind we up the heights;
Wait ye the warning?
Our low life was the level's and the night's;
He's for the morning.
Step to a tune, square chests, erect each head.
'Ware the beholders!
This is our master, famous, calm and dead.
Borne on our shoulders.

Sleep, crop and herd! sleep, darkling thorpe and croft,
　　Safe from the weather!
He, whom we convoy to his grave aloft,
　　Singing together,
He was a man born with thy face and throat,
　　Lyric Apollo!
Long he lived nameless: how should Spring take note
　　Winter would follow?
Till lo, the little touch, and youth was gone!
　　Cramped and diminished,
Moaned he, "New measures, other feet anon!
　　My dance is finished"?
No, that's the world's way: (keep the mountain-side,
　　Make for the city!)
He knew the signal, and stepped on with pride
　　Over men's pity;
Left play for work, and grappled with the world
　　Bent on escaping:
"What's in the scroll," quoth he, "thou keepest furled?
　　Show me their shaping,
Theirs who most studied man, the bard and sage,—
　　Give!"—So, he gowned him,
Straight got by heart that book to its last page:
　　Learnèd, we found him.
Yea, but we found him bald too, eyes like lead,
　　Accents uncertain:
"Time to taste life," another would have said,
　　"Up with the curtain!"
This man said rather, "Actual life comes next?
　　Patience a moment!
Grant I have mastered learning's crabbed text,
　　Still there's the comment.
Let me know all! Prate not of most or least,
　　Painful or easy!
Even to the crumbs I'd fain eat up the feast,
　　Ay, nor feel queasy."
Oh, such a life as he resolved to live,
　　When he had learned it,
When he had gathered all books had to give!
　　Sooner, he spurned it.

Image the whole, then execute the parts—
Fancy the fabric
Quite, ere you build, ere steel strike fire from quartz,
Ere mortar dab brick!

(Here's the town-gate reached: there's the market-place
Gaping before us.)
Yea, this in him was the peculiar grace
(Hearten our chorus!)
That before living he'd learn how to live—
No end to learning:
Earn the means first—God surely will contrive
Use for our earning.
Others mistrust and say, "But time escapes:
Live now or never!"
He said, "What's time? Leave Now for dogs and apes!
Man has Forever."
Back to his book then: deeper drooped his head:
*Calculus* racked him:
Leaden before, his eyes grew dross of lead:
*Tussis* attacked him.
"Now, master, take a little rest!"—not he!
(Caution redoubled,
Step two abreast, the way winds narrowly!)
Not a whit troubled,
Back to his studies, fresher than at first,
Fierce as a dragon
He (soul-hydroptic with a sacred thirst)
Sucked at the flagon.
Oh, if we draw a circle premature,
Heedless of far gain,
Greedy for quick returns of profit, sure
Bad is our bargain!
Was it not great? did not he throw on God,
(He loves the burthen)—
God's task to make the heavenly period
Perfect the earthen?
Did not he magnify the mind, show clear
Just what it all meant?
He would not discount life, as fools do here,
Paid by instalment.

He ventured neck or nothing—heaven's success
Found, or earth's failure:
"Wilt thou trust death or not?" He answered "Yes!
Hence with life's pale lure!"
That low man seeks a little thing to do,
Sees it and does it:
This high man, with a great thing to pursue,
Dies ere he knows it.
That low man goes on adding one to one,
His hundred's soon hit:
This high man, aiming at a million,
Misses an unit.
That, has the world here—should he need the next,
Let the world mind him!
This, throws himself on God, and unperplexed
Seeking shall find him.
So, with the throttling hands of death at strife,
Ground he at grammar;
Still, through the rattle, parts of speech were rife:
While he could stammer
He settled *Hoti's* business—let it be!—
Properly based *Oun*—
Gave us the doctrine of the enclitic *De*,
Dead from the waist down.
Well, here's the platform, here's the proper place:
Hail to your purlieus,
All ye highfliers of the feathered race,
Swallows and curlews!
Here's the top-peak; the multitude below
Live, for they can, there:
This man decided not to Live but Know—
Bury this man there?
Here—here's his place, where meteors shoot, clouds form,
Lightnings are loosened,
Stars come and go! Let joy break with the storm,
Peace let the dew send!
Lofty designs must close in like effects:
Loftily lying,
Leave him—still loftier than the world suspects,
Living and dying.

*Robert Browning* [1812–1889]

## THE RUBÁIYÁT OF OMAR KHAYYÁM

WAKE! For the Sun who scattered into flight
The Stars before him from the Field of Night,
Drives Night along with them from Heaven, and strikes
The Sultán's Turret with a Shaft of Light.

Before the phantom of False morning died,
Methought a Voice within the Tavern cried,
"When all the Temple is prepared within,
Why nods the drowsy Worshiper outside?"

And, as the Cock crew, those who stood before
The Tavern shouted—"Open then the Door!
You know how little while we have to stay,
And, once departed, may return no more."

Now the New Year reviving old Desires,
The thoughtful Soul to Solitude retires,
Where the WHITE HAND OF MOSES on the Bough
Puts out, and Jesus from the ground suspires.

Iram indeed is gone with all his Rose,
And Jamshyd's Seven-ringed Cup where no one knows;
But still a Ruby kindles in the Vine,
And many a Garden by the Water blows.

And David's lips are locked; but in divine
High-piping Pehleví, with "Wine! Wine! Wine!
Red Wine!"—the Nightingale cries to the Rose
That sallow cheek of hers t' incarnadine.

Come, fill the Cup, and in the fire of Spring
Your Winter-garment of Repentance fling:
The Bird of Time has but a little way
To flutter—and the Bird is on the Wing.

Whether at Naishápúr or Babylon,
Whether the Cup with sweet or bitter run,
The Wine of Life keeps oozing drop by drop,
The Leaves of Life keep falling one by one.

Each Morn a thousand Roses brings, you say;
Yes, but where leaves the Rose of Yesterday?
  And this first Summer month that brings the Rose
Shall take Jamshyd and Kaikobád away.

Well, let it take them! What have we to do
With Kaikobád the Great, or Kaikhosrú?
  Let Zál and Rustum bluster as they will,
Or Hátim call to Supper—heed not you.

With me along the strip of Herbage strown
That just divides the desert from the sown,
  Where name of Slave and Sultán is forgot—
And peace to Máhmúd on his golden Throne!

A Book of Verses underneath the Bough,
A Jug of Wine, a Loaf of Bread—and Thou
  Beside me singing in the Wilderness—
Oh, Wilderness were Paradise enow!

Some for the Glories of this World; and some
Sigh for the Prophet's Paradise to come;
  Ah, take the Cash, and let the Credit go,
Nor heed the rumble of a distant Drum!

Look to the blowing Rose about us—"Lo,
Laughing," she says, "into the world I blow,
  At once the silken tassel of my Purse
Tear, and its Treasure on the Garden throw."

And those who husbanded the Golden grain,
And those who flung it to the winds like Rain,
  Alike to no such aureate Earth are turned
As, buried once, Men want dug up again.

The Worldly Hope men set their Hearts upon
Turns Ashes—or it prospers; and anon,
  Like Snow upon the Desert's dusty Face,
Lighting a little hour or two—was gone.

Think, in this battered caravanserai
Whose Portals are alternate Night and Day,
  How Sultán after Sultán with his Pomp
Abode his destined Hour, and went his way.

They say the Lion and the Lizard keep
The Courts where Jamshyd gloried and drank deep:
  And Bahrám, that great Hunter—the Wild Ass
Stamps o'er his Head, but cannot break his Sleep.

I sometimes think that never blows so red
The Rose as where some buried Cæsar bled;
  That every Hyacinth the Garden wears
Dropped in her Lap from some once lovely Head.

And this reviving Herb whose tender Green
Fledges the River-Lip on which we lean—
  Ah, lean upon it lightly! for who knows
From what once lovely Lip it springs unseen!

Ah, my Beloved, fill the Cup that clears
TO-DAY of past Regret and future Fears:
  TO-MORROW!—Why, To-morrow I may be
Myself with Yesterday's Seven thousand Years.

For some we loved, the loveliest and the best
That from his Vintage rolling Time hath pressed,
  Have drunk their Cup a Round or two before,
And one by one crept silently to rest.

And we that now make merry in the Room
They left, and Summer dresses in new bloom,
  Ourselves must we beneath the Couch of Earth
Descend—ourselves to make a Couch—for whom?

Ah, make the most of what we yet may spend,
Before we too into the Dust descend;
  Dust into Dust, and under Dust, to lie,
Sans Wine, sans Song, sans Singer, and—sans End!

Alike for those who for To-day prepare,
And those that after some To-morrow stare,
A Muezzîn from the Tower of Darkness cries,
"Fools! your Reward is neither Here nor There!"

Why, all the Saints and Sages who discussed
Of the two Worlds so wisely—they are thrust
Like foolish Prophets forth; their Words to Scorn
Are scattered, and their Mouths are stopped with Dust.

Myself when young did eagerly frequent
Doctor and Saint, and heard great argument
About it and about: but evermore
Came out by the same door where in I went.

With them the seed of Wisdom did I sow,
And with mine own hand wrought to make it grow;
And this was all the Harvest that I reaped—
"I came like Water, and like Wind I go."

Into this Universe, and *Why* not Knowing
Nor *Whence*, like Water willy-nilly flowing;
And out of it, as Wind along the Waste,
I know not *Whither*, willy-nilly blowing.

What, without asking, hither hurried *Whence?*
And, without asking, *Whither* hurried hence!
Oh, many a Cup of this forbidden Wine
Must drown the memory of that insolence!

Up from Earth's Center through the Seventh Gate
I rose, and on the Throne of Saturn sate,
And many a Knot unraveled by the Road;
But not the Master-knot of Human Fate.

There was the Door to which I found no Key;
There was the Veil through which I might not see;
Some little talk awhile of Me and Thee
There was—and then no more of Thee and Me.

Earth could not answer; nor the Seas that mourn
In flowing Purple, of their Lord forlorn;
  Nor rolling Heaven, with all his Signs revealed
And hidden by the sleeve of Night and Morn.

Then of the THEE IN ME who works behind
The Veil, I lifted up my hands to find
  A Lamp amid the Darkness; and I heard,
As from Without—"THE ME WITHIN THEE BLIND!"

Then to the Lip of this poor earthen Urn
I leaned, the Secret of my Life to learn:
  And Lip to Lip it murmured—"While you live,
Drink!—for, once dead, you never shall return."

I think the Vessel, that with fugitive
Articulation answered, once did live,
  And drink; and ah! the passive Lip I kissed,
How many Kisses might it take—and give!

For I remember stopping by the way
To watch a Potter thumping his wet Clay:
  And with its all-obliterated Tongue
It murmured—"Gently, Brother, gently, pray!"

And has not such a Story from of Old
Down Man's successive generations rolled
  Of such a cloud of saturated Earth
Cast by the Maker into Human mold?

And not a drop that from our Cups we throw
For Earth to drink of, but may steal below
  To quench the fire of Anguish in some Eye
There hidden—far beneath, and long ago.

As then the Tulip for her morning sup
Of Heavenly Vintage from the soil looks up,
  Do you devoutly do the like, till Heaven
To Earth invert you—like an empty Cup.

Perplexed no more with Human or Divine,
To-morrow's tangle to the winds resign,
And lose your fingers in the tresses of
The Cypress-slender Minister of Wine.

And if the Wine you drink, the Lip you press,
End in what All begins and ends in—Yes;
Think then you are TO-DAY what YESTERDAY
You were—TO-MORROW you shall not be less.

So when the Angel of the darker Drink
At last shall find you by the river-brink,
And, offering his Cup, invite your Soul
Forth to your Lips to quaff—you shall not shrink.

Why, if the Soul can fling the Dust aside,
And naked on the Air of Heaven ride,
Wer't not a Shame—wer't not a Shame for him
In this clay carcase crippled to abide?

'Tis but a Tent where takes his one-day's rest
A Sultán to the realm of Death addressed;
The Sultán rises, and the dark Ferrásh
Strikes, and prepares it for another Guest.

And fear not lest Existence closing your
Account, and mine, should know the like no more
The Eternal Sákí from that Bowl has poured
Millions of Bubbles like us, and will pour.

When You and I behind the Veil are passed,
Oh, but the long, long while the World shall last,
Which of our Coming and Departure heeds
As the Sea's self should heed a pebble-cast.

A Moment's Halt—a momentary taste
Of BEING from the Well amid the Waste—
And Lo!—the phantom Caravan has reached
The NOTHING it set out from—Oh, make haste!

Would you that spangle of Existence spend
About THE SECRET—quick about it, Friend!
  A Hair perhaps divides the False and True—
And upon what, prithee, does life depend?

A Hair perhaps divides the False and True;
Yes; and a single Alif were the clue—
  Could you but find it—to the Treasure-house,
And peradventure to THE MASTER too:

Whose secret Presence, through Creation's veins
Running Quicksilver-like eludes your pains;
  Taking all shapes from Máh to Máhi; and
They change and perish all—but He remains;

A moment guessed—then back behind the Fold
Immersed of Darkness round the Drama rolled
  Which, for the Pastime of Eternity,
He doth Himself contrive, enact, behold.

But if in vain, down on the stubborn floor
Of Earth, and up to Heaven's unopening Door,
  You gaze TO-DAY, while You are You—how then
TO-MORROW, You when shall be You no more?

Waste not your Hour, nor in the vain pursuit
Of This and That endeavor and dispute;
  Better be jocund with the fruitful Grape
Than sadden after none, or bitter, Fruit.

You know, my Friends, with what a brave Carouse
I made a Second Marriage in my house;
  Divorced old barren Reason from my Bed,
And took the Daughter of the Vine to Spouse.

For "IS" and "IS-NOT" though with Rule and Line
And "UP-AND-DOWN" by Logic I define,
  Of all that one should care to fathom, I
Was never deep in anything but—Wine.

Ah, but my Computations, People say,
Reduced the Year to better reckoning?—Nay,
'Twas only striking from the Calendar
Unborn To-morrow, and dead Yesterday.

And lately, by the Tavern Door agape,
Came shining through the Dusk an Angel Shape
Bearing a Vessel on his Shoulder; and
He bid me taste of it; and 'twas—the Grape!

The Grape that can with Logic absolute
The Two-and-Seventy jarring Sects confute:
The sovereign Alchemist that in a trice
Life's leaden metal into Gold transmute:

The mighty Mahmúd, Allah-breathing Lord,
That all the misbelieving and black Horde
Of Fears and Sorrows that infest the Soul
Scatters before him with his whirlwind Sword.

Why, be this Juice the growth of God, who dare
Blaspheme the twisted tendril as a Snare?
A Blessing, we should use it, should we not?
And if a Curse—why, then, Who set it there?

I must abjure the Balm of Life, I must,
Scared by some After-reckoning ta'en on trust,
Or lured with Hope of some Diviner Drink,
To fill the Cup—when crumbled into Dust!

Oh threats of Hell and Hopes of Paradise!
One thing at least is certain—*This* Life flies:
One thing is certain and the rest is Lies;
The Flower that once has blown for ever dies.

Strange, is it not? that of the myriads who
Before us passed the door of Darkness through,
Not one returns to tell us of the Road,
Which to discover we must travel too.

The Revelations of Devout and Learned
Who rose before us, and as Prophets burned,
  Are all but Stories, which, awoke from Sleep,
They told their comrades and to Sleep returned.

I sent my Soul through the Invisible
Some letter of that After-life to spell:
  And by and by my Soul returned to me,
And answered, "I Myself am Heaven and Hell."

Heaven but the Vision of fulfilled Desire,
And Hell the Shadow from a Soul on fire
  Cast on the Darkness into which Ourselves
So late emerged from, shall so soon expire.

We are no other than a moving row
Of Magic Shadow-shapes that come and go
  Round with the Sun-illumined Lantern held
In Midnight by the Master of the Show;

But helpless Pieces of the Game He plays
Upon this Checker-board of Nights and Days;
  Hither and thither moves, and checks, and slays,
And one by one back in the Closet lays.

The Ball no question makes of Ayes and Noes,
But Here or There, as strikes the Player, goes;
  And He that tossed you down into the Field,
He knows about it all—HE knows—HE knows!

The Moving Finger writes; and, having writ,
Moves on: nor all your Piety nor Wit
  Shall lure it back to cancel half a Line
Nor all your Tears wash out a Word of it

And that inverted Bowl they call the Sky,
Whereunder crawling cooped we live and die
  Lift not your hands to *It* for help—for It
As impotently moves as you or I.

With Earth's first Clay They did the Last Man knead,
And there of the Last Harvest sowed the Seed;
  And the first Morning of Creation wrote
What the Last Dawn of Reckoning shall read.

YESTERDAY *This* Day's Madness did prepare;
TO-MORROW'S Silence, Triumph, or Despair:
  Drink! for you know not whence you came, nor why:
Drink! for you know not why you go, nor where.

I tell you this—When, started from the Goal,
Over the flaming shoulders of the Foal
  Of Heaven Parwín and Mushtarí they flung,
In my predestined Plot of Dust and Soul

The Vine had struck a fiber: which about
If clings my Being—let the Dervish flout;
  Of my Base metal may be filed a Key,
That shall unlock the Door he howls without.

And this I know: whether the one True Light
Kindle to Love, or Wrath consume me quite,
  One flash of It within the Tavern caught
Better than in the Temple lost outright.

What! out of senseless Nothing to provoke
A conscious Something to resent the yoke
  Of unpermitted Pleasure, under pain
Of Everlasting Penalties, if broke!

What! from his helpless Creature be repaid
Pure Gold for what he lent him dross-allayed—
  Sue for a Debt we never did contract,
And cannot answer—Oh the sorry trade!

Oh Thou, who didst with pitfall and with gin
Beset the Road I was to wander in,
  Thou wilt not with Predestined Evil round
Enmesh, and then impute my Fall to Sin!

Oh Thou, who Man of Baser Earth didst make,
And even with Paradise devise the Snake:
For all the Sin wherewith the Face of Man
Is blackened—Man's forgiveness give—and take!

. . . . . . . . .

As under cover of departing Day
Slunk hunger-stricken Ramazán away,
Once more within the Potter's house alone
I stood, surrounded by the Shapes of Clay.

Shapes of all Sorts and Sizes, great and small,
That stood along the floor and by the wall;
And some loquacious vessels were; and some
Listened perhaps, but never talked at all.

Said one among them—"Surely not in vain
My substance of the common Earth was ta'en
And to this Figure molded, to be broke,
Or trampled back to shapeless Earth again."

Then said a Second—"Ne'er a peevish Boy
Would break the Bowl from which he drank in Joy;
And He that with his hand the Vessel made
Will surely not in after Wrath destroy."

After a momentary silence spake
Some Vessel of a more ungainly make:
"They sneer at me for leaning all awry:
What! did the Hand then of the Potter shake?"

Whereat some one of the loquacious Lot—
I think a Súfi pipkin—waxing hot—
"All this of Pot and Potter—Tell me then,
Who is the Potter, pray, and who the Pot?"

"Why," said another, "Some there are who tell
Of one who threatens he will toss to Hell
The luckless Pots he marred in making—Pish!
He's a Good Fellow, and 'twill all be well."

"Well," murmured one, "let whoso make or buy,
My Clay with long Oblivion is gone dry;
  But fill me with the old familiar Juice,
Methinks I might recover by and by."

So while the Vessels one by one were speaking,
The little Moon looked in that all were seeking:
  And then they jogged each other, "Brother! Brother!
Now for the Porter's shoulder-knot a-creaking!"

. . . . . . . . .

Ah, with the Grape my fading Life provide,
And wash the Body whence the Life has died,
  And lay me, shrouded in the living Leaf,
By some not unfrequented Garden-side.

That even my buried Ashes such a snare
Of Vintage shall fling up into the Air
  As not a True-believer passing by
But shall be overtaken unaware.

Indeed the Idols I have loved so long
Have done my credit in the World much wrong:
  Have drowned my Glory in a shallow Cup,
And sold my reputation for a Song.

Indeed, indeed, Repentance oft before
I swore—but was I sober when I swore?
  And then, and then came Spring, and Rose-in-hand
My thread-bare Penitence apieces tore.

And much as Wine has played the Infidel,
And robbed me of my Robe of Honor—Well,
  I often wonder what the Vintners buy
One half so precious as the stuff they sell.

Yet Ah, that Spring should vanish with the Rose!
That Youth's sweet-scented manuscript should close!
  The Nightingale that in the branches sang,
Ah whence, and whither flown again, who knows!

Would but the Desert of the Fountain yield
One glimpse—if dimly, yet indeed, revealed,
  To which the fainting Traveler might spring,
As springs the trampled herbage of the field!

Would but some wingèd Angel ere too late
Arrest the yet unfolded Roll of Fate,
  And make the stern Recorder otherwise
Enregister, or quite obliterate!

Ah Love! could you and I with Him conspire
To grasp this sorry Scheme of Things entire,
  Would not we shatter it to bits—and then
Remold it nearer to the Heart's desire!

. . . . . . . . . . 

Yon rising Moon that looks for us again—
How oft hereafter will she wax and wane;
  How oft hereafter rising look for us
Through this same Garden—and for *one* in vain!

And when like her, oh Sákí, you shall pass
Among the Guests Star-scattered on the Grass,
  And in your joyous errand reach the spot
Where I made One—turn down an empty Glass!

*Edward Fitzgerald* [1809–1883]

## THE KASÎDAH

### THE LAY OF THE HIGHER LAW

II

In these drear wastes of sea-born land, these wilds where none may dwell but He,
What visionary Pasts revive, what process of the Years we see:

Gazing beyond the thin blue line that rims the far horizon-ring,
Our saddened sight why haunt these ghosts, whence do these spectral shadows spring?

What endless questions vex the thought, of Whence and Whither, When and How?
What fond and foolish strife to read the Scripture writ on human brow;

As stand we perched on point of Time, betwixt the two Eternities,
Whose awful secrets gathering round with black profound oppress our eyes.

"This gloomy night, these grisly waves, these winds and whirlpools loud and dread:
What reck they of our wretched plight who Safety's shore so lightly tread?"

Thus quoth the Bard of Love and Wine, whose dream of Heaven ne'er could rise
Beyond the brimming Kauser-cup and Houris with the white-black eyes.

Ah me! my race of threescore years is short, but long enough to pall
My sense with joyless joys as these, with Love and Houris, Wine and all.

Another boasts he would divorce old barren Reason from his bed,
And wed the Vine-maid in her stead;—fools who believe a word he said!

And "'Dust thou art to dust returning,' ne'er was spoke of human soul,"
The Soofi cries: 'tis well for him that hath such gift to ask its goal.

"And this is all, for this we're born to weep a little and to die!'
So sings the shallow bard whose life still labors at the letter "I".

"Ear never heard, Eye never saw the bliss of those who enter in

My heavenly kingdom," Isâ said, who wailed our sorrows
and our sin:
Too much of words or yet too few! What to thy Godhead
easier than
One little glimpse of Paradise to ope the eyes and ears of
man?

"I am the Truth! I am the Truth!" we hear the God-
drunk gnostic cry;
"The microcosm abides in Me; Eternal Allah's naught but
I!"

Mansûr was wise, but wiser they who smote him with the
hurlèd stones;
And, though his blood a witness bore, no wisdom-might
could mend his bones.

"Eat, drink, and sport; the rest of life's not worth a fillip,"
quoth the King;
Methinks the saying saith too much: the swine would say
the self-same thing!

Two-footed beasts that browse through life, by Death to
serve as soil designed,
Bow prone to Earth whereof they be, and there the proper
pleasures find:

But you of finer, nobler stuff, ye, whom to Higher leads the
High,
What binds your hearts in common bond with creatures
of the stall and sty?

"In certain hope of Life-to-come I journey through this
shifting scene,"
The Zâhid snarls and saunters down his Vale of Tears with
confident mien.

Wiser than Amrân's Son art thou, who ken'st so well the
world-to-be,
The Future when the Past is not, the Present merest dream-
ery.

What know'st thou, man, of Life? and yet, for ever twixt
the womb, the grave,
Thou pratest of the Coming Life, of Heaven and Hell thou
fain must rave.

The world is old and thou art young: the world is large
and thou art small:
Cease, atom of a moment's span, to hold thyself an All-in-All!

IX

How then shall man so order life that when his tale of years
is told,
Like sated guest he wend his way; how shall his even tenor
hold—

Despite the Writ that stores the skull; despite the Table
and the Pen;
Maugre the Fate that plays us down, her board the world,
her pieces men?

How when the light and glow of life wax dim in thickly
gathering gloom,
Shall mortal scoff at sting of Death, shall scorn the victory
of the Tomb?

One way, two paths, one end the grave. This runs athwart
the flowery plain,
That breasts the bush, the steep, the crag, in sun and wind
and snow and rain:

Who treads the first must look adown, must deem his life
an all in all;
Must see no heights where man may rise, must sight no
depths where man may fall.

Allah in Adam's form must view: adore the Maker in the
made,
Content to bask in Mâyâ's smile, in joys of pain, in lights
of shade.

He breaks the Law, he burns the Book, he sends the Moolah back to school;
Laughs at the beards of Saintly men, and dubs the Prophet dolt and fool;

Embraces Cypress' taper-waist; cools feet on wavy breast of rill;
Smiles in the Nargis' love-lorn eyes, and 'joys the dance of Daffodil;

Melts in the saffron light of Dawn to hear the moaning of the Dove;
Delights in Sundown's purpling hues when Bulbul woos the Rose's love;

Finds mirth and joy in Jamshid-bowl; toys with the Daughter of the vine;
And bids the beauteous cup-boy say, "Master, I bring thee ruby wine!"

Sips from the maiden's lips the dew; brushes the bloom from virgin brow:—
Such is his fleshly bliss that strives the Maker through the Made to know.

I've tried them all; I find them all so same and tame, so drear, so dry,
My gorge ariseth at the thought; I commune with myself and cry:—

Better the myriad toils and pains that make the man to manhood true;
This be the rule that guideth life; these be the laws for me and you:

With Ignorance wage eternal war, to know thy self for ever strain;
Thine ignorance of thine ignorance is thy fiercest foe, thy deadliest bane,

That blunts thy sense, and dulls thy taste: that deafs thine ears, and blinds thine eyes;
Creates the thing that never was, the Thing that ever is defies.

The finite Atom infinite that forms thy circle's centre-dot,
So full-sufficient for itself, for other selves existing not,

Finds the world mighty as 'tis small; yet must be fought the unequal fray;
A myriad giants here; and there a pinch of dust, a clod of clay.

Yes! maugre all thy dreams of peace, still must the fight unfair be fought;
Where thou mayest learn the noblest lore, to know that all we know is naught.

True to thy Nature, to Thy self, Fame and Disfame nor hope nor fear:
Enough to thee the small still voice aye thundering in thine inner ear.

From self-approval seek applause: what ken not men thou kennest, thou!
Spurn every idol others raise: before thine own Ideal bow:

Be thine own Deus: make self free, liberal as the circling air:
Thy Thought to thee an Empire be; break every prisoning lock and bar:

Do thou the Ought to self aye owed: here all the duties meet and blend,
In widest sense, withouten care of what began, for what shall end.

Thus, as thou view the Phantom-forms which in the misty Past were thine,
To be again the thing thou wast with honest pride thou mayest decline:

And, glancing down the range of years, fear not thy future self to see;
Resigned to life, to death resigned, as though the choice were naught to thee.

On Thought itself feed not thy Thought; nor turn from Sun and Light to gaze
At darkling cloisters paved with tombs, where rot the bones of bygone days:

"Eat not thy heart," the Sages said: "nor mourn the Past, the buried Past:"
Do what thou dost, be strong, be brave; and, like the Star, nor rest nor haste.

Pluck the old woman from thy breast: be stout in woe, be stark in weal;
Do good for Good is good to do: spurn bribe of Heaven and threat of Hell.

To seek the True, to glad the heart, such is of life the HIGHER LAW,
Whose difference is the Man's degree, the Man of gold, the Man of straw.

See not that something in Mankind that rouses hate or scorn or strife;
Better the worm of Izrâil than Death that walks in form of life.

Survey thy kind as One whose wants in the great Human Whole unite;
The Homo rising high from earth to seek the Heavens of Life-in-Light;

And hold Humanity one man, whose universal agony
Still strains and strives to gain the goal, where agonies shall cease to be.

Believe in all things; none believe; judge not nor warp by "Facts" the thought:

See clear, hear clear, though life may seem Mâyâ and Mirage, Dream and Naught.

Abjure the Why and seek the How: the God and gods enthroned on high,
Are silent all, are silent still; nor hear thy voice, nor deign reply.

The Now, that indivisible point which studs the length of infinite line
Whose ends are nowhere, is thine all, the puny all thou callest thine.

Perchance the law some Giver hath: Let be! let be! what canst thou know?
A myriad races came and went; this Sphinx hath seen them come and go.

Haply the Law that rules the world allows to man the widest range;
And haply Fate's a Theist-word, subject to human chance and change.

This "I" may find a future Life, a nobler copy of our own,
Where every riddle shall be ree'd, where every knowledge shall be known;

Where 'twill be man's to see the whole of what on Earth he sees in part;
Where change shall ne'er surcharge the thought; nor hope deferred shall hurt the heart.

But!—faded flower and fallen leaf no more shall deck the parent tree;
And man once dropped by Tree of Life what hope of other life has he?

The shattered bowl shall know repair; the riven lute shall sound once more;
But who shall mend the clay of man, the stolen breath to man restore?

The shivered clock again shall strike; the broken reed shall
pipe again;
But we, we die, and Death is one, the doom of brutes, the
doom of men.

Then, if Nirwânâ round our life with nothingness, 'tis haply
best;
Thy toils and troubles, want and woe, at length have won
their guerdon—Rest.

Cease, Abdû, cease! Thy song is sung, nor think the gain
the singer's prize;
Till men hold Ignorance deadly sin, till man deserves his
title "Wise:"

In Days to come, Days slow to dawn, when Wisdom deigns
to dwell with men,
These echoes of a voice long stilled haply shall wake responsive strain:

Wend now thy way with brow serene, fear not thy humble
tale to tell:—
The whispers of the Desert-wind; the Tinkling of the camel's-
bell.

*Richard Francis Burton* [1821-1890]

## GAUDEAMUS IGITUR *

Let us live, then, and be glad
While young life's before us!
After youthful pastime had,
After old age, hard and sad,
Earth will slumber o'er us.

Where are they who in this world,
Ere we kept, were keeping?
Go ye to the gods above;
Go to hell; inquire thereof:
They are not: they're sleeping.

* For the original of this poem see page 3829.

Brief is life, and brevity
  Briefly shall be ended:
Death comes like a whirlwind strong,
Bears us with his blast along;
  None shall be defended.

Live this university,
  Men that learning nourish!
Live each member of the same,
Long live all that bear its name;
  Let them ever flourish!

Live the commonwealth also,
  And the men that guide it!
Live our town in strength and health,
Founders, patrons, by whose wealth
  We are here provided!

Live all girls! A health to you,
  Melting maids and beauteous!
Live the wives and women too,
Gentle, loving, tender, true,
  Good, industrious, duteous!

Perish cares that pule and pine!
  Perish envious blamers!
Die the Devil, thine and mine!
Die the starch-neck Philistine!
  Scoffers and defamers!

*Translated from the Latin by*
*John Addington Symonds* [1840–1893]

## LAURIGER HORATIUS *

LAUREL-CROWNED Horatius,
  True, how true thy saying!
Swift as wind flies over us
  Time, devouring, slaying.

For the original of this poem see page 3832.

Where are, oh! those goblets full
  Of wine, honey-laden,
Strifes and loves and bountiful
  Lips of ruddy maiden?

Grows the young grape tenderly,
  And the maid is growing;
But the thirsty poet, see,
  Years on him are snowing!
What's the use on hoary curls
  Of the bays undying,
If we may not kiss the girls,
  Drink while time's a-flying?

*Translated from the Latin by*
*John Addington Symonds* [1840–1893]

## THE CONCLUSION OF THE WHOLE MATTER

**From "The House of a Hundred Lights"**

THE Great Sword Bearer only knows just when He'll wound
  my heart,—not I:
But since He is the one who gives the balm, what does it
  signify?

If my Control should lose its hold on Fortune's collar through
  some hurt,
What then?—Why then I'd simply cling to old gray Resignation's skirt.

Of all the languages of earth in which the human kind confer
The Master Speaker is the Tear: it is the Great Interpreter.

Man's life is like a tide that weaves the sea within its daily
  web.
It rises, surges, swells, and grows,—a pause—then comes the
  evening ebb.

In this rough field of earthly life I have reaped cause for
  tears enough,
Yet, after all, I think I've gleaned my modicum of Laughing-
  Stuff.

*Ridgely Torrence* [1875–1950]

## IN MEMORIAM

STRONG Son of God, immortal Love,
  Whom we, that have not seen thy face,
  By faith, and faith alone embrace,
Believing where we cannot prove;

Thine are these orbs of light and shade;
  Thou madest Life in man and brute;
  Thou madest Death; and lo, thy foot
Is on the skull which thou hast made.

Thou wilt not leave us in the dust:
  Thou madest man, he knows not why,
  He thinks he was not made to die;
And thou hast made him: thou art just.

Thou seemest human and divine,
  The highest, holiest manhood, thou.
  Our wills are ours, we know not how;
Our wills are ours, to make them thine.

Our little systems have their day;
  They have their day and cease to be;
  They are but broken lights of thee,
And thou, O Lord, art more than they.

We have but faith: we cannot know,
  For knowledge is of things we see;
  And yet we trust it comes from thee,
A beam in darkness: let it grow.

Let knowledge grow from more to more,
  But more of reverence in us dwell;
  That mind and soul, according well,
May make one music as before,

But vaster. We are fools and slight;
  We mock thee when we do not fear:
  But help thy foolish ones to bear;
Help thy vain worlds to bear thy light.

Forgive what seemed my sin in me,
  What seemed my worth since I began;

For merit lives from man to man,
And not from man, O Lord, to thee.

Forgive my grief for one removed,
Thy creature, whom I found so fair.
I trust he lives in thee, and there
I find him worthier to be loved.

Forgive these wild and wandering cries,
Confusions of a wasted youth;
Forgive them where they fail in truth,
And in thy wisdom make me wise.

I

I held it truth, with him who sings
To one clear harp in divers tones,
That men may rise on stepping-stones
Of their dead selves to higher things.

But who shall so forecast the years
And find in loss a gain to match?
Or reach a hand through time to catch
The far-off interest of tears?

Let Love clasp Grief lest both be drowned,
Let darkness keep her raven gloss.
Ah, sweeter to be drunk with loss,
To dance with Death, to beat the ground,

Than that the victor Hours should scorn
The long result of love, and boast,
"Behold the man that loved and lost,
But all he was is overworn '

XXVII

I envy not in any moods
The captive void of noble rage,
The linnet born within the cage,
That never knew the summer woods;

I envy not the beast that takes
His license in the field of time,
Unfettered by the sense of crime,
To whom a conscience never wakes;

Nor, what may count itself as blest,
  The heart that never plighted troth
  But stagnates in the weeds of sloth;
Nor any want-begotten rest.

I hold it true, whate'er befall;
  I feel it, when I sorrow most;
  'Tis better to have loved and lost
Than never to have loved at all.

LIV

O, yet we trust that somehow good
  Will be the final goal of ill,
  To pangs of nature, sins of will,
Defects of doubt, and taints of blood;

That nothing walks with aimless feet;
  That not one life shall be destroyed,
  Or cast as rubbish to the void,
When God hath made the pile complete.

That not a worm is cloven in vain;
  That not a moth with vain desire
  Is shrivelled in a fruitless fire,
Or but subserves another's gain.

Behold, we know not anything;
  I can but trust that good shall fall
  At last—far off—at last, to all,
And every winter change to spring.

So runs my dream; but what am I?
  An infant crying in the night;
  An infant crying for the light,
And with no language but a cry.

LV

The wish, that of the living whole
  No life may fail beyond the grave,
  Derives it not from what we have
The likest God within the soul?

Are God and Nature then at strife,
  That Nature lends such evil dreams?
  So careful of the type she seems,
So careless of the single life,

That I, considering everywhere
  Her secret meaning in her deeds,
  And finding that of fifty seeds
She often brings but one to bear,

I falter where I firmly trod,
  And falling with my weight of cares
  Upon the great world's altar-stairs
That slope through darkness up to God,

I stretch lame hands of faith, and grope,
  And gather dust and chaff, and call
  To what I feel is Lord of all,
And faintly trust the larger hope.

LVI

"So careful of the type?" but no.
  From scarped cliff and quarried stone
  She cries, "A thousand types are gone;
I care for nothing, all shall go.

"Thou makest thine appeal to me:
  I bring to life, I bring to death;
  The spirit does but mean the breath:
I know no more." And he, shall he,

Man, her last work, who seemed so fair,
  Such splendid purpose in his eyes,
  Who rolled the psalm to wintry skies,
Who built him fanes of fruitless prayer,

Who trusted God was love indeed
  And love Creation's final law—
  Though Nature, red in tooth and claw
With ravine, shrieked against his creed—

Who loved, who suffered countless ills,
  Who battled for the True, the Just,

Be blown about the desert dust,
Or sealed within the iron hills?

No more? A monster then, a dream,
A discord. Dragons of the prime,
That tare each other in their slime,
Were mellow music matched with him.

O life as futile, then, as frail!
O for thy voice to soothe and bless!
What hope of answer, or redress?
Behind the veil, behind the veil.

LXXIII

So many worlds, so much to do,
So little done, such things to be,
How know I what had need of thee,
For thou wert strong as thou wert true?

The fame is quenched that I foresaw,
The head hath missed an earthly wreath:
I curse not Nature, no, nor Death;
For nothing is that errs from law.

We pass; the path that each man trod
Is dim, or will be dim, with weeds.
What fame is left for human deeds
In endless age? It rests with God.

O hollow wraith of dying fame,
Fade wholly, while the soul exults,
And self-infolds the large results
Of force that would have forged a name.

CVI

Ring out, wild bells, to the wild sky,
The flying cloud, the frosty light:
The year is dying in the night;
Ring out, wild bells, and let him die.

Ring out the old, ring in the new,
Ring, happy bells, across the snow:
The year is going, let him go;
Ring out the false, ring in the true.

Ring out the grief that saps the mind,
  For those that here we see no more;
  Ring out the feud of rich and poor,
Ring in redress to all mankind.

Ring out a slowly dying cause,
  And ancient forms of party strife;
  Ring in the nobler modes of life,
With sweeter manners, purer laws.

Ring out the want, the care, the sin,
  The faithless coldness of the times;
  Ring out, ring out my mournful rhymes,
But ring the fuller minstrel in.

Ring out false pride in place and blood,
  The civic slander and the spite;
  Ring in the love of truth and right,
Ring in the common love of good.

Ring out old shapes of foul disease;
  Ring out the narrowing lust of gold;
  Ring out the thousand wars of old,
Ring in the thousand years of peace.

Ring in the valiant man and free,
  The larger heart, the kindlier hand;
  Ring out the darkness of the land,
Ring in the Christ that is to be.

CXVII

O days and hours, your work is this,
  To hold me from my proper place,
  A little while from his embrace,
For fuller gain of after bliss;

That out of distance might ensue
  Desire of nearness doubly sweet,
  And unto meeting, when we meet,
Delight a hundredfold accrue,

For every grain of sand that runs,
  And every span of shade that steals,
  And every kiss of toothed wheels,
And all the courses of the suns.

CXXVI

Love is and was my lord and king,
  And in his presence I attend
  To hear the tidings of my friend,
Which every hour his couriers bring.

Love is and was my king and lord,
  And will be, though as yet I keep
  Within the court on earth, and sleep
Encompassed by his faithful guard,

And hear at times a sentinel
  Who moves about from place to place,
  And whispers to the worlds of space,
In the deep night, that all is well.

CXXVII

And all is well, though faith and form
  Be sundered in the night of fear;
  Well roars the storm to those that hear
A deeper voice across the storm,

Proclaiming social truth shall spread,
  And justice, even though thrice again
  The red fool-fury of the Seine
Should pile her barricades with dead.

But ill for him that wears a crown,
  And him, the lazar, in his rags!
  They tremble, the sustaining crags;
The spires of ice are toppled down,

And molten up, and roar in flood;
  The fortress crashes from on high,
  The brute earth lightens to the sky,
And the great Æon sinks in blood,

And compassed by the fires of hell;
  While thou, dear spirit, happy star,
  O'erlook'st the tumult from afar,
And smilest, knowing all is well.

CXXX

Thy voice is on the rolling air;
  I hear thee where the waters run;
  Thou standest in the rising sun,
And in the setting thou art fair.

What art thou then? I cannot guess;
  But though I seem in star and flower
  To feel thee some diffusive power,
I do not therefore love thee less.

My love involves the love before;
  My love is vaster passion now;
  Though mixed with God and Nature thou,
I seem to love thee more and more.

Far off thou art, but ever nigh;
  I have thee still, and I rejoice;
  I prosper, circled with thy voice;
I shall not lose thee though I die.

CXXXI

O living will that shalt endure
  When all that seems shall suffer shock,
  Rise in the spiritual rock,
Flow through our deeds and make them pure,

That we may lift from out of dust
  A voice as unto him that hears,
  A cry above the conquered years
To one that with us works, and trust,

With faith that comes of self-control,
  The truths that never can be proved
  Until we close with all we loved,
And all we flow from, soul in soul.

*Alfred Tennyson* [1809–1892]

## DRIFTWOOD

I

HEAVEN is lovelier than the stars,
The sea is fairer than the shore;
I've seen beyond the sunset bars
A color more.

A thought is floating round my mind,
And there are words that will not come.
Do you believe, as I, the wind
Somewhere goes home?

II

In grassy paths my spirit walks.
The earth I travel speaks me fair
And still through many voices talks
Of that deep oneness which we are.

I love to see the rolling sod
Mixing and changing ever grow
To other forms,—and this is God
And all of God and all we know.

I love to feel the dead dust whirled
About my face, to touch the dust;
And this large muteness of the world
Gives me vitality of trust.

Here on the earth I lie a space,
The quiet earth that knows no strife.
I mix with her and take my place
In the dark matter that is life.

IV

Between the sun and moon
A voice, now vague, now clear—
Do you hear?—
Says, "Wander on."

And on the hearthstone black
The embers poignantly—
Do you see?—
Spell, "Come back."

*Trumbull Stickney* [1874–1904]

## "WHAT RICHES HAVE YOU"

What riches have you that you deem me poor,
Or what large comfort that you call me sad?
Tell me what makes you so exceeding glad:
Is your earth happy or your heaven sure?
I hope for heaven, since the stars endure
And bring such tidings as our fathers had.
I know no deeper doubt to make me mad,
I need no brighter love to keep me pure.
To me the faiths of old are daily bread;
I bless their hope, I bless their will to save,
And my deep heart still meaneth what they said.
It makes me happy that the soul is brave,
And, being so much kinsman to the dead,
I walk contented to the peopled grave.

*George Santayana* [1863–1952]

## "O WORLD"

O world, thou choosest not the better part!
It is not wisdom to be only wise,
And on the inward vision close the eyes,
But it is wisdom to believe the heart.
Columbus found a world, and had no chart,
Save one that faith deciphered in the skies;
To trust the soul's invincible surmise
Was all his science and his only art.
Our knowledge is a torch of smoky pine
That lights the pathway but one step ahead
Across a void of mystery and dread.
Bid, then, the tender light of faith to shine
By which alone the mortal heart is led
Unto the thinking of the thought divine.

*George Santayana* [1863–1952]

## THE RUSTIC AT THE PLAY

OUR youth is like a rustic at the play
That cries aloud in simple-hearted fear,
Curses the villain, shudders at the fray,
And weeps before the maiden's wreathèd bier.
Yet once familiar with the changeful show,
He starts no longer at a brandished knife,
But, his heart chastened at the sight of woe,
Ponders the mirrored sorrows of his life.

So tutored too, I watch the moving art
Of all this magic and impassioned pain
That tells the story of the human heart
In a false instance, such as poets feign;
I smile, and keep within the parchment furled
That prompts the passions of this strutting world.

*George Santayana* [1863–1952]

## TO HASEKAWA

PERHAPS it is no matter that you died.
Life's an *incognito* which you saw through:
You never told on life—you had your pride;
But life has told on you.

*Walter Conrad Arensberg* [1861–1954]

## LIFE, A QUESTION

LIFE? and worth living?
Yes, with each part of us—
Hurt of us, help of us, hope of us, heart of us,
Life is worth living.
Ah! with the whole of us,
Will of us, brain of us, senses and soul of us.
Is life worth living?
Aye, with the best of us,
Heights of us, depths of us,—
Life is the test of us!

*Corinne Roosevelt Robinson* [1861–1933]

## THE EARTH AND MAN

A LITTLE sun, a little rain,
A soft wind blowing from the west—
And woods and fields are sweet again,
And warmth within the mountain's breast.

So simple is the earth we tread,
So quick with love and life her frame:
Ten thousand years have dawned and fled,
And still her magic is the same.

A little love, a little trust,
A soft impulse, a sudden dream—
And life as dry as desert dust
Is fresher than a mountain stream.

So simple is the heart of man,
So ready for new hope and joy:
Ten thousand years since it began
Have left it younger than a boy.

*Stopford Augustus Brooke* [1832–1916]

## DESERVINGS

THIS is the height of our deserts:
A little pity for life's hurts;
A little rain, a little sun,
A little sleep when work is done.

A little righteous punishment,
Less for our deeds than their intent;
A little pardon now and then,
Because we are but struggling men.

A little light to show the way,
A little guidance where we stray;
A little love before we pass
To rest beneath the kirkyard grass.

A little faith, in days of change,
When life is stark and bare and strange;
A solace when our eyes are wet
With tears of longing and regret.

True it is that we cannot claim
Unmeasured recompense or blame,
Because our way of life is small:
A little is the sum of all. *Unknown*

## "A LITTLE WORK" *

From "Trilby"

A LITTLE work, a little play
To keep us going—and so, good-day!

A little warmth, a little light
Of love's bestowing—and so, good-night!

A little fun, to match the sorrow
Of each day's growing—and so, good-morrow.

A little trust that when we die
We reap our sowing! And so—good-bye!
*George du Maurier* [1834–1896]

## MAN'S DAYS

A SUDDEN wakin', a sudden weepin',
A li'l suckin', a li'l sleepin';
A cheel's full joys an' a cheel's short sorrows,
Wi' a power o' faith in gert to-morrows.

Young blood red-hot an' the love of a maid,
One glorious day as'll never fade;
Some shadows, some sunshine, some triumphs, some tears,
And a gatherin' weight o' the flyin' years.

Then old man's talk o' the days behind 'e,
Your darter's youngest darter to mind 'e;
A li'l dreamin', a li'l dyin':
A li'l lew corner o' airth to lie in.
*Eden Phillpotts* [1862–1960]

* For the original of this poem see page 3848.

## A LITTLE WHILE

A LITTLE while the tears and laughter,
The willow and the rose;
A little while, and what comes after
No man knows.

An hour to sing, to love and linger,
Then lutanist and lute
Will fall on silence, song and singer
Both be mute.

Our gods from our desires we fashion,
Exalt our baffled lives,
And dream their vital bloom and passion
Still survives;

But when we're done with mirth and weeping,
With myrtle, rue, and rose,
Shall Death take Life into his keeping?
No man knows.

What heart hath not, through twilight places,
Sought for its dead again
To gild with love their pallid faces?
Sought in vain!

Still mounts the Dream on shining pinion,
Still broods the dull distrust:
Which shall have ultimate dominion,
Dream, or dust?

A little while with grief and laughter,
And then the day will close;
The shadows gather . . . what comes after
No man knows!

*Don Marquis* [1878–1937]

# THE CONDUCT OF LIFE

## INTEGER VITÆ *

THE man of life upright,
  Whose guiltless heart is free
From all dishonest deeds,
  Or thought of vanity;

The man whose silent days
  In harmless joys are spent
Whom hope cannot delude,
  Nor sorrow discontent;

That man needs neither towers
  Nor armor for defense,
Nor secret vaults to fly
  From thunder's violence:

He only can behold
  With unaffrighted eyes
The horrors of the deep
  And terrors of the skies.

Thus, scorning all the cares
  That fate or fortune brings,
He makes the heaven his book,
  His wisdom heavenly things;

Good thoughts his only friends,
  His wealth a well-spent age,
The earth his sober inn
  And quiet pilgrimage.

*After Horace, by Thomas Campion* [?–1619]

* For the original of this poem see page 3828

## THE CHAMBERED NAUTILUS

From "The Autocrat of the Breakfast Table"

THIS is the ship of pearl, which, poets feign,
Sails the unshadowed main,—
The venturous bark that flings
On the sweet summer wind its purpled wings
In gulfs enchanted, where the Siren sings,
And coral reefs lie bare,
Where the cold sea-maids rise to sun their streaming hair.

Its webs of living gauze no more unfurl;
Wrecked is the ship of pearl!
And every chambered cell,
Where its dim dreaming life was wont to dwell,
As the frail tenant shaped his growing shell,
Before thee lies revealed,—
Its irised ceiling rent, its sunless crypt unsealed!

Year after year beheld the silent toil
That spread his lustrous coil;
Still, as the spiral grew,
He left the past year's dwelling for the new,
Stole with soft step its shining archway through,
Built up its idle door,
Stretched in his last-found home, and knew the old no more.

Thanks for the heavenly message brought by thee,
Child of the wandering sea,
Cast from her lap, forlorn!
From thy dead lips a clearer note is born
Than ever Triton blew from wreathèd horn!
While on mine ear it rings,
Through the deep caves of thought I hear a voice that sings—

Build thee more stately mansions, O my soul,
As the swift seasons roll!
Leave thy low-vaulted past!

Let each new temple, nobler than the last,
Shut thee from heaven with a dome more vast,
Till thou at length art free,
Leaving thine outgrown shell by life's unresting sea!

*Oliver Wendell Holmes* [1809–1894]

## A PSALM OF LIFE

WHAT THE HEART OF THE YOUNG MAN SAID TO THE PSALMIST

Tell me not, in mournful numbers,
Life is but an empty dream!—
For the soul is dead that slumbers,
And things are not what they seem.

Life is real! Life is earnest!
And the grave is not its goal;
Dust thou art, to dust returnest,
Was not spoken of the soul.

Not enjoyment, and not sorrow,
Is our destined end or way;
But to act, that each to-morrow
Find us farther than to-day.

Art is long, and Time is fleeting,
And our hearts, though stout and brave,
Still, like muffled drums, are beating
Funeral marches to the grave.

In the world's broad field of battle,
In the bivouac of Life,
Be not like dumb, driven cattle!
Be a hero in the strife!

Trust no Future, howe'er pleasant!
Let the dead Past bury its dead!
Act,—act in the living Present!
Heart within, and God o'erhead!

Lives of great men all remind us
We can make our lives sublime,
And, departing, leave behind us
Footprints on the sands of time;

Footprints, that perhaps another,
  Sailing o'er life's solemn main,
A forlorn and shipwrecked brother,
  Seeing, shall take heart again.

Let us, then, be up and doing,
  With a heart for any fate;
Still achieving, still pursuing,
  Learn to labor and to wait.

*Henry Wadsworth Longfellow* [1807–1882]

## EXCELSIOR

The shades of night were falling fast,
As through an Alpine village passed
A youth, who bore, 'mid snow and ice,
A banner with the strange device,
  Excelsior!

His brow was sad; his eye beneath,
Flashed like a falchion from its sheath,
And like a silver clarion rung
The accents of that unknown tongue,
  Excelsior!

In happy homes he saw the light
Of household fires gleam warm and bright;
Above, the spectral glaciers shone,
And from his lips escaped a groan,
  Excelsior!

"Try not the Pass!" the old man said;
"Dark lowers the tempest overhead,
The roaring torrent is deep and wide!"
And loud that clarion voice replied,
  Excelsior!

"Oh stay," the maiden said, "and rest
Thy weary head upon this breast!"
A tear stood in his bright blue eye,
But still he answered, with a sigh,
  Excelsior!

"Beware the pine-tree's withered branch!
Beware the awful avalanche!"
This was the peasant's last Good-night,
A voice replied, far up the height,
Excelsior!

At break of day, as heavenward
The pious monks of Saint Bernard
Uttered the oft-repeated prayer,
A voice cried through the startled air,
Excelsior!

A traveler, by the faithful hound,
Half buried in the snow was found,
Still grasping in his hand of ice
That banner with the strange device,
Excelsior!

There in the twilight cold and gray,
Lifeless, but beautiful, he lay,
And from the sky, serene and far,
A voice fell, like a falling star,
Excelsior!

*Henry Wadsworth Longfellow* [1807-1882]

## THE VILLAGE BLACKSMITH

UNDER a spreading chestnut-tree
The village smithy stands;
The smith, a mighty man is he,
With large and sinewy hands;
And the muscles of his brawny arms
Are strong as iron bands.

His hair is crisp, and black, and long,
His face is like the tan;
His brow is wet with honest sweat,
He earns whate'er he can,
And looks the whole world in the face,
For he owes not any man.

Week in, week out, from morn till night,
  You can hear his bellows blow;
You can hear him swing his heavy sledge
  With measured beat and slow,
Like a sexton ringing the village bell,
  When the evening sun is low.

And children coming home from school
  Look in at the open door;
They love to see the flaming forge,
  And hear the bellows roar,
And catch the burning sparks that fly
  Like chaff from a threshing-floor.

He goes on Sunday to the church,
  And sits among his boys;
He hears the parson pray and preach,
  He hears his daughter's voice,
Singing in the village choir,
  And it makes his heart rejoice.

It sounds to him like her mother's voice,
  Singing in Paradise!
He needs must think of her once more,
  How in the grave she lies;
And with his hard, rough hand he wipes
  A tear out of his eyes.

Toiling,—rejoicing,—sorrowing,
  Onward through life he goes;
Each morning sees some task begin,
  Each evening sees it close;
Something attempted, something done,
  Has earned a night's repose.

Thanks, thanks to thee, my worthy friend,
  For the lesson thou hast taught!
Thus at the flaming forge of life
  Our fortunes must be wrought;
Thus on its sounding anvil shaped
  Each burning deed and thought!

*Henry Wadsworth Longfellow* [1807–1882]

## FOUR THINGS

FOUR things a man must learn to do
If he would make his record true:
To think without confusion clearly;
To love his fellow-men sincerely;
To act from honest motives purely;
To trust in God and Heaven securely.

*Henry Van Dyke* [1852–1933]

## LABOR AND LOVE

LABOR and love! there are no other laws
To rule the liberal action of that soul
Which fate hath set beneath thy brief control,
Or lull the empty fear that racks and gnaws;
Labor! then like a rising moon, the cause
Of life shall light thine hour from pole to pole,
Thou shalt taste health of purpose, and the roll
Of simple joys unwind without a pause.
Love! and thy heart shall cease to question why
Its beating pulse was set to rock and rave;
Find but another heart this side the grave
To soothe and cling to,—thou hast life's reply.
Labor and love! then fade without a sigh,
Submerged beneath the inexorable wave.

*Edmund Gosse* [1849–1928]

## WHAT IS GOOD

"WHAT is the real good?"
I asked in musing mood.

Order, said the law court;
Knowledge, said the school;
Truth, said the wise man;
Pleasure, said the fool;
Love, said the maiden;
Beauty, said the page;

Freedom, said the dreamer;
Home, said the sage;
Fame, said the soldier;
Equity, the seer;—

Spake my heart full sadly,
"The answer is not here."

Then within my bosom
Softly this I heard:
"Each heart holds the secret;
Kindness is the word."

*John Boyle O'Reilly* [1844-1890]

## FAITH

Better trust all and be deceived,
And weep that trust and that deceiving,
Than doubt one heart that, if believed,
Had blessed one's life with true believing.

Oh, in this mocking world, too fast
The doubting fiend o'ertakes our youth;
Better be cheated to the last
Than lose the blessed hope of truth.

*Frances Anne Kemble* [1809-1893]

## A CHARGE

If thou hast squandered years to grave a gem
Commissioned by thy absent Lord, and while
'Tis incomplete,
Others would bribe thy needy skill to them—
Dismiss them to the street!

Should'st thou at last discover Beauty's grove,
At last be panting on the fragrant verge,
But in the track,
Drunk with divine possession, thou meet Love—
Turn, at her bidding, back.

When round thy ship in tempest Hell appears,
And every specter mutters up more dire
To snatch control
And loose to madness thy deep-kenneled Fears—
Then to the helm, O Soul!

Last, if upon the cold, green-mantling sea,
Thou cling, alone with Truth, to the last spar,
Both castaway,
And one must perish—let it not be he
Whom thou art sworn to obey.

*Herbert Trench* [1865–1923]

## TO-DAY

So here hath been dawning
Another blue Day:
Think, wilt thou let it
Slip useless away?

Out of Eternity
This new Day is born;
Into Eternity,
At night, will return.

Behold it aforetime
No eye ever did:
So soon it for ever
From all eyes is hid.

Here hath been dawning
Another blue Day:
Think, wilt thou let it
Slip useless away?

*Thomas Carlyle* [1795–1881]

## "MY DAYS AMONG THE DEAD ARE PASSED"

My days among the Dead are passed,
Around me I behold,
Where'er these casual eyes are cast,
The mighty minds of old:

My never-failing friends are they,
With whom I converse day by day.

With them I take delight in weal,
And seek relief in woe;
And while I understand and feel
How much to them I owe,
My cheeks have often been bedewed
With tears of thoughtful gratitude.

My thoughts are with the Dead; with them
I live in long-past years,
Their virtues love, their faults condemn,
Partake their hopes and fears;
And from their lessons seek and find
Instruction with an humble mind.

My hopes are with the Dead; anon
My place with them will be,
And I with them shall travel on
Through all Futurity;
Yet leaving here a name, I trust,
That will not perish in the dust.

*Robert Southey* [1774–1843]

## OPPORTUNITY

MASTER of human destinies am I!
Fame, love, and fortune on my footsteps wait.
Cities and fields I walk; I penetrate
Deserts and seas remote, and passing by
Hovel and mart and palace—soon or late
I knock unbidden once at every gate!

If sleeping, wake—if feasting, rise before
I turn away. It is the hour of fate,
And they who follow me reach every state
Mortals desire, and conquer every foe

Save death; but those who doubt or hesitate,
Condemned to failure, penury, and woe,
Seek me in vain and uselessly implore.
I answer not, and I return no more!

*John James Ingalls* [1833–1900]

## OPPORTUNITY

They do me wrong who say I come no more
When once I knock and fail to find you in;
For every day I stand outside your door
And bid you wake, and rise to fight and win.

Wail not for precious chances passed away!
Weep not for golden ages on the wane!
Each night I burn the records of the day—
At sunrise every soul is born again!

Dost thou behold thy lost youth all aghast?
Dost reel from righteous Retribution's blow?
Then turn from blotted archives of the past
And find the future's pages white as snow.

Art thou a mourner? Rouse thee from thy spell;
Art thou a sinner? Sins may be forgiven;
Each morning gives thee wings to flee from hell,
Each night a star to guide thy feet to heaven.

Laugh like a boy at splendors that have sped,
To vanished joys be blind and deaf and dumb;
My judgments seal the dead past with its dead,
But never bind a moment yet to come.

Though deep in mire, wring not your hands and weep;
I lend my arm to all who say "I can!"
No shame-faced outcast ever sank so deep
But yet might rise and be again a man!

*Walter Malone* [1866–1915]

## OPPORTUNITY

THIS I beheld, or dreamed it in a dream:—
There spread a cloud of dust along a plain;
And underneath the cloud, or in it, raged
A furious battle, and men yelled, and swords
Shocked upon swords and shields. A prince's banner
Wavered, then staggered backward, hemmed by foes.
A craven hung along the battle's edge,
And thought, "Had I a sword of keener steel—
That blue blade that the king's son bears,—but this
Blunt thing!" he snapped and flung it from his hand,
And lowering crept away and left the field.
Then came the king's son, wounded, sore bestead,
And weaponless, and saw the broken sword,
Hilt-buried in the dry and trodden sand,
And ran and snatched it, and with battle-shout
Lifted afresh he hewed his enemy down,
And saved a great cause that heroic day.

*Edward Rowland Sill* [1841-1887]

## THE ARROW AND THE SONG

I SHOT an arrow into the air,
It fell to earth, I knew not where;
For, so swiftly it flew, the sight
Could not follow it in its flight.

I breathed a song into the air,
It fell to earth, I knew not where;
For who has sight so keen and strong,
That it can follow the flight of song?

Long, long afterward, in an oak
I found the arrow, still unbroke;
And the song, from beginning to end,
I found again in the heart of a friend.

*Henry Wadsworth Longfellow* [1807-1882]

## CALUMNY

A WHISPER woke the air,
A soft, light tone, and low,
Yet barbed with shame and woe.
Ah! might it only perish there,
Nor farther go!

But no! a quick and eager ear
Caught up the little, meaning sound;
Another voice has breathed it clear;
And so it wandered round
From ear to lip, from lip to ear,
Until it reached a gentle heart
That throbbed from all the world apart
And that—it broke!

It was the only heart it found,—
The only heart 'twas meant to find,
When first its accents woke.
It reached that gentle heart at last,
And that—it broke!

*Frances Sargent Osgood* [1811-1850]

## THE EFFECT OF EXAMPLE

WE scatter seeds with careless hand,
And dream we ne'er shall see them more;
But for a thousand years
Their fruit appears,
In weeds that mar the land,
Or healthful shore.

The deeds we do, the words we say,—
Into still air they seem to fleet.
We count them ever past;
But they shall last,—
In the dread judgment they
And we shall meet.

I charge thee by the years gone by,
For the love's sake of brethren dear,
Keep thou the one true way,
In work and play,
Lest in that world their cry
Of woe thou hear.

*John Keble* [1792-1866]

## LITTLE AND GREAT

A TRAVELER on a dusty road
Strewed acorns on the lea;
And one took root and sprouted up,
And grew into a tree.
Love sought its shade at evening-time,
To breathe its early vows;
And Age was pleased, in heats of noon,
To bask beneath its boughs.
The dormouse loved its dangling twigs,
The birds sweet music bore—
It stood a glory in its place,
A blessing evermore.

A little spring had lost its way
Amid the grass and fern;
A passing stranger scooped a well
Where weary men might turn;
He walled it in, and hung with care
A ladle at the brink;
He thought not of the deed he did,
But judged that Toil might drink.
He passed again; and lo! the well,
By summer never dried,
Had cooled ten thousand parchèd tongues,
And saved a life beside.

A dreamer dropped a random thought;
'Twas old, and yet 'twas new;
A simple fancy of the brain,
But strong in being true.

It shone upon a genial mind,
And, lo! its light became
A lamp of life, a beacon ray,
A monitory flame:
The thought was small; its issue great;
A watch-fire on the hill,
It sheds its radiance far adown,
And cheers the valley still.

A nameless man, amid the crowd
That thronged the daily mart,
Let fall a word of hope and love,
Unstudied from the heart;—
A whisper on the tumult thrown,
A transitory breath,—
It raised a brother from the dust,
It saved a soul from death.
O germ! O fount! O word of love!
O thought at random cast!
Ye were but little at the first,
But mighty at the last.

*Charles Mackay* [1814-1889]

## THE SIN OF OMISSION

It isn't the thing you do, dear;
It's the thing you leave undone,
Which gives you a bit of heartache
At the setting of the sun.
The tender word forgotten,
The letter you did not write,
The flower you might have sent, dear,
Are your haunting ghosts to-night.

The stone you might have lifted
Out of a brother's way,
The bit of heartsome counsel
You were hurried too much to say;

The loving touch of the hand, dear,
  The gentle and winsome tone,
That you had no time nor thought for,
  With troubles enough of your own.

The little acts of kindness,
  So easily out of mind;
Those chances to be angels
  Which every one may find—
They come in night and silence—
  Each chill, reproachful wraith—
When hope is faint and flagging
  And a blight has dropped on faith.

For life is all too short, dear,
  And sorrow is all too great;
To suffer our great compassion
  That tarries until too late;
And it's not the thing you do, dear,
  It's the thing you leave undone,
Which gives you the bit of heartache
  At the setting of the sun.

*Margaret Sangster* [1838-1912]

## THE FLOWER

Once in a golden hour
  I cast to earth a seed.
Up there came a flower,
  The people said, a weed.

To and fro they went
  Through my garden-bower,
And muttering discontent
  Cursed me and my flower.

Then it grew so tall
  It wore a crown of light,
But thieves from o'er the wall
  Stole the seed by night;

Sowed it far and wide
  By every town and tower,
Till all the people cried,
  "Splendid is the flower."

Read my little fable:
  He that runs may read.
Most can raise the flowers now,
  For all have got the seed.

And some are pretty enough,
  And some are poor indeed;
And now again the people
  Call it but a weed.

*Alfred Tennyson* [1809–1892]

## STANZAS

Often rebuked, yet always back returning
  To those first feelings that were born with me,
And leaving busy chase of wealth and learning
  For idle dreams of things that cannot be:

To-day, I will seek not the shadowy region;
  Its unsustaining vastness waxes drear;
And visions rising, legion after legion,
  Bring the unreal world too strangely near.

I'll walk, but not in old heroic traces,
  And not in paths of high morality,
And not among the half-distinguished faces,
  The clouded forms of long-past history.

I'll walk where my own nature would be leading:
  It vexes me to choose another guide:
Where the gray flocks in ferny glens are feeding;
  Where the wild wind blows on the mountain side.

What have those lonely mountains worth revealing?
  More glory and more grief than I can tell:
The earth that wakes *one* human heart to feeling
  Can center both the worlds of Heaven and Hell.

*Emily Brontë* [1818–1848]

## SOLITUDE

LAUGH, and the world laughs with you;
  Weep, and you weep alone,
For the sad old earth must borrow its mirth,
  But has trouble enough of its own.
Sing, and the hills will answer;
  Sigh, it is lost on the air,
The echoes bound to a joyful sound,
  But shrink from voicing care.

Rejoice, and men will seek you;
  Grieve, and they turn and go.
They want full measure of all your pleasure,
  But they do not need your woe.
Be glad, and your friends are many;
  Be sad, and you lose them all,—
There are none to decline your nectared wine,
  But alone you must drink life's gall.

Feast, and your halls are crowded;
  Fast, and the world goes by.
Succeed and give, and it helps you live,
  But no man can help you die.
There is room in the halls of pleasure
  For a long and lordly train,
But one by one we must all file on
  Through the narrow aisles of pain.

*Ella Wheeler Wilcox* [1850–1919]

## RECOMPENSE

THE gifts that to our breasts we fold
  Are brightened by our losses.
The sweetest joys a heart can hold
  Grow up between its crosses.
And on life's pathway many a mile
  Is made more glad and cheery,
Because, for just a little while,
  The way seemed dark and dreary.

*Nixon Waterman* [1859–1944]

## THE LESSON OF THE WATER-MILL

Listen to the Water-Mill;
Through the live-long day
How the clicking of its wheel
Wears the hours away!
Languidly the Autumn wind
Stirs the forest leaves,
From the field the reapers sing,
Binding up their sheaves;
And a proverb haunts my mind
As a spell is cast,
"The mill cannot grind
With the water that is past."

Autumn winds revive no more
Leaves that once are shed,
And the sickle cannot reap
Corn once gatherèd;
Flows the ruffled streamlet on,
Tranquil, deep, and still,
Never gliding back again
To the water-mill;
Truly speaks the proverb old,
With a meaning vast,—
"The mill cannot grind
With the water that is past."

Take the lesson to thyself
True and loving heart;
Golden youth is fleeting by,
Summer hours depart;
Learn to make the most of life,
Lose no happy day,
Time will never bring thee back
Chances swept away!
Leave no tender word unsaid,
Love while love shall last;
"The mill cannot grind
With the water that is past."

Work while yet the daylight shines,
Man of strength and will!
Never does the streamlet glide
Useless by the mill;
Wait not till to-morrow's sun
Beams upon thy way,
All that thou canst call thine own
Lies in thy "to-day";
Power and intellect and health
May not always last,
"The mill cannot grind
With the water that is past."

O the wasted hours of life
That have drifted by!
O the good that might have been,—
Lost, without a sigh!
Love, that we might once have saved
By a single word,
Thoughts conceived, but never penned,
Perishing unheard;—
Take the proverb to thine heart,
Take, and hold it fast,—
"The mill cannot grind
With the water that is past."

*Sarah Doudney* [1843–1926]

## LIFE

I MADE a posy, while the day ran by:
Here will I smell my remnant out, and tie
My life within this band.
But Time did beckon to the flowers, and they
By noon most cunningly did steal away,
And withered in my hand.

My hand was next to them, and then my heart;
I took, without more thinking, in good part
Time's gentle admonition;

Who did so sweetly Death's sad taste convey,
Making my mind to smell my fatal day,
Yet sugaring the suspicion.

Farewell, dear flowers! sweetly your time ye spent,
Fit, while ye lived, for smell or ornament,
And after death for cures.
I follow straight, without complaints or grief;
Since, if my scent be good, I care not if
It be as short as yours.

*George Herbert* [1593-1633]

## BE TRUE

THOU must be true thyself,
If thou the truth wouldst teach;
Thy soul must overflow, if thou
Another's soul wouldst reach!
It needs the overflow of heart
To give the lips full speech.

Think truly, and thy thoughts
Shall the world's famine feed;
Speak truly, and each word of thine
Shall be a fruitful seed;
Live truly, and thy life shall be
A great and noble creed.

*Horatius Bonar* [1808-1889]

## TO-DAY

WHY fear to-morrow, timid heart?
Why tread the future's way?
We only need to do our part
To-day, dear child, to-day.

The past is written! Close the book
On pages sad and gay;
Within the future do not look,
But live to-day—to-day.

'Tis this one hour that God has given;
His Now we must obey;
And it will make our earth his heaven
To live to-day—to-day.

*Lydia Avery Coonley Ward* [1845–1924]

## THE VALLEY OF VAIN VERSES

The grief that is but feigning,
And weeps melodious tears
Of delicate complaining
From self-indulgent years;
The mirth that is but madness,
And has no inward gladness
Beneath its laughter, straining
To capture thoughtless ears;

The love that is but passion
Of amber-scented lust;
The doubt that is but fashion;
The faith that has no trust;—
These Thamyris disperses,
In the Valley of Vain Verses
Below the Mount Parnassian,
And they crumble into dust.

*Henry Van Dyke* [1852–1933]

## A THANKSGIVING

Lord, for the erring thought
Not unto evil wrought;
Lord, for the wicked will
Betrayed and baffled still;
For the heart from itself kept:
Our Thanksgiving accept!

For ignorant hopes that were
Broken to our blind prayer;
For pain, death, sorrow—sent
Unto our chastisement;

For all loss of seeming good:
Quicken our gratitude!

*William Dean Howells* [1837–1920]

## THE LADY POVERTY

THE Lady Poverty was fair:
But she has lost her looks of late,
With change of times and change of air.
Ah slattern, she neglects her hair,
Her gown, her shoes. She keeps no state
As once when her pure feet were bare.

Or—almost worse, if worse can be—
She scolds in parlors; dusts and trims,
Watches and counts. Oh, is this she
Whom Francis met, whose step was free,
Who with Obedience caroled hymns,
In Umbria walked with Chastity?

Where is her ladyhood? Not here,
Not among modern kinds of men;
But in the stony fields, where clear
Through the thin trees the skies appear;
In delicate spare soil and fen,
And slender landscape and austere.

*Alice Meynell* [1850–1922]

## THE LADY POVERTY

I MET her on the Umbrian Hills,
  Her hair unbound, her feet unshod;
As one whom secret glory fills
  She walked—alone with God.

I met her in the city street;
  Oh, how changed was her aspect then!
With heavy eyes and weary feet
  She walked alone—with men.

*Evelyn Underhill* [1875–1941]

## CHARACTER OF THE HAPPY WARRIOR

Who is the happy Warrior? Who is he
That every man in arms should wish to be?

It is the generous spirit, who, when brought
Among the tasks of real life, hath wrought
Upon the plan that pleased his boyish thought:
Whose high endeavors are an inward light
That makes the path before him always bright:
Who, with a natural instinct to discern
What knowledge can perform, is diligent to learn;
Abides by this resolve, and stops not there,
But makes his moral being his prime care;
Who, doomed to go in company with pain,
And fear, and bloodshed, miserable train!
Turns his necessity to glorious gain;
In face of these doth exercise a power
Which is our human nature's highest dower;
Controls them and subdues, transmutes, bereaves
Of their bad influence, and their good receives:
By objects, which might force the soul to abate
Her feeling, rendered more compassionate;
Is placable—because occasions rise
So often that demand such sacrifice;
More skilful in self-knowledge, even more pure,
As tempted more; more able to endure,
As more exposed to suffering and distress;
Thence, also, more alive to tenderness.

'Tis he whose law is reason; who depends
Upon that law as on the best of friends;
Whence, in a state where men are tempted still
To evil for a guard against worse ill,
And what in quality or act is best
Doth seldom on a right foundation rest,
He labors good on good to fix, and owes
To virtue every triumph that he knows:
Who, if he rise to station of command,
Rises by open means; and there will stand

On honorable terms, or else retire,
And in himself possess his own desire;
Who comprehends his trust, and to the same
Keeps faithful with a singleness of aim;
And therefore does not stoop, nor lie in wait
For wealth, or honors, or for worldly state;
Whom they must follow; on whose head must fall,
Like showers of manna, if they come at all:
Whose powers shed round him in the common strife,
Or mild concerns of ordinary life,
A constant influence, a peculiar grace;
But who, if he be called upon to face
Some awful moment to which Heaven has joined
Great issues, good or bad for human kind,
Is happy as a lover; and attired
With sudden brightness, like a man inspired;
And, through the heat of conflict, keeps the law
In calmness made, and sees what he foresaw;
Or if an unexpected call succeed,
Come when it will, is equal to the need:
He who, though thus endued as with a sense
And faculty for storm and turbulence,
Is yet a soul whose master-bias leans
To homefelt pleasures and to gentle scenes;
Sweet images! which, wheresoe'er he be,
Are at his heart; and such fidelity
It is his darling passion to approve;
More brave for this, that he hath much to love.
'Tis, finally, the Man, who, lifted high,
Conspicuous object in a Nation's eye,
Or left unthought-of in obscurity,—
Who, with a toward or untoward lot,
Prosperous or adverse, to his wish or not—
Plays, in the many games of life, that one
Where what he most doth value must be won.
Whom neither shape of danger can dismay,
Nor thought of tender happiness betray;
Who, not content that former worth stand fast,
Looks forward, persevering to the last,
From well to better, daily self-surpassed:

Who, whether praise of him must walk the earth
For ever, and to noble deeds give birth,
Or he must fall, to sleep without his fame,
And leave a dead unprofitable name—
Finds comfort in himself and in his cause;
And, while the mortal mist is gathering, draws
His breath in confidence of Heaven's applause.

This is the happy Warrior; this is he
That every man in arms should wish to be.

*William Wordsworth* [1770–1850]

## THE GREAT ADVENTURE

'Tis sweet to hear of heroes dead,
To know them still alive;
But sweeter if we earn their bread,
And in us they survive.

Ye skies, drop gently round my breast
And be my corselet blue;
Ye earth, receive my lance in rest,
My faithful charger you:

Ye stars my spear-heads in the sky,
My arrow-tips ye are:
I see the routed foemen fly
My bright spears fixed [for war].

Give me an angel for a foe!
Fix now the place and time!
And straight to meet him I will go
Above the starry chime:

And with our clashing bucklers' clang
The heavenly spheres shall ring,
While bright the northern lights shall hang
Beside our tourneying.

And if she lose her champion true,
Tell Heaven not to despair,
For I will be her champion new,
Her fame I will repair.

*Henry David Thoreau* [1817–1862]

## "HE WHOM A DREAM HATH POSSESSED"

He whom a dream hath possessed knoweth no more of doubting,
For mist and the blowing of winds and the mouthing of words he scorns;
Not the sinuous speech of schools he hears, but a knightly shouting,
And never comes darkness down, yet he greeteth a million morns.

He whom a dream hath possessed knoweth no more of roaming;
All roads and the flowing of waves and the speediest flight he knows,
But wherever his feet are set, his soul is forever homing,
And going, he comes, and coming he heareth a call and goes.

He whom a dream hath possessed knoweth no more of sorrow,
At death and the dropping of leaves and the fading of suns he smiles,
For a dream remembers no past and scorns the desire of a morrow,
And a dream in a sea of doom sets surely the ultimate isles.

He whom a dream hath possessed treads the impalpable marches,
From the dust of the day's long road he leaps to a laughing star,
And the ruin of worlds that fall he views from eternal arches,
And rides God's battle-field in a flashing and golden car.

*Shaemas O'Sheel* [1886–1954]

## MASTERY

I would not have a god come in
To shield me suddenly from sin,
And set my house of life to rights;
Nor angels with bright burning wings
Ordering my earthly thoughts and things;

Rather my own frail guttering lights
Wind-blown and nearly beaten out,
Rather the terror of the nights
And long sick groping after doubt,
Rather be lost than let my soul
Slip vaguely from my own control—
Of my own spirit let me be
In sole though feeble mastery.

*Sara Teasdale* [1884–1933]

## A PRAYER

I KNEEL not now to pray that thou
Make white one single sin,—
I only kneel to thank thee, Lord,
For what I have not been;

For deeds which sprouted in my heart
But ne'er to bloom were brought,
For monstrous vices which I slew
In the shambles of my thought—

Dark seeds the world has never guessed
By hell and passion bred,
Which never grew beyond the bud
That cankered in my head.

Some said I was a righteous man—
Poor fools! The gallow's tree
(If thou hadst let one foot to slip)
Had grown a limb for me.

So for the Man I might have been
My heart must cease to mourn—
'Twere best to praise the living Lord
For monsters never born,

To bend the spiritual knee
(Knowing myself within)
And thank the kind, benignant God
For what I have not been.

*Harry Kemp* [1883–1960]

## "OF WOUNDS AND SORE DEFEAT"

Pandora's Song from "The Fire-Bringer"

Of wounds and sore defeat
I made my battle stay;
Wingèd sandals for my feet
I wove of my delay;
Of weariness and fear
I made my shouting spear;
Of loss, and doubt, and dread,
And swift oncoming doom
I made a helmet for my head
And a floating plume.
From the shutting mist of death,
From the failure of the breath,
I made a battle-horn to blow
Across the vales of overthrow.
O hearken, love, the battle-horn!
The triumph clear, the silver scorn!
O hearken where the echoes bring,
Down the gray disastrous morn,
Laughter and rallying!

*William Vaughn Moody* [1869-1910]

## PRAYER FOR PAIN

I do not pray for peace nor ease,
Nor truce from sorrow:
No suppliant on servile knees
Begs here against to-morrow!

Lean flame against lean flame we flash,
O Fates that meet me fair;
Blue steel against blue steel we clash—
Lay on, and I shall dare!

But Thou of deeps the awful Deep,
Thou breather in the clay,

Grant this my only prayer—Oh keep
My soul from turning gray!

For until now, whatever wrought
Against my sweet desires,
My days were smitten harps strung taut,
My nights were slumbrous lyres.

And howsoe'er the hard blow rang
Upon my battered shield,
Some lark-like, soaring spirit sang
Above my battle-field;

And through my soul of stormy night
The zigzag blue flame ran.
I asked no odds—I fought my fight—
Events against a man.

But now—at last—the gray mist chokes
And numbs me. *Leave me pain!*
*Oh, let me feel the biting strokes*
*That I may fight again!*

*John G. Neihardt* [1881-

## CARRY ON!

It's easy to fight when everything's right,
And you're mad with the thrill and the glory;
It's easy to cheer when victory's near,
And wallow in fields that are gory.
It's a different song when everything's wrong,
When you're feeling infernally mortal;
When it's ten against one, and hope there is none,
Buck up, little soldier, and chortle:

Carry on! Carry on!
There isn't much punch in your blow.
You're glaring and staring and hitting out blind;
You're muddy and bloody, but never you mind.
Carry on! Carry on!
You haven't the ghost of a show.
It's looking like death, but while you've a breath,
Carry on, my son! Carry on!

And so in the strife of the battle of life
It's easy to fight when you're winning;
It's easy to slave, and starve and be brave,
When the dawn of success is beginning.
But the man who can meet despair and defeat
With a cheer, there's the man of God's choosing;
The man who can fight to Heaven's own height
Is the man who can fight when he's losing.

Carry on! Carry on!
Things never were looming so black.
But show that you haven't a cowardly streak,
And though you're unlucky you never are weak.
Carry on! Carry on!
Brace up for another attack.
It's looking like hell, but—you never can tell:
Carry on, old man! Carry on!

There are some who drift out in the deserts of doubt,
And some who in brutishness wallow;
There are others, I know, who in piety go
Because of a Heaven to follow.
But to labor with zest, and to give of your best,
For the sweetness and joy of the giving;
To help folks along with a hand and a song;
Why, there's the real sunshine of living.

Carry on! Carry on!
Fight the good fight and true;
Believe in your mission, greet life with a cheer;
There's big work to do, and that's why you are here.
Carry on! Carry on!
Let the world be the better for you;
And at last when you die, let this be your cry:
*Carry on, my soul! Carry on!*

*Robert W. Service* [1874–1958]

## THE FIGHTING FAILURE

He has come the way of the fighting men and fought by the rules of the Game.
And out of Life he has gathered—what? A living—and little fame.

Ever and ever the Goal looms near—seeming each time
worth while,
But ever it proves a mirage fair—ever the grim gods smile.
And so, with lips hard set and white, he buries the hope
that is gone—
His fight is lost—and he knows it is lost—and yet he is
fighting on.

Out of the smoke of the battle-line, watching men win their
way
And cheering with those who cheer success, he enters again
the fray,
Licking the blood and dust from his lips, wiping the sweat
from his eyes,
He does the work he is set to do, and—"therein honor lies."
Brave they were, those men he cheered, theirs is the winners'
thrill;
His fight is lost—and he knows it is lost—and yet he is
fighting still.

And those who have won, have rest and peace; and those
who have died, have more;
But weary and spent, he cannot stop, seeking the ultimate
score.
Courage was theirs for a little time—but what of the man
who sees
That lose he must, yet will not beg, for mercy, upon his knees?
Side by side with grim Defeat, he struggles at dusk or dawn;
His fight is lost—and he knows it is lost—and yet, he is
fighting on.

Praise for the warriors who succeed, and tears for the vanquished dead.
The world will hold them close to Her heart, wreathing
each honored head;
But there in the ranks, soul-sick, time-tried, he battles
against the odds,
*Sans* hope, but true to his colors torn, the plaything of the
gods!
Uncover when he goes by at last! Held to his task by *will*—
The fight is lost—and he knows it is lost—and yet he is
fighting still!

*Everard John Appleton* [1872–1931]

## THE PRAYER OF BEATEN MEN

From "The House of Broken Swords"

WE are the fallen, who, with helpless faces
 Low in the dust, in stiffening ruin lay,
Felt the hoof's beat, and heard the rattling traces
 As o'er us drove the chariots of the fray.

We are the fallen, who by ramparts gory,
 Awaiting death, heard the far shouts begin,
And with our last glance glimpsed the victor's glory
 For which we died, but dying might not win.

We were but men. Always our eyes were holden,
 We could not read the dark that walled us round,
Nor deem our futile plans with thine enfolden—
 We fought, not knowing God was on the ground.

Give us our own; and though in realms eternal
 The potsherd and the pot, belike, are one,
Make our old world to know that with supernal
 Powers we were matched, and by the stars o'erthrown.

Ay, grant our ears to hear the foolish praising
 Of men—old voices of our lost home-land,
Or else, the gateways of this dim world raising,
 Give us our swords again, and hold thy hand.

*William Hervey Woods* [1852–

## THE LAST WORD

CREEP into thy narrow bed,
Creep, and let no more be said!
Vain thy onset! all stands fast.
Thou thyself must break at last.

Let the long contention cease!
Geese are swans, and swans are geese,
Let them have it how they will!
Thou art tired; best be still.

They out-talked thee, hissed thee, tore thee?
Better men fared thus before thee;
Fired their ringing shot and passed,
Hotly charged—and sank at last.

Charge once more, then, and be dumb!
Let the victors, when they come,
When the forts of folly fall,
Find thy body by the wall!

*Matthew Arnold* [1822–1888]

## IO VICTIS

**From "He and She"**

I SING the hymn of the conquered, who fell in the Battle of Life,
The hymn of the wounded, the beaten, who died overwhelmed in the strife;
Not the jubilant song of the victors, for whom the resounding acclaim
Of nations was lifted in chorus, whose brows wore the chaplet of fame,
But the hymn of the low and the humble, the weary, the broken in heart,
Who strove and who failed, acting bravely a silent and desperate part;
Whose youth bore no flower on its branches, whose hopes burned in ashes away,
From whose hands slipped the prize they had grasped at, who stood at the dying of day
With the wreck of their life all around them, unpitied, unheeded, alone,
With Death swooping down o'er their failure, and all but their faith overthrown,
While the voice of the world shouts its chorus—its pæan for those who have won;
While the trumpet is sounding triumphant and high to the breeze and the sun

Glad banners are waving, hands clapping and hurrying feet
Thronging after the laurel-crowned victors, I stand on the
field of defeat
In the shadow, with those who are fallen, and wounded, and
dying, and there
Chant a requiem low, place my hand on their pain-knotted
brows, breathe a prayer,
Hold the hand that is helpless and whisper, "They only the
victory win
Who have fought the good fight and have vanquished the
demon that tempts us within,
Who have held to their faith unseduced by the prize that the
world holds on high,
Who have dared for a high cause to suffer, resist, fight—if
need be, to die."
Speak, History! Who are life's victors? Unroll thy long
annals and say,
Are they those whom the world called the victors,—who
won the success of a day?
The martyrs, or Nero? The Spartans who fell at Ther-
mopylæ's tryst,
Or the Persians and Xerxes? His judges, or Socrates?
Pilate, or Christ?

*William Wetmore Story* [1819–1895]

## "THEY WENT FORTH TO BATTLE BUT THEY ALWAYS FELL"

THEY went forth to battle but they always fell;
Their eyes were fixed above the sullen shields;
Nobly they fought and bravely, but not well,
And sank heart-wounded by a subtle spell.
They knew not fear that to the foeman yields,
They were not weak, as one who vainly wields
A futile weapon; yet the sad scrolls tell
How on the hard-fought field they always fell.

It was a secret music that they heard,
A sad sweet plea for pity and for peace;
And that which pierced the heart was but a word,
Though the white breast was red-lipped where the sword

Pressed a fierce cruel kiss, to put surcease
On its hot thirst, but drank a hot increase.
Ah, they by some strange troubling doubt were stirred,
And died for hearing what no foeman heard.

They went forth to battle but they always fell:
Their might was not the might of lifted spears;
Over the battle-clamor came a spell
Of troubling music, and they fought not well.
Their wreaths are willows and their tribute, tears;
Their names are old sad stories in men's ears;
Yet they will scatter the red hordes of Hell,
Who went to battle forth and always fell.

*Shaemas O'Sheel* [1886–1954]

## THE MASTERS

Oh, Masters, you who rule the world,
Will you not wait with me awhile,
When swords are sheathed and sails are furled,
And all the fields with harvest smile?
I would not waste your time for long,
I ask you but, when you are tired,
To read how by the weak, the strong
Are weighed and worshiped and desired.

When weary of the Mart, the Loom,
The Withering-house, the Riffle-blocks,
The Barrack-square, the Engine-room,
The pick-axe, ringing on the rocks,—
When tents are pitched and work is done,
While restful twilight broods above,
By fresh-lit lamp, or dying sun,
See in my songs how women love.

We shared your lonely watch by night,
We knew you faithful at the helm,
Our thoughts went with you through the fight
That saved a soul,—or wrecked a realm:

Ah, how our hearts leapt forth to you,
In pride and joy, when you prevailed,
And when you died, serene and true:
—We wept in silence when you failed!

Oh, brain, that did not gain the gold!
Oh, arm, that could not wield the sword,
Here is the love, that is not sold,
Here are the hearts to hail you Lord!

You played and lost the game? What then?
The rules are harsh and hard, we know;
You, still, oh, brothers, are the men
Whom we in secret reverence so.
Your work was waste? Maybe your share
Lay in the hour you laughed and kissed;
Who knows but that your son shall wear
The laurels that his father missed?

Ay, you who win, and you who lose,
Whether you triumph,—or despair,—
When your returning footsteps choose
The homeward track, our love is there.
For, since the world is ordered thus,
To you, the fame, the stress, the sword,
We can but wait, until to us
You give yourselves, for our reward.

To Whaler's deck and Coral beach,
To lonely Ranch and Frontier-Fort,
Beyond the narrow bounds of speech
I lay the cable of my thought.
I fain would send my thanks to you,
(Though who am I, to give you praise?)
Since what you are, and work you do
Are lessons for our easier ways.

'Neath alien stars your camp-fires glow,
I know you not,—your tents are far.
My hope is but in song to show
How honored and how dear you are.

*Laurence Hope* [1865–1904]

## THE KINGS

A MAN said unto his Angel:
"My spirits are fallen low,
And I cannot carry this battle:
O brother! where might I go?

"The terrible Kings are on me
With spears that are deadly bright;
Against me so from the cradle
Do fate and my fathers fight."

Then said to the man his Angel:
"Thou wavering witless soul,
Back to the ranks! What matter
To win or to lose the whole,

"As judged by the little judges
Who hearken not well, nor see?
Not thus, by the outer issue,
The Wise shall interpret thee.

"Thy will is the sovereign measure
And only event of things:
The puniest heart, defying,
Were stronger than all these Kings.

"Though out of the past they gather,
Mind's Doubt and Bodily Pain,
And pallid Thirst of the Spirit
That is kin to the other twain,

"And Grief, in a cloud of banners,
And ringleted Vain Desires,
And Vice with the spoils upon him
Of thee and thy beaten sires,—

"While Kings of eternal evil
Yet darken the hills about,
Thy part is with broken saber
To rise on the last redoubt;

"To fear not sensible failure,
Nor covet the game at all,
But fighting, fighting, fighting,
Die, driven against the wall!"

*Louise Imogen Guiney* [1861–1920]

## FAILURES

THEY bear no laurels on their sunless brows,
Nor aught within their pale hands as they go;
They look as men accustomed to the slow
And level onward course 'neath drooping boughs.
Who may these be no trumpet doth arouse,
These of the dark processionals of woe,
Unpraised, unblamed, but whom sad Acheron's flow
Monotonously lulls to leaden drowse?
These are the Failures. Clutched by Circumstance,
They were—say not too weak!—too ready prey
To their own fear whose fixèd Gorgon glance
Made them as stone for aught of great essay;—
Or else they nodded when their Master-Chance
Wound his one signal, and went on his way.

*Arthur Upson* [1877–1908]

## DON QUIXOTE

BEHIND thy pasteboard, on thy battered hack,
Thy lean cheek striped with plaster to and fro,
Thy long spear leveled at the unseen foe,
And doubtful Sancho trudging at thy back,
Thou wert a figure strange enough, good lack!
To make Wiseacredom, both high and low,
Rub purblind eyes, and (having watched thee go),
Dispatch its Dogberrys upon thy track:
Alas! poor Knight! Alas! poor soul possessed!
Yet would to-day, when Courtesy grows chill,
And life's fine loyalties are turned to jest,
Some fire of thine might burn within us still!
Ah! would but one might lay his lance in rest,
And charge in earnest—were it but a mill.

*Austin Dobson* [1840–1921]

## A PRAYER

LORD, not for light in darkness do we pray,
Not that the veil be lifted from our eyes,
Nor that the slow ascension of our day
Be otherwise.

Not for a clearer vision of the things
Whereof the fashioning shall make us great,
Nor for remission of the peril and stings
Of time and fate.

Not for a fuller knowledge of the end
Whereto we travel, bruised yet unafraid,
Nor that the little healing that we lend
Shall be repaid.

Not these, O Lord. We would not break the bars
Thy wisdom sets about us; we shall climb
Unfettered to the secrets of the stars
In thy good time.

We do not crave the high perception swift
When to refrain were well, and when fulfil,
Nor yet the understanding strong to sift
The good from ill.

Not these, O Lord. For these thou hast revealed.
We know the golden season when to reap
The heavy-fruited treasure of the field,
The hour to sleep.

Not these. We know the hemlock from the rose,
The pure from stained, the noble from the base,
The tranquil holy light of truth that glows
On Pity's face.

We know the paths wherein our feet should press,
Across our hearts are written thy decrees.
Yet now, O Lord, be merciful to bless
With more than these.

Grant us the will to fashion as we feel,
Grant us the strength to labor as we know,
Grant us the purpose, ribbed and edged with steel,
    To strike the blow.

Knowledge we ask not—knowledge thou hast lent;
But Lord, the will—there lies our bitter need.
Give us to build above the deep intent
    The deed, the deed.

*John Drinkwater* [1882–1937]

## IF—

If you can keep your head when all about you
  Are losing theirs and blaming it on you,
If you can trust yourself when all men doubt you,
  But make allowance for their doubting too;
If you can wait and not be tired by waiting,
  Or being lied about, don't deal in lies,
Or being hated don't give way to hating,
  And yet don't look too good, nor talk too wise:

If you can dream—and not make dreams your master;
  If you can think—and not make thoughts your aim,
If you can meet with Triumph and Disaster
  And treat those two imposters just the same;
If you can bear to hear the truth you've spoken
  Twisted by knaves to make a trap for fools,
Or watch the things you gave your life to, broken,
  And stoop and build 'em up with worn-out tools:

If you can make one heap of all your winnings;
  And risk it on one turn of pitch-and-toss,
And lose, and start again at your beginnings
  And never breathe a word about your loss;
If you can force your heart and nerve and sinew
  To serve your turn long after they are gone,
And so hold on when there is nothing in you
  Except the Will which says to them: "Hold on!"

If you can talk with crowds and keep your virtue,
Or walk with Kings—nor lose the common touch,
If neither foes nor loving friends can hurt you,
If all men count with you, but none too much;
If you can fill the unforgiving minute
With sixty seconds' worth of distance run,
Yours is the Earth and everything that's in it,
And—which is more—you'll be a Man, my son!

*Rudyard Kipling* [1865–1936]

## RABIA

Rabia, sick upon her bed,
By two saints was visited,—

Holy Malik, Hassan wise—
Men of mark in Moslem eyes.

Hassan says, "Whose prayer is pure,
Will God's chastisement endure."

Malik, from a deeper sense
Uttered his experience:

"He who loves his Master's choice
Will in chastisement rejoice."

Rabia saw some selfish will
In their maxims lingering still,

And replied, "O men of grace!
He who sees his Master's face

Will not, in his prayer, recall
That he is chastised at all."

*From the Arabic, by James Freeman Clarke* [1810–1888]

## THE JOYFUL WISDOM

From "The Angel in the House"

Would Wisdom for herself be wooed,
And wake the foolish from his dream.
She must be glad as well as good,
And must not only be, but seem.

Beauty and joy are hers by right;
  And, knowing this, I wonder less
That she's so scorned, when falsely dight
  In misery and ugliness.
What's that which Heaven to man endears,
  And that which eyes no sooner see
Than the heart says, with floods of tears,
  "Ah, that's the thing which I would be!"
Not childhood, full of frown and fret;
  Not youth, impatient to disown
Those visions high, which to forget
  Were worse than never to have known;
Not worldlings, in whose fair outside,
  Nor courtesy nor justice fails,
Thanks to cross-pulling vices tied,
  Like Samson's foxes, by the tails;
Not poets; real things are dreams,
  When dreams are as realities,
And boasters of celestial gleams
  Go stumbling aye for want of eyes;
Not patriots nor people's men,
  In whom two worse-matched evils meet
Than ever sought Adullam's den,
  Base conscience and a high conceit;
Not new-made saints, their feelings iced,
  Their joy in man and nature gone,
Who sing "O easy yoke of Christ!"
  But find 'tis hard to get it on;
Not great men, even when they're good;
  The good man whom the time makes great,
By some disgrace of chance or blood,
  God fails not to humiliate;
Not these: but souls, found here and there,
  Oases in our waste of sin,
Where everything is well and fair,
  And Heaven remits its discipline;
Whose sweet subdual of the world
  The worldling scarce can recognize,
And ridicule, against it hurled,
  Drops with a broken sting, and dies;

Who nobly, if they cannot know
  Whether a 'scutcheon's dubious field
Carries a falcon or a crow,
  Fancy a falcon on the shield;
Yet, ever careful not to hurt
  God's honor, who creates success,
Their praise of even the best desert
  Is but to have presumed no less;
Who, should their own life plaudits bring,
  Are simply vexed at heart that such
An easy, yea, delightful thing
  Should move the minds of men so much.
They live by law, not like the fool,
  But like the bard, who freely sings
In strictest bonds of rhyme and rule,
  And finds in them, not bonds, but wings.
Postponing still their private ease
  To courtly custom, appetite,
Subjected to observances,
  To banquet goes with full delight;
Nay, continence and gratitude
  So cleanse their lives from earth's alloy,
They taste, in Nature's common food,
  Nothing but spiritual joy.
They shine like Moses in the face,
  And teach our hearts, without the rod,
That God's grace is the only grace,
  And all grace is the grace of God.

*Coventry Patmore* [1823–1896]

## ODE TO DUTY

STERN Daughter of the Voice of God!
O Duty! if that name thou love,
Who art a light to guide, a rod
To check the erring and reprove;
Thou, who art victory and law
When empty terrors overawe;
From vain temptations dost set free;
And calm'st the weary strife of frail humanity!

There are who ask not if thine eye
Be on them; who, in love and truth,
Where no misgiving is, rely
Upon the genial sense of youth:
Glad Hearts! without reproach or blot,
Who do thy work, and know it not:
O, if through confidence misplaced
They fail, thy saving arms, dread Power! around them cast.

Serene will be our days and bright,
And happy will our nature be,
When love is an unerring light,
And joy its own security.
And they a blissful course may hold
Even now, who, not unwisely bold,
Live in the spirit of this creed;
Yet seek thy firm support, according to their need.

I, loving freedom, and untried;
No sport of every random gust,
Yet being to myself a guide,
Too blindly have reposed my trust:
And oft, when in my heart was heard
Thy timely mandate, I deferred
The task, in smoother walks to stray;
But thee I now would serve more strictly, if I may.

Through no disturbance of my soul,
Or strong compunction in me wrought,
I supplicate for thy control;
But in the quietness of thought:
Me this unchartered freedom tires;
I feel the weight of chance-desires;
My hopes no more must change their name,
I long for a repose that ever is the same.

Stern Lawgiver! yet thou dost wear
The Godhead's most benignant grace;
Nor know we anything so fair
As is the smile upon thy face:

Flowers laugh before thee on their beds,
And fragrance in thy footing treads;
Thou dost preserve the stars from wrong;
And the most ancient heavens, through Thee, are fresh and
strong.

To humbler functions, awful Power!
I call thee: I myself commend
Unto thy guidance from this hour;
O, let my weakness have an end!
Give unto me, made lowly wise,
The spirit of self-sacrifice;
The confidence of reason give;
And in the light of truth thy Bondman let me live!

*William Wordsworth* [1770-1850]

## CHANT ROYAL OF HIGH VIRTUE

WHO lives in suit of armor pent,
And hides himself behind a wall,
For him is not the great event,
The garland, nor the Capitol.
And is God's guerdon less than they?
Nay, moral man, I tell thee Nay:
Nor shall the flaming forts be won
By sneaking negatives alone,
By Lenten fast or Ramazàn,
But by the challenge proudly thrown—
*Virtue is that beseems a Man!*

God, in his Palace resident
Of Bliss, beheld our sinful ball,
And charged His own Son innocent
Us to redeem from Adam's fall.
—"Yet must it be that men Thee slay."
—"Yea, though it must, must I obey,"
Said Christ,—and came, His royal Son,
To die, and dying to atone
For harlot and for publican.
Read on that rood He died upon—
*Virtue is that beseems a Man!*

And by that rood where He was bent
  I saw the world's great captains all
Go riding to the tournament—
  Cyrus the Great and Hannibal,
Cæsar of Rome and Attila,
Lord Charlemagne and his array,
Lord Alisaundre of Macedon—
With flaming lance and habergeon
  They passed, and to the rataplan
Of drums gave salutation—
  *Virtue is that beseems a Man!*

Had tall Achilles lounged in tent
  For aye, and Xanthus neighed in stall,
The towers of Troy had ne'er been shent,
  Nor stayed the dance in Priam's hall.
Bend o'er thy book till thou be gray,
Read, mark, perpend, digest, survey—
Instruct thee deep as Solomon—
One only chapter thou shalt con,
  One lesson learn, one sentence scan,
One title and one colophon—
  *Virtue is that beseems a Man!*

High Virtue's hest is eloquent
  With spur and not with martingall:
Sufficeth not thou'rt continent:
  BE COURTEOUS, BRAVE, AND LIBERAL.
God fashioned thee of chosen clay
For service, nor did ever say
"Deny thee this," "Abstain from yon,"
Save to inure thee, thew and bone,
  To be confirmèd of the clan
That made immortal Marathon—
  *Virtue is that beseems a Man!*

ENVOY

Young Knight, the lists are set to-day:
Hereafter shall be long to pray
In sepulture with hands of stone.
Ride, then! outride the bugle blown!

And gaily dinging down the van
Charge with a cheer—Set on! Set on!
*Virtue is that beseems a Man!*

*Arthur T. Quiller-Couch* [1863–1944]

## THE SPLENDID SPUR

NOT on the neck of prince or hound,
Nor on a woman's finger twined,
May gold from the deriding ground
Keep sacred that we sacred bind:
Only the heel
Of splendid steel
Shall stand secure on sliding fate,
When golden navies weep their freight.

The scarlet hat, the laureled stave
Are measures, not the springs, of worth;
In a wife's lap, as in a grave,
Man's airy notions mix with earth.
Seek other spur
Bravely to stir
The dust in this loud world, and tread
Alp-high among the whispering dead.

*Trust in thyself*,—then spur amain:
So shall Charybdis wear a grace,
Grim Ætna laugh, the Libyan plain
Take roses to her shriveled face.
This orb—this round
Of sight and sound—
Count it the lists that God hath built
For haughty hearts to ride a-tilt.

*Arthur T. Quiller-Couch* [1863–1944]

## SACRIFICE

THOUGH love repine, and reason chafe,
There came a voice without reply,—
"'Tis man's perdition to be safe,
When for the truth he ought to die."

*Ralph Waldo Emerson* [1803–1882]

# THE TRANSCENDENTALISTS

## CONSCIENCE

From "A Week on the Concord and Merrimack Rivers"

CONSCIENCE is instinct bred in the house,
Feeling and Thinking propagate the sin
By an unnatural breeding in and in.
I say, Turn it out of doors,
Into the moors.
I love a life whose plot is simple,
And does not thicken with every pimple,
A soul so sound no sickly conscience binds it,
That makes the universe no worse than 't finds it.
I love an earnest soul,
Whose mighty joy and sorrow
Are not drowned in a bowl,
And brought to life to-morrow;
That lives one tragedy,
And not seventy;
A conscience worth keeping,
Laughing not weeping;
A conscience wise and steady,
And forever ready;
Not changing with events,
Dealing in compliments;
A conscience exercised about
Large things, which one *may* doubt.
I love a soul not all of wood,
Predestined to be good,
But true to the backbone
Unto itself alone
And false to none;
Born to its own affairs,
Its own joys and own cares;
By whom the work which God begun
Is finished, and not undone;

Taken up where he left off,
Whether to worship or to scoff;
If not good, why then evil,
If not good god, good devil.
Goodness!—you hypocrite, come out of that,
Live your life, do your work, then take your hat.
I have no patience towards
Such conscientious cowards.
Give me simple laboring folk,
Who love their work,
Whose virtue is a song
To cheer God along.

*Henry David Thoreau* [1817–1862]

## MY PRAYER

Great God, I ask thee for no meaner pelf
Than that I may not disappoint myself;
That in my action I may soar as high
As I can now discern with this clear eye.

And next in value, which thy kindness lends,
That I may greatly disappoint my friends,
Howe'er they think or hope that it may be,
They may not dream how thou'st distinguished me.

That my weak hand may equal my firm faith,
And my life practise more than my tongue saith;
That my low conduct may not show,
Nor my relenting lines,
That I thy purpose did not know,
Or overrated thy designs.

*Henry David Thoreau* [1817–1862]

## INSPIRATION

If with light head erect I sing,
Though all the Muses lend their force,
From my poor love of anything,
The verse is weak and shallow as its source.

But if with bended neck I grope
Listening behind me for my wit,
With faith superior to hope,
More anxious to keep back than forward it,—

Making my soul accomplice there
Unto the flame my heart hath lit,
Then will the verse forever wear,—
Time cannot bend the line which God has writ.

I hearing get, who had but ears,
And sight, who had but eyes before;
I moments live, who lived but years,
And truth discern, who knew but learning's lore.

Now chiefly is my natal hour,
And only now my prime of life;
Of manhood's strength it is the flower,
'Tis peace's end, and war's beginning strife.

It comes in summer's broadest noon,
By a gray wall, or some chance place,
Unseasoning time, insulting June,
And vexing day with its presuming face.

I will not doubt the love untold
Which not my worth nor want hath bought,
Which wooed me young, and wooes me old,
And to this evening hath me brought.

*Henry David Thoreau* [1817–1862]

## EACH AND ALL

LITTLE thinks, in the field, yon red-cloaked clown
Of thee from the hill-top looking down;
The heifer that lows in the upland farm,
Far-heard, lows not thine ear to charm;
The sexton, tolling his bell at noon,
Deems not that great Napoleon
Stops his horse, and lists with delight,
Whilst his files sweep round yon Alpine height;

Nor knowest thou what argument
Thy life to thy neighbor's creed has lent.
All are needed by each one;
Nothing is fair or good alone.
I thought the sparrow's note from heaven,
Singing at dawn on the alder bough;
I brought him home, in his nest, at even;
He sings the song, but it cheers not now,
For I did not bring home the river and sky;—
He sang to my ear,—they sang to my eye.

The delicate shells lay on the shore;
The bubbles of the latest wave
Fresh pearls to their enamel gave,
And the bellowing of the savage sea
Greeted their safe escape to me.
I wiped away the weeds and foam,
I fetched my sea-born treasures home;
But the poor, unsightly, noisome things
Had left their beauty on the shore,
With the sun and the sand and the wild uproar.

The lover watched his graceful maid,
As 'mid the virgin train she strayed;
Nor knew her beauty's best attire
Was woven still by the snow-white choir.
At last she came to his hermitage,
Like the bird from the woodlands to the cage;—
The gay enchantment was undone,
A gentle wife, but fairy none.

Then I said, "I covet truth;
Beauty is unripe childhood's cheat;
I leave it behind with the games of youth:"—
As I spoke, beneath my feet
The ground-pine curled its pretty wreath,
Running over the club-moss burrs;
I inhaled the violet's breath;
Around me stood the oaks and firs;
Pine-cones and acorns lay on the ground;

Over me soared the eternal sky,
Full of light and of deity;
Again I saw, again I heard,
The rolling river, the morning bird;—
Beauty through my senses stole;
I yielded myself to the perfect whole.

*Ralph Waldo Emerson* [1803–1882]

## BRAHMA

If the red slayer think he slays,
Or if the slain think he is slain,
They know not well the subtle ways
I keep, and pass, and turn again.

Far or forgot to me is near;
Shadow and sunlight are the same;
The vanished gods to me appear;
And one to me are shame and fame.

They reckon ill who leave me out;
When me they fly, I am the wings;
I am the doubter and the doubt,
And I the hymn the Brahmin sings.

The strong gods pine for my abode,
And pine in vain the sacred Seven;
But thou, meek lover of the good!
Find me, and turn thy back on heaven.

*Ralph Waldo Emerson* [1803–1882]

## BACCHUS

Bring me wine, but wine which never grew
In the belly of the grape,
Or grew on vine whose tap-roots, reaching through
Under the Andes to the Cape,
Suffered no savor of the earth to 'scape.

Let its grapes the morn salute
From a nocturnal root,
Which feels the acrid juice
Of Styx and Erebus;
And turns the woe of Night,
By its own craft, to a more rich delight.

We buy ashes for bread;
We buy diluted wine;
Give me of the true,—
Whose ample leaves and tendrils curled
Among the silver hills of heaven
Draw everlasting dew;
Wine of wine,
Blood of the world,
Form of forms, and mold of statures,
That I intoxicated,
And by the draught assimilated,
May float at pleasure through all natures;
The bird-language rightly spell,
And that which roses say so well.

Wine that is shed
Like the torrents of the sun
Up the horizon walls,
Or like the Atlantic streams, which run
When the South Sea calls.

Water and bread,
Food which needs no transmuting,
Rainbow-flowering, wisdom-fruiting,
Wine which is already man,
Food which teach and reason can.

Wine which Music is,—
Music and wine are one,—
That I, drinking this,
Shall hear far Chaos talk with me;
Kings unborn shall walk with me,

And the poor grass shall plot and plan
What it will do when it is man.
Quickened so, will I unlock
Every crypt of every rock.

I thank the joyful juice
For all I know;—
Winds of remembering
Of the ancient being blow,
And seeming-solid walls of use
Open and flow.

Pour, Bacchus! the remembering wine;
Retrieve the loss of me and mine!
Vine for vine be antidote,
And the grape requite the lote!
Haste to cure the old despair;—
Reason in Nature's lotus drenched,
The memory of ages quenched;
Give them again to shine;
Let wine repair what this undid;
And where the infection slid,
A dazzling memory revive;
Refresh the faded tints,
Recut the agèd prints,
And write my old adventures with the pen
Which on the first day drew,
Upon the tablets blue,
The dancing Pleiads and eternal men.

*Ralph Waldo Emerson* [1803-1882]

## THE PROBLEM

I LIKE a church; I like a cowl;
I love a prophet of the soul;
And on my heart monastic aisles
Fall like sweet strains, or pensive smiles:
Yet not for all his faith can see
Would I that cowlèd churchman be.

Why should the vest on him allure,
Which I could not on me endure?

Not from a vain or shallow thought
His awful Jove young Phidias brought;
Never from lips of cunning fell
The thrilling Delphic oracle;
Out from the heart of nature rolled
The burdens of the Bible old;
The litanies of nations came,
Like the volcano's tongue of flame,
Up from the burning core below,—
The canticles of love and woe:
The hand that rounded Peter's dome,
And groined the aisles of Christian Rome,
Wrought in a sad sincerity;
Himself from God he could not free;
He builded better than he knew;—
The conscious stone to beauty grew.

Know'st thou what wove yon woodbird's nest
Of leaves, and feathers from her breast?
Or how the fish outbuilt her shell,
Painting with morn each annual cell?
Or how the sacred pine-tree adds
To her old leaves new myriads?
Such and so grew these holy piles,
Whilst love and terror laid the tiles.
Earth proudly wears the Parthenon,
As the best gem upon her zone,
And Morning opes with haste her lids,
To gaze upon the Pyramids;
O'er England's abbeys bends the sky,
As on its friends, with kindred eye;
For, out of Thought's interior sphere,
These wonders rose to upper air;
And Nature gladly gave them place,
Adopted them into her race,
And granted them an equal date
With Andes and with Ararat.

These temples grew as grows the grass;
Art might obey, but not surpass.
The passive Master lent his hand
To the vast soul that o'er him planned;
And the same power that reared the shrine
Bestrode the tribes that knelt within.
Ever the fiery Pentecost
Girds with one flame the countless host,
Trances the heart through chanting choirs,
And through the priest the mind inspires.
The word unto the prophet spoken
Was writ on tables yet unbroken;
The word by seers or sibyls told,
In groves of oak, or fanes of gold,
Still floats upon the morning wind,
Still whispers to the willing mind.
One accent of the Holy Ghost
The heedless world hath never lost.
I know what say the fathers wise,—
The Book itself before me lies,—
Old *Chrysostom*, best Augustine,
And he who blent both in his line,
The younger *Golden Lips* or mines,
Taylor, the Shakespeare of divines.
His words are music in my ear,
I see his cowlèd portrait dear;
And yet, for all his faith could see,
I would not the good bishop be.

*Ralph Waldo Emerson* [1803–1882]

## EVENING HYMN

Slowly by God's hand unfurled,
Down around the weary world
Falls the darkness; oh, how still
Is the working of Thy will!

Mighty Maker! Here am I,—
Work in me as silently,

Veil the day's distracting sights,
Show me heaven's eternal lights.

From the darkened sky come forth
Countless stars, a wondrous birth!
So may gleams of glory dart
Through the dim abyss, my heart;

Living worlds to view be brought,
In the boundless realms of thought,
High and infinite desires,
Burning like those upper fires.

Holy truth, eternal right,
Let them break upon my sight,
Let them shine unclouded, still,
And with light my being fill.

Thou art there. Oh, let me know,
Thou art here within me too;
Be the perfect peace of God
Here as there now shed abroad.

May my soul attunèd be
To that perfect harmony,
Which, beyond the power of sound,
Fills the universe around.

*William Henry Furness* [1802–1896]

## THE HIGHER GOOD

FATHER, I will not ask for wealth or fame,
Though once they would have joyed my carnal sense:
I shudder not to bear a hated name,
Wanting all wealth, myself my sole defense.
But give me, Lord, eyes to behold the truth;
A seeing sense that knows the eternal right;
A heart with pity filled, and gentlest ruth;
A manly faith that makes all darkness light:

Give me the power to labor for mankind;
Make me the mouth of such as cannot speak;
Eyes let me be to groping men and blind;
A conscience to the base; and to the weak
Let me be hands and feet; and to the foolish, mind;
And lead still further on such as thy kingdom seek.

*Theodore Parker* [1810–1860]

## THE IDLER

I IDLE stand that I may find employ,
Such as my Master when He comes will give;
I cannot find in mine own work my joy,
But wait, although in waiting I must live;
My body shall not turn which way it will,
But stand till I the appointed road can find,
And journeying so his messages fulfil,
And do at every step the work designed.
Enough for me, still day by day to wait
Till Thou who form'st me find'st me too a task,
A cripple lying at the rich man's gate,
Content for the few crumbs I get to ask,
A laborer but in heart, while bound my hands
Hang idly down still waiting thy commands.

*Jones Very* [1813–1880]

## QUESTIONINGS

HATH this world, without me wrought,
Other substance than my thought?
Lives it by my sense alone,
Or by essence of its own?
Will its life, with mine begun,
Cease to be when that is done,
Or another consciousness
With the self-same forms impress?

Doth yon fire-ball, poised in air,
Hang by my permission there?

Are the clouds that wander by
But the offspring of mine eye,
Born with every glance I cast,
Perishing when that is past?
And those thousand, thousand eyes,
Scattered through the twinkling skies,
Do they draw their life from mine,
Or of their own beauty shine?

Now I close my eyes, my ears,
And creation disappears;
Yet if I but speak the word,
All creation is restored.
Or, more wonderful, within
New creations do begin;
Hues more bright and forms more rare
Than reality doth wear
Flash across my inward sense,
Born of the mind's omnipotence.

Soul! that all informest, say!
Shall these glorics pass away?
Will those planets cease to blaze
When these eyes no longer gaze?
And the life of things be o'er
When these pulses beat no more?

Thought! that in me works and lives,—
Life to all things living gives,—
Art thou not thyself, perchance,
But the universe in trance?
A reflection inly flung
By that world thou fanciedst sprung
From thyself—thyself a dream—
Of the world's thinking thou the theme?

Be it thus, or be thy birth
From a source above the earth—
Be thou matter, be thou mind,
In thee alone myself I find,

And through thee alone, for me,
Hath this world reality.
Therefore, in thee will I live,
To thee all myself will give,
Losing still, that I may find
This bounded self in boundless Mind.

*Frederic Henry Hedge* [1805–1890]

## THE GREAT VOICES

A VOICE from the sea to the mountains,
From the mountains again to the sea;
A call from the deep to the fountains:
O spirit! be glad and be free!

A cry from the floods to the fountains,
And the torrents repeat the glad song
As they leap from the breast of the mountains:
O spirit! be free and be strong!

The pine forests thrill with emotion
Of praise as the spirit sweeps by;
With a voice like the murmur of ocean
To the soul of the listener they cry.

Oh, sing, human heart, like the fountains,
With joy reverential and free;
Contented and calm as the mountains,
And deep as the woods and the sea.

*Charles Timothy Brooks* [1813–1883]

## BEAUTY AND DUTY

I SLEPT, and dreamed that life was beauty;
I woke, and found that life was duty.
Was thy dream then a shadowy lie?
Toil on, sad heart, courageously,
And thou shalt find thy dream to be
A noonday light and truth to thee.

*Ellen Hooper* [1816–1841]

## THE STRAIGHT ROAD

Beauty may be the path to highest good,
And some successfully have it pursued.
Thou, who wouldst follow, be well warned to see
That way prove not a curvèd road to thee.
The straightest path perhaps which may be sought,
Lies through the great highway men call "I ought."

*Ellen Hooper* [1816–1841]

## THE WAY

They find the way who linger where
The soul finds fullest life;
The battle brave is carried on
By all who wait, and waiting, dare
Deem each day's least that's fitly done
A victory worthy to be won,
Nor seek their gain with strife.

*Sidney Henry Morse* [18 –

## INSPIRATION

Life of Ages, richly poured,
Love of God, unspent and free,
Flowing in the Prophet's word
And the People's liberty!

Never was to chosen race
That unstinted tide confined;
Thine is every time and place,
Fountain sweet of heart and mind!

Secret of the morning stars,
Motion of the oldest hours,
Pledge through elemental wars
Of the coming spirit's powers!

Rolling planet, flaming sun,
  Stand in nobler man complete;
Prescient laws Thine errands run,
  Frame the shrine for Godhead meet.

Homeward led, the wondering eye
  Upward yearned in joy or awe,
Found the love that waited nigh,
  Guidance of Thy guardian Law.

In the touch of earth it thrilled;
  Down from mystic skies it burned;
Right obeyed and passion stilled
  Its eternal gladness earned.

Breathing in the thinker's creed,
  Pulsing in the hero's blood,
Nerving simplest thought and deed,
  Freshening time with truth and good,

Consecrating art and song,
  Holy book and pilgrim track,
Hurling floods of tyrant wrong
  From the sacred limits back,—

Life of Ages, richly poured,
  Love of God, unspent and free,
Flow still in the Prophet's word
  And the People's liberty!

*Samuel Johnson* [1822–1882]

## I IN THEE, AND THOU IN ME

I AM but clay in thy hands; but thou art the all-loving artist;
  Passive I lie in thy sight, yet in my selfhood I strive
So to embody the life and love thou ever impartest
  That in my spheres of the finite I may be truly alive.

Knowing thou needest this form, as I thy divine inspiration,
  Knowing thou shapest the clay with a vision and purpose divine,
So would I answer each touch of thy hand in its loving creation,
  That in my conscious life thy power and beauty may shine.

Reflecting the noble intent thou hast in forming thy creatures;
Waking from sense into life of the soul, and the image of thee;
Working with thee in thy work to model humanity's features
Into the likeness of God, myself from myself I would free.

One with all human existence, no one above or below me;
Lit by thy wisdom and love, as roses are steeped in the morn;
Growing from clay to statue, from statue to flesh, till thou know me
Wrought into manhood celestial, and in thine image reborn.

So in thy love will I trust, bringing me sooner or later
Past the dark screen that divides these shows of the finite from thee.
Thine, thine only, this warm dear life, O loving Creator!
Thine the invisible future, born of the present, must be.

*Christopher Pearse Cranch* [1813–1892]

## GNOSIS

THOUGHT is deeper than all speech,
Feeling deeper than all thought;
Souls to souls can never teach
What unto themselves was taught

We are spirits clad in veils;
Man by man was never seen;
All our deep communing fails
To remove the shadowy screen.

Heart to heart was never known;
Mind with mind did never meet:
We are columns left alone
Of a temple once complete.

Like the stars that gem the sky,
  Far apart, though seeming near,
In our light we scattered lie;
  All is thus but starlight here.

What is social company
  But a babbling summer stream?
What our wise philosophy
  But the glancing of a dream?

Only when the sun of love
  Melts the scattered stars of thought,
Only when we live above
  What the dim-eyed world hath taught,

Only when our souls are fed
  By the fount which gave them birth,
And by inspiration led
  Which they never drew from earth,

We, like parted drops of rain,
  Swelling till they meet and run,
Shall be all absorbed again,
  Melting, flowing into one.

*Christopher Pearse Cranch* [1813–1892]

## THE FUTURE

WHAT may we take into the vast Forever?
    That marble door
Admits no fruit of all our long endeavor,
    No fame-wreathed crown we wore,
    No garnered lore.

What can we bear beyond the unknown portal?
    No gold, no gains
Of all our toiling: in the life immortal
    No hoarded wealth remains,
    Nor gilds, nor stains.

Naked from out that far abyss behind us
We entered here:
No word came with our coming, to remind us
What wondrous world was near,
No hope, no fear.

Into the silent, starless Night before us,
Naked we glide:
No hand has mapped the constellations o'er us,
No comrade at our side,
No chart, no guide.

Yet fearless toward that midnight, black and hollow,
Our footsteps fare;
The beckoning of a Father's hand we follow—
His love alone is there,
No curse, no care.

*Edward Rowland Sill* [1841–1887]

## TWICE FED

THANK God we do not live by bread alone
But by all loveliness that we have known,
By each fair color and by each soft tone.

Far to the west the golden wheat fields spread,
And from this beauty soul and sense are fed;
For so God gives us twice our daily bread.

*A. A. Bassett* [

## LOVE'S LORD

WHEN weight of all the garnered years
Bows me, and praise must find relief
In harvest-song, and smiles and tears
Twist in the band that binds my sheaf;

Thou known Unknown, dark, radiant sea
In whom we live, in whom we move,
My spirit must lose itself in Thee,
Crying a name—Life, Light, or Love.

*Edward Dowden* [1843-1913]

# A MIND CONTENT

## "JOG ON, JOG ON"

From "The Winter's Tale"

Jog on, jog on the foot-path way,
And merrily hent the stile-a;
A merry heart goes all the day,
Your sad tires in a mile-a.

*William Shakespeare* [1564–1616]

## ON A CONTENTED MIND

When all is done and said,
In the end this shall you find:
He most of all doth bathe in bliss
That hath a quiet mind;
And, clear from worldly cares,
To deem can be content
The sweetest time in all his life
In thinking to be spent.

The body subject is
To fickle Fortune's power,
And to a million of mishaps
Is casual every hour;
And Death in time doth change
It to a clod of clay;
When as the mind, which is divine,
Runs never to decay.

Companion none is like
Unto the mind alone,
For many have been harmed by speech,–
Through thinking, few, or none.

Fear oftentimes restraineth words,
But makes not thoughts to cease;
And he speaks best that hath the skill
When for to hold his peace.

Our wealth leaves us at death,
Our kinsmen at the grave;
But virtues of the mind unto
The heavens with us we have;
Wherefore, for virtue's sake,
I can be well content
The sweetest time of all my life
To deem in thinking spent.

*Thomas Vaux* [1510–1556]

## MÆSIA'S SONG

From "Farewell to Folly"

Sweet are the thoughts that savor of content,
The quiet mind is richer than a crown,
Sweet are the nights in careless slumber spent,
The poor estate scorns Fortune's angry frown:
Such sweet content, such minds, such sleep, such bliss,
Beggars enjoy, when princes oft do miss.

The homely house that harbors quiet rest,
The cottage that affords no pride nor care,
The mean that 'grees with country music best,
The sweet consort of mirth and modest fare,
Obscurèd life sets down a type of bliss:
A mind content both crown and kingdom is.

*Robert Greene* [1560?–1592]

## THE MEANS TO ATTAIN HAPPY LIFE

Martial, the things that do attain
The happy life be these, I find:
The riches left, not got with pain;
The fruitful ground; the quiet mind;

The equal friend; no grudge, no strife;
No charge of rule, no governance;
Without disease, the healthful life;
The household of continuance;
The mean diet, no delicate fare;
True wisdom joined with simpleness;
The night dischargèd of all care,
Where wine the wit may not oppress;
The faithful wife, without debate;
Such sleeps as may beguile the night:
Contented with thine own estate,
Nor wish for death, nor fear his might.

*After Martial, by Henry Howard* [1517?–1547]

## RISPOSTA

There is a jewel which no Indian mines
Can buy, no chemic art can counterfeit;
It makes men rich in greatest poverty;
Makes water wine, turns wooden cups to gold,
The homely whistle to sweet music's strain:
Seldom it comes, to few from heaven sent,
That much in little, all in naught—Content.

*John Wilbye* [fl. 1598–1614]

## A CONTENTED MIND

I weigh not fortune's frown or smile;
I joy not much in earthly joys;
I seek not state, I reck not style;
I am not fond of fancy's toys:
I rest so pleased with what I have,
I wish no more, no more I crave.

I quake not at the thunder's crack;
I tremble not at news of war;
I swound not at the news of wrack;
I shrink not at a blazing star;
I fear not loss, I hope not gain,
I envy none, I none disdain.

I see ambition never pleased;
  I see some Tantals starved in store;
I see gold's dropsy seldom eased;
  I see even Midas gape for more;
I neither want nor yet abound,—
Enough's a feast, content is crowned.

I feign not friendship where I hate;
  I fawn not on the great (in show);
I prize, I praise a mean estate,—
  Neither too lofty nor too low:
This, this is all my choice, my cheer,—
A mind content, a conscience clear.

*Joshua Sylvester* [1563–1618]

## THE HAPPY HEART

From "Patient Grissell"

ART thou poor, yet hast thou golden slumbers?
    O sweet content!
Art thou rich, yet is thy mind perplexèd?
    O punishment!
Dost thou laugh to see how fools are vexèd
To add to golden numbers, golden numbers?
O sweet content! O sweet, O sweet content!
  Work apace, apace, apace, apace;
  Honest labor bears a lovely face;
Then hey nonny nonny, hey nonny nonny!

Canst drink the waters of the crispèd spring?
    O sweet content!
Swimm'st thou in wealth, yet sink'st in thine own tears?
    O punishment!
Then he that patiently want's burden bears
No burden bears, but is a king, a king!
O sweet content! O sweet, O sweet content!
  Work apace, apace, apace, apace;
  Honest labor bears a lovely face;
Then hey nonny nonny, hey nonny nonny!

*Thomas Dekker* [1570?–1641?]

## THE MILLER OF THE DEE

THERE dwelt a miller, hale and bold,
  Beside the River Dee;
He wrought and sang from morn till night,
  No lark more blithe than he;
And this the burden of his song
  Forever used to be,
"I envy no man, no, not I,
  And no one envies me!"

"Thou'rt wrong, my friend!" said old King Hal,
  "As wrong as wrong can be;
For could my heart be light as thine,
  I'd gladly change with thee.
And tell me now what makes thee sing
  With voice so loud and free,
While I am sad, though I'm the King,
  Beside the River Dee?"

The miller smiled and doffed his cap:
  "I earn my bread," quoth he;
"I love my wife, I love my friend,
  I love my children three.
I owe no one I cannot pay,
  I thank the River Dee,
That turns the mill that grinds the corn
  To feed my babes and me!"

"Good friend," said Hal, and sighed the while,
  "Farewell! and happy be;
But say no more, if thou'dst be true,
  That no one envies thee.
Thy mealy cap is worth my crown;
  Thy mill my kingdom's fee!
Such men as thou are England's boast,
  Oh, miller of the Dee!"

*Charles Mackay* [1814–1889]

## A PHILOSOPHER

To take things as they be—
That's my philosophy.
No use to holler, mope, or cuss—
If they was changed they might be wuss.

If rain is pourin' down,
An' lightnin's buzzin' roun',
I ain't a-fearin' we'll be hit,
But grin that I ain't out in it.

If I got deep in debt—
It hasn't happened yet—
And owed a man two dollars, Gee!
Why, I'd be glad it wasn't three!

If some one come along,
And tried to do me wrong,
Why I should sort of take a whim
To thank the Lord I wasn't him.

I never seen a night
So dark there wasn't light
Somewheres about if I took care
To strike a match and find out where.

*John Kendrick Bangs* [1862–1922]

## THE GOOD DAY

When the golden sun he knelt
On the far horizon's brim,
Casting off the cloaks of night,
At my bed I bowed with him,

Said my prayer, and, as he rose,
Rose up too, and went my way,
Fed the beast and cleaned the byre,
Bent my back above the hay.

When at noon full hot he paused.
Then I spread my cloth, and ate
Meat that had its life from him,
Meat and fruit from his estate,

Rose refreshed, and took my scythe,
Toiled until, as dusk drew nigh,
Passing hence, the moon his bride,
Held her glowing monstrance high,

Bade me see him still, then, blessed,
Sent me home with joyful tread,
Where the two dear hands I love
Poured the wine, and broke the bread.

*Henry Howarth Bashford* [1880-

## "I SAW THE CLOUDS"

I SAW the clouds among the hills
  Trailing their plumes of rainy gray.
The purple of the woods behind
  Fell down to where the valley lay
In sweet satiety of rain,
With ripened fruit, and full filled grain.

I saw the graves, upon the plain,
  Of pioneers, who took the land,
And tamed the stubborn elements
  Till they were gentle to the hand.
Their children, now in fortune's ways,
Dwell in their father's palaces.

I saw some old forgotten lays;
  And treasured volumes I passed by.
They were but repetitions cheap
  For any hucksterer to buy.
The clouds, the graves, the worn old song,
I bear them in my heart along.

*Hervey White* [1866-1944]

## CORONATION

At the king's gate the subtle noon
  Wove filmy yellow nets of sun;
Into the drowsy snare too soon
  The guards fell one by one.

Through the king's gate, unquestioned then,
  A beggar went, and laughed, "This brings
Me chance, at last, to see if men
  Fare better, being kings."

The king sat bowed beneath his crown,
  Propping his face with listless hand;
Watching the hour-glass sifting down
  Too slow its shining sand.

"Poor man, what wouldst thou have of me?"
  The beggar turned, and pitying,
Replied, like one in dream, "Of thee,
  Nothing. I want the king."

Uprose the king, and from his head
  Shook off the crown, and threw it by.
"O man, thou must have known," he said,
  "A greater king than I."

Through all the gates, unquestioned then,
  Went king and beggar hand in hand.
Whispered the king, "Shall I know when
  Before *his* throne I stand?"

The beggar laughed. Free winds in haste
  Were wiping from the king's hot brow
The crimson lines the crown had traced.
  "This is his presence now."

At the king's gate, the crafty noon
  Unwove its yellow nets of sun;
Out of their sleep in terror soon
  The guards waked one by one.

"Ho here! Ho there! Has no man seen
The king?" The cry ran to and fro;
Beggar and king, they laughed, I ween,
The laugh that free men know.

On the king's gate the moss grew gray;
The king came not. They called him dead;
And made his eldest son one day
Slave in his father's stead.

*Helen Hunt Jackson* [1831–1885]

## THE CHARACTER OF A HAPPY LIFE

How happy is he born and taught
That serveth not another's will;
Whose armor is his honest thought,
And simple truth his utmost skill!

Whose passions not his masters are;
Whose soul is still prepared for death,
Not tied unto the world by care
Of public fame or private breath;

Who envies none that chance doth raise,
Nor vice; who never understood
How deepest wounds are given by praise;
Nor rules of state, but rules of good;

Who hath his life from rumors freed;
Whose conscience is his strong retreat;
Whose state can neither flatterers feed,
Nor ruin make oppressors great;

Who God doth late and early pray
More of His grace than gifts to lend;
And entertains the harmless day
With a religious book, or friend;

—This man is freed from servile bands
Of hope to rise, or fear to fall:
Lord of himself, though not of lands,
And having nothing, yet hath all.

*Henry Wotton* [1568–1639]

## "MY MIND TO ME A KINGDOM IS"

My mind to me a kingdom is,
  Such present joys therein I find,
That it excels all other bliss
  That earth affords or grows by kind:
Though much I want which most would have,
Yet still my mind forbids to crave.

No princely pomp, no wealthy store,
  No force to win the victory,
No wily wit to salve a sore,
  No shape to feed a loving eye;
To none of these I yield as thrall:
For why? My mind doth serve for all.

I see how plenty [surfeits] oft,
  And hasty climbers soon do fall;
I see that those which are aloft
  Mishap doth threaten most of all;
They get with toil, they keep with fear:
Such cares my mind could never bear.

Content to live, this is my stay;
  I seek no more than may suffice;
I press to bear no haughty sway;
  Look, what I lack my mind supplies:
Lo, thus I triumph like a king,
Content with that my mind doth bring.

Some have too much, yet still do crave;
  I little have, and seek no more.
They are but poor, though much they have,
  And I am rich with little store:
They poor, I rich; they beg, I give;
They lack, I leave; they pine, I live.

I laugh not at another's loss;
  I grudge not at another's gain;
No worldly waves my mind can toss;
  My state at one doth still remain:

I fear no foe, I fawn no friend;
I loathe not life, nor dread my end.

Some weigh their pleasure by their lust,
  Their wisdom by their rage of will;
Their treasure is their only trust;
  A cloakèd craft their store of skill:
But all the pleasure that I find
Is to maintain a quiet mind.

My wealth is health and perfect ease;
  My conscience clear my chief defense;
I neither seek by bribes to please,
  Nor by deceit to breed offense:
Thus do I live; thus will I die;
Would all did so as well as I!

*Edward Dyer* [1550?-1607]

## WRITTEN AT AN INN AT HENLEY

To thee, fair freedom! I retire
  From flattery, cards, and dice, and din;
Nor art thou found in mansions higher
  Than the low cot, or humble inn.

'Tis here with boundless power I reign;
  And every health which I begin,
Converts dull port to bright champagne;
  Such freedom crowns it, at an inn.

I fly from pomp, I fly from plate!
  I fly from falsehood's specious grin!
Freedom I love, and form I hate,
  And choose my lodgings at an inn.

Here, waiter! take my sordid ore,
  Which lackeys else might hope to win;
It buys, what courts have not in store;
  It buys me freedom at an inn.

Whoe er has traveled life's dull round,
  Where'er his stages may have been,
May sigh to think he still has found
  The warmest welcome, at an inn.

*William Shenstone* [1714-1763]

## CARELESS CONTENT

I AM content, I do not care,
  Wag as it will the world for me!
When fuss and fret was all my fare
  It got no ground that I could see;
So when away my caring went
I counted cost and was content.

With more of thanks and less of thought
  I strive to make my matters meet;
To seek what ancient sages sought,
  Physic and food in sour and sweet;
To take what passes in good part
And keep the hiccups from the heart.

With good and gently-humored hearts
  I choose to chat where'er I come,
Whate'er the subject be that starts;
  But if I get among the glum
I hold my tongue to tell the troth,
And keep my breath to cool my broth.

For chance or change of peace or pain,
  For Fortune's favor or her frown,
For lack or glut, for loss or gain,
  I never dodge nor up nor down,
But swing what way the ship shall swim,
Or tack about with equal trim.

I suit not where I shall not speed,
  Nor trace the turn of every tide.
If simple sense will not succeed
  I made no bustling, but abide.

For shining wealth or scaring woe
I force no friend, I fear no foe.

Of ups and downs, of ins and outs,
  Of they're-i'-th'-wrong and we're-i'-th'-right,
I shun the rancors and the routs;
  And, wishing well to every wight,
Whatever turn the matter takes,
I deem it all but ducks and drakes.

With whom I feast I do not fawn,
  Nor if the folks should flout me, faint.
If wonted welcome be withdrawn
  I cook no kind of a complaint.
With none disposed to disagree,
I like them best who best like me.

Not that I rate myself the rule
  How all my betters should behave;
But fame shall find me no man's fool,
  Nor to a set of men a slave;
I love a friendship free and frank,
But hate to hang upon a hank.

Fond of a true and trusty tie,
  I never loose where'er I link,
Though if a business budges by
  I talk thereon just as I think;
My word, my work, my heart, my hand,
Still on a side together stand.

If names or notions make a noise,
  Whatever hap the question hath
The point impartially I poise,
  And read and write, but without wrath
For, should I burn or break my brains,
Pray, who will pay me for my pains?

I love my neighbor as myself—
  Myself like him too, by his leave!
Nor to his pleasure, power or pelf
  Came I to crouch, as I conceive!

Dame Nature doubtless has designed
A man the monarch of his mind.

Now taste and try this temper, sirs,
  Mood it and brood it in your breast;
Or, if ye ween for worldly stirs
  That man does right to mar his rest,
Let me be deft and debonair,
I am content, I do not care!

*John Byrom* [1692–1763]

## THE GOLDEN MEAN*

RECEIVE, dear friend, the truths I teach,
So shalt thou live beyond the reach
  Of adverse Fortune's power;
Not always tempt the distant deep,
Nor always timorously creep
  Along the treacherous shore.

He that holds fast the golden mean,
And lives contentedly between
  The little and the great,
Feels not the wants that pinch the poor,
Nor plagues that haunt the rich man's door,
  Imbittering all his state.

The tallest pines feel most the power
Of wintry blasts; the loftiest tower
  Comes heaviest to the ground;
The bolts, that spare the mountain's side,
His cloud-capped eminence divide,
  And spread the ruin round.

The well-informed philosopher
Rejoices with a wholesome fear,

* For the original of this poem see page 3829.

And hopes, in spite of pain;
If Winter bellow from the north,
Soon the sweet Spring comes dancing forth,
And Nature laughs again.

What if thine heaven be overcast?
The dark appearance will not last;
Expect a brighter sky.
The God, that strings the silver bow,
Awakes sometimes the Muses too,
And lays his arrows by.

If hindrances obstruct thy way,
Thy magnanimity display,
And let thy strength be seen;
But O! if Fortune fill thy sail
With more than a propitious gale,
Take half thy canvas in.

*After Horace, by William Cowper* [1731-1800]

## "ITS AIN DRAP O' DEW"

Confide ye aye in Providence,
For Providence is kind:
An' bear ye a' life's changes
Wi' a calm an' tranquil mind.
Though pressed and hemmed on every side,
Ha'e faith, an' ye'll win through;
For ilka blade o' grass
Keps its ain drap o' dew.

Gin reft frae friends, or crossed in love,
As whiles nae doubt ye've been,
Grief lies deep-hidden in your heart,
Or tears flow frae your e'en,
Believe it for the best, and trow
There's good in store for you;
For ilka blade o' grass
Keps its ain drap o' dew.

In lang, lang days o' simmer,
When the clear and cloudless sky
Refuses ae wee drap o' rain
To nature, parched and dry,
The genial night, with balmy breath,
Gars verdure spring anew,
An' ilka blade o' grass
Keps its ain drap o' dew.

Sae lest 'mid fortune's sunshine
We should feel owre proud an' hie,
An' in our pride forget to wipe
The tear frae poortith's e'e,
Some wee dark clouds o' sorrow come,
We ken na whence nor hoo;
But ilka blade o' grass
Keps its ain drap o' dew.

*James Ballantine* [1808–1877]

## RESIGNATION

Why, why repine, my pensive friend,
At pleasures slipped away?
Some the stern Fates will never lend,
And all refuse to stay.

I see the rainbow in the sky,
The dew upon the grass;
I see them, and I ask not why
They glimmer or they pass.

With folded arms I linger not
To call them back; 'twere vain:
In this, or in some other spot,
I know they'll shine again.

*Walter Savage Landor* [1775–1864]

## "EN VOYAGE"

Whichever way the wind doth blow,
Some heart is glad to have it so;
Then blow it east or blow it west,
The wind that blows, that wind is best.

My little craft sails not alone:
A thousand fleets from every zone
Are out upon a thousand seas;
And what for me were favoring breeze
Might dash another, with the shock
Of doom, upon some hidden rock.

And so I do not care to pray
For winds to waft me on my way,
But leave it to a Higher Will
To stay or speed me; trusting still
That all is well, and sure that He
Who launched my bark will sail with me
Through storm and calm, and will not fail,
Whatever breezes may prevail,
To land me, every peril past,
Within his sheltering haven at last.

Then, whatsoever wind doth blow,
My heart is glad to have it so;
And blow it east or blow it west,
The wind that blows, that wind is best.

*Caroline Atwater Mason* [1853-1939]

## THE HAPPIEST HEART

Who drives the horses of the sun
Shall lord it but a day;
Better the lowly deed were done,
And kept the humble way.

The rust will find the sword of fame,
The dust will hide the crown;
Ay, none shall nail so high his name
Time will not tear it down.

The happiest heart that ever beat
Was in some quiet breast
That found the common daylight sweet,
And left to Heaven the rest.

*John Vance Cheney* [1848-1922]

## GOOD-BYE

GOOD-BYE, proud world! I'm going home:
Thou art not my friend, and I'm not thine.
Long through thy weary crowds I roam;
A river-ark on the ocean brine,
Long I've been tossed like the driven foam;
But now, proud world! I'm going home.

Good-bye to Flattery's fawning face;
To Grandeur with his wise grimace;
To upstart Wealth's averted eye;
To supple Office, low and high;
To crowded halls, to court and street;
To frozen hearts and hasting feet;
To those who go, and those who come;
Good-bye, proud world! I'm going home.

I am going to my own hearth-stone,
Bosomed in yon green hills alone,—
A secret nook in a pleasant land,
Whose groves the frolic fairies planned;
Where arches green, the livelong day,
Echo the blackbird's roundelay,
And vulgar feet have never trod—
A spot that is sacred to thought and God.

O, when I am safe in my sylvan home,
I tread on the pride of Greece and Rome;
And when I am stretched beneath the pines,
Where the evening star so holy shines,
I laugh at the lore and the pride of man,
At the sophist schools, and the learned clan;
For what are they all, in their high conceit,
When man in the bush with God may meet?

*Ralph Waldo Emerson* [1803-1882]

## SAPIENTIA LUNÆ

THE wisdom of the world said unto me:
"*Go forth and run, the race is to the brave;*
*Perchance some honor tarrieth for thee!*"
"As tarrieth," I said, "for sure, the grave."

For I had pondered on a rune of roses,
Which to her votaries the moon discloses.

The wisdom of the world said: "*There are bays:*
*Go forth and run, for victory is good,*
*After the stress of the laborious days.*"
"Yet," said I, "shall I be the worms' sweet food,"
As I went musing on a rune of roses,
Which in her hour, the pale, soft moon discloses.

Then said my voices: "*Wherefore strive or run,*
*On dusty highways ever, a vain race?*
*The long night cometh, starless, void of sun,*
*What light shall serve thee like her golden face?*"
For I had pondered on a rune of roses,
And knew some secrets which the moon discloses.

"Yea," said I, "for her eyes are pure and sweet
As lilies, and the fragrance of her hair
Is many laurels; and it is not meet
To run for shadows when the prize is here";
And I went reading in that rune of roses
Which to her votaries the moon discloses.

*Ernest Dowson* [1867–1900]

## THE BEASTS

From "Song of Myself"

I THINK I could turn and live with animals, they are so placid
and self-contained;
I stand and look at them long and long.

They do not sweat and whine about their condition;
They do not lie awake in the dark and weep for their sins;
They do not make me sick discussing their duty to God;
Not one is dissatisfied—not one is demented with the mania
of owning things;
Not one kneels to another, nor to his kind that lived thousands of years ago;
Not one is respectable or industrious over the whole earth.

*Walt Whitman* [1819–1892]

## IMMORAL

I KEEP walking around myself, mouth open with amazement:
For by all the ethical rules of life, I ought to be solemn and sad,
But, look you, I am bursting with joy.

I scold myself:
I say: Boy, your work has gone to pot:
You have scarcely enough money to last out the week:
And think of your responsibilities!
Whereupon, my heart bubbles over,
I puff on my pipe, and think how solemnly the world goes by my window,
And how childish people are, wrinkling their foreheads over groceries and rent.

For here jets life fresh and stinging in the vivid air:
The winds laugh to the jovial Earth:
The day is keen with Autumn's fine flavor of having done the year's work.
Earth, in her festival, calls her children to the crimson revels.
The trees are a drunken riot: the sunshine is dazzling . . .

Yes, I ought, I suppose, to be saddened and tragic:
But joy drops from me like ripe apples.

*James Oppenheim* [1882–1932]

## DIOGENES

A HUT, and a tree,
And a hill for me,
And a piece of a weedy meadow.
I'll ask no thing,
Of God or king,
But to clear away his shadow.

*Max Eastman* [1883-

## LEISURE

WHAT is this life if, full of care,
We have no time to stand and stare.

No time to stand beneath the boughs
And stare as long as sheep or cows.

No time to see, when woods we pass,
Where squirrels hide their nuts in grass.

No time to see, in broad daylight,
Streams full of stars, like skies at night.

No time to turn at Beauty's glance,
And watch her feet, how they can dance.

No time to wait till her mouth can
Enrich that smile her eyes began.

A poor life this if, full of care,
We have no time to stand and stare.

*William H. Davies* [1870–1940]

## POOR KINGS

GOD'S pity on poor kings,
They know no gentle rest;
The North and South cry out,
Cries come from East and West—
"Come, open this new Dock,
Building, Bazaar or Fair."
Lord, what a wretched life
Such men must bear.

They're followed, watched and spied,
No liberty they know;
Some eye will watch them still,
No matter where they go.
When in green lanes I muse,
Alone, and hear birds sing,
God's pity then, say I,
On some poor king.

*William H. Davies* [1870–1940]

# FRIENDSHIP AND BROTHERHOOD

## SALVE!

To live within a cave—it is most good;
    But, if God make a day,
    And some one come, and say,
"Lo! I have gathered fagots in the wood!"
    E'en let him stay,
And light a fire, and fan a temporal mood!

So sit till morning! when the light is grown
    That he the path can read,
    Then bid the man God-speed!
His morning is not thine: yet must thou own
They have a cheerful warmth—those ashes on the stone.

*Thomas Edward Brown* [1830–1897]

## ABOU BEN ADHEM

Abou Ben Adhem (may his tribe increase!)
Awoke one night from a deep dream of peace,
And saw, within the moonlight in his room,
Making it rich, and like a lily in bloom,
An angel writing in a book of gold:—
Exceeding peace had made Ben Adhem bold,
And to the Presence in the room he said,
"What writest thou?"—The vision raised its head,
And with a look made of all sweet accord,
Answered, "The names of those who love the Lord."
"And is mine one?" said Abou. "Nay, not so,"
Replied the Angel. Abou spoke more low,
But cheerly still; and said, "I pray thee, then,
Write me as one that loves his fellow-men."

The angel wrote, and vanished. The next night
It came again with a great wakening light,
And showed the names whom love of God had blessed,
And lo! Ben Adhem's name led all the rest.

*Leigh Hunt* [1784–1859]

## ENVOY

From "More Songs from Vagabondia"

I

WHOSE furthest footstep never strayed
Beyond the village of his birth,
Is but a lodger for the night
In this old wayside inn of earth.

To-morrow he shall take his pack,
And set out for the ways beyond,
On the old trail from star to star,
An alien and a vagabond.

II

If any record of our names
Be blown about the hills of time,
Let no one sunder us in death,—
The man of paint, the men of rhyme.

Of all our good, of all our bad,
This one thing only is of worth,—
We held the league of heart to heart
The only purpose of the earth.

*Richard Hovey* [1864–1900]

## FRIENDS

YOU ask me "why I like him." Nay,
I cannot; nay, I would not, say.
I think it vile to pigeonhole
The pros and cons of a kindred soul.

You "wonder he should be my friend."
But then why should you comprehend?
Thank God for this—a new—surprise:
My eyes, remember, are not your eyes.

Cherish this one small mystery;
And marvel not that love can be
"In spite of all his many flaws."
In spite? Supposing I said "Because."

A truce, a truce to questioning:
"We two are friends" tells everything.
Yet if you *must* know, this is why:
Because he is he and I am I.

*Edward Verrall Lucas* [1868–1938]

## A FRIEND

All that he came to give,
He gave and went again:
I have seen one man live,
I have seen one man reign,
With all the graces in his train.

As one of us, he wrought
Things of the common hour:
Whence was the charmed soul brought,
That gave each act such power;
The natural beauty of a flower?

Magnificence and grace,
Excellent courtesy:
A brightness on the face,
Airs of high memory:
Whence came all these, to such as he?

Like young Shakespearean kings,
He won the adoring throng:
And as Apollo sings,
He triumphed with a song:
Triumphed, and sang, and passed along.

With a light word, he took
The hearts of men in thrall:
And, with a golden look,
Welcomed them, at his call
Giving their love, their strength, their all.

No man less proud than he,
Nor cared for homage less:
Only, he could not be
Far off from happiness:
Nature was bound to his success.

Weary, the cares, the jars,
The lets, of every day:
But the heavens filled with stars,
Chanced he upon the way:
And where he stayed, all joy would stay.

Now when the night draws down,
When the austere stars burn;
Roaming the vast live town,
My thoughts and memories yearn
Toward him, who never will return.

Yet have I seen him live,
And owned my friend, a king:
All that he came to give,
He gave and I, who sing
His praise, bring all I have to bring.

*Lionel Johnson* [1867-1902]

## BILL AND JOE

Come, dear old comrade, you and I
Will steal an hour from days gone by,
The shining days when life was new,
And all was bright with morning dew,
The lusty days of long ago,
When you were Bill and I was Joe:

Your name may flaunt a titled trail,
Proud as a cockerel's rainbow tail;
And mine as brief appendix wear
As Tam O'Shanter's luckless mare;
To-day, old friend, remember still
That I am Joe and you are Bill.

You've won the great world's envied prize,
And grand you look in people's eyes,
With H O N. and L L. D.
In big brave letters, fair to see,—
Your fist, old fellow! off they go!—
How are you, Bill? How are you, Joe?

You've worn the judge's ermined robe;
You've taught your name to half the globe;
You've sung mankind a deathless strain;
You've made the dead past live again:
The world may call you what it will,
But you and I are Joe and Bill.

The chaffing young folks stare and say,
"See those old buffers, bent and gray,—
They talk like fellows in their teens!
Mad, poor old boys! That's what it means,"—
And shake their heads; they little know
The throbbing hearts of Bill and Joe!—

How Bill forgets his hour of pride,
While Joe sits smiling at his side;
How Joe, in spite of time's disguise,
Finds the old schoolmate in his eyes,—
Those calm, stern eyes that melt and fill
As Joe looks fondly up at Bill.

Ah, pensive scholar, what is fame?
A fitful tongue of leaping flame;
A giddy whirlwind's fickle gust,
That lifts a pinch of mortal dust;
A few swift years, and who can show
Which dust was Bill and which was Joe?

The weary idol takes his stand,
Holds out his bruised and aching hand,
While gaping thousands come and go,—
How vain it seems, this empty show!
Till all at once his pulses thrill;—
'Tis poor old Joe's "God bless you, Bill!"

And shall we breathe in happier spheres
The names that pleased our mortal ears;
In some sweet lull of harp and song,
For earth-born spirits none too long,
Just whispering of the world below
Where this was Bill and that was Joe?

No matter; while our home is here
No sounding name is half so dear;
When fades at length our lingering day,
Who cares what pompous tombstones say?
Read on the hearts that love us still,
*Hic jacet* Joe. *Hic jacet* Bill.

*Oliver Wendell Holmes* [1809–1894]

## "AS TOILSOME I WANDERED VIRGINIA'S WOODS"

As toilsome I wandered Virginia's woods,
To the music of rustling leaves kicked by my feet, (for 'twas autumn,)
I marked at the foot of a tree the grave of a soldier;
Mortally wounded he and buried on the retreat, (easily all could I understand,)
The halt of a mid-day hour, when up! no time to lose—yet this sign left,
On a tablet scrawled and nailed on the tree by the grave,
*Bold, cautious, true, and my loving comrade.*

Long, long I muse, then on my way go wandering,
Many a changeful season to follow, and many a scene of life,
Yet at times through changeful season and scene, abrupt, alone, or in the crowded street,
Comes before me the unknown soldier's grave, comes the inscription rude in Virginia's woods,
*Bold, cautious, true, and my loving comrade.*

*Walt Whitman* [1819–1892]

## GONE

About the little chambers of my heart
Friends have been coming—going—many a year.
The doors stand open there.
Some, lightly stepping, enter; some depart.

Freely they come and freely go, at will.
The walls give back their laughter; all day long
They fill the house with song.
One door alone is shut, one chamber still.

*Mary E. Coleridge* [1861–1907]

## COMRADES

Where are the friends that I knew in my Maying,
In the days of my youth, in the first of my roaming?
We were dear; we were leal; O, far we went straying;
Now never a heart to my heart comes homing!—
Where is he now, the dark boy slender
Who taught me bare-back, stirrup and reins?
I loved him; he loved me; my beautiful, tender
Tamer of horses on grass-grown plains.

Where is he now whose eyes swam brighter,
Softer than love, in his turbulent charms;
Who taught me to strike, and to fall, dear fighter,
And gathered me up in his boyhood arms;
Taught me the rifle, and with me went riding,
Suppled my limbs to the horseman's war;
Where is he now, for whom my heart's biding,
Biding, biding—but he rides far?

O love that passes the love of woman!
Who that hath felt it shall ever forget,
When the breath of life with a throb turns human
And a lad's heart is to a lad's heart set?
Ever, forever, lover and rover—
They shall cling, nor each from other shall part
Till the reign of the stars in the heavens be over,
And life is dust in each faithful heart!—

They are dead, the American grasses under;
There is no one now who presses my side;
By the African chotts I am riding asunder,
And with great joy ride I the last great ride.
I am fey; I am fain of sudden dying;
Thousands of miles there is no one near;
And my heart—all the night it is crying, crying
In the bosoms of dead lads darling-dear.

Hearts of my music—them dark earth covers;
Comrades to die, and to die for, were they;—
In the width of the world there were no such rovers—
Back to back, breast to breast, it was ours to stay;
And the highest on earth was the vow that we cherished,
To spur forth from the crowd and come back never more,
And to ride in the track of great souls perished
Till the nests of the lark shall roof us o'er.

Yet lingers a horseman on Altai highlands,
Who hath joy of me, riding the Tartar glissade;
And one, far faring o'er orient islands
Whose blood yet glints with my blade's accolade;
North, west, east, I fling you my last hallooing,
Last love to the breasts where my own has bled;
Through the reach of the desert my soul leaps pursuing
My star where it rises a Star of the Dead.

*George Edward Woodberry* [1855–1930]

## COMRADES

At least, it was a life of swords,
Our life! nor lived in vain:
We fought the fight with mighty lords,
Nor dastards have we slain.

We stirred at morn, and through bright air
Swept to the trysting place:
Winds of the mountains in our hair,
And sunrise on each face.

No need to spur! our horses knew
The joy, to which we went:
Over the brightening lands they flew
Forward, and were content.

On each man's lips, an happy smile;
In each man's eyes, delight:
So, fired with foretaste, mile on mile,
We thundered to the fight.

Let death come now, and from the sun
Hide me away: what then?
My days have seen more prowess done,
Than years of other men.

Oh, warriors of the rugged heights,
We, where the eagles nest:
They, courtly soldiers, gentle knights,
By kings and dames caressed.

Not theirs, the passion of the sword,
The fire of living blades!
Like men, they fought: and found reward
In dance and feast, like maids.

We, on the mountain lawns encamped,
Close under the great stars,
Turned, when the horses hard by stamped,
And dreamed again, of wars:

Or, if one woke, he saw the gleam
Of moonlight, on each face,
Touch its tumultuary dream
With moments of mild grace.

We hated no man; but we fought
With all men: the fierce wind
Lashes the wide earth without thought;
Our tempest scourged mankind.

They cursed us, living without laws!
They, in their pride of peace:
Who bared no blade, but in just cause:
Nor grieved, that war should cease.

O spirit of the wild hill-side!
O spirit of the steel!
We answered nothing, when they cried,
But challenged with a peal.

And, when the battle blood had poured
To slake our souls' desire:
Oh, brave to hear, how torrents roared
Beside the pinewood fire!

My brothers, whom in warrior wise
The death of deaths hath stilled!
Ah, you would understand these eyes,
Although with strange tears filled!

*Lionel Johnson* [1867-1902

## COMRADES

I ROSE up when the battle was dead,
I, the most wounded man of us all!
From the slain that fell, to the living that fled,
Over the waste one name I call.

Thou whose strength was an oak that branched,
Thou whose voice was a fire that burned,
Thine the face that the fighting blanched,
Thine the heart that the tumult turned!

Had I, beloved, when swords swept measure,
Had I but reached thee, and slain thee then:
Then in thy death had my soul found pleasure,
Counting thee dead as a man with men.

Then with the peace, when the fight was ended,
Men would have asked, and I would have said
"Yonder he lies whom once I befriended,
Sharing his rest in the ranks of the dead"

Ghosts of the riders, ghosts of the ridden,
  Here keep tryst for the loves that died;
Thou alone of all loves art hidden,
  Never again to be near my side.

Here, beloved, when the fight has slackened,
  I rise up, and a sword is mine!
Over the mounds with dead men blackened,
  Ever my soul makes haste for thine.

Though thou lurk in the caverns beneath,
  Though thou crouch by the moaning sea,
I am a sword that leaps to its sheath,
  Never at rest till I find out thee!

Oh, poor soul, all the night unstanched,
  Poor heart, couched in a shameful breast,
Thou, whose face at the fighting blanched,
  Out of the battle I bring thee—rest.

*Laurence Housman* [1867–1959]

## AT THE CROSSROADS

You to the left and I to the right,
For the ways of men must sever—
And it well may be for a day and a night,
And it well may be forever.
But whether we meet or whether we part
(For our ways are past our knowing),
A pledge from the heart to its fellow heart
On the ways we all are going!
Here's luck!
For we know not where we are going.

We have striven fair in love and war,
But the wheel was always weighted!
We have lost the prize that we struggled for,
We have won the prize that was fated.
We have met our loss with a smile and a song,

And our gains with a wink and a whistle,—
For, whether we're right or whether we're wrong,
There's a rose for every thistle.
Here's luck!
And a drop to wet your whistle!

Whether we win or whether we lose
With the hands that life is dealing,
It is not we nor the ways we choose
But the fall of the cards that's sealing.
There's a fate in love and a fate in fight,
And the best of us all go under—
And whether we're wrong or whether we're right,
We win, sometimes, to our wonder.
Here's luck!
That we may not yet go under!

With a steady swing and an open brow
We have tramped the ways together,
But we're clasping hands at the crossroads now
In the Fiend's own night for weather;
And whether we bleed or whether we smile
In the leagues that lie before us,
The ways of life are many a mile
And the dark of Fate is o'er us.
Here's luck!
And a cheer for the dark before us!

You to the left and I to the right,
For the ways of men must sever,
And it well may be for a day and a night,
And it well may be forever!
But whether we live or whether we die
(For the end is past our knowing),
Here's two frank hearts and the open sky,
Be a fair or an ill wind blowing!
Here's luck!
In the teeth of all winds blowing.

*Richard Hovey* [1864-1900]

## TWILIGHT SONG

THROUGH the shine, through the rain
We have shared the day's load;
To the old march again
We have tramped the long road;
We have laughed, we have cried,
And we've tossed the King's crown;
We have fought, we have died,
And we've trod the day down.
So it's lift the old song
Ere the night flies again,
Where the road leads along
Through the shine, through the rain.

Long ago, far away,
Came a sign from the skies;
And we feared then to pray
For the new sun to rise:
With the King there at hand,
Not a child stepped or stirred—
Where the light filled the land
And the light brought the word;
For we knew then the gleam
Though we feared then the day,
And the dawn smote the dream
Long ago, far away.

But the road leads us all,
For the King now is dead;
And we know, stand or fall,
We have shared the day's bread.
We can laugh down the dream,
For the dream breaks and flies;
And we trust now the gleam,
For the gleam never dies;—
So it's off now the load,
For we know the night's call,
And we know now the road
And the road leads us all.

Through the shine, through the rain,
We have wrought the day's quest;
To the old march again
We have earned the day's rest;
We have laughed, we have cried,
And we've heard the King's groans;
We have fought, we have died,
And we've burned the King's bones,
And we lift the old song
Ere the night flies again,
Where the road leads along
Through the shine, through the rain.

*Edwin Arlington Robinson* [1869–1935]

## THE ADVENTURERS

They sit at home and they dream and dally,
Raking the embers of long-dead years—
But ye go down to the haunted Valley,
Light-hearted pioneers.
They have forgotten they ever were young,
They hear your songs as an unknown tongue . . .
But the Flame of God through your spirit stirs,
Adventurers—O Adventurers!

They weigh and ponder, and shilly-shally,
Wielding the pen, who are past the sword—
But ye go down to the mystic Valley,
That never was yet explored.
They brood over obsolete ways and means,
Their eyes confusing the grays and greens, . . .
But no tradition your vision blurs,
Adventurers—O Adventurers!

They tithe their herbs and they count their tally,
Choosing their words that a phrase may live—
But ye cast down in the hungry Valley
All that a man can give.
They prophesy smoothly, with weary smile
Fulfilling their feeble appointed while,
But Death himself to your pride defers,
Adventurers—O Adventurers!

*May Byron* [1861–1936]

## "FAME IS A FOOD THAT DEAD MEN EAT"

Fame is a food that dead men eat,—
I have no stomach for such meat.
In little light and narrow room,
They eat it in the silent tomb,
With no kind voice of comrade near
To bid the feaster be of cheer.

But Friendship is a nobler thing,—
Of Friendship it is good to sing.
For truly, when a man shall end,
He lives in memory of his friend,
Who doth his better part recall
And of his fault make funeral.

*Austin Dobson* [1840–1921]

## JAFFÀR

*Shelley, take this to thy dear memory;—*
*To praise the generous, is to think of thee.*

Jaffàr, the Barmecide, the good Vizier,
The poor man's hope, the friend without a peer,
Jaffàr was dead, slain by a doom unjust;
And guilty Hàroun, sullen with mistrust
Of what the good, and e'en the bad, might say,
Ordained that no man living from that day
Should dare to speak his name on pain of death.
All Araby and Persia held their breath;
All but the brave Mondeer: he, proud to show
How far for love a grateful soul could go,
And facing death for very scorn and grief
(For his great heart wanted a great relief),
Stood forth in Bagdad daily, in the square
Where once had stood a happy house, and there
Harangued the tremblers at the scimitar
On all they owed to the divine Jaffàr.

"Bring me this man," the caliph cried. The man
Was brought, was gazed upon. The mutes began
To bind his arms. "Welcome, brave cords," cried he;
"From bonds far worse Jaffàr delivered me;
From wants, from shames, from loveless household fears;
Made a man's eyes friends with delicious tears;
Restored me, loved me, put me on a par
With his great self. How can I pay Jaffàr?"

Haroun, who felt that on a soul like this
The mightiest vengeance could but fall amiss,
Now deigned to smile, as one great lord of fate
Might smile upon another half as great.
He said, "Let worth grow frenzied if it will;
The caliph's judgment shall be master still.
Go: and since gifts so move thee, take this gem,
The richest in the Tartar's diadem,
And hold the giver as thou deemest fit!"

"Gifts!" cried the friend; he took, and holding it
High toward the heavens, as though to meet his star,
Exclaimed, "This, too, I owe to thee, Jaffàr!"

*Leigh Hunt* [1784-1859]

## COUNSEL

If thou shouldst bid thy friend farewell,
  But for one night though that farewell may be,
Press thou his hand in thine; thou canst not tell
    How far from thee

Fate or caprice may lead his feet
  Ere that to-morrow come. Men have been known
Lightly to turn the corner of a street,
  And days have grown

To months, and months to lagging years,
  Before they look on loving eyes again.
Parting, at best, is underlaid with tears,
    With tears and pain,

Therefore, lest sudden death should come between,
Or time, or distance, clasp with pressure true
The palm of him who goeth forth; unseen,
Fate goeth too!

Yea, find thou always time to say
Some earnest word betwixt the idle talk,
Lest with thee henceforth ever, night and day,
Regret should walk.

*Mary Evelyn Moore Davis* [1852–1909]

## TO A FRIEND

When we were idlers with the loitering rills,
The need of human love we little noted:
Our love was nature; and the peace that floated
On the white mist, and dwelt upon the hills,
To sweet accord subdued our wayward wills:
One soul was ours, one mind, one heart devoted,
That, wisely doting, asked not why it doted,
And ours the unknown joy, which knowing kills.
But now I find how dear thou wert to me;
That man is more than half of nature's treasure,
Of that fair beauty which no eye can see,
Of that sweet music which no ear can measure;
And now the streams may sing for others' pleasure,
The hills sleep on in their eternity.

*Hartley Coleridge* [1796–1849]

## "FAREWELL! BUT WHENEVER"

Farewell!—but whenever you welcome the hour
That awakens the night-song of mirth in your bower,
Then think of the friend who once welcomed it too,
And forgot his own griefs, to be happy with you.
His griefs may return,—not a hope may remain
Of the few that have brightened his pathway of pain,—
But he ne'er will forget the short vision that threw
Its enchantment around him, while ling'ring with you!

And still on that evening, when Pleasure fills up
To the highest top sparkle each heart and each cup,
Where'er my path lies, be it gloomy or bright,
My soul, happy friends, shall be with you that night;

Shall join in your revels, your sports, and your wiles,
And return to me, beaming all o'er with your smiles,—
Too blest if it tell me that, 'mid the gay cheer,
Some kind voice had murmured, "I wish he were here!"

Let Fate do her worst, there are relics of joy,
Bright dreams of the past, which she cannot destroy;
Which come, in the night-time of sorrow and care,
And bring back the features that joy used to wear.
Long, long be my heart with such memories filled!
Like the vase in which roses have once been distilled,—
You may break, you may shatter the vase, if you will,
But the scent of the roses will hang round it still.

*Thomas Moore* [1779–1852]

## "AWAKE! AWAKE!"

From "Song of the Dawn"

Awake! awake! the stars are pale, the east is russet gray;
They fade, behold the phantoms fade, that keep the gates of Day;
Throw wide the burning valves, and let the golden streets be free,
The morning watch is past—the watch of evening shall not be.

Put off, put off your mail, ye kings, and beat your brands to dust;
A surer grasp your hands must know, your hearts a better trust;
Nay, bend aback the lance's point, and break the helmet bar,—
A noise is on the morning winds; but not the noise of war!

For aye, the time of wrath is past, and near the time of rest,
And honor binds the brow of man, and faithfulness his breast,
Behold, the time of wrath is past, and righteousness shall be,
And the Wolf is dead in Arcady and the Dragon in the sea!

*John Ruskin* [1819–1900]

## THE VOICE OF TOIL

I HEARD men saying, Leave hope and praying.
All days shall be as all have been;
To-day and to-morrow bring fear and sorrow,
The never-ending toil between.

When Earth was young 'mid toil and hunger,
In hope we strove, and our hands were strong;
Then great men led us, with words they fed us,
And bade us right the earthly wrong.

Go read in story their deeds and glory,
Their names amidst the nameless dead;
Turn then from lying to us slow-dying
In that good world to which they led;

Where fast and faster our iron master,
The thing we made, for ever drives,
Bids us grind treasure and fashion pleasure
For other hopes and other lives;

Where home is a hovel and dull we grovel,
Forgetting that the world is fair;
Where no babe we cherish, lest its very soul perish;
Where mirth is crime, and love a snare.

Who now shall lead us, what god shall heed us
As we lie in the hell our hands have won?
For us are no rulers but fools and befoolers,
The great are fallen, the wise men gone.

I heard men saying, Leave tears and praying,
The sharp knife heedeth not the sheep;
Are we not stronger than the rich and the wronger,
When day breaks over dreams and sleep?

Come, shoulder to shoulder ere the world grows older!
Help lies in naught but thee and me;
Hope is before us, and the long years that bore us
Bore leaders more than men may be.

Let dead hearts tarry and trade and marry,
And trembling nurse their dreams of mirth,
While we the living our lives are giving
To bring the bright new world to birth.

Come, shoulder to shoulder ere earth grows older!
The Cause spreads over land and sea;
Now the world shaketh, and fear awaketh,
And joy at last for thee and me.

*William Morris* [1834-1896]

## TOM DUNSTAN, OR, THE POLITICIAN

Now poor Tom Dunstan's cold,
  Our shop is duller;
Scarce a story is told,
And our chat has lost the old
  Red-republican color!
Though he was sickly and thin,
  'Twas a sight to see his face—
While, sick of the country's sin,
With bang of the fist, and chin
  Thrust out, he argued the case!
He prophesied folk should be free,
  And the money-bags be bled—
"She's coming, she's coming!" said he;
"Courage, boys! wait and see!
  Freedom's ahead!"

All day we sat in the heat,
  Like spiders spinning,
Stitching full fine and fleet,
While the old Jew on his seat
  Sat greasily grinning:
And there Tom said his say,
  And prophesied Tyranny's death,
And the tallow burnt all day,
And we stitched and stitched away
  In the thick smoke of our breath,
Wearily, wearily,

With hearts as heavy as lead—
But "Patience, she's coming!" said he;
"Courage, boys! wait and see!
Freedom's ahead!"

And at night, when we took here
The rest allowed to us,
The paper came with the beer,
And Tom read, sharp and clear,
The news out loud to us;
And then, in his witty way,
He threw the jests about—
The cutting things he'd say
Of the wealthy and the gay!
How he turned them inside out!
And it made our breath more free
To hearken to what he said—
"She's coming, she's coming!" said he;
"Courage, boys! wait and see!
Freedom's ahead!"

But grim Jack Hart, with a sneer,
Would mutter, "Master,
If Freedom means to appear,
I think she might step here
A little faster!"
Then it was fine to see Tom flame,
And argue and prove and preach,
Till Jack was silent for shame,
Or a fit of coughing came
O' sudden to spoil Tom's speech.
Ah! Tom had the eyes to see,
When Tyranny should be sped;
"She's coming, she's coming!" said he;
"Courage, boys! wait and see!
Freedom's ahead!"

But Tom was little and weak;
The hard hours shook him;
Hollower grew his cheek,
And when he began to speak

The coughing took him.
Ere long the cheery sound
Of his chat among us ceased,
And we made a purse all round,
That he might not starve, at least;
His pain was sorry to see,
Yet there, on his poor sick-bed,
"She's coming, in spite of me!
Courage, and wait!" cried he,
"Freedom's ahead!"

A little before he died,
To see his passion!
"Bring me a paper!" he cried,
And then to study it tried
In his old sharp fashion;
And with eyeballs glittering
His look on me he bent,
And said that savage thing
Of the lords of the Parliament.
Then, darkening, smiling on me,
"What matter if one be dead?
She's coming, at last!" said he;
"Courage, boys! wait and see!
Freedom's ahead!"

Ay, now Tom Dunstan's cold,
The shop feels duller;
Scarce a story is told,
And our talk has lost the old
Red-republican color.
But we see a figure gray,
And we hear a voice of death,
And the tallow burns all day,
And we stitch and stitch away,
In the thick smoke of our breath;
Ay, while in the dark sit we,
Tom seems to call from the dead—
"She's coming, she's coming!" says he;
"Courage, boys! wait and see!
"Freedom's ahead!"

How long, O Lord, how long
  Doth Thy handmaid linger?
She who shall right the wrong?
Make the oppressèd strong?—
  Sweet morrow, bring her!
Hasten her over the sea,
  O Lord, ere hope be fled—
Bring her to men and to me!
O slave, pray still on thy knee—
  "Freedom's ahead!"

*Robert Buchanan* [1841–1901]

## THE COMMON STREET

THE common street climbed up against the sky,
Gray meeting gray; and wearily to and fro
I saw the patient common people go,
Each, with his sordid burden, trudging by.
And the rain dropped; there was not any sigh
Or stir of a live wind; dull, dull and slow
All motion; as a tale told long ago
The faded world; and creeping night drew nigh.

Then burst the sunset, flooding far and fleet,
Leavening the whole of life with magic leaven.
Suddenly down the long wet glistening hill
Pure splendor poured—and lo! the common street,
A golden highway into golden heaven,
With the dark shapes of men ascending still.

*Helen Gray Cone* [1859–1934]

## TO A NEW YORK SHOP-GIRL DRESSED FOR SUNDAY

TO-DAY I saw the shop-girl go
Down gay Broadway to meet her beau.

Conspicuous, splendid, conscious, sweet,
She spread abroad and took the street.

And all that niceness would forbid,
Superb, she smiled upon and did.

Let other girls, whose happier days
Preserve the perfume of their ways,

Go modestly. The passing hour
Adds splendor to their opening flower.

But from this child too swift a doom
Must steal her prettiness and bloom,

Toil and weariness hide the grace
That pleads a moment from her face.

So blame her not if for a day
She flaunts her glories while she may.

She half perceives, half understands,
Snatching her gifts with both her hands.

The little strut beneath the skirt
That lags neglected in the dirt,

The indolent swagger down the street—
Who can condemn such happy feet!

Innocent! vulgar—that's the truth!
Yet with the darling wiles of youth!

The bright, self-conscious eyes that stare
With such hauteur, beneath such hair!
*Perhaps the men will find me fair!*

Charming and charmed, flippant, arrayed,
Fluttered and foolish, proud, displayed,
Infinite pathos of parade!

The bangles and the narrowed waist—
The tinseled boa—forgive the taste!

Oh, the starved nights she gave for that,
And bartered bread to buy her hat!

She flows before the reproachful sage
And begs her woman's heritage.

Dear child, with the defiant eyes,
Insolent with the half surmise
We do not quite admire, I know
How foresight frowns on this vain show!

And judgment, wearily sad, may see
No grace in such frivolity.

Yet which of us was ever bold
To worship Beauty, hungry and cold!

Scorn famine down, proudly expressed
Apostle to what things are best.

Let him who starves to buy the food
For his soul's comfort find her good,

Nor chide the frills and furbelows
That are the prettiest things she knows.

Poet and prophet in God's eyes
Make no more perfect sacrifice.

Who knows before what inner shrine
She eats with them the bread and wine?

Poor waif! One of the sacred few
That madly sought the best they knew!

Dear—let me lean my cheek to-night
Close, close to yours. Ah, that is right.

How warm and near! At last I see
One beauty shines for thee and me.

So let us love and understand—
Whose hearts are hidden in God's hand.

And we will cherish your brief Spring
And all its fragile flowering.

God loves all prettiness, and on this
Surely his angels lay their kiss.

*Anna Hempstead Branch* [18 –1937]

## SATURDAY NIGHT

THE lights of Saturday night beat golden, golden over the pillared street;
The long plate-glass of a Dream-World olden is as the foot-lights shining sweet.
Street-lamp—flambeau—glamor of trolley—comet-trail of the trains above,
Splash where the jostling crowds are jolly with echoing laughter and human love.

This is the City of the Enchanted, and these are her Enchanted People;
Far and far is Daylight, haunted with whistle of mill and bell of steeple.
The Eastern tenements loose the women, the Western flats release the wives
To touch, where all the ways are common, a glory to their sweated lives.

The leather of shoes in the brilliant casement sheds a luster over the heart;
The high-heaped fruit in the flaring basement glows with the tints of Turner's art.
Darwin's dream and the eye of Spencer saw not such a gloried race
As here, in copper light intenser than desert sun, glides face by face.

The drab washwoman dazed and breathless, ray-chiseled in the golden stream,
Is a magic statue standing deathless—her tub and soap-suds touched with Dream.

Yea, in this people, glamor-sunnied, democracy wins heaven
again;
Here the unlearned and the unmoneyed laugh in the lights
of Lover's Lane!

O Dream-World lights that lift through the ether millions
of miles to the Milky Way!
To-night Earth rolls through a golden weather that lights
the Pleiades where they play!
Yet . . . God? Does he lead these sons and daughters?
Yea, do they feel with a passion that stills,
God on the face of the moving waters, God in the quiet of
the hills?

Yet . . . what if the million-mantled mountains, and what
if the million-moving sea
Are here alone in façades and fountains—our deep stone-
world of humanity—
We builders of cities and civilizations walled away from the
sea and the sod
Must reach, dream-led, for our revelations through one another—as far as God.

Through one another—through one another—no more the
gleam on sea or land
But so close that we see the Brother—and understand—and
understand!
Till, drawn in swept crowd closer, closer, we see the gleam in
the human clod,
And clerk and foreman, peddler and grocer, are in our
Family of God!

*James Oppenheim* [1882–1932]

## THE BARREL-ORGAN

THERE'S a barrel-organ caroling across a golden street,
In the City as the sun sinks low;
And the music's not immortal; but the world has made it
sweet
And fulfilled it with the sunset glow;

And it pulses through the pleasures of the City and the pain
  That surround the singing organ like a large eternal light;
And they've given it a glory and a part to play again
  In the Symphony that rules the day and night.

And now it's marching onward through the realms of old romance,
  And trolling out a fond familiar tune,
And now it's roaring cannon down to fight the King of France,
  And now it's prattling softly to the moon,
And all around the organ there's a sea without a shore
  Of human joys and wonders and regrets;
To remember and to recompense the music evermore
  For what the cold machinery forgets. . . .

Yes; as the music changes,
  Like a prismatic glass,
It takes the light and ranges
  Through all the moods that pass;
Dissects the common carnival
  Of passions and regrets,
And gives the world a glimpse of all
  The colors it forgets.

And there *La Traviata* sighs
  Another sadder song;
And there *Il Trovatore* cries
  A tale of deeper wrong;
And bolder knights to battle go
  With sword and shield and lance,
Than ever here on earth below
  Have whirled into—*a dance!*—

Go down to Kew in lilac-time, in lilac-time, in lilac-time;
Go down to Kew in lilac-time (it isn't far from London!)
And you shall wander hand in hand with love in summer's wonderland;
Go down to Kew in lilac-time (it isn't far from London!)

The cherry-trees are seas of bloom and soft perfume and sweet perfume,
The cherry-trees are seas of bloom (and oh, so near to London!)
And there they say, when dawn is high and all the world's a blaze of sky
The cuckoo, though he's very shy, will sing a song for London.

The nightingale is rather rare and yet they say you'll hear him there
At Kew, at Kew in lilac-time (and oh, so near to London!)
The linnet and the throstle, too, and after dark the long halloo
And golden-eyed *tu-whit, tu-whoo* of owls that ogle London.

Nor Noah hardly knew a bird of any kind that isn't heard
At Kew, at Kew in lilac-time (and oh, so near to London!)
And when the rose begins to pout and all the chestnut spires are out
You'll hear the rest without a doubt, all chorusing for London:—

*Come down to Kew in lilac-time, in lilac-time, in lilac-time;*
*Come down to Kew in lilac-time (it isn't far from London!)*
*And you shall wander hand in hand with Love in summer's wonderland;*
*Come down to Kew in lilac-time (it isn't far from London!)*

And then the troubadour begins to thrill the golden street,
In the City as the sun sinks low;
And in all the gaudy busses there are scores of weary feet
Marking time, sweet time, with a dull mechanic beat,
And a thousand hearts are plunging to a love they'll never meet,
Through the meadows of the sunset, through the poppies and the wheat,
In the land where the dead dreams go.

Verdi, Verdi, when you wrote *Il Trovatore* did you dream
  Of the City when the sun sinks low
Of the organ and the monkey and the many-colored stream
On the Piccadilly pavement, of the myriad eyes that seem
To be litten for a moment with a wild Italian gleam
As *A che la morte* parodies the world's eternal theme
  And pulses with the sunset-glow?

There's a thief, perhaps, that listens with a face of frozen stone
  In the City as the sun sinks low;
There's a portly man of business with a balance of his own,
There's a clerk and there's a butcher of a soft reposeful tone,
And they're all of them returning to the heavens they have known:
They are crammed and jammed in busses and—they're each of them alone
  In the land where the dead dreams go.

There's a very modish woman and her smile is very bland
  In the City as the sun sinks low;
And her hansom jingles onward, but her little jeweled hand
Is clenched a little tighter and she cannot understand
What she wants or why she wanders to that undiscovered land,
For the parties there are not at all the sort of thing she planned,
  In the land where the dead dreams go.

There's an Oxford man that listens and his heart is crying out
  In the City as the sun sinks low;
For the barge, the eight, the Isis, and the coach's whoop and shout,
For the minute-gun, the counting and the long disheveled rout,
For the howl along the tow-path and a fate that's still in doubt,
For a roughened oar to handle and a race to think about
  In the land where the dead dreams go.

There's a laborer that listens to the voices of the dead
In the City as the sun sinks low;
And his hand begins to tremble and his face to smoulder red
As he sees a loafer watching him and—there he turns his head
And stares into the sunset where his April love is fled,
For he hears her softly singing and his lonely soul is led
Through the land where the dead dreams go.

There's an old and hardened demi-rep, it's ringing in her ears,
In the City as the sun sinks low;
With the wild and empty sorrow of the love that blights and sears,
Oh, and if she hurries onward, then be sure, be sure she hears,
Hears and bears the bitter burden of the unforgotten years,
And her laugh's a little harsher and her eyes are brimmed with tears
For the land where the dead dreams go.

There's a barrel-organ carolling across a golden street
In the City as the sun sinks low;
Though the music's only Verdi there's a world to make it sweet
Just as yonder yellow sunset where the earth and heaven meet
Mellows all the sooty City! Hark, a hundred thousand feet
Are marching on to glory through the poppies and the wheat
In the land where the dead dreams go.

So it's Jeremiah, Jeremiah,
What have you to say
When you meet the garland girls
Tripping on their way?

All around my gala hat
I wear a wreath of roses
(A long and lonely year it is
I've waited for the May!)

If any one should ask you,
  The reason why I wear it is—
My own love, my true love
  Is coming home to-day.

And it's buy a bunch of violets for the lady
  (*It's lilac-time in London; it's lilac-time in London!*)
Buy a bunch of violets for the lady
  While the sky burns blue above:

On the other side the street you'll find it shady
  (*It's lilac-time in London; it's lilac-time in London!*)
But buy a bunch of violets for the lady,
  And tell her she's your own true love.

There's a barrel-organ carolling across a golden street
  In the City as the sun sinks glittering and slow;
And the music's not immortal; but the world has made it sweet
And enriched it with the harmonies that make a song complete
In the deeper heavens of music where the night and morning meet,
  As it dies into the sunset glow;
And it pulses through the pleasures of the City and the pain
  That surround the singing organ like a large eternal light,
And they've given it a glory and a part to play again
  In the Symphony that rules the day and night.

And there, as the music changes,
  The song runs round again;
Once more it turns and ranges
  Through all its joy and pain:
Dissects the common carnival
  Of passions and regrets;
And the wheeling world remembers all
  The wheeling song forgets.

Once more *La Traviata* sighs
  Another sadder song:
Once more *Il Trovatore* cries
  A tale of deeper wrong;

Once more the knights to battle go
With sword and shield and lance,
Till once, once more, the shattered foe
Has whirled into—*a dance!*

*Come down to Kew in lilac-time, in lilac-time, in lilac-time;*
*Come down to Kew in lilac-time (it isn't far from London!)*
*And you shall wander hand in hand with Love in summer's wonderland,*
*Come down to Kew in lilac-time (it isn't far from London!)*

*Alfred Noyes* [1880–1958]

## AMANTIUM IRÆ

From "The Paradise of Dainty Devices"

In going to my naked bed, as one that would have slept,
I heard a wife sing to her child, that long before had wept.
She sighèd sore, and sang full sweet to bring the babe to rest,
That would not cease, but crièd still, in sucking at her breast.
She was full weary of her watch, and grievèd with her child;
She rockèd it, and rated it, till that on her it smiled.
Then did she say, "Now have I found this proverb true to prove,
*The falling out of faithful friends, renewing is of love.*"

Then took I paper, pen, and ink, this proverb for to write,
In register for to remain of such a worthy wight.
As she proceeded thus in song unto her little brat
Much matter uttered she of weight, in place whereas she sat:
And provèd plain there was no beast, nor creature bearing life
Could well be known to live in love, without discord and strife.
Then kissèd she her little babe, and sware, by God above,
*The falling out of faithful friends, renewing is of love.*

She said that neither king, nor prince, nor lord could live aright,
Until their puissance they did prove, their manhood, and their might,
When manhood shall be matchèd so, that fear can take no place,
Then weary works make warriors each other to embrace,
And leave their force that failèd them; which did consume the rout
That might before have lived their time, their strength and nature out.
Then did she sing, as one that thought no man could her reprove,
*The falling out of faithful friends, renewing is of love.*

She said she saw no fish, nor fowl, nor beast within her haunt
That met a stranger in their kind, but could give it a taunt.
Since flesh might not endure, but rest must wrath succeed,
And force the fight to fall to play, in pasture where they feed,
So noble Nature can well end the work she hath begun;
And bridle well that will not cease her tragedy in some.
Thus in her song she oft rehearsed, as did her well behove,
*The falling out of faithful friends, renewing is of love.*

"I marvel much, pardy," quoth she, "for to behold the rout,
To see man, woman, boy, and beast, to toss the world about;
Some kneel, some crouch, some beck, some check, and some can smoothly smile,
And some embrace others in arms, and there think many a wile.
Some stand aloof at cap and knee, some humble, and some stout,
Yet are they never friends in deed, until they once fall out."
Thus ended she her song, and said before she did remove,
"*The falling out of faithful friends, renewing is of love.*"

*Richard Edwards* [1523?–1566]

## QUA CURSUM VENTUS

As ships, becalmed at eve, that lay
  With canvas drooping, side by side,
Two towers of sail at dawn of day
  Are scarce long leagues apart descried;

When fell the night, upsprung the breeze,
  And all the darkling hours they plied,
Nor dreamt but each the self-same seas
  By each was cleaving, side by side:

E'en so—but why the tale reveal
  Of those, whom year by year unchanged,
Brief absence joined anew to feel,
  Astounded, soul from soul estranged?

At dead of night their sails were filled,
  And onward each rejoicing steered—
Ah, neither blame, for neither willed,
  Or wist, what first with dawn appeared!

To veer, how vain! On, onward strain,
  Brave barks! In light, in darkness too,
Through winds and tides one compass guides—
  To that, and your own selves, be true.

But O blithe breeze! and O great seas,
  Though ne'er, that earliest parting past,
On your wide plain they join again,
  Together lead them home at last.

One port, methought, alike they sought,
  One purpose hold where'er they fare,—
O bounding breeze, O rushing seas!
  At last, at last, unite them there!

*Arthur Hugh Clough* [1819–1861]

## "FOR A' THAT AND A' THAT"

Is there, for honest Poverty,
  That hangs his head, and a' that!
The coward slave, we pass him by,
  We dare be poor for a' that!
For a' that, and a' that,
  Our toil's obscure, and a' that;
The rank is but the guinea's stamp,
  The Man's the gowd for a' that.

What though on hamely fare we dine,
  Wear hoddin gray, and a' that;
Gie fools their silks, and knaves their wine,
  A Man's a Man for a' that.
For a' that, and a' that,
  Their tinsel show, and a' that;
The honest man, though e'er sae poor,
  Is king o' men for a' that.

Ye see yon birkie, ca'd a lord,
  Wha struts, and stares, and a' that;
Though hundreds worship at his word,
  He's but a coof for a' that;
For a' that, and a' that,
  His ribbon, star, and a' that;
The man o' independent mind,
  He looks and laughs at a' that.

A prince can mak a belted knight,
  A marquis, duke, and a' that;
But an honest man's aboon his might,
  Guid faith, he maunna fa' that!
For a' that, and a' that,
  Their dignities, and a' that,
The pith o' sense, and pride o' worth,
  Are higher rank than a' that.

Then let us pray that come it may,—
As come it will for a' that,—
That Sense and Worth, o'er a' the earth,
May bear the gree, and a' that.
For a' that, and a' that,
It's coming yet, for a' that,—
That Man to Man, the warld o'er,
Shall brothers be for a' that!

*Robert Burns* [1759–1796]

## "WE ARE BRETHREN A'"

A HAPPY bit hame this auld world would be
If men, when they're here, could make shift to agree,
An' ilk said to his neebor, in cottage an' ha',
"Come, gi'e me your hand,—we are brethren a'."

I ken na why ane wi' anither should fight,
When to 'gree would make a' body cosie an' right,
When man meets wi' man, 'tis the best way ava,
To say, "Gi'e me your hand,—we are brethren a'."

My coat is a coarse ane, an' yours may be fine,
And I maun drink water, while you may drink wine;
But we baith ha'e a leal heart, unspotted to shaw:
Sae gi'e me your hand,—we are brethren a'.

The knave ye would scorn, the unfaithfu' deride;
Ye would stand like a rock, wi' the truth on your side;
Sae would I, an' naught else would I value a straw:
Then gi'e me your hand,—we are brethren a'.

Ye would scorn to do fausely by woman or man;
I haud by the right aye, as well as I can;
We are ane in our joys, our affections, an' a':
Come, gi'e me your hand,—we are brethren a'.

Your mother has lo'ed you as mithers can lo'e;
An' mine has done for me what mithers can do;
We are ane high an' laigh, an' we shouldna be twa:
Sae gi'e me your hand,—we are brethren a'.

We love the same simmer day, sunny an' fair;
Hame! oh, how we love it, an' a' that are there!
Frae the pure air o' heaven the same life we draw:
Come, gi'e me your hand,—we are brethren a'.

Frail shakin' auld age will soon come o'er us baith,
An' creepin' alang at his back will be death;
Syne into the same mither-yird we will fa':
Come, gi'e me your hand,—we are brethren a'.

*Robert Nicoll* [1814-1837]

## FRATERNITY

I KNOW not but in every leaf
  That sprang to life along with me,
Were written all the joy and grief
  Thenceforth my fate to be.

The wind that whispered to the earth,
  The bird that sang its earliest lay,
The flower that blossomed at my birth—
  My kinsmen all were they.

Ay, but for fellowship with these
  I had not been—nay, might not be;
Nor they but vagrant melodies
  Till harmonized by me.

*John Banister Tabb* [1845-1909]

## SONNET

MOST men know love but as a part of life;
They hide it in some corner of the breast,
Even from themselves; and only when they rest
In the brief pauses of that daily strife,
Wherewith the world might else be not so rife,
They draw it forth (as one draws forth a toy
To soothe some ardent, kiss-exacting boy)
And hold it up to sister, child, or wife.

Ah me! why may not love and life be one?
Why walk we thus alone, when by our side,
Love, like a visible God, might be our guide?
How would the marts grow noble! and the street,

Worn like a dungeon-floor by weary feet,
Seem then a golden court-way of the Sun!

*Henry Timrod* [1843–1867]

## IF I SHOULD DIE TO-NIGHT*

If I should die to-night,
My friends would look upon my quiet face
Before they laid it in its resting-place,
And deem that death had left it almost fair;
And, laying snow-white flowers against my hair,
Would smooth it down with tearful tenderness,
And fold my hands with lingering caress,—
Poor hands, so empty and so cold to-night!

If I should die to-night,
My friends would call to mind with loving thought
Some kindly deed the icy hands had wrought,
Some gentle word the frozen lips had said,
Errands on which the willing feet had sped;
The memory of my selfishness and pride,
My hasty words would all be put aside,
And so I should be loved and mourned to-night.

If I should dic to-night,
Even hearts estranged would turn once more to me,
Recalling other days remorsefully;
The eyes that chill me with averted glance
Would look upon me as of yore, perchance,
And soften in the old familiar way,
For who could war with dumb, unconscious clay?
So I might rest, forgiven of all to-night.

Oh, friends! I pray to-night,
Keep not your kisses for my dead, cold brow:
The way is lonely; let me feel them now.
Think gently of me; I am travel-worn;
My faltering feet are pierced with many a thorn.
Forgive, oh, hearts estranged, forgive, I plead!
When dreamless rest is mine I shall not need
The tenderness for which I long to-night.

*Arabella Eugenia Smith* [1844–1916]

* For a parody of this poem see page 1950.

## VERSES

### SUPPOSED TO BE WRITTEN BY ALEXANDER SELKIRK DURING HIS SOLITARY ABODE ON THE ISLAND OF JUAN FERNANDEZ

I AM monarch of all I survey;
My right there is none to dispute;
From the center all round to the sea
I am lord of the fowl and the brute.
O Solitude! where are the charms
That sages have seen in thy face?
Better dwell in the midst of alarms,
Than reign in this horrible place.

I am out of humanity's reach,
I must finish my journey alone,
Never hear the sweet music of speech;
I start at the sound of my own.
The beasts that roam over the plain
My form with indifference see;
They are so unacquainted with man,
Their tameness is shocking to me.

Society, Friendship, and Love,
Divinely bestowed upon man,
O, had I the wings of a dove
How soon would I taste you again!
My sorrows I then might assuage
In the ways of religion and truth,
Might learn from the wisdom of age,
And be cheered by the sallies of youth.

Religion! what treasure untold
Resides in that heavenly word!
More precious than silver and gold,
Or all that this earth can afford.
But the sound of the church-going bell
These valleys and rocks never heard,
Nor sighed at the sound of a knell,
Or smiled when a Sabbath appeared.

Ye winds, that have made me your sport,
Convey to this desolate shore
Some cordial endearing report
Of a land I shall visit no more:
My friends,—do they now and then send
A wish or a thought after me?
O tell me I yet have a friend,
Though a friend I am never to see.

How fleet is a glance of the mind!
Compared with the speed of its flight,
The tempest itself lags behind,
And the swift-wingèd arrows of light.
When I think of my own native land,
In a moment I seem to be there;
But alas! recollection at hand
Soon hurries me back to despair.

But the sea-fowl is gone to her nest,
The beast is laid down in his lair;
Even here is a season of rest,
And I to my cabin repair.
There's mercy in every place,
And mercy, encouraging thought!
Gives even affliction a grace
And reconciles man to his lot.

*William Cowper* [1731–1800]

## "BLOW, BLOW, THOU WINTER WIND"

From "As You Like It"

Blow, blow, thou winter wind,
Thou art not so unkind
As man's ingratitude;
Thy tooth is not so keen,
Because thou art not seen,
Although thy breath be rude.
Heigh-ho! sing heigh-ho! unto the green holly;
Most friendship is feigning, most loving mere folly:
Then, heigh-ho, the holly!
This life is most jolly!

Freeze, freeze, thou bitter sky,
Thou dost not bite so nigh
As benefits forgot:
Though thou the waters warp,
Thy sting is not so sharp
As friend remembered not.
Heigh-ho! sing heigh-ho! unto the green holly;
Most friendship is feigning, most loving mere folly:
Then, heigh-ho, the holly!
This life is most jolly!

*William Shakespeare* [1564-1616]

## THE HOUSE BY THE SIDE OF THE ROAD

THERE are hermit souls that live withdrawn
In the place of their self-content;
There are souls like stars, that dwell apart,
In a fellowless firmament;
There are pioneer souls that blaze their paths
Where highways never ran—
But let me live by the side of the road
And be a friend to man.

Let me live in a house by the side of the road
Where the race of men go by—
The men who are good and the men who are bad,
As good and as bad as I.
I would not sit in the scorner's seat
Or hurl the cynic's ban—
Let me live in a house by the side of the road
And be a friend to man.

I see from my house by the side of the road,
By the side of the highway of life,
The men who press with the ardor of hope,
The men who are faint with the strife,
But I turn not away from their smiles nor their tears,
Both parts of an infinite plan—
Let me live in a house by the side of the road
And be a friend to man.

I know there are brook-gladdened meadows ahead,
  And mountains of wearisome height;
That the road passes on through the long afternoon
  And stretches away to the night.
And still I rejoice when the travelers rejoice
  And weep with the strangers that moan,
Nor live in my house by the side of the road
  Like a man who dwells alone.

Let me live in my house by the side of the road,
  It's here the race of men go by—
They are good, they are bad, they are weak, they are strong,
  Wise, foolish—so am I.
Then why should I sit in the scorner's seat,
  Or hurl the cynic's ban?
Let me live in my house by the side of the road
  And be a friend to man.

*Sam Walter Foss* [1858–1911]

## THE MAN WITH THE HOE

WRITTEN AFTER SEEING MILLET'S WORLD-FAMOUS PAINTING.

God made man in His own image in the image of God made He him.
—GENESIS

BOWED by the weight of centuries he leans
Upon his hoe and gazes on the ground,
The emptiness of ages in his face,
And on his back the burden of the world.
Who made him dead to rapture and despair,
A thing that grieves not and that never hopes,
Stolid and stunned, a brother to the ox?
Who loosened and let down this brutal jaw?
Whose was the hand that slanted back this brow?
Whose breath blew out the light within this brain?

Is this the Thing the Lord God made and gave
To have dominion over sea and land;
To trace the stars and search the heavens for power;
To feel the passion of Eternity?

Is this the Dream He dreamed who shaped the suns
And marked their ways upon the ancient deep?
Down all the stretch of Hell to its last gulf
There is no shape more terrible than this—
More tongued with censure of the world's blind greed-
More filled with signs and portents for the soul—
More fraught with menace to the universe.

What gulfs between him and the seraphim!
Slave of the wheel of labor, what to him
Are Plato and the swing of Pleiades?
What the long reaches of the peaks of song,
The rift of dawn, the reddening of the rose?
Through this dread shape the suffering ages look;
Time's tragedy is in that aching stoop;
Through this dread shape humanity betrayed,
Plundered, profaned and disinherited,
Cries protest to the Judges of the World,
A protest that is also prophecy.

O masters, lords and rulers in all lands,
Is this the handiwork you give to God,
This monstrous thing distorted and soul-quenched?
How will you ever straighten up this shape;
Touch it again with immortality;
Give back the upward looking and the light;
Rebuild in it the music and the dream;
Make right the immemorial infamies,
Perfidious wrongs, immedicable woes?

O masters, lords and rulers in all lands,
How will the Future reckon with this Man?
How answer his brute question in that hour
When whirlwinds of rebellion shake the world?
How will it be with kingdoms and with kings—
With those who shaped him to the thing he is—
When this dumb Terror shall reply to God,
After the silence of the centuries?

*Edwin Markham* [1852-1940]

## THE MAN WITH THE HOE

### A REPLY

Let us a little permit Nature to take her own way: she better understands her own affairs than we.—MONTAIGNE

NATURE reads not our labels, "great" and "small";
Accepts she one and all

Who, striving, win and hold the vacant place;
All are of royal race.

Him, there, rough-cast, with rigid arm and limb,
The Mother molded him,

Of his rude realm ruler and demigod,
Lord of the rock and clod.

With Nature is no "better" and no "worse,"
On this bared head no curse.

Humbled it is and bowed; so is he crowned
Whose kingdom is the ground.

Diverse the burdens on the one stern road
Where bears each back its load;

Varied the toil, but neither high nor low.
With pen or sword or hoe,

He that has put out strength, lo, he is strong;
Of him with spade or song

Nature but questions,—"This one, shall he stay?"
She answers "Yea," or "Nay,"

"Well, ill, he digs, he sings"; and he bides on,
Or shudders, and is gone.

Strength shall he have, the toiler, strength and grace,
So fitted to his place

As he leaned, there, an oak where sea winds blow,
Our brother with the hoe.

No blot, no monster, no unsightly thing,
The soil's long-lineaged king;

His changeless realm, he knows it and commands;
Erect enough he stands,

Tall as his toil. Nor does he bow unblest:
Labor he has, and rest.

Need was, need is, and need will ever be
For him and such as he;

Cast for the gap, with gnarlèd arm and limb,
The Mother molded him,—

Long wrought, and molded him with mother's care,
Before she set him there.

And aye she gives him, mindful of her own,
Peace of the plant, the stone;

Yea, since above his work he may not rise,
She makes the field his skies.

See! she that bore him, and metes out the lot,
He serves her. Vex him not

To scorn the rock whence he was hewn, the pit
And what was digged from it;

Lest he no more in native virtue stand,
The earth-sword in his hand,

But follow sorry phantoms to and fro,
And let a kingdom go.

*John Vance Cheney* [1848-1922]

## THE SINGING MAN

HE sang above the vineyards of the world.
And after him the vines with woven hands
Clambered and clung, and everywhere unfurled
Triumphing green above the barren lands;
Till high as gardens grow, he climbed, he stood,
Sun-crowned with life and strength, and singing toil,
And looked upon his work; and it was good:
The corn, the wine, the oil.

He sang above the noon. The topmost cleft
That grudged him footing on the mountain scars
He planted and despaired not; till he left
His vines soft breathing to the host of stars.
He wrought, he tilled; and even as he sang,
The creatures of his planting laughed to scorn
The ancient threat of deserts where there sprang
The wine, the oil, the corn!

He sang not for abundance.—Over-lords
Took of his tilth. Yet was there still to reap,
The portion of his labor; dear rewards
Of sunlit day, and bread, and human sleep.
He sang for strength; for glory of the light.
He dreamed above the furrows, "They are mine!"
When all he wrought stood fair before his sight
With corn, and oil, and wine.

*Truly, the light is sweet*
*Yea, and a pleasant thing*
*It is to see the Sun.*
*And that a man should eat*
*His bread that he hath won;—*
*(So is it sung and said),*
*That he should take and keep,*
*After his laboring,*
*The portion of his labor in his bread,*
*His bread that he hath won;*
*Yea, and in quiet sleep,*
*When all is done.*

He sang; above the burden and the heat,
Above all seasons with their fitful grace;
Above the chance and change that led his feet
To this last ambush of the Market-place.
" Enough for him," they said—and still they say—
" A crust, with air to breathe, and sun to shine;
He asks no more!"—Before they took away
The corn, the oil, the wine.

He sang. No more he sings now, anywhere.
Light was enough, before he was undone.
They knew it well, who took away the air,
—Who took away the sun;
Who took, to serve their soul-devouring greed,
Himself, his breath, his bread—the goad of toil;—
Who have and hold, before the eyes of Need,
The corn, the wine,—the oil!

*Truly, one thing is sweet*
*Of things beneath the Sun;*
*This, that a man should earn his bread and eat,*
*Rejoicing in his work which he hath done.*
*What shall be sung or said*
*Of desolate deceit,*
*When others take his bread;*
*His and his children's bread?—*
*And the laborer hath none.*
*This, for his portion now, of all that he hath done.*
*He earns; and others eat.*
*He starves;—they sit at meat*
*Who have taken away the Sun.*

II

Seek him now, that singing Man.
Look for him,
Look for him
In the mills,
In the mines;
Where the very daylight pines,—
He, who once did walk the hills!

You shall find him, if you scan
Shapes all unbefitting Man,
Bodies warped, and faces dim.
In the mines; in the mills
Where the ceaseless thunder fills
Spaces of the human brain
Till all thought is turned to pain.
Where the skirl of wheel on wheel,
Grinding him who is their tool,
Makes the shattered senses reel
To the numbness of the fool.
Perished thought, and halting tongue—
(Once it spoke;—once it sung!)
Live to hunger, dead to song.
Only heart-beats loud with wrong
Hammer on,—*How long?*
. . . *How long?—How long?*

Search for him;
Search for him;
Where the crazy atoms swim
Up the fiery furnace-blast.
You shall find him, at the last,—
He whose forehead braved the sun,—
Wrecked and tortured and undone.
Where no breath across the heat
Whispers him that life was sweet;
But the sparkles mock and flare,
Scattering up the crooked air.
(Blackened with that bitter mirk,—
Would God know His handiwork?)

Thought is not for such as he;
Naught but strength, and misery;
Since, for just the bite and sup,
Life must needs be swallowed up.
Only, reeling up the sky,
Hurtling flames that hurry by,
Gasp and flare, with *Why—Why,*
. . . *Why?* . . .

Why the human mind of him
Shrinks, and falters and is dim
When he tries to make it out:
What the torture is about.—
Why he breathes, a fugitive
Whom the World forbids to live.
Why he earned for his abode,
Habitation of the toad!
Why his fevered day by day
Will not serve to drive away
Horror that must always haunt:—
. . . *Want* . . . *Want!*
Nightmare shot with waking pangs;—
Tightening coil, and certain fangs,
Close and closer, always nigh . . .
. . . *Why?* . . . *Why?*

Why he labors under ban
That denies him for a man.
Why his utmost drop of blood
Buys for him no human good;
Why his utmost urge of strength
Only lets Them starve at length;—
Will not let him starve alone;
He must watch, and see his own
Fade and fail, and starve, and die.

. . . . . .

. . . *Why?* . . . *Why?*

. . . . . .

Heart-beats, in a hammering song,
Heavy as an ox may plod,
Goaded—goaded—faint with wrong,
Cry unto some ghost of God
. . . *How long?* . . . *How long?*
. . . . . . . *How long?*

III

Seek him yet. Search for him!
You shall find him, spent and grim;

In the prisons, where we pen
These unsightly shards of men.
Sheltered fast;
Housed at length;
Clothed and fed, no matter how!—
Where the householders, aghast,
Measure in his broken strength
Naught but power for evil, now.
Beast-of-burden drudgeries
Could not earn him what was his:
He who heard the world applaud
Glories seized by force and fraud,
He must break,—he must take!—
Both for hate and hunger's sake.
He must seize by fraud and force;
He must strike, without remorse!
Seize he might; but never keep.
Strike, his once!—Behold him here.
(Human life we buy so cheap,
Who should know we held it dear?)

No denial,—no defence
From a brain bereft of sense,
Any more than penitence.
But the heart-beats now, that plod
Goaded—goaded—dumb with wrong,
Ask not even a ghost of God
. . . . . . . *How long?*

*When the Sea gives up its dead,*
*Prison caverns, yield instead*
*This, rejected and despised;*
*This, the Soiled and Sacrificed!*
*Without form or comeliness;*
*Shamed for us that did transgress;*
*Bruised, for our iniquities,*
*With the stripes that are all his!*
*Face that wreckage, you who can.*
*It was once the Singing Man.*

IV

Must it be?—Must we then
Render back to God again
This His broken work, this thing,
For His man that once did sing?
Will not all our wonders do?
Gifts we stored the ages through,
(Trusting that He had forgot)—
Gifts the Lord requirèd not?

Would the all-but-human serve!
Monsters made of stone and nerve;
Towers to threaten and defy
Curse or blessing of the sky;
Shafts that blot the stars with smoke;
Lightnings harnessed under yoke;
Sea-things, air-things, wrought with steel,
That may smite, and fly, and feel!
Oceans calling each to each;
Hostile hearts, with kindred speech.
Every work that Titans can;
Every marvel: save a man,
Who might rule without a sword.—
  Is a man more precious, Lord?

Can it be?—Must we then
Render back to Thee again
Million, million wasted men?
Men, of flickering human breath,
Only made for life and death?

Ah, but see the sovereign Few,
Highly favored, that remain!
These, the glorious residue,
Of the cherished race of Cain.
These, the magnates of the age,
High above the human wage,
Who have numbered and possessed
All the portion of the rest!

What are all despairs and shames,
What the mean, forgotten names
Of the thousand more or less,
For one surfeit of success?

For those dullest lives we spent,
Take these Few magnificent!
For that host of blotted ones,
Take these glittering central suns.
Few;—but how their lustre thrives
On the million broken lives!
Splendid, over dark and doubt,
For a million souls gone out!
These, the holders of our hoard,—
Wilt thou not accept them, Lord?

V

Oh, in the wakening thunders of the heart,
—The small lost Eden, troubled through the night,
Sounds there not now,—forboded and apart,
Some voice and sword of light?

Some voice and portent of a dawn to break?—
Searching like God, the ruinous human shard
Of that lost Brother-man Himself did make,
And Man himself hath marred?

It sounds!—And may the anguish of that birth
Seize on the world; and may all shelters fail,
Till we behold new Heaven and new Earth
Through the rent Temple-vail!

When the high-tides that threaten near and far
To sweep away our guilt before the sky,—
Flooding the waste of this dishonored Star,
Cleanse, and o'erwhelm, and cry!—

Cry, from the deep of world-accusing waves,
With longing more than all since Light began,
Above the nations,—underneath the graves,—
"Give back the Singing Man!"

*Josephine Preston Peabody* [1874–1922]

## "SCUM O' THE EARTH"

I

AT the gate of the West I stand,
On the isle where the nations throng.
We call them "scum o' the earth";

Stay, are we doing you wrong,
Young fellow from Socrates' land?—
You, like a Hermes so lissome and strong
Fresh from the master Praxiteles' hand?
So you're of Spartan birth?
Descended, perhaps, from one of the band—
Deathless in story and song—
Who combed their long hair at Thermopylæ's pass? . . .
Ah, I forgot what straits, (alas!),
More tragic than theirs, more compassion-worth,
That have doomed you to march in our "immigrant class"
Where you're nothing but "scum o' the earth."

II

You Pole with a child on your knee,
What dower bring you to the land of the free?
Hark! does she croon
That sad little tune
That Chopin once found on his Polish lea
And mounted in gold for you and for me?
Now a ragged young fiddler answers
In wild Czeck melody
That Dvořak took whole from the dancers.
And the heavy faces bloom
In the wonderful Slavic way;
The little, dull eyes, the brows a-gloom,
Suddenly dawn like the day.
While, watching these folks and their mystery,
I forget that they're nothing worth;
That Bohemians, Slovaks, Croatians,
And men of all Slavic nations
Are "polacks"—and "scum o' the earth."

III

Genoese boy of the level brow,
Lad of the lustrous, dreamy eyes
Astare at Manhattan's pinnacles now
In the first, sweet shock of a hushed surprise;
Within your far-rapt seer's eyes
I catch the glow of the wild surmise
That played on the Santa Maria's prow
In that still gray dawn,
Four centuries gone,
When a world from the wave began to rise.
Oh, who shall foretell what high emprise
Is the goal that gleams
When Italy's dreams
Spread wing and sweep into the skies?
Cæsar dreamed him a world ruled well;
Dante dreamed Heaven out of Hell;
Angelo brought us there to dwell;
And you, are you of a different birth?—
You're only a "dago,"—and "scum o' the earth"!

IV

Stay, are we doing you wrong
Calling you "scum o' the earth,"
Man of the sorrow-bowed head,
Of the features tender yet strong,—
Man of the eyes full of wisdom and mystery
Mingled with patience and dread?
Have not I known you in history,
Sorrow-bowed head?
Were you the poet-king, worth
Treasures of Ophir unpriced?
Were you the prophet, perchance, whose art
Foretold how the rabble would mock
That shepherd of spirits, ere long,
Who should gather the lambs to his heart
And tenderly feed his flock?
Man—lift that sorrow-bowed head.
Behold the face of the Christ!

The vision dies at its birth.
You're merely a butt for our mirth.
You're a "sheeny"—and therefore despised
And rejected as "scum o' the earth."

V

Countrymen, bend and invoke
Mercy for us blasphemers,
For that we spat on these marvelous folk,
Nations of darers and dreamers,
Scions of singers and seers,
Our peers, and more than our peers.
"Rabble and refuse," we name them
And "scum o' the earth," to shame them.
Mercy for us of the few, young years,
Of the culture so callow and crude,
Of the hands so grasping and rude,
The lips so ready for sneers
At the sons of our ancient more-than-peers.
Mercy for us who dare despise
Men in whose loins our Homer lies;
Mothers of men who shall bring to us
The glory of Titian, the grandeur of Huss;
Children in whose frail arms may rest
Prophets and singers and saints of the West.

Newcomers all from the eastern seas,
Help us incarnate dreams like these.
Forget, and forgive, that we did you wrong.
Help us to father a nation strong
In the comradeship of an equal birth,
In the wealth of the richest bloods of earth.

*Robert Haven Schauffler* [1879-

## THE SECOND COMING

The Saviour came. With trembling lips
He counted Europe's battleships.
"Yet millions lack their daily bread.
So much for Calvary!" He said.

*Norman Gale* [1862–1942]

## THE NIGHT COURT

"CALL Rose Costara!"
Insolent she comes.
The watchers, practised, keen, turn down their thumbs.
The walk, the talk, the face,—that sea-shell tint,—
It is old stuff; they read her like coarse print.
Here is no hapless innocence waylaid.
This is a stolid worker at her trade.
Listening, she yawns, half smiling, undismayed,
Shrugging a little at the law's delay,
Bored and impatient to be on her way.
It is her eighth conviction. Out beyond the rail
A lady novelist in search of types turns pale.
She meant to write of them just as she found them,
And with no tears or maudlin glamor round them,
In forceful, virile words, harsh, true words, without shame,
Calling an ugly thing, boldly, an ugly name;
Sympathy, velvet glove, on purpose, iron hand.
But *eighth conviction!* All the phrases she had planned
Fail; "sullen," "vengeful," no, she isn't that.
No, the pink face beneath the hectic hat
Gives back her own aghast and sickened stare
With a detached and rather cheerful air,
And then the little novelist sees red.
From her chaste heart all clemency is fled.
"Oh, loathsome! venomous! Off with her head!
*Call* Rose Costara!" But before you stop,
And shelve your decent rage,
Let's call the cop.

Let's call the plain-clothes cop who brought her in.
The weary-eyed night watchman of the law,
A shuffling person with a hanging jaw,
Loose-lipped and sallow, rather vague of chin,
Comes rubber-heeling at His Honor's rap.
He set and baited and then sprung the trap—
The *trap*—by his unsavory report.
Let's ask him why—but first
Let's call the court.

Not only the grim figure in the chair,
Sphinx-like above the waste and wreckage there,
Skeptical, tired of a retold tale,
But the whole humming hive, the false, the frail,—
An old young woman with a weasel face,
A lying witness waiting in his place,
Two ferret lawyers nosing out a case,
Reporters questioning a Mexican,
Sobbing her silly heart out for her man,
Planning to feature her, "lone, desperate, pretty,"—
Yes, call the court. But wait!
Let's call the city.

Call the community! Call up, call down,
Call all the speeding, mad, unheeding town!
Call rags and tags and then call velvet gown!
Go, summon them from tenements and clubs,
On office floors and over steaming tubs!
Shout to the boxes and behind the scenes,
Then to the push-carts and the limousines!
Arouse the lecture-room, the cabaret!
Confound them with a trumpet blast and say,
"Are you so dull, so deaf and blind indeed,
That you mistake the harvest for the seed?"
Condemn them for—but stay!
Let's call the code—

That facile thing they've fashioned to their mode.
Smug sophistries that smother and befool,
That numb and stupefy; that clumsy thing
That measures mountains with a three-foot rule,
And plumbs the ocean with a pudding string—
The little, brittle code. Here is the root,
Far out of sight and buried safe and deep,
And Rose Costara is the bitter fruit.
On every limb and leaf, death, ruin, creep.

So, lady novelist, go home again.
Rub biting acid on your little pen.
Look back and out and up and in, and then

Write that it is no job for pruning-shears.
Tell them to dig for years and years and years
The twined and twisted roots. Blot out the page;
Invert the blundering order of the age;
Reverse the scheme: the last shall be the first.
Summon the system, starting with the worst—
The lying, dying code! On, down the line,
The city and the court, the cop. Assign
The guilt, the blame, the shame! Sting, lash, and spur!
Call each and all! Call us! And *then* call her!

*Ruth Comfort Mitchell* [18 -1953]

## THE FACTORIES

I HAVE shut my little sister in from life and light
(For a rose, for a ribbon, for a wreath across my hair),
I have made her restless feet still until the night,
Locked from sweets of summer and from wild spring air;
I who ranged the meadowlands, free from sun to sun,
Free to sing and pull the buds and watch the far wings fly,
I have bound my sister till her playing-time was done—
Oh, my little sister, was it I? Was it I?

I have robbed my sister of her day of maidenhood
(For a robe, for a feather, for a trinket's restless spark),
Shut from Love till dusk shall fall, how shall she know good,
How shall she go scatheless through the sin-lit dark?
I who could be innocent, I who could be gay,
I who could have love and mirth before the light went by,
I have put my sister in her mating-time away—
Sister, my young sister, was it I? Was it I?

I have robbed my sister of the lips against her breast,
(For a coin, for the weaving of *my* children's lace and lawn),
Feet that pace beside the loom, hands that cannot rest—
How can she know motherhood, whose strength is gone?
I who took no heed of her, starved and labor-worn,
I, against whose placid heart my sleepy gold-heads lie,
Round my path they cry to me, little souls unborn—
*God of Life! Creator! It was I! It was I!*

*Margaret Widdemer* [18

## BLACK SHEEP

FROM their folded mates they wander far,
Their ways seem harsh and wild;
They follow the beck of a baleful star,
Their paths are dream beguiled.

Yet haply they sought but a wider range,
Some loftier mountain-slope,
And little recked of the country strange
Beyond the gates of hope.

And haply a bell with a luring call
Summoned their feet to tread
Midst the cruel rocks, where the deep pitfall
And the lurking snare are spread.

Maybe, in spite of their tameless days
Of outcast liberty,
They're sick at heart for the homely ways
Where their gathered brothers be.

And oft at night, when the plains fall dark
And the hills loom large and dim,
For the Shepherd's voice they mutely hark,
And their souls go out to him.

Meanwhile, "Black sheep! black sheep!" we cry,
Safe in the inner fold;
And maybe, they hear, and wonder why,
And marvel, out in the cold.

*Richard Burton* [1861-1940]

## IN MEN WHOM MEN CONDEMN AS ILL

From "Byron"

IN men whom men condemn as ill
I find so much of goodness still,
In men whom men pronounce divine
I find so much of sin and blot,
I do not dare to draw a line
Between the two, where God has not.

*Joaquin Miller* [1839-1913]

## SUNDAY EVENING IN THE COMMON

Look—on the topmost branches of the world
  The blossoms of the myriad stars are thick;
  Over the huddled rows of stone and brick
A few sad wisps of empty smoke are curled
  Like ghosts, languid and sick.

One breathless moment now the city's moaning
  Fades, and the endless streets seem vague and dim;
  There is no sound around the whole world's rim,
Save in the distance a small band is droning
  Some desolate old hymn.

Van Wyck, how often have we been together
  When this same moment made all mysteries clear—
  The infinite stars that brood above us here,
And the gray city in the soft June weather,
  So tawdry and so dear!

*John Hall Wheelock* [1886-     ]

## CALIBAN IN THE COAL MINES

God, we don't like to complain
  We know that the mine is no lark—
But—there's the pools from the rain;
But—there's the cold and the dark.

God, You don't know what it is—
  You, in Your well-lighted sky,
Watching the meteors whizz;
  Warm, with the sun always by.

God, if You had but the moon
  Stuck in Your cap for a lamp,
Even You'd tire of it soon,
  Down in the dark and the damp.

Nothing but blackness above,
  And nothing that moves but the cars—
God, if You wish for our love,
  Fling us a handful of stars!

*Louis Untermeyer* [1885-

## LANDSCAPES

THE rain was over, and the brilliant air
Made every little blade of grass appear
Vivid and startling—everything was there
With sharpened outlines, eloquently clear,
As though one saw it in a crystal sphere.
The rusty sumac with its struggling spires;
The golden-rod with all its million fires;
(A million torches swinging in the wind)
A single poplar, marvellously thinned,
Half like a naked boy, half like a sword;
Clouds, like the haughty banners of the Lord;
A group of pansies with their shrewish faces
Little old ladies cackling over laces;
The quaint, unhurried road that curved so well;
The prim petunias with their rich, rank smell;
The lettuce-birds, the creepers in the field—
How bountifully were they all revealed!
How arrogantly each one seemed to thrive—
So frank and strong, so radiantly alive!

And over all the morning-minded earth
There seemed to spread a sharp and kindling mirth,
Piercing the stubborn stones until I saw
The toad face heaven without shame or awe,
The ant confront the stars, and every weed
Grow proud as though it bore a royal seed;
While all the things that die and decompose
Sent forth their bloom as richly as the rose . . .
Oh, what a liberal power that made them thrive
And keep the very dirt that died, alive.

And now I saw the slender willow-tree
No longer calm and drooping listlessly,
Letting its languid branches sway and fall
As though it danced in some sad ritual;
But rather like a young, athletic girl,
Fearless and gay, her hair all out of curl,
And flying in the wind—her head thrown back,
Her arms flung up, her garments flowing slack,

And all her rushing spirits running over. . . .
What made a sober tree seem such a rover—
Or made the staid and stalwart apple-trees,
That stood for years knee-deep in velvet peace,
Turn all their fruit to little worlds of flame,
And burn the trembling orchard there below.
What lit the heart of every golden-glow—
Oh, why was nothing weary, dull or tame? . . .
Beauty it was, and keen, compassionate mirth
That drives the vast and energetic earth.

And, with abrupt and visionary eyes,
I saw the huddled tenements arise.
Here where the merry clover danced and shone
Sprang agonies of iron and of stone;
There, where green Silence laughed or stood enthralled,
Cheap music blared and evil alleys sprawled.
The roaring avenues, the shrieking mills;
Brothels and prisons on those kindly hills—
The menace of these things swept over me;
A threatening, unconquerable sea. . . .

A stirring landscape and a generous earth!
Freshening courage and benevolent mirth—
And then the city, like a hideous sore. . . .
*Good God, and what is all this beauty for?*

*Louis Untermeyer* [1885-

## STUPIDITY STREET

I SAW with open eyes
Singing birds sweet
Sold in the shops
For the people to eat,
Sold in the shops of
Stupidity Street.

I saw in vision
The worm in the wheat,
And in the shops nothing
For people to eat;
Nothing for sale in
Stupidity Street.

*Ralph Hodgson* [1871-

## A TROOP OF THE GUARD

[HARVARD CLASS POEM]

THERE'S trampling of hoofs in the busy street,
There's clanking of sabres on floor and stair,
There's sound of restless, hurrying feet,
Of voices that whisper, of lips that entreat,
Will they live, will they die, will they strive, will they dare?
The houses are garlanded, flags flutter gay,
For a Troop of the Guard rides forth to-day.

Oh, the troopers will ride and their hearts will leap,
When it's shoulder to shoulder and friend to friend—
But it's some to the pinnacle, some to the deep,
And some in the glow of their strength to sleep,
And for all it's a fight to the tale's far end.
And it's each to his goal, nor turn nor sway,
When the Troop of the Guard rides forth to-day.
The dawn is upon us, the pale light speeds
To the zenith with glamor and golden dart.
On, up! Boot and saddle! Give spurs to your steeds!
There's a city beleaguered that cries for men's deeds,
With the pain of the world in its cavernous heart.
Ours be the triumph! Humanity calls!
Life's not a dream in the clover!
On to the walls, on to the walls,
On to the walls, and over!

The wine is spent, the tale is spun,
The revelry of youth is done.
The horses prance, the bridles clink,
While maidens fair in bright array
With us the last sweet goblet drink,
Then bid us "Mount and ride away!"
Into the dawn, we ride, we ride,
Fellow and fellow, side by side;
Galloping over the field and hill,

Over the marshland, stalwart still;
Into the forest's shadowy hush,
Where spectres walk in sunless day,
And in dark pools and branch and bush
The treacherous will-o'-the-wisp lights play.
Out of the wood 'neath the risen sun,
Weary we gallop, one and one,
To a richer hope and a stronger foe
And a hotter fight in the fields below—
Each man his own slave, each his lord,
For the golden spurs and the victor's sword!

Friends of the great, the high, the perilous years,
Upon the brink of mighty things we stand—
Of golden harvests and of silver tears,
And griefs and pleasures that like grains of sand
Gleam in the hour-glass, yield their place, and die.
Like a dark sea our lives before us lie,
And we, like divers o'er a pearl-strewn deep,
Stand yet an instant in the warm, young sun,
Plunge, and are gone,
And over pearl and diver the restless breakers sweep.
On to the quest! To-day
In joyful revelry we still may play
With the last golden phantoms of dead years;
Hearing above the stir
The old protecting music in our ears
Of fluttering pinions and the voice of her,
The Mighty Mother, watching o'er her sons.
To-day we still may crouch beneath her wings,
Dreaming of unimagined things;
To-morrow we are part
Of the world's depthless, palpitating heart,
One with the living, striving millions
Whose lives beat out the ceaseless, rhythmic song
Of joy and pain and peace and love and wrong.
We may not dwell on solitary heights.
There is a force that draws men breast to breast
In the hot swirl of never-ending fights,
When man—enriched, despoiled, oppressed,

By the great titans of the earth who hold
The nations in their hands as boys a swallow's nest—
Leaps from the sodden mass through loves and feuds
And tumult of hot strife and tempest blast,
Until he stands, free of the depths at last,
A titan in his turn, to mould
The pliable clay of the world's multitudes.

An anxious generation sends us forth
On the far conquest of the thrones of might.
From West and East, from South and North,
Earth's children, weary-eyed with too much light,
Cry from their dream-forsaken vales of pain,
"Give us our gods, give us our gods again!"
A lofty and relentless century,
Gazing with Argus eyes,
Has pierced the very inmost halls of faith,
And left no shelter whither man may flee
From the cold storms of night and lovelessness and death
Old gods have fallen and the new must rise!
Out of the dust of doubt and broken creeds,
The sons of those who cast men's idols low
Must build up for a hungry people's needs
New gods, new hopes, new strength to toil and grow;
Knowing that naught that ever lived can die,
No act, no dream but spreads its sails, sublime,
Sweeping across the visible seas of Time,
Into the treasure-haven of eternity.

The portals are open, the white road leads
  Through thicket and garden, o'er stone and sod:
On, up! Boot and saddle! Give spurs to your steeds!
There's a city beleaguered that cries for men's deeds,
  For the faith that is strength and the love that is God!
    On through the dawning! Humanity calls!
      Life's not a dream in the clover!
    On to the walls, on to the walls,
      On to the walls, and over!

*Hermann Hagedorn* [1882-

## THE GOD-MAKER, MAN

NEVERMORE
Shall the shepherds of Arcady follow
Pan's moods as he lolls by the shore
Of the mere, or lies hid in the hollow;
Nevermore
Shall they start at the sound of his reed-fashioned flute;

Fallen mute
Are the strings of Apollo,
His lyre and his lute;
And the lips of the Memnons are mute
Evermore;
And the gods of the North,—are they dead or forgetful,
Our Odin and Baldur and Thor?
Are they drunk, or grown weary of worship and fretful,
Our Odin and Baldur and Thor?

And into what night have the Orient deities strayed?
Swart gods of the Nile, in dusk splendors arrayed,
Brooding Isis and somber Osiris,
You were gone ere the fragile papyrus,
(That bragged you eternal!) decayed.

The avatars
But illumine their limited evens
And vanish like plunging stars;
They are fixed in the whirling heavens
No firmer than falling stars;
Brief lords of the changing soul, they pass
Like a breath from the face of a glass,
Or a blossom of summer blown shallop-like over
The clover
And tossed tides of grass.

Sink to silence the psalms and the pæans,
The shibboleths shift, and the faiths,
And the temples that challenged the æons
Are tenanted only by wraiths;
Swoon to silence the cymbals and psalters,
The worships grow senseless and strange

And the mockers ask, "*Where be thy altars?*"
   Crying, "*Nothing is changeless—but Change!*"

Yes, nothing seems changeless, but Change.
And yet, through the creed-wrecking years,
One story for ever appears;
The tale of a City Supernal—
The whisper of Something eternal—
A passion, a hope, and a vision
   That peoples the silence with Powers;
A fable of meadows Elysian
   Where Time enters not with his Hours;—
Manifold are the tale's variations,
   Race and clime ever tinting the dreams,
Yet its essence, through endless mutations,
   Immutable gleams.

Deathless, though godheads be dying,
   Surviving the creeds that expire,
Illogical, reason-defying,
   Lives that passionate, primal desire;
Insistent, persistent, forever
Man cries to the silences, "*Never*
*Shall Death reign the lord of the soul,*
*Shall the dust be the ultimate goal—*
*I will storm the black bastions of Night!*
   *I will tread where my vision has trod,*
*I will set in the darkness a light,*
   *In the vastness, a god!*"

As the forehead of Man grows broader, so do his creeds;
And his gods they are shaped in his image, and mirror his needs;
And he clothes them with thunders and beauty, he clothes them with music and fire;
Seeing not, as he bows by their altars, that he worships his own desire;
And mixed with his trust there is terror, and mixed with his madness is ruth,
And every man grovels in error, yet every man glimpses a truth.

For all of the creeds are false, and all of the creeds are true;
And low at the shrines where my brothers bow, there will I
bow, too;
For no form of a god, and no fashion
Man has made in his desperate passion
But is worthy some worship of mine;—
Not too hot with a gross belief,
Nor yet too cold with pride,
I will bow me down where my brothers bow,
Humble—but open-eyed!

*Don Marquis* [1878–1937]

## THE FIELD OF GLORY

WAR shook the land where Levi dwelt,
And fired the dismal wrath he felt,
That such a doom was ever wrought
As his, to toil while others fought;
To toil, to dream—and still to dream,
With one day barren as another;
To consummate, as it would seem,
The dry despair of his old mother.

Far off one afternoon began
The sound of man destroying man;
And Levi, sick with nameless rage,
Condemned again his heritage,
And sighed for scars that might have come,
And would, if once he could have sundered
Those harsh, inhering claims of home
That held him while he cursed and wondered.

Another day, and then there came,
Rough, bloody, ribald, hungry, lame,
But yet themselves, to Levi's door,
Two remnants of the day before.
They laughed at him and what he sought;
They jeered him, and his painful acre;
But Levi knew that they had fought,
And left their manners to their Maker.

That night, for the grim widow's ears,
With hopes that hid themselves in fears,
He told of arms, and fiery deeds,
Whereat one leaps the while he reads,
And said he'd be no more a clown,
While others drew the breath of battle.—
The mother looked him up and down,
And laughed—a scant laugh with a rattle.

She told him what she found to tell,
And Levi listened, and heard well
Some admonitions of a voice
That left him no cause to rejoice.—
He sought a friend, and found the stars,
And prayed aloud that they should aid him;
But they said not a word of wars,
Or of a reason why God made him.

And who's of this or that estate
We do not wholly calculate,
When baffling shades that shift and cling
Are not without their glimmering;
When even Levi, tired of faith,
Beloved of none, forgot by many,
Dismissed as an inferior wraith,
Reborn may be as great as any.

*Edwin Arlington Robinson* [1869–1935]

## THE CONQUERORS

I SAW the Conquerors riding by
  With trampling feet of horse and men:
Empire on empire like the tide
  Flooded the world and ebbed again;

A thousand banners caught the sun,
  And cities smoked along the plain,
And laden down with silk and gold
  And heaped-up pillage groaned the wain.

I saw the Conquerors riding by,
  Splashing through loathsome floods of war—

The Crescent leaning o'er its hosts,
And the barbaric scimitar,—

And continents of moving spears,
And storms of arrows in the sky,
And all the instruments sought out
By cunning men that men may die!

I saw the Conquerors riding by
With cruel lips and faces wan:
Musing on kingdoms sacked and burned
There rode the Mongol Ghengis Khan;

And Alexander, like a god,
Who sought to weld the world in one;
And Cæsar with his laurel wreath;
And like a thing from Hell the Hun;

And, leading like a star the van,
Heedless of upstretched arm and groan,
Inscrutable Napoleon went
Dreaming of empire, and alone. . . .

Then all they perished from the earth
As fleeting shadows from a glass,
And, conquering down the centuries,
Came Christ, the Swordless, on an ass!

*Harry Kemp* [1883–1960]

## THE ARSENAL AT SPRINGFIELD

THIS is the Arsenal. From floor to ceiling,
Like a huge organ, rise the burnished arms;
But from their silent pipes no anthem pealing
Startles the villages with strange alarms.

Ah! what a sound will rise, how wild and dreary,
When the death-angel touches those swift keys!
What loud lament and dismal Miserere
Will mingle with their awful symphonies!

I hear even now the infinite fierce chorus,
The cries of agony, the endless groan,

Which, through the ages that have gone before us,
  In long reverberations reach our own.

On helm and harness rings the Saxon hammer,
  Through Cimbric forest roars the Norseman's song,
And loud, amid the universal clamor,
  O'er distant deserts sounds the Tartar gong.

I hear the Florentine, who from his palace
  Wheels out his battle-bell with dreadful din,
And Aztec priests upon their teocallis
  Beat the wild war-drums made of serpent's skin;

The tumult of each sacked and burning village;
  The shout that every prayer for mercy drowns;
The soldiers' revels in the midst of pillage;
  The wail of famine in beleaguered towns;

The bursting shell, the gateway wrenched asunder,
  The rattling musketry, the clashing blade;
And ever and anon, in tones of thunder,
  The diapason of the cannonade.

Is it, O man, with such discordant noises,
  With such accursed instruments as these,
Thou drownest Nature's sweet and kindly voices,
  And jarrest the celestial harmonies?

Were half the power that fills the world with terror,
  Were half the wealth bestowed on camps and courts,
Given to redeem the human mind from error,
  There were no need of arsenals or forts:

The warrior's name would be a name abhorrèd!
  And every nation, that should lift again
Its hand against a brother, on its forehead
  Would wear forevermore the curse of Cain!

Down the dark future, through long generations,
  The echoing sounds grow fainter and then cease;
And like a bell, with solemn, sweet vibrations,
  I hear once more the voice of Christ say, "Peace!"

Peace! and no longer from its brazen portals
The blast of War's great organ shakes the skies!
But beautiful as songs of the immortals,
The holy melodies of love arise.

*Henry Wadsworth Longfellow* [1807-1882]

## THE LITTLE SISTER OF THE PROPHET

"If there arise among you a prophet or dreamer . . . ."

I HAVE left a basket of dates
In the cool dark room that is under the vine,
Some curds set out in two little crimson plates
And a flask of amber wine,
And cakes most cunningly beaten
Of savory herbs, and spice, and the delicate wheaten
Flour that is best,
And all to lighten his spirit and sweeten his rest.

This morning he cried, "Awake,
And see what the wonderful grace of the Lord hath revealed!"
And we ran for his sake,
But 'twas only the dawn outspread o'er our father's field,
And the house of the potter white in the valley below.
But his hands were upraised to the east and he cried to us, "So
Ye may ponder and read
The strength and the beauty of God out-rolled in a fiery screed!"

Then the little brown mother smiled,
As one does on the words of a well-loved child,
And, "Son," she replied, "have the oxen been watered and fed?
For work is to do, though the skies be never so red,
And already the first sweet hours of the day are spent."
And he sighed, and went.

Will he come from the byre
With his head all misty with dreams, and his eyes on fire,
Shaking us all with the weight of the words of his passion?

I will give him raisins instead of dates,
And wreathe young leaves on the little red plates.
I will put on my new head-tyre,
And braid my hair in a comelier fashion.
Will he note? Will he mind?
Will he touch my cheek as he used to, and laugh and be kind?

*Marjorie L. C. Pickthall* [1883–1922]

## THE SONS OF MARTHA

The Sons of Mary seldom bother, for they have inherited that good part;
But the Sons of Martha favor their Mother of the careful soul and the troubled heart.
And because she lost her temper once, and because she was rude to the Lord, her Guest,
Her Sons must wait upon Mary's Sons, world without end, reprieve, or rest.

It is their care in all the ages to take the buffet and cushion the shock.
It is their care that the gear engages; it is their care that the switches lock.
It is their care that the wheels run truly; it is their care to embark and entrain,
Tally, transport, and deliver duly the Sons of Mary by land and main.

They say to mountains, "Be ye removèd." They say to the lesser floods "Be dry."
Under their rods are the rocks reprovèd—they are not afraid of that which is high.
Then do the hill-tops shake to the summit—then is the bed of the deep laid bare,
That the Sons of Mary may overcome it, pleasantly sleeping and unaware.

They finger death at their gloves' end where they piece and repiece the living wires.
He rears against the gates they tend: they feed him hungry behind their fires.

Early at dawn, ere men see clear, they stumble into his terrible stall,
And hale him forth like a haltered steer, and goad and turn him till evenfall.

To these from birth is Belief forbidden; from these till death is Relief afar.
They are concerned with matters hidden—under the earthline their altars are:
The secret fountains to follow up, waters withdrawn to restore to the mouth,
And gather the floods as in a cup, and pour them again at a city's drouth.

They do not preach that their God will rouse them a little before the nuts work loose.
They do not teach that His Pity allows them to leave their job when they damn-well choose.
As in the thronged and the lighted ways, so in the dark and the desert they stand,
Wary and watchful all their days that their brethren's days may be long in the land.

Raise ye the stone or cleave the wood to make a path more fair or flat;
Lo, it is black already with blood some Son of Martha spilled for that!
Not as a ladder from earth to Heaven, not as a witness to any creed,
But simple service simply given to his own kind in their common need.

And the Sons of Mary smile and are blessèd—they know the angels are on their side.
They know in them is the Grace confessèd, and for them are the Mercies multiplied.
They sit at the Feet—they hear the Word—they see how truly the Promise runs.
They have cast their burden upon the Lord, and—the Lord He lays it on Martha's Sons!

*Rudyard Kipling* [1865–1936]

## THE TUFT OF FLOWERS

I WENT to turn the grass once after one
Who mowed it in the dew before the sun.

The dew was gone that made his blade so keen
Before I came to view the levelled scene.

I looked for him behind an isle of trees;
I listened for his whetstone on the breeze.

But he had gone his way, the grass all mown,
And I must be, as he had been,—alone,

"As all must be," I said within my heart,
"Whether they work together or apart."

But as I said it, swift there passed me by
On noiseless wing a 'wildered butterfly,

Seeking with memories grown dim o'er night
Some resting flower of yesterday's delight.

And once I marked his flight go round and round,
As where some flower lay withering on the ground

And then he flew as far as eye could see,
And then on tremulous wing came back to me.

I thought of questions that have no reply,
And would have turned to toss the grass to dry;

But he turned first, and led my eye to look
At a tall tuft of flowers beside a brook,

A leaping tongue of bloom the scythe had spared
Beside a reedy brook the scythe had bared.

I left my place to know them by their name,
Finding them butterfly weed when I came.

The mower in the dew had loved them thus
By leaving them to flourish, not for us,

Nor yet to draw one thought of ours to him,
But from sheer morning gladness at the brim.

The butterfly and I had lit upon,
Nevertheless, a message from the dawn,

That made me hear the wakening birds around,
And hear his long scythe whispering to the ground,

And feel a spirit kindred to my own;
So that henceforth I worked no more alone;

But glad with him, I worked as with his aid,
And weary, sought at noon with him the shade;

And dreaming, as it were, held brotherly speech
With one whose thought I had not hoped to reach.

"Men work together," I told him from the heart,
"Whether they work together or apart."

*Robert Frost* [1875–

## MENDING WALL

SOMETHING there is that doesn't love a wall,
That sends the frozen-ground-swell under it,
And spills the upper boulders in the sun;
And makes gaps even two can pass abreast.
The work of hunters is another thing:
I have come after them and made repair
Where they have left not one stone on stone,
But they would have the rabbit out of hiding,
To please the yelping dogs. The gaps I mean,
No one has seen them made or heard them made,
But at spring mending-time we find them there.
I let my neighbor know beyond the hill;
And on a day we meet to walk the line
And set the wall between us once again.
We keep the wall between us as we go.
To each the boulders that have fallen to each.
And some are loaves and some so nearly balls
We have to use a spell to make them balance

"Stay where you are until our backs are turned!"
We wear our fingers rough with handling them.
Oh, just another kind of out-door game,
One on a side. It comes to little more:
There where it is we do not need the wall:
He is all pine and I am apple orchard.
My apple trees will never get across
And eat the cones under his pines, I tell him.
He only says, "Good fences make good neighbors."
Spring is the mischief in me, and I wonder
If I could put a notion in his head:
"*Why* do they make good neighbors? Isn't it
Where there are cows? But here there are no cows.
Before I built a wall I'd ask to know
What I was walling in or walling out,
And to whom I was like to give offence.
Something there is that doesn't love a wall,
That wants it down." I could say "Elves" to him,
But it's not elves exactly, and I'd rather
He said it for himself. I see him there
Bringing a stone grasped firmly by the top
In each hand, like an old-stone savage armed.
He moves in darkness as it seems to me,
Not of woods only and the shade of trees.
He will not go behind his father's saying,
And he likes having thought of it so well
He says again, "Good fences make good neighbors."

*Robert Frost* [1875-

## FORBEARANCE

HAST thou named all the birds without a gun?
Loved the wood-rose, and left it on its stalk?
At rich men's tables eaten bread and pulse?
Unarmed, faced danger with a heart of trust?
And loved so well a high behavior,
In man or maid, that thou from speech refrained,
Nobility more nobly to repay?
O, be my friend, and teach me to be thine!

*Ralph Waldo Emerson* [1803-1882]

# THE MUSIC-MAKERS

## ISRAFEL

**And the angel Israfel, whose heart-strings are a lute, and who has the sweetest voice of all God's creatures.—KORAN**

IN Heaven a spirit doth dwell
Whose heart-strings are a lute;
None sing so wildly well
As the angel Israfel,
And the giddy stars (so legends tell),
Ceasing their hymns, attend the spell
Of his voice, all mute.

Tottering above
In her highest noon,
The enamoured moon
Blushes with love,
While, to listen, the red levin
(With the rapid Pleiads, even,
Which were seven)
Pauses in Heaven.

And they say (the starry choir
And the other listening things)
That Israfeli's fire
Is owing to that lyre
By which he sits and sings,
The trembling living wire
Of those unusual strings.

But the skies that angel trod,
Where deep thoughts are a duty,
Where Love's a grown-up God,
Where the Houri glances are
Imbued with all the beauty
Which we worship in a star.

Therefore thou art not wrong,
  Israfeli, who despisest
An unimpassioned song;
To thee the laurels belong,
  Best bard, because the wisest:
Merrily live, and long!

The ecstasies above
  With thy burning measures suit:
Thy grief, thy joy, thy hate, thy love,
  With the fervor of thy lute:
  Well may the stars be mute!

Yes, Heaven is thine; but this
  Is a world of sweets and sours;
  Our flowers are merely—flowers,
And the shadow of thy perfect bliss
  Is the sunshine of ours.

If I could dwell
Where Israfel
  Hath dwelt, and he where I,
He might not sing so wildly well
  A mortal melody,
While a bolder note than this might swell
  From my lyre within the sky.

*Edgar Allan Poe* [1809–1849]

## PROEM

WRITTEN TO INTRODUCE THE FIRST GENERAL COLLECTION OF HIS POEMS)

I LOVE the old melodious lays
Which softly melt the ages through,
  The songs of Spenser's golden days,
  Arcadian Sidney's silvery phrase,
Sprinkling our noon of time with freshest morning dew.

Yet, vainly in my quiet hours
To breathe their marvellous notes I try;
I feel them, as the leaves and flowers
In silence feel the dewy showers,
And drink with glad, still lips the blessing of the sky.

The rigor of a frozen clime,
The harshness of an untaught ear,
The jarring words of one whose rhyme
Beat often Labor's hurried time,
Or Duty's rugged march through storm and strife, are here.

Of mystic beauty, dreamy grace,
No rounded art the lack supplies;
Unskilled the subtle lines to trace,
Or softer shades of Nature's face,
I view her common forms with unanointed eyes.

Nor mine the seer-like power to show
The secrets of the heart and mind;
To drop the plummet-line below
Our common world of joy and woe,
A more intense despair or brighter hope to find.

Yet here at least an earnest sense
Of human right and weal is shown;
A hate of tyranny intense,
And hearty in its vehemence,
As if my brother's pain and sorrow were my own.

O Freedom! if to me belong
Nor mighty Milton's gift divine,
Nor Marvell's wit and graceful song,
Still with a love as deep and strong
As theirs, I lay, like them, my best gifts on thy shrine!

*John Greenleaf Whittier* [1807–1892]

## EMBRYO

I FEEL a poem in my heart to-night,
A still thing growing,—
As if the darkness to the outer light
A song were owing:

A something strangely vague, and sweet, and sad,
Fair, fragile, slender;
Not tearful, yet not daring to be glad,
And oh, so tender!

It may not reach the outer world at all,
Despite its growing;
Upon a poem-bud such cold winds fall
To blight its blowing.
But, oh, whatever may the thing betide,
Free life or fetter,
My heart, just to have held it till it died,
Will be the better!

*Mary Ashley Townsend* [1832–1901]

## THE SINGER'S PRELUDE

From "The Earthly Paradise"

Of Heaven or Hell I have no power to sing,
I cannot ease the burden of your fears,
Or make quick-coming death a little thing,
Or bring again the pleasure of past years,
Nor for my words shall ye forget your tears,
Or hope again for aught that I can say,
The idle singer of an empty day.

But rather, when aweary of your mirth,
From full hearts still unsatisfied ye sigh,
And, feeling kindly unto all the earth,
Grudge every minute as it passes by,
Made the more mindful that the sweet days die,—
Remember me a little then, I pray,
The idle singer of an empty day.

The heavy trouble, the bewildering care
That weighs us down who live and earn our bread,
These idle verses have no power to bear;
So let me sing of names rememberèd,
Because they, living not, can ne'er be dead,
Or long time take their memory quite away
From us poor singers of an empty day.

Dreamer of dreams, born out of my due time,
Why should I strive to set the crooked straight?
Let it suffice me that my murmuring rhyme
Beats with light wing against the ivory gate,
Telling a tale not too importunate
To those who in the sleepy region stay,
Lulled by the singer of an empty day.

Folk say, a wizard to a northern king
At Christmas-tide such wondrous things did show,
That through one window men beheld the spring,
And through another saw the summer glow,
And through a third the fruited vines a-row,
While still, unheard, but in its wonted way,
Piped the drear wind of that December day.

So with this Earthly Paradise it is,
If ye will read aright, and pardon me,
Who strive to build a shadowy isle of bliss
Midmost the beating of the steely sea,
Where tossed about all hearts of men must be;
Whose ravening monsters mighty men shall slay,
Not the poor singer of an empty day.

*William Morris* [1834–1896]

## A PRELUDE

Spirit that moves the sap in spring,
When lusty male birds fight and sing,
Inform my words, and make my lines
As sweet as flowers, as strong as vines.

Let mine be the freshening power
Of rain on grass, of dew on flower;
The fertilizing song be mine,
Nut-flavored, racy, keen as wine.

Let some procreant truth exhale
From me, before my forces fail;
Or ere the ecstatic impulse go,
Let all my buds to blossoms blow.

If quick, sound seed be wanting where
The virgin soil feels sun and air,
And longs to fill a higher state,
There let my meanings germinate.

Let not my strength be spilled for naught,
But, in some fresher vessel caught,
Be blended into sweeter forms,
And fraught with purer aims and charms.

Let bloom-dust of my life be blown
To quicken hearts that flower alone;
Around my knees let scions rise
With heavenward-pointed destinies.

And when I fall, like some old tree,
And subtile change makes mould of me,
There let earth show a fertile line
Whence perfect wild-flowers leap and shine!

*Maurice Thompson* [1844–1901]

## ON FIRST LOOKING INTO CHAPMAN'S HOMER

Much have I travelled in the realms of gold,
And many goodly states and kingdoms seen;
Round many western islands have I been
Which bards in fealty to Apollo hold.
Oft of one wide expanse had I been told
That deep-browed Homer ruled as his demesne:
Yet did I never breathe its pure serene
Till I heard Chapman speak out loud and bold:
Then felt I like some watcher of the skies
When a new planet swims into his ken;
Or like stout Cortez, when with eagle eyes
He stared at the Pacific—and all his men
Looked at each other with a wild surmise—
Silent, upon a peak in Darien.

*John Keats* [1795–1821]

## THE ODYSSEY

As one that for a weary space has lain
  Lulled by the song of Circe and her wine
  In gardens near the pale of Proserpine,
Where that Ææan isle forgets the main,
And only the low lutes of love complain,
  And only shadows of wan lovers pine,
  As such an one were glad to know the brine
Salt on his lips, and the large air again,—
So gladly, from the songs of modern speech
  Men turn, and see the stars, and feel the free
    Shrill wind beyond the close of heavy flowers,
    And through the music of the languid hours,
They hear like ocean on a western beach
  The surge and thunder of the Odyssey.

*Andrew Lang* [1844-1912]

## HOMERIC UNITY

The sacred keep of Ilion is rent
With trench and shaft; foiled waters wander slow
Through plains where Simois and Scamander went
To war with Gods and heroes long ago.
Not yet to tired Cassandra, lying low
In rich Mycenae, do the Fates relent:
The bones of Agamemnon are a show,
And ruined is his royal monument.
The dust and awful treasures of the Dead,
Hath Learning scattered wide, but vainly thee,
Homer, she meteth with her tool of lead,
And strives to rend thy songs; too blind to see
The crown that burns on thine immortal head
Of indivisible supremacy!

*Andrew Lang* [1844-1912]

## "ENAMORED ARCHITECT OF AIRY RHYME"

Enamored architect of airy rhyme,
Build as thou wilt, heed not what each man says:
Good souls, but innocent of dreamers' ways,
Will come, and marvel why thou wastest time:

Others, beholding how thy turrets climb
'Twixt theirs and heaven, will hate thee all thy days;
But most beware of those who come to praise.
O Wondersmith, O worker in sublime
And heaven-sent dreams, let art be all in all;
Build as thou wilt, unspoiled by praise or blame,
Build as thou wilt, and as thy light is given;
Then, if at last the airy structure fall,
Dissolve, and vanish—take thyself no shame.
They fail, and they alone, who have not striven.

*Thomas Bailey Aldrich* [1839-1907]

## DIVINA COMMEDIA

Oft have I seen at some cathedral door
A laborer, pausing in the dust and heat,
Lay down his burden, and with reverent feet
Enter, and cross himself, and on the floor
Kneel to repeat his paternoster o'er;
Far off the noises of the world retreat;
The loud vociferations of the street
Become an indistinguishable roar.
So, as I enter here from day to day,
And leave my burden at this minster gate,
Kneeling in prayer, and not ashamed to pray,
The tumult of the time disconsolate
To inarticulate murmurs dies away,
While the eternal ages watch and wait.

*Henry Wadsworth Longfellow* [1807-1882]

## "A MAN CALLED DANTE, I HAVE HEARD"

A man called Dante, I have heard,
Once ranged the country-side,
He knew to dawn's mysterious word
What drowsy birds replied;

He knew the deep sea's voice, its gleams
And tremulous lights afar.
When he lay down at night, in dreams
He tramped from star to star.

*Georgiana Goddard King* [1871-1939]

## THE SONGS I SING

THE songs I sing at morning
I never sing at eve;
Oh, not through any scorning,
For tears regret may leave;
But that our radiant pleasures
Suit not the shadowed hour,
For which I have such measures
As mourn the withered flower.

The songs I sing at twilight
I never sing at morn;
I would not mar the highlight
With any note forlorn;
My path made gay and sunny,
With joy I fill my heart;
The hyssop from the honey—
I keep them wide apart.

*Charles G. Blanden* [1857–1933]

## THE DEAREST POETS

WERE I to name, out of the times gone by,
The poets dearest to me, I should say,
Pulci for spirits, and a fine, free way;
Chaucer for manners, and close, silent eye;
Milton for classic taste, and harp strung high;
Spenser for luxury, and sweet, sylvan play;
Horace for chatting with, from day to day;
Shakespeare for all, but most, society.
But which take with me, could I take but one?
Shakespeare,—as long as I was unoppressed
With the world's weight, making sad thoughts intenser
But did I wish, out of the common sun
To lay a wounded heart in leafy rest,
And dream of things far off and healing,—Spenser.

*Leigh Hunt* [1784–1859]

## FALSE POETS AND TRUE

LOOK how the lark soars upward and is gone,
Turning a spirit as he nears the sky!
His voice is heard, but body there is none
To fix the vague excursions of the eye.

So, poets' songs are with us, though they die
Obscured, and hid by death's oblivious shroud,
And Earth inherits the rich melody
Like raining music from the morning cloud.
Yet few there be who pipe so sweet and loud
Their voices reach us through the lapse of space:
The noisy day is deafened by a crowd
Of undistinguished birds, a twittering race;
But only lark and nightingale forlorn
Fill up the silences of night and morn.

*Thomas Hood* [1799-1845]

## A SINGING LESSON

Far-fetched and dear bought, as the proverb rehearses,
Is good, or was held so, for ladies: but naught
In a song can be good if the turn of the verse is
Far-fetched and dear bought.

As the turn of a wave should it sound, and the thought
Ring smooth, and as light as the spray that disperses
Be the gleam of the words for the garb thereof wrought.

Let the soul in it shine through the sound as it pierces
Men's hearts with possession of music unsought;
For the bounties of song are no jealous god's mercies,
Far-fetched and dear bought.

*Algernon Charles Swinburne* [1837–1909]

## POETRY

I am the reality of things that seem;
The great transmuter, melting loss to gain,
Languor to love, and fining joy from pain.
I am the waking, who am called the dream;
I am the sun, all light reflects my gleam;
I am the altar-fire within the fane;
I am the force of the refreshing rain;
I am the sea to which flows every stream;
I am the utmost height there is to climb:

I am the truth, mirrored in fancy's glass;
I am stability, all else will pass;
I am eternity, encircling time;
Kill me, none may; conquer me, nothing can—
I am God's soul, fused in the soul of man.

*Ella Heath* [18 -

## THE INNER VISION

Most sweet it is with unuplifted eyes
To pace the ground, if path be there or none,
While a fair region round the traveller lies
Which he forbears again to look upon;
Pleased rather with some soft ideal scene,
The work of Fancy, or some happy tone
Of meditation, slipping in between
The beauty coming and the beauty gone.
—If Thought and Love desert us, from that day
Let us break off all commerce with the Muse:
With Thought and Love companions of our way—
Whate'er the senses take or may refuse,—
The Mind's internal heaven shall shed her dews
Of inspiration on the humblest lay.

*William Wordsworth* [1770–1850]

## ON AN OLD SONG

Little snatch of ancient song,
What has made thee live so long?
Flying on thy wings of rhyme
Lightly down the depths of time,
Telling nothing strange or rare,
Scarce a thought or image there,
Nothing but the old, old tale
Of a hapless lover's wail;
Offspring of an idle hour,
Whence has come thy lasting power?
By what turn of rhythm or phrase,
By what subtle careless grace,
Can thy music charm our ears
After full three hundred years?

Landmarks of the human mind
One by one are left behind,
And a subtle change is wrought
In the mould and cast of thought;
Modes of reasoning pass away,
Types of beauty lose their sway;
Creeds and causes that have made
Many noble lives must fade,
And the words that thrilled of old
Now seem hueless, dead, and cold;
Fancy's rainbow tints are flying,
Thoughts, like men, are slowly dying;
All things perish, and the strongest
Often do not last the longest;
The stately ship is seen no more,
The fragile skiff attains the shore;
And while the great and wise decay,
And all their trophies pass away,
Some sudden thought, some careless rhyme,
Still floats above the wrecks of Time.

*William Edward Hartpole Lecky* [1838–1903]

## TO SONG

Here shall remain all tears for lovely things
And here enshrined the longing of great hearts,
Caught on a lyre whence waking wonder starts,
To mount afar upon immortal wings;
Here shall be treasured tender wonderings,
The faintest whisper that the soul imparts,
All silent secrets and all gracious arts,
Where nature murmurs of her hidden springs.

O magic of a song! here loveliness
May sleep unhindered of life's mortal toll,
And noble things stand towering o'er the tide;
Here mid the years, untouched by time or stress,
Shall sweep on every wind that stirs the soul
The music of a voice that never died!

*Thomas S. Jones, Jr.* [1882–1932]

## VERSE

Past ruined Ilion Helen lives,
Alcestis rises from the shades;
Verse calls them forth; 'tis verse that gives
Immortal youth to mortal maids.

Soon shall Oblivion's deepening veil
Hide all the peopled hills you see,
The gay, the proud, while lovers hail
These many summers you and me.

*Walter Savage Landor* [1775–1864]

## AN OLD-FASHIONED POET

In simpler verse than triolets,
Rondeau, or deft quatrain,
With breath of morning violets
In every dewy strain,
He sang from overflowing heart
His sweet old songs unspoiled by art.

Progressive years have passed since then—
The Muse has changed her ways;
No more through flowery mead and glen
A rustic maid she strays;
Amid the traffic of the town
We catch the flutter of her gown.

But one who knows her virgin grace
Gives back the songs she sung
And brings with glimpses of her face
The days when love was young.
O Muse immortal, singer true,
What harmonies unite the two!

*Ada Foster Murray* [1857–1936]

## POET AND LARK

When leaves turn outward to the light,
And all the roads are fringed with green,
When larks are pouring, high, unseen,
The joy they find in song and flight,

Then I, too, with the lark would wing
My little flight, and, soaring, sing

When larks drop downward to the nest,
  And day drops downward to the sea,
And song and wing are fain to rest,
  The lark's dear wisdom guideth me,
And I too turn within my door,
Content to dream, and sing no more.

*Mary Ainge de Vere* [1844–1920]

## A HINT FROM HERRICK

No slightest golden rhyme he wrote
That held not something men must quote;
Thus by design or chance did he
Drop anchors to posterity.

*Thomas Bailey Aldrich* [1836–1907]

## TO THE POETS

Bards of Passion and of Mirth,
Ye have left your souls on earth!
Have ye souls in heaven too,
Double-lived in regions new?
Yes, and those of heaven commune
With the spheres of sun and moon;
With the noise of fountains wondrous
And the parle of voices thund'rous;
With the whisper of heaven's trees
And one another, in soft ease
Seated on Elysian lawns,
Browsed by none but Dian's fawns;
Underneath large blue-bells tented,
Where the daisies are rose-scented.
And the rose herself has got
Perfume which on earth is not,
Where the nightingale doth sing,
Not a senseless, trancèd thing,
But divine, melodious truth,
Philosophic numbers smooth;
Tales and golden histories
Of heaven and its mysteries

Thus ye live on high, and then
On the earth ye live again;
And the souls ye left behind you
Teach us, here, the way to find you,
Where your other souls are joying,
Never slumbered, never cloying.
Here, your earth-born souls still speak
To mortals, of their little week;
Of their sorrows and delights;
Of their passions and their spites;
Of their glory and their shame;
What doth strengthen and what maim.
Thus ye teach us, every day,
Wisdom, though fled far away.

Bards of Passion and of Mirth,
Ye have left your souls on earth!
Ye have souls in heaven too,
Double-lived in regions new!

*John Keats* [1795–1821]

## THE PROGRESS OF POESY

### A PINDARIC ODE

AWAKE, Æolian lyre, awake,
And give to rapture all thy trembling strings.
From Helicon's harmonious springs
A thousand rills their mazy progress take:
The laughing flowers, that round them blow,
Drink life and fragrance as they flow.
Now the rich stream of music winds along
Deep, majestic, smooth and strong,
Through verdant vales, and Ceres' golden reign:
Now rolling down the steep amain,
Headlong, impetuous, see it pour;
The rocks and nodding groves rebellow to the roar.

O Sovereign of the willing soul,
Parent of sweet and solemn-breathing airs,
Enchanting shell! the sullen Cares
And frantic Passions hear thy soft control.

On Thracia's hills the Lord of War
Has curbed the fury of his car,
And dropped his thirsty lance at thy command.
Perching on the sceptered hand
Of Jove, thy magic lulls the feathered king
With ruffled plumes and flagging wing:
Quenched in dark clouds of slumber lie
The terror of his beak, and lightnings of his eye.

Thee the voice, the dance, obey,
Tempered to thy warbled lay.
  O'er Idalia's velvet-green
  The rosy-crownèd Loves are seen
On Cytherea's day,
  With antic Sports, and blue-eyed Pleasures,
  Frisking light in frolic measures;
Now pursuing, now retreating,
  Now in circling troops they meet:
To brisk notes in cadence beating,
  Glance their many-twinkling feet.
Slow melting strains their Queen's approach declare:
  Where'er she turns, the Graces homage pay.
With arms sublime, that float upon the air,
  In gliding state she wins her easy way:
O'er her warm cheek and rising bosom move
The bloom of young Desire and purple light of Love.

  Man's feeble race what ills await!
Labor, and Penury, the racks of Pain,
Disease, and Sorrow's weeping train,
  And Death, sad refuge from the storms of fate!
The fond complaint, my song, disprove,
And justify the laws of Jove.
Say, has he given in vain the heavenly Muse?
Night, and all her sickly dews,
Her specters wan, and birds of boding cry,
He gives to range the dreary sky:
Till down the eastern cliffs afar
Hyperion's march they spy, and glittering shafts of
  war.

In climes beyond the solar road,
Where shaggy forms o'er ice-built mountains roam,
The Muse has broke the twilight gloom
To cheer the shivering native's dull abode.
And oft, beneath the odorous shade
Of Chili's boundless forests laid,
She deigns to hear the savage youth repeat
In loose numbers wildly sweet
Their feather-cinctured chiefs, and dusky loves.
Her track, where'er the Goddess roves,
Glory pursue and generous Shame,
The unconquerable Mind, and Freedom's holy flame

Woods, that wave o'er Delphi's steep,
Isles, that crown the Ægean deep,
Fields, that cool Ilissus laves,
Or where Mæander's amber waves
In lingering labyrinths creep,
How do your tuneful echoes languish,
Mute, but to the voice of anguish?
Where each old poetic mountain
Inspiration breathed around:
Every shade and hallowed fountain
Murmured deep a solemn sound:
Till the sad Nine, in Greece's evil hour,
Left their Parnassus for the Latian plains.
Alike they scorn the pomp of tyrant Power,
And coward Vice, that revels in her chains.
When Latium had her lofty spirit lost,
They sought, O Albion! next thy sea-encircled coast.

Far from the sun and summer gale,
In thy green lap was Nature's darling laid,
What time, where lucid Avon strayed,
To him the mighty mother did unveil
Her awful face: the dauntless child
Stretched forth his little arms, and smiled.
This pencil take (she said), whose colors clear
Richly paint the vernal year:
Thine too these golden keys, immortal boy!
This can unlock the gates of joy;

Of horror that, and thrilling fears,
Or ope the sacred source of sympathetic tears.

Nor second he, that rode sublime
Upon the seraph-wings of Ecstasy,
The secrets of the abyss to spy.
He passed the flaming bounds of place and time:
The living Throne, the sapphire-blaze,
Where Angels tremble while they gaze,
He saw; but, blasted with excess of light,
Closed his eyes in endless night.
Behold, where Dryden's less presumptuous car,
Wide o'er the fields of glory bear
Two coursers of ethereal race,
With necks in thunder clothed, and long-resounding pace

Hark, his hands the lyre explore!
Bright-eyed Fancy, hovering o'er,
Scatters from her pictured urn
Thoughts that breathe, and words that burn.
But ah, 'tis heard no more!
O Lyre divine! what daring Spirit
Wakes thee now? Though he inherit
Nor the pride, nor ample pinion,
That the Theban Eagle bear,
Sailing with supreme dominion
Through the azure deep of air:
Yet oft before his infant eyes would run
Such forms as glitter in the Muse's ray,
With orient hues, unborrowed of the Sun:
Yet shall he mount, and keep his distant way
Beyond the limits of a vulgar fate,
Beneath the Good how far—but far above the Great.

*Thomas Gray* [1716-1771.

## SEAWEED

When descends on the Atlantic
The gigantic
Storm-wind of the equinox.

Landward in his wrath he scourges
 The toiling surges,
Laden with seaweed from the rocks:

From Bermuda's reefs; from edges
 Of sunken ledges,
In some far-off, bright Azore;
From Bahama, and the dashing,
 Silver-flashing
Surges of San Salvador;

From the tumbling surf, that buries
 The Orkneyan skerries,
Answering the hoarse Hebrides;
And from wrecks of ships, and drifting
 Spars, uplifting
On the desolate, rainy seas,—

Ever drifting, drifting, drifting
 On the shifting
Currents of the restless main;
Till in sheltered coves, and reaches
 Of sandy beaches,
All have found repose again.

So when storms of wild emotion
 Strike the ocean
Of the poet's soul, ere long,
From each cave and rocky fastness
 In its vastness,
Floats some fragment of a song:

From the far-off isles enchanted
 Heaven has planted
With the golden fruit of Truth;
From the flashing surf, whose vision
 Gleams Elysian
In the tropic clime of Youth;

From the strong Will, and the Endeavor
 That for ever
Wrestles with the tides of Fate;

From the wreck of Hopes far-scattered,
Tempest-shattered,
Floating waste and desolate;—

Ever drifting, drifting, drifting
On the shifting
Currents of the restless heart;
Till at length in books recorded,
They, like hoarded
Household words, no more depart.

*Henry Wadsworth Longfellow* [1807–1882]

## TO THE MUSES

Whether on Ida's shady brow,
Or in the chambers of the East,
The chambers of the Sun, that now
From ancient melody have ceased;

Whether in heaven ye wander fair,
Or the green corners of the earth,
Or the blue regions of the air
Where the melodious winds have birth;

Whether on crystal rocks ye rove,
Beneath the bosom of the sea,
Wandering in many a coral grove;
Fair Nine, forsaking Poetry;

How have you left the ancient love
That bards of old enjoyed in you!
The languid strings do scarcely move,
The sound is forced, the notes are few.

*William Blake* [1757–1827]

## "WHITHER IS GONE THE WISDOM AND THE POWER"

Whither is gone the wisdom and the power
That ancient sages scattered with the notes
Of thought-suggesting lyres? The music floats
In the void air; e'en at this breathing hour,

In every cell and every blooming bower
The sweetness of old lays is hovering still:
But the strong soul, the self-constraining will,
The rugged root which bare the winsome flower
Is weak and withered. Were we like the fays
That sweetly nestle in the fox-glove bells,
Or lurk and murmur in the rose-lipped shells
Which Neptune to the earth for quit-rent pays,
Then might our pretty modern Philomels
Sustain our spirits with their roundelays.

*Hartley Coleridge* [1796–1849]

## THE MUSES

Of old the Muses sat on high,
And heard and judged the songs of men;
On one they smiled, who loitered by;
Of toiling ten, they slighted ten.

"They lightly serve who serve us best,
Nor know they how the task was done;
We Muses love a soul at rest,
But violence and toil we shun."

If men say true, the Muses now
Have changed their ancient habitude,
And would be served with knitted brow,
And stress and toil each day renewed.

So each one with the other vies,
Of those who weave romance or song:
"On us, O Muse, bestow thy prize,
For we have striven well and long!"

And yet methinks I hear the hest
Come murmuring down from Helicon:
"They lightly serve who serve us best,
Nor know they how the task was done!"

*Edith M. Thomas* [1854–1925]

## EVOE!

"Many are the wand-bearers, few are the true bacchanals."

MANY are the wand-bearers;
  Their windy shouts I hear
Along the hillside vineyard,
  And where the wine runs clear;
They show the vine-leaf chaplet,
  The ivy-wreathen spear,
But the god, the true Iacchus,
  He does not hold them dear.

Many are the wand-bearers,
  And bravely are they clad;
Yes, they have all the tokens
  His early lovers had.
They sing the master passions,
  Themselves unsad, unglad;
And the god, the true Iacchus—
  He knows they are not mad!

Many are the wand-bearers;
  The fawn-skin bright they wear;
There are among them mænads
  That rave with unbound hair.
They toss the harmless firebrand—
  It spends itself in air:
And the god, the true Iacchus,
  He smiles—and does not care.

Many are the wand-bearers,
  And who (ye ask) am I?
One who was born in madness,
  "Evoe!" my first cry—
Who dares, before your spear-points,
  To challenge and defy;
And the god, the true Iacchus,
  So keep me till I die!

Many are the wand-bearers.
I bear with me no sign;
Yet, I was mad, was drunken,
Ere yet I tasted wine;
Nor bleeding grape can slacken
The thirst wherewith I pine;
And the god, the true Iacchus,
Hears now this song of mine.

*Edith M. Thomas* [1854-1925]

## AN INVOCATION

I NEVER prayed for Dryads, to haunt the woods again;
More welcome were the presence of hungering, thirsting men,
Whose doubts we could unravel, whose hopes we could fulfil,
Our wisdom tracing backward, the river to the rill;
Were such beloved forerunners one summer day restored,
Then, then we might discover the Muse's mystic hoard.

Oh, dear divine Comatas, I would that thou and I
Beneath this broken sunlight this leisure day might lie;
Where trees from distant forests, whose names were strange to thee,
Should bend their amorous branches within thy reach to be,
And flowers thine Hellas knew not, which art hath made more fair,
Should shed their shining petals upon thy fragrant hair.

Then thou shouldst calmly listen with ever-changing looks
To songs of younger minstrels and plots of modern books,
And wonder at the daring of poets later born,
Whose thoughts are unto thy thoughts as noon-tide is to morn;
And little shouldst thou grudge them their greater strength of soul,
Thy partners in the torch-race, though nearer to the goal.

As when ancestral portraits look gravely from the walls
Upon the youthful baron who treads their echoing halls;

And whilst he builds new turrets, the thrice ennobled heir
Would gladly wake his grandsire his home and feast to share;
So from Ægean laurels that hide thine ancient urn
I fain would call thee hither, my sweeter lore to learn.

Or in thy cedarn prison thou waitest for the bee:
Ah, leave that simple honey, and take thy food from me!
My sun is stooping westward. Entrancèd dreamer, haste:
There's fruitage in my garden, that I would have thee taste.
Now lift the lid a moment: now, Dorian shepherd, speak:
Two minds shall flow together, the English and the Greek.

*William Johnson-Cory* [1823-1892]

## INVENTION

I ENVY not the Lark his song divine,
Nor thee, O Maid, thy beauty's faultless mould.
Perhaps the chief felicity is mine,
Who hearken and behold.

The joy of the Artificer Unknown
Whose genius could devise the Lark and thee—
This, or a kindred rapture, let me own,
I covet ceaselessly!

*William Watson* [1858-1935]

## JOY OF THE MORNING

I HEAR you, little bird,
Shouting aswing above the broken wall.
Shout louder yet: no song can tell it all.
Sing to my soul in the deep still wood:
'Tis wonderful beyond the wildest word:
I'd tell it, too, if I could.

Oft when the white, still dawn
Lifted the skies and pushed the hills apart,
I've felt it like a glory in my heart—
(The world's mysterious stir)
But had no throat like yours, my bird,
Nor such a listener.

*Edwin Markham* [1852-1940]

## CRICKET

CRICKET, chirring in the autumn twilight,
Little kinsman,
I, like you, the unknown path must follow
Into darkness,—
One day into darkness.
Would I might, with your ecstatic buoyance,
Fare forth singing!

*Clinton Scollard* [1860–1932]

## TO A POET A THOUSAND YEARS HENCE

I WHO am dead a thousand years,
And wrote this sweet archaic song,
Send you my words for messengers
The way I shall not pass along.

I care not if you bridge the seas,
Or ride secure the cruel sky,
Or build consummate palaces
Of metal or of masonry.

But have you wine and music still,
And statues and a bright-eyed love,
And foolish thoughts of good and ill,
And prayers to them that sit above?

How shall we conquer? Like a wind
That falls at eve our fancies blow,
And old Mæonides the blind
Said it three thousand years ago.

O friend unseen, unborn, unknown,
Student of our sweet English tongue,
Read out my words at night, alone:
I was a poet, I was young.

Since I can never see your face,
And never shake you by the hand,
I send my soul through time and space
To greet you. You will understand.

*James Elroy Flecker* [1884–1915]

## THE MOODS

(AFTER READING CERTAIN OF THE IRISH POETS)

THE Moods have laid their hands across my hair:
The Moods have drawn their fingers through my heart;
My hair shall nevermore lie smooth and bright,
But stir like tide-worn sea-weed, and my heart
Shall nevermore be glad of small, sweet things,—
A wild rose, or a crescent moon,—a book
Of little verses, or a dancing child.
My heart turns crying from the rose and brook,
My heart turns crying from the thin bright moon,
And weeps with useless sorrow for the child.
The Moods have loosed a wind to vex my hair,
And made my heart too wise, that was a child.

Now I shall blow like smitten candle-flame;
I shall desire all things that may not be:
The years, the stars, the souls of ancient men,
All tears that must, and smiles that may not be,—
Yes, glimmering lights across a windy ford,
And vagrant voices on a darkened plain,
And holy things, and outcast things, and things
Far too remote, frail-bodied, to be plain.

My pity and my joy are grown alike;
I cannot sweep the strangeness from my heart.
The Moods have laid swift hands across my hair:
The Moods have drawn swift fingers through my heart.

*Fannie Stearns Davis* [1884-

## THE PASSIONATE READER TO HIS POET

DOTH it not thrill thee, Poet,
Dead and dust though thou art,
To feel how I press thy singing
Close to my heart?

Take it at night to my pillow,
Kiss it before I sleep,
And again when the delicate morning
Beginneth to peep?

See how I bathe thy pages
Here in the light of the sun;
Through thy leaves, as a wind among roses,
The breezes shall run.

Feel how I take thy poem
And bury within it my face,
As I pressed it last night in the heart of a flower,
Or deep in a dearer place.

Think, as I love thee, Poet,
A thousand love beside,
Dear women love to press thee too
Against a sweeter side.

Art thou not happy, Poet?
I sometimes dream that I
For such a fragrant fame as thine
Would gladly sing and die.

Say, wilt thou change thy glory
For this same youth of mine?
And I will give my days i' the sun
For that great song of thine.

*Richard Le Gallienne* [1886–1947]

## THE FLIGHT OF THE GODDESS

A MAN should live in a garret aloof,
And have few friends, and go poorly clad,
With an old hat stopping the chink in the roof
To keep the Goddess constant and glad.

Of old, when I walked on a rugged way,
And gave much work for but little bread,
The Goddess dwelt with me night and day,
Sat at my table, haunted my bed.

The narrow, mean attic, I see it now!—
Its window o'erlooking the city's tiles,
The sunset's fires, and the clouds of snow,
And the river wandering miles and miles.

Just one picture hung in the room,
The saddest story that Art can tell—
Dante and Virgil in lurid gloom
Watching the Lovers float through Hell.

Wretched enough was I sometimes,
Pinched, and harassed with vain desires;
But thicker than clover sprung the rhymes
As I dwelt like a sparrow among the spires.

Midnight filled my slumbers with song;
Music haunted my dreams by day.
Now I listen and wait and long,
But the Delphian airs have died away.

I wonder and wonder how it befell:
Suddenly I had friends in crowds;
I bade the house-tops a long farewell;
"Good-by," I cried, "to the stars and clouds!

"But thou, rare soul, thou hast dwelt with me,
Spirit of Poesy! thou divine
Breath of the morning, thou shalt be,
Goddess! for ever and ever mine."

And the woman I loved was now my bride,
And the house I wanted was my own;
I turned to the Goddess satisfied—
But the Goddess had somehow flown.

Flown, and I fear she will never return;
I am much too sleek and happy for her,
Whose lovers must hunger and waste and burn,
Ere the beautiful heathen heart will stir.

I call—but she does not stoop to my cry;
I wait—but she lingers, and ah! so long!
It was not so in the years gone by,
When she touched my lips with chrism of song.

I swear I will get me a garret again,
And adore, like a Parsee, the sunset's fires,
And lure the Goddess, by vigil and pain,
Up with the sparrows among the spires.

For a man should live in a garret aloof,
And have few friends, and go poorly clad,
With an old hat stopping the chink in the roof,
To keep the Goddess constant and glad.

*Thomas Bailey Aldrich* [1837–1907]

## THE SOVEREIGNS

THEY who create rob death of half its stings;
Their life is given for the Muse's sake;
Of thought they build their palaces, and make
Enduring entities and beauteous things;
They are the Poets—they give airy wings
To shapes marmorean; or they overtake
The Ideal with the brush, or, soaring, wake
Far in the rolling clouds their glorious strings.
The Poet is the only potentate;
His sceptre reaches o'er remotest zones;
His thought remembered and his golden tones
Shall, in the ears of nations uncreate,
Roll on for ages and reverberate
When Kings are dust beside forgotten thrones.

*Lloyd Mifflin* [1846–1921]

## THE ARGUMENT OF HIS BOOK

I SING of brooks, of blossoms, birds, and bowers,
Of April, May, of June, and July flowers;
I sing of May-poles, hock-carts, wassails, wakes,
Of bridegrooms, brides, and of their bridal cakes.
I write of Youth, of Love, and have access
By these, to sing of cleanly wantonness;
I sing of dews, of rains, and, piece by piece,
Of balm, of oil, of spice, and ambergris.
I sing of times trans-shifting; and I write
How roses first came red, and lilies white;

I write of groves, of twilights, and I sing
The court of Mab, and of the Fairy King.
I write of Hell; I sing, and ever shall,
Of Heaven, and hope to have it after all.

*Robert Herrick* [1591–1674]

## ENVOY

Go, little book, and wish to all
Flowers in the garden, meat in the hall,
A bit of wine, a spice of wit,
A house with lawns enclosing it,
A living river by the door,
A nightingale in the sycamore!

*Robert Louis Stevenson* [1850–1894]

## ENVOY

Go, songs, for ended is our brief, sweet play;
  Go, children of swift joy and tardy sorrow:
And some are sung, and that was yesterday,
  And some unsung, and that may be to-morrow.

Go forth; and if it be o'er stony way,
  Old joy can lend what newer grief must borrow:
And it was sweet, and that was yesterday,
  And sweet is sweet, though purchasèd with sorrow.

Go, songs, and come not back from your far way:
  And if men ask you why ye smile and sorrow,
Tell them ye grieve, for your hearts know To-day,
  Tell them ye smile, for your eyes know To-morrow.

*Francis Thompson* [1859?–1907]

## THE SONNET'S VOICE

### A METRICAL LESSON BY THE SEASHORE

Yon silvery billows breaking on the beach
Fall back in foam beneath the star-shine clear,
The while my rhymes are murmuring in your ear
A restless lore like that the billows teach;
For on these sonnet-waves my soul would reach

From its own depths, and rest within you, dear,
As, through the billowy voices yearning here,
Great nature strives to find a human speech.
A sonnet is a wave of melody:
From heaving waters of the impassioned soul
A billow of tidal music one and whole
Flows, in the "octave"; then, returning free,
Its ebbing surges in the "sestet" roll
Back to the deeps of Life's tumultuous sea.

*Theodore Watts-Dunton* [1836–1914]

## THE SONNET

A SONNET is a moment's monument,—
Memorial from the Soul's eternity
To one dead deathless hour. Look that it be,
Whether for lustral rite or dire portent,
Of its own arduous fulness reverent:
Carve it in ivory or in ebony,
As Day or Night may rule; and let Time see
Its flowering crest impearled and orient.
A Sonnet is a coin: its face reveals
The soul,—its converse, to what Power 'tis due:—
Whether for tribute to the august appeals
Of Life, or dower in Love's high retinue,
It serve; or, 'mid the dark wharf's cavernous breath,
In Charon's palm it pay the toll to Death.

*Dante Gabriel Rossetti* [1828–1882]

## THE SONNET

WHAT is a sonnet? 'Tis the pearly shell
That murmurs of the far-off murmuring sea;
A precious jewel carved most curiously;
It is a little picture painted well.
What is a sonnet? 'Tis the tear that fell
From a great poet's hidden ecstasy;
A two-edged sword, a star, a song,—ah me!
Sometimes a heavy-tolling funeral bell.
This was the flame that shook with Dante's breath,
The solemn organ whereon Milton played,

And the clear glass where Shakespeare's shadow falls;
A sea this is,—beware who ventureth!
For like a fiord the narrow floor is laid
Mid-ocean deep sheer to the mountain walls.

*Richard Watson Gilder* [1844-1909]

## THE SONNET

### I

The Sonnet is a fruit which long hath slept
And ripened on life's sun-warmed orchard-wall;
A gem which, hardening in the mystical
Mine of man's heart, to quenchless flame hath leapt;
A medal of pure gold art's nympholept
Stamps with love's lips and brows imperial;
A branch from memory's briar, whereon the fall
Of thought-eternalizing tears hath wept:
A star that shoots athwart star-steadfast heaven;
A fluttering aigrette of tossed passion's brine;
A leaf from youth's immortal missal torn;
A bark across dark seas of anguish driven;
A feather dropped from breast-wings aquiline;
A silvery dream shunning red lips of morn.

### II

There is no mood, no heart-throb fugitive,
No spark from man's imperishable mind,
No moment of man's will, that may not find
Form in the Sonnet; and thenceforward live
A potent elf, by art's imperative
Magic to crystal spheres of song confined:
As in the moonstone's orb pent spirits wind
'Mid dungeon depths day-beams they take and give.
Spare thou no pains; carve thought's pure diamond
With fourteen facets, scattering fire and light:—
Uncut, what jewel burns but darkly bright?
And Prospero vainly waves his runic wand,
If, spurning art's inexorable law,
In Ariel's prison-sphere he leave one flaw.

III

The Sonnet is a world, where feelings caught
In webs of phantasy, combine and fuse
Their kindred elements 'neath mystic dews
Shed from the ether round man's dwelling wrought;
Distilling heart's content, star-fragrance fraught
With influences from the breathing fires
Of heaven in everlasting endless gyres
Enfolding and encircling orbs of thought.
Our Sonnet's world hath two fixed hemispheres:
This, where the sun with fierce strength masculine
Pours his keen rays and bids the noonday shine;
That, where the moon and the stars, concordant powers,
Shed milder rays, and daylight disappears
In low melodious music of still hours.

*John Addington Symonds* [1840-1893]

## "SCORN NOT THE SONNET"

SCORN not the Sonnet; Critic, you have frowned,
Mindless of its just honors; with this key
Shakespeare unlocked his heart; the melody
Of this small lute gave ease to Petrarch's wound;
A thousand times this pipe did Tasso sound;
With it Camöens soothed an exile's grief;
The Sonnet glittered a gay myrtle leaf
Amid the cypress with which Dante crowned
His visionary brow; a glow-worm lamp,
It cheered mild Spenser, called from Faery-land
To struggle through dark ways; and, when a damp
Fell round the path of Milton, in his hand
The Thing became a trumpet, whence he blew
Soul-animating strains—alas, too few!

*William Wordsworth* [1770-1850]

## VENDOR'S SONG

MY songs to sell, good sir!
  I pray you buy.
Here's one will win a lady's tears,
  Here's one will make her gay,

Here's one will charm your true love true
  Forever and a day;
Good sir, I pray you buy!

*Oh, no, he will not buy.*

My songs to sell, sweet maid!
  I pray you buy.
This one will teach you Lilith's lore,
  And this what Helen knew,
And this will keep your gold hair gold,
  And this your blue eyes blue;
Sweet maid, I pray you buy!

*Oh, no, she will not buy.*

*If I'd as much money as I could tell,*
*I never would cry my songs to sell,*
*I never would cry my songs to sell.*

*Adelaide Crapsey* [1878–1914]

## THUNDERSTORMS

My mind has thunderstorms,
  That brood for heavy hours:
Until they rain me words;
  My thoughts are drooping flowers
And sulking, silent birds.

Yet come, dark thunderstorms,
  And brood your heavy hours;
For when you rain me words,
  My thoughts are dancing flowers
And joyful singing birds.

*William H. Davies* [1870–1940]

## GENIUS LOCI

Peace, Shepherd, peace! What boots it singing on?
  Since long ago grace-giving Phœbus died,
  And all the train that loved the stream-bright side
Of the poetic mount with him are gone

Beyond the shores of Styx and Acheron,
  In unexplorèd realms of night to hide.
  The clouds that strew their shadows far and wide
Are all of Heaven that visits Helicon.
Yet here, where never muse or god did haunt,
  Still may some nameless power of Nature stray,
Pleased with the reedy stream's continual chant
  And purple pomp of these broad fields in May.
The shepherds meet him where he herds the kine,
And careless pass him by whose is the gift divine.

*Margaret Woods* [1856–1945]

## THE RONDEAU

You bid me try, Blue Eyes, to write
A Rondeau. What! Forthwith?—To-night?
  Reflect. Some skill I have, 'tis true;
  But thirteen lines!—and rhymed on two!—
"Refrain," as well. Ah, hapless plight!

Still, there are five lines—ranged aright.
These Gallic bonds, I feared, would fright
  My easy Muse. They did, till you—
    You bid me try!

That makes them eight.—The port's in sight:
'Tis all because your eyes are bright!
  Now just a pair to end in "oo,"—
  When maids command, what can't we do!
Behold!—the Rondeau, tasteful, light,
    You bid me try!

*After the French of Voiture by Austin Dobson* [1840–1921]

## METRICAL FEET

### LESSON FOR A BOY

TROCHEE trips from long to short;
From long to long in solemn sort

Slow Spondee stalks; strong foot! yet ill able
Ever to come up with dactyl trisyllable.
Iambics march from short to long;—
With a leap and a bound the swift Anapæsts throng;
One syllable long, with one short at each side,
Amphibrachys hastes with a stately stride;—
First and last being long, middle short, Amphimacer
Strikes his thundering hoofs like a proud highbred racer.

*Samuel Taylor Coleridge* [1772–1834]

## ACCIDENT IN ART

WHAT painter has not with a careless smutch
Accomplished his despair?—one touch revealing
All he had put of life, thought, vigor, feeling,
Into the canvas that without that touch
Showed of his love and labor just so much
Raw pigment, scarce a scrap of soul concealing!
What poet has not found his spirit kneeling
A-sudden at the sound of such or such
Strange verses staring from his manuscript,
Written he knows not how, but which will sound
Like trumpets down the years? So Accident
Itself unmasks the likeness of Intent,
And even in blind Chance's darkest crypt
The shrine-lamp of God's purposing is found.

*Richard Hovey* [1864–1900]

## A SONG FOR ST. CECILIA'S DAY, 1687

FROM harmony, from heavenly harmony,
This universal frame began:
When nature underneath a heap
Of jarring atoms lay,
And could not heave her head,
The tuneful voice was heard from high,
"Arise, ye more than dead!"
Then cold, and hot, and moist, and dry,
In order to their stations leap,
And Music's power obey.

From harmony, from heavenly harmony,
This universal frame began:
From harmony to harmony
Through all the compass of the notes it ran,
The diapason closing full in Man.

What passion cannot Music raise and quell?
When Jubal struck the chorded shell,
His listening brethren stood around,
And, wondering, on their faces fell
To worship that celestial sound:
Less than a God they thought there could not dwell
Within the hollow of that shell
That spoke so sweetly and so well.
What passion cannot Music raise and quell?

The trumpet's loud clangor
Excites us to arms,
With shrill notes of anger,
And mortal alarms.
The double double double beat
Of the thundering drum
Cries Hark! the foes come;
Charge, charge, 'tis too late to retreat!

The soft complaining flute,
In dying notes, discovers
The woes of hopeless lovers,
Whose dirge is whispered by the warbling lute

Sharp violins proclaim
Their jealous pangs and desperation,
Fury, frantic indignation,
Depth of pains, and height of passion,
For the fair, disdainful dame.

But O, what art can teach,
What human voice can reach,
The sacred organ's praise?

Notes inspiring holy love,
Notes that wing their heavenly ways
To mend the choirs above.

Orpheus could lead the savage race;
And trees uprooted left their place,
Sequacious of the lyre;
But bright Cecilia raised the wonder higher:
When to her organ vocal breath was given,
An angel heard, and straight appeared
Mistaking Earth for Heaven.

GRAND CHORUS

As from the power of sacred lays
The spheres began to move,
And sung the great Creator's praise
To all the Blest above;
So when the last and dreadful hour
This crumbling pageant shall devour,
The trumpet shall be heard on high,
The dead shall live, the living die,
And Music shall untune the sky!

*John Dryden* [1631–1700]

## ALEXANDER'S FEAST, OR, THE POWER OF MUSIC; AN ODE IN HONOR OF ST. CECILIA'S DAY, 1697

I

'Twas at the royal feast for Persia won
By Philip's warlike son—
Aloft in awful state
The godlike hero sate
On his imperial throne;
His valiant peers were placed around,
Their brows with roses and with myrtles bound,
(So should desert in arms be crowned);
The lovely Thais by his side
Sate like a blooming Eastern bride
In flower of youth and beauty's pride:—

Happy, happy, happy pair!
None but the brave
None but the brave
None but the brave deserves the fair!

CHORUS—*Happy, happy, happy pair!*
*None but the brave*
*None but the brave*
*None but the brave deserves the fair!*

II

Timotheus, placed on high
Amid the tuneful choir,
With flying fingers touched the lyre:
The trembling notes ascend the sky
And heavenly joys inspire.
The song began from Jove
Who left his blissful seats above—
Such is the power of mighty love!
A dragon's fiery form belied the god;
Sublime on radiant spires he rode
When he to fair Olympia pressed,
And while he sought her snowy breast,
Then round her slender waist he curled,
And stamped an image of himself, a sovereign of the world.
—The listening crowd admire the lofty sound!
A present deity! they shout around:
A present deity! the vaulted roofs rebound:
With ravished ears
The monarch hears,
Assumes the god,
Affects to nod
And seems to shake the spheres.

CHORUS—*With ravished ears*
*The monarch hears,*
*Assumes the god,*
*Affects to nod*
*And seems to shake the spheres.*

III

The praise of Bacchus then the sweet musician sung,
Of Bacchus ever fair and ever young:
The jolly god in triumph comes!
Sound the trumpets, beat the drums!
Flushed with a purple grace
He shows his honest face:
Now give the hautboys breath; he comes, he comes!
Bacchus, ever fair and young,
Drinking joys did first ordain;
Bacchus' blessings are a treasure,
Drinking is the soldier's pleasure:
Rich the treasure,
Sweet the pleasure,
Sweet is pleasure after pain.

CHORUS—*Bacchus' blessings are a treasure,*
*Drinking is the soldier's pleasure:*
*Rich the treasure,*
*Sweet the pleasure,*
*Sweet is pleasure after pain.*

IV

Soothed with the sound, the king grew vain;
Fought all his battles o'er again,
And thrice he routed all his foes, and thrice he slew the slain!
The master saw the madness rise,
His glowing cheeks, his ardent eyes;
And, while he Heaven and Earth defied,
Changed his hand and checked his pride.
He chose a mournful Muse
Soft pity to infuse:
He sung Darius great and good,
By too severe a fate
Fallen, fallen, fallen, fallen,
Fallen from his high estate,
And weltering in his blood;
Deserted at his utmost need
By those his former bounty fed;

On the bare earth exposed he lies
With not a friend to close his eyes.
—With downcast looks the joyless victor sate,
Revolving, in his altered soul,
The various turns of Chance below;
And, now and then, a sigh he stole,
And tears began to flow.

CHORUS—*Revolving, in his altered soul,*
*The various turns of Chance below;*
*And, now and then, a sigh he stole,*
*And tears began to flow.*

V

The mighty master smiled to see
That love was in the next degree;
'Twas but a kindred-sound to move,
For pity melts the mind to love.
Softly sweet, in Lydian measures
Soon he soothed his soul to pleasures.
War, he sung, is toil and trouble,
Honor but an empty bubble;
Never ending, still beginning,
Fighting still, and still destroying;
If the world be worth thy winning,
Think, O think it worth enjoying:
Lovely Thais sits beside thee,
Take the good the gods provide thee!
—The many rend the skies with loud applause;
So Love was crowned, but Music won the cause.
The prince, unable to conceal his pain,
Gazed on the fair
Who caused his care,
And sighed and looked, sighed and looked,
Sighed and looked, and sighed again:
At length, with love and wine at once oppressed,
The vanquished victor sunk upon her breast.

CHORUS—*The prince, unable to conceal his pain,*
*Gazed on the fair*
*Who caused his care,*

*And sighed and looked, sighed and looked,*
*Sighed and looked, and sighed again:*
*At length, with love and wine at once oppressed,*
*The vanquished victor sunk upon her breast.*

VI

Now strike the golden lyre again:
A louder yet, and yet a louder strain!
Break his bands of sleep asunder
And rouse him, like a rattling peal of thunder.
Hark, hark! the horrid sound
Has raised up his head:
As awaked from the dead,
And amazed he stares around.
Revenge, revenge, Timotheus cries,
See the Furies arise!
See the snakes that they rear
How they hiss in their hair,
And the sparkles that flash from their eyes!
Behold a ghastly band,
Each a torch in his hand!
Those are Grecian ghosts, that in battle were slain
And unburied remain
Inglorious on the plain:
Give the vengeance due
To the valiant crew!
Behold how they toss their torches on high,
How they point to the Persian abodes
And glittering temples of their hostile gods.
—The princes applaud with a furious joy:
And the King seized a flambeau with zeal to destroy;
Thais led the way
To light him to his prey,
And, like another Helen, fired another Troy!

CHORUS—*And the King seized a flambeau with zeal to de-*
*stroy;*
*Thais led the way*
*To light him to his prey,*
*And, like another Helen, fired another Troy!*

VII

—Thus, long ago,
Ere heaving bellows learned to blow,
While organs yet were mute,
Timotheus, to his breathing flute
And sounding lyre,
Could swell the soul to rage, or kindle soft desire.
At last divine Cecilia came,
Inventress of the vocal frame;
The sweet enthusiast from her sacred store
Enlarged the former narrow bounds,
And added length to solemn sounds,
With Nature's mother-wit, and arts unknown before.
—Let old Timotheus yield the prize
Or both divide the crown;
He raised a mortal to the skies;
She drew an angel down!

GRAND CHORUS—*At last divine Cecilia came,*
*Inventress of the vocal frame;*
*The sweet enthusiast from her sacred store*
*Enlarged the former narrow bounds,*
*And added length to solemn sounds,*
*With Nature's mother-wit, and arts unknown before.*
*—Let old Timotheus yield the prize*
*Or both divide the crown;*
*He raised a mortal to the skies;*
*She drew an angel down!*

*John Dryden* [1631-1700]

## THE PASSIONS

### AN ODE FOR MUSIC

WHEN Music, heavenly maid, was young,
While yet in early Greece she sung,
The Passions oft, to hear her shell,
Thronged around her magic cell.

Exulting, trembling, raging, fainting,
Possessed beyond the Muse's painting;
By turns they felt the glowing mind
Disturbed, delighted, raised, refined:
Till once, 'tis said, when all were fired,
Filled with fury, rapt, inspired,
From the supporting myrtles round
They snatched her instruments of sound;
And, as they oft had heard apart
Sweet lessons of her forceful art,
Each (for madness ruled the hour),
Would prove his own expressive power.

First Fear his hand, its skill to try,
  Amid the chords bewildered laid,
And back recoiled, he knew not why,
  Even at the sound himself had made.

Next Anger rushed; his eyes, on fire,
  In lightnings owned his secret stings;
In one rude clash he struck the lyre,
  And swept with hurried hand the strings.

With woful measures wan Despair
  Low, sullen sounds his grief beguiled;
A solemn, strange, and mingled air;
  'Twas sad by fits, by starts 'twas wild.

But thou, O Hope, with eyes so fair,
  What was thy delightful measure?
Still it whispered promised pleasure,
  And bade the lovely scenes at distance hail!
Still would her touch the strain prolong,
  And from the rocks, the woods, the vale,
She called on Echo still, through all the song;
  And, where her sweetest theme she chose,
A soft responsive voice was heard at every close,
And Hope enchanted smiled, and waved her golden hair.

And longer had she sung,—but, with a frown,
Revenge impatient rose;
He threw his blood-stained sword in thunder down
And, with a withering look,
The war-denouncing trumpet took,
And blew a blast so loud and dread,
Were ne'er prophetic sounds so full of woe.
And ever and anon he beat
The doubling drum with furious heat;
And though sometimes, each dreary pause between,
Dejected Pity, at his side,
Her soul-subduing voice applied,
Yet still he kept his wild unaltered mien,
While each strained ball of sight seemed bursting from his head.

Thy numbers, Jealousy, to naught were fixed,
Sad proof of thy distressful state;
Of differing themes the veering song was mixed,
And now it courted Love, now raving called on Hate.

With eyes upraised, as one inspired,
Pale Melancholy sate retired,
And from her wild sequestered seat,
In notes by distance made more sweet,
Poured through the mellow horn her pensive soul:
And, dashing soft from rocks around,
Bubbling runnels joined the sound;
Through glades and glooms the mingled measure stole:
Or, o'er some haunted stream, with fond delay,
Round an holy calm diffusing,
Love of Peace and lonely musing,
In hollow murmurs died away.

But oh, how altered was its sprightlier tone,
When Cheerfulness, a nymph of healthiest hue,
Her bow across her shoulder flung,
Her buskins gemmed with morning dew,
Blew an inspiring air, that dale and thicket rung,
The hunter's call to faun and dryad known!

The oak-crowned sisters, and their chaste-eyed queen,
Satyrs, and sylvan boys, were seen,
Peeping from forth their alleys green;
Brown Exercise rejoiced to hear,
And Sport leapt up, and seized his beechen spear.

Last came Joy's ecstatic trial.
He, with viny crown advancing,
First to the lively pipe his hand addressed;
But soon he saw the brisk awakening viol,
Whose sweet entrancing voice he loved the best.
They would have thought, who heard the strain,
They saw in Tempe's vale her native maids
Amidst the vestal sounding shades,
To some unwearied minstrel dancing,
While, as his flying fingers kissed the strings,
Love framed with Mirth a gay fantastic round;
Loose were her tresses seen, her zone unbound,
And he, amidst his frolic play,
As if he would the charming air repay,
Shook thousand odors from his dewy wings.

O Music! sphere-descended maid,
Friend of Pleasure, Wisdom's aid!
Why, goddess, why, to us denied,
Lay'st thou thy ancient lyre aside?
As, in that loved Athenian bower,
You learned an all-commanding power,
Thy mimic soul, O Nymph endeared,
Can well recall what then it heard.
Where is thy native simple heart,
Devote to Virtue, Fancy, Art?
Arise, as in that elder time,
Warm, energic, chaste, sublime!
Thy wonders, in that godlike age,
Fill thy recording sister's page.—
'Tis said, and I believe the tale,
Thy humblest reed could more prevail,
Had more of strength, diviner rage,
Than all which charms this laggard age;

Even all at once together found,
Cecilia's mingled world of sound.
O bid our vain endeavors cease,
Revive the just designs of Greece:
Return in all thy simple state!
Confirm the tales her sons relate!

*William Collins* [1721-1759]

## TO MUSIC, TO BECALM HIS FEVER

Charm me asleep, and melt me so
With thy delicious numbers,
That, being ravished, hence I go
Away in easy slumbers.
Ease my sick head,
And make my bed,
Thou power that canst sever
From me this ill,
And quickly still,
Though thou not kill
My fever.

Thou sweetly canst convert the same
From a consuming fire
Into a gentle-licking flame,
And make it thus expire.
Then make me weep
My pains asleep;
And give me such reposes
That I, poor I,
May think thereby
I live and die
'Mongst roses.

Fall on me like a silent dew,
Or like those maiden showers
Which, by the peep of day, do strew
A baptism o'er the flowers.
Melt, melt my pains
With thy soft strains;

That, having ease me given,
With full delight
I leave this light,
And take my flight
For Heaven.

*Robert Herrick* [1591–1674]

## A MUSICAL INSTRUMENT

WHAT was he doing, the great god Pan,
Down in the reeds by the river?
Spreading ruin and scattering ban,
Splashing and paddling with hoofs of a goat,
And breaking the golden lilies afloat
With the dragon-fly on the river.

He tore out a reed, the great god Pan,
From the deep cool bed of the river:
The limpid water turbidly ran,
And the broken lilies a-dying lay,
And the dragon-fly had fled away,
Ere he brought it out of the river.

High on the shore sat the great god Pan,
While turbidly flowed the river;
And hacked and hewed as a great god can,
With his hard bleak steel at the patient reed,
Till there was not a sign of a leaf indeed
To prove it fresh from the river.

He cut it short, did the great god Pan,
(How tall it stood in the river!)
Then drew the pith, like the heart of a man,
Steadily from the outside ring,
And notched the poor dry empty thing
In holes, as he sat by the river.

"This is the way," laughed the great god Pan,
(Laughed while he sat by the river,)
"The only way, since gods began

To make sweet music, they could succeed."
Then, dropping his mouth to a hole in the reed,
He blew in power by the river.

Sweet, sweet, sweet, O Pan!
Piercing sweet by the river!
Blinding sweet, O great god Pan!
The sun on the hill forgot to die,
And the lilies revived, and the dragon fly
Came back to dream on the river.

Yet half a beast is the great god Pan,
To laugh as he sits by the river,
Making a poet out of a man:
The true gods sigh for the cost and pain,—
For the reed which grows nevermore again
As a reed with the reeds in the river.

*Elizabeth Barrett Browning* [1806–1861]

## AT A SOLEMN MUSIC

BLEST pair of Sirens, pledges of Heaven's joy,
Sphere-born harmonious Sisters, Voice and Verse!
Wed your divine sounds, and mixed power employ,
Dead things with inbreathed sense able to pierce,
And to our high-raised phantasy present
That undisturbèd Song of pure consent
Aye sung before the sapphire-colored throne
To Him that sits thereon,
With saintly shout and solemn jubilee;
Where the bright Seraphim in burning row
Their loud uplifted angel-trumpets blow;
And the Cherubic host in thousand choirs
Touch their immortal harps of golden wires,
With those just Spirits that wear victorious palms,
Hymns devout and holy psalms
Singing everlastingly:
That we on earth, with undiscording voice
May rightly answer that melodious noise;
As once we did, till disproportioned sin
Jarred against nature's chime, and with harsh din

Broke the fair music that all creatures made
To their great Lord, whose love their motion swayed
In perfect diapason, whilst they stood
In first obedience, and their state of good.
O may we soon again renew that Song,
And keep in tune with Heaven, till God ere long
To his celestial concert us unite,
To live with him, and sing in endless morn of light!

*John Milton* [1608–1674]

## WITH A GUITAR, TO JANE

Ariel to Miranda:—Take
This slave of Music, for the sake
Of him who is the slave of thee,
And teach it all the harmony
In which thou can'st, and only thou,
Make the delighted spirit glow,
Till joy denies itself again,
And, too intense, is turned to pain;
For by commission and command
Of thine own Prince Ferdinand,
Poor Ariel sends this silent token
Of more than ever can be spoken;
Your guardian spirit, Ariel, who,
From life to life, must still pursue
Your happiness;—for thus alone
Can Ariel ever find his own.
From Prospero's enchanted cell,
As the mighty verses tell,
To the throne of Naples, he
Lit you o'er the trackless sea,
Flitting on, your prow before,
Like a living meteor.
When you die, the silent Moon,
In her interlunar swoon,
Is not sadder in her cell
Than deserted Ariel.
When you live again on earth,
Like an unseen star of birth,

Ariel guides you o'er the sea
Of life from your nativity.
Many changes have been run
Since Ferdinand and you begun
Your course of love, and Ariel still
Has tracked your steps and served your will
Now, in humbler, happier lot,
This is all remembered not;
And now, alas! the poor sprite is
Imprisoned, for some fault of his,
In a body like a grave;—
From you he only dares to crave,
For his service and his sorrow,
A smile to-day, a song to-morrow.

The artist who this idol wrought
To echo all harmonious thought,
Felled a tree, while on the steep
The woods were in their winter sleep,
Rocked in that repose divine
On the wind-swept Apennine;
And dreaming, some of Autumn past,
And some of Spring approaching fast,
And some of April buds and showers,
And some of songs in July bowers,
And all of love; and so this tree—
Oh, that such our death may be!—
Died in sleep, and felt no pain,
To live in happier form again:
From which, beneath Heaven's fairest star,
The artist wrought this loved Guitar;
And taught it justly to reply
To all who question skilfully,
In language gentle as thine own;
Whispering in enamoured tone
Sweet oracles of woods and dells,
And summer winds in sylvan cells.
For it had learnt all harmonies
Of the plains and of the skies,

Of the forests and the mountains,
And the many-voicèd fountains;
The clearest echoes of the hills,
The softest notes of falling rills,
The melodies of birds and bees,
The murmuring of summer seas,
And pattering rain, and breathing dew,
And airs of evening; and it knew
That seldom-heard, mysterious sound
Which, driven on its diurnal round,
As it floats through boundless day,
Our world enkindles on its way.—
All this it knows; but will not tell
To those who cannot question well
The Spirit that inhabits it.
It talks according to the wit
Of its companions; and no more
Is heard than has been felt before,
By those who tempt it to betray
These secrets of an elder day:
But sweetly as its answers will
Flatter hands of perfect skill,
It keeps its highest, holiest tone
For our belovèd Jane alone.

*Percy Bysshe Shelley* [1792–1822]

## ODE

We are the music-makers,
  And we are the dreamers of dreams,
Wandering by lone sea-breakers,
  And sitting by desolate streams;
World-losers and world-forsakers,
  On whom the pale moon gleams:
Yet we are the movers and shakers
  Of the world for ever, it seems.

With wonderful deathless ditties
We build up the world's great cities,

And out of a fabulous story
  We fashion an empire's glory:
One man with a dream, at pleasure,
  Shall go forth and conquer a crown;
And three with a new song's measure
  Can trample an empire down.

We, in the ages lying
  In the buried past of the earth,
Built Nineveh with our sighing,
  And Babel itself with our mirth;
And o'erthrew them with prophesying
  To the old of the new world's worth;
For each age is a dream that is dying,
  Or one that is coming to birth.

A breath of our inspiration
Is the life of each generation;
  A wondrous thing of our dreaming
  Unearthly, impossible seeming—
The soldier, the king, and the peasant
  Are working together in one,
Till our dream shall become their present,
  And their work in the world be done.

They had no vision amazing
Of the goodly house they are raising;
  They had no divine foreshowing
  Of the land to which they are going:
But on one man's soul it hath broken,
  A light that doth not depart;
And his look, or a word he hath spoken,
  Wrought flame in another man's heart.

And therefore to-day is thrilling
With a past day's late fulfilling;
  And the multitudes are enlisted
  In the faith that their fathers resisted.

And, scorning the dream of tomorrow,
  And bringing to pass, as they may,
In the world, for its joy or its sorrow,
  The dream that was scorned yesterday.

But we, with our dreaming and singing,
  Ceaseless and sorrowless we!
The glory about us clinging
  Of the glorious futures we see,
Our souls with high music ringing:
  O men! it must ever be
That we dwell, in our dreaming and singing,
  A little apart from ye.

For we are afar with the dawning
  And the suns that are not yet high,
And out of the infinite morning
  Intrepid you hear us cry—
How, spite of your human scorning,
  Once more God's future draws nigh,
And already goes forth the warning
  That ye of the past must die.

Great hail! we cry to the comers
  From the dazzling unknown shore;
Bring us hither your sun and your summers,
  And renew our world as of yore;
You shall teach us your song's new numbers,
  And things that we dreamed not before:
Yea, in spite of a dreamer who slumbers.
  And a singer who sings no more.

*Arthur O'Shaughnessy* [1844–1881]

## MUSIC

THE God of Music dwelleth out of doors.
All seasons through his minstrelsy we meet,
Breathing by field and covert haunting-sweet:
From organ-lofts in forests old he pours
A solemn harmony: on leafy floors

To smooth Autumnal pipes he moves his feet,
Or with the tingling plectrum of the sleet
In Winter keen beats out his thrilling scores.
Leave me the reed unplucked beside the stream,
And he will stoop and fill it with the breeze;
Leave me the viol's frame in secret trees,
Unwrought, and it shall make a druid theme;
Leave me the whispering shell on Nereid shores:
The God of Music dwelleth out of doors.

*Edith M. Thomas* [1854-1925]

## ON MUSIC

Many love music but for music's sake,
Many because her touches can awake
Thoughts that repose within the breast half-dead,
And rise to follow where she loves to lead.
What various feelings come from days gone by!
What tears from far-off sources dim the eye!
Few, when light fingers with sweet voices play
And melodies swell, pause, and melt away,
Mind how at every touch, at every tone,
A spark of life hath glistened and hath gone.

*Walter Savage Landor* [1775-1864]

## MUSIC AT TWILIGHT

O Twilight, Twilight! evermore to hear
The wounded viols pleading to thy heart!
To dream we watch thy purple wings depart;
To wake, and know thy presence always near!

What dost thou on the pathway of the sun?
Abide thy sister Night, while grief so pure
Makes heaven and all its beauty seem too sure,
And all too certain her oblivion.

One star awakes to turn thee from the South.
Oh, linger in the shadows thou hast drawn,
Ere Night cast dew before the feet of Dawn,
Or Silence lay her kiss on Music's mouth!

*George Sterling* [1869-1926]

## THE KEY-BOARD

FIVE-AND-THIRTY black slaves,
Half-a-hundred white,
All their duty but to sing
For their Queen's delight,
Now with throats of thunder,
Now with dulcet lips,
While she rules them royally
With her finger-tips!

When she quits her palace,
All the slaves are dumb—
Dumb with dolor till the Queen
Back to Court is come:
Dumb the throats of thunder,
Dumb the dulcet lips,
Lacking all the sovereignty
Of her finger-tips.

Dusky slaves and pallid
Ebon slaves and white,
When the Queen was on her throne
How you sang to-night!
Ah, the throats of thunder!
Ah, the dulcet lips!
Ah, the gracious tyrannies
Of her finger-tips!

Silent, silent, silent,
All your voices now;
Was it then her life alone
Did your life endow?
Waken, throats of thunder!
Waken, dulcet lips!
Touched to immortality
By her finger-tips.

*William Watson* [1858–1935]

## A TOCCATA OF GALUPPI'S

Oh Galuppi, Baldassare, this is very sad to find!
I can hardly misconceive you; it would prove me deaf and blind;
But although I take your meaning, 'tis with such a heavy mind!

Here you come with your old music, and here's all the good it brings.
What, they lived once thus at Venice where the merchants were the kings,
Where St. Mark's is, where the Doges used to wed the sea with rings?

Ay, because the sea's the street there; and 'tis arched by . . . . what you call
. . . Shylock's bridge with houses on it, where they kept the carnival:
I was never out of England—it's as if I saw it all.

Did young people take their pleasure when the sea was warm in May?
Balls and masks begun at midnight, burning ever to mid-day,
When they made up fresh adventures for the morrow, do you say?

Was a lady such a lady, cheeks so round and lips so red,—
On her neck the small face buoyant, like a bell-flower on its bed,
O'er the breast's superb abundance where a man might base his head?

Well, and it was graceful of them—they'd break talk off and afford
—She, to bite her mask's black velvet—he, to finger on his sword,
While you sat and played Toccatas, stately at the clavichord?

What? Those lesser thirds so plaintive, sixths diminished, sigh on sigh,
Told them something? Those suspensions, those solutions—"Must we die?"
Those commiserating sevenths—"Life might last! we can but try!"

"Were you happy?"—"Yes"—"And are you still as happy?"—"Yes. And you?"
—"Then, more kisses!"—"Did *I* stop them, when a million seemed so few?"
Hark! the dominant's persistence, till it must be answered to!

So, an octave struck the answer. Oh, they praised you, I dare say!
"Brave Galuppi! that was music! good alike at grave and gay!
I can always leave off talking, when I hear a master play."

Then they left you for their pleasure: till in due time, one by one,
Some with lives that came to nothing, some with deeds as well undone,
Death came tacitly and took them where they never see the sun.

But when I sit down to reason, think to take my stand nor swerve,
While I triumph o'er a secret wrung from nature's close reserve,
In you come with your cold music, till I creep through every nerve.

Yes, you, like a ghostly cricket, creaking where a house was burned:
"Dust and ashes, dead and done with, Venice spent what Venice earned!
The soul, doubtless, is immortal—where a soul can be discerned.

"Yours for instance: you know physics, something of geology,
Mathematics are your pastime; souls shall rise in their degree;
Butterflies may dread extinction,—you'll not die, it cannot be!

"As for Venice and her people, merely born to bloom and drop,
Here on earth they bore their fruitage, mirth and folly were the crop:
What of soul was left, I wonder, when the kissing had to stop?

"Dust and ashes!" So you creak it, and I want the heart to scold.
Dear dead women, with such hair, too—what's become of all the gold
Used to hang and brush their bosoms? I feel chilly and grown old.

*Robert Browning* [1812–1889]

## ABT VOGLER

(AFTER HE HAS BEEN EXTEMPORIZING UPON THE MUSICAL INSTRUMENT OF HIS INVENTION)

WOULD that the structure brave, the manifold music I build,
Bidding my organ obey, calling its keys to their work,
Claiming each slave of the sound, at a touch, as when Solomon willed
Armies of angels that soar, legions of demons that lurk,
Man, brute, reptile, fly,—alien of end and of aim,
Adverse, each from the other heaven-high, hell-deep removed,—
Should rush into sight at once as he named the ineffable Name,
And pile him a palace straight, to pleasure the princess he loved!

Would it might tarry like his, the beautiful building of mine,
  This which my keys in a crowd pressed and importuned to raise!
Ah, one and all, how they helped, would dispart now and now combine,
  Zealous to hasten the work, heighten their master his praise!
And one would bury his brow with a blind plunge down to hell,
  Burrow awhile and build, broad on the roots of things,
Then up again swim into sight, having based me my palace well,
  Founded it, fearless of flame, flat on the nether springs.

And another would mount and march, like the excellent minion he was,
  Ay, another and yet another, one crowd but with many a crest,
Raising my rampired walls of gold as transparent as glass,
  Eager to do and die, yield each his place to the rest:
For higher still and higher (as a runner tips with fire,
  When a great illumination surprises a festal night—
Outlining round and round Rome's dome from space to spire)
  Up, the pinnacled glory reached, and the pride of my soul was in sight.

In sight? Not half! for it seemed, it was certain, to match man's birth,
  Nature in turn conceived, obeying an impulse as I;
And the emulous heaven yearned down, made effort to reach the earth,
  As the earth had done her best, in my passion, to scale the sky:
Novel splendors burst forth, grew familiar and dwelt with mine,
  Not a point nor peak but found and fixed its wandering star;
Meteor-moons, balls of blaze: and they did not pale nor pine,
  For earth had attained to heaven, there was no more near nor far.

Nay more; for there wanted not who walked in the glare
and glow,
Presences plain in the place; or, fresh from the Protoplast,
Furnished for ages to come, when a kindlier wind should
blow,
Lured now to begin and live, in a house to their liking at
last;
Or else the wonderful Dead who have passed through the
body and gone,
But were back once more to breathe in an old world worth
their new:
What never had been, was now; what was, as it shall be
anon;
And what is,—shall I say, matched both? for I was made
perfect too.

All through my keys that gave their sounds to a wish of my
soul,
All through my soul that praised as its wish flowed visibly
forth,
All through music and me! For think, had I painted the
whole,
Why, there it had stood, to see, nor the process so wonder-
worth.
Had I written the same, made verse—still, effect proceeds
from cause,
Ye know why the forms are fair, ye hear how the tale is
told;
It is all triumphant art, but art in obedience to laws,
Painter and poet are proud, in the artist-list enrolled:—

But here is the finger of God, a flash of the will that can,
Existent behind all laws, that made them, and, lo, they are!
And I know not if, save in this, such gift be allowed to man,
That out of three sounds he frame not a fourth sound
but a star.
Consider it well: each tone of our scale in itself is naught:
It is everywhere in the world—loud, soft, and all is said:
Give it to me to use! I mix it with two in my thought:
And there! Ye have heard and seen: consider and bow
the head!

Well, it is gone at last, the palace of music I reared;
  Gone! and the good tears start, the praises that come too slow;
For one is assured at first, one scarce can say that he feared,
  That he even gave it a thought, the gone thing was to go.
Never to be again! But many more of the kind
  As good, nay, better perchance: is this your comfort to me?
To me, who must be saved because I cling with my mind
  To the same, same self, same love, same God: ay, what was, shall be.

Therefore to whom turn I but to thee, the ineffable Name?
  Builder and maker, thou, of houses not made with hands!
What, have fear of change from thee who art ever the same?
  Doubt that thy power can fill the heart that thy power expands?
There shall never be one lost good! What was, shall live as before;
  The evil is null, is naught, is silence implying sound;
What was good shall be good, with, for evil, so much good more;
  On the earth the broken arcs; in the heaven a perfect round.

All we have willed or hoped or dreamed of good shall exist;
  Not its semblance, but itself; no beauty, nor good, nor power
Whose voice has gone forth, but each survives for the melodist
  When eternity affirms the conception of an hour.
The high that proved too high, the heroic for earth too hard,
  The passion that left the ground to lose itself in the sky,
Are music sent up to God by the lover and the bard;
  Enough that he heard it once: we shall hear it by and by.

And what is our failure here but a triumph's evidence
  For the fullness of the days? Have we withered or agonized?
Why else was the pause prolonged but that singing might issue thence?
  Why rushed the discords in, but that harmony should be prized?

Sorrow is hard to bear, and doubt is slow to clear,
Each sufferer says his say, his scheme of the weal and woe:
But God has a few of us whom he whispers in the ear;
The rest may reason and welcome: 'tis we musicians know.

Well, it is earth with me; silence resumes her reign:
I will be patient and proud, and soberly acquiesce.
Give me the keys. I feel for the common chord again,
Sliding by semitones till I sink to the minor,—yes,
And I blunt it into a ninth, and I stand on alien ground,
Surveying awhile the heights I rolled from into the deep;
Which, hark, I have dared and done, for my resting-place is found,
The C Major of this life: so, now I will try to sleep.

*Robert Browning* [1812–1889]

## HACK AND HEW

Hack and Hew were the sons of God
In the earlier earth than now:
One at his right hand, one at his left,
To obey as he taught them how.

And Hack was blind, and Hew was dumb,
But both had the wild, wild heart;
And God's calm will was their burning will,
And the gist of their toil was art.

They made the moon and the belted stars,
They set the sun to ride;
They loosed the girdle and veil of the sea,
The wind and the purple tide.

Both flower and beast beneath their hands
To beauty and speed outgrew,—
The furious, fumbling hand of Hack,
And the glorying hand of Hew.

Then, fire and clay, they fashioned a man,
And painted him rosy brown;
And God himself blew hard in his eyes:
"Let them burn till they smoulder down!"

And "There!" said Hack, and "There!" thought Hew,
"We'll rest, for our toil is done."
But "Nay," the Master Workman said,
"For your toil is just begun.

"And ye who served me of old as God
Shall serve me anew as man,
Till I compass the dream that is in my heart,
And perfect the vaster plan."

And still the craftsman over his craft,
In the vague white light of dawn,
With God's calm will for his burning will,
While the mounting day comes on,

Yearning, wind-swift, indolent, wild,
Toils with those shadowy two,—
The faltering, restless hand of Hack,
And the tireless hand of Hew.

*Bliss Carman* [1861–1929]

## ARS VICTRIX *

### IMITATED FROM THÉOPHILE GAUTIER

YES; when the ways oppose—
When the hard means rebel,
Fairer the work out-grows,—
More potent far the spell.

O POET, then, forbear
The loosely-sandalled verse,
Choose rather thou to wear
The buskin—strait and terse;

Leave to the tyro's hand
The limp and shapeless style;
See that thy form demand
The labor of the file.

* For the original of this poem see page 3842.

SCULPTOR, do thou discard
The yielding clay,—consign
To Paros marble hard
The beauty of thy line;—

Model thy Satyr's face
For bronze of Syracuse;
In the veined agate trace
The profile of thy Muse.

PAINTER, that still must mix
But transient tints anew,
Thou in the furnace fix
The firm enamel's hue;

Let the smooth tile receive
Thy dove-drawn Erycine;
Thy Sirens blue at eve
Coiled in a wash of wine.

All passes. ART alone
Enduring stays to us:
The Bust out-lasts the throne,—
The Coin, Tiberius;

Even the gods must go;
Only the lofty Rhyme
Not countless years o'erthrow,—
Not long array of time.

Paint, chisel, then, or write;
But, that the work surpass,
With the hard fashion fight,—
With the resisting mass.

*Austin Dobson* [1840–1921]

# FLOWER O' THE MIND

## TOM-A-BEDLAM'S POEM

FROM the hag and hungry goblin
That into rags would rend ye,
  And the spirits that stand
  By the naked man
In the Book of Moons, defend ye!
That of your five sound senses
You never be forsaken,
  Nor wander from yourself with Tom,
Abroad to beg your bacon.

With a thought I took for Maudlin,
And a cruse of cockle pottage
  With a thing thus tall,
  Sky bless you all,
I fell into this dotage.
I slept not since the Conquest,
Till then I never wakèd,
  Till the roguish boy of love where I lay
Me found and stripped me naked.

When I short have shorn my sow's face
And swigged my horny barrel,
  In an oaken inn
  I pawn my skin
As a suit of gilt apparel.
The Moon's my constant mistress,
And the lonely owl my marrow;
  The flaming drake and the night-crow make
Me music to my sorrow.

I know more than Apollo,
For oft, when he lies sleeping,
  I see the stars
  At mortal wars
And the rounded welkin weeping;
The Moon embrace her shepherd,
And the Queen of Love her warrior,
  While the first doth horn the star of morn,
And the next the heavenly farrier.

With an host of furious fancies
Whereof I am commander
  With a burning spear
  And a horse of air
To the wilderness I wander;
By a knight of ghosts and shadows
I summoned am to tourney
  Ten leagues beyond the wide world's end—
Methinks it is no journey

*Unknown*

## L'ALLEGRO

Hence loathèd Melancholy
Of Cerberus and blackest Midnight born,
In Stygian Cave forlorn
  'Mongst horrid shapes, and shrieks, and sights unholy!
Find out some uncouth cell,
  Where brooding Darkness spreads his jealous wings,
And the night-Raven sings;
  There, under Ebon shades, and low-browed Rocks,
As ragged as thy Locks,
  In dark Cimmerian desert ever dwell.
But come, thou Goddess fair and free,
In Heaven yclept Euphrosyne,
And by men, heart-easing Mirth,
Whom lovely Venus, at a birth,
With two sister Graces more,
To Ivy-crownèd Bacchus bore;
Or whether (as some Sager sing)
The frolic Wind that breathes the Spring,
Zephir with Aurora playing,
As he met her once a-Maying,
There, on Beds of Violets blue,
And fresh-blown Roses washed in dew,
Filled her with thee, a daughter fair,
So buxom, blithe, and debonair.
  Haste thee, Nymph, and bring with thee
Jest and youthful Jollity,

Quips and Cranks, and wanton Wiles,
Nods, and Becks, and Wreathèd Smiles,
Such as hang on Hebe's cheek,
And love to live in dimple sleek;
Sport that wrinkled Care derides,
And Laughter holding both his sides.
Come, and trip it as ye go
On the light fantastic toe,
And in thy right hand lead with thee,
The Mountain Nymph, sweet Liberty;
And if I give thee honor due,
Mirth, admit me of thy crew
To live with her, and live with thee,
In unreprovèd pleasures free;
To hear the Lark begin his flight,
And, singing, startle the dull night,
From his watch-tower in the skies,
Till the dappled dawn doth rise;
Then to come in spite of sorrow,
And at my window bid good-morrow,
Through the Sweet-Briar, or the Vine,
Or the twisted Eglantine.
While the Cock, with lively din,
Scatters the rear of darkness thin,
And to the stack, or the Barn-door,
Stoutly struts his Dames before,
Oft listening how the Hounds and horn
Clearly rouse the slumbering morn,
From the side of some Hoar Hill,
Through the high wood echoing shrill.
Some time walking not unseen
By Hedge-row Elms, on Hillocks green,
Right against the Eastern gate,
Where the great Sun begins his state,
Robed in flames, and Amber light,
The clouds in thousand Liveries dight.
While the Plowman, near at hand,
Whistles o'er the Furrowed Land,
And the Milkmaid singeth blithe,
And the Mower whets his scythe,

And every Shepherd tells his tale
Under the Hawthorn in the dale.
Straight mine eye hath caught new pleasures
Whilst the Landscape round it measures,
Russet Lawns, and Fallows Gray,
Where the nibbling flocks do stray,
Mountains on whose barren breast
The laboring clouds do often rest:
Meadows trim with Daisies pied,
Shallow Brooks, and Rivers wide.
Towers, and Battlements it sees
Bosomed high in tufted Trees,
Where perhaps some beauty lies,
The Cynosure of neighboring eyes.
Hard by a Cottage chimney smokes,
From betwixt two aged Oaks,
Where Corydon and Thyrsis met.
Are at their savory dinner set
Of Herbs, and other Country Messes,
Which the neat-handed Phillis dresses;
And then in haste her Bower she leaves,
With Thestylis to bind the Sheaves;
Or, if the earlier season lead,
To the tanned Haycock in the Mead.
Sometimes with secure delight
The up-land Hamlets will invite,
When the merry Bells ring round,
And the jocund rebecks sound
To many a youth, and many a maid,
Dancing in the Chequered shade;
And young and old come forth to play
On a Sunshine Holyday,
Till the live-long day-light fail;
Then to the Spicy Nut-brown Ale,
With stories told of many a feat,
How Faery Mab the junkets eat.
She was pinched, and pulled she said;
And he, by Friar's Lantern led,
Tells how the drudging Goblin sweat.
To earn his Cream-bowl duly set,

When in one night, ere glimpse of morn,
His shadowy Flail hath threshed the Corn
That ten day-laborers could not end,
Then lies him down, the Lubbar Fiend,
And stretched out all the Chimney's length,
Basks at the fire his hairy strength;
And Crop-full out of doors he flings,
Ere the first Cock his Matin rings.
Thus done the Tales, to bed they creep,
By whispering Winds soon lulled asleep.
  Towered Cities please us then,
And the busy hum of men,
Where throngs of Knights and Barons bold,
In weeds of Peace high triumphs hold,
With store of Ladies, whose bright eyes
Rain influence, and judge the prize
Of Wit, or Arms, while both contend
To win her Grace, whom all commend.
There let Hymen oft appear
In Saffron robe, with Taper clear,
And pomp, and feast, and revelry,
With mask, and antique Pageantry,
Such sights as youthful Poets dream
On Summer eves by haunted stream.
Then to the well-trod stage anon,
If Jonson's learnèd Sock be on,
Or sweetest Shakespeare, Fancy's child,
Warble his native Wood-notes wild;
And ever, against eating Cares,
Lap me in soft Lydian Airs,
Married to immortal verse
Such as the meeting soul may pierce
In notes, with many a winding bout
Of linkèd sweetness long drawn out,
With wanton heed, and giddy cunning,
The melting voice through mazes running;
Untwisting all the chains that tie
The hidden soul of harmony;
That Orpheus' self may heave his head
From golden slumber on a bed

Of heaped Elysian flowers, and hear
Such strains as would have won the ear
Of Pluto, to have quite set free
His half-regained Eurydice.
These delights, if thou canst give,
Mirth, with thee I mean to live.

*John Milton* [1608-1674]

## IL PENSEROSO

HENCE vain deluding Joys,
The brood of Folly without father bred!
How little you bestead,
Or fill the fixèd mind with all your toys;
Dwell in some idle brain,
And fancies fond with gaudy shapes possess,
As thick and numberless
As the gay motes that people the sun-beams,
Or likest hovering dreams
The fickle Pensioners of Morpheus' train.
But hail, thou Goddess, sage and holy,
Hail, divinest Melancholy!
Whose Saintly visage is too bright
To hit the Sense of human sight;
And therefore to our weaker view,
O'er-laid with black, staid Wisdom's hue.
Black, but such as in esteem,
Prince Memnon's sister might beseem,
Or that Starred Ethiope Queen that strove
To set her beauty's praise above
The Sea Nymphs, and their powers offended.
Yet thou art higher far descended:
Thee bright-haired Vesta long of yore,
To solitary Saturn bore;
His daughter she (in Saturn's reign,
Such mixture was not held a stain).
Oft in glimmering Bowers, and glades
He met her, and in secret shades
Of woody Ida's inmost grove,
Whilst yet there was no fear of Jove.

Come, pensive Nun, devout and pure,
Sober, steadfast, and demure,
All in a robe of darkest grain,
Flowing with majestic train,
And sable stole of Cypress Lawn,
Over thy decent shoulders drawn.
Come, but keep thy wonted state,
With even step, and musing gait,
And looks commercing with the skies,
Thy rapt soul sitting in thine eyes:
There, held in holy passion still,
Forget thy self to Marble, till
With a sad Leaden downward cast,
Thou fix them on the earth as fast.
And join with thee calm Peace, and Quiet,
Spare Fast, that oft with gods doth diet,
And hears the Muses in a ring,
Aye round about Jove's Altar sing.
And add to these retirèd Leisure,
That in trim Gardens takes his pleasure;
But first, and chiefest, with thee bring,
Him that yon soars on golden wing,
Guiding the fiery-wheelèd throne,
The Cherub Contemplation,
And the mute Silence hist along,
'Less Philomel will deign a Song,
In her sweetest, saddest plight,
Smoothing the rugged brow of Night,
While Cynthia checks her Dragon yoke,
Gently o'er th' accustomed Oak;
Sweet Bird, that shunn'st the noise of folly,
Most musical, most melancholy!
Thee, Chauntress, oft the Woods among,
I woo to hear thy even-song;
And missing thee, I walk unseen
On the dry smooth-shaven Green,
To behold the wandering Moon,
Riding near her highest noon,
Like one that had been led astray
Through the Heaven's wide pathless way;

And oft, as if her head she bowed,
Stooping through a fleecy cloud.
Oft on a Plat of rising ground,
I hear the far-off Curfew sound,
Over some wide-watered shore,
Swinging slow with sullen roar;
Or if the Air will not permit,
Some still removèd place will fit,
Where glowing Embers through the room
Teach light to counterfeit a gloom,
Far from all resort of mirth,
Save the Cricket on the hearth,
Or the Bellman's drowsy charm,
To bless the doors from nightly harm:
Or let my Lamp, at midnight hour,
Be seen in some high lonely Tower,
Where I may oft out-watch the Bear,
With thrice great Hermes, or unsphere
The spirit of Plato to unfold
What Worlds, or what vast Regions hold
The immortal mind that hath forsook
Her mansion in this fleshly nook:
And of those Dæmons that are found
In fire, air, flood, or under ground,
Whose power hath a true consent
With Planet, or with Element.
Some time let Gorgeous Tragedy
In Sceptered Pall come sweeping by,
Presenting Thebes, or Pelops' line,
Or the tale of Troy divine,
Or what (though rare) of later age,
Ennoblèd hath the Buskined stage.
But, O sad Virgin, that thy power
Might raise Musæus from his bower,
Or bid the soul of Orpheus sing
Such notes as, warbled to the string,
Drew Iron tears down Pluto's cheek,
And made Hell grant what Love did seek.
Or call up him that left half told
The story of Cambuscan bold,

Of Camball, and of Algarsife,
And who had Canace to wife,
That owned the virtuous Ring and Glass,
And of the wondrous Horse of Brass,
On which the Tartar King did ride;
And if aught else great Bards beside,
In sage and solemn tunes have sung,
Of Tourneys and of Trophies hung;
Of Forests, and enchantments drear,
Where more is meant than meets the ear.
Thus, Night, oft see me in thy pale career,
Till civil-suited Morn appear,
Not tricked and frounced as she was wont,
With the Attic Boy to hunt,
But Kerchiefed in a comely Cloud,
While rocking Winds are Piping loud,
Or ushered with a shower still,
When the gust hath blown his fill,
Ending on the rustling Leaves,
With minute-drops from off the Eaves.
And when the Sun begins to fling
His flaring beams, me, Goddess, bring
To archèd walks of twilight groves,
And shadows brown, that Sylvan loves,
Of Pine, or monumental Oak,
Where the rude Ax with heavèd stroke,
Was never heard the Nymphs to daunt,
Or fright them from their hallowed haunt.
There in close covert by some Brook,
Where no profaner eye may look,
Hide me from Day's garish eye,
While the Bee with Honied thigh,
That at her flowery work doth sing,
And the Waters murmuring
With such consort as they keep,
Entice the dewy-feathered Sleep;
And let some strange mysterious dream,
Wave at his Wings, in Airy stream
Of lively portraiture displayed,
Softly on my eye-lids laid.

And as I wake, sweet music breathe
Above, about, or underneath,
Sent by some Spirit to mortals good,
Or th' unseen Genius of the Wood.
But let my due feet never fail,
To walk the studious Cloister's pale,
And love the high embowèd Roof,
With antique Pillars massy proof,
And storied Windows richly dight.
Casting a dim religious light.
There let the pealing Organ blow,
To the full voiced choir below,
In Service high, and Anthems clear,
As may with sweetness, through mine ear,
Dissolve me into ecstasies,
And bring all Heaven before mine eyes.
And may at last my weary age
Find out the peaceful hermitage,
The Hairy Gown and Mossy Cell,
Where I may sit and rightly spell
Of every Star that Heaven doth shew,
And every Herb that sips the dew;
Till old experience do attain
To something like Prophetic strain.
These pleasures, Melancholy, give,
And I with thee will choose to live.

*John Milton* [1608-1674]

## KILMENY

From "The Queen's Wake"

BONNY Kilmeny gaed up the glen;
But it wasna to meet Duneira's men,
Nor the rosy monk of the isle to see,
For Kilmeny was pure as pure could be.
It was only to hear the yorlin sing,
And pu' the cress-flower round the spring;—
The scarlet hypp, and the hind-berrye,
And the nut that hung frae the hazel-tree;
For Kilmeny was pure as pure could be.

But lang may her minny look o'er the wa',
And lang may she seek i' the green-wood shaw;
Lang the laird o' Duneira blame,
And lang, lang greet or Kilmeny come hame!

When many a day had come and fled,
When grief grew calm, and hope was dead,
When mass for Kilmeny's soul had been sung,
When the bedesman had prayed, and the dead-bell rung:
Late, late in a gloamin', when all was still,
When the fringe was red on the westlin hill,
The wood was sere, the moon i' the wane,
The reek o' the cot hung over the plain,
Like a little wee cloud in the world its lane;
When the ingle lowed wi' an eiry leme,
Late, late in the gloamin' Kilmeny came hame!

"Kilmeny, Kilmeny, where have you been?
Lang hae we sought baith holt and den;
By burn, by ford, by green-wood tree,
Yet you are halesome and fair to see.
Where gat ye that joup o' the lily sheen?
That bonny snood o' the birk sae green?
And those roses, the fairest that ever was seen?
Kilmeny, Kilmeny, where have you been?"

Kilmeny looked up wi' a lovely grace,
But nae smile was seen on Kilmeny's face;
As still was her look, and as still was her e'e,
As the stillness that lay on the emerant lea,
Or the mist that sleeps on a waveless sea.
For Kilmeny had been she knew not where,
And Kilmeny had seen what she could not declare;
Kilmeny had been where the cock never crew,
Where the rain never fell, and the wind never blew;
But it seemed as the harp of the sky had rung,
And the airs of heaven played round her tongue,
When she spake of the lovely forms she had seen,
And a land where sin had never been;
A land of love, and a land of light,
Withouten sun, or moon, or night;

Where the river swa'd a living stream,
And the light a pure celestial beam;
The land of vision, it would seem,
A still, an everlasting dream.

In yon green-wood there is a waik,
And in that waik there is a wene,
And in that wene there is a maike,
That neither has flesh, nor blood, nor bane;
And down in yon green-wood he walks his lane

In that green wene Kilmeny lay,
Her bosom happed wi' the flowerets gay;
But the air was soft, and the silence deep,
And bonny Kilmeny fell sound asleep;
She kenned nae mair, nor opened her e'e,
Till waked by the hymns of a far countrye.

She woke on a couch of silk sae slim,
All striped wi' the bars of the rainbow's rim;
And lovely beings around were rife,
Who erst had travelled mortal life;
And aye they smiled, and 'gan to spier:
"What spirit has brought this mortal here?"

"Lang have I ranged the world wide,"
A meek and reverend fere replied;
"Baith night and day I have watched the fair
Eident a thousand years and mair.
Yes, I have watched o'er ilk degree,
Wherever blooms femenitye;
But sinless virgin, free of stain,
In mind and body, fand I nane.
Never, since the banquet of time,
Found I a virgin in her prime,
Till late this bonny maiden I saw,
As spotless as the morning snaw:
Full twenty years she has lived as free
As the spirits that sojourn in this countrye.
I have brought her away frae the snares of men,
That sin or death she never may ken."

They clasped her waist, and her hands sae fair;
They kissed her cheeks, and they kemmed her hair;
And round came many a blooming fere,
Saying, "Bonny Kilmeny, ye're welcome here!
Women are freed of the littand scorn;
O, blest be the day Kilmeny was born!
Now shall the land of the spirits see,
Now shall it ken, what a woman may be!
Many a lang year, in sorrow and pain,
Many a lang year through the world we've gane,
Commissioned to watch fair woman-kind,
For it's they who nurse the immortal mind.
We have watched their steps as the dawning shone,
And deep in the green-wood walks alone;
By lily bower and silken bed,
The viewless tears have been o'er them shed;
Have soothed their ardent minds to sleep,
Or left the couch of love to weep.
We have seen! we have seen! but the time maun come,
And the angels will weep at the day of doom!

"O, would the fairest of mortal kind
Aye keep these holy truths in mind,
That kindred spirits their motions see,
Who watch their ways with anxious e'e,
And grieve for the guilt of humanitye!
O, sweet to Heaven the maiden's prayer,
And the sigh that heaves a bosom sae fair!
And dear to Heaven the words of truth,
And the praise of virtue frae beauty's mouth!
And dear to the viewless forms of air
The minds that kythes as the body fair!

"O bonny Kilmeny! free frae stain,
If ever you seek the world again,
That world of sin, of sorrow and fear,
O, tell of the joys that are waiting here;
And tell of the signs you shall shortly see;
Of the times that are now, and the times that shall be."

They lifted Kilmeny, they led her away,
And she walked in the light of a sunless day;
The sky was a dome of crystal bright,
The fountain of vision, and fountain of light;
The emerald fields were of dazzling glow,
And the flowers of everlasting blow.
Then deep in the stream her body they laid,
That her youth and beauty never might fade;
And they smiled on Heaven, when they saw her lie
In the stream of life that wandered by.
And she heard a song,—she heard it sung,
She kenned not where; but sae sweetly it rung,
It fell on her ear like a dream of the morn,—
"O, blest be the day Kilmeny was born!
Now shall the land of the spirits see,
Now shall it ken, what a woman may be!
The sun that shines on the world sae bright,
A borrowed gleid frae the fountain of light;
And the moon that sleeks the sky sae dun,
Like a gouden bow, or a beamless sun,
Shall wear away, and be seen nae mair;
And the angels shall miss them, travelling the air.
But lang, lang after, baith night and day,
When the sun and the world have fled away,
When the sinner has gane to his waesome doom,
Kilmeny shall smile in eternal bloom!"

They bore her away, she wist not how,
For she felt not arm nor rest below;
But so swift they wained her through the light,
'Twas like the motion of sound or sight;
They seemed to split the gales of air,
And yet nor gale nor breeze was there.
Unnumbered groves below them grew;
They came, they passed, and backward flew,
Like floods of blossoms gliding on,
A moment seen, in a moment gone.
Ah, never vales to mortal view
Appeared like those o'er which they flew,

That land to human spirits given,
The lowermost vales of the storied heaven;
From thence they can view the world below,
And heaven's blue gates with sapphires glow,—
More glory yet unmeet to know.

They bore her far to a mountain green,
To see what mortal never had seen;
And they seated her high on a purple sward,
And bade her heed what she saw and heard,
And note the changes the spirits wrought;
For now she lived in the land of thought.—
She looked, and she saw nor sun nor skies,
But a crystal dome of a thousand dyes;
She looked, and she saw nae land aright,
But an endless whirl of glory and light;
And radiant beings went and came,
Far swifter than wind or the linkèd flame;
She hid her e'en frae the dazzling view;
She looked again, and the scene was new.

She saw a sun in a summer sky,
And clouds of amber sailing by;
A lovely land beneath her lay,
And that land had lakes and mountains gray:
And that land had valleys and hoary piles,
And marlèd seas, and a thousand isles;
Its fields were speckled, its forests green,
And its lakes were all of the dazzling sheen,
Like magic mirrors, where slumbering lay
The sun and the sky and the cloudlet gray,
Which heaved and trembled, and gently swung;
On every shore they seemed to be hung;
For there they were seen on their downward plain
A thousand times and a thousand again;
In winding lake and placid firth,
Little peaceful heavens in the bosom of earth.

Kilmeny sighed and seemed to grieve,
For she found her heart to that land did cleave;

She saw the corn wave on the vale;
She saw the deer run down the dale;
She saw the plaid and the broad claymore,
And the brows that the badge of freedom bore;
And she thought she had seen the land before.

She saw a lady sit on a throne,
The fairest that ever the sun shone on:
A lion licked her hand of milk,
And she held him in a leish of silk,
And a leifu' maiden stood at her knee,
With a silver wand and melting e'e;
Her sovereign shield, till love stole in,
And poisoned all the fount within.

Then a gruff, untoward bedesman came,
And hundit the lion on his dame;
And the guardian maid wi' the dauntless e'e,
She dropped a tear, and left her knee;
And she saw till the queen frae the lion fled,
Till the bonniest flower o' the world lay dead;
A coffin was set on a distant plain,
And she saw the red blood fall like rain.
Then bonny Kilmeny's heart grew sair,
And she turned away, and could look nae mair.

Then the gruff, grim carle girned amain,
And they trampled him down, but he rose again;
And he baited the lion to deeds of weir,
Till he lapped the blood to the kingdom dear;
And weening his head was danger-proof
When crowned with the rose and clover leaf,
He gowled at the carle, and chased him away
To feed wi' the deer on the mountain gray.
He gowled at the carle, and he gecked at heaven;
But his mark was set, and his arles given.
Kilmeny a while her e'en withdrew;
She looked again, and the scene was new.

She saw below her, fair unfurled,
One half of all the glowing world,

Where oceans rolled and rivers ran,
To bound the aims of sinful man.
She saw a people fierce and fell,
Burst frae their bounds like fiends of hell;
There lilies grew, and the eagle flew;
And she herked on her ravening crew,
Till the cities and towers were wrapped in a blaze,
And the thunder it roared o'er the lands and the seas.
The widows they wailed, and the red blood ran,
And she threatened an end to the race of man.
She never lened, nor stood in awe,
Till caught by the lion's deadly paw.
O, then the eagle swinked for life,
And brainzelled up a mortal strife;
But flew she north, or flew she south,
She met wi' the gowl of the lion's mouth.

With a mooted wing and waefu' maen,
The eagle sought her eiry again;
But lang may she cower in her bloody nest,
And lang, lang sleek her wounded breast,
Before she sey another flight,
To play wi' the norland lion's might.

But to sing the sights Kilmeny saw,
So far surpassing nature's law,
The singer's voice wad sink away,
And the string of his harp wad cease to play.
But she saw till the sorrows of man were by
And all was love and harmony;
Till the stars of heaven fell calmly away,
Like the flakes of snaw on a winter's day.

Then Kilmeny begged again to see
The friends she had left in her ain countrie,
To tell of the place where she had been,
And the glories that lay in the land unseen;
To warn the living maidens fair,
The loved of heaven, the spirits' care,
That all whose minds unmeled remain
Shall bloom in beauty when time is gane.

With distant music, soft and deep,
They lulled Kilmeny sound asleep;
And when she awakened, she lay her lane,
All happed wi' flowers in the green-wood wene.
When seven long years had come and fled,
When grief was calm, and hope was dead,
When scarce was remembered Kilmeny's name,
Late, late in a gloamin', Kilmeny came hame!
And O, her beauty was fair to see,
But still and steadfast was her e'e!
Such beauty bard may never declare,
For there was no pride nor passion there;
And the soft desire of maidens' e'en,
In that mild face could never be seen.
Her seymar was the lily flower,
And her cheek the moss-rose in the shower;
And her voice like the distant melody
That floats along the twilight sea.
But she loved to raike the lanely glen,
And keep afar frae the haunts of men;
Her holy hymns unheard to sing,
To suck the flowers and drink the spring.
But wherever her peaceful form appeared,
The wild beasts of the hills were cheered;
The wolf played blithely round the field;
The lordly byson lowed and kneeled;
The dun deer wooed with manner bland,
And cowered aneath her lily hand.
And when at eve the woodlands rung,
When hymns of other worlds she sung
In ecstasy of sweet devotion,
O, then the glen was all in motion!
The wild beasts of the forest came,
Broke from their bughts and faulds the tame,
And goved around, charmed and amazed;
Even the dull cattle crooned, and gazed,
And murmured, and looked with anxious pain
For something the mystery to explain.
The buzzard came with the throstle-cock,
The corby left her houf in the rock;

The blackbird alang wi' the eagle flew;
The hind came tripping o'er the dew;
The wolf and the kid their raike began;
And the kid, and the lamb, and the leveret ran;
The hawk and the hern attour them hung,
And the merle and the mavis forhooyed their young;
And all in a peaceful ring were hurled:
It was like an eve in a sinless world!

When a month and day had come and gane,
Kilmeny sought the green-wood wene;
There laid her down on the leaves sae green,
And Kilmeny on earth was never mair seen.
But O the words that fell frae her mouth
Were words of wonder, and words of truth!
But all the land were in fear and dread,
For they kendna whether she was living or dead.
It wasna her hame, and she couldna remain;
She left this world of sorrow and pain,
And returned to the land of thought again.

*James Hogg* [1770–1835]

## KUBLA KHAN

In Xanadu did Kubla Khan
A stately pleasure-dome decree:
Where Alph, the sacred river, ran
Through caverns measureless to man
Down to a sunless sea.
So twice five miles of fertile ground
With walls and towers were girdled round:
And there were gardens bright with sinuous rills,
Where blossomed many an incense-bearing tree;
And here were forests ancient as the hills,
Enfolding sunny spots of greenery.

But O! that deep romantic chasm which slanted
Down the green hill athwart a cedarn cover!
A savage place! as holy and enchanted
As e'er beneath a waning moon was haunted
By woman wailing for her demon-lover!

And from this chasm, with ceaseless turmoil seething,
As if this Earth in fast thick pants were breathing,
A mighty fountain momently was forced,
Amid whose swift half-intermitted burst
Huge fragments vaulted like rebounding hail,
Or chaffy grain beneath the thresher's flail:
And 'mid these dancing rocks at once and ever
It flung up momently the sacred river.
Five miles meandering with a mazy motion
Through wood and dale the sacred river ran,
Then reached the caverns measureless to man,
And sank in tumult to a lifeless ocean:
And 'mid this tumult Kubla heard from far
Ancestral voices prophesying war!

The shadow of the dome of pleasure
Floated midway on the waves;
Where was heard the mingled measure
From the fountain and the caves.
It was a miracle of rare device,
A sunny pleasure-dome with caves of ice!

A damsel with a dulcimer
In a vision once I saw:
It was an Abyssinian maid,
And on her dulcimer she played,
Singing of Mount Abora.
Could I revive within me
Her symphony and song,
To such a deep delight 'twould win me
That with music loud and long,
I would build that dome in air,
That sunny dome! those caves of ice!
And all who heard should see them there,
And all should cry, Beware! Beware!
His flashing eyes, his floating hair!
Weave a circle round him thrice,
And close your eyes with holy dread,
For he on honey-dew hath fed,
And drunk the milk of Paradise.

*Samuel Taylor Coleridge* [1772–1834]

## HYMN OF PAN

FROM the forests and highlands
We come, we come;
From the river-girt islands,
Where loud waves are dumb,
Listening my sweet pipings.
The wind in the reeds and the rushes,
The bees on the bells of thyme,
The birds on the myrtle bushes,
The cicale above in the lime,
And the lizards below in the grass,
Were as silent as ever old Tmolus was,
Listening my sweet pipings.

Liquid Penëus was flowing,
And all dark Tempe lay
In Pelion's shadow, outgrowing
The light of the dying day,
Speeded by my sweet pipings.
The Sileni, and Sylvans, and Fauns,
And the Nymphs of the woods and waves,
To the edge of the moist river-lawns,
And the brink of the dewy caves,
And all that did then attend and follow,
Were silent with love, as you now, Apollo,
With envy of my sweet pipings.

I sang of the dancing Stars,
I sang of the dædal Earth,
And of Heaven, and the giant wars,
And Love, and Death, and Birth.
And then I changed my pipings—
Singing how down the vale of Mænalus
I pursued a maiden, and clasped a reed:
Gods and men, we are all deluded thus;
It breaks in our bosom, and then we bleed.
All wept—as I think both ye now would,
If envy or age had not frozen your blood,
At the sorrow of my sweet pipings.

*Percy Bysshe Shelley* [1792–1822]

## ODE ON A GRECIAN URN

Thou still unravished bride of quietness,
Thou foster-child of Silence and slow Time,
Sylvan historian, who canst thus express
A flowery tale more sweetly than our rhyme:
What leaf-fringed legend haunts about thy shape
Of deities or mortals, or of both,
In Tempe or the dales of Arcady?
What men or gods are these? What maidens loth?
What mad pursuit? What struggle to escape?
What pipes and timbrels? What wild ecstasy?

Heard melodies are sweet, but those unheard
Are sweeter; therefore, ye soft pipes, play on;
Not to the sensual ear, but, more endeared,
Pipe to the spirit ditties of no tone:
Fair youth, beneath the trees, thou canst not leave
Thy song, nor ever can those trees be bare;
Bold Lover, never, never canst thou kiss,
Though winning near the goal—yet, do not grieve;
She cannot fade, though thou hast not thy bliss,
For ever wilt thou love, and she be fair!

Ah, happy, happy boughs! that cannot shed
Your leaves, nor ever bid the Spring adieu;
And, happy melodist, unwearièd,
For ever piping songs for ever new;
More happy love! more happy, happy love!
For ever warm and still to be enjoyed,
For ever panting and for ever young;
All breathing human passion far above,
That leaves a heart high-sorrowful and cloyed,
A burning forehead, and a parching tongue.

Who are these coming to the sacrifice?
To what green altar, O mysterious priest,
Lead'st thou that heifer lowing at the skies,
And all her silken flanks with garlands dressed?

What little town by river or sea-shore,
Or mountain-built with peaceful citadel,
Is emptied of its folk, this pious morn?
And, little town, thy streets for evermore
Will silent be; and not a soul, to tell
Why thou art desolate, can e'er return.

O Attic shape! fair attitude! with brede
Of marble men and maidens overwrought,
With forest branches and the trodden weed;
Thou, silent form! dost tease us out of thought
As doth eternity. Cold Pastoral!
When old age shall this generation waste,
Thou shalt remain, in midst of other woe
Than ours, a friend to man, to whom thou say'st,
" Beauty is truth, truth beauty,"—that is all
Ye know on earth, and all ye need to know.

*John Keats* [1795–1821]

## ODE TO PSYCHE

O GODDESS! hear these tuneless numbers, wrung
By sweet enforcement and remembrance dear,
And pardon that thy secrets should be sung
Even into thine own soft-conchèd ear:
Surely I dreamed to-day, or did I see
The wingèd Psyche with awakened eyes?
I wandered in a forest thoughtlessly,
And, on the sudden, fainting with surprise,
Saw two fair creatures, couchèd side by side
In deepest grass, beneath the whispering roof
Of leaves and trembled blossoms, where there ran
A brooklet, scarce espied:
'Mid hushed, cool-rooted flowers fragrant-eyed,
Blue, silver-white, and budded Tyrian,
They lay calm-breathing on the bedded grass;
Their arms embracèd, and their pinions too;
Their lips touched not, but had not bade adieu,
As if disjoinèd by soft-handed slumber,
And ready still past kisses to outnumber

At tender eye-dawn of aurorean love:
The wingèd boy I knew;
But who wast thou, O happy, happy dove?
His Psyche true!

O latest-born and loveliest vision far
Of all Olympus' faded hierarchy!
Fairer than Phœbe's sapphire-regioned star,
Or Vesper, amorous glow-worm of the sky;
Fairer than these, though temple thou hast none,
Nor altar heaped with flowers;
Nor Virgin-choir to make delicious moan
Upon the midnight hours;
No voice, no lute, no pipe, no incense sweet
From chain-swung censer teeming;
No shrine, no grove, no oracle, no heat
Of pale-mouthed prophet dreaming.

O brightest! though too late for antique vows,
Too, too late for the fond believing lyre,
When holy were the haunted forest boughs,
Holy the air, the water, and the fire;
Yet even in these days so far retired
From happy pieties, thy lucent fans,
Fluttering among the faint Olympians,
I see, and sing, by my own eyes inspired.
So let me be thy choir, and make a moan
Upon the midnight hours!
Thy voice, thy lute, thy pipe, thy incense sweet
From swingèd censer teeming:
Thy shrine, thy grove, thy oracle, thy heat
Of pale-mouthed prophet dreaming.

Yes, I will be thy priest, and build a fane
In some untrodden region of my mind,
Where branchèd thoughts, new-grown with pleasant pain,
Instead of pines shall murmur in the wind:
Far, far around shall those dark-clustered trees
Fledge the wild-ridgèd mountains steep by steep;
And there by zephyrs, streams, and birds, and bees,
The moss-lain Dryads shall be lulled to sleep;

And in the midst of this wide quietness
A rosy sanctuary will I dress
With the wreathed trellis of a working brain,
With buds, and bells, and stars without a name,
With all the gardener Fancy e'er could feign,
Who, breeding flowers, will never breed the same;
And there shall be for thee all soft delight
That shadowy thought can win,
A bright torch, and a casement ope at night,
To let the warm Love in!

*John Keats* [1795-1821]

## TO FANCY

EVER let the Fancy roam,
Pleasure never is at home:
At a touch sweet Pleasure melteth,
Like to bubbles when rain pelteth;
Then let wingèd Fancy wander
Through the thought still spread beyond her:
Open wide the mind's cage-door,
She'll dart forth, and cloudward soar.
O sweet Fancy! let her loose;
Summer's joys are spoilt by use,
And the enjoying of the Spring
Fades as does its blossoming;
Autumn's red-lipped fruitage too,
Blushing through the mist and dew,
Cloys with tasting: What do then?
Sit thee by the ingle, when
The sear faggot blazes bright,
Spirit of a winter's night;
When the soundless earth is muffled,
And the cakèd snow is shuffled
From the ploughboy's heavy shoon;
When the Night doth meet the Noon
In a dark conspiracy
To banish Even from her sky.
Sit thee there, and send abroad,
With a mind self-overawed,

Fancy, high-commissioned:—send her!
She has vassals to attend her:
She will bring, in spite of frost,
Beauties that the earth hath lost;
She will bring thee, all together,
All delights of summer weather;
All the buds and bells of May,
From dewy sward or thorny spray;
All the heapèd Autumn's wealth,
With a still, mysterious stealth:
She will mix these pleasures up
Like three fit wines in a cup,
And thou shalt quaff it:—thou shalt hear
Distant harvest-carols clear;
Rustle of the reapèd corn;
Sweet birds antheming the morn:
And, in the same moment—hark!
'Tis the early April lark,
Or the rooks, with busy caw,
Foraging for sticks and straw.
Thou shalt, at one glance, behold
The daisy and the marigold;
White-plumed lilies, and the first
Hedge-grown primrose that hath burst;
Shaded hyacinth, alway
Sapphire queen of the mid-May;
And every leaf, and every flower
Pearlèd with the self-same shower.
Thou shalt see the field-mouse peep
Meagre from its cellèd sleep;
And the snake all winter-thin
Cast on sunny bank its skin;
Freckled nest-eggs thou shalt see
Hatching in the hawthorn-tree,
When the hen-bird's wing doth rest
Quiet on her mossy nest;
Then the hurry and alarm
When the bee-hive casts its swarm;
Acorns ripe down-pattering,
While the autumn breezes sing.

Oh, sweet Fancy! let her loose;
Every thing is spoilt by use:
Where's the cheek that doth not fade,
Too much gazed at? Where's the maid
Whose lip mature is ever new?
Where's the eye, however blue,
Doth not weary? Where's the face
One would meet in every place?
Where's the voice, however soft,
One would hear so very oft?
At a touch sweet Pleasure melteth
Like to bubbles when rain pelteth.
Let, then, wingèd Fancy find
Thee a mistress to thy mind:
Dulcet-eyed as Ceres' daughter,
Ere the God of Torment taught her
How to frown and how to chide;
With a waist and with a side
White as Hebe's, when her zone
Slipped its golden clasp, and down
Fell her kirtle to her feet,
While she held the goblet sweet,
And Jove grew languid.—Break the mesh
Of the Fancy's silken leash;
Quickly break her prison-string,
And such joys as these she'll bring.—
Let the wingèd Fancy roam,
Pleasure never is at home.

*John Keats* [1795-1821]

## THE HAUNTED PALACE

In the greenest of our valleys
By good angels tenanted,
Once a fair and stately palace—
Radiant palace—reared its head.
In the monarch Thought's dominion,
It stood there;
Never seraph spread a pinion
Over fabric half so fair.

Banners yellow, glorious, golden,
  On its roof did float and flow
(This—all this—was in the olden
  Time long ago),
And every gentle air that dallied,
  In that sweet day,
Along the ramparts plumed and pallid,
  A wingèd odor went away.

Wanderers in that happy valley
  Through two luminous windows saw
Spirits moving musically,
  To a lute's well-tunèd law,
Round about a throne where, sitting
  (Porphyrogene),
In state his glory well befitting,
  The ruler of the realm was seen.

And all with pearl and ruby glowing
  Was the fair palace door,
Through which came flowing, flowing, flowing,
  And sparkling evermore,
A troop of Echoes, whose sweet duty
  Was but to sing,
In voices of surpassing beauty,
  The wit and wisdom of their king.

But evil things, in robes of sorrow,
  Assailed the monarch's high estate;
(Ah, let us mourn, for never morrow
  Shall dawn upon him desolate!)
And round about his home, the glory
  That blushed and bloomed,
Is but a dim-remembered story
  Of the old time entombed.

And travelers now, within that valley,
  Through the red-litten windows see
Vast forms that move fantastically
  To a discordant melody;

While, like a ghastly rapid river,
  Through the pale door
A hideous throng rush out forever,
  And laugh—but smile no more.

*Edgar Allan Poe* [1809-1849]

## THE RAVEN

ONCE upon a midnight dreary, while I pondered, weak and weary,
Over many a quaint and curious volume of forgotten lore,—
While I nodded, nearly napping, suddenly there came a tapping,
As of some one gently rapping, rapping at my chamber door.
"'Tis some visitor," I muttered, "tapping at my chamber door:
  Only this and nothing more."

Ah, distinctly I remember it was in the bleak December,
And each separate dying ember wrought its ghost upon the floor.
Eagerly I wished the morrow;—vainly I had sought to borrow
From my books surcease of sorrow—sorrow for the lost Lenore,
For the rare and radiant maiden whom the angels name Lenore:
  Nameless here for evermore.

And the silken sad uncertain rustling of each purple curtain
Thrilled me—filled me with fantastic terrors never felt before;
So that now, to still the beating of my heart, I stood repeating,
"'Tis some visitor entreating entrance at my chamber door,
Some late visitor entreating entrance at my chamber door:
  This it is and nothing more."

Presently my soul grew stronger; hesitating then no longer,
"Sir," said I, "or Madam, truly your forgiveness I implore;
But the fact is I was napping, and so gently you came rapping,
And so faintly you came tapping, tapping at my chamber door,
That I scarce was sure I heard you"—here I opened wide the door:—
Darkness there and nothing more.

Deep into that darkness peering, long I stood there wondering, fearing,
Doubting, dreaming dreams no mortals ever dared to dream before;
But the silence was unbroken, and the stillness gave no token,
And the only word there spoken was the whispered word, "Lenore!"
This I whispered, and an echo murmured back the word, "Lenore!"
Merely this and nothing more.

Back into the chamber turning, all my soul within me burning,
Soon again I heard a tapping somewhat louder than before.
"Surely," said I, "surely that is something at my window lattice;
Let me see, then, what thereat is, and this mystery explore;
Let my heart be still a moment and this mystery explore;
'Tis the wind and nothing more."

Open here I flung the shutter, when, with many a flirt and flutter,
In there stepped a stately Raven of the saintly days of yore.
Not the least obeisance made he; not a minute stopped or stayed he;
But, with mien of lord or lady, perched above my chamber door,
Perched upon a bust of Pallas just above my chamber door:
Perched, and sat, and nothing more.

Then this ebony bird beguiling my sad fancy into smiling
By the grave and stern decorum of the countenance it wore,—
"Though thy crest be shorn and shaven, thou," I said, "art sure no craven,
Ghastly grim and ancient Raven wandering from the Nightly shore:
Tell me what thy lordly name is on the Night's Plutonian shore!"
Quoth the Raven, "Nevermore."

Much I marvelled this ungainly fowl to hear discourse so plainly,
Though its answer little meaning—little relevancy bore;
For we cannot help agreeing that no living human being
Ever yet was blessed with seeing bird above his chamber door,
Bird or beast upon the sculptured bust above his chamber door,
With such name as "Nevermore."

But the Raven, sitting lonely on the placid bust, spoke only
That one word, as if his soul in that one word he did outpour.
Nothing further then he uttered, not a feather then he fluttered,
Till I scarcely more than muttered,—"Other friends have flown before;
On the morrow *he* will leave me, as my Hopes have flown before."
Then the bird said, "Nevermore."

Startled at the stillness broken by reply so aptly spoken,
"Doubtless," said I, "what it utters is its only stock and store,
Caught from some unhappy master whom unmerciful Disaster
Followed fast and followed faster till his songs one burden bore:
Till the dirges of his Hope that melancholy burden bore
Of 'Never—nevermore.'"

But the Raven still beguiling all my sad soul into smiling,
Straight I wheeled a cushioned seat in front of bird and bust
and door;
Then, upon the velvet sinking, I betook myself to linking
Fancy unto fancy, thinking what this ominous bird of yore,
What this grim, ungainly, ghastly, gaunt, and ominous bird
of yore
Meant in croaking "Nevermore."

This I sat engaged in guessing, but no syllable expressing
To the fowl whose fiery eyes now burned into my bosom's
core;
This and more I sat divining, with my head at ease reclin-
ing
On the cushion's velvet lining that the lamplight gloated
o'er,
But whose velvet violet lining with the lamp-light gloating
o'er
*She* shall press, ah, nevermore!

Then, methought, the air grew denser, perfumed from an un-
seen censer
Swung by seraphim whose foot-falls tinkled on the tufted
floor.
"Wretch," I cried, "thy God hath lent thee—by these
angels he hath sent thee
Respite—respite and nepenthe from thy memories of Lenore!
Quaff, oh quaff this kind nepenthe, and forget this lost
Lenore!"
Quoth the Raven, "Nevermore."

"Prophet!" said I, "thing of evil! prophet still, if bird or
devil!
Whether Tempter sent, or whether tempest tossed thee here
ashore,
Desolate, yet all undaunted, on this desert land enchanted—
On this home by Horror haunted—tell me truly, I implore:
Is there—*is* there balm in Gilead?—tell me—tell me, I im-
plore!"
Quoth the Raven, "Nevermore."

"Prophet!" said I, "thing of evil! prophet still, if bird or devil!
By that Heaven that bends above us, by that God we both adore,
Tell this soul with sorrow laden if, within the distant Aidenn,
It shall clasp a sainted maiden whom the angels name Lenore:
Clasp a rare and radiant maiden whom the angels name Lenore!"
Quoth the Raven, "Nevermore."

"Be that word our sign of parting, bird or fiend!" I shrieked, upstarting·
"Get thee back into the tempest and the Night's Plutonian shore!
Leave no black plume as a token of that lie thy soul hath spoken!
Leave my loneliness unbroken! quit the bust above my door!
Take thy beak from out my heart, and take thy form from off my door!"
Quoth the Raven, "Nevermore."

And the Raven, never flitting, still is sitting, still is sitting
On the pallid bust of Pallas just above my chamber door;
And his eyes have all the seeming of a demon's that is dreaming,
And the lamp-light o'er him streaming throws his shadow on the floor;
And my soul from out that shadow that lies floating on the floor
Shall be lifted—nevermore!

*Edgar Allan Poe* [1809-1849]

## THE BELLS

I

HEAR the sledges with the bells,
Silver bells!
What a world of merriment their melody foretells!

How they tinkle, tinkle, tinkle,
In the icy air of night!
While the stars that oversprinkle
All the heavens seem to twinkle
With a crystalline delight;
Keeping time, time, time,
In a sort of Runic rhyme,
To the tintinabulation that so musically wells
From the bells, bells, bells, bells,
Bells, bells, bells—
From the jingling and the tinkling of the bells.

II

Hear the mellow wedding bells,
Golden bells!
What a world of happiness their harmony foretells!
Through the balmy air of night
How they ring out their delight!
From the molten-golden notes,
And all in tune,
What a liquid ditty floats
To the turtle-dove that listens, while she gloats
On the moon!
Oh, from out the sounding cells,
What a gush of euphony voluminously wells!
How it swells!
How it dwells
On the future; how it tells
Of the rapture that impels
To the swinging and the ringing
Of the bells, bells, bells,
Of the bells, bells, bells, bells,
Bells, bells, bells—
To the rhyming and the chiming of the bells!

III

Hear the loud alarum bells—
Brazen bells!
What a tale of terror, now, their turbulency tells

In the startled ear of night
How they scream out their affright!
Too much horrified to speak,
They can only shriek, shriek,
Out of tune,
In a clamorous appealing to the mercy of the fire,
In a mad expostulation with the deaf and frantic fire.
Leaping higher, higher, higher,
With a desperate desire,
And a resolute endeavor
Now, now to sit, or never,
By the side of the pale-faced moon.
Oh, the bells, bells, bells!
What a tale their terror tells
Of despair!
How they clang, and clash, and roar!
What a horror they outpour
On the bosom of the palpitating air!
Yet the ear it fully knows,
By the twanging,
And the clanging,
How the danger ebbs and flows;
Yet the ear distinctly tells,
In the jangling,
And the wrangling,
How the danger sinks and swells,
By the sinking or the swelling in the anger of the bells;
Of the bells—
Of the bells, bells, bells, bells,
Bells, bells, bells—
In the clamor and the clangor of the bells!

IV

Hear the tolling of the bells,
Iron bells!
What a world of solemn thought their melody compels!
In the silence of the night,
How we shiver with affright
At the melancholy menace of their tone!

For every sound that floats
From the rust within their throats,
Is a groan.
And the people—ah, the people,
They that dwell up in the steeple,
All alone.
And who tolling, tolling, tolling,
In that muffled monotone,
Feel a glory in so rolling
On the human heart a stone—
They are neither man nor woman,
They are neither brute nor human,
They are ghouls:
And their king it is who tolls;
And he rolls, rolls, rolls,
Rolls
A pæan from the bells!
And his merry bosom swells
With the pæan of the bells!
And he dances, and he yells;
Keeping time, time, time,
In a sort of Runic rhyme,
To the pæan of the bells,
Of the bells;
Keeping time, time, time,
In a sort of Runic rhyme,
To the throbbing of the bells;
Of the bells, bells, bells—
To the sobbing of the bells;
Keeping time, time, time,
As he knells, knells, knells,
In a happy Runic rhyme,
To the rolling of the bells;
Of the bells, bells, bells—
To the tolling of the bells,
Of the bells, bells, bells, bells,
Bells, bells, bells—
To the moaning and the groaning of the bells.

*Edgar Allan Poe* [1809-1849]

## THE LOTOS-EATERS

"COURAGE!" he said, and pointed toward the land,
"This mounting wave will roll us shoreward soon."
In the afternoon they came unto a land
In which it seemèd always afternoon.
All round the coast the languid air did swoon,
Breathing like one that hath a weary dream.
Full-faced above the valley stood the moon;
And, like a downward smoke, the slender stream
Along the cliff to fall and pause and fall did seem.

A land of streams! some, like a downward smoke,
Slow-dropping veils of thinnest lawn, did go;
And some through wavering lights and shadows broke,
Rolling a slumberous sheet of foam below.
They saw the gleaming river seaward flow
From the inner land: far off, three mountain-tops,
Three silent pinnacles of agèd snow,
Stood sunset-flushed; and, dewed with showery drops,
Up-clomb the shadowy pine above the woven copse.

The charmèd sunset lingered low adown
In the red West: through mountain clefts the dale
Was seen far inland, and the yellow down
Bordered with palm, and many a winding vale
And meadow, set with slender galingale;
A land where all things always seemed the same!
And round about the keel with faces pale,
Dark faces pale against that rosy flame,
The mild-eyed melancholy Lotos-eaters came.

Branches they bore of that enchanted stem,
Laden with flower and fruit, whereof they gave
To each, but whoso did receive of them
And taste, to him the gushing of the wave
Far, far away did seem to mourn and rave
On alien shores; and if his fellow spake,
His voice was thin, as voices from the grave;
And deep-asleep he seemed, yet all awake,
And music in his ears his beating heart did make.

They sat them down upon the yellow sand,
Between the sun and moon upon the shore;
And sweet it was to dream of Fatherland,
Of child, and wife, and slave; but evermore
Most weary seemed the sea, weary the oar,
Weary the wandering fields of barren foam.
Then some one said, "We will return no more;"
And all at once they sang, "Our island home
Is far beyond the wave; we will no longer roam."

*Alfred Tennyson* [1809-1892]

## ULYSSES

It little profits that an idle king,
By this still hearth, among these barren crags,
Matched with an agèd wife, I mete and dole
Unequal laws unto a savage race,
That hoard, and sleep, and feed, and know not me.
I cannot rest from travel: I will drink
Life to the lees. All times I have enjoyed
Greatly, have suffered greatly, both with those
That loved me, and alone; on shore, and when
Through scudding drifts the rainy Hyades
Vexed the dim sea. I am become a name;
For always roaming with a hungry heart
Much have I seen and known,—cities of men
And manners, climates, councils, governments,
Myself not least, but honored of them all;
And drunk delight of battle with my peers,
Far on the ringing plains of windy Troy.
I am part of all that I have met;
Yet all experience is an arch wherethrough
Gleams that untravelled world, whose margin fades
For ever and for ever when I move.
How dull it is to pause, to make an end,
To rust unburnished, not to shine in use!
As though to breathe were life. Life piled on life
Were all too little, and of one to me
Little remains: but every hour is saved

From that eternal silence, something more,
A bringer of new things; and vile it were
For some three suns to store and hoard myself,
And this gray spirit yearning in desire
To follow knowledge like a sinking star,
Beyond the utmost bound of human thought.
  This is my son, mine own Telemachus,
To whom I leave the sceptre and the isle—
Well-loved of me, discerning to fulfil
This labor, by slow prudence to make mild
A rugged people, and through soft degrees
Subdue them to the useful and the good.
Most blameless is he, centred in the sphere
Of common duties, decent not to fail
In offices of tenderness, and pay
Meet adoration to my household gods,
When I am gone. He works his work, I mine.
  There lies the port; the vessel puffs her sail:
There gloom the dark, broad seas. My mariners,
Souls that have toiled, and wrought, and thought with me—
That ever with a frolic welcome took
The thunder and the sunshine, and opposed
Free hearts, free foreheads—you and I are old;
Old age hath yet his honor and his toil;
Death closes all: but something ere the end,
Some work of noble note, may yet be done,
Not unbecoming men that strove with gods.
The lights begin to twinkle from the rocks:
The long day wanes: the slow moon climbs: the deep
Moans round with many voices. Come, my friends,
'Tis not too late to seek a newer world.
Push off, and sitting well in order smite
The sounding furrows; for my purpose holds
To sail beyond the sunset, and the baths
Of all the western stars, until I die.
It may be that the gulfs will wash us down:
It may be we shall touch the Happy Isles,
And see the great Achilles, whom we knew.
Though much is taken, much abides; and though
We are not now that strength which in old days

Moved earth and heaven; that which we are, we are;—
One equal temper of heroic hearts,
Made weak by time and fate, but strong in will
To strive, to seek, to find, and not to yield.

*Alfred Tennyson* [1809–1892]

## MORTE D'ARTHUR

So all day long the noise of battle rolled
Among the mountains by the winter sea;
Until King Arthur's table, man by man,
Had fallen in Lyonesse about their Lord,
King Arthur: then, because his wound was deep,
The bold Sir Bedivere uplifted him,
Sir Bedivere, the last of all his knights,
And bore him to a chapel nigh the field,
A broken chancel with a broken cross,
That stood on a dark strait of barren land.
On one side lay the ocean, and on one
Lay a great water, and the moon was full.
Then spake King Arthur to Sir Bedivere:
"The sequel of to-day unsolders all
The goodliest fellowship of famous knights
Whereof this world holds record. Such a sleep
They sleep—the men I loved. I think that we
Shall never more, at any future time,
Delight our souls with talk of knightly deeds,
Walking about the gardens and the halls
Of Camelot, as in the days that were.
I perish by this people which I made,—
Though Merlin sware that I should come again
To rule once more—but let what will be, be,
I am so deeply smitten through the helm,
That without help I cannot last till morn.
Thou therefore take my brand Excalibur,
Which was my pride: for thou rememberest how
In those old days, one summer noon, an arm
Rose up from out the bosom of the lake,
Clothed in white samite, mystic, wonderful,
Holding the sword—and how I rowed across
And took it, and have worn it, like a king:

And, wheresoever I am sung or told
In after time, this also shall be known:
But now delay not: take Excalibur,
And fling him far into the middle mere:
Watch what thou seest, and lightly bring me word."
  To him replied the bold Sir Bedivere:
"It is not meet, Sir King, to leave thee thus,
Aidless, alone, and smitten through the helm.
A little thing may harm a wounded man.
Yet I thy hest will all perform at full,
Watch what I see, and lightly bring thee word."
  So saying, from the ruined shrine he stepped
And in the moon athwart the place of tombs,
Where lay the mighty bones of ancient men,
Old knights, and over them the sea-wind sang
Shrill, chill, with flakes of foam. He, stepping down
By zigzag paths, and juts of pointed rock,
Came on the shining levels of the lake.
  There drew he forth the brand Excalibur,
And o'er him, drawing it, the winter moon,
Brightening the skirts of a long cloud, ran forth
And sparkled keen with frost against the hilt:
For all the haft twinkled with diamond sparks,
Myriads of topaz-lights, and jacinth-work
Of subtlest jewelery. He gazed so long
That both his eyes were dazzled, as he stood,
This way and that dividing the swift mind,
In act to throw: but at the last it seemed
Better to leave Excalibur concealed
There in the many-knotted water-flags,
That whistled stiff and dry about the marge.
So strode he back slow to the wounded king.
  Then spake King Arthur to Sir Bedivere:
"Hast thou performed my mission which I gave?
What is it thou hast seen? or what hast heard?"
  And answer made the bold Sir Bedivere:
"I heard the ripple washing in the reeds,
And the wild water lapping on the crag."
  To whom replied King Arthur, faint and pale:
"Thou hast betrayed thy nature and thy name,

Not rendering true answer, as beseemed
Thy fealty, nor like a noble knight:
For surer sign had followed, either hand,
Or voice, or else a motion of the mere.
This is a shameful thing for men to lie.
Yet now, I charge thee, quickly go again
As thou art lief and dear, and do the thing
I bade thee, watch, and lightly bring me word."

Then went Sir Bedivere the second time
Across the ridge, and paced beside the mere,
Counting the dewy pebbles, fixed in thought;
But when he saw the wonder of the hilt,
How curiously and strangely chased, he smote
His palms together, and he cried aloud,
"And if indeed I cast the brand away,
Surely a precious thing, one worthy note,
Should thus be lost forever from the earth,
Which might have pleased the eyes of many men.
What good should follow this, if this were done?
What harm, undone? deep harm to disobey,
Seeing obedience is the bond of rule.
Were it well to obey then, if a king demand
An act unprofitable, against himself?
The king is sick, and knows not what he does.
What record, or what relic of my lord
Should be to aftertime, but empty breath
And rumors of a doubt? but were this kept,
Stored in some treasure-house of mighty kings,
Some one might show it at a joust of arms,
Saying, 'King Arthur's sword, Excalibur,
Wrought by the lonely maiden of the lake;
Nine years she wrought it, sitting in the deeps
Upon the hidden bases of the hills.'
So might some old man speak in the aftertime
To all the people, winning reverence;
But now much honor and much fame were lost."

So spake he, clouded with his own conceit,
And hid Excalibur, the second time,
And so strode back slow to the wounded king.

Then spoke King Arthur, breathing heavily:

"What is it thou hast seen? or what hast heard?"
 And answer made the bold Sir Bedivere:
"I heard the water lapping on the crag
And the long ripple washing in the reeds."
 To whom replied King Arthur, much in wrath:
"Ah, miserable and unkind, untrue,
Unknightly, traitor-hearted! Woe is me!
Authority forgets a dying king,
Laid widowed of the power in his eye
That bowed the will. I see thee what thou art,
For thou, the latest-left of all my knights,
In whom should meet the offices of all,
Thou would'st betray me for the precious hilt;
Either from lust of gold, or like a girl
Valuing the giddy pleasure of the eyes.
Yet, for a man may fail in duty twice,
And the third time may prosper, get thee hence:
But, if thou spare to fling Excalibur,
I will arise and slay thee with my hands."
 Then quickly rose Sir Bedivere, and ran,
And, leaping down the ridges lightly, plunged
Among the bulrush-beds, and clutched the sword,
And strongly wheeled and threw it. The great brand
Made lightnings in the splendor of the moon,
And flashing round and round, and whirled in an arch,
Shot like a streamer of the northern morn,
Seen where the moving isles of winter shock
By night, with noises of the northern sea.
So flashed and fell the brand Excalibur:
But ere he dipped the surface, rose an arm,
Clothed in white samite, mystic, wonderful,
And caught him by the hilt, and brandished him
Three times, and drew him under in the mere.
And lightly went the other to the king.
 Then spoke King Arthur, drawing thicker breath:
"Now see I by thine eyes that this is done.
Speak out: what is it thou hast heard, or seen?"
 And answer made the bold Sir Bedivere:
"Sir King, I closed mine eyelids, lest the gems
Should blind my purpose, for I never saw,

Nor shall see, here or elsewhere, till I die,
Not though I live three lives of mortal men,
So great a miracle as yonder hilt.
Then with both hands I flung him, wheeling him;
But when I looked again, behold an arm,
Clothed in white samite, mystic, wonderful,
That caught him by the hilt, and brandished him
Three times, and drew him under in the mere."
And answer made King Arthur, breathing hard:
"My end draws nigh; 'tis time that I were gone.
Make broad thy shoulders to receive my weight,
And bear me to the margin; yet I fear
My wound hath taken cold, and I shall die."
So saying, from the pavement he half rose,
Slowly, with pain, reclining on his arm,
And looking wistfully with wide blue eyes
As in a picture. Him Sir Bedivere
Remorsefully regarded through his tears,
And would have spoken, but he found not words,
Then took with care, and kneeling on one knee,
O'er both his shoulders drew the languid hands,
And rising bore him through the place of tombs.
But, as he walked, King Arthur panted hard,
Like one that feels a nightmare on his bed
When all the house is mute. So sighed the king,
Muttering and murmuring at his ear, "Quick, quick!
I fear it is too late, and I shall die."
But the other swiftly strode from ridge to ridge,
Clothed with his breath, and looking, as he walked,
Larger than human on the frozen hills.
He heard the deep behind him, and a cry
Before. His own thought drove him like a goad.
Dry clashed his harness in the icy caves
And barren chasms, and all to left and right
The bare black cliff clanged round him, as he based
His feet on juts of slippery crag that rang
Sharp-smitten with the dint of armèd heels—
And on a sudden, lo! the level lake,
And the long glories of the winter moon.
Then saw they how there hove a dusky barge,

Dark as a funeral scarf from stem to stern,
Beneath them; and descending they were ware
That all the decks were dense with stately forms
Black-stoled, black-hooded, like a dream—by these
Three queens with crowns of gold—and from them rose
A cry that shivered to the tingling stars,
And, as it were one voice, an agony
Of lamentation, like a wind, that shrills
All night in a waste land, where no one comes,
Or hath come, since the making of the world.
  Then murmured Arthur, "Place me in the barge,"
And to the barge they came. There those three queens
Put forth their hands, and took the king, and wept.
But she that rose the tallest of them all
And fairest, laid his head upon her lap,
And loosed the shattered casque, and chafed his hands,
And called him by his name, complaining loud,
And dropping bitter tears against his brow
Striped with dark blood: for all his face was white
And colorless, and like the withered moon
Smote by the fresh beam of the springing east;
And all his greaves and cuisses dashed with drops
Of onset; and the light and lustrous curls—
That made his forehead like a rising sun
High from the dais-throne—were parched with dust;
Or, clotted into points and hanging loose,
Mixed with the knightly growth that fringed his lips.
So like a shattered column lay the king;
Not like that Arthur who, with lance in rest,
From spur to plume a star of tournament,
Shot through the lists at Camelot, and charged
Before the eyes of ladies and of kings.
  Then loudly cried the bold Sir Bedivere:
"Ah! my Lord Arthur, whither shall I go?
Where shall I hide my forehead and my eyes?
For now I see the true old times are dead,
When every morning brought a noble chance,
And every chance brought out a noble knight.
Such times have been not since the light that led
The holy Elders with the gift of myrrh.

But now the whole ROUND TABLE is dissolved
Which was an image of the mighty world;
And I, the last, go forth companionless,
And the days darken round me, and the years,
Among new men, strange faces, other minds."
And slowly answered Arthur from the barge:
"The old order changeth, yielding place to new,
And God fulfils Himself in many ways,
Lest one good custom should corrupt the world.
Comfort thyself: what comfort is in me?
I have lived my life, and that which I have done
May He within Himself make pure! but thou,
If thou shouldst never see my face again,
Pray for my soul. More things are wrought by prayer
Than this world dreams of. Wherefore, let thy voice
Rise like a fountain for me night and day.
For what are men better than sheep or goats
That nourish a blind life within the brain,
If, knowing God, they lift not hands of prayer
Both for themselves and those who call them friend?
For so the whole round earth is every way
Bound by gold chains about the feet of God.
But now farewell. I am going a long way
With these thou seest—if indeed I go—
For all my mind is clouded with a doubt—
To the island-valley of Avilion;
Where falls not hail, or rain, or any snow,
Nor ever wind blows loudly; but it lies
Deep-meadowed, happy, fair with orchard-lawns
And bowery hollows crowned with summer sea,
Where I will heal me of my grievous wound."
So said he, and the barge with oar and sail
Moved from the brink, like some full-breasted swan
That, fluting a wild carol ere her death,
Ruffles her pure cold plume, and takes the flood
With swarthy webs. Long stood Sir Bedivere
Revolving many memories, till the hull
Looked one black dot against the verge of dawn,
And on the mere the wailing died away.

*Alfred Tennyson* [1809–1892]

## THE LADY OF SHALOTT

### PART I

On either side the river lie
Long fields of barley and of rye,
That clothe the wold and meet the sky;
And through the field the road runs by
To many-towered Camelot;
And up and down the people go,
Gazing where the lilies blow
Round an island there below,
The island of Shalott.

Willows whiten, aspens quiver,
Little breezes dusk and shiver
Through the wave that runs for ever
By the island in the river
Flowing down to Camelot.
Four gray walls, and four gray towers,
Overlook a space of flowers,
And the silent isle embowers
The Lady of Shalott.

By the margin, willow-veiled,
Slide the heavy barges trailed
By slow horses; and unhailed
The shallop flitteth silken-sailed
Skimming down to Camelot:
But who hath seen her wave her hand?
Or at the casement seen her stand?
Or is she known in all the land,
The Lady of Shalott?

Only reapers, reaping early
In among the bearded barley,
Hear a song that echoes cheerly
From the river winding clearly,
Down to towered Camelot:

And by the moon the reaper weary,
Piling sheaves in uplands airy,
Listening, whispers "'Tis the fairy
Lady of Shalott."

PART II

There she weaves by night and day
A magic web with colors gay.
She has heard a whisper say,
A curse is on her if she stay
To look down to Camelot.
She knows not what the curse may be,
And so she weaveth steadily,
And little other care hath she,
The Lady of Shalott.

And moving through a mirror clear
That hangs before her all the year,
Shadows of the world appear.
There she sees the highway near
Winding down to Camelot:
There the river eddy whirls,
And there the surly village-churls,
And the red cloaks of market girls,
Pass onward from Shalott.

Sometimes a troop of damsels glad,
An abbot on an ambling pad,
Sometimes a curly shepherd-lad,
Or long-haired page in crimson clad,
Goes by to towered Camelot;
And sometimes through the mirror blue
The knights come riding two and two:
She hath no loyal knight and true,
The Lady of Shalott.

But in her web she still delights
To weave the mirror's magic sights,
For often through the silent nights
A funeral, with plumes and lights
And music, went to Camelot:

Or when the moon was overhead,
Came two young lovers lately wed;
"I am half sick of shadows," said
The Lady of Shalott.

### PART III

A bow-shot from her bower-eaves,
He rode between the barley-sheaves,
The sun came dazzling through the leaves,
And flamed upon the brazen greaves
Of bold Sir Lancelot.
A red-cross knight for ever kneeled
To a lady in his shield,
That sparkled on the yellow field,
Beside remote Shalott.

The gemmy bridle glittered free,
Like to some branch of stars we see
Hung in the golden Galaxy.
The bridle bells rang merrily
As he rode down to Camelot;
And from his blazoned baldric slung
A mighty silver bugle hung,
And as he rode his armor rung,
Beside remote Shalott.

All in the blue unclouded weather
Thick-jeweled shone the saddle-leather,
The helmet and the helmet-feather
Burned like one burning flame together,
As he rode down to Camelot;
As often through the purple night,
Below the starry clusters bright,
Some bearded meteor, trailing light,
Moves over still Shalott.

His broad clear brow in sunlight glowed;
On burnished hooves his war-horse trode;
From underneath his helmet flowed
His coal-black curls as on he rode,
As he rode down to Camelot.

From the bank and from the river
He flashed into the crystal mirror,
"Tirra lirra," by the river
Sang Sir Lancelot.

She left the web, she left the loom,
She made three paces through the room,
She saw the water-lily bloom,
She saw the helmet and the plume,
She looked down to Camelot.
Out flew the web and floated wide;
The mirror cracked from side to side;
"The curse is come upon me!" cried
The Lady of Shalott.

PART IV

In the stormy east-wind straining,
The pale yellow woods were waning,
The broad stream in his banks complaining,
Heavily the low sky raining
Over towered Camelot;
Down she came and found a boat
Beneath a willow left afloat,
And round about the prow she wrote
*The Lady of Shalott.*

And down the river's dim expanse--
Like some bold seër in a trance,
Seeing all his own mischance—
With a glassy countenance
Did she look to Camelot.
And at the closing of the day
She loosed the chain, and down she lay;
The broad stream bore her far away,
The Lady of Shalott.

Lying, robed in snowy white
That loosely flew to left and right—
The leaves upon her falling light—
Through the noises of the night
She floated down to Camelot

And as the boat-head wound along
The willowy hills and fields among,
They heard her singing her last song,
The Lady of Shalott.

Heard a carol, mournful, holy,
Chanted loudly, chanted lowly,
Till her blood was frozen slowly,
And her eyes were darkened wholly,
Turned to towered Camelot;
For ere she reached upon the tide
The first house by the water-side,
Singing in her song she died,
The Lady of Shalott.

Under tower and balcony,
By garden-wall and gallery,
A gleaming shape she floated by,
Dead-pale between the houses high,
Silent into Camelot.
Out upon the wharfs they came,
Knight and burgher, lord and dame,
And round the prow they read her name,
*The Lady of Shalott.*

Who is this? and what is here?
And in the lighted palace near
Died the sound of royal cheer;
And they crossed themselves for fear,
All the knights at Camelot:
But Lancelot mused a little space;
He said, "She has a lovely face;
God in His mercy lend her grace,
The Lady of Shalott."

*Alfred Tennyson* [1809-1892]

## RENASCENCE

ALL I could see from where I stood
Was three long mountains and a wood;
I turned and looked the other way,
And saw three islands in a bay.
So with my eyes I traced the line
Of the horizon, thin and fine,

Straight around till I was come
Back to where I'd started from;
And all I saw from where I stood
Was three long mountains and a wood.
Over these things I could not see:
These were the things that bounded me;
And I could touch them with my hand,
Almost, I thought, from where I stand.
And all at once things seemed so small
My breath came short, and scarce at all.
But, sure, the sky is big, I said;
Miles and miles above my head;
So here upon my back I'll lie
And look my fill into the sky.
And so I looked, and, after all,
The sky was not so very tall.
The sky, I said, must somewhere stop,
And—sure enough!—I see the top!
The sky, I thought, is not so grand;
I 'most could touch it with my hand!
And, reaching up my hand to try,
I screamed to feel it touch the sky.
I screamed, and—lo!—Infinity
Came down and settled over me;
Forced back my scream into my chest,
Bent back my arm upon my breast,
And, pressing of the Undefined
The definition on my mind,
Held up before my eyes a glass
Through which my shrinking sight did pass
Until it seemed I must behold
Immensity made manifold;
Whispered to me a word whose sound
Deafened the air for worlds around,
And brought unmuffled to my ears
The gossiping of friendly spheres,
The creaking of the tented sky,
The ticking of Eternity.

I saw and heard, and knew at last
The How and Why of all things, past,

And present, and forevermore.
The Universe, cleft to the core,
Lay open to my probing sense
That, sickening, I would fain pluck thence
But could not,—nay! But needs must suck
At the great wound, and could not pluck
My lips away till I had drawn
All venom out.—Ah, fearful pawn!
For my omniscience paid I toll
In infinite remorse of soul.
All sin was of my sinning, all
Atoning mine, and mine the gall
Of all regret. Mine was the weight
Of every brooded wrong, the hate
That stood behind each envious thrust,
Mine every greed, mine every lust.
And all the while for every grief,
Each suffering, I craved relief
With individual desire,—
Craved all in vain! And felt fierce fire
About a thousand people crawl;
Perished with each,—then mourned for all!
A man was starving in Capri;
He moved his eyes and looked at me;
I felt his gaze, I heard his moan,
And knew his hunger as my own.
I saw at sea a great fog bank
Between two ships that struck and sank;
A thousand screams the heavens smote;
And every scream tore through my throat.
No hurt I did not feel, no death
That was not mine; mine each last breath
That, crying, met an answering cry
From the compassion that was I.
All suffering mine, and mine its rod;
Mine, pity like the pity of God.
Ah, awful weight! Infinity
Pressed down upon the finite Me!
My anguished spirit, like a bird,
Beating against my lips I heard;
Yet lay the weight so close about

There was no room for it without.
And so beneath the weight lay I
And suffered death, but could not die.

Long had I lain thus, craving death,
When quietly the earth beneath
Gave way, and inch by inch, so great
At last had grown the crushing weight,
Into the earth I sank till I
Full six feet under ground did lie,
And sank no more,—there is no weight
Can follow here, however great.
From off my breast I felt it roll,
And as it went my tortured soul
Burst forth and fled in such a gust
That all about me swirled the dust.

Deep in the earth I rested now;
Cool is its hand upon the brow
And soft its breast beneath the head
Of one who is so gladly dead.
And all at once, and over all
The pitying rain began to fall;
I lay and heard each pattering hoof
Upon my lowly, thatchèd roof,
And seemed to love the sound far more
Than ever I had done before.
For rain it hath a friendly sound
To one who's six feet under ground;
And scarce the friendly voice or face:
A grave is such a quiet place.

The rain, I said, is kind to come
And speak to me in my new home.
I would I were alive again
To kiss the fingers of the rain,
To drink into my eyes the shine
Of every slanting silver line,
To catch the freshened, fragrant breeze
From drenched and dripping apple-trees.
For soon the shower will be done,
And then the broad face of the sun
Will laugh above the rain-soaked earth

Until the world with answering mirth
Shakes joyously, and each round drop
Rolls, twinkling, from its grass-blade top.
How can I bear it; buried here,
While overhead the sky grows clear
And blue again after the storm?
O, multi-colored, multiform,
Belovèd beauty over me,
That I shall never, never see
Again! Spring-silver, autumn-gold,
That I shall never more behold!
Sleeping your myriad magics through,
Close-sepulchred away from you!
O God, I cried, give me new birth,
And put me back upon the earth!
Upset each cloud's gigantic gourd
And let the heavy rain, down-poured
In one big torrent, set me free,
Washing my grave away from me!

I ceased; and, through the breathless hush
That answered me, the far-off rush
Of herald wings came whispering
Like music down the vibrant string
Of my ascending prayer, and—crash!
Before the wild wind's whistling lash
The startled storm-clouds reared on high
And plunged in terror down the sky,
And the big rain in one black wave
Fell from the sky and struck my grave.
I know not how such things can be;
I only know there came to me
A fragrance such as never clings
To aught save happy living things;
A sound as of some joyous elf
Singing sweet songs to please himself,
And, through and over everything,
A sense of glad awakening.
The grass, a-tiptoe at my ear,
Whispering to me I could hear;
I felt the rain's cool finger-tips

Brushed tenderly across my lips,
Laid gently on my sealèd sight,
And all at once the heavy night
Fell from my eyes and I could see,—
A drenched and dripping apple-tree,
A last long line of silver rain,
A sky grown clear and blue again.
And as I looked a quickening gust
Of wind blew up to me and thrust
Into my face a miracle
Of orchard-breath, and with the smell,—
I know not how such things can be!—
I breathed my soul back into me.
Ah! Up then from the ground sprang I
And hailed the earth with such a cry
As is not heard save from a man
Who has been dead, and lives again.
About the trees my arms I wound;
Like one gone mad I hugged the ground;
I raised my quivering arms on high;
I laughed and laughed into the sky,
Till at my throat a strangling sob
Caught fiercely, and a great heart-throb
Sent instant tears into my eyes;
O God, I cried, no dark disguise
Can e'er hereafter hide from me
Thy radiant identity!
Thou canst not move across the grass
But my quick eyes will see Thee pass,
Nor speak, however silently,
But my hushed voice will answer Thee.
I know the path that tells Thy way
Through the cool eve of every day;
God, I can push the grass apart
And lay my finger on Thy heart!

The world stands out on either side
No wider than the heart is wide;
Above the world is stretched the sky,—
No higher than the soul is high.
The heart can push the sea and land

Farther away on either hand;
The soul can split the sky in two,
And let the face of God shine through.
But East and West will pinch the heart
That can not keep them pushed apart;
And he whose soul is flat—the sky
Will cave in on him by and by.

*Edna St. Vincent Millay* [1892–1950]

## THE BLESSED DAMOZEL

The blessed damozel leaned out
  From the gold bar of Heaven;
Her eyes were deeper than the depth
  Of waters stilled at even;
She had three lilies in her hand,
  And the stars in her hair were seven.

Her robe, ungirt from clasp to hem,
  No wrought flowers did adorn,
But a white rose of Mary's gift,
  For service sweetly worn;
Her hair that lay along her back
  Was yellow like ripe corn.

Herseemed she scarce had been a day
  One of God's choristers;
The wonder was not yet quite gone
  From that still look of hers;
Albeit, to them she left, her day
  Had counted as ten years.

(To one, it is ten years of years.
  . . . Yet now, and in this place,
Surely she leaned o'er me—her hair
  Fell all about my face. . . .
Nothing: the autumn fall of leaves.
  The whole year sets apace.)

It was the rampart of God's house
  That she was standing on;
By God built over the sheer depth
  The which is Space begun;
So high, that looking downward thence
  She scarce could see the sun.

It lies in Heaven, across the flood
  Of ether, as a bridge.
Beneath, the tides of day and night
  With flame and darkness ridge
The void, as low as where this earth
  Spins like a fretful midge.

Around her, lovers, newly met
  'Mid deathless love's acclaims,
Spoke evermore among themselves
  Their heart-remembered names;
And the souls mounting up to God
  Went by her like thin flames.

And still she bowed herself and stooped
  Out of the circling charm;
Until her bosom must have made
  The bar she leaned on warm,
And the lilies lay as if asleep
  Along her bended arm.

From the fixed place of Heaven she saw
  Time like a pulse shake fierce
Through all the worlds. Her gaze still strove
  Within the gulf to pierce
Its path; and now she spoke as when
  The stars sang in their spheres.

The sun was gone now; the curled moon
  Was like a little feather
Fluttering far down the gulf; and now
  She spoke through the still weather.
Her voice was like the voice the stars
  Had when they sang together.

(Ah sweet! Even now, in that bird's song,
  Strove not her accents there,
Fain to be hearkened? When those bells
  Possessed the mid-day air,
Strove not her steps to reach my side
  Down all the echoing stair?)

"I wish that he were come to me,
  For he will come," she said.
"Have not I prayed in Heaven?—on earth,
  Lord, Lord, has he not prayed?
Are not two prayers a perfect strength?
  And shall I feel afraid?

"When round his head the aureole clings,
  And he is clothed in white,
I'll take his hand and go with him
  To the deep wells of light;
As unto a stream we will step down,
  And bathe there in God's sight.

"We two will stand beside that shrine,
  Occult, withheld, untrod,
Whose lamps are stirred continually
  With prayer sent up to God;
And see our old prayers, granted, melt
  Each like a little cloud.

"We two will lie i' the shadow of
  That living mystic tree
Within whose secret growth the Dove
  Is sometimes felt to be,
While every leaf that His plumes touch
  Saith His Name audibly.

"And I myself will teach to him,
  I myself, lying so,
The songs I sing here; which his voice
  Shall pause in, hushed and slow,
And find some knowledge at each pause
  Or some new thing to know."

(Alas! we two, we two, thou say'st!
  Yea, one wast thou with me
That once of old. But shall God lift
  To endless unity
The soul whose likeness with thy soul
  Was but its love for thee?)

"We two," she said, "will seek the groves
  Where the lady Mary is,
With her five handmaidens, whose names
  Are five sweet symphonies,
Cecily, Gertrude, Magdalen,
  Margaret and Rosalys.

"Circlewise sit they, with bound locks
  And foreheads garlanded;
Into the fine cloth white like flame
  Weaving the golden thread,
To fashion the birth-robes for them
  Who are just born, being dead.

"He shall fear, haply, and be dumb:
  Then will I lay my cheek
To his, and tell about our love,
  Not once abashed or weak:
And the dear Mother will approve
  My pride, and let me speak.

"Herself shall bring us, hand in hand,
  To Him round whom all souls
Kneel, the clear-ranged unnumbered heads
  Bowed with their aureoles:
And angels meeting us shall sing
  To their citherns and citoles.

"There will I ask of Christ the Lord
  Thus much for him and me:—
Only to live as once on earth
  With Love, only to be,
As then awhile, for ever now
  Together, I and he."

She gazed and listened and then said,
  Less sad of speech than mild,—
"All this is when he comes." She ceased.
  The light thrilled towards her, filled
With angels in strong level flight.
  Her eyes prayed, and she smiled.

(I saw her smile.) But soon their path
Was vague in distant spheres:
And then she cast her arms along
The golden barriers,
And laid her face between her hands,
And wept. (I heard her tears.)

*Dante Gabriel Rossetti* [1828–1882]

## A SONG OF ANGIOLA IN HEAVEN

Flowers,—that have died upon my Sweet,
Lulled by the rhythmic dancing beat
Of her young bosom under you,—
Now will I show you such a thing
As never, through thick buds of Spring,
Betwixt the daylight and the dew,
The Bird whose being no man knows—
The voice that waketh all night through,
Tells to the Rose.

For lo,—a garden-place I found,
Well filled of leaves, and stilled of sound,
Well flowered, with red fruit marvelous;
And 'twixt the shining trunks would flit
Tall knights and silken maids, or sit
With faces bent and amorous;—
There, in the heart thereof, and crowned
With woodbine and amaracus,
My Love I found.

Alone she walked,—ah, well I wis,
My heart leapt up for joy of this!—
Then when I called to her her name,—
The name, that like a pleasant thing
Men's lips remember, murmuring,—
At once across the sward she came,—
Full fain she seemed, my own dear maid
And askèd ever as she came,
"Where hast thou stayed?"

"Where hast thou stayed?" she asked, as though
The long years were an hour ago;
  But I spake not, nor answerèd,
For, looking in her eyes, I saw
A light not lit of mortal law;
  And in her clear cheek's changeless red,
And sweet, unshaken speaking found
  That in this place the Hours were dead,
      And Time was bound.

"This is well done," she said, "in thee,
O Love, that thou art come to me,
  To this green garden glorious;
Now truly shall our life be sped
In joyance and all goodlihed,
  For here all things are fair to us,
And none with burden is oppressed,
  And none is poor or piteous,—
      For here is Rest.

"No formless Future blurs the sky;
Men mourn not here, with dull dead eye,
  By shrouded shapes of Yesterday;
Betwixt the Coming and the Past
The flawless life hangs fixen fast
  In one unwearying To-Day,
That darkens not; for Sin is shriven,
  Death from the doors is thrust away,
      And here is Heaven."

At "Heaven" she ceased;—and lifted up
Her fair head like a flower-cup,
  With rounded mouth, and eyes aglow;
Then set I lips to hers, and felt,—
Ah, God,—the hard pain fade and melt,
  And past things change to painted show;
The song of quiring birds outbroke;
  The lit leaves laughed—sky shook, and lo,
      I swooned,—and woke.

And now, O Flowers,
    —Ye that indeed are dead,—

Now for all waiting hours,
Well am I comforted;
For of a surety, now, I see,
That, without dim distress
Of tears, or weariness,
My Lady, verily, awaiteth me;
So that until with Her I be,
For my dear Lady's sake
I am right fain to make
Out from my pain a pillow, and to take
Grief for a golden garment unto me;
Knowing that I, at last, shall stand
In that green garden-land,
And, in the holding of my dear Love's hand,
Forget the grieving and the misery.

*Austin Dobson* [1840–1921]

## THE HOUND OF HEAVEN

I FLED Him, down the nights and down the days;
I fled Him, down the arches of the years;
I fled Him, down the labyrinthine ways
Of my own mind; and in the mist of tears
I hid from Him, and under running laughter.
Up vistaed hopes I sped;
And shot, precipitated
Adown Titanic glooms of chasmed fears,
From those strong Feet that followed, followed after.
But with unhurrying chase,
And unperturbèd pace,
Deliberate speed, majestic instancy,
They beat—and a Voice beat
More instant than the Feet—
"All things betray thee, who betrayest Me."

I pleaded, outlaw-wise,
By many a hearted casement, curtained red,
Trellised with intertwining charities;
(For, though I knew His love Who followèd,
Yet was I sore adread

Lest, having Him, I must have naught beside);
But, if one little casement parted wide,
  The gust of His approach would clash it to.
Fear wist not to evade, as Love wist to pursue.
Across the margent of the world I fled,
  And troubled the gold gateways of the stars,
  Smiting for shelter on their clangèd bars;
    Fretted to dulcet jars
And silvern chatter the pale ports o' the moon.
I said to dawn, Be sudden; to eve, Be soon;
  With thy young skiey blossoms heap me over
    From this tremendous Lover!
Float thy vague veil about me, lest He see!
  I tempted all His servitors, but to find
My own betrayal in their constancy,
In faith to Him their fickleness to me,
  Their traitorous trueness, and their loyal deceit.
To all swift things for swiftness did I sue;
  Clung to the whistling mane of every wind.
    But whether they swept, smoothly fleet,
  The long savannahs of the blue;
    Or whether, Thunder-driven,
    They clanged his chariot 'thwart a heaven
Plashy with flying lightnings round the spurn o' their feet:—
  Fear wist not to evade, as Love wist to pursue.
    Still with unhurrying chase,
    And unperturbèd pace,
  Deliberate speed, majestic instancy,
    Came on the following Feet,
    And a Voice above their beat—
  "Naught shelters thee, who wilt not shelter Me."

I sought no more that after which I strayed
  In face of man or maid;
But still within the little children's eyes
  Seems something, something that replies;
*They* at least are for me, surely for me!
I turned me to them very wistfully;
But, just as their young eyes grew sudden fair
  With dawning answers there,

Their angel plucked them from me by the hair.
"Come then, ye other children, Nature's—share
With me" (said I) "your delicate fellowship;
Let me greet you lip to lip,
Let me twine you with caresses,
Wantoning
With our Lady-Mother's vagrant tresses,
Banqueting
With her in her wind-walled palace,
Underneath her azure daïs,
Quaffing, as your taintless way is,
From a chalice
Lucent-weeping out of the dayspring."
So it was done:
I in their delicate fellowship was one—
Drew the bolt of Nature's secrecies.
I knew all the swift importings
On the wilful face of skies,
I knew how the clouds arise
Spumèd of the wild sea-snortings;
All that's born or dies
Rose and drooped with—made them shapers
Of mine own moods, or wailful or divine—
With them joyed and was bereaven.
I was heavy with the even,
When she lit her glimmering tapers
Round the day's dead sanctities.
I laughed in the morning's eyes.
I triumphed and I saddened with all weather,
Heaven and I wept together,
And its sweet tears were salt with mortal mine;
Against the red throb of its sunset-heart
I laid my own to beat,
And share commingling heat;
But not by that, by that, was eased my human smart.
In vain my tears were wet on Heaven's gray cheek.
For ah! we know not what each other says,
These things and I; in sound *I* speak—
*Their* sound is but their stir, they speak by silences.
Nature, poor stepdame, cannot slake my drouth;

Let her, if she would owe me,
Drop yon blue bosom-veil of sky, and show me
The breasts o' her tenderness:
Never did any milk of hers once bless
My thirsting mouth.
Nigh and dry draws the chase,
With unperturbèd pace,
Deliberate speed, majestic instancy;
And past those noisèd Feet
A voice comes yet more fleet—
"Lo! naught contents thee, who content'st not Me.'

Naked I wait Thy love's uplifted stroke!
My harness piece by piece Thou hast hewn from me,
And smitten me to my knee;
I am defenseless utterly.
I slept, methinks, and woke,
And, slowly gazing, find me stripped in sleep.
In the rash lustihood of my young powers,
I shook the pillaring hours
And pulled my life upon me; grimed with smears
I stand amid the dust o' the mounded years—
My mangled youth lies dead beneath the heap.
My days have crackled and gone up in smoke,
Have puffed and burst as sun-starts on a stream.
Yea, faileth now even dream
The dreamer, and the lute the lutanist;
Even the linked fantasies, in whose blossomy twist
I swung the earth a trinket at my wrist,
Are yielding; cords of all too weak account
For earth with heavy griefs so overplussed.
Ah! is Thy love indeed
A weed, albeit an amaranthine weed,
Suffering no flowers except its own to mount?
Ah! must—
Designer infinite!—
Ah! must Thou char the wood ere Thou canst limn with it?
My freshness spent its wavering shower i' the dust:
And now my heart is as a broken fount,

Wherein tear-drippings stagnate, spilt down ever
From the dank thoughts that shiver
Upon the sighful branches of my mind.
Such is; what is to be?
The pulp so bitter, how shall taste the rind?
I dimly guess what Time in mists confounds:
Yet ever and anon a trumpet sounds
From the hid battlements of Eternity;
Those shaken mists a space unsettle, then
Round the half-glimpsèd turrets slowly wash again.
But not ere him who summoneth
I first have seen, enwound
With glooming robes purpureal, cypress-crowned;
His name I know, and what his trumpet saith.
Whether man's heart or life it be which yields
Thee harvest, must Thy harvest fields
Be dunged with rotten death?

Now of that long pursuit
Comes on at hand the bruit;
That Voice is round me like a bursting sea:
"And is thy earth so marred,
Shattered in shard on shard?
Lo, all things fly thee, for thou flyest Me!
Strange, piteous, futile thing,
Wherefore should any set thee love apart?
Seeing none but I makes much of naught" (He said),
"And human love needs human meriting:
How hast thou merited—
Of all man's clotted clay the dingiest clot?
Alack, thou knowest not
How little worthy of any love thou art!
Whom wilt thou find to love ignoble thee
Save Me, save only Me?
All which I took from thee, I did but take,
Not for thy harms,
But just that thou might'st seek it in My arms.
All which thy child's mistake
Fancies as lost, I have stored for thee at home:
Rise, clasp My hand, and come!"

Halts by me that footfall:
Is my gloom, after all,
Shade of His hand, outstretched caressingly?
"Ah, fondest, blindest, weakest,
I am He Whom thou seekest!
Thou dravest love from thee, who dravest Me."

*Francis Thompson* [1859?–1907]

## WILD EDEN

THERE is a garden enclosed
In the high places,
But never hath love reposed
In its bowery spaces;
And the cedars there like shadows
O'er the moonlit champaign stand
Till light like an angel's hand
Touches Wild Eden.

Who told me the name of the garden
That lieth remote, apart,
I know not, nor whence was the music
That sang it into my heart;
But just as the loud robin tosses
His notes from the elm tops high,
As the violets come in the mosses
When south winds wake and sigh,
So on my lips I found it,
This name that is made my cry.

There, under the stars and the dawns
Of the virginal valleys,
White lilies flood the low lawns
And the rose lights the alleys;
But never are heard there the voices
That sweeten on lovers' lips,
And the wild bee never sips
Sweets of Wild Eden.

But who hath shown me the vision
  Of the roses and lilies in ranks
I would that I knew, that forever
  To him I might render thanks;
For a maiden grows there in her blossom,
  In the place of her maidenhood,
Nor knows how her virgin bosom
  Is stored with the giving of good,
For the truth is hidden from her
  That of love is understood.

No bird with his mate there hovers,
  Nor beside her has trilled or sung;
No bird in the dewy covers
  Has built a nest for his young;
And over the dark-leaved mountains
  The voice in the laurel sleeps;
  And the moon broods on the deeps
    Shut in Wild Eden.

O Love, if thou in thy hiding
  Art he who above me stands,
If thou givest wings to my spirit,
  If thou art my heart and my hands,—
Through the morn, through the noon, through the even
  That burns with thy planet of light,
Through the moonlit space of heaven,
  Guide thou my flight
Till, star-like on the dark garden,
  I fall in the night!

Fly, song of my bosom, unto it
  Wherever the earth breathes spring;
Though a thousand years were to rue it,
  Such a heart beats under thy wing,
Thou shalt dive, thou shalt soar, thou shalt find it,
  And forever my life be blest,
  Such a heart beats in my breast,—
    Fly to Wild Eden!

*George Edward Woodberry* [1855-1930]

## THE AZTEC CITY

THERE is a clouded city, gone to rest
Beyond the crest
Where cordilleras mar the mystic west.

There suns unheeded rise and re-arise;
And in the skies
The harvest moon unnoticed lives and dies.

And yet this clouded city has no night—
Volcanic light
Compels eternal noontide, redly bright.

A thousand wells, whence cooling waters came,
No more the same,
Now send aloft a thousand jets of flame.

This clouded city is enchanting fair,
For rich and rare
From sculptured frieze the gilded griffins stare.

With level look—with loving, hopeful face,
Fixed upon space,
Stand caryatides of unknown race,

And colonnades of dark green serpentine,
Of strange design,
Carved on whose shafts queer alphabets combine.

And there are lofty temples, rich and great,
And at the gate,
Carved in obsidian, the lions wait.

And from triumphant arches, looking down
Upon the town,
In porphyry, sad, unknown statesmen frown.

And there are palace homes, and stately walls,
And open halls
Where fountains are, with voiceless waterfalls.

The ruddy fire incessantly illumes
Temples and tombs,
And in its blaze the stone-wrought cactus blooms.

From clouds congealed the mercury distils,
And, forming rills,
Adown the streets in double streamlet trills.

As rains from clouds, that summer skies eclipse,
From turret-tips
And spire and porch the mobile metal drips.

No one that visited this fiery hive
Ever alive
Came out but me—I, I alone, survive.

*Eugene Fitch Ware* [1841-1911]

## BEFORE A STATUE OF ACHILLES

Behold Pelides with his yellow hair,
Proud child of Thetis, hero loved of Jove;
Above the frowning of his brows it wove
A crown of gold, well combed, with Spartan care.
Who might have seen him, sullen, great, and fair,
As with the wrongful world he proudly strove,
And by high deeds his wilder passion shrove,
Mastering love, resentment, and despair.
He knew his end, and Phoebus' arrow sure
He braved for fame immortal and a friend,
Despising life; and we, who know our end,
Know that in our decay he shall endure
And all our children's hearts to grief inure,
With whose first bitter battles his shall blend.

Who brought thee forth, immortal vision, who
In Pythia or in Tempe brought thee forth?
Out of the sunlight and the sapful earth
What god the simples of thy spirit drew?
A goddess rose from the green waves, and threw
Her arms about a king, to give thee birth;
A centaur, patron of thy boyish mirth,
Over the meadows in thy footsteps flew.
Now Thessaly forgets thee, and the deep
Thy keeled bark furrowed answers not thy prayer;
But far away new generations keep
Thy laurels fresh, where branching Isis hems

The lawns of Oxford round about, or where
Enchanted Eton sits by pleasant Thames.

I gaze on thee as Phidias of old
Or Polyclitus gazed, when first he saw
These hard and shining limbs, without a flaw,
And cast his wonder in heroic mould.
Unhappy me who only may behold,
Nor make immutable and fix in awe
A fair immortal form no worm shall gnaw,
A tempered mind whose faith was never told!
The godlike mien, the lion's lock and eye,
The well-knit sinew, utter a brave heart
Better than many words that part by part
Spell in strange symbols what serene and whole
In nature lives, nor can in marble die.
The perfect body is itself the soul.

*George Santayana* [1863–1952]

## "I FLUNG ME ROUND HIM"

From "The Water-nymph and the Boy"

I FLUNG me round him,
I drew him under;
I clung, I drowned him,
My own white wonder! . . .

Father and mother,
Weeping and wild,
Came to the forest,
Calling the child,
Came from the palace,
Down to the pool,
Calling my darling,
My beautiful!
Under the water,
Cold and so pale!
Could it be love made
Beauty to fail?

Ah me! for mortals:
In a few moons,

If I had left him,
After some Junes
He would have faded,
Faded away,
He, the young monarch, whom
All would obey,
Fairer than day;
Alien to springtime,
Joyless and gray,
He would have faded,
Faded away,
Moving a mockery,
Scorned of the day!
Now I have taken him
All in his prime,
Saved from slow poisoning
Pitiless Time,
Filled with his happiness,
One with the prime,
Saved from the cruel
Dishonor of Time.
Laid him, my beautiful,
Laid him to rest,
Loving, adorable,
Softly to rest,
Here in my crystalline,
Here in my breast! *Roden Noel* [1834-1894]

## THE QUEEN'S SONG

HAD I the power
To Midas given of old
To touch a flower
And leave the petals gold,
I then might touch thy face,
Delightful boy,
And leave a metal grace,
A graven joy.

Thus would I slay,—
Ah, desperate device!

The vital day
  That trembles in thine eyes,
And let the red lips close
  Which sang so well,
And drive away the rose
  To leave a shell.

Then I myself,
  Rising austere and dumb,
On the high shelf
  Of my half-lighted room
Would place the shining bust
  And wait alone,
Until I was but dust,
  Buried unknown.

Thus in my love
  For nations yet unborn,
I would remove
  From our two lives the morn,
And muse on loveliness
  In mine arm-chair,
Content should Time confess
  How sweet you were.

*James Elroy Flecker* [1884–1915]

## BALKIS

From "Emblems of Love"

BALKIS was in her marble town,
And shadow over the world came down.
Whiteness of walls, towers and piers,
That all day dazzled eyes to tears,
Turned from being white-golden flame,
And like the deep-sea blue became.
Balkis into her garden went;
Her spirit was in discontent
Like a torch in restless air.
Joylessly she wandered there,
And saw her city's azure white
Lying under the great night,
Beautiful as the memory
Of a worshipping world would be

In the mind of a god, in the hour
When he must kill his outward power;
And, coming to a pool where trees
Grew in double greeneries,
Saw herself, as she went by
The water, walking beautifully,
And saw the stars shine in the glance
Of her eyes, and her own fair countenance
Passing, pale and wonderful,
Across the night that filled the pool.
And cruel was the grief that played
With the queen's spirit; and she said:
"What do I hear, reigning alone?
For to be unloved is to be alone.
There is no man in all my land
Dare my longing understand;
The whole folk like a peasant bows
Lest its look should meet my brows
And be harmed by this beauty of mine.
I burn their brains as I were sign
Of God's beautiful anger sent
To master them with punishment
Of beauty that must pour distress
On hearts grown dark with ugliness.
But it is I am the punished one.
Is there no man, is there none,
In whom my beauty will but move
The lust of a delighted love;
In whom some spirit of God so thrives
That we may wed our lonely lives?
Is there no man, is there none?"—
She said, "I will go to Solomon."

*Lascelles Abercrombie* [1881–1938]

## THE GATES OF DREAMLAND

It's a lonely road through bogland to the lake at Carrowmore,
And a sleeper there lies dreaming where the water laps the shore;

Though the moth-wings of the twilight in their purples are
unfurled,
Yet his sleep is filled with music by the masters of the world.

There's a hand is white as silver that is fondling with his
hair:
There are glimmering feet of sunshine that are dancing by
him there:
And half-open lips of faery that were dyed a faery red
In their revels where the Hazel Tree its holy clusters shed.

"Come away," the red lips whisper, "all the world is weary
now;
'Tis the twilight of the ages and it's time to quit the plough.
Oh, the very sunlight's weary ere it lightens up the dew,
And its gold is changed and faded before it falls to you.

"Though your colleen's heart be tender, a tenderer heart is
near.
What's the starlight in her glances when the stars are shining
clear?
Who would kiss the fading shadow when the flower-face
glows above?
'Tis the Beauty of all Beauty that is calling for your love."

Oh, the great gates of the mountain have opened once again,
And the sound of song and dancing falls upon the ears of
men,
And the Land of Youth lies gleaming, flushed with rainbow
light and mirth,
And the old enchantment lingers in the honey-heart of
earth.

*A. E. (George William Russell)* [1867–1935]

## EDITH

Edith, the silent stars are coldly gleaming,
The night wind moans, the leafless trees are still.
Edith, there is a life beyond this seeming,
So sleeps the ice-clad lake beneath thy hill.

So silent beats the pulse of thy pure heart,
  So shines the thought of thy unquestioned eyes.
O life! why wert thou helpless in thy art?
  O loveliness! why seem'st thou but surprise?

Edith, the streamlets laugh to leap again;
  There is a spring to which life's pulses fly;
And hopes that are not all the sport of pain,
  Like lustres in the veil of that gray eye.

They say the thankless stars have answering vision,
  That courage sings from out the frost-bound ways;
Edith, I grant that olden time's decision—
  Thy beauty paints with gold the icy rays.

As in the summer's heat her promise lies,
  As in the autumn's seed his vintage hides,
Thus might I shape my moral from those eyes,
  Glass of thy soul, where innocence abides.

Edith, thy nature breathes of answered praying;
  If thou dost live, then not my grief is vain;
Beyond the nerves of woe, beyond delaying,
  Thy sweetness stills to rest the winter's pain.

*William Ellery Channing* [1818–1901]

## TENANTS

SUDDENLY, out of dark and leafy ways,
We came upon the little house asleep
In cold blind stillness, shadowless and deep,
In the white magic of the full moon-blaze:
Strangers without the gate, we stood agaze,
Fearful to break that quiet, and to creep
Into the house that had been ours to keep
Through a long year of happy nights and days.
So unfamiliar in the white moon-gleam,
So old and ghostly like a house of dream
It seemed, that over us there stole the dread
That even as we watched it, side by side,
The ghosts of lovers, who had lived and died
Within its walls, were sleeping in our bed.

*Wilfrid Wilson Gibson* [1878-

## THE LISTENERS

"Is there anybody there?" said the Traveller,
  Knocking on the moonlit door;
And his horse in the silence champed the grasses
  Of the forest's ferny floor:
And a bird flew up out of the turret,
  Above the Traveller's head:
And he smote upon the door again a second time;
  "Is there anybody there?" he said.
But no one descended to the Traveller;
  No head from the leaf-fringed sill
Leaned over and looked into his gray eyes,
  Where he stood perplexed and still.
But only a host of phantom listeners
  That dwelt in the lone house then
Stood listening in the quiet of the moonlight
  To that voice from the world of men:
Stood thronging the faint moonbeams on the dark stair,
  That goes down to the empty hall,
Hearkening in an air stirred and shaken
  By the lonely Traveller's call.
And he felt in his heart their strangeness,
  Their stillness answering his cry,
While his horse moved, cropping the dark turf,
  'Neath the starred and leafy sky;
For he suddenly smote on the door, even
  Louder, and lifted his head:—
"Tell them I came, and no one answered,
  That I kept my word," he said.
Never the least stir made the listeners,
  Though every word he spake
Fell echoing through the shadowiness of the still house
  From the one man left awake:
Ay, they heard his foot upon the stirrup,
  And the sound of iron on stone,
And how the silence surged softly backward,
  When the plunging hoofs were gone.

*Walter de la Mare* [1873–1956]

## "CARE-CHARMER SLEEP"

### SLEEP

From "The Woman-Hater"

COME, Sleep, and with thy sweet deceiving
Lock me in delight awhile;
Let some pleasing dreams beguile
All my fancies; that from thence
I may feel an influence
All my powers of care bereaving!

Though but a shadow, but a sliding,
Let me know some little joy!
We that suffer long annoy
Are contented with a thought
Through an idle fancy wrought:
O let my joys have some abiding!

*John Fletcher* [1579-1625]

### "SLEEP, SILENCE' CHILD"

SLEEP, Silence' child, sweet father of soft rest,
Prince, whose approach peace to all mortals brings,
Indifferent host to shepherds and to kings,
Sole comforter of minds with grief oppressed;
Lo, by thy charming rod all breathing things
Lie slumbering, with forgetfulness possessed,
And yet o'er me to spread thy drowsy wings
Thou sparest, alas! who cannot be thy guest.
Since I am thine, O come, but with that face
To inward light which thou art wont to show;
With feignèd solace ease a true-felt woe;
Or if, deaf god, thou do deny that grace,

Come as thou wilt, and what thou wilt bequeath:
I long to kiss the image of my death.

*William Drummond* [1585–1649]

## TO SLEEP

A FLOCK of sheep that leisurely pass by,
One after one; the sound of rain, and bees
Murmuring; the fall of rivers, winds and seas,
Smooth fields, white sheets of water, and pure sky;
I've thought of all by turns, and yet do lie
Sleepless; and soon the small birds' melodies
Must hear, first uttered from my orchard trees;
And the first cuckoo's melancholy cry.
Even thus last night, and two nights more, I lay,
And could not win thee, Sleep! by any stealth:
So do not let me wear to-night away:
Without Thee what is all the morning's wealth?
Come, blessed barrier between day and day,
Dear mother of fresh thoughts and joyous health!

*William Wordsworth* [1770–1850]

## VIXI

I HAVE lived and I have loved;
I have waked and I have slept;
I have sung and I have danced;
I have smiled and I have wept;
I have won and wasted treasure;
I have had my fill of pleasure;
And all these things were weariness,
And some of them were dreariness;—
And all these things, but two things,
Were emptiness and pain:
And Love—it was the best of them;
And Sleep—worth all the rest of them,
Worth everything but Love to my spirit and my brain.
Be still my friend, O Slumber,
Till my days complete their number,
For Love shall never, never return to me again!

(?) *Charles Mackay* [1814–1889]

## SLEEP

O happy Sleep! thou bear'st upon thy breast
The blood-red poppy of enchanting rest,
Draw near me through the stillness of this place
And let thy low breath move across my face,
As faint wind moves above a poplar's crest.

The broad seas darken slowly in the west;
The wheeling sea-birds call from nest to nest;
Draw near and touch me, leaning out of space,
O happy Sleep!

There is no sorrow hidden or confessed,
There is no passion uttered or suppressed,
Thou canst not for a little while efface;
Enfold me in thy mystical embrace,
Thou sovereign gift of God most sweet, most blest,
O happy Sleep!

*Ada Louise Martin* [18

## THE QUIET NIGHTS

Unmindful of my low desert
Who turn e'en blessings to my hurt,
God sends me graces o'er and o'er,
More than the sands on the seashore.

Among the blessings He doth give
My starveling soul that she may live,
I praise Him for my nights He kept
And all the quiet sleep I slept.

Since I was young, who now grow old,
For all those nights of heat, of cold,
I slept the sweet hours through, nor heard
Even the call of the first bird.

Nights when the darkness covered me
In a great peace like a great sea,
With waves of sweetness, who should lie
Wakeful for mine iniquity.

Cool nights of fragrance dripping sweet
After the sultriness of heat,
Amid gray meadows drenched with dew;
Sweet was the sleep my eyelids knew.

Surely some angel kept my bed
After I had knelt down and prayed;
Like a young child I slept until
The day stood at the window-sill.

I thank Him for the nights of stars,
Bright Saturn, with his rings, and Mars.
And overhead the Milky Way;
Nights when the Summer lightnings play.

How many a Milky Way I trod,
And through the mercy of my God
Drank milk and honey, wrapped in ease
Of darkness and sweet heaviness!

I thank Him for the wakening bird
And the struck hours I have not heard,
And for the morns so cool, so kind,
That found me fresh in heart and mind.

Among the gifts of His mercy,
More than the leaves upon the tree,
The sands upon the shore, I keep
And name my lovely nights of sleep.

*Katherine Tynan Hinkson* [1861–1931]

## THE NIGHT

Most Holy Night, that still dost keep
The keys of all the doors of sleep,
To me when my tired eyelids close
  Give thou repose.

And let the far lament of them
That chaunt the dead day's requiem
Make in my ears, who wakeful lie,
  Soft lullaby.

Let them that guard the hornèd Moon
By my bedside their memories croon.
So shall I have new dreams and blest
  In my brief rest.

Fold thy great wings about my face,
Hide day-dawn from my resting-place,
And cheat me with thy false delight,
  Most Holy Night.

*Hilaire Belloc* [1870–1953]

## O SLEEP

TAKE me upon thy breast,
  O river of rest.
Draw me down to thy side,
  Slow-moving tide.
Carry out beyond reach
  Of song or of speech
This body and soul forespent.
  To thy still continent,
Where silence hath his home,
  Where I would come,
Bear me now in thy deep
  Bosom, Sleep,
    O Sleep.

*Grace Fallow Norton* [18

## THE WHARF OF DREAMS

STRANGE wares are handled on the wharves of sleep:
  Shadows of shadows pass, and many a light
  Flashes a signal fire across the night;
Barges depart whose voiceless steersmen keep

Their way without a star upon the deep;
  And from lost ships, homing with ghostly crews,
  Come cries of incommunicable news,
While cargoes pile the piers, a moon-white heap—
Budgets of dream-dust, merchandise of song,
Wreckage of hope and packs of ancient wrong,
  Nepenthes gathered from a secret strand,
Fardels of heartache, burdens of old sins,
Luggage sent down from dim ancestral inns,
  And bales of fantasy from No-Man's Land.

*Edwin Markham* [1852-1940

# HOME AND FATHERLAND

## HAME, HAME, HAME

HAME, hame, hame, O hame fain wad I be—
O hame, hame, hame, to my ain countree!

When the flower is i' the bud and the leaf is on the tree,
The lark shall sing me hame in my ain countree;
Hame, hame, hame, O hame fain wad I be—
O hame, hame, hame, to my ain countree!

The green leaf o' loyaltie's beginning for to fa',
The bonnie White Rose it is withering an' a';
But I'll water 't wi' the blude of usurping tyrannie,
An' green it will graw in my ain countree.

O, there's nocht now frae ruin my country can save,
But the keys o' kind heaven, to open the grave;
That a' the noble martyrs wha died for loyaltie
May rise again an' fight for their ain countree.

The great now are gane, a' wha ventured to save,
The new grass is springing on the tap o' their grave;
But the sun through the mirk blinks blithe in my e'e,
"I'll shine on ye yet in your ain countree."

Hame, hame, hame, O hame fain wad I be—
O hame, hame, hame, to my ain countree!

*Allan Cunningham* [1784–1842]

## HOME, SWEET HOME!

From "Clari, the Maid of Milan"

'MID pleasures and palaces though we may roam,
Be it ever so humble, there's no place like home;
A charm from the sky seems to hallow us there,
Which, seek through the world, is ne'er met with elsewhere.
    Home, Home, sweet, sweet Home!
There's no place like Home! there's no place like Home!

An exile from home, splendor dazzles in vain;
O, give me my lowly thatched cottage again!
The birds singing gayly, that came at my call,—
Give me them,—and the peace of mind, dearer than all!
Home, Home, sweet, sweet Home!
There's no place like Home! there's no place like Home!

How sweet 'tis to sit 'neath a fond father's smile,
And the cares of a mother to soothe and beguile!
Let others delight mid new pleasures to roam,
But give me, oh, give me, the pleasures of home!
Home! Home! sweet, sweet Home!
There's no place like Home! there's no place like Home!

To thee I'll return, overburdened with care;
The heart's dearest solace will smile on me there;
No more from that cottage again will I roam;
Be it ever so humble, there's no place like home.
Home! Home! sweet, sweet Home!
There's no place like Home! there's no place like Home!

*John Howard Payne* [1792–1852]

## MY OLD KENTUCKY HOME

THE sun shines bright in the old Kentucky home;
'Tis summer, the darkeys are gay;
The corn-top's ripe, and the meadow's in the bloom,
While the birds make music all the day.
The young folks roll on the little cabin floor,
All merry, all happy and bright;
By-'n'-by hard times comes a-knocking at the door:—
Then my old Kentucky home, good-night!

Weep no more, my lady,
O, weep no more to-day!
We will sing one song for the old Kentucky home,
For the old Kentucky home, far away.

They hunt no more for the possum and the coon,
On the meadow, the hill, and the shore;
They sing no more by the glimmer of the moon,
On the bench by the old cabin door.

The day goes by like a shadow o'er the heart,
With sorrow, where all was delight;
The time has come when the darkeys have to part:—
Then my old Kentucky home, good-night!

The head must bow, and the back will have to bend,
Wherever the darkey may go;
A few more days and the troubles all will end,
In the field where the sugar-canes grow.
A few more days for to tote the weary load,—
No matter, 'twill never be light;
A few more days till we totter on the road:—
Then my old Kentucky home, good-night!

Weep no more, my lady,
O, weep no more to-day!
We will sing one song for the old Kentucky home,
For the old Kentucky home, far away.

*Stephen Collins Foster* [1826-1864]

## OLD FOLKS AT HOME

Way down upon de Swanee ribber,
Far, far away,
Dere's wha my heart is turning ebber,
Dere's wha de old folks stay.
All up and down de whole creation
Sadly I roam,
Still longing for de old plantation,
And for de old folks at home.

All de world am sad and dreary,
Eb'rywhere I roam;
Oh, darkeys, how my heart grows weary,
Far from de old folks at home!

All round de little farm I wandered
When I was young,
Den many happy days I squandered
Many de songs I sung.

When I was playing wid my brudder
  Happy was I;
Oh, take me to my kind old mudder!
  Dere let me live and die.

One little hut among de bushes,
  One dat I love,
Still sadly to my memory rushes,
  No matter where I rove.
When will I see de bees a-humming
  All around de comb?
When will I hear de banjo tumming,
  Down in my good old home?

*Stephen Collins Foster* [1826–1864]

## HOME

O, FALMOUTH is a fine town with ships in the bay,
And I wish from my heart it's there I was to-day;
I wish from my heart I was far away from here,
Sitting in my parlor and talking to my dear.
For it's home, dearie, home—it's home I want to be.
Our topsails are hoisted, and we'll away to sea.
O, the oak and the ash and the bonnie birken tree
They're all growing green in the old countrie.

In Baltimore a-walking a lady I did meet
With her babe on her arm as she came down the street;
And I thought how I sailed, and the cradle standing ready
For the pretty little babe that has never seen its daddie.
  And it's home, dearie, home,—

O, if it be a lass, she shall wear a golden ring;
And if it be a lad, he shall fight for his king;
With his dirk and his hat and his little jacket blue
He shall walk the quarter-deck as his daddie used to do.
  And it's home, dearie, home,—

O, there's a wind a-blowing, a-blowing from the west,
And that of all the winds is the one I like the best,

For it blows at our backs, and it shakes our pennon free,
And it soon will blow us home to the old countrie.
For it's home, dearie, home—it's home I want to be.
Our topsails are hoisted, and we'll away to sea.
O, the oak and the ash and the bonnie birken tree
They're all growing green in the old countrie.

*William Ernest Henley* [1849-1903]

## HOT WEATHER IN THE PLAINS—INDIA

FAR beyond the sky-line, where the steamers go,
There's a cool, green country, there's the land I know;
Where the gray mist rises from the hidden pool,
And the dew falls softly on the meadows cool.
When the exile's death has claimed me it is there my soul shall fly,
To the pleasant English country, when my time has come to die;
Where the west wind on the uplands echoes back the sea-bird's cry—
Oh! it's there my soul will hasten though it's here my bones must lie.

From the many temples, tinkling bells ring clear,
But a fairer music in my heart I hear—
Lilt of English skylark, plash of woodland streams,
Songs of thrush and blackbird fill my waking dreams.
In each pause from work and worry, it is there my thoughts will fly,
To the pleasant English country with the pearly, misty sky—
And the present's toil and trouble fade and cease and pass me by—
Oh! it's there I fain would wander, but it's here my bones must lie.

Hard and hot the sky spreads, one unchanging glare,
Far and wide the earth lies burnt and brown and bare,
Sunset brings no solace, night-time no redress,
Still the breathless silence mocks the land's distress.

So my thoughts recross the waters to the spring-times long
gone by,
Passed 'mid English woods and pastures, 'neath a softer,
sweeter sky;
For when death shall end my exile, thither will my spirit
fly—
Oh! it's there my soul shall wander, though it's here my
bones must lie.

*E. H. Tipple* [18 –

## HEART'S CONTENT

"A SAIL! a sail! Oh, whence away,
And whither, o'er the foam?
Good brother mariners, we pray,
God speed you safely home!"
"Now wish us not so foul a wind,
Until the fair be spent;
For hearth and home we leave behind:
We sail for Heart's Content."

"For Heart's Content! And sail ye so,
With canvas flowing free?
But, pray you, tell us, if ye know,
Where may that harbor be?
For we that greet you, worn of time,
Wave-racked, and tempest-rent,
By sun and star, in every clime,
Have searched for Heart's Content.

"In every clime the world around,
The waste of waters o'er;
An El Dorado have we found,
That ne'er was found before.
The isles of spice, the lands of dawn,
Where East and West are blent—
All these our eyes have looked upon,
But where is Heart's Content?

"Oh, turn again, while yet ye may,
And ere the hearths are cold,
And all the embers ashen-gray,
By which ye sat of old,
And dumb in death the loving lips
That mourned as forth ye went
To join the fleet of missing ships,
In quest of Heart's Content;

"And seek again the harbor-lights,
Which faithful fingers trim,
Ere yet alike the days and nights
Unto your eyes are dim!
For woe, alas! to those that roam
Till time and tide are spent,
And win no more the port of home—
The only Heart's Content!"

*Unknown*

## SONG

STAY, stay at home, my heart, and rest;
Home-keeping hearts are happiest,
For those that wander they know not where
Are full of trouble and full of care;
To stay at home is best.

Weary and homesick and distressed,
They wander east, they wander west,
And are baffled and beaten and blown about
By the winds of the wilderness of doubt;
To stay at home is best.

Then stay at home, my heart, and rest;
The bird is safest in its nest;
Over all that flutter their wings and fly
A hawk is hovering in the sky;
To stay at home is best.

*Henry Wadsworth Longfellow* [1807-1882]

## MY EARLY HOME

HERE sparrows build upon the trees,
  And stockdove hides her nest;
The leaves are winnowed by the breeze
  Into a calmer rest:
The black-cap's song was very sweet,
  That used the rose to kiss;
It made the Paradise complete:
  My early home was this.

The red-breast from the sweetbrier bush
  Dropped down to pick the worm;
On the horse-chestnut sang the thrush,
  O'er the house where I was born;
The moonlight, like a shower of pearls,
  Fell o'er this 'bower of bliss',
And on the bench sat boys and girls:
  My early home was this.

The old house stooped just like a cave,
  Thatched o'er with mosses green;
Winter around the walls would rave,
  But all was calm within;
The trees are here all green again,
  Here bees the flowers still kiss,
But flowers and trees seemed sweeter then:
  My early home was this.

*John Clare* [1793-1864]

## THE OLD HOME

AN old lane, an old gate, an old house by a tree;
A wild wood, a wild brook—they will not let me be;
In boyhood I knew them, and still they call to me.

Down deep in my heart's core I hear them and my eyes
Through tear-mists behold them beneath the oldtime skies
'Mid bee-boom and rose-bloom and orchard-lands arise.

I hear them; and heartsick with longing is my soul,
To walk there, to dream there, beneath the sky's blue bowl;
Around me, within me, the weary world made whole.

To talk with the wild brook of all the long ago;
To whisper the wood-wind of things we used to know
When we were old companions, before my heart knew woe.

To walk with the morning and watch its rose unfold;
To drowse with the noontide lulled in its heart of gold;
To lie with the night-time and dream the dreams of old.

To tell to the old trees, and to each listening leaf,
The longing, the yearning, as in my boyhood brief,
The old hope, the old love, would ease me of my grief.

The old lane, the old gate, the old house by the tree,
The wild wood, the wild brook—they will not let me be:
In boyhood I knew them, and still they call to me.

*Madison Cawein* [1865-1914]

## THE AULD HOUSE

Oh, the auld house, the auld house,—
What though the rooms were wee?
Oh, kind hearts were dwelling there,
And bairnies fu' o' glee;
The wild rose and the jessamine
Still hang upon the wa':
How mony cherished memories
Do they sweet flowers reca'!

Oh, the auld laird, the auld laird,
Sae canty, kind, and crouse,—
How mony did he welcome to
His ain wee dear auld house;
And the leddy too, sae genty,
There sheltered Scotland's heir,
And clipped a lock wi' her ain hand,
Frae his lang yellow hair.

The mavis still doth sweetly sing,
  The bluebells sweetly blaw,
The bonny Earn's clear winding still,
  But the auld house is awa'.
The auld house, the auld house,—
  Deserted though ye be,
There ne'er can be a new house
  Will seem sae fair to me.

Still flourishing the auld pear-tree
  The bairnies liked to see;
And oh, how often did they speir
  When ripe they a' wad be!
The voices sweet, the wee bit feet
  Aye rinnin' here and there,
The merry shout—oh! whiles we greet
  To think we'll hear nae mair.

For they are a' wide scattered now;
  Some to the Indies gane,
And ane, alas! to her lang hame;
  Not here we'll meet again.
The kirkyard, the kirkyard!
  Wi' flowers o' every hue,
Sheltered by the holly's shade
  An' the dark sombre yew.

The setting sun, the setting sun!
  How glorious it gaed doon;
The cloudy splendor raised our hearts
  To cloudless skies aboon.
The auld dial, the auld dial!
  It tauld how time did pass;
The wintry winds hae dung it doon,
  Now hid 'mang weeds and grass.

*Carolina Nairne* [1766–1845]

## THE ROWAN TREE

O ROWAN tree, O rowan tree! thou'lt aye be dear to me!
Intwined thou art wi' mony ties o' hame and infancy.
Thy leaves were aye the first o' spring, thy flowers the simmer's pride;
There wasna sic a bonnie tree in a' the country side.
O rowan tree!

How fair wert thou in simmer time, wi' a' thy clusters white,
How rich and gay thy autumn dress, wi' berries red and bright!
On thy fair stem were mony names which now nae mair I see,
But they're engraven on my heart—forgot they ne'er can be!
O rowan tree!

We sat aneath thy spreading shade, the bairnies round thee ran,
They pu'd thy bonnie berries red, and necklaces they strang.
My mother! O I see her still, she smiled our sports to see,
Wi' little Jeanie on her lap, and Jamie at her knee.
O rowan tree!

O there arose my father's prayer, in holy evening's calm;
How sweet was then my mother's voice in the Martyr's psalm!
Now a' are gane! we meet nae mair aneath the rowan tree!
But hallowed thoughts around thee twine o' hame and infancy,
O rowan tree!

*Carolina Nairne* [1766–1845]

## THE FIRE OF DRIFT-WOOD

WE sat within the farm-house old,
Whose windows, looking o'er the bay,
Gave to the sea-breeze damp and cold
An easy entrance, night and day.

Not far away we saw the port,
  The strange, old-fashioned, silent town,
The lighthouse, the dismantled fort,
  The wooden houses, quaint and brown.

We sat and talked until the night,
  Descending, filled the little room;
Our faces faded from the sight,
  Our voices only broke the gloom.

We spake of many a vanished scene,
  Of what we once had thought and said,
Of what had been, and might have been,
  And who was changed, and who was dead;

And all that fills the heart of friends,
  When first they feel, with secret pain,
Their lives thenceforth have separate ends,
  And never can be one again;

The first slight swerving of the heart,
  That words are powerless to express,
And leave it still unsaid in part,
  Or say it in too great excess.

The very tones in which we spake
  Had something strange, I could but mark;
The leaves of memory seemed to make
  A mournful rustling in the dark.

Oft died the words upon our lips,
  As suddenly, from out the fire
Built of the wreck of stranded ships,
  The flames would leap and then expire.

And, as their splendor flashed and failed,
  We thought of wrecks upon the main,
Of ships dismasted, that were hailed,
  And sent no answer back again.

The windows, rattling in their frames,
The ocean, roaring up the beach,
The gusty blast, the bickering flames,
All mingled vaguely in our speech;

Until they made themselves a part
Of fancies floating through the brain,
The long-lost ventures of the heart,
That send no answers back again.

O flames that glowed! O hearts that yearned!
They were indeed too much akin,
The drift-wood fire without that burned,
The thoughts that burned and glowed within.

*Henry Wadsworth Longfellow* [1807-1882]

## MY AIN FIRESIDE

I HAE seen great anes and sat in great ha's,
'Mang lords and fine ladies a' covered wi' braws,
At feasts made for princes wi' princes I've been,
When the grand shine o' splendor has dazzled my een;
But a sight sae delightfu' I trow I ne'er spied
As the bonny blithe blink o' my ain fireside.
My ain fireside, my ain fireside,
O, cheery's the blink o' my ain fireside;
My ain fireside, my ain fireside,
O, there's naught to compare wi' ane's ain fireside.

Ance mair, Gude be thankit, round my ain heartsome ingle
Wi' the friends o' my youth I cordially mingle;
Nae forms to compel me to seem wae or glad,
I may laugh when I'm merry, and sigh when I'm sad.
Nae falsehood to dread, and nae malice to fear,
But truth to delight me, and friendship to cheer;
Of a' roads to happiness ever were tried,
There's nane half so sure as ane's ain fireside.
My ain fireside, my ain fireside,
O, there's naught to compare wi' ane's ain fireside.

When I draw in my stool on my cozy hearthstane,
My heart loups sae light I scarce ken 't for my ain;
Care's down on the wind, it is clean out o' sight,
Past troubles they seem but as dreams o' the night.
I hear but kend voices, kend faces I see,
And mark saft affection glent fond frae ilk ee;
Nae fleechings o' flattery, nae boastings o' pride,
'Tis heart speaks to heart at ane's ain fireside.
  My ain fireside, my ain fireside,
  O, there's naught to compare wi' ane's ain fireside.

*Elizabeth Hamilton* [1758-1816]

## THE INGLE-SIDE

It's rare to see the morning bleeze
  Like a bonfire frae the sea,
It's fair to see the burnie kiss
  The lip o' the flowery lea;
An' fine it is on green hillside,
  Where hums the bonnie bee,
But rarer, fairer, finer far
  Is the ingle-side for me.

Glens may be gilt wi' gowans rare,
  The birds may fill the tree;
An' haughs hae a' the scented ware
  The simmer-growth can gie:
But the canty hearth where cronies meet,
  An' the darling o' our e'e,
That makes to us a warl' complete:
  Oh, the ingle-side for me!

*Hew Ainslee* [1792-1878]

## THE CANE-BOTTOMED CHAIR

In tattered old slippers that toast at the bars,
And a ragged old jacket perfumed with cigars,
Away from the world and its toils and its cares,
I've a snug little kingdom up four pair of stairs.

To mount to this realm is a toil, to be sure,
But the fire there is bright and the air rather pure;
And the view I behold on a sunshiny day
Is grand, through the chimney-pots over the way.

This snug little chamber is crammed in all nooks
With worthless old knicknacks and silly old books,
And foolish old odds and foolish old ends,
Cracked bargains from brokers, cheap keepsakes from friends.

Old armor, prints, pictures, pipes, china (all cracked),
Old rickety tables, and chairs broken-backed;
A twopenny treasury, wondrous to see;
What matter? 'tis pleasant to you, friend, and me.

No better divan need the Sultan require,
Than the creaking old sofa that basks by the fire,
And 'tis wonderful, surely, what music you get
From the rickety, ramshackle, wheezy spinet.

That praying-rug came from a Turcoman's camp;
By Tiber once twinkled that brazen old lamp;
A Mameluke fierce yonder dagger has drawn:
'Tis a murderous knife to toast muffins upon.

Long, long through the hours, and the night, and the chimes,
Here we talk of old books, and old friends, and old times:
As we sit in a fog made of rick Latakie,
This chamber is pleasant to you, friend, and me.

But of all the cheap treasures that garnish my nest,
There's one that I love and I cherish the best;
For the finest of couches that's padded with hair
I never would change thee, my cane-bottomed chair.

'Tis a bandy-legged, high-shouldered, worm-eaten seat,
With a creaking old back, and twisted old feet;
But since the fair morning when Fanny sat there,
I bless thee and love thee, old cane-bottomed chair.

If chairs have but feeling, in holding such charms,
A thrill must have passed through your withered old arms!

I looked, and I longed, and I wished in despair;
I wished myself turned to a cane-bottomed chair.

It was but a moment she sat in this place,
She'd a scarf on her neck, and a smile on her face!
A smile on her face, and a rose in her hair,
And she sat there, and bloomed in my cane-bottomed chair.

And so I have valued my chair ever since,
Like the shrine of a saint, or the throne of a prince;
Saint Fanny, my patroness sweet I declare,
The queen of my heart and my cane-bottomed chair.

When the candles burn low, and the company's gone,
In the silence of night as I sit here alone—
I sit here alone, but we yet are a pair—
My Fanny I see in my cane-bottomed chair.

She comes from the past, and revisits my room;
She looks as she then did, all beauty and bloom;
So smiling and tender, so fresh and so fair,
And yonder she sits in my cane-bottomed chair.

*William Makepeace Thackeray* [1811–1863]

## DUNA

When I was a little lad
With folly on my lips,
Fain was I for journeying
All the seas in ships.
But now across the southern swell,
Every dawn I hear
The little streams of Duna
Running clear.

When I was a young man,
Before my beard was gray,
All to ships and sailormen
I gave my heart away.
But I'm weary of the sea-wind,
I'm weary of the foam,
And the little stars of Duna
Call me home.

*Marjorie L. C. Pickthall* [1883–1922]

## THE OLD CLOCK ON THE STAIRS

Somewhat back from the village street
Stands the old-fashioned country-seat.
Across its antique portico
Tall poplar-trees their shadows throw;
And from its station in the hall
An ancient timepiece says to all,—
"Forever—never!
Never—forever!"

Half-way up the stairs it stands,
And points and beckons with its hands
From its case of massive oak,
Like a monk, who, under his cloak,
Crosses himself, and sighs, alas!
With sorrowful voice to all who pass,—
"Forever—never!
Never—forever!"

By day its voice is low and light;
But in the silent dead of night,
Distinct as a passing footstep's fall,
It echoes along the vacant hall,
Along the ceiling, along the floor,
And seems to say, at each chamber-door,—
"Forever—never!
Never—forever!"

Through days of sorrow and of mirth,
Through days of death and days of birth,
Through every swift vicissitude
Of changeful time, unchanged it has stood,
And as if, like God, it all things saw,
It calmly repeats those words of awe,—
"Forever—never!
Never—forever!"

In that mansion used to be
Free-hearted Hospitality;
His great fires up the chimney roared;
The stranger feasted at his board;

But, like the skeleton at the feast,
That warning timepiece never ceased,—
"Forever—never!
Never—forever!"

There groups of merry children played,
There youths and maidens dreaming strayed;
O precious hours! O golden prime,
And affluence of love and time!
Even as a miser counts his gold,
Those hours the ancient timepiece told,—
"Forever—never!
Never—forever!"

From that chamber, clothed in white,
The bride came forth on her wedding night;
There, in that silent room below,
The dead lay in his shroud of snow;
And in the hush that followed the prayer,
Was heard the old clock on the stair,—
"Forever—never!
Never—forever!"

All are scattered now and fled,
Some are married, some are dead;
And when I ask, with throbs of pain,
"Ah! when shall they all meet again?"
As in the days long since gone by,
The ancient timepiece makes reply,—
"Forever—never!
Never—forever!"

Never here, forever there,
Where all parting, pain, and care,
And death, and time shall disappear,—
Forever there, but never here!
The horologe of Eternity
Sayeth this incessantly,—
"Forever—never!
Never—forever!"

*Henry Wadsworth Longfellow* [1807–1882]

## "MOTHER, HOME, HEAVEN"

THREE words fall sweetly on my soul,
  As music from an angel's lyre,
That bid my spirit spurn control,
  And upward to its source aspire;
The sweetest sounds to mortals given
Are heard in Mother, Home, and Heaven.

Dear Mother!—ne'er shall I forget
  Thy brow, thine eye, thy pleasant smile;
Though in the sea of death hath set
  Thy star of life, my guide awhile,
Oh, never shall thy form depart
From the bright pictures in my heart.

And like a bird that from the flowers,
  Wing-weary seeks her wonted nest,
My spirit, e'en in manhood's hours,
  Turns back in childhood's Home to rest;
The cottage, garden, hill, and stream,
Still linger like a pleasant dream.

And while to one engulfing grave
  By Time's swift tide we're driven,
How sweet the thought that every wave
  But bears us nearer Heaven!
There we shall meet, when life is o'er,
In that blest Home, to part no more.

*William Goldsmith Brown* [1812–1906]

## THE HERO

MY hero is na decked wi' gowd,
  He has nae glittering state;
Renown upon a field o' blood
  In war he hasna met.
He has nae siller in his pouch,
  Nae menials at his ca';
The proud o' earth frae him would turn,
  And bid him stand awa'.

His coat is hame-spun hodden-gray,
His shoon are clouted sair,
His garments, maist unhero-like,
Are a' the waur o' wear:
His limbs are strong—his shoulders broad,
His hands were made to plow;
He's rough without, but sound within;
His heart is bauldly true.

He toils at e'en, he toils at morn,
His wark is never through;
A coming life o' weary toil
Is ever in his view.
But on he trudges, keeping aye
A stout heart to the brae,
And proud to be an honest man
Until his dying day.

His hame a hame o' happiness
And kindly love may be;
And monie a nameless dwelling-place
Like his we still may see.
His happy altar-hearth so bright
Is ever bleezing there;
And cheerfu' faces round it set
Are an unending prayer.

The poor man in his humble hame,
Like God, who dwells aboon,
Makes happy hearts around him there,
Sae joyfu' late and soon.
His toil is sair, his toil is lang;
But weary nights and days,
Hame—happiness akin to his—
A hunder-fauld repays.

Go, mock at conquerors and kings!
What happiness give they?
Go, tell the painted butterflies
To kneel them down and pray!

Go, stand erect in manhood's pride,
  Be what a man should be,
Then come, and to my hero bend
  Upon the grass your knee!

*Robert Nicoll* [1814-1837]

## THE COTTER'S SATURDAY NIGHT

### INSCRIBED TO ROBERT AIKEN, ESQ.

Let not Ambition mock their useful toil,
  Their homely joys, and destiny obscure;
Nor Grandeur hear with a disdainful smile
  The short and simple annals of the poor.—GRAY

My loved, my honored, much-respected friend!
  No mercenary bard his homage pays;
With honest pride, I scorn each selfish end;
  My dearest meed, a friend's esteem and praise.
  To you I sing, in simple Scottish lays,
The lowly train in life's sequestered scene;
  The native feelings strong, the guileless ways;
What Aiken in a cottage would have been;
Ah! though his worth unknown, far happier there, I ween.

November chill blaws loud wi' angry sugh;
  The shortening winter-day is near a close;
The miry beasts retreating frae the pleugh,
  The blackening trains o' craws to their repose:
  The toilworn cotter frae his labor goes,—
This night his weekly moil is at an end,—
  Collects his spades, his mattocks, and his hoes,
Hoping the morn in ease and rest to spend,
And weary, o'er the moor, his course does hameward bend.

At length his lonely cot appears in view,
  Beneath the shelter of an agèd tree;
The expectant wee things, toddlin', stacher through
  To meet their dad, wi' flichterin' noise an' glee.
  His wee bit ingle, blinking bonnily,
His clean hearthstane, his thriftie wifie's smile,
  The lisping infant prattling on his knee,
Does a' his weary kiaugh and care beguile,
And makes him quite forget his labor and his toil.

Belyve, the elder bairns come drapping in,
At service out, amang the farmers roun';
Some ca' the pleugh, some herd, some tentie rin
A cannie errand to a neibor town;
Their eldest hope, their Jenny, woman grown,
In youthfu' bloom, love sparkling in her e'e,
Comes hame, perhaps to shew a braw new gown,
Or deposit her sair-won penny-fee,
To help her parents dear, if they in hardship be.

With joy unfeigned, brothers and sisters meet,
And each for other's weelfare kindly spiers:
The social hours, swift-winged, unnoticed fleet:
Each tells the uncos that he sees or hears;
The parents, partial, eye their hopeful years;
Anticipation forward points the view.
The mother, wi' her needle and her shears,
Gars auld claes look amaist as weel's the new;
The father mixes a' wi' admonition due.

Their master's and their mistress's command,
The younkers a' are warnèd to obey;
And mind their labors wi' an eydent hand,
And ne'er, though out o' sight, to jauk or play:
"And oh! be sure to fear the Lord alway!
And mind your duty, duly, morn and night!
Lest in temptation's path ye gang astray,
Implore His counsel and assisting might:
They never sought in vain that sought the Lord aright!"

But, hark! a rap comes gently to the door;
Jenny, wha kens the meaning o' the same,
Tells how a neibor lad cam o'er the moor,
To do some errands, and convoy her hame.
The wily mother sees the conscious flame
Sparkle in Jenny's e'e, and flush her cheek;
With heart-struck anxious care inquires his name,
While Jenny hafflins is afraid to speak;
Weel pleased the mother hears it's nae wild, worthless rake

Wi' kindly welcome, Jenny brings him ben;
A strappin' youth; he taks the mother's eye;
Blithe Jenny sees the visit's no ill-ta'en;
The father cracks of horses, pleughs, and kye.
The youngster's artless heart o'erflows wi' joy,
But blate and lathefu', scarce can weel behave;
The mother, wi' a woman's wiles, can spy
What makes the youth sae bashfu' an' sae grave:
Weel pleased to think her bairn's respected like the lave.

O happy love! where love like this is found!
O heartfelt raptures! bliss beyond compare!
I've pacèd much this weary, mortal round,
And sage experience bids me this declare:—
If Heaven a draught of heavenly pleasure spare,
One cordial in this melancholy vale,
'Tis when a youthful, loving, modest pair
In other's arms breathe out the tender tale,
Beneath the milk-white thorn that scents the evening gale.

Is there, in human form, that bears a heart,
A wretch, a villain, lost to love and truth,
That can, with studied, sly, ensnaring art,
Betray sweet Jenny's unsuspecting youth?
Curse on his perjured arts! dissembling smooth!
Are honor, virtue, conscience, all exiled?
Is there no pity, no relenting ruth,
Points to the parents fondling o'er their child?
Then paints the ruined maid, and their distraction wild?

But now the supper crowns their simple board,
The halesome parritch, chief o' Scotia's food,
The soupe their only hawkie does afford,
That 'yont the hallan snugly chows her cood:
The dame brings forth, in complimental mood,
To grace the lad, her weel-hained kebbuck, fell,
And aft he's pressed, and aft he ca's it guid;
The frugal wifie, garrulous, will tell
How 'twas a towmond auld, sin' lint was i' the bell.

The cheerfu' supper done, wi' serious face,
They, round the ingle, form a circle wide;
The sire turns o'er, wi' patriarchal grace,
The big ha' Bible, ance his father's pride;
His bonnet reverently is laid aside,
His lyart haffets wearing thin and bare;
Those strains that once did sweet in Zion glide,
He wales a portion with judicious care;
And "Let us worship God!" he says, with solemn air.

They chant their artless notes in simple guise;
They tune their hearts, by far the noblest aim:
Perhaps "Dundee's" wild-warbling measures rise,
Or plaintive "Martyrs," worthy of the name,
Or noble "Elgin" beets the heavenward flame,
The sweetest far of Scotia's holy lays:
Compared with these, Italian trills are tame;
The tickled ear no heartfelt raptures raise;
Nae unison hae they with our Creator's praise.

The priest-like father reads the sacred page,—
How Abram was the friend of God on high;
Or Moses bade eternal warfare wage
With Amalek's ungracious progeny;
Or how the royal bard did groaning lie
Beneath the stroke of Heaven's avenging ire;
Or Job's pathetic plaint, and wailing cry;
Or rapt Isaiah's wild, seraphic fire;
Or other holy seers that tune the sacred lyre.

Perhaps the Christian volume is the theme,—
How guiltless blood for guilty man was shed;
How He, who bore in heaven the second name,
Had not on earth whereon to lay his head:
How his first followers and servants sped
The precepts sage they wrote to many a land;
How he, who lone in Patmos banishèd,
Saw in the sun a mighty angel stand,
And heard great Babylon's doom pronounced by Heaven's
command.

Then kneeling down to Heaven's Eternal King,
The saint, the father, and the husband prays:
Hope "springs exulting on triumphant wing,"
That thus they all shall meet in future days:
There ever bask in uncreated rays,
No more to sigh, or shed the bitter tear,
Together hymning their Creator's praise,
In such society, yet still more dear;
While circling Time moves round in an eternal sphere.

Compared with this, how poor Religion's pride,
In all the pomp of method and of art,
When men display to congregations wide,
Devotion's every grace, except the heart!
The Power, incensed, the pageant will desert,
The pompous strain, the sacerdotal stole;
But, haply, in some cottage far apart,
May hear, well pleased, the language of the soul;
And in His Book of Life the inmates poor enroll.

Then homeward all take off their several way;
The youngling cottagers retire to rest:
The parent-pair their secret homage pay,
And proffer up to Heaven the warm request,
That He, who stills the raven's clamorous nest,
And decks the lily fair in flowery pride,
Would, in the way His wisdom sees the best,
For them and for their little ones provide;
But, chiefly, in their hearts with grace divine preside.

From scenes like these old Scotia's grandeur springs,
That makes her loved at home, revered abroad;
Princes and lords are but the breath of kings,
"An honest man's the noblest work of God";
And certes, in fair Virtue's heavenly road,
The cottage leaves the palace far behind:
What is a lordling's pomp?—a cumbrous load,
Disguising oft the wretch of human kind,
Studied in arts of hell, in wickedness refined!

O Scotia! my dear, my native soil!
For whom my warmest wish to Heaven is sent,
Long may thy hardy sons of rustic toil
Be blest with health, and peace, and sweet content!
And, oh, may Heaven their simple lives prevent
From luxury's contagion, weak and vile!
Then, howe'er crowns and coronets be rent,
A virtuous populace may rise the while,
And stand a wall of fire around their much-loved isle.

O Thou! who poured the patriotic tide,
That streamed through Wallace's undaunted heart;
Who dared to nobly stem tyrannic pride,
Or nobly die, the second glorious part,
(The patriot's God peculiarly thou art,
His friend, inspirer, guardian, and reward!)
O, never, never Scotia's realm desert;
But still the patriot, and the patriot bard,
In bright succession raise, her ornament and guard!

*Robert Burns* [1759-1796]

## ON THE RECEIPT OF MY MOTHER'S PICTURE OUT OF NORFOLK

### THE GIFT OF MY COUSIN, ANN BODHAM

O THAT those lips had language! Life has passed
With me but roughly since I heard thee last.
Those lips are thine,—thy own sweet smile I see,
The same that oft in childhood solaced me;
Voice only fails, else how distinct they say,
"Grieve not, my child; chase all thy fears away!"
The meek intelligence of those dear eyes
(Blest be the art that can immortalize,
The art that baffles Time's tyrannic claim
To quench it!) here shines on me still the same.
Faithful remembrancer of one so dear!
O welcome guest, though unexpected here!
Who bid'st me honor with an artless song,
Affectionate. a mother lost so long,

I will obey, not willingly alone,
But gladly, as the precept were her own:
And, while that face renews my filial grief,
Fancy shall weave a charm for my relief,
Shall steep me in Elysian reverie,
A momentary dream that thou art she.
My mother! when I learned that thou wast dead,
Say, wast thou conscious of the tears I shed?
Hovered thy spirit o'er thy sorrowing son,
Wretch even then, life's journey just begun?
Perhaps thou gavest me, though unfelt, a kiss:
Perhaps a tear, if souls can weep in bliss—
Ah, that maternal smile! It answers—Yes.
I heard the bell tolled on thy burial day;
I saw the hearse that bore thee slow away;
And, turning from my nursery window, drew
A long, long sigh, and wept a last adieu!
But was it such?—It was.—Where thou art gone
Adieus and farewells are a sound unknown.
May I but meet thee on that peaceful shore,
The parting word shall pass my lips no more.
Thy maidens, grieved themselves at my concern,
Oft gave me promise of thy quick return.
What ardently I wished I long believed,
And, disappointed still, was still deceived.
By expectation every day beguiled,
Dupe of *to-morrow* even from a child.
Thus many a sad to-morrow came and went,
Till, all my stock of infant sorrow spent,
I learned at last submission to my lot;
But, though I less deplored thee, ne'er forgot.
Where once we dwelt our name is heard no more;
Children not thine have trod my nursery floor;
And where the gardener Robin, day by day,
Drew me to school along the public way,
Delighted with my bawble coach, and wrapped
In scarlet mantle warm, and velvet capped,
'Tis now become a history little known
That once we called the pastoral house our own.

Short-lived possession! but the record fair,
That memory keeps of all thy kindness there,
Still outlives many a storm that has effaced
A thousand other themes, less deeply traced.
Thy nightly visits to my chamber made,
That thou might'st know me safe and warmly laid;
Thy morning bounties ere I left my home,
The biscuit, or confectionery plum;
The fragrant waters on my cheek bestowed
By thy own hand, till fresh they shone and glowed;
All this, and, more endearing still than all,
Thy constant flow of love, that knew no fall,
Ne'er roughened by those cataracts and brakes
That humor interposed too often makes;
All this still legible in memory's page,
And still to be so to my latest age,
Adds joy to duty, makes me glad to pay
Such honors to thee as my numbers may;
Perhaps a frail memorial, but sincere,
Not scorned in heaven, though little noticed here.
  Could Time, his flight reversed, restore the hours,
When, playing with thy vesture's tissued flowers,
The violet, the pink, the jessamine,
I pricked them into paper with a pin
(And thou wast happier than myself the while,
Wouldst softly speak, and stroke my head and smile),
Could those few pleasant days again appear,
Might one wish bring them, would I wish them here?
I would not trust my heart,—the dear delight
Seems so to be desired, perhaps I might,—
But no,—what here we call our life is such,
So little to be loved, and thou so much,
That I should ill requite thee to constrain
Thy unbound spirit into bonds again.
  Thou, as a gallant bark, from Albion's coast
(The storms all weathered and the ocean crossed),
Shoots into port at some well-havened isle,
Where spices breathe, and brighter seasons smile;
There sits quiescent on the floods, that show
Her beauteous form reflected clear below,

While airs impregnated with incense play
Around her, fanning light her streamers gay;
So thou, with sails how swift! hast reached the shore,
"Where tempests never beat nor billows roar,"
And thy loved consort on the dangerous tide
Of life long since has anchored by thy side.
But me, scarce hoping to attain that rest,
Always from port withheld, always distressed,—
Me howling blasts drive devious, tempest-tossed,
Sails ripped, seams opening wide, and compass lost;
And day by day some current's thwarting force
Sets me more distant from a prosperous course.
Yet oh, the thought that thou art safe, and he!
That thought is joy, arrive what may to me.
My boast is not that I deduce my birth
From loins enthroned, and rulers of the earth;
But higher far my proud pretensions rise,—
The son of parents passed into the skies!
  And now, farewell!—Time, unrevoked, has run
His wonted course; yet what I wished is done.
By contemplation's help, not sought in vain,
I seem to have lived my childhood o'er again:
To have renewed the joys that once were mine,
Without the sin of violating thine;
And, while the wings of Fancy still are free,
And I can view this mimic show of thee,
Time has but half succeeded in his theft,—
Thyself removed, thy power to soothe me left.

*William Cowper* [1731-1800]

## THE CROWING OF THE RED COCK

ACROSS the Eastern sky has glowed
  The flicker of a blood-red dawn,
Once more the clarion cock has crowed,
  Once more the sword of Christ is drawn.
A million burning rooftrees light
The world-wide path of Israel's flight.

Where is the Hebrew's Fatherland?
  The folk of Christ is sore bestead;
The Son of Man is bruised and banned,
  Nor finds whereon to lay his head.
His cup is gall, his meat is tears,
His passion lasts a thousand years.

Each crime that wakes in man the beast,
  Is visited upon his kind.
The lust of mobs, the greed of priest,
  The tyranny of kings, combined
To root his seed from earth again;
His record is one cry of pain.

When the long roll of Christian guilt
  Against his sires and kin is known,
The flood of tears, the life-blood spilt,
  The agony of ages shown,
What oceans can the stain remove
From Christian law and Christian love?

Nay, close the book; not now, not here,
  The hideous tale of sin narrate,
Re-echoing in the martyr's ear
  Even he might nurse revengeful hate,
Even he might turn in wrath sublime,
With blood for blood and crime for crime.

Coward? Not he, who faces death,
  Who singly against worlds has fought,
For what? A name he may not breathe,
  For liberty of prayer and thought.
The angry sword he will not whet,
His nobler task is—to forget.

*Emma Lazarus* [1849–1887]

## THE WORLD'S JUSTICE

If the sudden tidings came
  That on some far, foreign coast,
Buried ages long from fame,
  Had been found a remnant lost

Of that hoary race who dwelt
  By the golden Nile divine,
Spake the Pharaoh's tongue and knelt
  At the moon-crowned Isis' shrine—
How at reverend Egypt's feet,
Pilgrims from all lands would meet!

If the sudden news were known,
  That anigh the desert-place
Where once blossomed Babylon,
  Scions of a mighty race
Still survived, of giant build,
  Huntsmen, warriors, priest and sage,
Whose ancestral fame had filled,
  Trumpet-tongued, the earlier age,
How at old Assyria's feet
Pilgrims from all lands would meet!

Yet when Egypt's self was young,
  And Assyria's bloom unworn,
Ere the mythic Homer sung,
  Ere the gods of Greece were born,
Lived the nation of one God,
  Priests of freedom, sons of Shem,
Never quelled by yoke or rod,
  Founders of Jerusalem—
Is there one abides to-day,
Seeker of dead cities, say!

Answer, now as then, *they are;*
  Scattered broadcast o'er the lands,
Knit in spirit nigh and far,
  With indissoluble bands.
Half the world adores their God,
  They the living law proclaim,
And their guerdon is—the rod,
  Stripes and scourgings, death and shame.
Still on Israel's head forlorn,
Every nation heaps its scorn.

*Emma Lazarus* [1849–1887]

## DOVER CLIFFS

On these white cliffs, that calm above the flood
Uplift their shadowing heads, and at their feet
Hear not the surge that has for ages beat,
How many a lonely wanderer has stood;
And, whilst the lifted murmur met his ear
And o'er the distant billows the still eve
Sailed slow, has thought of all his heart must leave
To-morrow; of the friends he loved most dear;
Of social scenes from which he wept to part.
Oh! if, like me, he knew how fruitless all
The thoughts that would full fain the past recall,
Soon would he quell the risings of his heart,
And brave the wild winds and unhearing tide,—
The World his country, and his God his guide.

*William Lisle Bowles* [1762–1850]

## THE BRIDGE

Across the foaming river
  The old bridge bends its bow;
My father's fathers built it
  In ages long ago.

They never left the farmstead
  Past which the waters curled,
Why should one ever wander
  When here is all the world:

Family, friends and garden;
  Small fields of rice and tea;
The cattle in the meadow;
  The birds in stream and tree;

The pageant of the seasons
  As the slow years go by;
Between the peaks above us
  An azure bridge of sky.

The dead they live and linger
  In each familiar place
With kindly thoughts to hearten
  The children of their race.

*Frederick Peterson* [1859–1938]

## THE EXILE'S SONG

Oh, why left I my hame?
  Why did I cross the deep?
Oh, why left I the land
  Where my forefathers sleep?
I sigh for Scotia's shore,
  And I gaze across the sea,
But I canna get a blink
  O' my ain countrie!

The palm-tree waveth high,
  And fair the myrtle springs;
And to the Indian maid
  The bulbul sweetly sings;
But I dinna see the broom
  Wi' its tassels on the lea,
Nor hear the lintie's sang
  O' my ain countrie!

Oh, here no Sabbath bell
  Awakes the Sabbath morn,
Nor song of reapers heard
  Amang the yellow corn:
For the tyrant's voice is here,
  And the wail o' slaverie;
But the sun of freedom shines
  In my ain countrie!

There's a hope for every woe,
  And a balm for every pain,
But the first joys o' our heart
  Come never back again.
There's a track upon the deep,
  And a path across the sea;
But the weary ne'er return
  To their ain countrie!

*Robert Gilfillan* [1798–1850]

## "THE SUN RISES BRIGHT IN FRANCE"

THE sun rises bright in France,
And fair sets he;
But he has tint the blithe blink he had
In my ain countrie.

O, it's nae my ain ruin
That saddens aye my e'e,
But the dear Marie I left behin'
Wi' sweet bairnies three.

My lanely hearth burned bonnie,
An' smiled my ain Marie;
I've left a' my heart behin'
In my ain countrie.

The bird comes back to summer,
And the blossom to the bee;
But I'll win back, O never,
To my ain countrie.

O, I am leal to high Heaven,
Which aye was leal to me,
An' there I'll meet ye a' soon
Frae my ain countrie!

*Allan Cunningham* [1784-1842]

## FATHER LAND AND MOTHER TONGUE

OUR Father Land! and wouldst thou know
Why we should call it Father Land?
It is that Adam here below
Was made of earth by Nature's hand;
And he, our father made of earth,
Hath peopled earth on every hand;
And we, in memory of his birth,
Do call our country Father Land.

At first, in Eden's bowers, they say,
  No sound of speech had Adam caught,
But whistled like a bird all day,—
  And maybe 'twas for want of thought:
But Nature, with resistless laws,
  Made Adam soon surpass the birds;
She gave him lovely Eve because
  If he'd a wife they must *have words.*

And so the native land, I hold,
  By male descent is proudly mine;
The language, as the tale hath told,
  Was given in the female line.
And thus we see on either hand
  We name our blessings whence they've sprung;
We call our country Father Land,
  We call our language Mother Tongue.

*Samuel Lover* [1797-1868]

## THE FATHERLAND

WHERE is the true man's fatherland?
  Is it where he by chance is born?
  Doth not the yearning spirit scorn
In such scant borders to be spanned?
Oh, yes! his fatherland must be
As the blue heaven wide and free!

Is it alone where freedom is,
  Where God is God and man is man?
  Doth he not claim a broader span
For the soul's love of home than this?
Oh, yes! his fatherland must be
As the blue heaven wide and free!

Where'er a human heart doth wear
  Joy's myrtle-wreath or sorrow's gyves,
  Where'er a human spirit strives

After a life more true and fair,
There is the true man's birthplace grand,
His is a world-wide fatherland!

Where'er a single slave doth pine,
  Where'er one man may help another,—
  Thank God for such a birthright, brother,—
That spot of earth is thine and mine!
There is the true man's birthplace grand,
His is a world-wide fatherland!

*James Russell Lowell* [1819–1891]

## THE CALL TO A SCOT

There came an ancient man and slow
  Who piped his way along our street—
How could the neighbors' children know
  That to her ears 'twas passing sweet?

With smiles they spoke the ragged kilt,
  And jeered the pipes, in mirthful file;
But, strangely moved, she heard the lilt
  That rallied Carrick and Argyle.

A stroller, playing in the street,
  Half-hearted, weary, out of place—
But his old measure stirred her feet,
  My baby with the Gaelic face:

She squared her shoulders as she stood
  To watch the piper 'round the turn—
Nor dreamed what beat within her blood
  Was Robert Bruce and Bannockburn!

*Ruth Guthrie Harding* [1882-

# NARRATIVE AND DESCRIPTIVE POEMS

## THE DESERTED VILLAGE

Sweet Auburn! loveliest village of the plain,
Where health and plenty cheered the laboring swain,
Where smiling spring its earliest visit paid,
And parting summer's lingering blooms delayed:
Dear lovely bowers of innocence and ease,
Seats of my youth, when every sport could please:
How often have I loitered o'er thy green,
Where humble happiness endeared each scene!
How often have I paused on every charm,
The sheltered cot, the cultivated farm,
The never-failing brook, the busy mill,
The decent church that topped the neighboring hill,
The hawthorn bush, with seats beneath the shade,
For talking age and whispering lovers made!
How often have I blessed the coming day,
When toil remitting lent its turn to play,
And all the village train, from labor free,
Led up their sports beneath the spreading tree:
While many a pastime circled in the shade,
The young contending as the old surveyed;
And many a gambol frolicked o'er the ground,
And sleights of art and feats of strength went round:
And still, as each repeated pleasure tired,
Succeeding sports the mirthful band inspired;
The dancing pair that simply sought renown,
By holding out, to tire each other down;
The swain mistrustless of his smutted face,
While secret laughter tittered round the place;
The bashful virgin's sidelong looks of love,
The matron's glance that would those looks reprove,—

These were thy charms, sweet village! sports like these,
With sweet succession, taught e'en toil to please;
These round thy bowers their cheerful influence shed,
These were thy charms,—but all these charms are fled.

Sweet smiling village, loveliest of the lawn,
Thy sports are fled, and all thy charms withdrawn;
Amidst thy bowers the tyrant's hand is seen,
And desolation saddens all thy green;
One only master grasps the whole domain,
And half a tillage stints thy smiling plain;
No more thy glassy brook reflects the day,
But, choked with sedges, works its weedy way;
Along thy glades, a solitary guest,
The hollow-sounding bittern guards its nest;
Amidst thy desert walks the lapwing flies,
And tires their echoes with unvaried cries.
Sunk are thy bowers in shapeless ruin all,
And the long grass o'ertops the moldering wall,
And, trembling, shrinking from the spoiler's hand,
Far, far away thy children leave the land.

Ill fares the land, to hastening ills a prey,
Where wealth accumulates, and men decay:
Princes and lords may flourish, or may fade;
A breath can make them, as a breath has made;
But a bold peasantry, their country's pride,
When once destroyed, can never be supplied.

A time there was, ere England's griefs began,
When every rood of ground maintained its man;
For him light labor spread her wholesome store,
Just gave what life required, but gave no more:
His best companions, innocence and health;
And his best riches, ignorance of wealth.

But times are altered: trade's unfeeling train
Usurp the land and dispossess the swain;
Along the lawn, where scattered hamlets rose,
Unwieldy wealth and cumbrous pomp repose,
And every want to opulence allied,
And every pang that folly pays to pride.

Those gentle hours that plenty bade to bloom,
Those calm desires that asked but little room,
Those healthful sports that graced the peaceful scene,
Lived in each look, and brightened all the green,—
These, far departing, seek a kinder shore,
And rural mirth and manners are no more.

Sweet Auburn! parent of the blissful hour,
Thy glades forlorn confess the tyrant's power.
Here, as I take my solitary rounds,
Amidst thy tangling walks and ruined grounds,
And, many a year elapsed, return to view
Where once the cottage stood, the hawthorn grew,
Remembrance wakes, with all her busy train,
Swells at my breast, and turns the past to pain.

In all my wanderings round this world of care,
In all my griefs—and God has given my share—
I still had hopes my latest hours to crown,
Amidst these humble bowers to lay me down;
To husband out life's taper at the close,
And keep the flame from wasting by repose;
I still had hopes—for pride attends us still—
Amidst the swains to show my book-learned skill,
Around my fire an evening group to draw,
And tell of all I felt, and all I saw;
And, as a hare, whom hounds and horns pursue,
Pants to the place from whence at first she flew,
I still had hopes, my long vexations past,
Here to return,—and die at home at last.

O blest retirement, friend to life's decline,
Retreats from care, that never must be mine,
How happy he who crowns, in shades like these,
A youth of labor with an age of ease;
Who quits a world where strong temptations try,
And, since 'tis hard to combat, learns to fly!
For him no wretches, born to work and weep,
Explore the mine, or tempt the dangerous deep;
No surly porter stands in guilty state,
To spurn imploring famine from the gate:

But on he moves to meet his latter end,
Angels around befriending Virtue's friend;
Bends to the grave with unperceived decay,
While Resignation gently slopes the way;
And, all his prospects brightening to the last,
His heaven commences ere the world be past.

Sweet was the sound, when oft, at evening's close,
Up yonder hill the village murmur rose;
There, as I passed with careless steps and slow,
The mingling notes came softened from below;
The swain responsive as the milkmaid sung,
The sober herd that lowed to meet their young;
The noisy geese that gabbled o'er the pool,
The playful children just let loose from school;
The watch-dog's voice that bayed the whispering wind,
And the loud laugh that spoke the vacant mind,—
These all in sweet confusion sought the shade,
And filled each pause the nightingale had made.
But now the sounds of population fail,
No cheerful murmurs fluctuate in the gale,
No busy steps the grass-grown foot-way tread,
For all the bloomy flush of life is fled—
All but yon widowed, solitary thing,
That feebly bends beside the plashy spring;
She, wretched matron, forced in age, for bread,
To strip the brook with mantling cresses spread,
To pick her wintry fagot from the thorn,
To seek her nightly shed, and weep till morn;
She only left of all the harmless train,
The sad historian of the pensive plain.

Near yonder copse, where once the garden smiled,
And still where many a garden-flower grows wild;
There, where a few torn shrubs the place disclose,
The village preacher's modest mansion rose.
A man he was to all the country dear,
And passing rich with forty pounds a year;
Remote from towns he ran his godly race,
Nor e'er had changed, nor wished to change, his place:

Unpractised he to fawn, or seek for power,
By doctrines fashioned to the varying hour;
Far other aims his heart had learned to prize,
More skilled to raise the wretched than to rise.
His house was known to all the vagrant train.
He chid their wanderings, but relieved their pain;
The long-remembered beggar was his guest,
Whose beard descending swept his aged breast;
The ruined spendthrift, now no longer proud,
Claimed kindred there, and had his claims allowed;
The broken soldier, kindly bade to stay,
Sat by his fire, and talked the night away;
Wept o'er his wounds, or, tales of sorrow done,
Shouldered his crutch, and showed how fields were won.
Pleased with his guests, the good man learned to glow,
And quite forgot their vices in their woe;
Careless their merits or their faults to scan,
His pity gave ere charity began.

Thus to relieve the wretched was his pride,
And e'en his failings leaned to Virtue's side;
But in his duty prompt at every call,
He watched and wept, he prayed and felt for all;
And, as a bird each fond endearment tries
To tempt its new-fledged offspring to the skies,
He tried each art, reproved each dull delay,
Allured to brighter worlds, and led the way.

Beside the bed where parting life was laid,
And sorrow, guilt, and pain, by turns dismayed,
The reverend champion stood. At his control,
Despair and anguish fled the struggling soul;
Comfort came down the trembling wretch to raise,
And his last faltering accents whispered praise.

At church, with meek and unaffected grace,
His looks adorned the venerable place;
Truth from his lips prevailed with double sway,
And fools, who came to scoff, remained to pray.
The service past, around the pious man,
With steady zeal, each honest rustic ran;

Even children followed, with endearing wile,
And plucked his gown, to share the good man's smile.
His ready smile a parent's warmth expressed,
Their welfare pleased him, and their cares distressed;
To them his heart, his love, his griefs were given,
But all his serious thoughts had rest in heaven.
As some tall cliff, that lifts its awful form,
Swells from the vale, and midway leaves the storm,
Though round its breast the rolling clouds are spread,
Eternal sunshine settles on its head.

Beside yon straggling fence that skirts the way,
With blossomed furze unprofitably gay,
There, in his noisy mansion, skilled to rule,
The village master taught his little school;
A man severe he was, and stern to view;
I knew him well, and every truant knew:
Well had the boding tremblers learned to trace
The day's disasters in his morning face;
Full well they laughed, with counterfeited glee,
At all his jokes, for many a joke had he;
Full well the busy whisper, circling round,
Conveyed the dismal tidings when he frowned;
Yet he was kind, or, if severe in aught,
The love he bore to learning was in fault.
The village all declared how much he knew;
'Twas certain he could write, and cipher too;
Lands he could measure, terms and tides presage,
And e'en the story ran that he could gauge;
In arguing, too, the parson owned his skill,
For, e'en though vanquished, he could argue still,
While words of learnèd length and thundering sound
Amazed the gazing rustics ranged around;
And still they gazed, and still the wonder grew
That one small head could carry all he knew.

But past is all his fame. The very spot
Where many a time he triumphed, is forgot.
Near yonder thorn, that lifts its head on high,
Where once the sign-post caught the passing eye,

Low lies that house where nut-brown draughts inspired,
Where graybeard mirth and smiling toil retired,
Where village statesmen talked with looks profound,
And news much older than their ale went round.
Imagination fondly stoops to trace
The parlor splendors of that festive place,—
The whitewashed wall; the nicely sanded floor;
The varnished clock that clicked behind the door;
The chest contrived a double debt to pay—
A bed by night, a chest of drawers by day;
The pictures placed for ornament and use;
The twelve good rules, the royal game of goose;
The hearth, except when winter chilled the day,
With aspen boughs and flowers and fennel gay;
While broken teacups, wisely kept for show,
Ranged o'er the chimney, glistened in a row.

Vain, transitory splendors! could not all
Reprieve the tottering mansion from its fall?
Obscure it sinks, nor shall it more impart
An hour's importance to the poor man's heart;
Thither no more the peasant shall repair
To sweet oblivion of his daily care;
No more the farmer's news, the barber's tale,
No more the woodman's ballad shall prevail;
No more the smith his dusky brow shall clear,
Relax his ponderous strength, and lean to hear;
The host himself no longer shall be found
Careful to see the mantling bliss go round;
Nor the coy maid, half willing to be pressed,
Shall kiss the cup to pass it to the rest.

Yes! let the rich deride, the proud disdain,
These simple blessings of the lowly train;
To me more dear, congenial to my heart,
One native charm, than all the gloss of art.
Spontaneous joys, where nature has its play,
The soul adopts, and owns their first-born sway;
Lightly they frolic o'er the vacant mind,
Unenvied, unmolested, unconfined:

But the long pomp, the midnight masquerade,
With all the freaks of wanton wealth arrayed,—
In these, ere triflers half their wish obtain,
The toiling pleasure sickens into pain;
And, e'en while fashion's brightest arts decoy,
The heart, distrusting, asks if this be joy.

Ye friends to truth, ye statesmen, who survey
The rich man's joys increase, the poor's decay,
'Tis yours to judge, how wide the limits stand
Between a splendid and a happy land.
Proud swells the tide with loads of freighted ore,
And shouting Folly hails them from her shore;
Hoards e'en beyond the miser's wish abound,
And rich men flock from all the world around.
Yet count our gains. This wealth is but a name
That leaves our useful products still the same.
Not so the loss. The man of wealth and pride
Takes up a space that many poor supplied;
Space for his lake, his park's extended bounds,
Space for his horses, equipage, and hounds:
The robe that wraps his limbs in silken sloth
Has robbed the neighboring fields of half their growth;
His seat, where solitary sports are seen,
Indignant spurns the cottage from the green;
Around the world each needful product flies,
For all the luxuries the world supplies:
While thus the land, adorned for pleasure all,
In barren splendor feebly waits the fall.

As some fair female, unadorned and plain,
Secure to please while youth confirms her reign,
Slights every borrowed charm that dress supplies,
Nor shares with art the triumph of her eyes,
But when those charms are past,—for charms are frail,—
When time advances, and when lovers fail,
She then shines forth, solicitous to bless,
In all the glaring impotence of dress;
Thus fares the land, by luxury betrayed,
In nature's simplest charms at first arrayed,

But verging to decline, its splendors rise,
Its vistas strike, its palaces surprise;
While, scourged by famine from the smiling land,
The mournful peasant leads his humble band;
And while he sinks, without one arm to save,
The country blooms,—a garden and a grave.

Where then, ah! where shall poverty reside,
To 'scape the pressure of contiguous pride?
If to some common's fenceless limits strayed,
He drives his flock to pick the scanty blade,
Those fenceless fields the sons of wealth divide,
And e'en the bare-worn common is denied.
If to the city sped,—what waits him there?
To see profusion that he must not share;
To see ten thousand baneful arts combined
To pamper luxury and thin mankind;
To see those joys the sons of pleasure know
Extorted from his fellow-creature's woe.
Here while the courtier glitters in brocade,
There the pale artist plies the sickly trade;
Here while the proud their long-drawn pomps display,
There the black gibbet glooms beside the way.
The dome where Pleasure holds her midnight reign,
Here, richly decked, admits the gorgeous train;
Tumultuous grandeur crowds the blazing square,
The rattling chariots clash, the torches glare.
Sure scenes like these no troubles e'er annoy!
Sure these denote one universal joy!
Are these thy serious thoughts?—Ah, turn thine eyes
Where the poor houseless shivering female lies.
She once, perhaps, in village plenty blest,
Has wept at tales of innocence distressed;
Her modest looks the cottage might adorn,
Sweet as the primrose peeps beneath the thorn;
Now lost to all, her friends, her virtue fled,
Near her betrayer's door she lays her head,
And, pinched with cold, and shrinking from the shower,
With heavy heart deplores that luckless hour,
When idly first, ambitious of the town,
She left her wheel and robes of country brown.

Do thine, sweet Auburn, thine, the loveliest train,
Do thy fair tribes participate her pain?
E'en now, perhaps, by cold and hunger led,
At proud men's doors they ask a little bread!

Ah, no! To distant climes, a dreary scene,
Where half the convex world intrudes between,
Through torrid tracts with fainting steps they go,
Where wild Altama murmurs to their woe.
Far different there from all that charmed before,
The various terrors of that horrid shore,—
Those blazing suns that dart a downward ray,
And fiercely shed intolerable day;
Those matted woods where birds forget to sing,
But silent bats in drowsy clusters cling;
Those poisonous fields with rank luxuriance crowned,
Where the dark scorpion gathers death around;
Where at each step the stranger fears to wake
The rattling terrors of the vengeful snake;
Where crouching tigers wait their hapless prey,
And savage men more murderous still than they;
While oft in whirls the mad tornado flies,
Mingling the ravaged landscape with the skies.
Far different these from every former scene,
The cooling brook, the grassy-vested green,
The breezy covert of the warbling grove,
That only sheltered thefts of harmless love.

Good Heaven! what sorrows gloomed that parting day
That called them from their native walks away;
When the poor exiles, every pleasure past,
Hung round their bowers, and fondly looked their last,
And took a long farewell, and wished in vain
For seats like these beyond the western main;
And, shuddering still to face the distant deep,
Returned and wept, and still returned to weep.
The good old sire the first prepared to go
To new-found worlds, and wept for others' woe;
But for himself, in conscious virtue brave,
He only wished for worlds beyond the grave.

His lovely daughter, lovelier in her tears,
The fond companion of his helpless years,
Silent went next, neglectful of her charms,
And left a lover's for a father's arms.
With louder plaints the mother spoke her woes,
And blessed the cot where every pleasure rose;
And kissed her thoughtless babes with many a tear,
And clasped them close, in sorrow doubly dear;
Whilst her fond husband strove to lend relief
In all the silent manliness of grief.

O Luxury! thou cursed by Heaven's decree,
How ill exchanged are things like these for thee!
How do thy potions, with insidious joy,
Diffuse their pleasures only to destroy!
Kingdoms by thee, to sickly greatness grown,
Boast of a florid vigor not their own.
At every draught more large and large they grow,
A bloated mass of rank, unwieldy woe;
Till, sapped their strength, and every part unsound,
Down, down they sink, and spread a ruin round.

E'en now the devastation is begun,
And half the business of destruction done;
Even now, methinks, as pondering here I stand,
I see the rural virtues leave the land.
Down where yon anchoring vessel spreads the sail
That idly waiting flaps with every gale,
Downward they move, a melancholy band,
Pass from the shore, and darken all the strand.
Contented toil, and hospitable care,
And kind connubial tenderness, are there;
And piety with wishes placed above,
And steady loyalty, and faithful love.
And thou, sweet Poetry, thou loveliest maid,
Still first to fly where sensual joys invade;
Unfit, in these degenerate times of shame,
To catch the heart, or strike for honest fame;
Dear charming nymph, neglected and decried,
My shame in crowds, my solitary pride;

Thou source of all my bliss and all my woe,
That found'st me poor at first, and keep'st me so;
Thou guide, by which the nobler arts excel,
Thou nurse of every virtue, fare thee well!
Farewell; and oh, where'er thy voice be tried,
On Torno's cliffs or Pambamarca's side,
Whether where equinoctial fervors glow,
Or winter wraps the polar world in snow,
Still let thy voice, prevailing over time,
Redress the rigors of the inclement clime;
Aid slighted truth; with thy persuasive strain
Teach erring man to spurn the rage of gain;
Teach him, that states of native strength possessed,
Though very poor, may still be very blest;
That trade's proud empire hastes to swift decay,
As ocean sweeps the labored mole away;
While self-dependent power can time defy,
As rocks resist the billows and the sky.

*Oliver Goldsmith* [1728–1774]

## THE PRISONER OF CHILLON: A FABLE

### SONNET ON CHILLON

ETERNAL Spirit of the chainless Mind!
Brightest in dungeons, Liberty, thou art,
For there thy habitation is the heart—
The heart which love of thee alone can bind;
And when thy sons to fetters are consigned—
To fetters, and the damp vault's dayless gloom—
Their country conquers with their martyrdom,
And Freedom's fame finds wings on every wind.
Chillon! thy prison is a holy place,
And thy sad floor an altar; for 'twas trod,
Until his very steps have left a trace
Worn, as if thy cold pavement were a sod,
By Bonnivard!—May none those marks efface!
For they appeal from tyranny to God.

I

My hair is gray, but not with years,
Nor grew it white
In a single night,
As men's have grown from sudden fears.
My limbs are bowed, though not with toil,
But rusted with a vile repose,
For they have been a dungeon's spoil,
And mine has been the fate of those
To whom the goodly earth and air
Are banned and barred—forbidden fare.
But this was for my father's faith,
I suffered chains and courted death.
That father perished at the stake
For tenets he would not forsake;
And for the same his lineal race
In darkness found a dwelling-place.
We were seven,—who now are one—
Six in youth, and one in age,
Finished as they had begun,
Proud of Persecution's rage:
One in fire, and two in field,
Their belief with blood have sealed—
Dying as their father died,
For the God their foes denied;
Three were in a dungeon cast,
Of whom this wreck is left the last.

II

There are seven pillars, of Gothic mold,
In Chillon's dungeons deep and old;
There are seven columns, massy and gray,
Dim with a dull imprisoned ray—
A sunbeam which hath lost its way,
And through the crevice and the cleft
Of the thick wall is fallen and left,
Creeping o'er the floor so damp,
Like a marsh's meteor-lamp.

And in each pillar there is a ring,
  And in each ring there is a chain:
That iron is a cankering thing,
  For in these limbs its teeth remain,
With marks that will not wear away
Till I have done with this new day,
Which now is painful to these eyes,
Which have not seen the sun so rise
For years—I cannot count them o'er;
I lost their long and heavy score
When my last brother drooped and died,
And I lay living by his side.

III

They chained us each to a column stone,
And we were three—yet, each alone;
We could not move a single pace;
We could not see each other's face,
But with that pale and livid light
That made us strangers in our sight;
And thus together, yet apart,
Fettered in hand, but joined in heart,
'Twas still some solace, in the dearth
Of the pure elements of earth,
To hearken to each other's speech,
And each turn comforter to each
With some new hope or legend old,
Or song heroically bold;
But even these at length grew cold.
Our voices took a dreary tone,
An echo of the dungeon-stone,
    A grating sound—not full and free,
    As they of yore were wont to be;
    It might be fancy—but to me
They never sounded like our own.

IV

I was the eldest of the three,
    And to uphold and cheer the rest
    I ought to do, and did, my best—
And each did well in his degree.

The youngest, whom my father loved,
Because our mother's brow was given
To him, with eyes as blue as heaven—
For him my soul was sorely moved;
And truly might it be distressed
To see such bird in such a nest;
For he was beautiful as day
(When day was beautiful to me
As to young eagles, being free),—
A polar day, which will not see
A sunset till its summer's gone—
Its sleepless summer of long light,
The snow-clad offspring of the sun:
And thus he was as pure and bright,
And in his natural spirit gay,
With tears for naught but others' ills;
And then they flowed like mountain rills,
Unless he could assuage the woe
Which he abhorred to view below.

V

The other was as pure of mind,
But formed to combat with his kind;
Strong in his frame, and of a mood
Which 'gainst the world in war had stood,
And perished in the foremost rank
With joy; but not in chains to pine.
His spirit withered with their clank;
I saw it silently decline—
And so, perchance, in sooth, did mine:
But yet I forced it on, to cheer
Those relics of a home so dear.
He was a hunter of the hills,
Had followed there the deer and wolf;
To him this dungeon was a gulf,
And fettered feet the worst of ills.

VI

Lake Leman lies by Chillon's walls,
A thousand feet in depth below,
Its massy waters meet and flow;

Thus much the fathom-line was sent
From Chillon's snow-white battlement,
  Which round about the wave enthralls;
A double dungeon wall and wave
Have made—and like a living grave,
Below the surface of the lake
The dark vault lies wherein we lay;
We heard it ripple night and day;
  Sounding o'er our heads it knocked.
And I have felt the winter's spray
Wash through the bars when winds were high,
And wanton in the happy sky;
    And then the very rock hath rocked,
    And I have felt it shake, unshocked;
Because I could have smiled to see
The death that would have set me free.

VII

I said my nearer brother pined;
I said his mighty heart declined.
He loathed and put away his food;
It was not that 'twas coarse and rude,
For we were used to hunters' fare,
And for the like had little care.
The milk drawn from the mountain goat
Was changed for water from the moat;
Our bread was such as captives' tears
Have moistened many a thousand years,
Since man first pent his fellow-men,
Like brutes, within an iron den.
But what were these to us or him?
These wasted not his heart or limb;
My brother's soul was of that mold
Which in a palace had grown cold,
Had his free breathing been denied
The range of the steep mountain's side.
But why delay the truth?—he died.
I saw, and could not hold his head,
Nor reach his dying hand—nor dead,—
Though hard I strove, but strove in vain,

To rend and gnash my bonds in twain.
He died—and they unlocked his chain,
And scooped for him a shallow grave
Even from the cold earth of our cave.
I begged them, as a boon, to lay
His corse in dust whereon the day
Might shine—it was a foolish thought;
But then within my brain it wrought,
That even in death his freeborn breast
In such a dungeon could not rest.
I might have spared my idle prayer—
They coldly laughed, and laid him there,
The flat and turfless earth above
The being we so much did love;
His empty chain above it leant—
Such murder's fitting monument!

VIII

But he, the favorite and the flower,
Most cherished since his natal hour,
His mother's image in fair face,
The infant love of all his race,
His martyred father's dearest thought,
My latest care, for whom I sought
To hoard my life, that his might be
Less wretched now, and one day free—
He too, who yet had held untired
A spirit natural or inspired—
He, too, was struck, and day by day
Was withered on the stalk away.
Oh, God! it is a fearful thing
To see the human soul take wing
In any shape, in any mood:
I've seen it rushing forth in blood;
I've seen it on the breaking ocean
Strive with a swoln, convulsive motion;
I've seen the sick and ghastly bed
Of Sin, delirious with its dread;
But these were horrors,—this was woe
Unmixed with such,—but sure and slow.

He faded, and so calm and meek,
So softly worn, so sweetly weak,
So tearless, yet so tender,—kind,
And grieved for those he left behind;
With all the while a cheek whose bloom
Was as a mockery of the tomb,
Whose tints as gently sunk away
As a departing rainbow's ray;
An eye of most transparent light,
That almost made the dungeon bright;
And not a word of murmur, not
A groan o'er his untimely lot—
A little talk of better days,
A little hope my own to raise;
For I was sunk in silence, lost
In this last loss, of all the most.
And then the sighs he would suppress
Of fainting nature's feebleness,
More slowly drawn, grew less and less.
I listened, but I could not hear—
I called, for I was wild with fear;
I knew 'twas hopeless, but my dread
Would not be thus admonishèd;
I called, and thought I heard a sound—
I burst my chain with one strong bound,
And rushed to him:—I found him not.
*I* only stirred in this black spot;
*I* only lived—*I* only drew
The accursèd breath of dungeon-dew;
The last, the sole, the dearest link
Between me and the eternal brink,
Which bound me to my failing race,
Was broken in this fatal place.
One on the earth, and one beneath—
My brothers—both had ceased to breathe.
I took that hand which lay so still—
Alas! my own was full as chill;
I had not strength to stir, or strive,
But felt that I was still alive—
A frantic feeling, when we know

That what we love shall ne'er be so.
I know not why
I could not die,
I had no earthly hope,—but faith,
And that forbade a selfish death.

IX

What next befell me then and there
I know not well,—I never knew.
First came the loss of light and air,
And then of darkness too.
I had no thought, no feeling—none:
Among the stones I stood a stone;
And was, scarce conscious what I wist,
As shrubless crags within the mist;
For all was blank, and bleak, and gray;
It was not night—it was not day;
It was not even the dungeon-light,
So hateful to my heavy sight;
But vacancy absorbing space,
And fixedness,—without a place;
There were no stars, no earth, no time,
No check, no change, no good, no crime,—
But silence, and a stirless breath
Which neither was of life nor death—
A sea of stagnant idleness,
Blind, boundless, mute and motionless!

X

A light broke in upon my brain—
It was the carol of a bird;
It ceased, and then it came again—
The sweetest song ear ever heard;
And mine was thankful till my eyes
Ran over with the glad surprise,
And they that moment could not see
I was the mate of misery;
But then, by dull degrees, came back

My senses to their wonted track:
I saw the dungeon walls and floor
Close slowly round me as before;
I saw the glimmer of the sun
Creeping as it before had done;
But through the crevice where it came
That bird was perched, as fond and tame,
  And tamer than upon the tree—
A lovely bird, with azure wings,
And song that said a thousand things,
  And seemed to say them all for me!
I never saw its like before—
I ne'er shall see its likeness more.
It seemed, like me, to want a mate,
But was not half so desolate;
And it was come to love me when
None lived to love me so again,
And, cheering from my dungeon's brink,
Had brought me back to feel and think.
I know not if it late were free,
  Or broke its cage to perch on mine;
But knowing well captivity,
  Sweet bird! I could not wish for thine!
Or if it were, in wingèd guise,
A visitant from Paradise;
For—Heaven forgive that thought, the while
Which made me both to weep and smile!—
I sometimes deemed that it might be
My brother's soul come down to me;
But then at last away it flew,
And then 'twas mortal—well I knew;
For he would never thus have flown,
And left me twice so doubly lone—
Lone—as the corse within its shroud,
Lone—as a solitary cloud,
  A single cloud on a sunny day,
While all the rest of heaven is clear,
A frown upon the atmosphere,
That hath no business to appear
  When skies are blue, and earth is gay.

XI

A kind of change came in my fate—
My keepers grew compassionate.
I know not what had made them so—
They were inured to sights of woe;
But so it was—my broken chain
With links unfastened did remain;
And it was liberty to stride
Along my cell from side to side,
And up and down, and then athwart,
And tread it over every part;
And round the pillars one by one,
Returning where my walk begun—
Avoiding only, as I trod,
My brothers' graves without a sod;
For if I thought with heedless tread
My step profaned their lowly bed,
My breath came gaspingly and thick,
And my crushed heart fell blind and sick.

XII

I made a footing in the wall:
  It was not therefrom to escape,
For I had buried one and all
  Who loved me in a human shape;
And the whole earth would henceforth be
A wider prison unto me;
No child, no sire, no kin had I,
No partner in my misery.
I thought of this, and I was glad,
For thought of them had made me mad;
But I was curious to ascend
To my barred windows, and to bend
Once more, upon the mountains high,
The quiet of a loving eye.

XIII

I saw them—and they were the same;
They were not changed, like me, in frame;

I saw their thousand years of snow
On high—their wide, long lake below,
And the blue Rhone in fullest flow;
I heard the torrents leap and gush
O'er channeled rock and broken bush;
I saw the white-walled distant town,
And whiter sails go skimming down;
And then there was a little isle,
Which in my very face did smile—
  The only one in view;
A small, green isle, it seemed no more,
Scarce broader than my dungeon floor;
But in it there were three tall trees,
And o'er it blew the mountain breeze,
And by it there were waters flowing,
And on it there were young flowers growing
  Of gentle breath and hue.
The fish swam by the castle wall,
And they seemed joyous, each and all;
The eagle rode the rising blast—
Methought he never flew so fast
As then to me he seemed to fly;
And then new tears came in my eye,
And I felt troubled, and would fain
I had not left my recent chain;
And when I did descend again,
The darkness of my dim abode
Fell on me as a heavy load;
It was as is a new-dug grave,
Closing o'er one we sought to save;
And yet my glance, too much oppressed,
Had almost need of such a rest.

XIV

It might be months, or years, or days—
  I kept no count, I took no note—
I had no hope my eyes to raise,
  And clear them of their dreary mote;
At last men came to set me free,
  I asked not why, and recked not where;

It was at length the same to me,
Fettered or fetterless to be;
  I learned to love despair.
And thus, when they appeared at last,
And all my bonds aside were cast,
These heavy walls to me had grown
A hermitage—and all my own!
And half I ſelt as they were come
To tear me from a second home.
With spiders I had friendship made,
And watched them in their sullen trade;
Had seen the mice by moonlight play—
And why should I feel less than they?
We were all inmates of one place,
And I, the monarch of each race,
Had power to kill; yet, strange to tell!
In quiet we had learned to dwell.
My very chains and I grew friends,
So much a long communion tends
To make us what we are:—even I
Regained my freedom with a sigh.

*George Gordon Byron* [1788–1824]

## THE EVE OF ST. AGNES

St. Agnes' Eve—Ah, bitter chill it was!
The owl, for all his feathers, was a-cold;
The hare limped trembling through the frozen grass,
And silent was the flock in woolly fold:
Numb were the Beadsman's fingers, while he told
His rosary, and while his frosted breath,
Like pious incense from a censer old,
Seemed taking flight for heaven, without a death,
Past the sweet Virgin's picture, while his prayer he saith.

His prayer he saith, this patient, holy man;
Then takes his lamp, and riseth from his knees,
And back returneth, meager, barefoot, wan,
Along the chapel aisle by slow degrees:
The sculptured dead, on each side, seem to freeze,

Emprisoned in black, purgatorial rails:
Knights, ladies, praying in dumb orat'ries,
He passeth by; and his weak spirit fails
To think how they may ache in icy hoods and mails.

Northward he turneth through a little door,
And scarce three steps, ere Music's golden tongue
Flattered to tears this agèd man and poor;
But no—already had his death-bell rung;
The joys of all his life were said and sung;
His was harsh penance on St. Agnes' Eve:
Another way he went, and soon among
Rough ashes sat he for his soul's reprieve,
And all night kept awake, for sinners' sake to grieve.

That ancient Beadsman heard the prelude soft;
And so it chanced, for many a door was wide,
From hurry to and fro. Soon, up aloft,
The silver, snarling trumpets 'gan to chide:
The level chambers, ready with their pride,
Were glowing to receive a thousand guests:
The carvèd angels, ever eager-eyed,
Stared, where upon their heads the cornice rests,
With hair blown back, and wings put cross-wise on their breasts.

At length burst in the argent revelry,
With plume, tiara, and all rich array,
Numerous as shadows haunting faerily
The brain, newstuffed in youth, with triumphs gay
Of old romance. These let us wish away,
And turn, sole-thoughted, to one Lady there,
Whose heart had brooded, all that wintry day,
On love, and winged St. Agnes' saintly care,
As she had heard old dames full many times declare.

They told her how, upon St. Agnes' eve,
Young virgins might have visions of delight,
And soft adorings from their loves receive
Upon the honeyed middle of the night,

If ceremonies due they did aright;
As, supperless to bed they must retire,
And couch supine their beauties, lily white;
Nor look behind, nor sideways, but require
Of Heaven with upward eyes for all that they desire.

Full of this whim was thoughtful Madeline:
The music, yearning like a God in pain,
She scarcely heard: her maiden eyes divine
Fixed on the floor, saw many a sweeping train
Pass by—she heeded not at all: in vain
Came many a tiptoe, amorous cavalier,
And back retired; not cooled by high disdain,
But she saw not: her heart was otherwhere:
She sighed for Agnes' dreams, the sweetest of the year

She danced along with vague, regardless eyes,
Anxious her lips, her breathing quick and short:
The hallowed hour was near at hand: she sighs
Amid the timbrels, and the thronged resort
Of whisperers in anger, or in sport;
'Mid looks of love, defiance, hate, and scorn,
Hoodwinked with faery fancy; all amort,
Save to St. Agnes and her lambs unshorn,
And all the bliss to be before to-morrow morn.

So, purposing each moment to retire,
She lingered still. Meantime, across the moors,
Had come young Porphyro, with heart on fire
For Madeline. Beside the portal doors,
Buttressed from moonlight, stands he, and implores
All saints to give him sight of Madeline,
But for one moment in the tedious hours,
That he might gaze and worship all unseen;
Perchance speak, kneel, touch, kiss—in sooth such things
have been.

He ventures in: let no buzzed whisper tell:
All eyes be muffled, or a hundred swords
Will storm his heart, Love's feverous citadel:
For him, those chambers held barbarian hordes,

Hyena foemen, and hot-blooded lords,
Whose very dogs would execrations howl
Against his lineage: not one breast affords
Him any mercy, in that mansion foul,
Save one old beldame, weak in body and in soul.

Ah, happy chance! the agèd creature came,
Shuffling along with ivory-headed wand,
To where he stood, hid from the torch's flame,
Behind a broad hall-pillar, far beyond
The sound of merriment and chorus bland:
He startled her; but soon she knew his face,
And grasped his fingers in her palsied hand,
Saying, "Mercy, Porphyro! hie thee from this place;
They are all here to-night, the whole blood-thirsty race!

"Get hence! get hence! there's dwarfish Hildebrand:
He had a fever late, and in the fit
He cursèd thee and thine, both house and land:
Then there's that old Lord Maurice, not a whit
More tame for his gray hairs—Alas me! flit!
Flit like a ghost away."—"Ah, Gossip, dear,
We're safe enough; here in this armchair sit,
And tell me how"—"Good Saints! not here, not here:
Follow me, child, or else these stones will be thy bier."

He followed through a lowly archèd way,
Brushing the cobwebs with his lofty plume,
And as she muttered "Well-a-well-a-day!"
He found him in a little moonlight room,
Pale, latticed, chill, and silent as a tomb.
"Now tell me where is Madeline," said he,
"O tell me, Angela, by the holy loom,
Which none but secret sisterhood may see,
When they St. Agnes' wool are weaving piously."

"St. Agnes! Ah! it is St. Agnes' Eve—
Yet men will murder upon holy days:
Thou must hold water in a witch's sieve,
And be liege-lord of all the Elves and Fays,

To venture so: it fills me with amaze
To see thee, Porphyro!—St. Agnes' Eve!
God's help! my lady fair the conjurer plays
This very night: good angels her deceive!
But let me laugh awhile,—I've mickle time to grieve."

Feebly she laugheth in the languid moon,
While Porphyro upon her face doth look,
Like puzzled urchin on an agèd crone
Who keepeth closed a wondrous riddle-book,
As spectacled she sits in chimney nook.
But soon his eyes grew brilliant, when she told
His lady's purpose; and he scarce could brook
Tears, at the thought of those enchantments cold,
And Madeline asleep in lap of legends old.

Sudden a thought came like a full-blown rose,
Flushing his brow, and in his painèd heart
Made purple riot: then doth he propose
A stratagem, that makes the beldame start:
"A cruel man and impious thou art:
Sweet lady! let her pray, and sleep, and dream
Alone with her good angels, far apart
From wicked men like thee. Go, go!—I deem
Thou canst not surely be the same that thou didst seem."

"I will not harm her, by all saints I swear,"
Quoth Porphyro: "O may I ne'er find grace
When my weak voice shall whisper its last prayer,
If one of her soft ringlets I displace,
Or look with ruffian passion in her face.
Good Angela, believe me, by these tears;
Or I will, even in a moment's space,
Awake, with horrid shout, my foemen's ears,
And beard them, though they be more fanged than wolves and bears."

"Ah! why wilt thou affright a feeble soul?
A poor, weak, palsy-stricken, churchyard thing,
Whose passing-bell may ere the midnight toll;
Whose prayers for thee, each morn and evening,

Were never missed."—Thus plaining, doth she bring
A gentler speech from burning Porphyro;
So woeful, and of such deep sorrowing,
That Angela gives promise she will do
Whatever he shall wish, betide her weal or woe.

Which was, to lead him, in close secrecy,
Even to Madeline's chamber, and there hide
Him in a closet, of such privacy
That he might see her beauty unespied,
And win perhaps that night a peerless bride,
While legioned fairies paced the coverlet,
And pale enchantment held her sleepy-eyed.
Never on such a night have lovers met,
Since Merlin paid his Demon all the monstrous debt.

"It shall be as thou wishest," said the Dame:
"All cates and dainties shall be storèd there
Quickly on this feast-night: by the tambour frame
Her own lute thou wilt see: no time to spare,
For I am slow and feeble, and scarce dare
On such a catering trust my dizzy head.
Wait here, my child, with patience; kneel in prayer
The while: Ah! thou must needs the lady wed,
Or may I never leave my grave among the dead."

So saying, she hobbled off with busy fear.
The lover's endless minutes slowly passed;
The dame returned and whispered in his ear
To follow her; with agèd eyes aghast
From fright of dim espial. Safe at last,
Through many a dusky gallery, they gain
The maiden's chamber, silken, hushed, and chaste;
Where Porphyro took covert, pleased amain.
His poor guide hurried back with agues in her brain.

Her faltering hand upon the balustrade,
Old Angela was feeling for the stair,
When Madeline, St. Agnes' charmèd maid,
Rose, like a missioned spirit, unaware:
With silver taper's light, and pious care,

She turned, and down the agèd gossip led
To a safe level matting. Now prepare,
Young Porphyro, for gazing on that bed;
She comes, she comes again, like ring-dove frayed and fled.

Out went the taper as she hurried in;
Its little smoke, in pallid moonshine, died:
She closed the door, she panted, all akin
To spirits of the air, and visions wide:
No uttered syllable, or, woe betide!
But to her heart, her heart was voluble,
Paining with eloquence her balmy side;
As though a tongueless nightingale should swell
Her throat in vain, and die, heart-stifled, in her dell.

A casement high and triple-arched there was,
All garlanded with carven imageries
Of fruits, and flowers, and bunches of knot-grass,
And diamonded with panes of quaint device,
Innumerable of stains and splendid dyes,
As are the tiger-moth's deep-damasked wings;
And in the midst, 'mong thousand heraldries,
And twilight saints, and dim emblazonings,
A shielded scutcheon blushed with blood of queens and kings.

Full on this casement shone the wintry moon,
And threw warm gules on Madeline's fair breast,
As down she knelt for Heaven's grace and boon;
Rose-bloom fell on her hands, together pressed,
And on her silver cross soft amethyst,
And on her hair a glory, like a saint:
She seemed a splendid angel, newly dressed,
Save wings, for heaven:—Porphyro grew faint:
She knelt, so pure a thing, so free from mortal taint.

Anon his heart revives: her vespers done,
Of all its wreathèd pearls her hair she frees;
Unclasps her warmèd jewels one by one;
Loosens her fragrant bodice; by degrees
Her rich attire creeps rustling to her knees:

Half-hidden, like a mermaid in seaweed,
Pensive awhile she dreams awake, and sees,
In fancy, fair St. Agnes in her bed,
But dares not look behind, or all the charm is fled.

Soon, trembling in her soft and chilly nest,
In sort of wakeful swoon, perplexed she lay,
Until the poppied warmth of sleep oppressed
Her soothèd limbs, and soul fatigued away;
Flown, like a thought, until the morrow-day;
Blissfully havened both from joy and pain;
Clasped like a missal where swart Paynims pray;
Blinded alike from sunshine and from rain,
As though a rose should shut, and be a bud again.

Stolen to this paradise, and so entranced,
Porphyro gazed upon her empty dress,
And listened to her breathing, if it chanced
To wake into a slumberous tenderness;
Which when he heard, that minute did he bless
And breathed himself: then from the closet crept
Noiseless as fear in a wide wilderness,
And over the hushed carpet, silent, stept,
And 'tween the curtains peeped, where, lo—how fast she slept.

Then by the bed-side, where the faded moon
Made a dim, silver twilight, soft he set
A table, and, half anguished, threw thereon
A cloth of woven crimson, gold, and jet:—
O for some drowsy Morphean amulet!
The boisterous, midnight, festive clarion,
The kettle-drum, and far-heard clarionet,
Affray his ears, though but in dying tone:—
The hall-door shuts again, and all the noise is gone.

And still she slept an azure-lidded sleep,
In blanchèd linen, smooth and lavendered,
While he forth from the closet brought a heap
Of candied apple, quince, and plum, and gourd;
With jellies soother than the creamy curd,

And lucent syrops, tinct with cinnamon;
Manna and dates, in argosy transferred
From Fez; and spicèd dainties, every one,
From silken Samarcand to cedared Lebanon.

These delicates he heaped with glowing hand
On golden dishes and in baskets bright
Of wreathèd silver: sumptuous they stand
In the retirèd quiet of the night,
Filling the chilly room with perfume light—
"And now, my love, my seraph fair, awake!
Thou art my heaven, and I thine eremite:
Open thine eyes, for meek St. Agnes' sake,
Or I shall drowse beside thee, so my soul doth ache."

Thus whispering, his warm, unnervèd arm
Sank in her pillow. Shaded was her dream
By the dusk curtains:—'twas a midnight charm
Impossible to melt as icèd stream:
The lustrous salvers in the moonlight gleam;
Broad golden fringe upon the carpet lies:
It seemed he never, never could redeem
From such a steadfast spell his lady's eyes;
So mused awhile, entoiled in woofèd phantasies.

Awakening up, he took her hollow lute,—
Tumultuous,—and, in chords that tenderest be,
He played an ancient ditty, long since mute,
In Provence called, "La belle dame sans merci":
Close to her ear touching the melody;—
Wherewith disturbed, she uttered a soft moan:
He ceased—she panted quick—and suddenly
Her blue affrayèd eyes wide open shone:
Upon his knees he sank, pale as smooth-sculptured stone

Her eyes were open, but she still beheld,
Now wide awake, the vision of her sleep:
There was a painful change, that nigh expelled
The blisses of her dream so pure and deep:
At which fair Madeline began to weep,

And moan forth witless words with many a sigh,
While still her gaze on Porphyro would keep;
Who knelt, with joinèd hands and piteous eye,
Fearing to move or speak, she looked so dreamingly.

"Ah, Porphyro!" said she, "but even now
Thy voice was at sweet tremble in mine ear,
Made tuneable with every sweetest vow;
And those sad eyes were spiritual and clear;
How changed thou art! how pallid, chill, and drear!
Give me that voice again, my Porphyro,
Those looks immortal, those complainings dear!
Oh leave me not in this eternal woe,
For if thou diest, my Love, I know not where to go."

Beyond a mortal man impassioned far
At these voluptuous accents, he arose,
Ethereal, flushed, and like a throbbing star
Seen 'mid the sapphire heaven's deep repose;
Into her dream he melted, as the rose
Blendeth its odor with the violet,—
Solution sweet: meantime the frost-wind blows
Like Love's alarum, pattering the sharp sleet
Against the window-panes; St. Agnes' moon hath set.

'Tis dark, quick pattereth the flaw-blown sleet:
"This is no dream, my bride, my Madeline!"
'Tis dark: the icèd gusts still rave and beat:
"No dream, alas! alas! and woe is mine!
Porphyro will leave me here to fade and pine.—
Cruel! what traitor could thee hither bring?
I curse not, for my heart is lost in thine,
Though thou forsakest a deceivèd thing;—
A dove forlorn and lost with sick unprunèd wing."

"My Madeline! sweet dreamer! lovely bride!
Say, may I be for aye thy vassal blest?
Thy beauty's shield, heart-shaped and vermeil-dyed?
Ah, silver shrine, here will I take my rest
After so many hours of toil and quest,

A famished pilgrim,—saved by miracle.
Though I have found, I will not rob thy nest
Saving of thy sweet self; if thou thinkest well
To trust, fair Madeline, to no rude infidel.

"Hark! 'tis an elfin-storm from faery land,
Of haggard seeming, but a boon indeed:
Arise—arise! the morning is at hand;—
The bloated wassailers will never heed:—
Let us away, my love, with happy speed;
There are no ears to hear, or eyes to see,—
Drowned all in Rhenish and the sleepy mead:
Awake! arise! my love, and fearless be,
For o'er the southern moors I have a home for thee."

She hurried at his words, beset with fears,
For there were sleeping dragons all around,
At glaring watch, perhaps, with ready spears.—
Down the wide stairs a darkling way they found.—
In all the house was heard no human sound.
A chain-drooped lamp was flickering by each door;
The arras, rich with horsemen, hawk, and hound,
Fluttered in the besieging wind's uproar;
And the long carpets rose along the gusty floor.

They glide, like phantoms, into the wide hall;
Like phantoms, to the iron porch, they glide;
Where lay the Porter, in uneasy sprawl,
With a huge empty flagon by his side:
The wakeful bloodhound rose, and shook his hide,
But his sagacious eye an inmate owns:
By one, and one, the bolts full easy slide:—
The chains lie silent on the footworn stones;—
The key turns, and the door upon its hinges groans.

And they are gone: ay, ages long ago
These lovers fled away into the storm
That night the Baron dreamt of many a woe,
And all his warrior-guests, with shade and form
Of witch, and demon, and large coffin-worm,

Were long be-nightmared. Angela the old
Died palsy-twitched, with meager face deform;
The Beadsman, after thousand aves told,
For aye unsought-for slept amongst his ashes cold.

*John Keats* [1795--1821]

## LOCKSLEY HALL

COMRADES, leave me here a little, while as yet 'tis early morn;
Leave me here, and when you want me, sound upon the bugle horn.

'Tis the place, and all around it, as of old, the curlews call,
Dreary gleams about the moorland, flying over Locksley Hall:

Locksley Hall, that in the distance overlooks the sandy tracts,
And the hollow ocean-ridges roaring into cataracts.

Many a night from yonder ivied casement, ere I went to rest,
Did I look on great Orion sloping slowly to the west.

Many a night I saw the Pleiads, rising through the mellow shade,
Glitter like a swarm of fireflies tangled in a silver braid.

Here about the beach I wandered, nourishing a youth sublime
With the fairy tales of science, and the long result of time;

When the centuries behind me like a fruitful land reposed;
When I clung to all the present for the promise that it closed;

When I dipped into the future far as human eye could see,
Saw the vision of the world, and all the wonder that would be.

In the spring a fuller crimson comes upon the robin's breast;
In the spring the wanton lapwing gets himself another crest;

In the spring a livelier iris changes on the burnished dove;
In the spring a young man's fancy lightly turns to thoughts of love.

Then her cheek was pale and thinner than should be for one so young,
And her eyes on all my motions with a mute observance hung.

And I said, "My cousin Amy, speak, and speak the truth to me;
Trust me, cousin, all the current of my being sets to thee."

On her pallid cheek and forehead came a color and a light,
As I have seen the rosy red flushing in the northern night.

And she turned,—her bosom shaken with a sudden storm of sighs;
All the spirit deeply dawning in the dark of hazel eyes,—

Saying, "I have hid my feelings, fearing they should do me wrong;"
Saying, "Dost thou love me, cousin?" weeping, "I have loved thee long."

Love took up the glass of Time, and turned it in his glowing hands;
Every moment, lightly shaken, ran itself in golden sands.

Love took up the harp of Life, and smote on all the chords with might;
Smote the chord of Self, that, trembling, passed in music out of sight.

Many a morning on the moorland did we hear the copses ring,
And her whisper thronged my pulses with the fulness of the spring.

Many an evening by the waters did we watch the stately ships,
And our spirits rushed together at the touching of the lips.

O my cousin, shallow-hearted! O my Amy, mine no more!
O the dreary, dreary moorland! O the barren, barren shore!

Falser than all fancy fathoms, falser than all songs have sung,
Puppet to a father's threat, and servile to a shrewish tongue!

Is it well to wish thee happy?—having known me; to decline
On a range of lower feelings and a narrower heart than mine!

Yet it shall be: thou shalt lower to his level day by day,
What is fine within thee growing coarse to sympathize with clay.

As the husband is, the wife is; thou art mated with a clown,
And the grossness of his nature will have weight to drag thee down.

He will hold thee, when his passion shall have spent its novel force,
Something better than his dog, a little dearer than his horse.

What is this? his eyes are heavy,—think not they are glazed with wine.
Go to him; it is thy duty,—kiss him, take his hand in thine.

It may be my lord is weary, that his brain is overwrought,—
Soothe him with thy finer fancies, touch him with thy lighter thought.

He will answer to the purpose, easy things to understand,—
Better thou wert dead before me, though I slew thee with my hand.

Better thou and I were lying, hidden from the heart's disgrace,
Rolled in one another's arms, and silent in a last embrace.

Cursed be the social wants that sin against the strength of youth!
Cursed be the social lies that warp us from the living truth!

Cursed be the sickly forms that err from honest Nature's
rule!
Cursed be the gold that gilds the straitened forehead of the
fool!

Well—'tis well that I should bluster!—Hadst thou less
unworthy proved,
Would to God—for I have loved thee more than ever wife
was loved.

Am I mad, that I should cherish that which bears but bitter
fruit?
I will pluck it from my bosom, though my heart be at the
root.

Never! though my mortal summers to such length of years
should come
As the many-wintered crow that leads the clanging rookery
home.

Where is comfort? in division of the records of the mind?
Can I part her from herself, and love her, as I knew her,
kind?

I remember one that perished; sweetly did she speak and
move;
Such a one do I remember, whom to look at was to love.

Can I think of her as dead, and love her for the love she bore?
No,—she never loved me truly; love is love for evermore.

Comfort? comfort scorned of devils! this is truth the poet
sings,
That a sorrow's crown of sorrow is remembering happier
things.

Drug thy memories, lest thou learn it, lest thy heart be put
to proof,
In the dead, unhappy night, and when the rain is on the roof.

Like a dog, he hunts in dreams; and thou art staring at the wall,
Where the dying night-lamp flickers, and the shadows rise and fall.

Then a hand shall pass before thee, pointing to his drunken sleep,
To thy widowed marriage-pillows, to the tears that thou wilt weep.

Thou shalt hear the "Never, never," whispered by the phantom years,
And a song from out the distance in the ringing of thine ears.

And an eye shall vex thee, looking ancient kindness on thy pain.
Turn thee, turn thee on thy pillow; get thee to thy rest again.

Nay, but Nature brings thee solace; for a tender voice will cry;
'Tis a purer life than thine, a lip to drain thy trouble dry.

Baby lips will laugh me down; my latest rival brings thee rest,—
Baby fingers, waxen touches, press me from the mother's breast.

O, the child too clothes the father with a dearness not his due.
Half is thine and half is his: it will be worthy of the two.

O, I see thee old and formal, fitted to thy petty part,
With a little hoard of maxims preaching down a daughter's heart.

"They were dangerous guides, the feelings—she herself was not exempt—
Truly, she herself had suffered"—Perish in thy self-contempt!

Overlive it—lower yet—be happy! wherefore should I care?
I myself must mix with action, lest I wither by despair.

What is that which I should turn to, lighting upon days like these?
Every door is barred with gold, and opens but to golden keys.

Every gate is thronged with suitors, all the markets overflow.
I have but an angry fancy: what is that which I should do?

I had been content to perish, falling on the foeman's ground,
When the ranks are rolled in vapor, and the winds are laid with sound.

But the jingling of the guinea helps the hurt that Honor feels,
And the nations do but murmur, snarling at each other's heels.

Can I but relive in sadness? I will turn that earlier page.
Hide me from my deep emotion, O thou wondrous Mother-Age!

Make me feel the wild pulsation that I felt before the strife,
When I heard my days before me, and the tumult of my life;

Yearning for the large excitement that the coming years would yield,
Eager-hearted as a boy when first he leaves his father's field,

And at night along the dusky highway near and nearer drawn,
Sees in heaven the light of London flaring like a dreary dawn;

And his spirit leaps within him to be gone before him then,
Underneath the light he looks at, in among the throngs of men;

Men, my brothers, men the workers, ever reaping something new:
That which they have done but earnest of the things that they shall do.

For I dipped into the future, far as human eye could see,
Saw the Vision of the world, and all the wonder that would be;

Saw the heavens fill with commerce, argosies of magic sails,
Pilots of the purple twilight, dropping down with costly bales;

Heard the heavens fill with shouting, and there rained a ghastly dew
From the nations' airy navies grappling in the central blue;

Far along the world-wide whisper of the south-wind rushing warm,
With the standards of the peoples plunging through the thunder-storm;

Till the war-drum throbbed no longer, and the battle-flags were furled
In the Parliament of man, the Federation of the world.

There the common sense of most shall hold a fretful realm in awe,
And the kindly earth shall slumber, lapped in universal law.

So I triumphed ere my passion sweeping through me left me dry,
Left me with the palsied heart, and left me with the jaundiced eye;

Eye, to which all order festers, all things here are out of joint.
Science moves, but slowly, slowly, creeping on from point to point:

Slowly comes a hungry people, as a lion, creeping nigher,
Glares at one that nods and winks behind a slowly-dying fire.

Yet I doubt not through the ages one increasing purpose runs,
And the thoughts of men are widened with the process of the suns.

What is that to him that reaps not harvest of his youthful joys,
Though the deep heart of existence beat forever like a boy's?

Knowledge comes, but wisdom lingers; and I linger on the shore,
And the individual withers, and the world is more and more.

Knowledge comes, but wisdom lingers, and he bears a laden breast,
Full of sad experience, moving toward the stillness of his rest.

Hark! my merry comrades call me, sounding on the bugle-horn,—
They to whom my foolish passion were a target for their scorn.

Shall it not be scorn to me to harp on such a moldered string?
I am shamed through all my nature to have loved so slight a thing.

Weakness to be wroth with weakness! woman's pleasure, woman's pain—
Nature made them blinder motions bounded in a shallower brain.

Woman is the lesser man, and all thy passions, matched with mine,
Are as moonlight unto sunlight, and as water unto wine—

Here at least, where nature sickens, nothing. Ah, for some retreat
Deep in yonder shining Orient, where my life began to beat!

Where in wild Mahratta-battle fell my father, evil-starred;
I was left a trampled orphan, and a selfish uncle's ward.

Or to burst all links of habit,—there to wander far away,
On from island unto island at the gateways of the day,—

Larger constellations burning, mellow moons and happy skies,
Breadths of tropic shade and palms in cluster, knots of Paradise.

Never comes the trader, never floats an European flag,—
Slides the bird o'er lustrous woodland, swings the trailer from the crag,—

Droops the heavy-blossomed bower, hangs the heavy-fruited tree,—
Summer isles of Eden lying in dark-purple spheres of sea.

There, methinks, would be enjoyment more than in this march of mind—
In the steamship, in the railway, in the thoughts that shake mankind.

There the passions, cramped no longer, shall have scope and breathing-space;
I will take some savage woman, she shall rear my dusky race.

Iron-jointed, supple-sinewed, they shall dive, and they shall run,
Catch the wild goat by the hair, and hurl their lances in the sun,

Whistle back the parrot's call, and leap the rainbows of the brooks,
Not with blinded eyesight poring over miserable books—

Fool, again the dream, the fancy! but I *know* my words are wild,
But I count the gray barbarian lower than the Christian child.

I, to herd with narrow foreheads, vacant of our glorious gains,
Like a beast with lower pleasures, like a beast with lower pains!

Mated with a squalid savage,—what to me were sun or clime?
I, the heir of all the ages, in the foremost files of time,—

I, that rather held it better men should perish one by one,
Than that earth should stand at gaze like Joshua's moon in Ajalon!

Not in vain the distance beacons. Forward, forward let us range;
Let the great world spin for ever down the ringing grooves of change.

Through the shadow of the globe we sweep into the younger day;
Better fifty years of Europe than a cycle of Cathay.

Mother-Age,—for mine I knew not,—help me as when life begun,—
Rift the hills, and roll the waters, flash the lightnings, weigh the sun.

O, I see the crescent promise of my spirit hath not set;
Ancient founts of inspiration well through all my fancy yet.

Howsoever these things be, a long farewell to Locksley Hall!
Now for me the woods may wither, now for me the roof-tree fall.

Comes a vapor from the margin, blackening over heath and holt,
Cramming all the blast before it, in its breast a thunderbolt.

Let it fall on Locksley Hall, with rain or hail, or fire or snow;
For the mighty wind arises, roaring seaward, and I go.

*Alfred Tennyson* [1809–1892]

## THE SCHOLAR-GIPSY

Go, for they call you, Shepherd, from the hill;
Go, Shepherd, and untie the wattled cotes:
No longer leave thy wistful flock unfed,
Nor let thy bawling fellows rack their throats,
Nor the cropped grasses shoot another head.
But when the fields are still,
And the tired men and dogs all gone to rest,
And only the white sheep are sometimes seen
Cross and recross the strips of moon-blanched green;
Come, Shepherd, and again begin the quest.

Here, where the reaper was at work of late,
In this high field's dark corner, where he leaves
His coat, his basket, and his earthen cruse,
And in the sun all morning binds the sheaves,
Then here, at noon, comes back his stores to use;
Here will I sit and wait,
While to my ear from uplands far away
The bleating of the folded flocks is borne,
With distant cries of reapers in the corn—
All the live murmur of a summer's day.

Screened is this nook o'er the high, half-reaped field,
And here till sundown, Shepherd, will I be.
Through the thick corn the scarlet poppies peep,
And round green roots and yellowing stalks I see
Pale blue convolvulus in tendrils creep:
And air-swept lindens yield
Their scent, and rustle down their perfumed showers
Of bloom on the bent grass where I am laid,
And bower me from the August sun with shade;
And the eye travels down to Oxford's towers:

And near me on the grass lies Glanvil's book—
Come, let me read the oft-read tale again:
The story of that Oxford scholar poor,
Of pregnant parts and quick inventive brain,

Who, tired of knocking at Preferment's door,
One summer morn forsook
His friends, and went to learn the Gipsy lore,
And roamed the world with that wild brotherhood,
And came, as most men deemed, to little good,
But came to Oxford and his friends no more.

But once, years after, in the country lanes,
Two scholars, whom at college erst he knew,
Met him, and of his way of life inquired.
Whereat he answered that the Gipsy crew,
His mates, had arts to rule as they desired
The workings of men's brains;
And they can bind them to what thoughts they will:
"And I," he said, "the secret of their art,
When fully learned, will to the world impart:
But it needs Heaven-sent moments for this skill!"

This said, he left them, and returned no more,
But rumors hung about the country-side,
That the lost Scholar long was seen to stray,
Seen by rare glimpses, pensive and tongue-tied,
In hat of antique shape, and cloak of gray,
The same the Gipsies wore.
Shepherds had met him on the Hurst in spring;
At some lone alehouse in the Berkshire moors,
On the warm ingle-bench, the smock-frocked boors
Had found him seated at their entering,

But, 'mid their drink and clatter, he would fly:
And I myself seem half to know thy looks,
And put the shepherds, Wanderer, on thy trace;
And boys who in lone wheatfields scare the rooks
I ask if thou hast passed their quiet place;
Or in my boat I lie
Moored to the cool bank in the summer heats,
'Mid wide grass meadows which the sunshine fills,
And watch the warm green-muffled Cumnor hills,
And wonder if thou haunt'st their shy retreats.

For most, I know, thou lov'st retirèd ground.
Thee, at the ferry, Oxford riders blithe,
Returning home on summer nights, have met
Crossing the stripling Thames at Bablock-hithe,
Trailing in the cool stream thy fingers wet,
As the slow punt swings round:
And leaning backwards in a pensive dream,
And fostering in thy lap a heap of flowers
Plucked in shy fields and distant Wychwood bowers,
And thine eyes resting on the moonlit stream:

And then they land, and thou art seen no more.
Maidens who from the distant hamlets come
To dance around the Fyfield elm in May,
Oft through the darkening fields have seen thee roam,
Or cross a stile into the public way.
Oft thou hast given them store
Of flowers—the frail-leafed, white anemone—
Dark bluebells drenched with dews of summer eves,
And purple orchises with spotted leaves—
But none has words she can report of thee.

And, above Godstow Bridge, when hay-time's here
In June, and many a scythe in sunshine flames,
Men who through those wide fields of breezy grass
Where black-winged swallows haunt the glittering Thames,
To bathe in the abandoned lasher pass,
Have often passed thee near
Sitting upon the river bank o'ergrown:
Marked thine outlandish garb, thy figure spare,
Thy dark vague eyes, and soft abstracted air;
But, when they came from bathing, thou wert gone

At some lone homestead in the Cumnor hills,
Where at her open door the housewife darns,
Thou hast been seen, or hanging on a gate
To watch the threshers in the mossy barns.
Children, who early range these slopes and late
For cresses from the rills,

Have known thee watching, all an April day,
The springing pastures and the feeding kine;
And marked thee, when the stars come out and shine,
Through the long dewy grass move slow away.

In autumn, on the skirts of Bagley Wood,
Where most the Gipsies by the turf-edged way
Pitch their smoked tents, and every bush you see
With scarlet patches tagged and shreds of gray,
Above the forest-ground called Thessaly—
The blackbird picking food
Sees thee, nor stops his meal, nor fears at all;
So often has he known thee past him stray
Rapt, twirling in thy hand a withered spray,
And waiting for the spark from Heaven to fall.

And once, in winter, on the causeway chill
Where home through flooded fields foot-travelers go,
Have I not passed thee on the wooden bridge
Wrapped in thy cloak and battling with the snow,
Thy face towards Hinksey and its wintry ridge?
And thou hast climbed the hill
And gained the white brow of the Cumnor range;
Turned once to watch, while thick the snowflakes fall,
The line of festal light in Christ Church hall—
Then sought thy straw in some sequestered grange.

But what—I dream! Two hundred years are flown
Since first thy story ran through Oxford halls,
And the grave Glanvil did the tale inscribe
That thou wert wandered from the studious walls
To learn strange arts, and join a Gipsy tribe:
And thou from earth art gone
Long since, and in some quiet churchyard laid;
Some country nook, where o'er thy unknown grave
Tall grasses and white flowering nettles wave—
Under a dark red-fruited yew-tree's shade.

—No, no, thou hast not felt the lapse of hours.
For what wears out the life of mortal men?
'Tis that from change to change their being rolls
'Tis that repeated shocks, again, again,
Exhaust the energy of strongest souls,
And numb the elastic powers.
Till having used our nerves with bliss and teen,
And tired upon a thousand schemes our wit,
To the just-pausing Genius we remit
Our worn-out life, and are—what we have been.

Thou hast not lived, why shouldst thou perish, so?
Thou hadst *one* aim, *one* business, *one* desire:
Else wert thou long since numbered with the dead
Else hadst thou spent, like other men, thy fire.
The generations of thy peers are fled,
And we ourselves shall go;
But thou possessest an immortal lot,
And we imagine thee exempt from age
And living as thou liv'st on Glanvil's page,
Because thou hadst—what we, alas, have not!

For early didst thou leave the world, with powers
Fresh, undiverted to the world without,
Firm to their mark, not spent on other things;
Free from the sick fatigue, the languid doubt,
Which much to have tried, in much been baffled, brings.
O Life unlike to ours!
Who fluctuate idly without term or scope,
Of whom each strives, nor knows for what he strives,
And each half lives a hundred different lives;
Who wait like thee, but not, like thee, in hope.

Thou waitest for the spark from Heaven: and we,
Vague half-believers of our casual creeds,
Who never deeply felt, nor clearly willed,
Whose insight never has borne fruit in deeds,
Whose weak resolves never have been fulfilled;
For whom each year we see

Breeds new beginnings, disappointments new;
Who hesitate and falter life away,
And lose to-morrow the ground won to-day—
Ah, do not we, Wanderer, await it too?

Yes, we await it, but it still delays,
And then we suffer; and amongst us One,
Who most has suffered, takes dejectedly
His seat upon the intellectual throne;
And all his store of sad experience he
Lays bare of wretched days;
Tells us his misery's birth and growth and signs,
And how the dying spark of hope was fed,
And how the breast was soothed, and how the head,
And all his hourly varied anodynes.

This for our wisest: and we others pine,
And wish the long unhappy dream would end,
And waive all claim to bliss, and try to bear,
With close-lipped Patience for our only friend,
Sad Patience, too near neighbor to Despair:
But none has hope like thine.
Thou through the fields and through the woods dost stray,
Roaming the country-side, a truant boy,
Nursing thy project in unclouded joy,
And every doubt long blown by time away.

O born in days when wits were fresh and clear,
And life ran gaily as the sparkling Thames;
Before this strange disease of modern life,
With its sick hurry, its divided aims,
Its heads o'ertaxed, its palsied hearts, was rife—
Fly hence, our contact fear!
Still fly, plunge deeper in the bowering wood!
Averse, as Dido did with gesture stern
From her false friend's approach in Hades turn,
Wave us away, and keep thy solitude.

Still nursing the unconquerable hope,
Still clutching the inviolable shade,
With a free onward impulse brushing through,
By night, the silvered branches of the glade—
Far on the forest-skirts, where none pursue,
On some mild pastoral slope
Emerge, and resting on the moonlit pales,
Freshen thy flowers, as in former years,
With dew, or listen with enchanted ears,
From the dark dingles, to the nightingales.

But fly our paths, our feverish contact fly!
For strong the infection of our mental strife,
Which, though it gives no bliss, yet spoils for rest;
And we should win thee from thy own fair life,
Like us distracted, and like us unblest.
Soon, soon thy cheer would die,
Thy hopes grow timorous, and unfixed thy powers,
And thy clear aims be cross and shifting made:
And then thy glad perennial youth would fade,
Fade, and grow old at last, and die like ours.

Then fly our greetings, fly our speech and smiles!
—As some grave Tyrian trader, from the sea,
Descried at sunrise an emerging prow
Lifting the cool-haired creepers stealthily,
The fringes of a southward-facing brow
Among the Ægean isles;
And saw the merry Grecian coaster come,
Freighted with amber grapes, and Chian wine,
Green bursting figs, and tunnies steeped in brine;
And knew the intruders on his ancient home,

The young light-hearted Masters of the waves;
And snatched his rudder, and shook out more sail,
And day and night held on indignantly
O'er the blue Midland waters with the gale,
Betwixt the Syrtes and soft Sicily,
To where the Atlantic raves

Outside the Western Straits, and unbent sails
There, where down cloudy cliffs, through sheets of foam,
Shy traffickers, the dark Iberians come;
And on the beach undid his corded bales.

*Matthew Arnold* [1822-1888]

## JUGGLING JERRY

PITCH here the tent, while the old horse grazes:
By the old hedge-side we'll halt a stage.
It's nigh my last above the daisies:
My next leaf'll be man's blank page.
Yes, my old girl! and it's no use crying:
Juggler, constable, king, must bow.
One that outjuggles all's been spying
Long to have me, and he has me now.

We've traveled times to this old common
Often we've hung our pots in the gorse.
We've had a stirring life, old woman!
You, and I, and the old gray horse.
Races, and fairs, and royal occasions,
Found us coming to their call:
Now they'll miss us at our stations:
There's a Juggler outjuggles all!

Up goes the lark, as if all were jolly!
Over the duck-pond the willow shakes.
Easy to think that grieving's folly,
When the hand's firm as driven stakes!
Ay, when we're strong, and braced, and manful,
Life's a sweet fiddle: but we're a batch
Born to become the Great Juggler's han'ful:
Balls he shies up, and is safe to catch.

Here's where the lads of the village cricket:
I was a lad not wide from here:
Couldn't I whip off the bale from the wicket?
Like an old world those days appear!

Donkey, sheep, geese, and thatched ale-house—I know them!
They are old friends of my halts, and seem,
Somehow, as if kind thanks I owe them:
Juggling don't hinder the heart's esteem.

Juggling's no sin, for we must have victual:
Nature allows us to bait for the fool.
Holding one's own makes us juggle no little;
But, to increase it, hard juggling's the rule.
You that are sneering at my profession,
Haven't you juggled a vast amount?
There's the Prime Minister, in one Session,
Juggles more games than my sins'll count.

I've murdered insects with mock thunder:
Conscience, for that, in men don't quail.
I've made bread from the bump of wonder:
That's my business, and there's my tale.
Fashion and rank all praised the professor:
Ay! and I've had my smile from the Queen:
Bravo, Jerry! she meant: God bless her!
Ain't this a sermon on that scene?

I've studied men from my topsy-turvy
Close, and, I reckon, rather true.
Some are fine fellows: some, right scurvy:
Most, a dash between the two.
But it's a woman, old girl, that makes me
Think more kindly of the race:
And it's a woman, old girl, that shakes me
When the Great Juggler I must face.

We two were married, due and legal:
Honest we've lived since we've been one.
Lord! I could then jump like an eagle:
You danced bright as a bit o' the sun.
Birds in a May-bush we were! right merry!
All night we kissed, we juggled all day.
Joy was the heart of Juggling Jerry!
Now from his old girl he's juggled away.

It's past parsons to console us:
  No, nor no doctor fetch for me:
I can die without my bolus;
  Two of a trade, lass, never agree!
Parson and Doctor!—don't they love rarely,
  Fighting the devil in other men's fields!
Stand up yourself and match him fairly:
  Then see how the rascal yields!

I, lass, have lived no gipsy, flaunting
  Finery while his poor helpmate grubs:
Coin I've stored, and you won't be wanting:
  You shan't beg from the troughs and tubs.
Nobly you've stuck to me, though in his kitchen
  Many a Marquis would hail you Cook!
Palaces you could have ruled and grown rich in,
  But your old Jerry you never forsook.

Hand up the chirper! ripe ale winks in it;
  Let's have comfort and be at peace.
Once a stout draught made me light as a linnet.
  Cheer up! the Lord must have his lease.
May be—for none see in that black hollow—
  It's just a place where we're held in pawn,
And, when the Great Juggler makes as to swallow,
  It's just the sword-trick—I ain't quite gone!

Yonder came smells of the gorse, so nutty,
  Gold-like and warm: it's the prime of May.
Better than mortar, brick and putty,
  Is God's house on a blowing day.
Lean me more up the mound; now I feel it:
  All the old heath-smells! Ain't it strange?
There's the world laughing, as if to conceal it,
  But He's by us, juggling the change.

I mind it well, by the sea-beach lying,
  Once—it's long gone—when two gulls we beheld,
Which, as the moon got up, were flying
  Down a big wave that sparked and swelled.

Crack, went a gun: one fell; the second
    Wheeled round him twice, and was off for new luck:
There in the dark her white wing beckoned:—
    Drop me a kiss—I'm the bird dead-struck!

*George Meredith* [1828–1909]

## A COURT LADY

Her hair was tawny with gold, her eyes with purple were
    dark,
Her cheeks' pale opal burnt with a red and restless spark

Never was lady of Milan nobler in name and in race;
Never was lady of Italy fairer to see in the face.

Never was lady on earth more true as woman and wife,
Larger in judgment and instinct, prouder in manners and
    life.

She stood in the early morning, and said to her maidens,
    "Bring
That silken robe made ready to wear at the Court of the
    King.

"Bring me the clasps of diamond, lucid, clear of the mote,
Clasp me the large at the waist, and clasp me the small at
    the throat.

"Diamonds to fasten the hair, and diamonds to fasten the
    sleeves,
Laces to drop from their rays, like a powder of snow from
    the eaves."

Gorgeous she entered the sunlight which gathered her up in
    a flame,
While, straight in her open carriage, she to the hospital came.

In she went at the door, and gazing from end to end,
"Many and low are the pallets, but each is the place of a
    friend."

Up she passed through the wards, and stood at a young man's bed:
Bloody the band on his brow, and livid the droop of his head.

"Art thou a Lombard, my brother? Happy art thou," she cried,
And smiled like Italy on him: he dreamed in her face and died.

Pale with his passing soul, she went on still to a second:
He was a grave hard man, whose years by dungeons were reckoned.

Wounds in his body were sore, wounds in his life were sorer.
"Art thou a Romagnole?" Her eyes drove lightnings before her.

"Austrian and priest had joined to double and tighten the cord
Able to bind thee, O strong one,—free by the stroke of a sword.

"Now be grave for the rest of us, using the life overcast
To ripen our wine of the present, (too new) in glooms of the past."

Down she stepped to a pallet where lay a face like a girl's,
Young, and pathetic with dying,—a deep black hole in the curls.

"Art thou from Tuscany, brother? and seest thou, dreaming in pain,
Thy mother stand in the piazza, searching the list of the slain?"

Kind as a mother herself, she touched his cheeks with her hands:
"Blessed is she who has borne thee, although she should weep as she stands."

On she passed to a Frenchman, his arm carried off by a ball:
Kneeling,—"O more than my brother! how shall I thank thee for all?

"Each of the heroes around us has fought for his land and line,
But *thou* hast fought for a stranger, in hate of a wrong not thine.

"Happy are all free peoples, too strong to be dispossessed:
But blessed are those among nations, who dare to be strong for the rest!"

Ever she passed on her way, and came to a couch where pined
One with a face from Venetia, white with a hope out of mind.

Long she stood and gazed, and twice she tried at the name,
But two great crystal tears were all that faltered and came.

Only a tear for Venice?—she turned as in passion and loss,
And stooped to his forehead and kissed it, as if she were kissing the cross.

Faint with that strain of heart she moved on then to another,
Stern and strong in his death. "And dost thou suffer, my brother?"

Holding his hands in hers:—"Out of the Piedmont lion
Cometh the sweetness of freedom! sweetest to live or to die on."

Holding his cold rough hands,—"Well, oh, well have ye done
In noble, noble Piedmont, who would not be noble alone."

Back he fell while she spoke. She rose to her feet with a spring,—
"That was a Piedmontese! and this is the Court of the King."

*Elizabeth Barrett Browning* [1806–1861]

## THE HIGH TIDE ON THE COAST OF LINCOLNSHIRE

(1571)

THE old mayor climbed the belfry tower,
The ringers ran by two, by three;
"Pull, if ye never pulled before;
Good ringers, pull your best," quoth he.
"Play uppe, play uppe, O Boston bells!
Play all your changes, all your swells,
Play uppe, 'The Brides of Enderby'."

Men say it was a stolen tyde—
The Lord that sent it, He knows all;
But in myne ears doth still abide
The message that the bells let fall:
And there was naught of strange, beside
The flight of mews and peewits pied
By millions crouched on the old sea wall.

I sat and spun within the doore,
My thread brake off, I raised myne eyes;
The level sun, like ruddy ore,
Lay sinking in the barren skies;
And dark against day's golden death
She moved where Lindis wandereth,
My sonne's faire wife, Elizabeth.

"Cusha! Cusha! Cusha!" calling,
Ere the early dews were falling,
Farre away I heard her song,
"Cusha! Cusha!" all along;
Where the reedy Lindis floweth,
Floweth, floweth,
From the meads where melick groweth
Faintly came her milking song—

"Cusha! Cusha! Cusha!" calling,
"For the dews will soone be falling;
Leave your meadow grasses mellow,
Mellow, mellow;

Quit your cowslips, cowslips yellow;
Come uppe, Whitefoot, come uppe, Lightfoot;
Quit the stalks of parsley hollow,
Hollow, hollow;
Come uppe, Jetty, rise and follow,
From the clovers lift your head;
Come uppe, Whitefoot, come uppe, Lightfoot,
Come uppe, Jetty, rise and follow,
Jetty, to the milking shed."

If it be long, ay, long ago,
When I beginne to think howe long,
Againe I hear the Lindis flow,
Swift as an arrowe, sharpe and strong;
And all the aire, it seemeth mee,
Bin full of floating bells (sayth shee),
That ring the tune of Enderby.

Alle fresh the level pasture lay,
And not a shadowe mote be seene,
Save where full fyve good miles away
The steeple towered from out the greene;
And lo! the great bell farre and wide
Was heard in all the country side
That Saturday at eventide.

The swanherds where their sedges are
Moved on in sunset's golden breath,
The shepherde lads I heard afarre,
And my sonne's wife, Elizabeth;
Till floating o'er the grassy sea
Came downe that kyndly message free,
The "Brides of Mavis Enderby."

Then some looked uppe into the sky,
And all along where Lindis flows
To where the goodly vessels lie,
And where the lordly steeple shows.
They sayde, "And why should this thing be?
What danger lowers by land or sea?
They ring the tune of Enderby!

"For evil news from Mablethorpe,
  Of pyrate galleys warping down;
For shippes ashore beyond the scorpe,
  They have not spared to wake the towne:
But while the west bin red to see,
And storms be none, and pyrates flee,
Why ring 'The Brides of Enderby'?"

I looked without, and lo! my sonne
  Came riding downe with might and main:
He raised a shout as he drew on,
  Till all the welkin rang again,
"Elizabeth! Elizabeth!"
(A sweeter woman ne'er drew breath
Than my sonne's wife, Elizabeth.)

"The olde sea wall (he cried) is downe,
  The rising tide comes on apace,
And boats adrift in yonder towne
  Go sailing uppe the market-place."
He shook as one that looks on death:
"God save you, mother!" straight he saith;
"Where is my wife, Elizabeth?"

"Good sonne, where Lindis winds her way,
  With her two bairns I marked her long;
And ere yon bells beganne to play,
  Afar I heard her milking song."
He looked across the grassy lea,
To right, to left, "Ho, Enderby!"
They rang "The Brides of Enderby!"

With that he cried and beat his breast;
  For, lo! along the river's bed
A mighty eygre reared his crest,
  And uppe the Lindis raging sped.
It swept with thunderous noises loud;
Shaped like a curling snow-white cloud,
Or like a demon in a shroud.

And rearing Lindis backward pressed,
  Shook all her trembling bankes amaine;
Then madly at the eygre's breast
  Flung uppe her weltering walls again.
Then bankes came downe with ruin and rout—
Then beaten foam flew round about—
Then all the mighty floods were out.

So farre, so fast the eygre drave,
  The heart had hardly time to beat
Before a shallow seething wave
  Sobbed in the grasses at oure feet:
The feet had hardly time to flee
Before it brake against the knee,
And all the world was in the sea.

Upon the roofe we sate that night,
  The noise of bells went sweeping by;
I marked the lofty beacon light
  Stream from the church tower, red and high—
A lurid mark and dread to see;
And awsome bells they were to mee,
That in the dark rang "Enderby."

They rang the sailor lads to guide
  From roofe to roofe who fearless rowed;
And I—my sonne was at my side,
  And yet the ruddy beacon glowed:
And yet he moaned beneath his breath,
"O come in life, or come in death!
O lost! my love, Elizabeth!"

And didst thou visit him no more?
  Thou didst, thou didst, my daughter deare;
The waters laid thee at his doore,
  Ere yet the early dawn was clear.
Thy pretty bairns in fast embrace,
The lifted sun shone on thy face,
Downe drifted to thy dwelling-place.

That flow strewed wrecks about the grass,
  That ebbe swept out the flocks to sea;
A fatal ebbe and flow, alas!
  To manye more than myne and mee;
But each will mourn his own (she saith);
And sweeter woman ne'er drew breath
Than my sonne's wife, Elizabeth.

I shall never hear her more
By the reedy Lindis shore,
"Cusha! Cusha! Cusha!" calling,
Ere the early dews be falling;
I shall never hear her song,
"Cusha! Cusha!" all along
Where the sunny Lindis floweth,
    Goeth, floweth;
From the meads where melick groweth,
  When the water winding down,
  Onward floweth to the town.

I shall never see her more
Where the reeds and rushes quiver,
    Shiver, quiver;
Stand beside the sobbing river,
Sobbing, throbbing, in its falling
To the sandy lonesome shore;
I shall never hear her calling,
"Leave your meadow grasses mellow,
    Mellow, mellow;
Quit your cowslips, cowslips yellow;
Come uppe, Whitefoot, come uppe, Lightfoot;
Quit your pipes of parsley hollow,
    Hollow, hollow;
Come uppe, Lightfoot, rise and follow;
    Lightfoot, Whitefoot,
From your clovers lift the head;
Come uppe, Jetty, follow, follow,
Jetty, to the milking shed."

*Jean Ingelow* [1820–1897]

## THE SKELETON IN ARMOR

"Speak! speak! thou fearful guest!
Who, with thy hollow breast
Still in rude armor dressed,
Comest to daunt me!
Wrapped not in Eastern balms,
But with thy fleshless palms
Stretched, as if asking alms,
Why dost thou haunt me?"

Then, from those cavernous eyes
Pale flashes seemed to rise,
As when the Northern skies
Gleam in December;
And, like the water's flow
Under December's snow,
Came a dull voice of woe
From the heart's chamber.

"I was a Viking old!
My deeds, though manifold,
No Skald in song has told,
No Saga taught thee!
Take heed, that in thy verse
Thou dost the tale rehearse,
Else dread a dead man's curse;
For this I sought thee.

"Far in the Northern Land,
By the wild Baltic's strand,
I, with my childish hand,
Tamed the gerfalcon;
And, with my skates fast-bound,
Skimmed the half-frozen Sound,
That the poor whimpering hound
Trembled to walk on.

"Oft to his frozen lair
Tracked I the grisly bear,
While from my path the hare
Fled like a shadow;

Oft through the forest dark
Followed the were-wolf's bark,
Until the soaring lark
  Sang from the meadow.

"But when I older grew,
Joining a corsair's crew,
O'er the dark sea I flew
  With the marauders.
Wild was the life we led;
Many the souls that sped,
Many the hearts that bled,
  By our stern orders.

"Many a wassail-bout
Wore the long Winter out;
Often our midnight shout
  Set the cocks crowing,
As we the Berserk's tale
Measured in cups of ale,
Draining the oaken pail,
  Filled to o'erflowing.

"Once as I told in glee
Tales of the stormy sea,
Soft eyes did gaze on me,
  Burning yet tender;
And as the white stars shine
On the dark Norway pine,
On that dark heart of mine
  Fell their soft splendor.

"I wooed the blue-eyed maid,
Yielding, yet half afraid,
And in the forest's shade
  Our vows were plighted.
Under its loosened vest
Fluttered her little breast,
Like birds within their nest
  By the hawk frighted.

"Bright in her father's hall
Shields gleamed upon the wall,
Loud sang the minstrels all,
Chanting his glory;
When of old Hildebrand
I asked his daughter's hand,
Mute did the minstrels stand
To hear my story.

"While the brown ale he quaffed,
Loud then the champion laughed,
And as the wind-gusts waft
The sea-foam brightly,
So the loud laugh of scorn,
Out of those lips unshorn,
From the deep drinking-horn
Blew the foam lightly.

"She was a Prince's child,
I but a Viking wild,
And though she blushed and smiled,
I was discarded!
Should not the dove so white
Follow the sea-mew's flight,
Why did they leave that night
Her nest unguarded?

"Scarce had I put to sea,
Bearing the maid with me,
Fairest of all was she
Among the Norsemen!
When on the white sea-strand,
Waving his armèd hand,
Saw we old Hildebrand,
With twenty horsemen.

"Then launched they to the blast,
Bent like a reed each mast,
Yet we were gaining fast,
When the wind failed us;

And with a sudden flaw
Came round the gusty Skaw,
So that our foe we saw
Laugh as he hailed us.

"And as to catch the gale
Round veered the flapping sail,
'Death!' was the helmsman's hail,
'Death without quarter!'
Mid-ships with iron keel
Struck we her ribs of steel;
Down her black hulk did reel
Through the black water!

"As with his wings aslant,
Sails the fierce cormorant,
Seeking some rocky haunt,
With his prey laden,—
So toward the open main,
Beating to sea again,
Through the wild hurricane,
Bore I the maiden.

"Three weeks we westward bore,
And when the storm was o'er,
Cloud-like we saw the shore
Stretching to leeward;
There for my lady's bower
Built I the lofty tower,
Which, to this very hour,
Stands looking seaward.

'There lived we many years;
Time dried the maiden's tears;
She had forgot her fears,
She was a mother;
Death closed her mild blue eyes,
Under that tower she lies;
Ne'er shall the sun arise
On such another!

"Still grew my bosom then,
Still as a stagnant fen!
Hateful to me were men,
The sunlight hateful!
In the vast forest here,
Clad in my warlike gear,
Fell I upon my spear,
Oh, death was grateful!

"Thus, seamed with many scars,
Bursting these prison bars,
Up to its native stars
My soul ascended!
There from the flowing bowl
Deep drinks the warrior's soul,
*Skoal!* to the Northland! *skoal!*"
Thus the tale ended.

*Henry Wadsworth Longfellow* [1807–1882]

## DANIEL GRAY

If I shall ever win the home in heaven
For whose sweet rest I humbly hope and pray,
In the great company of the forgiven
I shall be sure to find old Daniel Gray.

I knew him well; in truth, few knew him better;
For my young eyes oft read for him the Word,
And saw how meekly from the crystal letter
He drank the life of his beloved Lord.

Old Daniel Gray was not a man who lifted
On ready words his freight of gratitude,
Nor was he called upon among the gifted,
In the prayer-meetings of his neighborhood.

He had a few old-fashioned words and phrases,
Linked in with sacred texts and Sunday rhymes;
And I suppose that in his prayers and graces
I've heard them all at least a thousand times.

I see him now—his form, his face, his motions,
His homespun habit, and his silver hair,—
And hear the language of his trite devotions,
Rising behind the straight-backed kitchen chair.

I can remember how the sentence sounded—
"Help us, O Lord, to pray and not to faint!"
And how the "conquering-and-to-conquer" rounded
The loftier aspirations of the saint.

He had some notions that did not improve him,
He never kissed his children—so they say;
And finest scenes and fairest flowers would move him
Less than a horseshoe picked up in the way.

He had a hearty hatred of oppression,
And righteous words for sin of every kind;
Alas, that the transgressor and transgression
Were linked so closely in his honest mind!

He could see naught but vanity in beauty,
And naught but weakness in a fond caress,
And pitied men whose views of Christian duty
Allowed indulgence in such foolishness.

Yet there was love and tenderness within him;
And I am told that when his Charley died,
Nor nature's need nor gentle words could win him
From his fond vigils at the sleeper's side.

And when they came to bury little Charley,
They found fresh dewdrops sprinkled in his hair,
And on his breast a rose-bud gathered early,
And guessed, but did not know who placed it there.

Honest and faithful, constant in his calling,
Strictly attendant on the means of grace,
Instant in prayer, and fearful most of falling,
Old Daniel Gray was always in his place.

A practical old man, and yet a dreamer,
He thought that in some strange, unlooked-for way
His mighty Friend in Heaven, the great Redeemer,
Would honor him with wealth some golden day.

This dream he carried in a hopeful spirit
Until in death his patient eye grew dim,
And his Redeemer called him to inherit
The heaven of wealth long garnered up for him.

So, if I ever win the home in Heaven
For whose sweet rest I humbly hope and pray,
In the great company of the forgiven
I shall be sure to find old Daniel Gray.

*Josiah Gilbert Holland* [1819-1881]

## "CURFEW MUST NOT RING TO-NIGHT"

SLOWLY England's sun was setting o'er the hilltops far away,
Filling all the land with beauty at the close of one sad day,
And the last rays kissed the forehead of a man and maiden fair,—
He with footsteps slow and weary, she with sunny floating hair;
He with bowed head, sad and thoughtful, she with lips all cold and white,
Struggling to keep back the murmur,—
"Curfew must not ring to-night."

"Sexton," Bessie's white lips faltered, pointing to the prison old,
With its turrets tall and gloomy, with its walls dark, damp, and cold,
"I've a lover in that prison, doomed this very night to die,
At the ringing of the Curfew, and no earthly help is nigh;
Cromwell will not come till sunset," and her lips grew strangely white
As she breathed the husky whisper:—
"Curfew must not ring to-night."

"Bessie," calmly spoke the sexton,—every word pierced her young heart
Like the piercing of an arrow, like a deadly poisoned dart,—
"Long, long years I've rung the Curfew from that gloomy, shadowed tower;
Every evening, just at sunset, it has told the twilight hour;
I have done my duty ever, tried to do it just and right,
Now I'm old I will not falter,—
Curfew, it must ring to-night."

Wild her eyes and pale her features, stern and white her thoughtful brow,
As within her secret bosom Bessie made a solemn vow.
She had listened while the judges read, without a tear or sigh:
"At the ringing of the Curfew, Basil Underwood must die."
And her breath came fast and faster, and her eyes grew large and bright;
In an undertone she murmured:—
"Curfew must not ring to-night."

With quick step she bounded forward, sprang within the old church door,
Left the old man threading slowly paths he'd trod so oft before;
Not one moment paused the maiden, but with eye and cheek aglow
Mounted up the gloomy tower, where the bell swung to and fro:
As she climbed the dusty ladder, on which fell no ray of light,
Up and up,—her white lips saying:—
"Curfew must not ring to-night!"

She has reached the topmost ladder; o'er her hangs the great, dark bell;
Awful is the gloom beneath her, like the pathway down to hell.
Lo, the ponderous tongue is swinging,—'tis the hour of Curfew now,
And the sight has chilled her bosom, stopped her breath, and paled her brow.

Shall she let it ring? No, never! flash her eyes with sudden light,
As she springs, and grasps it firmly,—
"Curfew shall not ring to-night!"

Out she swung—far out; the city seemed a speck of light below,
There 'twixt heaven and earth suspended as the bell swung to and fro,
And the half-deaf sexton ringing (years he had not heard the bell),
Sadly thought the twilight Curfew rang young Basil's funeral knell.
Still the maiden clung more firmly, and with trembling lips so white,
Said to hush her heart's wild throbbing:—
"Curfew shall not ring to-night!"

It was o'er, the bell ceased swaying, and the maiden stepped once more
Firmly on the dark old ladder where for hundred years before
Human foot had not been planted. The brave deed that she had done
Should be told long ages after: as the rays of setting sun
Crimson all the sky with beauty, aged sires, with heads of white,
Tell the eager, listening children,
"Curfew did not ring that night."

O'er the distant hills came Cromwell; Bessie sees him, and her brow,
Lately white with fear and anguish, has no anxious traces now.
At his feet she tells her story, shows her hands all bruised and torn;
And her face so sweet and pleading, yet with sorrow pale and worn,
Touched his heart with sudden pity, lit his eyes with mist light:
"Go! your lover lives," said Cromwell,
"Curfew shall not ring to-night."

Wide they flung the massive portal; led the prisoner forth to
die,—
All his bright young life before him. 'Neath the darkening
English sky
Bessie comes with flying footsteps, eyes aglow with love-
light sweet;
Kneeling on the turf beside him, lays his pardon at his feet.
In his brave, strong arms he clasped her, kissed the face up-
turned and white,
Whispered, "Darling, you have saved me,—
Curfew will not ring to-night!"

*Rose Hartwick Thorpe* [1850–1939]

## THE FACE UPON THE FLOOR

'Twas a balmy summer evening, and a goodly crowd was
there,
Which well nigh filled Joe's bar-room on the corner of the
square;
And as songs and witty stories came through the open door,
A vagabond crept slowly in and posed upon the floor.

"Where did it come from?" some one said. "The wind
has blown it in."
"What does it want?" another cried. "Some whiskey, rum,
or gin."
"Here, Toby, sic him if your stomach's equal to the work—
I wouldn't touch him with a fork, he's as filthy as a Turk."

This badinage the poor wretch took with stoical good grace;
In fact he smiled, as though he thought he'd struck the
proper place.
"Come, boys, I know there's burly hearts among so good a
crowd,
To be in such good company would make a deacon proud.

"Give me a drink—that's what I want—I'm out of funds
you know;
When I had cash to treat the gang this hand was never slow.

What? You laugh as though you thought this pocket never held a sou!
I once was fixed as well, my boys, as any one of you.

"There, thanks! that's braced me nicely! God bless you one and all!
Next time I pass this good saloon I'll make another call.
Give you a song? No, I can't do that; my singing days are past;
My voice is cracked, my throat's worn out, and my lungs are going fast.

"Say! give me another whiskey, and I tell you what I'll do—
I'll tell you a funny story, and a fact, I promise, too.
That I was ever a decent man not one of you would think;
But I was, some four or five years back. Say, give me another drink.

"Fill her up, Joe; I want to put some life into my frame—
Such little drinks to a bum like me are miserably tame;
Five fingers—there, that's the scheme—and corking whiskey, too.
Well, here's luck, boys! and, landlord, my best regards to you!

"You've treated me pretty kindly, and I'd like to tell you how
I came to be the dirty sot you see before you now.
As I told you, once I was a man, with muscles, frame and health,
And but for a blunder ought to have made considerable wealth.

"I was a painter—not one that daubs on bricks and wood,
But an artist, and for my age was rated pretty good.
I worked hard at my canvas, and was bidding fair to rise,
For gradually I saw the star of fame before my eyes.

"I made a picture perhaps you've seen; 'tis called 'The Chase of Fame'.

It brought me fifteen hundred pounds and added to my
name.
And then I met a woman—now comes the funny part—
With eyes that petrified my brain and sunk into my heart.

"Why don't you laugh? 'Tis funny that the vagabond you
see
Could ever love a woman and expect her love for me;
But 'twas so, and for a month or so her smiles were freely
given,
And when her lovely lips touched mine it carried me to heaven.

"Did you ever see a woman for whom your soul you'd give,
With a form like the Milo Venus, too beautiful to live;
With eyes that would beat the Koh-i-noor, and a wealth of
chestnut hair?
If so, 'twas she, for there never was another half so fair.

"I was working on a portrait, one afternoon in May,
Of a fair-haired boy, a friend of mine, who lived across the
way;
And Madeleine admired it, and, much to my surprise,
Said that she'd like to know the man that had such dreamy
eyes.

"It didn't take long to know him, and before the month
had flown
My friend had stolen my darling, and I was left alone;
And ere a year of misery had passed above my head,
The jewel I had treasured so had tarnished, and was dead!

"That's why I took to drink, boys. Why, I never saw you
smile!
I thought you'd be amused, and laughing all the while.
Why, what's the matter, friend? There's a tear-drop in
your eye!
Come, laugh like me; 'tis only babes and women that should
cry.

"Say, boys, if you give me just another whiskey I'll be glad,
And I'll draw right here a picture of the face that drove me
mad.

Give me that piece of chalk with which you mark the base-
ball score,
You shall see the lovely Madeleine upon the bar-room
floor."

Another drink, and with chalk in hand the vagabond began
To sketch a face that well might buy the soul of any man;
Then, as he placed another lock upon the shapely head,
With a fearful shriek he leaped and fell across the picture—
dead.

*Hugh A. D'Arcy* [1843–1925]

## 'OSTLER JOE

I STOOD at eve, as the sun went down, by a grave where a
woman lies,
Who lured men's souls to the shores of sin with the light of
her wanton eyes;
Who sang the song that the siren sang on the treacherous
Lorelei height;
Whose face was as fair as a summer day, and whose heart
was as black as night.

Yet a blossom I fain would pluck to-day from the garden
above her dust—
Not the languorous lily of soulless sin, nor the blood-red
rose of lust,
But a sweet, white blossom of holy love that grew in the
one green spot
In the arid desert of Phryne's life, where all else was parched
and hot.

In the summer, when the meadows were aglow with blue
and red,
Joe, the 'ostler of "The Magpie," and fair Annie Smith
were wed;
Plump was Annie, plump and pretty, with a cheek as white
as snow;
He was anything but handsome, was "The Magpie's"
'ostler, Joe.

But he won the winsome lassie; they'd a cottage and a cow,
And her matronhood sat lightly on the village beauty's brow.
Sped the months, and came a baby—such a blue-eyed baby
boy!
Joe was working in the stables when they told him of his joy.

He was rubbing down the horses, and he gave them, then
and there,
All a special feed of clover, just in honor of his heir.
It had been his great ambition, and he told the horses so,
That the Fates would send a baby who might bear the name
of Joe.

Little Joe the child was christened, and, like babies, grew
apace;
He'd his mother's eyes of azure, and his father's honest face.
Swift the happy years went over, years of blue and cloudless
sky;
Love was lord of that small cottage, and the tempest passed
them by.

Passed them by for years, then swiftly burst in fury o'er
their home.
Down the lane by Annie's cottage chanced a gentleman
to roam;
Thrice he came and saw her sitting by the window with her
child,
And he nodded to the baby, and the baby laughed and
smiled.

So at last it grew to know him (little Joe was nearly four);
He would call the "pretty gemplum" as he passed the open
door;
And one day he ran and caught him, and in child's play
pulled him in;
And the baby Joe had prayed for brought about the mother's
sin.

'Twas the same old wretched story that for ages bards have
sung;
'Twas a woman weak and wanton, and a villain's tempting
tongue;

'Twas a picture deftly painted for a silly creature's eyes
Of the Babylonian wonders and the joy that in them lies.

Annie listened and was tempted; she was tempted and she fell,
As the angels fell from heaven to the blackest depths of hell;
She was promised wealth and splendor, and a life of gentle sloth,
Yellow gold for child and husband—and the woman left them both.

Home one eve came Joe, the 'ostler, with a cheery cry of "Wife!"
Finding that which blurred forever all the story of his life:
She had left a silly letter—through the cruel scrawl he spelt;
Then he sought the lonely bedroom, joined his horny hands and knelt.

"Now, O Lord, O God, forgive her, for she ain't to blame," he cried;
"For I ought 'a' seen her trouble and 'a' gone away and died.
Why, a girl like her, God bless her!—'twasn't likely as her'd rest
With her bonny head forever on a 'ostler's ragged vest.

"It was kind 'o her to bear me all this long and happy time;
So, for my sake, please to bless her, though you count her deed a crime;
If so be I don't pray proper, Lord, forgive me, for you see
I can talk all right to 'osses, but I'm nervous like with Thee."

Ne'er a line came to the cottage from the woman who had flown;
Joe, the baby, died that winter, and the man was left alone.
Ne'er a bitter word he uttered, but in silence kissed the rod,
Saving what he told his horses, saving what he told his God.

Far away in mighty London rose the wanton into fame,
For her beauty won men's homage, and she prospered in her shame;

Quick from lord to lord she flitted, higher still each prize
she won,
And her rivals paled beside her as the stars beside the sun.

Next she trod the stage half-naked, and she dragged Art's
temple down
To the level of a market for the women of the town,
And the kisses she had given to poor 'Ostler Joe for naught,
With their gold and priceless jewels rich and titled lovers
bought.

Went the years with flying footsteps while her star was at
its height;
Then the darkness came on swiftly, and the gloaming turned
to night.
Shattered strength and faded beauty tore the laurels from
her brow;
Of the thousands who had worshipped, never one came near
her now.

Broken down in health and fortune, men forgot her very
name,
Till the news that she was dying woke the echoes of her
fame;
And the papers in their gossip mentioned how an "actress"
lay
Sick to death in humble lodgings, growing weaker every day.

One there was who read the story in a far-off country place,
And that night the dying woman woke and looked upon his
face.
Once again the strong arms clasped her that had clasped her
long ago,
And the weary head lay pillowed on the breast of 'Ostler Joe.

All the past had he forgiven, all the sorrow and the shame;
He had found her sick and lonely, and his wife he now could
claim;
Since the grand folks who had known her one and all had
slunk away,
He could clasp his long-lost darling, and no man could say
him nay.

In his arms death found her lying; from his arms her spirit fled,
And his tears came down in torrents as he knelt beside his dead.
Never once his love had faltered through her sad, unhallowed life,
And the stone above her ashes bears the sacred name of wife.

That's the blossom I fain would pluck to-day from the garden above her dust;
Not the languorous lily of soulless sin, nor the blood-red rose of lust,
But a sweet, white blossom of holy love that grew in the one green spot
In the arid desert of Phryne's life, where all else was parched and hot.

*George R. Sims* [1847–1922]

## LASCA

It's all very well to write reviews,
And carry umbrellas, and keep dry shoes,
And say what everyone's saying here,
And wear what everyone else must wear;
But to-night I'm sick of the whole affair,
I want free life, and I want fresh air;
And I sigh for the canter after the cattle,
The crack of the whips like shots in a battle,
The mellay of hoofs and horns and heads
That wars and wrangles and scatters and spreads;
The green beneath, and the blue above,
And dash and danger, and life and love—
And Lasca!

Lasca used to ride
On a mouse-gray mustang close to my side,
With blue *serape* and bright-belled spur;
I laughed with joy as I looked at her!
Little knew she of books or creeds;
An *Ave Maria* sufficed her needs;
Little she cared, save to be at my side,

To ride with me, and ever to ride,
From San Saba's shore to Lavaca's tide.
She was as bold as the billows that beat,
She was as wild as the breezes that blow:
From her little head to her little feet,
She was swayed in her suppleness to and fro
By each gust of passion; a sapling pine,
That grows on the edge of a Kansas bluff,
And wars with the wind when the weather is rough,
Is like this Lasca, this love of mine.

She would hunger that I might eat,
Would take the bitter and leave me the sweet;
But once, when I made her jealous for fun,
At something I'd whispered, or looked, or done,
One Sunday, in San Antonio,
To a glorious girl on the Alamo,
She drew from her garter a dear little dagger,
And—sting of a wasp!—it made me stagger!
An inch to the left, or an inch to the right,
And I shouldn't be maundering here to-night;
But she sobbed, and, sobbing, so swiftly bound
Her torn *rebosa* about the wound,
That I quickly forgave her. Scratches don't count
In Texas, down by the Rio Grande.

Her eye was brown—a deep, deep brown;
Her hair was darker than her eye;
And something in her smile and frown,
Curled crimson lip and instep high,
Showed that there ran in each blue vein,
Mixed with the milder Aztec strain,
The vigorous vintage of Old Spain.
She was alive in every limb
With feeling, to the finger-tips;
And when the sun is like a fire,
And sky one shining, soft sapphire,
One does not drink in little sips.

Why did I leave the fresh and the free,
That suited her and suited me?

Listen awhile, and you will see;
But this be sure—in earth or air,
God and God's laws are everywhere,
And Nemesis comes with a foot as fleet
On the Texas trail as in Regent Street.

. . . . . . . . . . . . .

The air was heavy, the night was hot,
I sat by her side and forgot,—forgot:
Forgot the herd that were taking their rest,
Forgot that the air was close oppressed,
That the Texas norther comes sudden and soon,
In the dead of night, or the blaze of noon;
That once let the herd at its breath take fright,
Nothing on earth can stop their flight;
And woe to the rider, and woe to the steed,
Who fall in front of their mad stampede!

. . . . . . . . . . . . .

Was that thunder? No, by the Lord!
I sprang to my saddle without a word.
One foot on mine, and she clung behind.
Away! on a wild chase down the wind!
But never was fox-hunt half so hard,
And never was steed so little spared;
For we rode for our lives. You shall hear how we fared
In Texas, down by the Rio Grande.

The mustang flew, and we urged him on;
There was one chance left, and you have but one—
Halt! jump to the ground, and shoot your horse;
Crouch under his carcass, and take your chance;
And if the steers in their frantic course
Don't batter you both to pieces at once,
You may thank your star; if not, goodbye
To the quickening kiss and the long-drawn sigh,
And the open air and the open sky,
In Texas, down by the Rio Grande.

The cattle gained on us, and, just as I felt
For my old six-shooter behind in my belt,
Down came the mustang, and down came we,
Clinging together, and,—what was the rest?

A body that spread itself on my breast,
Two arms that shielded my dizzy head,
Two lips that hard to my lips were pressed;
Then came thunder in my ears,
As over us surged the sea of steers,
Blows that beat blood into my eyes;
And when I could rise—
Lasca was dead!

. . . . . . . . . . . . . . .

I hollowed a grave a few feet deep,
And there in Earth's arms I laid her to sleep;
And there she is lying, and no one knows;
And the summer shines, and the winter snows;
For many a day the flowers have spread
A pall of petals over her head;
And the little gray hawk hangs aloft in the air,
And the sly coyote trots here and there,
And the black-snake glides and glitters and slides
Into a rift in a cottonwood tree;
And the buzzard sails on,
And comes and is gone,
Stately and still, like a ship at sea;
And I wonder why I do not care
For the things that are, like the things that were.
Does half my heart lie buried there
In Texas, down by the Rio Grande?

*Frank Desprez* [1853–1916]

## JIM BLUDSO OF THE PRAIRIE BELLE

WALL, no! I can't tell whar he lives,
Becase he don't live, you see;
Leastways, he's got out of the habit
Of livin' like you and me.
Whar have you been for the last three year
That you haven't heard folks tell
How Jimmy Bludso passed in his checks
The night of the Prairie Belle?

He weren't no saint,—them engineers
Is all pretty much alike,—

One wife in Natchez-under-the-Hill
  And another one here, in Pike;
A keerless man in his talk, was Jim,
  And an awkward hand in a row,
But he never flunked, and he never lied,—
  I reckon he never knowed how.

And this was all the religion he had,—
  To treat his engine well;
Never be passed on the river;
  To mind the pilot's bell;
And if ever the Prairie Bell took fire,—
  A thousand times he swore
He'd hold her nozzle agin the bank
  Till the last soul got ashore.

All boats has their day on the Mississip,
  And her day come at last,—
The Movastar was a better boat,
  But the Belle she *wouldn't* be passed.
And so she come tearin' along that night—
  The oldest craft on the line—
With a nigger squat on her safety-valve,
  And her furnace crammed, rosin and pine.

The fire bust out as she clared the bar,
  And burnt a hole in the night,
And quick as a flash she turned, and made
  For that willer-bank on the right.
There was runnin' and cursin', but Jim yelled out,
  Over all the infernal roar,
"I'll hold her nozzle agin the bank
  Till the last galoot's ashore."

Through the hot, black breath of the burnin' boat
  Jim Bludso's voice was heard,
And they all had trust in his cussedness,
  And knowed he would keep his word.
And, sure's you're born, they all got off
  Afore the smoke-stacks fell,—
And Bludso's ghost went up alone
  In the smoke of the Prairie Belle.

He weren't no saint,—but at jedgment
  I'd run my chance with Jim,
'Longside of some pious gentlemen
  That wouldn't shook hands with him.
He seen his duty, a dead-sure thing,—
  And went for it thar and then;
And Christ ain't a going to be too hard
  On a man that died for men.

*John Hay* [1838–1905]

## LITTLE BREECHES

I DON'T go much on religion,
  I never ain't had no show;
But I've got a middlin' tight grip, sir,
  On the handful o' things I know.
I don't pan out on the prophets
  And free-will, and that sort of thing,—
But I b'lieve in God and the angels,
  Ever sence one night last spring.

I came into town with some turnips,
  And my little Gabe come along,—
No four-year-old in the county
  Could beat him for pretty and strong,
Peart and chipper and sassy,
  Always ready to swear and fight,—
And I'd larnt him to chaw terbacker,
  Jest to keep his milk-teeth white.

The snow come down like a blanket
  As I passed by Taggart's store;
I went in for a jug of molasses
  And left the team at the door.
They scared at something and started,—
  I heard one little squall,
And hell-to-split over the prairie
  Went team, Little Breeches and all.

Hell-to-split over the prairie!
  I was almost froze with skeer;

But we rousted up some torches,
  And sarched for 'em far and near.
At last we struck hosses and wagon,
  Snowed under a soft white mound,
Upsot, dead beat,—but of little Gabe
  No hide nor hair was found.

And here all hope soured on me
  Of my fellow-critter's aid,—
I jest flopped down on my marrow-bones,
  Crotch-deep in the snow, and prayed.

. . . . . . . .

By this, the torches was played out,
  And me and Isrul Parr
Went off for some wood to a sheepfold
  That he said was somewhar thar.

We found it at last, and a little shed
  Where they shut up the lambs at night.
We looked in, and seen them huddled thar,
  So warm and sleepy and white;
And thar sot Little Breeches and chirped,
  As peart as ever you see,
"I want a chaw of terbacker,
  And that's what the matter of me."

How did he get thar? Angels.
  He could never have walked in that storm.
They jest scooped down and toted him
  To whar it was safe and warm.
And I think that saving a little child,
  And fotching him to his own,
Is a derned sight better business
  Than loafing around the Throne.

*John Hay* [1838–1905]

## THE TREE-TOP ROAD

BEYOND the narrow window
  Of my dull House of Care
One road is always beckoning
  When days are gray and bare.

And then I spurn the dusty street,
The struggle and the load —
I pin my wings upon my feet
And take the Tree-top Road.

The joy of life is hidden
In unsubstantial things;
An April rain, a fragrance,
A vision of blue wings!
And what are memory and hope
But dreams? and yet the bread
On which these little lives of ours
Are fed and comforted!

Without imagination
Man sinks into a clod;
Missing the trail of beauty —
Losing the way to God,
And I have built a temple-stair
Out of a lilac's bloom,
And climbed to Heaven with purple pomp,
And censer, and perfume!

Philosophers and Sages
Seeking to find out God,
With puzzling chart and compass,
And strange divining-rod,
I think if you put on your wings
And take the Tree-top Way
You'll meet Him, coming down to see
His orchards bloom in May.

I have no feud with labor,
But at the Gates of June,
My dusty pack forsaking
I join in Youth's glad tune;
And just forgetting for a while
That I am worn and gray,
Go sailing off with Peter Pan
Along the Tree-top Way!

*May Riley Smith* [1842–1927]

# PART VII

# POEMS OF SORROW, DEATH AND IMMORTALITY

## "DEATH, BE NOT PROUD"

From "Holy Sonnets"

DEATH, be not proud, though some have callèd thee
Mighty and dreadful, for thou art not so:
For those whom thou think'st thou dost overthrow
Die not, poor Death; nor yet canst thou kill me.
From Rest and Sleep, which but thy picture be,
Much pleasure, then from thee much more must flow;
And soonest our best men with thee do go—
Rest of their bones and souls' delivery!
Thou'rt slave to fate, chance, kings, and desperate men,
And dost with poison, war, and sickness dwell;
And poppy or charms can make us sleep as well
And better than thy stroke. Why swell'st thou then?
  One short sleep past, we wake eternally,
  And Death shall be no more: Death, thou shalt die!

*John Donne* [1573-1631]

# IN THE SHADOW

## MELANCHOLY

From "The Nice Valor"

HENCE, all you vain delights,
As short as are the nights,
Wherein you spend your folly:
There's naught in this life sweet
If man were wise to see't,
But only melancholy,
O sweetest Melancholy!
Welcome, folded arms, and fixèd eyes,
A sigh that piercing mortifies,
A look that's fastened to the ground,
A tongue chained up without a sound!
Fountain-heads and pathless groves,
Places which pale passion loves!
Moonlight walks, when all the fowls
Are warmly housed save bats and owls!
A midnight bell, a parting groan!
These are the sounds we feed upon;
Then stretch our bones in a still gloomy valley;
Nothing's so dainty sweet as lovely melancholy.

*John Fletcher* [1579–1625]

## ON MELANCHOLY

No, no! go not to Lethe, neither twist
Wolf's-bane, tight-rooted, for its poisonous wine;
Nor suffer thy pale forehead to be kissed
By nightshade, ruby grape of Proserpine;
Make not your rosary of yew-berries,

Nor let the beetle, nor the death-moth be
Your mournful Psyche, nor the downy owl
A partner in your sorrow's mysteries;
For shade to shade will come too drowsily,
And drown the wakeful anguish of the soul.

But when the melancholy fit shall fall
Sudden from heaven like a weeping cloud,
That fosters the droop-headed flowers all,
And hides the green hill in an April shroud;
Then glut thy sorrow on a morning rose,
Or on the rainbow of the salt sand-wave,
Or on the wealth of globèd peonies;
Or if thy mistress some rich anger shows,
Emprison her soft hand, and let her rave,
And feed deep, deep upon her peerless eyes.

She dwells with Beauty—Beauty that must die;
And Joy, whose hand is ever at his lips
Bidding adieu; and aching Pleasure nigh,
Turning to poison while the bee-mouth sips:
Ay, in the very temple of Delight
Veiled Melancholy has her sovereign shrine,
Though seen of none save him whose strenuous tongue
Can burst Joy's grape against his palate fine:
His soul shall taste the sadness of her might,
And be among her cloudy trophies hung.

*John Keats* [1795–1821]

## THE RAINY DAY

The day is cold, and dark, and dreary;
It rains, and the wind is never weary;
The vine still clings to the moldering wall,
But at every gust the dead leaves fall,
And the day is dark and dreary.

My life is cold, and dark, and dreary;
It rains, and the wind is never weary;

My thoughts still cling to the moldering Past,
But the hopes of youth fall thick in the blast
And the days are dark and dreary.

Be still, sad heart! and cease repining;
Behind the clouds is the sun still shining;
Thy fate is the common fate of all,
Into each life some rain must fall,
Some days must be dark and dreary.

*Henry Wadsworth Longfellow* [1807–1882]

## THE PRECEPT OF SILENCE

I KNOW you: solitary griefs,
Desolate passions, aching hours!
I know you: tremulous beliefs,
Agonized hopes, and ashen flowers!

The winds are sometimes sad to me;
The starry spaces full of fear:
Mine is the sorrow on the sea,
And mine the sigh of places drear.

Some players upon plaintive strings
Publish their wistfulness abroad:
I have not spoken of these things,
Save to one man, and unto God.

*Lionel Johnson* [1867–1902]

## "MOAN, MOAN, YE DYING GALES"

MOAN, moan, ye dying gales!
The saddest of your tales
Is not so sad as life;
Nor have you e'er began
A theme so wild as man,
Or with such sorrow rife.

Fall, fall, thou withered leaf!
Autumn sears not like grief,
Nor kills such lovely flowers;
More terrible the storm,
More mournful the deform,
When dark misfortune lowers.

Hush! hush! thou trembling lyre,
Silence, ye vocal choir,
And thou, mellifluous lute,
For man soon breathes his last,
And all his hope is past,
And all his music mute.

Then, when the gale is sighing,
And when the leaves are dying,
And when the song is o'er,
O, let us think of those
Whose lives are lost in woes,
Whose cup of grief runs o'er.

*Henry Neele* [1798–1828]

## SORROW

Count each affliction, whether light or grave,
God's messenger sent down to thee; do thou
With courtesy receive him; rise and bow;
And, ere his shadow pass thy threshold, crave
Permission first his heavenly feet to lave;
Then lay before him all thou hast; allow
No cloud of passion to usurp thy brow,
Or mar thy hospitality; no wave
Of mortal tumult to obliterate
The soul's marmoreal calmness. Grief should be,
Like joy, majestic, equable, sedate;
Confirming, cleansing, raising, making free;
Strong to consume small troubles; to commend
Great thoughts, grave thoughts, thoughts lasting to the end.

*Aubrey Thomas De Vere* [1814–1902]

## TIME AND GRIEF

O time! who know'st a lenient hand to lay
Softest on Sorrow's wound, and slowly thence
(Lulling to sad repose the weary sense)
The faint pang stealest unperceived away;

On thee I rest my only hope at last,
And think, when thou hast dried the bitter tear
That flows in vain o'er all my soul held dear,
I may look back on every sorrow past,
And meet life's peaceful evening with a smile:
As some lone bird, at day's departing hour,
Sings in the sunbeam, of the transient shower
Forgetful, though its wings are wet the while:—
Yet ah! how much must that poor heart endure,
Which hopes from thee, and thee alone, a cure!

*William Lisle Bowles* [1762–1850]

## GRIEF

I TELL you, hopeless grief is passionless;
That only men incredulous of despair,
Half-taught in anguish, through the midnight air
Beat upward to God's throne in loud access
Of shrieking and reproach. Full desertness,
In souls as countries, lieth silent-bare
Under the blanching, vertical eye-glare
Of the absolute Heavens. Deep-hearted man, express
Grief for thy Dead in silence like to death—
Most like a monumental statue set
In everlasting watch and moveless woe
Till itself crumble to the dust beneath.
Touch it; the marble eyelids are not wet:
If it could weep, it could arise and go.

*Elizabeth Barrett Browning* [1806–1861]

## PAIN

DISMAL and purposeless and gray
The world and all its woe, we say,
Poor slaves! who in hot hours of pain
Yearn for the night to come again.

Like tortured men at length set free,
We stagger from our misery,
And watch with foolish, pain-dimmed eyes
Vague lands and unremembered skies.

When lo! what sudden splendor spreads
Its heaven of rose above our heads!
What soft winds visit our despair;
What lights, what voices everywhere!

Ere sorrow taught us, knew we these
Stupendous hills, amazing seas?
Shone there such moonlight on the lawn;
So deep a secret in the dawn?

What wandering hue from Paradise
Has found a home in children's eyes?
What women these, whose faces bless
Life with such tranquil tenderness?

When earth and sky and man seem fair,
Be this my watchword, this my prayer:
Grant me, O Gods, to prize aright
Sorrow, since sorrow gives me sight.

*St. John Lucas* [1879–1934]

## A FAREWELL

Flow down, cold rivulet, to the sea,
  Thy tribute wave deliver
No more by thee my steps shall be,
  For ever and for ever.

Flow, softly flow, by lawn and lea,
  A rivulet, then a river:
No where by thee my steps shall be,
  For ever and for ever.

But here will sigh thine alder-tree,
  And here thine aspen shiver;
And here by thee will hum the bee,
  For ever and for ever.

A thousand suns will stream on thee,
  A thousand moons will quiver;
But not by thee my steps shall be,
  For ever and for ever.

*Alfred Tennyson* [1809–1892]

## "THE DAY IS DONE"

THE day is done, and the darkness
  Falls from the wings of Night,
As a feather is wafted downward
  From an eagle in his flight.

I see the lights of the village
  Gleam through the rain and the mist,
And a feeling of sadness comes o'er me
  That my soul cannot resist:

A feeling of sadness and longing,
  That is not akin to pain,
And resembles sorrow only
  As the mist resembles the rain.

Come, read to me some poem,
  Some simple and heartfelt lay,
That shall soothe this restless feeling,
  And banish the thoughts of day.

Not from the grand old masters,
  Not from the bards sublime,
Whose distant footsteps echo
  Through the corridors of Time.

For, like strains of martial music,
  Their mighty thoughts suggest
Life's endless toil and endeavor;
  And to-night I long for rest.

Read from some humbler poet,
  Whose songs gushed from his heart,
As showers from the clouds of summer,
  Or tears from the eyelids start;

Who, through long days of labor,
  And nights devoid of ease,
Still heard in his soul the music
  Of wonderful melodies

Such songs have power to quiet
  The restless pulse of care,
And come like the benediction
  That follows after prayer.

Then read from the treasured volume
  The poem of thy choice,
And lend to the rhyme of the poet
  The beauty of thy voice.

And the night shall be filled with music,
  And the cares, that infest the day,
Shall fold their tents, like the Arabs,
  And as silently steal away.

*Henry Wadsworth Longfellow* [1807-1882]

## THE BRIDGE

I STOOD on the bridge at midnight,
  As the clocks were striking the hour,
And the moon rose o'er the city,
  Behind the dark church-tower.

I saw her bright reflection
  In the waters under me,
Like a golden goblet falling
  And sinking into the sea.

And far in the hazy distance
  Of that lovely night in June,
The blaze of the flaming furnace
  Gleamed redder than the moon.

Among the long, black rafters
  The wavering shadows lay,
And the current that came from the ocean
  Seemed to lift and bear them away,

As, sweeping and eddying through them,
  Rose the belated tide,
And, streaming into the moonlight,
  The seaweed floated wide.

And like those waters rushing
  Among the wooden piers,
A flood of thoughts came o'er me
  That filled my eyes with tears.

How often, oh, how often,
  In the days that had gone by,
I had stood on that bridge at midnight
  And gazed on that wave and sky!

How often, oh, how often,
  I had wished that the ebbing tide
Would bear me away on its bosom
  O'er the ocean wild and wide!

For my heart was hot and restless,
  And my life was full of care,
And the burden laid upon me
  Seemed greater than I could bear.

But now it has fallen from me,
  It is buried in the sea;
And only the sorrow of others
  Throws its shadow over me.

Yet whenever I cross the river
  On its bridge with wooden piers,
Like the odor of brine from the ocean
  Comes the thought of other years.

And I think how many thousands
  Of care-encumbered men,
Each bearing his burden of sorrow,
  Have crossed the bridge since then.

I see the long procession
  Still passing to and fro,
The young heart hot and restless,
  And the old subdued and slow!

And forever and forever,
As long as the river flows,
As long as the heart has passions,
As long as life has woes;

The moon and its broken reflection
And its shadow shall appear,
As the symbol of love in heaven,
And its wavering image here.

*Henry Wadsworth Longfellow* [1807-1882]

## "MY LIFE IS LIKE THE SUMMER ROSE"

My life is like the summer rose
That opens to the morning sky,
But, ere the shades of evening close,
Is scattered on the ground—to die!
Yet on the rose's humble bed
The sweetest dews of night are shed,
As if she wept the waste to see,—
But none shall weep a tear for me!

My life is like the autumn leaf
That trembles in the moon's pale ray;
Its hold is frail,—its date is brief,
Restless,—and soon to pass away!
Yet, ere that leaf shall fall and fade,
The parent tree will mourn its shade,
The winds bewail the leafless tree,—
But none shall breathe a sigh for me!

My life is like the prints, which feet
Have left on Tampa's desert strand;
Soon as the rising tide shall beat,
All trace will vanish from the sand;
Yet, as if grieving to efface
All vestige of the human race,
On that lone shore loud moans the sea,—
But none, alas! shall mourn for me!

*Richard Henry Wilde* [1789-1847]

## "AS I LAYE A-THYNKYNGE"

As I laye a-thynkynge, a-thynkynge, a-thynkynge,
Merrie sang the Birde as she sat upon the spraye;
There came a noble Knyghte,
With his hauberke shynynge brighte,
And his gallant heart was lyghte,
Free and gaye;
As I laye a-thynkynge, he rode upon his waye.

As I laye a-thynkynge, a-thynkynge, a-thynkynge,
Sadly sang the Birde as she sat upon the tree!
There seemed a crimson plain,
Where a gallant Knyghte lay slayne,
And a steed with broken rein
Ran free,
As I laye a-thynkynge, most pitiful to see!

As I laye a-thynkynge, a-thynkynge, a-thynkynge,
Merrie sang the Birde as she sat upon the boughe;
A lovely maide came by,
And a gentil youthe was nyghe,
And he breathed many a syghe
And a vowe;
As I laye a-thynkynge, her hearte was gladsome now.

As I laye a-thynkynge, a-thynkynge, a-thynkynge,
Sadly sang the Birde as she sat upon the thorne;
No more a youth was there,
But a Maiden rent her haire,
And cried in sad despaire
"That I was borne!"
As I laye a-thynkynge, she perishèd forlorne.

As I laye a-thynkynge, a-thynkynge, a-thynkynge,
Sweetly sang the Birde as she sat upon the briar;
There came a lovely Childe,
And his face was meek and mild,
Yet joyously he smiled
On his sire;
As I laye a-thynkynge, a Cherub mote admire.

But I laye a-thynkynge, a-thynkynge, a-thynkynge,
And sadly sang the Birde as it perched upon a bier;
That joyous smile was gone,
And the face was white and wan,
As the downe upon the Swan
Doth appear,
As I laye a-thynkynge—oh! bitter flowed the tear!

As I laye a-thynkynge, the golden sun was sinking,
O merrie sang that Birde as it glittered on her breast
With a thousand glorious dyes,
While, soaring to the skies,
'Mid the stars she seemed to rise,
As to her nest;

As I laye a-thynkynge, a-thynkynge, a-thynkynge,
As I laye a-thynkynge, her meaning was expressed:—
"Follow, follow me away,
It boots not to delay,"—
'Twas so she seemed to saye,
"Here is rest!"

*Richard Harris Barham* [1788–1845

## THE HARP OF SORROW

Sorrow has a harp of seven strings
And plays on it unceasing all the day;
The first string sings of love that is long dead,
The second sings of lost hopes burièd;
The third of happiness forgot and fled.
Of vigil kept in vain the fourth cord sings,
And the fifth string of roses dropped away.
The sixth string calls and is unanswerèd,
The seventh with your name for ever rings—
I listen for its singing all the day!

*Ethel Clifford* [18 -

## THE JOURNEY ONWARDS

As slow our ship her foamy track
Against the wind was cleaving,
Her trembling pennant still looked back

To that dear Isle 'twas leaving.
So loth we part from all we love,
From all the links that bind us;
So turn our hearts, as on we rove,
To those we've left behind us!

When, round the bowl, of vanished years
We talk with joyous seeming,
With smiles, that might as well be tears,
So faint, so sad their beaming;
While memory brings us back again
Each early tie that twined us,
Oh, sweet's the cup that circles then
To those we've left behind us!

And when, in other climes, we meet
Some isle, or vale enchanting,
Where all looks flowery, wild, and sweet,
And naught but love is wanting;
We think how great had been our bliss
If Heaven had but assigned us
To live and die in scenes like this,
With some we've left behind us!

As travelers oft look back at eve
When eastward darkly going,
To gaze upon that light they leave
Still faint behind them glowing,—
So, when the close of pleasure's day
To gloom hath near consigned us,
We turn to catch one fading ray
Of joy that's left behind us.

*Thomas Moore* [1779–1852]

## SONG

IN LEINSTER

I TRY to knead and spin, but my life is low the while.
Oh, I long to be alone, and walk abroad a mile;
Yet if I walk alone, and think of naught at all,
Why from me that's young should the wild tears fall?

The shower-sodden earth, the earth-colored streams,
They breathe on me awake, and moan to me in dreams,
And yonder ivy fondling the broke castle-wall,
It pulls upon my heart till the wild tears fall.

The cabin-door looks down a furze-lighted hill,
And far as Leighlin Cross the fields are green and still;
But once I hear the blackbird in Leighlin hedges call,
The foolishness is on me, and the wild tears fall!

*Louise Imogen Guiney* [1861–1920]

## MY SORROW

My sorrow that I am not by the little dun,
By the lake of the starlings at Rosses under the hill—
And the larks there, singing over the fields of dew,
Or evening there, and the sedges still!
For plain I see now the length of the yellow sand,
And Lissadell far off and its leafy ways,
And the holy mountain whose mighty heart
Gathers into it all the colored days.
My sorrow that I am not by the little dun,
By the lake of the starlings at evening when all is still—
And still in whispering sedges the herons stand.
'Tis there I would nestle at rest till the quivering moon
Uprose in the golden quiet over the hill.

*Seumas O'Sullivan* [1879–1958]

## SPIRIT OF SADNESS

She loved the Autumn, I the Spring,
Sad all the songs she loved to sing;
And in her face was strangely set
Some great inherited regret.

Some look in all things made her sigh,
Yea! sad to her the morning sky:
"So sad! so sad its beauty seems"—
I hear her say it still in dreams.

But when the day grew gray and old,
And rising stars shone strange and cold,
Then only in her face I saw
A mystic glee, a joyous awe.

Spirit of Sadness, in the spheres
Is there an end of mortal tears?
Or is there still in those great eyes
That look of lonely hills and skies?

*Richard Le Gallienne* [1866–1947]

## "'TIS BUT A LITTLE FADED FLOWER"

'Tis but a little faded flower,
  But oh, how fondly dear!
'Twill bring me back one golden hour,
  Through many a weary year.
I may not to the world impart
  The secret of its power,
But treasured in my inmost heart,
  I keep my faded flower.

Where is the heart that doth not keep,
  Within its inmost core,
Some fond remembrance, hidden deep,
  Of days that are no more?
Who hath not saved some trifling thing
  More prized than jewels rare—
A faded flower, a broken ring,
  A tress of golden hair?

*Ellen Clementine Howarth* [1827–1899]

## TO EACH HIS OWN

Each hath his drug for Sorrow
  (Or else the pain would slay!)
For one, it is "To-morrow";
  For one, 'tis "Yesterday."

"And hast thou lost, my Brother?"
  "Yea, but in dreams I find."
"And I" (so saith another)
  "Leave buried dead behind!"

For each, when gyves are fretting,
  A different balm must be.
Some find it in forgetting,
  And some in memory.

*Margaret Root Garvin* [18 –1949]

## SONG

RARELY, rarely comest thou,
  Spirit of Delight!
Wherefore hast thou left me now
  Many a day and night?
Many a weary night and day
'Tis since thou art fled away.

How shall ever one like me
  Win thee back again?
With the joyous and the free
  Thou wilt scoff at pain.
Spirit false! thou hast forgot
All but those who need thee not.

As a lizard with the shade
  Of a trembling leaf,
Thou with sorrow art dismayed;
  Even the sighs of grief
Reproach thee, that thou art not near,
And reproach thou wilt not hear.

Let me set my mournful ditty
  To a merry measure:
Thou wilt never come for pity,
  Thou wilt come for pleasure;
Pity then will cut away
Those cruel wings, and thou wilt stay.

I love all that thou lovest,
  Spirit of Delight!
The fresh Earth in new leaves dressed,
  And the starry night,
Autumn evening, and the morn
When the golden mists are born.

I love snow, and all the forms
  Of the radiant frost;
I love waves, and winds, and storms—
  Everything almost
Which is Nature's, and may be
Untainted by man's misery.

I love tranquil solitude,
  And such society
As is quiet, wise, and good;
  Between thee and me
What difference? But thou dost possess
The things I seek, not love them less.

I love Love—though he has wings,
  And like light can flee;
But above all other things,
  Spirit, I love thee!—
Thou art love and life! Oh, come,
Make once more my heart thy home!

*Percy Bysshe Shelley* [1792-1822]

## THE NAMELESS ONE

ROLL forth, my song, like the rushing river,
  That sweeps along to the mighty sea;
God will inspire me while I deliver
    My soul of thee!

Tell thou the world, when my bones lie whitening
  Amid the last homes of youth and eld,
That once there was one whose veins ran lightning
    No eye beheld.

Tell how his boyhood was one drear night-hour,
How shone for him, through his griefs and gloom,
No star of all heaven sends to light our
Path to the tomb.

Roll on, my song, and to after ages
Tell how, disdaining all earth can give,
He would have taught men, from wisdom's pages,
The way to live.

And tell how trampled, derided, hated,
And worn by weakness, disease, and wrong,
He fled for shelter to God, who mated
His soul with song.

—With song which alway, sublime or vapid,
Flowed like a rill in the morning beam,
Perchance not deep, but intense and rapid:
A mountain stream.

Tell how this Nameless, condemned for years long
To herd with demons from hell beneath,
Saw things that made him, with groans and tears, long
For even death.

Go on to tell how, with genius wasted,
Betrayed in friendship, befooled in love,
With spirit shipwrecked, and young hopes blasted,
He still, still strove;

Till, spent with toil, dreeing death for others
(And some whose hands should have wrought for him,
If children live not for sires and mothers),
His mind grew dim;

And he fell far through that pit abysmal,
The gulf and grave of Maginn and Burns,
And pawned his soul for the devil's dismal
Stock of returns.

But yet redeemed it in days of darkness,
And shapes and signs of the final wrath,

When death, in hideous and ghastly starkness,
Stood on his path.

And tell how now, amid wreck and sorrow,
And want, and sickness, and houseless nights,
He bides in calmness the silent morrow,
That no ray lights.

And lives he still, then? Yes! Old and hoary
At thirty-nine, from despair and woe,
He lives, enduring what future story
Will never know.

Him grant a grave to, ye pitying noble,
Deep in your bosoms: there let him dwell!
He, too, had tears for all souls in trouble,
Here and in hell.

*James Clarence Mangan* [1803-1849]

## "DE MORTUIS NIL NISI BONUM"

(WRITTEN ON THE NIGHT OF HIS SUICIDE)

"*De mortuis nil nisi bonum.*" When
For me this end has come and I am dead,
And the little voluble, chattering daws of men
Peck at me curiously, let it then be said
By some one brave enough to speak the truth:
Here lies a great soul killed by cruel wrong.
Down all the balmy days of his fresh youth
To his bleak, desolate noon, with sword and song,
And speech that rushed up hotly from the heart,
He wrought for liberty, till his own wound
(He had been stabbed), concealed with painful art
Through wasting years, mastered him, and he swooned,
And sank there where you see him lying now
With the word "Failure" written on his brow.

But say that he succeeded. If he missed
World's honors, and world's plaudits, and the wage
Of the world's deft lacqueys, still his lips were kissed
Daily by those high angels who assuage

The thirstings of the poets—for he was
 Born unto singing—and a burthen lay
Mightily on him, and he moaned because
 He could not rightly utter to the day
What God taught in the night. Sometimes, nathless,
 Power fell upon him, and bright tongues of flame,
And blessings reached him from poor souls in stress;
 And benedictions from black pits of shame,
And little children's love, and old men's prayers,
And a Great Hand that led him unawares.

So he died rich. And if his eyes were blurred
 With big films—silence! he is in his grave.
Greatly he suffered; greatly, too, he erred;
 Yet broke his heart in trying to be brave.
Nor did he wait till Freedom had become
 The popular shibboleth of courtier's lips;
He smote for her when God Himself seemed dumb
 And all His arching skies were in eclipse.
He was a-weary, but he fought his fight,
 And stood for simple manhood; and was joyed
To see the august broadening of the light
 And new earths heaving heavenward from the void.
He loved his fellows, and their love was sweet—
Plant daisies at his head and at his feet.

*Richard Realf* [1834–1878]

## HOPE AND DESPAIR

Said God, "You sisters, ere ye go
Down among men, my work to do,
I will on each a badge bestow:
Hope I love best, and gold for her,
Yet a silver glory for Despair,
For she is my angel too."

Then like a queen, Despair
Put on the stars to wear.
But Hope took ears of corn, and round
Her temples in a wreath them bound.—
Which think ye looked the more fair?

*Lascelles Abercrombie* [1881–1938]

## DEJECTION: AN ODE

Late, late yestreen I saw the new Moon,
With the old Moon in her arms;
And I fear, I fear, my Master dear!
We shall have a deadly storm.
Ballad of Sir Patrick Spence.

I

WELL! If the Bard was weather-wise, who made
The grand old ballad of Sir Patrick Spence,
This night, so tranquil now, will not go hence
Unroused by winds, that ply a busier trade
Than those which mould yon cloud in lazy flakes,
Or the dull sobbing draft, that moans and rakes
Upon the strings of this Æolian lute,
Which better far were mute.
For lo! the New-moon winter-bright!
And overspread with phantom light,
(With swimming phantom light o'erspread
But rimmed and circled by a silver thread)
I see the old Moon in her lap, foretelling
The coming-on of rain and squally blast.
And oh! that even now the gust were swelling,
And the slant night-shower driving loud and fast!
Those sounds which oft have raised me, whilst they awed,
And sent my soul abroad,
Might now perhaps their wonted impulse give,
Might startle this dull pain, and make it move and live!

II

A grief without a pang, void, dark, and drear,
A stifled, drowsy, unimpassioned grief,
Which finds no natural outlet, no relief,
In word, or sigh, or tear—
O Lady! in this wan and heartless mood,
To other thoughts by yonder throstle wooed,
All this long eve, so balmy and serene,
Have I been gazing on the western sky,
And its peculiar tint of yellow green:
And still I gaze—and with how blank an eye!

And those thin clouds above, in flakes and bars,
That give away their motion to the stars;
Those stars, that glide behind them or between,
Now sparkling, now bedimmed, but always seen:
Yon crescent Moon, as fixed as if it grew
In its own cloudless, starless lake of blue;
I see them all so excellently fair,
I see, not feel, how beautiful they are!

III

My genial spirits fail;
And what can these avail
To lift the smothering weight from off my breast?
It were a vain endeavor,
Though I should gaze for ever
On that green light that lingers in the west:
I may not hope from outward forms to win
The passion and the life, whose fountains are within.

IV

O Lady! we receive but what we give,
And in our life alone does Nature live:
Ours is her wedding garment, ours her shroud!
And would we aught behold, of higher worth,
Than that inanimate cold world allowed
To the poor loveless ever-anxious crowd,
Ah! from the soul itself must issue forth
A light, a glory, a fair luminous cloud
Enveloping the Earth—
And from the soul itself must there be sent
A sweet and potent voice, of its own birth,
Of all sweet sounds the life and element!

V

O pure of heart! thou need'st not ask of me
What this strong music in the soul may be!
What, and wherein it doth exist,
This light, this glory, this fair luminous mist,
This beautiful and beauty-making power.

Joy, virtuous Lady! Joy that ne'er was given,
Save to the pure, and in their purest hour,
Life, and Life's effluence, cloud at once and shower,
Joy, Lady! is the spirit and the power,
Which wedding Nature to us gives in dower
A new Earth and new Heaven,
Undreamt of by the sensual and the proud—
Joy is the sweet voice, Joy the luminous cloud—
We in ourselves rejoice!
And thence flows all that charms or ear or sight,
All melodies the echoes of that voice,
All colors a suffusion from that light.

VI

There was a time when, though my path was rough,
This joy within me dallied with distress,
And all misfortunes were but as the stuff
Whence Fancy made me dreams of happiness:
For hope grew round me, like the twining vine,
And fruits, and foliage, not my own, seemed mine.
But now afflictions bow me down to earth:
Nor care I that they rob me of my mirth;
But oh! each visitation
Suspends what nature gave me at my birth,
My shaping spirit of Imagination.
For not to think of what I needs must feel,
But to be still and patient, all I can;
And haply by abstruse research to steal
From my own nature all the natural man—
This was my sole resource, my only plan:
Till that which suits a part infects the whole,
And now is almost grown the habit of my soul.

VII

Hence, viper thoughts, that coil around my mind,
Reality's dark dream!
I turn from you, and listen to the wind,
Which long has raved unnoticed. What a scream
Of agony by torture lengthened out
That lute sent forth! Thou Wind, that rav'st without,
Bare crag, or mountain-tairn, or blasted tree,

Or pine-grove whither woodman never clomb,
Or lonely house, long held the witches' home,
    Methinks were fitter instruments for thee,
Mad Lutanist! who in this month of showers,
Of dark-brown gardens, and of peeping flowers,
Mak'st Devils' yule, with worse than wintry song,
The blossoms, buds, and timorous leaves among.
    Thou Actor, perfect in all tragic sounds!
Thou mighty Poet, e'en to frenzy bold!
        What tell'st thou now about?
        'Tis of the rushing of an host in rout,
    With groans, of trampled men, with smarting wounds—
At once they groan with pain, and shudder with the cold!
But hush! there is a pause of deepest silence!
    And all that noise, as of a rushing crowd,
With groans, and tremulous shudderings—all is over—
    It tells another tale, with sounds less deep and loud!
        A tale of less affright,
        And tempered with delight,
As Otway's self had framed the tender lay,—
        'Tis of a little child
        Upon a lonesome wild,
Not far from home, but she hath lost her way:
And now moans low in bitter grief and fear,
And now screams loud, and hopes to make her mother hear.

VIII

'Tis midnight, but small thoughts have I of sleep:
Full seldom may my friend such vigils keep!
Visit her, gentle Sleep! with wings of healing,
    And may this storm be but a mountain-birth,
May all the stars hang bright above her dwelling,
    Silent as though they watched the sleeping Earth!
        With light heart may she rise,
        Gay fancy, cheerful eyes,
    Joy lift her spirit, joy attune her voice;
To her may all things live, from pole to pole,
Their life the eddying of her living soul!
    O simple spirit, guided from above,
Dear Lady! friend devoutest of my choice,
Thus mayest thou ever, evermore rejoice.

*Samuel Taylor Coleridge* [1772–1834]

## WORK WITHOUT HOPE

All Nature seems at work. Slugs leave their lair—
The bees are stirring—birds are on the wing—
And Winter slumbering in the open air,
Wears on his smiling face a dream of Spring!
And I the while, the sole unbusy thing,
Nor honey make, nor pair, nor build, nor sing.

Yet well I ken the banks where amaranths blow,
Have traced the fount whence streams of nectar flow.
Bloom, O ye amaranths! bloom for whom ye may,
For me ye bloom not! Glide, rich streams, away!
With lips unbrightened, wreathless brow, I stroll:
And would you learn the spells that drowse my soul?
Work without Hope draws nectar in a sieve,
And Hope without an object cannot live.

*Samuel Taylor Coleridge* [1772–1834]

## CARE

All in the leafy darkness, when sleep had passed me by,
I knew the surging of the sea—
Though never wave were nigh.
All in the leafy darkness, unbroken by a star,
There came the clamorous call of day,
While yet the day was far.
All in the leafy darkness, woven with hushes deep,
I heard the vulture wings of Fear
Above me tireless sweep;
The sea of Doubt, the dread of day, upon me surged and swept
All in the leafy darkness,
And while the whole world slept.

*Virginia Woodward Cloud* [18 –1938]

## AT THE SALON

Brave as the firstborn flame upsprings the statue,
A worshiper of the Sun:
With arms and lips and vital hair he praises
The Dawn begun.

Buoyancy, adoration of beginnings,
He soars tiptoe,

Nor heeds he that his plinth was wreathed with cypress
An hour ago,

Memorial of the maker of the statue
Who in his ultimate pain
Set free the spirit in the block of marble,
—Child of his brain.

The men and women pacing through the Salon
By that grave challenge are stopped,
Pondering on him from whose arrested fingers
The tool has dropped.

For him black weeds are draped and just one moment
Chatter is mute,
While, like a skylark, sings his last glad sculpture
Its flame salute.

*Florence Wilkinson* [18

## THE WIND'S WAY

A WHITE way is the wind's way,
The silver side o' the leaf:
Follow the wind, heart of mine,
Heart of grief!

Wind of the dawn, wind of the dusk,
Wingèd wind of the day,
Who would follow the wind must go
The wind's way.

*Grace Hazard Conkling* [1878–1958]

## TROPICAL TOWN

BLUE, pink and yellow houses, and, afar,
The cemetery, where the green trees are.

Sometimes you see a hungry dog pass by,
And there are always buzzards in the sky,
Sometimes you hear the big cathedral bell;
A blind man rings it; and sometimes you hear
A rumbling ox-cart that brings wood to sell.
Else nothing ever breaks the ancient spell

That holds the town asleep, save, once a year,
The Easter Festival. . .

I come from there,
And when I tire of hoping, and despair
Is heavy over me, my thoughts go far,
Beyond that length of lazy street, to where
The lonely green trees and the white graves are

*Salomôn de la Selva* [1893-

## SUNSET WINGS

To-night this sunset spreads two golden wings
Cleaving the western sky;
Winged too with wind it is, and winnowings
Of birds; as if the day's last hour in rings
Of strenuous flight must die.

Sun-steeped in fire, the homeward pinions sway
Above the dovecote-tops;
And clouds of starlings, ere they rest with day,
Sink, clamorous like mill-waters, at wild play,
By turns in every copse:

Each tree heart-deep the wrangling rout receives,—
Save for the whirr within,
You could not tell the starlings from the leaves;
Then one great puff of wings, and the swarm heaves
Away with all its din.

Even thus Hope's hours, in ever-eddying flight,
To many a refuge tend;
With the first light she laughed, and the last light
Glows round her still; who natheless in the night
At length must make an end.

And now the mustering rooks innumerable
Together sail and soar,
While for the day's death, like a tolling knell,
Unto the heart they seem to cry, Farewell,
No more, farewell, no more!

Is Hope not plumed, as 'twere a fiery dart?
And oh! thou dying day,
Even as thou goest must she too depart,
And Sorrow fold such pinions on the heart
As will not fly away?

*Dante Gabriel Rossetti* [1828–1882]

## MORALITY

We cannot kindle when we will
The fire which in the heart resides·
The spirit bloweth and is still,
In mystery our soul abides.
But tasks in hours of insight willed
Can be through hours of gloom fulfilled.

With aching hands and bleeding feet
We dig and heap, lay stone on stone;
We bear the burden and the heat
Of the long day, and wish 'twere done.
Not till the hours of light return
All we have built do we discern.

Then, when the clouds are off the soul,
When thou dost bask in Nature's eye,
Ask, how *she* viewed thy self-control,
Thy struggling, tasked morality—
Nature, whose free, light, cheerful air,
Oft made thee, in thy gloom, despair.

And she, whose answer thou dost dread
Whose eye thou wast afraid to seek,
See, on her face a glow is spread,
A strong emotion on her cheek!
"Ah, child," she cries, "that strife divine,
Whence was it, for it is not mine?

"There is no effort on *my* brow—
I do not strive, I do not weep;
I rush with the swift spheres and glow
In joy, and when I will, I sleep.
Yet that severe, that earnest air,
I saw, I felt it once—but where?

"I knew not yet the gauge of time,
Nor wore the manacles of space;
I felt it in some other clime,
I saw it in some other place.
'Twas when the heavenly house I trod,
And lay upon the breast of God.

*Matthew Arnold* [1822–1888]

## CUI BONO

WHAT is Hope? A smiling rainbow
Children follow through the wet;
'Tis not here, still yonder, yonder:
Never urchin found it yet.

What is Life? A thawing iceboard
On a sea with sunny shore;
Gay we sail; it melts beneath us;
We are sunk, and seen no more.

What is Man? A foolish baby,
Vainly strives, and fights, and frets;
Demanding all, deserving nothing;
One small grave is what he gets.

*Thomas Carlyle* [1795–1881]

## MUTABILITY

THE flower that smiles to-day
To-morrow dies;
All that we wish to stay
Tempts, and then flies.
What is this world's delight?
Lightning that mocks the night,
Brief even as bright.

Virtue, how frail it is!
Friendship how rare!
Love, how it sells poor bliss
For proud despair!
But we, though soon they fall,
Survive their joy, and all
Which ours we call.

Whilst skies are blue and bright,
  Whilst flowers are gay,
Whilst eyes that change ere night
  Make glad the day,
Whilst yet the calm hours creep,
Dream thou—and from thy sleep
Then wake to weep.

*Percy Bysshe Shelley* [1792–1822]

## A FANCY FROM FONTENELLE

***De mêmoires de Roses on n'a point vu mourir le Jardinier***

The Rose in the garden slipped her bud,
And she laughed in the pride of her youthful blood,
As she thought of the Gardener standing by—
"He is old—so old! And he soon must die!"

The full Rose waxed in the warm June air,
And she spread and spread till her heart lay bare;
And she laughed once more as she heard his tread—
"He is older now! He will soon be dead!"

But the breeze of the morning blew, and found
That the leaves of the blown Rose strewed the ground;
And he came at noon, that Gardener old,
And he raked them gently under the mold.

*And I wove the thing to a random rhyme:*
*For the Rose is Beauty; the Gardener, Time.*

*Austin Dobson* [1840–1921]

## "OH, EARLIER SHALL THE ROSEBUDS BLOW"

Oh, earlier shall the rosebuds blow,
  In after years, those happier years,
And children weep, when we lie low,
  Far fewer tears, far softer tears.

Oh, true shall boyish laughter ring,
  Like tinkling chimes, in kinder times!
And merrier shall the maiden sing:
  And I not there, and I not there.

Like lightning in the summer night
  Their mirth shall be, so quick and free;
And oh! the flash of their delight
  I shall not see, I may not see.

In deeper dream, with wider range,
  Those eyes shall shine, but not on mine:
Unmoved, unblest, by worldly change,
  The dead must rest, the dead shall rest.

*William Johnson Cory* [1823–1892]

## THE DOVE

I HAD a dove, and the sweet dove died;
  And I have thought it died of grieving:
O, what could it grieve for? Its feet were tied
  With a silken thread of my own hand's weaving;
Sweet little red feet! why should you die—
Why would you leave me, sweet bird! why?
You lived alone in the forest tree,
Why, pretty thing! would you not live with me?
I kissed you oft and gave you white peas;
Why not live sweetly, as in the green trees?

*John Keats* [1795–1821]

## THE WHISPERERS

As beneath the moon I walked,
Dog-at-heel my shadow stalked,
Keeping ghostly company:
And as we went gallantly
Down the fell-road, dusty-white,
Round us in the windy night
Bracken, rushes, bent and heather
Whispered ceaselessly together:
"Would he ever journey more,
Ever stride so carelessly,
If he knew what lies before,
And could see what we can see?"

As I listened, cold with dread,
Every hair upon my head

Strained to hear them talk of me,
Whispering, whispering ceaselessly:
"Folly's fool the man must be,
Surely, since, though where he goes
He knows not, his shadow knows:
And his secret shadow never
Utters warning words, or ever
Seeks to save him from his fate,
Reckless, blindfold, and unknown,
Till death tells him all, too late,
And his shadow walks alone."

*Wilfrid Wilson Gibson* [1878-

## ON A TEAR

O THAT the chemist's magic art
  Could crystallize this sacred treasure!
Long should it glitter near my heart,
  A secret source of pensive pleasure.

The little brilliant, ere it fell,
  Its luster caught from Chloe's eye;
Then, trembling, left its coral cell,—
  The spring of Sensibility!

Sweet drop of pure and pearly light!
  In thee the rays of Virtue shine,
More calmly clear, more mildly bright,
  Than any gem that gilds the mine.

Benign restorer of the soul!
  Who ever fliest to bring relief,
When first we feel the rude control
  Of Love or Pity, Joy or Grief.

The sage's and the poet's theme,
  In every clime, in every age,
Thou charm'st in Fancy's idle dream,
  In Reason's philosophic page.

That very law which molds a tear,
  And bids it trickle from its source,—
That law preserves the earth a sphere,
  And guides the planets in their course.

*Samuel Rogers* [1763-1855]

## THE ROSARY OF MY TEARS

SOME reckon their age by years,
  Some measure their life by art;
But some tell their days by the flow of their tears,
  And their lives by the moans of their heart.

The dials of earth may show
  The length, not the depth, of years—
Few or many they come, few or many they go,
  But time is best measured by tears.

Ah! not by the silver gray
  That creeps through the sunny hair,
And not by the scenes that we pass on our way,
  And not by the furrows the fingers of care

On forehead and face have made,—
  Not so do we count our years;
Not by the sun of the earth, but the shade
  Of our souls, and the fall of our tears.

For the young are oft-times old,
  Though their brows be bright and fair;
While their blood beats warm, their hearts are cold—
  O'er them the spring—but winter is there;

And the old are oft-times young
  When their hair is thin and white;
And they sing in age, as in youth they sung,
  And they laugh, for their cross was light.

But, bead by bead, I tell
  The rosary of my years;
From a cross to a cross they lead; 'tis well,
  And they're blest with a blessing of tears.

Better a day of strife
  Than a century of sleep;
Give me instead of a long stream of life
  The tempests and tears of the deep.

A thousand joys may foam
  On the billows of all the years;
But never the foam brings the lone back home,—
  He reaches the haven through tears.

*Abram J. Ryan* [1839–1888]

## ENDURANCE

How much the heart may bear, and yet not break!
  How much the flesh may suffer, and not die!
I question much if any pain or ache
  Of soul or body brings our end more nigh:
Death chooses his own time; till that is sworn,
    All evils may be borne.

We shrink and shudder at the surgeon's knife,
  Each nerve recoiling from the cruel steel
Whose edge seems searching for the quivering life;
  Yet to our sense the bitter pangs reveal,
That still, although the trembling flesh be torn,
    This also can be borne.

We see a sorrow rising in our way,
  And try to flee from the approaching ill;
We seek some small escape: we weep and pray;
  But when the blow falls, then our hearts are still;
Not that the pain is of its sharpness shorn,
    But that it can be borne.

We wind our life about another life;
  We hold it closer, dearer than our own:
Anon it faints and fails in deathly strife,
  Leaving us stunned and stricken and alone;
But ah! we do not die with those we mourn,—
    This also can be borne.

Behold, we live through all things,—famine, thirst,
  Bereavement, pain; all grief and misery,
All woe and sorrow; life inflicts its worst
  On soul and body,—but we can not die.
Though we be sick, and tired, and faint, and worn,—
    Lo, all things can be borne!

*Elizabeth Akers* [1832–1911]

## LANGLEY LANE

In all the land, range up, range down,
  Is there ever a place so pleasant and sweet,
As Langley Lane in London town,
  Just out of the bustle of square and street?
Little white cottages all in a row,
Gardens where bachelors'-buttons grow,
  Swallows' nests in roof and wall,
And up above the still blue sky,
Where the woolly white clouds go sailing by—
  I seem to be able to see it all!

For now, in summer, I take my chair,
  And sit outside in the sun, and hear
The distant murmur of street and square,
  And the swallows and sparrows chirping near;
And Fanny, who lives just over the way,
Comes running many a time each day,
  With her little hand's-touch so warm and kind,
And I smile and talk, with the sun on my cheek,
And the little live hand seems to stir and speak—
  For Fanny is dumb and I am blind.

Fanny is sweet thirteen, and she
  Has fine black ringlets and dark eyes clear,
And I am older by summers three,—
  Why should we hold one another so dear?
Because she cannot utter a word,
Nor hear the music of bee or bird,
  The water-cart's splash or the milkman's call.
Because I have never seen the sky,
Nor the little singers that hum and fly,—
  Yet know she is gazing upon them all!

For the sun is shining, the swallows fly,
  The bees and the blueflies murmur low,
And I hear the water-cart go by,
  With its cool splash-splash down the dusty row;
And the little one, close at my side, perceives
Mine eyes upraised to the cottage eaves,

Where birds are chirping in summer shine,
And I hear, though I cannot look, and she,
Though she cannot hear, can the singers see,—
And the little soft fingers flutter in mine.

Hath not the dear little hand a tongue,
When it stirs on my palm for the love of me?
Do I not know she is pretty and young?
Hath not my soul an eye to see?
'Tis pleasure to make one's bosom stir,
To wonder how things appear to her,
That I only hear as they pass around;
And as long as we sit in the music and light,
She is happy to keep God's sight,
And I am happy to keep God's sound.

Why, I know her face, though I am blind—
I made it of music long ago:
Strange large eyes and dark hair twined
Round the pensive light of a brow of snow;
And when I sit by my little one,
And hold her hand and talk in the sun,
And hear the music that haunts the place,
I know she is raising her eyes to me,
And guessing how gentle my voice must be,
And seeing the music upon my face.

Though, if ever the Lord should grant me a prayer
(I know the fancy is only vain),
I should pray: Just once, when the weather is fair,
To see little Fanny and Langley Lane;
Though Fanny, perhaps, would pray to hear
The voice of the friend she holds so dear,
The song of the birds, the hum of the street,—
It is better to be as we have been,—
Each keeping up something, unheard, unseen,
To make God's heaven more strange and sweet!

Ah, life is pleasant in Langley Lane!
There is always something sweet to hear!
Chirping of birds or patter of rain;
And Fanny, my little one, always near;

And though I am weakly and can't live long,
And Fanny my darling is far from strong,
  And though we can never married be,—
What then?—since we hold one another so dear,
For the sake of the pleasure one cannot hear,
  And the pleasure that only one can see?

*Robert Buchanan* [1841–1901]

## THE WEAKEST THING

WHICH is the weakest thing of all
  Mine heart can ponder?
The sun, a little cloud can pall
  With darkness yonder?
The cloud, a little wind can move
  Where'er it listeth?
The wind, a little leaf above,
  Though sere, resisteth?

What time that yellow leaf was green,
  My days were gladder;
But now, whatever Spring may mean,
  I must grow sadder.
Ah me! a *leaf* with sighs can wring
  My lips asunder?
Then is mine heart the weakest thing
  Itself can ponder.

Yet, Heart, when sun and cloud are pined
  And drop together,
And at a blast which is not wind
  The forests wither,
Thou, from the darkening deathly curse
  To glory breakest,—
The Strongest of the universe
  Guarding the weakest!

*Elizabeth Barrett Browning* [1806–1861]

## SONG

We only ask for sunshine,
  We did not want the rain;
But see the flowers that spring from showers
  All up and down the plain.

We beg the gods for laughter,
  We shrink, we dread the tears;
But grief's redress is happiness,
  Alternate through the years.

*Helen Hay Whitney* [18 –1944]

## THE HOUSE OF PAIN

Unto the Prison House of Pain none willingly repair—
  The bravest who an entrance gain
Reluctant linger there—
For Pleasure, passing by that door, stays not to cheer the sight,
And Sympathy but muffles sound and banishes the light.

Yet in the Prison House of Pain things full of beauty blow—
  Like Christmas roses, which attain
Perfection 'mid the snow—
Love entering, in his mild warmth the darkest shadows melt,
And often, where the hush is deep, the waft of wings is felt.

Ah, me! the Prison House of Pain!—what lessons there are bought!
  Lessons of a sublimer strain
Than any elsewhere taught;
Amid its loneliness and gloom, grave meanings grow more clear,
For to no earthly dwelling-place seems God so strangely near!

*Florence Earle Coates* [1850–1927]

## WISE

AN apple orchard smells like wine;
  A succory flower is blue;
Until Grief touched these eyes of mine,
  Such things I never knew.

And now indeed I know so plain
  Why one would like to cry
When spouts are full of April rain—
  Such lonely folk go by!

So wise, so wise—that my tears fall
  Each breaking of the dawn;
That I do long to tell you all—
  But you are dead and gone.

*Lizette Woodworth Reese* [1856–1935]

## "MULTUM DILEXIT"

SHE sat and wept beside His feet; the weight
Of sin oppressed her heart; for all the blame,
And the poor malice of the worldly shame,
To her was past, extinct, and out of date:
Only the sin remained,—the leprous state;
She would be melted by the heat of love,
By fires far fiercer than are blown to prove
And purge the silver ore adulterate.

She sat and wept, and with her untressed hair
Still wiped the feet she was so blessed to touch;
And He wiped off the soiling of despair
From her sweet soul, because she loved so much.
I am a sinner, full of doubts and fears:
Make me a humble thing of love and tears.

*Hartley Coleridge* [1796–1849]

## PIERRETTE IN MEMORY

PIERRETTE has gone, but it was not
  Exactly that she died,
So much as vanished and forgot
  To say where she would hide.

To keep a sudden rendezvous,
  It came into her mind
That she was late. What could she do
  But leave distress behind?

Afraid of being in disgrace,
  And hurrying to dress,
She heard there was another place
  In need of loveliness.

She went so softly and so soon,
  She hardly made a stir;
But going, took the stars and moon
  And sun away with her.

*William Griffith* [1876–1936]

## "WIND ME A SUMMER CROWN"

"WIND me a summer crown," she said,
  "And set it on my brows;
For I must go, while I am young,
  Home to my Father's house.

"And make me ready for the day,
  And let me not be stayed;
I would not linger on the way
  As if I was afraid.

"O, will the golden courts of heaven,
  When I have paced them o'er,
Be lovely as the lily walks
  Which I must see no more?

"And will the seraph hymns and harps,
When they have filled my ear,
Be tender as my mother's voice,
Which I must never hear?

"And shall I lie where sunsets drift,
Or where the stars are born,
Or where the living tints are mixed
To paint the clouds of morn?"

Your mother's tones shall reach you still,
Even sweeter than they were;
And the false love that broke your heart
Shall be forgotten there:

And not a star or flower is born
The beauty of that shore;
There is a face which you shall see
And wish for nothing more.

*Menella Bute Smedley* [1820–1877]

## TO THE HARPIES

You who with birch or laurel
Are swift to scourge or bless—
Silence your foolish quarrel
Before her loveliness.

What though she went a-travel
Down paths you do not know?
Your words shall not unravel
Webs that allured her so.

Hush now your foolish babble
Around her golden head.
Shut out the prying rabble.
Be happy. She is dead.

Now give one final kindness
That late you dreamed not of—
Silence, to cloak your blindness—
Peace, since you know not love.

*Arthur Davison Ficke* [1883–1945]

## THE BRIDGE OF SIGHS

ONE more Unfortunate,
Weary of breath,
Rashly importunate,
Gone to her death!

Take her up tenderly,
Lift her with care;
Fashioned so slenderly,
Young, and so fair!

Look at her garments
Clinging like cerements:
Whilst the wave constantly
Drips from her clothing;
Take her up instantly,
Loving, not loathing.

Touch her not scornfully;
Think of her mournfully,
Gently and humanly;
Not of the stains of her;
All that remains of her
Now is pure womanly.

Make no deep scrutiny
Into her mutiny
Rash and undutiful;
Past all dishonor,
Death has left on her
Only the beautiful.

Still, for all slips of hers,
One of Eve's family—
Wipe those poor lips of hers
Oozing so clammily.

Loop up her tresses
Escaped from the comb,
Her fair auburn tresses;
Whilst wonderment guesses
Where was her home?

Who was her father?
  Who was her mother?
Had she a sister?
  Had she a brother?
Or was there a dearer one
Still, and a nearer one
  Yet, than all other?

Alas! for the rarity
Of Christian charity
  Under the sun!
O, it was pitiful!
Near a whole city full,
  Home she had none.

Sisterly, brotherly,
Fatherly, motherly
  Feelings had changed:
Love, by harsh evidence,
Thrown from its eminence;
Even God's providence
  Seeming estranged.

Where the lamps quiver
So far in the river,
  With many a light
From window and casement,
From garret to basement,
She stood, with amazement,
  Houseless by night.

The bleak wind of March
  Made her tremble and shiver;
But not the dark arch
Or the black flowing river:
Mad from life's history,
Glad to death's mystery,
  Swift to be hurled—
Anywhere, anywhere
  Out of the world!

In she plunged boldly—
No matter how coldly
  The rough river ran—
Over the brink of it,
Picture it,—think of it,
  Dissolute Man!
Lave in it,—drink of it,
  Then, if you can!

Take her up tenderly,
  Lift her with care;
Fashioned so slenderly,
  Young, and so fair!

Ere her limbs frigidly
Stiffen too rigidly,
  Decently, kindly,
Smooth and compose them;
And her eyes, close them,
  Staring so blindly!

Dreadfully staring
  Through muddy impurity,
As when with the daring
Last look of despairing,
  Fixed on futurity.

Perishing gloomily,
Spurred by contumely,
Cold inhumanity,
Burning insanity,
  Into her rest.—
Cross her hands humbly
As if praying dumbly,
  Over her breast!

Owning her weakness,
  Her evil behavior,
And leaving, with meekness,
  Her sins to her Saviour!

*Thomas Hood* [1799–1845]

## THE SONG OF THE SHIRT

WITH fingers weary and worn,
With eyelids heavy and red,
A woman sat, in unwomanly rags,
Plying her needle and thread,—
Stitch—stitch—stitch!
In poverty, hunger, and dirt;
And still with a voice of dolorous pitch
She sang the "Song of the Shirt!"

"Work—work—work
While the cock is crowing aloof!
And work—work—work
Till the stars shine through the roof!
It's oh! to be a slave
Along with the barbarous Turk,
Where woman has never a soul to save,
If this is Christian work!

"Work—work—work
Till the brain begins to swim!
Work—work—work
Till the eyes are heavy and dim!
Seam, and gusset, and band,
Band, and gusset, and seam,—
Till over the buttons I fall asleep,
And sew them on in a dream!

"O men with sisters dear!
O men with mothers and wives!
It is not linen you're wearing out,
But human creatures' lives!
Stitch—stitch—stitch,
In poverty, hunger and dirt,—
Sewing at once, with a double thread,
A shroud as well as a shirt!

"But why do I talk of death,—
That phantom of grisly bone?
I hardly fear his terrible shape,
It seems so like my own,—

It seems so like my own
   Because of the fasts I keep;
O God! that bread should be so dear,
   And flesh and blood so cheap!

"Work—work—work!
   My labor never flags;
And what are its wages? A bed of straw,
   A crust of bread—and rags.
That shattered roof—and this naked floor—
   A table—a broken chair—
And a wall so blank my shadow I thank
   For sometimes falling there!

"Work—work—work
   From weary chime to chime!
Work—work—work
   As prisoners work for crime!
Band, and gusset, and seam,
   Seam, and gusset, and band,—
Till the heart is sick and the brain benumbed,
   As well as the weary hand.

"Work—work—work
   In the dull December light!
And work—work—work
   When the weather is warm and bright!
While underneath the eaves
   The brooding swallows cling,
As if to show me their sunny backs,
   And twit me with the Spring.

"Oh but to breathe the breath
   Of the cowslip and primrose sweet,—
With the sky above my head,
   And the grass beneath my feet!
For only one short hour
   To feel as I used to feel,
Before I knew the woes of want
   And the walk that costs a meal!

"Oh but for one short hour,—
  A respite, however brief!
No blessèd leisure for love or hope,
  But only time for grief!
A little weeping would ease my heart;
  But in their briny bed
My tears must stop, for every drop
  Hinders needle and thread!"

With fingers weary and worn,
  With eyelids heavy and red,
A woman sat, in unwomanly rags,
  Plying her needle and thread,—
    Stitch—stitch—stitch!
  In poverty, hunger, and dirt;
And still with a voice of dolorous pitch—
Would that its tone could reach the rich!—
  She sang this "Song of the Shirt!"

*Thomas Hood* [1799-1845]

## STANZAS

In a drear-nighted December,
  Too happy, happy tree,
Thy branches ne'er remember
  Their green felicity:
The north cannot undo them,
With a sleety whistle through them;
Nor frozen thawings glue them
  From budding at the prime.

In a drear-nighted December,
  Too happy, happy brook,
Thy bubblings ne'er remember
  Apollo's summer look;
But with a sweet forgetting,
They stay their crystal fretting,
Never, never petting
  About the frozen time.

Ah! would 'twere so with many
  A gentle girl and boy!
But were there ever any
  Writhed not at passèd joy?
To know the change and feel it,
When there is none to heal it,
Nor numbèd sense to steal it,
  Was never said in rhyme.

*John Keats* [1795–1821]

## THE DEAD FAITH

She made a little shadow-hidden grave
  The day Faith died;
Therein she laid it, heard the clod's sick fall,
  And smiled aside—
"If less I ask," tear-blind, she mocked, "I may
  Be less denied."

She set a rose to blossom in her hair,
  The day Faith died—
"Now glad," she said, "and free at last, I go,
  And life is wide."
But through long nights she stared into the dark,
  And knew she lied.

*Fannie Heaslip Lea* [1884–1955]

## THE BALLAD OF THE BOAT

The stream was smooth as glass, we said, "Arise and let's away":
The Siren sang beside the boat that in the rushes lay;
And spread the sail, and strong the oar, we gaily took our way.
When shall the sandy bar be crossed? When shall we find the bay?

The broadening flood swells slowly out o'er cattle-dotted plains,
The stream is strong and turbulent, and dark with heavy rains;

The laborer looks up to see our shallop speed away.
When shall the sandy bar be crossed? When shall we find
the bay?

Now are the clouds like fiery shrouds; the sun, superbly
large,
Slow as an oak to woodman's stroke sinks flaming at their
marge.
The waves are bright with mirrored light as jacinths on our
way.
When shall the sandy bar be crossed? When shall we find
the bay?

The moon is high up in the sky, and now no more we see
The spreading river's either bank, and surging distantly
There booms a sullen thunder as of breakers far away.
Now shall the sandy bar be crossed, now shall we find the
bay!

The sea-gull shrieks high overhead, and dimly to our sight
The moonlit crests of foaming waves gleam towering through
the night.
We'll steal upon the mermaid soon, and start her from her
lay,
When once the sandy bar is crossed, and we are in the bay.

What rises white and awful as a shroud-enfolded ghost?
What roar of rampant tumult bursts in clangor on the coast?
Pull back! pull back! The raging flood sweeps every oar
away.
O stream, is this thy bar of sand? O boat, is this the bay?

*Richard Garnett* [1835–1906]

## ELDORADO

GAILY bedight,
A gallant knight
In sunshine and in shadow
Had journeyed long,
Singing a song,
In search of Eldorado.

  But he grew old—
  This knight so bold—
And o'er his heart a shadow
  Fell, as he found
  No spot of ground
That looked like Eldorado.

  And, as his strength
  Failed him at length,
He met a pilgrim shadow:
  "Shadow," said he,
  "Where can it be—
This land of Eldorado?"

  "Over the mountains
  Of the moon,
Down the valley of the Shadow
  Ride, boldly ride,"
  The shade replied,
"If you seek for Eldorado!"

*Edgar Allan Poe* [1809–1849]

## A LOST CHORD

SEATED one day at the Organ,
  I was weary and ill at ease,
And my fingers wandered idly
  Over the noisy keys.

I do not know what I was playing,
  Or what I was dreaming then;
But I struck one chord of music,
  Like the sound of a great Amen.

It flooded the crimson twilight,
  Like the close of an Angel's Psalm,
And it lay on my fevered spirit
  With a touch of infinite calm.

It quieted pain and sorrow,
  Like love overcoming strife;
It seemed the harmonious echo
  From our discordant life.

It linked all perplexèd meanings
  Into one perfect peace,
And trembled away into silence
  As if it were loth to cease.

I have sought, but I seek it vainly,
  That one lost chord divine,
Which came from the soul of the Organ,
  And entered into mine.

It may be that Death's bright angel
  Will speak in that chord again,—
It may be that only in Heaven
  I shall hear that grand Amen.

*Adelaide Anne Procter* [1825–1864]

## LITTLE GRAY SONGS FROM ST. JOSEPH'S

### XXX

WITH cassock black, baret and book,
  Father Saran goes by;
I think he goes to say a prayer
  For one who has to die.

Even so, some day, Father Saran
  May say a prayer for me;
Myself meanwhile, the Sister tells,
  Should pray unceasingly.

They kneel who pray: how may I kneel
  Who face to ceiling lie,
Shut out by all that man has made
  From God who made the sky?

They lift who pray—the low earth-born—
  A humble heart to God:
But O, my heart of clay is proud—
  True sister to the sod.

I look into the face of God,
  They say bends over me;
I search the dark, dark face of God—
  O what is it I see?

I see—who lie fast bound, who may
Not kneel, who can but seek—
I see mine own face over me,
With tears upon its cheek.

XLVII

My little soul I never saw,
Nor can I count its days;
I do not know its wondrous law
And yet I know its ways.

Oh, it is young as morning-hours,
And old as is the night;
Oh, it has growth of budding flowers,
Yet tastes my body's blight.

And it is silent and apart,
And far and fair and still,
Yet ever beats within my heart,
And cries within my will.

And it is light and bright and strange,
And sees life far away,
Yet far with near can interchange
And dwell within the day.

My soul has died a thousand deaths,
And yet it does not die;
My soul has broke a thousand faiths,
And yet it cannot lie;

My soul—there's naught can make it less;
My soul—there's naught can mar;
Yet here it weeps with loneliness
Within its lonely star.

My soul—not any dark can bind,
Nor hinder any hand,
Yet here it weeps—long blind, long blind—
And cannot understand.

*Grace Fallow Norton* [18

## BIRTHRIGHT

Lord Rameses of Egypt sighed
Because a summer evening passed;
And little Ariadne cried
That summer fancy fell at last
To dust; and young Verona died
When beauty's hour was overcast.

Theirs was the bitterness we know
Because the clouds of hawthorn keep
So short a state, and kisses go
To tombs unfathomably deep,
While Rameses and Romeo
And little Ariadne sleep.

*John Drinkwater* [1882–1937]

## IMMORTALIS

All loved and lovely women dear to rhyme:
Thais, Cassandra, Helen and their fames,
Burn like tall candles through forgotten time,
Lighting the Past's dim arras with their names.
Around their faces wars the eager dark
Wherein all other lights are sunken now,
Yet, casting back, the seeker still may mark
A flame of hair, a bright immortal brow.

Surely, where they have passed, one after one,
Wearing their radiance to the darkened room,—
Surely, newcomers to Oblivion
May still descry in that all-quenching gloom,
Rare faces lovely, lifted and alight,
Like tapers burning through the windy night.

*David Morton* [18 –1957]

## SONNETS

Long, long ago, when all the glittering earth
Was heaven itself, when drunkards in the street
Were like mazed kings shaking at giving birth
To acts of war that sickle men like wheat,
When the white clover opened Paradise
And God lived in a cottage up the brook,
Beauty, you lifted up my sleeping eyes

And filled my heart with longing with a look;
And all the day I searched but could not find
The beautiful dark-eyed who touched me there,
Delight in her made trouble in my mind,
She was within all Nature, everywhere,
The breath I breathed, the brook, the flower, the grass,
Were her, her word, her beauty, all she was.

If I could come again to that dear place
Where once I came, where Beauty lived and moved,
Where, by the sea, I saw her face to face,
That soul alive by which the world has loved;
If, as I stood at gaze among the leaves,
She would appear again, as once before,
While the red herdsman gathered up his sheaves
And brimming waters trembled up the shore;
If, as I gazed, her Beauty that was dumb,
In that old time, before I learned to speak,
Would lean to me and revelation come,
Words to the lips and color to the cheek,
Joy with its searing-iron would burn me wise,
I should know all; all powers, all mysteries.

Roses are beauty, but I never see
Those blood drops from the burning heart of June
Glowing like thought upon the living tree,
Without a pity that they die so soon,
Die into petals, like those roses old,
Those women, who were summer in men's hearts
Before the smile upon the Sphinx was cold,
Or sand had hid the Syrian and his arts.
O myriad dust of beauty that lies thick
Under our feet that not a single grain
But stirred and moved in beauty and was quick
For one brief moon and died nor lived again;
But when the moon rose lay upon the grass
Pasture to living beauty, life that was.

O little self, within whose smallness lies
All that man was, and is, and will become,
Atom unseen that comprehends the skies
And tells the tracks by which the planets roam.

That, without moving, knows the joys of wings,
The tiger's strength, the eagle's secrecy,
And in the hovel can consort with kings,
Or clothe a god with his own mystery.
O with what darkness do we cloak thy light,
What dusty folly gather thee for food,
Thou who alone art knowledge and delight,
The heavenly bread, the beautiful, the good.
O living self, O god, O morning star,
Give us thy light, forgive us what we are.

There is no God, as I was taught in youth,
Though each, according to his stature, builds
Some covered shrine for what he thinks the truth,
Which day by day his reddest heart-blood gilds.
There is no God; but death, the clasping sea,
In which we move like fish, deep over deep
Made of men's souls that bodies have set free,
Floods to a Justice though it seems asleep.
There is no God, but still, behind the veil,
The hurt thing works, out of its agony.
Still, like a touching of a brimming Grail,
Return the pennies given to passers by.
There is no God, but we, who breathe the air,
Are God ourselves and touch God everywhere.

Let that which is to come be as it may,
Darkness, extinction, justice, life intense,
The flies are happy in the summer day,
Flies will be happy many summers hence.
Time with his antique breeds that built the Sphinx
Time with her men to come whose wings will tower,
Poured and will pour, not as the wise man thinks,
But with blind force, to each his little hour.
And when the hour has struck, comes death or change,
Which, whether good or ill, we cannot tell,
But the blind planet will wander through her range
Bearing men like us who will serve as well.
The sun will rise, the winds that ever move
Will blow our dust that once were men in love.

*John Masefield* [1878-

## "THE DESPOT'S DESPOT"

### VITAE SUMMA BREVIS SPEM NOS VETAT INCOHARE LONGAM

THEY are not long, the weeping and the laughter,
  Love and desire and hate;
I think they have no portion in us after
  We pass the gate.

They are not long, the days of wine and roses:
  Out of a misty dream
Our path emerges for a while, then closes
  Within a dream.

*Ernest Dowson* [1867–1900]

### DEATH'S FINAL CONQUEST

From "The Contention of Ajax and Ulysses"

THE glories of our blood and state
  Are shadows, not substantial things;
There is no armor against fate;
  Death lays his icy hand on kings:
    Scepter and Crown
    Must tumble down,
And in the dust be equal made
With the poor crooked scythe and spade.

Some men with swords may reap the field,
  And plant fresh laurels where they kill:
But their strong nerves at last must yield;
  They tame but one another still:
    Early or late
    They stoop to fate,
And must give up their murmuring breath
When they, pale captives, creep to death.

The garlands wither on your brow;
Then boast no more your mighty deeds;
Upon Death's purple altar now
See where the victor-victim bleeds:
Your heads must come
To the cold tomb;
Only the actions of the just
Smell sweet, and blossom in their dust.

*James Shirley* [1596–1666]

## DEATH'S SUBTLE WAYS

From "Cupid and Death"

VICTORIOUS men of earth, no more
Proclaim how wide your empires are:
Though you bind in every shore,
And your triumphs reach as far
As night or day,
Yet you, proud monarchs, must obey,
And mingle with forgotten ashes when
Death calls ye to the crowd of common men.

Devouring famine, plague, and war,
Each able to undo mankind,
Death's servile emissaries are;
Nor to these alone confined,
He hath at will
More quaint and subtle ways to kill:
A smile or kiss, as he will use the art,
Shall have the cunning skill to break a heart.

*James Shirley* [1596–1666]

## MAN'S MORTALITY

From "Microbiblion"

LIKE as the damask rose you see,
Or like the blossom on the tree,
Or like the dainty flower of May,
Or like the morning of the day,

Or like the sun, or like the shade,
Or like the gourd which Jonas had;
Even such is man, whose thread is spun,
Drawn out, and cut, and so is done.
The rose withers, the blossom blasteth,
The flower fades, the morning hasteth,
The sun sets, the shadow flies,
The gourd consumes, and man—he dies!

Like to the grass that's newly sprung,
Or like a tale that's new begun,
Or like a bird that's here to-day,
Or like the pearlèd dew of May,
Or like an hour, or like a span,
Or like the singing of a swan;
Even such is man, who lives by breath,
Is here, now there: so life, and death.
The grass withers, the tale is ended,
The bird is flown, the dew's ascended,
The hour is short, the span not long,
The swan near death,—man's life is done!

Like to a bubble in the brook,
Or in a glass much like a look,
Or like a shuttle in weaver's hand,
Or like a writing on the sand,
Or like a thought, or like a dream,
Or like the gliding of a stream;
Even such is man, who lives by breath,
Is here, now there: so life, and death.
The bubble's cut, the look's forgot,
The shuttle's flung, the writing's blot,
The thought is past, the dream is gone,
The water glides,—man's life is done!

Like to a blaze of fond delight,
Or like a morning clear and bright,
Or like a frost, or like a shower,
Or like the pride of Babel's tower,
Or like the hour that guides the time,
Or like to Beauty in her prime;

Even such is man, whose glory lends
That life a blaze or two, and ends.
The morn's o'ercast, joy turned to pain,
The frost is thawed, dried up the rain,
The tower falls, the hour is run,
The beauty lost,—man's life is done!

Like to an arrow from the bow,
Or like swift course of water-flow,
Or like the time 'twixt flood and ebb,
Or like the spider's tender web,
Or like a race, or like a goal,
Or like the dealing of a dole;
Even such is man, whose brittle state
Is always subject unto Fate.
The arrow's shot, the flood soon spent,
The time no time, the web soon rent,
The race soon run, the goal soon won,
The dole soon dealt,—man's life is done!

Like to the lightning from the sky,
Or like a post that quick doth hie,
Or like a quaver in short song,
Or like a journey three days long,
Or like the snow when summer's come,
Or like the pear, or like the plum;
Even such is man, who heaps up sorrow,
Lives but this day, and dies to-morrow.
The lightning's past, the post must go,
The song is short, the journey's so,
The pear doth rot, the plum doth fall,
The snow dissolves,—and so must all!

? *Simon Wastell* [ ? -1632]

## TO DEATH

O KING of Terrors! whose unbounded sway
All that have life must certainly obey;
The king, the priest, the prophet, all are thine,
Nor would even God (in flesh) thy stroke decline.

My name is on thy roll, and sure I must
Increase thy gloomy kingdom in the dust.
My soul at this no apprehension feels,
But trembles at thy swords, thy racks, thy wheels,
Thy scorching fevers, which distract the sense,
And snatch us raving, unprepared, from hence;
At thy contagious darts, that wound the heads
Of weeping friends who wait at dying beds.—
Spare these, and let thy time be when it will;
My office is to die, and thine to kill.
Gently thy fatal scepter on me lay,
And take to thy cold arms, insensibly, thy prey.

*Anne Finch* [ ? –1720]

## THE GENIUS OF DEATH

WHAT is death? 'Tis to be free,
  No more to love or hope or fear,
To join the great equality;
  All, all alike are humbled there.
    The mighty grave
    Wraps lord and slave;
Nor pride nor poverty dares come
Within that refuge-house,—the tomb.

Spirit with the drooping wing
  And the ever-weeping eye,
Thou of all earth's kings art king;
  Empires at thy footstool lie;
    Beneath thee strewed,
    Their multitude
Sink like waves upon the shore;
Storms shall never raise them more.

What's the grandeur of the earth
  To the grandeur round thy throne?
Riches, glory, beauty, birth,
  To thy kingdom all have gone.
    Before thee stand
    The wondrous band,—

Bards, heroes, sages, side by side,
Who darkened nations when they died.

Earth has hosts, but thou canst show
  Many a million for her one;
Through thy gates the mortal flow
  Hath for countless years rolled on.
    Back from the tomb
    No step has come,
There fixed till the last thunder's sound
Shall bid thy prisoners be unbound.

*George Croly* [1780–1860]

## "OH, WHY SHOULD THE SPIRIT OF MORTAL BE PROUD?"

Oh, why should the spirit of mortal be proud?
Like a swift-flitting meteor, a fast-flying cloud,
A flash of the lightning, a break of the wave,
He passeth from life to his rest in the grave.

The leaves of the oak and the willow shall fade,
Be scattered around, and together be laid;
As the young and the old, the low and the high,
Shall crumble to dust and together shall lie.

The child that a mother attended and loved,
The mother that infant's affection who proved,
The husband that mother and infant who blessed,—
Each, all, are away to their dwellings of rest.

The maid on whose brow, on whose cheek, in whose eye,
Shone beauty and pleasure,—her triumphs are by;
And alike from the minds of the living erased
Are the memories of mortals who loved her and praised.

The hand of the king, that the scepter hath borne;
The brow of the priest, that the mitre hath worn;
The eyes of the sage, and the heart of the brave,—
Are hidden and lost in the depths of the grave.

The peasant, whose lot was to sow and to reap;
The herdsman, who climbed with his goats up the steep;
The beggar, who wandered in search of his bread,—
Have faded away like the grass that we tread.

The saint who enjoyed the communion of heaven,
The sinner who dared to remain unforgiven,
The wise and the foolish, the guilty and just,
Have quietly mingled their bones in the dust.

So the multitude goes, like the flower or weed,
That withers away to let others succeed;
So the multitude comes, even those we behold,
To repeat every tale that has often been told.

For we are the same things our fathers have been;
We see the same sights our fathers have seen;
We drink the same stream, we feel the same sun,
And run the same course our fathers have run.

The thoughts we are thinking our fathers did think;
From the death we are shrinking our fathers did shrink;
To the life we are clinging our fathers did cling,
But it speeds from us all like the bird on the wing.

They loved,—but the story we cannot unfold;
They scorned,—but the heart of the haughty is cold;
They grieved,—but no wail from their slumbers will come;
They joyed,—but the tongue of their gladness is dumb.

They died,—ah! they died;—we, things that are now,
That walk on the turf that lies over their brow,
And make in their dwellings a transient abode,
Meet the changes they met on their pilgrimage road.

Yea, hope and despondency, pleasure and pain,
Are mingled together in sunshine and rain:
And the smile and the tear, the song and the dirge,
Still follow each other like surge upon surge.

'Tis the wink of an eye; 'tis the draught of a breath
From the blossom of health to the paleness of death,
From the gilded saloon to the bier and the shroud;
Oh, why should the spirit of mortal be proud?

*William Knox* [1789-1825]

## THE HOUR OF DEATH

LEAVES have their time to fall,
And flowers to wither at the north-wind's breath,
And stars to set,—but all,
Thou hast all seasons for thine own, O Death!

Day is for mortal care:
Eve for glad meetings round the joyous hearth;
Night, for the dreams of sleep, the voice of prayer,
But all for thee, thou Mightiest of the earth.

The banquet hath its hour—
Its feverish hour—of mirth and song and wine;
There comes a day for grief's o'erwhelming power,
A time for softer tears,—but all are thine.

Youth and the opening rose
May look like things too glorious for decay,
And smile at thee,—but thou art not of those
That wait the ripened bloom to seize their prey.

Leaves have their time to fall,
And flowers to wither at the north-wind's breath,
And stars to set,—but all,
Thou hast all seasons for thine own, O Death!

We know when moons shall wane,
When summer birds from far shall cross the sea,
When autumn's hue shall tinge the golden grain,—
But who shall teach us when to look for thee?

Is it when Spring's first gale
Comes forth to whisper where the violets lie?
Is it when roses in our paths grow pale?
They have *one* season—*all* are ours to die!

Thou art where billows foam;
Thou art where music melts upon the air;
Thou art around us in our peaceful home;
And the world calls us forth—and thou art there.

Thou art where friend meets friend,
Beneath the shadow of the elm to rest;
Thou art where foe meets foe, and trumpets rend
The skies, and swords beat down the princely crest.

Leaves have their time to fall,
And flowers to wither at the north-wind's breath,
And stars to set,—but all,
Thou hast all seasons for thine own, O Death!

*Felicia Dorothea Hemans* [1793-1835]

## THE SLEEP

**"He giveth his belovèd sleep."—*Psalm* cxxvii. 2**

Of all the thoughts of God that are
Borne inward into souls afar,
Along the Psalmist's music deep,
Now tell me if that any is,
For gift or grace, surpassing this:
"He giveth his belovèd—sleep"?

What would we give to our beloved?
The hero's heart to be unmoved,
The poet's star-tuned harp to sweep,
The patriot's voice to teach and rouse,
The monarch's crown, to light the brows?
He giveth *his* belovèd—sleep.

What do we give to our beloved?
A little faith all undisproved,
A little dust to overweep,
And bitter memories to make
The whole earth blasted for our sake:
He giveth *his* belovèd—sleep.

"Sleep soft," beloved! we sometimes say,
Who have no tune to charm away
Sad dreams that through the eyelids creep:
But never doleful dream again
Shall break the happy slumber when
He giveth *his* belovèd—sleep.

O earth, so full of dreary noises!
O men, with wailing in your voices!
O delvèd gold, the wailers heap!
O strife, O curse, that o'er it fall!
God strikes a silence through you all,
And giveth his belovèd—sleep.

His dews drop mutely on the hill,
His cloud above it saileth still,
Though on its slope men sow and reap:
More softly than the dew is shed,
Or cloud is floated overhead,
He giveth his belovèd—sleep.

Ay, men may wonder while they scan
A living, thinking, feeling man
Confirmed in such a rest to keep;
But Angels say, and through the word
I think their happy smile is *heard*—
"He giveth his belovèd—sleep."

For me, my heart, that erst did go
Most like a tired child at a show,
That sees through tears the mummers leap,
Would now its wearied vision close,
Would childlike on his love repose
Who giveth his belovèd—sleep.

And friends, dear friends, when it shall be
That this low breath is gone from me,
And round my bier ye come to weep,
Let One, most loving of you all,
Say "Not a tear must o'er her fall!
He giveth his belovèd sleep."

*Elizabeth Barrett Browning* [1806–1861]

## AZRAEL

The angels in high places
  Who minister to us,
Reflect God's smile,—their faces
  Are luminous;
Save one, whose face is hidden,
  (The Prophet saith),
The unwelcome, the unbidden,
  Azrael, Angel of Death.
And yet that veilèd face, I know
  Is lit with pitying eyes,
Like those faint stars, the first to glow,
  Through cloudy winter skies.

That they may never tire,
  Angels, by God's decree,
Bear wings of snow and fire,—
  Passion and purity;
Save one, all unavailing,
  (The Prophet saith),
His wings are gray and trailing,
  Azrael, Angel of Death.
And yet the souls that Azrael brings
  Across the dark and cold,
Look up beneath those folded wings,
  And find them lined with gold.

*Robert Gilbert Welsh* [1869–1924]

## "WHERE LIES THE LAND"

From "Songs in Absence"

Where lies the land to which the ship would go?
Far, far ahead, is all her seamen know.
And where the land she travels from? Away,
Far, far behind, is all that they can say.

On sunny noons upon the deck's smooth face,
Linked arm in arm, how pleasant here to pace;
Or, o'er the stern reclining, watch below
The foaming wake far widening as we go.

On stormy nights, when wild north-westers rave,
How proud a thing to fight with wind and wave!
The dripping sailor on the reeling mast
Exults to bear, and scorns to wish it past.

Where lies the land to which the ship would go?
Far, far ahead, is all her seamen know.
And where the land she travels from? Away,
Far, far behind, is all that they can say.

*Arthur Hugh Clough* [1819–1861]

## UP-HILL

Does the road wind up-hill all the way?
Yes, to the very end.
Will the day's journey take the whole long day?
From morn to night, my friend.

But is there for the night a resting-place?
A roof for when the slow, dark hours begin.
May not the darkness hide it from my face?
You cannot miss that inn.

Shall I meet other wayfarers at night?
Those who have gone before.
Then must I knock, or call when just in sight?
They will not keep you waiting at that door.

Shall I find comfort, travel-sore and weak?
Of labor you shall find the sum.
Will there be beds for me and all who seek?
Yea, beds for all who come.

*Christina Georgina Rossetti* [1830–1894]

## THE BOURNE

Underneath the growing grass,
Underneath the living flowers,
Deeper than the sound of showers:
There we shall not count the hours
By the shadows as they pass.

Youth and health will be but vain,
  Beauty reckoned of no worth:
  There a very little girth
  Can hold round what once the earth
Seemed too narrow to contain.

*Christina Georgina Rossetti* [1830–1894]

## THE CONQUEROR WORM

Lo! 'tis a gala night
  Within the lonesome latter years.
An angel throng, bewinged, bedight
  In veils, and drowned in tears,
Sit in a theater to see
  A play of hopes and fears,
While the orchestra breathes fitfully
  The music of the spheres.

Mimes, in the form of God on high,
  Mutter and mumble low,
And hither and thither fly;
  Mere puppets they, who come and go
At bidding of vast formless things
  That shift the scenery to and fro,
Flapping from out their condor wings
  Invisible Woe.

That motley drama—oh, be sure
  It shall not be forgot!
With its Phantom chased for evermore
  By a crowd that seize it not,
Through a circle that ever returneth in
  To the self-same spot;
And much of Madness, and more of Sin,
  And Horror the soul of the plot.

But see amid the mimic rout
  A crawling shape intrude:
A blood-red thing that writhes from out
  The scenic solitude!

It writhes!—it writhes!—with mortal pangs!
  The mimes become its food,
And seraphs sob at vermin fangs
  In human gore imbued.

Out—out are the lights—out all!
  And, over each quivering form,
The curtain, a funeral pall,
  Comes down with the rush of a storm,
While the angels, all pallid and wan,
  Uprising, unveiling, affirm
That the play is the tragedy, "Man,"
  And its hero, the Conqueror Worm.

*Edgar Allan Poe* [1809-1849]

## THE CITY IN THE SEA

Lo! Death has reared himself a throne
In a strange city lying alone
Far down within the dim West,
Where the good and the bad and the worst and the best
Have gone to their eternal rest.
There shrines and palaces and towers
(Time-eaten towers that tremble not)
Resemble nothing that is ours.
Around, by lifting winds forgot,
Resignedly beneath the sky
The melancholy waters lie.

No rays from the holy heaven come down
On the long night-time of that town;
But light from out the lurid sea
Streams up the turrets silently,
Gleams up the pinnacles far and free:
Up domes, up spires, up kingly halls,
Up fanes, up Babylon-like walls,
Up shadowy, long-forgotten bowers
Of sculptured ivy and stone flowers,
Up many and many a marvelous shrine,
Whose wreathèd friezes intertwine
The viol, the violet, and the vine.

Resignedly beneath the sky
The melancholy waters lie.
So blend the turrets and shadows there
That all seem pendulous in air,
While from a proud tower in the town
Death looks gigantically down.

There open fanes and gaping graves
Yawn level with the luminous waves;
But not the riches there that lie
In each idol's diamond eye,—
Not the gaily-jeweled dead
Tempt the waters from their bed;
For no ripples curl, alas,
Along that wilderness of glass;
No swellings tell that winds may be
Upon some far-off happier sea;
No heavings hint that winds have been
On seas less hideously serene!

But lo, a stir is in the air!
The wave—there is a movement there!
As if the towers had thrust aside,
In slightly sinking, the dull tide;
As if their tops had feebly given
A void within the filmy Heaven!
The waves have now a redder glow,
The hours are breathing faint and low;
And when, amid no earthly moans,
Down, down that town shall settle hence,
Hell, rising from a thousand thrones,
Shall do it reverence.

*Edgar Allan Poe* [1809-1849]

## THE REAPER AND THE FLOWERS

THERE is a Reaper, whose name is Death,
And, with his sickle keen,
He reaps the bearded grain at a breath,
And the flowers that grow between.

"Shall I have naught that is fair?" saith he;
  "Have naught but the bearded grain?
Though the breath of these flowers is sweet to me,
  I will give them all back again."

He gazed at the flowers with tearful eyes,
  He kissed their drooping leaves;
It was for the Lord of Paradise
  He bound them in his sheaves.

"My Lord has need of these flowerets gay,"
  The Reaper said, and smiled;
"Dear tokens of the earth are they,
  Where He was once a child.

"They shall all bloom in fields of light,
  Transplanted by my care,
And saints, upon their garments white,
  These sacred blossoms wear."

And the mother gave, in tears and pain,
  The flowers she most did love;
She knew she should find them all again
  In the fields of light above.

Oh, not in cruelty, not in wrath,
  The Reaper came that day;
'Twas an angel visited the green earth,
  And took the flowers away.

*Henry Wadsworth Longfellow* [1807-1882]

## THE CLOSING SCENE

Within his sober realm of leafless trees,
  The russet year inhaled the dreamy air;
Like some tanned reaper in his hour of ease,
  When all the fields are lying brown and bare.

The gray barns looking from their hazy hills
  O'er the dim waters widening in the vales,
Sent down the air a greeting to the mills,
  On the dull thunder of alternate flails.

All sights were mellowed and all sounds subdued,
The hills seemed farther and the streams sang low;
As in a dream the distant woodman hewed
His winter log with many a muffled blow.

The embattled forests, erewhile armed in gold,
Their banners bright with every martial hue,
Now stood, like some sad, beaten host of old,
Withdrawn afar in Time's remotest blue.

On slumbrous wings the vulture held his flight;
The dove scarce heard his sighing mate's complaint,
And like a star slow drowning in the light,
The village church-vane seemed to pale and faint.

The sentinel-cock upon the hillside crew,—
Crew thrice, and all was stiller than before,—
Silent till some replying warder blew
His alien horn, and then was heard no more.

Where erst the jay, within the elm's tall crest,
Made garrulous trouble round her unfledged young,
And where the oriole hung her swaying nest,
By every light wind like a censer swung—

Where sang the noisy masons of the eaves,
The busy swallows, circling ever near,
Foreboding, as the rustic mind believes,
An early harvest and a plenteous year;—

Where every bird which charmed the vernal feast,
Shook the sweet slumber from its wings at morn,
To warn the reaper of the rosy east,—
All now was songless, empty, and forlorn.

Alone from out the stubble piped the quail,
And croaked the crow through all the dreamy gloom;
Alone the pheasant, drumming in the vale,
Made echo to the distant cottage loom.

There was no bud, no bloom upon the bowers;
  The spiders wove their thin shrouds night by night;
The thistle-down, the only ghost of flowers,
  Sailed slowly by, passed noiseless out of sight.

Amid all this, in this most cheerless air,
  And where the woodbine shed upon the porch
Its crimson leaves, as if the Year stood there
  Firing the floor with his inverted torch;—

Amid all this, the center of the scene,
  The white-haired matron, with monotonous tread,
Plied the swift wheel, and with her joyless mien,
  Sat, like a Fate, and watched the flying thread.

She had known Sorrow,—he had walked with her,
  Oft supped, and broke the bitter ashen crust;
And in the dead leaves still she heard the stir
  Of his black mantle trailing in the dust.

While yet her cheek was bright with summer bloom,
  Her country summoned and she gave her all;
And twice War bowed to her his sable plume,—
  Re-gave the swords to rust upon the wall.

Re-gave the swords,—but not the hand that drew
  And struck for Liberty its dying blow,
Nor him who, to his sire and country true,
  Fell 'mid the ranks of the invading foe.

Long, but not loud, the droning wheel went on,
  Like the low murmur of a hive at noon;
Long, but not loud, the memory of the gone
  Breathed through her lips a sad and tremulous tune.

At last the thread was snapped,—her head was bowed;
  Life dropped the distaff through his hands serene;—
And loving neighbors smoothed her careful shroud,
  While Death and Winter closed the autumn scene.

*Thomas Buchanan Read* [1822–1872]

## MORS ET VITA

WE know not yet what life shall be,
What shore beyond earth's shore be set;
What grief awaits us, or what glee,
We know not yet.

Still, somewhere in sweet converse met,
Old friends, we say, beyond death's sea
Shall meet and greet us, nor forget

Those days of yore, those years when we
Were loved and true,—but will death let
Our eyes the longed-for vision see?
We know not yet.

*Samuel Waddington* [1844–1923]

## "WHAT IS TO COME"

WHAT is to come we know not. But we know
That what has been was good—was good to show,
Better to hide, and best of all to bear.
We are the masters of the days that were:
We have lived, we have loved, we have suffered . . .
even so.

Shall we not take the ebb who had the flow?
Life was our friend. Now, if it be our foe—
Dear, though it spoil and break us!—need we care
What is to come?

Let the great winds their worst and wildest blow,
Or the gold weather round us mellow slow:
We have fulfilled ourselves, and we can dare,
And we can conquer, though we may not share
In the rich quiet of the after-glow
What is to come.

*William Ernest Henley* [1849–1903]

## A ROUNDEL OF REST

IF rest is sweet at shut of day
For tired hands and tired feet,
How sweet at last to rest for aye,
If rest is sweet!

We work or work not through the heat:
Death bids us soon our labors lay
In lands where night and twilight meet.

When the last dawns are fallen gray
And all life's toil and ease complete,
They know who work, not they who play,
If rest is sweet.

*Arthur Symons* [1865–1945]

## "WHEN THE MOST IS SAID"

WHAT'S love, when the most is said? The flash of the lightning fleet,
Then, darkness that shrouds the soul,—but the earth is firm to my feet;
The rocks and the tides endure, the grasses and herbs return,
The path to my foot is sure, and the sods to my bosom yearn.

What's fame, when the truth is told? A shout to a distant hill,
The crags may echo a while, but fainter, and fainter still;
Yet forever the wind blows wide the sweetness of all the skies,
The rain cries and the snow flies, and the storm in its bosom lies.

What's life, what's life, little heart? A dream when the nights are long,
Toil in the waking days,—tears, and a kiss, a song.

What's life, what's life, little heart? To beat and be glad
of breath
While death waits on either side,—before and behind us
Death!

*Mary Ainge De Vere* [1844–1920]

## THE GARDEN OF PROSERPINE

HERE, where the world is quiet,
Here, where all trouble seems
Dead winds' and spent waves' riot
In doubtful dreams of dreams,
I watch the green field growing
For reaping folk and sowing,
For harvest-time and mowing,
A sleepy world of streams.

I am tired of tears and laughter,
And men that laugh and weep;
Of what may come hereafter
For men that sow to reap:
I am weary of days and hours,
Blown buds of barren flowers,
Desires and dreams and powers,
And everything but sleep.

Here life has death for neighbor,
And far from eye or ear
Wan waves and wet winds labor,
Weak ships and spirits steer;
They drive adrift, and whither
They wot not who make thither;
But no such winds blow hither,
And no such things grow here.

No growth of moor or coppice,
No heather-flower or vine,
But bloomless buds of poppies,
Green grapes of Proserpine,

Pale beds of blowing rushes,
Where no leaf blooms or blushes
Save this whereout she crushes
  For dead men deadly wine.

Pale, without name or number,
  In fruitless fields of corn,
They bow themselves and slumber
  All night till light is born;
And like a soul belated,
In hell and heaven unmated,
By cloud and mist abated
  Comes out of darkness morn.

Though one were strong as seven,
  He too with death shall dwell,
Nor wake with wings in heaven,
  Nor weep for pains in hell;
Though one were fair as roses,
His beauty clouds and closes;
And well though love reposes,
  In the end it is not well.

Pale, beyond porch and portal,
  Crowned with calm leaves, she stands
Who gathers all things mortal
  With cold immortal hands;
Her languid lips are sweeter
Than Love's, who fears to greet her,
To men that mix and meet her
  From many times and lands.

She waits for each and other,
  She waits for all men born;
Forgets the earth her mother,
  The life of fruits and corn;
And spring and seed and swallow
Take wing for her and follow
Where summer song rings hollow
  And flowers are put to scorn.

There go the loves that wither,
  The old loves with wearier wings;
And all dead years draw thither,
  And all disastrous things;
Dead dreams of days forsaken,
Blind buds that snows have shaken,
Wild leaves that winds have taken,
  Red strays of ruined springs.

We are not sure of sorrow,
  And joy was never sure;
To-day will die to-morrow;
  Time stoops to no man's lure;
And Love, grown faint and fretful,
With lips but half regretful
Sighs, and with eyes forgetful
  Weeps that no loves endure.

From too much love of living,
  From hope and fear set free,
We thank with brief thanksgiving
  Whatever gods may be,
That no life lives forever;
That dead men rise up never;
That even the weariest river
  Winds somewhere safe to sea.

Then star nor sun shall waken,
  Nor any change of light:
Nor sound of waters shaken,
  Nor any sound or sight:
Nor wintry leaves nor vernal,
Nor days nor things diurnal;
Only the sleep eternal
  In an eternal night.

*Algernon Charles Swinburne* [1837-1909]

## THE CHANGING ROAD

BENEATH the softly falling snow,
The wood whose shy anemones
We plucked such little while ago
Becomes a wood of Christmas trees.

Our paths of rustling silken grass
Will soon be ermine bands of white
Spotted with tiny steps that pass
On silent errands in the night.

The river will be locked in hush,
But frosted like a fairy lawn
With knots of crystal flowers that flush
By moonlight, blanching in the dawn.

Flown are our minstrels, golden-wing
And rosy-breast and ruby-throat,
But all the pines are murmuring
A sweet, orchestral under-note.

So trustfully our hands we lay
Within the old, kind hands of Time,
Who holds on his mysterious way
From rime to bloom, from bloom to rime,

And lets us run beside his knee
O'er rough and smooth, and touch his load,
And play we bear the burden, we,
And revel in the changing road,

Till ivory dawn and purple noon
And dove-gray eve have one by one
Traced on the skies their ancient rune,
And all our little strength is done.

Then Time shall lift a starry torch
In signal to his gentle Twin,
Who, stooping from a shining porch,
Gathers the drowsy children in.

I wonder if, through that strange sleep,
 Unstirred by clock or silver chime,
Our dreams will not the cadence keep
 Of those unresting feet of Time,

And follow on his beauteous path
 From snow to flowers, from flowers to snow,
And marvel what high charge he hath,
 Whither the fearless footsteps go.

*Katharine Lee Bates* [1859–1929]

## THE GREAT MISGIVING

"Not ours," say some, "the thought of death to dread;
 Asking no heaven, we fear no fabled hell:
Life is a feast, and we have banqueted—
 Shall not the worms as well?

"The after-silence, when the feast is o'er,
 And void the places where the minstrels stood,
Differs in naught from what hath been before,
 And is nor ill nor good."

Ah, but the Apparition—the dumb sign—
 The beckoning finger bidding me forgo
The fellowship, the converse, and the wine,
 The songs, the festal glow!

And ah, to know not, while with friends I sit,
 And while the purple joy is passed about,
Whether 'tis ampler day divinelier lit
 Or homeless night without;

And whether, stepping forth, my soul shall see
 New prospects, or fall sheer—a blinded thing!
*There* is, O grave, thy hourly victory,
 And there, O death, thy sting.

*William Watson* [1858–1935]

## THE DEAD COACH

AT night when sick folk wakeful lie,
I heard the dead coach passing by,
And heard it passing wild and fleet,
And knew my time was come not yet.

Click-clack, click-clack, the hoofs went past,
Who takes the dead coach travels fast,
On and away through the wild night,
The dead must rest ere morning light.

If one might follow on its track
The coach and horses, midnight black,
Within should sit a shape of doom
That beckons one and all to come.

God pity them to-night who wait
To hear the dead coach at their gate,
And him who hears, though sense be dim,
The mournful dead coach stop for him.

He shall go down with a still face,
And mount the steps and take his place,
The door be shut, the order said!
How fast the pace is with the dead!

Click-clack, click-clack, the hour is chill,
The dead coach climbs the distant hill.
Now, God, the Father of all us,
Wipe Thou the widow's tears that fall!

*Katherine Tynan Hinkson* [1861–1931]

## L'ENVOI

WHERE are the loves that we loved before,
When once we are alone, and shut the door?
No matter whose the arms that held me fast,
The arms of Darkness hold me at the last.

No matter down what primrose path I tend,
I kiss the lips of Silence in the end.
No matter on what heart I found delight,
I come again unto the breast of Night.
No matter when or how Love did befall,
'Tis loneliness that loves me best of all.
And in the end she claims me, and I know
That she will stay, though all the rest may go.
No matter whose the eyes that I would keep
Near in the dark, 'tis in the eyes of Sleep
That I must look and look forevermore,
When once I am alone and shut the door.

*Willa Sibert Cather* [1875-1947]

## DEATH

I AM the key that parts the gates of Fame;
I am the cloak that covers cowering Shame;
I am the final goal of every race;
I am the storm-tossed spirit's resting-place:

The messenger of sure and swift relief,
Welcomed with wailings and reproachful grief;
The friend of those that have no friend but me,
I break all chains, and set all captives free.

I am the cloud that, when Earth's day is done,
An instant veils an unextinguished sun;
I am the brooding hush that follows strife,
The waking from a dream that Man calls—Life!

*Florence Earle Coates* [1850-1927]

## A DIRGE

From "The White Devil"

CALL for the robin-redbreast and the wren,
Since o'er shady groves they hover,
And with leaves and flowers do cover
The friendless bodies of unburied men.

Call unto his funeral dole
The ant, the field-mouse, and the mole,
To rear him hillocks that shall keep him warm,
And (when gay tombs are robbed) sustain no harm;
But keep the wolf far thence, that's foe to men,
For with his nails he'll dig them up again.

*John Webster* [1580?–1625?]

## DIRGE

From "Cymbeline"

Fear no more the heat o' the sun
  Nor the furious winter's rages;
Thou thy worldly task hast done,
  Home art gone and ta'en thy wages:
Golden lads and girls all must,
As chimney-sweepers, come to dust.

Fear no more the frown o' the great,
  Thou art past the tyrant's stroke;
Care no more to clothe and eat;
  To thee the reed is as the oak:
The scepter, learning, physic, must
All follow this, and come to dust.

Fear no more the lightning-flash
  Nor the all-dreaded thunder-stone;
Fear not slander, censure rash;
  Thou hast finished joy and moan:
All lovers young, all lovers must
Consign to thee, and come to dust.

*William Shakespeare* [1564–1616]

## DIRGE IN CYMBELINE

*Sung by Guiderus and Arviragus over Fidele, supposed to be dead*

To fair Fidele's grassy tomb
  Soft maids and village hinds shall bring
Each opening sweet, of earliest bloom,
  And rifle all the breathing spring.

No wailing ghost shall dare appear,
  To vex with shrieks this quiet grove;
But shepherd lads assemble here,
  And melting virgins own their love.

No withered witch shall here be seen,
  No goblins lead their nightly crew;
The female fays shall haunt the green,
  And dress thy grave with pearly dew.

The redbreast oft at evening hours
  Shall kindly lend his little aid,
With hoary moss, and gathered flowers,
  To deck the ground where thou art laid.

When howling winds, and beating rain,
  In tempests shake the sylvan cell,
Or midst the chase on every plain,
  The tender thought on thee shall dwell,

Each lonely scene shall thee restore,
  For thee the tear be duly shed:
Beloved, till life could charm no more;
  And mourned, till Pity's self be dead.

*William Collins* [1721–1759]

## HALLOWED GROUND

WHAT's hallowed ground? Has earth a clod
Its Maker meant not should be trod
By man, the image of his God,
  Erect and free,
Unscourged by Superstition's rod
  To bow the knee?

That's hallowed ground where, mourned and missed
The lips repose our love has kissed;—
But where's their memory's mansion? Is't
  Yon churchyard's bowers?
No! in ourselves their souls exist,
  A part of ours.

A kiss can consecrate the ground
Where mated hearts are mutual bound:
The spot where love's first links were wound,
That ne'er are riven,
Is hallowed down to earth's profound,
And up to Heaven!

For time makes all but true love old;
The burning thoughts that then were told
Run molten still in memory's mold;
And will not cool
Until the heart itself be cold
In Lethe's pool.

What hallows ground where heroes sleep?
'Tis not the sculptured piles you heap!
In dews that heavens far distant weep
Their turf may bloom;
Or Genii twine beneath the deep
Their coral tomb.

But strew his ashes to the wind
Whose sword or voice has served mankind,—
And is he dead, whose glorious mind
Lifts thine on high?—
To live in hearts we leave behind
Is not to die.

Is't death to fall for Freedom's right?
He's dead alone that lacks her light!
And murder sullies in Heaven's sight
The sword he draws:—
What can alone ennoble fight?
A noble cause!

Give that!—and welcome War to brace
Her drums! and rend Heaven's reeking space!
The colors planted face to face,
The charging cheer,
Though Death's pale horse lead on the chase
Shall still be dear.

And place our trophies where men kneel
To Heaven!—but Heaven rebukes my zeal
The cause of Truth and human weal,
  O God above!
Transfer it from the sword's appeal
  To Peace and Love.

Peace, Love! the cherubim, that join
Their spread wings o'er Devotion's shrine,
Prayers sound in vain, and temples shine,
  Where they are not,—
The heart alone can make divine
  Religion's spot.

To incantations dost thou trust,
And pompous rites in domes august?
See moldering stones and metal's rust
  Belie the vaunt,
That man can bless one pile of dust
  With chime or chaunt.

The ticking wood-worm mocks thee, man!
Thy temples,—creeds themselves grow wan!
But there's a dome of nobler span,
  A temple given
Thy faith, that bigots dare not ban,—
  Its space is Heaven!

Its roof, star-pictured Nature's ceiling,
Where, trancing the rapt spirit's feeling,
And God himself to man revealing,
  The harmonious spheres
Make music, though unheard their pealing
  By mortal ears.

Fair stars! are not your beings pure?
Can sin, can death, your worlds obscure?
Else why so swell the thoughts at your
  Aspect above?
Ye must be Heavens that make us sure
  Of heavenly love!

And in your harmony sublime
I read the doom of distant time:
That man's regenerate soul from crime
Shall yet be drawn,
And reason on his mortal clime
Immortal dawn.

What's hallowed ground? 'Tis what gives birth
To sacred thoughts in souls of worth!—
Peace! Independence! Truth! go forth
Earth's compass round;
And your high-priesthood shall make earth
*All hallowed ground.*

*Thomas Campbell* [1777–1844]

## THE CHURCHYARD

How slowly creeps the hand of Time
On the old clock's green-mantled face!
Yea, slowly as those ivies climb,
The hours roll round with patient pace;
The drowsy rooks caw on the tower,
The tame doves hover round and round;
Below, the slow grass hour by hour
Makes green God's sleeping-ground.

All moves, but nothing here is swift;
The grass grows deep, the green boughs shoot;
From east to west the shadows drift;
The earth feels heavenward underfoot;
The slow stream through the bridge doth stray
With water-lilies on its marge,
And slowly, piled with scented hay,
Creeps by the silent barge.

All stirs, but nothing here is loud:
The cushat broods, the cuckoo cries;
Faint, far up, under a white cloud,
The lark trills soft to earth and skies;

And underneath the green graves rest;
  And through the place, with slow footfalls,
With snowy cambric on his breast,
  The old gray Vicar crawls.

And close at hand, to see him come,
  Clustering at the playground gate,
The urchins of the school-house, dumb
  And bashful, hang the head and wait;
The little maidens curtsey deep,
  The boys their forelocks touch meanwhile,
The Vicar sees them, half asleep,
  And smiles a sleepy smile.

Slow as the hand on the clock's face,
  Slow as the white cloud in the sky,
He cometh now with tottering pace
  To the old vicarage hard by;
Smothered it stands in ivy leaves,
  Laurels and yews make dark the ground;
The swifts that build beneath the eaves
  Wheel in still circles round.

And from the portal, green and dark,
  He glances at the church-clock old—
Gray soul! why seek his eyes to mark
  The creeping of that finger cold?
He cannot see, but still as stone
  He pauses, listening for the chime,
And hears from that green tower intone
  The eternal voice of Time.

*Robert Buchanan* [1841-1901]

## THE OLD CHURCHYARD OF BONCHURCH

The churchyard leans to the sea with its dead,—
It leans to the sea with its dead so long.
Do they hear, I wonder, the first bird's song,
When the winter's anger is all but fled;

The high, sweet voice of the west wind,
The fall of the warm, soft rain,
When the second month of the year
Puts heart in the earth again?

Do they hear, through the glad April weather,
The green grasses waving above them?
Do they think there are none left to love them,
They have lain for so long there together?
Do they hear the note of the cuckoo,
The cry of gulls on the wing,
The laughter of winds and waters,
The feet of the dancing Spring?

Do they feel the old land slipping seaward,—
The old land, with its hills and its graves,—
As they gradually slide to the waves,
With the wind blowing on them from leaward?
Do they know of the change that awaits them,—
The sepulcher vast and strange?
Do they long for the days to go over,
And bring that miraculous change?

Or love they their night with no moonlight,
With no starlight, no dawn to its gloom?
Do they sigh: "'Neath the snow, or the bloom
Of the wild things that wave from our night,
We are warm, through winter and summer;
We hear the winds rave, and we say:
'The storm-wind blows over our heads,
But we, here, are out of its way'"?

Do they mumble low, one to another
With a sense that the waters that thunder
Shall ingather them all, draw them under:
"Ah, how long to our moving, my brother?
How long shall we quietly rest here,
In graves of darkness and ease?
The waves even now, may be on us
To draw us down under the seas!"

Do they think 'twill be cold when the waters
That they love not, that neither can love them,
Shall eternally thunder above them?
Have they dread of the sea's shining daughters,
That people the bright sea-regions
And play with the young sea-kings?
Have they dread of their cold embraces,
And dread of all strange sea-things?

But their dread or their joy,—it is bootless:
They shall pass from the breast of their mother;
They shall lie low, dead brother by brother,
In a place that is radiant and fruitless;
And the folk that sail over their heads
In violent weather
Shall come down to them, haply, and all
They shall lie there, together.

*Philip Bourke Marston* [1850–1887]

## THE INDIAN BURYING-GROUND

In spite of all the learned have said,
  I still my old opinion keep;
The posture that we give the dead
  Points out the soul's eternal sleep.

Not so the ancients of these lands;—
  The Indian, when from life released,
Again is seated with his friends,
  And shares again the joyous feast.

His imaged birds, and painted bowl,
  And venison, for a journey dressed,
Bespeak the nature of the soul,
  Activity, that wants no rest.

His bow for action ready bent,
  And arrows with a head of stone,
Can only mean that life is spent,
  And not the old ideas gone.

Thou, stranger, that shalt come this way,
  No fraud upon the dead commit,—
Observe the swelling turf, and say,
  They do not lie, but here they sit.

Here still a lofty rock remains,
  On which the curious eye may trace
(Now wasted half by wearing rains)
  The fancies of a ruder race.

Here still an aged elm aspires,
  Beneath whose far projecting shade
(And which the shepherd still admires)
  The children of the forest played.

There oft a restless Indian queen
  (Pale Shebah with her braided hair),
And many a barbarous form is seen
  To chide the man that lingers there.

By midnight moons, o'er moistening dews,
  In habit for the chase arrayed,
The hunter still the deer pursues,
  The hunter and the deer—a shade!

And long shall timorous Fancy see
  The painted chief, and pointed spear,
And Reason's self shall bow the knee
  To shadows and delusions here.

*Philip Freneau* [1752–1832]

## GOD'S-ACRE

I LIKE that ancient Saxon phrase, which calls
  The burial-ground God's-Acre! It is just;
It consecrates each grave within its walls,
  And breathes a benison o'er the sleeping dust.

God's-Acre! Yes, that blessed name imparts
  Comfort to those who in the grave have sown
The seed that they had garnered in their hearts,
  Their bread of life, alas! no more their own.

Into its furrows shall we all be cast,
 In the sure faith, that we shall rise again
At the great harvest, when the archangel's blast
 Shall winnow, like a fan, the chaff and grain.

Then shall the good stand in immortal bloom,
 In the fair garden of that second birth;
And each bright blossom mingle its perfume
 With that of flowers, which never bloomed on earth.

With thy rude plowshare, Death, turn up the sod,
 And spread the furrow for the seed we sow;
This is the field and Acre of our God,
 This is the place where human harvests grow.

*Henry Wadsworth Longfellow* [1807–1882]

## THE CITY OF THE DEAD

They do neither plight nor wed
In the city of the dead,
In the city where they sleep away the hours;
But they lie, while o'er them range
Winter blight and Summer change,
And a hundred happy whisperings of flowers.
No, they neither wed nor plight,
And the day is like the night,
For their vision is of other kind than ours.

They do neither sing nor sigh
In that burg of by and by,
Where the streets have grasses growing cool and long;
But they rest within their bed,
Leaving all their thoughts unsaid,
Deeming silence better far than sob or song.
No, they neither sigh nor sing,
Though the robin be a-wing,
Though the leaves of Autumn march a million strong.

There is only rest and peace
In the City of Surcease
From the failings and the wailings 'neath the sun,
And the wings of the swift years
Beat but gently o'er the biers,

Making music to the sleepers every one.
There is only peace and rest;
But to them it seemeth best,
For they lie at ease and know that life is done.

*Richard Burton* [1861–1940]

## THE GARDEN THAT I LOVE

THE Garden that I love is full of Light;
It lies upon the sloping of a hill,
Where Dawn first stirs the curtains of the Night,
And the breeze whispers when the Noon is still.

The garden that I love is full of Peace;
The voices of the vale are faint and far,
The busy murmurs of the highway cease,
And silently, at evening, comes the Star.

The garden that I love is full of Dreams;
Visions of joy gone by, and bliss that waits,
Beyond the furthest verge of sunset gleams,
With the wide opening of the Golden Gates.

The garden that I love is full of Rest;
God's own fair Acre, where His dear ones lie,
In the safe shelter of the kind earth's breast,
Waiting His Easter dawning up the sky.

There may I rest, asleep with them awhile,
There may I wake, with them, that glorious Day,
When, in the sunshine of the Master's smile,
Sorrow and sighing shall be swept away!

*Florence L. Henderson* [18 –

## THE OLD SEXTON

NIGH to a grave that was newly made,
Leaned a sexton old on his earth-worn spade;
His work was done, and he paused to wait
The funeral-train at the open gate.

A relic of by-gone days was he,
And his locks were gray as the foamy sea;
And these words came from his lips so thin:
"I gather them in—I gather them in—
Gather—gather—gather them in.

"I gather them in; for man and boy,
Year after year of grief and joy,
I've builded the houses that lie around
In every nook of this burial-ground,
Mother and daughter, father and son,
Come to my solitude, one by one;
But come they stranger, or come they kin,
I gather them in—I gather them in.

"Many are with me, yet I'm alone;
I'm King of the Dead, and I make my throne
On a monument slab of marble cold—
My scepter of rule is the spade I hold.
Come they from cottage, or come they from hall
Mankind are my subjects, all, all, all!
May they loiter in pleasure, or toilfully spin,
I gather them in—I gather them in.

"I gather them in, and their final rest
Is here, down here, in the earth's dark breast!"
And the sexton ceased as the funeral-train
Wound mutely over that solemn plain;
And I said to myself: When time is told,
A mightier voice than that sexton's old,
Will sound o'er the last trump's dreadful din:
"I gather them in—I gather them in—
Gather—gather—gather them in."

*Park Benjamin* [1809–1864]

## THE TWO VILLAGES

Over the river, on the hill,
Lieth a village white and still;
All around it the forest-trees
Shiver and whisper in the breeze;
Over it sailing shadows go
Of soaring hawk and screaming crow,

And mountain grasses, low and sweet,
Grow in the middle of every street.

Over the river, under the hill,
Another village lieth still;
There I see in the cloudy night
Twinkling stars of household light,
Fires that gleam from the smithy's door,
Mists that curl on the river-shore;
And in the roads no grasses grow,
For the wheels that hasten to and fro.

In that village on the hill
Never is sound of smithy or mill;
The houses are thatched with grass and flowers;
Never a clock to toll the hours;
The marble doors are always shut,
You cannot enter in hall or hut;
All the villagers lie asleep;
Never a grain to sow or reap;
Never in dreams to moan or sigh;
Silent and idle and low they lie.

In that village under the hill,
When the night is starry and still,
Many a weary soul in prayer
Looks to the other village there,
And weeping and sighing, longs to go
Up to that home from this below;
Longs to sleep in the forest wild,
Whither have vanished wife and child,
And heareth, praying, this answer fall:
"Patience! that village shall hold ye all!"

*Rose Terry Cooke* [1827-1892]

## DAYBREAK

A WIND came up out of the sea,
And said, "O mists, make room for me!"

It hailed the ships, and cried, "Sail on,
Ye mariners, the night is gone!"

And hurried landward far away,
Crying, "Awake! it is the day!"

It said unto the forest, "Shout!
Hang all your leafy banners out!"

It touched the wood-bird's folded wing,
And said, "O bird, awake and sing!"

And o'er the farms, "O chanticleer,
Your clarion blow, the day is near!"

It whispered to the fields of corn,
"Bow down, and hail the coming morn!"

It shouted through the belfry-tower,
"Awake, O bell! proclaim the hour."

It crossed the churchyard with a sigh,
And said, "Not yet! in quiet lie."

*Henry Wadsworth Longfellow* [1807-1882]

## THANATOPSIS

To him who in the love of Nature holds
Communion with her visible forms, she speaks
A various language; for his gayer hours
She has a voice of gladness, and a smile
And eloquence of beauty, and she glides
Into his darker musings, with a mild
And healing sympathy, that steals away
Their sharpness, ere he is aware. When thoughts
Of the last bitter hour come like a blight
Over thy spirit, and sad images
Of the stern agony, and shroud, and pall,
And breathless darkness, and the narrow house,
Make thee to shudder and grow sick at heart;—
Go forth, under the open sky, and list
To Nature's teachings, while from all around—
Earth and her waters, and the depths of air—
Comes a still voice:—

Yet a few days, and thee
The all-beholding sun shall see no more
In all his course; nor yet in the cold ground,
Where thy pale form was laid, with many tears,
Nor in the embrace of ocean, shall exist
Thy image. Earth, that nourished thee, shall claim
Thy growth, to be resolved to earth again,
And, lost each human trace, surrendering up
Thine individual being, shalt thou go
To mix forever with the elements,
To be a brother to the insensible rock
And to the sluggish clod, which the rude swain
Turns with his share, and treads upon. The oak
Shall send his roots abroad, and pierce thy mold.

Yet not to thine eternal resting-place
Shalt thou retire alone, nor couldst thou wish
Couch more magnificent. Thou shalt lie down
With patriarchs of the infant world—with kings,
The powerful of the earth—the wise, the good,
Fair forms, and hoary seers of ages past,
All in one mighty sepulcher. The hills
Rock-ribbed and ancient as the sun,—the vales
Stretching in pensive quietness between;
The venerable woods—rivers that move
In majesty, and the complaining brooks
That make the meadows green; and, poured round all,
Old Ocean's gray and melancholy waste,—
Are but the solemn decorations all
Of the great tomb of man. The golden sun,
The planets, all the infinite host of heaven,
Are shining on the sad abodes of death
Through the still lapse of ages. All that tread
The globe are but a handful to the tribes
That slumber in its bosom.—Take the wings
Of morning, pierce the Barcan wilderness,
Or lose thyself in the continuous woods
Where rolls the Oregon, and hears no sound,
Save his own dashings—yet the dead are there:
And millions in those solitudes, since first

The flight of years began, have laid them down
In their last sleep—the dead reign there alone.
So shalt thou rest, and what if thou withdraw
In silence from the living, and no friend
Take note of thy departure? All that breathe
Will share thy destiny. The gay will laugh
When thou art gone, the solemn brood of care
Plod on, and each one as before will chase
His favorite phantom; yet all these shall leave
Their mirth and their employments, and shall come
And make their bed with thee. As the long train
Of ages glides away, the sons of men—
The youth in life's fresh spring, and he who goes
In the full strength of years, matron and maid,
The speechless babe, and the gray-headed man—
Shall one by one be gathered to thy side,
By those, who in their turn shall follow them.

So live, that when thy summons comes to join
The innumerable caravan, which moves
To that mysterious realm, where each shall take
His chamber in the silent halls of death,
Thou go not, like the quarry-slave at night,
Scourged to his dungeon, but, sustained and soothed
By an unfaltering trust, approach thy grave
Like one who wraps the drapery of his couch
About him, and lies down to pleasant dreams.

*William Cullen Bryant* [1794–1878]

## THE DANCE OF DEATH

(AFTER HOLBEIN)

*" Contra vim Mortis*
*Non est medicamen in hortis."*

HE is the despots' Despot. All must bide,
Later or soon, the message of his might;
Princes and potentates their heads must hide,
Touched by the awful sigil of his right;
Beside the Kaiser he at eve doth wait

And pours a potion in his cup of state;
The stately Queen his bidding must obey;
No keen-eyed Cardinal shall him affray;
And to the Dame that wantoneth he saith—
"Let be, Sweet-heart, to junket and to play."
There is no King more terrible than Death.

The lusty Lord, rejoicing in his pride,
He draweth down; before the armèd Knight
With jingling bridle-rein he still doth ride;
He crosseth the strong Captain in the fight;
The Burgher grave he beckons from debate;
He hales the Abbot by his shaven pate,
Nor for the Abbess' wailing will delay;
No bawling Mendicant shall say him nay;
E'en to the pyx the Priest he followeth,
Nor can the Leech his chilling finger stay . . .
There is no King more terrible than Death.

All things must bow to him. And woe betide
The Wine-bibber,—the Roisterer by night;
Him the feast-master, many bouts defied,
Him 'twixt the pledging and the cup shall smite;
Woe to the Lender at usurious rate,
The hard Rich Man, the hireling Advocate;
Woe to the Judge that selleth Law for pay;
Woe to the Thief that like a beast of prey
With creeping tread the traveller harryeth:—
These, in their sin, the sudden sword shall slay . . .
There is no King more terrible than Death.

He hath no pity,—nor will be denied.
When the low hearth is garnishèd and bright,
Grimly he flingeth the dim portal wide,
And steals the Infant in the Mother's sight;
He hath no pity for the scorned of fate:—
He spares not Lazarus lying at the gate,
Nay, nor the Blind that stumbleth as he may;
Nay, the tired Ploughman,—at the sinking ray,—
In the last furrow,—feels an icy breath,
And knows a hand hath turned the team astray . . .
There is no King more terrible than Death.

He hath no pity. For the new-made Bride,
Blithe with the promise of her life's delight,
That wanders gladly by her Husband's side,
He with the clatter of his drum doth fright;
He scares the Virgin at the convent grate;
The Maid half-won, the Lover passionate;
He hath no grace for weakness and decay:
The tender Wife, the Widow bent and gray,
The feeble Sire whose footstep faltereth,—
All these he leadeth by the lonely way . . .
There is no King more terrible than Death.

ENVOY

YOUTH, for whose ear and monishing of late,
I sang of Prodigals and lost estate,
Have thou thy joy of living and be gay;
But know not less that there must come a day,—
Aye, and perchance e'en now it hasteneth,—
When thine own heart shall speak to thee and say,—
There is no King more terrible than Death.

*Austin Dobson* [1840–1921]

## FACING THE SUNSET

### THE LIE

Go, Soul, the Body's guest,
  Upon a thankless arrant;
Fear not to touch the best;
  The truth shall be thy warrant:
Go, since I needs must die,
And give the World the lie.

Say to the Court, it glows
  And shines like rotten wood·
Say to the Church, it shows
  What's good, and doth no good:
If Court and Church reply
Then give them both the lie.

Tell Potentates, they live
  Acting by others' action,
Not loved unless they give,
  Not strong but by a faction:
If Potentates reply,
Give Potentates the lie.

Tell men of high condition
  That manage the Estate,
Their purpose is ambition,
  Their practice, only hate:
And if they once reply,
Then give them all the lie.

Tell them that brave it most,
  They beg for more by spending,
Who in their greatest cost,
  Seek nothing but commending:
And if they make reply,
Then give them all the lie.

Tell Zeal it wants devotion;
  Tell Love it is but lust;
Tell Time it is but motion;
  Tell Flesh it is but dust:
And wish them not reply,
For thou must give the lie.

Tell Age it daily wasteth;
  Tell Honor how it alters;
Tell Beauty how she blasteth;
  Tell Favor how it falters:
And as they shall reply,
Give every one the lie.

Tell Wit how much it wrangles
  In tickle points of niceness;
Tell Wisdom she entangles
  Herself in over-wiseness:
And when they do reply,
Straight give them both the lie.

Tell Physic of her boldness;
  Tell Skill it is pretension;
Tell Charity of coldness;
  Tell Law it is contention:
And as they do reply,
So give them still the lie.

Tell Fortune of her blindness;
  Tell Nature of decay;
Tell Friendship of unkindness;
  Tell Justice of delay:
And if they will reply,
Then give them all the lie.

Tell Arts they have no soundness,
  But vary by esteeming;
Tell Schools they want profoundness,
  And stand too much on seeming:
If Arts and Schools reply,
Give Arts and Schools the lie.

Tell Faith it's fled the City;
  Tell how the Country erreth,
Tell Manhood shakes off pity;
  Tell Virtue least preferreth:
And if they do reply,
Spare not to give the lie.

So when thou hast, as I
  Commanded thee, done blabbing,—
Although to give the lie
  Deserves no less than stabbing,—
Yet, stab at thee that will,
No stab the soul can kill!

*Walter Raleigh* [1552?–1618]

## HIS PILGRIMAGE

GIVE me my scallop-shell of quiet,
  My staff of faith to walk upon,
My scrip of joy, immortal diet,
  My bottle of salvation,
My gown of glory, hope's true gage;
And thus I'll take my pilgrimage.

Blood must be my body's balmer,
No other balm will there be given;
Whilst my soul, like quiet palmer,
Traveleth towards the land of Heaven;
Over the silver mountains
Where spring the nectar fountains:
    There will I kiss
    The bowl of bliss,
And drink mine everlasting fill
Upon every milken hill.
My soul will be a-dry before;
But after, it will thirst no more.

Then by that happy, blissful day,
More peaceful pilgrims I shall see,
That have cast off their rags of clay,
And walk appareled fresh like me.
    I'll take them first
    To quench their thirst,

And taste of nectar's suckets
At those clear wells
Where sweetness dwells
Drawn up by saints in crystal buckets.

And when our bottles and all we
Are filled with immortality,
Then the blessèd paths we'll travel,
Strowed with rubies thick as gravel;—
Ceilings of diamonds, sapphire floors,
High walls of coral, and pearly bowers.
From thence to Heaven's bribeless hall,
Where no corrupted voices brawl;
No conscience molten into gold,
No forged accuser bought or sold,
No cause deferred, no vain-spent journey,
For there Christ is the King's Attorney,
Who pleads for all without degrees,
And He hath angels, but no fees.
And when the grand twelve-million jury
Of our sins, with direful fury,
Against our souls black verdicts give,
Christ pleads His death, and then we live.

Be Thou my speaker, taintless pleader,
Unblotted lawyer, true proceeder!
Thou giv'st salvation even for alms;
Not with a bribèd lawyer's palms.
And this is mine eternal plea
To Him that made heaven, earth, and sea,
That, since my flesh must die so soon,
And want a head to dine next noon,
Just at the stroke, when my veins start and spread,
Set on my soul an everlasting head!
Then am I ready, like a palmer, fit
To tread those blest paths which before I writ.

O death and judgment, heaven and hell,
Who oft doth think, must needs die well.

*Walter Raleigh* [1552?–1618]

## THE CONCLUSION

Even such is Time, that takes in trust
  Our youth, our joys, our all we have,
And pays us but with earth and dust;
  Who in the dark and silent grave,
When we have wandered all our ways,
Shuts up the story of our days;
But from this earth, this grave, this dust,
My God shall raise me up, I trust.

*Walter Raleigh* [1552?–1618]

## DEATH'S SUMMONS

Adieu, farewell, earth's bliss!
This world uncertain is:
Fond are life's lustful joys,
Death proves them all but toys.
None from his darts can fly:
I am sick, I must die.
  Lord, have mercy on us!

Rich men, trust not in wealth,
Gold cannot buy you health;
Physic himself must fade;
All things to end are made;
The plague full swift goes by:
I am sick, I must die.
  Lord, have mercy on us!

Beauty is but a flower,
Which wrinkles will devour:
Brightness falls from the air;
Queens have died young and fair;
Dust hath closed Helen's eye:
I am sick, I must die.
  Lord, have mercy on us!

Strength stoops unto the grave;
Worms feed on Hector brave;

Swords may not fight with fate;
Earth still holds ope her gate;
Come, come, the bells do cry.
I am sick, I must die.
  Lord, have mercy on us!

Wit with his wantonness,
Tasteth death's bitterness;
Hell's executioner
Hath no ears for to hear
What vain art can reply;
I am sick, I must die.
  Lord, have mercy on us!

Haste therefore each degree
To welcome destiny!
Heaven is our heritage,
Earth but a player's stage;
Mount we unto the sky:
I am sick, I must die.
  Lord, have mercy on us!

*Thomas Nashe* [1567–1601]

## HIS WINDING-SHEET

Come thou, who art the wine and wit
  Of all I've writ:
The grace, the glory, and the best
  Piece of the rest.
Thou art of what I did intend
  The all and end;
And what was made, was made to meet
  Thee, thee, my sheet.
Come then, and be to my chaste side
  Both bed and bride:
We two, as reliques left, will have
  One rest, one grave:
And, hugging close, we will not fear
  Lust entering here:
Where all desires are dead and cold
  As is the mold;

And all affections are forgot,
  Or trouble not.
Here, here, the slaves and prisoners be
  From shackles free:
And weeping widows, long oppressed,
  Do here find rest.
The wrongèd client ends his laws
  Here, and his cause.
Here those long suits of Chancery lie
  Quiet, or die:
And all Star-Chamber bills do cease
  Or hold their peace.
Here needs no Court for our Request
  Where all are best,
All wise, all equal, and all just
  Alike i' th' dust.
Nor need we here to fear the frown
  Of court or crown:
Where Fortune bears no sway o'er things,
  There all are kings.
In this securer place we'll keep
  As lulled asleep;
Or for a little time we'll lie
  As robes laid by;
To be another day re-worn,
  Turned, but not torn:
Or like old testaments engrossed,
  Locked up, not lost.
And for a while lie here concealed,
  To be revealed
Next at that great Platonic Year,
  And then meet here.

*Robert Herrick* [1591–1674]

## A PRAYER IN THE PROSPECT OF DEATH

O Thou unknown, Almighty Cause
  Of all my hope and fear!
In whose dread presence, ere an hour,
  Perhaps I must appear!

If I have wandered in those paths
  Of life I ought to shun,
As something, loudly, in my breast,
  Remonstrates I have done;

Thou know'st that Thou hast formèd me
  With passions wild and strong;
And listening to their witching voice
  Has often led me wrong.

Where human weakness has come short,
  Or frailty stepped aside,
Do Thou, All-Good!—for such Thou art,—
  In shades of darkness hide.

Where with intention I have erred,
  No other plea I have,
But, Thou art good; and Goodness still
  Delighteth to forgive.

*Robert Burns* [1759-1796]

## SONG OF THE SILENT LAND *

INTO the Silent Land!
Ah! who shall lead us thither?
Clouds in the evening sky more darkly gather,
And shattered wrecks lie thicker on the strand.
Who leads us with a gentle hand
Thither, oh, thither,
Into the Silent Land?

Into the Silent Land!
To you, ye boundless regions
Of all perfection! Tender morning-visions
Of beauteous souls! The Future's pledge and band
Who in Life's battle firm doth stand,
Shall bear Hope's tender blossoms
Into the Silent Land!

* For the original of this poem see page 3832.

O Land! O Land!
For all the broken-hearted
The mildest herald by our fate allotted,
Beckons, and with inverted torch doth stand
To lead us with a gentle hand
To the land of the great Departed,
Into the Silent Land!

*After von Salis-Seewis, by*
*Henry Wadsworth Longfellow* [1807-1882]

## JUNE

I GAZED upon the glorious sky
And the green mountains round,
And thought that when I came to lie
At rest within the ground,
'Twere pleasant that, in flowery June,
When brooks send up a cheerful tune,
And groves a joyous sound,
The sexton's hand, my grave to make,
The rich, green mountain-turf should break.

A cell within the frozen mould,
A coffin borne through sleet,
And icy clods above it rolled,
While fierce the tempests beat—
Away!—I will not think of these—
Blue be the sky and soft the breeze,
Earth green beneath the feet,
And be the damp mould gently pressed
Into my narrow place of rest.

There through the long, long summer hours,
The golden light should lie,
And thick young herbs and groups of flowers
Stand in their beauty by.
The oriole should build and tell
His love-tale close beside my cell;
The idle butterfly
Should rest him there, and there be heard
The housewife bee and humming-bird.

And what if cheerful shouts at noon
Come, from the village sent,
Or songs of maids, beneath the moon
With fairy laughter blent?
And what if, in the evening light,
Betrothèd lovers walk in sight
Of my low monument?
I would the lovely scene around
Might know no sadder sight nor sound.

I know that I no more should see
The season's glorious show,
Nor would its brightness shine for me,
Nor its wild music flow;
But if, around my place of sleep,
The friends I love should come to weep,
They might not haste to go.
Soft airs, and song, and light, and bloom
Should keep them lingering by my tomb.

These to their softened hearts should bear
The thought of what has been,
And speak of one who cannot share
The gladness of the scene;
Whose part, in all the pomp that fills
The circuit of the summer hills,
Is that his grave is green;
And deeply would their hearts rejoice
To hear again his living voice.

*William Cullen Bryant* [1794-1878]

## LOVE, TIME AND DEATH

Ah me, dread friends of mine,—Love, Time, and Death:
Sweet Love, who came to me on shining wing,
And gave her to my arms,—her lips, her breath,
And all her golden ringlets clustering:
And Time, who gathers in the flying years,
He gave me all, but where is all he gave?
He took my love and left me barren tears:
Weary and lone I follow to the grave.

There Death will end this vision half-divine.
Wan Death, who waits in shadow evermore,
And silent, ere he give the sudden sign;
Oh, gently lead me through thy narrow door,
Thou gentle Death, thou trustieth friend of mine—
Ah me, for Love—will Death my Love restore?

*Frederick Locker-Lampson* [1821–1895]

## A WISH

I ASK not that my bed of death
From bands of greedy heirs be free;
For these besiege the latest breath
Of fortune's favored sons, not me.

I ask not each kind soul to keep
Tearless, when of my death he hears.
Let those who will, if any, weep!
There are worse plagues on earth than tears.

I ask but that my death may find
The freedom to my life denied;
Ask but the folly of mankind
Then, then at last, to quit my side.

Spare me the whispering, crowded room,
The friends who come, and gape, and go;
The ceremonious air of gloom—
All, which makes death a hideous show!

Nor bring, to see me cease to live,
Some doctor full of phrase and fame,
To shake his sapient head, and give
The ill he cannot cure a name.

Nor fetch, to take the accustomed toll,
Of the poor sinner bound for death,
His brother-doctor of the soul,
To canvass with official breath

The future and its viewless things—
That undiscovered mystery
Which one who feels death's winnowing wings
Must needs read clearer, sure, than he!

Bring none of these; but let me be,
While all around in silence lies,
Moved to the window near, and see
Once more, before my dying eyes,

Bathed in the sacred dews of morn
The wide aërial landscape spread—
The world which was ere I was born,
The world which lasts when I am dead;

Which never was the friend of *one*,
Nor promised love it could not give,
But lit for all its generous sun,
And lived itself, and made us live.

There let me gaze, till I become
In soul, with what I gaze on, wed!
To feel the universe my home;
To have before my mind—instead

Of the sick room, the mortal strife,
The turmoil for a little breath—
The pure eternal course of life,
Not human combatings with death!

Thus feeling, gazing, might I grow
Composed, refreshed, ennobled, clear;
Then willing let my spirit go
To work or wait elsewhere or here!

*Matthew Arnold* [1822–1888]

## NEXT OF KIN

THE shadows gather round me, while you are in the sun:
My day is almost ended, but yours is just begun:
The winds are singing to us both and the streams are singing still,
And they fill your heart with music, but mine they cannot fill.

Your home is built in sunlight, mine in another day:
Your home is close at hand, sweet friend, but mine is far away:
Your bark is in the haven where you fain would be:
I must launch out into the deep, across the unknown sea.

You, white as dove or lily or spirit of the light:
I, stained and cold and glad to hide in the cold dark night:
You, joy to many a loving heart and light to many eyes:
I, lonely in the knowledge earth is full of vanities.

Yet when your day is over, as mine is nearly done,
And when your race is finished, as mine is almost run,
You, like me, shall cross your hands and bow your graceful head:
Yea, we twain shall sleep together in an equal bed.

*Christina Georgina Rossetti* [1830–1894]

## A BETTER RESURRECTION

I HAVE no wit, no words, no tears;
My heart within me like a stone
Is numbed too much for hopes or fears;
Look right, look left, I dwell alone;
I lift mine eyes, but dimmed with grief
No everlasting hills I see;
My life is in the falling leaf:
O Jesu, quicken me!

My life is like a faded leaf,
My harvest dwindled to a husk;
Truly my life is void and brief
And tedious in the barren dusk;
My life is like a frozen thing,
No bud nor greenness can I see:
Yet rise it shall,—the sap of Spring;
O Jesu, rise in me!

My life is like a broken bowl,
A broken bowl that cannot hold
One drop of water for my soul
Or cordial in the searching cold;

Cast in the fire the perished thing,
  Melt and remold it, till it be
A royal cup for Him my King:
    O Jesu, drink of me!

*Christina Georgina Rossetti* [1830–1894]

## THE SUMMER IS ENDED

WREATHE no more lilies in my hair,
For I am dying, Sister sweet:
Or, if you will for the last time
    Indeed, why make me fair
    Once for my winding-sheet.

Pluck no more roses for my breast,
For I like them fade in my prime:
Or, if you will, why pluck them still,
    That they may share my rest
    Once more for the last time.

Weep not for me when I am gone,
Dear tender one, but hope and smile:
Or, if you cannot choose but weep,
    A little while weep on,
    Only a little while.

*Christina Georgina Rossetti* [1830–1894]

## A LITTLE PARABLE

I MADE the cross myself whose weight
  Was later laid on me.
This thought is torture as I toil
  Up life's steep Calvary.

To think mine own hands drove the nails!
  I sang a merry song,
And chose the heaviest wood I had
  To build it firm and strong.

If I had guessed—if I had dreamed
Its weight was meant for me,
I should have made a lighter cross
To bear up Calvary!

*Anne Reeve Aldrich* [1866–1892]

## MY CROSS

My Lord would make a cross for me
But I would none of His,—
I thought I better knew than He
To bear my pain or bliss.

My Lord would make a cross for me
But I would make my own,—
In fashion light as cross could be
But now it weighs like stone.

If I had only bowed me low
To take the cross He laid,
It never would have galled me so
As this, the one I made.

For aye, His cross is true and sure
In all its breadth and length,
Just what His children can endure
And measured to their strength.

But I had fainted 'neath the load
I on myself did lay,
Had He not met me on the road
And helped me on the way!

*Zitella Cocke* [1847–1929

## IN THE HOSPITAL

I lay me down to sleep,
With little thought or care
Whether my waking find
Me here, or there.

A bowing, burdened head,
That only asks to rest,
Unquestioning, upon
A loving breast.

My good right hand forgets
Its cunning now;
To march the weary march
I know not how.

I am not eager, bold,
Nor strong—all that is past;
I am ready not to do
At last, at last.

My half day's work is done,
And this is all my part—
I give a patient God
My patient heart,

And grasp His banner still,
Though all the blue be dim;
These stripes as well as stars
Lead after Him.

*Mary Woolsey Howland* [1832–1864]

## WHEN

If I were told that I must die to-morrow,
That the next sun
Which sinks would bear me past all fear and sorrow
For any one,
All the fight fought, all the short journey through,
What should I do?

I do not think that I should shrink or falter,
But just go on,
Doing my work, nor change nor seek to alter
Aught that is gone;
But rise and move and love and smile and pray
For one more day.

And, lying down at night for a last sleeping,
Say in that ear
Which hearkens ever: "Lord, within Thy keeping
How should I fear?
And when to-morrow brings Thee nearer still,
Do thou Thy will."

I might not sleep for awe; but peaceful, tender,
My soul would lie
All the night long; and when the morning splendor
Flushed o'er the sky,
I think that I could smile—could calmly say,
"It is His day."

But if a wondrous hand from the blue yonder
Held out a scroll
On which my life was writ, and I with wonder
Beheld unroll
To a long century's end its mystic clue,
What should I do?

What *could* I do, O blessed Guide and Master,
Other than this:
Still to go on as now, not slower, faster,
Nor fear to miss
The road, although so very long it be,
While led by Thee?

Step after step, feeling Thee close beside me,
Although unseen,
Through thorns, through flowers, whether the tempest hide Thee,
Or heavens serene,
Assured Thy faithfulness cannot betray,
Thy love decay.

I may not know; my God, no hand revealeth
Thy counsels wise;
Along the path a deepening shadow stealeth,
No voice replies
To all my questioning thought, the time to tell;
And it is well.

Let me keep on, abiding and unfearing
Thy will always,
Through a long century's ripening fruition
Or a short day's;
Thou canst not come too soon; and I can wait
If Thou come late.

*Sarah Chauncey Woolsey* [1835–1905]

## "EX LIBRIS"

In an old book at even as I read
Fast fading words adown my shadowy page,
I crossed a tale of how, in other age,
At Arqua, with his books around him, sped
The word to Petrarch; and with noble head
Bowed gently o'er his volume that sweet sage
To Silence paid his willing seigniorage.
And they who found him whispered, "He is dead!"
Thus timely from old comradeships would I
To Silence also rise. Let there be night,
Stillness, and only these staid watchers by,
And no light shine save my low study light—
Lest of his kind intent some human cry
Interpret not the Messenger aright.

*Arthur Upson* [1877–1908]

## IN EXTREMIS

Till dawn the Winds' insuperable throng
Passed over like archangels in their might,
With roar of chariots from their stormy height,
And broken thunder of mysterious song—
By mariner or sentry heard along
The star-usurping battlements of night—
And wafture of immeasurable flight,
And high-blown trumpets mutinous and strong.
Till louder on the dreadful dark I heard
The shrieking of the tempest-tortured tree,
And deeper on immensity the call
And tumult of the empire-forging sea;

But near the eternal Peace I lay, nor stirred,
Knowing the happy dead hear not at all.

*George Sterling* [1869–1926]

## SPINNING

Like a blind spinner in the sun,
I tread my days;
I know that all the threads will run
Appointed ways;
I know each day will bring its task,
And, being blind, no more I ask.

I do not know the use or name
Of that I spin:
I only know that some one came,
And laid within
My hand the thread, and said, "Since you
Are blind, but one thing you can do."

Sometimes the threads so rough and fast
And tangled fly,
I know wild storms are sweeping past,
And fear that I
Shall fall; but dare not try to find
A safer place, since I am blind.

I know not why, but I am sure
That tint and place,
In some great fabric to endure
Past time and race,
My threads will have; so from the first,
Though blind, I never felt accurst.

I think, perhaps, this trust has sprung
From one short word
Said over me when I was young,—
So young, I heard
It, knowing not that God's name signed
My brow, and sealed me His, though blind.

But whether this be seal or sign
Within, without,
It matters not. The bond divine
I never doubt.
I know He set me here, and still,
And glad, and blind, I wait His will;

But listen, listen, day by day,
To hear their tread
Who bear the finished web away,
And cut the thread,
And bring God's message in the sun,
"Thou poor blind spinner, work is done."

*Helen Hunt Jackson* [1831-1885]

## "SOME TIME AT EVE"

Some time at eve when the tide is low,
I shall slip my mooring and sail away,
With no response to the friendly hail
Of kindred craft in the busy bay.
In the silent hush of the twilight pale,
When the night stoops down to embrace the day,
And the voices call in the waters' flow—
Some time at eve when the tide is low,
I shall slip my mooring and sail away.

Through the purpling shadows that darkly trail
O'er the ebbing tide of the Unknown Sea,
I shall fare me away, with a dip of sail
And a ripple of waters to tell the tale
Of a lonely voyager, sailing away
To the Mystic Isles where at anchor lay
The crafts of those who have sailed before
O'er the Unknown Sea to the Unseen Shore.

A few who have watched me sail away
Will miss my craft from the busy bay;
Some friendly barks that were anchored near,
Some loving souls that my heart held dear,
In silent sorrow will drop a tear—

But I shall have peacefully furled my sail
In moorings sheltered from storm or gale,
And greeted the friends who have sailed before
O'er the Unknown Sea to the Unseen Shore.

*Elizabeth Clark Hardy* [18

## NIGHT

When the time comes for me to die,
To-morrow, or some other day,
If God should bid me make reply,
"What would'st thou?" I shall say,

O God, Thy world was great and fair;
Yet give me to forget it clean!
Vex me no more with things that were,
And things that might have been.

I loved, I toiled, throve ill or well,
—Lived certain years and murmured not.
Now grant me in that land to dwell
Where all things are forgot.

For others, Lord, Thy purging fires,
The loves reknit the crown, the palm.
For me, the death of all desires
In deep, eternal calm.

*Thomas William Rolleston* [1857–1920]

## Afterwards

I know that these poor rags of womanhood,—
This oaten pipe, whereon the wild winds played
Making sad music,—tattered and outfrayed,
Cast off, played out,—can hold no more of good,
Of love, or song, or sense of sun and shade.

What homely neighbors elbow me (hard by
'Neath the black yews) I know I shall not know,
Nor take account of changing winds that blow,
Shifting the golden arrow, set on high
On the gray spire, nor mark who come and go.

Yet would I lie in some familiar place,
  Nor share my rest with uncongenial dead,—
  Somewhere, may be, where friendly feet will tread,—
As if from out some little chink of space
  Mine eyes might see them tripping overhead.

And though too sweet to deck a sepulcher
  Seem twinkling daisy-buds and meadow-grass;
  And so would more than serve me, lest they pass
Who fain would know what woman rested there,
  What her demeanor, or her story was,—

For these I would that on a sculptured stone
  (Fenced round with ironwork to keep secure)
  Should sleep a form with folded palms demure,
In aspect like the dreamer that was gone,
  With these words carved, "*I hoped, but was not sure*"

*Violet Fane* [1843–1905]

## A HUNDRED YEARS TO COME

Oh, where will be the birds that sing,
  A hundred years to come?
The flowers that now in beauty spring,
  A hundred years to come?
The rosy lip, the lofty brow,
The heart that beats so gaily now,—
Oh, where will be love's beaming eye,
Joy's pleasant smile, and sorrow's sigh,
  A hundred years to come?

Who'll press for gold this crowded street,
  A hundred years to come?
Who'll tread yon church with willing feet,
  A hundred years to come?
Pale, trembling age, and fiery youth,
And childhood with its brow of truth,
The rich and poor, on land and sea,—
Where will the mighty millions be,
  A hundred years to come?

We all within our graves shall sleep,
  A hundred years to come;
No living soul for us will weep
  A hundred years to come;
But other men our lands shall till,
And others then our streets shall fill,
While other birds shall sing as gay,
As bright the sunshine as to-day,
  A hundred years to come!

*William Goldsmith Brown* [1812–1906] *or*
*Hiram Ladd Spencer* [1829–1915]. *Said to have been published anonymously in a paper Brown edited, and erroneously attributed to him.*

## THE LAST CAMP-FIRE

SCAR not earth's breast that I may have
Somewhere above her heart a grave;
Mine was a life whose swift desire
Bent ever less to dust than fire;
Then through the swift white path of flame
Send back my soul to whence it came;
From some great peak, storm challenging,
My death-fire to the heavens fling;
The rocks my altar, and above
The still eyes of the stars I love;
No hymn, save as the midnight wind
Comes whispering to seek his kind.

Heap high the logs of spruce and pine,
Balsam for spices and for wine;
Brown cones, and knots a golden blur
Of hoarded pitch, more sweet than myrrh;
Cedar, to stream across the dark
Its scented embers spark on spark;
Long, shaggy boughs of juniper,
And silvery, odorous sheaves of fir;
Spice-wood, to die in incense smoke
Against the stubborn roots of oak,
Red to the last for hate or love
As that red stubborn heart above.

Watch till the last pale ember dies,
Till wan and low the dead pyre lies,
Then let the thin white ashes blow
To all earth's winds a finer snow;
There is no wind of hers but I
Have loved it as it whistled by;
No leaf whose life I would not share,
No weed that is not some way fair;
Hedge not my dust in one close urn,
It is to these I would return,—
The wild, free winds, the things that know
No master's rule, no ordered row,—

To be, if Nature will, at length
Part of some great tree's noble strength;
Growth of the grass; to live anew
In many a wild-flower's richer hue;
Find immortality, indeed,
In ripened heart of fruit and seed.
Time grants not any man redress
Of his broad law, forgetfulness;
I parley not with shaft and stone,
Content that in the perfume blown
From next year's hillsides something sweet
And mine, shall make earth more complete

*Sharlot M. Hall* [1870–1944]

## INTERLUDE

THE days grow shorter, the nights grow longer,
The headstones thicken along the way;
And life grows sadder, but love grows stronger
For those who walk with us, day by day.

The tear comes quicker, the laugh comes slower,
The courage is lesser to do and dare;
And the tide of joy in the heart runs lower
And seldom covers the reefs of care.

But all true things in the world seem truer,
And the better things of the earth seem best;

And friends are dearer as friends are fewer,
And love is all as our sun dips west.

Then let us clasp hands as we walk together,
And let us speak softly, in love's sweet tone,
For no man knows, on the morrow, whether
We two pass by, or but one alone.

*Ella Wheeler Wilcox* [1850–1919]

## THE ONE HOPE

When vain desire at last and vain regret
Go hand in hand to death, and all is vain,
What shall assuage the unforgotten pain
And teach the unforgetful to forget?
Shall Peace be still a sunk stream long unmet,—
Or may the soul at once in a green plain
Stoop through the spray of some sweet life-fountain
And cull the dew-drenched flowering amulet?
Ah! when the wan soul in that golden air
Between the scriptured petals softly blown
Peers breathless for the gift of grace unknown,—
Ah! let none other alien spell soe'er
But only the one Hope's one name be there,—
Not less nor more, but even that word alone.

*Dante Gabriel Rossetti* [1828–1882[

## THE LAMP IN THE WEST

Venus has lit her silver lamp
Low in the purple West,
Casting a soft and mellow light
Upon the sea's full breast;
In one clear path—as if to guide
Some pale, wayfaring guest.

Far out, far out the restless bar
Starts from a troubled sleep,
Where, roaring through the narrow straits,
The meeting waters leap;
But still that shining pathway leads
Across the lonely deep.

When I sail out the narrow straits
  Where unknown dangers be,
And cross the troubled, moaning bar
  To the mysterious sea,
Dear God, wilt thou not set a lamp
  Low in the West for me?

*Ella Higginson* [1862–1940]

## THE DYING RESERVIST

I SHALL not see the faces of my friends,
Nor hear the songs the rested reapers sing
After the labors of the harvesting,
In those dark nights before the summer ends;
Nor see the floods of spring, the melting snow,
Nor in the autumn twilight hear the stir
Of reedy marshes, when the wild ducks whir
And circle black against the afterglow.
My mother died; she shall not have to weep;
My wife will find another home; my child,
Too young, will never grieve or know; but I
Have found my brother, and contentedly
I'll lay my head upon his knees and sleep.
O brother Death,—I knew you when you smiled.

*Maurice Baring* [1874–1945]

## "IF LOVE WERE JESTER AT THE COURT OF DEATH"

IF Love were jester at the court of Death,
And Death the king of all, still would I pray,
"For me the motley and the bauble, yea,
Though all be vanity, as the Preacher saith,
The mirth of love be mine for one brief breath!"
Then would I kneel the monarch to obey,
And kiss that pale hand, should it spare or slay;
Since I have tasted love, what mattereth!
But if, dear God, this heart be dry as sand,
And cold as Charon's palm holding Hell's toll,

How worse! how worse! Scorch it with sorrow's brand!
Haply, though dead to joy, 'twould feel *that* coal;
Better a cross, and nails through either hand,
Than Pilate's palace and a frozen soul!

*Frederic Lawrence Knowles* [1869-1905]

## CONSTANCY

"DEAR as remembered kisses after death"—
We read and pause, toying the pliant page
With absent fingers while we question slow,
By whom remembered? Not by those that live,
And love again, and wed, and know fresh joys,
Forgetting the pale past. Ah, no! for them,
The sudden stirring of such long-whelmed thought
Means shock and pain, and swift reburial.
But it may be, that with the dreaming dead,
Who sank away quick piercèd by despair,
It may be that their stillness is aglow
Through soft recalling of each loved caress;
Perchance it is of them the poet saith
"Dear as remembered kisses after death."

*Minor Watson* [18 -

## THE WILD RIDE

*I hear in my heart, I hear in its ominous pulses*
*All day, on the road, the hoofs of invisible horses,*
*All night, from their stalls, the importunate pawing and neighing.*

Let cowards and laggards fall back! but alert to the saddle
Weatherworn and abreast, go men of our galloping legion,
With a stirrup-cup each to the lily of women that loves him.

The trail is through dolor and dread, over crags and morasses;
There are shapes by the way, there are things that appal or entice us:
What odds? We are Knights of the Grail, we are vowed to the riding.

Thought's self is a vanishing wing, and joy is a cobweb,
And friendship a flower in the dust, and glory a sunbeam:
Not here is our prize, nor, alas! after these our pursuing.

A dipping of plumes, a tear, a shake of the bridle,
A passing salute to this world and her pitiful beauty:
We hurry with never a word in the track of our fathers.

*I hear in my heart, I hear in its ominous pulses*
*All day, on the road, the hoofs of invisible horses,*
*All night, from their stalls, the importunate pawing and neighing.*

We spur to a land of no name, outracing the storm-wind;
We leap to the infinite dark like sparks from the anvil.
Thou leadest, O God! All's well with Thy troopers that follow.

*Louise Imogen Guiney* [1861–1920]

## "I WOULD NOT LIVE ALWAY"

I WOULD not live alway—live alway below!
Oh no, I'll not linger when bidden to go:
The days of our pilgrimage granted us here
Are enough for life's woes, full enough for its cheer:
Would I shrink from the path which the prophets of God,
Apostles, and martyrs, so joyfully trod?
Like a spirit unblest, o'er the earth would I roam,
While brethren and friends are all hastening home?

I would not live alway: I ask not to stay
Where storm after storm rises dark o'er the way;
Where seeking for rest we but hover around,
Like the patriarch's bird, and no resting is found;
Where Hope, when she paints her gay bow in the air,
Leaves its brilliance to fade in the night of despair,
And joy's fleeting angel ne'er sheds a glad ray,
Save the gleam of the plumage that bears him away.

I would not live alway—thus fettered by sin,
Temptation without and corruption within;
In a moment of strength if I sever the chain,
Scarce the victory's mine, ere I'm captive again;
E'en the rapture of pardon is mingled with fears,
And the cup of thanksgiving with penitent tears:
The festival trump calls for jubilant songs,
But my spirit her own *miserere* prolongs.

I would not live alway—no, welcome the tomb,
Since Jesus hath lain there I dread not its gloom;
Where He deigned to sleep, I'll too bow my head,
All peaceful to slumber on that hallowed bed.
Then the glorious daybreak, to follow that night,
The orient gleam of the angels of light,
With their clarion call for the sleepers to rise
And chant forth their matins, away to the skies.

Who, who would live alway? away from his God,
Away from yon heaven, that blissful abode,
Where the rivers of pleasure flow o'er the bright plains,
And the noontide of glory eternally reigns;
Where the saints of all ages in harmony meet,
Their Saviour and brethren transported to greet,
While the songs of salvation exultingly roll
And the smile of the Lord is the feast of the soul.

That heavenly music! what is it I hear?
The notes of the harpers ring sweet in mine ear!
And see, soft unfolding those portals of gold,
The King all arrayed in His beauty behold!
Oh give me, oh give me, the wings of a dove,
To adore Him—be near Him—enwrapped with his love;
I but wait for the summons, I list for the word—
Alleluia—Amen—evermore with the Lord!

*William Augustus Muhlenberg* [1796–1877]

## TRAVELLER'S HOPE

LAY me to rest in some fair spot
  Where sound of waters near,
And songs of sailors in their ships
  Shall reach my waiting ear:

Where I shall catch the Captain's call:
  "All hands again to sea!"
When swift embarking, I may fare
  To founts of life to be;

Fare to the dreamed-of lands that lie
  Beyond the Port of Death;
Fare to the Dawn of whose glad realms
  God sometimes whispereth;

With hope of flowers that lift their heads
  After the night is past,
And joy of sailors in their ships
  When home's in sight at last.

*Charles Granville* [18

## SEALED ORDERS

WE bear sealed orders o'er Life's weltered sea,
  Our haven dim and far;
We can but man the helm right cheerily,
  Steer by the brightest star,

And hope that when at last the Great Command
  Is read, we then may hear
Our anchor song, and see the longed-for land
  Lie, known and very near.

*Richard Burton* [1861-1940]

## SONG

I MAKE my shroud but no one knows,
So shimmering fine it is and fair,
With stitches set in even rows.
I make my shroud but no one knows.

In door-way where the lilac blows,
Humming a little wandering air,
I make my shroud and no one knows,
So shimmering fine it is and fair.

*Adelaide Crapsey* [1878-1914]

## A SONG OF LIVING

Because I have loved life, I shall have no sorrow to die.
I have sent up my gladness on wings, to be lost in the blue of the sky.
I have run and leaped with the rain, I have taken the wind to my breast.
My cheek like a drowsy child to the face of the earth I have pressed.
Because I have loved life, I shall have no sorrow to die.
I have kissed young Love on the lips, I have heard his song to the end.
I have struck my hand like a seal in the loyal hand of a friend.
I have known the peace of heaven, the comfort of work done well.
I have longed for death in the darkness and risen alive out of hell.
Because I have loved life, I shall have no sorrow to die.
I give a share of my soul to the world where my course is run.
I know that another shall finish the task I must leave undone.
I know that no flower, no flint was in vain on the path I trod.
As one looks on a face through a window, through life I have looked on God.
Because I have loved life, I shall have no sorrow to die.

*Amelia Josephine Burr* [1878-

## COMPENSATION

Because I had loved so deeply,
Because I had loved so long,
God in His great compassion
Gave me the gift of song.

Because I have loved so vainly,
  And sung with such faltering breath,
The Master, in infinite mercy,
  Offers the boon of Death.

*Paul Laurence Dunbar* [1872-1906]

## THE RECESSIONAL

Now along the solemn heights
Fade the Autumn's altar-lights;
  Down the great earth's glimmering chancel
Glide the days and nights.

Little kindred of the grass,
Like a shadow in a glass
  Falls the dark and falls the stillness;
We must rise and pass.

We must rise and follow, wending
Where the nights and days have ending,—
  Pass in order pale and slow
Unto sleep extending.

Little brothers of the clod,
Soul of fire and seed of sod,
  We must fare into the silence
At the knees of God.

Little comrades of the sky,
Wing to wing we wander by,
  Going, going, going, going,
Softly as a sigh.

Hark, the moving shapes confer,
Globe of dew and gossamer,
  Fading and ephemeral spirits
In the dusk astir.

Moth and blossom, blade and bee,
Worlds must go as well as we,
  In the long procession joining
Mount and star and sea.

Toward the shadowy brink we climb
Where the round year rolls sublime,
  Rolls, and drops, and falls forever
In the vast of time.

Like a plummet plunging deep
Past the utmost reach of sleep,
  Till remembrance has no longer
Care to laugh or weep.

*Charles G. D. Roberts* [1860–1943]

## MOUNTAIN SONG

I HAVE not where to lay my head:
  Upon my breast no child shall lie;
For me no marriage feast is spread:
  I walk alone under the sky.

My staff and scrip I cast away—
  Light-burdened to the mountain height!
Climbing the rocky steep by day,
  Kindling my fire against the night.

The bitter hail shall flower the peak,
  The icy wind shall dry my tears.
Strong shall I be, who am but weak,
  When bright Orion spears my fears

Under the horned moon I shall rise
  Up-swinging on the scarf of dawn.
The sun, searching with level eyes,
  Shall take my hand and lead me on.

Wide flaming pinions veil the West—
  Ah, shall I find? and shall I know?
My feet are bound upon the Quest—
  Over the Great Divide I go.

*Harriet Monroe* [1860–1936]

## TO M. E. W.

WORDS, for alas my trade is words, a barren burst of rhyme,
Rubbed by a hundred rhymesters, battered a thousand times,
Take them, you, that smile on strings, those nobler sounds than mine,
The words that never lie, or brag, or flatter, or malign.

I give a hand to my lady, another to my friend,
To whom you too have given a hand; and so before the end
We four may pray, for all the years, whatever suns be set,
The sole two prayers worth praying—to live and not forget.

The pale leaf falls in pallor, but the green leaf turns to gold;
We that have found it good to be young shall find it good to be old;
Life that bringeth the marriage bell, the cradle and the grave,
Life that is mean to the mean of heart, and only brave to the brave.

In the calm of the last white winter, when all the past is ours,
Old tears are frozen as jewels, old storms frosted as flowers,
Dear Lady, may we meet again, stand up again, we four,
Beneath the burden of the years, and praise the earth once more.

*Gilbert Keith Chesterton* [1874–1936]

## RETURNING

NEVER sings a city-robin on the gray-stone window-ledges
But I dream the long, cool meadows where the yellow cowslips be;
To his call I guess an answer from the grass and tangled hedges—
There's a thrill of other springtimes in the country soul of me!

Never falls light rain above me but I hear its gentle patter
On a lonely roof at even, as I heard it years ago;
Through the music, warmth, and fragrance, past the sound of careless chatter,
Throbs the silence of far places where the pines and birches grow.

I shall see a few more springtimes, then shall heed no answer lilted
To that first full-throated robin, hear no rain above my head . . .
Give me, God, the meadow-blossoms when my formal wreaths have wilted—
Let me lie till Thine Own Springtime with the pines beside my bed!

*Ruth Guthrie Harding* [1882-

## "O WORLD, BE NOT SO FAIR"

O MOON, O hide thy golden light,
O night, be not so fair;
O ye dear stars, shine not so bright:
I would for sleep prepare.
Mine eyes are closing wearily
That watched the slow day's flight,
And yet there is no rest for me
In this enchanted night.

O fellow-men, be not too good!
O world, be not too fair!
Wake no new life-glow in my blood—
I would for sleep prepare.
My day is dim; there beckons clear
A star of other air;
And yet, and yet, my heart is here!
O world, be not so fair.

*From the German of Maria Jäger by*
*Grace Fallow Norton* [18

## "ONE FIGHT MORE"

### PROSPICE

FEAR death?—to feel the fog in my throat,
  The mist in my face,
When the snows begin, and the blasts denote
  I am nearing the place,
The power of the night, the press of the storm,
  The post of the foe;
Where he stands, the Arch Fear in a visible form,
  Yet the strong man must go:
For the journey is done and the summit attained,
  And the barriers fall,
Though a battle's to fight ere the guerdon be gained,
  The reward of it all.
I was ever a fighter, so—one fight more,
  The best and the last!
I would hate that death bandaged my eyes, and forbore
  And bade me creep past.
No! let me taste the whole of it, fare like my peers
  The heroes of old,
Bear the brunt, in a minute pay glad life's arrears
  Of pain, darkness and cold.
For sudden the worst turns the best to the brave,
  The black minute's at end,
And the elements' rage, the fiend-voices that rave,
  Shall dwindle, shall blend,
Shall change, shall become first a peace out of pain,
  Then a light, then thy breast,
O thou soul of my soul! I shall clasp thee again,
  And with God be the rest!

*Robert Browning* [1812–1889]

## REQUIEM

UNDER the wide and starry sky
Dig the grave and let me lie.
Glad did I live and gladly die,
And I laid me down with a will.

This be the verse you grave for me:
*Here he lies where he longed to be;*
*Home is the sailor, home from sea,*
*And the hunter home from the hill.*

*Robert Louis Stevenson* [1850–1894]

## "OH MAY I JOIN THE CHOIR INVISIBLE"

Longum illud tempus, quum non ero, magis me movet, quam hoc exiguum.—*Cicero, ad Att.*, xii. 18.

OH MAY I join the choir invisible
Of those immortal dead who live again
In minds made better by their presence: live
In pulses stirred to generosity,
In deeds of daring rectitude, in scorn
For miserable aims that end with self,
In thoughts sublime that pierce the night like stars,
And with their mild persistence urge man's search
To vaster issues.
So to live is heaven:
To make undying music in the world,
Breathing as beauteous order that controls
With growing sway the growing life of man.
So we inherit that sweet purity
For which we struggled, failed, and agonized,
With widening retrospect that bred despair.
Rebellious flesh that would not be subdued,
A vicious parent shaming still its child,
Poor anxious penitence, is quick dissolved;
Its discords, quenched by meeting harmonies,
Die in the large and charitable air.
And all our rarer, better, truer self,

That sobbed religiously in yearning song,
That watched to ease the burden of the world,
Laboriously tracing what must be,
And what may yet be better,—saw within
A worthier image for the sanctuary,
And shaped it forth before the multitude,
Divinely human, raising worship so
To higher reverence more mixed with love,—
That better self shall live till human Time
Shall fold its eyelids, and the human sky
Be gathered like a scroll within the tomb
Unread forever.
This is life to come,
Which martyred men have made more glorious
For us who strive to follow. May I reach
That purest heaven, be to other souls
The cup of strength in some great agony,
Enkindle generous ardor, feed pure love,
Beget the smiles that have no cruelty,
Be the sweet presence of a good diffused,
And in diffusion ever more intense.
So shall I join the choir invisible
Whose music is the gladness of the world.

*George Eliot* [1819-1880]

## LAST LINES

No coward soul is mine,
No trembler in the world's storm-troubled sphere.
I see Heaven's glories shine,
And faith shines equal, arming me from fear.

O God within my breast,
Almighty, ever-present Deity!
Life—that in me has rest,
As I—undying Life—have power in Thee!

Vain are the thousand creeds
That move men's hearts: unutterably vain;
Worthless as withered weeds,
Or idlest froth amid the boundless main,

To waken doubt in one
Holding so fast by Thine infinity;
So surely anchored on
The steadfast rock of immortality.

With wide-embracing love
Thy Spirit animates eternal years,
Pervades and broods above,
Changes, sustains, dissolves, creates, and rears.

Though earth and man were gone,
And suns and universes cease to be,
And Thou were left alone,
Every existence would exist in Thee.

There is not room for Death,
Nor atom that his might could render void:
Thou—Thou art Being and Breath,
And what Thou art may never be destroyed.

*Emily Brontë* [1818–1848]

## LAUS MORTIS

NAY, why should I fear Death,
Who gives us life, and in exchange takes breath?

He is like cordial Spring
That lifts above the soil each buried thing;—

Like Autumn, kind and brief—
The frost that chills the branches frees the leaf;—

Like Winter's stormy hours
That spread their fleece of snow to save the flowers

The lordliest of all things,—
Life lends us only feet, Death gives us wings!

Fearing no covert thrust,
Let me walk onward, armed with valiant trust,

Dreading no unseen knife,
Across Death's threshold step from life to life!

O all ye frightened folk,
Whether ye wear a crown or bear a yoke,

Laid in one equal bed,
When once your coverlet of grass is spread,

What daybreak need you fear?
The Love will rule you there which guides you here!

Where Life, the Sower, stands,
Scattering the ages from his swinging hand

Thou waitest, Reaper lone,
Until the multitudinous grain hath grown

Scythe-bearer, when thy blade
Harvests my flesh, let me be unafraid!

God's husbandman thou art!—
In His unwithering sheaves, O bind my heart!

*Frederic Lawrence Knowles* [1869-1905]

## "WHEN I HAVE FEARS"

When I have fears that I may cease to be
Before my pen has gleaned my teeming brain,
Before high-pilèd books, in charact'ry
Hold like rich garners the full-ripened grain;
When I behold, upon the night's starred face,
Huge cloudy symbols of a high romance,
And think that I may never live to trace
Their shadows, with the magic hand of chance;
And when I feel, fair creature of an hour!
That I shall never look upon thee more,
Never have relish in the fairy power
Of unreflecting love!—then on the shore
Of the wide world I stand alone, and think
Till Love and Fame to nothingness do sink.

*John Keats* [1795-1821]

## LAST SONNET

Bright Star! would I were steadfast as thou art—
Not in lone splendor hung aloft the night,
And watching, with eternal lids apart,
Like Nature's patient, sleepless Eremite,
The moving waters at their priest-like task
Of pure ablution round earth's human shores,
Or gazing on the new soft-fallen mask
Of snow upon the mountains and the moors—
No—yet still steadfast, still unchangeable,
Pillowed upon my fair love's ripening breast,
To feel for ever its soft fall and swell,
Awake for ever in a sweet unrest,
Still, still to hear her tender-taken breath,
And so live ever—or else swoon to death.

*John Keats* [1795–1821]

## THE DYING CHRISTIAN TO HIS SOUL

*Animula, vagula, blandula,*
*Hospes Comesque Corporis,*
*Quæ nunc abibis in loca,*
*Pallidula, rigida, nudula?*
*Nec, ut soles, dabis joca.*
ADRIANI MORIENTIS, AD ANIMAM SUAM

Vital spark of heavenly flame,
Quit, O quit this mortal frame!
Trembling, hoping, lingering, flying,
O the pain, the bliss of dying!
Cease, fond Nature, cease thy strife,
And let me languish into life.

Hark! they whisper; angels say,
Sister Spirit, come away!
What is this absorbs me quite,
Steals my senses, shuts my sight,
Drowns my spirits, draws my breath?
Tell me, my soul, can this be death?

The world recedes; it disappears!
Heaven opens on my eyes; my ears

With sounds seraphic ring!
Lend, lend your wings! I mount! I fly!
O Grave! where is thy victory?
O Death! where is thy sting?

*Alexander Pope* [1688-1744]

## "BEYOND THE SMILING AND THE WEEPING"

Beyond the smiling and the weeping
I shall be soon;
Beyond the waking and the sleeping,
Beyond the sowing and the reaping,
I shall be soon.
Love, rest, and home!
Sweet hope!
Lord, tarry not, but come.

Beyond the blooming and the fading
I shall be soon;
Beyond the shining and the shading,
Beyond the hoping and the dreading,
I shall be soon.

Beyond the rising and the setting
I shall be soon;
Beyond the calming and the fretting,
Beyond remembering and forgetting,
I shall be soon.

Beyond the gathering and the strowing
I shall be soon;
Beyond the ebbing and the flowing,
Beyond the coming and the going,
I shall be soon.

Beyond the parting and the meeting
I shall be soon;
Beyond the farewell and the greeting,
Beyond this pulse's fever beating,
I shall be soon.

Beyond the frost chain and the fever
I shall be soon;
Beyond the rock waste and the river,
Beyond the ever and the never,
I shall be soon.
Love, rest, and home!
Sweet hope!
Lord, tarry not, but come.

*Horatius Bonar* [1808–1889]

## "I STROVE WITH NONE"

I STROVE with none; for none was worth my strife.
Nature I loved and, next to Nature, Art;
I warmed both hands before the fire of life;
It sinks, and I am ready to depart.

*Walter Savage Landor* [1775–1864]

## DEATH

DEATH stands above me, whispering low
I know not what into my ear;
Of his strange language all I know
Is, there is not a word of fear.

*Walter Savage Landor* [1775–1864]

## LIFE

LIFE! I know not what thou art,
But know that thou and I must part;
And when, or how, or where we met,
I own to me's a secret yet.
But this I know, when thou art fled,
Where'er they lay these limbs, this head,
No clod so valueless shall be
As all that then remains of me.

O whither, whither dost thou fly?
Where bend unseen thy trackless course?
And in this strange divorce,
Ah, tell where I must seek this compound I?
To the vast ocean of empyreal flame
From whence thy essence came
Dost thou thy flight pursue, when freed
From matter's base encumbering weed?
Or dost thou, hid from sight,
Wait, like some spell-bound knight,
Through blank oblivious years the appointed hour
To break thy trance and reassume thy power?
Yet canst thou without thought or feeling be?
O say, what art thou, when no more thou'rt thee?

Life! we have been long together,
Through pleasant and through cloudy weather;
'Tis hard to part when friends are dear;
Perhaps 'twill cost a sigh, a tear;—
Then steal away, give little warning,
Choose thine own time;
Say not Good-night, but in some brighter clime
Bid me Good-morning!

*Anna Letitia Barbauld* [1743-1825]

## DYING HYMN

Earth, with its dark and dreadful ills,
Recedes, and fades away;
Lift up your heads, ye heavenly hills;
Ye gates of death, give way!

My soul is full of whispered song,
My blindness is my sight;
The shadows that I feared so long
Are all alive with light.

The while my pulses faintly beat,
My faith doth so abound,
I feel grow firm beneath my feet
The green immortal ground.

That faith to me a courage gives
  Low as the grave, to go:
I know that my Redeemer lives:
  That I shall live, I know.

The palace walls I almost see,
  Where dwells my Lord and King;
O grave, where is thy victory!
  O death, where is thy sting!

*Alice Cary* [1820–1871]

## IN HARBOR

I THINK it is over, over,
  I think it is over at last;
Voices of foeman and lover,
  The sweet and the bitter, have passed:
Life, like a tempest of ocean,
Hath outblown its ultimate blast:
There's but a faint sobbing seaward
While the calm of the tide deepens leeward,
And behold! like the welcoming quiver
Of heart-pulses throbbed through the river,
  Those lights in the harbor at last,
  The heavenly harbor at last!

I feel it is over! over!
  For the winds and the waters surcease;
Ah, few were the days of the rover
  That smiled in the beauty of peace!
And distant and dim was the omen
That hinted redress or release:—
From the ravage of life, and its riot,
What marvel I yearn for the quiet
  Which bides in the harbor at last,—
For the lights, with their welcoming quiver,
That throb through the sanctified river,
  Which girdle the harbor at last,
  This heavenly harbor at last?

I know it is over, over,
  I know it is over at last!
Down sail! the sheathed anchor uncover,
  For the stress of the voyage has passed:
Life, like a tempest of ocean,
  Hath outbreathed its ultimate blast:
There's but a faint sobbing to seaward,
While the calm of the tide deepens leeward;
And behold! like the welcoming quiver
Of heart-pulses throbbed through the river,
  Those lights in the harbor at last,
  The heavenly harbor at last!

*Paul Hamilton Hayne* [1830–1886]

## THE LAST INVOCATION

At the last, tenderly,
From the walls of the powerful, fortressed house,
From the clasp of the knitted locks, from the keep of the well-closed doors,
Let me be wafted.

Let me glide noiselessly forth;
With the key of softness unlock the locks—with a whisper
Set ope the doors, O soul!

Tenderly—be not impatient!
(Strong is your hold, O mortal flesh!
Strong is your hold, O love!)

*Walt Whitman* [1819–1892]

## "DAREST THOU NOW, O SOUL"

Darest thou now, O soul,
Walk out with me toward the unknown region,
Where neither ground is for the feet nor any path to follow?

No map there, nor guide,
Nor voice sounding, nor touch of human hand,
Nor face with blooming flesh, nor lips, nor eyes, are in that land.

I know it not, O soul,
Nor dost thou, all is a blank before us,—
All waits undreamed of in that region, that inaccessible land.

Till when the ties loosen,
All but the ties eternal, Time and Space,
Nor darkness, gravitation, sense, nor any bounds bounding
us.

Then we burst forth, we float,
In Time and Space, O soul! prepared for them,
Equal, equipped at last (O joy! O fruit of all!), them to fulfill,
O soul!

*Walt Whitman* [1819–1892]

## WAITING

SERENE, I fold my hands and wait,
Nor care for wind, or tide, or sea;
I rave no more 'gainst Time or Fate,
For, lo! my own shall come to me.

I stay my haste, I make delays,
For what avails this eager pace?
I stand amid the eternal ways,
And what is mine shall know my face.

Asleep, awake, by night or day,
The friends I seek are seeking me;
No wind can drive my bark astray,
Nor change the tide of destiny.

What matter if I stand alone?
I wait with joy the coming years;
My heart shall reap where it hath sown,
And garner up its fruits of tears.

The waters know their own and draw
The brook that springs in yonder heights;
So flows the good with equal law
Unto the soul of pure delights.

The stars come nightly to the sky;
The tidal wave unto the sea;
Nor time, nor space, nor deep, nor high,
Can keep my own away from me.

*John Burroughs* [1837–1921]

## IN THE DARK

All moveless stand the ancient cedar-trees
Along the drifted sand-hills where they grow;
And from the dark west comes a wandering breeze,
And waves them to and fro.

A murky darkness lies along the sand,
Where bright the sunbeams of the morning shone,
And the eye vainly seeks, by sea and land,
Some light to rest upon.

No large, pale star its glimmering vigil keeps;
An inky sea reflects an inky sky;
And the dark river, like a serpent, creeps
To where its black piers lie.

Strange salty odors through the darkness steal,
And through the dark, the ocean-thunders roll;
Thick darkness gathers, stifling, till I feel
Its weight upon my soul.

I stretch my hands out in the empty air;
I strain my eyes into the heavy night;
Blackness of darkness!—Father, hear my prayer!
Grant me to see the light!

*George Arnold* [1834–1865]

## LAST VERSES

When I beneath the cold red earth am sleeping,
Life's fever o'er,
Will there for me be any bright eye weeping
That I'm no more?
Will there be any heart still memory keeping
Of heretofore?

When the great winds through leafless forests rushing
Sad music make;
When the swollen streams, o'er crag and gully gushing,
Like full hearts break,—
Will there then one, whose heart despair is crushing,
Mourn for my sake?

When the bright sun upon that spot is shining,
With purest ray,
And the small flowers, their buds and blossoms twining,
Burst through that clay,—
Will there be one still on that spot repining
Lost hopes all day?

When no star twinkles with its eye of glory
On that low mound,
And wintry storms have, with their ruins hoary,
Its loneness crowned,—
Will there be then one, versed in misery's story,
Pacing it round?

It may be so,—but this is selfish sorrow
To ask such meed,—
A weakness and a wickedness to borrow,
From hearts that bleed,
The wailings of to-day for what to-morrow
Shall never need.

Lay me then gently in my narrow dwelling,
Thou gentle heart;
And though thy bosom should with grief be swelling,
Let no tear start:
It were in vain,—for Time hath long been knelling,—
"Sad one, depart!"

*William Motherwell* [1797-1835]

## THE RUBICON

One other bitter drop to drink,
And then—no more!
One little pause upon the brink,
And then—go o'er!

One sigh—and then the lib'rant morn
  Of perfect day,
When my free spirit, newly born,
  Will soar away!

One pang—and I shall rend the thrall
  Where grief abides,
And generous Death will show me all
  That now he hides;
And, lucid in that second birth,
  I shall discern
What all the sages of the earth
  Have died to learn.

One motion—and the stream is crossed,
  So dark, so deep!
And I shall triumph, or be lost
  In endless sleep.
Then, onward! Whatsoe'er my fate,
  I shall not care!
Nor Sin nor Sorrow, Love nor Hate
  Can touch me there.

*William Winter* [1836–1917]

## WHEN I HAVE GONE WEIRD WAYS

When I have finished with this episode,
Left the hard, uphill road,
And gone weird ways to seek another load,
  O Friend, regret me not, nor weep for me—
  Child of Infinity!

Nor dig a grave, nor rear for me a tomb
To say with lying writ: "Here in the gloom
He who loved bigness takes a narrow room,
  Content to pillow here his weary head—
  For he is dead."

But give my body to the funeral pyre,
And bid the laughing fire,
Eager and strong and swift as my desire,
  Scatter my subtle essence into Space—
  Free me of Time and Place.

Sweep up the bitter ashes from the hearth!
Fling back the dust I borrowed from the Earth
Unto the chemic broil of Death and Birth—
  The vast Alembic of the cryptic Scheme,
  Warm with the Master-Dream.

And thus, O little House that sheltered me,
Dissolve again in wind and rain, to be
Part of the cosmic weird Economy:
  And Oh, how oft with new life shalt thou lift
  Out of the atom-drift!

*John G. Neihardt* [1881–

## A RHYME OF LIFE

If life be as a flame that death doth kill,
  Burn, little candle, lit for me,
  With a pure flame, that I may rightly see
  To word my song, and utterly
    God's plan fulfil.

If life be as a flower that blooms and dies,
  Forbid the cunning frost that slays
  With Judas kiss, and trusting love betrays;
  Forever may my song of praise
    Untainted rise.

If life be as a voyage, foul or fair,
  Oh, bid me not my banners furl
  For adverse gale, or wave in angry whirl,
  Till I have found the gates of pearl,
    And anchored there.

*Charles Warren Stoddard* [1843–1909]

## "THALATTA! THALATTA!"

### CRY OF THE TEN THOUSAND

I stand upon the summit of my years;
Behind, the toil, the camp, the march, the strife,
The wandering and the desert; vast, afar,
Beyond this weary way, behold! the Sea!

The sea o'erswept by clouds and winds and wings,
By thoughts and wishes manifold, whose breath
Is freshness and whose mighty pulse is peace.
Palter no question of the dim Beyond;
Cut loose the bark; such voyage itself is rest,
Majestic motion, unimpeded scope,
A widening heaven, a current without care.
Eternity!—Deliverance, Promise, Course!
Time-tired souls salute thee from the shore.

*Joseph Brownlee Brown* [1824–1888]

## REQUIEM

Hush your prayers, 'tis no saintly soul
Comes fainting back from the foughten field;
Carry me forth on my broken shield;
Trumpet and drum shall my requiem yield—
Silence the bells that toll.

Dig no hole in the ground for me:
Though my body be made of mold and must,
Ne'er in the earth shall my dead bones rust;
Give my corse to the flame's white lust,
And sink my ashes at sea.

Reeking still with the sweat of the strife,
Never a prayer have I to say
(My lips long since have forgotten the way)
Save this: "I have sorrowed sore in my day—
But I thank Thee, God, for my life!"

*F. Norreys Connell* [1874–1948]

## INVICTUS

Out of the night that covers me,
  Black as the pit from pole to pole,
I thank whatever gods may be
  For my unconquerable soul.

In the fell clutch of circumstance
I have not winced nor cried aloud.
Under the bludgeonings of chance
My head is bloody, but unbowed.

Beyond this place of wrath and tears
Looms but the Horror of the shade,
And yet the menace of the years
Finds and shall find me unafraid.

It matters not how strait the gate,
How charged with punishments the scroll,
I am the master of my fate:
I am the captain of my soul.

*William Ernest Henley* [1849–1903]

## "A LATE LARK TWITTERS FROM THE QUIET SKIES"

A LATE lark twitters from the quiet skies;
And from the west,
Where the sun, his day's work ended,
Lingers as in content,
There falls on the old, gray city
An influence luminous and serene,
A shining peace.

The smoke ascends
In a rosy-and-golden haze. The spires
Shine, and are changed. In the valley
Shadows rise. The lark sings on. The sun,
Closing his benediction,
Sinks, and the darkening air
Thrills with a sense of the triumphing night—
Night with her train of stars
And her great gift of sleep.

So be my passing!
My task accomplished and the long day done.

My wages taken, and in my heart
Some late lark singing,
Let me be gathered to the quiet west,
The sundown splendid and serene,
Death.

*William Ernest Henley* [1849–1903]

## "IN AFTER DAYS"

In after days when grasses high
O'er-top the stone where I shall lie,
Though ill or well the world adjust
My slender claim to honored dust,
I shall not question or reply.

I shall not see the morning sky;
I shall not hear the night-wind sigh;
I shall be mute, as all men must
In after days!

But yet, now living, fain were I
That some one then should testify,
Saying—"He held his pen in trust
To Art, not serving shame or lust."
Will none?—Then let my memory die
In after days!

*Austin Dobson* [1840–1921]

## "CALL ME NOT DEAD"

Call me not dead when I, indeed, have gone
Into the company of the everliving
High and most glorious poets! Let thanksgiving
Rather be made. Say: "He at last hath won
Rest and release, converse supreme and wise,
Music and song and light of immortal faces;
To-day, perhaps, wandering in starry places,
He hath met Keats, and known him by his eyes.

To-morrow (who can say?) Shakespeare may pass,
And our lost friend just catch one syllable
Of that three-centuried wit that kept so well;
Or Milton; or Dante, looking on the grass
Thinking of Beatrice, and listening still
To chanted hymns that sound from the heavenly hill."

*Richard Watson Gilder* [1844–1909]

## EPILOGUE

**From "Asolando"**

At the midnight in the silence of the sleep-time,
When you set your fancies free,
Will they pass to where—by death, fools think, imprisoned—
Low he lies who once so loved you, whom you loved so,
—Pity me?

Oh to love so, be so loved, yet so mistaken!
What had I on earth to do
With the slothful, with the mawkish, the unmanly?
Like the aimless, helpless, hopeless, did I drivel
—Being—who?

One who never turned his back but marched breast forward,
Never doubted clouds would break,
Never dreamed, though right were worsted, wrong would triumph,
Held we fall to rise, are baffled to fight better,
Sleep to wake.

No, at noonday in the bustle of man's work-time
Greet the unseen with a cheer!
Bid him forward, breast and back as either should be,
"Strive and thrive!" cry "Speed,—fight on, fare ever
There as here!"

*Robert Browning* [1812–1889]

## CROSSING THE BAR

SUNSET and evening star,
And one clear call for me!
And may there be no moaning of the bar,
When I put out to sea,

But such a tide as moving seems asleep,
Too full for sound and foam,
When that which drew from out the boundless deep
Turns again home.

Twilight and evening bell,
And after that the dark!
And may there be no sadness of farewell,
When I embark;

For though from out our bourne of Time and Place
The flood may bear me far,
I hope to see my Pilot face to face
When I have crossed the bar.

*Alfred Tennyson* [1809–1892]

## L'ENVOI

WHEN Earth's last picture is painted, and the tubes are twisted and dried,
When the oldest colors have faded, and the youngest critic has died,
We shall rest, and, faith, we shall need it—lie down for an eon or two,
Till the Master of All Good Workmen shall set us to work anew!

And those that were good shall be happy: they shall sit in a golden chair;
They shall splash at a ten-league canvas with brushes of comets' hair;

They shall find real saints to draw from—Magdalene, Peter, and Paul;
They shall work for an age at a sitting and never be tired at all!

And only the Master shall praise us, and only the Master shall blame;
And no one shall work for money, and no one shall work for fame;
But each for the joy of the working, and each, in his separate star
Shall draw the Thing as he sees It for the God of Things as They Are!

*Rudyard Kipling* [1865-1936]

## ENVOI

Oh seek me not within a tomb;
Thou shalt not find me in the clay!
I pierce a little wall of gloom
To mingle with the Day!

I brothered with the things that pass,
Poor giddy Joy and puckered Grief;
I go to brother with the Grass
And with the sunning Leaf.

Not Death can sheathe me in a shroud;
A joy-sword whetted keen with pain,
I join the armies of the Cloud,
The Lightning and the Rain.

Oh subtle in the sap athrill,
Athletic in the glad uplift,
A portion of the Cosmic Will,
I pierce the planet-drift.

My God and I shall interknit
As rain and Ocean, breath and Air;
And Oh, the luring thought of it
Is prayer!

*John G. Neihardt* [1881-

## A CYPRIAN WOMAN

UNDER dusky laurel leaf,
 Scarlet leaf of rose,
I lie prone, who have known
 All a woman knows.

Love and grief and motherhood,
 Fame and mirth and scorn—
These are all shall befall
 Any woman born.

Jewel-laden are my hands,
 Tall my stone above—
Do not weep that I sleep,
 Who was wise in love.

Where I walk, a shadow gray
 Through gray asphodel,
I am glad, who have had
 All that Life could tell.

*Margaret Widdemer* [18

## "WHEN I AM DEAD AND SISTER TO THE DUST"

WHEN I am dead and sister to the dust;
 When no more avidly I drink the wine
 Of human love; when the pale Proserpine
Has covered me with poppies, and cold rust
Has cut my lyre-strings, and the sun has thrust
 Me underground to nourish the world-vine,
 Men shall discover these old songs of mine,
And say: This woman lived—as poets must!
This woman lived and wore life as a sword
 To conquer wisdom; this dead woman read
In the sealed Book of Love and underscored
 The meanings. Then the sails of faith she spread,
And faring out for regions unexplored,
 Went singing down the River of the Dead.

*Elsa Barker* [18 –1954]

## A PARTING GUEST

WHAT delightful hosts are they—
 Life and Love!
Lingeringly I turn away,
 This late hour, yet glad enough
They have not withheld from me
 Their high hospitality.
So, with face lit with delight
 And all gratitude, I stay
 Yet to press their hands and say,
"Thanks.—So fine a time! Good night."

*James Whitcomb Riley* [1849-1916]

## THE STIRRUP CUP

MY short and happy day is done,
The long and dreary night comes on;
And at my door the Pale Horse stands,
To carry me to unknown lands.

His whinny shrill, his pawing hoof,
Sound dreadful as a gathering storm;
And I must leave this sheltering roof,
And joys of life so soft and warm.

Tender and warm the joys of life,—
Good friends, the faithful and the true;
My rosy children and my wife,
So sweet to kiss, so fair to view.

So sweet to kiss, so fair to view,—
The night comes down, the lights burn blue;
And at my door the Pale Horse stands,
To bear me forth to unknown lands.

*John Hay* [1838-1905]

## "THEY ARE ALL GONE"

### FRIENDS DEPARTED

THEY are all gone into the world of light,
And I alone sit lingering here;
Their very memory is fair and bright,
And my sad thoughts doth clear.

It glows and glitters in my cloudy breast,
Like stars upon some gloomy grove,
Or those faint beams in which this hill is dressed
After the sun's remove.

I see them walking in an air of glory,
Whose light doth trample on my days:
My days, which are at best but dull and hoary,
Mere glimmering and decays.

O holy Hope! and high Humility,
High as the heavens above!
These are your walks, and you have showed them me,
To kindle my cold love.

Dear, beauteous Death! the jewel of the Just!
Shining nowhere, but in the dark;
What mysteries do lie beyond thy dust,
Could man outlook that mark!

He that hath found some fledged bird's nest may know,
At first sight, if the bird be flown;
But what fair dell or grove he sings in now,
That is to him unknown.

And yet, as Angels in some brighter dreams
Call to the soul, when man doth sleep,
So some strange thoughts transcend our wonted themes,
And into glory peep.

If a star were confined into a tomb,
Her captive flames must needs burn there;
But when the hand that locked her up gives room,
She'll shine through all the sphere.

O Father of eternal life, and all
Created glories under Thee!
Resume Thy spirit from this world of thrall
Into true liberty.

Either disperse these mists, which blot and fill
My perspective still as they pass:
Or else remove me hence unto that hill,
Where I shall need no glass.

*Henry Vaughan* [1622–1695]

## "OVER THE RIVER"

OVER the river they beckon to me,—
Loved ones who've crossed to the farther side;
The gleam of their snowy robes I see,
But their voices are drowned in the rushing tide.
There's one with ringlets of sunny gold,
And eyes the reflection of heaven's own blue;
He crossed in the twilight gray and cold,
And the pale mist hid him from mortal view.
We saw not the angels who met him there,
The gates of the city we could not see:
Over the river, over the river,
My brother stands waiting to welcome me.

Over the river the boatman pale
Carried another, the household pet;
Her brown curls waved in the gentle gale,—
Darling Minnie! I see her yet.
She crossed on her bosom her dimpled hands,
And fearlessly entered the phantom bark;
We watched it glide from the silver sands,
And all our sunshine grew strangely dark.

We know she is safe on the farther side,
  Where all the ransomed and angels be:
Over the river, the mystic river,
  My childhood's idol is waiting for me.

For none return from those quiet shores,
  Who cross with the boatman cold and pale;
We hear the dip of the golden oars,
  And catch a gleam of the snowy sail;
And lo! they have passed from our yearning hearts,
  They cross the stream and are gone for aye.
We may not sunder the veil apart
  That hides from our vision the gates of day;
We only know that their barks no more
  May sail with us o'er life's stormy sea;
Yet somewhere, I know, on the unseen shore,
  They watch, and beckon, and wait for me.

And I sit and think, when the sunset's gold
  Is flushing river and hill and shore,
I shall one day stand by the water cold,
  And list for the sound of the boatman's oar;
I shall watch for a gleam of the flapping sail,
  I shall hear the boat as it gains the strand,
I shall pass from sight with the boatman pale,
  To the better shore of the spirit land.
I shall know the loved who have gone before,
  And joyfully sweet will the meeting be,
When over the river, the peaceful river,
  The angel of death shall carry me.

*Nancy Woodbury Priest* [1836–1870]

## RESIGNATION

THERE is no flock, however watched and tended,
  But one dead lamb is there!
There is no fireside, howsoe'er defended,
  But has one vacant chair!

The air is full of farewells to the dying,
And mournings for the dead;
The heart of Rachel, for her children crying,
Will not be comforted!

Let us be patient! These severe afflictions
Not from the ground arise,
But oftentimes celestial benedictions
Assume this dark disguise.

We see but dimly through the mists and vapors;
Amid these earthly damps
What seem to us but sad, funereal tapers
May be heaven's distant lamps.

There is no Death! What seems so is transition;
This life of mortal breath
Is but a suburb of the life elysian
Whose portal we call Death

She is not dead,—the child of our affection,—
But gone unto that school
Where she no longer needs our poor protection,
And Christ himself doth rule.

In that great cloister's stillness and seclusion,
By guardian angels led,
Safe from temptation, safe from sin's pollution,
She lives, whom we call dead.

Day after day we think what she is doing
In those bright realms of air;
Year after year, her tender steps pursuing,
Behold her grown more fair.

Thus do we walk with her and keep unbroken
The bond which nature gives,
Thinking that our remembrance, though unspoken,
May reach her where she lives.

Not as a child shall we again behold her;
For when with raptures wild
In our embraces we again enfold her,
She will not be a child;

But a fair maiden, in her Father's mansion,
Clothed with celestial grace;
And beautiful with all the soul's expansion
Shall we behold her face.

And though at times impetuous with emotion
And anguish long suppressed,
The swelling heart heaves moaning like the ocean,
That cannot be at rest,—

We will be patient, and assuage the feeling
We may not wholly stay;
By silence sanctifying, not concealing,
The grief that must have way.

*Henry Wadsworth Longfellow* [1807–1882

## AFTERWARD

THERE *is* no vacant chair. The loving meet,
A group unbroken—smitten, who knows how?
One sitteth silent only, in his usual seat;
We gave him once that freedom. Why not now?

Perhaps he is too weary, and needs rest;
He needed it so often, nor could we
Bestow. God gave it, knowing how to do so best.
Which of us would disturb him? Let him be.

There is no vacant chair. If he will take
The mood to listen mutely, be it done.
By his least mood we crossed, for which the heart must ache,
Plead not nor question! Let him have this one.

Death is a mood of life. It is no whim
By which life's Giver mocks a broken heart.
Death is life's reticence. Still audible to Him,
The hushed voice, happy, speaketh on, apart.

There is no vacant chair. To love is still
To have. Nearer to memory than to eye.
And dearer yet to anguish than to comfort, will
We hold by our love, that shall not die.

For while it doth not, thus he cannot. Try!
Who can put out the motion or the smile?
The old ways of being noble all with him laid by?
Because we love, he is. Then trust awhile.

*Elizabeth Stuart Phelps Ward* [1844–1911]

## SOMETIME

SOMETIME, when all life's lessons have been learned,
And sun and stars forevermore have set,
The things which our weak judgments here have spurned,
The things o'er which we grieved with lashes wet,
Will flash before us out of life's dark night,
As stars shine most in deeper tints of blue;
And we shall see how all God's plans are right,
And how what seemed reproof was love most true.

And we shall see how, while we frown and sigh,
God's plans go on as best for you and me;
How, when we called, He heeded not our cry,
Because His wisdom to the end could see.
And e'en as prudent parents disallow
Too much of sweet to craving babyhood,
So God, perhaps, is keeping from us now
Life's sweetest things, because it seemeth good.

And if, sometimes, commingled with life's wine,
We find the wormwood, and rebel and shrink,
Be sure a wiser hand than yours or mine
Pours out the potion for our lips to drink;

And if some friend you love is lying low,
Where human kisses cannot reach his face,
Oh, do not blame the loving Father so,
But wear your sorrow with obedient grace!

And you shall shortly know that lengthened breath
Is not the sweetest gift God sends His friend,
And that, sometimes, the sable pall of death
Conceals the fairest boon His love can send.
If we could push ajar the gates of life,
And stand within and all God's workings see,
We could interpret all this doubt and strife
And for each mystery could find a key.

But not to-day. Then be content, poor heart;
God's plans, like lilies pure and white, unfold;
We must not tear the close-shut leaves apart,—
Time will reveal the chalices of gold.
And if, through patient toil, we reach the land
Where tired feet, with sandals loosed, may rest,
When we shall clearly see and understand,
I think that we will say, "God knew the best!"

*May Riley Smith* [1842–1927]

## "THE MOURNERS CAME AT BREAK OF DAY"

The mourners came at break of day
Unto the garden-sepulcher;
With darkened hearts to weep and pray,
For Him, the loved one buried there.
What radiant light dispels the gloom?
An angel sits beside the tomb.

The earth doth mourn her treasures lost,
All sepulchered beneath the snow;
When wintry winds, and chilling frost
Have laid her summer glories low:
The spring returns, the flowerets bloom—
An angel sits beside the tomb.

Then mourn we not belovèd dead,
E'en while we come to weep and pray;
The happy spirit far hath fled
To brighter realms of endless day:
Immortal Hope dispels the gloom!
An angel sits beside the tomb.

*Sarah Flower Adams* [1805–1848]

## WHAT OF THE DARKNESS?

### TO THE HAPPY DEAD PEOPLE

WHAT of the darkness? Is it very fair?
Are there great calms? and find we silence there?
Like soft-shut lilies, all your faces glow
With some strange peace our faces never know,
With some strange faith our faces never dare,—
Dwells it in Darkness? Do you find it there?

Is it a Bosom where tired heads may lie?
Is it a Mouth to kiss our weeping dry?
Is it a Hand to still the pulse's leap?
Is it a Voice that holds the runes of sleep?
Day shows us not such comfort anywhere—
Dwells it in Darkness? Do you find it there?

Out of the Day's deceiving light we call—
Day that shows man so great, and God so small,
That hides the stars, and magnifies the grass—
O is the Darkness too a lying glass!
Or undistracted, do you find truth there?
What of the Darkness? Is it very fair?

*Richard Le Gallienne* [1866–1947]

## A SEA DIRGE

### From "The Tempest"

FULL fathom five thy father lies:
Of his bones are coral made;
Those are pearls that were his eyes:
Nothing of him that doth fade,

But doth suffer a sea-change
Into something rich and strange,
Sea-nymphs hourly ring his knell:
Hark! now I hear them,—
Ding, dong, Bell.

*William Shakespeare* [1564–1616]

## EPITAPHS

### I—ON ELIZABETH L. H.

WOULDST thou hear what Man can say
In a little? Reader, stay.
Underneath this stone doth lie
As much Beauty as could die:
Which in life did harbor give
To more Virtue than doth live.
If at all she had a fault,
Leave it buried in this vault.
One name was *Elizabeth*,
The other, let it sleep with death:
Fitter, where it died, to tell
Than that it lived at all. Farewell.

### II—ON SALATHIEL PAVY, A CHILD OF QUEEN ELIZABETH'S CHAPEL

WEEP with me, all you that read
This little story;
And know, for whom a tear you shed
Death's self is sorry.
'Twas a child that so did thrive
In grace and feature,
As Heaven and Nature seemed to strive
Which owned the creature.
Years he numbered scarce thirteen
When Fates turned cruel,
Yet three filled zodiacs had he been
The stage's jewel;
And did act (what now we moan)
Old men so duly,
As sooth the Parcæ thought him one,
He played so truly.

So, by error, to his fate
They all consented;
But, viewing him since, alas, too late!
They have repented;
And have sought, to give new birth,
In baths to steep him;
But, being so much too good for earth,
Heaven vows to keep him.

*Ben Jonson* [1573?–1637]

## SONG

From "The Devil's Law Case"

All the flowers of the spring
Meet to perfume our burying;
These have but their growing prime,
And man does flourish but his time:
Survey our progress from our birth—
We are set, we grow, we turn to earth.
Courts adieu, and all delights,
All bewitching appetites!
Sweetest breath and clearest eye
Like perfumes go out and die;
And consequently this is done
As shadows wait upon the sun.
Vain the ambition of kings
Who seek by trophies and dead things
To leave a living name behind,
And weave but nets to catch the wind.

*John Webster* [1580?–1625?]

## ON THE TOMBS IN WESTMINSTER

Mortality, behold and fear!
What a change of flesh is here!
Think how many royal bones
Sleep within this heap of stones;
Here they lie had realms and lands,
Who now want strength to stir their hands;
Where from their pulpits sealed with dust
They preach, "In greatness is no trust."

Here's an acre sown indeed
With the richest royal'st seed
That the earth did e'er suck in,
Since the first man died for sin;
Here the bones of birth have cried,
"Though gods they were, as men they died."
Here are sands, ignoble things,
Dropped from the ruined sides of kings.
Here's a world of pomp and state,
Buried in dust, once dead by fate.

*Francis Beaumont* [1584–1616]

## EPITAPH ON THE COUNTESS DOWAGER OF PEMBROKE

UNDERNEATH this sable hearse
Lies the subject of all verse:
Sidney's sister, Pembroke's mother:
Death, ere thou hast slain another,
Fair, and learned, and good as she,
Time shall throw a dart at thee.

Marble piles let no man raise
To her name: in after days,
Some kind woman born as she,
Reading this, like Niobe
Shall turn marble, and become
Both her mourner and her tomb.

*William Browne* [1591–1643]

## AN EPITAPH INTENDED FOR HIMSELF

LIKE thee I once have stemmed the sea of life,
Like thee have languished after empty joys,
Like thee have labored in the stormy strife,
Been grieved for trifles, and amused with toys

Forget my frailties; thou art also frail:
Forgive my lapses; for thyself may'st fall:
Nor read unmoved my artless tender tale—
I was a friend, O man, to thee, to all.

*James Beattie* [1735–1803]

## LYCIDAS

### A LAMENT FOR A FRIEND DROWNED IN HIS PASSAGE FROM CHESTER ON THE IRISH SEAS, 1637

YET once more, O ye Laurels, and once more
Ye Myrtles brown, with Ivy never sere,
I come to pluck your Berries harsh and crude,
And with forced fingers rude,
Shatter your leaves before the mellowing year.
Bitter constraint, and sad occasion dear,
Compels me to disturb your season due:
For Lycidas is dead, dead ere his prime,
Young Lycidas, and hath not left his peer:
Who would not sing for Lycidas? he knew
Himself to sing, and build the lofty rhyme.
He must not float upon his watery bier
Unwept, and welter to the parching wind,
Without the meed of some melodious tear.
  Begin, then, Sisters of the sacred well,
That from beneath the seat of Jove doth spring;
Begin, and somewhat loudly sweep the string.
Hence with denial vain, and coy excuse,
So may some gentle Muse
With lucky words favor *my* destined Urn,
And as he passes turn,
And bid fair peace be to my sable shroud.
For we were nursed upon the self-same hill,
Fed the same flock, by fountain, shade, and rill;
Together both, ere the high Lawns appeared
Under the opening eye-lids of the Morn,
We drove a-field, and both together heard
What time the Gray-fly winds her sultry horn,
Battening our flocks with the fresh dews of night,
Oft till the Star that rose, at Evening, bright
Toward Heaven's descent had sloped his westering wheel.
Meanwhile the Rural ditties were not mute,
Tempered to the Oaten Flute;
Rough Satyrs danced, and Fauns with cloven heel,

From the glad sound would not be absent long,
And old Damætas loved to hear our song.
  But O the heavy change, now thou art gone,
Now thou art gone, and never must return!
Thee, Shepherd, thee the Woods, and desert Caves,
With wild Thyme and the gadding Vine o'ergrown,
And all their echoes mourn.
The Willows, and the Hazel Copses green,
Shall now no more be seen,
Fanning their joyous Leaves to thy soft lays.
As killing as the Canker to the Rose,
Or Taint-worm to the weanling Herds that graze,
Or Frost to Flowers, that their gay wardrobe wear,
When first the White-thorn blows;
Such, Lycidas, thy loss to Shepherd's ear.
  Where were ye, Nymphs, when the remorseless deep
Closed o'er the head of your loved Lycidas?
For neither were ye playing on the steep,
Where your old Bards, the famous Druids, lie,
Nor on the shaggy top of Mona high,
Nor yet where Deva spreads her wizard stream:
Aye me, I fondly dream!
Had ye been there—for what could that have done?
What could the Muse herself that Orpheus bore,
The Muse herself, for her enchanting son
Whom Universal nature did lament,
When, by the rout that made the hideous roar,
His gory visage down the stream was sent,
Down the swift Hebrus to the Lesbian shore?
  Alas! What boots it with uncessant care
To tend the homely slighted Shepherd's trade,
And strictly meditate the thankless Muse,
Were it not better done, as others use,
To sport with Amaryllis in the shade,
Or with the tangles of Neæra's hair?
Fame is the spur that the clear spirit doth raise
(That last infirmity of Noble mind)
To scorn delights, and live laborious days;
But the fair Guerdon when we hope to find,
And think to burst out into sudden blaze,

Comes the blind Fury with the abhorrèd shears,
And slits the thin-spun life. "But not the praise,"
Phœbus replied, and touched my trembling ears;
"Fame is no plant that grows on mortal soil,
Nor in the glistering foil
Set off to the world, nor in broad rumor lies,
But lives and spreads aloft by those pure eyes,
And perfect witness of all-judging Jove;
As he pronounces lastly on each deed,
Of so much fame in Heaven expect thy meed."
O fountain Arethuse, and thou honored flood,
Smooth-sliding Mincius, crowned with vocal reeds,
That strain I heard was of a higher mood:
But now my Oat proceeds,
And listens to the Herald of the Sea
That came in Neptune's plea.
He asked the Waves, and asked the Felon winds,
What hard mishap hath doomed this gentle swain?
And questioned every gust of rugged wings
That blows from off each beakèd Promontory.
They knew not of his story,
And sage Hippotades their answer brings,
That not a blast was from his dungeon strayed,
The Air was calm, and on the level brine,
Sleek Panope with all her sisters played.
It was that fatal and perfidious Bark
Built in the eclipse, and rigged with curses dark,
That sunk so low that sacred head of thine.
Next Camus, reverend Sire, went footing slow,
His Mantle hairy, and his Bonnet sedge,
Inwrought with figures dim, and on the edge
Like to that sanguine flower inscribed with woe.
"Ah, who hath reft," (quoth he) "my dearest pledge?
Last come, and last did go,
The Pilot of the Galilean Lake.
Two massy Keys he bore of metals twain,
(The Golden opes, the Iron shuts amain).
He shook his Mitered locks, and stern bespake,
"How well could I have spared for thee, young swain,
Enow of such as, for their bellies' sake,

Creep and intrude, and climb into the fold!
Of other care they little reckoning make,
Than how to scramble at the shearers' feast,
And shove away the worthy bidden guest.
Blind mouths! that scarce themselves know how to hold
A Sheep-hook, or have learned aught else the least
That to the faithful Herdman's art belongs!
What recks it them? What need they? They are sped;
And when they list, their lean and flashy songs
Grate on their scrannel Pipes of wretched straw,
The hungry Sheep look up, and are not fed,
But swoln with wind, and the rank mist they draw,
Rot inwardly, and foul contagion spread:
Besides what the grim Wolf with privy paw
Daily devours apace, and nothing said.
But that two-handed engine at the door,
Stands ready to smite once, and smite no more."
 Return Alpheus, the dread voice is past,
That shrunk thy streams; return Sicilian Muse,
And call the Vales, and bid them hither cast
Their Bells, and Flowerets of a thousand hues.
Ye valleys low, where the mild whispers use,
Of shades and wanton winds, and gushing brooks,
On whose fresh lap the swart Star sparely looks,
Throw hither all your quaint enameled eyes,
That on the green turf suck the honied showers,
And purple all the ground with vernal flowers.
Bring the rathe Primrose that forsaken dies,
The tufted Crow-toe, and pale Jessamine,
The white Pink, and the Pansy freaked with jet,
The glowing Violet,
The Musk-rose, and the well-attired Woodbine,
With Cowslips wan that hang the pensive head,
And every flower that sad embroidery wears:
Bid Amaranthus all his beauty shed,
And Daffadillies fill their cups with tears,
To strew the Laureate Hearse where Lycid lies.
For so to interpose a little ease,
Let our frail thoughts dally with false surmise.
Ay me! Whilst thee the shores, and sounding Seas

Wash far away, where e'er thy bones are hurled,
Whether beyond the stormy Hebrides,
Where thou perhaps under the whelming tide
Visit'st the bottom of the monstrous world;
Or whether thou, to our moist vows denied,
Sleep'st by the fable of Bellerus old,
Where the great vision of the guarded Mount
Looks toward Namancos and Bayona's hold;
Look homeward, Angel, now, and melt with ruth:
And, O ye Dolphins, waft the hapless youth.
Weep no more, woful Shepherds, weep no more,
For Lycidas your sorrow is not dead,
Sunk though he be beneath the watery floor.
So sinks the day-star in the Ocean bed,
And yet anon repairs his drooping head,
And tricks his beams, and with new-spangled Ore,
Flames in the forehead of the morning sky:
So Lycidas sunk low, but mounted high,
Through the dear might of Him that walked the waves
Where, other groves and other streams along,
With Nectar pure his oozy Locks he laves,
And hears the unexpressive nuptial Song,
In the blest Kingdoms meek of joy and love.
There entertain him all the Saints above,
In solemn troops, and sweet Societies,
That sing, and singing in their glory move,
And wipe the tears for ever from his eyes.
Now, Lycidas, the Shepherds weep no more;
Henceforth thou art the Genius of the shore,
In thy large recompense, and shalt be good
To all that wander in that perilous flood.
Thus sang the uncouth Swain to the Oaks and rills,
While the still morn went out with Sandals gray,
He touched the tender stops of various Quills,
With eager thought warbling his Doric lay:
And now the Sun had stretched out all the hills,
And now was dropt into the Western bay;
At last he rose, and twitched his Mantle blue:
To-morrow to fresh Woods, and Pastures new.

*John Milton* [1608–1674]

## TO THE PIOUS MEMORY OF THE ACCOMPLISHED YOUNG LADY, MRS. ANNE KILLIGREW, EXCELLENT IN THE TWO SISTER-ARTS OF POESIE AND PAINTING

I

THOU youngest Virgin-Daughter of the skies,
Made in the last promotion of the blest;
Whose palms, new plucked from Paradise,
In spreading branches more sublimely rise,
Rich with immortal green above the rest:
Whether, adopted to some neighboring star,
Thou roll'st above us in thy wandering race,
Or, in procession fixed and regular,
Moved with the heavens' majestic pace;
Or, called to more superior bliss,
Thou tread'st, with seraphims, the vast abyss:
Whatever happy region is thy place,
Cease thy celestial song a little space;
(Thou wilt have time enough for hymns divine,
Since Heaven's eternal year is thine.)
Hear then a mortal muse thy praise rehearse
In no ignoble verse;
But such as thy own voice did practice here,
When thy first fruits of poesie were given,
To make thyself a welcome inmate there;
While yet a young probationer,
And candidate of Heaven.

II

If by traduction came thy mind,
Our wonder is the less to find
A soul so charming from a stock so good;
Thy father was transfused into thy blood:
So wert thou born into the tuneful strain,
(An early, rich, and inexhausted vein.)
But if thy pre-existing soul
Was formed, at first, with myriads more,
It did through all the mighty poets roll

Who Greek or Latin laurels wore,
And was that Sappho last, which once it was before.
If so, then cease thy flight, O Heaven-born mind!
Thou hast no dross to purge from thy rich ore:
Nor can thy soul a fairer mansion find
Than was the beauteous frame she left behind:
Return, to fill or mend the choir of thy celestial kind.

May we presume to say, that at thy birth
New joy was sprung in Heaven as well as here on earth?
For sure the milder planets did combine
On thy auspicious horoscope to shine,
And even the most malicious were in trine.
Thy brother-angels at thy birth
Strung each his lyre, and tuned it high,
That all the people of the sky
Might know a poetess was born on earth.
And then if ever, mortal ears
Had heard the music of the spheres!
And if no clustering swarm of bees
On thy sweet mouth distilled their golden dew,
'Twas that, such vulgar miracles
Heaven had not leisure to renew:
For all the blest fraternity of love
Solemnized there thy birth, and kept thy holyday above

IV

O gracious God! How far have we
Profaned thy Heavenly gift of poesy!
Made prostitute and profligate the muse,
Debased to each obscene and impious use,
Whose harmony was first ordained above,
For tongues of angels and for hymns of love!
Oh wretched we! why were we hurried down
This lubrique and adulterate age,
(Nay, added fat pollutions of our own)
To increase the steaming ordures of the stage?
What can we say to excuse our second fall?
Let this thy vestal, Heaven, atone for all:

Her Arethusian stream remains unsoiled,
Unmixed with foreign filth and undefiled,
Her wit was more than man, her innocence a child.

V

Art she had none, yet wanted none,
For nature did that want supply:
So rich in treasures of her own,
She might our boasted stores defy:
Such noble vigor did her verse adorn,
That it seemed borrowed, where 'twas only born.
Her morals too were in her bosom bred
By great examples daily fed,
What in the best of books, her father's life, she read.
And to be read her self she need not fear;
Each test, and every light, her muse will bear,
Though Epictetus with his lamp were there.
Even love (for love sometimes her muse expressed),
Was but a lambent-flame which played about her breast:
Light as the vapors of a morning dream,
So cold herself, whilst she such warmth expressed,
'Twas Cupid bathing in Diana's stream.

VI

Born to the spacious empire of the Nine,
One would have thought, she should have been content
To manage well that mighty government;
But what can young ambitious souls confine?
To the next realm she stretched her sway,
For painting near adjoining lay,
A plenteous province, and alluring prey.
A chamber of dependences was framed,
(As conquerors will never want pretence,
When armed, to justify the offence),
And the whole fief, in right of poetry she claimed.
The country open lay without defence;
For poets frequent inroads there had made,
And perfectly could represent
The shape, the face, with every lineament;

And all the large domains which the dumb-sister swayed;
All bowed beneath her government,
Received in triumph wheresoe'er she went.
Her pencil drew whate'er her soul designed
And oft the happy draught surpassed the image in her mind.
The sylvan scenes of herds and flocks
And fruitful plains and barren rocks,
Of shallow brooks that flowed so clear,
The bottom did the top appear;
Of deeper too and ampler floods
Which as in mirrors, showed the woods;
Of lofty trees, with sacred shades
And perspectives of pleasant glades,
Where nymphs of brightest form appear,
And shaggy satyrs standing near,
Which them at once admire and fear.
The ruins too of some majestic piece,
Boasting the power of ancient Rome or Greece,
Whose statues, friezes, columns, broken lie,
And, though defaced, the wonder of the eye;
What nature, art, bold fiction, e'er durst frame,
Her forming hand gave feature to the name.
So strange a concourse ne'er was seen before,
But when the peopled ark the whole creation bore.

VII

The scene then changed; with bold erected look
Our martial King the sight with reverence strook:
For, not content to express his outward part,
Her hand called out the image of his heart,
His warlike mind, his soul devoid of fear,
His high-designing thoughts were figured there,
As when, by magic, ghosts are made appear.
Our phœnix Queen was portrayed too so bright,
Beauty alone could beauty take so right:
Her dress, her shape, her matchless grace,
Were all observed, as well as heavenly face.
With such a peerless majesty she stands,
As in that day she took the crown from sacred hands.

Before a train of heroines was seen,
In beauty foremost, as in rank, the Queen!
  Thus nothing to her genius was denied,
But like a ball of fire, the farther thrown,
Still with a greater blaze she shone,
  And her bright soul broke out on every side.
What next she had designed, Heaven only knows:
To such immoderate growth her conquest rose
That Fate alone its progress could oppose.

VIII

Now all those charms, that blooming grace,
The well-proportioned shape and beauteous face,
Shall never more be seen by mortal eyes;
In earth the much-lamented virgin lies!
  Not wit nor piety could Fate prevent;
  Nor was the cruel destiny content
  To finish all the murder at a blow,
  To sweep at once her life and beauty too;
But, like a hardened felon, took a pride
  To work more mischievously slow,
And plundered first, and then destroyed.
O double sacrilege on things divine,
To rob the relique, and deface the shrine!
  But thus Orinda died:
Heaven, by the same disease, did both translate,
As equal were their souls, so equal was their fate.

IX

Mean time, her warlike brother on the seas
His waving streamers to the winds displays,
And vows for his return, with vain devotion, pays.
Ah, generous youth! that wish forbear,
  The winds too soon will waft thee here!
  Slack all thy sails, and fear to come,
Alas, thou know'st not, thou art wrecked at home!
No more shalt thou behold thy sister's face,
Thou hast already had her last embrace.
But look aloft, and if thou ken'st from far,

Among the Pleiades, a new-kindled star,
If any sparkles, than the rest, more bright,
'Tis she that shines in that propitious light.

X

When in mid-air the golden trump shall sound,
  To raise the nations under ground;
  When in the valley of Jehosaphat
The judging God shall close the book of Fate;
  And there the last assizes keep
  For those who wake and those who sleep;
  When rattling bones together fly
  From the four corners of the sky,
When sinews o'er the skeletons are spread,
Those clothed with flesh, and life inspires the dead;
The sacred poets first shall hear the sound,
And foremost from the tomb shall bound:
For they are covered with the lightest ground;
And straight, with in-born vigor, on the wing,
Like mounting larks to the New Morning sing.
There thou, sweet Saint, before the choir shalt go,
As harbinger of Heaven, the way to show,
The way which thou so well hast learned below.

*John Dryden* [1631–1700]

## HERACLITUS

They told me, Heraclitus, they told me you were dead,
They brought me bitter news to hear and bitter tears to shed
I wept as I remembered how often you and I
Had tired the sun with talking and sent him down the sky.

And now that thou art lying, my dear old Carian guest
A handful of gray ashes, long, long ago at rest,
Still are thy pleasant voices, thy nightingales, awake;
For Death, he taketh all away, but them he cannot take.

*After Callimachus by William Johnson-Cory* [1823–1892]

## ELEGY

### TO THE MEMORY OF AN UNFORTUNATE LADY

WHAT beckoning ghost along the moonlight shade
Invites my steps, and points to yonder glade?
'Tis she!—but why that bleeding bosom gored?
Why dimly gleams the visionary sword?
O ever beauteous, ever friendly! tell,
Is it in heaven a crime to love too well,
To bear too tender or too firm a heart,
To act a lover's or a Roman's part?
Is there no bright reversion in the sky,
For those who greatly think or bravely die?
  Why bade ye else, ye Powers! her soul aspire
Above the vulgar flight of low desire?
Ambition first sprung from your blest abodes,
The glorious fault of angels and of gods;
Thence to their images on earth it flows,
And in the breasts of kings and heroes glows.
Most souls, 'tis true, but peep out once an age,
Dull sullen prisoners in the body's cage:
Dim lights of life, that burn a length of years,
Useless, unseen, as lamps in sepulchres;
Like Eastern kings a lazy state they keep,
And, close confined to their own palace, sleep.
  From these perhaps (ere Nature bade her die),
Fate snatched her early to the pitying sky.
As into air the purer spirits flow,
And separate from their kindred dregs below,
So flew the soul to its congenial place,
Nor left one virtue to redeem her race.
  But thou, false guardian of a charge too good!
Thou, mean deserter of thy brother's blood!
See on these ruby lips the trembling breath,
These cheeks now fading at the blast of Death.
Cold is that breast which warmed the world before,
And those love-darting eyes must roll no more.
Thus, if eternal Justice rules the ball,
Thus shall your wives, and thus your children fall;

On all the line a sudden vengeance waits,
And frequent hearses shall besiege your gates.
There passengers shall stand, and pointing say
(While the long funerals blacken all the way),
"Lo! these were they whose souls the Furies steeled,
And cursed with hearts unknowing how to yield."
Thus unlamented pass the proud away,
The gaze of fools, and pageant of a day!
So perish all whose breast ne'er learned to glow
For others' good, or melt at others' woe!
What can atone (O ever-injured shade!)
Thy fate unpitied, and thy rites unpaid?
No friend's complaint, no kind domestic tear
Pleased thy pale ghost, or graced thy mournful bier.
By foreign hands thy dying eyes were closed,
By foreign hands thy decent limbs composed,
By foreign hands thy humble grave adorned,
By strangers honored, and by strangers mourned!
What though no friends in sable weeds appear,
Grieve for an hour, perhaps, then mourn a year,
And bear about the mockery of woe
To midnight dances, and the public show?
What though no weeping Loves thy ashes grace,
Nor polished marble emulate thy face?
What though no sacred earth allow thee room,
Nor hallowed dirge be muttered o'er thy tomb?
Yet shall thy grave with rising flowers be dressed,
And the green turf lie lightly on thy breast:
There shall the morn her earliest tears bestow,
There the first roses of the year shall blow;
While angels with their silver wings o'ershade
The ground now sacred by thy reliques made.
So peaceful rests, without a stone, a name,
What once had beauty, titles, wealth, and fame.
How loved, how honored once, avails thee not,
To whom related, or by whom begot;
A heap of dust alone remains of thee,
'Tis all thou art, and all the proud shall be!
Poets themselves must fall, like those they sung,
Deaf the praised ear, and mute the tuneful tongue.

Even he whose soul now melts in mournful lays
Shall shortly want the generous tear he pays;
Then from his closing eyes thy form shall part,
And the last pang shall tear thee from his heart:
Life's idle business at one gasp be o'er,
The Muse forgot, and thou beloved no more!

*Alexander Pope* [1688–1744]

## ELEGY WRITTEN IN A COUNTRY CHURCHYARD

THE curfew tolls the knell of parting day,
  The lowing herd winds slowly o'er the lea,
The plowman homeward plods his weary way,
  And leaves the world to darkness and to me.

Now fades the glimmering landscape on the sight,
  And all the air a solemn stillness holds,
Save where the beetle wheels his droning flight,
  And drowsy tinklings lull the distant folds:

Save that from yonder ivy-mantled tower
  The moping owl does to the moon complain
Of such as, wandering near her secret bower,
  Molest her ancient solitary reign.

Beneath those rugged elms, that yew-tree's shade,
  Where heaves the turf in many a moldering heap,
Each in his narrow cell for ever laid,
  The rude forefathers of the hamlet sleep.

The breezy call of incense-breathing morn,
  The swallow twittering from the straw-built shed,
The cock's shrill clarion, or the echoing horn,
  No more shall rouse them from their lowly bed.

For them no more the blazing hearth shall burn,
  Or busy housewife ply her evening care:
No children run to lisp their sire's return,
  Or climb his knees the envied kiss to share.

Oft did the harvest to their sickle yield,
  Their furrow oft the stubborn glebe has broke:
How jocund did they drive their team afield!
  How bowed the woods beneath their sturdy stroke!

Let not Ambition mock their useful toil,
  Their homely joys, and destiny obscure;
Nor Grandeur hear with a disdainful smile
  The short and simple annals of the poor.

The boast of heraldry, the pomp of power,
  And all that beauty, all that wealth e'er gave,
Awaits alike the inevitable hour:
  The paths of glory lead but to the grave.

Nor you, ye proud, impute to these the fault
  If Memory o'er their tomb no trophies raise,
Where through the long-drawn aisle and fretted vault
  The pealing anthem swells the note of praise.

Can storied urn or animated bust
  Back to its mansion call the fleeting breath?
Can Honor's voice provoke the silent dust,
  Or Flattery soothe the dull cold ear of death?

Perhaps in this neglected spot is laid
  Some heart once pregnant with celestial fire;
Hands, that the rod of empire might have swayed
  Or waked to ecstasy the living lyre.

But Knowledge to their eyes her ample page
  Rich with the spoils of time did ne'er unroll;
Chill Penury repressed their noble rage,
  And froze the genial current of the soul.

Full many a gem of purest ray serene
  The dark unfathomed caves of ocean bear:
Full many a flower is born to blush unseen,
  And waste its sweetness on the desert air.

Some village Hampden that, with dauntless breast,
The little tyrant of his fields withstood,
Some mute inglorious Milton here may rest,
Some Cromwell guiltless of his country's blood.

The applause of listening senates to command,
The threats of pain and ruin to despise,
To scatter plenty o'er a smiling land,
And read their history in a nation's eyes,

Their lot forbade: nor circumscribed alone
Their growing virtues, but their crimes confined;
Forbade to wade through slaughter to a throne,
And shut the gates of mercy on mankind;

The struggling pangs of conscious truth to hide,
To quench the blushes of ingenuous shame,
Or heap the shrine of Luxury and Pride
With incense kindled at the Muse's flame.

Far from the madding crowd's ignoble strife,
Their sober wishes never learned to stray;
Along the cool, sequestered vale of life
They kept the noiseless tenor of their way.

Yet even these bones from insult to protect
Some frail memorial still erected nigh,
With uncouth rhymes and shapeless sculpture decked,
Implores the passing tribute of a sigh.

Their name, their years, spelt by the unlettered Muse,
The place of fame and elegy supply:
And many a holy text around she strews,
That teach the rustic moralist to die.

For who, to dumb Forgetfulness a prey,
This pleasing anxious being e'er resigned,
Left the warm precincts of the cheerful day,
Nor cast one longing lingering look behind?

On some fond breast the parting soul relies,
  Some pious drops the closing eye requires;
E'en from the tomb the voice of Nature cries,
  E'en in our ashes live their wonted fires.

For thee, who, mindful of the unhonored dead,
  Dost in these lines their artless tale relate;
If chance, by lonely contemplation led,
  Some kindred spirit shall inquire thy fate,—

Haply some hoary-headed swain may say,
  "Oft have we seen him at the peep of dawn
Brushing with hasty steps the dews away
  To meet the sun upon the upland lawn.

"There at the foot of yonder nodding beech
  That wreathes its old fantastic roots so high,
His listless length at noontide would he stretch,
  And pore upon the brook that babbles by.

"Hard by yon wood, now smiling as in scorn,
  Muttering his wayward fancies he would rove,
Now drooping, woeful-wan, like one forlorn,
  Or crazed with care, or crossed in hopeless love.

"One morn I missed him on the 'customed hill,
  Along the heath, and near his favorite tree;
Another came; nor yet beside the rill,
  Nor up the lawn, nor at the wood was he:

"The next, with dirges due in sad array,
  Slow through the church-way path we saw him borne
Approach and read (for thou canst read) the lay
  Graved on the stone beneath yon aged thorn:"

THE EPITAPH

*Here rests his head upon the lap of Earth*
  *A Youth, to Fortune and to Fame unknown.*
*Fair Science frowned not on his humble birth,*
  *And Melancholy marked him for her own.*

*Large was his bounty, and his soul sincere,*
*Heaven did a recompense as largely send:*
*He gave to Misery (all he had) a tear,*
*He gained from Heaven ('twas all he wished) a friend.*

*No farther seek his merits to disclose,*
*Or draw his frailties from their dread abode,*
*(There they alike in trembling hope repose,)*
*The bosom of his Father and his God.*

*Thomas Gray* [1716–1771]

## THE SETTLERS

How green the earth, how blue the sky,
How pleasant all the days that pass,
Here where the British settlers lie
Beneath their cloaks of grass!

Here ancient peace resumes her round,
And rich from toil stand hill and plain;
Men reap and store; but they sleep sound,
The men who sowed the grain.

Hard to the plough their hands they put,
And wheresoe'er the soil had need
The furrow drave, and underfoot
They sowed themselves for seed.

Ah! not like him whose hand made yield
The brazen kine with fiery breath,
And over all the Colchian field
Strewed far the seeds of death;

Till, as day sank, awoke to war
The seedlings of the dragon's teeth,
And death ran multiplied once more
Across the hideous heath.

But rich in flocks be all these farms,
And fruitful be the fields which hide
Brave eyes that loved the light, and arms
That never clasped a bride!

O willing hearts turned quick to clay,
Glad lovers holding death in scorn,
Out of the lives ye cast away
The coming race is born.

*Laurence Housman* [1867–1959]

## "HE BRINGETH THEM UNTO THEIR DESIRED HAVEN"

I KNEW a much-loved mariner,
Who lies a fathom underground;
Above him now the grasses stir,
Two rose-trees set a bound.

From a high hill his grave looks out
Through sighing larches to the sea;
Now for the ocean's raucous rout
All June the humblebee

Drones round him on the lonely steeps,
And shy wood-creatures come and go
Above the green mound where he keeps
His silent watch below.

An elemental man was he—
Loved God, his wife, his children dear,
And fared through dangers of the sea
Without a sense of fear.

And, loving nature, he was wise
In all the moods of wave and cloud;
Before the pageant of the skies
Nightly his spirit bowed;

Yet reckoned shrewdly with the gale,
And felt the viking's fierce delight
To face the north wind's icy hail,
Unmoved to thought of flight.

But wheresoe'er his prow was turned,
His thoughts, like homing pigeons, came
Back where his casement candle burned
Through many a league its flame.

Exiled from all he loved, at last
  The summer gale has brought him home,
Where on the hillsides thickly massed
  The elders break in foam.

The lonely highways that he knew
  No longer hold him, nor the gale,
Sweeping the desolated blue,
  Roars in his slanting sail.

For he has grown a part of all
  The winter silence of the hills;
For him the stately twilights fall,
  The hemlock softly shrills

In mimicry of gales that woke
  His vigilance off many a shore
Whereon the vibrant billows broke.
  Now he awakes no more.

He wakes no more! Ah, me! his grief
  Was ever that the sea had power
To hold from him the budding leaf,
  The opening of the flower.

And so he hungered for the spring—
  The hissing, furrow-turning plow,
The first thin notes the bluebirds sing,
  The reddening of the bough.

Wave-deafened, many a night he stood
  Upon his watery deck, and dreamed
Of thrushes singing in the wood,
  And murmurous brooks that streamed

Through silver shallows, and of bees
  Lulling the summer afternoon
With mellow trumpetings of ease,
  Of drowsiness the boon.

And dreamed of growing old at home,
  The wise Ulysses of his crew

Of children's children, who would roam
  With him the lands he knew;

And, wide-eyed, face with him the gale,
  And hear the slanting billows roar
Their diapason round his rail—
  All safe beside his door.

Now he has come into his own,—
  Sunshine and bird-song round the spot,
And scents from spicy woodlands blown,—
  Yet haply knows it not.

But round the grave where he doth keep,
  Unsolaced by regret or woe,
His narrowed heritage in sleep,
  The little children go.

They shyly go without a sound,
  And read in reverent awe his name,
Until for them the very ground
  Doth blossom with his fame.

*L. Frank Tooker* [1855-1925]

## IN THE LILAC-RAIN

All in the lilac-rain,
  Tender and sweet,
Brushing the window-pane
  Sudden—and fleet!
Came the dear wraith of her
  Out of lost Mays—
(Ah, but the faith of her,
  True to old ways!)

Scarcely her face I knew
  Dim in the wet;
Only her eyes of blue
  Who could forget!
Hands full of lilacs too—
  Lilac crowned, yet!

These were the flowers she loved
  In the far years;
These were the showers she loved—
  Light as her tears!
These were the hours she loved—
  Hope chasing fears!

Veiled in the lilac-rain
  Comes she—and goes. . . .
Sun through the clouds again,
  Fresh the wind blows.
Mine, a swift pleasure-pain
  None other knows.

*Edith M. Thomas* [1854–1925]

## A DEAD MARCH

PLAY me a march, low-toned and slow—a march for a silent tread,
Fit for the wandering feet of one who dreams of the silent dead,
Lonely, between the bones below and the souls that are overhead.

Here for a while they smiled and sang, alive in the interspace,
Here with the grass beneath the foot, and the stars above the face,
Now are their feet beneath the grass, and whither has flown their grace?

Who shall assure us whence they come, or tell us the way they go?
Verily, life with them was joy, and, now they have left us, woe.
Once they were not, and now they are not, and this is the sum we know.

Orderly range the seasons due, and orderly roll the stars.
How shall we deem the soldier brave who frets of his wounds and scars?
Are we as senseless brutes that we should dash at the well-seen bars?

No, we are here, with feet unfixed, but ever as if with lead,
Drawn from the orbs which shine above to the orb on which
we tread,
Down to the dust from which we came and with which we
shall mingle dead.

No, we are here to wait, and work, and strain our banished
eyes,
Weary and sick of soil and toil, and hungry and fain for
skies,
Far from the reach of wingless men, and not to be scaled
with cries.

No, we are here to bend our necks to the yoke of tyrant
Time,
Welcoming all the gifts he gives us—glories of youth and
prime,
Patiently watching them all depart as our heads grow white
as rime.

Why do we mourn the days that go—for the same sun shines
each day,
Ever a spring her primrose hath, and ever a May her may;
Sweet as the rose that died last year is the rose that is born
to-day.

Do we not too return, we men, as ever the round earth
whirls?
Never a head is dimmed with gray but another is sunned with
curls;
She was a girl and he was a boy, but yet there are boys and
girls.

Ah, but alas for the smile of smiles that never but one face
wore;
Ah, for the voice that has flown away like a bird to an unseen shore;
Ah, for the face—the flower of flowers—that blossoms on
earth no more.

*Cosmo Monkhouse* [1840–1901]

## TOMMY'S DEAD

You may give over plow, boys,
You may take the gear to the stead,
All the sweat o' your brow, boys,
Will never get beer and bread.
The seed's waste, I know, boys,
There's not a blade will grow, boys,
'Tis cropped out, I trow, boys,
And Tommy's dead.

Send the colt to fair, boys,
He's going blind, as I said,
My old eyes can't bear, boys,
To see him in the shed;
The cow's dry and spare, boys,
She's neither here nor there, boys,
I doubt she's badly bred;
Stop the mill to-morn, boys,
There'll be no more corn, boys,
Neither white nor red;
There's no sign of grass, boys,
You may sell the goat and the ass, boys,
The land's not what it was, boys,
And the beasts must be fed:
You may turn Peg away, boys,
You may pay off old Ned,
We've had a dull day, boys,
And Tommy's dead.

Move my chair on the floor, boys,
Let me turn my head:
She's standing there in the door, boys
Your sister Winifred!
Take her away from me, boys,
Your sister Winifred!
Move me round in my place, boys,
Let me turn my head,

Take her away from me, boys,
As she lay on her death-bed,
The bones of her thin face, boys,
As she lay on her death-bed!
I don't know how it be, boys,
When all's done and said,
But I see her looking at me, boys,
Wherever I turn my head;
Out of the big oak-tree, boys,
Out of the garden-bed,
And the lily as pale as she, boys,
And the rose that used to be red.

There's something not right, boys,
But I think it's not in my head,
I've kept my precious sight, boys—
The Lord be hallowèd!
Outside and in
The ground is cold to my tread,
The hills are wizen and thin,
The sky is shriveled and shred,
The hedges down by the loan
I can count them bone by bone,
The leaves are open and spread,
But I see the teeth of the land,
And hands like a dead man's hand,
And the eyes of a dead man's head.
There's nothing but cinders and sand,
The rat and the mouse have fed,
And the summer's empty and cold;
Over valley and wold
Wherever I turn my head
There's a mildew and a mold,
The sun's going out overhead,
And I'm very old,
And Tommy's dead.

What am I staying for, boys?
You're all born and bred,
'Tis fifty years and more, boys,
Since wife and I were wed,

And she's gone before, boys,
And Tommy's dead.

She was always sweet, boys,
Upon his curly head,
She knew she'd never see't, boys,
And she stole off to bed;
I've been sitting up alone, boys,
For he'd come home, he said,
But it's time I was gone, boys,
For Tommy's dead.

Put the shutters up, boys,
Bring out the beer and bread,
Make haste and sup, boys,
For my eyes are heavy as lead;
There's something wrong i' the cup, boys,
There's something ill wi' the bread,
I don't care to sup, boys,
And Tommy's dead.

I'm not right, I doubt, boys,
I've such a sleepy head,
I shall never more be stout, boys,
You may carry me to bed.
What are you about, boys?
The prayers are all said,
The fire's raked out, boys,
And Tommy's dead.

The stairs are too steep, boys,
You may carry me to the head,
The night's dark and deep, boys,
Your mother's long in bed,
'Tis time to go to sleep, boys,
And Tommy's dead.

I'm not used to kiss, boys,
You may shake my hand instead.
All things go amiss, boys,
You may lay me where she is, boys,

And I'll rest my old head:
'Tis a poor world, this, boys,
And Tommy's dead.

*Sydney Dobell* [1824–1874]

## IN MEMORIAM

'Tis right for her to sleep between
Some of those old Cathedral walls,
And right too that her grave is green
With all the dew and rain that falls.

'Tis well the organ's solemn sighs
Should soar and sink around her rest,
And almost in her ear should rise
The prayers of those she loved the best.

'Tis also well this air is stirred
By Nature's voices loud and low,
By thunder and the chirping bird,
And grasses whispering as they grow.

For all her spirit's earthly course
Was as a lesson and a sign
How to o'errule the hard divorce
That parts things natural and divine.

Undaunted by the clouds of fear,
Undazzled by a happy day,
She made a Heaven about her here,
And took how much! with her away.

*Richard Monckton Milnes* [1809–1885]

## HER EPITAPH

The handful here, that once was Mary's earth,
Held, while it breathed, so beautiful a soul,
That, when she died, all recognized her birth,
And had their sorrow in serene control.

"Not here! not here!" to every mourner's heart
  The wintry wind seemed whispering round her bier;
And when the tomb-door opened, with a start
  We heard it echoed from within,—"Not here!"

Shouldst thou, sad pilgrim, who mayst hither pass,
  Note in these flowers a delicater hue,
Should spring come earlier to this hallowed grass,
  Or the bee later linger on the dew,—

Know that her spirit to her body lent
  Such sweetness, grace, as only goodness can;
That even her dust, and this her monument,
  Have yet a spell to stay one lonely man,—

Lonely through life, but looking for the day
  When what is mortal of himself shall sleep,
When human passion shall have passed away,
  And Love no longer be a thing to weep.

*Thomas William Parsons* [1819-1892]

## THE DEATH-BED

We watched her breathing through the night,
  Her breathing soft and low,
As in her breast the wave of life
  Kept heaving to and fro.

So silently we seemed to speak,
  So slowly moved about,
As we had lent her half our powers
  To eke her living out.

Our very hopes belied our fears,
  Our fears our hopes belied—
We thought her dying when she slept,
  And sleeping when she died.

For when the morn came dim and sad,
  And chill with early showers,
Her quiet eyelids closed—she had
  Another morn than ours.

*Thomas Hood* [1799-1845]

## HESTER

WHEN maidens such as Hester die,
Their place ye may not well supply,
Though ye among a thousand try,
With vain endeavor.
A month or more hath she been dead,
Yet cannot I by force be led
To think upon the wormy bed,
And her together.

A springy motion in her gait,
A rising step, did indicate
Of pride and joy no common rate,
That flushed her spirit:
I know not by what name beside
I shall it call;—if 'twas not pride,
It was a joy to that allied,
She did inherit.

Her parents held the Quaker rule,
Which doth the human feeling cool;
But she was trained in Nature's school,
Nature had blessed her.
A waking eye, a prying mind,
A heart that stirs, is hard to bind;
A hawk's keen sight ye cannot blind,—
Ye could not Hester.

My sprightly neighbor, gone before
To that unknown and silent shore,
Shall we not meet, as heretofore,
Some summer morning,
When from thy cheerful eyes a ray
Hath struck a bliss upon the day,—
A bliss that would not go away,—
A sweet forewarning?

*Charles Lamb* [1775–1834]

## "SOFTLY WOO AWAY HER BREATH"

Softly woo away her breath,
  Gentle Death!
Let her leave thee with no strife,
  Tender, mournful, murmuring Life!
She hath seen her happy day:—
  She hath had her bud and blossom:
Now she pales and shrinks away,
  Earth, into thy gentle bosom!

She hath done her bidding here,
  Angels dear!
Bear her perfect soul above,
  Seraph of the skies,—sweet Love!
Good she was, and fair in youth,
  And her mind was seen to soar,
And her heart was wed to truth:
  Take her, then, for evermore,—
    For ever—evermore.

*Bryan Waller Procter* [1787–1874]

## A DEATH-BED

Her suffering ended with the day,
  Yet lived she at its close,
And breathed the long, long night away
  In statue-like repose.

But when the sun in all his state
  Illumed the eastern skies,
She passed through Glory's morning gate
  And walked in Paradise.

*James Aldrich* [1810–1856]

## "SHE DIED IN BEAUTY"

She died in beauty,—like a rose
  Blown from its parent stem;
She died in beauty,—like a pearl
  Dropped from some diadem.

She died in beauty,—like a lay
  Along a moonlit lake;
She died in beauty,—like the song
  Of birds amid the brake.

She died in beauty,—like the snow
  On flowers dissolved away;
She died in beauty,—like a star
  Lost on the brow of day.

She lives in glory,—like night's gems
  Set round the silver moon;
She lives in glory,—like the sun
  Amid the blue of June.

*Charles Doyne Sillery* [1807–1837]

## THE WHITE JESSAMINE

I KNEW she lay above me,
  Where the casement all the night
Shone, softened with a phosphor glow
  Of sympathetic light,
And that her fledgling spirit pure
  Was pluming fast for flight.

Each tendril throbbed and quickened
  As I nightly climbed apace,
And could scarce restrain the blossoms
  When, anear the destined place,
Her gentle whisper thrilled me
  Ere I gazed upon her face.

I waited, darkling, till the dawn
  Should touch me into bloom,
While all my being panted
  To outpour its first perfume,
When, lo! a paler flower than mine
  Had blossomed in the gloom!

*John Banister Tabb* [1845–1909]

## EARLY DEATH

SHE passed away like morning dew
Before the sun was high;
So brief her time, she scarcely knew
The meaning of a sigh.

As round the rose its soft perfume,
Sweet love around her floated;
Admired she grew—while mortal doom
Crept on, unfeared, unnoted.

Love was her guardian Angel here,
But Love to Death resigned her;
Though Love was kind, why should we fear
But holy Death is kinder?

*Hartley Coleridge* [1796–1849]

## THE MOSS-ROSE

WALKING to-day in your garden, O gracious lady,
Little you thought, as you turned in that alley remote and shady
And gave me a rose, and asked if I knew its savor—
The old-world scent of the moss-rose, flower of a bygone favor—

Little you thought, as you waited the word of appraisement,
Laughing at first, and then amazed at my amazement,
That the rose you gave was a gift already cherished,
And the garden whence you plucked it a garden long perished.

But I—I saw that garden, with its one treasure
The tiny moss-rose, tiny even by childhood's measure.
And the long morning shadow of the rusty laurel,
And a boy and a girl beneath it, flushed with a childish quarrel.

She wept for her one little bud; but he, outreaching
The hand of brotherly right, would take it for all her beseeching;

And she flung her arms about him, and gave like a sister,
And laughed at her own tears, and wept again when he kissed her.

So the rose is mine since, and whenever I find it
And drink again the sharp sweet scent of the moss behind it,
I remember the tears of a child, and her love and her laughter,
And the morning shadows of youth, and the night that fell thereafter.

*Henry Newbolt* [1862–1938]

## A REQUIEM

Thou hast lived in pain and woe,
Thou hast lived in grief and fear;
Now thine heart can dread no blow,
Now thine eyes can shed no tear:
Storms round us shall beat and rave;
Thou art sheltered in the grave.

Thou for long, long years hast borne,
Bleeding through Life's wilderness,
Heavy loss and wounding scorn;
Now thine heart is burdenless:
Vainly rest for ours we crave;
Thine is quiet in the grave.

We must toil with pain and care,
We must front tremendous Fate,
We must fight with dark Despair:
Thou dost dwell in solemn state,
Couched triumphant, calm and brave,
In the ever-holy grave.

*James Thomson* [1834–1882]

## DIRGE

Calm on the bosom of thy God,
Fair spirit, rest thee now!
E'en while with ours thy footsteps trod,
His seal was on thy brow.

Dust, to its narrow house beneath!
  Soul, to its place on high!
They that have seen thy look in death
  No more may fear to die.

Lone are the paths, and sad the bowers,
  Whence thy meek smile is gone;
But oh! a brighter home than ours
  In heaven, is now thine own.

*Felicia Dorothea Hemans* [1793–1835]

## THE LAMP OF POOR SOULS

Above my head the shields are stained with rust,
The wind has taken his spoil, the moth his part;
Dust of dead men beneath my knees, and dust,
Lord, in my heart.

Lay Thou the hand of faith upon my fears;
The priest has prayed, the silver bell has rung,
But not for him. O unforgotten tears,
He was so young!

Shine, little lamp, nor let thy light grow dim.
Into what vast, dread dreams, what lonely lands,
Into what griefs hath death delivered him,
Far from my hands?

Cradled is he, with half his prayers forgot.
I cannot learn the level way he goes.
He whom the harvest hath remembered not
Sleeps with the rose.

Shine, little lamp, fed with sweet oil of prayers.
Shine, little lamp, as God's own eyes may shine,
When He treads softly down His starry stairs
And whispers, "Thou art Mine."

Shine, little lamp, for love hath fed thy gleam.
Sleep, little soul, by God's own hands set free.
Cling to His arms and sleep, and sleeping, dream,
And dreaming, look for me.

*Marjorie L. C. Pickthall* [1883–1922]

## SENTENCE

SHALL I say that what heaven gave
  Earth has taken?—
Or that sleepers in the grave
  Reawaken?

One sole sentence can I know,
  Can I say:
You, my comrade, had to go,
  I to stay.

*Witter Bynner* [1881-

## RESURRECTION

I HOPE there is a resurrection day
For bodies, as the ancient prophets say,
When Helen's naked limbs again will gleam
Regathered from the dust of death's long dream,—
When those who thrilled the ages, being fair,
Will take the singing angels unaware
And make God's perfect meadows doubly sweet
With rosy vagrancy of little feet.

*Harry Kemp* [1883–1960]

## THE SLEEPER

ABOVE the cloistral valley,
  Above the druid rill,
There lies a quiet sleeper
  Upon a lonely hill.

All the long days of summer
  The low winds whisper by,
And the soft voices of the leaves
  Make murmurous reply.

All the long eves of autumn
  The loving shadows mass
Round this sequestered slumbering-place
  Beneath the cool hill grass.

All the long nights of winter
The white drifts heap and heap
To form a fleecy coverlet
Above the dreamer's sleep.

All the long morns of springtime
The tear-drops of the dew
Gleam in the violets' tender eyes
As if the blossoms knew.

Ah, who would break the rapture
Brooding and sweet and still,
The great peace of the sleeper
Upon the lonely hill!

*Clinton Scollard* [1860–1932]

## THE WIDOW'S MITE

A WIDOW—she had only one!
A puny and decrepit son;
But, day and night,
Though fretful oft, and weak and small,
A loving child, he was her all—
The Widow's Mite.

The Widow's Mite! ay, so sustained,
She battled onward, nor complained,
Though friends were fewer:
And while she toiled for daily fare,
A little crutch upon the stair
Was music to her.

I saw her then,—and now I see
That, though resigned and cheerful, she
Has sorrowed much:
She has, He gave it tenderly,
Much faith; and, carefully laid by,
A little crutch.

*Frederick Locker-Lampson* [1821–1895]

## MOTHER AND POET

TURIN, AFTER NEWS FROM GAETA, 1861

DEAD! One of them shot by the sea in the east,
And one of them shot in the west by the sea.
Dead! both my boys! When you sit at the feast
And are wanting a great song for Italy free,
Let none look at *me!*

Yet I was a poetess only last year,
And good at my art, for a woman, men said;
But *this* woman, *this*, who is agonized here,
—The east sea and west sea rhyme on in her head
For ever instead.

What art can a woman be good at? Oh, vain!
What art *is* she good at, but hurting her breast
With the milk-teeth of babes, and a smile at the pain?
Ah boys, how you hurt! you were strong as you pressed,
And I proud, by that test.

What art's for a woman! To hold on her knees
Both darlings! to feel all their arms round her throat
Cling, strangle a little! to sew by degrees
And 'broider the long-clothes and neat little coat;
To dream and to dote.

To teach them. . . It stings there! *I* made them indeed
Speak plain the word "country." *I* taught them, no doubt,
That a country's a thing men should die for at need.
*I* prated of liberty, rights, and about
The tyrant cast out.

And when their eyes flashed . . . O my beautiful eyes! . . .
*I* exulted; nay, let them go forth at the wheels
Of the guns, and denied not. But then the surprise
When one sits quite alone! Then one weeps, then one kneels!
God! how the house feels!

At first, happy news came, in gay letters moiled
With my kisses,—of camp-life and glory, and how
They both loved me; and, soon coming home to be spoiled,
In return would fan off every fly from my brow
With their green laurel-bough.

Then was triumph at Turin: "Ancona was free!"
And some one came out of the cheers in the street,
With a face pale as stone, to say something to me.
My Guido was dead! I fell down at his feet,
While they cheered in the street.

I bore it; friends soothed me; my grief looked sublime
As the ransom of Italy. One boy remained
To be leant on and walked with, recalling the time
When the first grew immortal, while both of us strained
To the height he had gained.

And letters still came, shorter, sadder, more strong,
Writ now but in one hand, "I was not to faint,—
One loved me for two . . . would be with me erelong:
And *Viva l'Italia!—he* died for, our saint,
Who forbids our complaint."

My Nanni would add, "he was safe, and aware
Of a presence that turned off the balls . . . was impressed
It was Guido himself, who knew what I could bear,
And how 'twas impossible, quite dispossessed,
To live on for the rest."

On which, without pause, up the telegraph-line
Swept smoothly the next news from Gaeta:—*Shot.*
*Tell his mother.* Ah, ah, "his," "their" mother;—not "mine,"
No voice says "*My* mother" again to me. What!
You think Guido forgot?

Are souls straight so happy that, dizzy with Heaven,
They drop earth's affections, conceive not of woe?
I think not. Themselves were too lately forgiven
Through THAT Love and Sorrow which reconciled so
The Above and Below.

O Christ of the five wounds, who look'dst through the dark
To the face of thy mother! consider, I pray,
How we common mothers stand desolate, mark,
Whose sons, not being Christs, die with eyes turned away,
And no last word to say!

Both boys dead? but that's out of nature. We all
Have been patriots, yet each house must always keep one.
'Twere imbecile, hewing out roads to a wall;
And when Italy's made, for what end is it done
If we have not a son?

Ah, ah, ah! when Gaeta's taken, what then?
When the fair wicked queen sits no more at her sport
Of the fire-balls of death crashing souls out of men?
When the guns of Cavalli with final retort
Have cut the game short?

When Venice and Rome keep their new jubilee,
When your flag takes all heaven for its white, green and red,
When *you* have your country from mountain to sea,
When King Victor has Italy's crown on his head,
(And *I* have my Dead)—

What then? Do not mock me. Ah, ring your bells low,
And burn your lights faintly! *My* country is *there*,
Above the star pricked by the last peak of snow:
My Italy's THERE, with my brave civic Pair,
To disfranchise despair!

Forgive me. Some women bear children in strength,
And bite back the cry of their pain in self-scorn;
But the birth-pangs of nations will wring us at length
Into wail such as this—and we sit on forlorn
When the man-child is born.

Dead! One of them shot by the sea in the east,
And one of them shot in the west by the sea.
Both! both my boys! If in keeping the feast
You want a great song for your Italy free,
Let none look at *me!*

*Elizabeth Barrett Browning* [1806–1861]

## A MOTHER IN EGYPT

"About midnight will I go out into the midst of Egypt: and all the first-born in the land of Egypt shall die, from the first-born of Pharaoh that sitteth upon his throne, even unto the first-born of the maid-servant that is behind the mill."

Is the noise of grief in the palace over the river
For this silent one at my side?
There came a hush in the night, and he rose with his hands
 a-quiver
Like lotus petals adrift on the swing of the tide.
O small cold hands, the day groweth old for sleeping!
O small still feet, rise up, for the hour is late!
Rise up, my son, for I hear them mourning and weeping
In the temple down by the gate!

Hushed is the face that was wont to brighten with laughter
When I sang at the mill;
And silence unbroken shall greet the sorrowful dawns here-
 after,—
The house shall be still.
Voice after voice takes up the burden of wailing—
Do you heed, do you hear?—in the high priest's house by the
 wall.
But mine is the grief, and their sorrow is all unavailing.
Will he wake at their call?

Something I saw of the broad dim wings half folding
The passionless brow.
Something I saw of the sword that the shadowy hands were
 holding,—
What matters it now?
I held you close, dear face, as I knelt and harkened
To the wind that cried last night like a soul in sin,
When the broad bright stars dropped down and the soft sky
 darkened
And the Presence moved therein.

I have heard men speak in the market-place of the city,
Low-voiced, in a breath,
Of a God who is stronger than ours, and who knows not
 changing nor pity,
Whose anger is death.

Nothing I know of the lords of the outland races,
But Amun is gentle and Hathor the mother is mild,
And who would descend from the light of the Peaceful Places
To war on a child?

Yet here he lies, with a scarlet pomegranate petal
Blown down on his cheek.
The slow sun sinks to the sand like a shield of some burnished
metal,
But he does not speak.
I have called, I have sung, but he neither will hear nor waken;
So lightly, so whitely, he lies in the curve of my arm,
Like a feather let fall from the bird that the arrow hath
taken,—
Who could see him, and harm?

"The swallow flies home to her sleep in the eaves of the altar,
And the crane to her nest."—
So do we sing o'er the mill, and why, ah, why should I falter,
Since he goes to his rest?
Does he play in their flowers as he played among these with
his mother?
Do the gods smile downward and love him and give him
their care?
Guard him well, O ye gods, till I come; lest the wrath of that
Other
Should reach to him there.

*Marjorie L. C. Pickthall* [1883-1922]

## THE DARK ROAD

There is no light in any path of Heaven,
Every star is folded in dark sleep;
The clouds hang heavily, the moon is hidden,
How will she know the road her soul must keep?

She did not ask for heavenly palaces,
A little human home was her desire;
The intimate, close touch of human hands—
To love and watch beside a human fire.

As tears will be remembrance in her heart
  If she recall her lamp's familiar light,
And as a sword vain pity in her heart
  If she should hear her children's cry to-night.

Ah Mary, Mother, stand by Heaven's gate
  And watch the road for one who comes to find
In loneliness and fear what Heaven holds
  To comfort her who leaves the earth behind.

*Ethel Clifford* [18 –

## OUT OF HEARING

No need to hush the children for her sake,
  Or fear their play:
She will not wake, mavrone, she will not wake.
'Tis the long sleep, the deep long sleep she'll take,
  Betide what may.
No need to hush the children for her sake;
Even if their glee could yet again outbreak
  So loud and gay,
She will not wake, mavrone, she will not wake.
But sorrow a thought have they of merry-make
  This many a day:
No need to hush the children. For her sake
So still they bide and sad, her heart would ache
  At their dismay.
She will not wake, mavrone, she will not wake
To bid them laugh, and if some angel spake
  Small heed they'd pay.
No need to hush the children for her sake:
She will not wake, mavrone, she will not wake.

*Jane Barlow* [18 –1917]

## "JOHN ANDERSON, MY JO"

"John Anderson, my jo, John,"
  How cold you are, and still;
You hear me not, nor see me,
  Ah, no, and never will.

Your hands are resting now, John;
The heart that loved me so
Against my breast shall beat no more,
"John Anderson, my jo."

"John Anderson, my jo, John,"
I'll tarry but a while;
I've still some work to do, John,
To go a weary mile;
And then I'll take your path, John,
And win you soon, I know,
For you will wait for your old wife,
"John Anderson, my jo."

*Charles G. Blanden* [1857–1933]

## THE SPRING OF THE YEAR

GONE were but the winter cold,
And gone were but the snow,
I could sleep in the wild woods
Where primroses blow.

Cold's the snow at my head,
And cold at my feet;
And the finger of death's at my e'en,
Closing them to sleep.

Let none tell my father
Or my mother so dear,—
I'll meet them both in heaven
At the spring of the year.

*Allan Cunningham* [1784–1842

## THE GRAVES OF A HOUSEHOLD

THEY grew in beauty, side by side,
They filled one home with glee;
Their graves are severed far and wide
By mount, and stream, and sea.

The same fond mother bent at night
  O'er each fair sleeping brow;
She had each folded flower in sight—
  Where are those dreamers now?

One 'mid the forests of the West,
  By a dark stream is laid;
The Indian knows his place of rest,
  Far in the cedar shade.
The sea, the blue lone sea, hath one—
  He lies where pearls lie deep;
He was the loved of all, yet none
  O'er his low bed may weep.

One sleeps where southern vines are dressed
  Above the noble slain;
He wrapped his colors round his breast
  On a blood-red field of Spain.
And one—o'er her the myrtle showers
  Its leaves, by soft winds fanned;
She faded 'mid Italian flowers,
  The last of that bright band.

And, parted thus, they rest who played
  Beneath the same green tree,
Whose voices mingled as they prayed
  Around one parent-knee!
They that with smiles lit up the hall,
  And cheered with song the hearth;
Alas for love, if thou wert all,
  And naught beyond, O Earth!

*Felicia Dorothea Hemans* [1793-1835]

## THE FAMILY MEETING

We are all here,
Father, mother,
Sister, brother,
All who hold each other dear.
Each chair is filled, we are all at home!
To-night let no cold stranger come;

It is not often thus around
Our old familiar hearth we're found.
Bless, then, the meeting and the spot,
For once be every care forgot;
Let gentle peace assert her power,
And kind affection rule the hour.
We're all—all here.

We're not all here!
Some are away,—the dead ones dear,
Who thronged with us this ancient hearth,
And gave the hour to guileless mirth.
Fate, with a stern, relentless hand,
Looked in and thinned our little band;
Some like a night-flash passed away,
And some sank lingering day by day;
The quiet grave-yard—some lie there,—
And cruel ocean has his share.
We're not all here!

We are all here.
Even they—the dead—though dead, so dear,
Fond memory, to her duty true,
Brings back their faded forms to view.
How life-like, through the mist of years,
Each well-remembered face appears!
We see them, as in times long past;
From each to each kind looks are cast;
We hear their words, their smiles behold,
They're 'round us as they were of old.
We are all here!

We are all here:
Father, mother,
Sister, brother,
You that I love with love so dear.
This may not long of us be said;
Soon must we join the gathered dead,
And by the hearth we now sit 'round
Some other circle will be found.

Oh, then, that wisdom may we know
Which yields a life of peace below;
So, in the world to follow this,
May each repeat, in words of bliss,
We're all—all here.

*Charles Sprague* [1791–1875]

## THE TWO APRIL MORNINGS

We walked along, while bright and red
Uprose the morning sun;
And Matthew stopped, he looked, and said,
"The will of God be done!"

A village schoolmaster was he,
With hair of glittering gray;
As blithe a man as you could see
On a spring holiday.

And on that morning, through the grass,
And by the steaming rills,
We traveled merrily, to pass
A day among the hills.

"Our work," said I, "was well begun;
Then, from thy breast what thought,
Beneath so beautiful a sun,
So sad a sigh has brought?"

A second time did Matthew stop;
And fixing still his eye
Upon the eastern mountain-top,
To me he made reply:

"Yon cloud with that long purple cleft
Brings fresh into my mind
A day like this which I have left
Full thirty years behind.

"And just above yon slope of corn
Such colors, and no other,
Were in the sky, that April morn,
Of this the very brother.

"With rod and line I sued the sport
Which that sweet season gave,
And, to the church-yard come, stopped short
Beside my daughter's grave.

"Nine summers had she scarcely seen,
The pride of all the vale;
And then she sang;—she would have been
A very nightingale.

"Six feet in earth my Emma lay;
And yet I loved her more,
For so it seemed, than till that day
I e'er had loved before.

"And, turning from her grave, I met,
Beside the church-yard yew,
A blooming girl, whose hair was wet
With points of morning dew.

"A basket on her head she bare;
Her brow was smooth and white:
To see a child so very fair
It was a pure delight!

"No fountain from its rocky cave
E'er tripped with foot so free;
She seemed as happy as a wave
That dances on the sea.

"There came from me a sigh of pain
Which I could ill confine;
I looked at her, and looked again,
And did not wish her mine!"

Matthew is in his grave, yet now,
  Methinks, I see him stand,
As at that moment, with a bough
  Of wilding in his hand.

*William Wordsworth* [1770–1850]

## "SURPRISED BY JOY"

SURPRISED by joy—impatient as the Wind—
I turned to share the transport—O! with whom
But Thee, deep buried in the silent tomb,
That spot which no vicissitude can find?
Love, faithful love, recalled thee to my mind—
But how could I forget thee? Through what power,
Even for the least division of an hour,
Have I been so beguiled as to be blind
To my most grievous loss?—That thought's return
Was the worst pang that sorrow ever bore,
Save one, one only, when I stood forlorn,
Knowing my heart's best treasure was no more;
That neither present time, nor years unborn
Could to my sight that heavenly face restore.

*William Wordsworth* [1770–1850]

## THE REVEL

### EAST INDIA

WE meet 'neath the sounding rafter,
  And the walls around are bare;
As they shout back our peals of laughter
  It seems that the dead are there.
Then stand to your glasses, steady!
  We drink in our comrades' eyes:
One cup to the dead already—
  Hurrah for the next that dies!

Not here are the goblets glowing,
  Not here is the vintage sweet;
'Tis cold, as our hearts are growing,
  And dark as the doom we meet.

But stand to your glasses, steady!
  And soon shall our pulses rise:
A cup to the dead already—
  Hurrah for the next that dies!

There's many a hand that's shaking,
  And many a cheek that's sunk;
But soon, though our hearts are breaking,
  They'll burn with the wine we've drunk.
Then stand to your glasses, steady!
  'Tis here the revival lies:
Quaff a cup to the dead already—
  Hurrah for the next that dies!

Time was when we laughed at others;
  We thought we were wiser then;
Ha! ha! let them think of their mothers,
  Who hope to see them again.
No! stand to your glasses, steady!
  The thoughtless is here the wise:
One cup to the dead already—
  Hurrah for the next that dies!

Not a sigh for the lot that darkles,
  Not a tear for the friends that sink;
We'll fall, 'midst the wine-cup's sparkles,
  As mute as the wine we drink.
Come, stand to your glasses, steady!
  'Tis this that the respite buys:
A cup to the dead already—
  Hurrah for the next that dies!

There's a mist on the glass congealing,
  'Tis the hurricane's sultry breath;
And thus does the warmth of feeling
  Turn ice in the grasp of Death.
But stand to your glasses, steady!
  For a moment the vapor flies:
Quaff a cup to the dead already—
  Hurrah for the next that dies!

Who dreads to the dust returning?
  Who shrinks from the sable shore,
Where the high and haughty yearning
  Of the soul can sting no more?
No, stand to your glasses, steady!
  The world is a world of lies:
A cup to the dead already—
  And hurrah for the next that dies!

Cut off from the land that bore us,
  Betrayed by the land we find,
When the brightest have gone before us,
  And the dullest are most behind—
Stand, stand to your glasses, steady!
  'Tis all we have left to prize:
One cup to the dead already—
  Hurrah for the next that dies!

*Bartholomew Dowling* [1823–1863]

## THE CHOICE

From "The House of Life"

I

EAT thou and drink; to-morrow thou shalt die.
Surely the earth, that's wise being very old,
Needs not our help. Then loose me, love, and hold
Thy sultry hair up from my face; that I
May pour for thee this golden wine, brim-high,
Till round the glass thy fingers glow like gold.
We'll drown all hours: thy song, while hours are tolled,
Shall leap, as fountains veil the changing sky.
Now kiss, and think that there are really those,
My own high-bosomed beauty, who increase
Vain gold, vain lore, and yet might choose our way!
Through many years they toil; then on a day
They die not,—for their life was death,—but cease;
And round their narrow lips the mold falls close.

II

Watch thou and fear; to-morrow thou shalt die.
Or art thou sure thou shalt have time for death?
Is not the day which God's word promiseth
To come man knows not when? In yonder sky,
Now while we speak, the sun speeds forth: can I
Or thou assure him of his goal? God's breath
Even at this moment haply quickeneth
The air to a flame; till spirits, always nigh
Though screened and hid, shall walk the daylight here.
And dost thou prate of all that man shall do?
Canst thou, who hast but plagues, presume to be
Glad in his gladness that comes after thee?
Will *his* strength slay *thy* worm in Hell? Go to:
Cover thy countenance, and watch, and fear.

III

Think thou and act; to-morrow thou shalt die.
Outstretched in the sun's warmth upon the shore,
Thou say'st: "Man's measured path is all gone o'er;
Up all his years, steeply, with strain and sigh,
Man clomb until he touched the truth; and I,
Even I, am he whom it was destined for."
How should this be? Art thou then so much more
Than they who sowed, that thou shouldst reap thereby?
Nay, come up hither. From this wave-washed mound
Unto the furthest flood-brim look with me;
Then reach on with thy thought till it be drowned.
Miles and miles distant though the last line be,
And though thy soul sail leagues and leagues beyond,—
Still, leagues beyond those leagues, there is more sea.

*Dante Gabriel Rossetti* [1828–1882]

## READÈN OV A HEAD-STWONE

As I wer readèn ov a stwone
In Grenley church-yard all alwone,
A little maïd ran up, wi' pride
To zee me there, an' pushed a-zide

A bunch o' bennets that did hide
  A verse her father, as she zaïd,
  Put up above her mother's head,
    To tell how much he loved her.

The verse wer short, but very good,
I stood an' larned en where I stood:—
"Mid God, dear Meäry, gi'e me greäce,
To vind, lik' thee, a better pleäce,
Where I woonce mwore mid zee thy feäce;
  An' bring thy children up to know
  His word, that they mid come an' show
    Thy soul how much I loved thee."

"Where's father, then," I zaid, "my chile?"
"Dead too," she answered wi' a smile;
"An' I an' brother Jim do bide
At Betty White's, o' t'other side
O' road." "Mid He, my chile," I cried,
  "That's father to the fatherless,
  Become thy father now, an' bless,
    An' keep, an' leäd, an' love thee."

Though she've a-lost, I thought, so much,
Still He don't let the thoughts o't touch
Her litsome heart by day or night;
An' zoo, if we could teäke it right,
Do show He'll meäke His burdens light
  To weaker souls, an' that His smile
  Is sweet upon a harmless chile,
    When they be dead that loved it.

*William Barnes* [1801-1886]

## THE TWO MYSTERIES

We know not what it is, dear, this sleep so deep and still;
The folded hands, the awful calm, the cheek so pale and chill;
The lids that will not lift again, though we may call and call;
The strange, white solitude of peace that settles over all.

We know not what it means, dear, this desolate heart-pain;
This dread to take our daily way, and walk in it again;
We know not to what other sphere the loved who leave us
go,
Nor why we're left to wonder still, nor why we do not know.

But this we know: Our loved and dead, if they should come
this day—
Should come and ask us, "What is life?" not one of us could
say.
Life is a mystery as deep as ever death can be;
Yet, oh, how dear it is to us, this life we live and see!

Then might they say—these vanished ones—and blessed
is the thought,
"So death is sweet to us, beloved! though we may show you
naught;
We may not to the quick reveal the mystery of death—
Ye cannot tell us, if ye would, the mystery of breath."

The child who enters life comes not with knowledge or in-
tent,
So those who enter death must go as little children sent.
Nothing is known. But I believe that God is overhead;
And as life is to the living, so death is to the dead.

*Mary Mapes Dodge* [1831–1905]

## FOREVER

THOSE we love truly never die,
Though year by year the sad memorial wreath,
A ring and flowers, types of life and death,
Are laid upon their graves.

For death the pure life saves,
And life all pure is love; and love can reach
From heaven to earth, and nobler lessons teach
Than those by mortals read.

Well blest is he who has a dear one dead:
A friend he has whose face will never change—
A dear communion that will not grow strange;
The anchor of a love is death.

The blessed sweetness of a loving breath
Will reach our cheek all fresh through weary years.
For her who died long since, ah! waste not tears,
She's thine unto the end.

Thank God for one dear friend,
With face still radiant with the light of truth,
Whose love comes laden with the scent of youth,
Through twenty years of death.

*John Boyle O'Reilly* [1844-1890]

## NOW AND AFTERWARDS

"Two hands upon the breast, and labor is past"—RUSSIAN PROVERB

Two hands upon the breast,
And labor's done;
Two pale feet crossed in rest,—
The race is won;
Two eyes with coin-weights shut,
And all tears cease,
Two lips where grief is mute,
Anger at peace;—
So pray we oftentimes, mourning our lot;
God in His kindness answereth not.

Two hands to work addressed
Aye for His praise;
Two feet that never rest
Walking His ways;
Two eyes that look above
Through all their tears;
Two lips still breathing love,
Not wrath, nor fears;—
So pray we afterwards, low on our knees;
Pardon those erring prayers! Father, hear these!

*Dinah Maria Mulock Craik* [1826-1887]

## "NOW THE LABORER'S TASK IS O'ER"

Now the laborer's task is o'er;
  Now the battle day is past;
Now upon the farther shore
  Lands the voyager at last.
Father, in Thy gracious keeping
Leave we now Thy servant sleeping.

There the tears of earth are dried;
  There its hidden things are clear;
There the work of life is tried
  By a juster Judge than here.
Father, in Thy gracious keeping
Leave we now Thy servant sleeping.

There the penitents, that turn
  To the cross their dying eyes,
All the love of Jesus learn
  At His feet in Paradise.
Father, in Thy gracious keeping
Leave we now Thy servant sleeping.

There no more the powers of hell
  Can prevail to mar their peace;
Christ the Lord shall guard them well,
  He who died for their release.
Father, in Thy gracious keeping
Leave we now Thy servant sleeping.

"Earth to earth, and dust to dust,"
  Calmly now the words we say,
Left behind, we wait in trust
  For the resurrection day.
Father, in Thy gracious keeping
Leave we now Thy servant sleeping.

*John Lodge Ellerton* [1801–1873]

## LOVE AND DEATH

ALAS! that men must see
  Love, before Death!
Else they content might be
  With their short breath;
Aye, glad, when the pale sun
Showed restless day was done,
And endless Rest begun.

Glad, when with strong, cool hand
  Death clasped their own,
And with a strange command
  Hushed every moan;
Glad to have finished pain,
And labor wrought in vain,
Blurred by Sin's deepening stain.

But Love's insistent voice
  Bids self to flee—
"Live that I may rejoice,
  Live on, for me!"
So, for Love's cruel mind,
Men fear this Rest to find,
Nor know great Death is kind!

*Margaret Deland* [1857–1945]

## VAN ELSEN

GOD spake three times and saved Van Elsen's soul;
He spake by sickness first and made him whole;
  Van Elsen heard him not,
  Or soon forgot.

God spake to him by wealth, the world outpoured
Its treasures at his feet, and called him Lord;
  Van Elsen's heart grew fat
  And proud thereat.

God spake the third time when the great World smiled,
And in the sunshine slew his little child;
  Van Elsen like a tree
  Fell hopelessly.

Then in the darkness came a voice which said,
"As thy heart bleedeth, so my heart hath bled,
As I have need of thee,
Thou needest me."

That night Van Elsen kissed the baby feet,
And, kneeling by the narrow winding-sheet,
Praised Him with fervent breath
Who conquered death.

*Frederick George Scott* [1861–1944]

## THE FLIGHT

Upon a cloud among the stars we stood:
The angel raised his hand, and looked, and said,
"Which world, of all yon starry myriad
Shall we make wing to?" The still solitude
Became a harp whereon his voice and mood
Made spheral music round his haloed head.
I spake—for then I had not long been dead—
"Let me look round upon the vasts, and brood
A moment on these orbs ere I decide. . . .
What is yon lower star that beauteous shines
And with soft splendor now incarnadines
Our wings?—*There* would I go and there abide."
Then he, as one who some child's thought divines:
"That is the world where yesternight you died."

*Lloyd Mifflin* [1846–1921]

## RIPE GRAIN

O still, white face of perfect peace,
Untouched by passion, freed from pain,—
He who ordained that work should cease
Took to Himself the ripened grain.

O noble face! your beauty bears
The glory that is wrung from pain,—
The high, celestial beauty wears
Of finished work, of ripened grain.

Of human care you left no trace,
  No lightest trace of grief or pain,—
On earth an empty form and face—
  In Heaven stands the ripened grain.

*Dora Reed Goodale* [1866–

## "THE LAND WHICH NO ONE KNOWS"

DARK, deep, and cold the current flows
Unto the sea where no wind blows,
Seeking the land which no one knows.

O'er its sad gloom still comes and goes
The mingled wail of friends and foes,
Borne to the land which no one knows.

Why shrieks for help yon wretch, who goes
With millions, from a world of woes,
Unto the land which no one knows?

Though myriads go with him who goes,
Alone he goes where no wind blows,
Unto the land which no one knows.

For all must go where no wind blows,
And none can go for him who goes;
None, none return whence no one knows.

Yet why should he who shrieking goes
With millions, from a world of woes,
Reunion seek with it or those?

Alone with God, where no wind blows,
And Death, his shadow—doomed, he goes:
That God is there the shadow shows.

O shoreless Deep, where no wind blows!
And thou, O Land, which no one knows!
That God is all, His shadow shows.

*Ebenezer Elliott* [1781–1849]

## THE HILLS OF REST

BEYOND the last horizon's rim,
Beyond adventure's farthest quest,
Somewhere they rise, serene and dim,
The happy, happy Hills of Rest.

Upon their sunlit slopes uplift
The castles we have built in Spain—
While fair amid the summer drift
Our faded gardens flower again.

Sweet hours we did not live go by
To soothing note, on scented wing;
In golden-lettered volumes lie
The songs we tried in vain to sing.

They all are there: the days of dream
That build the inner lives of men;
The silent, sacred years we deem
The might be, and the might have been.

Some evening when the sky is gold
I'll follow day into the west;
Nor pause, nor heed, till I behold
The happy, happy Hills of Rest.

*Albert Bigelow Paine* [1861–1937]

## AT THE TOP OF THE ROAD

"BUT, Lord," she said, "my shoulders still are strong—
I have been used to bear the load so long;

"And see, the hill is passed, and smooth the road . . ."
"Yet," said the Stranger, "yield me now thy load."

Gently he took it from her, and she stood
Straight-limbed and lithe, in new-found maidenhood,

Amid long, sunlit fields; around them sprang
A tender breeze, and birds and rivers sang.

"My Lord," she said, "the land is very fair!"
Smiling, he answered: " Was it not so there?"

"There?" In her voice a wondering question lay:
"Was I not always here, then, as to-day?"

He turned to her with strange, deep eyes aflame:
"Knowest thou not this kingdom, nor my name?"

"Nay," she replied: "but this I understand—
That thou art Lord of Life in this dear land!"

"Yea, child," he murmured, scarce above his breath:
"Lord of the Land! but men have named me Death."

*Charles Buxton Going* [1863-

## SHEMUEL

SHEMUEL, the Bethlehemite,
Watched a fevered guest at night;
All his fellows fared afield
Saw the angel host revealed;
He nor caught the mystic story,
Heard the song, nor saw the glory.

Through the night they gazing stood,
Heard the holy multitude;
Back they came in wonder home,
Knew the Christmas kingdom come,
Eyes aflame and hearts elated;
Shemuel sat alone, and waited.

Works of mercy now, as then,
Hide the angel host from men;
Hearts attuned to earthly love
Miss the angel notes above;
Deeds at which the world rejoices,
Quench the sound of angel voices.

So they thought, nor deemed from whence
His celestial recompense.
Shemuel, by the fever bed,
Touched by beckoning hands that led,
Died, and saw the Uncreated;
All his fellows lived, and waited.

*Edward Ernest Bowen* [1836–1901]

## SHE AND HE

"SHE is dead!" they said to him. "Come away;
Kiss her and leave her!—thy love is clay!"

They smoothed her tresses of dark brown hair;
On her forehead of marble they laid it fair;

Over her eyes, that gazed too much,
They drew the lids with a gentle touch;

With a tender touch they closed up well
The sweet thin lips that had secrets to tell:

About her brows, and her dear, pale face,
They tied her veil and her marriage-lace·

And drew on her white feet her white silk shoes;—
Which were the whiter no eye could choose!

And over her bosom they crossed her hands;
"Come away," they said,—"God understands!"

And then there was Silence;—and nothing there
But the Silence—and scents of eglantere,

And jasmine, and roses, and rosemary;
And they said, "As a lady should lie, lies she!"

And they held their breath till they left the room,
With a shudder to glance at its stillness and gloom.

But he—who loved her too well to dread
The sweet, the stately, the beautiful dead,—

He lit his lamp, and took the key,
And turned it!—Alone again—he and she!

He and she; but she would not speak,
Though he kissed, in the old place, the quiet cheek;

He and she; yet she would not smile,
Though he called her the name that was fondest erewhile.

He and she; and she did not move
To any one passionate whisper of love!

Then he said, "Cold lips! and breast without breath!
Is there no voice?—no language of death

"Dumb to the ear and still to the sense,
But to heart and to soul distinct,—intense?

"See, now,—I listen with soul, not ear,—
What was the secret of dying, Dear?

"Was it the infinite wonder of all
That you ever could let life's flower fall?

"Or was it a greater marvel to feel
The perfect calm o'er the agony steal?

"Was the miracle greatest to find how deep,
Beyond all dreams, sank downward that sleep?

"Did life roll backward its record, Dear,
And show, as they say it does, past things clear?

"And was it the innermost heart of the bliss
To find out so what a wisdom love is?

"Oh, perfect Dead! Oh, Dead most dear,
I hold the breath of my soul to hear;

"I listen—as deep as to horrible hell,
As high as to heaven!—and you do not tell!

"There must be pleasures in dying, Sweet,
To make you so placid from head to feet!

"I would tell *you*, Darling, if I were dead,
And 'twere your hot tears upon *my* brow shed.

"I would say, though the angel of death had laid
His sword on my lips to keep it unsaid.

"*You* should not ask, vainly, with streaming eyes,
Which in Death's touch was the chiefest surprise;

"The very strangest and suddenest thing
Of all the surprises that dying must bring."

. . . . . . .

Ah! foolish world! Oh! most kind Dead!
Though he told me, who will believe it was said?

Who will believe that he heard her say,
With the soft rich voice, in the dear old way:—

"The utmost wonder is this,—I hear,
And see you, and love you, and kiss you, Dear;

"I can speak, now you listen with soul alone;
If your soul could see, it would all be shown

"What a strange delicious amazement is Death,
To be without body and breathe without breath.

"I should laugh for joy if you did not cry;
Oh, listen! Love lasts!—Love never will die.

"I am only your Angel, who was your Bride;
And I know, that though dead, I have never died."

*Edwin Arnold* [1832–1904]

## AFTER DEATH IN ARABIA

He who died at Azan sends
This to comfort all his friends:

Faithful friends! It lies, I know,
Pale and white and cold as snow:
And ye say, "Abdallah's dead!"
Weeping at the feet and head.
I can see your falling tears,
I can hear your sighs and prayers;
Yet I smile and whisper this:
"*I* am not the thing you kiss;
Cease your tears, and let it lie;
It *was* mine—it is not I."

Sweet friends! what the women lave
For its last bed of the grave,
Is a tent which I am quitting,
Is a garment no more fitting,
Is a cage from which, at last,
Like a hawk my soul hath passed.
Love the inmate, not the room,—
The wearer, not the garb;—the plume
Of the falcon, not the bars
That kept him from these splendid stars!

Loving friends! be wise, and dry
Straightway every weeping eye.
What ye lift upon the bier
Is not worth a wistful tear.
'Tis an empty sea-shell,—one
Out of which the pearl is gone.
The shell is broken, it lies there;
The pearl, the all, the soul, is here.
'Tis an earthen jar, whose lid
Allah sealed, the while it hid
That treasure of his treasury,
A mind that loved him: let it lie!
Let the shard be earth's once more,
Since the gold shines in his store!

Allah glorious! Allah good!
Now Thy world is understood;
Now the long, long wonder ends!
Yet ye weep, my erring friends,
While the man whom ye call dead,
In unspoken bliss, instead,
Lives and loves you; lost, 'tis true,
By such light as shines for you;
But in light ye cannot see
Of unfulfilled felicity,—
In enlarging paradise,
Lives a life that never dies.

Farewell, friends! yet not farewell;—
Where I am, ye, too, shall dwell.
I am gone before your face,
A moment's time, a little space.
When ye come where I have stepped,
Ye will wonder why ye wept;
Ye will know, by wise love taught,
That here is all, and there is naught.
Weep awhile, if ye are fain,—
Sunshine still must follow rain;
Only not at death,—for death,
Now I know, is that first breath
Which our souls draw when we enter
Life, which is of all life center.

Be ye certain all seems love,
Viewed from Allah's throne above;
Be ye stout of heart, and come
Bravely onward to your home!
*La Allah illa Allah!* yea!
Thou love divine! Thou Love alway!

He that died at Azan gave
This to those who made his grave.

*Edwin Arnold* [1832–1904]

# SENTINEL SONGS

## TO THE EARL OF WARWICK, ON THE DEATH OF MR. ADDISON

[1672–1719]

If, dumb too long, the drooping Muse hath stayed,
And left her debt to Addison unpaid,
Blame not her silence, Warwick, but bemoan,
And judge, O, judge my bosom by your own.
What mourner ever felt poetic fires?
Slow comes the verse that real woe inspires:
Grief unaffected suits but ill with art,
Or flowing numbers with a bleeding heart.
Can I forget the dismal night that gave
My soul's best part forever to the grave?
How silent did his old companions tread,
By midnight lamps, the mansions of the dead,
Through breathing statues, then unheeded things,
Through rows of warriors and through walks of kings!
What awe did the slow, solemn knell inspire;
The pealing organ, and the pausing choir;
The duties by the lawn-robed prelate paid;
And the last words, that dust to dust conveyed!
While speechless o'er thy closing grave we bend,
Accept these tears, thou dear, departed friend.
O, gone forever! take this long adieu;
And sleep in peace next thy loved Montague.
To strew fresh laurels let the task be mine,
A frequent pilgrim at thy sacred shrine;
Mine with true sighs thy absence to bemoan,
And grave with faithful epitaphs thy stone.
If e'er from me thy loved memorial part,
May shame afflict this alienated heart;
Of thee forgetful, if I form a song,
My lyre be broken, and untuned my tongue,
My grief be doubled, from thy image free,
And mirth a torment, unchastised by thee!
Oft let me range the gloomy aisles alone.

Sad luxury! to vulgar minds unknown;
Along the walls where speaking marbies show
What worthies form the hallowed mold below;
Proud names, who once the reins of empire held;
In arms who triumphed, or in arts excelled;
Chiefs, graced with scars, and prodigal of blood;
Stern patriots, who for sacred freedom stood;
Just men, by whom impartial laws were given;
And saints, who taught and led the way to heaven;
Ne'er to these chambers, where the mighty rest,
Since their foundation came a nobler guest;
Nor e'er was to the bowers of bliss conveyed
A fairer spirit or more welcome shade.
  In what new region, to the just assigned,
What new employments please the unbodied mind?
A wingèd Virtue, through the ethereal sky,
From world to world unwearied does he fly?
Or curious trace the long laborious maze
Of Heaven's decrees, where wondering angels gaze?
Does he delight to hear bold seraphs tell
How Michael battled and the dragon fell,
Or, mixed with milder cherubim, to glow
In hymns of love, not ill-essayed below?
Or dost thou warn poor mortals left behind,—
A task well suited to thy gentle mind?
O, if sometimes thy spotless form descend,
To me thy aid, thou guardian genius, lend!
When rage misguides me, or when fear alarms,
When pain distresses, or when pleasure charms,
In silent whisperings purer thoughts impart,
And turn from ill a frail and feeble heart;
Lead through the paths thy virtue trod before,
Till bliss shall join, nor death can part us more.
  That awful form which, so the heavens decree,
Must still be loved and still deplored by me,
In nightly visions seldom fails to rise,
Or, roused by fancy, meets my waking eyes.
If business calls, or crowded courts invite,
The unblemished statesman seems to strike my sight
If in the stage I seek to soothe my care,
I meet his soul which breathes in Cato there;

If pensive to the rural shades I rove,
His shape o'ertakes me in the lonely grove;
'Twas there of just and good he reasoned strong,
Cleared some great truth, or raised some serious song:
There patient showed us the wise course to steer,
A candid censor and a friend severe;
There taught us how to live, and (O, too high
The price for knowledge!) taught us how to die.
Thou Hill, whose brow the antique structures grace,
Reared by bold chiefs of Warwick's noble race,
Why, once so loved, whene'er thy bower appears,
O'er my dim eyeballs glance the sudden tears?
How sweet were once thy prospects fresh and fair,
Thy sloping walks, and unpolluted air!
How sweet the glooms beneath thy aged trees,
Thy noontide shadow, and thy evening breeze!
His image thy forsaken bowers restore;
Thy walks and airy prospects charm no more;
No more the summer in thy glooms allayed,
Thy evening breezes, and thy noonday shade.
From other hills, however fortune frowned,
Some refuge in the Muse's art I found;
Reluctant now I touch the trembling string,
Bereft of him who taught me how to sing;
And these sad accents, murmured o'er his urn,
Betray that absence they attempt to mourn.
O, must I then (now fresh my bosom bleeds,
And Craggs in death to Addison succeeds)
The verse, begun to one lost friend, prolong,
And weep a second in the unfinished song!
These works divine, which, on his death-bed laid,
To thee, O Craggs! the expiring sage conveyed,
Great, but ill-omened, monument of fame,
Nor he survived to give, nor thou to claim.
Swift after him thy social spirit flies,
And close to his, how soon! thy coffin lies.
Blest pair! whose union future bards shall tell
In future tongues: each other's boast! farewell!
Farewell! whom, joined in fame, in friendship tried,
No chance could sever, nor the grave divide.

*Thomas Tickell* [1686–1740]

## THE EAGLE THAT IS FORGOTTEN

[JOHN P. ALTGELD, 1847–1902]

SLEEP softly . . . eagle forgotten . . . under the stone.
Time has its way with you there, and the clay has its own.
"We have buried him now," thought your foes, and in secret rejoiced.
They made a brave show of their mourning, their hatred unvoiced.
They had snarled at you, barked at you, foamed at you, day after day,
Now you were ended. They praised you . . . and laid you away.
The others, that mourned you in silence and terror and truth,
The widow bereft of her crust, and the boy without youth,
The mocked and the scorned and the wounded, the lame and the poor,
That should have remembered forever, . . . remember no more.
Where are those lovers of yours, on what name do they call,
The lost, that in armies wept over your funeral pall?
They call on the names of a hundred high-valiant ones,
A hundred white eagles have risen, the sons of your sons.
The zeal in their wings is a zeal that your dreaming began,
The valor that wore out your soul in the service of man.
Sleep softly . . . eagle forgotten . . . under the stone.
Time has its way with you there, and the clay has its own.
Sleep on, O brave-hearted, O wise man that kindled the flame—
To live in mankind is far more than to live in a name,
To live in mankind, far, far more than to live in a name!—

*Vachel Lindsay* [1879–1931]

## ELEGIAC STANZAS

SUGGESTED BY A PICTURE OF PEELE CASTLE IN A STORM, PAINTED BY SIR GEORGE BEAUMONT

[1753–1827]

I WAS thy neighbor once, thou rugged Pile!
Four summer weeks I dwelt in sight of thee:
I saw thee every day; and all the while
Thy Form was sleeping on a glassy sea.

So pure the sky, so quiet was the air!
So like, so very like, was day to day!
Whene'er I looked, thy image still was there;
It trembled, but it never passed away.

How perfect was the calm! It seemed no sleep,
No mood, which season takes away, or brings:
I could have fancied that the mighty Deep
Was even the gentlest of all gentle things.

Ah! THEN—if mine had been the Painter's hand
To express what then I saw; and add the gleam,
The light that never was, on sea or land,
The consecration, and the Poet's dream,—

I would have planted thee, thou hoary Pile,
Amid a world how different from this!
Beside a sea that could not cease to smile;
On tranquil land, beneath a sky of bliss.

Thou shouldst have seemed a treasure-house divine
Of peaceful years; a chronicle of heaven;—
Of all the sunbeams that did ever shine
The very sweetest had to thee been given.

A Picture had it been of lasting ease,
Elysian quiet, without toil or strife;
No motion but the moving tide, a breeze,
Or merely silent Nature's breathing life.

Such, in the fond illusion of my heart,
Such Picture would I at that time have made;
And seen the soul of truth in every part,
A steadfast peace that might not be betrayed.

So once it would have been,—'tis so no more;
I have submitted to a new control:
A power is gone, which nothing can restore;
A deep distress hath humanized my soul.

Not for a moment could I now behold
A smiling sea, and be what I have been:
The feeling of my loss will ne'er be old;
This, which I know, I speak with mind serene.

Then, Beaumont, Friend! who would have been the friend
If he had lived, of Him whom I deplore,
This work of thine I blame not, but commend;
This sea in anger, and that dismal shore.

O 'tis a passionate Work!—yet wise and well,
Well chosen is the spirit that is here;
That Hulk which labors in the deadly swell,
This rueful sky, this pageantry of fear!

And this huge Castle, standing here sublime,
I love to see the look with which it braves,
—Cased in the unfeeling armor of old time—
The lightning, the fierce wind, and trampling waves.

—Farewell, farewell the heart that lives alone,
Housed in a dream, at distance from the Kind!
Such happiness, wherever it be known,
Is to be pitied; for 'tis surely blind.

But welcome fortitude, and patient cheer,
And frequent sights of what is to be borne!
Such sights, or worse, as are before me here:—
Not without hope we suffer and we mourn.

*William Wordsworth* [1770–1850]

## WILLIAM BLAKE

[1757–1827]

He came to the desert of London town,
 Gray miles long;
He wandered up and he wandered down
 Singing a quiet song.

He came to the desert of London town,
Mirk miles broad;
He wandered up and he wandered down,
Ever alone with God.

There were thousands and thousands of human kind
In this desert of brick and stone:
But some were deaf and some were blind,
And he was there alone.

At length the good hour came; he died
As he had lived, alone:
He was not missed from the desert wide,
Perhaps he was found at the Throne.

*James Thomson* [1834–1882]

## EDWIN BOOTH

[1833–1893]

*" Ay, every inch a king "*

Now is the night, foreshadowed of our fears;
The curtain falls, the lights fade, one by one.
Darkness and silence from the widowed stage
Proclaim the great and final act is done.
Vain are the thundered plaudits of the house,
The laurel wreath, the players' loud acclaim;
Thou art grown dumb to clamoring for response,
Deaf to the ringing of thy jewelled name.
Thy crystal soul hath traversed back the pathway whence it came.

They who the virtues of the mighty dead
Enwrap in majesty of broidered verse,
Call upon Nature, in her solitude,
His beauties and her sorrow to rehearse.
The forest and the field, the fitful wind
They challenge, and the ever-sounding wave,
To seek his spirit in the vast afar,
And drop their dews on his enrichèd grave,
Crowning the poet's lyric woe with some forlorner stave.

Greater than all the universe of space
The mimic world thou didst thyself create:
The subtile sphere, compact of passion's breath,
Where Nature bade thee hold imperial state.
There shall the mourning garments be outworn;
There shall the desolate their dirges sing;
No princeling may ascend the vacant throne,
Laying new triumph's gall to sorrow's sting.
"The King is dead!" we cry, but nevermore, "Long live the King!"

Of all the stops of mortal harmony
Master thou art forever, though in death.
The melancholy of the Dane is thine,
The poisonous blighting of Iago's breath.
Thou didst take on foul Richard's humpbacked soul,
And clasp it close, yet do thine own no wrong:
As 'twere the mantle of Sir Caradoc,
Unerring witness sung in ancient song,
Destined to prove the pure of heart more pure, the strong more strong.

Slave of self-conjured evil, Cawdor's thane!
The jester, bitter-hearted, striking home!
The fox-robed cardinal, creating France,
And launching forth the curse of sovereign Rome!
Gallant Don César, lord of ragged lace!
These wert thou in their turn, and sorrow-blind,
Alas! thou wert the doited father, too,
Pelted by heaven, and stabbed by human kind:
Heartbreakingly confessed, "I am not in my perfect mind!"

Such was thy Protean form, but what wert thou?
A changing cloud, content to borrow hue
From lordly sun-rays that o'errule it quite,
And thus with color and with form endue?
Nay, rather let the time's remembrancing,
When it doth con anew thy mortal span,
Ignore thine art, if such despite may be,
But bow in awe before thy nature's plan,
Crying with trumpet tone, to alien ears, "This was a man!"

Thine was the guilt of filching heavenly fire;
Wherefore Jove's eagle fed upon thy heart.
Yet never word nor strangled cry betrayed
Responsive agony beneath the smart.
A thousand hovering spectres menaced thee
Bound, by eternal fiat, on the rock
Of mortal languishment: yet unappalled
As gallant bird beneath the tempest shock;
For still thy soul soared free, thy silence met each hideous
mock.

And can such glory pass? Nay, thus thou art,
Where'er in world diviner thou dost walk,
Mated with love celestial, that doth spring,
Fragrant and fair, from life's divided stalk.
But we who knew thee may not cease to mourn
The moment's grief, the time's perpetual loss.
Not ours to pluck from thine engravèd name
Oblivion's cold and memory-choking moss:
Blest are we for so noble sake to bear affliction's cross.

Henceforward nevermore may Denmark's Prince
Pace through his tragic hour in sabled pride,
But thou, the sceptre's rightful heir, wilt walk,
Eclipsing all his grandeur, by his side.
And dally as we may with pageantry
Wherein some newer actor plays a part,
The scene will fade, while thine enshadowed form
Doth from the slumbrous aisles of memory start,—
Again the lost but ever-reigning monarch of the heart.

Farewell! farewell indeed! But take with thee
Our true allegiance to that orient land,—
The laurels and the rosemary of life
Lying unnoted in thy nerveless hand.
Take with thee, too, our bond of gratitude,
That in a cynic and a tattling age
Thou didst consent to write, in missal script,
Thy name on the poor players' slandered page,
And teach the lords of empty birth a king may walk the
stage.

*Alice Brown* [1857–1948]

## GENERAL WILLIAM BOOTH ENTERS INTO HEAVEN

(1829–1912)

(To be sung to the tune of "The Blood of the Lamb" with indicated instrument)

I

(*Bass drum beaten loudly*)
Booth led boldly with his big bass drum—
(Are you washed in the blood of the Lamb?)
The Saints smiled gravely and they said: "He's come."
(Are you washed in the blood of the Lamb?)
Walking lepers followed, rank on rank,
Lurching bravos from the ditches dank,
Drabs from the alleyways and drug fiends pale—
Minds still passion-ridden, soul-powers frail:—
Vermin-eaten saints with moldy breath,
Unwashed legions with the ways of Death—
(Are you washed in the blood of the Lamb?)

(*Banjos*)
Every slum had sent its half-a-score
The round world over. (Booth had groaned for more.)
Every banner that the wide world flies
Bloomed with glory and transcendent dyes.
Big-voiced lasses made their banjos bang,
Tranced, fanatical they shrieked and sang:—
"Are you washed in the blood of the Lamb?"
Hallelujah! It was queer to see
Bull-necked convicts with that land make free.
Loons with trumpets blowed a blare, blare, blare
On, on upward through the golden air!
(Are you washed in the blood of the Lamb?)

II

(*Bass drum slower and softer*)
Booth died blind and still by faith he trod,
Eyes still dazzled by the ways of God.
Booth led boldly, and he looked the chief,
Eagle countenance in sharp relief,
Beard a-flying, air of high command
Unabated in that holy land.

(*Sweet flute music*)
Jesus came from out the court-house door,
Stretched his hands above the passing poor.
Booth saw not, but led his queer ones there
Round and round the mighty court-house square.
Yet in an instant all that blear review
Marched on spotless, clad in raiment new.
The lame were straightened, withered limbs uncurled
And blind eyes opened on a new, sweet world.
(*Bass drum louder*)
Drabs and vixens in a flash made whole!
Gone was the weasel-head, the snout, the jowl!
Sages and sibyls now, and athletes clean,
Rulers of empires, and of forests green!
(*Chorus of all instruments. Tambourines to foreground*)
The hosts were sandalled, and their wings were fire!
(Are you washed in the blood of the Lamb?)
But their noise played havoc with the angel-choir.
(Are you washed in the blood of the Lamb?)
Oh, shout Salvation! It was good to see
Kings and Princes by the Lamb set free.
The banjos rattled and the tambourines
Jing-jing-jingled in the hands of Queens.
(*Reverently sung, no instruments*)
And when Booth halted by the curb for prayer
He saw his Master through the flag-filled air.
Christ came gently with a robe and crown
For Booth the soldier, while the throng knelt down.
He saw King Jesus. They were face to face,
And he knelt a-weeping in that holy place.
Are you washed in the blood of the Lamb?

*Vachel Lindsay* [1879–1931]

## E. B. B.
[1806–1861]

THE white-rose garland at her feet,
The crown of laurel at her head,
Her noble life on earth complete,
Lay her in the last low bed

For the slumber calm and deep:
"He giveth His belovèd sleep."

Soldiers find their fittest grave
In the field whereon they died;
So her spirit pure and brave
Leaves the clay it glorified
To the land for which she fought
With such grand impassioned thought.

Keats and Shelley sleep at Rome,
She in well-loved Tuscan earth;
Finding all their death's long home
Far from their old home of birth.
Italy, you hold in trust
Very sacred English dust.

Therefore this one prayer I breathe,—
That you yet may worthy prove
Of the heirlooms they bequeath
Who have loved you with such love:
Fairest land while land of slaves
Yields their free souls no fit graves.

*James Thomson* [1834-1882]

## ROBERT BURNS

[1759-1796]

All Scottish legends did his fancy fashion,
All airs that richly flow,
Laughing with frolic, tremulous with passion,
Broken with love-lorn woe;

Ballads whose beauties years have long been stealing
And left few links of gold,
Under his quaint and subtle touch of healing
Grew fairer, not less old.

Gray Cluden, and the vestal's choral cadence,
His spell awoke therewith;
Till boatmen hung their oars to hear the maidens
Upon the banks of Nith.

His, too, the strains of battle nobly coming
From Bruce, or Wallace wight,
Such as the Highlander shall oft be humming
Before some famous fight.

Nor only these—for him the hawthorn hoary
Was with new wreaths enwrought,
The "crimson-tippèd daisy" wore fresh glory,
Born of poetic thought.

From the "wee cowering beastie" he could borrow
A moral strain sublime,
A noble tenderness of human sorrow,
In wondrous wealth of rhyme.

Oh, but the mountain breeze must have been pleasant
Upon the sunburnt brow
Of that poetic and triumphant peasant
Driving his laureled plow!

*William Alexander* [1824–1911]

## ON A FLY-LEAF OF BURNS'S SONGS

These are the best of him,
Pathos and jest of him;
Earth holds the rest of him.

Passions were strong in him,—
Pardon the wrong in him;
Hark to the song in him!—

Each little lyrical
Grave or satirical
Musical miracle!

*Frederic Lawrence Knowles* [1869–1905]

## ON THE DEATHS OF THOMAS CARLYLE AND GEORGE ELIOT

Two souls diverse out of our human sight
Pass, followed one with love and each with wonder:
The stormy sophist with his mouth of thunder,
Clothed with loud words and mantled in the might

Of darkness and magnificence of night;
And one whose eye could smite the night in sunder,
Searching if light or no light were thereunder,
And found in love of loving-kindness light.
Duty divine and Thought with eyes of fire
Still following Righteousness with deep desire
Shone sole and stern before her and above,
Sure stars and sole to steer by; but more sweet
Shone lower the loveliest lamp for earthly feet,
The light of little children, and their love.

*Algernon Charles Swinburne* [1837-1909]

## AT THE GRAVE OF CHAMPERNOWNE

[1614-1687]

HERE poise, like flowers on flowers, the butterflies;
The grasshopper on crookèd crutch leaps up,
The wild bees hum above the clover cup,
The fox-grape wreathes the fence in green disguise
Of ruin; and antique plants set out in tears,
Pink, guelder-rose, and myrtle's purple bells
Struggle 'mid grass and their own wasting years
To show the grave that no inscription tells.
Here rest the bones of Francis Champernowne;
The blazonry of Norman kings he bore;
His fathers builded many a tower and town,
And after Senlac England's lords. Now o'er
His island cairn the lonesome forests frown,
And sailless seas beat the untrodden shore.

*John Albee* [1833-1915]

## THE OPENING OF THE TOMB OF CHARLEMAGNE

[742-814]

AMID the cloistered gloom of Aachen's aisle
Stood Otho, Germany's imperial lord,
Regarding, with a melancholy smile,
A simple stone, where, fitly to record

A world of action by a single word,
Was graven "Carlo-Magno." Regal style
Was needed none; that name such thoughts restored
As sadden, yet make nobler, men the while.
They rolled the marble back. With sudden gasp,
A moment o'er the vault the Kaiser bent,
Where still a mortal monarch seemed to reign.
Crowned on his throne, a scepter in his grasp,
Perfect in each gigantic lineament,
Otho looked face to face on Charlemagne.

*Aubrey De Vere* [1788–1846]

## BY THE STATUE OF KING CHARLES AT CHARING CROSS

[1600–1649]

Sombre and rich, the skies;
Great glooms, and starry plains.
Gently the night wind sighs;
Else a vast silence reigns.

The splendid silence clings
Around me: and around
The saddest of all kings
Crowned, and again discrowned.

Comely and calm, he rides
Hard by his own Whitehall:
Only the night wind glides:
No crowds, nor rebels, brawl.

Gone, too, his Court: and yet,
The stars his courtiers are:
Stars in their stations set;
And every wandering star.

Alone he rides, alone,
The fair and fatal king:
Dark night is all his own,
That strange and solemn thing.

Which are more full of fate:
The stars; or those sad eyes?
Which are more still and great:
Those brows; or the dark skies?

Although his whole heart yearn
In passionate tragedy:
Never was face so stern
With sweet austerity.

Vanquished in life, his death
By beauty made amends:
The passing of his breath
Won his defeated ends.

Brief life, and hapless? Nay:
Through death, life grew sublime.
*Speak after sentence?* Yea:
And to the end of time.

Armored he rides, his head
Bare to the stars of doom:
He triumphs now, the dead,
Beholding London's gloom.

Our wearier spirit faints,
Vexed in the world's employ:
His soul was of the saints;
And art to him was joy.

King, tried in fires of woe!
Men hunger for thy grace:
And through the night I go,
Loving thy mournful face.

Yet, when the city sleeps;
When all the cries are still:
The stars and heavenly deeps
Work out a perfect will.

*Lionel Johnson* [1867-1902]

## CHAVEZ

(Georges Chavez, after crossing the Alps in his aëroplane, fell and was killed Sept. 23, 1919.)

So hath he fallen, the Endymion of the air,
And so lies down in slumber lapped for aye.
Diana, passing, found his youth too fair,
His soul too fleet and willing to obey.
She swung her golden moon before his eyes—
Dreaming, he rose to follow—and ran—and was away.

His foot was wingèd as the mounting sun.
Earth he disdained—the dusty ways of men
Not yet had learned. His spirit longed to run
With the bright clouds, his brothers, to answer when
The airs were fleetest and could give him hand
Into the starry fields beyond our plodding ken.

All wittingly that glorious way he chose,
And loved the peril when it was most bright.
He tried anew the long-forbidden snows
And like an eagle topped the dropping height
Of Nagenhorn, and still toward Italy
Past peak and cliff pressed on, in glad, unerring flight.

Oh when the bird lies low with golden wing
Bruisèd past healing by some bitter chance,
Still must its tireless spirit mount and sing
Of meadows green with morning, of the dance
On windy trees, the darting flight away,
And of that last, most blue, triumphant downward glance.

So murmuring of the snow: "*The snow, and more,
O God, more snow!*" on that last field he lay.
Despair and wonder spent their passionate store
In his great heart, through heaven gone astray,
And early lost. Too far the golden moon
Had swung upon that bright, that long, untraversed way.

Now to lie ended on the murmuring plain—
Ah, this for his bold heart was not the loss,
But that those windy fields he ne'er again
Might try, nor fleet and shimmering mountains cross,
Unfollowed, by a path none other knew:
His bitter woe had here its deep and piteous cause.

Dear toils of youth unfinished! And songs unwritten left
By young and passionate hearts! O melodies
Unheard, whereof we ever stand bereft!
Clear-singing Schubert, boyish Keats—with these
He roams henceforth, one with the starry band,
Still paying to fairy call and far command
His spirit heed, still winged with golden prophecies.

*Mildred McNeal Sweeney* [1871-

## COLERIDGE

[1772-1834]

I SEE thee pine like her in golden story
Who, in her prison, woke and saw, one day,
The gates thrown open—saw the sunbeams play,
With only a web 'tween her and summer's glory;
Who, when that web—so frail, so transitory
It broke before her breath—had fallen away,
Saw other webs and others rise for aye
Which kept her prisoned till her hair was hoary.
Those songs half-sung that yet were all divine—
That woke Romance, the queen, to reign afresh—
Had been but preludes from that lyre of thine,
Could thy rare spirit's wings have pierced the mesh
Spun by the wizard who compels the flesh,
But lets the poet see how heaven can shine.

*Theodore Watts-Dunton* [1836-1914]

## COWPER'S GRAVE

[1731-1800]

IT is a place where poets crowned may feel the heart's decaying;
It is a place where happy saints may weep amid their praying;

Yet let the grief and humbleness as low as silence languish.
Earth surely now may give her calm to whom she gave her anguish.

O poets, from a maniac's tongue was poured the deathless singing!
O Christians, at your cross of hope a hopeless hand was clinging!
O men, this man in brotherhood your weary paths beguiling,
Groaned inly while he taught you peace, and died while ye were smiling!

And now, what time ye all may read through dimming tears his story,
How discord on the music fell and darkness on the glory,
And how when, one by one, sweet sounds and wandering lights departed,
He wore no less a loving face, because so broken-hearted.

He shall be strong to sanctify the poet's high vocation,
And bow the meekest Christian down in meeker adoration;
Nor ever shall he be, in praise, by wise or good forsaken,
Named softly as the household name of one whom God hath taken.

With quiet sadness and no gloom, I learn to think upon him,
With meekness that is gratefulness to God whose heaven hath won him,
Who suffered once the madness-cloud to his own love to blind him,
But gently led the blind along where breath and bird could find him;

And wrought within his shattered brain such quick poetic senses
As hills have language for, and stars, harmonious influences;
The pulse of dew upon the grass kept his within its number,
And silent shadows from the trees refreshed him like a slumber.

Wild timid hares were drawn from woods to share his home-caresses,
Uplooking to his human eyes with sylvan tendernesses:
The very world, by God's constraint, from falsehood's ways removing,
Its women and its men became, beside him, true and loving.

And though, in blindness, he remained unconscious of that guiding,
And things provided came without the sweet sense of providing,
He testified this solemn truth, while frenzy desolated,
—Nor man nor nature satisfies, whom only God created.

Like a sick child that knoweth not his mother while she blesses
And drops upon his burning brow the coolness of her kisses,—
That turns his fevered eyes around,—"My mother! where's my mother?"—
As if such tender words and deeds could come from any other!—

The fever gone, with leaps of heart, he sees her bending o'er him,
Her face all pale from watchful love, the unweary love she bore him!
Thus woke the poet from the dream his life's long fever gave him,
Beneath those deep, pathetic Eyes which closed in death to save him!

Thus? oh, not *thus!* no type of earth can image that awaking,
Wherein he scarcely heard the chant of seraphs, round him breaking,
Or felt the new immortal throb of soul from body parted,
But felt those eyes alone, and knew—"*My* Saviour! *not* deserted!"

Deserted! Who hath dreamt that when the cross in darkness rested,
Upon the Victim's hidden face no love was manifested?
What frantic hands outstretched have e'er the atoning drops averted?
What tears have washed them from the soul, that *one* should be deserted?

Deserted! God could separate from His own essence rather;
And Adam's sins *have* swept between the righteous Son and Father:
Yea, once, Immanuel's orphaned cry his universe hath shaken—
It went up single, echoless, "My God, I am forsaken!"

It went up from the Holy's lips amid His lost creation,
That, of the lost, no son should use those words of desolation!
That Earth's worst frenzies, marring hope, should mar not hope's fruition,
And I, on Cowper's grave, should see his rapture in a vision.

*Elizabeth Barrett Browning* [1806–1861]

## ON A BUST OF DANTE

[1265–1321]

SEE, from this counterfeit of him
Whom Arno shall remember long,
How stern of lineament, how grim,
The father was of Tuscan song:
There but the burning sense of wrong,
Perpetual care, and scorn, abide—
Small friendship for the lordly throng;
Distrust of all the world beside.

Faithful if this wan image be,
No dream his life was—but a fight;
Could any Beatrice see
A lover in that anchorite?

To that cold Ghibelline's gloomy sight
Who could have guessed the visions came
Of Beauty, veiled with heavenly light,
In circles of eternal flame?

The lips as Cumæ's cavern close,
The cheeks with fast and sorrow thin,
The rigid front, almost morose,
But for the patient hope within,
Declare a life whose course hath been
Unsullied still, though still severe,
Which, through the wavering days of sin,
Kept itself icy-chaste and clear.

Not wholly such his haggard look
When wandering once, forlorn, he strayed,
With no companion save his book,
To Corvo's hushed monastic shade;
Where, as the Benedictine laid
His palm upon the convent's guest,
The single boon for which he prayed
Was peace, that pilgrim's one request.

Peace dwells not here—this rugged face
Betrays no spirit of repose;
The sullen warrior sole we trace,
The marble man of many woes.
Such was his mien when first arose
The thought of that strange tale divine—
When hell he peopled with his foes,
Dread scourge of many a guilty line.

War to the last he waged with all
The tyrant canker-worms of earth;
Baron and duke, in hold and hall,
Cursed the dark hour that gave him birth;
He used Rome's harlot for his mirth;
Plucked bare hypocrisy and crime;
But valiant souls of knightly worth
Transmitted to the rolls of Time.

O Time! whose verdicts mock our own,
The only righteous judge art thou;
That poor, old exile, sad and lone,
Is Latium's other Virgil now.
Before his name the nations bow;
His words are parcel of mankind,
Deep in whose hearts, as on his brow,
The marks have sunk of Dante's mind.

*Thomas William Parsons* [1819–1892]

## DICKENS IN CAMP

[1812–1870]

Above the pines the moon was slowly drifting,
The river sang below;
The dim Sierras, far beyond, uplifting
Their minarets of snow.

The roaring camp-fire, with rude humor, painted
The ruddy tints of health
On haggard face and form that drooped and fainted
In the fierce race for wealth;

Till one arose, and from his pack's scant treasure
A hoarded volume drew,
And cards were dropped from hands of listless leisure
To hear the tale anew.

And then, while round them shadows gathered faster,
And as the firelight fell,
He read aloud the book wherein the Master
Had writ of "Little Nell."

Perhaps 'twas boyish fancy,—for the reader
Was youngest of them all,—
But, as he read, from clustering pine and cedar
A silence seemed to fall;

The fir-trees, gathering closer in the shadows,
Listened in every spray,

While the whole camp, with "Nell," on English meadows
  Wandered and lost their way.

And so in mountain solitudes—o'ertaken
  As by some spell divine—
Their cares dropped from them like the needles shaken
  From out the gusty pine.

Lost is that camp, and wasted all its fire:
  And he who wrought that spell?—
Ah, towering pine and stately Kentish spire,
  Ye have one tale to tell!

Lost is that camp, but let its fragrant story
  Blend with the breath that thrills
With hop-vine's incense all the pensive glory
  That fills the Kentish hills.

And on that grave where English oak and holly
  And laurel wreaths entwine,
Deem it not all a too presumptuous folly—
  This spray of Western pine!

*Bret Harte* [1839–1902]

## DRAKE'S DRUM

[SIR FRANCIS DRAKE, 1540?–1596]

DRAKE he's in his hammock an' a thousand mile away,
  (Capten, art tha sleepin' there below?),
Slung atween the round shot in Nombre Dios Bay,
  An' dreamin' arl the time o' Plymouth Hoe.
Yarnder lumes the Island, yarnder lie the ships,
  Wi' sailor lads a-dancin' heel-an'-toe,
An' the shore-lights flashin', an' the night-tide dashin',
  He sees et arl so plainly as he saw et long ago.

Drake he was a Devon man, an' ruled the Devon seas,
  (Capten, art tha sleepin' there below?),
Rovin' though his death fell, he went wi' heart at ease
  An' dreamin' arl the time o' Plymouth Hoe.

"Take my drum to England, hang et by the shore,
  Strike et when your powder's runnin' low;
If the Dons sight Devon, I'll quit the port o' Heaven,
  An' drum them up the Channel as we drummed them long ago."

Drake he's in his hammock till the great Armadas come,
  (Capten, art tha sleepin' there below?),
Slung atween the round shot, listenin' for the drum,
  An' dreamin' arl the time o' Plymouth Hoe.
Call him on the deep sea, call him up the Sound,
  Call him when ye sail to meet the foe;
Where the old trade's plyin' an' the old flag flyin',
  They shall find him ware an' wakin', as they found him long ago!

*Henry Newbolt* [1862–1938]

## ON THE DEATH OF JOSEPH RODMAN DRAKE

[1795–1820]

GREEN be the turf above thee,
  Friend of my better days!
None knew thee but to love thee,
  Nor named thee but to praise.

Tears fell, when thou wert dying,
  From eyes unused to weep,
And long where thou art lying,
  Will tears the cold turf steep.

When hearts, whose truth was proven,
  Like thine, are laid in earth,
There should a wreath be woven
  To tell the world their worth;

And I, who woke each morrow
  To clasp thy hand in mine,
Who shared thy joy and sorrow,
  Whose weal and woe were thine:

It should be mine to braid it
  Around thy faded brow,
But I've in vain essayed it,
  And feel I cannot now.

While memory bids me weep thee,
  Nor thoughts nor words are free,
The grief is fixed too deeply
  That mourns a man like thee.

*Fitz-Greene Halleck* [1790–1867]

## "OH, BREATHE NOT HIS NAME!"

[ROBERT EMMET, 1778–1803]

Oh, breathe not his name! let it sleep in the shade,
Where cold and unhonored his relics are laid;
Sad, silent, and dark be the tears that we shed,
As the night-dew that falls on the grave o'er his head.

But the night-dew that falls, though in silence it weeps,
Shall brighten with verdure the grave where he sleeps;
And the tear that we shed, though in secret it rolls,
Shall long keep his memory green in our souls.

*Thomas Moore* [1779–1852]

## VANQUISHED

[ULYSSES S. GRANT, 1822–1885]

Not by the ball or brand
Sped by a mortal hand,
Not by the lightning stroke
When fiery tempests broke,—
Not mid the ranks of war
Fell the great Conqueror.

Unmoved, undismayed,
In the crash and carnage of the cannonade,—
Eye that dimmed not, hand that failed not,

Brain that swerved not, heart that quailed not,
Steel nerve, iron form,—
The dauntless spirit that o'erruled the storm.

While the Hero peaceful slept
A foeman to his chamber crept,
Lightly to the slumberer came,
Touched his brow and breathed his name:
O'er the stricken form there passed
Suddenly an icy blast.

The Hero woke: rose undismayed:
Saluted Death, and sheathed his blade.

The Conqueror of a hundred fields
To a mightier Conqueror yields;
No mortal foeman's blow
Laid the great Soldier low;
Victor in his latest breath—
Vanquished but by Death.

*Francis Fisher Browne* [1843–1913]

## THE KNIGHT IN DISGUISE

[WILLIAM SIDNEY PORTER (O. HENRY), 1862–1910]

*"He could not forget that he was a Sidney."*

Is this Sir Philip Sidney, this loud clown,
The darling of the glad and gaping town?

This is that dubious hero of the press
Whose slangy tongue and insolent address
Were spiced to rouse on Sunday afternoon
The man with yellow journals round him strewn.
We laughed and dozed, then roused and read again
And vowed O. Henry funniest of men.
He always worked a triple-hinged surprise
To end the scene and make one rub his eyes

He comes with vaudeville, with stare and leer.
He comes with megaphone and specious cheer.
His troupe, too fat or short or long or lean,
Step from the pages of the magazine
With slapstick or sombrero or with cane,
The rube, the cowboy or the masher vain.
They overact each part. But at the height
Of banter and of canter and delight
The masks fall off for one queer instant there
And show real faces: faces full of care
And desperate longing; love that's hot or cold;
And subtle thoughts, and countenances bold.
The masks go back. 'Tis one joke more. Laugh on!
The goodly grown-up company is gone.

No doubt, had he occasion to address
The brilliant court of purple-clad Queen Bess,
He would have wrought for them the best he knew
And led more loftily his actor-crew.
How coolly he misquoted. 'Twas his art:
Slave-scholar, who misquoted—from the heart!
So when he slapped his back with friendly roar
Æsop awaited him, without the door,—
Æsop the Greek, who made dull masters laugh
With little tales of fox and dog and calf.

And, be it said, 'mid these his pranks so odd,
With something nigh to chivalry he trod,
And oft the drear and driven would defend—
The little shop-girl's knight, unto the end.
Yea, he had passed, ere we could understand
The blade of Sidney glimmered in his hand.
Yea, ere we knew, Sir Philip's sword was drawn
With valiant cut and thrust, and he was gone.

*Vachel Lindsay* [1879–1931]

## ADONAIS

[JOHN KEATS, 1795–1821]

I WEEP for Adonais—he is dead!
Oh, weep for Adonais! though our tears
Thaw not the frost which binds so dear a head!
And thou, sad Hour, selected from all years
To mourn our loss, rouse thy obscure compeers,
And teach them thine own sorrow. Say: "With me
Died Adonais; till the Future dares
Forget the Past, his fate and fame shall be
An echo and a light unto eternity!"

Where wert thou, mighty Mother, when he lay,
When thy Son lay, pierced by the shaft which flies
In darkness? where was lorn Urania
When Adonais died? With veilèd eyes,
'Mid listening Echoes, in her Paradise
She sate, while one, with soft enamored breath,
Rekindled all the fading melodies,
With which, like flowers that mock the corse beneath,
He had adorned and hid the coming bulk of death.

Oh, weep for Adonais—he is dead!
Wake, melancholy Mother, wake and weep!
Yet wherefore? Quench within their burning bed
Thy fiery tears, and let thy loud heart keep
Like his, a mute and uncomplaining sleep;
For he is gone where all things wise and fair
Descend. Oh, dream not that the amorous Deep
Will yet restore him to the vital air;
Death feeds on his mute voice, and laughs at our despair.

Most musical of mourners, weep again!
Lament anew, Urania!—He died,
Who was the Sire of an immortal strain,
Blind, old, and lonely, when his country's pride

The priest, the slave, and the liberticide
Trampled and mocked with many a loathèd rite
Of lust and blood; he went, unterrified,
Into the gulf of death; but his clear Sprite
Yet reigns o'er earth, the third among the sons of light.

Most musical of mourners, weep anew!
Not all to that bright station dared to climb;
And happier they their happiness who knew,
Whose tapers yet burn through that night of time
In which suns perished; others more sublime,
Struck by the envious wrath of man or God,
Have sunk, extinct in their refulgent prime;
And some yet live, treading the thorny road,
Which leads, through toil and hate, to Fame's serene abode.

But now, thy youngest, dearest one has perished,
The nursling of thy widowhood, who grew,
Like a pale flower by some sad maiden cherished,
And fed with true-love tears, instead of dew;
Most musical of mourners, weep anew!
Thy extreme hope, the loveliest and the last,
The bloom, whose petals, nipped before they blew,
Died on the promise of the fruit, is waste;
The broken lily lies—the storm is overpast.

To that high Capital, where kingly Death
Keeps his pale court in beauty and decay,
He came; and bought, with price of purest breath,
A grave among the eternal.—Come away!
Haste, while the vault of blue Italian day
Is yet his fitting charnel-roof! while still
He lies, as if in dewy sleep he lay;
Awake him not! surely he takes his fill
Of deep and liquid rest, forgetful of all ill.

He will awake no more, oh, never more!
Within the twilight chamber spreads apace
The shadow of white Death, and at the door
Invisible Corruption waits to trace

His extreme way to her dim dwelling-place;
The eternal Hunger sits, but pity and awe
Soothe her pale rage, nor dares she to deface
So fair a prey, till darkness and the law
Of change, shall o'er his sleep the mortal curtain draw.

Oh, weep for Adonais!—The quick Dreams,
The passion-wingèd ministers of thought,
Who were his flocks, whom near the living streams
Of his young spirit he fed, and whom he taught
The love which was its music, wander not,—
Wander no more, from kindling brain to brain,
But droop there, whence they sprung; and mourn their lot
Round the cold heart, where, after their sweet pain,
They ne'er will gather strength, or find a home again.

And one with trembling hands clasps his cold head,
And fans him with her moonlight wings, and cries,
"Our love, our hope, our sorrow, is not dead;
See, on the silken fringe of his faint eyes,
Like dew upon a sleeping flower, there lies
A tear some Dream has loosened from his brain."
Lost Angel of a ruined Paradise!
She knew not 'twas her own; as with no stain
She faded, like a cloud which had outwept its rain.

One from a lucid urn of starry dew
Washed his light limbs as if embalming them;
Another clipped her profuse locks, and threw
The wreath upon him, like an anadem,
Which frozen tears instead of pearls begem;
Another in her wilful grief would break
Her bow and wingèd reeds, as if to stem
A greater loss with one which was more weak;
And dull the barbèd fire against his frozen cheek.

Another Splendor on his mouth alit,
That mouth, whence it was wont to draw the breath
Which gave it strength to pierce the guarded wit,
And pass into the panting heart beneath

With lightning and with music: the damp death
Quenched its caress upon his icy lips;
And, as a dying meteor stains a wreath
Of moonlight vapor, which the cold night clips,
It flushed through his pale limbs, and passed to its eclipse.

And others came . . . Desires and Adorations,
Wingèd Persuasions and veiled Destinies,
Splendors, and Glooms, and glimmering Incarnations
Of hopes and fears, and twilight Fantasies;
And Sorrow, with her family of Sighs,
And Pleasure, blind with tears, led by the gleam
Of her own dying smile instead of eyes,
Came in slow pomp;—the moving pomp might seem
Like pageantry of mist on an autumnal stream.

All he had loved, and molded into thought,
From shape, and hue, and odor, and sweet sound,
Lamented Adonais. Morning sought
Her eastern watch-tower, and her hair unbound,
Wet with the tears which should adorn the ground,
Dimmed the aërial eyes that kindle day;
Afar the melancholy thunder moaned,
Pale Ocean in unquiet slumber lay,
And the wild winds flew round, sobbing in their dismay.

Lost Echo sits amid the voiceless mountains,
And feeds her grief with his remembered lay,
And will no more reply to winds or fountains,
Or amorous birds perched on the young green spray,
Or herdsman's horn, or bell at closing day;
Since she can mimic not his lips, more dear
Than those for whose disdain she pined away
Into a shadow of all sounds:—a drear
Murmur, between their songs, is all the woodmen hear.

Grief made the young Spring wild, and she threw down
Her kindling buds, as if she Autumn were,
Or they dead leaves; since her delight is flown,
For whom should she have waked the sullen year?

To Phœbus was not Hyacinth so dear,
Nor to himself Narcissus, as to both
Thou, Adonais; wan they stand and sere
Amid the faint companions of their youth,
With dew all turned to tears; odor, to sighing ruth

Thy spirit's sister, the lorn nightingale,
Mourns not her mate with such melodious pain;
Not so the eagle, who like thee could scale
Heaven, and could nourish in the sun's domain
Her mighty youth with morning, doth complain,
Soaring and screaming round her empty nest,
As Albion wails for thee: the curse of Cain
Light on his head who pierced thy innocent breast,
And scared the angel soul that was its earthly guest!

Ah woe is me! Winter is come and gone,
But grief returns with the revolving year;
The airs and streams renew their joyous tone;
The ants, the bees, the swallows reappear;
Fresh leaves and flowers deck the dead Seasons' bier;
The amorous birds now pair in every brake,
And build their mossy homes in field and brere;
And the green lizard and the golden snake,
Like unimprisoned flames, out of their trance awake.

Through wood and stream and field and hill and Ocean
A quickening life from the Earth's heart has burst,
As it has ever done, with change and motion,
From the great morning of the world when first
God dawned on Chaos; in its stream immersed
The lamps of Heaven flash with a softer light;
All baser things pant with life's sacred thirst,
Diffuse themselves, and spend in love's delight,
The beauty and the joy of their renewèd might.

The leprous corpse, touched by this spirit tender,
Exhales itself in flowers of gentle breath;
Like incarnations of the stars, when splendor
Is changed to fragrance, they illumine death

And mock the merry worm that wakes beneath.
Naught we know, dies. Shall that alone which knows
Be as a sword consumed before the sheath
By sightless lightning?—the intense atom glows
A moment, then is quenched in a most cold repose.

Alas! that all we loved of him should be,
But for our grief, as if it had not been,
And grief itself be mortal! Woe is me!
Whence are we, and why are we? of what scene
The actors or spectators? Great and mean
Meet massed in death, who lends what life must borrow.
As long as skies are blue, and fields are green,
Evening must usher night, night urge the morrow,
Month follow month with woe, and year wake year to sorrow.

*He* will awake no more, oh, never more!
"Wake thou," cried Misery, "childless Mother, rise
Out of thy sleep, and slake, in thy heart's core,
A wound more fierce than his with tears and sighs."
And all the Dreams that watched Urania's eyes,
And all the Echoes whom their sister's song
Had held in holy silence, cried, "Arise!"
Swift as a Thought by the snake Memory stung,
From her ambrosial rest the fading Splendor sprung.

She rose like an autumnal Night, that springs
Out of the East, and follows wild and drear
The golden Day, which, on eternal wings,
Even as a ghost abandoning a bier,
Had left the Earth a corpse.—Sorrow and fear
So struck, so roused, so rapt Urania;
So saddened round her like an atmosphere
Of stormy mist; so swept her on her way
Even to the mournful place where Adonais lay.

Out of her secret Paradise she sped,
Through camps and cities rough with stone, and steel,
And human hearts which, to her airy tread

Yielding not, wounded the invisible
Palms of her tender feet where'er they fell;
And barbèd tongues, and thoughts more sharp than they,
Rent the soft Form they never could repel,
Whose sacred blood, like the young tears of May,
Paved with eternal flowers that undeserving way.

In the death-chamber for a moment Death,
Shamed by the presence of that living Might,
Blushed to annihilation, and the breath
Revisited those lips, and life's pale light
Flashed through those limbs, so late her dear delight.
"Leave me not wild and drear and comfortless,
As silent lightning leaves the starless night!
Leave me not!" cried Urania; her distress
Roused Death; Death rose and smiled, and met her vain caress.

"Stay yet awhile! speak to me once again;
Kiss me, so long but as a kiss may live;
And in my heartless breast and burning brain
That word, that kiss, shall all thoughts else survive,
With food of saddest memory kept alive,
Now thou art dead, as if it were a part
Of thee, my Adonais! I would give
All that I am to be as thou now art!
But I am chained to Time, and cannot thence depart!

"O gentle child, beautiful as thou wert,
Why didst thou leave the trodden paths of men
Too soon, and with weak hands though mighty heart
Dare the unpastured dragon in his den?
Defenseless as thou wert, oh, where was then
Wisdom the mirrored shield, or scorn the spear?
Or hadst thou waited the full cycle, when
Thy spirit should have filled its crescent sphere,
The monsters of life's waste had fled from thee like deer.

"The herded wolves, bold only to pursue;
The obscene ravens, clamorous o'er the dead;
The vultures, to the conqueror's banner true,

Who feed where Desolation first has fed,
And whose wings rain contagion;—how they fled,
When, like Apollo, from his golden bow
The Pythian of the age one arrow sped
And smiled!—The spoilers tempt no second blow,
They fawn on the proud feet that spurn them lying low.

"The sun comes forth, and many reptiles spawn;
He sets, and each ephemeral insect then
Is gathered into death without a dawn,
And the immortal stars awake again;
So is it in the world of living men:
A godlike mind soars forth, in its delight
Making earth bare and veiling heaven, and when
It sinks, the swarms that dimmed or shared its light
Leave to its kindred lamps the spirit's awful night."

Thus ceased she: and the mountain shepherds came,
Their garlands sere, their magic mantles rent;
The Pilgrim of Eternity, whose fame
Over his living head like Heaven is bent,
An early but enduring monument,
Came, veiling all the lightnings of his song
In sorrow; from her wilds Ierne sent
The sweetest lyrist of her saddest wrong,
And love taught grief to fall like music from his tongue.

Midst others of less note, came one frail Form,
A phantom among men; companionless
As the last cloud of an expiring storm
Whose thunder is its knell; he, as I guess,
Had gazed on Nature's naked loveliness,
Actæon-like, and now he fled astray
With feeble steps o'er the world's wilderness,
And his own thoughts, along that rugged way,
Pursued, like raging hounds, their father and their prey.

A pardlike Spirit beautiful and swift—
A Love in desolation masked;—a Power
Girt round with weakness;—it can scarce uplift

The weight of the superincumbent hour;
It is a dying lamp, a falling shower,
A breaking billow;—even whilst we speak
Is it not broken? On the withering flower
The killing sun smiles brightly: on a cheek
The life can burn in blood, even while the heart may break.

His head was bound with pansies overblown,
And faded violets, white, and pied, and blue;
And a light spear topped with a cypress cone,
Round whose rude shaft dark ivy tresses grew
Yet dripping with the forest's noonday dew,
Vibrated, as the ever-beating heart
Shook the weak hand that grasped it; of that crew
He came the last, neglected and apart;
A herd-abandoned deer struck by the hunter's dart.

All stood aloof, and at his partial moan
Smiled through their tears; well knew that gentle band
Who in another's fate now wept his own,
As in the accents of an unknown land
He sung new sorrow; sad Urania scanned
The Stranger's mien, and murmured: "Who art thou?"
He answered not, but with a sudden hand
Made bare his branded and ensanguined brow,
Which was like Cain's or Christ's—oh! that it should be so!

What softer voice is hushed over the dead?
Athwart what brow is that dark mantle thrown?
What form leans sadly o'er the white death-bed,
In mockery of monumental stone,
The heavy heart heaving without a moan?
If it be He, who, gentlest of the wise,
Taught, soothed, loved, honored the departed one;
Let me not vex with inharmonious sighs
The silence of that heart's accepted sacrifice.

Our Adonais has drunk poison—oh,
What deaf and viperous murderer could crown
Life's early cup with such a draught of woe?

The nameless worm would now itself disown;
It felt, yet could escape the magic tone
Whose prelude held all envy, hate and wrong,
But what was howling in one breast alone,
Silent with expectation of the song,
Whose master's hand is cold, whose silver lyre unstrung.

Live thou, whose infamy is not thy fame!
Live! fear no heavier chastisement from me,
Thou noteless blot on a remembered name!
But be thyself, and know thyself to be!
And ever at thy season be thou free
To spill the venom when thy fangs o'erflow;
Remorse and Self-contempt shall cling to thee;
Hot Shame shall burn upon thy secret brow,
And like a beaten hound tremble thou shalt—as now.

Nor let us weep that our delight is fled
Far from these carrion kites that scream below;
He wakes or sleeps with the enduring dead;
Thou canst not soar where he is sitting now.
Dust to the dust! but the pure spirit shall flow
Back to the burning fountain whence it came,
A portion of the Eternal, which must glow
Through time and change, unquenchably the same,
Whilst thy cold embers choke the sordid hearth of shame

Peace, peace! he is not dead, he doth not sleep—
He hath awakened from the dream of life—
'Tis we, who, lost in stormy visions, keep
With phantoms an unprofitable strife,
And in mad trance, strike with our spirit's knife
Invulnerable nothings. *We* decay
Like corpses in a charnel; fear and grief
Convulse us and consume us day by day,
And cold hopes swarm like worms within our living clay.

He has outsoared the shadow of our night;
Envy and calumny and hate and pain,
And that unrest which men miscall delight,

Can touch him not and torture not again;
From the contagion of the world's slow stain
He is secure, and now can never mourn
A heart grown cold, a head grown gray in vain;
Nor, when the spirit's self has ceased to burn,
With sparkless ashes load an unlamented urn.

He lives, he wakes—'tis Death is dead, not he;
Mourn not for Adonais.—Thou young Dawn,
Turn all thy dew to splendor, for from thee
The spirit thou lamentest is not gone;
Ye caverns and ye forests, cease to moan!
Cease, ye faint flowers and fountains, and thou Air,
Which like a mourning veil thy scarf hadst thrown
O'er the abandoned Earth, now leave it bare
Even to the joyous stars which smile on its despair!

He is made one with Nature: there is heard
His voice in all her music, from the moan
Of thunder, to the song of night's sweet bird;
He is a presence to be felt and known
In darkness and in light, from herb and stone,
Spreading itself where'er that Power may move
Which has withdrawn his being to its own;
Which wields the world with never-wearied love,
Sustains it from beneath, and kindles it above.

He is a portion of the loveliness
Which once he made more lovely: he doth bear
His part, while the one Spirit's plastic stress
Sweeps through the dull dense world, compelling there,
All new successions to the forms they wear;
Torturing the unwilling dross that checks its flight
To its own likeness, as each mass may bear,
And bursting in its beauty and its might
From trees and beasts and men into the Heaven's light.

The splendors of the firmament of time
May be eclipsed, but are extinguished not;
Like stars to their appointed height they climb,

And death is a low mist which cannot blot
The brightness it may veil. When lofty thought
Lifts a young heart above its mortal lair,
And love and life contend in it, for what
Shall be its earthly doom, the dead live there
And move like winds of light on dark and stormy air.

The inheritors of unfulfilled renown
Rose from their thrones, built beyond mortal thought,
Far in the Unapparent. Chatterton
Rose pale,—his solemn agony had not
Yet faded from him; Sidney, as he fought
And as he fell and as he lived and loved,
Sublimely mild, a Spirit without spot,
Arose; and Lucan, by his death approved;
Oblivion as they rose shrank like a thing reproved.

And many more, whose names on Earth are dark,
But whose transmitted effluence cannot die
So long as fire outlives the parent spark,
Rose, robed in dazzling immortality.
"Thou art become as one of us," they cry;
"It was for thee yon kingless sphere has long
Swung blind in unascended majesty,
Silent alone amid an Heaven of song.
Assume thy wingèd throne, thou Vesper of our throng!"

Who mourns for Adonais? oh, come forth,
Fond wretch! and know thyself and him aright.
Clasp with thy panting soul the pendulous Earth;
As from a center, dart thy spirit's light
Beyond all worlds, until its spacious might
Satiate the void circumference; then shrink
Even to a point within our day and night;
And keep thy heart light lest it make thee sink
When hope has kindled hope, and lured thee to the brink

Or go to Rome, which is the sepulchre
Oh, not of him, but of our joy: 'tis naught
That ages, empires, and religions there
Lie buried in the ravage they have wrought;
For such as he can lend,—they borrow not

Glory from those who made the world their prey;
And he is gathered to the kings of thought
Who waged contention with their time's decay,
And of the past are all that cannot pass away.

Go thou to Rome,—at once the Paradise,
The grave, the city, and the wilderness;
And where its wrecks like shattered mountains rise,
And flowering weeds, and fragrant copses dress
The bones of Desolation's nakedness,
Pass, till the Spirit of the spot shall lead
Thy footsteps to a slope of green access,
Where, like an infant's smile, over the dead
A light of laughing flowers along the grass is spread.

And gray walls molder round, on which dull Time
Feeds, like slow fire upon a hoary brand;
And one keen pyramid with wedge sublime,
Pavilioning the dust of him who planned
This refuge for his memory, doth stand
Like flame transformed to marble; and beneath
A field is spread, on which a newer band
Have pitched in Heaven's smile their camp of death.
Welcoming him we lose with scarce extinguished breath.

Here pause: these graves are all too young as yet
To have outgrown the sorrow which consigned
Its charge to each; and if the seal is set,
Here, on one fountain of a mourning mind,
Break it not thou! too surely shalt thou find
Thine own well full, if thou returnest home,
Of tears and gall. From the world's bitter wind
Seek shelter in the shadow of the tomb.
What Adonais is, why fear we to become?

The One remains, the many change and pass;
Heaven's light forever shines, Earth's shadows fly;
Life, like a dome of many-colored glass,
Stains the white radiance of Eternity,
Until Death tramples it to fragments.—Die,
If thou wouldst be with that which thou dost seek!
Follow where all is fled!—Rome's azure sky,

Flowers, ruins, statues, music, words, are weak
The glory they transfuse with fitting truth to speak.

Why linger, why turn back, why shrink, my Heart?
Thy hopes are gone before; from all things here
They have departed; thou shouldst now depart!
A light is passed from the revolving year,
And man, and woman; and what still is dear
Attracts to crush, repels to make thee wither.
The soft sky smiles,—the low wind whispers near;
'Tis Adonais calls! oh, hasten thither,
No more let Life divide what Death can join together.

That Light whose smile kindles the Universe,
That Beauty in which all things work and move,
That Benediction which the eclipsing Curse
Of birth can quench not, that sustaining Love
Which through the web of being blindly wove
By man and beast and earth and air and sea,
Burns bright or dim, as each are mirrors of
The fire for which all thirst, now beams on me,
Consuming the last clouds of cold mortality.

The breath whose might I have invoked in song
Descends on me; my spirit's bark is driven
Far from the shore, far from the trembling throng
Whose sails were never to the tempest given;
The massy earth and spherèd skies are riven!
I am borne darkly, fearfully, afar;
Whilst, burning through the inmost veil of Heaven,
The soul of Adonais, like a star,
Beacons from the abode where the Eternal are.

*Percy Bysshe Shelley* [1792-1822]

## TO THE SISTER OF ELIA

[CHARLES LAMB, 1775-1834]

COMFORT thee, O thou mourner, yet awhile!
Again shall Elia's smile
Refresh thy heart, where heart can ache no more.
What is it we deplore?

He leaves behind him, freed from griefs and years,
  Far worthier things than tears.
The love of friends without a single foe:
  Unequaled lot below!

His gentle soul, his genius, these are thine;
  For these dost thou repine?
He may have left the lowly walks of men;
  Left them he has; what then?

Are not his footsteps followed by the eyes
  Of all the good and wise?
Though the warm day is over, yet they seek
  Upon the lofty peak

Of his pure mind the roseate light that glows
  O'er death's perennial snows.
Behold him! from the region of the blest
  He speaks: he bids thee rest.

*Walter Savage Landor* [1775-1864]

## IN MEMORY OF WALTER SAVAGE LANDOR

[1775-1864]

BACK to the flower-town, side by side,
    The bright months bring,
New-born, the bridegroom and the bride,
    Freedom and spring.

The sweet land laughs from sea to sea,
    Filled full of sun;
All things come back to her, being free;
    All things but one.

In many a tender wheaten plot
    Flowers that were dead
Live, and old suns revive; but not
    That holier head.

By this white wandering waste of sea,
Far north, I hear
One face shall never turn to me
As once this year:

Shall never smile and turn and rest
On mine as there,
Nor one most sacred hand be pressed
Upon my hair.

I came as one whose thoughts half linger,
Half run before;
The youngest to the eldest singer
That England bore.

I found him whom I shall not find
Till all grief end,
In holiest age our mightiest mind,
Father and friend.

But thou, if anything endure,
If hope there be,
O spirit that man's life left pure,
Man's death set free,

Not with disdain of days that were
Look earthward now;
Let dreams revive the reverend hair,
The imperial brow;

Come back in sleep, for in the life
Where thou art not
We find none like thee. Time and strife
And the world's lot

Move thee no more; but love at least
And reverent heart
May move thee, royal and released
Soul, as thou art.

And thou, his Florence, to thy trust
Receive and keep,
Keep safe his dedicated dust,
His sacred sleep.

So shall thy lovers, come from far
Mix with thy name
As morning-star with evening-star
His faultless fame.

*Algernon Charles Swinburne* [1837-1909]

## ON THE DEATH OF MR. ROBERT LEVET, A PRACTISER IN PHYSIC

[1701-1782]

CONDEMNED to Hope's delusive mine,
As on we toil from day to day,
By sudden blasts or slow decline
Our social comforts drop away.

Well tried through many a varying year,
See Levet to the grave descend,
Officious, innocent, sincere,
Of every friendless name the friend.

Yet still he fills affection's eye,
Obscurely wise and coarsely kind;
Nor, lettered Arrogance, deny
Thy praise to merit unrefined.

When fainting nature called for aid,
And hovering death prepared the blow,
His vigorous remedy displayed
The power of art without the show.

In Misery's darkest cavern known,
His useful care was ever nigh,
Where hopeless Anguish poured his groan,
And lonely Want retired to die.

No summons mocked by chill delay,
No petty gain disdained by pride;
The modest wants of every day
The toil of every day supplied.

His virtues walked their narrow round,
Nor made a pause, nor left a void;
And sure the Eternal Master found
The single talent well employed.

The busy day, the peaceful night,
Unfelt, uncounted, glided by;
His frame was firm—his powers were bright,
Though now his eightieth year was nigh.

Then with no fiery throbbing pain,
No cold gradations of decay
Death broke at once the vital chain,
And freed his soul the nearest way.

*Samuel Johnson* [1709–1784]

## "O CAPTAIN! MY CAPTAIN!"

[ABRAHAM LINCOLN, 1809–1865]

O CAPTAIN! my Captain! our fearful trip is done,
The ship has weathered every rack, the prize we sought is won,
The port is near, the bells I hear, the people all exulting,
While follow eyes the steady keel, the vessel grim and daring
But O heart! heart! heart!
O the bleeding drops of red,
Where on the deck my Captain lies,
Fallen cold and dead.

O Captain! my Captain! rise up and hear the bells;
Rise up—for you the flag is flung—for you the bugle trills,
For you bouquets and ribboned wreaths—for you the shores a-crowding,
For you they call, the swaying mass, their eager faces turning;
Here Captain! dear father!
This arm beneath your head!
It is some dream that on the deck
You've fallen cold and dead.

My Captain does not answer, his lips are pale and still,
My father does not feel my arm, he has no pulse nor will,
The ship is anchored safe and sound, its voyage closed and done,
From fearful trip the victor ship comes in with object won;
Exult O shores, and ring O bells!
But I with mournful tread,
Walk the deck my Captain lies,
Fallen cold and dead.

*Walt Whitman* [1819-1892]

## "WHEN LILACS LAST IN THE DOORYARD BLOOMED"

I

WHEN lilacs last in the dooryard bloomed,
And the great star early drooped in the western sky in the night,
I mourned, and yet shall mourn with ever-returning spring.

Ever-returning spring, trinity sure to me you bring,
Lilac blooming perennial and drooping star in the west,
And thought of him I love.

II

O powerful western fallen star!
O shades of night—O moody, tearful night!
O great star disappeared—O the black murk that hides the star!

O cruel hands that hold me powerless—O helpless soul of me!
O harsh surrounding cloud that will not free my soul!

III

In the dooryard fronting an old farmhouse, near the whitewashed palings,
Stands the lilac-bush tall-growing with heart-shaped leaves
of rich green,
With many a pointed blossom rising delicate, with the perfume strong I love,
With every leaf a miracle—and from this bush in the
dooryard,
With delicate-colored blossoms and heart-shaped leaves of
rich green,
A sprig with its flower I break.

IV

In the swamp in secluded recesses,
A shy and hidden bird is warbling a song.

Solitary the thrush,
The hermit withdrawn to himself, avoiding the settlements,
Sings by himself a song.

Song of the bleeding throat,
Death's outlet song of life—(for well, dear brother, I know
If thou wast not gifted to sing thou wouldst surely die).

V

Over the breast of the spring, the land, amid cities,
Amid lanes and through old woods, where lately the violets
peeped from the ground, spotting the gray debris,
Amid the grass in the fields each side of the lanes, passing the
endless grass,
Passing the yellow-speared wheat, every grain from its
shroud in the dark-brown fields uprisen,
Passing the apple-tree blows of white and pink in the orchards,

Carrying a corpse to where it shall rest in the grave,
Night and day journeys a coffin.

VI

Coffin that passes through lanes and streets,
Through day and night, with the great cloud darkening the land,
With the pomp of the inlooped flags, with the cities draped in black,
With the show of the States themselves as of crape-veiled women standing,
With processions long and winding and the flambeaus of the night,
With the countless torches lit, with the silent sea of faces and the unbared heads,
With the waiting depot, the arriving coffin, and the somber faces,
With dirges through the night, with the thousand voices rising strong and solemn,
With all the mournful voices of the dirges poured around the coffin,
The dim-lit churches and the shuddering organs—where amid these you journey,
With the tolling tolling bells' perpetual clang,
Here, coffin that slowly passes,
I give you my sprig of lilac.

VII

(Nor for you, for one alone,
Blossoms and branches green to coffins all I bring,
For fresh as the morning, thus would I chant a song for you,
O sane and sacred death.

All over bouquets of roses,
O death, I cover you over with roses and early lilies,
But mostly and now the lilac that blooms the first,
Copious I break, I break the sprigs from the bushes,
With loaded arms I come, pouring for you,
For you and the coffins all of you, O death.)

VIII

O western orb sailing the heaven,
Now I know what you must have meant as a month since I walked,
As I walked in silence the transparent shadowy night,
As I saw you had something to tell as you bent to me night after night,
As you drooped from the sky low down as if to my side, (while the other stars all looked on,)
As we wandered together the solemn night, (for something, I know not what, kept me from sleep,)
As the night advanced, and I saw on the rim of the west how full you were of woe,
As I stood on the rising ground in the breeze in the cool transparent night,
As I watched where you passed, and was lost in the netherward black of the night,
As my soul in its trouble dissatisfied sank, as where yon sad orb,
Concluded, dropped in the night, and was gone.

IX

Sing on there in the swamp,
O singer bashful and tender, I hear your notes, I hear your call,
I hear, I come presently, I understand you,
But a moment I linger, for the lustrous star has detained me,
The star my departing comrade holds and detains me.

X

O how shall I warble myself for the dead one there I loved?
And how shall I deck my song for the large sweet soul that has gone?
And what shall my perfume be for the grave of him I love?

Sea-winds blown from east and west,
Blown from the Eastern sea and blown from the Western sea, till there on the prairies meeting,
These and with these and the breath of my chant,
I'll perfume the grave of him I love.

XI

O what shall I hang on the chamber walls?
And what shall the pictures be that I hang on the walls,
To adorn the burial-house of him I love?

Pictures of growing spring and farms and homes,
With the Fourth-month eve at sundown, and the gray smoke lucid and bright,
With floods of the yellow gold of the gorgeous, indolent, sinking sun, burning, expanding the air,
With the fresh spring herbage under foot, and the pale green leaves of the trees prolific,
In the distance the flowing glaze, the breast of the river, with a wind-dapple here and there,
With ranging hills on the banks, with many a line against the sky, and shadows,
And the city at hand with dwellings so dense, and stacks of chimneys,
And all the scenes of life and the workshops, and the workmen homeward returning.

XII

Lo, body and soul—this land,
My own Manhattan with spires, and the sparkling and hurrying tides, and the ships,
The varied and ample land, the South and the North in the light, Ohio's shores and flashing Missouri,
And ever the far-spreading prairies covered with grass and corn.

Lo, the most excellent sun so calm and haughty,
The violet and purple morn with just-felt breezes,
The gentle soft-born measureless light,
The miracle spreading bathing all, the fulfilled noon,
The coming eve delicious, the welcome night and the stars,
Over my cities shining all, enveloping man and land.

XIII

Sing on, sing on, you gray-brown bird,
Sing from the swamps, the recesses, pour your chant from the bushes,
Limitless out of the dusk, out of the cedars and pines

Sing on, dearest brother, warble your reedy song,
Loud human song, with voice of uttermost woe.

O liquid and free and tender!
O wild and loose to my soul—O wondrous singer!
You only I hear—yet the star holds me, (but will soon depart,)
Yet the lilac with mastering odor holds me.

XIV

Now while I sat in the day and looked forth,
In the close of the day with its light and the fields of spring, and the farmers preparing their crops,
In the large unconscious scenery of my land with its lakes and forests,
In the heavenly aerial beauty, (after the perturbed winds and the storms,)
Under the arching heavens of the afternoon swift passing, and the voices of children and women,
The many-moving sea-tides, and I saw the ships how they sailed,
And the summer approaching with richness, and the fields all busy with labor,
And the infinite separate houses, how they all went on, each with its meals and minutia of daily usages,
And the streets how their throbbings throbbed, and the cities pent—lo, then and there,
Falling upon them all and among them all, enveloping me with the rest,
Appeared the cloud, appeared the long black trail,
And I knew death, its thought, and the sacred knowledge of death.

Then with the knowledge of death as walking one side of me,
And the thought of death close-walking the other side of me,
And I in the middle as with companions, and as holding the hands of companions,
I fled forth to the hiding receiving night that talks not,
Down to the shores of the water, the path by the swamp in the dimness,
To the solemn shadowy cedars and ghostly pines so still.

And the singer so shy to the rest received me,
The gray-brown bird I know received us comrades three,
And he sang the carol of death, and a verse for him I love.

From deep secluded recesses,
From the fragrant cedars and the ghostly pines so still,
Came the carol of the bird.

And the charm of the carol rapt me,
As I held as if by their hands my comrades in the night,
And the voice of my spirit tallied the song of the bird.

*Come, lovely and soothing death,*
*Undulate round the world, serenely arriving, arriving,*
*In the day, in the night, to all, to each,*
*Sooner or later delicate death.*

*Praised be the fathomless universe,*
*For life and joy, and for objects and knowledge curious,*
*And for love, sweet love—but praise! praise! praise!*
*For the sure-enwinding arms of cool-enfolding death.*

*Dark mother always gliding near with soft feet,*
*Have none chanted for thee a chant of fullest welcome?*
*Then I chant it for thee, I glorify thee above all,*
*I bring thee a song that when thou must indeed come, come unfalteringly.*

*Approach, strong deliveress,*
*When it is so, when thou hast taken them I joyously sing the dead,*
*Lost in the loving floating ocean of thee,*
*Laved in the flood of thy bliss, O death.*

*From me to thee glad serenades,*
*Dances for thee I propose, saluting thee, adornments and feastings for thee,*
*And the sights of the open landscape and the high-spread sky are fitting,*
*And life and the fields, and the huge and thoughtful night.*

*The night in silence under many a star,*
*The ocean shore and the husky whispering wave whose voice I know,*
*And the soul turning to thee, O vast and well-veiled death,*
*And the body gratefully nestling close to thee.*

*Over the tree-tops I float thee a song,*
*Over the rising and sinking waves, over the myriad fields and the prairies wide,*
*Over the dense-packed cities all and the teeming wharves and ways,*
*I float this carol with joy, with joy to thee, O death.*

XV

To the tally of my soul,
Loud and strong kept up the gray-brown bird,
With pure deliberate notes spreading filling the night.

Loud in the pines and cedars dim,
Clear in the freshness moist and the swamp-perfume,
And I with my comrades there in the night.

While my sight that was bound in my eyes unclosed,
As to long panoramas of visions.

And I saw askant the armies,
I saw as in noiseless dreams hundreds of battle-flags,
Borne through the smoke of the battles and pierced with missiles I saw them,
And carried hither and yon through the smoke, and torn and bloody,
And at last but a few shreds left on the staffs, (and all in silence,)
And the staffs all splintered and broken.

I saw battle-corpses, myriads of them,
And the white skeletons of young men, I saw them,
I saw the debris and debris of all the slain soldiers of the war.

But I saw they were not as was thought,
They themselves were fully at rest, they suffered not,
The living remained and suffered, the mother suffered,
And the wife and the child and the musing comrade suffered,
And the armies that remained suffered.

XVI

Passing the visions, passing the night,
Passing, unloosing the hold of my comrades' hands,
Passing the song of the hermit bird, and the tallying song of my soul,
Victorious song, death's outlet song, yet varying ever-altering song,
As low and wailing, yet clear the notes, rising and falling, flooding the night,
Sadly sinking and fainting, as warning and warning, and yet again bursting with joy,
Covering the earth and filling the spread of the heaven,
As that powerful psalm in the night I heard from recesses,
Passing, I leave thee lilac with heart-shaped leaves,
I leave thee there in the dooryard, blooming, returning with spring.

I cease from my song for thee,
From my gaze on thee in the west, fronting the west, communing with thee,
O comrade lustrous with silver face in the night.

Yet each to keep and all, retrievements out of the night,
The song, the wondrous chant of the gray-brown bird,
And the tallying chant, the echo aroused in my soul,
With the lustrous and drooping star with the countenance full of woe,
With the holders holding my hand nearing the call of the bird,
Comrades mine and I in the midst, and their memory ever to keep, for the dead I loved so well,
For the sweetest, wisest soul of all my days and lands—and this for his dear sake,
Lilac and star and bird twined with the chant of my soul,
There in the fragrant pines and the cedars dusk and dim.

*Walt Whitman* [1819–1892]

## LINCOLN, THE MAN OF THE PEOPLE

When the Norn Mother saw the Whirlwind Hour
Greatening and darkening as it hurried on,
She left the Heaven of Heroes and came down
To make a man to meet the mortal need.
She took the tried clay of the common road—
Clay warm yet with the genial heat of Earth,
Dashed through it all a strain of prophecy;
Tempered the heap with thrill of human tears;
Then mixed a laughter with the serious stuff.
Into the shape she breathed a flame to light
That tender, tragic, ever-changing face.
Here was a man to hold against the world,
A man to match the mountains and the sea.

The color of the ground was in him, the red earth;
The smack and tang of elemental things:
The rectitude and patience of the cliff;
The good-will of the rain that loves all leaves;
The friendly welcome of the wayside well;
The courage of the bird that dares the sea;
The gladness of the wind that shakes the corn;
The pity of the snow that hides all scars;
The secrecy of streams that make their way
Beneath the mountain to the rifted rock;
The tolerance and equity of light
That gives as freely to the shrinking flower
As to the great oak flaring to the wind—
To the grave's low hill as to the Matterhorn
That shoulders out the sky.

Sprung from the West,
The strength of virgin forests braced his mind,
The hush of spacious prairies stilled his soul.
Up from log cabin to the Capitol,
One fire was on his spirit, one resolve—
To send the keen ax to the root of wrong,
Clearing a free way for the feet of God.
And evermore he burned to do his deed

With the fine stroke and gesture of a king:
He built the rail-pile as he built the State,
Pouring his splendid strength through every blow,
The conscience of him testing every stroke,
To make his deed the measure of a man.

So came the Captain with the mighty heart;
And when the judgment thunders split the house,
Wrenching the rafters from their ancient rest,
He held the ridgepole up, and spiked again
The rafters of the Home. He held his place—
Held the long purpose like a growing tree—
Held on through blame and faltered not at praise.
And when he fell in whirlwind, he went down
As when a lordly cedar, green with boughs,
Goes down with a great shout upon the hills,
And leaves a lonesome place against the sky.

*Edwin Markham* [1852–1940]

## THE MASTER

**Supposed to have been written not long after the Civil War**

A FLYING word from here and there
Had sown the name at which we sneered,
But soon the name was everywhere,
To be reviled and then revered:
A presence to be loved and feared,
We cannot hide it, or deny
That we, the gentlemen who jeered,
May be forgotten by and by.

He came when days were perilous
And hearts of men were sore beguiled;
And having made his note of us,
He pondered and was reconciled.
Was ever master yet so mild
As he, and so untamable?
We doubted, even when he smiled,
Not knowing what he knew so well.

He knew that undeceiving fate
Would shame us whom he served unsought;
He knew that he must wince and wait—
The jest of those for whom he fought;
He knew devoutly what he thought
Of us and of our ridicule;
He knew that we must all be taught
Like little children in a school.

We gave a glamor to the task
That he encountered and saw through,
But little of us did he ask,
And little did we ever do.
And what appears if we review
The season when we railed and chaffed?
It is the face of one who knew
That we were learning while we laughed.

The face that in our vision feels
Again the venom that we flung,
Transfigured to the world reveals
The vigilance to which we clung.
Shrewd, hallowed, harassed, and among
The mysteries that are untold,
The face we see was never young
Nor could it wholly have been old.

For he, to whom we had applied
Our shopman's test of age and worth,
Was elemental when he died,
As he was ancient at his birth:
The saddest among kings of earth,
Bowed with a galling crown, this man
Met rancor with a cryptic mirth,
Laconic—and Olympian.

The love, the grandeur, and the fame,
Are bounded by the world alone;
The calm, the smoldering, and the flame
Of awful patience were his own:

With him they are forever flown
Past all our fond self-shadowings,
Wherewith we cumber the Unknown
As with inept, Icarian wings.

For we were not as other men:
'Twas ours to soar and his to see:
But we are coming down again,
And we shall come down pleasantly;
Nor shall we longer disagree
On what it is to be sublime,
But flourish in our perigee
And have one Titan at a time.

*Edwin Arlington Robinson* [1869–1935]

## ON THE LIFE-MASK OF ABRAHAM LINCOLN

THIS bronze doth keep the very form and mold
Of our great martyr's face. Yes, this is he:
That brow all wisdom, all benignity;
That human, humorous mouth; those cheeks that hold
Like some harsh landscape all the summer's gold;
That spirit fit for sorrow, as the sea
For storms to beat on; the lone agony
Those silent, patient lips too well foretold.
Yes, this is he who ruled a world of men
As might some prophet of the elder day,—
Brooding above the tempest and the fray
With deep-eyed thought and more than mortal ken.
A power was his beyond the touch of art
Or armèd strength—his pure and mighty heart.

*Richard Watson Gilder* [1844–1909]

## ABRAHAM LINCOLN

[Written by the editor of London *Punch*, as that journal's apology and atonement]

YOU lay a wreath on murdered Lincoln's bier,
*You*, who, with mocking pencil, wont to trace,
Broad for the self-complaisant British sneer,
His length of shambling limb, his furrowed face.

His gaunt, gnarled hands, his unkempt, bristling hair,
His garb uncouth, his bearing ill at ease,
His lack of all we prize as debonair,
Of power or will to shine, of art to please;

*You*, whose smart pen backed up the pencil's laugh,
Judging each step as though the way were plain;
Reckless, so it could point its paragraph
Of chief's perplexity, or people's pain,—

Beside this corpse, that bears for winding-sheet
The Stars and Stripes he lived to rear anew,
Between the mourners at his head and feet,
Say, scurrile jester, is there room for *you?*

Yes, he had lived to shame me from my sneer,
To lame my pencil, and confute my pen;
To make me own this hind of Princes peer,
This rail-splitter a true-born king of men.

My shallow judgment I had learned to rue,
Noting how to occasion's height he rose,
How his quaint wit made home-truth seem more true,
How, iron-like, his temper grew by blows;

How humble, yet how hopeful, he could be;
How, in good fortune and in ill, the same;
Nor bitter in success, nor boastful he,
Thirsty for gold, nor feverish for fame.

He went about his work—such work as few
Ever had laid on head and heart and hand—
As one who knows, where there's a task to do,
Man's honest will must Heaven's good grace command;

Who trusts the strength will with the burden grow,
That God makes instruments to work His will,
If but that will we can arrive to know,
Nor tamper with the weights of good and ill.

So he went forth to battle, on the side
  That he felt clear was Liberty's and Right's,
As in his peasant boyhood he had plied
  His warfare with rude Nature's thwarting mights,-

The uncleared forest, the unbroken soil,
  The iron bark that turns the lumberer's ax,
The rapid, that o'erbears the boatman's toil,
  The prairie, hiding the mazed wanderer's tracks,

The ambushed Indian, and the prowling bear,—
  Such were the needs that helped his youth to train:
Rough culture—but such trees large fruit may bear,
  If but their stocks be of right girth and grain.

So he grew up, a destined work to do,
  And lived to do it: four long-suffering years'
Ill-fate, ill-feeling, ill-report, lived through,
  And then he heard the hisses change to cheers,

The taunts to tribute, the abuse to praise,
  And took both with the same unwavering mood;
Till, as he came on light, from darkling days,
  And seemed to touch the goal from where he stood,

A felon hand, between the goal and him
  Reached from behind his back, a trigger pressed—
And those perplexed and patient eyes were dim,
  Those gaunt, long-laboring limbs were laid to rest.

The words of mercy were upon his lips,
  Forgiveness in his heart and on his pen,
When this vile murderer brought swift eclipse
  To thoughts of peace on earth, good will to men.

The Old World and the New, from sea to sea,
  Utter one voice of sympathy and shame.
Sore heart, so stopped when it at last beat high!
  Sad life, cut short just as its triumph came!

A deed accursed! Strokes have been struck before
By the assassin's hand, whereof men doubt
If more of horror or disgrace they bore;
But thy foul crime, like Cain's, stands darkly out,

Vile hand, that brandest murder on a strife,
Whate'er its grounds, stoutly and nobly striven,
And with the martyr's crown, crownest a life
With much to praise, little to be forgiven.

*Tom Taylor* [1817–1880]

## HENRY WADSWORTH LONGFELLOW

[1807–1882]

Nec turpem senectam
Degere, nec cithara carentem.—Hor. i. 31

"Not to be tuneless in old age!"
Ah! surely blest his pilgrimage,
Who, in his Winter's snow,
Still sings with note as sweet and clear
As in the morning of the year
When the first violets blow.

Blest!—but more blest, whom Summer's heat,
Whom Spring's impulsive stir and beat,
Have taught no feverish lure;
Whose Muse, benignant and serene,
Still keeps his Autumn chaplet green
Because his verse is pure!

Lie calm, O white and laureate head!
Lie calm, O Dead, that art not dead,
Since from the voiceless grave,
Thy voice shall speak to old and young
While song yet speaks an English tongue
By Charles' or Thamis' wave!

*Austin Dobson* [1840–1921]

## MARY QUEEN OF SCOTS

[1542–1587]

When the young hand of Darnley locked in hers
Had knit her to her northern doom—amid
The spousal pomp of flags and trumpeters,
Her fate looked forth and was no longer hid;
A jealous brain beneath a southern crown
Wrought spells upon her; from afar she felt
The waxen image of her fortunes melt
Beneath the Tudor's eye, while the grim frown
Of her own lords o'ermastered her sweet smiles,
And nipped her growing gladness, till she mourned,
And sank, at last, beneath their cruel wiles;
But, ever since, all generous hearts have burned
To clear her fame, yea, very babes have yearned
Over this saddest story of the isles.

*Charles Tennyson Turner* [1808–1879]

## THE ANGELUS

[Jean François Millet, 1814–1875]

Not far from Paris, in fair Fontainebleau,
  A lovely memory-haunted hamlet lies,
  Whose tender spell makes captive, and defies
Forgetfulness. The peasants come and go—
Their backs too used to stoop, and patient sow
  The harvest which a narrow want supplies—
  Even as when, Earth's pathos in his eyes,
Millet dwelt here, companion of their woe.

Ah, Barbizon! With thorns, not laurels, crowned,
He looked thy sorrows in the face, and found—
  Vital as seed warm-nestled in the sod—
The hidden sweetness at the heart of pain;
Trusting thy sun and dew, thy wind and rain—
  At home with Nature, and at one with God!

*Florence Earle Coates* [1850–1927]

## UNDER THE PORTRAIT OF MILTON

IN TONSON'S FOLIO EDITION OF PARADISE LOST, 1688

[1608–1674]

THREE Poets, in three distant ages born,
Greece, Italy, and England did adorn.
The first in loftiness of thought surpassed;
The next in majesty; in both the last.
The force of Nature could no further go:
To make a third she joined the former two.

*John Dryden* [1631–1700]

## IN MEMORY OF "BARRY CORNWALL"

[BRYAN WALLER PROCTER, 1787–1874]

IN the garden of death, where the singers whose names are deathless,
One with another make music unheard of men,
Where the dead sweet roses fade not of lips long breathless,
And the fair eyes shine that shall weep not or change again,
Who comes now crowned with the blossom of snow-white years?
What music is this that the world of the dead men hears?

Beloved of men, whose words on our lips were honey,
Whose name in our ears and our fathers' ears was sweet,
Like summer gone forth of the land his songs made sunny,
To the beautiful veiled bright world where the glad ghosts meet,
Child, father, bridegroom and bride, and anguish and rest,
No soul shall pass of a singer than this more blest.

Blest for the years' sweet sake that were filled and brightened,
As a forest with birds, with the fruit and the flower of his song;
For the souls' sake blest that heard, and their cares were lightened,
For the hearts' sake blest that have fostered his name so long;

By the living and dead lips blest that have loved his name,
And clothed with their praise and crowned with their love
for fame.

Ah, fair and fragrant his fame as flowers that close not,
That shrink not by day for heat or for cold by night,
As a thought in the heart shall increase when the heart's
self knows not,
Shall endure in our ears as a sound, in our eyes as a light;
Shall wax with the years that wane and the seasons' chime,
As a white rose thornless that grows in the garden of time.

The same year calls, and one goes hence with another,
And men sit sad that were glad for their sweet songs' sake;
The same year beckons, and elder with younger brother
Takes mutely the cup from his hand that we all shall take.
They pass ere the leaves be past or the snows be come;
And the birds are loud, but the lips that outsang them dumb.

Time takes them home that we loved, fair names and famous,
To the soft long sleep, to the broad sweet bosom of death;
But the flower of their souls he shall take not away to shame
us,
Nor the lips lack song forever that now lack breath.
For with us shall the music and perfume that die not dwell,
Though the dead to our dead bid welcome, and we farewell.

*Algernon Charles Swinburne* [1837–1909]

## GREAT-HEART

[Theodore Roosevelt, 1858–1919]

"The Interpreter then called for a man-servant of his, one Great-Heart."
Bunyan's *Pilgrim's Progress.*

CONCERNING brave Captains
Our age hath made known
For all men to honor,
One standeth alone,
Of whom, o'er both oceans
Both Peoples may say:
"Our realm is diminished,
With Great-Heart away."

In purpose unsparing,
  In action no less,
The labors he praised
  He would seek and profess
Through travail and battle,
  At hazard and pain. . . .
And our world is none the braver
  Since Great-Heart was ta'en.

Plain speech with plain folk,
  And plain words for false things,
Plain faith in plain dealing
  'Twixt neighbors or kings
He used and he followed,
  However it sped. . . .
Oh, our world is none more honest
  Now Great-Heart is dead!

The heat of his spirit
  Struck warm through all lands;
For he loved such as showed
  'Emselves men of their hands;
In love, as in hate,
  Paying home to the last. . . .
But our world is none the kinder
  Now Great-Heart has passed!

Hard-schooled by long power,
  Yet most humble of mind
Where aught that he was
  Might advantage mankind.
Leal servant, loved master,
  Rare comrade, sure guide. . . .
Oh, our world is none the safer
  Now Great-Heart hath died!

Let those who would handle
  Make sure they can wield
His far-reaching sword
  And his close-guarding shield;
For those who must journey
  Henceforward alone
Have need of stout convoy
  Now Great-Heart is gone.

*Rudyard Kipling* [1865–1936]

## TO THE MEMORY OF MY BELOVED MASTER WILLIAM SHAKESPEARE, AND WHAT HE HATH LEFT US

[1564–1616]

To draw no envy, Shakespeare, on thy name,
Am I thus ample to thy book and fame;
While I confess thy writings to be such
As neither Man, nor Muse, can praise too much.
'Tis true, and all men's suffrage. But these ways
Were not the paths I meant unto thy praise;
For silliest ignorance on these may light,
Which, when it sounds at best, but echoes right;
Or blind affection, which doth ne'er advance
The truth, but gropes, and urgeth all by chance;
Or crafty malice might pretend this praise,
And think to ruin, where it seemed to raise.
These are, as some infamous bawd or whore
Should praise a matron. What could hurt her more?
But thou art proof against them, and, indeed,
Above the ill fortune of them, or the need.
I therefore will begin: Soul of the age!
The applause, delight, the wonder of our stage!
My Shakespeare, rise! I will not lodge thee by
Chaucer, or Spenser, or bid Beaumont lie
A little further, to make thee a room:
Thou art a monument without a tomb,
And art alive still while thy book doth live
And we have wits to read and praise to give.
That I not mix thee so, my brain excuses,
I mean with great, but disproportioned Muses;
For if I thought my judgment were of years,
I should commit thee surely with thy peers,
And tell how far thou didst our Lyly outshine,
Or sporting Kyd, or Marlowe's mighty line.
And though thou hadst small Latin and less Greek,
From thence to honor thee, I would not seek
For names; but call forth thundering Æschylus,
Euripides, and Sophocles to us;

Pacuvius, Accius, him of Cordova dead,
To life again, to hear thy buskin tread,
And shake a stage; or, when thy socks were on,
Leave thee alone for the comparison
Of all that insolent Greece or haughty Rome
Sent forth, or since did from their ashes come.
Triumph, my Britain, thou hast one to show
To whom all scenes of Europe homage owe.
He was not of an age, but for all time!
And all the Muses still were in their prime,
When, like Apollo, he came forth to warm
Our ears, or like a Mercury to charm!
Nature herself was proud of his designs
And joyed to wear the dressing of his lines!
Which were so richly spun, and woven so fit,
As, since, she will vouchsafe no other wit.
The merry Greek, tart Aristophanes,
Neat Terence, witty Plautus, now not please;
But antiquated and deserted lie,
As they were not of Nature's family.
Yet must I not give Nature all; thy Art
My gentle Shakespeare, must enjoy a part.
For though the poet's matter nature be,
His art doth give the fashion; and, that he
Who casts to write a living line, must sweat,
(Such as thine are) and strike the second heat
Upon the Muses' anvil; turn the same
(And himself with it) that he thinks to frame,
Or, for the laurel, he may gain a scorn;
For a good poet's made, as well as born.
And such wert thou! Look how the father's face
Lives in his issue, even so the race
Of Shakespeare's mind and manners brightly shines
In his well-turnèd, and true-filèd lines;
In each of which he seems to shake a lance,
As brandished at the eyes of ignorance.
Sweet Swan of Avon! what a sight it were
To see thee in our waters yet appear,
And make those flights upon the banks of Thames,
That so did take Eliza, and our James!

But stay, I see thee in the hemisphere
Advanced, and made a constellation there!
Shine forth, thou Star of Poets, and with rage
Or influence, chide or cheer the drooping stage,
Which, since thy flight from hence, hath mourned like night,
And despairs day, but for thy volume's light.

*Ben Jonson* [1573?–1637]

## ON THE PORTRAIT OF SHAKESPEARE PREFIXED TO THE FIRST FOLIO EDITION, 1623

This figure, that thou here seest put,
It was for gentle Shakespeare cut;
Wherein the Graver had a strife
With Nature to outdo the life:
O, could he but have drawn his wit
As well in brass, as he hath hit
His face; the Print would then surpass
All that was ever writ in brass.
But since he cannot, Reader, look
Not at his picture, but his book.

*Ben Jonson* [1573?–1637]

## SHAKESPEARE

O let me leave the plains behind,
And let me leave the vales below!
Into the highlands of the mind,
Into the mountains let me go.

My Keats, my Spenser, loved I well;
Gardens and statued lawns were these;
Yet not for ever could I dwell
In arbors and in pleasances.

Here are the heights, crest beyond crest,
With Himalayan dews impearled;
And I will watch from Everest
The long heave of the surging world.

*William Watson* [1858–1935]

## SHAKESPEARE

OTHERS abide our question. Thou art free.
We ask and ask—Thou smilest and art still,
Out-topping knowledge. For the loftiest hill,
Who to the stars uncrowns his majesty,
Planting his steadfast footsteps in the sea,
Making the heaven of heavens his dwelling-place,
Spares but the cloudy border of his base
To the foiled searching of mortality;
And thou, who didst the stars and sunbeams know,
Self-schooled, self-scanned, self-honored, self-secure,
Didst tread on earth unguessed at.—Better so!
All pains the immortal spirit must endure,
All weakness which impairs, all griefs which bow,
Find their sole speech in that victorious brow.

*Matthew Arnold* [1822–1888]

## AN EPITAPH ON THE ADMIRABLE DRAMATIC POET, W. SHAKESPEARE

WHAT needs my Shakespeare for his honored bones
The labor of an age in pilèd stones?
Or that his hallowed relics should be hid
Under a star-ypointing pyramid?
Dear son of memory, great heir of fame,
What need'st thou such weak witness of thy name?
Thou in our wonder and astonishment
Hast built thyself a livelong monument.
For whilst, to the shame of slow-endeavoring art,
Thy easy numbers flow, and that each heart
Hath from the leaves of thy unvalued book
Those Delphic lines with deep impression took,
Then thou, our fancy of itself bereaving,
Dost make *us* marble with too much conceiving;
And so sepùlchered in such pomp dost lie,
That kings for such a tomb would wish to die.

*John Milton* [1608–1674]

## TO WILLIAM SHARP

### FIONA MACLEOD

[1856–1905]

THE waves about Iona dirge,
  The wild winds trumpet over Skye;
Shrill around Arran's cliff-bound verge
  The gray gulls cry.

Spring wraps its transient scarf of green,
  Its heathery robe, round slope and scar;
And night, the scudding wrack between,
  Lights its lone star.

But you who loved these outland isles,
  Their gleams, their glooms, their mysteries,
Their eldritch lures, their druid wiles,
  Their tragic seas,

Will heed no more, in mortal guise,
  The potent witchery of their call,
If dawn be regnant in the skies,
  Or evenfall.

Yet, though where suns Sicilian beam
  The loving earth enfolds your form,
I can but deem these coasts of dream
  And hovering storm

Still thrall your spirit—that it bides
  By far Iona's kelp-strewn shore,
There lingering till time and tides
  Shall surge no more.

*Clinton Scollard* [1860–1932]

## AN ODE

### ON THE UNVEILING OF THE SHAW MEMORIAL ON BOSTON COMMON, MAY THIRTY-FIRST, 1897

[ROBERT GOULD SHAW, 1837-1863]

I

Not with slow, funereal sound
Come we to this sacred ground;
Not with wailing fife and solemn muffled drum,
Bringing a cypress wreath
To lay, with bended knee,
On the cold brows of Death—
Not so, dear God, we come,
But with the trumpets' blare
And shot-torn battle-banners flung to air,
As for a victory!

Hark to the measured tread of martial feet,
The music and the murmurs of the street!
No bugle breathes this day
Disaster and retreat!—
Hark, how the iron lips
Of the great battle-ships
Salute the City from her azure Bay!

II

Time was—time was, ah, unforgotten years!—
We paid our hero tribute of our tears.
But now let go
All sounds and signs and formulas of woe:
'Tis Life, not Death, we celebrate;
To Life, not Death, we dedicate
This storied bronze, whereon is wrought
The lithe immortal figure of our thought,
To show forever to men's eyes,
Our children's children's children's eyes,
How once he stood
In that heroic mood,

He and his dusky braves
So fain of glorious graves!—
One instant stood, and then
Drave through that cloud of purple steel and flame,
Which wrapped him, held him, gave him not again,
But in its trampled ashes left to Fame
An everlasting name!

III

That was indeed to live—
At one bold swoop to wrest
From darkling death the best
That death to life can give.
He fell as Roland fell
That day at Roncevaux,
With foot upon the ramparts of the foe!
A pæan, not a knell,
For heroes dying so!
No need for sorrow here,
No room for sigh or tear,
Save such rich tears as happy eyelids know.
See where he rides, our Knight!
Within his eyes the light
Of battle, and youth's gold about his brow;
Our Paladin, our Soldier of the Cross,
Not weighing gain with loss—
World-loser, that won all
Obeying duty's call!
Not his, at peril's frown,
A pulse of quicker beat;
Not his to hesitate
And parley hold with Fate,
But proudly to fling down
His gauntlet at her feet.
O soul of loyal valor and white truth,
Here, by this iron gate,
Thy serried ranks about thee as of yore,
Stand thou for evermore
In thy undying youth!

The tender heart, the eagle eye!
Oh, unto him belong
The homages of Song;
Our praises and the praise
Of coming days
To him belong—
To him, to him, the dead that shall not die!

*Thomas Bailey Aldrich* [1837-1907]

## MEMORABILIA

[1792-1822]

Ah, did you once see Shelley plain,
And did he stop and speak to you,
And did you speak to him again?
How strange it seems and new!

But you were living before that,
And also you were living after;
And the memory I started at—
My starting moves your laughter!

I crossed a moor, with a name of its own
And a certain use in the world no doubt,
Yet a hand's-breadth of it shines alone
'Mid the blank miles round about:

For there I picked up on the heather
And there I put inside my breast
A molted feather, an eagle-feather!
Well, I forget the rest.

*Robert Browning* [1816-1889]

## ROBERT LOUIS STEVENSON

[1850-1894]

In his old gusty garden of the North,
He heard lark-time the uplifting Voices call;
Smitten through with Voices was the evenfall--
At last they drove him forth.

Now there were two rang silverly and long;
And of Romance, that spirit of the sun,
And of Romance, Spirit of Youth, was one;
And one was that of Song.

Gold-belted sailors, bristling buccaneers,
The flashing soldier, and the high, slim dame,
These were the Shapes that all around him came,—
That we let go with tears.

His was the unstinted English of the Scot,
Clear, nimble, with the scriptural tang of Knox
Thrust through it like the far, sweet scent of box,
To keep it unforgot.

No frugal Realist, but quick to laugh,
To see appealing things in all he knew,
He plucked the sun-sweet corn his fathers grew,
And would have naught of chaff.

David and Keats, and all good singing men,
Take to your heart this Covenanter's son,
Gone in mid-years, leaving our years undone,
Where you do sing again!

*Lizette Woodworth Reese* [1856–1935]

## BAYARD TAYLOR

[1825–1878]

"And where now, Bayard, will thy footsteps tend?"
My sister asked our guest one winter's day.
Smiling he answered in the Friends' sweet way
Common to both: "Wherever thou shalt send!
What wouldst thou have me see for thee?" She laughed,
Her dark eyes dancing in the wood-fire's glow:
"Loffoden isles, the Kilpis, and the low
Unsetting sun on Finmark's fishing-craft."
"All these and more I soon shall see for thee!"
He answered cheerily: and he kept his pledge
On Lapland snows, the North Cape's windy wedge,
And Tromsö freezing in its winter sea.
He went and came. But no man knows the track
Of his last journey, and he comes not back!

He brought us wonders of the new and old;
We shared all climes with him. The Arab's tent
To him its story-telling secret lent,
And, pleased, we listened to the tales he told.
His task, beguiled with songs that shall endure,
In manly, honest thoroughness he wrought;
From humble home-lays to the heights of thought
Slowly he climbed, but every step was sure.
How, with the generous pride that friendship hath,
We, who so loved him, saw at last the crown
Of civic honor on his brows pressed down,
Rejoiced, and knew not that the gift was death.
And now for him, whose praise in deafened ears
Two nations speak, we answer but with tears!

O Vale of Chester! trod by him so oft,
Green as thy June turf keep his memory. Let
Nor wood, nor dell, nor storied stream forget,
Nor winds that blow round lonely Cedarcroft;
Let the home voices greet him in the far,
Strange lands that hold him; let the messages
Of love pursue him o'er the chartless seas
And unmapped vastness of his unknown star!
Love's language, heard beyond the loud discourse
Of perishable fame, in every sphere
Itself interprets; and its utterance here
Somewhere in God's unfolding universe
Shall reach our traveler, softening the surprise
Of his rapt gaze on unfamiliar skies!

*John Greenleaf Whittier* [1807–1892]

## LACRIMÆ MUSARUM

[ALFRED TENNYSON, 1809–1892]

Low, like another's, lies the laureled head:
The life that seemed a perfect song is o'er:
Carry the last great bard to his last bed.
Land that he loved, thy noblest voice is mute.
Land that he loved, that loved him! nevermore
Meadow of thine, smooth lawn or wild sea-shore,
Gardens of odorous bloom and tremulous fruit,

Or woodlands old, like Druid couches spread,
The master's feet shall tread.
Death's little rift hath rent the faultless lute:
The singer of undying songs is dead.

Lo, in this season pensive-hued and grave,
While fades and falls the doomed, reluctant leaf
From withered Earth's fantastic coronal,
With wandering sighs of forest and of wave
Mingles the murmur of a people's grief
For him whose leaf shall fade not, neither fall.
He hath fared forth, beyond these suns and showers
For us, the autumn glow, the autumn flame,
And soon the winter silence shall be ours:
Him the eternal spring of fadeless fame
Crowns with no mortal flowers.

What needs his laurel our ephemeral tears,
To save from visitation of decay?
Not in this temporal light alone, that bay
Blooms, nor to perishable mundane ears
Sings he with lips of transitory clay.
Rapt though he be from us,
Virgil salutes him, and Theocritus;
Catullus, mightiest-brained Lucretius, each
Greets him, their brother, on the Stygian beach;
Proudly a gaunt right hand doth Dante reach;
Milton and Wordsworth bid him welcome home;
Keats, on his lips the eternal rose of youth,
Doth in the name of Beauty that is Truth
A kinsman's love beseech;
Coleridge, his locks aspersed with fairy foam,
Calm Spenser, Chaucer suave,
His equal friendship crave:
And godlike spirits hail him guest, in speech
Of Athens, Florence, Weimar, Stratford, Rome.

Nay, he returns to regions whence he came.
Him doth the spirit divine

Of universal loveliness reclaim.
All nature is his shrine.
Seek him henceforward in the wind and sea,
In earth's and air's emotion or repose,
In every star's august serenity,
And in the rapture of the flaming rose.
There seek him if ye would not seek in vain,
There, in the rhythm and music of the Whole;
Yea, and for ever in the human soul
Made stronger and more beauteous by his strain.

For lo! creation's self is one great choir,
And what is nature's order but the rhyme
Whereto in holiest unanimity
All things with all things move unfalteringly,
Infolded and communal from their prime?
Who shall expound the mystery of the lyre?
In far retreats of elemental mind
Obscurely comes and goes
The imperative breath of song, that as the wind
Is trackless, and oblivious whence it blows.
Demand of lilies wherefore they are white,
Extort her crimson secret from the rose,
But ask not of the Muse that she disclose
The meaning of the riddle of her might:
Somewhat of all things sealed and recondite,
Save the enigma of herself, she knows.
The master could not tell, with all his lore,
Wherefore he sang, or whence the mandate sped:
Even as the linnet sings, so I, he said:
Ah, rather as the imperial nightingale,
That held in trance the ancient Attic shore,
And charms the ages with the notes that o'er
All woodland chants immortally prevail!
And now, from our vain plaudits greatly fled,
He with diviner silence dwells instead,
And on no earthly sea with transient roar,
Unto no earthly airs, he sets his sail,
But far beyond our vision and our hail
Is heard for ever and is seen no more.

No more, O never now,
Lord of the lofty and the tranquil brow,
Shall men behold those wizard locks where Time
Let fall no wintry rime.
Once, in his youth obscure,
The weaver of this verse, that shall endure
By splendor of its theme which cannot die,
Beheld thee eye to eye,
And touched through thee the hand
Of every hero of thy race divine,
Even to the sire of all the laureled line,
The sightless wanderer on the Ionian strand.
Yea, I beheld thee, and behold thee yet:
Thou hast forgotten, but can I forget?
Are not thy words all goldenly impressed
On memory's palimpsest?
I hear the utterance of thy sovereign tongue,
I tread the floor thy hallowing feet have trod;
I see the hands a nation's lyre that strung,
The eyes that looked through life and gazed on God.

The seasons change, the winds they shift and veer;
The grass of yesteryear
Is dead; the birds depart, the groves decay:
Empires dissolve and peoples disappear:
Song passes not away.
Captains and conquerors leave a little dust,
And kings a dubious legend of their reign;
The swords of Cæsars, they are less than rust:
The poet doth remain.
Dead is Augustus, Maro is alive;
And thou, the Mantuan of this age and soil,
With Virgil shalt survive.
Enriching Time with no less honeyed spoil,
The yielded sweet of every Muse's hive;
Heeding no more the sound of idle praise
In that great calm our tumults cannot reach,—
Master who crown'st our immelodious days
With flower of perfect speech.

*William Watson* [1858–1935]

## TENNYSON

[WESTMINSTER ABBEY: OCTOBER TWELFTH, 1892]

GIB DIESEN TODTEN MIR HERAUS!

(*The Minster speaks*)

BRING me my dead!
To me that have grown,
Stone laid upon stone,
As the stormy brood
Of English blood
Has waxed and spread
And filled the world,
With sails unfurled;
With men that may not lie;
With thoughts that cannot die.

Bring me my dead!
Into the storied hall,
Where I have garnered all
My harvest without weed;
My chosen fruits of goodly seed,
And lay him gently down among
The men of state, the men of song:
The men that would not suffer wrong:
The thought-worn chieftains of the mind:
Head-servants of the human kind.

Bring me my dead!
The autumn sun shall shed
Its beams athwart the bier's
Heaped blooms: a many tears
Shall flow; his words, in cadence sweet and strong,
Shall voice the full hearts of the silent throng.
Bring me my dead!
And oh! sad wedded mourner, seeking still
For vanished hand-clasp: drinking in thy fill
Of holy grief; forgive, that pious theft
Robs thee of all, save memories, left:

Not thine to kneel beside the grassy mound
While dies the western glow; and all around
Is silence; and the shadows closer creep
And whisper softly: All must fall asleep.

*Thomas Henry Huxley* [1825–1895]

## FOR A COPY OF THEOCRITUS

[C. 270 B. C.]

O SINGER of the field and fold,
Theocritus! Pan's pipe was thine,—
Thine was the happier Age of Gold.

For thee the scent of new-turned mold,
The bee-hives, and the murmuring pine,
O Singer of the field and fold

Thou sang'st the simple feasts of old,—
The beechen bowl made glad with wine . . .
Thine was the happier Age of Gold.

Thou bad'st the rustic loves be told,—
Thou bad'st the tuneful reeds combine,
O Singer of the field and fold!

And round thee, ever-laughing, rolled
The blithe and blue Sicilian brine . . .
Thine was the happier Age of Gold.

Alas for us! Our songs are cold;
Our Northern suns too sadly shine:—
O Singer of the field and fold,
Thine was the happier Age of Gold!

*Austin Dobson* [1840–1921]

## THEOCRITUS

O SINGER of Persephone!
  In the dim meadows desolate,
Dost thou remember Sicily?

Still through the ivy flits the bee
   Where Amaryllis lies in state;
O Singer of Persephone!

Simætha calls on Hecate
   And hears the wild dogs at the gate:
Dost thou remember Sicily?

Still by the light and laughing sea
   Poor Polypheme bemoans his fate:
O Singer of Persephone!

And still in boyish rivalry
   Young Daphnis challenges his mate:
Dost thou remember Sicily?

Slim Lacon keeps a goat for thee,
   For thee the jocund shepherds wait,
O singer of Persephone!
Dost thou remember Sicily?

*Oscar Wilde* [1856–1900]

## THE QUIET SINGER

[AVE! FRANCIS THOMPSON,—1859–1907]

He had been singing—but I had not heard his voice;
He had been weaving lovely dreams of song,
O many a morning long.
But I, remote and far,
Under an alien star,
Listened to other singers, other birds,
And other silver words.
But does the skylark, singing sweet and clear,
Beg the cold world to hear?
Rather he sings for very rapture of singing,
At dawn, or in the blue, mild Summer noon,
Knowing that, late or soon,
His wealth of beauty, and his high notes, ringing
Above the earth, will make some heart rejoice.

He sings, albeit alone,
Spendthrift of each pure tone,
Hoarding no single song,
No cadence wild and strong.
But one day, from a friend far overseas,
As if upon the breeze,
There came the teeming wonder of his words—
A golden troop of birds,
Caged in a little volume made to love;
Singing, singing,
Flinging, flinging
Their breaking hearts on mine, and swiftly bringing
Tears, and the peace thereof.

How the world woke anew!
How the days broke anew!
Before my tear-blind eyes a tapestry
I seemed to see,
Woven of all the dreams dead or to be.
Hills, hills of song, Springs of eternal bloom,
Autumns of golden pomp and purple gloom
Were hung upon his loom.
Winters of pain, roses with awful thorns,
Yet wondrous faith in God's dew-drenchèd morns—
These, all these I saw,
With that ecstatic awe
Wherewith one looks into Eternity.

And then I knew that, though I had not heard
His voice before,
His quiet singing, like some quiet bird
At some one's distant docr,
Had made my own more sweet; and made it more
Lovely, in one of God's miraculous ways.
I knew then why the days
Had seemed more perfect to me when the Spring
Came with old burgeoning;
For somewhere in the world his voice was raised,
And somewhere in the world his heart was breaking;
And never a flower but knew it, sweetly taking

Beauty more high and noble for his sake,
As a whole wood grows lovelier for the wail
Of one sad nightingale.

Yet, if the Springs long past
Seemed wonderful before I heard his voice,
I tremble at the beauty I shall see
In seasons still to be,
Now that his songs are mine while Life shall last.
O now for me
New floods of visions open suddenly. . . .
Rejoice, my heart! Rejoice
That you have heard the Quiet Singer's voice!

*Charles Hanson Towne* [1877-

## THOREAU'S FLUTE

[HENRY DAVID THOREAU, 1817-1862]

We, sighing, said, "Our Pan is dead;
His pipe hangs mute beside the river;
Around it wistful sunbeams quiver,
But Music's airy voice is fled.
Spring mourns as for untimely frost;
The bluebird chants a requiem;
The willow-blossom waits for him:—
The Genius of the wood is lost."

Then from the flute, untouched by hands,
There came a low, harmonious breath:
"For such as he there is no death;
His life the eternal life commands;
Above man's aims his nature rose:
The wisdom of a just content
Made one small spot a continent,
And turned to poetry Life's prose.

"Haunting the hills, the stream, the wild,
Swallow and aster, lake and pine,
To him grew human or divine,—
Fit mates for this large-hearted child.

Such homage Nature ne'er forgets,
And yearly on the coverlid
'Neath which her darling lieth hid
Will write his name in violets.

"To him no vain regrets belong,
Whose soul, that finer instrument,
Gave to the world no poor lament,
But wood-notes ever sweet and strong.
O lonely friend! he still will be
A potent presence, though unseen,—
Steadfast, sagacious, and serene:
Seek not for him,—he is with thee."

*Louisa May Alcott* [1832–1888]

## AVE ATQUE VALE

### IN MEMORIAM ARTHUR UPSON

[1877–1908]

I

You found the green before the Spring was sweet
And in the boughs the color of a rose,
The haunting fragrance that the south-wind knows
When May has wandered far on questing feet;
And in your heart—a wild note, full and fleet,
The first cry of a gladdened bird that goes
North to the fields of winter-laden snows,
Joyous against the blast and stinging sleet.

And now the Spring is here, the snows are gone,
The apple-blossoms fall from every tree
And all the branches throb with love and Spring;
But never comes one note to greet the dawn,
Never again a wild-glad melody—
God speed, great soul, your valiant wandering!

II

Your hand that traced these lines, and now is dust!
How strange, to-night, this thing of life and death
Where my low candle-flame o'ershadoweth
What once knew youth in its first joyous trust;
So simple and so near, as if you must
Still linger somewhere—yet no answer saith
Its golden word, no magic-freighted breath,
Only a heart-beat stilled in rainbow-rust.

Stilled in the music of a yester-year
That ever echoes its sweet instrument,
And richly sings across an unknown sea;
But these dim lines—so vital they appear,
So full of youth and joy and life's intent.
Ah, this it is that seems so strange to me!

III

How quiet are their voices on the wind
As they toss sadly in a darkened sky,
And yet, mayhap, to you old words imply
That all my questing days I shall not find;
For never more may earthly vestures bind,
But stripped away from things that needs must die,
Deep in that youth where death's strange secrets lie
And whose faint whispers fall on us behind.

Therefore to you the voices harbor peace,
Their ancient patience do you know at last,—
Yet more, the inmost murmuring of these;
And in that mystic lore beyond release,
In one full instant from a treasured past,
Mayhap, you heard the Message of the Trees!

IV

I stood to-day upon time's border-land
And looked far off across each rolling year,
Yet scarcely their great thunder did I hear
Nor marked the wreckage of the changing sand;

For one soft note persuasive did command
  All other tones that reached my quickened ear,
  And in that note a message low and clear
That I so plainly seemed to understand.

As in the saddened passing of fair things,
  The sorrow of the sunset and the dawn,
    For death that comes when life's hour least should
      fail—
Ever the moment's hush of lifted wings,
  A gleam of wonder ere the flood is gone. . . .
    The host uncovered from its mortal veil!

V

October almost holds her golden sway
  Across these hills and through the slopes between,
  As if for you some sacrament unseen
Were now unfolded in a silent way,—
As if for you pale memory astray
  Had touched each spot of misted summer green,
  And in the coolness where the shadows lean
Had whispered of a cherished yesterday.

For one to whom you gave your youth's full praise
  Now takes you back into her hallowed rest
    With all the loveliness that is your due,
Yielding the precious beauty of her days
  To your deep sleep upon her tranquil breast,—
    Giving you back her deathless love of you!

*Thomas S. Jones, Jr.* [1882–1932]

## THE WARDEN OF THE CINQUE PORTS

[THE DUKE OF WELLINGTON, 1769–1852]

A MIST was driving down the British Channel,
  The day was just begun,
And through the window-panes, on floor and panel,
  Streamed the red autumn sun.

It glanced on flowing flag and rippling pennon,
  And the white sails of ships;
And, from the frowning rampart, the black cannon
  Hailed it with feverish lips.

Sandwich and Romney, Hastings, Hithe, and Dover,
  Were all alert that day,
To see the French war-steamers speeding over
  When the fog cleared away.

Sullen and silent, and like couchant lions,
  Their cannon, through the night,
Holding their breath, had watched, in grim defiance
  The seacoast opposite.

And now they roared at drum-beat from their stations
  On every citadel;
Each answering each, with morning salutations,
  That all was well.

And down the coast, all taking up the burden,
  Replied the distant forts,
As if to summon from his sleep the Warden
  And Lord of the Cinque Ports.

Him shall no sunshine from the fields of azure,
  No drum-beat from the wall,
No morning gun from the black fort's embrasure,
  Awaken with its call!

No more, surveying with an eye impartial
  The long line of the coast,
Shall the gaunt figure of the old Field Marshal
  Be seen upon his post!

For in the night, unseen, a single warrior,
  In somber harness mailed,
Dreaded of man, and surnamed the Destroyer,
  The rampart wall had scaled.

He passed into the chamber of the sleeper,
   The dark and silent room;
And, as he entered, darker grew, and deeper,
   The silence and the gloom.

He did not pause to parley or dissemble,
   But smote the Warden hoar;
Ah! what a blow! that made all England tremble
   And groan from shore to shore.

Meanwhile, without, the surly cannon waited,
   The sun rose bright o'erhead;
Nothing in Nature's aspect intimated
   That a great man was dead.

*Henry Wadsworth Longfellow* [1807-1882]

## ODE ON THE DEATH OF THE DUKE OF WELLINGTON

I

   Bury the Great Duke
      With an empire's lamentation;
Let us bury the Great Duke
   To the noise of the mourning of a mighty nation;
Mourning when their leaders fall,
Warriors carry the warrior's pall,
And sorrow darkens hamlet and hall.

II

Where shall we lay the man whom we deplore?
Here, in streaming London's central roar.
Let the sound of those he wrought for,
And the feet of those he fought for,
Echo round his bones for evermore.

III

Lead out the pageant: sad and slow,
As fits an universal woe,

Let the long, long procession go,
And let the sorrowing crowd about it grow,
And let the mournful martial music blow;
The last great Englishman is low.

IV

Mourn, for to us he seems the last,
Remembering all his greatness in the past.
No more in soldier fashion will hc greet
With lifted hand the gazer in the street.
O friends, our chief state-oracle is mute!
Mourn for the man of long-enduring blood,
The statesman-warrior, moderate, resolute,
Whole in himself, a common good.
Mourn for the man of amplest influence,
Yet clearest of ambitious crime,
Our greatest yet with least pretence,
Great in council and great in war,
Foremost captain of his time,
Rich in saving common-sense,
And, as the greatest only are,
In his simplicity sublime.
O good gray head which all men knew,
O voice from which their omens all men drew,
O iron nerve to true occasion true,
O fallen at length that tower of strength
Which stood four-square to all the winds that blew!
Such was he whom we deplore.
The long self-sacrifice of life is o'er.
The great World-victor's victor will be seen no more.

V

All is over and done.
Render thanks to the Giver,
England, for thy son.
Let the bell be tolled.
Render thanks to the Giver,
And render him to the mould.
Under the cross of gold

That shines over city and river,
There he shall rest for ever
Among the wise and the bold.
Let the bell be tolled,
And a reverent people behold
The towering car, the sable steeds.
Bright let it be with its blazoned deeds,
Dark in its funeral fold.
Let the bell be tolled,
And a deeper knell in the heart be knolled;
And the sound of the sorrowing anthem rolled
Through the dome of the golden cross;
And the volleying cannon thunder his loss;
He knew their voices of old.
For many a time in many a clime
His captain's ear has heard them boom
Bellowing victory, bellowing doom.
When he with those deep voices wrought,
Guarding realms and kings from shame,
With those deep voices our dead captain taught
The tyrant, and asserts his claim
In that dread sound to the great name
Which he has worn so pure of blame,
In praise and in dispraise the same,
A man of well-attempered frame.
O civic muse, to such a name,
To such a name for ages long,
To such a name,
Preserve a broad approach of fame,
And ever-echoing avenues of song!

VI

"Who is he that cometh, like an honored guest,
With banner and with music, with soldier and with priest,
With a nation weeping, and breaking on my rest?"—
Mighty Seaman, this is he
Was great by land as thou by sea.
Thine island loves thee well, thou famous man,
The greatest sailor since our world began.

Now, to the roll of muffled drums,
To thee the greatest soldier comes;
For this is he
Was great by land as thou by sea.
His foes were thine; he kept us free;
Oh, give him welcome, this is he
Worthy of our gorgeous rites,
And worthy to be laid by thee;
For this is England's greatest son,
He that gained a hundred fights,
Nor ever lost an English gun;
This is he that far away
Against the myriads of Assaye
Clashed with his fiery few and won;
And underneath another sun,
Warring on a later day,
Round affrighted Lisbon drew
The treble works, the vast designs
Of his labored rampart-lines,
Where he greatly stood at bay,
Whence he issued forth anew,
And ever great and greater grew,
Beating from the wasted vines
Back to France her banded swarms,
Back to France with countless blows,
Till o'er the hills her eagles flew
Beyond the Pyrenean pines,
Followed up in valley and glen
With blare of bugle, clamor of men,
Roll of cannon and clash of arms,
And England pouring on her foes.
Such a war had such a close.
Again their ravening eagle rose
In anger, wheeled on Europe-shadowing wings,
And barking for the thrones of kings;
Till one that sought but Duty's iron crown
On that loud Sabbath shook the spoiler down;
A day of onsets of despair!
Dashed on every rocky square,

Their surging charges foamed themselves away;
Last, the Prussian trumpet blew;
Through the long-tormented air
Heaven flashed a sudden jubilant ray,
And down we swept and charged and overthrew.
So great a soldier taught us there
What long-enduring hearts could do
In that world-earthquake, Waterloo!
Mighty Seaman, tender and true,
And pure as he from taint of craven guile,
O saviour of the silver-coasted isle,
O shaker of the Baltic and the Nile,
If aught of things that here befall
Touch a spirit among things divine,
If love of country move thee there at all,
Be glad, because his bones are laid by thine!
And through the centuries let a people's voice
In full acclaim,
A people's voice,
The proof and echo of all human fame,
A people's voice, when they rejoice
At civic revel and pomp and game,
Attest their great commander's claim
With honor, honor, honor, honor to him,
Eternal honor to his name.

VII

A people's voice! we are a people yet.
Though all men else their nobler dreams forget,
Confused by brainless mobs and lawless Powers,
Thank Him who isled us here, and roughly set
His Briton in blown seas and storming showers,
We have a voice with which to pay the debt
Of boundless love and reverence and regret
To those great men who fought, and kept it ours.
And keep it ours, O God, from brute control!
O Statesmen, guard us, guard the eye, the soul
Of Europe, keep our noble England whole,

And save the one true seed of freedom sown
Betwixt a people and their ancient throne,
That sober freedom out of which there springs
Our loyal passion for our temperate kings!
For, saving that, ye help to save mankind
Till public wrong be crumbled into dust,
And drill the raw world for the march of mind,
Till crowds at length be sane and crowns be just.
But wink no more in slothful overtrust.
Remember him who led your hosts;
He bade you guard the sacred coasts.
Your cannons moulder on the seaward wall;
His voice is silent in your council-hall
For ever; and whatever tempests lour
For ever silent; even if they broke
In thunder, silent; yet remember all
He spoke among you, and the Man who spoke;
Who never sold the truth to serve the hour,
Nor paltered with Eternal God for power;
Who let the turbid streams of rumor flow
Through either babbling world of high and low;
Whose life was work, whose language rife
With rugged maxims hewn from life;
Who never spoke against a foe;
Whose eighty winters freeze with one rebuke
All great self-seekers trampling on the right.
Truth-teller was our England's Alfred named;
Truth-lover was our English Duke;
Whatever record leap to light
He never shall be shamed.

VIII

Lo! the leader in these glorious wars
Now to glorious burial slowly borne
Followed by the brave of other lands,
He, on whom from both her open hands
Lavish Honor showered all her stars,
And affluent Fortune emptied all her horn.

Yea, let all good things await
Him who cares not to be great
But as he saves or serves the state.
Not once or twice in our rough island-story
The path of duty was the way to glory.
He that walks it, only thirsting
For the right, and learns to deaden
Love of self, before his journey closes,
He shall find the stubborn thistle bursting
Into glossy purples, which outredden
All voluptuous garden-roses.
Not once or twice in our fair island-story
The path of duty was the way to glory.
He, that ever following her commands,
On with toil of heart and knees and hands,
Through the long gorge to the far light has won
His path upward, and prevailed,
Shall find the toppling crags of Duty scaled
Are close upon the shining table-lands
To which our God Himself is moon and sun.
Such was he: his work is done.
But while the races of mankind endure
Let his great example stand
Colossal, seen of every land,
And keep the soldier firm, the statesman pure;
Till in all lands and through all human story
The path of duty be the way to glory.
And let the land whose hearths he saved from shame
For many and many an age proclaim
At civic revel and pomp and game,
And when the long-illumined cities flame,
Their ever-loyal iron leader's fame,
With honor, honor, honor, honor to him,
Eternal honor to his name.

IX

Peace, his triumph will be sung
By some yet unmoulded tongue

Far on in summers that we shall not see.
Peace, it is a day of pain
For one about whose patriarchal knee
Late the little children clung.
O peace, it is a day of pain
For one upon whose hand and heart and brain
Once the weight and fate of Europe hung.
Ours the pain, be his the gain!
More than is of man's degree
Must be with us, watching here
At this, our great solemnity.
Whom we see not we revere;
We revere, and we refrain
From talk of battles loud and vain,
And brawling memories all too free
For such a wise humility
As befits a solemn fane:
We revere, and while we hear
The tide of Music's golden sea
Setting toward eternity,
Uplifted high in heart and hope are we,
Until we doubt not that for one so true
There must be other nobler work to do
Than when he fought at Waterloo,
And Victor he must ever be.
For though the Giant Ages heave the hill
And break the shore, and evermore
Make and break, and work their will,
Though world on world in myriad myriads roll
Round us, each with different powers,
And other forms of life than ours,
What know we greater than the soul?
On God and Godlike men we build our trust.
Hush, the Dead March wails in the people's ears;
The dark crowd moves, and there are sobs and tears;
The black earth yawns; the mortal disappears;
Ashes to ashes, dust to dust;
He is gone who seemed so great.—
Gone, but nothing can bereave him
Of the force he made his own

Being here, and we believe him
Something far advanced in State,
And that he wears a truer crown
Than any wreath that man can weave him.
Speak no more of his renown,
Lay your earthly fancies down,
And in the vast cathedral leave him,
God accept him, Christ receive him!

*Alfred Tennyson* [1809-1892]

## MEMORIAL VERSES

[WILLIAM WORDSWORTH, 1770-1850]

GOETHE in Weimar sleeps, and Greece,
Long since, saw Byron's struggle cease.
But one such death remained to come;
The last poetic voice is dumb—
We stand to-day by Wordsworth's tomb.

When Byron's eyes were shut in death,
We bowed our head and held our breath.
He taught us little; but our soul
Had *felt* him like the thunder's roll.
With shivering heart the strife we saw
Of passion with eternal law;
And yet with reverential awe
We watched the fount of fiery life
Which served for that Titanic strife.

When Goethe's death was told, we said
Sunk, then, is Europe's sagest head.
Physician of the iron age,
Goethe has done his pilgrimage

He took the suffering human race,
He read each wound, each weakness clear:
And struck his finger on the place,
And said: *Thou ailest here, and here!*
He looked on Europe's dying hour
Of fitful dream and feverish power;
His eye plunged down the weltering strife,
The turmoil of expiring life—
He said: *The end is everywhere,*
*Art still has truth, take refuge there!*
And he was happy, if to know
Causes of things, and far below
His feet to see the lurid flow
Of terror, and insane distress,
And headlong fate, be happiness.

And Wordsworth!—Ah, pale ghosts, rejoice!
For never has such soothing voice
Been to your shadowy world conveyed,
Since erst, at morn, some wandering shade
Heard the clear song of Orpheus come
Through Hades, and the mournful gloom.
Wordsworth has gone from us—and ye,
Ah, may ye feel his voice as we!
He too upon a wintery clime
Had fallen—on this iron time
Of doubts, disputes, distractions, fears.
He found us when the age had bound
Our souls in its benumbing round;
He spoke, and loosed our hearts in tears.
He laid us as we lay at birth
On the cool flowery lap of earth,
Smiles broke from us, and we had ease;
The hills were round us, and the breeze
Went o'er the sun-lit fields again;
Our foreheads felt the wind and rain.
Our youth returned; for there was shed
On spirits that had long been dead,
Spirits dried up and closely furled,
The freshness of the early world.

Ah! since dark days still bring to light
Man's prudence and man's fiery might,
Time may restore us in his course
Goethe's sage mind and Byron's force;
But where will Europe's latter hour
Again find Wordsworth's healing power?
Others will teach us how to dare,
And against fear our breast to steel;
Others will strengthen us to bear—
But who, ah! who, will make us feel?
The cloud of mortal destiny,
Others will front it fearlessly—
But who, like him, will put it by?

Keep fresh the grass upon his grave,
O Rotha, with thy living wave!
Sing him thy best! for few or none
Hears thy voice right, now he is gone.

*Matthew Arnold* [1822–1888]

## WORDSWORTH'S GRAVE

I

The old rude church, with bare, bald tower, is here;
Beneath its shadow high-born Rotha flows;
Rotha, remembering well who slumbers near,
And with cool murmur lulling his repose.

Rotha, remembering well who slumbers near.
His hills, his lakes, his streams are with him yet.
Surely the heart that reads her own heart clear
Nature forgets not soon: 'tis we forget.

We that with vagrant soul his fixity
Have slighted; faithless, done his deep faith wrong;
Left him for poorer loves, and bowed the knee
To misbegotten strange new gods of song.

Yet, led by hollow ghost or beckoning elf
Far from her homestead to the desert bourn,
The vagrant soul returning to herself
Wearily wise, must needs to him return.

To him and to the powers that with him dwell:—
  Inflowings that divulged not whence they came;
And that secluded Spirit unknowable,
  The mystery we make darker with a name;

The Somewhat which we name but cannot know,
  Even as we name a star and only see
His quenchless flashings forth, which ever show
  And ever hide him, and which are not he.

II

Poet who sleepest by this wandering wave!
  When thou wast born, what birth-gift hadst thou then?
To thee what wealth was that the Immortals gave,
  The wealth thou gavest in thy turn to men?

Not Milton's keen, translunar music thine;
  Not Shakespeare's cloudless, boundless human view;
Not Shelley's flush of rose on peaks divine;
  Nor yet the wizard twilight Coleridge knew.

What hadst thou that could make so large amends
  For all thou hadst not and thy peers possessed,
Motion and fire, swift means to radiant ends?—
  Thou hadst, for weary feet, the gift of rest.

From Shelley's dazzling glow or thunderous haze,
  From Byron's tempest-anger, tempest-mirth,
Men turned to thee and found—not blast and blaze,
  Tumult of tottering heavens, but peace on earth.

Nor peace that grows by Lethe, scentless flower,
  There in white languors to decline and cease;
But peace whose names are also rapture, power,
  Clear sight, and love: for these are parts of peace.

III

I hear it vowed the Muse is with us still;
  If less divinely frenzied than of yore,
In lieu of feelings she has wondrous skill
  To simulate emotion felt no more.

Not such the authentic Presence pure, that made
This valley vocal in the great days gone!—
In *his* great days, while yet the spring-time played
About him, and the mighty morning shone.

No word-mosaic artificer, he sang
A lofty song of lowly weal and dole.
Right from the heart, right to the heart it sprang,
Or from the soul leapt instant to the soul.

He felt the charm of childhood, grace of youth,
Grandeur of age, insisting to be sung.
The impassioned argument was simple truth
Half-wondering at its own melodious tongue.

Impassioned? ay, to the song's ecstatic core!
But far removed were clangor, storm, and feud;
For plenteous health was his, exceeding store
Of joy, and an impassioned quietude.

IV

A hundred years ere he to manhood came,
Song from celestial heights had wandered down,
Put off her robe of sunlight, dew, and flame,
And donned a modish dress to charm the Town.

Thenceforth she but festooned the porch of things;
Apt at life's lore, incurious what life meant.
Dextrous of hand, she struck her lute's few strings;
Ignobly perfect, barrenly content.

Unflushed with ardor and unblanched with awe,
Her lips in profitless derision curled,
She saw with dull emotion—if she saw—
The vision of the glory of the world.

The human masque she watched, with dreamless eyes
In whose clear shallows lurked no trembling shade:
The stars, unkenned by her, might set and rise;
Unmarked by her, the daisies bloom and fade.

The age grew sated with her sterile wit.
  Herself waxed weary on her loveless throne.
Men felt life's tide, the sweep and surge of it,
  And craved a living voice, a natural tone.

For none the less, though song was but half true,
  The world lay common, one abounding theme.
Man joyed and wept, and fate was ever new,
  And love was sweet, life real, death no dream.

In sad, stern verse the rugged scholar-sage
  Bemoaned his toil unvalued, youth uncheered.
His numbers wore the vesture of the age,
  But, 'neath it beating, the great heart was heard.

From dewy pastures, uplands sweet with thyme,
  A virgin breeze freshened the jaded day.
It wafted Collins' lonely vesper-chime,
  It breathed abroad the frugal note of Gray.

It fluttered here and there, nor swept in vain
  The dusty haunts where futile echoes dwell,—
Then, in a cadence soft as summer rain,
  And sad from Auburn voiceless, drooped and fell.

It drooped and fell, and one 'neath northern skies,
  With southern heart, who tilled his father's field,
Found Poesy a-dying, bade her rise
  And touch quick Nature's hem and go forth healed.

On life's broad plain the plowman's conquering share
  Upturned the fallow lands of truth anew,
And o'er the formal garden's trim parterre
  The peasant's team a ruthless furrow drew.

Bright was his going forth, but clouds ere long
  Whelmed him; in gloom his radiance set, and those
Twin morning stars of the new century's song,
  Those morning stars that sang together, rose.

In elvish speech the *Dreämer* told his tale
  Of marvelous oceans swept by fateful wings.—
The *Seër* strayed not from earth's human pale
  But the mysterious face of common things

He mirrored as the moon in Rydal Mere
  Is mirrored, when the breathless night hangs blue:
Strangely remote she seems and wondrous near,
  And by some nameless difference born anew.

V

Peace—peace—and rest! Ah, how the lyre is loth,
  Or powerless now, to give what all men seek!
Either it deadens with ignoble sloth
  Or deafens with shrill tumult, loudly weak.

Where is the singer whose large notes and clear
  Can heal, and arm, and plenish, and sustain?
Lo, one with empty music floods the ear,
  And one, the heart refreshing, tires the brain.

And idly tuneful, the loquacious throng
  Flutter and twitter, prodigal of time,
And little masters make a toy of song,
  Till grave men weary of the sound of rhyme.

And some go pranked in faded antique dress,
  Abhorring to be hale and glad and free;
And some parade a conscious naturalness,
  The scholar's not the child's simplicity.

Enough;—the wisest who from words forbear
  The gentle river rails not as it glides;
And suave and charitable, the winsome air
  Chides not at all, or only him who chides.

VI

Nature! we storm thine ear with choric notes.
  Thou answerest through the calm great nights and days,
"Laud me who will: not tuneless are your throats;
  Yet if ye paused I should not miss the praise."

We falter, half-rebuked, and sing again.
  We chant thy desertness and haggard gloom,
Or with thy splendid wrath inflate the strain,
  Or touch it with thy color and perfume.

One, his melodious blood aflame for thee,
  Wooed with fierce lust, his hot heart world-defiled.
One, with the upward eye of infancy,
  Looked in thy face, and felt himself thy child.

Thee he approached without distrust or dread—
  Beheld thee throned, an awful queen, above—
Climbed to thy lap and merely laid his head
  Against thy warm wild heart of mother-love.

He heard that vast heart beating—thou didst press
  Thy child so close, and lov'dst him unaware.
Thy beauty gladdened him; yet he scarce less
  Had loved thee, had he never found thee fair!

For thou wast not as legendary lands
  To which with curious eyes and ears we roam.
Nor wast thou as a fane 'mid solemn sands,
  Where palmers halt at evening. Thou wast home.

And here, at home, still bides he; but he sleeps;
  Not to be wakened even at thy word;
Though we, vague dreamers, dream he somewhere keeps
  An ear still open to thy voice still heard,—

Thy voice, as heretofore, about him blown,
  For ever blown about his silence now;
Thy voice, though deeper, yet so like his own
  That almost, when he sang, we deemed 'twas thou!

VII

Behind Helm Crag and Silver Howe the sheen
  Of the retreating day is less and less.
Soon will the lordlier summits, here unseen,
  Gather the night about their nakedness.

The half-heard bleat of sheep comes from the hill.
  Faint sounds of childish play are in the air.
The river murmurs past. All else is still.
  The very graves seem stiller than they were.

Afar though nation be on nation hurled,
  And life with toil and ancient pain depressed,
Here one may scarce believe the whole wide world
  Is not at peace, and all man's heart at rest.

Rest! 'twas the gift *he* gave, and peace! the shade
  *He* spread, for spirits fevered with the sun.
To him his bounties are come back—here laid
  In rest, in peace, his labor nobly done.

*William Watson* [1858–1935]

# JERUSALEM THE GOLDEN

## JERUSALEM *

For thee, O dear dear Country!
  Mine eyes their vigils keep;
For very love, beholding
  Thy happy name, they weep:
The mention of thy glory
  Is unction to the breast,
And medicine in sickness,
  And love, and life, and rest.

O come, O onely Mansion!
  O Paradise of Joy!
Where tears are ever banished,
  And smiles have no alloy;
Beside thy living waters
  All plants are, great and small,
The cedar of the forest,
  The hyssop of the wall:
With jaspers glow thy bulwarks;
  Thy streets with emeralds blaze;
The sardius and the topaz
  Unite in thee their rays:
Thine ageless walls are bonded
  With amethyst unpriced:
Thy Saints build up its fabric,
  And the corner-stone is Christ.

The Cross is all thy splendor,
  The Crucified thy praise:
His laud and benediction
  Thy ransomed people raise:

* For the original of this poem see page 3824.

Jesus, the Gem of Beauty,
  True God and Man, they sing:
The never-failing Garden,
  The ever-golden Ring:
The Door, the Pledge, the Husband,
  The Guardian of his Court:
The Day-star of Salvation,
  The Porter and the Port.
Thou hast no shore, fair ocean!
  Thou hast no time, bright day!
Dear fountain of refreshment
  To pilgrims far away!

Upon the Rock of Ages
  They raise thy holy tower:
Thine is the victor's laurel,
  And thine the golden dower:
Thou feel'st in mystic rapture,
  O Bride that know'st no guile,
The Prince's sweetest kisses,
  The Prince's loveliest smile:

Unfading lilies, bracelets
  Of living pearl thine own:
The Lamb is ever near thee,
  The Bridegroom thine alone:
The Crown is He to guerdon,
  The Buckler to protect,
And He Himself the Mansion,
  And He the Architect.
The only art thou needest,
  Thanksgiving for thy lot:
The only joy thou seekest,
  The Life where Death is not.
And all thine endless leisure
  In sweetest accents sings,
The ill that was thy merit,—
  The wealth that is thy King's!

*Jerusalem the golden,*
*With milk and honey blest,*
*Beneath thy contemplation*
*Sink heart and voice oppressed;*
*I know not, O I know not,*
*What social joys are there!*
*What radiancy of glory,*
*What light beyond compare!*

And when I fain would sing them
My spirit fails and faints,
And vainly would it image
The assembly of the Saints.

*They stand, those halls of Syon,*
*Conjubilant with song,*
*And bright with many an angel,*
*And all the martyr throng:*
*The Prince is ever in them;*
*The daylight is serene:*
*The pastures of the Blessèd*
*Are decked in glorious sheen.*

*There is the Throne of David,—*
*And there, from care released,*
*The song of them that triumph,*
*The shout of them that feast:*
*And they who, with their Leader*
*Have conquered in the fight,*
*For ever and for ever*
*Are clad in robes of white!*

O holy, placid harp-notes
Of that eternal hymn!
O sacred, sweet refection,
And peace of Seraphim!
O thirst, for ever ardent,
Yet evermore content!
O true, peculiar vision
Of God cunctipotent!

Ye know the many mansions
  For many a glorious name
And divers retributions
  That divers merits claim:
For midst the constellations
  That deck our earthly sky,
This star than that is brighter,—
  And so it is on high.

Jerusalem the glorious!
  The glory of the Elect!
O dear and future vision
  That eager hearts expect:
Even now by faith I see thee
  Even here thy walls discern:
To thee my thoughts are kindled,
  And strive and pant and yearn:
Jerusalem the onely,
  That look'st from heaven below,
In thee is all my glory;
  In me is all my woe!
And though my body may not,
  My spirit seeks thee fain,
Till flesh and earth return me
  To earth and flesh again.
O none can tell thy bulwarks,
  How gloriously they rise:
O none can tell thy capitals
  Of beautiful device:
Thy loveliness oppresses
  All human thought and heart:
And none, O peace, O Syon,
  Can sing thee as thou art.
New mansion of new people,
  Whom God's own love and light
Promote, increase, make holy,
  Identify, unite.
Thou City of the Angels!
  Thou City of the Lord!

Whose everlasting music
  Is the glorious decachord!
And there the band of Prophets
  United praise ascribes,
And there the twelvefold chorus
  Of Israel's ransomed tribes:
The lily-beds of virgins,
  The roses' martyr-glow,
The cohort of the Fathers
  Who kept the faith below!
And there the Sole-Begotten
  Is Lord in regal state;
He, Judah's mystic Lion,
  He, Lamb Immaculate.

O fields that know no sorrow!
  O state that fears no strife!
O princely bowers! O land of flowers!
  O realm and home of life!

*John Mason Neale* [1818-1866]

## THE NEW JERUSALEM *

From "Song of Mary the Mother of Christ"

JERUSALEM, my happy home,
  When shall I come to thee?
When shall my sorrows have an end?
  Thy joys when shall I see?

O happy harbor of the Saints!
  O sweet and pleasant soil!
In thee no sorrow may be found,
  No grief, no care, no toil.

There lust and lucre cannot dwell,
  There envy bears no sway;
There is no hunger, heat, nor cold,
  But pleasure every way.

* For the original of this poem see page 3826.

Thy walls are made of precious stones,
Thy bulwarks diamonds square;
Thy gates are of right orient pearl,
Exceeding rich and rare.

Thy turrets and thy pinnacles
With carbuncles do shine;
Thy very streets are paved with gold,
Surpassing clear and fine.

Ah, my sweet home, Jerusalem,
Would God I were in thee!
Would God my woes were at an end,
Thy joys that I might see!

Thy gardens and thy gallant walks
Continually are green;
There grow such sweet and pleasant flowers
As nowhere else are seen.

Quite through thy streets, with silver sound,
The flood of Life doth flow;
Upon whose banks on every side
The wood of Life doth grow.

There trees for evermore bear fruit,
And evermore do spring;
There evermore the angels sit,
And evermore do sing.

Our Lady sings *Magnificat*
With tones surpassing sweet;
And all the virgins bear their part,
Sitting about her feet.

Jerusalem, my happy home,
Would God I were in thee!
Would God my woes were at an end,
Thy joys that I might see!

***Unknown***

## PEACE

My soul, there is a country
  Afar beyond the stars,
Where stands a wingèd sentry
  All skilful in the wars:
There, above noise and danger,
  Sweet Peace sits crowned with smiles,
And One born in a manger
  Commands the beauteous files.
He is thy gracious Friend,
  And—O my soul, awake!—
Did in pure love descend
  To die here for thy sake.
If thou canst get but thither,
  There grows the flower of Peace,
The Rose that cannot wither,
  Thy fortress, and thy ease.
Leave then thy foolish ranges;
  For none can thee secure
But One who never changes—
  Thy God, thy Life, thy Cure.

*Henry Vaughan* [1622-1695]

## PARADISE

O Paradise, O Paradise,
  Who doth not crave for rest,
Who would not seek the happy land
  Where they that loved are blest?
    Where loyal hearts and true
      Stand ever in the light,
    All rapture through and through,
      In God's most holy sight.

O Paradise, O Paradise,
  The world is growing old;
Who would not be at rest and free
  Where love is never cold?

O Paradise, O Paradise,
Wherefore doth death delay?
Bright death, that is the welcome dawn
Of our eternal day.

O Paradise, O Paradise,
'Tis weary waiting here;
I long to be where Jesus is,
To feel, to see Him near.

O Paradise, O Paradise,
I want to sin no more,
I want to be as pure on earth
As on thy spotless shore.

O Paradise, O Paradise,
I greatly long to see
The special place my dearest Lord
Is destining for me.

O Paradise, O Paradise,
I feel 'twill not be long;
Patience! I almost think I hear
Faint fragments of thy song;
Where loyal hearts and true
Stand ever in the light,
All rapture through and through,
In God's most holy sight.

*Frederick William Faber* [1814–1863]

## THE WORLD

I SAW Eternity the other night,
Like a great ring of pure and endless light,
All calm, as it was bright;
And round beneath it, Time in hours, days, years,
Driven by the spheres,
Like a vast shadow moved; in which the world
And all her train were hurled.

The doting lover in his quaintest strain
Did there complain;
Near him, his lute, his fancy, and his flights,
Wit's sour delights;
With gloves, and knots and silly snares of pleasure,
Yet his dear treasure
All scattered lay, while he his eyes did pour
Upon a flower.

The darksome statesman, hung with weights and woe,
Like a thick midnight-fog. moved there so slow,
He did nor stay, nor go;
Condemning thoughts—like sad eclipses—scowl
Upon his soul,
And clouds of crying witnesses without
Pursued him with one shout.
Yet digged the mole, and lest his ways be found,
Worked under ground,
Where he did clutch his prey; but one did see
That policy:
Churches and altars fed him; perjuries
Were gnats and flies;
It rained about him blood and tears, but he
Drank them as free.

The fearful miser on a heap of rust
Sate pining all his life there, did scarce trust
His own hands with the dust,
Yet would not place one piece above, but lives
In fear of thieves.
Thousands there were as frantic as himself,
And hugged each one his pelf;
The down-right epicure placed heaven in sense,
And scorned pretense;
While others, slipped into a wide excess,
Said little less;
The weaker sort slight, trival wares enslave,
Who think them brave;
And poor, despisèd Truth sate counting by
Their victory.

Yet some, who all this while did weep and sing,
And sing and weep, soared up into the ring;
But most would use no wing.
O fools—said I—thus to prefer dark night
Before true light!
To live in grots and caves, and hate the day
Because it shows the way;
The way, which from this dead and dark abode
Leads up to God;
A way where you might tread the sun, and be
More bright then he!
But as I did their madness so discuss,
One whispered thus,
"This ring the Bride-groom did for none provide,
But for His Bride."

*Henry Vaughan* [1622–1695]

## THE WHITE ISLAND

### OR, PLACE OF THE BLEST

In this world, the Isle of Dreams,
While we sit by sorrow's streams,
Tears and terrors are our themes
Reciting:

But when once from hence we fly,
More and more approaching nigh
Unto young Eternity
Uniting:

In that whiter island, where
Things are evermore sincere;
Candor here, and luster there
Delighting:

There no monstrous fancies shall
Out of Hell an horror call,
To create (or cause at all)
Affrighting.

There in calm and cooling sleep
We our eyes shall never steep;
But eternal watch shall keep
Attending

Pleasures such as shall pursue
Me immortalized, and you;
And fresh joys, as never too
Have ending.

*Robert Herrick* [1591–1674]

## "THIS WORLD IS ALL A FLEETING SHOW"

This world is all a fleeting show,
For man's illusion given;
The smiles of joy, the tears of woe,
Deceitful shine, deceitful flow,—
There's nothing true but Heaven!

And false the light on glory's plume,
As fading hues of even;
And love, and hope, and beauty's bloom
Are blossoms gathered for the tomb,—
There's nothing bright but Heaven!

Poor wanderers of a stormy day,
From wave to wave we're driven,
And fancy's flash and reason's ray
Serve but to light the troubled way,—
There's nothing calm but Heaven!

*Thomas Moore* [1779–1852]

## THE LAND O' THE LEAL

I'm wearin' awa', John,
Like snaw-wreaths in thaw, John.
I'm wearin' awa'
To the land o' the leal.

There's nae sorrow there, John,
There's neither cauld nor care, John,
The day is aye fair
In the land o' the leal.

Our bonnie bairn's there, John,
She was baith gude and fair, John;
And O! we grudged her sair
To the land o' the leal.
But sorrow's sel' wears past, John,
And joy's a-comin' fast, John,
The joy that's aye to last
In the land o' the leal.

Sae dear's that joy was bought, John,
Sae free the battle fought, John,
That sinfu' man e'er brought
To the land o' the leal.
O, dry your glistening e'e, John!
My saul langs to be free, John,
And angels beckon me
To the land o' the leal.

O, haud ye leal and true, John!
Your day it's wearin' through, John,
And I'll welcome you
To the land o' the leal.
Now fare-ye-weel, my ain John,
This warld's cares are vain, John,
We'll meet, and we'll be fain,
In the land o' the leal.

*Carolina Nairne* [1766–1845]

## HEAVENWARD

WOULD you be young again?
So would not I—
One tear to memory given,
Onward I'd hie.

Life's dark flood forded o'er,
All but at rest on shore,
Say, would you plunge once more,
With home so nigh?

If you might, would you now
Retrace your way?
Wander through thorny wilds,
Faint and astray?
Night's gloomy watches fled,
Morning all beaming red,
Hope's smiles around us shed,
Heavenward—away.

Where are they gone, of yore
My best delight?
Dear and more dear, though now
Hidden from sight.
Where they rejoice to be,
There is the land for me;
Fly time—fly speedily,
Come life and light.

*Carolina Nairne* [1766- 1845]

## "REST IS NOT HERE"

WHAT'S this vain world to me?
Rest is not here;
False are the smiles I see,
The mirth I hear.
Where is youth's joyful glee?
Where all once dear to me?
Gone as the shadows flee—
Rest is not here.

Why did the morning shine
Blithely and fair?
Why did those tints so fine
Vanish in air?

Does not the vision say,
Faint lingering heart, away,
Why in this desert stay—
Dark land of care!

Where souls angelic soar,
Thither repair:
Let this vain world no more
Lull and ensnare.
That heaven I love so well
Still in my heart shall dwell;
All things around me tell
Rest is found there.

*Carolina Nairne* [1766-1845]

## AT HOME IN HEAVEN

### PART I

"FOR EVER with the Lord!"
Amen! so let it be!
Life from the dead is in that word,
'Tis immortality.

Here in the body pent,
Absent from Him I roam,
Yet nightly pitch my moving tent
A day's march nearer home.

My Father's house on high,
Home of my soul! how near,
At times, to faith's foreseeing eye,
Thy golden gates appear!

Ah! then my spirit faints
To reach the land I love,
The bright inheritance of saints,
Jerusalem above!

Yet clouds will intervene,
And all my prospect flies;
Like Noah's dove, I flit between
Rough seas and stormy skies.

Anon the clouds depart,
  The winds and waters cease;
While sweetly o'er my gladdened heart
  Expands the bow of peace!

Beneath its glowing arch,
  Along the hallowed ground,
I see cherubic armies march,
  A camp of fire around.

I hear at morn and even,
  At noon and midnight hour,
The choral harmonies of heaven
  Earth's Babel-tongues o'erpower.

Then, then I feel that He,
  (Remembered or forgot,)
The Lord, is never far from me,
  Though I perceive Him not.

PART II

In darkness as in light,
  Hidden alike from view,
I sleep, I wake, as in His sight
  Who looks all nature through.

From the dim hour of birth,
  Through every changing state
Of mortal pilgrimage on earth,
  Till its appointed date;

All that I am, have been,
  All that I yet may be,
He sees at once, as He hath seen,
  And shall forever see.

How can I meet His eyes?
  Mine on the cross I cast,
And own my life a Saviour's prize
  Mercy from first to last

"Forever with the Lord:"
Father, if 'tis Thy will,
The promise of that faithful word
Even here to me fulfil!

So, when my latest breath
Shall rend the veil in twain,
By death I shall escape from death,
And life eternal gain.

Knowing as I am known
How shall I love that word,
And oft repeat before the throne,
"For ever with the Lord!"

Then though the soul enjoy
Communion high and sweet,
While worms this body must destroy,
Both shall in glory meet.

The trump of final doom
Will speak the self-same word,
And heaven's voice thunder through the tomb,
"For ever with the Lord!"

The tomb shall echo deep
That death-awakening sound;
The saints shall hear it in their sleep
And answer from the ground.

Then upward as they fly,
That resurrection-word
Shall be their shout of victory,
"For ever with the Lord!"

That resurrection-word,
That shout of victory,
Once more,—"For ever with the Lord!"
Amen, so let it be.

*James Montgomery* [1771–1854]

## PARADISE

ONCE in a dream I saw the flowers
That bud and bloom in Paradise;
More fair they are than waking eyes
Have seen in all this world of ours,
And faint the perfume-bearing rose,
And faint the lily on its stem,
And faint the perfect violet,
Compared with them.

I heard the songs of Paradise;
Each bird sat singing in its place;
A tender song so full of grace
It soared like incense to the skies.
Each bird sat singing to its mate
Soft cooing notes among the trees:
The nightingale herself were cold
To such as these.

I saw the fourfold River flow,
And deep it was, with golden sand;
It flowed between a mossy land
With murmured music grave and low.
It hath refreshment for all thirst,
For fainting spirit strength and rest:
Earth holds not such a draught as this
From east to west.

The Tree of Life stood budding there,
Abundant with its twelvefold fruits;
Eternal sap sustains its roots,
Its shadowing branches fill the air.
Its leaves are healing for the world,
Its fruit the hungry world can feed,
Sweeter than honey to the taste
And balm indeed.

I saw the Gate called Beautiful;
And looked, but scarce could look within;
I saw the golden streets begin,
And outskirts of the glassy pool.

Oh harps, oh crowns of plenteous stars,
  Oh green palm branches, many-leaved--
Eye hath not seen, nor ear hath heard,
  Nor heart conceived.

I hope to see these things again,
  But not as once in dreams by night;
  To see them with my very sight,
And touch and handle and attain:
To have all heaven beneath my feet
  For narrow way that once they trod;
To have my part with all the saints,
  And with my God.

*Christina Georgina Rossetti* [1830-1894]

## "HEAVEN OVERARCHES EARTH AND SEA"

HEAVEN overarches earth and sea,
  Earth-sadness and sea-bitterness.
Heaven overarches you and me:
A little while and we shall be—
Please God—where there is no more sea
  Nor barren wilderness.

Heaven overarches you and me,
  And all earth's gardens and her graves.
Look up with me, until we see
The day break and the shadows flee.
What though to-night wrecks you and me,
  If so to-morrow saves?

*Christina Georgina Rossetti* [1830-1894]

## THE SUNSET CITY

THERE'S a city that lies in the Kingdom of Clouds,
  In the glorious country on high,
Which an azure and silvery curtain enshrouds,
  To screen it from mortal eye;

A city of temples and turrets of gold,
  That gleam by a sapphire sea,
Like jewels more splendid than earth may behold,
  Or are dreamed of by you and by me.

And about it are highlands of amber that reach
  Far away till they melt in the gloom;
And waters that hem an immaculate beach
  With fringes of luminous foam.

Aerial bridges of pearl there are,
  And belfries of marvelous shapes,
And lighthouses lit by the evening star,
  That sparkle on violet capes;

And hanging gardens that far away
  Enchantedly float aloof;
Rainbow pavilions in avenues gay,
  And banners of glorious woof!

When the Summer sunset's crimsoning fires
  Are aglow in the western sky,
The pilgrim discovers the domes and spires
  Of this wonderful city on high;

And gazing enrapt as the gathering shade
  Creeps over the twilight lea,
Sees palace and pinnacle totter and fade,
  And sink in the sapphire sea;

Till the vision loses by slow degrees
  The magical splendor it wore;
The silvery curtain is drawn, and he sees
  The beautiful city no more!

*Henry Sylvester Cornwell* [1831–1886]

## GRADATIM

HEAVEN is not reached at a single bound;
  But we build the ladder by which we rise
  From the lowly earth to the vaulted skies,
And we mount to its summit round by round.

I count this thing to be grandly true:
That a noble deed is a step toward God,
Lifting the soul from the common clod
To a purer air and a broader view.

We rise by the things that are under feet;
By what we have mastered of good and gain;
By the pride deposed and the passion slain,
And the vanquished ills that we hourly meet.

We hope, we aspire, we resolve, we trust,
When the morning calls us to life and light,
But our hearts grow weary, and, ere the night,
Our lives are trailing the sordid dust.

We hope, we resolve, we aspire, we pray,
And we think that we mount the air on wings
Beyond the recall of sensual things,
While our feet still cling to the heavy clay.

Wings for the angels, but feet for men!
We may borrow the wings to find the way—
We may hope, and resolve, and aspire, and pray;
But our feet must rise, or we fall again.

Only in dreams is a ladder thrown
From the weary earth to the sapphire walls;
But the dreams depart, and the vision falls,
And the sleeper wakes on his pillow of stone.

Heaven is not reached at a single bound;
But we build the ladder by which we rise
From the lowly earth to the vaulted skies,
And we mount to its summit, round by round.

*Josiah Gilbert Holland* [1819–1881]

## THE OTHER WORLD

It lies around us like a cloud—
The world we do not see;
Yet the sweet closing of an eye
May bring us there to be.

Its gentle breezes fan our cheeks
Amid our worldly cares;
Its gentle voices whisper love,
And mingle with our prayers.

Sweet hearts around us throb and beat,
Sweet helping hands are stirred,
And palpitates the veil between
With breathings almost heard.

The silence—awful, sweet, and calm
They have no power to break;
For mortal words are not for them
To utter or partake.

So thin, so soft, so sweet they glide,
So near to press they seem,
They lull us gently to our rest,
And melt into our dream.

And, in the hush of rest they bring,
'Tis easy now to see
How lovely and how sweet a pass
The hour of death may be!

To close the eye and close the ear,
Wrapped in a trance of bliss,
And, gently drawn in loving arms,
To swoon to that—from this.

Scarce knowing if we wake or sleep,
Scarce asking where we are,
To feel all evil sink away,
All sorrow and all care.

Sweet souls around us! watch us still,
Press nearer to our side,
Into our thoughts, into our prayers,
With gentle helping glide.

Let death between us be as naught,
A dried and vanished stream;
Your joy be the reality,
Our suffering life the dream.

*Harriet Beecher Stowe* [1811-1896]

## MY AIN COUNTREE

I AM far frae my hame, an' I'm weary often whiles
For the longed-for hame-bringing an' my Father's welcome smiles;
I'll ne'er be fu' content until my een do see
The gowden gates o' heaven, an' my ain countree.

The earth is flecked wi' flowers, mony-tinted, fresh an' gay,
The birdies warble blithely, for my Father made them sae;
But these sights an' these soun's will as naething be to me,
When I hear the angels singing in my ain countree.

I've his gude word of promise, that some gladsome day the King
To his ain royal palace his banished hame will bring;
Wi' een an' wi' heart running over we shall see
"The King in his beauty," an' our ain countree.

My sins hae been mony an' my sorrows hae been sair,
But there they'll never vex me, nor be remembered mair,
His bluid has made me white, his hand shall wipe mine ee,
When he brings me hame at last to my ain countree.

Like a bairn to his mither, a wee birdie to its nest,
I wud fain be ganging noo unto my Saviour's breast;
For he gathers in his bosom witless, worthless lambs like me,
An' he carries them himsel' to his ain countree.

He's faithfu' that hath promised, he'll surely come again;
He'll keep his tryst wi' me, at what hour I dinna ken;
But he bids me still to watch, an' ready aye to be
To gang at ony moment to my ain countree.

So I'm watching aye an' singing o' my hame as I wait,
For the soun'ing o' his footsteps this side the gowden gate.
God gie his grace to ilka ane wha listens noo to me,
That we may a' gang in gladness to our ain countree.

*Mary Lee Demarest* [1838–1888]

## HOME

THERE lies a little city in the hills;
White are its roofs, dim is each dwelling's door,
And peace with perfect rest its bosom fills.

There the pure mist, the pity of the sea,
Comes as a white, soft hand, and reaches o'er
And touches its still face most tenderly.

Unstirred and calm, amid our shifting years,
Lo! where it lies, far from the clash and roar,
With quiet distance blurred, as if through tears.

O heart that prayest so for God to send
Some loving messenger to go before
And lead the way to where thy longings end,

Be sure, be very sure, that soon will come
His kindest angel, and through that still door
Into the Infinite love will lead thee home.

*Edward Rowland Sill* [1841–1887]

## CHARTLESS

I NEVER saw a moor,
I never saw the sea;
Yet know I how the heather looks,
And what a wave must be.

I never spoke with God,
Nor visited in heaven;
Yet certain am I of the spot
As if the chart were given.

*Emily Dickinson* [1830–1886]

## "IT CANNOT BE"

It cannot be that He who made
  This wondrous world for our delight,
Designed that all its charms should fade
  And pass forever from our sight;
That all shall wither and decay,
  And know on earth no life but this,
With only one finite survey
  Of all its beauty and its bliss.

It cannot be that all the years
  Of toil and care and grief we live
Shall find no recompense but tears,
  No sweet return that earth can give;
That all that leads us to aspire,
  And struggle onward to achieve,
And every unattained desire
  Were given only to deceive.

It cannot be that, after all
  The mighty conquests of the mind,
Our thoughts shall pass beyond recall
  And leave no record here behind;
That all our dreams of love and fame,
  And hopes that time has swept away,—
All that enthralled this mortal frame,—
  Shall not return some other day.

It cannot be that all the ties
  Of kindred souls and loving hearts
Are broken when this body dies,
  And the immortal mind departs;
That no serener light shall break
  At last upon our mortal eyes,
To guide us as our footsteps make
  The pilgrimage to Paradise.

*David Banks Sickels* [1837-1918]

## A THANKSGIVING TO GOD FOR HIS HOUSE

Lord, Thou hast given me a cell
Wherein to dwell;
A little house, whose humble roof
Is weather-proof;
Under the spars of which I lie
Both soft and dry;
Where Thou, my chamber for to ward,
Hast set a guard
Of harmless thoughts, to watch and keep
Me, while I sleep.
Low is my porch, as is my fate;
Both void of state;
And yet the threshold of my door
Is worn by the poor,
Who thither come, and freely get
Good words, or meat.
Like as my parlor, so my hall
And kitchen's small;
A little buttery, and therein
A little bin,
Which keeps my little loaf of bread
Unchipped, unflead;
Some brittle sticks of thorn or briar
Make me a fire,
Close by whose living coal I sit,
And glow like it.
Lord, I confess too, when I dine,
The pulse is Thine,
And all those other bits that be
There placed by Thee:
The worts, the purslain, and the mess
Of water-cress;
Which of Thy kindness Thou hast sent;
And my content
Makes those, and my belovèd beet,
To be more sweet.
'Tis Thou that crown'st my glittering hearth
With guiltless mirth,

And giv'st me wassail bowls to drink,
Spiced to the brink.
Lord, 'tis Thy plenty-dropping hand
That soils my land,
And giv'st me, for my bushel sown,
Twice ten for one;
Thou mak'st my teeming hen to lay
Her egg each day;
Besides, my healthful ewes to bear
Me twins each year;
The while the conduits of my kine
Run cream, for wine:
All these, and better, Thou dost send
Me, to this end,—
That I should render, for my part,
A thankful heart;
Which, fired with incense, I resign,
As wholly Thine;
—But the acceptance, that must be,
My Christ, by Thee.

*Robert Herrick* [1591–1674]

## THE SHEPHERD BOY SINGS IN THE VALLEY OF HUMILIATION

From "The Pilgrim's Progress"

He that is down needs fear no fall,
He that is low, no pride;
He that is humble ever shall
Have God to be his guide.

I am content with what I have,
Little be it or much:
And, Lord, contentment still I crave,
Because Thou savest such.

Fullness to such a burden is
That go on pilgrimage:
Here little, and hereafter bliss,
Is best from age to age.

*John Bunyan* [1628–1688]

## THE PILGRIM

From "The Pilgrim's Progress"

WHO would true valor see,
  Let him come hither!
One here will constant be,
  Come wind, come weather;
There's no discouragement
Shall make him once relent
His first-avowed intent
  To be a Pilgrim.

Whoso beset him round
  With dismal stories,
Do but themselves confound;
  His strength the more is.
No lion can him fright;
He'll with a giant fight;
But he will have a right
  To be a Pilgrim.

Hobgoblin, nor foul fiend,
  Can daunt his spirit;
He knows he at the end
  Shall Life inherit:—
Then, fancies, fly away;
He'll not fear what men say;
He'll labor, night and day,
  To be a Pilgrim.

*John Bunyan* [1628–1688]

## "THE BIRD, LET LOOSE IN EASTERN SKIES"

THE bird, let loose in eastern skies,
  When hastening fondly home,
Ne'er stoops to earth her wing, nor flies
  Where idle warblers roam;

But high she shoots through air and light,
  Above all low delay,
Where nothing earthly bounds her flight,
  Nor shadow dims her way.

So grant me, God! from every care
  And stain of passion free,
Aloft, through virtue's purer air,
  To hold my course to Thee!
No sin to cloud,—no lure to stay
  My soul, as home she springs;—
Thy sunshine on her joyful way,
  Thy freedom in her wings!

*Thomas Moore* [1779–1852]

## "HE LIVETH LONG WHO LIVETH WELL"

He liveth long who liveth well!
  All other life is short and vain;
He liveth longest who can tell
  Of living most for heavenly gain.

He liveth long who liveth well!
  All else is being flung away;
He liveth longest who can tell
  Of true things truly done each day.

Waste not thy being; back to Him
  Who freely gave it, freely give;
Else is that being but a dream;
  'Tis but to *be*, and not to *live*.

Be what thou seemest! live thy creed!
  Hold up to earth the torch divine;
Be what thou prayest to be made;
  Let the great Master's steps be thine,

Fill up each hour with what will last;
  Buy up the moments as they go;
The life above, when this is past,
  Is the ripe fruit of life below.

Sow truth, if thou the truth wouldst reap:
  Who sows the false shall reap the vain;
Erect and sound thy conscience keep;
  From hollow words and deeds refrain.

Sow love, and taste its fruitage pure;
  Sow peace, and reap its harvests bright;
Sow sunbeams on the rock and moor,
  And find a harvest-home of light.

*Horatius Bonar* [1808-1889]

## THE MASTER'S TOUCH

In the still air the music lies unheard;
  In the rough marble beauty hides unseen:
To wake the music and the beauty needs
  The master's touch, the sculptor's chisel keen.

Great Master, touch us with thy skilful hand;
  Let not the music that is in us die!
Great Sculptor, hew and polish us; nor let,
  Hidden and lost, thy form within us lie!

Spare not the stroke! do with us as thou wilt!
  Let there be naught unfinished, broken, marred;
Complete thy purpose, that we may become
  Thy perfect image, O our God and Lord!

*Horatius Bonar* [1808-1889]

## HOW WE LEARN

Great truths are dearly bought. The common truth,
  Such as men give and take from day to day,
Comes in the common walks of easy life,
  Blown by the careless wind across our way.

Bought in the market, at the current price,
  Bred of the smile, the jest, perchance the bowl,
It tells no tale of daring or of worth,
  Nor pierces even the surface of a soul.

Great truths are greatly won. Not found by chance,
Nor wafted on the breath of summer dream,
But grasped in the great struggle of the soul,
Hard buffeting with adverse wind and stream.

Not in the general mart, 'mid corn and wine,
Not in the merchandise of gold and gems,
Not in the world's gay halls of midnight mirth,
Not 'mid the blaze of regal diadems,

But in the day of conflict, fear, and grief,
When the strong hand of God, put forth in might,
Plows up the subsoil of the stagnant heart,
And brings the imprisoned truth-seed to the light.

Wrung from the troubled spirit in hard hours
Of weakness, solitude, perchance of pain,
Truth springs, like harvest, from the well-plowed field,
And the soul feels it has not wept in vain.

*Horatius Bonar* [1808–1889]

## LOVE

Love bade me welcome; yet my soul drew back,
Guilty of dust and sin.
But quick-eyed Love, observing me grow slack
From my first entrance in,
Drew nearer to me, sweetly questioning
If I lack anything.

"A guest," I answered, "worthy to be here:"
Love said, "You shall be he."
"I, the unkind, ungrateful? Ah, my dear,
I cannot look on Thee."
Love took my hand and, smiling, did reply,
"Who made the eyes but I?"

"Truth, Lord; but I have marred them: let my shame
Go where it doth deserve."
"And know you not," says Love, "Who bore the blame?"
"My dear, then I will serve."
"You must sit down," says Love, "and taste my meat."
So I did sit and eat.

*George Herbert* [1593–1633]

## THE COLLAR

I STRUCK the board, and cried, "No more;
I will abroad.
What, shall I ever sigh and pine?
My lines and life are free; free as the road,
Loose as the wind, as large as store.
Shall I be still in suit?
Have I no harvest but a thorn
To let me blood and not restore
What I have lost with cordial fruit?
Sure there was wine,
Before my sighs did dry it; there was corn
Before my tears did drown it;
Is the year only lost to me?
Have I no bays to crown it,
No flowers, no garlands gay? all blasted,
All wasted?
Not so, my heart; but there is fruit,
And thou hast hands.
Recover all thy sigh-blown age
On double pleasures; leave thy cold dispute
Of what is fit and not; forsake thy cage,
Thy rope of sands
Which petty thoughts have made; and made to thee
Good cable, to enforce and draw,
And be thy law,
While thou didst wink and wouldst not see.
Away! take heed;
I will abroad.
Call in thy death's-head there, tie up thy fears;
He that forbears
To suit and serve his need
Deserves his load."
But as I raved and grew more fierce and wild
At every word,
Methought I heard one calling, "Child!"
And I replied, "My Lord!"

*George Herbert* [1593–1633]

## VIRTUE

SWEET day, so cool, so calm, so bright!
The bridal of the earth and sky—
The dew shall weep thy fall to-night;
    For thou must die.

Sweet rose, whose hue angry and brave
Bids the rash gazer wipe his eye,
Thy root is ever in its grave,
    And thou must die.

Sweet spring, full of sweet days and roses,
A box where sweets compacted lie,
My music shows ye have your closes,
    And all must die.

Only a sweet and virtuous soul,
Like seasoned timber, never gives;
But though the whole world turn to coal
    Then chiefly lives.

*George Herbert* [1593–1633]

## DISCIPLINE

THROW away Thy rod,
Throw away Thy wrath;
    O my God,
Take the gentle path!

For my heart's desire
Unto Thine is bent:
    I aspire
To a full consent.

Not a word or look
I affect to own,
    But by book,
And Thy Book alone.

Though I fail, I weep;
Though I halt in pace,
Yet I creep
To the throne of grace.

Then let wrath remove;
Love will do the deed;
For with love
Stony hearts will bleed.

Love is swift of foot;
Love's a man of war,
And can shoot,
And can hit from far.

Who can 'scape his bow?
That which wrought on Thee,
Brought Thee low,
Needs must work on me.

Throw away Thy rod;
Though man frailties hath,
Thou art God:
Throw away Thy wrath.

*George Herbert* [1593–1633]

## HOLY BAPTISM

SINCE, Lord, to Thee
A narrow way and little gate
Is all the passage, on my infancy
Thou didst lay hold, and antedate
My faith in me.

O, let me still
Write Thee "great God," and me "a child";
Let me be soft and supple to Thy will,
Small to myself, to others mild,
Behither ill.

Although by stealth
My flesh get on; yet let her sister,
My soul, bid nothing, but preserve her wealth:
The growth of flesh is but a blister;
Childhood is health.

*George Herbert* [1593–1633]

## UNKINDNESS

Lord, make me coy and tender to offend:
In friendship first, I think, if that agree
Which I intend
Unto my friend's intent and end;
I would not use a friend as I use Thee.

If any touch my friend or his good name,
It is my honor and my love to free
His blasted fame
From the least spot or thought of blame;
I could not use a friend as I use Thee.

My friend may spit upon my curious floor.
Would he have gold? I lend it instantly;
But let the poor,
And Thee within them, starve at door;
I cannot use a friend as I use Thee.

When that my friend pretendeth to a place,
I quit my interest, and leave it free;
But when Thy grace
Sues for my heart, I Thee displace;
Nor would I use a friend as I use Thee.

Yet can a friend what Thou hast done fulfil?
O, write in brass, "My God upon a tree
His blood did spill,
Only to purchase my good-will";
Yet use I not my foes as I use Thee.

*George Herbert* [1593–1633]

## PRAYER

### AN ODE WHICH WAS PREFIXED TO A LITTLE PRAYER-BOOK GIVEN TO A YOUNG GENTLEWOMAN

Lo, here a little volume, but great book!
(Fear it not, sweet,
It is no hypocrite),
Much larger in itself than in its look.
A nest of new-born sweets,
Whose native fires, disdaining
To lie thus folded, and complaining
Of these ignoble sheets,
Affect more comely bands,
Fair one, from thy kind hands,
And confidently look
To find the rest
Of a rich binding in your breast!
It is, in one choice handful, heaven; and all
Heaven's royal host, encamped thus small
To prove that true, schools use to tell,
Ten thousand angels in one point can dwell.
It is love's great artillery,
Which here contracts itself, and comes to lie
Close-couched in your white bosom; and from thence,
As from a snowy fortress of defense,
Against the ghostly foe to take your part,
And fortify the hold of your chaste heart.
It is the armory of light;
Let constant use but keep it bright,
You'll find it yields
To holy hands and humble hearts
More swords and shields
Than sin hath snares, or hell hath darts.
Only be sure
The hands be pure
That hold these weapons; and the eyes
Those of turtles, chaste and true,
Wakeful and wise,
Here is a friend shall fight for you;

Hold but this book before your heart,—
Let prayer alone to play his part.
But, O! the heart
That studies this high art
Must be a sure house-keeper,
And yet no sleeper.
Dear soul, be strong;
Mercy will come ere long,
And bring her bosom fraught with blessings,—
Flowers of never-fading graces,
To make immortal dressings
For worthy souls, whose wise embraces
Store up themselves for Him Who is alone
The Spouse of virgins, and the Virgin's Son.
But if the noble Bridegroom, when He come,
Shall find the wandering heart from home,
Leaving her chaste abode
To gad abroad,
Amongst the gay mates of the god of flies
To take her pleasure, and to play
And keep the Devil's holiday;
To dance in the sunshine of some smiling,
But beguiling
Spheres of sweet and sugared lies,
Some slippery pair
Of false, perhaps, as fair,
Flattering, but forswearing, eyes;
Doubtless some other heart
Will get the start
Meanwhile, and, stepping in before,
Will take possession of that sacred store
Of hidden sweets, and holy joys—
Words which are not heard with ears
(These tumultuous shops of noise),
Effectual whispers, whose still voice
The soul itself more feels than hears;
Amorous languishments, luminous trances,
Sights which are not seen with eyes,
Spiritual and soul-piercing glances,
Whose pure and subtle lightning flies

Home to the heart, and sets the house on fire,
And melts it down in sweet desire;
Yet doth not stay
To ask the window's leave to pass that way;
Delicious deaths, soft exhalations
Of soul, dear and divine annihilations;
A thousand unknown rites
Of joys, and rarefied delights;
An hundred thousand loves and graces,
And many a mystic thing,
Which the divine embraces
Of the dear Spouse of spirits, with them will bring,
For which it is no shame
That dull mortality must not know a name.
Of all this store
Of blessings, and ten thousand more,
If, when He come,
He find the heart from home,
Doubtless He will unload
Himself some otherwhere,
And pour abroad
His precious sweets
On the fair soul whom first He meets.
O fair! O fortunate! O rich! O dear!
O happy and thrice-happy she,
Selected dove,
Whoe'er she be,
Whose early love
With wingèd vows
Makes haste to meet her morning Spouse,
And close with His immortal kisses!
Happy, indeed, who never misses
To improve that precious hour,
And every day
Seize her sweet prey,
All fresh and fragrant as He rises,
Dropping, with a balmy shower,
A delicious dew of spices.
O, let the blissful heart hold fast
Her heavenly armful; she shall taste

At once ten thousand paradises!
She shall have power
To rifle and deflower
The rich and roseal spring of those rare sweets
Which, with a swelling bosom, there she meets;
Boundless and infinite, bottomless treasures
Of pure inebriating pleasures;
Happy proof! she shall discover
What joy, what bliss,
How many heavens at once it is
To have her God become her lover.

*Richard Crashaw* [1613?–1649]

## PROVIDENCE

Lo, the lilies of the field,
How their leaves instruction yield!
Hark to Nature's lesson given
By the blessed birds of heaven!
Every bush and tufted tree
Warbles sweet philosophy:
Mortal, fly from doubt and sorrow,
God provideth for the morrow.

Say, with richer crimson glows
The kingly mantle than the rose?
Say, have kings more wholesome fare
Than we citizens of air?
Barns nor hoarded grain have we,
Yet we carol merrily.
Mortal, fly from doubt and sorrow,
God provideth for the morrow.

One there lives, whose guardian eye
Guides our humble destiny;
One there lives, who, Lord of all,
Keeps our feathers lest they fall.
Pass we blithely then the time,
Fearless of the snare and lime,
Free from doubt and faithless sorrow:
God provideth for the morrow.

*Reginald Heber* [1783–1826]

## THE BELOVED

Blow gently over my garden,
  Wind of the Southern sea,
In the hour that my Love cometh
  And calleth me!
My Love shall entreat me sweetly,
  With voice like the wood-pigeon;
"I am here at the gate of thy garden,
  Here in the dawn."

Then I shall rise up swiftly
  All in the rose and gray,
And open the gate to my Lover
  At dawning of day.
He hath crowns of pain on His forehead,
  And wounds in His hands and feet;
But here mid the dews of my garden
  His rest shall be sweet.

Then blow not out of your forests,
  Wind of the icy North;
But Wind of the South that is healing,
  Rise and come forth!
And shed your musk and your honey,
  And spill your odors of spice,
For one who forsook for my garden
  His Paradise!

*Katherine Tynan Hinkson* [1861–1931]

## MY LEGACY

They told me I was heir: I turned in haste,
And ran to seek my treasure,
And wondered, as I ran, how it was placed,—
If I should find a measure
Of gold, or if the titles of fair lands
And houses would be laid within my hands.

I journeyed many roads; I knocked at gates;
I spoke to each wayfarer
I met, and said, "A heritage awaits
Me. Art not thou the bearer

Of news? Some message sent to me whereby
I learn which way my new possessions lie?"

Some asked me in; naught lay beyond their door;
Some smiled, and would not tarry,
But said that men were just behind who bore
More gold than I could carry;
And so the morn, the noon, the day, were spent,
While empty-handed up and down I went.

At last one cried, whose face I could not see,
As through the mists he hasted:
"Poor child, what evil ones have hindered thee
Till this whole day is wasted?
Hath no man told thee that thou art joint heir
With one named Christ, who waits the goods to share?'

The one named Christ I sought for many days,
In many places vainly;
I heard men name his name in many ways;
I saw his temples plainly;
But they who named him most gave me no sign
To find him by, or prove the heirship mine.

And when at last I stood before his face,
I knew him by no token
Save subtle air of joy which filled the place;
Our greeting was not spoken;
In solemn silence I received my share,
Kneeling before my brother and "joint heir."

My share! No deed of house or spreading lands,
As I had dreamed; no measure
Heaped up with gold; my elder brother's hands
Had never held such treasure.
Foxes have holes, and birds in nests are fed:
My brother had not where to lay his head.

My share! The right like him to know all pain
Which hearts are made for knowing;
The right to find in loss the surest gain;
To reap my joy from sowing

In bitter tears; the right with him to keep
A watch by day and night with all who weep.

My share! To-day men call it grief and death;
I see the joy and life to-morrow;
I thank my Father with my every breath,
For this sweet legacy of sorrow;
And through my tears I call to each, "Joint heir
With Christ make haste to ask him for thy share."

*Helen Hunt Jackson* [1831–1885]

## THE STARRY HOST

From "God and the Soul"

The countless stars, which to our human eye
Are fixed and steadfast, each in proper place,
Forever bound to changeless points in space,
Rush with our sun and planets through the sky,
And like a flock of birds still onward fly;
Returning never whence began their race,
They speed their ceaseless way with gleaming face
As though God bade them win Infinity.
Ah whither, whither is their forward flight
Through endless time and limitless expanse?
What power with unimaginable might
First hurled them forth to spin in tireless dance?
What beauty lures them on through primal night,
So that for them to be is to advance?

*John Lancaster Spalding* [1840–1916]

## THE CELESTIAL SURGEON

If I have faltered more or less
In my great task of happiness;
If I have moved among my race
And shown no glorious morning face;
If beams from happy human eyes
Have moved me not; if morning skies,
Books, and my food, and summer rain
Knocked on my sullen heart in vain,—

Lord, Thy most pointed pleasure take,
And stab my spirit broad awake;
Or, Lord, if too obdurate I,
Choose Thou, before that spirit die,
A piercing pain, a killing sin,
And to my dead heart run them in!

*Robert Louis Stevenson* [1850–1894]

## THE WAY, THE TRUTH, AND THE LIFE

O THOU great Friend to all the sons of men,
Who once appeared in humblest guise below,
Sin to rebuke, to break the captive's chain,
And call thy brethren forth from want and woe,—

We look to thee! thy truth is still the Light
Which guides the nations, groping on their way,
Stumbling and falling in disastrous night,
Yet hoping ever for the perfect day.

Yes; thou art still the Life, thou art the Way
The holiest know; Light, Life, the Way of heaven!
And they who dearest hope and deepest pray,
Toil by the Light, Life, Way, which thou hast given.

*Theodore Parker* [1810–1860]

## THE INNER LIGHT

Lo, if some pen should write upon your rafter
MENE and MENE in the folds of flame,
Think you could any memories thereafter
Wholly retrace the couplet as it came?

Lo, if some strange, intelligible thunder
Sang to the earth the secret of a star,
Scarce could ye catch, for terror and for wonder,
Shreds of the story that was pealed so far.

Scarcely I catch the words of His revealing,
Hardly I hear Him, dimly understand,
Only the Power that is within me pealing
Lives on my lips and beckons to my hand.

Whoso has felt the Spirit of the Highest
Cannot confound nor doubt Him nor deny:
Yea, with one voice, O world, though thou deniest,
Stand thou on that side, for on this am I.

Rather the earth shall doubt when her retrieving
Pours in the rain and rushes from the sod,
Rather than he for whom the great conceiving
Stirs in his soul to quicken into God.

Ay, though thou then shouldst strike from him his glory,
Blind and tormented, maddened and alone,
Even on the cross would he maintain his story,
Yes, and in hell would whisper, I have known.

*Frederic William Henry Myers* [1843–1901]

## HEREDITY

Why bowest thou, O soul of mine,
Crushed by ancestral sin?
Thou hast a noble heritage,
That bids thee victory win.

The tainted past may bring forth flowers,
As blossomed Aaron's rod;
No legacy of sin annuls
Heredity from God.

*Lydia Avery Coonley Ward* [1845–1924]

## BRINGING OUR SHEAVES

The time for toil is past, and night has come,
The last and saddest of the harvest eves;
Worn out with labor long and wearisome,
Drooping and faint, the reapers hasten home,
Each laden with his sheaves.

Last of the laborers, Thy feet I gain,
Lord of the harvest! and my spirit grieves
That I am burdened not so much with grain
As with a heaviness of heart and brain;
Master, behold my sheaves!

Full well I know I have more tares than wheat,
  Brambles and flowers, dry stalks and withered leaves;
Wherefore I blush and weep, as at thy feet
I kneel down reverently and repeat:
  "Master, behold my sheaves!"

Few, light and worthless; yet their trifling weight
  Through all my frame a weary aching leaves;
For long I struggled with my hapless fate,
And stayed and toiled till it was dark and late,
  But these are all my sheaves.

And yet I gather strength and hope anew,
  For well I know thy patient love perceives
Not what I did, but what I strove to do;
And though the full, ripe ears be sadly few,
  Thou wilt accept my sheaves.

*Elizabeth Akers* [1832-1911]

## TAKE HEART

All day the stormy wind has blown
  From off the dark and rainy sea;
No bird has past the window flown,
The only song has been the moan
  The wind made in the willow-tree.

This is the summer's burial-time:
  She died when dropped the earliest leaves;
And, cold upon her rosy prime,
Fell direful autumn's frosty rime;
  Yet I am not as one that grieves,—

For well I know o'er sunny seas
  The bluebird waits for April skies;
And at the roots of forest trees
The May-flowers sleep in fragrant ease,
  And violets hide their azure eyes.

O thou, by winds of grief o'erblown
  Beside some golden summer's bier,—

Take heart! Thy birds are only flown,
Thy blossoms sleeping, tearful sown,
To greet thee in the immortal year!

*Edna Dean Proctor* [1838–1923]

## FORWARD

DREAMER, waiting for darkness with sorrowful, drooping eyes,
Linger not in the valley, bemoaning the day that is done!
Climb the hills of morning and welcome the rosy skies—
Never yet was the setting so fair as the rising sun!

Dear is the past; its treasures we hold in our hearts for aye;
Woe to the hand that would scatter one wreath of its garnered flowers;
But larger blessing and honor will come with the waking day—
Hail, then, To-morrow, nor tarry with Yesterday's ghostly hours!

Mark how the summers hasten through blossoming fields of June
To the purple lanes of the vintage and levels of golden corn;
"Splendors of life I lavish," runs nature's exultant rune,
"For myriads press to follow, and the rarest are yet unborn."

Think how eager the earth is, and every star that shines,
To circle the grander spaces about God's throne that be;
Never the least moon loiters nor the largest sun declines—
Forward they roll forever those glorious depths to see.

Dreamer, waiting for darkness with sorrowful, drooping eyes,
Summers and suns go gladly, and wherefore dost thou repine?

Climb the hills of morning and welcome the rosy skies—
The joy of the boundless future—nay, God himself is thine!

*Edna Dean Proctor* [1838–1923]

## "THE HARVEST WAITS"

God hath been patient long. In eons past
He plowed the waste of Chaos. He hath sown
The furrows with His worlds, and from His throne
Showered, like grain, planets upon the Vast.
What meed of glory hath He from the past?
Shall He not reap, who hears but prayer and groan?
The harvest waits. . . . He cometh to His own,—
He who shall scythe the starry host at last.
When the accumulated swarms of Death
Glut the rank worlds as rills are choked by leaves,
Then shall God flail the million orbs, as sheaves
Unfruitful gleaned; and, in His age sublime,
Winnow the gathered stars, and with a breath
Whirl the spurned chaff adown the void of Time!

*Lloyd Mifflin* [1846–1921]

## ONE GIFT I ASK

Through weary days and sleepless nights
I fast and pray;
And of my listening Lord I ask
The same alway—
That He will to His child impart
Pureness of heart.

The pure in heart God's face shall see.
And does not this
Include the whole ecstatic scale
Of promised bliss?
Can souls which His dear presence gain
More joy attain?

I need not plead with Him to give
  Me every grace
That makes the spirit beautiful;
  For, if God's face
I am to see, He will bestow
  All else, I know.

And so, through days of prayer and fast,
  I only try
To win that purity of heart
  Which, by and by,
The wondrous boon will gain for me,
  God's face to see.

*Virginia Bioren Harrison* [1847-

## MAGDALEN

MAGDALEN at Michael's gate
  Tirlèd at the pin;
On Joseph's thorn sang the blackbird,
  "Let her in! Let her in!"

"Hast thou seen the wounds?" said Michael,
  "Know'st thou thy sin?"
"It is evening, evening," sang the blackbird,
  "Let her in! Let her in!"

"Yes, I have seen the wounds,
  And I know my sin."
"She knows it well, well, well," sang the blackbird,
  "Let her in! Let her in!"

"Thou bringest no offerings," said Michael,
  "Naught save sin."
And the blackbird sang, "She is sorry, sorry, sorry,
  Let her in! Let her in!"

When he had sung himself to sleep,
  And night did begin,
One came and opened Michael's gate,
  And Magdalen went in.

*Henry Kingsley* [1830-1876]

## GOD'S WILL

God meant me to be hungry,
So I should seek to find
Wisdom, and truth, and beauty,
To satisfy my mind.

God meant me to be lonely,
Lest I should wish to stay
In some green earthly Eden
Too long from heaven away.

God meant me to be weary,
That I should yearn to rest
This feeble, aching body
Deep in the earth's dark breast.

*Mildred Howells* [1872- ]

## AFTER THE MARTYRDOM

They threw a stone, you threw a stone,
I threw a stone that day.
Although their sharpness bruised his flesh
He had no word to say.

But for the moan he did not make
To-day I make my moan;
And for the stone I threw at him
My heart must bear a stone.

*Scharmel Iris* [18

## THE BURIAL OF MOSES

" And he buried him in a valley in the land of Moab, over against Beth-peor; but no man knoweth of his sepulcher unto this day."—Deut. xxxiv, 6.

By Nebo's lonely mountain,
On this side Jordan's wave,
In a vale in the land of Moab,
There lies a lonely grave;
But no man built that sepulcher,
And no man saw it e'er;
For the angels of God upturned the sod
And laid the dead man there.

That was the grandest funeral
That ever passed on earth;
Yet no man heard the trampling,
Or saw the train go forth:
Noiselessly as the daylight
Comes when the night is done,
And the crimson streak on ocean's cheek
Grows into the great sun;

Noiselessly as the spring-time
Her crown of verdure weaves,
And all the trees on all the hills
Unfold their thousand leaves:
So without sound of music
Or voice of them that wept,
Silently down from the mountain's crown
The great procession swept.

Perchance the bald old eagle
On gray Beth-peor's height
Out of his rocky eyrie
Looked on the wondrous sight;
Perchance the lion stalking
Still shuns that hallowed spot;
For beast and bird have seen and heard
That which man knoweth not.

But, when the warrior dieth,
His comrades of the war,
With arms reversed and muffled drums,
Follow the funeral car:
They show the banners taken;
They tell his battles won;
And after him lead his masterless steed,
While peals the minute-gun.

Amid the noblest of the land
Men lay the sage to rest,
And give the bard an honored place
With costly marble dressed.

In the great minster transept
Where lights like glories fall,
And the sweet choir sings, and the organ rings
Along the emblazoned wall.

This was the bravest warrior
That ever buckled sword;
This the most gifted poet
That ever breathed a word;
And never earth's philosopher
Traced with his golden pen
On the deathless page truths half so sage
As he wrote down for men.

And had he not high honor?—
The hillside for a pall!
To lie in state, while angels wait,
With stars for tapers tall!
And the dark rock-pines, like tossing plumes,
Over his bier to wave,
And God's own hand, in that lonely land,
To lay him in the grave!—

In that strange grave without a name,
Whence his uncoffined clay
Shall break again—O wondrous thought!—
Before the judgment-day,
And stand, with glory wrapped around,
On the hills he never trod
And speak of the strife that won our life
With the incarnate Son of God.

O lonely tomb in Moab's land!
O dark Beth-peor's hill!
Speak to these curious hearts of ours,
And teach them to be still:
God hath His mysteries of grace,
Ways that we cannot tell;
He hides them deep, like the secret sleep
Of him He loved so well.

*Cecil Frances Alexander* [1818-1895]

## THE CROOKED FOOTPATH

From "The Professor at the Breakfast Table"

Ah, here it is! the sliding rail
  That marks the old remembered spot,—
The gap that struck our schoolboy trail,—
  The crooked path across the lot.

It left the road by school and church,
  A penciled shadow, nothing more,
That parted from the silver birch
  And ended at the farm-house door.

No line or compass traced its plan;
  With frequent bends to left or right,
In aimless, wayward curves it ran
  But always kept the door in sight.

The gabled porch, with woodbine green,—
  The broken millstone at the sill,—
Though many a rood might stretch between
  The truant child could see them still.

No rocks across the pathway lie,—
  No fallen trunk is o'er it thrown,—
And yet it winds, we know not why,
  And turns as if for tree or stone.

Perhaps some lover trod the way
  With shaking knees and leaping heart,—
And so it often runs astray
  With sinuous sweep or sudden start.

Or one, perchance, with clouded brain
  From some unholy banquet reeled,—
And since, our devious steps maintain
  His track across the trodden field.

Nay, deem not thus,—no earthborn will
  Could ever trace a faultless line;
Our truest steps are human still,—
  To walk unswerving were divine!

Truants from love, we dream of wrath;—
  Oh, rather, let us trust the more!
Through all the wanderings of the path,
  We still can see our Father's door!

*Oliver Wendell Holmes* [1809–1894]

## ALLAH'S TENT

WITH fore-cloth smoothed by careful hands
The night's serene pavilion stands,
And many cressets hang on high
Against its arching canopy.

Peace to His children God hath sent,
We are at peace within His tent.
Who knows without these guarded doors
What wind across the desert roars?

*Arthur Colton* [1868–1943]

## ST. JOHN BAPTIST

I THINK he had not heard of the far towns;
Nor of the deeds of men, nor of kings' crowns;
  Before the thought of God took hold of him,
As he was sitting dreaming in the calm
  Of one first noon, upon the desert's rim,
Beneath the tall fair shadows of the palm,
All overcome with some strange inward balm.

He numbered not the changes of the year,
The days, the nights, and he forgot all fear
  Of death: each day he thought there should have been
A shining ladder set for him to climb
  Athwart some opening in the heavens, e'en
To God's eternity, and see, sublime—
His face whose shadow passing fills all time.

But he walked through the ancient wilderness.
O, there the prints of feet were numberless
And holy all about him! And quite plain
He saw each spot an angel silvershod
Had lit upon; where Jacob too had lain
The place seemed fresh,—and, bright and lately trod,
A long track showed where Enoch walked with God.

And often, while the sacred darkness trailed
Along the mountains smitten and unveiled
By rending lightnings,—over all the noise
Of thunders and the earth that quaked and bowed
From its foundations—he could hear the voice
Of great Elias prophesying loud
To Him whose face was covered by a cloud.

*Arthur O'Shaughnessy* [1844-1881]

## FOR THE BAPTIST

THE last and greatest Herald of Heaven's King,
Girt with rough skins, hies to the deserts wild,
Among that savage brood the woods forth bring,
Which he than man more harmless found and mild.
His food was locusts, and what there doth spring,
With honey that from virgin hives distilled;
Parched body, hollow eyes, some uncouth thing
Made him appear, long since from earth exiled.
There burst he forth: "All ye whose hopes rely
On God, with me amidst these deserts mourn,
Repent, repent, and from old errors turn!"
—Who listened to his voice, obeyed his cry?
Only the echoes, which he made relent,
Rung from their flinty caves, "Repent! Repent!"

*William Drummond* [1585-1649]

## "THE SPRING IS LATE"

SHE stood alone amidst the April fields,—
Brown, sodden fields, all desolate and bare,—
"The spring is late," she said,—"the faithless spring,
That should have come to make the meadows fair.

"Their sweet South left too soon, among the trees
The birds, bewildered, flutter to and fro;
For them no green boughs wait,—their memories
Of last year's April had deceived them so.

"From 'neath a sheltering pine some tender buds
Looked out, and saw the hollows filled with snow;
On such a frozen world they closed their eyes;
When spring is cold, how can the blossoms blow?"

She watched the homeless birds, the slow, sad spring,
The barren fields, and shivering, naked trees:
"Thus God has dealt with me, his child," she said,—
"I wait my spring-time, and am cold like these.

"To them will come the fulness of their time;
Their spring, though late, will make the meadows fair;
Shall I, who wait like them, like them be blest?
I am His own,—doth not my Father care?"

*Louise Chandler Moulton* [1835-1908]

## THE QUESTION

I SAW the Son of God go by
Crowned with the crown of Thorn.
"Was It not finished, Lord?" I said,
"And all the anguish borne?"

He turned on me His awful eyes:
"Hast thou not understood?
Lo! Every soul is Calvary,
And every sin a Rood."

*Rachel Annand Taylor* [18

## A DIVINE RAPTURE

E'EN like two little bank-dividing brooks,
That wash the pebbles with their wanton streams,
And having ranged and searched a thousand nooks,
Meet both at length in silver-breasted Thames,
Where in a greater current they conjoin:
So I my Best-belovèd's am; so He is mine.

E'en so we met; and after long pursuit,
  E'en so we joined; we both became entire;
No need for either to renew a suit,
  For I was flax, and He was flames of fire:
    Our firm-united souls did more than twine;
So I my Best-belovèd's am; so He is mine.

If all those glittering Monarchs, that command
  The servile quarters of this earthly ball,
Should tender in exchange their shares of land,
  I would not change my fortunes for them all:
    Their wealth is but a counter to my coin:
The world's but theirs; but my Belovèd's mine.

*Francis Quarles* [1592–1644]

## "IF I COULD SHUT THE GATE AGAINST MY THOUGHTS"

If I could shut the gate against my thoughts,
  And keep out sorrow from this room within,
Or memory could cancel all the notes
  Of my misdeeds, and I unthink my sin:
How free, how clear, how clean my soul should lie,
Discharged of such a loathsome company.

Or were there other rooms within my heart
  That did not to my conscience join so near,
Where I might lodge the thoughts of sin apart,
  That I might not their clamorous crying hear;
What peace, what joy, what ease should I possess,
Freed from their horrors that my soul oppress.

But, O my Saviour, who my refuge art,
  Let Thy dear mercies stand 'twixt them and me,
And be the wall to separate my heart
  So that I may at length repose me free;
That peace, and joy, and rest may be within,
And I remain divided from my sin.

*John Daniel* [fl. 1625]

## HIS LITANY TO THE HOLY SPIRIT

In the hour of my distress,
When temptations me oppress,
And when I my sins confess,
Sweet Spirit, comfort me!

When I lie within my bed,
Sick in heart and sick in head,
And with doubts discomforted,
Sweet Spirit, comfort me!

When the house doth sigh and weep,
And the world is drowned in sleep,
Yet mine eyes the watch do keep,
Sweet Spirit, comfort me!

When the artless doctor sees
No one hope, but of his fees,
And his skill runs on the lees,
Sweet Spirit, comfort me!

When his potion and his pill,
His, or none, or little skill,
Meet for nothing, but to kill,
Sweet Spirit, comfort me!

When the passing-bell doth toll,
And the furies in a shoal
Come to fright a parting soul,
Sweet Spirit, comfort me!

When the tapers now burn blue,
And the comforters are few,
And that number more than true,
Sweet Spirit, comfort me!

When the priest his last hath prayed,
And I nod to what is said
'Cause my speech is now decayed,
Sweet Spirit, comfort me!

When, God knows, I'm tossed about
Either with despair or doubt,
Yet, before the glass be out,
Sweet Spirit, comfort me!

When the tempter me pursu'th
With the sins of all my youth,
And half damns me with untruth,
Sweet Spirit, comfort me!

When the flames and hellish cries
Fright mine ears and fright mine eyes,
And all terrors me surprise,
Sweet Spirit, comfort me!

When the Judgment is revealed,
And that opened which was sealed,
When to Thee I have appealed,
Sweet Spirit, comfort me!

*Robert Herrick* [1591–1674]

## TO KEEP A TRUE LENT

Is this a fast, to keep
The larder lean,
And clean
From fat of veals and sheep?

Is it to quit the dish
Of flesh, yet still
To fill
The platter high with fish?

Is it to fast an hour,
Or ragged to go,
Or show
A downcast look, and sour?

No; 'tis a fast to dole
Thy sheaf of wheat
And meat
Unto the hungry soul.

It is to fast from strife,
From old debate
And hate;
To circumcise thy life.

To show a heart grief-rent;
To starve thy sin,
Not bin;
And that's to keep thy Lent.

*Robert Herrick* [1591-1674]

## THE FALLEN STAR

A STAR is gone! a star is gone!
There is a blank in Heaven;
One of the cherub choir has done
His airy course this even.

He sat upon the orb of fire
That hung for ages there,
And lent his music to the choir
That haunts the nightly air.

But when his thousand years are passed,
With a cherubic sigh
He vanished with his car at last,
For even cherubs die!

Hear how his angel-brothers mourn—
The minstrels of the spheres—
Each chiming sadly in his turn
And dropping splendid tears.

The planetary Sisters all
Join in the fatal song.
And weep this hapless brother's fall,
Who sang with them so long.

But deepest of the choral band
The Lunar Spirit sings,
And with a bass-according hand
Sweeps all her sullen strings.

From the deep chambers of the dome
Where sleepless Uriel lies,
His rude harmonic thunders come
Mingled with mighty sighs.

The thousand car-borne cherubim,
The wandering Eleven,
All join to chant the dirge of him
Who fell just now from Heaven.

*George Darley* [1795–1846]

## "WE NEED NOT BID, FOR CLOISTERED CELL"

We need not bid, for cloistered cell,
Our neighbor and our work farewell,
Nor strive to wind ourselves too high
For sinful man beneath the sky:

The trivial round, the common task,
Would furnish all we ought to ask;
Room to deny ourselves; a road
To bring us, daily, nearer God.

Seek we no more; content with these
Let present Rapture, Comfort, Ease,
As Heaven shall bid them, come and go:—
The secret this of Rest below

*John Keble* [1792–1866]

## "A CHILD MY CHOICE"

Let folly praise that fancy loves, I praise and love that Child
Whose heart no thought, whose tongue no word, whose hand no deed defiled.
I praise Him most, I love Him best, all praise and love is His,
While Him I love, in Him I live, and cannot live amiss.

Love's sweetest mark, laud's highest theme, man's most desired light,
To love Him life, to leave Him death, to live in Him delight.
He mine by gift, I His by debt, thus each to other due,
First friend He was, best friend He is, all times will try Him true.
Though young, yet wise, though small, yet strong; though man, yet God He is;
As wise He knows, as strong He can, as God He loves to bliss.
His knowledge rules, His strength defends, His love doth cherish all;
His birth our joy, His life our light, His death our end of thrall.
Alas! He weeps, He sighs, He pants, yet do His angels sing;
Out of His tears, His sighs and throbs, doth bud a joyful spring.
Almighty Babe, whose tender arms can force all foes to fly,
Correct my faults, protect my life, direct me when I die!

*Robert Southwell* [1561?–1595]

## AN UPPER CHAMBER

I CAME into the City and none knew me;
None came forth, none shouted "He is here!"
Not a hand with laurel would bestrew me,
All the way by which I drew anear—
Night my banner, and my herald Fear.

But I knew where one so long had waited
In the low room at the stairway's height,
Trembling lest my foot should be belated,
Singing, sighing for the long hours' flight
Towards the moment of our dear delight.

I came into the City when you hailed me
Saviour, and again your chosen Lord:—
Not one guessing what it was that failed me,
While along the way as they adored
Thousands, thousands, shouted in accord.

But through all the joy I knew—I only—
  How the hostel of my heart lay bare and cold,
Silent of its music, and how lonely!
  Never, though you crown me with your gold,
  Shall I find that little chamber as of old!

*Frances Bannerman* [18 -

## THE SECOND CRUCIFIXION

Loud mockers in the roaring street
  Say Christ is crucified again:
Twice pierced His gospel-bearing feet,
  Twice broken His great heart in vain.

I hear, and to myself I smile,
For Christ talks with me all the while.

No angel now to roll the stone
  From off His unawaking sleep,
In vain shall Mary watch alone,
  In vain the soldiers vigil keep.

Yet while they deem my Lord is dead
My eyes are on His shining head.

Ah! never more shall Mary hear
  That voice exceeding sweet and low
Within the garden calling clear:
  Her Lord is gone, and she must go.

Yet all the while my Lord I meet
In every London lane and street.

Poor Lazarus shall wait in vain,
  And Bartimæus still go blind;
The healing hem shall ne'er again
  Be touched by suffering humankind.

Yet all the while I see them rest,
The poor and outcast, on His breast.

No more unto the stubborn heart
With gentle knocking shall He plead,
No more the mystic pity start,
For Christ twice dead is dead indeed.

So in the street I hear men say,
Yet Christ is with me all the day.

*Richard Le Gallienne* [1866–1947]

## THE VOICE OF CHRISTMAS

I CANNOT put the Presence by, of Him, the Crucified,
Who moves men's spirits with His Love as doth the moon the tide;
Again I see the Life He lived, the godlike Death He died.

Again I see upon the cross that great Soul-battle fought,
Into the texture of the world the tale of which is wrought
Until it hath become the woof of human deed and thought,—

And, joining with the cadenced bells that all the morning fill,
His cry of agony doth yet my inmost being thrill,
Like some fresh grief from yesterday that tears the heart-strings still.

I cannot put His Presence by, I meet Him everywhere;
I meet Him in the country town, the busy market-square;
The Mansion and the Tenement attest His Presence there.

Upon the funneled ships at sea He sets His shining feet;
The Distant Ends of Empire not in vain His Name repeat,—
And, like the presence of a rose, He makes the whole world sweet.

He comes to break the barriers down raised up by barren creeds;
About the globe from zone to zone like sunlight He proceeds;
He comes to give the World's starved heart the perfect love it needs,

The Christ Whose friends have played Him false, Whom
Dogmas have belied,
Still speaking to the hearts of men—though shamed and
crucified,
The Master of the Centuries Who will not be denied!

*Harry Kemp* [1883–1960]

## TE MARTYRUM CANDIDATUS

Ah, see the fair chivalry come, the companions of Christ!
White Horsemen, who ride on white horses, the Knights of
God!
They, for their Lord and their Lover who sacrificed
All, save the sweetness of treading where He first trod!

These through the darkness of death, the dominion of night,
Swept, and they woke in white places at morning tide:
They saw with their eyes, and sang for joy of the sight,
They saw with their eyes the Eyes of the Crucified.

Now, whithersoever He goeth, with Him they go:
White Horsemen, who ride on white horses, oh fair to see!
They ride, where the Rivers of Paradise flash and flow,
White Horsemen, with Christ their Captain: for ever He!

*Lionel Johnson* [1867–1902]

## ON A SCULPTURED HEAD OF THE CHRIST

I saw it once where myriad works adorn
Encloistered walls as with a Cloth of Gold;
Then did I see, still fair in every fold,
Still jewel-strewn, the robe a king had worn.
I glimpsed a god, of antique glory born;
A boasted picture, and a carven gem,—
Soul-sick, the while, to view, unvexed of them,
That simple Christus with its crown of thorn!
The World is old; she hath seen many wars;
And states and kingdoms crowd her courts like grass;
Princes in pride she watches where they pass
Unnumbered and innumerable as the stars;

Then turns, a child with tired feet homeward set,
Back to the Cross, and lo! her lids are wet.

*Mahlon Leonard Fisher* [1874–1947]

## GOOD KING WENCESLAS

Good King Wenceslas looked out,
On the Feast of Stephen,
When the snow lay round about,
Deep, and crisp, and even:
Brightly shone the moon that night,
Though the frost was cruel,
When a poor man came in sight,
Gathering winter fuel.

"Hither, page, and stand by me,
If thou know'st it, telling,
Yonder peasant, who is he?
Where and what his dwelling?"
"Sire, he lives a good league hence,
Underneath the mountain;
Right against the forest fence,
By Saint Agnes' fountain."

"Bring me flesh, and bring me wine,
Bring me pine logs hither;
Thou and I will see him dine,
When we bear them thither."
Page and monarch forth they went,
Forth they went together;
Through the rude wind's wild lament,
And the bitter weather.

"Sire, the night is darker now,
And the wind blows stronger;
Fails my heart, I know not how,
I can go no longer."
"Mark my footsteps, good my page!
Tread thou in them boldly;
Thou shalt find the winter's rage
Freeze thy blood less coldly."

In his master's steps he trod,
  Where the snow lay dinted;
Heat was in the very sod
  Which the saint had printed.
Therefore, Christian men, be sure,
  Wealth or rank possessing,
Ye who now will bless the poor,
  Shall yourselves find blessing.

*John Mason Neale* [1818-1866]

## SIMON THE CYRENEAN

"And as they came out they found a man of Cyrene, Simon by name; him they compelled to bear his cross."

THIS is the tale from first to last;—
  Outside Jerusalem
I saw them lead a prisoner past
  With thorns for diadem.
Broken and weak and driven fast
  He fell at my garment's hem.

There stood no other stranger by
  On me they laid his load.
The Cross whereon he was to die
  I bore along the road,
I saw him nailed, I heard him cry
  Forsaken of his God.

Now I am dead as well as he,
  And, marvel strange to tell,
But him they nailed upon the tree
  Is Lord of Heaven and Hell,
And judgeth who doth wickedly,
  Rewardeth who doth well.

He has given to me the beacons four,
  A Cross in the southern sky,

In token that his Cross I bore
  In his extremity;
For one I never knew before
  The day he came to die.

*Lucy Lyttleton* [1884-

THE WINGED WORSHIPPERS

  Gay, guiltless pair,
What seek ye from the fields of Heaven?
  Ye have no need of prayer,
Ye have no sins to be forgiven.

  Why perch ye here,
Where mortals to their Maker bend?
  Can your pure spirits fear
The God ye never could offend?

  Ye never knew
The crimes for which we come to weep.
  Penance is not for you,
Blessed wanderers of the upper deep.

  To you 'tis given
To wake sweet Nature's untaught lays,
  Beneath the arch of Heaven
To chirp away a life of praise.

  Then spread each wing,
Far, far above, o'er lakes and lands,
  And join the choirs that sing
In yon blue dome not reared with hands.

  Or, if ye stay
To note the consecrated hour,
  Teach me the airy way,
And let me try your envied power.

Above the crowd,
On upward wings could I but fly,
I'd bathe in yon bright cloud,
And seek the stars that gem the sky.

'Twere Heaven indeed
Through fields of trackless light to soar,
On nature's charms to feed,
And Nature's own great God adore.

*Charles Sprague* [1791–1875]

## DE SHEEPFOL'

De massa ob de sheepfol',
Dat guards de sheepfol' bin,
Look out in de gloomerin' meadows,
Wha'r de long night rain begin—
So he call to de hirelin' shepa'd,
"Is my sheep, is dey all come in?—
My sheep, is dey all come in?"

Oh den, says de hirelin' shepa'd:
"Dey's some, dey's black and thin,
And some, dey's po' ol' wedda's,
Dat can't come home agin.
Dey's some black sheep an' ol' wedda's,
But de res', dey's all brung in.—
De res', dey's all brung in."

Den de massa ob de sheepfol',
Dat guards de sheepfol' bin,
Goes down in de gloomerin' meadows,
Wha'r de long night rain begin—
So he le' down de ba's ob de sheepfol',
Callin' sof', "Come in. Come in."
Callin' sof', "Come in. Come in."

Den up t'ro' de gloomerin' meadows,
T'ro' de col' night rain and win',
And up t'ro' de gloomerin' rain-paf',
Wha'r de sleet fa' pie'cin' thin,

De po' los' sheep ob de sheepfol',
Dey all comes gadderin' in.
De po' los' sheep ob de sheepfol',
Dey all comes gadderin' in.

*Sarah Pratt McLean Greene* [1856-1935]

## THE LOST SHEEP

("THE NINETY AND NINE")

THERE were ninety and nine that safely lay
In the shelter of the fold;
But one was out on the hills away,
Far off from the gates of gold,—
Away on the mountains wild and bare,
Away from the tender Shepherd's care.

"Lord, thou hast here thy ninety and nine:
Are they not enough for thee?"
But the Shepherd made answer: "'Tis of mine
Has wandered away from me;
And although the road be rough and steep
I go to the desert to find my sheep."

But none of the ransomed ever knew
How deep were the waters crossed,
Nor how dark was the night that the Lord passed through
Ere he found his sheep that was lost.
Out in the desert he heard its cry—
Sick and helpless, and ready to die.

"Lord, whence are those blood-drops all the way,
That mark out the mountain-track?"
"They were shed for one who had gone astray
Ere the Shepherd could bring him back."
"Lord, whence are thy hands so rent and torn?"
"They are pierced to-night by many a thorn."

But all through the mountains, thunder-riven,
And up from the rocky steep,
There rose a cry to the gate of heaven,
"Rejoice! I have found my sheep!"

And the angels echoed around the throne,
"Rejoice, for the Lord brings back his own!"
*Elizabeth Cecilia Clephane* [1830-1869]

## LOST BUT FOUND

I WAS a wandering sheep,
I did not love the fold;
I did not love my Shepherd's voice,
I would not be controlled.
I was a wayward child,
I did not love my home,
I did not love my Father's voice,
I loved afar to roam.

The Shepherd sought his sheep;
The Father sought his child;
They followed me o'er vale and hill,
O'er deserts waste and wild.
They found me nigh to death,
Famished, and faint, and lone;
They bound me with the bands of love;
They saved the wandering one.

They spoke in tender love,
They raised my drooping head;
They gently closed my bleeding wounds,
My fainting soul they fed.
They washed my filth away,
They made me clean and fair;
They brought me to my home in peace,
The long-sought wanderer.

Jesus my Shepherd is,
'Twas he that loved my soul;
'Twas he that washed me in his blood,
'Twas he that made me whole;
'Twas he that sought the lost,
That found the wandering sheep;
'Twas he that brought me to the fold,
'Tis he that still doth keep.

I was a wandering sheep,
I would not be controlled;
But now I love my Shepherd's voice,
I love, I love the fold.
I was a wayward child,
I once preferred to roam;
But now I love my Father's voice,
I love, I love his home.

*Horatius Bonar* [1808-1889]

## STAINS

The three ghosts on the lonesome road
Spake each to one another,
"Whence came that stain about your mouth
No lifted hand may cover?"
"From eating of forbidden fruit,
Brother, my brother."

The three ghosts on the sunless road
Spake each to one another,
"Whence came that red burn on your foot
No dust nor ash may cover?"
"I stamped a neighbor's hearth-flame out,
Brother, my brother."

The three ghosts on the windless road
Spake each to one another,
"Whence came that blood upon your hand
No other hand may cover?"
"From breaking of a woman's heart,
Brother, my brother."

"Yet on the earth clean men we walked,
Glutton and Thief and Lover;
White flesh and fair it hid our stains
That no man might discover."
"Naked the soul goes up to God,
Brother, my brother."

*Theodosia Garrison* [1874-

### A HYMN TO GOD THE FATHER

Wilt Thou forgive that sin where I begun,
  Which was my sin, though it were done before?
Wilt Thou forgive that sin through which I run,
  And do run still, though still I do deplore?
When Thou hast done, Thou hast not done;
    For I have more.

Wilt Thou forgive that sin which I have won
  Others to sin, and made my sin their door?
Wilt Thou forgive that sin which I did shun
  A year or two, but wallowed in a score?
When Thou hast done, Thou hast not done;
    For I have more.

I have a sin of fear, that when I've spun
  My last thread, I shall perish on the shore;
But swear by Thyself that at my death Thy Son
  Shall shine as He shines now and heretofore:
And having done that, Thou hast done;
    I fear no more.

*John Donne* [1573-1631]

### SHEEP AND LAMBS

All in the April evening,
  April airs were abroad;
The sheep with their little lambs
  Passed me by on the road.

The sheep with their little lambs
  Passed me by on the road;
All in the April evening
  I thought on the Lamb of God.

The lambs were weary, and crying
  With a weak human cry,
I thought on the Lamb of God
  Going meekly to die.

Up in the blue, blue mountains
Dewy pastures are sweet:
Rest for the little bodies,
Rest for the little feet.

But for the Lamb of God
Up on the hill-top green,
Only a Cross of shame
Two stark crosses between.

All in the April evening,
April airs were abroad;
I saw the sheep with their lambs,
And thought on the Lamb of God.

*Katherine Tynan Hinkson* [1861–1931]

## "ALL'S WELL!"

EIGHT bells! Eight bells! their clear tone tells
The midnight hour is here,
And as they cease, these words of peace
Fall gently on my ear:
"All's well! All's well!"

Fond thoughts fly far, where loved ones are,
Though distant, ever near,
From those dear homes the echo comes,
Our longing hearts to cheer:
"All's well! All's well!"

Swift through the deep our course we keep,
To shores unseen we steer,
No thought of ill our souls shall chill,
Nor wind nor wave we fear:
"All's well! All's well!"

Thus o'er life's sea our voyage may be
A pathway lone and drear,
Through tempest loud and sorrow's cloud,
Faith still shall whisper near:
"All's well! All's well!"

And when for me, earth, sky, and sea
Shall fade and disappear,

May this sweet note still downward float,
From some undying sphere:
"All's well! All's well!"

*William Allen Butler* [1825–1902]

## LIVING WATERS

THERE are some hearts like wells, green-mossed and deep
As ever Summer saw;
And cool their water is,—yea, cool and sweet;—
But you must come to draw.
They hoard not, yet they rest in calm content,
And not unsought will give;
They can be quiet with their wealth unspent,
So self-contained they live.

And there are some like springs, that bubbling burst
To follow dusty ways,
And run with offered cup to quench his thirst
Where the tired traveller strays;
That never ask the meadows if they want
What is their joy to give;—
Unasked, their lives to other life they grant,
So self-bestowed they live!

And One is like the ocean, deep and wide,
Wherein all waters fall;
That girdles the broad earth, and draws the tide,
Feeding and bearing all;
That broods the mists, that sends the clouds abroad,
That takes, again to give;—
Even the great and loving heart of God,
Whereby all love doth live.

*Caroline Spencer* [1848–1898]

## ONE BY ONE

ONE by one the sands are flowing,
One by one the moments fall;
Some are coming, some are going;
Do not strive to grasp them all.

One by one thy duties wait thee—
  Let thy whole strength go to each,
Let no future dreams elate thee,
  Learn thou first what these can teach

One by one (bright gifts from heaven)
  Joys are sent thee here below;
Take them readily when given—
  Ready, too, to let them go.

One by one thy griefs shall meet thee;
  Do not fear an armèd band;
One will fade as others greet thee—
  Shadows passing through the land.

Do not look at life's long sorrow;
  See how small each moment's pain;
God will help thee for to-morrow,
  So each day begin again.

Every hour that fleets so slowly
  Has its task to do or bear;
Luminous the crown, and holy,
  When each gem is set with care.

Do not linger with regretting,
  Or for passing hours despond;
Nor, thy daily toil forgetting,
  Look too eagerly beyond.

Hours are golden links, God's token,
  Reaching heaven; but, one by one,
Take them, lest the chain be broken
  Ere the pilgrimage be done.

*Adelaide Anne Procter* [1825-1864]

## "THERE IS NO UNBELIEF"

    THERE is no unbelief;
Whoever plants a seed beneath the sod
And waits to see it push away the clod,
    He trusts in God.

There is no unbelief;
Whoever says, when clouds are in the sky,
"Be patient, heart; light breaketh by and by,"
Trusts the Most High.

There is no unbelief;
Whoever sees, 'neath winter's field of snow,
The silent harvest of the future grow—
God's power must know.

There is no unbelief;
Whoever lies down on his couch to sleep,
Content to lock each sense in slumber deep,
Knows God will keep.

There is no unbelief;
Whoever says "to-morrow," "the unknown,"
"The Future," trusts that power alone
He dares disown.

There is no unbelief;
The heart that looks on when dear eyelids close,
And dares to live when life has only woes,
God's comfort knows.

There is no unbelief;
For thus by day and night unconsciously
The heart lives by the faith the lips deny.
God knoweth why.

*Lizzie York Case* [18 -1911]

## "THERE IS NO DEATH"

There is no death! The stars go down
To rise upon some other shore,
And bright in heaven's jeweled crown
They shine for evermore.

There is no death! The dust we tread
Shall change beneath the summer showers
To golden grain or mellow fruit
Or rainbow-tinted flowers.

The granite rocks disorganize
To feed the hungry moss they bear;
The forest leaves drink daily life
From out the viewless air.

There is no death! The leaves may fall,
The flowers may fade and pass away—
They only wait, through wintry hours,
The coming of the May.

There is no death! An angel form
Walks o'er the earth with silent tread;
He bears our best loved things away,
And then we call them "dead."

He leaves our hearts all desolate—
He plucks our fairest, sweetest flowers;
Transplanted into bliss, they now
Adorn immortal bowers.

The bird-like voice, whose joyous tones
Made glad this scene of sin and strife,
Sings now an everlasting song,
Amid the tree of life.

Where'er He sees a smile too bright,
Or soul too pure for taint of vice,
He bears it to that world of light,
To dwell in Paradise.

Born into that undying life,
They leave us but to come again;
With joy we welcome them—the same
Except in sin and pain.

And ever near us, though unseen,
The dear immortal spirits tread;
For all the boundless universe
Is life—there are no dead!

*John Luckey McCreery* [1835–1906]

## THE FOOL'S PRAYER

THE royal feast was done; the King
Sought some new sport to banish care,
And to his jester cried: "Sir Fool,
Kneel now, and make for us a prayer!"

The jester doffed his cap and bells,
  And stood the mocking court before;
They could not see the bitter smile
  Behind the painted grin he wore.

He bowed his head, and bent his knee
  Upon the monarch's silken stool;
His pleading voice arose: "O Lord,
  Be merciful to me, a fool!

"No pity, Lord, could change the heart
  From red with wrong to white as wool;
The rod must heal the sin: but Lord,
  Be merciful to me, a fool!

"'Tis not by guilt the onward sweep
  Of truth and right, O Lord, we stay;
'Tis by our follies that so long
  We hold the earth from heaven away.

"These clumsy feet, still in the mire,
  Go crushing blossoms without end;
These hard, well-meaning hands we thrust
  Among the heart-strings of a friend.

"The ill-timed truth we might have kept—
  Who knows how sharp it pierced and stung?
The word we had not sense to say—
  Who knows how grandly it had rung!

"Our faults no tenderness should ask,
  The chastening stripes must cleanse them all;
But for our blunders—oh, in shame
  Before the eyes of heaven we fall.

"Earth bears no balsam for mistakes;
  Men crown the knave, and scourge the tool
That did his will; but Thou, O Lord,
  Be merciful to me, a fool!"

The room was hushed; in silence rose
  The King, and sought his gardens cool,
And walked apart, and murmured low,
  "Be merciful to me, a fool!"

*Edward Rowland Sill* [1841–1887]

## THE ECLIPSE

WHITHER, O whither didst Thou fly?
When did I grieve Thine holy eye?
When Thou didst mourn to see me lost,
And all Thy care and counsels crossed.
O do not grieve, where'er Thou art!
Thy grief is an undoing smart,
Which doth not only pain, but break
My heart, and makes me blush to speak.
Thy anger I could kiss, and will;
But O Thy grief, Thy grief, doth kill!

*Henry Vaughan* [1622–1695]

## COMFORT

SPEAK low to me, my Saviour, low and sweet
From out the hallelujahs, sweet and low,
Lest I should fear and fall, and miss Thee so,
Who art not missed by any that entreat.
Speak to me as to Mary at Thy feet!
And if no precious gums my hands bestow,
Let my tears drop like amber, while I go
In reach of Thy divinest voice complete
In humanest affection—thus, in sooth,
To lose the sense of losing. As a child,
Whose song-bird seeks the wood for evermore,
Is sung to in its stead by mother's mouth,
Till, sinking on her breast, love-reconciled,
He sleeps the faster that he wept before.

*Elizabeth Barrett Browning* [1806–1861]

## ST. AGNES' EVE

DEEP on the convent-roof the snows
Are sparkling to the moon:
My breath to heaven like vapor goes:
May my soul follow soon!
The shadows of the convent-towers
Slant down the snowy sward,
Still creeping with the creeping hours
That lead me to my Lord:
Make Thou my spirit pure and clear
As are the frosty skies,
Or this first snowdrop of the year
That in my bosom lies.

As these white robes are soiled and dark,
To yonder shining ground;
As this pale taper's earthly spark,
To yonder argent round;
So shows my soul before the Lamb,
My spirit before Thee;
So in mine earthly house I am,
To that I hope to be.
Break up the heavens, O Lord! and far,
Through all yon starlight keen,
Draw me, thy bride, a glittering star,
In raiment white and clean.

He lifts me to the golden doors;
The flashes come and go;
All heaven bursts her starry floors,
And strows her lights below,
And deepens on and up! the gates
Roll back, and far within
For me the Heavenly Bridegroom waits,
To make me pure of sin.
The Sabbaths of Eternity,
One Sabbath deep and wide—
A light upon the shining sea—
The Bridegroom with his bride!

*Alfred Tennyson* [1809-1892]

## HIS BANNER OVER ME

SURROUNDED by unnumbered foes,
Against my soul the battle goes!
Yet though I weary, sore distressed,
I know that I shall reach my rest:
  I lift my tearful eyes above,—
  His banner over me is love.

Its sword my spirit will not yield,
Though flesh may faint upon the field;
He waves before my fading sight
The branch of palm,—the crown of light;
  I lift my brightening eyes above,—
  His banner over me is love.

My cloud of battle-dust may dim,
His veil of splendor curtain him!
And in the midnight of my fear
I may not feel him standing near;
  But, as I lift mine eyes above,
  His banner over me is love.

*Gerald Massey* [1828-1907]

## JESUS THE CARPENTER

"ISN'T this Joseph's son?"—ay, it is He;
Joseph the carpenter—same trade as me—
I thought as I'd find it—I knew it was here—
  But my sight's getting queer.

I don't know right where as His shed must ha' stood-
But often, as I've been a-planing my wood,
I've took off my hat, just with thinking of He
  At the same work as me,

He warn't that set up that He couldn't stoop down
And work in the country for folks in the town;
And I'll warrant He felt a bit pride, like I've done,
  At a good job begun.

The parson he knows that I'll not make too free,
But on Sunday I feels as pleased as can be,
When I wears my clean smock, and sits in a pew,
And has thoughts a few.

I think of as how not the parson hissen,
As is teacher and father and shepherd o' men,
Not he knows as much of the Lord in that shed,
Where He earned His own bread.

And when I goes home to my missus, says she,
"Are ye wanting your key?"
For she knows my queer ways, and my love for the shed,
(We've been forty years wed.)

So I comes right away by mysen, with the Book,
And I turns the old pages and has a good look
For the text as I've found, as tells me as He
Were the same trade as me.

Why don't I mark it? Ah, many says so,
But I think I'd as lief, with your leaves, let it go:
It do seem that nice when I fall on it sudden—
Unexpected, you know!

*Catharine C. Liddell* [1848-

## "I SAW THEE"

**"When thou wast under the fig-tree, I saw thee"**

I SAW thee when, as twilight fell,
And evening lit her fairest star,
Thy footsteps sought yon quiet dell,
The world's confusion left afar.

I saw thee when thou stood'st alone,
Where drooping branches thick o'erhung,
Thy still retreat to all unknown,
Hid in deep shadows darkly flung.

I saw thee when, as died each sound
 Of bleating flock or woodland bird,
Kneeling, as if on holy ground,
 Thy voice the listening silence heard.

I saw thy calm, uplifted eyes,
 And marked the heaving of thy breast,
When rose to heaven thy heartfelt sighs
 For purer life, for perfect rest.

I saw the light that o'er thy face
 Stole with a soft, suffusing glow,
As if, within, celestial grace
 Breathed the same bliss that angels know.

I saw—what thou didst not—above
 Thy lowly head an open heaven;
And tokens of thy Father's love
 With smiles to thy rapt spirit given.

I saw thee from that sacred spot
 With firm and peaceful soul depart,
I, Jesus, saw thee,—doubt it not,—
 And read the secrets of thy heart!

*Ray Palmer* [1808-1887]

## THE VETERAN OF HEAVEN

O CAPTAIN of the wars, whence won Ye so great scars?
 In what fight did Ye smite, and what manner was the foe?
Was it on a day of rout they compassed Thee about,
 Or gat Ye these adornings when Ye wrought their overthrow?

"'Twas on a day of rout they girded Me about,
 They wounded all My brow, and they smote Me through the side:
My hand held no sword when I met their armèd horde,
 And the conqueror fell down, and the conquered bruised his pride."

What is this, unheard before, that the unarmed make war,
And the slain hath the gain, and the victor hath the rout?
What wars, then, are these, and what the enemies,
Strange Chief, with the scars of Thy conquest trenched about?

"The Prince I drave forth held the Mount of the North,
Girt with the guards of flame that roll around the pole.
I drave him with My wars from all his fortress-stars,
And the sea of death divided that My march might strike its goal.

"In the keep of Northern Guard, many a great demonian sword
Burns as it turns round the Mount occult, apart:
There is given power and place still for some certain days,
And his Name would turn the Sun's blood back upon its heart."

What is *Thy* Name? O show!—"My Name ye may not know;
'Tis a going forth with banners, and a baring of much swords:
But my titles that are high, are they not upon my thigh?
'King of Kings!' are the words, 'Lord of Lords';
It is written 'King of Kings, Lord of Lords.'"

*Francis Thompson* [1859?–1907]

## LUCIFER IN STARLIGHT

On a starred night Prince Lucifer uprose.
Tired of his dark dominion swung the fiend
Above the rolling ball in cloud part screened,
Where sinners hugged their specter of repose.
Poor prey to his hot fit of pride were those.
And now upon his western wing he leaned,
Now his huge bulk o'er Afric's sands careened,
Now the black planet shadowed Arctic snows.
Soaring through wider zones that pricked his scars

With memory of the old revolt from Awe,
He reached a middle height, and at the stars,
Which are the brain of Heaven, he looked, and sank.
Around the ancient track marched, rank on rank,
The army of unalterable law.

*George Meredith* [1828–1909]

## HORA CHRISTI

Sweet is the time for joyous folk
Of gifts and minstrelsy;
Yet I, O lowly-hearted One,
Crave but Thy company.
On lonesome road, beset with dread,
My questing lies afar.
I have no light, save in the east
The gleaming of Thy star.

In cloistered aisles they keep to-day
Thy feast, O living Lord!
With pomp of banner, pride of song,
And stately-sounding word.
Mute stand the kings of power and place,
While priests of holy mind
Dispense Thy blessed heritage
Of peace to all mankind.

I know a spot where budless twigs
Are bare above the snow,
And where sweet winter-loving birds
Flit softly to and fro;
There with the sun for altar-fire,
The earth for kneeling-place,
The gentle air for Chorister,
Will I adore Thy face.

Loud, underneath the great blue sky,
My heart shall pæan sing,
The gold and myrrh of meekest love
Mine only offering.

Bliss of Thy birth shall quicken me,
And for Thy pain and dole
Tears are but vain, so I will keep
The silence of the soul.

*Alice Brown* [1857–1948]

## CHRISTUS CONSOLATOR

BESIDE the dead I knelt for prayer,
And felt a presence as I prayed.
Lo! it was Jesus standing there.
He smiled: "Be not afraid!"

"Lord, thou hast conquered death we know;
Restore again to life," I said,
"This one who died an hour ago."
He smiled: "She is not dead!"

"Asleep then, as thyself did say;
Yet thou canst lift the lids that keep
Her prisoned eyes from ours away!"
He smiled: "She doth not sleep!"

"Nay then, though haply she do wake,
And look upon some fairer dawn,
Restore her to our hearts that ache!"
He smiled: "She is not gone!"

"Alas! too well we know our loss,
Nor hope again our joy to touch,
Until the stream of death we cross."
He smiled: "There is no such!"

"Yet our belovèd seem so far,
The while we yearn to feel them near,
Albeit with Thee we trust they are."
He smiled: "And I am here!"

"Dear Lord, how shall we know that they
Still walk unseen with us and Thee,
Nor sleep, nor wander far away?"
He smiled: "Abide with me."

*Rossiter Worthington Raymond* [1840–1918]

## THAT HOLY THING

From "Paul Faber"

THEY all were looking for a king
  To slay their foes and lift them high:
Thou cam'st, a little baby thing
    That made a woman cry.

O Son of Man, to right my lot
  Naught but Thy presence can avail;
Yet on the road Thy wheels are not,
    Nor on the sea Thy sail!

My how or when Thou wilt not heed,
  But come down Thine own secret stair,
That Thou mayst answer all my need--
    Yea, every bygone prayer.

*George Macdonald* [1824-1905]

## WHAT CHRIST SAID

I SAID, "Let me walk in the fields;"
  He said, "Nay, walk in the town;"
I said, "There are no flowers there;"
  He said, "No flowers, but a crown."

I said, "But the sky is black,
  There is nothing but noise and din;"
But He wept as He sent me back—
  "There is more," He said, "there is sin."

I said, "But the air is thick,
  And fogs are veiling the sun;"
He answered, "Yet hearts are sick,
  And souls in the dark undone."

I said, "I shall miss the light,
  And friends will miss me, they say;"
He answered me, "Choose to-night
  If I am to miss you or they."

I pleaded for time to be given;
He said, "Is it hard to decide?
It will not seem hard in heaven
To have followed the steps of your Guide."

I cast one look at the field,
Then set my face to the town;
He said, "My child, do you yield?
Will you leave the flowers for the crown?"

Then into His hand went mine.
And into my heart came He.
And I walk in a light divine
The path I had feared to see.

*George Macdonald* [1824–1905]

## SAN LORENZO GIUSTINIANI'S MOTHER

"And we the shadows of the dream"—SHELLEY

I HAD not seen my son's dear face
(He chose the cloister by God's grace)
Since it had come to full flower-time.
I hardly guessed at its perfect prime,
That folded flower of his dear face.

Mine eyes were veiled by mists of tears
When on a day in many years
One of his Order came. I thrilled,
Facing, I thought, that face fulfilled.
I doubted, for my mists of tears.

His blessing be with me forever!
My hope and doubt were hard to sever.
—That altered face, those holy weeds.
I filled his wallet and kissed his beads,
And lost his echoing feet for ever.

If to my son my alms were given
I know not, and I wait for Heaven.
He did not plead for child of mine,
But for another Child divine,
And unto Him it was surely given.

There is One alone who cannot change;
Dreams are we, shadows, visions strange;
And all I give is given to One.
I might mistake my dearest son,
But never the Son who cannot change.

*Alice Meynell* [1850-1922]

## A BALLAD OF TREES AND THE MASTER

Into the woods my Master went,
Clean forspent, forspent.
Into the woods my Master came,
Forspent with love and shame.
But the olives they were not blind to Him;
The little gray leaves were kind to Him;
The thorn-tree had a mind to Him
When into the woods He came.

Out of the woods my Master went,
And He was well content.
Out of the woods my Master came,
Content with death and shame.
When Death and Shame would woo Him last,
From under the trees they drew Him last:
'Twas on a tree they slew Him—last
When out of the woods He came.

*Sidney Lanier* [1842-1881]

## THE MYSTERY

He came and took me by the hand
Up to a red rose tree,
He kept His meaning to Himself
But gave a rose to me.

I did not pray Him to lay bare
The mystery to me;
Enough the rose was Heaven to smell,
And His own face to see.

*Ralph Hodgson* [1871-

# SONGS OF PRAISE

## DIES IRÆ *

DAY of wrath, that day of burning,
Seer and Sibyl speak concerning,
All the world to ashes turning.

Oh, what fear shall it engender,
When the Judge shall come in splendor
Strict to mark and just to render!

Trumpet, scattering sounds of wonder,
Rending sepulchers asunder,
Shall resistless summons thunder.

All aghast then Death shall shiver,
And great Nature's frame shall quiver,
When the graves their dead deliver.

Volume, from which nothing's blotted,
Evil done nor evil plotted,
Shall be brought and dooms allotted.

When shall sit the Judge unerring,
He'll unfold all here occurring,
Vengeance then no more deferring.

What shall *I* say, that time pending?
Ask what advocate's befriending,
When the just man needs defending?

Dreadful King, all power possessing,
Saving freely those confessing,
Save thou me, O Fount of Blessing!

* For the original of this poem see page 3819

Think, O Jesus, for what reason,
Thou didst bear earth's spite and treason,
Nor me lose in that dread season!

Seeking me Thy worn feet hasted,
On the cross Thy soul death tasted:
Let such travail not be wasted!

Righteous Judge of retribution!
Make me gift of absolution
Ere that day of execution!

Culprit-like, I plead, heart-broken,
On my cheek shame's crimson token:
Let the pardoning word be spoken!

Thou, who Mary gav'st remission,
Heard'st the dying Thief's petition,
Cheer'st with hope my lost condition.

Though my prayers be void of merit,
What is needful, Thou confer it,
Lest I endless fire inherit.

Be there, Lord, my place decided
With Thy sheep, from goats divided,
Kindly to Thy right hand guided!

When the accursed away are driven,
To eternal burnings given,
Call me with the blessed to heaven!

I beseech Thee, prostrate lying,
Heart as ashes, contrite, sighing,
Care for me when I am dying!

Day of tears and late repentance,
Man shall rise to hear his sentence:
Him, the child of guilt and error,
Spare, Lord, in that hour of terror!

*Translated from the Latin of Tommåso di Celano by*
*Abraham Coles* [1813–1891]

## STABAT MATER DOLOROSA *

Stood the afflicted mother weeping,
Near the cross her station keeping
Whereon hung her Son and Lord;
Through whose spirit sympathizing,
Sorrowing and agonizing,
Also passed the cruel sword.

Oh! how mournful and distressèd
Was that favored and most blessèd
Mother of the only Son,
Trembling, grieving, bosom heaving,
While perceiving, scarce believing,
Pains of that Illustrious One!

Who the man, who, called a brother,
Would not weep, saw he Christ's mother
In such deep distress and wild?
Who could not sad tribute render
Witnessing that mother tender
Agonizing with her child?

For His people's sins atoning,
Him she saw in torments groaning,
Given to the scourger's rod;
Saw her darling offspring dying,
Desolate, forsaken, crying,
Yield His spirit up to God.

Make me feel thy sorrow's power,
That with thee I tears may shower,
Tender mother, fount of love!
Make my heart with love unceasing
Burn toward Christ the Lord, that pleasing
I may be to Him above.

Holy mother, this be granted,
That the slain one's wounds be planted
Firmly in my heart to bide.

* For the original of this poem see page 3821.

Of Him wounded, all astounded—
Depths unbounded for me sounded—
All the pangs with me divide.

Make me weep with thee in union;
With the Crucified, communion
In His grief and suffering give;
Near the cross, with tears unfailing,
I would join thee in thy wailing
Here as long as I shall live.

Maid of maidens, all excelling!
Be not bitter, me repelling;
Make thou me a mourner too;
Make me bear about Christ's dying,
Share His passion, shame defying;
All His wounds in me renew.

Wound for wound be there created;
With the cross intoxicated
For thy Son's dear sake, I pray—
May I, fired with pure affection,
Virgin, have through thee protection
In the solemn Judgment Day.

Let me by the cross be warded,
By the death of Christ be guarded,
Nourished by divine supplies.
When the body death hath riven,
Grant that to the soul be given
Glories bright of Paradise.

*Translated from the Latin of Jacopone da Todi by*
*Abraham Coles* [1813–1891]

## VENI, SANCTE SPIRITUS *

Come, Holy Ghost! thou fire divine!
From highest heaven on us shine!
Comforter, be Thy comfort mine!

* For the original of this poem see page 3822.

Come, Father of the poor, to earth;
Come, with Thy gifts of precious worth;
Come, Light of all of mortal birth!

Thou rich in comfort! Ever blest
The heart where Thou art constant guest,
Who giv'st the heavy-laden rest.

Come, Thou in whom our toil is sweet,
Our shadow in the noonday heat,
Before whom mourning flieth fleet.

Bright Sun of Grace! Thy sunshine dart
On all who cry to Thee apart,
And fill with gladness every heart.

Whate'er without Thy aid is wrought,
Or skilful deed, or wisest thought,
God counts it vain and merely naught.

O cleanse us that we sin no more,
O'er parchèd souls Thy waters pour;
Heal the sad heart that acheth sore.

Thy will be ours in all our ways;
O melt the frozen with Thy rays;
Call home the lost in error's maze.

And grant us, Lord, who cry to Thee.
And hold the Faith in unity,
Thy precious gifts of charity;

That we may live in holiness,
And find in death our happiness,
And dwell with Thee in lasting bliss!

*Translated from the Latin of Robert II. of France by*
*Catharine Winkworth* [1827–1878]

## VENI, CREATOR SPIRITUS *

Creator Spirit, by whose aid
The world's foundations first were laid,
Come visit every pious mind,
Come pour thy joys on human-kind;
From sin and sorrow set us free,
And make thy temples worthy thee.

O source of uncreated light,
The Father's promised Paraclete!
Thrice holy fount, thrice holy fire,
Our hearts with heavenly love inspire;
Come, and thy sacred unction bring,
To sanctify us while we sing.

Plenteous of grace, descend from high,
Rich in thy seven-fold energy!
Thou strength of His Almighty hand,
Whose power does heaven and earth command!
Proceeding Spirit, our defense,
Who dost the gifts of tongues dispense,
And crown'st thy gift with eloquence!

Refine and purge our earthly parts;
But, O, inflame and fire our hearts!
Our frailties help, our vice control,
Submit the senses to the soul;
And when rebellious they are grown,
Then lay thy hand and hold them down.

Chase from our minds the infernal foe,
And peace, the fruit of love, bestow;
And, lest our feet should step astray,
Protect and guide us in the way.

Make us eternal truths receive,
And practise all that we believe;
Give us thyself, that we may see
The Father, and the Son, by thee.

* For the original of this poem see page 3823.

Immortal honor, endless fame,
Attend the Almighty Father's name;
The Saviour Son be glorified,
Who for lost man's redemption died;
And equal adoration be,
Eternal Paraclete, to thee.

*Translated from the Latin of St. Gregory the Great(?) by*
*John Dryden* [1631–1700]

## STANZAS FROM "SONG TO DAVID"

SUBLIME—invention ever young,
Of vast conception, towering tongue
To God the eternal theme;
Notes from yon exaltations caught,
Unrivaled royalty of thought
O'er meaner strains supreme.

His muse, bright angel of his verse,
Gives balm for all the thorns that pierce,
For all the pangs that rage;
Blest light still gaining on the gloom,
The more than Michal of his bloom,
The Abishag of his age.

He sang of God—the mighty source
Of all things—the stupendous force
On which all strength depends;
From whose right arm, beneath whose eyes,
All period, power, and enterprise
Commences, reigns, and ends.

Tell them, I AM, Jehovah said
To Moses; while earth heard in dread,
And, smitten to the heart,
At once above, beneath, around,
All Nature, without voice or sound,
Replied, O LORD, THOU ART.

The world, the clustering spheres, He made;
The glorious light, the soothing shade,
  Dale, champaign, grove, and hill;
The multitudinous abyss,
Where Secrecy remains in bliss,
  And Wisdom hides her skill.

The pillars of the Lord are seven,
Which stand from earth to topmost heaven;
  His Wisdom drew the plan;
His Word accomplished the design,
From brightest gem to deepest mine;
  From Christ enthroned, to Man.

For Adoration all the ranks
Of Angels yield eternal thanks,
  And David in the midst;
With God's good poor, which, last and least
In man's esteem, Thou to Thy feast,
  O blessèd Bridegroom, bidd'st!

For Adoration, David's Psalms
Lift up the heart to deeds of alms;
  And he, who kneels and chants,
Prevails his passions to control,
Finds meat and medicine to the soul,
  Which for translation pants.

For Adoration, in the dome
Of Christ, the sparrows find a home,
  And on His olives perch:
The swallow also dwells with thee,
O man of God's humility,
  Within his Saviour's church.

Sweet is the dew that falls betimes,
And drops upon the leafy limes;
  Sweet, Hermon's fragrant air:
Sweet is the lily's silver bell,
And sweet the wakeful tapers' smell
  That watch for early prayer.

Sweet the young nurse, with love intense,
Which smiles o'er sleeping innocence;
Sweet, when the lost arrive:
Sweet the musician's ardor beats,
While his vague mind's in quest of sweets,
The choicest flowers to hive.

Strong is the horse upon his speed;
Strong in pursuit the rapid glede,
Which makes at once his game:
Strong the tall ostrich on the ground;
Strong through the turbulent profound
Shoots Xiphias to his aim.

Strong is the lion—like a coal
His eyeball,—like a bastion's mole
His chest against the foes:
Strong the gier-eagle on his sail;
Strong against tide the enormous whale
Emerges as he goes.

But stronger still, in earth and air,
And in the sea, the man of prayer,
And far beneath the tide:
And in the seat to fate assigned,
Where ask is have, where seek is find,
Where knock is open wide.

Precious the penitential tear;
And precious is the sigh sincere,
Acceptable to God:
And precious are the winning flowers,
In gladsome Israel's feast of bowers
Bound on the hallowed sod.

Glorious the sun in mid career;
Glorious the assembled fires appear;
Glorious the comet's train:
Glorious the trumpet and alarm;
Glorious the Almighty's stretched-out arm;
Glorious the enraptured main;

Glorious the northern lights astream;
Glorious the song, when God's the theme;
Glorious the thunder's roar:
Glorious Hosanna from the den;
Glorious the catholic Amen;
Glorious the martyr's gore:

Glorious—more glorious—is the crown
Of Him that brought salvation down,
By meekness called thy Son:
Thou that stupendous truth believed;—
And now the matchless deed's achieved,
Determined, dared, and done!

*Christopher Smart* [1722-1771]

## NOX NOCTI INDICAT SCIENTIAM

When I survey the bright
Celestial sphere;
So rich with jewels hung, that night
Doth like an Ethiop bride appear:

My soul her wings doth spread
And heavenward flies,
The Almighty's mysteries to read
In the large volumes of the skies.

For the bright firmament
Shoots forth no flame
So silent, but is eloquent
In speaking the Creator's name.

No unregarded star
Contracts its light
Into so small a character,
Removed far from our human sight,

But if we steadfast look
We shall discern
In it, as in some holy book,
How man may heavenly knowledge learn.

It tells the conqueror
That far-stretched power,
Which his proud dangers traffic for,
Is but the triumph of an hour;

That from the farthest North,
Some nation may,
Yet undiscovered, issue forth,
And o'er his new-got conquest sway:

Some nation yet shut in
With hills of ice
May be let out to scourge his sin,
Till they shall equal him in vice.

And then they likewise shall
Their ruin have;
For as yourselves your empires fall,
And every kingdom hath a grave.

Thus those celestial fires,
Though seeming mute,
The fallacy of our desires
And all the pride of life confute:—

For they have watched since first
The world had birth;
And found sin in itself accurst,
And nothing permanent on earth.

*William Habington* [1605-1654]

## "THE SPACIOUS FIRMAMENT ON HIGH"

From "The Spectator," No. 465

The spacious firmament on high,
With all the blue ethereal sky,
And spangled heavens, a shining frame,
Their great Original proclaim.
The unwearied Sun, from day to day,
Does his Creator's power display;

And publishes to every land
The work of an Almighty hand.

Soon as the evening shades prevail,
The Moon takes up the wondrous tale;
And nightly to the listening Earth
Repeats the story of her birth:
Whilst all the stars that round her burn,
And all the planets in their turn,
Confirm the tidings as they roll
And spread the truth from pole to pole.

What though, in solemn silence, all
Move round the dark terrestrial ball?
What though nor real voice nor sound
Amidst their radiant orbs be found?
In Reason's ear they all rejoice,
And utter forth a glorious voice;
For ever singing as they shine,
"The Hand that made us is divine."

*Joseph Addison* [1672–1719]

## UNIVERSAL PRAYER

DEO. OPT. MAX.

Father of all! in every age,
  In every clime adored,
By saint, by savage, and by sage,
  Jehovah, Jove, or Lord!

Thou Great First Cause, least understood,
  Who all my sense confined
To know but this, that Thou art good,
  And that myself am blind;

Yet gave me, in this dark estate,
  To see the good from ill;
And, binding nature fast in fate,
  Left free the human will.

What conscience dictates to be done,
  Or warns me not to do,
This, teach me more than hell to shun,
  That, more than heaven pursue.

What blessings Thy free bounty gives
  Let me not cast away;
For God is paid when man receives,
  To enjoy is to obey.

Yet not to earth's contracted span
  Thy goodness let me bound,
Or think Thee Lord alone of man,
  When thousand worlds are round:

Let not this weak, unknowing hand
  Presume Thy bolts to throw
And deal damnation round the land
  On each I judge Thy foe.

If I am right, Thy grace impart
  Still in the right to stay;
If I am wrong, O, teach my heart
  To find that better way!

Save me alike from foolish pride
  And impious discontent
At aught Thy wisdom has denied,
  Or aught Thy goodness lent.

Teach me to feel another's woe,
  To hide the fault I see;
That mercy I to others show,
  That mercy show to me.

Mean though I am, not wholly so,
  Since quickened by Thy breath;
O, lead me, whereso'er I go,
  Through this day's life or death!

This day be bread and peace my lot;
  All else beneath the sun,
Thou know'st if best bestowed or not,
  And let Thy will be done.

To Thee, whose temple is all space,
  Whose altar earth, sea, skies,
One chorus let all Being raise,
  All Nature's incense rise!

*Alexander Pope* [1688–1744]

## "O GOD! OUR HELP IN AGES PAST"

O God! our help in ages past,
  Our hope for years to come,
Our shelter from the stormy blast,
  And our eternal home!

Under the shadow of Thy Throne
  Thy saints have dwelt secure;
Sufficient is Thine arm alone,
  And our defense is sure.

Before the hills in order stood,
  Or earth received her fame,
From everlasting Thou art God,
  To endless years the same.

A thousand ages in Thy sight
  Are like an evening gone;
Short as the watch that ends the night
  Before the rising sun.

Time, like an ever-rolling stream,
  Bears all its sons away;
They fly, forgotten, as a dream
  Dies at the opening day.

O God! our help in ages past,
  Our hope for years to come,
Be Thou our guide when troubles last,
  And our eternal home!

*Isaac Watts* [1674–1748]

## "JESUS, LOVER OF MY SOUL"

JESUS lover of my soul,
  Let me to Thy bosom fly,
While the nearer waters roll,
  While the tempest still is high!
Hide me, O my Saviour, hide,
  Till the storm of life is past;
Safe into the haven guide,
  Oh receive my soul at last!

Other refuge have I none,
  Hangs my helpless soul on Thee;
Leave, ah! leave me not alone,
  Still support and comfort me!
All my trust on Thee is stayed,
  All my help from Thee I bring;
Cover my defenseless head
  With the shadow of Thy wing.

Wilt Thou not regard my call?
  Wilt Thou not accept my prayer?
Lo! I sink, I faint, I fall,—
  Lo! on Thee I cast my care;
Reach me out Thy gracious hand,
  While I of Thy strength receive!
Hoping against hope I stand,—
  Dying, and behold I live!

Thou, O Christ, art all I want;
  More than all in Thee I find:
Raise the fallen, cheer the faint,
  Heal the sick, and lead the blind!
Just and holy is Thy Name;
  I am all unrighteousness;
False and full of sin I am,
  Thou art full of truth and grace.

Plenteous grace with Thee is found,-
  Grace to cover all my sin;
Let the healing streams abound,
  Make and keep me pure within:—

Thou of life the Fountain art,
Freely me let take of Thee;
Spring Thou up within my heart,
Rise to all eternity!

*Charles Wesley* [1707–1788]

## "A CHARGE TO KEEP I HAVE"

A CHARGE to keep I have,
A God to glorify,
A never-dying soul to save,
And fit it for the sky.

From youth to hoary age,
My calling to fulfil,
Oh, may it all my powers engage
To do my Master's will!

Arm me with jealous care
As in Thy sight to live;
And oh, Thy servant, Lord, prepare
A strict account to give!

Help me to watch and pray,
And on Thyself rely,
Assured, if I my trust betray,
I shall forever die.

*Charles Wesley* [1707–1788]

## CORONATION

ALL hail the power of Jesus' name!
Let angels prostrate fall;
Bring forth the royal diadem,
To crown Him Lord of all!

Let high-born seraphs tune the lyre,
And, as they tune it, fall
Before His face who tunes their choir,
And crown Him Lord of all!

Crown Him, ye morning stars of light,
  Who fixed this floating ball;
Now hail the Strength of Israel's might,
  And crown Him Lord of all!

Crown Him, ye martyrs of your God,
  Who from His altar call;
Extol the stem of Jesse's rod,
  And crown Him Lord of all!

Ye seed of Israel's chosen race,
  Ye ransomed of the fall,
Hail Him who saves you by His grace,
  And crown Him Lord of all!

Hail Him, ye heirs of David's line,
  Whom David Lord did call,
The God incarnate, Man divine,
  And crown Him Lord of all!

Sinners, whose love can ne'er forget
  The wormwood and the gall,
Go spread your trophies at His feet,
  And crown Him Lord of all!

Let every tribe and every tongue
  That bound creation's call,
Now shout, in universal song,
  The Crownèd Lord of all!

*Edward Perronet* [1721–1792]

## "HOLY, HOLY, HOLY"

Holy, holy, holy, Lord God Almighty!
  Early in the morning our songs shall rise to Thee;
Holy, holy, holy! merciful and mighty!
  God in Three Persons, Blessed Trinity!

Holy, holy, holy! all the saints adore Thee,
  Casting down their golden crowns around the glassy sea,
Cherubim and seraphim falling down before Thee,
  Who wert, and art, and evermore shalt be!

Holy, holy, holy! though the darkness hide Thee,
Though the eye of sinful man Thy glory may not see,
Only Thou art holy, there is none beside Thee,
Perfect in power, in love, and purity!

Holy, holy, holy, Lord God Almighty!
All Thy works shall praise Thy name in earth and sky and sea;
Holy, holy, holy! merciful and mighty!
God in Three Persons, Blessed Trinity!

*Reginald Heber* [1783–1826]

## "THE SON OF GOD GOES FORTH TO WAR"

The Son of God goes forth to war,
A kingly crown to gain;
His blood-red banner streams afar!
Who follows in His train?
Who best can drink his cup of woe,
Triumphant over pain,
Who patient bears his cross below,
He follows in His train!

Thy martyr first, whose eagle eye
Could pierce beyond the grave;
Who saw his Master in the sky,
And called on Him to save:
Like Him, with pardon on his tongue,
In midst of mortal pain,
He prayed for them that did the wrong!
Who follows in His train?

A glorious band, the chosen few,
On whom the Spirit came;
Twelve valiant saints, their hope they knew,
And mocked the cross and flame!
They met the tyrant's brandished steel
The lion's gory mane:
They bowed their necks, the death to feel!
Who follows in their train?

A noble army—men and boys,
The matron and the maid,—
Around the Saviour's throne rejoice
In robes of light arrayed.
They climbed the steep ascent of Heaven,
Through peril, toil, and pain!
O God! to us may grace be given
To follow in their train!

*Reginald Heber* [1783–1826]

## "FROM GREENLAND'S ICY MOUNTAINS"

From Greenland's icy mountains,
From India's coral strand;
Where Afric's sunny fountains
Roll down their golden sand:
From many an ancient river,
From many a palmy plain,
They call us to deliver
Their land from error's chain.

What though the spicy breezes
Blow soft o'er Ceylon's isle;
Though every prospect pleases,
And only man is vile:
In vain with lavish kindness
The gifts of God are strown;
The heathen, in his blindness,
Bows down to wood and stone.

Can we, whose souls are lighted
With wisdom from on high—
Can we, to men benighted,
The lamp of life deny?
Salvation! oh, salvation!
The joyful sound proclaim;
Till each remotest nation
Has learnt Messiah's Name.

Waft, waft, ye winds, His story,
And you, ye waters, roll,
Till, like a sea of glory,
It spreads from pole to pole;
Till o'er our ransomed nature,
The Lamb for sinners slain,
Redeemer, King, Creator,
In bliss returns to reign.

*Reginald Heber* [1783–1826]

## LIGHT SHINING OUT OF DARKNESS

God moves in a mysterious way,
His wonders to perform;
He plants His footsteps in the sea,
And rides upon the storm.

Deep in unfathomable mines
Of never-failing skill
He treasures up His bright designs,
And works His sovereign will.

Ye fearful saints, fresh courage take;
The clouds ye so much dread
Are big with mercy, and shall break
In blessings on your head.

Judge not the Lord by feeble sense,
But trust Him for His grace;
Behind a frowning Providence
He hides a smiling face.

His purposes will ripen fast,
Unfolding every hour;
The bud may have a bitter taste,
But sweet will be the flower.

Blind unbelief is sure to err,
And scan His work in vain;
God is His own interpreter,
And He will make it plain.

*William Cowper* [1731–1800]

## ROCK OF AGES

Rock of Ages, cleft for me,
Let me hide myself in Thee!
Let the water and the blood,
From Thy riven side which flowed,
Be of sin the double cure—
Cleanse me from its guilt and power.

Not the labors of my hands
Can fulfil Thy law's demands;
Could my zeal no respite know,
Could my tears for ever flow,
All for sin could not atone—
Thou must save, and Thou alone.

Nothing in my hand I bring—
Simply to Thy Cross I cling;
Naked come to Thee for dress—
Helpless look to Thee for grace;
Foul, I to the Fountain fly—
Wash me, Saviour, or I die!

While I draw this fleeting breath,
When my eye-strings break in death,
When I soar to worlds unknown,
See Thee on Thy judgment-throne,
Rock of Ages, cleft for me,
Let me hide myself in Thee!

*Augustus Montague Toplady* [1740–1778]

## LOVE TO THE CHURCH

I love Thy kingdom, Lord,
The house of Thine abode,
The church our blest Redeemer saved
With His own precious blood.

I love Thy church, O God!
Her walls before Thee stand,
Dear as the apple of Thine eye,
And graven on Thy hand.

If e'er to bless Thy sons
My voice or hands deny,
These hands let useful skill forsake,
This voice in silence die.

For her my tears shall fall,
For her my prayers ascend;
To her my cares and toils be given
Till toils and cares shall end.

Beyond my highest joy
I prize her heavenly ways,
Her sweet communion, solemn vows,
Her hymns of love and praise.

Jesus, Thou Friend divine,
Our Saviour and our King,
Thy hand from every snare and foe
Shall great deliverance bring.

Sure as thy Truth shall last,
To Zion shall be given
The brightest glories earth can yield,
And brighter bliss of heaven.

*From the Latin of St. Ambrose by Timothy Dwight* [1752–1817]

## GOOD TIDINGS OF GREAT JOY TO ALL PEOPLE

ANGELS from the realms of glory,
Wing your flight o'er all the earth;
Ye who sang creation's story
Now proclaim Messiah's birth;
Come and worship,
Worship Christ, the new-born King.

Shepherds, in the fields abiding,
  Watching o'er your flocks by night,
God with man is now residing,
  Yonder shines the infant-light;
    Come and worship;
Worship Christ, the new-born King.

Sages, leave your contemplations,
  Brighter visions beam afar;
Seek the great Desire of Nations;
  Ye have seen His natal-star;
    Come and worship;
Worship Christ, the new-born King.

Saints, before the altar bending,
  Watching long in hope and fear
Suddenly, the Lord descending,
  In His temple shall appear;
    Come and worship;
Worship Christ, the new-born King.

Sinners, wrung with true repentance,
  Doomed, for guilt, to endless pains,
Justice now revokes the sentence,
  Mercy calls you—break your chains;
    Come and worship;
Worship Christ, the new-born King.

*James Montgomery* [1771-1854]

## CHRIST OUR EXAMPLE IN SUFFERING

Go to dark Gethsemane,
  Ye that feel the tempter's power;
Your Redeemer's conflict see,
  Watch with Him one bitter hour;
Turn not from His griefs away,
Learn of Jesus Christ to pray!

Follow to the judgment hall,
  View the Lord of Life arraigned;
O the wormwood and the gall!
  O the pangs His soul sustained!

Shun not suffering, shame, or loss,—
Learn of Him to bear the cross!

Calvary's mournful mountain climb;
There, adoring at His feet,
Mark that miracle of time,
God's own sacrifice complete!
"It is finished!" hear the cry;
Learn of Jesus Christ to die!

Early hasten to the tomb
Where they laid His breathless clay;
All is solitude and gloom;
Who hath taken Him away?
Christ is risen! He meets our eyes!
Saviour, teach us so to rise!

*James Montgomery* [1771-1854]

## "JUST AS I AM"

Just as I am, without one plea
But that Thy blood was shed for me,
And that Thou bid'st me come to Thee,
O Lamb of God, I come!

Just as I am, and waiting not
To rid my soul of one dark blot,
To Thee, whose blood can cleanse each spot,
O Lamb of God, I come!

Just as I am, though tossed about,
With many a conflict, many a doubt,
Fightings and fears within, without,
O Lamb of God, I come!

Just as I am, poor, wretched, blind;
Sight, riches, healing of the mind,
Yea, all I need, in Thee to find,
O Lamb of God, I come!

Just as I am, Thou wilt receive,
Wilt welcome, pardon, cleanse, relieve;
Because Thy promise I believe,
O Lamb of God, I come!

Just as I am—Thy love unknown
Has broken every barrier down;
Now to be Thine, yea, Thine alone,
O Lamb of God, I come!

Just as I am, of that free love,
The breadth, length, depth, and height to prove,
Here for a season, then above,
O Lamb of God, I come!

*Charlotte Elliott* [1789–1871]

## "BLEST BE THE TIE THAT BINDS"

Blest be the tie that binds
Our hearts in Jesus' love;
The fellowship of Christian minds
Is like to that above.

Before our Father's throne
We pour united prayers;
Our fears, our hopes, our aims, are one,
Our comforts, and our cares.

We share our mutual woes,
Our mutual burdens bear,
And often for each other flows
The sympathizing tear.

When we at death must part,
Not like the world's our pain;
But one in Christ, and one in heart,
We part to meet again.

From sorrow, toil, and pain,
And sin, we shall be free;
And perfect love and friendship reign
Throughout eternity.

*John Fawcett* [1740–1817]

## "IN THE CROSS OF CHRIST I GLORY"

In the Cross of Christ I glory,
Towering o'er the wrecks of time,
All the light of sacred story
Gathers round its head sublime.

When the woes of life o'ertake me,
Hopes deceive, and fears annoy,
Never shall the Cross forsake me—
Lo! it grows with peace and joy.

When the sun of bliss is beaming
Light and love upon my way,
From the Cross the radiance streaming
Adds more luster to the day.

Bane and blessing, pain and pleasure,
By the Cross are sanctified;
Peace is there that knows no measure,
Joys, that through all time abide.

In the Cross of Christ I glory,
Towering o'er the wrecks of time,
All the light of sacred story
Gathers round its head sublime.

*John Bowring* [1792-1872]

## "ABIDE WITH ME"

Abide with me! Fast falls the eventide;
The darkness deepens: Lord, with me abide!
When other helpers fail, and comforts flee,
Help of the helpless, O abide with me!

Swift to its close ebbs out life's little day;
Earth's joys grow dim; its glories pass away:
Change and decay in all around I see;
O Thou, who changest not, abide with me!

Not a brief glance, I beg, a passing word,
But, as Thou dwell'st with Thy disciples, Lord,
Familiar, condescending, patient, free,—
Come, not to sojourn, but abide, with me!

Come not in terrors, as the King of kings;
But kind and good, with healing in Thy wings:
Tears for all woes, a heart for every plea;
Come, Friend of sinners, and abide with me!

Thou on my head in early youth didst smile,
And, though rebellious and perverse meanwhile,
Thou hast not left me, oft as I left Thee:
On to the close, O Lord, abide with me!

I need Thy presence every passing hour.
What but Thy grace can foil the tempter's power?
Who like Thyself my guide and stay can be?
Through cloud and sunshine, O abide with me!

I fear no foe with Thee at hand to bless:
Ills have no weight, and tears no bitterness.
Where is death's sting, where, grave, thy victory?
I triumph still, if Thou abide with me.

Hold then Thy cross before my closing eyes;
Shine through the gloom, and point me to the skies:
Heaven's morning breaks, and earth's vain shadows flee:
In life and death, O Lord, abide with me!

*Henry Francis Lyte* [1793–1847]

## THE HOUR OF PEACEFUL REST

THERE is an hour of peaceful rest
To mourning wanderers given:
There is a joy for souls distressed,
A balm for every wounded breast,
'Tis found alone in heaven.

There is a soft, a downy bed,
Far from these shades of even—
A couch for weary mortals spread,
Where they may rest the aching head,
And find repose, in heaven.

There is a home for weary souls
By sin and sorrow driven;
When tossed on life's tempestuous shoals,
Where storms arise, and ocean rolls,
And all is drear but heaven.

There faith lifts up her cheerful eye,
To brighter prospects given;
And views the tempest passing by,
The evening shadows quickly fly,
And all serene in heaven.

There fragrant flowers immortal bloom,
And joys supreme are given;
There rays divine disperse the gloom:
Beyond the confines of the tomb
Appears the dawn of heaven.

*William Bingham Tappan* [1794–1849]

## THE PILLAR OF THE CLOUD

LEAD, kindly Light, amid the encircling gloom,
Lead Thou me on!
The night is dark, and I am far from home—
Lead Thou me on!
Keep Thou my feet; I do not ask to see
The distant scene,—one step enough for me.

I was not ever thus, nor prayed that Thou
Shouldst lead me on.
I loved to choose and see my path; but now
Lead Thou me on!
I loved the garish day, and, spite of fears,
Pride ruled my will: remember not past years

So long Thy power hath blessed me, sure it still
  Will lead me on,
O'er moor and fen, o'er crag and torrent, till
  The night is gone;
And with the morn those angel faces smile
Which I have loved long since, and lost awhile.

*John Henry Newman* [1801–1890]

## "NEARER TO THEE"

NEARER, my God, to Thee,
  Nearer to Thee!
E'en though it be a cross
  That raiseth me;
Still all my song shall be,
Nearer, my God, to Thee,
  Nearer to Thee!

Though like the wanderer,
  The sun gone down,
Darkness be over me,
  My rest a stone;
Yet in my dreams I'd be
Nearer, my God, to Thee,
  Nearer to Thee!

There let the way appear
  Steps unto heaven;
All that Thou send'st to me
  In mercy given;
Angels to beckon me
Nearer, my God, to Thee,
  Nearer to Thee!

Then, with my waking thoughts
  Bright with Thy praise,
Out of my stony griefs
  Bethel I'll raise;
So by my woes to be
Nearer, my God, to Thee,
  Nearer to Thee!

Or if on joyful wing
  Cleaving the sky,
Sun, moon, and stars forgot,
  Upward I fly,
Still all my song shall be,
Nearer, my God, to Thee,
  Nearer to Thee!

*Sarah Flower Adams* [1805-1848]

## "A MIGHTY FORTRESS IS OUR GOD" *

A MIGHTY fortress is our God,
  A bulwark never failing;
Our helper He amid the flood
  Of mortal ills prevailing.
    For still our ancient foe
    Doth seek to work us woe;
    His craft and power are great,
    And, armed with cruel hate,
  On earth is not his equal.

Did we in our own strength confide,
  Our striving would be losing,—
Were not the right man on our side,
  The man of God's own choosing.
    Dost ask who that may be?
    Christ Jesus, it is He,
    Lord Sabaoth His name,
    From age to age the same,
  And He must win the battle.

And though this world, with devils filled,
  Should threaten to undo us,
We will not fear, for God hath willed
  His truth to triumph through us.
    The Prince of Darkness grim,—
    We tremble not for him;
    His rage we can endure,
    For lo! his doom is sure:
  One little word shall fell him.

* For the original of this poem, see page 3831.

That word above all earthly powers,
No thanks to them, abideth;
The spirit and the gifts are ours
Through Him who with us sideth.
Let goods and kindred go,
This mortal life also;
The body they may kill,
God's truth abideth still,
His Kingdom is forever.

*From the German of Martin Luther, by*
*Frederick Henry Hedge* [1805-1890]

## PRAYER TO THE TRINITY

Lead us, heavenly Father, lead us
O'er the world's tempestuous sea;
Guard us, guide us, keep us, feed us,
For we have no help but Thee;
Yet possessing
Every blessing,
If our God our Father be.

Saviour, breathe forgiveness o'er us;
All our weakness Thou dost know;
Thou didst tread this earth before us,
Thou didst feel its keenest woe;
Lone and dreary,
Faint and weary,
Through the desert Thou didst go.

Spirit of our God, descending,
Fill our hearts with heavenly joy,
Love with every passion blending,
Pleasure that can never cloy:
Thus provided,
Pardoned, guided,
Nothing can our peace destroy.

*James Edmeston* [1791-1867]

## IN SORROW

Gently, Lord, oh, gently lead us,
  Pilgrims in this vale of tears,
Through the trials yet decreed us,
  Till our last great change appears.
When temptation's darts assail us,
  When in devious paths we stray,
Let Thy goodness never fail us,
  Lead us in Thy perfect way.

In the hour of pain and anguish,
  In the hour when death draws near,
Suffer not our hearts to languish,
  Suffer not our souls to fear;
And, when mortal life is ended,
  Bid us in Thine arms to rest,
Till, by angel bands attended,
  We awake among the blest.

*Thomas Hastings* [1784-1872]

## "JUST FOR TO-DAY"

Lord, for to-morrow and its needs,
  I do not pray:
Keep me, my God, from stain of sin,
  Just for to-day;
Let me no wrong or idle word
  Unthinking say:
Set Thou a seal upon my lips,
  Just for to-day.

Let me both diligently work,
  And duly pray;
Let me be kind in word and deed
  Just for to-day;
Let me in season, Lord, be grave,
  In season, gay;
Let me be faithful to Thy grace.
  Just for to-day.

In pain and sorrow's cleansing fires,
  Brief be my stay;
Oh, bid me if to-day I die,
  Come home to-day;
So, for to-morrow and its needs,
  I do not pray;
But keep me, guide me, love me, Lord,
  Just for to-day.

*Sybil F Partridge* [18 -

## LOVEST THOU ME?

HARK, my soul! it is the Lord;
'Tis thy Saviour, hear his word;
Jesus speaks, and speaks to thee;
"Say, poor sinner, lov'st thou me?

"I delivered thee when bound,
And, when wounded, healed thy wound;
Sought thee wandering, set thee right,
Turned thy darkness into light.

"Can a woman's tender care
Cease, towards the child she bare?
Yes, she may forgetful be,
Yet will I remember thee.

"Mine is an unchanging love,
Higher than the heights above;
Deeper than the depths beneath,
Free and faithful, strong as death.

"Thou shalt see my glory soon,
When the work of grace is done;
Partner of my throne shalt be;
Say, poor sinner, lov'st thou me?"

Lord, it is my chief complaint,
That my love is weak and faint;
Yet I love thee and adore,
Oh for grace to love thee more!

*William Cowper* [1731-1800]

## THE VOICE FROM GALILEE

I HEARD the voice of Jesus say,
"Come unto Me and rest;
Lay down, thou weary one, lay down
Thy head upon My breast."
I came to Jesus as I was,
Weary, and worn, and sad,
I found in Him a resting-place,
And He has made me glad.

I heard the voice of Jesus say,
"Behold, I freely give
The living water,—thirsty one,
Stoop down, and drink, and live."
I came to Jesus and I drank
Of that life-giving stream;
My thirst was quenched, my soul revived,
And now I live in Him.

I heard the voice of Jesus say,
"I am this dark world's Light;
Look unto Me, thy morn shall rise,
And all thy day be bright."
I looked to Jesus, and I found
In Him, my Star, my Sun;
And in that Light of life I'll walk
Till traveling days be done.

*Horatius Bonar* [1808--1889]

## FAITH

MY faith looks up to Thee,
Thou Lamb of Calvary,
Saviour divine!
Now hear me while I pray,
Take all my guilt away,
O let me from this day
Be wholly Thine!

May Thy rich grace impart
Strength to my fainting heart,
My zeal inspire;
As Thou hast died for me,
O may my love for Thee
Pure, warm, and changeless be.—
A living fire!

While life's dark maze I tread,
And griefs around me spread,
Be Thou my guide;
Bid darkness turn to day,
Wipe sorrow's tears away,
Nor let me ever stray
From Thee aside.

When ends life's transient dream,
When death's cold, sullen stream
Shall o'er me roll;
Blest Saviour, then, in love,
Fear and distrust remove;
O bear me safe above,
A ransomed soul!

*Ray Palmer* [1808-1887]

## HE STANDETH AT THE DOOR

In the silent midnight watches,
List—thy bosom door!
How it knocketh—knocketh—knocketh
Knocketh evermore!
Say not 'tis thy pulse's beating:
'Tis thy heart of sin;
'Tis thy Saviour knocks, and crieth,
"Rise, and let Me in!"

Death comes on with reckless footsteps,
To the hall and hut:
Think you Death will tarry, knocking,
Where the door is shut?

Jesus waiteth—waiteth—waiteth,
  But the door is fast;
Grieved, away my Saviour goeth;
  Death breaks in at last.

Then 'tis time to stand entreating
  Christ to let thee in:
At the gate of Heaven beating,
  Wailing for thy sin.
Nay!—alas, thou guilty creature!
  Hast thou, then, forgot?
Jesus waited long to know thee;
  Now He knows thee not.

*Arthur Cleveland Coxe* [1818–1896]

## "THERE IS A GREEN HILL"

There is a green hill far away,
  Without a city wall,
Where the dear Lord was crucified,
  Who died to save us all.

We may not know, we cannot tell
  What pains He had to bear,
But we believe it was for us
  He hung and suffered there.

He died that we might be forgiven,
  He died to make us good,
That we might go at last to heaven,
  Saved by His precious blood.

There was no other good enough
  To pay the price of sin;
He only could unlock the gate
  Of heaven, and let us in.

O dearly, dearly has He loved,
  And we must love Him too,
And trust in His redeeming blood,
  And try His works to do.

*Cecil Frances Alexander* [1818–1895]

## NEARER HOME

ONE sweetly solemn thought
 Comes to me o'er and o'er;
I am nearer home to-day
 Than I ever have been before;

Nearer my Father's house,
 Where the many mansions be;
Nearer the great white throne,
 Nearer the crystal sea;

Nearer the bound of life,
 Where we lay our burdens down;
Nearer leaving the cross!
 Nearer gaining the crown!

But lying darkly between,
 Winding down through the night,
Is the silent, unknown stream,
 That leads at last to the light.

Closer and closer my steps
 Come to the dread abysm:
Closer Death to my lips
 Presses the awful chrism.

Oh, if my mortal feet
 Have almost gained the brink;
If it be I am nearer home
 Even to-day than I think;

Father, perfect my trust;
 Let my spirit feel in death,
That her feet are firmly set
 On the rock of a living faith!

*Phoebe Cary* [1824-1871]

## "ONWARD, CHRISTIAN SOLDIERS!"

ONWARD, Christian soldiers!
  Marching as to war,
With the Cross of Jesus
  Going on before.
Christ the Royal Master
  Leads against the foe;
Forward into battle,
  See, His banners go!
    Onward, Christian soldiers!
      Marching as to war,
    With the Cross of Jesus
      Going on before.

At the sign of triumph
  Satan's host doth flee;
On, then, Christian soldiers,
  On to victory!
Hell's foundations quiver
  At the shout of praise;
Brothers, lift your voices,
  Loud your anthems raise!

Like a mighty army
  Moves the Church of God;
Brothers, we are treading
  Where the Saints have trod;
We are not divided
  All one body we,
One in hope and doctrine,
  One in charity.

Crowns and thrones may perish,
  Kingdoms rise and wane,
But the Church of Jesus
  Constant will remain;
Gates of hell can never
  'Gainst that Church prevail;
We have Christ's own promise,
  And that cannot fail.

Onward, then, ye people!
  Join our happy throng,
Blend with ours your voices
  In the triumph song;
Glory, laud, and honor
  Unto Christ the King,
This through countless ages
  Men and angels sing.
    Onward, Christian soldiers!
      Marching as to war,
    With the Cross of Jesus
      Going on before.

*Sabine Baring-Gould* [1834–1924]

## EVENING

Softly now the light of day
Fades upon my sight away;
Free from care, from labor free,
Lord, I would commune with Thee:

Thou, whose all-pervading eye
Naught escapes, without, within,
Pardon each infirmity,
Open fault, and secret sin.

Soon, for me, the light of day
Shall for ever pass away;
Then, from sin and sorrow free,
Take me, Lord, to dwell with Thee:

Thou, who, sinless, yet hast known
All of man's infirmity;
Then, from Thine eternal throne,
Jesus, look with pitying eye.

*George Washington Doane* [1799–1859]

## A DEDICATION

My new-cut ashlar takes the light
Where crimson-blank the windows flare.
By my own work before the night,
Great Overseer, I make my prayer.

If there be good in that I wrought
Thy Hand compelled it, Master, Thine—
Where I have failed to meet Thy Thought
I know, through Thee, the blame was mine.

The depth and dream of my desire,
The bitter paths wherein I stray—
Thou knowest Who hast made the Fire,
Thou knowest Who hast made the Clay.

Who, lest all thought of Eden fade,
Bring'st Eden to the craftsman's brain—
Godlike to muse o'er his own trade
And manlike stand with God again!

One stone the more swings into place
In that dread Temple of Thy worth.
It is enough that, through Thy Grace,
I saw naught common on Thy Earth.

Take not that vision from my ken—
Oh whatsoe'er may spoil or speed.
Help me to need no aid from men
That I may help such men as need!

*Rudyard Kipling* [1865–1936]

# APPENDIX

## CONTAINING A FEW OF THE MORE FAMOUS POEMS IN OTHER LANGUAGES, OF WHICH TRANSLATIONS OR PARAPHRASES OCCUR IN THE FOREGOING PAGES

# APPENDIX

## DIES IRÆ *

DIES IRÆ, DIES ILLA, *dies tribulationis et angustiæ, dies calamitatis et miseriæ, dies tenebrarum et caliginis, dies nebulæ et turbinis, dies tubæ et clangoris super civitates munitas et super angulos excelsos!*—Sophonias i. 15, 16.

DIES iræ, dies illa!
Solvet sæclum in faviliâ,
Teste David cum Sybillâ.

Quantus tremor est futurus.
Quando Judex est venturus.
Cuncta stricte discussurus!

Tuba mirum spargens sonum
Per sepulcra regionum,
Coget omnes ante thronum.

Mors stupebit, et natura.
Quum resurget creatura,
Judicanti responsura.

Liber scriptus proferetur,
In quo totum continetur.
Unde mundus judicetur.

Judex ergo cum sedebit,
Quidquid latet, apparebit:
Nil inultum remanebit.

Quid sum, miser! tunc dicturus,
Quem patronum rogaturus,
Quum vix justus sit securus?

Rex tremendæ majestatis,
Qui salvandos salvas gratis,
Salva me, fons pietatis!

* For a translation of this poem see page 3777.

Recordare, Jesu pie,
Quod sum causa tuæ viæ;
Ne me perdas illâ die!

Quærens me, sedisti lassus,
Redemisti, crucem passus:
Tantus labor non sit cassus!

Juste Judex ultionis,
Donum fac remissionis
Ante diem rationis!

Ingemisco tanquam reus,
Culpâ rubet vultus meus;
Supplicanti parce, Deus!

Qui Mariam absolvisti,
Et latronem exaudisti,
Mihi quoque spem dedisti.

Preces meæ non sunt dignæ,
Sed tu bonus fac benigne
Ne perenni cremer igne!

Inter oves locum præsta,
Et ab hædis me sequestra,
Statuens in parte dextrâ

Confutatis maledictis,
Flammis acribus addictis,
Voca me cum benedictis!

Oro supplex et acclinis,
Cor contritum quasi cinis,
Gere curam mei finis!

Lacrymosa dies illa,
Qua resurget ex favillâ
Judicandus homo reus;
Huic ergo parce, Deus!

*Tommâso di Celano* [1185?–1255?]

## STABAT MATER DOLOROSA *

STABAT Mater dolorosa
Juxta crucem lacrymosa,
    Dum pendebat filius;
Cujus animam gementem,
Contristatam et dolentem,
    Pertransivit gladius.

O quam tristis et afflicta
Fuit illa benedicta
    Mater unigeniti,
Quæ mœrebat et dolebat,
Pia mater, dum videbat
    Nati pœnas inclyti!

Quis est homo qui non fleret,
Christi matrem si videret
    In tanto supplicio?
Quis non posset contristari
Piam matrem contemplari
    Dolentem cum filio?

Pro peccatis suæ gentis,
Vidit Jesum in tormentis,
    Et flagellis subditum.
Vidit suum dulcem natum,
Morientem, desolatum,
    Dum emisit spiritum.

Eia mater, fons amoris,
Me sentire vim doloris
    Fac, ut tecum lugeam.
Fac ut ardeat cor meum
In amando Christum Deum,
    Ut illi complaceam.

Sancta Mater, istud agas,
Crucifixi fige plagas
    Cordi meo valide.

* For a translation of this poem see page 3779.

Tui nati vulnerati,
Tam dignati pro me pati,
Pœnas mecum divide.

Fac me vere tecum flere,
Crucifixo condolere,
Donec ego vixero;
Juxta crucem tecum stare,
Et tibi me sociare
In planctu desidero.

Virgo virginum præclara,
Mihi jam non sis amara;
Fac me tecum plangere;
Fac ut portem Christi mortem,
Passionis fac consortem,
Et plagas recolere.

Fac me plagis vulnerari,
Cruce hac inebriari,
Et cruore filii;
Inflammatus et accensus,
Per te, Virgo, sum defensus
In die judicii.

Fac me cruce custodiri,
Morte Christi præmuniri,
Confoveri gratia.
Quando corpus morietur,
Fac ut animæ donetur
Paradisi gloria.

*Jacopone da Todi* [ ? –1306]

## VENI, SANCTE SPIRITUS *

Veni, Sancte Spiritus,
Et emitte cœlitus
Lucis tuæ radium.

* For a translation of this poem see page 3780

Veni, pater pauperum,
Veni, dator munerum,
Veni, lumen cordium.

Consolator optime,
Dulcis hospes animæ,
Dulce refrigerium.

In labore requies,
In æstu temperies,
In fletu solatium.

O lux beatissima!
Reple cordis intima,
Tuorum fidelium.

Sine tuo numine,
Nihil est in homine,
Nihil est innoxium.

Lava quod est sordidum,
Riga quod est aridum,
Sana quod est saucium,

Flecte quod est rigidum,
Fove quod est frigidum,
Rege quod est devium.

Da tuis fidelibus,
In te confidentibus,
Sacrum septenarium;

Da virtutis meritum,
Da salutis exitum,
Da perenne gaudium!

*Robert II. of France* [971-1031]

## VENI, CREATOR SPIRITUS *

VENI, Creator Spiritus,
Mentes tuorum visita,
Imple superna gratia,
Quæ tu creasti pectora.

* For a translation of this poem see page 3782.

Qui diceris Paraclitus,
Altissimi donum Dei,
Fons vivus, ignis, caritas,
Et spiritalis unctio.

Tu septiformis munere,
Dextræ Dei tu digitus,
Tu rite promissum Patris,
Sermone ditans guttura.

Accende lumen sensibus,
Infunde amorem cordibus,
Infirma nostri corporis
Virtute firmans perpeti.

Hostem repellas longius,
Pacemque dones protinus:
Ductore sic te prævio
Vitemus omne noxium.

Per te sciamus da Patrem,
Noscamus atque Filium;
Te utriusque Spiritum
Credamus omni tempore.

Deo Patri sit gloria
Et Filio qui a mortuis
Surrexit, ac Paraclito,
In sæculorum sæcula.

*St. Gregory the Great (?)* [540?–604]

## URBS SYON AUREA *

From "Hora Novissima"

URBS Syon aurea, patria lactea, cive decora,
Omne cor obruis, omnibus obstruis et cor et ora.
Nescio, nescio, quæ jubilatio, lux tibi qualis,
Quam socialia gaudia, gloria quam specialis:
Laude studens ea tollere, mens mea victa fatiscit:
O bona gloria, vincor; in omnia laus tua vicit.

* For a paraphrase of this poem see page 3689.

Sunt Syon atria conjubilantia, martyre plena,
Cive micantia, Principe stantia, luce serena:
Est ibi pascua, mitibus afflua, præstita sanctis,
Regis ibi thronus, agminis et sonus est epulantis.
Gens duce splendida, concio candida vestibus albis
Sunt sine fletibus in Syon ædibus, ædibus almis;
Sunt sine crimine, sunt sine turbine, sunt sine lite
In Syon ædibus editioribus Israëlitae.
Urbs Syon inclyta, gloria debita glorificandis,
Tu bona visibus interioribus intima pandis:
Intima lumina, mentis acumina te speculantur,
Pectora flammea spe modo, postea forte lucrantur.
Urbs Syon unica, mansio mystica, condita cælo,
Nunc tibi gaudeo, nunc mihi lugeo, tristor, anhelo:
Te qui corpore non queo, pectore sæpe penetro,
Sed caro terrea, terraque carnea, mox cado retro.
Nemo retexere nemoque promere sustinet ore,
Quo tua mœnia, quo capitalia plena decore;
Opprimit omne cor ille tuus decor, o Syon, o pax,
Urbs sine tempore, nulla potest fore laus tibi mendax;
O sine luxibus, o sine luctibus, o sine lite
Splendida curia, florida patria, patria vitæ!

Urbs Syon inclyta, turris et edita littore tuto,
Te peto, te colo, te flagro, te volo, canto, saluto;
Nec meritis peto, nam meritis meto morte perire,
Nec reticens tego, quod meritis ego fillius iræ:
Vita quidem mea, vita nimis rea, mortua vita,
Quippe reatibus exitialibus obruta, trita.
Spe tamen ambulo, præmia postulo speque fideque,
Illa perennia postulo præmia nocte dieque.
Me Pater optimus atque piissimus ille creavit;
In lue pertulit, ex lue sustulit, a lue lavit.
Gratia cælica sustinet unica totius orbis
Parcere sordibus, interioribus unctio morbis;
Diluit omnia cælica gratia, fons David undans
Omnia diluit, omnibus affluit, omnia mundans:
O pia gratia, celsa palatia cernere præsta,
Ut videam bona, festaque consona, cælica festa.
O mea, spes mea, tu Syon aurea, clarior auro,

Agmine splendida, stans duce, florida perpete lauro,
O bona patria, num tua guadia teque videbo?
O bona patria, num tua præmia plena tenebo?
Dic mihi, flagito, verbaque reddito, dicque, Videbis:
Spem solidam gero; remne tenens ero? dic, Retinebis.
O sacer, o pius, o ter et amplius ille beatus,
Cui sua pars Deus: o miser, o reus, hâc viduatus.

*Bernard of Cluny* [1122?–1156?]

## URBS BEATA HIERUSALEM *

Urbs beata Hierusalem,
Dicta Pacis Visio,
Quæ construitur in cœlis
Vivis ex lapidibus,
Et ab angelis ornata,
Ut sponsata comite.

Nova veniens e cœlo,
Nuptiali thalamo
Præparata, ut sponsata
Copuletur Domino;
Plateæ et muri ejus
Ex auro purissimo.

Portæ nitent margaritis,
Adytis patentibus;
Et virtute meritorum
Illuc introducitur
Omnis qui ob Christi Nomen
Hoc in mundo premitur.

Tunsionibus, pressuris
Expoliti lapides
Suis coaptantur locis
Per Manum Artificis;
Disponuntur permansuri
Sacris ædificiis.

* For a paraphrase of this poem see page 3693.

Gloria et honor Deo
  Usquequo Altissimo,
Una Patri, Filioque,
  Inclyto Paraclito,
Cui laus est et potestas
  Per æterna sæcula.

*Unknown*

## VIVAMUS, MEA LESBIA *

Vivamus, mea Lesbia, atque amemus,
Rumoresque senum severiorum
Omnes unius æstimemus assis.
Soles occidere et redire possunt:
Nobis, cum semel occidit brevis lux,
Nox est perpetua una dormienda.
Da mi basia mille, deinde centum,
Dein mille altera, dein secunda centum,
Deinde usque altera mille, deinde centum.
Dein, cum milia multa fecerimus,
Conturbabimus illa, ne sciamus,
Aut nequis malus invidere possit,
Cum tantum sciat esse basiorum.

*Gaius Valerius Catullus* [87 B. C.?–54 B. C.?]

## PERSICOS ODI †

(*Odes*, Bk. i, No. 38)

Persicos odi, puer, apparatus,
Displicent nexæ philyrâ coronæ;
Mitte sectari, rosa quo locorum
  Sera moretur.

Simplici myrto nihil allabores
Sedulus, curo: neque te ministrum
Dedecet myrtus neque me sub arctâ
  Vite bibentem.

*Quintus Horatius Flaccus* [65 B. C.–8 B. C.]

* For a paraphrase of this poem see page 588.
† For a paraphrase of this poem see page 1987.

## INTEGER VITÆ *

(*Odes*, Bk. i, No. 22)

INTEGER vitæ scelerisque purus
Non eget Mauris jaculis neque arcu
Nec venenatis gravida sagittis,
Fusce, pharetra,

Sive per Syrtes iter æstuosas
Sive facturus per inhospitalem
Caucasum, vel quæ loca fabulosus
Lambit Hydaspes.

Namque me silva lupus in Sabina,
Dum meam canto Lalagen et ultra
Terminum curis vagor expeditis,
Fugit inermem;

Quale portentum neque militaris
Daunias latis alit æsculetis
Nec Jubæ tellus generat, leonum
Arida nutrix.

Pone me pigris ubi nulla campis
Arbor æstiva recreatur aura,
Quod latus mundi nebulæ malusque
Juppiter urget;

Pone sub curru nimium propinqui
Solis in terra domibus negata:
Dulce ridentem Lalagen amabo,
Dulce loquentem.

*Quintus Horatius Flaccus* [65 B. C.–8 B. C.]

* For a paraphrase of this poem see page 2912.

## RECTIUS VIVES *

(*Odes*, Bk. ii, No. 10)

RECTIUS vives, Licini, neque altum
Semper urgendo neque, dum procellas
Cautus horrescis, nimium premendo
Litus iniquum.

Auream quisquis mediocritatem
Diligit, tutus caret obsoleti
Sordibus tecti, caret invidenda
Sobrius aula.

Sæpius ventis agitatur ingens
Pinus et celsæ graviore casu
Decidunt turres feriuntque summos
Fulgura montis.

Sperat infestis, metuit secundis
Alteram sortem bene præparatum
Pectus. Informis hiemes reducit
Juppiter, idem

Submovet; non, si male nunc, et olim
Sic erit; quondam cithara tacentem
Suscitat musam neque semper arcum
Tendit Apollo.

Rebus angustis animosus atque
Fortis appare; sapienter idem
Contrahes vento nimium secundo
Turgida vela.

*Quintus Horatius Flaccus* [65 B. C.–8 B. C.]

## DE BREVITATE VITÆ †

(CARMEN AMŒBÆUM)

GAUDEAMUS igitur,
Juvenes dum sumus;

* For a paraphrase of this poem see page 2991.
† For a paraphrase of this poem see page 2895.

Post jucundam juventutem,
Post molestam senectutem
Nos habebit humus.

Ubi sunt, qui ante nos
In mundo fuere?
Vadite ad superos,
Transite ad inferos,
Ubi jam fuere.

Vita nostra brevis est,
Brevi finietur,
Venit mors velociter,
Rapit nos atrociter,
Nemini parcetur.

Vivat academia,
Vivant professores,
Vivat membrum quodlibet,
Vivant membra quaelibet,
Semper sint in flore!

Vivant omnes virgines,
Faciles, formosæ,
Vivant et mulieres,
Teneræ, amabiles,
Bonæ, laboriosæ!

Vivat et respublica
Et qui illam regit,
Vivat nostra civitas,
Mæcenatum caritas,
Quæ nos hic protegit!

Pereat tristitia,
Pereant osores,
Pereat diabolus,
Quivis antiburschius,
Atque irrisores.

*Unknown*

## LAURIGER HORATIUS *

LAURIGER HORATIUS,
Quàm dixisti verum;
Fugit Euro citius
Tempus edax rerum!
Ubi sunt, o pocula
Dulciora melle!
Rixæ, pax et oscula
Rubentis puellæ?

Crescit uva molliter
Et puella crescit,
Sed poeta turpiter
Sitiens canescit.
Quid juvat æternitas
Nominis, amare
Nisi terræ filias
Licet, et potare.

*Unknown*

## EIN FESTE BURG †

EIN feste Burg ist unser Gott,
Ein gute Wehr und Waffen,
Er hilft uns frei aus aller Not,
Die uns jetzt hat betroffen.
Der alt böse Feind
Mit Ernst ers jetzt meint,
Gross Macht und viel List
Sein grausam Rüstung ist,
Auf Erd ist nicht seins Gleichen.

Mit unsrer Macht ist nichts getan,
Wir sind gar bald verloren;
Es streit für uns der rechte Mann,
Den Gott hat selbst erkoren.

* For a paraphrase of this poem see page 2896.
† For a translation of this poem see page 3806.

Fragst du, wer der ist!
Er heisst Jesus Christ,
Der Herr Zebaoth,
Und ist kein andrer Gott,
Das Feld muss er behalten.

Und wenn die Welt voll Teufel wär
Und wollt uns gar verschlingen,
So fürchten wir uns nicht so sehr,
Es soll uns doch gelingen.
Der Fürst dieser Welt,
Wie saur er sich stellt,
Tut er uns doch nicht;
Das macht, er ist gericht,
Ein Wörtlein kann ihn fällen.

Das Wort sie sollen lassen stan
Und kein Dank dazu haben.
Er ist bei uns wohl auf dem Plan
Mit seinem Geist und Gaben.
Nehmen sie den Leib,
Gut, Ehr, Kind und Weib,
Lass fahren dahin,
Sie habens kein Gewinn:
Das Reich muss uns doch bleiben.

*Martin Luther* [1483–1546]

## LIED *

Ins stille Land!
Wer leitet uns hinüber?
Schon wölkt sich uns der Abendhimmel trüber,
Und immer trümmervoller wird der Strand.
Wer leitet uns mit sanfter Hand
Hinüber, ach! hinüber
Ins stille Land?

Ins stille Land!
Zu euch, ihr freien Räume
Für die Veredlung! Zarte Morgenträume

* For a paraphrase of this poem see page 3456.

Der schönen Seelen! künftgen Daseins Pfand.
Wer treu des Lebens Kampf bestand,
Trägt seiner Hoffnung Keime
Ins stille Land.

Ach Land! ach Land!
Für alle Sturmbedrohten
Der mildeste von unsers Schicksals Boten
Winkt uns, die Fackel umgewandt,
Und leitet uns mit sanfter Hand
Ins Land der grossen Toten,
Ins stille Land.

*Johann Gaudenz von Salis-Seewis* [1762–1834]

## DIE WACHT AM RHEIN *

Es braust ein Ruf wie Donnerhall,
Wie Schwertgeklirr und Wogenprall:
"Zum Rhein, zum Rhein, zum deutschen Rhein!
Wer will des Stromes Hüter sein?"

*Chorus*—Lieb Vaterland, magst ruhig sein,
Fest steht und treu die Wacht am Rhein!

Durch Hunderttausend zuckt es schnell,
Und aller Augen blitzen hell.
Der deutsche Jüngling fromm und stark
Beschirmt die heil'ge Landesmark.

Er blickt hinauf in Himmelsau'n,
Wo Heldengeister niederschaun,
Und schwört mit stolzer Kampfeslust:
"Du, Rhein, bleibst deutsch wie meine Brust!

"Und ob mein Herz im Tode bricht,
Wirst du doch drum ein Welscher nicht.
Reich wie an Wasser deine Flut,
Ist Deutschland ja an Heldenblut.

* For a translation of this poem see page 2269.

"So lang ein Tropfen Blut noch glüht,
Noch eine Faust den Degen zieht,
Und noch ein Arm die Büchse spannt,
Betritt kein Feind hier deinen Strand."

Der Schwur erschallt, die Woge rinnt,
Die Fahnen flattern hoch im Wind:
Zum Rhein, zum Rhein, zum deutschen Rhein!
Wir alle wollen Hüter sein!

*Max Schneckenburger* [1819–1849]

## DES DEUTSCHEN VATERLAND *

WAS ist des Deutschen Vaterland?
Ist's Preussenland? ist's Schwabenland?
Ist's, wo am Rhein die Rebe blüht?
Ist's, wo am Belt die Möve zieht?
O nein! nein! nein!
Sein Vaterland muss grösser sein.

Was ist des Deutschen Vaterland?
Ist's Baierland? ist's Steierland?
Ist's, wo des Marsen Rind sich streckt?
Ist's, wo der Märker Eisen reckt?
O nein! nein! nein!
Sein Vaterland muss grösser sein.

Was ist des Deutschen Vaterland?
Ist's Pommerland, Westfalenland?
Ist's, wo der Sand der Dünen weht?
Ist's, wo die Donau brausend geht?
O nein! nein! nein!
Sein Vaterland muss grösser sein.

Was ist des Deutschen Vaterland?
So nenne mir das grosse Land!

* For a translation of this poem see page 2270

Ist's Land der Schweitzer? ist's Tirol?
Das Land und Volk gefiel mir wohl;
Doch nein! nein! nein!
Sein Vaterland muss grösser sein.

Was ist des Deutschen Vaterland?
So nenne mir das grosse Land!
Gewiss es ist das Oesterreich,
An Ehren und an Siegen reich?
O nein! nein! nein!
Sein Vaterland muss grösser sein.

Was ist des Deutschen Vaterland?
So nenne mir das grosse Land!
So weit die deutsche Zunge klingt
Und Gott im Himmel Lieder singt,
Das soll es sein!
Das, wackrer Deutscher, nenne dein!

Das ist des Deutschen Vaterland,
Wo Eide schwört der Druck der Hand,
Wo Treue hell vom Auge blitzt
Und Liebe warm im Herzen sitzt—
Das soll es sein!
Das, wackrer Deutscher, nenne dein!

Das ist des Deutschen Vaterland,
Wo Zorn vertilgt den wälschen Tand,
Wo jeder Franzmann heisset Feind,
Wo jeder Deutsche heisset Freund—
Das soll es sein!
Das ganze Deutschland soll es sein!

Das ganze Deutschland soll es sein!
O Gott vom Himmel sieh' darein,
Und gieb uns rechten deutschen Muth,
Dass wir es lieben treu und gut.
Das soll es sein!
Das *ganze Deutschland* soll es sein!

*Ernst Moritz Arndt* [1769-1860]

## LA MARSEILLAISE*

Allons, enfants de la patrie!
Le jour de gloire est arrivé!
Contre nous de la tyrannie
L'étendard sanglant est levé,
Entendez-vous dans les campagnes
Mugir ces féroces soldats?
Ils viennent, jusque dans nos bras,
Égorger nos fils, nos compagnes! . . .
Aux armes, citoyens! formez vos bataillons!
Marchons, marchons, qu'un sang impur abreuve nos sillons!

Que veut cette horde d'esclaves,
De traîtres, de rois conjurés?
Pour qui ces ignobles entraves,
Ces fers dès longtemps préparés?
Français! pour vous, ah quel outrage!
Quels transports il doit exciter!
C'est vous qu'on ose méditer
De rendre à l'antique esclavage!

Quoi! ces cohortes étrangères
Feraient la loi dans nos foyers!
Quoi! ces phalanges mercenaires
Terrasseraient nos fiers guerriers!
Grand Dieu! par des mains enchaînées
Nos fronts sous le joug se ploieraient!
De vils despotes deviendraient
Les moteurs de nos destinées!

Tremblez, tyrans! et vous, perfides,
L'opprobre de tous les partis,
Tremblez! vos projets parricides
Vont enfin recevoir leur prix!
Tout est soldat pour vous combattre.
S'ils tombent, nos jeunes héros,
La terre en produit de nouveaux
Contre vous tous prêts à se battre!

*For a paraphrase of this poem see page 2271.

Français! en guerriers magnanimes
Portez ou retenez vos coups;
Épargnez ces tristes victimes
A regret s'armant contre nous.
Mais le despote sanguinaire,
Mais les complices de Bouillé,
Tous ces tigres qui sans pitié
Dechirent le sein de leur mère! . . .

Amour sacré de la patrie,
Conduis, soutiens nos bras vengeurs:
Liberté, Liberté chérie,
Combats avex tes défenseurs.
Sous nos drapeaux que la Victoire
Accoure à tes mâles accents;
Que tes ennemis expirants
Voient ton triomphe et notre gloire! . .
Aux armes, citoyens! formez vos bataillons!
Marchons, marchons, qu'un sang impur abreuve nos sillons!

*Claude Joseph Rouget de Lisle* [1760–1836]

*La strophe des enfants:*

Nous entrerons dans la carrière
Quand nos aînés n'y seront plus;
Nos y trouverons leur poussière
Et la trace de leurs vertus!
Bien moins jaloux de leur survivre
Que de partager leur cercueil,
Nous aurons le sublime orgueil
De les venger ou de les suivre! . . .

*Louis François Dubois* [1773–1855]

## BALLADE DES DAMES DU TEMPS JADIS*

Dictes-moy où, n'en quel pays,
Est Flora, la belle Romaine;
Archipiada, ne Thaïs,
Qui fut sa cousine germaine;

*For translations of this poem see pages 1783, 1784, 1785.

Echo, parlant quand bruyt on maine
Dessus riviere ou sus estan,
Qui beauté eut trop plus qu'humaine?
Mais où sont les neiges d'antan!

Où est la tres sage Heloïs,
Pour qui fut blessé et puis moyne
Pierre Esbaillart à Sainct-Denys
(Pour son amour eut cest essoyne)?
Semblablement, où est la royne
Qui commanda que Buridan
Fust jetté en ung sac en Seine? . . .
Mais où sont les neiges d'antan?

La royne Blanche comme ung lys,
Qui chantoit à voix de sereine;
Berthe au grand pied, Bietris, Allys;
Harembourges, qui tint le Mayne,
Et Jehanne, la bonne Lorraine,
Qu'Angloys bruslerent à Rouen;
Où sont-ils, Vierge souveraine? . . .
Mais où sont les neiges d'antan!

ENVOI

Prince, n'enquerez de sepmaine
Où elles sont, ne de cest an,
Que ce refrain ne vous remaine:
Mais où sont les neiges d'antan?

*François Villon* [1431–14?]

## BALLADE DE FRÈRE LUBIN *

POUR courir en poste à la ville
Vingt fois, cent fois, ne sçai combien,
Pour faire quelque chose vile,
Frère Lubin le fera bien;
Mais d'avoir honneste entretien,
Ou mener vie salutaire,
C'est à faire à un bon chrestien,
Frère Lubin ne le peut faire.

* For a translation of this poem see page 1874.

Pour mettre (comme un homme habile)
Le bien d'autruy avec le sien,
Et vous laisser sans croix ne pile,
Frère Lubin le fera bien.
On a beau dire, je le tien,
Et le presser de satisfaire,
Jamais ne vous en rendra rien;
Frère Lubin ne le peut faire.

Pour desbaucher par un doux stile
Quelque fille de bon maintien,
Point ne faut de vieille subtile,
Frère Lubin le fera bien.
Il presche en theologien;
Mais pour boire de belle eau claire,
Faites la boire à vostre chien,
Frère Lubin ne le peut faire.

ENVOI

Pour faire plus tost mal que bien,
Frère Lubin le fera bien,
Et si c'est quelque bon affaire,
Frère Lubin ne le peut faire.

*Clément Marot* [1495-1544]

## LE GRENIER *

Je viens revoir l'asile où ma jeunesse
De la misère a subi les leçons.
J'avais vingt ans, une folle maîtresse,
De francs amis et l'amour des chansons.
Bravant le monde et les sots et les sages,
Sans avenir, riche de mon printemps,
Leste et joyeux, je montais six étages.
Dans un grenier qu'on est bien à vingt ans!

C'est un grenier, point ne veux qu'on l'ignore.
Là fut mon lit, bien chétif et bien dur;
Là fut ma table; et je retrouve encore
Trois pieds d'un vers charbonnés sur le mur

* For a translation of this poem see page 463.

Apparaissez, plaisirs de mon bel âge,
  Que d'un coup d'aile a fustigés le temps,
Vingt fois pour vous j'ai mis ma montre en gage,
  Dans un grenier qu'on est bien à vingt ans!

Lisette ici doit surtout apparaître,
  Vive, jolie, avec un frais chapeau;
Déjà sa main à l'étroite fenêtre
  Suspend son schal, en guise de rideau.
Sa robe aussi va parer ma couchette;
  Respecte, Amour, ses plis longs et flottans.
J'ai su depuis qui payait sa toilette.
  Dans un grenier qu'on est bien à vingt ans!

À table un jour, jour de grande richesse,
  De mes amis les voix brillaient en chœur,
Quand jusqu'ici monte un cri d'allégresse:
  À Marengo Bonaparte est vainqueur.
Le canon gronde; un autre chant commence·
  Nous célébrons tant de faits éclatans.
Les rois jamais n'envahiront la France.
  Dans un grenier qu'on est bien à vingt ans!

Quittons ce toit où ma raison s'enivre.
  Oh! qu'ils sont loin ces jours si regrettés!
J'échangerais ce qu'il me reste à vivre
  Contre un des mois qu'ici Dieu m'a comptés,
Pour rêver gloire, amour, plaisir, folie,
  Pour dépenser sa vie en peu d'instans,
D'un long espoir pour la voir embellie.
  Dans un grenier qu'on est bien à vingt ans!

*Pierre-Jean de Béranger* [1780–1857]

## LE ROI D'YVETOT *

Il était un roi d'Yvetot
  Peu connu dans l'histoire,
Se levant tard, se couchant tôt,
  Dormant fort bien sans gloire,

* For a paraphrase of this poem see page 1848

Et couronné par Jeanneton
D'un simple bonnet de coton,
Dit-on.
Oh! oh! oh! oh! ah! ah! ah! ah!
Quel bon petit roi c'était là!
La, la.

Il faisait ses quatre repas
Dans son palais de chaume,
Et sur un âne, pas à pas,
Parcourait son royaume.
Joyeux, simple et croyant le bien,
Pour toute garde il n'avait rien
Qu'un chien.

Il n'avait de goût onéreux
Qu'une soif un peu vive;
Mais, en rendant son peuple heureux,
Il faut bien qu'un roi vive.
Lui-même, à table et sans suppôt,
Sur chaque muid levait un pot
D'impôt.

Aux filles de bonnes maisons
Comme il avait su plaire,
Ses sujets avaient cent raisons
De le nommer leur père.
D'ailleurs il ne levait de ban
Que pour tirer, quatre fois l'an,
Au blanc.

Il n'agrandit point ses états,
Fut un voisin commode,
Et, modèle des potentats,
Prit le plaisir pour code.
Ce n'est que lorsqu'il expira
Que le peuple, qui l'enterra,
Pleura.

On conserve encor le portrait
De ce digne et bon prince:

C'est l'enseigne d'un cabaret
  Fameux dans la province.
Les jours de fête, bien souvent,
La foule s'écrie en buvant
          Devant:
Oh! oh! oh! oh! ah! ah! ah! ah!
Quel bon petit roi c'était là!
          La, la.

*Pierre-Jean de Béranger* [1780–1857]

## FANTAISIE *

Il est un air pour qui je donnerais
  Tout Rossini, tout Mozart, tout Weber,
Un air très vieux, languissant et funèbre,
  Qui pour moi seul a des charmes secrets.

Or, chaque fois que je viens à l'entendre,
  De deux cents ans mon âme rajeunit;
C'est sous Louis treize . . . et je crois voir s'étendre
  Un coteau vert que le couchant jaunit.

Puis un château de brigue à coins de pierres,
  Aux vitraux teints de rougeâtres couleurs,
Ceint de grands parcs, avec une rivière
  Baignant ses pieds, qui coule entre les fleurs.

Puis une dame à sa haute fenêtre,
  Blonde, aux yeux noirs, en ses habits anciens . . .
Que dans une autre existence, peut-être,
  J'ai déjà vue! . . . et dont je me souviens.

*Gérard de Nerval* [1808–1855]

## L'ART †

Oui, l'œuvre sort plus belle
D'une forme au travail
      Rebelle,
Vers, marbre, onyx, émail.

* For a translation of this poem see page 920.
† For a paraphrase of this poem see page 3140.

Point de contraintes fausses!
Mais que, pour marcher droit,
Tu chausses,
Muse, un cothurne étroit.

Fi du rhythme commode,
Comme un soulier trop grand,
Du mode
Que tout pied quitte et prend!

Statuaire, repousse
L'argile que pétrit
Le pouce
Quand flotte ailleurs l'esprit.

Lutte avec le carrare,
Avec le paros dur
Et rare,
Gardiens du contour pur;

Emprunte à Syracuse
Son bronze où fermement
S'accuse
Le trait fier et charmant;

D'une main délicate
Poursuis dans un filon
D'agate
Le profil d'Apollon.

Peintre, fuis l'aquarelle,
Et fixe la couleur
Trop frêle
Au four de l'émailleur.

Fais les sirènes bleues,
Tordant de cent façons
Leurs queues,
Les monstres des blasons

Dans son nimbe trilobe
La Vierge et son Jésus,
Le globe
Avec la croix dessus.

Tout passe.—L'art robuste
Seul a l'éternité.
Le buste.
Survit à la cité.

Et la médaille austère
Que trouve un laboureur
Sous terre
Révèle un empereur.

Les dieux eux-mêmes meurent.
Mais les vers souverains
Demeurent
Plus fort que les airains.

Sculpte, lime, cisèle;
Que ton rêve flottant
Se scelle
Dans le bloc résistant!

*Théophile Gautier* [1811–1872]

## CARCASSONNE *

Je me fais vieux, j'ai soixante ans;
J'ai travaillé toute ma vie
Sans avoir, durant ce temps,
Pu satisfaire mon envie.
Je vois bien qu'il n'est ici-bas
De bonheur complet pour personne.
Mon voeu ne s'accomplira pas:
Je n'ai jamais vu Carcassonne!

On voit la ville de là-haut
Derrière les montagnes bleues,
Mais, pour y parvenir, il faut,
Il faut faire cinq grandes lieues,
En faire autant pour revenir;
Ah, si la vendange était bonne!
Le raisin ne veut pas jaunir:
Je ne verrai pas Carcassonne!

* For a translation of this poem see page 438.

On dit qu'on y voit tous les jours,
  Ni plus ni moins que les dimanches,
Des gens s'en aller sur les cours,
  En habits neufs, en robes blanches.
On dit qu'on y voit des châteaux
  Grands commes ceux de Babylone,
Un évêque et deux généraux!
  Je ne connais pas Carcassonne!

Le vicaire a cent fois raison:
  C'est des imprudents que nous sommes.
Il disait dans son oraison
  Que l'ambition perd les hommes.
Si je pouvois trouver pourtant
  Deux jours sur la fin de l'automne—
Mon Dieu, que je mourrais content
  Après avoir vu Carcassonne!

Mon Dieu, mon Dieu, pardonnez-moi
  Si ma prière vous offense;
On voit toujours plus haut que soi,
  En vieillesse comme en enfance.
Ma femme, avec mon fils Aignan,
  A voyagé jusqu'à Narbonne;
Mon filleul a vu Perpignan,
  Et je n'ai pas vu Carcassonne!

Ainsi chantait près de Limoux
  Un paysan courbé par l'âge.
Je lui dis: "Ami, levez-vous;
  Nous allons faire le voyage."
Nous partîmes le lendemain,
  Mais, que le Bon Dieu lui pardonne,
Il mourut à moitié chemin:
  Il n'a jamais vu Carcassonne!

*Gustave Nadaud* [1820–1893]

## HASSGESANG GEGEN ENGLAND *

WAS schiert uns Russe und Franzos?
Schuss wider Schuss und Stoss um Stoss,
Wir lieben sie nicht,
Wir hassen sie nicht.
Wir schützen Weichsel und Wasgaupass,—
Wir haben nur einen einzigen Hass,
Wir lieben vereint, wir hassen vereint,
Wir haben nur einen einzigen Feind:—

Den ihr alle wisst, den ihr alle wisst,
Er sitzt geduckt hinter der grauen Flut,
Voll Neid, voll Wut, voll Schläue, voll List,
Durch Wasser getrennt, die sind dicker als Blut.
Wir wollen treten in ein Gericht,
Einen Schwur zu schwören, Gesicht in Gesicht.
Einen Schwur von Erz, den verbläst kein Wind,
Einen Schwur für Kind und für Kindeskind.
Vernehmt das Wort, sagt nach das Wort,
Es wälze sich durch ganz Deutschland fort:
Wir wollen nicht lassen von unserem Hass,
Wir haben alle nur einen Hass,
Wir lieben vereint, wir hassen vereint,
Wir haben alle nur einen Feind:
*ENGLAND!*

In der Bordkajüte, in Feiersaal,
Sassen Schiffsoffiziere beim Liebesmahl,—
Wie ein Säbelhieb, wie ein Segelschwung,
Einer riss grüssend empor den Trunk;
Knap hinknallend wie Ruderschlag
Drei Worte sprach er: "Auf den Tag!"

Wem galt das Glas?
Sie hatten alle nur einen Hass.
Wer war gemeint?
Sie hatten alle nur einen Feind:
*ENGLAND!*

* For a translation of this poem see page 2549.

Nimm du die Völker der Erde in Sold,
Baue Wälle aus Barren von Gold,
Bedecke die Meerflut mit Bug bei Bug,
Du rechnetest klug, doch nicht klug genug.
Was schiert uns Russe und Franzos?
Schuss wider Schuss, und Stoss um Stoss.
Wir kämpfen den Kampf mit Bronze und Stahl
Und schliessen Frieden irgend einmal,
Dich werden wir hassen mit langem Hass,
Wir werden nicht lassen von unserem Hass.
Hass zu Wasser und Hass zu Land,
Hass des Hauptes und Hass der Hand,
Hass der Hammer und Hass der Kronen,
Drosselnder Hass von siebzig Millionen,
Sie lieben vereint, sie hassen vereint,
Sie haben alle nur einen Feind:
*ENGLAND!*

*Ernst Lissauer* [1882–1937]

## "QUAND VOUS SEREZ VIEILLE"*

Quand vous serez bien vieille, au soir, à la chandelle,
Assise auprès du feu, devidant et filant,
Direz chantant mes vers, en vous émerveillant:
"Ronsard me célébrait du temps que j'étais belle."
Lors vous n'aurez servante, oyant telle nouvelle,
Déjà sous le labeur à demi sommeillant,
Qui au bruit de mon nom ne s'aille réveillant,
Bénissant votre nom de louange immortelle.
Je serai sous la terre, et fantôme sans os,
Par les ombres myrteux je prendrai mon repos:
Vous serez au foyer, une vieille accroupie,
Regrettant mon amour et votre fier dédain.
Vivez, si m'en croyez, n'attendez à demain:
Cueillez dès aujourd'hui les roses de la vie.

*Pierre de Ronsard* [1524–1585]

*For a paraphrase of this sonnet see page 636.

## PEU DE CHOSE ET PRESQUE TROP *

La vie est vaine:
Un peu d'amour,
Un peu de haine . . .
Et puis—bon jour!

La vie est brève:
Un peu d'espoir,
Un peu de rêve . . .
Et puis—bon soir!

La vie est telle
Que Dieu la fit;
Et, telle quelle,
Elle suffit!

*Léon van Montenaeken* [1859–

* For a paraphrase of this poem see page 2910.

# INDEX OF AUTHORS

*See also Corrigenda, p. 4011.*

**Selections from the later work of the poets whose names are starred will be found in THE HOME BOOK OF MODERN VERSE.**

## A

# INDEX OF FIRST LINES

## A

## C

H

## I

N

P

T

W

# INDEX OF TITLES

## A

M

U

## Y

# CORRIGENDA TO INDEX OF AUTHORS

(The years given are those of the authors' deaths.)

Adams, Charles Follen, 1918.
Akins, Zoë, 1958.
Arensberg, Walter Conrad, 1954.
Ashburton, Robert Offley, 1945.

Bacon, Josephine Daskam, 1961.
Banning, Kendall, 1944.
Baring, Maurice, 1945.
Barker, Elsa, 1954.
Beesly, A. H., 1909.
Belloc, Hilaire, 1953.
Bennett, John, 1956.
Benson, Margaret, 1916.
Binyon, Laurence, 1943.
Bird, Robert Montgomery, 1938.
Blanden, Charles Granger, 1933.
Bowen, Robert Adger, 1958.
Branch, Anna Hempstead, 1937.
Brown, Alice, 1948.
Buck, Richard Henry, 1937.
Burgess, Frank Gelett, 1951.
Byers, Samuel Hawkins Marshall, 1933.
Byron, May, 1936.

Canton, William, 1936.
Cather, Willa Sibert, 1947.
Chalmers, Patrick R., 1942.
Cleghorn, Sarah N., 1959.
Cloud, Virginia Woodward, 1938.
Cochrane, Alfred, 1948.
Cocke, Zitella, 1929.
Colton, Arthur Willis, 1943.
Cone, Helen Gray, 1934.
Conkling, Grace Hazard, 1958.
Connell, F. Norreys, 1948.
Coogler, J. Gordon, 1901.
Cortissoz, Ellen Mackay Hutchinson, 1933.
Custance, Olive, 1944.

Daly, Thomas Augustin, 1948.
De la Mare, Walter, 1956.
Deland, Margaretta Wade, 1945.
Dickinson, Martha Gilbert, 1943.
Doty, Walter G., 1920.
Doudney, Sarah, 1926.
Driscoll, Louise, 1957.

Eastman, Elaine Goodale, 1953.

Ficke, Arthur Davison, 1945.
Fisher, A. Hugh, 1945.
Fisher, Mahlon Leonard, 1947.
Ford, Ford Madox, 1939.
Fuller, Margaret, 1954.

Gale, Norman, 1942.
Garrison, Theodosia, 1944.
Garvin, Margaret Root, 1949.
Gibson, Wilfred Wilson, 1962.
Gorman, Herbert S., 1954.
Gosse, Edmund William, 1938.
Guiterman, Arthur, 1943.
Gwynne, Stephen Lucius, 1950.

Hall, Sharlot, 1944.
Hawley, Charles B., 1915.
Hawthorne, Hildegard, 1952.
Helburn, Theresa, 1959.
Henderson, Daniel, 1955.
Higginson, Ella Rhoades, 1940.
Hooker, William Brian, 1946.
Horne, Herbert P., 1916.
Housman, Laurence, 1959.

Irwin, Wallace, 1959.

Johns, Orrick, 1946.
Johnson, Robert Underwood, 1937.
Jones, Frederick Scheetz, 1944.
Joyce, James, 1941.

Kauffmann, Reginald Wright, 1959.
Kemp, Harry, 1960.

La Coste, Marie Ravenel de, 1936.
Lea, Fannie Heaslip, 1955.
Ledoux, Louis Vernon, 1948.
LeGallienne, Richard, 1947.
Lippman, Julie Mathilde, 1952.
Litchfield, Grace Denio, 1944.
Lucas, Edward Verrall, 1938.
Lucas, St. John, 1934.

McGroarty, John Steven, 1944.
Mackay, Isabel Ecclestone, 1928.
Mackintosh, Newton, 1938.
Manning, Frederic, 1935.
Millay, Edna St. Vincent, 1950.
Mitchell, Ruth Comfort, 1953.
Morris, Harrison Smith, 1958.
Morton, David, 1957.

Noyes, Alfred, 1958.

Opdyke, Oliver, 1956.
O'Sheel, Shaemas, 1954.
O'Sullivan, Seumas, 1958.

Packard, Winthrop, 1943.
Percy, William Alexander, 1942.
Phillpotts, Eden, 1960.
Plarr, Victor Gustave, 1946.
Plunkett, Edward J. M. D., 1957.

Quiller-Couch, Arthur Thomas, 1944.

Raymond, Rossiter Worthington, 1918.
Rhys, Ernest, 1946.
Rice, Cale Young, 1943.
Richards, Laura E., 1943.